# PUNCTUATION

T4-APS-893

## COMMA

# UNIFIED
# *ENGLISH*
# *COMPOSITION*

# UNIFIED
# *ENGLISH*
# *COMPOSITION*

[*Second Edition*]

## Gerald D. Sanders
*Michigan State Normal College*

## Hoover H. Jordan
*Michigan State Normal College*

## Wallace H. Magoon
*Ball State Teachers College*

## Robert M. Limpus
*Western Michigan College of Education*

*APPLETON–CENTURY–CROFTS, INC.*
*New York*

COPYRIGHT 1942, 1947, BY F. S. CROFTS & CO., INC.

*No part of the material covered by this copyright may be reproduced in any form without permission in writing from the publisher.*

MANUFACTURED IN THE UNITED STATES OF AMERICA

4129

# PREFACE TO THE FIRST EDITION

THIS BOOK was planned by one of the publishers and one of the authors some years ago when, because of hard times, students sometimes found it difficult to buy several textbooks for one course. Many things intervened, however, to prevent its being written till now, when again, because of the limited supply of white paper, it is well to economize. But aside from economy, there is an advantage in having within the covers of one volume all the materials for a year's work in composition: theory, handbook, readings, and worksheets.[1]

We may be old-fashioned in believing that the fundamental purpose of a course in composition is to give students instruction in the correct use of their language. It should not, for instance, be primarily a course for making students think. All courses should do that, the composition course as much as the history or the chemistry course—but no more. It is a primary responsibility of the course, however, to teach students how to organize and present their thoughts clearly and cogently, and to help them think straight; and to this end we have directed our aim in the text. But since a problem inseparable from that of writing well is reading well, we have included a special section on reading, as well as adequate selections, with somewhat detailed suggestions for study.

A word may be said about the reading selections. No effort has been made to select purple patches or to represent only the best that has been written. Many selections are from contemporary periodicals, and are the sort of writing which better students may well hope to equal in their own work. We are not among those, however, who believe nothing old is good; hence we have tried to make a judicious selection from the older writers as well as contemporary ones. Because our experience has taught us that a teacher can waste much time in trying to integrate readings with theory in a composition course, we have made the integration in the text; but teachers with different ideas about how to use the readings need have no trouble in adapting the readings to their own scheme. We may add that since the selections are meant to serve as models, we have taken the liberty of making spelling, punctuation, and mechanics conform to the best contemporary American practices.

1. Instructors are asked to note that whereas a workbook, integrated with the text through cross references, has been provided at the back of the text for those who use workbooks, an edition omitting the workbook is available at a cheaper cost, and that a separate edition of the workbook is also available for those who would find that arrangement more convenient.

A word also may be said about the divisions of the book. We have tried to organize the materials so that any section may be omitted without detracting from what remains. Many institutions, for instance, require a study of grammar, and many do not. But even those so fortunate as to have students who do not need to study grammar may find it useful to have such a section present for reference. There is of course more matter in the volume than can be taught adequately in one year, but we have included nothing that students will not be the better for knowing; and although a teacher may put the major emphasis on certain parts, he may find it helpful to have his students read such parts as cannot be covered adequately in class. Our chief aim has been to make a book that will save the teacher every effort possible in organization and class procedure so that he can concentrate on his relationship with the students themselves in their attempts to write better.

We are indebted for suggestions and help to our colleagues, especially to Professors Estabrooke Rankin and Elisabeth Carey, who have been generous in their aid with the grammar section. We are also greatly indebted to the authors and publishers who have kindly permitted the use of material held in copyright. To these we have made acknowledgment at the proper places in the text.

## PREFACE TO THE SECOND EDITION

THE PLAN of this edition follows, in the main, that of the original edition. The chief differences consist of (1) the inclusion of many more reading selections and a greater unity among these within sections, (2) greater exactness in the rules to which numbers are assigned—to aid students in finding their errors more easily, and (3) a thorough rewriting of most of the Workbook.

It would please us as much as it would honor us to list here the names of those professors—authorities in the teaching of rhetoric—who generously made suggestions for this revision, but we hesitate to associate their names with a book with which they might not agree at all points. They know, of course, how deeply we appreciate their kindnesses.

A word about the numbering of footnotes may be in order. We number our own footnotes consecutively throughout a whole section, but retain the numbering of the author's own footnotes as in the original. This will explain such apparent discrepancies as that, for instance, on page 428.

THE AUTHORS

*Ypsilanti, Michigan*
*May 6, 1947*

# CONTENTS

# CONTENTS

# CONTENTS

# CONTENTS

# READING SELECTIONS

[BY SUBJECTS]

# ORIENTATION

## I

## A FOREWORD TO STUDENTS

BOTH evidence and experience prove that a student of average intelligence can master any subject in which he takes enough interest. That many students at the time they enter college are miserably prepared in the use of their own language indicates, then, that they have never become convinced of the value of knowing how to use language correctly and effectively in speaking and writing. If you are one of these and your attitude in the past has been one of repugnance or indifference towards the work of learning to write and speak well, you are asked to give thoughtful consideration to the following remarks.

Perhaps your reason for entering college was to prepare for a profession—that of engineering, dentistry, medicine, or some other—or to become a superior farmer or businessman, and you are impatient at having to spend time learning the skills and techniques of composition. It may therefore be important to you to learn that there is a direct relationship between ability to use English well and achievement in all your college work. This is not just the idea of some English professor. Many investigations, in various places and at different times, each conducted with scientific objectivity, prove its truth. We have space to report just a few of these, but all similar tests show like results.

(1) M. E. Gladfelter concluded after a study of the grades of freshmen at Temple University that a diagnostic English test, plus a psychological test, would reveal so clearly a student's ability to do college work that the high-school record need not be consulted, except to check upon desirable prerequisites.[1] (2) W. D. Templeman, of the University of Illinois, after

1. "The Value of the Cooperative English Test in Prediction for Success in College," *School and Society*, XLIV (September 19, 1936), 384.

studying the record of 2,430 freshmen, reached a similar conclusion. His study verified a belief in the office of the Dean of Liberal Arts and Sciences at the University of Illinois "that, generally speaking, a student's grade in freshman rhetoric is a good index of his entire future academic ranking." [2] Among his findings were the following: of sixty-five engineering students who received E (the lowest grade) in rhetoric, all but three were below C in their general average. Likewise, of sixty-eight engineers who received A or B in rhetoric, all but nineteen were above B in all subjects. This relationship held in every college of the university—Engineering, Agriculture, Commerce, Physical Education, and Liberal Arts. (3) Johnson O'Connor conducted a survey which demonstrated that a close relationship exists between the size of a student's vocabulary and his success after graduation. In reporting on his survey, he stated: "An extensive knowledge of the exact meanings of English words accompanies outstanding success more often than any other single characteristic which the Human Engineering Laboratories have been able to isolate and measure. . . . The balance of the evidence at the moment suggests that such a consciously, even laboriously, achieved vocabulary is an active asset." [3]

Now unless you have a closed mind, you will accept the weight of such evidence; and if you are intelligent and ambitious, you will determine to make the best use possible of the chance to learn the fundamental skills and techniques of communication, so that you will benefit in the ways these surveys indicated. You will be in a better position to do this, however, if you understand and accept two requisites: first, the responsibility of learning to write and speak well is yours alone; and second, the task entails hard, consistent, and intelligent effort.

You will, of course, have the help of a specialist—your instructor—who understands the principles and techniques of good communication. He can explain difficulties to you and advise you how to eliminate errors and better your style, but he cannot teach you to write well without your cooperation. If you are in earnest, you will strive diligently to follow his instructions. You will not wait for assignments before exploring sections of your text that treat of matters about which you are ignorant or on which you have become rusty. You will make it a rule to add something each day to your store of knowledge about how to write well.

You will be better fortified, moreover, if you keep in mind the fact that mastery of the skills and techniques of good writing and speaking will not come easily. Even the most expert and polished writers find composition difficult. The most fluent and smoothly flowing passages are often the ones over which a writer has labored longest. In his essay "Self-Cultivation in English," G. H. Palmer says, "I must write with pains that he may read with ease." If you find it necessary, therefore, to spend an undue amount of time on the course in order to perfect your skill in communication, you must not begrudge the time nor skimp your work. Just as the football player endures long, tedious hours of drill to win the plaudits of the crowd on Saturday afternoon, so you must spend long, trying hours in learning the principles set forth in your text, in studying the work of master writers, and in practicing the art of writing itself. This is the price you pay for being in arrears. But if you do learn the principles, if you make progress in applying them, your dividends will be great, both in the quality of all your college work and in your intellectual growth generally, for if you learn to express your ideas clearly, correctly, and logically, you will find this an aid in everything you do.

Nor will the advantage end with your college days. If you acquire the skill to write and speak well, you will find numerous ways to employ your ability after you leave college. You may need to explain your ideas or defend your opinions or actions to your business or professional colleagues or your community. You may have to talk at civic clubs, write reports of investigations you conduct, contribute material to your local newspaper; and always you will have to write letters—letters of application, business letters, and friendly letters. How well you do these tasks will in part determine your professional and social success. In this connection, Edward Menge makes a pertinent remark concerning one profession, that of engineering: "Every leader in engineering without exception places heavy emphasis upon the necessity of a thorough knowledge of English. J. A. W. Waddell, the famous civil engineer, justly says that an American engineer's greatest asset is his ability to write and speak correctly, elegantly, and vigorously." [4]

Writing is one of the best means, moreover, of achieving recognition in whatever profession you enter. Almost every business and profession has its publications, and if you are able to contribute to one of these, you can reach an audience far beyond your immediate circle and can bring to this audience your ideas and the results of your experiments and research. A teacher describes successful classroom techniques; a doctor analyzes his case histories; an engineer presents his methods of overcoming technical difficulties; a merchant describes successful advertising and merchandising programs. By doing this, each becomes better known and wins recog-

4. *Jobs for the College Graduate in Science,* The Bruce Publishing Company, N. Y., 1932, p. 72.

nition for himself in a way that would not be possible if he lacked the ability to present his information to others.

But in an even more significant way than in economic success, social success depends on the ability to speak and write well. Ben Jonson wrote: "No glass renders a man's form and image so true as his speech." And it is true that a man's breeding and social grace are evident as soon as he speaks or writes. No one, of course, expects a person to write and speak correctly who has had no educational opportunities, but few will condone flagrant errors in the speech and writing of college students. Bad grammar, wrong idioms, faulty sentences, and like errors handicap a college graduate not only because they hinder precise transmission of thought from one mind to another, but because educated men and women do not make such errors. To do so makes one as suspect as a man who wears high yellow shoes or a woman who wears slacks to a formal ball.

But in a more profound sense than in any discussed so far is it important that you know how to use your language well. As the means of communication tend to make the world smaller, and as Americans are called on more and more to assume responsibilities in many parts of the earth, it is important that every educated citizen of the country become increasingly conscious of the value of language in general and of his own in particular, and that he take pride in it and in his knowledge of it. In this connection, consider the following pertinent statement by John Milton:

> Whoever in a state knows how to form wisely the manners of men, and to rule them at home and in war with excellent institutes, him in the first place, above others, I should esteem worthy of all honor; but next to him the man who strives to establish in maxims and rules the method and habit of speaking and writing received from a good age of the nation, and, as it were, to fortify the same round with a kind of wall, any attempt to overleap which ought to be prevented by a law only short of that of Romulus. . . . The one, as I believe, supplies a noble courage and intrepid counsels against an enemy invading the territory; the other takes to himself the task of extirpating and defeating by means of a learned detective police of ears and a light cavalry of good authors, that barbarism which makes large inroads upon the minds of men, and is a destructive intestine enemy to genius. Nor is it to be considered of small consequence what language, pure or corrupt, a people has, or what is their customary degree of propriety in speaking it. . . . For, let the words of a country be in part unhandsome and offensive in themselves, in part debased by wear and wrongly uttered, and what do they declare but, by no light indication, that the inhabitants of that country are an indolent, idly-yawning race, with minds already long prepared for any amount of servility? On the other hand, we have never heard that any empire, any state, did not flour-

ish moderately at least, as long as liking and care for its own language lasted.[5]

If, then, being able to communicate correctly and effectively will benefit you in so many ways, and if you are interested in your development and achievements, no urging should be needed to induce you to determine to master the rules and principles of correct communication. If as the result of past experiences you believe you lack the aptitude to communicate your ideas intelligibly to others, be assured that no special aptitude in language is requisite in order to learn to write and speak clearly and correctly. You will need intelligence, diligence, patience, and persistence; but these are needed for any sort of attainment. Just as through practice you can learn to play bridge or tennis with acceptable skill, though you may never become a Culbertson or a Budge, so by diligent application and conscientious practice you can learn to write in a workmanlike manner.

You will benefit most from this course by considering it for what it is— a foundation course in which to learn the best means of transmitting all the ideas you will ever have on any subject. To think of it as intended primarily for those who will make a profession of writing, and therefore not as your concern, is to mistake its whole purpose. The future creative writer will derive benefit from it, to be sure, for it contains the principles of his craft; but for him it is only the beginning of a long apprenticeship. For many others, it is the only course they will take that is devoted specifically to the best means of transmitting ideas. If these should treat it as "just another course" and fail to learn what it attempts to teach, they are very likely to remain handicapped in their thinking, talking, and writing; for if their medium of expression is poor, how can their ideas appear in a favorable light? But if they should accept the chance to learn to use their language effectively, and be willing to devote whatever time is required to bring this about, they will find both in college and afterwards ample rewards for their decision and efforts.

## The Open Mind [6]

### NICHOLAS MURRAY BUTLER

In what spirit and in what attitude of mind the problems of practical life shall be approached by men and women who have had the benefit of the discipline and the instruction of a university are matters of grave con-

5. D. Masson, *The Life of John Milton,* 1881, I, 790.

6. (This is an address given to the entering class at Columbia University.) From *Scholarship and Service* by Nicholas Murray Butler (copyright, 1921). Reprinted by permission of Charles Scribner's Sons, the publishers.

cern to those charged with the university's oversight and direction. It is quite possible that one may be so assiduous in negligence and so skillful as to carry away from his college or university study little or nothing that will aid him to take a just, a sympathetic, and a helpful attitude toward the questions which life insistently asks. On the other hand, it is easily possible, and it should be normal and most usual, for the student to take with him from his college and university residence very much that will give him important advantage over his less fortunate fellows in estimating and in passing judgment upon men, upon tendencies, upon ideas, and upon human institutions. If he has gained from his study and discipline a mastery over method, a trained habit of withholding judgment until the evidence has been heard, a moral standard that knows instinctively the difference between right and wrong and that leads him to turn to the one as surely as it causes him to recoil from the other, then the university has furnished him well.

But granted the possession of these habits and traits, it is essential to beware of the closed mind. The closed mind is not of itself conservative or radical, destructive or constructive; it is merely a mental attitude which may be any one of these or all of them in turn. By the closed mind I mean a mind which has a fixed formula with which to reach a quick and certain answer to every new question, and a mind for which all the great issues of life are settled once for all and their settlements organized into carefully ordered dogma. To the closed mind the world is a finished product and nothing remains but its interested contemplation. The closed mind may be jostled, but it cannot have experience. The name of a notable historic family, the house of Bourbon, has passed into familiar speech with the definition of one who forgets nothing and who learns nothing. The Bourbon typifies the closed mind.

There is another type of mind equally to be shunned. To be sure this type of mind is not closed, for, unfortunately, it is quite open at both ends. This is the type which remembers nothing and which learns nothing. To it the name of no historic family has yet been given. There is every prospect, however, that some contemporary name may, through constant association with this type of mind, yet become as distinguished and as familiar in the speech of our grandchildren as the name of the house of Bourbon is distinguished and familiar to us.

Open-mindedness is a trait greatly to be desired. It differs both from the closed mind and from the mind which consists wholly of openings. The open mind is ready to receive freely and fairly, and to estimate new facts, new ideas, new movements, new teachings, new tendencies; but while it receives these it also estimates them. It does not yield itself wholly to the new until it has assured itself that the new is also true. It does not reject that which is old and customary and usual until it is certain that it is also false or futile.

The power to estimate implies the existence of standards of worth and their application to the new experiences of the open mind. These standards are themselves the product of older and longer experiences than ours, and they form the subject-matter of the lesson which the whole past teaches the immediate present.

History offers a third dimension to the superficial area of knowledge that each individual acquires through his own experience. When one proclaims that he is not bound by any trammels of the past, he reveals the fact that he is both very young and very foolish. Such an one would, if he could, reduce himself to the intellectual level of the lower animals. He can only mean by such a declaration that he proposes to set out to discover and to explain the world of nature and of man on his own account and as if nothing had been done before him. He also jauntily assumes his own certain competence for this mighty and self-imposed task. His egotism is as magnificent as his wisdom is wanting. Such an one possesses neither an open mind nor a closed mind, but a mind open at both ends through which a stream of sensation and feeling will pour without leaving any more permanent conscious impression than the lapping waves leave on the sandy shore.

The man of open mind, on the contrary, while keenly alive to the experiences of the present, will eagerly search the records of the past for their lessons, in order that he may be spared from trying to do over again what has once been proved useless, wasteful, or wrong. The man of open mind will watch the rise and fall of nations; the struggle of human ambition, greed, and thirst for power; the loves and hates of men and women as these have affected the march of events; the migrations of peoples; the birth, development, and application of ideas; the records of human achievement in letters, in the arts, and in science; the speculations and the beliefs of man as to what lies beyond the horizon of sense, with a view to seeking a firm foundation for the fabric of his own knowledge and his own faith. His open-mindedness will manifest itself in hearkening to the testimony of other men, other peoples, and other ages, as well as in reflecting upon and weighing the evidence of his own short-lived and very limited senses.

There is a great difference between being intellectual and being intelligent. Not a few intellectual persons are quite unintelligent, and very many intelligent persons would hardly be classed as intellectual. One of the chief manifestations of intelligence is open-mindedness. The intelligent man is open-minded enough to see the point of view of those who do not agree with him and to enter in some measure into their feelings and convictions. He is able, also, to view the conflicting arguments and phenomena in proportion to each other and to rank the less significant of these below the more significant. It is quite possible to be intellectual and to manifest the closed mind; but it is not possible to do so and to be intelligent.

It is the constant aim of this college and university, by act and by precept, to hold up the value of open-mindedness and to train students in ways of intelligence. This university is the product of liberty, and it is passionately devoted to liberty. It finds in liberty the justification and the ground for open-mindedness, and also the source of those dangers which it is the business of the educated man to avoid. Open-mindedness in the university teaches the habit of open-mindedness in later life. Genuine open-mindedness guides to progress based upon wisdom.

*Suggestions for Study*

1. What advantages should a college graduate have over others?
2. What is the author's definition of "a closed mind"?
3. In what way did the Bourbon family exemplify the closed mind? (Look up the term *Bourbon* first in a dictionary. If that does not give you the answer, try an encyclopaedia.)
4. What are the characteristics of an open mind?
5. Where can we find standards of worth by which to make our estimates?
6. Explain the author's differentiation between an intellectual person and an intelligent one.
7. Find five words in the article that you could not define, look up their definitions, copy these, and bring them to class.

## The Durable Satisfactions of Life [7]

### CHARLES W. ELIOT

For educated men what are the sources of the solid and durable satisfactions of life? I hope you are all aiming at the solid, durable satisfactions of life, not primarily the gratifications of this moment or of tomorrow, but the satisfactions that are going to last and grow. So far as I have seen, there is one indispensable foundation for the satisfactions of life—health. A young man ought to be a clean, wholesome, vigorous animal. That is the foundation for everything else, and I hope you will all be that, if you are nothing more. We have to build everything in this world of domestic joy and professional success, everything of a useful, honorable career, on

7. An address given to an entering class at Harvard University. Reprinted by permission of the Reverend Samuel A. Eliot.

bodily wholesomeness and vitality. This being a clean, wholesome, vigorous animal involves a good deal. It involves not condescending to the ordinary barbaric vices. One must avoid drunkenness, gluttony, licentiousness, and getting into dirt of any kind, in order to be a clean, wholesome, vigorous animal. Still, none of you would be content with this achievement as the total outcome of your lives. It is a happy thing to have in youth what are called animal spirits—a very descriptive phrase; but animal spirits do not last even in animals; they belong to the kitten or puppy stage. It is a wholesome thing to enjoy for a time, or for a time each day all through life, sports and active bodily exercise. These are legitimate enjoyments, but if made the main object of life, they tire. They cease to be a source of durable satisfaction. Play must be incidental in a satisfactory life.

What is the next thing, then, that we want in order to make sure of durable satisfactions in life? We need a strong mental grip, a wholesome capacity for hard work. It is intellectual power and aims that we need. In all the professions—learned, scientific, or industrial—large mental enjoyments should come to educated men. The great distinction between the privileged class to which you belong, the class that has opportunity for prolonged education, and the much larger class that has not that opportunity, is that the educated class lives mainly by the exercise of intellectual powers and gets therefore much greater enjoyment out of life than the much larger class that earns a livelihood chiefly by the exercise of bodily powers. You ought to obtain here, therefore, the trained capacity for mental labor, rapid, intense, and sustained. That is the great thing to get in college, long before the professional school is entered. Get it now. Get it in the years of college life. It is the main achievement of college life to win this mental force, this capacity for keen observation, just inference, and sustained thought, for everything that we mean by the reasoning power of man. That capacity will be the main source of intellectual joys and of happiness and content throughout a long and busy life.

But there is something more, something beyond this acquired power of intellectual labor. As Shakespeare puts it, "the purest treasure mortal times afford is spotless reputation." How is that treasure won? It comes by living with honor, on honor. Most of you have begun already to live honorably and honored, for the life of honor begins early. Some things the honorable man cannot do, never does. He never wrongs or degrades a woman. He never oppresses or cheats a person weaker or poorer than himself. He never betrays a trust. He is honest, sincere, candid, and generous. It is not enough to be honest. An honorable man must be generous, and I do not mean generous with money only. I mean generous in his judgments of men and women, and of the nature and prospects of mankind. Such generosity is a beautiful attribute of the man of honor.

How does honor come to a man? What is the evidence of the honorable life? What is the tribunal which declares at last, "This was an honorable man"? You look now for the favorable judgment of your elders—of parents and teachers and older students; but these elders will not be your final judges, and you had better get ready now in college to appear before the ultimate tribunal, the tribunal of your contemporaries and the younger generations. It is the judgment of your contemporaries that is most important to you; and you will find that the judgment of your contemporaries is made up alarmingly early—it may be made up this year in a way that sometimes lasts for life and beyond. It is made up in part by persons to whom you have never spoken, by persons who in your view do not know you, and who get only a general impression of you; but always it is contemporaries whose judgment is formidable and unavoidable. Live now in the fear of that tribunal—not an abject fear, because independence is an indispensable quality in the honorable man. There is an admirable phrase in the Declaration of Independence, a document which it was a good fashion of my time for boys to commit to memory. I doubt if that fashion still obtains. Some of our public action looks as if it did not. "When, in the course of human events, it becomes necessary for one people to dissolve the political bands which have connected them with another, and to assume among the powers of the earth the separate and equal station to which the laws of nature and of nature's God entitle them, a decent respect to the opinions of mankind requires that they should declare the causes which impel them to the separation." That phrase—"a decent respect"—is a very happy one. Cherish "a decent respect to the opinions of mankind," but never let that interfere with your personal declaration of independence. Begin now to prepare for the judgment of the ultimate tribunal.

Look forward to the important crises of your life. They are nearer than you are apt to imagine. It is a very safe protective rule to live today as if you were going to marry a pure woman within a month. That rule you will find a safeguard for worthy living. It is a good rule to endeavor hour by hour and week after week to learn to work hard. It is not well to take four minutes to do what you can accomplish in three. It is not well to take four years to do what you can perfectly accomplish in three. It is well to learn to work intensely. You will hear a good deal of advice about letting your soul grow and breathing in without effort the atmosphere of a learned society or place of learning. Well, you cannot help breathing and you cannot help growing; those processes will take care of themselves.

The question for you from day to day is how to learn to work to advantage, and college is the place and now is the time to win mental power. And, lastly, live today and every day like a man of honor.

*Suggestions for Study*

1. Name the things which, according to the author, one must have in order to find lasting satisfaction. Is the order in which he lists these things important?
2. What is the chief distinction between those who have the opportunity of a college education and those who do not?
3. What should be the main achievement of college life?
4. In what sense must an educated man be generous?
5. Whose judgment of us is most important? What is the best way to secure a favorable judgment?
6. On what two immediate matters does the author offer advice?
7. Define the following words from the article: condescending, barbaric, gluttony, incidental, candid, attribute, tribunal, abject, indispensable, ultimate.

## Work Your Way Through College? [8]

### RALPH COOPER HUTCHISON

There are great values to be had from the experience of earning one's way through college. There would be great values for my physician if he would close his office and build an automobile by hand. There would be great values for the leading lawyer in my community if he would build a barn, doing all the work with his own hands. But there are still higher values for these men if they will stay at their first tasks.

The physician might learn a lot about iron, steel, motors, and the composition of rubber, but it would be better for him to restore health and save lives. The lawyer would learn a great deal about bricks, woodwork, and construction, but there are higher values if he will perform his function in society. Surely a college student gains much when he sweeps floors in the Elks Hall, washes dishes at the dormitory, shovels coal in the professor's house, or acts as bellhop at the hotel. But there are higher values which he should be gaining and serving with every minute of his time and every ounce of strength. If these menial functions have such high value, why go to college? A boy can sweep floors, press suits, drive delivery wagons, and shovel coal without going to college and paying for the privilege.

Yes, working one's way through college has its values. It is better than

8. Reprinted by permission of the *Rotarian*. The author, then president of Washington and Jefferson College, wrote the article as an answer to one which argued the advantages of working one's way through college.

not going to college. It is also better than playing one's way through college. But it is not better than studying one's way through college.

The widespread illusion on this subject is due to several misconceptions. The first of these is the popular idea that the great objective is "to get through college." Getting through college is of no value whatsoever. Many men have "gotten through" college who would be better off if they had never seen a college. So would society. Which is to say that there are many ways of getting through college and some of them mean nothing. What counts is what a man gets out of college as he goes through. If he gets what he should, he will be immediately enriched and society will be blessed by his ability and his service. But if he does not get these proper values, he has nothing. The fact therefore that a man earned his way through college means nothing unless the man got something as he went through. Many of the earning men get little or nothing. They are in some cases like the playboys. In one case play interferes with education. In the other, menial, driving, all-absorbing remunerative work does the same.

What are the values of a college education in general terms? Well, men come to college having never used 70 per cent of their mental "muscles." They have never had to use them. Mentally they are as soft as a fat baby is physically. The college begins the process of exercising the unused and flabby 70 per cent. It is a long, slow, difficult process, much slower than the training of the physical muscles in athletics. New academic tasks and achievements, advanced problems and speeds, are used to bring into play mental muscles, abilities, and capacities heretofore only suspected in the mind of the student. To succeed under this training requires the most prodigious effort of the student's life, and that effort is mental in the highest degree. His failure or success depends on whether he makes that effort consistently and earnestly until he gets results.

Waiving aside this sentimental bosh about college jobs, we must recognize the fact that 90 per cent of the jobs available to college men make little or no contribution to this intellectual achievement characterizing the college experience. Most of the jobs are menial, requiring abilities which are elementary. Some require a certain commercial ability, but, even so, are no serious contribution to the intellectual training of college. Students themselves are under no illusion on this subject. The jobs they get in college are to earn money, not to develop their mental abilities, train their minds, or open the windows of their souls, and well they know it.

The second great value of the college is social, in the higher meaning of the term. The college man is concentrating into four years a social experience and training which he might possibly obtain in twelve years outside. By the benefit of the phenomenon known as the college, he is placed in a peculiar society. This society is a complete world in itself. Superficial educational writers regret this, but it is one of the chief values of college. Here is created for a student a concentrated world, an epitome of life, isolated from general society to a degree, complete in itself. The citizens are his contemporaries, but they are picked by that eliminating and sifting process which college is. These contemporaries are strong men from the best homes with rich heritage and the highest purposes.

In a world of such men he must make his way. Here he must learn the art of following or of leading. He must choose friends and develop friendships. He must match wits, struggle for recognition, protect his rights, serve those in need—keep pace with these eager men, physically, mentally, and spiritually. The vastly complicated activities of the college campus are not a happenstance. They are an achievement. They constitute a complete little world, and in it the student begins to learn that which takes much longer outside. He learns to walk upright among men and make his way.

If he is to succeed in this social problem and training, he will need every ounce of strength, every vestige of enthusiasm, and every moment of time. Everything which draws him out of his college world is an interference and relatively a loss. Earning his way through college does two wrongs. It takes his time and strength from this larger experience. Secondly, it frequently puts him out into the other world. The transition from the college world to that of the downtown hotel or the filling station is not a helpful event in this peculiar social experience. It is right if he has to, wrong if he does not have to do it. It has values which he can get all the rest of his life. College has values which he can never get again.

The second popular illusion in this matter is to the effect that the men who work their way through are the men who are subsequently successful. This is an optical illusion. We have talked so proudly of those who have earned their way and who have made good that we have overlooked those who earned their way and didn't amount to the proverbial row of pins. We do not count them and I hope we never shall. Nor, on the other hand, do we make special note of the fact that many of our finest and greatest college men are men who did not earn their way, who fully appreciated the values of college, who made distinguished records, and who have been giants subsequently. As a matter of fact, there are no scientific statistics which prove that those who earn their way do better than those who study their way. The chances are the second group would show the higher score. Both would score, of course, over those who "play their way."

Take again these men who earn their way and then make fine records in life. There is yet another optical illusion as we look at them. We say he is a success because he had to earn his way. No, all too often the reverse is true. He earned his way because he was a success before he started. That's why some go to college when others don't go. That's why they work like slaves to get through college. That's why they go hungry for an education. That's why they stick when others quit. They are the kind of people that make good, anytime, anywhere, college or no college.

When such a determined, able person does go to college, earns his way through, makes good in life, then a great chorus of praise is raised as to the virtues of dishwashing in the collegiate years. No, with such a man the dishwashing was a means to an end, the way to earn money. So far as the education he was seeking, the necessity was an interference, and he would of all men most thank God had he been able to put all that indomitable determination, all that time and strength into the larger opportunities for which he was fighting.

And such persons do more with those opportunities if they have them, do even better if they do not have to earn. Such persons invariably determine later that their sons, if qualified, shall not be tied down to such stern necessities, but shall go a step further and put all their strength into the herculean task of becoming educated for the exactions of life.

Finally, no man who does not have to earn his way has a right to earn his way. We have plenty of students who work in college and do not need to do so. In the first place, they take jobs which others should have. In the second place, they are self-deluded. They have been inculcated with the idea of working their way through college. They get this from storybooks and from well-intentioned parents. They work at their jobs with such a sense of satisfaction that they neglect their social development or their mental equipment. They make earning achievements an alibi for intellectual mediocrity. In their reverence for financial earnings they become intellectual sluggards. Their hard outside work exalts the ego while the mind atrophies. Slovenly workmanship in studies is accepted imperturbably because of the manly satisfaction of working half the night in the local steel mill.

Earning work in college is like many other things in life—a virtue only when a necessity. Robinson Crusoe did some remarkable things on that lonely island. Hollowing out a log for a canoe was magnificent. But to have done the same thing in London would have been an absurdity. So in college there are immeasurable opportunities for the development of the mind and the enrichment of the soul, for the growing of the bigger man. Let no student be denied these privileges save by stern necessity.

## Suggestions for Study

1. Under what circumstance does the author consider it right to earn one's way through college? Why is it wrong for any other reason? (Gather all his arguments in answering the latter question.)

2. What is an illusion? State the various illusions that make some consider it an advantage to work one's way through college.

3. What is better than working one's way through college?

4. In general terms, what are the values of a college education?

5. Does the author consider it an advantage while in college to have contact with the world of business? Summarize his argument on this point.

6. Make an orderly summary of his arguments against working while in college.

7. Define the following words from the article: menial, remunerative, prodigious, epitome, vestige, indomitable, imperturbably, atrophies.

## Suggestions for Writing

1. The three articles in this section contain advice and suggestions by three college presidents. Organize what they say into one unified paper, making a synthesis of their most important points, and make this an address for a group of freshmen.

2. Explain why you have entered college, what specific and general advantages you expect to get from attending college, and the immediate steps you propose to take to attain your ends.

3. Explain what you believe to be the chief values of a college education.

4. Explain the attitude you think a freshman entering college should have towards the matter of higher education.

# II
# FIRST CONSIDERATIONS

## A. The Manuscript

FEW who study freshman composition will ever be professional writers; hence such a course does not aim primarily at training students to become creative artists, but to use their language effectively in the ordinary affairs of life. Yet in many fundamentals, the standards are the same for the college student writing a letter home and the great novelist composing a masterpiece of fiction. The rules and practices commonly employed in all forms of writing are not the results of some individual's idiosyncrasies, but have been accepted for reasons of logic, convenience, common sense, or good taste. And a student who learns and adheres to them in his writing may have the satisfaction of knowing that he is using methods which are correct for all his written work, whether it be a class report, a term paper, a master's thesis, an address, a novel, or a poem.

**Form and Appearance.** The basic rules for the form and appearance of manuscripts depend on good taste and courtesy rather than on grammatical or rhetorical principles. If a person has good taste and courtesy, for instance, he will not expect someone to read a manuscript that is slovenly in appearance and partly illegible. Neatness and legibility are prerequisites in any manuscript. Almost no one, of course, prepares a first draft which is perfect in these respects; hence when the ideas are stated as well as a writer is capable of stating them, and all corrections have been made, it is essential to make a fair copy of the manuscript before submitting it to a reader. The following directions, if learned and followed, will insure a manuscript's being neat in appearance and conforming to the best practices of professional writers.

1. *Paper.* Use standard-size (8½ x 11 inches), white, unruled typewriting paper, unless your instructor requires another kind. If he does, write his specifications in this blank.

―――――――――――――――――――――――――――――――――――

―――――――――――――――――――――――――――――――――――

NOTE: Since ruled paper forces a student to leave margins of the required width and to space properly, it will probably save an instructor some time and a student some effort if regulation "theme" paper is stipulated; but since such paper is never used for ordinary business or professional purposes, and since a person would be thought lacking in taste who wrote letters on ruled paper, it is better that a student use unruled paper, thus accustoming himself to leave the proper margins, to keep straight lines, and to leave the proper spaces. This as much as learning the use of capitals, commas, or subordinate clauses is part of his training as a writer.

2. *Ink.* Use black or blue-black ink; or, if a typewriter is employed, use a black ribbon.

3. *Title.* Center the title, leaving equal space between it and each margin. If it is more than a line in length, fill up the first line and center the second. Place the title about two inches from the top of the page. Leave about an inch between the title and first line of the composition. Capitalize the first word of the title and all the other words except articles, conjunctions, and prepositions. Do not underline or use quotation marks unless these marks are required according to rules for italics and quotation marks (see pp. 288, 274 ff). Do not use a period after a title, but use a

question mark if the title is a question, and an exclamation point if it is exclamatory.

In typescript capitalize all letters in the title. All other directions are the same as in the preceding paragraph.

4. *Indention.* Indent the first line of each paragraph about an inch.

5. *Margins.* The left margin should be perfectly even and about 1½ inches wide, to allow plenty of room for the instructor's comments and marks. The right margin should be fairly even and about an inch wide. When possible, avoid dividing words at the end of lines, but if it is necessary to divide a long word to insure a good-looking margin, use the hyphen in accordance with the required rules (see page 281). Never divide a short word. Never leave a wide space at the end of a line, except at the end of a paragraph, and never crowd letters together towards the right margin. A very little skill will soon insure even lines and margins.

Leave margins of about an inch at the top and bottom of the page. Always write to the end of a line at the bottom of a page unless it is at the end of a paragraph.

6. *Erasures and corrections.* If there are several erasures or additions on a page of manuscript, the page should be recopied; but it is not necessary to recopy a page for an occasional change after the final draft is written. For an addition, use the caret, and write the omitted word in the space above, thus:

> spent
> Six of us ∧ the night at the camp.

To erase a passage, run two or three straight lines through the words to be omitted.

NOTE: The method of denoting a passage to be omitted by enclosing it in parentheses is incorrect. Parentheses have a very definite function which has nothing to do with marking an omitted passage. This erroneous usage seems to derive from the elementary grades, where for some obscure reason an occasional teacher requires pupils to denote an omission by placing it in parentheses. If you were one of those so taught, unlearn the practice now.

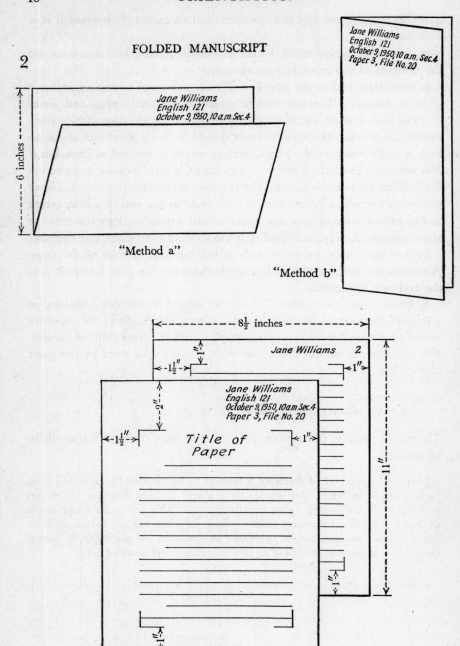

**FOLDED MANUSCRIPT**

2

Jane Williams
English 121
October 9, 1950, 10 a.m. Sec. 4

6 inches

"Method a"

Jane Williams
English 121
October 9, 1950, 10 a.m. Sec. 4
Paper 3, File No. 20

"Method b"

8½ inches

Jane Williams    2

1½"    1"

2"

Jane Williams
English 121
October 9, 1950, 10 a.m. Sec. 4
Paper 3, File No. 20

1½"    *Title of Paper*    1"

11"

1"

1"

**APPEARANCE OF MANUSCRIPT**
("Method a" of paging and endorsing)

3    7. *Paging and endorsing.* Write on one side of the page only. Check each manuscript carefully to see that the pages are not jumbled. Then, beginning with the second page, number each page in the upper righthand corner—using arabic numerals—and after the page number, write your last name or the title of your paper, as your instructor prefers, so that if the manuscript becomes disarranged, the instructor can reassemble it without undue trouble.

There are two commonly accepted methods of folding and endorsing college compositions. Check the one your instructor prefers, and delete the other.

(a) Fold the paper once, horizontally, so that the crease runs across the page about six inches from the top. When folded, the back of the lower half of the last sheet lies uppermost, and there is a margin at the top which allows the endorsement on the first page to show. In the upper righthand corner of the first page, write your name, the name and number of the course for which the paper is written, the date, the hour and section, the number of the composition, and your file number, thus:

> Jane Williams
> English 121
> April 9, 1950, 10 a.m., Sec. 4
> Paper 3, File No. 20

(b) Fold the paper vertically in the center. Place the endorsement, as given above, in the upper right corner on the back of the last sheet, so that after the paper is folded, the endorsement will appear as does a title on the front cover of a book; that is, the fold will be at the left of the endorsement.

NOTE: Method *b* should never be used elsewhere than in college classes. When submitting a manuscript for publication, do not fold the manuscript at all if it has many pages. If it consists of a few pages only, fold as noted in method *a,* or fold twice in the manner of a business letter. If the manuscript is one submitted for publication, the endorsement should be made according to method *a* except that the address is used instead of the number of the course, the date, and the other details required in college courses.

8. *Legibility.* In preparing manuscripts, use a typewriter if one is available. If no typewriter is available, however, the writer is obligated to see that his manuscript is legible. The following directions, if faithfully observed, will aid even a poor scribe in preparing a more legible manuscript.

(a) Do not crowd lines close together so that the letters of one line overrun those of another. On the other hand, do not leave a noticeable space between lines.

(b) Leave space enough between words so that a reader can distinguish one word from another without hesitation. Leave a slightly greater space between sentences. Do not leave a gap between letters of the same word.

(c) Avoid idiosyncrasies of handwriting, such as making certain letters with curlicues or large flourishes, writing certain words—as *and*—slantwise across the line, making a circle instead of a dot over *i's* and for periods. Cultivate a simple, clear style of handwriting, and leave the fancy trimming for cake icings.

(d) Take pains in forming your letters. Especially, write *m's* and *n's* and *u's* and *v's, a's* and *o's,* and *e's* and *i's* so that they are distinguishable. A little effort will do wonders to make a poor handwriting legible.

9. *Instructions for typing.* When using a typewriter, double-space the lines, except for footnotes and for quotations of several lines, which are single-spaced.

Underline—to designate italics—by using the interlinear mark, which on standard keyboards is on the key with the figure 6.

Use a single hyphen mark for the hyphen and two of these for the dash, with no space before or after the mark, whether it designates a hyphen or a dash.

Leave one space between words and after commas, semicolons, colons, parentheses, question marks, and the like within a sentence, but two spaces between sentences, regardless of what mark closes the sentence.

**Proofreading and Revising.** A writer's job is only half done when he is satisfied that he has stated and arranged his ideas to the best of his ability and has completed the draft of the whole composition. The remaining half of the job consists of going over the manuscript with care in order to correct errors, to test the sentences for correctness and clearness, and to revise awkward or faulty elements. Until one has become expert at revising, it is best to go over the manuscript for one thing at a time— once for spelling, once for punctuation, once for fragmentary and run-together sentences, once for the correct use of words, and so on. When this is done, make a final copy, read it for minor errors made in copying, and turn the manuscript in.

*Corrections.* When an instructor returns a manuscript, it will contain his criticisms and directions for revising or rewriting. Your final task is to consider these notations, keep in your notebook a list of the more obvious errors which you must avoid in future papers, and make all the corrections called for, or rewrite the paper, as directed. (See inside back cover for list of marks used by the instructor in calling attention to errors.) When the error is not at once obvious to you, refer to the proper section of this book for information as to what is wrong and how to correct it.

In making the final corrections, use ink of a different color from that employed in the original manuscript and from that used by the instructor, so that your final corrections may be distinguished easily. If, for instance, you used black ink originally, and the instructor made his criticisms in red ink, you might make the corrections in light blue ink. If your instructor has a preference in this matter, copy his instructions here.

---

---

**Literary Indebtedness.** The vast resources of man's thought up to the present are at the disposal of every college freshman, and may be used by him to enrich his ideas, to illustrate something he is saying, or in many other ways. The specific idea of another person, however, is his property, just as much as a piece of silverware he might own, and must not be appropriated without proper acknowledgment. In the matter of ideas, convention allows a writer to use what another has said if he makes the right acknowledgment, and this right acknowledgment means using quotation marks for every statement of another which is quoted exactly, and giving credit either in a footnote or in the body of the manuscript to the source of the quotation. It also means giving credit in similar manner when one uses the ideas of another, even when not quoting the exact words.

Using specific ideas or the words of another without acknowledgment is plagiarism, a matter usually dealt with severely by college authorities. Since plagiarism is more often the result of thoughtlessness or ignorance than downright dishonesty, a student should learn at the very outset of his college career the difference between legitimate and illegitimate copying. It is legitimate to use any source, written or oral, for ideas, and even to use the exact words of another; it is illegitimate to use these without making due note of the source, and putting within quotation marks words taken directly from another. Since instructors generally like to see a student use sources intelligently, and will rarely criticize such use unless the student makes his whole paper a patchwork of others' ideas, it is sheer lack of intelligence to use matter from an outside source without making proper note of the fact.

For the proper use of quotation marks, see page 274. It is sufficient here to note that when a quotation of more than a sentence or two is used, it should be set off from a writer's own work by an indention of about an inch from the margins of his own work, so that the quotation will stand out clearly on the page. If the manuscript is handwritten, it is best to use quotation marks, even for long passages, so that the quotation will be unmistakably apparent; but if the manuscript is typewritten, the conventional manner of noting a quotation is to set it off from the writer's own work, which is double spaced, by wider margins and single spacing. When this is done, the quotation marks are usually omitted, since the indention and single spacing is sufficient notice that the excerpt is a quotation.

## B. Preliminary Planning

A student who wishes to write interesting and successful papers instead of the dreary, formless ones that are too common a feature of the freshman composition course must do a certain amount of planning before he even starts to write. The minimum initial planning for a reasonably satisfactory result consists of choosing a subject you know something about or have some interest in, narrowing the scope of your paper to one or two topics that can be treated adequately in a short article, writing to a specific audience, and having in mind a specific purpose as you write.

**Subject.** Do not make a big problem of choosing a subject on which to write. No one expects you to have world-shaking ideas or to report sensational experiences. Settle on something about which you have information already at hand or about which you have ideas of your own. You should spend the bulk of your time in organizing your ideas and trying to present them correctly, not in worrying about a subject on which to write.

Your instructor may allow you to choose all your subjects, he may assign all subjects, or he may vary the procedure by assigning some and allowing you to choose some. But even when he assigns the subjects, he will usually allow a choice among several, or permit you to adapt the subject to your own knowledge and experience. The assignment, for instance, might be to explain how you secured spending money when attending high school. In this assignment, there is leeway enough to allow any student to write on the subject. One with a definite experience in finding and working at a job whereby he secured his spending money might perhaps have less trouble getting started than one who never had a job; yet even a girl who never earned a penny by working might write a very interesting paper on how she wheedled an allowance from an unwilling parent; and another who managed to go through high school without having any spending money might write a whimsical and interesting explanation of how such a feat was accomplished. It is good practice, incidentally, to write from assigned subjects, since one often is required to make reports, to give talks, and to write articles on specified topics.

When a writer has to choose a subject himself, he should select one he knows something about or is sufficiently interested in to investigate. A person, for instance, who was born and bred in a city, who never visited a farm, and whose interest in pigs is confined to the crispness of his breakfast bacon, would hardly be the one to write on "The Best Method of Feeding a Pig Which Is Being Prepared for Exhibit at a Fair"; and an article on "Recreational Facilities in Blank City" would probably have little value, and be a difficult chore besides, if it were undertaken by one born and brought up on a farm and with no interest in or knowledge of life in a city.

Once you have selected a general subject, the next step is to narrow it so that in a short paper you can treat adequately and fully the point you are making. Unless one has the skill of a Francis Bacon, it is difficult to say anything interesting in a brief article on such broad topics as "Truth," "Nature," "Patriotism," "Football," "College Athletics," and the like. One of the most common faults of inexperienced writers is that they say so little on such broad and general topics as those noted. "Recreational Facilities in Chicago," for instance, is much too broad a subject to be treated adequately in five hundred words. You might write a good short paper on such a topic as "Turning a Weed-patch into a Playground" or "A Needed Improvement for the Playground at Jackson Park" or "Where to Build a Playground on the North Side." For short papers, narrowly restricted subjects are imperative; for long papers, more inclusive subjects of varying complexity are in order.

**Audience.** Highly important, yet rarely considered by inexperienced writers, is the audience for which a given paper is written. The normal practice of writing a composition that will get a nod of acceptance from the instructor, and which has no other aim, is about the most stultifying a student could hit upon. *Every piece of writing should be directed at some specific person or group.* An article on college athletics for the Sunday section of a newspaper would probably be very different from one written for the *American Scholar,* the Phi Beta Kappa journal. And a youth wishing to explain his hobby of building airship models would produce very different articles in writing for a group of enthusiastic boys with the same hobby, for a group of sorority girls, and for his grandmother. A composition written for a definite audience will be more circumscribed and more unified, and therefore more likely to attain its end than if the author has no special reader in mind. A notably successful newspaperman explained his success by stating that in editing his newspaper he had always kept in mind one specific family he knew and had produced his journal with an idea of pleasing this family; since this family was typical of many in that community, by pleasing its members he pleased others. But note how much the editor simplified his problem by trying to please one specific family instead of trying to please that vague abstraction, the public. A writer with no definite audience in mind, indeed, is like a woman buying a wardrobe without thought of its purpose or use, or like a fisherman without the least notion of what kind of fish he is angling for, and therefore without any idea of what bait to use. Probably much of the dullness of student manuscripts results from this failure to have a definite audience in mind.

**Purpose.** In a general sense, every piece of writing you undertake will be to inform, to persuade, or to entertain your audience; and obviously you must know which you are trying to do, or you are likely to start out to do one and end by doing another. You might, for example, begin a paper with the intention of telling how to make a camp (to inform) and end by relating the story of a camping trip on which you had an exciting adventure (to entertain), or begin by explaining the T-formation in football (to inform) and end by arguing that the team needs a new coach who will develop more versatile players (to persuade). It is important, then, to know your *general purpose* in any piece of writing and not to waver from it.

But in each thing you write, you will also have a *specific purpose*. Suppose that in a letter home your specific purpose is to coax an extra allowance from a reluctant parent: you will, of course, direct the whole letter to that end, omitting any reference to extravagancies on your part, stressing extra calls on your purse, and so on. Again suppose that you have chosen as the topic for a paper the general subject "Bee Farming": your specific purpose might be to inform young veterans who are looking for ways to set up in business of the economic advantages of keeping bees, or to inform gardeners and fruit growers of the importance of having a few hives of bees near their gardens or orchards, or to entertain your audience with the humorous situations into which trying to keep bees has brought you.

**Thesis.** The next step preliminary to writing is to formulate a concise, one-sentence statement which will contain the central idea of your whole paper. This is your *thesis sentence*. It tells what your specific purpose is. It is like the beam which guides airplane pilots, for if you state your thesis sentence well and keep it in mind all the while you are writing, it will keep you from rambling off the topic and will "bring you safely into port"—that is, to a clear and logical conclusion.

Suppose your paper is written to persuade the city council or park commission of your city to locate a proposed playground at a certain spot. Your thesis sentence would read, "The playground which the city proposes to lay out should be located on the North Side on the vacant lot at Lake and Huron streets." Note these points concerning the thesis sentence: (1) it is a declarative sentence; (2) it contains the idea which the readers are to take away on completing the reading of the paper; (3) it is intimately related to the specific purpose of the paper (if it is not so related, your logic is faulty, and you probably have two distinct topics in mind); (4) the grammatical subject of the thesis sentence is the subject of the entire paper (the thesis sentence simply adds a predicate to that subject so that the audience will know what to think concerning the topic under consideration).

If you were writing on the subject we have just been considering, you would have a form somewhat like the following:

Subject: a playground for Haysville
Audience: city officials (mayor, city council, park commission)
Purpose:
General: to persuade
Specific: to induce the city authorities to locate the proposed playground on the North Side on the vacant lot at Lake and Huron streets.
Thesis sentence: The proposed playground for Haysville should be located on the North Side on the vacant lot at Lake and Huron streets.

**Tone.** Very early in the process of planning an article, a writer should decide on the tone he will employ in developing it. Will it be serious, whimsical, gay, pathetic, satirical, or what will it be? His decision will rest in part on the audience to which he is appealing, in part on his own abilities and interests, and in part on his purpose. It would of course be a grave mistake to write in a gay and mirthful mood on the subject of death to one lately bereaved, or to use a deeply serious tone in writing on women's make-up for a group of college students. It would also be an error for a heavy, plodding youth to attempt a playful tone in his writing, or, except in burlesque, for the campus clown to assume a mood of pathos. Some versatile students can adopt a tone suitable to any audience and theme, but those who lack such versatility should recognize their limitations, and choose their subjects and define their specific purpose on the basis of their ability, so that their tone will not conflict with their matter. Whatever the tone a writer employs, it should be chosen consciously, and should be appropriate to his subject, his audience, and his purpose.

**Title.** Subject and title must not be confused: the former is the general matter with which a writer is dealing; the latter is the name given to his composition. The chief purpose of a title is to give a reader an immediate idea of the substance of a piece of writing, or to attract his notice and make him wish to read it. The choosing of an interesting or expressive title, therefore, is an important, if minor, element in the production of a successful manuscript, and should not be done haphazardly or carelessly, as is so often true in student compositions. Some writers have a particular aptitude in choosing interesting titles. How much more interesting is such a title as *Life Is My Song,* which the poet John Gould Fletcher chose for his autobiography, than *The Story of My Life.* A good exercise would be to look at the index of a dozen contemporary magazines, and study the appropriateness and effectiveness of the titles. But whether he does this or not, a writer should give careful attention to his own titles, for the selection of an exact, expressive title is an important initial step in the production of a successful composition.

6    An important suggestion about choosing a title is not to make it too broad or too general. The title "Crows," for instance, is too broad for an article of five hundred words. But if a writer had made a careful study of the habits of crows, or had owned a pet crow and had taught it to speak, or had been interested in the mischievous pranks of a pet crow, he might use such titles as: "The Value of the Crow to the Farmer," "Should Crows Be Destroyed by State Decree?" "How to Teach a Crow to Talk," "How to Keep a Pet Crow without Going Crazy," "Johnny Crow—Conversationalist," "Johnny Crow—Problem Child among Birds," "Are Crows Reincarnations of Peck's Bad Boy?"

From the foregoing titles, another point emerges: the title should not only be narrowed to fit the scope of a paper; it should indicate the tone of the paper. Although it might be possible to write a humorous article on the subject, "The Value of the Crow to the Farmer," this title suggests a serious treatment of the subject. "How to Teach a Crow to Talk," suggests an informative article, giving specific advice. "How to Keep a Pet Crow without Going Crazy" suggests a paper perhaps informative, but certainly humorous. "Johnny Crow—Conversationalist" might be the title of a narrative about a specific crow, or a light essay on the extent and ability of a crow to talk. "Are Crows Reincarnations of Peck's Bad Boy?" suggests a whimsical, pseudoscientific article, treating the subject humorously.

The title should be simple, natural, and reasonably short. It should aim to attract a reader unless the sole function of the article is to inform, in which case it should give an idea of the nature of the information which the article contains; and in any event, it should suggest the tone of the article.

## Should Students Study? [1]

### WILLIAM TRUFANT FOSTER

"Do not let your studies interfere with your college education." This motto adorns the walls of many a student's room. It is his semihumorous way of expressing his semiconviction that studies do not count—that the thing to go in for is—"College Life." This thing, made up of intercollegiate athletics and lesser diversions, is spelled with capitals—with big capitals in the student's mind. This frequenter of college walks and halls and tombs and grandstands I call a "student" for want of a safer term, though it sometimes does him injustice. He has sundry answers to the question whether students should study.

In academic circles, this is not merely an academic question. The boy who goes to college faces it, in one form or another, again and again. Indeed, before he dons his freshman togs, his father has told him to get an all-round education, and may even have given him to understand that deficiencies in scholarship which do not end his college career will be overlooked if he makes the football team. He observes the boys who return from college; he finds that their language and their clothes bear marks of a higher education. He hears accounts of initiations and celebrations. His chum's big brother takes him aside and tells him confidentially just how he must conduct himself in order to be rushed for the right fraternity. Everybody tells him he must be a "good fellow"; few discourse upon the joys of the curriculum. Whether students should study may remain with him an open question, but he begins to doubt whether students do study.

With his mind set on going to college, he reads all that comes to hand on the subject. The newspapers give him vivid details of the games, big and little, with full-page pictures of the heroes. They report nightshirt parades, student riots, dances, beer nights—anything but studies. Now and then they do give space to a professor, if he has been indiscreet, or has appeared to say something scandalous, which everybody in college knows he did not say, or if he is sued for divorce. They even spare him an inch or two if he is awarded a Nobel prize.

1. Reprinted by permission of *Harper's Magazine*.

The lad reads stories of College Life. How they glow with escapades! His mind becomes a moving picture of thrilling escapes, of goats enthroned on professorial chairs, of freshies ducked in chilling waters, of battalions of rooters yelling with the precision of a cash register. Now and then there is mention of lectures and examinations, for it appears that the sophisticated youth knows many devices for "getting by" these impediments to the unalloyed enjoyment of College Life. Surely the high school teacher who spoke with such enthusiasm about the lectures of "Old Socrates" must be hopelessly behind the times. Surely nobody goes to college nowadays for lectures.

After entering college the boy continues his studies in the philosophy of education under the tutelage of a sophomore. His tutor informs him that the object of education is the all-round man. The faculty and the curriculum, he explains, are obstacles, but the upper classes rescue the poor freshman from pentagonal and other primitive shapes and round him out with smokers, hazing, initiations, jamborees, and visits to the big city, where he makes the acquaintance of drinks and ladies far more brilliant-hued than those of his somber native town. He is told that he is "seeing life," and that college will make an all-round man of him yet, if the faculty do not interfere with his education.

If this sophomoric philosophy leaves any doubts to puzzle the freshman, they may be cleared away by the alumni who return to warm up the fraternity house with stories of the good old days. And, of course, the lad joins a fraternity before giving his course of study a thought. For what is college to a non-fraternity man? Merely an institution of learning. To the man with the Greek-lettered pin the fraternity is the *sine qua non* of higher education, the radiant whole of which the college is a convenient part, providing for the fraternity a local habitation.

And so the undergraduate stretches his legs before the hearth and hears the wisdom of the "Old Grad." In his day, it seems, things were different. The students were not such mollycoddles, the beer flowed more freely, and the faculty did not try to run things. No, sir, in the good old days the faculty did not spoil College Life. What a glorious celebration after that 56 to 0 game, when every window in old West Hall was broken and the stoves were thrown downstairs!

"I tell you, boys," cries the Old Grad, warming his feet by the fire and his imagination by the wonder of the freshman, "it is not what you learn in your classes that counts. It is the College Life. Books, lectures, recitations—you will forget all that. Nobody cares after you graduate whether you know any Latin or algebra, unless you are a teacher, and no man can afford to be a teacher nowadays. But you will remember the College Life as long as you live."

Some of the alumni would have a different story to tell, no doubt, but they do not get back often for fraternity initiations. Perhaps they are too busy. And, again, they may have been nothing but "grinds" during their college days. . . .

Is high scholarship worth the effort? In other words, have colleges devised courses of study which bear any relation to the probable careers of their students? Is there any evidence that a man who attains high marks is more likely to achieve success after graduation than a man who is content with passing marks?

If there is any such connection between success in studies and success in life, it should be possible to measure it by approved statistical methods, and thus arrive at conclusions of more value as guidance to the undergraduate than the opinion of any man. Both the professor and the sport are in danger of arguing from exceptional instances—each is likely to find striking cases in proof of his preconceived notions; each is inclined to scorn the opinion of the other.

But conclusions drawn from large numbers of cases, not subject to invalidating processes of selection, and employing terms that are adequately defined for the purpose at hand, must command the respect of all men. If such conclusions do not support the contention that it pays to study, there is something radically wrong with the professor's part of college affairs; different kinds of achievement should receive academic distinction and new tests should be devised. If, on the other hand, present standards for rating students predict their future success with any degree of accuracy, the facts should be discovered and used everywhere to combat the prevalent undergraduate opinion. Whatever the outcome of such studies, we should have them in larger numbers, in many places, protected by every safeguard of scientific method. We may well ask, first, whether promise in the studies of one period becomes performance in the studies of a later period.

Are good students in high school more likely than others to become good students in college? Prof. Walter F. Dearborn tried to answer that question for the State of Wisconsin. He compared the records of hundreds of students at the University of Wisconsin with their records in various high schools. He found that above eighty per cent of those who were in the first quarter of their high school classes remained in the upper half of their classes throughout the four years of their university course, and that above eighty per cent of those who were in the lowest quarter in their high school classes failed to rise above the line of mediocre scholarship in the university. The parallelism is so striking that we are justified in concluding that, except in scattering cases, promise in the high school becomes performance in the college. Indeed, only one student out of nearly five hundred in this investigation who fell among the lowest quarter in the high school attained the highest rank in the university. Of course, a boy may loaf in high school and take his chance of being the one exception among five hundred. But he would hardly be taking a sporting chance; it would be rather a fool's chance. The risk would be less in going over Niagara Falls in a barrel.

The University of Chicago found that high school students who failed to attain an average rank higher than the passing mark, by at least twenty-five per cent of the difference between that passing mark and one hundred, failed in their college classes. The faculty therefore decided not to admit such students. Exceptions were made of the most meritorious cases, but few of these exceptions made satisfactory records in the college.

Basing its policy upon such evidence as this, Reed College, at the beginning of its work five years ago, decided to admit, as a rule, only students who ranked in the first third of their preparatory-school classes. Some exceptions have been made. Twenty per cent of those admitted were known to be below the first third, and two per cent below the median line. In all cases these candidates were regarded as the most promising of those who fell below the first third in high school rank, yet almost without exception they have failed to rise above the lowest quarter of their college classes. Thus, it appears that in Oregon, as in Wisconsin and Illinois, those who get the best start in the lower schools maintain their advantage in the upper schools; few of their classmates overtake them.

But why strive for high rank in college? Why not wait for the more "practical" studies of the professional school? Hundreds of boys the country over declare today that it makes little difference whether they win high grades or merely passable grades in the liberal arts, since these courses have no definite bearing on their intended lifework. Almost invariably they are ready to admit that they must settle down to serious effort in the studies of law, medicine, engineering—that is to say, in professional schools. Even the sport who makes the grade of mediocrity his highest aim as a college undergraduate, fully intends to strive for high scholarship in his professional studies. Does he often attain that aim? That is the question.

And that, fortunately, is a question we may answer with more than opinions. We may take, for example, all the students who graduated from Harvard College during a period of twelve years and entered the Harvard Medical School. Of the 239 who received no distinction as undergraduates,

36 per cent graduated with honor from the Medical School. Of the 41 who received degrees of A.B. with high honor, more than 92 per cent took their medical degrees with honor.

Still more conclusive are the records of the graduates of Harvard College who during a period of twenty years entered the Harvard Law School. Of those who graduated from college with no special honor, only 6½ per cent attained distinction in the Law School. Of those who graduated with honor from the college, 22 per cent attained distinction in the Law School; of those who graduated with great honor, 40 per cent; and of those who graduated with highest honor, 60 per cent. Sixty per cent! Bear that figure in mind a moment, while we consider the 340 who entered college "with conditions"—that is to say, without having passed all their entrance examinations—and graduated from college with plain degrees. Of these men, not 3 per cent won honor degrees in law.

If a college undergraduate is ready to be honest with himself, he must say, "If I am content with mediocre work in college, it is likely that the men in my class who graduate with honor will have three times my chances of success in the Law School, and the men who graduate in my class with highest honor will have nearly ten times my chances of success." So difficult is it for a student to change his habits of life after the crucial years of college that not one man in twenty years—not one man in twenty years—who was satisfied in Harvard College with grades of "C" and lower gained distinction in the studies of the Harvard Law School.

The same relation appears to persist between the promise of Yale undergraduates and their performance in the Harvard Law School. If we divide the 250 graduates of Yale who received their degrees in law at Cambridge between 1900 and 1915 into nine groups, according to undergraduate scholarship, beginning with those who won the highest "Senior Appointments" at Yale and ending with those who received no graduation honors, we find that the first group did the best work in their studies of law, the second group next, the third group next, and so on, in the same order, with but a single exception, to the bottom of the list. The performance at Harvard of each of the eight groups of Yale honor graduates was in precise accordance with the promise of their records at Yale.

Apparently the "good fellow" in college, the sport who does not let his studies interfere with his education, but who intends to settle down to hard work later on, and who later on actually does completely change his habits of life, is almost a myth. At least his record does not appear among those of thousands of students whose careers have been investigated under the direction of President Lowell and others. It seems that results are legal tender, but you cannot cash in good intentions.

"Dignified credit to all," cries the billboard. "Enjoy your new suit now, and pay for it later." Many a boy, lured by the installment plan, expects to get an education on deferred payments in effort, only to find that there is no credit for him, dignified or otherwise. What his honest effort has paid for in full is his today; nothing more by any chance whatever.

But why strive for the highest standing in professional school? Let us pursue the inquiry one step further. Let us ask whether success in studies gives promise of success in life. As far as the study of law is concerned, we may answer at once that the known success of the honor graduates of the Harvard Law School is one reason why even college undergraduates at Cambridge believe that law students should study law—hard and seriously. For the same reason, leading law offices the country over give preference to honor graduates of law schools.

But what is success in life? That is the first problem. It is one difficulty that confronts everyone who attempts to speak with certainty about the meaning of education. There is no accepted definition of the aim of education. The philosopher has been likened to a blind man in a dark cellar hunting for a black cat that isn't there. The aim of education seems as elusive as the proverbial black cat. Nevertheless, we do not close our schools. We strive for concrete ends, such as proficiency in handwriting, aware that any particular end may soon be regarded as not worth the effort to attain it. Until recently we could not say even what we meant by proficiency in handwriting, for we had not attempted to define our aim or devise a measure of our progress toward it. We still speak of educational processes and results about as accurately as the Indians spoke of temperature. We still speak of the science of education without seeming to understand that there is no science without precise measurement. From our fragmentary beginnings to an adequate science of education is a long journey, and the road is beset with difficulties. While we struggle along this road, generations will come and go. We will help them to attain what seem, for the time, the proper aims of education. And each individual will strive for what seems to him success in life.

As one measure of success in life, we may take the judgment of certain men. In so far as we accept their judgment our findings concerning the relation between college studies and this kind of success will seem important to us. Here, as in most questions of educational aim, we can do no better for the present than take the consensus of opinion of competent judges.

Using this measure for success, I endeavored to find out whether the members of the class of 1894 of Harvard College who had become notable in their lifework had been notable in their studies. I therefore asked three judges to select, independently, the most successful men from that class. I chose as judges the dean of the college, the secretary of the Alumni Association, and a professor in Columbia University who is a member of the class, because I thought that these men came nearer than any others to knowing all members of the class. I left each judge free to use his own definition of success, but I asked them not to select men whose achievements appeared to be due principally to family wealth or position. The judges agreed in naming twenty-three successful men. I then had the entire undergraduate records of these men accurately copied from the college records and compared with the standing of twenty-three men chosen at random from the same class.

The result was striking. The men who were thus named as most successful attained in their college studies nearly four times as many highest grades as the random selection. To the credit of the successful men are 196 "A's"; to the credit of the other men, only 56.

Following a similar plan, three judges selected the most successful men among the graduates of the first twenty-four (1878–1901) classes from the University of Oregon. An examination of the scholarship records of these men showed that 53 per cent had been good students and 17 per cent had been weak students. Of the graduates who were not regarded as successful, 52 per cent had been weak students and only 12 per cent had been good students.

Similar results have been found by Prof. A. A. Potter, Dean of the Kansas State Agricultural College, in an unpublished study of the relationship between superiority in undergraduate scholarship and success in the practice of engineering as indicated by salaries received. The Director of the School of Forestry of Yale University has collected evidence of the same kind in an unpublished study of the graduates of the Yale School of Forestry. It appears that about ninety per cent of the men who have had conspicuous success in the field of forestry were among the better students in their professional studies. President Thwing of Western Reserve University, the historian of higher education in America, says that he has found no exception, in the records of any American college, to the general rule that those who achieve most before graduation are likely to achieve most after graduation.

The list of the first ten scholars of each of the classes that graduated from Harvard College in the sixth decade of the last century, as presented by William Roscoe Thayer, is a list of men eminent in every walk of life. Indeed, it is likely that the first quarter in scholarship of any school or college class will give to the world as many distinguished men as the other three quarters.

What can we say in this connection of the 420 living graduates of the ten Wesleyan University classes from 1890 to 1899? Just this: Of the men in that group who graduated with highest honors, 60 per cent are now regarded as distinguished either by *Who's Who in America* or by the judgment of their classmates; of those who were elected to Phi Beta Kappa—the scholarship society—30 per cent; of those who won no superior honors in scholarship, only 11 per cent. Of the men now living who graduated from Wesleyan University between 1860 and 1889, 16 per cent are listed in *Who's Who;* of those who received high honors in scholarship during this period, 50 per cent; of those who attained no distinction as scholars, only 10 per cent.

From the records of 1,667 graduates of Wesleyan University, Professor Nicholson concludes that of the highest-honor graduates (the two or three leading scholars of each class) one out of two will become distinguished; of Phi Beta Kappa men, one out of three; of the rest, one out of ten.

Concerning the value of *Who's Who* as a criterion of success in life, we may say at least this, that it is a genuine effort, unwarped by commercial motives, to include the men and women who have achieved most worthy leadership in all reputable walks of life. Whatever flaws it may have, it is acknowledged to be the best list of names for such uses as we are now making of it—and such changes in the list as any group of competent judges might make would not materially affect the general conclusions we have drawn. . . .

In much that I have said about success I have used the mathematical term "chance," a term as far removed as any term could be from the popular notion of luck. If all these studies prove anything, they prove that there is a long chain of causal connections binding together the achievements of a man's life and explaining the success of a given moment. That is the nonskid chain that keeps him safe in slippery places. Luck is about as likely to strike a man as lightning, and about as likely to do him any good. The best luck a young man can have is the firm conviction that there is no such thing as luck, and that he will gain in life just about what he deserves, and no more. The man who is waiting around for something lucky to turn up has time to see a preparedness parade pass by him—the procession of those who have formed the habit of turning things up. In a saloon at a prairie station in Montana I saw the sign, "Luck beats science every time." That is the motto of the gambler and of every other fool. But all men who have won durable distinction are proof that science beats luck—science operating through the laws of heredity and habit. . . .

Ruskin had no patience with people who talk about "the thoughtlessness of youth" indulgently. "I had infinitely rather hear of thoughtless old age," he declared, "and the indulgence due to *that*. When a man has done his work, and nothing can any way be materially altered in his fate, let him forget his toil, and jest with his fate, if he will; but what excuse can you find for willfulness of thought at the very time when every crisis of future fortune hangs on your decisions? A youth thoughtless! when all the happiness of his home forever depends on the chances or the passions of an hour! A youth thoughtless! when the career of all his days depends on the opportunity of a moment. A youth thoughtless! when his every act is a foundation stone of future conduct, and every imagination a fountain of life or death! Be thoughtless in *any* afteryears, rather than now."

Now let the student profit by the experiences of the thousands who have gone before and greet his next task with the words of Hotspur before the battle of Shrewsbury:

> Oh, gentlemen, the time of life is short;
> To spend that shortness basely were too long,
> If life did ride upon a dial's point,
> Still ending at the arrival of an hour.

## Suggestions for Study

1. This article was written in the "flapper-and-coonskin-coat" age after World War I. From your own experience and observation, have you found the attitudes described in the first nine paragraphs true today?

2. What method did the author use to demonstrate that it is worth a student's while to study? Is he fair in the method he used? Can you suggest a better method?

3. Summarize the investigations which the author reports—methods used, results found.

4. State briefly the basic conclusions which the investigations throughout the article seem to prove.

5. By what means did the author determine what is success in life? Do you consider this a fair method of determining success? If you had this problem, what method would you use?

6. What is the author's attitude concerning luck? Do you consider his conclusions sound on this point? If you disagree, give several instances to show that he is wrong.

7. Explain the meaning of the following words from the article: curriculum, tutelage, sophomoric, meritorious, criterion.

## How to Learn [2]

### EDWARD S. ROBINSON

The old saw says that *Practice makes perfect*. And certainly perfection is unattainable in any of the complex forms of human activity without practice. Mere practice, however, is not enough. There are circumstances when much practice will produce either very little learning or none at all.

A man may pass along a street day after day for years without learning the order of the houses or all the details of their color and shape. Many things along this route he does learn, yet many others he does not learn, even though he is often conscious of them. Of course, if he were told that he had to pass an examination on these familiar scenes, his attitude in passing them would undergo a decisive change. He would now look upon the places that he passed in the attitude of actively intending to remember them. The distinction is between what psychologists call *incidental learning* on the one hand, and *intentional learning* on the other.

The difference in effectiveness of these two types of learning has been brought out by many experiments. Learning is frequently studied by means of an instrument known as the stylus-maze—a labyrinth cut as a groove in a metal sheet. The subject, who is blindfolded, pushes the stylus through the groove until he is able to find the shortest route, the route not involving culs-de-sac. Dr. Louis W. Gellerman recently put two groups of subjects through such a task. The members of one group were told that they were to learn the pattern. Those in the other group were instructed to "run" the maze, but they were not told to learn its pattern. Those who had the conscious intent to learn did learn in about one-fifth the practice required by those without this intent. Some of the latter never did learn the maze. A number of experiments have brought out the same facts for memorization. William McDougall and May Smith, his collaborator, once found that the reading, with no intent to learn, of a list of meaningless syllables would produce learning only after eleven times as many trials as would be required if the intent to learn were consciously present.

The presence of the intent to learn is, then, a prime requisite for effective learning. In much of our reading, typewriting, tennis playing, we are careless in this regard. We put too much faith in sheer repetition and fail to keep in mind the fact that we are trying to improve our knowledge or skill. Any kind of motivation that keeps us conscious that we are

---

2. From *Man as Psychology Sees Him*, by Edward S. Robinson (copyright, 1932). Reprinted by permission of The Macmillan Company, the publishers.

seeking to increase our efficiency is likely to be helpful. Competition, which encourages us to compare our own performance with that of others, is an especially good device for establishing and maintaining a strong intention to learn.

Another important supplement to sheer practice is an understanding of the task before us. Students frequently underscore what they consider important in the text. But too often they underscore almost every line. This indicates that they have not made clear to themselves the exact nature of the task. They hope that they will learn enough, but they do not think over the nature of the lesson. If they did they would not give equal importance to so many items. They would see the relations of parts to whole; they would see a logical structure. Suppose that one is trying to learn about Russia, the gold standard, or the Republican party. He reads books in order to acquire information. But he is likely to learn little unless he thinks as he reads—unless he constantly raises in his own mind the question as to what is important and therefore worthy of special attention and what is unimportant and a proper subject for neglect. Rarely, indeed, does one have reason to learn all that is in a book. But unless one decides on rational grounds what he wants to learn, he will acquire only a few scattered fragments of information which, because of their lack of logical coherence, will soon be forgotten.

There are various ways in which an act of skill or a body of knowledge can be understood, and not all of these are equally useful in aiding the learning process. We have pointed out that the golfer may become concerned with too many features of his play, so that his very understanding constitutes a distraction. Similarly in the acquisition of information, it is possible to understand what one is trying to learn, but at the same time to lay out for oneself a wholly impracticable task. The difficulty is not a lack of understanding of the subject to be mastered, but a lack of *selective* understanding based upon a realistic judgment of the time available and of one's capacity for the task. For adults who wish to go on acquiring useful and interesting knowledge, the importance of the selection in connection with learning can hardly be overestimated. Many a man who has decided to inform himself in regard to the banking system, tariff legislation, or modern painting has soon given up in discouragement; his progress has been impeded by a lack of any clear conception of what he wants to learn.

True, there are difficulties in the way of selecting the critical points in relatively unfamiliar materials. How can one know what parts of a book may safely be neglected until after one has mastered the text as a whole? Unless one is concerned with exceedingly close-knit and technical material, where a thorough understanding of each point is necessary before its successor can be met, the best plan is to begin by reading the entire book as rapidly as is comfortable. This will give one a reasonably accurate idea of the general framework, which in most cases is fairly simple. Then one can go back to the text and pick out and emphasize to oneself the essential ideas. An initial perspective can often be gained by reading the first and last chapters and then proceeding to the middle ones.

Especially in the case of informational learning, a principal cause of inefficiency lies in the fact that the first impression is not adequately supplemented. In one of the most important scientific studies of memory Hermann Ebbinghaus, in 1887, showed that forgetting proceeds very rapidly for material that has been just barely learned. He found that 42% of a list of meaningless syllables were forgotten within twenty minutes. Two days after learning, 72% had been forgotten. After that, forgetting proceeded very slowly, but of course most of the possible loss had occurred. Forgetting of meaningful facts does not take place so rapidly as that of meaningless materials, but the general nature of the process is much the same. Immediately following reading there is typically a swift disintegration of a considerable part of what has been learned. The application of this principle is simple. If one hears a simple fact like a name or a complex set of facts like a play, the time to reënforce the first impression and to cut off the normal process of rapid disintegration is as soon as possible after impression. A number of years ago Harold E. Jones, then at Columbia University, conducted a pretty demonstration of the importance of checking the progress of forgetting. He found that eight weeks after a lecture a college class remembered only 24% of the material that had been presented. But some of the students had been forced to use their knowledge by taking a test right after the lecture. Eight weeks later these students remembered approximately twice as much as did those who had not reënforced their first impression.

There are two important methods of reënforcement. In the case of material that has been read, we may simply turn back to the printed pages and read them over again. Or we may attempt, by our own efforts, to recall what we have read. In most instances the latter is by far the more effective procedure. It may be well to check the correctness of one's recall by referring to the printed page, but this should be done only after the effort to recall has been made. One reason for the difference between these two methods of reënforcement is to be found in the fact that the second involves the kind of use that one will ultimately want to make of one's knowledge. And the sooner the knowledge is put to such active use, the better adapted it will be to that purpose. Another important feature of reënforcement through active recall is that one is forced to put his whole attention upon the facts involved. If one simply reads and re-reads, his rehearsals are likely to become half-hearted.

There is some evidence that skills like golfing and typewriting, which involve adjustments among muscular movements, are not so readily forgotten as is newly acquired information. It is nevertheless important that each lesson be followed by a reënforcing practice and that the practice be of the best kind. As a result of a number of laboratory studies at the University of Chicago, Professor Harvey Carr and his students have shown that, just as in the case of intellectual acquisitions, the person acquiring a motor skill must be put upon his own. It is possible to learn a maze pattern, if through the blocking of the blind alleys, one is forced to go through the correct pathway again and again. This is a good deal like learning a lesson by going over it time after time while looking at the printed page. But this is not an efficient learning method. One will learn more quickly if he is forced to go through the maze while the blind alleys are open. If the performance of a certain task in actual practice involves the temptation to make certain errors, then it is desirable during at least part of the practice to expose the person to some of the errors. In complex skills learning consists quite as much in weakening the wrong acts as it does in strengthening the right ones.

There are applications of this principle in the realm of character building. A schoolmaster was known far and wide for his dominating personality and for his almost complete control over the boys in his school. Yet this sequel is also told. These boys were especially prone to get into trouble of one kind or another after their entrance into university life, where they were thrown upon their own resources. They might have been better prepared to control themselves if, during school days, they had had a little better acquaintance with their own propensities for mischief.

There are certain formal aspects of practice or rehearsal that have to be taken into account in arriving at the conditions of most efficient learning. How long is one to practice at one time, and how frequently is one to repeat the practice sessions? In the early days of experimental psychology there was hope of discovering some single simple formula regarding the optimal distribution of practice. But as this problem has been worked over, it appears that the best distribution of practice varies for the act or material being learned. Unless we are dealing with a very complicated act or a very large body of material, it is better to have the rehearsal period long enough to enable the learner to go through the task as a whole. If, for example, one is trying to learn a speech which is to take a half hour for delivery, it would surely be better not to curtail the single learning period to less than a half hour. The same principle would probably hold for considerably longer units of material. In other words, if the task to be learned has any real unity, it is best to preserve that unity by going through the task as a whole rather than through part of it at one session and another part at another session. There are, of course, limits to this rule. One cannot get all of American history or all of typewriting into a single study period. In such cases, however, it is always possible to find smaller subordinate unities within the larger subject matter. It is probably never justifiable to determine the length of the practice period simply in terms of time. The time element should always be brought into relation to the question of natural divisions within the task. Early investigators, studying the acquisition of fairly simple habits, found that very short practice periods were usually advantageous and their findings were undoubtedly sound for the tasks studied, but when we consider the complexity of a large part of our learning in practical life, we can see that one must reject the simple rule that practice should be interrupted as frequently as possible.

As to the optimal interval between rehearsals, this depends upon the rate at which the material being learned is forgotten. It is desirable, as we have seen, to reënforce the early impressions fairly promptly, because otherwise their influence will be rapidly lost. Later in the learning the intervals may be increased without harm and sometimes with actual advantage. In the main, muscular habits like golfing or typing do well with considerable periods between rehearsals, while ideational habits such as poems or language lessons require earlier repetitions for the best results.

## Suggestions for Study

1. Distinguish incidental learning from intentional learning.

2. How much more effective is intentional learning than incidental learning?

3. What is wrong with trying to memorize everything in a given assignment? After reading this article, select from it those main principles which should be learned.

4. State two important methods of reënforcing initial impressions. Which method is the more valuable?

5. Are skills which involve muscular movement likely to be retained longer than those which involve the acquisition of information?

6. Is it better in learning to follow just the right pattern each time or to strike out on your own and expose yourself to possible errors?

7. Are short periods of practice usually advantageous? What limitations are imposed upon this rule?

8. Formulate a rule for determining the time intervals to elapse between repetitions of a skill to be learned.

9. Write down as succinctly as possible the three major principles of learning formulated here. Then under each principle add the significant minor suggestions that will assist you in learning.

10. Write a thesis sentence for the article. What is the author's general purpose? his specific purpose? For what audience did he write this?

11. Define the following words from this article: stylus, cul-de-sac, impracticable, disintegration, prone, optimal, collaborator.

# The Usefulness of Useless Knowledge[3]

## ABRAHAM FLEXNER

Is it not a curious fact that in a world steeped in irrational hatreds which threaten civilization itself, men and women—old and young—detach themselves wholly or partly from the angry current of daily life to devote themselves to the cultivation of beauty, to the extension of knowledge, to the cure of disease, to the amelioration of suffering, just as though fanatics were not simultaneously engaged in spreading pain, ugliness, and suffering? The world has always been a sorry and confused sort of place —yet poets and artists and scientists have ignored the factors that would, if attended to, paralyze them. From a practical point of view, intellectual and spiritual life is, on the surface, a useless form of activity, in which men indulge because they procure for themselves greater satisfactions than are otherwise obtainable. In this paper I shall concern myself with the question of the extent to which the pursuit of these useless satisfactions proves unexpectedly the source from which undreamed-of utility is derived.

We hear it said with tiresome iteration that ours is a materialistic age, the main concern of which should be the wider distribution of material goods and worldly opportunities. The justified outcry of those who through no fault of their own are deprived of opportunity and a fair share of worldly goods therefore diverts an increasing number of students from the studies which their fathers pursued to the equally important and no less urgent study of social, economic, and governmental problems. I have no quarrel with this tendency. The world in which we live is the only world about which our senses can testify. Unless it is made a better world, a fairer world, millions will continue to go to their graves silent, saddened, and embittered. I have myself spent many years pleading that our schools should become more acutely aware of the world in which their pupils and students are destined to pass their lives. Now I sometimes won-

3. From *Harper's Magazine*. Reprinted by permission of the author.

der whether that current has not become too strong and whether there would be sufficient opportunity for a full life if the world were emptied of some of the useless things that give it spiritual significance; in other words, whether our conception of what is useful may not have become too narrow to be adequate to the roaming and capricious possibilities of the human spirit.

We may look at this question from two points of view: the scientific and the humanistic or spiritual. Let us take the scientific first. I recall a conversation which I had some years ago with Mr. George Eastman on the subject of use. Mr. Eastman, a wise and gentle far-seeing man, gifted with taste in music and art, had been saying to me that he meant to devote his vast fortune to the promotion of education in useful subjects. I ventured to ask him whom he regarded as the most useful worker in science in the world. He replied instantaneously: "Marconi." I surprised him by saying, "Whatever pleasure we derive from the radio or however wireless and the radio may have added to human life, Marconi's share was practically negligible."

I shall not forget his astonishment on this occasion. He asked me to explain. I replied to him somewhat as follows:

"Mr. Eastman, Marconi was inevitable. The real credit for everything that has been done in the field of wireless belongs, as far as such fundamental credit can be definitely assigned to anyone, to Professor Clerk Maxwell, who in 1865 carried out certain abstruse and remote calculations in the field of magetism and electricity. Maxwell reproduced his abstract equations in a treatise published in 1873. At the next meeting of the British Association Professor H. J. S. Smith of Oxford declared that 'no mathematician can turn over the pages of these volumes without realizing that they contain a theory which has already added largely to the methods and resources of pure mathematics.' Other discoveries supplemented Maxwell's theoretical work during the next fifteen years. Finally in 1887 and 1888 the scientific problem still remaining—the detection and demonstration of the electromagnetic waves which are the carriers of wireless signals—was solved by Heinrich Hertz, a worker in Helmholtz's laboratory in Berlin. Neither Maxwell nor Hertz had any concern about the utility of their work; no such thought ever entered their minds. They had no practical objective. The inventor in the legal sense was of course Marconi, but what did Marconi invent? Merely the last technical detail, mainly the now obsolete receiving device called coherer, almost universally discarded."

Hertz and Maxwell could invent nothing, but it was their useless theoretical work which was seized upon by a clever technician and which has created new means for communication, utility, and amusement by which men whose merits are relatively slight have obtained fame and earned millions. Who were the useful men? Not Marconi, but Clerk Maxwell and Heinrich Hertz. Hertz and Maxwell were geniuses without thought of use. Marconi was a clever inventor with no thought but use.

The mention of Hertz's name recalled to Mr. Eastman the Hertzian waves, and I suggested that he might ask the physicists of the University of Rochester precisely what Hertz and Maxwell had done; but one thing I said he could be sure of, namely, that they had done their work without thought of use and that throughout the whole history of science most of the really great discoveries which had ultimately proved to be beneficial to mankind had been made by men and women who were driven not by the desire to be useful but merely the desire to satisfy their curiosity.

"Curiosity?" asked Mr. Eastman.

"Yes," I replied, "curiosity, which may or may not eventuate in something useful, is probably the outstanding characteristic of modern thinking. It is not new. It goes back to Galileo, Bacon, and to Sir Isaac Newton, and it must be absolutely unhampered. Institutions of learning should be devoted to the cultivation of curiosity and the less they are deflected by considerations of immediacy of application, the more likely they are to contribute not only to human welfare but to the equally important satisfaction of intellectual interest which may indeed be said to have become the ruling passion of intellectual life in modern times."

What is true of Heinrich Hertz working quietly and unnoticed in a corner of Helmholtz's laboratory in the later years of the nineteenth century may be said of scientists and mathematicians the world over for several centuries past. We live in a world that would be helpless without electricity. Called upon to mention a discovery of the most immediate and far-reaching practical use we might well agree upon electricity. But who made the fundamental discoveries out of which the entire electrical development of more than one hundred years has come?

The answer is interesting. Michael Faraday's father was a blacksmith; Michael himself was apprenticed to a bookbinder. In 1812, when he was already twenty-one years of age, a friend took him to the Royal Institution where he heard Sir Humphrey Davy deliver four lectures on chemical subjects. He kept notes and sent a copy of them to Davy. The very next year, 1813, he became an assistant in Davy's laboratory, working on chemical problems. Two years later he accompanied Davy on a trip to the Continent. In 1825, when he was thirty-four years of age, he became Director of the Laboratory of the Royal Institution where he spent fifty-four years of his life.

Faraday's interest soon shifted from chemistry to electricity and magnetism, to which he devoted the rest of his active life. Important but puzzling work in this field had been previously accomplished by Oersted, Ampère, and Wollaston. Faraday cleared away the difficulties which they had left unsolved and by 1841 had succeeded in the task of induction of the electric current. Four years later a second and equally brilliant epoch in his career opened when he discovered the effect of magetism on polarized light. His earlier discoveries have led to the infinite number of practical applications by means of which electricity has lightened the burdens and increased the opportunities of modern life. His later discoveries have thus far been less prolific of practical results. What difference did this make to Faraday? Not the least. At no period of his unmatched career was he interested in utility. He was absorbed in disentangling the riddles of the universe, at first chemical riddles, in later periods, physical riddles. As far as he cared, the question of utility was never raised. Any suspicion of utility would have restricted his restless curiosity. In the end, utility resulted, but it was never a criterion to which his ceaseless experimentation could be subjected.

In the atmosphere which envelopes the world today it is perhaps timely to emphasize the fact that the part played by science in making war more destructive and more horrible was an unconscious and unintended by-product of scientific activity. Lord Rayleigh, president of the British Association for the Advancement of Science, in a recent address points out in detail how the folly of man, not the intention of the scientists, is responsible for the destructive use of the agents employed in modern warfare. The innocent study of the chemistry of carbon compounds, which has led to infinite beneficial results, showed that the action of nitric acid on substances like benzene, glycerine, cellulose, etc., resulted not only in the beneficent aniline dye industry but in the creation of nitro-glycerine, which has uses good and bad. Somewhat later Alfred Nobel, turning to the same subject, showed that by mixing nitro-glycerine with other substances, solid explosives which could be safely handled could be produced —among others, dynamite. It is to dynamite that we owe our progress in mining, in the making of such railroad tunnels as those which now pierce the Alps and other mountain ranges; but of course dynamite has been abused by politicians and soldiers. Scientists are, however, no more to blame than they are to blame for an earthquake or a flood. The same thing can be said of poison gas. Pliny was killed by breathing sulphur dioxide in the eruption of Vesuvius almost two thousand years ago. Chlorine was not isolated by scientists for warlike purposes, and the same is true of mustard gas. These substances could be limited to beneficent use, but when the airplane was perfected, men whose hearts were poisoned and whose brains were addled perceived that the airplane, an innocent invention, the result of long disinterested and scientific effort, could be made an instrument of destruction, of which no one had ever dreamed and at which no one had ever deliberately aimed.

In the domain of higher mathematics almost innumerable instances can be cited. For example, the most abstruse mathematical work of the eighteenth and nineteenth centuries was the "Non-Euclidian Geometry." Its inventor, Gauss, though recognized by his contemporaries as a distinguished mathematician, did not dare to publish his work on "Non-Euclidian Geometry" for a quarter of a century. As a matter of fact, the theory of relativity itself with all its infinite practical bearings would have been utterly impossible without the work which Gauss did at Göttingen.

Again, what is known now as "group theory" was an abstract and inapplicable mathematical theory. It was developed by men who were curious and whose curiosity and puttering led them into strange paths; but "group theory" is today the basis of the quantum theory of spectroscopy, which is in daily use by people who have no idea as to how it came about.

The whole calculus of probability was discovered by mathematicians whose real interest was the rationalization of gambling. It has failed of the practical purpose at which they aimed, but it has furnished a scientific basis for all types of insurance, and vast stretches of nineteenth century physics are based upon it.

From a recent number of *Science* I quote the following:

> The stature of Professor Albert Einstein's genius reached new heights when it was disclosed that the learned mathematical physicist developed mathematics fifteen years ago which are now helping to solve the mysteries of the amazing fluidity of helium near the absolute zero of the temperature scale. Before the symposium on intermolecular action of the American Chemical Society Professor F. London, of the University of Paris, now visiting professor at Duke University, credited Professor Einstein with the concept of an "ideal" gas which appeared in papers published in 1924 and 1925.
>
> The Einstein 1925 reports were not about relativity theory, but discussed problems seemingly without any practical significance at the time. They described the degeneracy of an "ideal" gas near the lower limits of the scale of temperature. Because all gases were known to be condensed to liquids at the temperatures in question, scientists rather overlooked the Einstein work of fifteen years ago.
>
> However, the recently discovered behavior of liquid helium has brought the side-tracked Einstein concept to new usefulness. Most liquids increase in viscosity, become stickier and flow less easily, when they become

colder. The phrase "colder than molasses in January" is the layman's concept of viscosity and a correct one.

Liquid helium, however, is a baffling exception. At the temperature
known as the "delta" point, only 2.19 degrees above absolute zero, liquid
helium flows better than it does at higher temperatures and, as a matter
of fact, the liquid helium is about as nebulous as a gas. Added puzzles in
its strange behavior include its enormous ability to conduct heat. At the
delta point it is about 500 times as effective in this respect as copper at
room temperature. Liquid helium, with these and other anomalies, has
posed a major mystery for physicists and chemists.

Professor London stated that the interpretation of the behavior of
liquid helium can best be explained by considering it as a Bose-Einstein
"ideal" gas, by using the mathematics worked out in 1924–25, and by
taking over also some of the concepts of the electrical conduction of
metals. By simple analogy, the amazing fluidity of liquid helium can be
partially explained by picturing the fluidity as something akin to the
wandering of electrons in metals to explain electrical conduction.

Let us look in another direction. In the domain of medicine and public
health the science of bacteriology has played for half a century the leading
role. What is its story? Following the Franco-Prussian War of 1870, the
German Government founded the great University of Strasbourg. Its first
professor of anatomy was Wilhelm von Waldeyer, subsequently professor
of anatomy in Berlin. In his *Reminiscences* he relates that among the
students who went with him to Strasbourg during his first semester there
was a small, inconspicuous, self-contained youngster of seventeen by name
Paul Ehrlich. The usual course in anatomy then consisted of dissection
and microscopic examination of tissues. Ehrlich paid little or no attention
to dissection, but, as Waldeyer remarks in his *Reminiscences:*

> I noticed quite early that Ehrlich would work long hours at his desk,
> completely absorbed in microscopic observation. Moreover, his desk grad-
> ually became covered with colored spots of every description. As I saw
> him sitting at work one day, I went up to him and asked what he was
> doing with all his rainbow array of colors on his table. Thereupon this
> young student in his first semester supposedly pursuing the regular course
> in anatomy looked up at me and blandly remarked, *"Ich probiere."* This
> might be freely translated, "I am trying" or "I am just fooling." I replied
> to him, "Very well. Go on with your fooling." Soon I saw that without
> any teaching or direction whatsoever on my part I possessed in Ehrlich
> a student of unusual quality.

Waldeyer wisely left him alone. Ehrlich made his way precariously
through the medical curriculum and ultimately procured his degree
mainly because it was obvious to his teachers that he had no intention of
ever putting his medical degree to practical use. He went subsequently to

Breslau where he worked under Professor Cohnheim, the teacher of our own Dr. Welch, founder and maker of the Johns Hopkins Medical School. I do not suppose that the idea of use ever crossed Ehrlich's mind. He was interested. He was curious; he kept on fooling. Of course his fooling was guided by a deep instinct, but it was a purely scientific, not an utilitarian motivation. What resulted? Koch and his associates established a new science, the science of bacteriology. Ehrlich's experiments were now applied by a fellow student, Weigert, to staining bacteria and thereby assisting in their differentiation. Ehrlich himself developed the staining of the blood film with the dyes on which our modern knowledge of the morphology of the blood corpuscles, red and white, is based. Not a day passes but that in thousands of hospitals the world over Ehrlich's technic is employed in the examination of the blood. Thus the apparently aimless fooling in Waldeyer's dissecting room in Strasbourg has become a main factor in the daily practice of medicine.

I shall give one example from industry, one selected at random; for there are scores besides. Professor Berl, of the Carnegie Institute of Technology (Pittsburgh) writes as follows:

> The founder of the modern rayon industry was the French Count Chardonnet. It is known that he used a solution of nitro cotton in ether-alcohol, and that he pressed this viscous solution through capillaries into water which served to coagulate the cellulose nitrate filament. After the coagulation, this filament entered the air and was wound up on bobbins. One day Chardonnet inspected his French factory at Besançon. By an accident the water which should coagulate the cellulose nitrate filament was stopped. The workmen found that the spinning operation went much better without water than with water. This was the birthday of the very important process of dry spinning, which is actually carried out on the greatest scale.

I am not for a moment suggesting that everything that goes on in laboratories will ultimately turn to some unexpected practical use or that an ultimate practical use is its actual justification. Much more am I pleading for the abolition of the word "use," and for the freeing of the human spirit. To be sure, we shall thus free some harmless cranks. To be sure, we shall thus waste some precious dollars. But what is infinitely more important is that we shall be striking the shackles off the human mind and setting it free for the adventures which in our own day have, on the one hand, taken Hale and Rutherford and Einstein and their peers millions upon millions of miles into the uttermost realms of space and, on the other, loosed the boundless energy imprisoned in the atom. What Rutherford and others like Bohr and Millikan have done out of sheer curiosity in the effort to understand the construction of the atom has released forces which may transform human life; but this ultimate and unforeseen and unpredictable practical result is not offered as a justification for Rutherford or Einstein or Millikan or Bohr or any of their peers. Let them alone. No educational administrator can possibly direct the channels in which these or other men shall work. The waste, I admit again, looks prodigious. It is not really so. All the waste that could be summed up in developing the science of bacteriology is as nothing compared to the advantages which have accrued from the discoveries of Pasteur, Koch, Ehrlich, Theobald Smith, and scores of others—advantages that could never have accrued if the idea of possible use had permeated their minds. These great artists—for such are scientists and bacteriologists—disseminated the spirit which prevailed in laboratories in which they were simply following the line of their own natural curiosity.

I am not criticising institutions like schools of engineering or law in which the usefulness motive necessarily predominates. Not infrequently the tables are turned, and practical difficulties encountered in industry or in laboratories stimulate theoretical inquiries which may or may not solve the problems by which they were suggested, but may also open up new vistas, useless at the moment, but pregnant with future achievements, practical and theoretical.

With the rapid accumulation of "useless" or theoretic knowledge a situation has been created in which it has become increasingly possible to attack practical problems in a scientific spirit. Not only inventors, but "pure" scientists have indulged in this sport. I have mentioned Marconi, an inventor, who, while a benefactor to the human race, as a matter of fact merely "picked other men's brains." Edison belongs to the same category. Pasteur was different. He was a great scientist; but he was not averse to attacking practical problems—such as the condition of French grapevines or the problems of beer-brewing—and not only solving the immediate difficulty, but also wresting from the practical problem some far-reaching theoretic conclusion, "useless" at the moment, but likely in some unforeseen manner to be "useful" later. Ehrlich, fundamentally speculative in his curiosity, turned fiercely upon the problem of syphilis and doggedly pursued it until a solution of immediate practical use—the discovery of salvarsan—was found. The discoveries of insulin by Banting for use in diabetes and of liver extract by Minot and Whipple for use in pernicious anemia belong in the same category: both were made by thoroughly scientific men, who realized that much "useless" knowledge had been piled up by men unconcerned with its practical bearings, but that the time was now ripe to raise practical questions in a scientific manner.

Thus it becomes obvious that one must be wary in attributing scientific discovery wholly to any one person. Almost every discovery has a long and precarious history. Someone finds a bit here, another a bit there. A third step succeeds later and thus onward till a genius pieces the bits together and makes the decisive contribution. Science, like the Mississippi, begins in a tiny rivulet in the distant forest. Gradually other streams swell its volume. And the roaring river that bursts the dikes is formed from countless sources.

I cannot deal with this aspect exhaustively, but I may in passing say this: over a period of one or two hundred years the contributions of professional schools to their respective activities will probably be found to lie, not so much in the training of men who may tomorrow become practical engineers or practical lawyers or practical doctors, but rather in the fact that even in the pursuit of strictly practical aims an enormous amount of apparently useless activity goes on. Out of this useless activity there come discoveries which may well prove of infinitely more importance to the human mind and to the human spirit than the accomplishment of the useful ends for which the schools were founded.

The considerations upon which I have touched emphasize—if emphasis were needed—the overwhelming importance of spiritual and intellectual freedom. I have spoken of experimental science; I have spoken of mathematics; but what I say is equally true of music and art and of every other expression of the untrammeled human spirit. The mere fact that they bring satisfaction to an individual soul bent upon its own purification and elevation is all the justification that they need. And in justifying these without any reference whatsoever, implied or actual, to usefulness we justify colleges, universities, and institutes of research. An institution which sets free successive generations of human souls is amply justified whether or not this graduate or that makes a so-called useful contribution to human knowledge. A poem, a symphony, a painting, a mathematical truth, a new scientific fact, all bear in themselves all the justification that universities, colleges, and institutes of research need or require. . . .

## Suggestions for Study

1. What is the general purpose of the author in this article? What is the specific purpose? Write a thesis sentence for the article.

2. What change does he note in his own thinking (paragraph 2)?

3. Show how the author's conversation with Mr. Eastman corroborates the title of the article.

4. What did the author think the outstanding characteristic of modern thinking?

5. What quality did Paul Ehrlich have as a student? To what did this ultimately lead?

6. Are the great scientific discoveries usually the product of one man's work?

7. On what basis is an institution justified?

8. Define the following words from the article: humanistic, obsolete, prolific, beneficent, spectroscopy, anomalies, prodigious.

### Suggestions for Writing

1. List the graduates of your high school for any three-year period five years ago or longer. Find out their grades while in the high school, and compare the present success of those receiving D's and failure with those receiving A's and B's. (Include your basis of measuring success.)

2. Talk with some upperclassman who is recognized as an exceptionally good student, find out from this student his methods of study, and write a paper on the information you obtain.

3. Talk with as many "old grads" and upperclassmen of different interests as you can, ask their advice on what attitude you should have towards your studies, and write a paper embodying the results.

4. Write an article for high-school seniors, giving your own attitude towards college work and advising them on the way in which they should act in college.

# III
# READING

FROM all sides on college campuses come complaints about the reading ability of students. The science teacher is irritated by the inability of his students to read laboratory instructions correctly; the history teacher finds that his class is powerless to derive the essential truth from a few pages of an only moderately difficult assignment; the teacher of literature is horrified at the failure of upperclassmen to comprehend Dryden or Arnold. If this is true in colleges and universities, it is certainly more true in the world at large.

The tragedy of the situation is that the majority of poor readers do not know the source of their difficulty. A student who spends three hours on an assignment and then fails on a test or is unable to recite in class may conclude that the reading was extraordinarily difficult or that the test was unfair or that he himself is stupid. Of course, one or all of these things may be true, but there is a great possibility that the student has never learned to read efficiently. What he could not accomplish in three hours he might be able to accomplish in an hour and a half if he could diagnose his faults and remedy them intelligently.

The sensible attitude to have about reading is that it represents a group of techniques that can be learned and improved upon. The person who, upon learning that he is a poor reader, shrugs his shoulders and says, "I guess that's the way I'm made" is not facing the facts. Although he may have to unlearn some bad habits and learn some new ones, if he has normal eyesight, moderately good health, and fair intelligence, he can become a good reader.

**Methods for Different Types of Reading.** The first consideration in learning to be a good reader is to recognize that the nature of the printed material should determine the method to be used. For a person to peruse an article in a Sunday newspaper supplement with the same minute attention that he focuses on a chapter in his textbook on economics is as foolish as to try to mow a lawn with a pair of grass shears. Francis Bacon wrote, "Some books are to be tasted, others to be swallowed, and some few to be chewed and digested; that is, some books are to be read only in parts; others to be read, but not curiously [i.e., with close scrutiny]; and some few to be read wholly, and with diligence and attention." A girl student may be a very rapid and efficient reader of current fiction, but perform badly when given an assignment in her biology textbook, even though she may like biology. A boy who is majoring in biology and handles his textbook assignments admirably may be so slow and clumsy in reading fiction that he deems it a waste of time. If the girl and the boy could combine their abilities, they would make one all-round reader. Her difficulty is that she has never mastered the technique of thoughtful, word-for-word and line-for-line following of a passage. He, on the other hand, tries to use the same method for fiction that he uses for his science texts, and is equally a failure. He has tried to chew and digest that which should only be tasted or swallowed.

When one reads a novel, he wants to know what happens, to understand the motivations of the characters, and to get the flavor of the author's style. Rarely is it important or necessary in novel-reading to weigh and analyze each word and phrase and to check painstakingly one's comprehension of the material for fear some detail has been overlooked. Actually, such a method is probably a deterrent to effective reading of fiction, because movement and change are fundamental factors in every story. Unless one can read rapidly enough to perceive these factors, his appreciation of the book is stunted. On the other hand, when an attorney reads the statement of a legal decision, he pays minute attention to the smallest details, looking for possible ambiguities and loopholes. The reading which an ordinary college student does runs the gamut between these extremes. If he is a good reader, he discovers what methods to apply to each situation.

Perhaps a reading test was given you when you entered college. If not, perhaps tests are available for students who ask for them. The diagnostic value of these tests is considerable: they may reveal to you peculiarities in your reading habits which handicap you in competition with other students. But if tests are not given and are not available, you can perform some experiments for yourself which may be just as illuminating. Make a number of charts like Chart I on page 53. Keep on a single chart a record of a week's reading. By the time you have done this for several weeks, you will have a fairly accurate idea of your rate of reading for different kinds of material. Determine the rate by dividing the number of pages by the time required.

Another testing device which any student can use for himself is this: Get a book (preferably not from the library, since you would then have to return it in two weeks or less) containing material which is not fiction, but which is not so difficult nor so dry but that you can maintain some interest in it for a long time, perhaps three months. Such a book might be Zweig's *Marie Antoinette,* Zinsser's *Rats, Lice, and History,* or Van Loon's *The Arts.* Divide it into sections which are approximately of such length that you are sure you can read each of them in less than thirty minutes. Do not simply count off arbitrarily a fixed number of pages for each section, but try to make each unit more or less independent, perhaps using chapter divisions or subdivisions. Read a section every day, *without interruptions.* Read steadily and as fast as you can without sacrificing comprehension. Keep a record of your experiment on a form similar to Chart II.

If you attempt these exercises conscientiously, they will show you where you stand as a reader; and Chart II may surprise you by showing an increase in rate over a period of time.

**Rate of Reading.** Let it be understood always that of the two factors in good reading, speed and comprehension, the latter is by far the more important. If you are a slow reader, but capable of understanding and evaluating what you read, you are much better off than the person who can skim rapidly but understands little of the content. However, there is no virtue in slowness. Good comprehension is by no means concomitant with a low rate, and with that only. A slow, methodical, careful, and conscientious carpenter will, other things being equal, build a better house than the fast and unscrupulous workman; but the person who pays for the job would prefer a fast carpenter who is also methodical, careful, and conscientious. As a matter of fact, a low rate of reading, as was said before, may be an obstacle in the way of good comprehension, because it tends to admit boredom and fatigue. A good rate of speed for the college student

| Kind (intensive, supplemental, recreational) | Subject Matter | Number of pages | Time | Rate (in pages) |
|---|---|---|---|---|
|  |  |  |  |  |

CHART I

| Author and title of book | | | | | | | |
|---|---|---|---|---|---|---|---|
| Pages | Time begun | Time finished | Time used | Number of lines | Rate | Increase or decrease | Date |
| 1-7 | 5:00 | 5:18 | 18 | 224 | 12+ |  | 10-21-48 |
| 8-16 | 5:00 | 5:21 | 21 | 288 | 14- | +1:2- | 10-22-48 |

CHART II

is approximately three hundred words of ordinary material per minute. Probably most "A" students do considerably better.

*General directions.* Although you cannot add a cubit to your stature by merely taking thought, you can increase your reading speed by nothing more than conscious attention. Pay attention first of all to the physical aspects of the problem. Do your reading in a quiet place. In general, make use of your own room. It will be necessary to work in the library part of the time, especially when assignments are made in reserve books, but even the best supervised college library is full of distracting influences. If your room is not quiet, it is your right and obligation to make it such. See that the light is good. The source of the light should be over your shoulder rather than directly above, nor should it be such as to form a glare in front of you. Reserve the easy chair by the radio for recreational reading only; do your serious study while sitting erect at your desk or study table. Even if it requires severe self-discipline, refrain from getting up and attending to something else every few minutes. A few minutes' relaxation at the end of an hour or an hour and a half should be sufficient. The next suggestion many college students will deride as hopelessly utopian; nevertheless it is based on good psychological principles. It is that if you are in need of sleep or rest, you should get sleep and rest and do your reading when you are physically fit. Forcing yourself to stay awake and read when you should be sleeping is not only to work inefficiently, but also to establish bad emotional attitudes toward the subject matter of the book—perhaps toward studying itself.

When sitting in an upright position, keep your muscles relaxed. Incessant fingering of things on the desk, crossing and uncrossing your legs, and swaying the head or body should be avoided. Also, from the very beginning of the process of consciously improving your reading habits, try to conquer any tendency to vocalize. A great many people are slow readers because they never learned to read silently. There should be a considerable difference between the spoken rate and the silent rate, and if you pronounce the words on the page audibly or under your breath, or even make small movements of the tongue or throat muscles, you have not learned good habits of silent reading and consequently are unnecessarily slow. Semi-illiterate people use all or part of their speech mechanism while reading, mumbling or working their lips, sometimes pointing with their fingers at the words on the page. The student who has habits like these should break them immediately, however difficult it may be to do so. Conscious effort is necessary. Cut down your reading periods to units of ten or fifteen minutes or less. Watch yourself closely during these periods and guard against muscular tension of various kinds. When ability to read easily without any kind of vocalization has been achieved, lengthen the periods.

*Eye movements.* A good deal of emphasis has been placed on eye movements in remedial reading classes, and expensive apparatus has been contrived to chart the progress of a reader's eyes down the page of a book. But without costly apparatus, an observant individual can determine approximately the efficiency of his own method of focusing on the printed page. The chart for the poor reader is likely to show that his eyes move unevenly back and forth, up and down, instead of progressing fairly steadily from left to right through each line.

After the initial stages of learning to read in the primary grades, a person should not have to let his eyes rest on each letter, or even each word, separately; he should be able to take in a *span* of words with each glance. The length of the span will vary, of course, with the reader and with the relative difficulty of the material. The eyes travel, therefore, in a series of jerks, or *fixations,* across the page. It is only during these slight pauses that clear images are made on the retina, and therefore the number of these pauses in a line indicates the span which the reader takes in at each fixation. Sometimes the eyes move backward to get a second or third look at something which was not clearly seen before or which has been forgotten. This is called a *regression.* Obviously, in normal reading, a large number of regressions means inefficiency. By paying attention to the movements of his eyes during reading, a person can gain an approximate knowledge of his own habits. If a second person can be found to assist in the experiment, he can stand behind the reader and observe the reader's eyes in a mirror which has been fixed just above the book. By watching closely, he can count the fixations and regressions which the reader makes as he follows the lines of print.

It cannot be repeated too many times that mere speed in covering the lines on a printed page does not constitute good reading. If a person needs to glance back at something which he did not read carefully enough or does not remember, he certainly should do so. The sole purpose of reading is to comprehend what the page says. A positive correlation exists, however, between speed and comprehension, especially in the reading of easy material. If the images and ideas can be carried to the brain in the coherent manner that they are presented on the page, without hesitation, stumbling, or repetition, comprehension is likely to be better than if the eyes pick up words and phrases in a pattern different from that intended by the author.

**Comprehending the Structure of the Whole.** Good comprehension of anything designed to be read, from a sentence to a book, is a result of three factors: comprehending the structure of the whole, understanding the relation of the parts to the whole, and evaluating the whole and its parts in terms of one's own experience and knowledge. If a book is particularly difficult, complete comprehension may come only after several readings. An inefficient reader may have to read even easy material two or more times. A good reader, however, is able to combine all three techniques in one perusal. In this discussion, the three factors will be treated separately, but it should be remembered that they do not necessarily occur separately. Ideally, they occur almost simultaneously.

*Purpose.* Comprehension of the structure of the whole book or passage is arrived at by three steps: understanding the purpose of the author, grasping the problems with which the author is dealing, and knowing the parts into which the whole is divided. The first two steps are closely related, but it should be clear that the reader will never arrive at anything like comprehension until he knows whether the author is going to try to define a problem, argue about it, tell a story about it, give some practical advice about it, or state its emotional connotations. It is impossible to criticize, or even understand, a book until one is clear as to what it tries to do.

Some of the noteworthy guides to the purpose of a book are so obvious that many people hardly notice them. The title, for example, is frequently very helpful. A book written by the eighteenth-century philosopher and historian, David Hume, is entitled *Enquiry Concerning Human Understanding*. Of the two key terms in this title, one (*Enquiry*) states the purpose, and the other (*Human Understanding*) states the problem. An enquiry is a questioning or an investigation for the purpose of learning something. Therefore, the title of this book indicates that the author is not primarily arguing, advising, or emotionalizing; he is investigating.

The preface of a book is commonly overlooked by hasty readers, but it is often a very important part of the work. In the preface the author is likely to explain his own attitude toward his book and tell why he happened to write it. He may attempt to differentiate his book from other works on the same subject; he may even state his purpose explicitly, as Mortimer Adler does in his preface to *How to Read a Book:* "I have tried to write a light book about heavy reading."

Even the table of contents may give hints about the author's purpose. But generally the opening chapter will clarify the reader's knowledge of the author's intention when everything else has failed. It is the most logical place for the author to define his problem and state what he intends to do with it. The opening chapter of an expository book, therefore, should be read with special care, since the information imparted in it is basic to a complete understanding of what follows.

On page 24 of this textbook, under "Preliminary Planning," a distinction is made between the *general purpose* and the *specific purpose* which the writer should have in mind. This distinction may be more useful to the writer than to the reader; yet the reader should bear in mind that, with some books, the particular attitude toward the subject which is taken by the author has a good deal to do with the critical appraisal which is made by the reader. It is plain that Mr. Adler's general purpose in the book mentioned above is expository, but that the exposition is pleasingly informative, not weightily scientific.

Writing a thesis sentence, to refer again to "Preliminary Planning," is an excellent device to force a writer to hold himself strictly to the point which he wants to make. It is also useful to enable the reader to test his own knowledge of the purpose and the main ideas in the book. A thesis sentence which is made for as long a piece of reading as a full-length book must, of course, be very general; yet, if carefully done, it can do a great deal toward cataloguing the book in a reader's mind and helping him understand the main ideas. A thesis sentence for Albert Carr's *Juggernaut* might be stated thus: The dictatorship form of government, from that of England under Cromwell to those of the present time, follows a fairly regular cycle: first, a "strong man" is placed in power because of the collapse of a previous form of government; second, a temporary period of efficiency and military success follows; finally, the exhaustion of internal resources to support a huge standing army leads to insurrection on the part of a large body of the populace.

*Problem.* If one is clear as to the purpose of a book, he may be clear also as to the problem which the author is attacking. The same guides (title, preface, table of contents, and opening chapter) are useful for both purposes. Thus, in the book by David Hume, the title indicates that the author's purpose was to make an enquiry or investigation, and that the problem which he intended to investigate was human understanding. Very often, however, it is not enough to be able to name the problem of a book by means of a phrase or caption. One must also know the meaning of the word or group of words which the author uses to name the problem, and have an understanding of the obligations and limits which such a problem places on the writer. Sometimes the author goes to considerable pains to explain the meaning of his problem to the reader, usually in the preface or first chapter; but more often, especially if he is writing for a fairly select audience, he assumes that the reader will understand without explanation.

To demonstrate the ways in which different kinds of writing impose different kinds of problems upon authors, let us look briefly at history, science, and philosophy.

Students are sometimes amazed to discover that accounts of an incident in history written by two historians differ radically. They have always assumed that the problem of the historian is merely to discover and re-count facts which took place in the past, not realizing that on any day of any year at any place so many things are happening at once that a his-torian of that day is forced to exercise processes of selection and interpre-tation. He must choose for his narrative those occurrences which seem to him to have been most important and tell why they were important in terms of other occurrences. For example, one person who writes an account of one of the big national political conventions may present a graphic and exciting picture of the convention hall, with bunting draped from the roof, orators pounding the speaker's desk, and frenzied delegates stampeding on the floor. Another person may write his account in terms of what happened in obscure hotel rooms and offices far from the more obvious center of activities. The facts in both accounts may be correct, but the two writers have selected different aspects of the convention as the most significant. The person who desires to read history with full com-prehension, then, must realize that the chief problem which the writing of history sets for the author is one of selecting and interpreting significant events. If a student can understand why, for instance, one historian con-siders battles and military campaigns of prime significance while another chooses to emphasize the spread of industry and the rise of unions and strikes, he is one step nearer to being a good reader of history.

Similarly, the student who reads a book of science should have a clear idea of the particular problem or problems with which the author is con-cerned. Stated in general terms, the problem of the writer of a scientific book or article is to describe accurately a set of observed phenomena and state a logical conclusion with respect to their meaning. It is a task in the collecting and interpreting of evidence. The reader must approach the evidence in the same way that the author does; that is, he must appreciate the importance of knowing what kind of evidence he is dealing with and its significance with regard to a possible conclusion. Darwin's *Origin of Species* is a tiresome mass of observation unless one realizes the problem which Darwin set for himself: to note the variations which take place in certain species and state the most logical conclusion which can be drawn concerning what these variations mean.

The reading of philosophy seems particularly difficult for students at the present time largely because they are unaware of the problems of philosophy. Perhaps this is because most of our education is unphilosophical; it is composed of answers to questions instead of the questions themselves. In a classroom we are likely to say this idea or institution is good, instead of asking what is good about this idea or institution. The problem in most philosophy is to ask pertinent questions about man and his universe and to try to answer them, making use of what factual knowledge we possess and substituting logical deduction when facts are not known. Really, the questions which philosophers ask are as old as the race and, if stated in simple terms, would look familiar to almost everybody. The reader of philosophy must know what the question or problem is and what instruments, factual or logical, are being used to arrive at a conclusion.

Although it may appear that this discussion is concerned wholly with expository writing, the principles which have been stated apply equally to the reading of fiction. The writer of fiction certainly has a purpose. Stated in the most general terms, his purpose is to entertain, but there are various ways of entertaining; and furthermore entertainment is sometimes like the sugar coating on a pill—it puts in attractive form an attempt to convince or persuade or to open a reader's eyes to a situation which he might otherwise miss. Every piece of fiction also has a problem. In a mystery story the problem is to focus the reader's attention on discovering the identity of a criminal. In *The Forsyte Saga* it is to show what changes the modern world is making in the wealthy middle classes. The reader who does not discover the purpose and the problem of Sinclair Lewis's *Main Street* cannot read the novel with full comprehension.

*Organization.* The third step, that of discovering the parts into which the whole book or article is divided, is an exercise in outlining, for a discussion of which see pages 367–372 of this book. Sometimes the table of contents is so orderly that the reader will need only to refer to it for the information he desires. Or, again, the author may outline his scheme at the beginning of the book. In a work of some length, the reader should be aware not only of the major classifications of the whole body of material, but also of the organization of subordinate points under the main headings, noting possible parallel methods of procedure which, if grasped in one major division, will assist in the comprehension of others.

Finally, a good exercise to test one's comprehension of the structure of the book is writing out one's discoveries in the following form:

General purpose: . . . . . . . . . . . . . . . . . .
Specific purpose: . . . . . . . . . . . . . . . . . .
Thesis sentence: . . . . . . . . . . . . . . . . . .
Problem (or problems): . . . . . . . . . . . . . . . .
Organization:
    I.   . . . . . . . . . . . . . . . . . . . . .
        A. . . . . . . . . . . . . . . . . . . . .
        B. . . . . . . . . . . . . . . . . . . . .
           1. . . . . . . . . . . . . . . . . . . .
           2. . . . . . . . . . . . . . . . . . . .
    II. (etc.)   . . . . . . . . . . . . . . . . . .

## Understanding the Relation of the Parts to the Whole

*Words (Semantics).* The first procedure in acquiring a complete comprehension in reading is recognizing the purpose, problem, and organization of the whole body of material. The second procedure is relating the parts to the whole. The smallest parts, and frequently the most difficult to understand, are the words. The importance and intricacy of the study of words may be indicated by the fact that *semantics,* the science of meanings, has, in recent years, been suggested by certain people as the basic element in the teaching of rhetoric. We can here consider only a few of the major aspects of semantics.

It is possible for people in conversation or debate to use the same vocabulary and yet not mean at all the same thing. Anyone who is familiar with student discussions in dormitories and rooming houses will recall numerous instances when the discussion came round to the question, "But what do you mean by . . . ?" The words in question were probably common ones in the vocabularies of those present, but the argument hinged on the interpretation of the words in a particular person's vocabulary. A student who was caught using a "pony" during an examination was asked by the dean, "Did you cheat during that examination?" The culprit replied indignantly, "No!"

"But," insisted the dean, "you brought to the examination and used material which had been written and prepared beforehand, did you not?"

"Yes."

"Isn't that cheating?"

"No, I don't call that cheating."

"Then what is cheating?"

"Well . . ." Obviously, the student had no very clear idea as to just what he did mean by cheating. At least, his mind had never associated, in any very active way, the word with the act which he had committed. "Cheating," which had been in his vocabulary since early childhood, had never been attached to the use of a "pony" during an examination.

One of the greatest errors which even educated people make is to suppose that words have necessary and eternally fixed connections with meanings. Among primitive peoples this superstition is particularly prevalent. The savage believes that possessing the name of an object, animal, or spirit gives him magical power over it. As late as the Middle Ages, it was supposed that devils could be called up by merely pronouncing their names. Rumpelstiltskin, a rascal in European folklore, was powerless when his right name was pronounced. In much the same way, modern people unconsciously assume that when they have applied a label they are possessed of some indisputable knowledge about the person or thing to which the label is attached. Just as the small boy says that "pigs are called pigs because they are such dirty animals," the adult thinks, "This man is a banker, and that means that he is rich and stingy" or "This man is a professor, and that means that he is narrow and unsociable." Propagandists are well aware of this tendency of most of us to think in terms of labels instead of the contexts in which labels are used, and make use of "name-calling" as their most effective device.

*The three classes of terms.* Intelligent reading is largely a matter of critical examination of terminology, and the critical approach to words must take into consideration three main classes of terms (exclusive of prepositions, conjunctions, and interjections). The first class is comparatively easy to deal with, since the words in it refer directly to things in nature, or to simple experience with nature. *Sky, sea, table, chair, automobile, theater,* and *bread* are words in this first class. They correspond to concrete experiences in the natural world about which every reader will have somewhat the same idea. Since this is true, it is seldom that they offer much difficulty to the reader; or, if one of these words is unfamiliar, the dictionary will give all the help that is necessary for all practical purposes. Thus, a chair is a piece of furniture, usually with four legs, designed to be sat in; we would all agree with that.

Real difficulty begins to arise when we use words of the second class, those which refer to *classes* of things. Here we advance a step from concrete experience. There need be no confusion when we mention *a* tennis player (say, Bill Tilden) and call him by name. But when we mention tennis players, as a class of human beings, we have departed from an exact, concrete referent. What do we mean? Can all people who ever handled a racket be called tennis players? Do we mean only good tennis players, or only professional tennis players? Again, what do we mean by such words as *society, students, professional men, teachers?* If the context in which such a word is used gives no clue as to what is meant by it, the result is likely to be misunderstanding. For example, in order to understand the old lady who said, "There are no such things as bad boys; only mischievous boys," one would need to make an almost occult analysis of her mind; and certainly there is no world-wide understanding as to who are "Aryans" and who are "Non-Aryans."

The third class of words is by far the most difficult. This class comprises abstractions, such as *goodness, evil, hospitality, justice, democracy, patriotism, religion, wisdom,* which do not correspond to anything in our concrete experience with the world of nature. The student of semantics will say that these terms have no referents, unless such are given in the context. If someone disagrees with us as to what *hospitality* means, or has never heard of the word and wants to know about it, we cannot go and point to *a* hospitality and say, "This is what we mean." We can merely talk about it as relative to other things about which we do agree. Since we cannot refer to any concrete experience to check on the exact meaning of these words, but are dependent on only a kind of gentleman's agreement concerning them, they are the source of much grief. The dictionary will help in defining them, but frequently the dictionary gives many meanings for the same word, and even within the dictionary meanings there are shades of expression which make these words most elusive.

However, we must be continually using these words—and continually reading them, also. The reader who is unfamiliar with the shades of meaning intended by the abstract vocabulary of an author is facing a difficulty which is ruinous unless overcome. As a matter of fact, a person's ability to use and understand words concerned with abstract experience is one of the chief factors which make him a person whom it is possible to educate. (Incidentally, unless the student who reads this chapter knows what is meant by the word *educate,* the preceding sentence is without much meaning. The writer's assumption about the word is that it implies, to a large extent, at least, training in the handling of ideas and values rather than training in mechanical skills. But there, again, at least three more words have been used which should be looked at twice: *skills, values,* and *ideas.*)

Professional publicity writers and propaganda experts find it easy to influence the opinions and arouse the emotions of people who are not aware of the dangers lying in wait for those who read and listen to abstract terminology. In *Ends and Means,* Mr. Aldous Huxley lays a great responsibility on educators to train young people to be on their guard against careless and unscrupulous users of this kind of diction. For example, the words *state, nation,* and *national honor* are used in every issue of a newspaper without clear referents. What is meant when we use the word *nation:* a constitution? a form of government? the Smiths and Browns and Joneses who are in positions of political leadership? Who, asks Mr. Huxley, is entitled to speak for this "nation" and determine when the "national honor" has been stained? Inasmuch as most people have no clear understanding as to what is meant by many of the stirring words in our patriotic vocabulary, such words offer convenient and effective instruments to the hands of men who wish to sway emotions in behalf of partisan interests. Students should learn to look behind these "thick veils of misleading verbiage"; they should be taught to search for the referents which make abstract terminology meaningful or empty.

*Comprehending difficult terminology.* Few mechanical rules can be prescribed for developing the ability to comprehend abstract terminology. One needs, first of all, to be able to recognize these bothersome words when he comes to them. Practice, close attention, and the comparing of one person's interpretation with another's should help the reader to recognize them. If a student finds that his interpretation of a passage is different from that of his instructor, instead of attributing the difference to the instructor's superior intelligence, he should reread the passage to see if he has missed something. Of course, it may be the student who is right and the instructor who is wrong, but the chances are that the student read the passage wrongly because he lacked comprehension of the words.

Having recognized, in something he is reading, a word which belongs in these categories of slippery terminology, the student must do whatever he can to give it the kind of meaning which the author intended. The different meanings given by the dictionary should be tested. Some of these meanings will obviously be inapplicable; of those meanings which *might* apply, which should be chosen? This is the place for considering the word in its context—that is, considering the word against the background of the other words and sentences which surround it, taking into account, also, the author and his purpose. This may sound like reasoning in a circle: in order to read well, you have to know the exact meaning of words; but to know the exact meaning of words, you must be able to read other words well. In a way, this criticism is good, but learning to read well is like any other complex learning process; the various techniques support one another, and the learner is likely to take several steps simultaneously.

Let us take, for example, the adjective *middle-class.* In a very strict sense, middle-class people are those with average incomes (figured on a basis including the very lowest as well as the very highest in a very large group, such as a nation), who enjoy an average standard of living, and whose ideals and ideas are commensurate with those of other people in the same economic range. The term, in itself, is one of neither approbation nor disparagement.

However, read the following sentences carefully:

> Our candidate is a middle-class American who knows what the people want and who will support sane legislative measures.
> He came from a middle-class home, from which he inherited his smug conservatism.

The speaker of the first sentence is trying to appeal to a mass of voters; consequently, he uses *middle-class* in a way which connotes soundness and democratic feeling; there is a loosely implied relationship to sanity. The second speaker uses the term with a sneer. *Smug conservatism* is evidently a characteristic of a middle-class home, according to his usage. Note, however, that it is the context in both instances which gives the reader the clue. Take the first clause in each sentence ("Our candidate is a middle-class American . . ." "He came from a middle-class home . . .") and there is no indication that the term is used differently, but add the modifying clauses and it appears that two sets of meanings are in operation.

This is what is meant by reading words in their contexts. Like people, words change with the company they keep. A man sitting in a quiet church on Sunday morning will function quite differently from the same man sitting in the bleachers on a Saturday afternoon watching a baseball game. The function and personality of a word may change just as radically in different contexts.

Let it be noted also that a word should be judged not only by the other words about it, but also by the author and his purpose. In the example in the second paragraph above, the author of the first sentence is evidently a politician whose purpose is to solicit votes for a candidate whom he is supporting. The class which wields the greatest voting power is the *middle* class, the common people. In identifying his candidate with this class, the author would certainly not use the term disparagingly. On the other hand, the second writer is attempting to analyze someone's character. In so doing, he assumes the role of an intellectual speaking to other intellectuals, and consequently uses the term in question in a way which implies a disparaging criticism.

The problem, then, which a person faces in trying to read accurately terminology of the second and third classes is to find *in the context* clues which will enable him to supply the missing referent. Stated from the point of view of the writer, the problem is to avoid the use of abstractions the exact meaning of which will not be clear to a person who reads his work with reasonable care. The obligation placed upon both reader and writer to come to terms with each other has been a heavy one since the early days of communication, but it is particularly heavy in these modern times when ideas and values are suffering a heavy bombardment and when propaganda experts have learned to play insidiously upon our tendency to be lazy about words. As instruments for motivating conduct, words contain dynamite. Like all high explosives, they should be approached with caution and used with care.

*Shifts in meaning.* While it is a common experience to misunderstand someone because we do not use his vocabulary with exactly the same meanings that he attaches to it, the student who believes that words and their meanings live in a kind of divinely ordained matrimony sometimes experiences a jolt when he realizes the enormous number of words which neither have nor have had the same meanings for everybody. While some words remain stable for thousands of years, their number is comparatively small. From the beginning of language, the meanings of words have been a matter of convention. There is nothing immutable or sacred about words. They are instruments of communication which are subject to changes in culture, technology, thought, and mere habits of usage; and the sooner one understands the impermanence of meanings, the sooner he will lay the foundation for good comprehension of the printed page. Mark Sullivan, in Volume Four of *Our Times,* notes how the general emphasis on material values during the 1920's affected the meanings of the words *sell, publicity,* and *propaganda.* Although *Webster's Dictionary* for 1929 still defined *sell* as a verb meaning to transfer goods at a price, the word was actually being used in a variety of situations connected only figuratively with merchandising. Any attempt to attract another's attention favorably was likely to be called "selling yourself to him"; a politician would try to "sell the League of Nations" to the people; and a missionary, instead of converting the heathen, might be said to be "selling religion to the heathen." As late as the administration of Woodrow Wilson, *publicity* meant letting in the light of day upon public corruption, but it soon came to be a synonym for *advertising.* At the end of the nineteenth century *propaganda* was limited almost entirely to the propagating of religious faith; during World War I it meant disseminating deceitful information; but during the 1920's the word was taken over by business and became, ironically, nearly synonymous with *advertising* and *publicity.*

Although we are discussing the acquiring of techniques for reading present-day English, it may serve to quicken the sense of changes in meaning in modern English to examine briefly some of the ways by which changes have taken place in the past. Two of the most common kinds of semantic change have been generalization and specialization. In the process of generalization, a word is extended to embrace more than it did originally; in specialization, a word is restricted to include less than it did before. Through generalization, the Old English word *berem* (barley) became Present English *barn;* the Old English *thing* (legal gathering) became Present English *thing;* the word *picture* originally meant only a painting, but now it means any representation of an object on a flat surface, such as a painting, a drawing, or a photograph. Through specialization, the Shakespearean word *deer* (animal) became Present English *deer* (a particular kind of animal); the German *hund* (dog) became Present English *hound;* and *corn,* which in British usage means *grain,* has come to mean a special kind of grain in America.

Two other kinds of semantic change have been labeled degeneration and elevation. Illustrations of words affected by these processes should be sufficient to show what the terms mean. By degeneration, the Old English *saelig* (fortunate, happy) became Present English *silly;* Old English *hūs-wīf* (housewife) became Present English *hussy; villain* originally meant the occupant of a villa, or country house; and Present English *stink* was once Old English *stincan,* meaning *"smell."* By elevation, Old English *cnicht* (servant or retainer) became Present English *knight;* the Latin *nescius* (not knowing) became Present English *nice;* and Old English *cwēn* (wife) became Present English *queen.*

Among other kinds of change, only two need be mentioned, and an appreciation of these pertains more to critical reading than to accurate reading. *Euphemization* is the tendency to cushion one's meaning by using a falsely pretty word for the plain one which fits more exactly. It usually connotes sentimentality, an overdelicate desire to avoid unpleasant facts. We are notoriously adept at concocting euphemisms for the verb *died; passed away, passed on, passed to the great beyond* are a very few of them. Even *kicked the bucket* seems preferable in some quarters to *died.* By the same process, the insurance agent becomes an "assessor of life values," and the beauty parlor operator becomes a "beautician." Like euphemization, *hyperbolization,* the tendency to use a word which is too strong for its context ("terribly" happy, "awfully" pleased), tends to weaken and confuse original meanings. The student should avoid these tendencies in his writing, and when he finds them in his reading, he should be aware of the kind of sentimental or impulsive thinking they represent.

The point to be remembered chiefly, however, is that these processes of change not only have been taking place since men first began to communicate by means of words, but are at work at the present time. Far from being static, words are constantly being stretched or limited, are unexpectedly going uphill or downhill. As a result of a recent semantic change, we may cite the term *genteel tradition* as used by critics and historians of nineteenth century American literature. Now, *genteel,* in the vocabularies of many persons, particularly persons of the nineteenth century, was a "good" word; that is, it meant something admirable and worth emulating: refined, gentlemanly, courteous, in harmony with well-bred society. But in the term *genteel tradition* it is a "bad" word, meaning refined beyond naturalness, ornate, mincing, squeamish, pertaining to a veneer of culture hiding a shoddy interior.

Before leaving this brief discussion of the method of reading words, one should know that he has really been studying the *denotations* and *connotations* of words. The denotation of a word is its meaning as given by the dictionary; to arrive at it is comparatively easy. The connotation of a word is an implied meaning—probably one of a number of possible implied meanings, the exact one to be determined by an examination of the context. In the discussion of *middle-class,* the denotation was given first; then two possible connotations of the word were explained. Connotations are subtle and slippery. Practice in placing words intelligently in their contexts is the only prescription for increasing one's ability to read words with a full appreciation of their true meanings.

*Sentences and Paragraphs.* From understanding words in their contexts to reading sentences efficiently is a short step. Like words, sentences also may have denotative and connotative functions; and if one understands the principles underlying these functions with regard to words, with a little practice he should be able to apply them to groups of words.

The denotation of a sentence is, of course, the factual information or opinions which are communicated. With a sentence as simple as "The cat ate the mouse" the reader has no difficulty. The statement could not be made more simply or directly; it is, one might say, completely denotative. But a poor reader will profit by making a short summary of such a sentence as that which opens the *Declaration of Independence:* "When in the course of human events, it becomes necessary for one people to dissolve the political bands which have connected them with another, and to assume among the powers of the earth, the separate and equal station to which the laws of nature and of nature's God entitle them, a decent respect to the opinions of mankind requires that they should declare the causes which impel them to the separation." Such a summary may resemble the following: "When a group of people find it necessary to secede from a government, and become an independent state, they are obligated to communicate to the rest of mankind the causes of the separation." If you can make an accurate paraphrase of a difficult sentence, you are master of at least its denotation. However, do not be content with the first paraphrase which comes into your head. The object of the exercise is to determine what the sentence means, not what you think it means.

There are key words in every sentence, and one should acquire the habit of finding them at a glance. The two most important key words are the subject and the verb. Next in importance are the complements. Thus, in the simple sentence quoted above, the three key words are *cat, ate,* and *mouse.* Finding such words immediately and, if the sentence is particularly difficult, underlining them, will provide a solid basis for comprehending the whole. In addition to key words, many sentences contain what might be called pivot words and phrases. These are conjunctions or other transitional devices upon which a sentence swings from one direction to another, the direction depending on the kind of pivot which is used. In the sentence "The weather was brisk this morning, just right for a hike, but George moped in his room," the meaning swings like a teeter-totter on the conjunction *but.* Notice the difference which the choice of conjunctions makes in this sentence:

and
but
Jack fell down and broke his crown, (;) then Jill came tumbling after.
nevertheless
moreover

Inasmuch as student writing is frequently deficient in the proper use of transitional words and phrases, it is logical to suspect that student readers are none too observant of these small but exceedingly important elements.

So much for the denotation of the sentence, the basic meaning which is modified or amplified by the connotation. As in words, connotations in sentences are likely to be more subtle and elusive than denotations. In spoken language, the inflections of the voice provide a great deal of the connotative value. Test this by repeating to yourself "He is a thief," placing the emphasis on different words and changing the pattern of pitch. But, except for italicizing emphatic words, written language must depend for connotative value on the choice of words and their position in the sentence. In both spoken and written communication, the *manner* in which something is said has a great deal to do with the full meaning of the information or the opinion which is expressed.

Let us refer again to the first sentence in the *Declaration of Independence,* which we shall repeat, along with the paraphrase which was made of it.

> When in the course of human events, it becomes necessary for one people to dissolve the political bands which have connected them with another, and to assume among the powers of the earth, the separate and equal station to which the laws of nature and of nature's God entitle them, a decent respect to the opinions of mankind requires that they should declare the causes which impel them to the separation.
>
> When a group of people find it necessary to secede from a government, and become an independent state, they are obligated to communicate to the rest of mankind the causes of the separation.

What is implied in the first statement that is not expressed in the second? In the first place, the diction of the original sentence is more stately than that of the paraphrase. Why did Thomas Jefferson write, "When in the course of human events" instead of just "when"; "dissolve the political bands" instead of "secede"; "assume among the powers of the earth, the separate and equal station" instead of "become an independent state"; "a decent respect to the opinions of mankind requires" instead of "they are obligated"? Was it not because he felt the great importance of the document he was writing and wished it to be couched in language which fitted the occasion? It is as if he were saying, at the same time that he expressed the idea stated in the paraphrase, "I want you to know that this is an extremely important document written for a very momentous occasion." This, then, is one of the connotations of the sentence.

Another connotation is this: "It should be understood that this is not an unconsidered or rash decision; we have done a great deal of serious thinking before making it." This the reader infers from the slow and weighty movement of the sentence and from such phrases as "the course of human events," "the laws of nature and of nature's God," and "a decent respect to the opinions of mankind." Still a third connotation is, "This decision has been made in a spirit of reverence," a meaning which is evoked by the reference to "the laws of nature and of nature's God." These are only a few of the many little gleams of meaning which the carefully prepared manner of the sentence connotes. Perhaps they will be of help in understanding why the original sentence seems so rich and important, whereas the paraphrase is so commonplace and uninspiring. Perhaps, also, they will indicate that, if it is the power of connotation which constitutes much of the difference between good writing and ordinary writing, it is the ability to grasp connotation which, to a great extent, distinguishes a good reader from a merely average one.

A final suggestion, as an aid to understanding both denotation and connotation, is to keep aware of the speaker, the audience, the purpose, the place, and the time. These elements may seem too obvious to deserve much consideration; yet they are of prime value in comprehending the meaning and evaluating the effectiveness of any communication. The speaker, or writer, of the *Declaration of Independence* was Thomas Jefferson, a young man suddenly placed in the midst of great events. His audience included, as he implied, all mankind, but particularly the people of America (divided bitterly over the question of independence) and the people of England (many of whom believed that the British government was unjust). His purpose was two-fold: to stimulate into activity the colonists who were in favor of separation; and to state the case for separation in as dignified and favorable a light as possible in order to win friends, at home and abroad, among those who were as yet undecided. The place was Philadelphia, the seat of the Continental Congress, and the time was the momentous year 1776. All these elements, especially the speaker, the audience, and the purpose, contribute specifically to an understanding of the reasons for the document being exactly what it is—and the reasons for there being a *Declaration of Independence* at all.

While the principles of denotation and connotation have thus far been applied only to words and sentences, it should not require a great deal of insight to discover that they apply also to paragraphs and even longer units. Indeed, the larger the unit, the more evidence there is from which to derive a proper understanding of the meanings. As with the sentence, the short paraphrase is useful in determining the denotation of a paragraph and segregating from the basic words, phrases, and sentences those which have connotative values.

The connotative meanings are derived from the choice of words, the characteristic sentence patterns, and the structure of the paragraph as a whole. Is the diction formal, colloquial, or slangy; does it connote severity, earnestness, whimsicality, loquacity, irony, humor, geniality, or bumptiousness? Do the sentences give a feeling of stiffness, awkwardness, scholarly thoroughness, or easy familiarity? Is the paragraph well organized, showing orderly thinking about the subject, or is it indicative of chaotic thinking? Is the paragraph so brief that it appears to have been ripped out of its context in the heat of excitement, or does its length connote a leisurely and careful examination of ideas? These are a few of the questions which can be asked with respect to units longer than a sentence.

Thus, an attempt has been made to show that words, sentences, and larger units can communicate in different ways and on different levels. The reader who cannot grasp all the meanings can be likened to a partially deaf person who cannot hear sounds high in the scale of pitch, except that the inefficient reader can, in all probability, remedy his difficulty by his own efforts, whereas the deaf man must remain incapacitated.

**Evaluating the Whole.** The statement was made earlier in this discussion that good comprehension is a result of three factors: comprehending the structure of the whole, understanding the relation of the parts to the whole, and evaluating the whole in terms of one's own knowledge or experience. The first two factors have been discussed, and only a brief word need be said about the third factor, inasmuch as it is treated at some length in the part of this book devoted to the book review.

Never be content with saying merely "I like this book" or "I don't like this book." Inability to give satisfactory reasons for a judgment indicates inattentive or untrained reading methods. Reading with a full understanding of purpose, problem, and instruments should provide something which can be compared with one's own knowledge of the subject matter and general experience with life. This little outline may serve in evaluating something which has been read:

1. What is the author's purpose?
2. What means does he use to achieve his purpose?
3. To what extent are his methods successful and why?
4. Is the author's purpose worthy of the effort?

The habit of critical reading is chiefly, as Mortimer Adler says, the habit of "talking back" to a book. Keep asking questions and demanding answers to them. Subject statements and situations to the test of your own common sense and experience with living. Check the reliability of the author's information. Examine the logic of his argument. In other words, be the master of what you read.

*Exercises in Reading*

A selection by Stevenson is analyzed below to illustrate a method for the analysis of sentences and paragraphs. Following the example are six selections. Using the suggestions of the sample analysis, analyze each of the six selections. (Since questions on literal meaning differ for each selection, these are given after each selection; for suggestions B to G refer to the sample analysis.)

## An Apology for Idlers

### R. L. STEVENSON

Just now, when everyone is bound, under pain of a decree in absence convicting him of *lèse*-respectability, to enter on some lucrative profession, and labor therein with something not far short of enthusiasm, a cry from the opposite party who are content when they have enough, and like to look on and enjoy in the meanwhile, savors a little of bravado and gasconade. And yet this should not be. Idleness, so-called, which does not consist in doing nothing, but in doing a great deal not recognized in the dogmatic formularies of the ruling class, has as good a right to state its position as industry itself. It is admitted that the presence of people who refuse to enter in the great handicap race for sixpenny pieces, is at once an insult and a disenchantment for those who do. A fine fellow (as we see so many) takes his determination, votes for the sixpences, and in the emphatic Americanism, "goes for" them. And while such a one is plowing distressfully up the road, it is not hard to understand his resentment, when he perceives cool persons in the meadows by the wayside, lying with a handkerchief over their ears and a glass at their elbow. Alexander is touched in a very delicate place by the disregard of Diogenes. Where was the glory of having taken Rome for these tumultuous barbarians who poured into the Senate house and found the Fathers sitting silent and unmoved by their success? It is a sore thing to have labored along and scaled the arduous hilltops, and when all is done, find humanity indifferent to your achievement. Hence physicists condemn the unphysical; financiers have only a superficial toleration for those who know little of stocks; literary persons despise the unlettered; and people of all pursuits combine to disparage those who have none.

A. Questions on literal meaning. Underline the correct elements.

1. The ideas which are about to be stated may sound like (a) foolish and excessive talking, (b) excessive respectability, (c) sober wisdom.

2. The idleness which is going to be discussed consists in (a) engaging in no activity, (b) engaging in activity which is not generally recognized as profitable, (c) engaging in bustling and money-grabbing.

3. People who are energetically engaged in a particular activity are annoyed by people who disparage that activity because of (a) fear that the government will be overthrown, (b) fear that the stock market will be upset, (c) injury to their self-esteem.

B. Manner of expression.

1. Choice of words: The language used in this passage is distinctly liter-

ary. The author makes use of a large vocabulary, but his choice of words is not that of common speech or ordinary direct expression, indicating that he is consciously trying to produce unusual effects with his language. (Examples: *bravado and gasconade, dogmatic formularies, an insult and a disenchantment, takes his determination, plowing distressfully, tumultuous barbarians, arduous hilltops*.) The figures of speech (*decree in absence, great handicap race for sixpenny pieces, scaled the arduous hilltops*) are ingenious and show imagination. The references to American slang, Alexander, and the sack of Rome indicate wide reading.

2. Sentence patterns: The characteristic sentence structure is long and rhythmical, but short sentences (such as "And yet this should not be.") spaced among the long ones prevent the style from seeming heavy. The sentences are artistically varied as to the positions of the various elements, flow smoothly, and give the effect of long experience in the use of literary English.

3. Structure of the paragraph: The paragraph proceeds logically from a statement of the leading idea to a restatement of it and then to a set of illustrations. The paragraph is well integrated. The last sentence, with its balanced series of independent clauses, the last of which returns to a statement of the leading idea, produces an effect of good craftsmanship and finality.

C. The speaker: Robert Louis Stevenson, a professional English author of the latter half of the nineteenth century, was particularly successful with romantic stories of action and adventure and with informal essays of a leisurely type. A chronic invalid, he spent some time in the United States and lived his last years on an island in the South Seas in pursuit of simple living and colorful romance.

D. The audience: Judged on the basis of vocabulary, sentence structure, and allusions, the audience for which Stevenson was writing was composed of educated, well-read people with time and a taste for considering ideas for their own sake.

E. The purpose: To explain and defend an attitude toward life which does not set the ordinary high premium on a busy pursuit of money.

F. The place: A British magazine devoted to literary and political writing.

G. The time: The year 1877, a time when industrial expansion, in both the United States and England, was reaching a high point in its history.

*Denotation:* In spite of its unpopularity at the present time, owing largely to the tendency of human beings to be annoyed by modes of living different from their own, the point of view of the person who does not wish to join in the busy pursuit of money deserves to be stated.

*Connotations:* I, an artist in words, find this era of industrialism in which I live uncongenial to my tastes. As an artist, a connoisseur of things which cannot be valued in money, I resent being looked down upon by those who consider money and the activities which procure it of highest value. I like to think that those whose lives are consumed in lucrative industry are not as bad as they seem, but that they have made an unwise choice, and, having made the choice, find it necessary to disparage people like me in order to protect their own self-esteem.

# I. The Diffusion of Cultural Traits [1]

### FRANZ BOAS

We are too much inclined to consider the development of civilization in Europe as an achievement of Europe alone, and to assume that Europe has always been the giver, not the recipient of new ideas. We are likely to forget that in antiquity the exchange of inventions and ideas extended from China all over the continent to Europe, and that the indirect contact between the Far East and Europe contributed much to the development of European civilization. We are likely to forget the immense service that Arab scientists did to Europe in re-establishing the contact with Greek thought. Later on, when contact with the Far East was interrupted by the Turkish invasion of eastern Europe and the development of the Mongolian empire, the need for contact with the East led to maritime discoveries, and the discovery of America brought inventions to Europe which modified life in many parts of the Old World. I need only mention the introduction of Indian corn, which in an incredibly short time found its way to all parts of the Old World that were adapted to its cultivation, or the use of tobacco, which has reached all parts of the inhabitable world.

Questions on literal meaning. Underline the correct elements.

1. Ideas and inventions (a) have always originated in Europe, (b) have always originated in Asia, (c) have, since the discovery of America, invariably originated in this hemisphere, (d) have filtered into Europe from all parts of the world.
2. Arab scientists (a) helped to revive Greek thought in Europe, (b) did much to confuse our knowledge of what the Greeks thought, (c) were the means of bringing Chinese culture to Europe.
3. The development of the Mongol empire (a) caused the Turkish invasion of Europe, (b) temporarily halted traffic between Europe and China, (c) caused Americans to raise tobacco for European consumption.
4. Indian corn was introduced to Europe from (a) America, (b) the East Indies, (c) Arabia, (d) China.

1. From *Social Research, an International Quarterly of Political and Social Science*. Reprinted by permission of the publisher.

## II. Jay Gould

HENRY ADAMS

Mr. Jay Gould was a partner in the firm of Smith, Gould and Martin, brokers, in Wall Street. He had been engaged before now in railway enterprises, and his operations had not been of a nature to encourage public confidence in his ideas of fiduciary relations. He was a broker, and a broker is almost by nature a gambler, perhaps the very last profession suitable for a railway manager. In character he was strongly marked by his disposition for silent intrigue. He preferred as a rule to operate on his own account, without admitting others into his confidence, and he seemed never to be satisfied except when deceiving everyone as to his intentions. There was a reminiscence of the spider in his nature. He spun huge webs, in the corners and in the dark, which were seldom strong enough to resist a serious strain at the critical moment. His disposition to this subtlety and elaboration of intrigue was irresistible. It is scarcely necessary to say that he had not a conception of moral principle. In speaking of this class of men it must be fairly assumed at the outset that they do not and cannot understand how there can be a distinction between right and wrong in matters of speculation, so long as the daily settlements are punctually effected. In this respect Mr. Gould was probably as honest as the mass of his fellows, according to the moral standard of the street; but without entering upon the technical questions of roguery, it is enough to say that he was an uncommonly fine and unscrupulous intriguer, skilled in the processes of stock-gambling, and passably indifferent to the praise or censure of society.

Questions on literal meaning. Underline the correct elements.

1. Jay Gould's previous relations with the railway business had been (a) questionable, (b) indicative of stupidity, (c) strictly honorable.
2. He was by disposition (a) frank, (b) genial, (c) secretive, (d) irascible.
3. He was like a spider because he (a) devoured his victims, (b) built flimsy structures of finance, (c) seemed to crawl when he walked.
4. In his speculations Gould was (a) less honorable than, (b) as honorable as, (c) more honorable than most of the other men engaged in the same activities.
5. He (a) liked the approbation of the public, (b) cared nothing about it, (c) disliked it.

## III. Of Education

### JOHN MILTON

The end then of learning is to repair the ruins of our first parents by regaining to know God aright, and out of that knowledge to love him, to imitate him, to be like him, as we may the nearest by possessing our souls of true virtue, which being united to the heavenly grace of faith, makes up the highest perfection. But because our understanding cannot in this body found itself but on sensible things, nor arrive so clearly to the knowledge of God and things invisible, as by orderly conning over the visible and inferior creature, the same method is necessarily to be followed in all discreet teaching. And seeing every nation affords not experience and tradition enough for all kinds of learning, therefore we are chiefly taught the languages of those people who at any time have been most industrious after wisdom; so that language is but the instrument conveying to us things useful to be known. And though a linguist should pride himself to have all the tongues that Babel cleft the world into, yet if he have not studied the solid things in them, as well as the words and lexicons, he were nothing so much to be esteemed a learned man, as any yeoman or tradesman competently wise in his mother dialect only.

Questions on literal meaning. Underline the correct elements.

1. The ultimate purpose of education is (a) to make a person better than his father and mother, (b) to remedy the evil which Adam and Eve brought upon mankind, (c) to teach a person to imitate his elders.
2. Human understanding is gained (a) by studying men and the physical world, (b) by faith and prayer, (c) by unexpected flashes of intuition.
3. The principal method of education is (a) to teach the student the language of his native land, (b) to teach the languages of the wisest nations, (c) to teach reading, writing, and arithmetic.
4. The study of languages is useful (a) in itself, (b) because it marks one as a cultured person, (c) because it opens the way to learning other things.

## IV. Speech at the Cooper Institute

### ABRAHAM LINCOLN

. . . If slavery is right, all words, acts, laws, and constitutions against it are themselves wrong and should be silenced and swept away. If it is right, we cannot justly object to its nationality—its universality; if it is wrong, they cannot justly insist upon its extension—its enlargement. All they ask we could readily grant, if we thought slavery right; all we ask they could as readily grant, if they thought it wrong. Their thinking it right and our thinking it wrong is the precise fact upon which depends the whole controversy. Thinking it right as they do, they are not to blame for desiring its full recognition as being right; but thinking it wrong as we do, can we yield to them? Can we cast our votes with their view and against our own? In view of our moral, social, and political responsibilities, can we do this?

Wrong as we think slavery is, we can yet afford to let it alone where it is, because that much is due to the necessity arising from its actual presence in the nation; but can we while our votes will prevent it allow it to spread into the national Territories and to overrun us here in these free States? If our sense of duty forbids this, then let us stand by our duty fearlessly and effectively. Let us be diverted by none of those sophistical contrivances wherewith we are so industriously plied and belabored— contrivances such as groping for some middle ground between the right and the wrong, vain as the search for a man who should be neither a living nor a dead man; such as a policy of "don't care" on a question about which all true men do care. . . .

Neither let us be slandered from our duty by false accusations against us nor frightened from it by menaces of destruction to the government or of dungeons to ourselves. Let us have faith that right makes might, and in that faith let us to the end dare to do our duty as we understand it.

Questions on literal meaning. Underline the correct elements.

1. The question of slavery is one on which (a) both sides may be right, (b) one side must be right and the other wrong, (c) it is the part of wisdom to take no sides.
2. Lincoln believes that (a) slavery should be immediately abolished, (b) slavery should not be allowed to spread, (c) slavery should be disregarded as a national issue.

## V. First Inaugural Address

### THOMAS JEFFERSON

During the contest of opinion through which we have passed, the animation of discussions and of exertions has sometimes worn an aspect which might impose on strangers unused to think freely and to speak and write what they think; but this being now decided by the voice of the nation, announced according to the rules of the Constitution, all will, of course, arrange themselves under the will of the law, and unite in common efforts for the common good. All, too, will bear in mind this sacred principle, that though the will of the majority is in all cases to prevail, that will, to be rightful, must be reasonable; that the minority possess their equal rights, which equal laws must protect, and to violate would be oppression. Let us, then, fellow citizens, unite with one heart and one mind; let us restore to social intercourse that harmony and affection without which liberty, and even life itself, are but dreary things. And let us reflect, that, having banished from our land that religious intolerance under which mankind so long bled and suffered, we have yet gained little, if we countenance a political intolerance as despotic, as wicked, and capable of as bitter and bloody persecutions. During the throes and convulsions of the ancient world, during the agonized spasms of infuriated man, seeking through blood and slaughter his long-lost liberty, it was not wonderful that the agitation of the billows should reach even this distant and peaceful shore . . . and should divide opinions as to measures of safety; but every difference of opinion is not a difference of principle. We have called by different names brethren of the same principle. We are all Republicans; we are all Federalists. If there be any among us who would wish to dissolve this Union, or to change its republican form, let them stand undisturbed as monuments of the safety with which error of opinion may be tolerated, where reason is left free to combat it. I know, indeed, that some honest men fear that a republican government cannot be strong; that this government is not strong enough. But would the honest patriot, in the full tide of successful experiment, abandon a government which has so far kept us free and firm, on the theoretic and visionary fear that this government, the world's best hope, may, by possibility, want energy to preserve itself? I trust not. I believe this, on the contrary, the strongest government on earth. I believe it the only one where man, at the call of the law, would fly to the standard of the law, and would meet invasions of the public order as his own personal concern. Sometimes it is said that man cannot be trusted with the government of himself. Can he, then, be trusted with the government of others? Or have we found angels in the form of kings to govern him? Let history answer this question.

Questions on literal meaning. Underline the correct elements.

1. A stranger to American ways who witnessed the presidential campaign of 1800 might think that (a) Americans were not interested in politics, (b) the country was on the verge of civil war, (c) there was no freedom of speech in this country.
2. In a republic, the majority must (a) respect the rights and opinions of the minority, (b) adopt the opinions of the minority, (c) pay no attention to the minority.
3. The turmoil in Europe has (a) caused division of opinion in America, (b) been successfully kept from our coasts, (c) caused a wave of immigration.
4. Members of the Federalist and Republican parties are (a) inalienably

separated with respect to their beliefs, (b) in danger of throwing the nation into civil war, (c) people of fundamentally the same principles.

5. Those who wish to destroy the government should (a) be imprisoned, (b) be let alone, (c) be deported to wherever they came from.

6. A government based on republican principles is (a) weaker than, (b) stronger than, (c) as strong as any other kind.

7. History has shown that (a) only angels can govern men well, (b) men can never govern themselves, (c) men have always been governed by men.

## VI. *Prospice*

### ROBERT BROWNING

Fear death?—to feel the fog in my throat,
    The mist in my face,
When the snows begin, and the blasts denote
    I am nearing the place,
The power of the night, the press of the storm,
    The post of the foe;
Where he stands, the Arch Fear in a visible form,
    Yet the strong man must go:
For the journey is done and the summit attained,
    And the barriers fall,
Though a battle's to fight ere the guerdon be gained,
    The reward of it all.
I was ever a fighter, so—one fight more,
    The best and the last!
I would hate that death bandaged my eyes, and forebore,
    And bade me creep past.
No! let me taste the whole of it, fare like my peers
    The heroes of old,
Bear the brunt, in a minute pay glad life's arrears
    Of pain, darkness, and cold.
For sudden the worst turns the best to the brave,
    The black minute's at end,
And the elements' rage, the fiend-voices that rave,
    Shall dwindle, shall blend,
Shall change, shall become first a peace out of pain,
    Then a light, then thy breast,
O thou soul of my soul! I shall clasp thee again,
    And with God be the rest!

Questions on literal meaning. Underline the correct elements.

1. Browning believes that death is (a) an easy transition from one state to another, (b) a terrible experience which he hates to face, (c) a terrible experience which he will face boldly.
2. The "foe" in line 6 is (a) death, (b) Satan, (c) the speaker's conscience.
3. Browning (a) relishes, (b) is resigned to, (c) cannot bear the thought of the last and greatest fight.
4. Browning thinks of himself as (a) an ordinary person, (b) a great sinner, (c) a hero.
5. The most desirable result of death will be (a) light, (b) the presence of a loved person, (c) peace out of pain.

## From *The Hero as Man of Letters*

### THOMAS CARLYLE

Our pious fathers, feeling well what importance lay in the speaking of man to men, founded churches, made endowments, regulations; everywhere in the civilized world there is a pulpit, environed with all manner of complex dignified appurtenances and furtherances, that therefrom a man with the tongue may, to best advantage, address his fellow men. They felt that this was the most important thing; that without this there was no good thing. It is a right pious work, that of theirs; beautiful to behold! But now with the art of writing, with the art of printing, a total change has come over that business. The writer of a book, is not he a preacher preaching not to this parish or that, on this day or that, but to all men in all times and places? Surely it is of the last importance that *he* do his work right, whoever do it wrong—that the *eye* report not falsely, for then all the other members are astray! Well; how he may do his work, whether he do it right or wrong, or do it at all, is a point which no man in the world has taken the pains to think of. To a certain shopkeeper, trying to get some money for his books, if lucky, he is of some importance; to no other man of any. Whence he came, whither he is bound, by what ways he arrived, by what he might be furthered on his course, no one asks. He is an accident in society. He wanders like a wild Ishmaelite, in a world of which he is as the spiritual light, either the guidance or the misguidance!

Certainly the art of writing is the most miraculous of all things man has devised. Odin's *Runes* were the first form of the work of a hero; *books,* written words, are still miraculous *runes,* the latest form! In books lies the *soul* of the whole past time; the articulate audible voice of the past, when the body and material substance of it has altogether vanished like a dream. Mighty fleets and armies, harbors and arsenals, vast cities, high-domed, many-engined—they are precious, great; but what do they become? Agamemnon, the many Agamemnons, Pericleses, and their Greece—all is gone now to some ruined fragments, dumb mournful wrecks and blocks; but the books of Greece! There Greece, to every thinker, still very literally lives; can be called up again into life. No magic *rune* is stranger than a book. All that mankind has done, thought, gained, or been—it is lying as in magic preservation in the pages of books. They are the chosen possession of men.

Do not books still accomplish *miracles,* as *runes* were fabled to do? They persuade men. Not the wretchedest circulating-library novel, which foolish girls thumb and con in remote villages, but will help to regulate the actual practical weddings and households of those foolish girls. So "Celia" felt, so "Clifford" acted: the foolish theorem of life, stamped into those young brains, comes out as a solid practice one day. Consider whether any *rune* in the wildest imagination of mythologist ever did such wonders as, on the actual firm earth, some books have done! What built St. Paul's Cathedral? Look at the heart of the matter, it was that divine Hebrew BOOK—the word partly of the man Moses, an outlaw tending his Midianitish herds, four thousand years ago, in the wilderness of Sinai! It is the strangest of things, yet nothing is truer. With the art of writing, of which printing is a simple, an inevitable and comparatively insignificant corollary, the true reign of miracles for mankind commenced. It related, with a wondrous new contiguity and perpetual closeness, the past and distant with the present in time and place; all times and all places with this our actual here and now. All things were altered for men, all modes of important work of men: teaching, preaching, governing, and all else.

To look at teaching, for instance. Universities are a notable, respectable product of the modern ages. Their existence too is modified, to the very basis of it, by the existence of books. Universities arose while there were yet no books procurable; while a man, for a single book, had to give an estate of land. That, in those circumstances, when a man had some knowledge to communicate, he should do it by gathering the learners round him, face to face, was a necessity for him. If you wanted to know what Abelard knew, you must go and listen to Abelard. Thousands, as many as thirty thousand, went to hear Abelard and that metaphysical theology of his. And now for any other teacher who had also something of his own to teach, there was a great convenience opened: so many thousands eager to learn were already assembled yonder; of all places the best place for him was that. For any third teacher it was better still; and grew ever the better, the more teachers there came. It only needed now that the king took notice of this new phenomenon; combined or agglomerated the various schools into one school; gave it edifices, privileges, encouragements, and named it *Universitas,* or School of all Sciences: the University of Paris, in its essential characters, was there. The model of all subsequent universities, which down even to these days, for six centuries now, have gone on to found themselves. Such, I conceive, was the origin of universities.

It is clear, however, that with this simple circumstance, facility of getting books, the whole conditions of the business from top to bottom were changed. Once invent printing, you metamorphosed all universities, or superseded them! The teacher needed not now to gather men personally round him, that he might *speak* to them what he knew: print it in a book, and all learners far and wide, for a trifle, had it each at his own fireside, much more effectually to learn it!—Doubtless there is still peculiar virtue in speech; even writers of books may still, in some circumstances, find it convenient to speak also—witness our present meeting here! There is, one would say, and must ever remain while man has a tongue, a distinct province for speech as well as for writing and printing. In regard to all things this must remain; to universities among others. But the limits of the two have nowhere yet been pointed out, ascertained, much less put in practice; the university which would completely take in that great new fact, of the existence of printed books, and stand on a clear footing for the nineteenth century as the Paris one did for the thirteenth, has not yet come into existence. If we think of it, all that a university or final highest school can do for us, is still but what the first school began doing—teach us to *read*. We learn to *read,* in various languages, in various sciences; we learn the alphabet and letters of all manner of books. But the place where we are to get knowledge, even theoretic knowledge, is the books themselves! It depends on what we read, after all manner of professors have done their best for us. The true university of these days is a collection of books. . . .

On all sides, are we not driven to the conclusion that, of the things which man can do or make here below, by far the most momentous, wonderful, and worthy are the things we call books! Those poor bits of rag paper with black ink on them—from the daily newspaper to the sacred Hebrew BOOK, what have they not done, what are they not doing! For . . . whatever be the outward form of the thing (bits of paper, as we say, and black ink), is it not verily, at bottom, the highest act of man's faculty that produces a book? It is the *thought* of man; the true thaumaturgic virtue; by which man works all things whatsoever. All that he does and brings to pass, is the vesture of a thought. This London City, with

all its houses, palaces, steam engines, cathedrals, and huge immeasurable
traffic and tumult, what is it but a thought, but millions of thoughts
made into one—a huge immeasurable spirit of a THOUGHT, embodied in
brick, in iron, smoke, dust, palaces, parliaments, hackney coaches, Kath-
erine docks, and the rest of it! Not a brick was made but some man had
to *think* of the making of that brick. The thing we called "bits of paper
with traces of black ink," is the *purest* embodiment a thought of man
can have. No wonder it is, in all ways, the activest and noblest.

*Suggestions for Study*

1. What change have books and reading made between our time and that
before books existed?
2. What were Odin's runes? (See dictionary.) In what sense were they
miracles?
3. In what sense are books greater than fleets, armies, cities?
4. List the specific "miracles" which Carlyle attributes to books.
5. Explain how universities came into being, according to Carlyle.
6. What is the main use of schools?
7. Define these words from the article: appurtenances, corollary, contiguity,
procurable, metaphysical, theology, agglomerated, edifices, metamorphosed,
superseded, thaumaturgic.

## From *Of Kings' Treasuries*

### JOHN RUSKIN

My first duty this evening is to ask your pardon for the ambiguity of
title under which the subject of this lecture has been announced: for indeed I am not going to talk of kings, known as regnant, nor of treasuries,
understood to contain wealth; but of quite another order of royalty, and
another material of riches, than those usually acknowledged. I had even
intended to ask your attention for a little while on trust, and (as sometimes one contrives, in taking a friend to see a favorite piece of scenery)
to hide what I wanted most to show, with such imperfect cunning as I
might, until we unexpectedly reached the best point of view by winding
paths. But—and as also I have heard it said, by men practiced in public
address, that hearers are never so much fatigued as by the endeavor to
follow a speaker who gives them no clue to his purpose—I will take the
slight mask off at once, and tell you plainly that I want to speak to you
about the treasures hidden in books; and about the way we find them,
and the way we lose them. . . .

Granting that we had both the will and the sense to choose our friends
well, how few of us have the power! or, at least, how limited, for most,

is the sphere of choice! Nearly all our associations are determined by chance, or necessity; and restricted within a narrow circle. We cannot know whom we would; and those whom we know, we cannot have at our side when we most need them. All the higher circles of human intelligence are, to those beneath, only momentarily and partially open. We may, by good fortune, obtain a glimpse of a great poet, and hear the sound of his voice; or put a question to a man of science, and be answered good-humoredly. We may intrude ten minutes' talk on a cabinet minister, answered probably with words worse than silence, being deceptive; or snatch, once or twice in our lives, the privilege of throwing a bouquet in the path of a princess, or arresting the kind glance of a queen. And yet these momentary chances we covet; and spend our years, and passions, and powers in pursuit of little more than these; while, meantime, there is a society, continually open to us, of people who will talk to us as long as we like, whatever our rank or occupation—talk to us in the best words they can choose, and of the things nearest their hearts. And this society, because it is so numerous and so gentle, and can be kept waiting round us all day long—kings and statesmen lingering patiently, not to grant audience, but to gain it!—in those plainly furnished and narrow ante-rooms, our bookcase shelves—we make no account of that company—perhaps never listen to a word they would say, all day long!

You may tell me, perhaps, or think within yourselves, that the apathy with which we regard this company of the noble, who are praying us to listen to them; and the passion with which we pursue the company, probably of the ignoble, who despise us, or who have nothing to teach us, are grounded in this—that we can see the faces of the living men, and it is themselves, and not their sayings, with which we desire to become familiar. But it is not so. Suppose you never were to see their faces—suppose you could be put behind a screen in the statesman's cabinet, or the prince's chamber, would you not be glad to listen to their words, though you were forbidden to advance beyond the screen? And when the screen is only a little less, folded in two instead of four, and you can be hidden behind the cover of the two boards that bind a book, and listen all day long, not to the casual talk, but to the studied, determined, chosen addresses of the wisest of men—this station of audience, and honorable privy council, you despise!

But perhaps you will say that it is because the living people talk of things that are passing, and are of immediate interest to you, that you desire to hear them. Nay, that cannot be so, for the living people will themselves tell you about passing matters, much better in their writings than in their careless talk. But I admit that this motive does influence you, so far as you prefer those rapid and ephemeral writings to slow and enduring writings—books, properly so called. For all books are divisible into two classes: the books of the hour, and the books of all time. Mark this distinction—it is not one of quality only. It is not merely the bad book that does not last, and the good one that does. It is a distinction of species. There are good books for the hour, and good ones for all time; bad books for the hour, and bad ones for all time. I must define the two kinds before I go farther.

The good book of the hour, then—I do not speak of the bad ones—is simply the useful or pleasant talk of some person whom you cannot otherwise converse with, printed for you. Very useful often, telling you what you need to know; very pleasant often, as a sensible friend's present talk would be. These bright accounts of travels; good-humored and witty discussions of questions; lively or pathetic storytelling in the form of novel; firm fact-telling by the real agents concerned in the events of passing history—all these books of the hour, multiplying among us as education becomes more general, are a peculiar possession of the present age: we ought to be entirely thankful for them, and entirely ashamed of ourselves if we make no good use of them. But we make the worst possible use if we allow them to usurp the place of true books: for, strictly speaking, they are not books at all, but merely letters or newspapers in good print. Our friend's letter may be delightful, or necessary, today: whether worth keeping or not, is to be considered. The newspaper may be entirely proper at breakfast time, but assuredly it is not reading for all day. So, though bound up in a volume, the long letter which gives you so pleasant an account of the inns and roads and weather last year at such a place, or which tells you that amusing story, or gives you the real circumstances of such and such events, however valuable for occasional reference, may not be, in the real sense of the word, a "book" at all, nor in the real sense, to be "read." A book is essentially not a talked thing, but a written thing; and written not with a view of mere communication, but of permanence. The book of talk is printed only because its author cannot speak to thousands of people at once; if he could, he would—the volume is mere *multiplication* of his voice. You cannot talk to your friend in India; if you could, you would; you write instead: that is mere *conveyance* of voice. But a book is written, not to multiply the voice merely, not to carry it merely, but to perpetuate it. The author has something to say which he perceives to be true and useful, or helpfully beautiful. So far as he knows, no one has yet said it; so far as he knows, no one else can say it. He is bound to say it, clearly and melodiously if he may; clearly, at all events. In the sum of his life he finds this to be the thing, or group of things, manifest to him—this, the piece of true knowledge, or sight, which his share of sunshine and earth has permitted him to seize. He would fain set it down forever; engrave it on rock, if he could; saying, "This is the best of me; for the rest, I ate, and drank, and slept, loved and hated, like another; my life was as the vapor, and is not; but this I saw and knew: this if anything of mine, is worth your memory." That is his "writing"; it is, in his small human way, and with whatever degree of true inspiration is in him, his inscription, or scripture. That is a "Book."

Perhaps you think no books were ever so written?

But, again, I ask you, do you at all believe in honesty, or at all in kindness? or do you think there is never any honesty or benevolence in wise people? None of us, I hope, are so unhappy as to think that. Well, whatever bit of a wise man's work is honestly and benevolently done, that bit is his book, or his piece of art. It is mixed always with evil fragments—ill-done, redundant, affected work. But if you read rightly, you will easily discover the true bits, and those *are* the book.

Now, books of this kind have been written in all ages by their greatest men—by great readers, great statesmen, and great thinkers. These are all at your choice; and life is short. You have heard as much before; yet, have you measured and mapped out this short life and its possibilities? Do you know, if you read this, that you cannot read that—that what you lose today you cannot gain tomorrow? Will you go and gossip with your housemaid, or your stableboy, when you may talk with queens and kings; or flatter yourselves that it is with any worthy consciousness of your own claims to respect that you jostle with the hungry and common crowd for *entrée* here, and audience there, when all the while this eternal court is open to you, with its society, wide as the world, multitudinous as its days, the chosen and the mighty of every place and time? Into that you may enter always; in that you may take fellowship and rank according to your wish; from that, once entered into it, you can never be an outcast but by your own fault; by your aristocracy of companionship there, your own inherent aristocracy will be assuredly tested, and the motives with which you strive to take high place in the society of the living, measured, as to all the truth and sincerity that are in them, by the place you desire to take in this company of the Dead.

"The place you desire," and the place *you fit yourself for,* I must also say; because, observe, this court of the past differs from all living aristocracy in this—it is open to labor and to merit, but to nothing else. No wealth will bribe, no name overawe, no artifice deceive, the guardian of those Elysian gates. In the deep sense, no vile or vulgar person ever enters there. At the portières of that silent Faubourg St. Germain,[2] there is but brief question: "Do you deserve to enter? Pass. Do you ask to be the companion of nobles? Make yourself noble, and you shall be. Do you long for the conversation of the wise? Learn to understand it, and you shall hear it. But on other terms?—no. If you will not rise to us, we cannot stoop to you. The living lord may assume courtesy, the living philosopher explain his thought to you with considerate pain; but here we neither feign nor interpret; you must rise to the level of our thoughts if you would be gladdened by them, and share our feelings if you would recognize our presence."

This, then, is what you have to do, and I admit that it is much. You must, in a word, love these people, if you are to be among them. No ambition is of any use. They scorn your ambition. You must love them, and show your love in these two following ways.

I. First, by a true desire to be taught by them, and to enter into their thoughts. To enter into theirs, observe; not to find your own expressed by them. If the person who wrote the book is not wiser than you, you need not read it; if he be, he will think differently from you in many respects.

Very ready we are to say of a book, "How good this is—that's exactly what I think!" But the right feeling is, "How strange that is! I never thought of that before, and yet I see it is true; or if I do not now, I hope I shall, some day." But whether thus submissively or not, at least be sure that you go to the author to get at *his* meaning, not to find yours. Judge it afterwards if you think yourself qualified to do so; but ascertain it first. And be sure also, if the author is worth anything, that you will not get at his meaning all at once—nay, that at his whole meaning you will not for a long time arrive in any wise. Not that he does not say what he means, and in strong words too; but he cannot say it all; and what is more strange, *will* not, but in a hidden way and in parable, in order that he may be sure you want it. I cannot quite see the reason of this, nor analyze that cruel reticence in the breasts of wise men which makes them always hide their deeper thought. They do not give it you by way of help, but of reward; and will make themselves sure that you deserve it before they allow you to reach it. But it is the same with the physical type of wisdom, gold. There seems, to you and me, no reason why the electric forces of the earth should not carry whatever there is of gold within it at once to the mountaintops, so that kings and people might know that all the gold they could get was there; and without any trouble of digging, or anxiety, or chance, or waste of time, cut it away, and coin

2. A quarter in Paris where the nobility lived.

as much as they needed. But Nature does not manage it so. She puts it in little fissures in the earth, nobody knows where; you may dig long and find none; you must dig painfully to find any.

And it is just the same with men's best wisdom. When you come to a good book, you must ask yourself, "Am I inclined to work as an Australian miner would? Are my pickaxes and shovels in good order, and am I in good trim myself, my sleeves well up to the elbow, and my breath good, and my temper?" And, keeping the figure a little longer, even at cost of tiresomeness, for it is a thoroughly useful one, the metal you are in search of being the author's mind or meaning, his words are as the rock which you have to crush and smelt in order to get at it. And your pickaxes are your own care, wit, and learning; your smelting furnace is your own thoughtful soul. Do not hope to get at any good author's meaning without those tools and that fire; often you will need sharpest, finest chiseling, and patientest fusing, before you can gather one grain of the metal.

And, therefore, first of all, I tell you earnestly and authoritatively (I *know* I am right in this), you must get into the habit of looking intensely at words, and assuring yourself of their meaning, syllable by syllable—nay, letter by letter. For though it is only by reason of the opposition of letters in the function of signs, to sounds in the function of signs, that the study of books is called "literature," and that a man versed in it is called, by the consent of nations, a man of letters instead of a man of books, or of words, you may yet connect with that accidental nomenclature this real fact— that you might read all the books in the British Museum (if you could live long enough), and remain an utterly "illiterate," uneducated person; but that if you read ten pages of a good book, letter by letter—that is to say, with real accuracy—you are forevermore in some measure an educated person. The entire difference between education and noneducation (as regards the merely intellectual part of it) consists in this accuracy. A well-educated gentleman may not know many languages—may not be able to speak any but his own—may have read very few books. But whatever language he knows, he knows precisely; whatever word he pronounces, he pronounces rightly; above all, he is learned in the *peerage* of words; knows the words of true descent and ancient blood, at a glance, from words of modern canaille; remembers all their ancestry, their intermarriages, distant relationships, and the extent to which they were admitted, and offices they held, among the national noblesse of words at any time, and in any country. But an uneducated person may know, by memory, many languages, and talk them all, and yet truly know not a word of any—not a word even of his own. An ordinarily clever and sensible seaman will be able to make his way ashore at most ports; yet he has only to speak a sentence of any language to be known for an illiterate person; so also the accent, or turn of expression of a single sentence, will at once mark a scholar. And this is so strongly felt, so conclusively admitted, by educated persons, that a false accent or a mistaken syllable is enough, in the parliament of any civilized nation, to assign to a man a certain degree of inferior standing forever.

And this is right; but it is a pity that the accuracy insisted on is not greater, and required to a serious purpose. It is right that a false Latin quantity should excite a smile in the House of Commons; but it is wrong that a false English *meaning* should *not* excite a frown there. Let the accent of words be watched, and closely; let their meaning be watched more closely still, and fewer will do the work. A few words, well chosen and distinguished, will do work that a thousand cannot, when every one is acting, equivocally, in the function of another. Yes; and words, if they are not watched, will do deadly work sometimes. There are masked words droning and skulking about us in Europe just now—(there never were so many, owing to the spread of a shallow, blotching, blundering, infectious "information," or rather deformation, everywhere, and to the teaching of catechisms and phrases at schools instead of human meanings)—there are masked words abroad, I say, which nobody understands, but which everybody uses, and most people will also fight for, live for, or even die for, fancying they mean this or that, or the other, of things dear to them: for such words wear chameleon cloaks—"ground-lion" cloaks, of the color of the ground of any man's fancy: on that ground they lie in wait, and rend him with a spring from it. There never were creatures of prey so mischievous, never diplomatists so cunning, never poisoners so deadly, as these masked words; they are the unjust stewards of all men's ideas: whatever fancy or favorite instinct a man most cherishes, he gives it to his favorite masked word to take care of for him; the word at last comes to have an infinite power over him—you cannot get at him but by its ministry. . . .

And now, merely for example's sake, I will, with your permission, read a few lines of a true book with you carefully; and see what will come out of them. I will take a book perfectly known to you all. No English words are more familiar to us, yet few perhaps have been read with less sincerity. I will take these few following lines of "Lycidas."

> Last came, and last did go,
> The Pilot of the Galilean lake.
> Two massy keys he bore of metals twain
> (The golden opes, the iron shuts amain).

He shook his mitred locks, and stern bespake:—
"How well could I have spared for thee, young swain,
Enow of such as, for their bellies' sake,
Creep, and intrude, and climb into the fold!
Of other care they little reckoning make
Than how to scramble at the shearers' feast,
And shove away the worthy bidden guest.
Blind mouths! that scarce themselves know how to hold
A sheep-hook, or have learned aught else the least
That to the faithful Herdman's art belongs!
What recks it them? What need they? They are sped,
And when they list, their lean and flashy songs
Grate on their scrannel pipes of wretched straw;
The hungry sheep look up, and are not fed,
But swoln with wind and the rank mist they draw,
Rot inwardly, and foul contagion spread;
Besides what the grim Wolf with privy paw
Daily devours apace, and nothing said."

Let us think over this passage, and examine its words.

First, is it not singular to find Milton assigning to St. Peter, not only his full episcopal function, but the very types of it which Protestants usually refuse most passionately? His "mitred" locks! Milton was no bishop-lover; how comes St. Peter to be "mitred"? "Two massy keys he bore." Is this, then, the power of the keys claimed by the Bishops of Rome, and is it acknowledged here by Milton only in a poetical license, for the sake of its picturesqueness, that he may get the gleam of the golden keys to help his effect?

Do not think it. Great men do not play stage tricks with the doctrines of life and death: only little men do that. Milton means what he says; and means it with his might too—is going to put the whole strength of his spirit presently into the saying of it. For though not a lover of false bishops, he *was* a lover of true ones; and the lake pilot is here, in his thoughts, the type and head of true episcopal power. For Milton reads that text, "I will give unto thee the keys of the kingdom of Heaven," quite honestly. Puritan though he be, he would not blot it out of the book because there have been bad bishops; nay, in order to understand *him*, we must understand that verse first; it will not do to eye it askance, or whisper it under our breath, as if it were a weapon of an adverse sect. It is a solemn, universal assertion, deeply to be kept in mind by all sects. But perhaps we shall be better able to reason on it if we go on a little farther, and come back to it. For clearly this marked insistence on the power of the true episcopate is to make us feel more weightily what is to be charged against the false claimants of . . . power and rank in the body of the clergy: they who, "for their bellies' sake, creep, and intrude, and climb into the fold."

Never think Milton uses those three words to fill up his verse, as a loose writer would. He needs all the three—specially those three, and no more than those—"creep," and "intrude," and "climb"; no other words would or could serve the turn, and no more could be added. For they exhaustively comprehend the three classes, correspondent to the three characters, of men who dishonestly seek ecclesiastical power. First, those who "creep" into the fold; who do not care for office, nor name, but for secret influence, and do all things occultly and cunningly, consenting to any servility of office or conduct, so only that they may intimately discern, and unawares direct, the minds of men. Then those who "intrude" (thrust, that is) themselves into the fold, who by natural insolence of heart, and stout eloquence of tongue, and fearlessly perseverant self-assertion, obtain hearing and authority with the common crowd. Lastly, those who "climb," who, by labor and learning, both stout and sound, but selfishly exerted in the cause of their own ambition, gain high dignities and authorities, and become "lords over the heritage," though not "ensamples to the flock."

Now go on:

> "Of other care they little reckoning make,
> Than how to scramble at the shearers' feast.
> *Blind mouths*"—

I pause again, for this is a strange expression: a broken metaphor, one might think, careless and unscholarly.

Not so; its very audacity and pithiness are intended to make us look close at the phrase and remember it. Those two monosyllables express the precisely accurate contraries of right character, in the two great offices of the Church—those of bishop and pastor.

A "bishop" means "a person who sees."

A "pastor" means "a person who feeds."

The most unbishoply character a man can have is therefore to be Blind.

The most unpastoral is, instead of feeding, to want to be fed—to be a Mouth.

Take the two reverses together, and you have "blind mouths." We may advisably follow out this idea a little. Nearly all the evils in the Church have arisen from bishops desiring *power* more than *light*. They want authority, not outlook. Whereas their real office is not to rule; though it may be vigorously to exhort and rebuke; it is the king's office to rule; the bishop's office is to *oversee* the flock; to number it, sheep by sheep; to be ready always to give full account of it. Now, it is clear he cannot give account of the souls, if he has not so much as numbered the bodies of his flock. The first thing, therefore, that a bishop has to do is at least to put himself in a position in which, at any moment, he can obtain the history, from childhood, of every living soul in his diocese, and of its present state. Down in that back street, Bill and Nancy, knocking each other's teeth out! Does the bishop know all about it? Has he his eye upon them? Has he *had* his eye upon them? Can he circumstantially explain to us how Bill got into the habit of beating Nancy about the head? If he cannot, he is no bishop, though he had a mitre as high as Salisbury steeple; he is no bishop—he has sought to be at the helm instead of the masthead; he has no sight of things. "Nay," you say, "it is not his duty to look after Bill in the back street." What! the fat sheep that have full fleeces—you think it is only those he should look after, while (go back to your Milton) "the hungry sheep look up, and are not fed, besides what the grim Wolf, with privy paw" (bishops knowing nothing about it), "daily devours apace, and nothing said"?

"But that's not our idea of a bishop." Perhaps not; but it was St. Paul's; and it was Milton's. They may be right, or we may be; but we must not think we are reading either one or the other by putting our meaning into their words.

I go on.

"But swoln with wind and the rank mist they draw."

This is to meet the vulgar answer that "if the poor are not looked after in their bodies, they are in their souls; they have spiritual food."

And Milton says, "They have no such thing as spiritual food; they are only swollen with wind." At first you may think that is a coarse type, and an obscure one. But again, it is a quite literally accurate one. Take up your Latin and Greek dictionaries, and find out the meaning of "Spirit." It is only a contraction of the Latin word "breath," and an indistinct translation of the Greek word for "wind." The same word is used in writing, "The wind bloweth where it listeth"; and in writing, "So is every one that is born of the Spirit"; born of the *breath,* that is; for it means the breath of God, in soul and body. We have the true sense of it in our words "inspiration" and "expire." Now, there are two kinds of breath with which the flock may be filled: God's breath and man's. The breath of God is health, and life, and peace to them, as the air of heaven is to the flocks on the hills; but man's breath—the word which *he* calls spiritual—is disease and contagion to them, as the fog of the fen. They rot inwardly with it; they are puffed up by it, as a dead body by the vapors of its own decomposition. This is literally true of all false religious teaching; the first, and last, and fatalest sign of it is that "puffing up." Your converted children, who teach their parents; your converted convicts, who teach honest men; your converted dunces, who, having lived in cretinous stupefaction half their lives, suddenly awaking to the fact of there being a God, fancy themselves therefore his peculiar people and messengers; your sectarians of every species, small and great, Catholic or Protestant, of high church or low, in so far as they think themselves exclusively in the right and others wrong; and pre-eminently, in every sect, those who hold that men can be saved by thinking rightly instead of doing rightly, by word instead of act, and wish instead of work—these are the true fog children—clouds, these, without water; bodies, these, of putrescent vapor and skin, without blood or flesh: blown bagpipes for the fiends to pipe with—corrupt, and corrupting—"Swoln with wind and the rank mist they draw."

Lastly, let us return to the lines respecting the power of the keys, for now we can understand them. Note the difference between Milton and Dante in their interpretation of this power; for once, the latter is weaker in thought; he supposes *both* the keys to be of the gate of heaven; one is of gold, the other of silver: they are given by St. Peter to the sentinel angel; and it is not easy to determine the meaning either of the substances of the three steps of the gate, or of the two keys. But Milton makes one, of gold, the key of heaven; the other, of iron, the key of the prison in which the wicked teachers are to be bound who "have taken away the key of knowledge, yet entered not in themselves."

We have seen that the duties of bishop and pastor are to see, and feed; and of all who do so it is said, "He that watereth, shall be watered also himself." But the reverse is truth also. He that watereth not, shall be *withered* himself; and he that seeth not, shall himself be shut out of sight —shut into the perpetual prisonhouse. And that prison opens here, as well as hereafter; he who is to be bound in heaven must first be bound on earth. That command to the strong angels, of which the rock-apostle is the image, "Take him, and bind him hand and foot, and cast him out," issues, in its measure, against the teacher, for every help withheld, and for every truth refused, and for every falsehood enforced; so that he is more strictly fettered the more he fetters, and farther outcast, as he more and more misleads, till at last the bars of the iron cage close upon him, and as "the golden opes, the iron shuts amain."

We have got something out of the lines, I think, and much more is yet to be found in them; but we have done enough by way of example of the kind of word-by-word examination of your author which is rightly called "reading"; watching every accent and expression, and putting our-selves always in the author's place, annihilating our own personality, and seeking to enter into his, so as to be able assuredly to say, "Thus Milton thought," not "Thus *I* thought, in misreading Milton." And by this proc-ess you will gradually come to attach less weight to your own "Thus I thought" at other times. You will begin to perceive that what *you* thought was a matter of no serious importance; that your thoughts on any sub-ject are not perhaps the clearest and wisest that could be arrived at there-upon: in fact, that unless you are a very singular person, you cannot be said to have any "thoughts" at all; that you have no materials for them, in any serious matters—no right to "think," but only to try to learn more of the facts. Nay, most probably all your life (unless, as I said, you are a singular person) you will have no legitimate right to an "opinion" on any business, except that instantly under your hand. What must of neces-sity be done, you can always find out, beyond question, how to do. Have you a house to keep in order, a commodity to sell, a field to plough, a ditch to cleanse? There need be no two opinions about these proceed-ings; it is at your peril if you have not much more than an "opinion" on the way to manage such matters. And also, outside of your own business, there are one or two subjects on which you are bound to have but one opinion. That roguery and lying are objectionable, and are instantly to be flogged out of the way whenever discovered; that covetousness and love of quarreling are dangerous dispositions even in children, and deadly dispositions in men and nations; that in the end, the God of heaven and earth loves active, modest, and kind people, and hates idle, proud, greedy, and cruel ones;—on these general facts you are bound to have but one, and that a very strong opinion. For the rest, respecting religions, gov-ernments, sciences, arts, you will find that, on the whole, you can know NOTHING—judge nothing; that the best you can do, even though you may be a well-educated person, is to be silent, and strive to be wiser every day, and to understand a little more of the thoughts of others, which so soon as you try to do honestly, you will discover that the thoughts even of the wisest are very little more than pertinent questions. To put the dif-ficulty into a clear shape, and exhibit to you the grounds for *in*decision, that is all they can generally do for you!—and well for them and for us, if indeed they are able "to mix the music with our thoughts, and sadden us with heavenly doubts." This writer, from whom I have been reading to you, is not among the first or wisest: he sees shrewdly as far as he sees, and therefore it is easy to find out his full meaning; but with the greater men, you cannot fathom their meaning; they do not even wholly measure it themselves, it is so wide. Suppose I had asked you, for instance, to seek for Shakespeare's opinion, instead of Milton's, on this matter of Church authority?—or for Dante's? Have any of you, at this instant, the least idea what either thought about it? Have you ever balanced the scene with the bishops in Richard III against the character of Cranmer? the description of St. Francis and St. Dominic against that of him who made Virgil wonder to gaze upon him—*"disteso, tanto vilmente, nell' eterno esilio"*;[3] or of him whom Dante stood beside, *"come 'l frate che confessa lo perfido assassin"?* Shakespeare and Alighieri knew men better than most of us, I presume! They were both in the midst of the main struggle between the temporal and spiritual powers. They had an opinion, we may guess. But where is it? Bring it into court! Put Shakespeare's or Dante's creed into articles, and send *it* up for trial by the Ecclesiastical Courts!

You will not be able, I tell you again, for many and many a day, to come at the real purposes and teaching of these great men; but a very little honest study of them will enable you to perceive that what you took for your own "judgment" was mere chance prejudice, and drifted, helpless, entangled weed of castaway thought; nay, you will see that most men's minds are indeed little better than rough heath wilderness, neglected and stubborn, partly barren, partly overgrown with pestilent brakes, and venomous, windsown herbage of evil surmise; that the first thing you have to do for them, and yourself, is eagerly and scornfully to set fire to *this;* burn all the jungle into wholesome ash heaps, and then plough and sow. All the true literary work before you, for life, must begin with obedience to that order, "Break up your fallow ground, and *sow not among thorns."* [4]

*Suggestions for Study*

1. Into what main classes can books be divided?
2. Would you rather listen to the "studied, determined, chosen addresses of the wisest of men" or to their "casual talk"? Why?
3. Are the books written for all time to be read by anybody and everybody? What bearing might Ruskin's answer to this question have on educational practices?

3. Longfellow translates this and the quotation in the next line as follows:
"O'er him who was extended on the cross
So vilely in eternal banishment."

"I stood even as the friar who is confessing
The false assassin."

4. Having made his first point—that a reader must enter into the thoughts of an author —Ruskin continues in the part of the essay here omitted to expound his second point— that a reader must enter into the author's heart.

4. What, according to Ruskin, is the proper spirit in which to approach a great book? Does this spirit exclude critical reading?

5. In what respects is Ruskin's interpretation of the lines from "Lycidas" likely to be different from that of the ordinary reader? What causes this difference?

6. What are "masked words"?

7. Explain the meaning of redundant, entrée, inherent, circumstantially, cretinous, Elysian, equivocally, catechism, chameleon, episcopate, ecclesiastical, servility, sectarians.

# IV
## THE PRÉCIS

An excellent aid in learning to read long paragraphs and difficult articles correctly is making a précis. This is a device which, as the name indicates, came from France. It is a condensed summary of the original article in which the writer of the précis preserves the essential ideas, organization, tone, and point of view of the original, but uses his own words in the condensation. Thus it differs from an abstract in that the latter, using the words of the original, achieves brevity by omission only, whereas the précis not only omits ideas of secondary importance, illustrative material, and the like, but expresses the main ideas in a condensed form.

The chief value to a student of making a précis is that it forces him to look for and find the fundamental idea of the whole article and of each part, and to follow the main thread of the author's reasoning throughout the article. It insures his discarding examples and asides and points of secondary interest, and thus brings the main ideas into prominence in his mind. It is therefore an excellent aid to intelligent reading. But it is also useful in another way. A college student soon finds that much more is required of him than was required in the high school. His assignments are longer; he is often expected to supplement his classroom work with outside reading. The student who learns to write a good précis will steer between the extremes of taking fragmentary notes and copying the assignment so copiously that he is as badly off after the copying as he was before. If he has a good précis of what he has read, moreover, he possesses a handy condensation of the assignment which he can file for use in reviewing later on.

A good précis keeps as close as possible to the spirit, if not the words, of the original. This means if the original is written in the first person, the précis is also written in the first person; if the tone of the original is ironical or whimsical, the irony or whimsicality must not be lost in the précis. Nor must the writer inject ideas or information of his own in the précis (unless he puts it in brackets, as explained on page 274).

Ability to write a good précis is evidence of capacity both to read intelligently and to write concisely. It is good practice, therefore, to write précis as frequently as possible in the freshman year, whether you are required to do so or not. An example of a précis follows. From this you may get a better idea of how to write one yourself, and you can use the selections which follow to try your own hand at this form of writing.

## Example of a Précis of Two Paragraphs from Macaulay

### Original

The progress of elegant literature and of the fine arts was proportioned to that of the public prosperity. Under the despotic successors of Augustus, all the fields of the intellect had been turned into arid wastes, still marked out by formal boundaries, still retaining the traces of old cultivation, but yielding neither flowers nor fruit. The deluge of barbarism came. It swept away all the landmarks. It obliterated all the signs of former tillage. But it fertilized while it devastated. When it receded, the wilderness was as the garden of God, rejoicing on every side, laughing, clapping its hands, pouring forth, in spontaneous abundance, everything brilliant, or fragrant, or nourishing. A new language, characterized by simple sweetness and simple energy, had attained perfection. No tongue ever furnished more gorgeous or vivid tints to poetry; nor was it long before a poet appeared, who knew how to employ them. Early in the fourteenth century came forth the *Divine Comedy,* beyond comparison the greatest work of imagination which had appeared since the poems of Homer. The following generation produced indeed no second Dante: but it was eminently distinguished by general intellectual activity. The study of the Latin writers had never been wholly neglected in Italy. But Petrarch introduced a more profound, liberal, and elegant scholarship, and communicated to his countrymen that enthusiasm for the literature, the history, and the antiquities of Rome, which divided his own heart with a frigid mistress and a more frigid Muse. Boccaccio turned their attention to the more subtle and graceful models of Greece.

From this time, the admiration of learning and genius became almost an idolatry among the people of Italy. Kings and republics, cardinals and doges, vied with each other in honoring and flattering Petrarch. Embassies from rival states solicited the honor of his instructions. His coronation agitated the Court of Naples and the people of Rome as much as the most important political transaction could have done. To collect books and antiques, to found professorships, to patronize men of learning, became almost universal fashions among the great. The spirit of literary research allied itself to that of commercial enterprise. Every place to which the merchant princes of Florence extended their gigantic traffic, from the bazaars of the Tigris to the monasteries of the Clyde, was ransacked for medals and manuscripts. Architecture, painting, and sculpture were munificently encouraged. Indeed, it would be difficult to name an Italian of eminence, during the period of which we speak, who, whatever may have been his general character, did not at least affect a love of letters and of the arts.—Macaulay, "Machiavelli."

### Précis

In early Renaissance Italy, prosperity, literature, and fine arts progressed simultaneously. Under the emperors after Augustus, intellectual culture degenerated, but it began to flourish spontaneously when the country had recovered from the barbarian invasions. The Italian language, simple, sweet, and energetic, was used by Dante for the greatest poem since those of Homer. Later scholars, such as Petrarch and Boccaccio, revived the enthusiastic study of Latin and Greek writers.

Learning and genius were so much admired that Petrarch was the object of almost unbelievable honor and flattery. All great men were patrons of scholarship and the arts, and search for manuscripts and other remnants of the ancient world extended as far as Italian commerce.

## Selections for Précis Writing

### A

The method of scientific investigation is nothing but the expression of the necessary mode of working of the human mind. It is simply the mode at which all phenomena are reasoned about, rendered precise and exact. There is no more difference, but there is just the same kind of difference, between the mental operations of a man of science and those of an ordinary person, as there is between the operations and methods of a baker or of a butcher weighing out his goods in common scales, and the operations of a chemist in performing a difficult and complex analysis by means of his balance and finely graduated scales. It is not that the action of the scales in the one case, and the balance in the other, differ in the principles of their construction or manner of working; but the beam of one is set on an infinitely finer axis than the other, and of course turns by the addition of a much smaller weight.— T. H. Huxley, "The Method of Scientific Investigation."

### B

It seems to me that it can be only in some such way, carried out in all departments of our national life, that the American dream can be wrought into an abiding reality. I have little trust in the wise paternalism of politicians or in the infinite wisdom of business leaders. We can look neither to the government nor to the heads of the great corporations to guide us into the paths of a satisfying and humane existence as a great nation unless we, as multitudinous individuals, develop some greatness in our own individual souls. Unless countless men and women have decided in their own hearts, through experience and sometimes disillusion, what is a genuinely satisfying life, a "good life" in the old Greek sense, we need look to neither political nor business leaders. Under our political system it is useless, save by the rarest of happy accidents, to expect a politician to rise higher than the source of his power. So long also as we are ourselves content with a mere extension of the material basis of existence, with the multiplying of our material possessions, it is absurd to think that the men who can utilize that power for themselves will abandon both to become spiritual leaders of a democracy that despises spiritual things. Just so long as wealth and power are our sole badges of success, so long will ambitious men strive to attain them.—James Truslow Adams, *The Epic of America.* (Used by permission of the publishers, Little, Brown and Co.)

## C

It follows, from what has been stated, that it is a great and dangerous error to suppose that all people are equally entitled to liberty. It is a reward to be earned, not a blessing to be lavished on all alike—a reward reserved for the intelligent, the patriotic, the virtuous and deserving—and not a boon to be bestowed upon a people too ignorant, degraded, and vicious to be capable either of appreciating it or of enjoying it. Nor is it any disparagement to liberty that such is and ought to be the case. On the contrary, its greatest praise, its proudest distinction is, that an all-wise providence has reserved it as the noblest and highest reward for the development of our faculties, moral and intellectual. A reward more appropriate than liberty could not be conferred on the deserving—nor a punishment more just, than to be subject to lawless and despotic rule. This dispensation seems to be the result of some fixed law; and every effort made to disturb or defeat it, by attempting to elevate a people in the scale of liberty above the point to which they are entitled to rise, must ever prove abortive and end in disappointment.—John C. Calhoun, "A Disquisition on Government."

## Classicism and Romanticism [1]

### ALLARDYCE NICOLL

For long centuries up to the time of the Renaissance men had moved unadventuresomely along a great highway, like a dog watchfully and faithfully following its master. Then in that period of spiritual awakening which in England is known as the age of Elizabeth a thousand objects on all sides flaunted their attractions and summoned men to freedom. It was as though the dog which so long had followed at heel, brought now to some vast fair ground, dazzled by its captivating excitements and by the seemingly endless opportunities offered for adventure and delight, were starting to move independently—greeting a friend here, menacing an enemy there, now snapping up some unconsidered trifle, now distract and alert at some unwonted and hitherto inexperienced sight or sound.

1. Used by permission of the author and of the *English Journal,* College Edition (now *College English*). The extract is from an essay, "Mr. T. S. Eliot and the Revival of Classicism."

In the joys of liberty, the very image of his master vanishes from his mind; he has suddenly become aware of his own personality; he exists solely for himself and takes no heed of the outside world save as a series of objects which have meaning and significance only in their temporary relationship to himself. All the old traditional supports and comfortable conventions are cast aside; into the variegated, multicolored life of the fair, men are swept, daring everything in their careless, emancipated bravery. With Marlowe they vaunt their own individualities, for the moment they take no heed of aught beyond themselves, richly experiencing and deeming nothing of value or interest save what can give them joy.

Inevitably there is a reaction. To the dog comes a surging wave of terror as suddenly he realizes he is lost. The crowds, which had appeared so friendly and so delightfully exciting, assume monstrous and menacing proportions; he is desolate and alone in a forest of giant legs each of which seems to threaten his very being. More and more frenziedly he dashes around, panting, losing courage with each interminable moment, seeking only for that stay and support which is his master. And then, just as the whole world about him seems reeling in a delirious nightmare, through the dark terrors of the awesome forest his master is espied. Amply content with certitude again, he follows meekly wherever this guardian power chooses to lead him, faithfully, watchfully treading at his heels along the miles of roadway homewards. Such fear and such horror came to England at the beginning of the seventeenth century. The melancholy which settled on literature and life about 1600 was no chance thing; it permeated the whole of society. Men spoke bitterly in satire because they were afraid, while dramatists such as Tourneur and Webster shuddered miserably in their imaginative charnel houses of skulls and rotting bones as they listened trembling to the gibbering of lunatics without. At the same time others sought for escape. The beautiful had become transmogrified into the terrifying; the source of delight had been wrought into an object of gigantic fear; some stable power was required which man might follow lest his liberated loneliness should drive him mad. Throughout the whole course of the seventeenth century this search was pursued, meeting and often becoming confused with the moods of tormented melancholy and surging terror. It was thus that a new classicism was accepted—not a vague formalist creed adopted only by pedantic critics and half unwillingly pursued by a few minor writers, but a genuine desire to find in the monuments of classic simplicity a support for erring and faltering steps, a deep-felt willingness to abandon personal freedom in favor of a comforting tradition, a recognition that the imitation of established models may be safer than the rioting of unbridled fancies. With this, the growth of a new intellectualism. Insanity has come dangerously near and passion has led to abnormality and decadence; to counter these, men try to impose control and seek rationally for images which before had been found in unfettered emotion. Amid the chaos of a world disrupted by personal freedom, men sought for an intellectual classicism in literature and welcomed later a royalist control in politics; both provided a buttress demanded, after the blackness of long despair, to keep men sane and erect.

The period of untrammeled delight was but a short one; the age of questing among fears and torments lasted through the greater part of the seventeenth century. Thereafter came a journey during the eighteenth century, when mankind remained once more watchful and faithful to the master it had found. With ruthless inevitability, however, the joys of the fair reintruded, and in the period of romanticism, man shook off the fetters that had once been supports and reveled in a new-found liberty. Masterless, Shelley and Byron lived for themselves alone. Renouncing outside aid, they demanded freedom to sip at this pleasure and to exult in that delight. For some brief span of years men tasted all the dangerous thrills of utter emancipation. And once again came disintegration, decadent chaos, fear, and disruption of spirit.

Within this period of disintegration we now are. To trace even its main outlines were a difficult—even an impossible—task; too many voices sound on all sides of us—pleading voices, dogmatic, despairing, hortatory —to make such an effort capable of fruition; yet there are clear indications showing how the main currents of thought, of emotion, and of expression are tending and to demonstrate how closely akin we are to those who, in the seventeenth century, sank dejectedly amid the ruins of their hopes or strove in anxious effort to secure a fresh foothold in time and space by cultivating ancient tradition.

## Suggestions for Study

1. In making a précis of this selection, concentrate on finding the essential definitions and the subdivisions thereof amid the illustrations. Then reproduce that content in your own words.

2. What characterizes the Elizabethan period of England?

3. What is the reaction which follows it? Define the new classicism.

4. Did the spirit of the eighteenth century accord with that of the late seventeenth century?

5. When did a spirit akin to that of the Elizabethans return to England?

6. Why is the illustration of the dog included in this explanation? Would the writing be as clear without it?

7. Define the following words from the selection: unwonted, variegated, emancipated, interminable, certitude, permeated, pedantic, decadent, untrammeled.

## The Retreat of the Humanities [2]

### LOUIS B. WRIGHT

That the humanities—which I take to mean literature, philosophy, and history—are being driven out of modern education we all know. English literature, once considered essential in secondary education, is packing up its baggage, ready for flight. History is in a precarious position. Sometimes now the two are lumped together with varied oddments of information and offered to unsuspecting youth as a course in "social studies." Greek is as unknown as a Bantu dialect. In most curriculums Latin has followed Greek into oblivion. Philosophy, except for a superficial acquaintance with modern ideologies implicit in social study, is of course unknown. In place of the humanities strange altars have been erected in our schools, while our professional educators religiously bow thrice daily to their particular Mecca in the East whence comes inspiration if not learning. A newspaper account, giving news of the progress of education in Southern California, announces that a class in a school which had discarded history for a course in "transportation" had substituted for the lesson concerned with transportation in Holland an "Edam cheese party." Products of Holland were prominent at the party. All this of course is pleasant, jolly, and vaguely informative. Undoubtedly the class found Edam cheese more to their taste than, let us say, Motley's *Rise of the Dutch Republic*. The only question for us to ask is whether we wish to stress calories or learning. On the college level conditions are much the same. Gradually humanistic studies are disappearing as the popular trend sweeps students by the thousands into fields that promise more practical and more immediate "results."

The god that first pushed the humanities from the ancient throne of learning was natural science; it rose, glittering and proud as young Hyperion, and for a season promised to be civilization's savior. All the world wanted to be scientists. The methods of natural science were regarded not only as infallible in their own field but as applicable to all other fields of human reason. Literary scholars applied the technique of the biologist to the study of artistic creation so zealously that for years no other method was in good standing. But the signs of the retreat of science

2. Used by permission of the author and of the *English Journal*, College Edition (now *College English*).

also are abundant. Man's blind faith in the utility of science has gone. There is even a suspicion that science has created Frankenstein monsters about to destroy civilization. As Ortega y Gasset puts it, science "which spreads its peacock feathers at academic gatherings, . . . this same science, once a living social faith, is now almost looked down upon by society in general." [1] Natural science has not yet of course conceded defeat. But only its more utilitarian branches seem destined to maintain the enthusiastic support which the public until recently has vouchsafed theoretical research in the sciences. Natural science is being rapidly demoted from a god in the temple of learning to a household drudge. As science has "lost face" it has had recourse to a vast amount of drum-beating to keep up its morale, but, even so, the great foundations are gradually liquidating their projects in "pure" science and turning to more practical objectives.

The newest god to challenge the older Titans is social study, in its infinite Protean shapes, under innumerable plain and fancy names. Pupils in the first grade now begin with social studies. In one school that has come to my attention, nothing so antiquated as a reading lesson is offered, but instead the primary children study "illumination," learning about the history of lighting from candles to the latest thing in indirect electrical lamps. From the cradle to the university, social studies are not only offered but prescribed. In one university a course in "marriage problems" now counts toward graduation in place of a more conventional but less titillating course in history. Our professional educators are fairly beside themselves with zeal to induce "social consciousness" in everybody. From the correspondence schools, ever a significant barometer of popular taste, syllabi, outlines, handbooks, graphs, and statistics are being scattered thicker than leaves in Vallombrosa. The hopeful pursuer of self-education, who a few years ago would have been taking a home-study course in elementary physics, is now laboriously studying graphs about population distribution or a handbook on problems in social adjustment. The come-on literature of some of these correspondence schools implies that the millennium will dawn when enough of us have mastered the twelve-week course and are thereby prepared to be socially adjusted.

What is of more concern to higher learning than the activities of the correspondence schools, or even our secondary schools, is the attitude of the great foundations and the men who give the money. With a few notable exceptions, the foundations are investing their money in studies looking toward the present relief of man's estate. Subsidies for non-utilitarian science—what we sometimes call "pure science"—and for the

1. José Ortega y Gasset, "History as a System," in *Philosophy and History,* ed. Raymond Klibansky and H. J. Paton (Oxford, 1936), p. 290.

support of humanistic studies are rapidly dwindling. While scientists and humanists stand like Oliver Twist with an empty bowl, the cup of the social investigator runneth over.

Why, we may ask ourselves, have the humanities been so completely eclipsed—first by science and then by sociology? The answer to that question ought to lie heavily on our souls. It may be that the humanities have not always had wise or energetic advocates. Destiny, the time-spirit, economic conditions—all these may be invoked to explain why men no longer reverence the old cultural tradition, but we might also ask whether we who set up to bear the humanistic torch have not let our lights burn dim.

Certain vulgar errors about the humanities have gained currency in the popular mind, and in turn have affected our own thinking. There is, for example, a heretical notion abroad that the chief end of the humanities, of the study of literature in particular, is merely to provide entertainment. Humanistic learning as a training of both the intellect and the emotions we seem to have forgotten. Readers of a pedagogical journal will find, among its helpful hints and tricks of the trade, articles by teachers who plume themselves over persuading their pupils to read Mr. Burroughs' notable books on Tarzan, or some other work of similar merit. In justification of such "literature" one teacher pointed out that she found it much easier to interest students in these books than in the classics; that she could always get a lively discussion about the movie versions of the books! If the purpose of literary education is to be able to report that a good time was had by all, then Tarzan may be just as good provender for adolescents as Shakespeare.

But even among those of us who teach literature in the universities, the notion that literature should serve chiefly to provide superficial amusement is not unknown. One ought to add, however, that the dullness of many of our courses would seem to give the lie to this belief. Instead of emphasizing the deepening of emotional experience and intellectual understanding that comes from humanistic training, we have let it be implied that the humanities are a luxury for those who can afford them, something on a par with concerts and theater parties.

This assumption is not only indicative of our failure to appreciate fundamental values in our subject but is also a grave tactical error. For the humanities cannot put on so good a show as some of the competitors. Even if the public no longer has an awestruck respect for science, nevertheless science can still pull more rabbits out of the hat than we can, and thereby provide more entertainment for the multitude. When a scientific institution recently held open house, twenty-three thousand visitors came to see the wonders. They stood open-mouthed before a million-volt machine that made lightning to order, and they were vastly entertained when a laboratory stagehand, with studied carelessness, dropped a frankfurter, frozen so hard by liquid air that it shattered like glass. If professors of the humanities believe they have any tricks in their show equal in box-office appeal to a lightning machine or a frankfurter freezer, they are destined to disappointment. Let no one make any mistake. The twenty-three thousand who came to see these scientific marvels were not moved by the implications of the utility of science; they came because it was a free show, a cut above a vaudeville magician. What old Pharoah said about Moses in *Green Pastures* can be said about science: "You is a good tricker." If the defenders of the humanities expect to base their appeal primarily on the entertainment value of their subjects, they must acquire another bag of tricks.

Paradoxically, another popular belief that has helped to rout the humanities is a confirmed notion that they are dead, and consequently dull. We who stand as advocates for literature, history, and philosophy have ourselves largely to blame for this deep-rooted opinion, for we assume the manner and technique of the curator of a natural history museum. Painstakingly we catalogue and arrange the bones of our literary dinosaurs, but if our specimens ever breathed and lived as creative artists, our students never get any inkling of it. Teachers of the humanities do not have to be "entertainers," nor do they need to use any factitious tricks to whip up interest in their subjects, provided they themselves are alive and have the imagination necessary to see that literature, philosophy, and history bring back to life the thoughts and deeds of men who have ruled the world of emotion, intellect, and action. . . . Another reason for the retreat of the humanities . . . is the confident assurance among those who profess the newer studies that they are the inspired bearers of the torch. If humanistic training succeeds, it tends to produce an objective calm that makes a man a poor drum-beater. The student who surveys the past successes and failures of the world, and meditates philosophically upon them, does not make a good banner-bearer. While some of our colleagues in other fields, with the assurance of inexperience, assert that they alone have the true salvation, we are inclined to speculate skeptically rather than raise an outcry in our own defense. As science earlier, and as social studies more recently, have claimed public attention and support, we have been content to grow cynically aloof, and have retreated farther into our isolation.

Ironically, one of the virtues of the humanities has also been responsible for the loss of influence. With decent modesty in a period of blatancy, the humanities have neglected to be "impressive," to develop a front, and to window-dress their subjects. Not that I mean to imply that they should. But it does not diminish our cynical pessimism to realize that the subjects which have talked loudest and, I fear, most unintelligibly have often impressed the public with their vigor and their importance. The humanities have not made a mystery of themselves. For example, everyone feels that he could understand literature and history if it were worth the trouble. But social studies, particularly those having to do with the techniques of modern education, have become a technical mystery, with a particular language understandable only to the initiated. In the opinion of the public, a technical language, plus statistics and graphs, makes a learned science to be approached with respect and to be interpreted only by its high priests. Although some may reason that modern "education" (meaning our contemporary theory and practice of pedagogy) has succeeded in spite of its jargon, it is doubtful if the speeches and articles of some of its more prominent apostles would merit anything but pity if their ideas were translated into lucid English. It is a revealing experience to go through the leading pedagogical journals—a task that I set myself at intervals, perhaps as a sort of subconscious duty in penance for my sins. That experience always convinces me that a jargon has enabled the little pedagogical fish to talk like great whales, to be impressive in the councils of the mighty. For example, an article in a leading pedagogical journal on "Supervising the Creative Teaching of Poetry" makes the profound observation that the supervisor of poetry-teaching should first "become conscious and convinced of the functional definitions of supervision in general." After that his task is easy. He merely sees to it that there is "wise, effective, and constructive release of teaching and learning initiatives and energies directed toward adjustments and achievements within the frame of creative society." Just what this has to do with poetry is apparent when our authority lucidly explains:

The teaching of poetry divides itself naturally into two areas of enterprise, each with essential conditioning validities. . . . Comprehending a poem need not involve any intellectual or formal concern with its technique, prose content, type, moral, diction, analysis, social implications, etc. Comprehending a poem is essentially an organic experience, essentially a response to the poetic stimulus of the author. Poetic comprehension may be verbalized or it may not.

That's it in a nutshell. With such sounding brass and tinkling cymbals, pedagogical leaders have made a great noise in the world, won votes for bond issues, created vast systems, and have come to be writ down as learned scientists. If one may digress long enough to translate the foregoing quotation into simple language, it seems to mean that the student's response to poetry should be about equivalent to the emotion that comes from being tickled on the ear with a feather, and it shows how simple and easy poetry can be if we do not confuse ourselves and our students with learning. Before such ideas and such jargon, sincere advocates of learning sometimes retreat in despair. It is hard to present the cause of the humanities to those high priests of our educational system because, having received a pentecostal gift of tongues, they meet our reasoning with the language of Babel. The humanities may have cause to thank the gods of reason for protecting them from any temptation to imitate the mysteries of the educationists. . . .

The humanities have also suffered because they do not hold out the promise of immediate, tangible results. At the present moment social studies seem to promise infinite good things for the relief of man's estate. The humanities can only say that perhaps its students may be made more intelligent and wiser, better able to live in whatever world they find. But that is almost as vague as the hope of heaven when compared with the definite and fascinating themes encountered by the student of sociological problems. A survey of the living conditions of mariners, or the incidence of measles among miners, or the social adjustments among the wives of milkmen (to mention only three problems that have recently come to my attention) offer concrete material for study, with the possibility of social uplift as a probable result. When such themes as these are weighed against a study of Greek philosophy, or the history of the Roman Empire, or the poetry of the Elizabethans, they take precedence because of their immediacy.

The effectiveness of the humanities in a practical world has been diminished because the humanities themselves have not realized their actual utility, their dollars-and-cents value to the everyday citizen. Although we hear at times that a specialist cannot waste time with irrelevant studies, and that the humanities make no direct contribution to efficient action, the more intelligent professional men and businessmen are quick to refute this heresy. The votaries of the humanities likewise ought to be conscious of the practical utility of their subjects. By the standards of the marketplace, the humanities have extraordinary utility. An executive of a California telephone company, with ten thousand employees under his direction, insists that preference be given job-hunters with liberal arts training. Of these, the applicants who have majored in English have the advantage; next after them come the history majors. "We give them technical training," this executive explains, "but we want men already trained to think." Another businessman, employing many engineers in an industrial plant, prescribes a course of reading for his technicians. It is not an outline of engineering or a handbook on the engineer's social responsibilities that his men must read. The first book on his list is Plutarch's *Lives*. "These men must learn to think outside of their little specialties," he coldly insists. No sentimental motives inspire the respect these business leaders have for humanistic learning. They are not academic theorists. Experience has proved to them that this discipline, by increasing intellectual capabilities, has practical, financial value. . . .

Yet, despite the recognition of the value of the humanities by intelligent leaders in various professions, the continuous fight upon humanistic learning by obscurantists and opportunists has profoundly affected teachers of those subjects. For one thing, the cumulative effect of neglect and disdain has produced a curiously apologetic attitude, an attitude of conscious inferiority, among some of the spokesmen for the humanities. Even while assuming a defensive air to outsiders, some teachers of the humanities have come to believe the worst the critics have said. No real defense can come from them or any sound interpretation of the value of humanistic training. They are insincere apologists, murmuring weak platitudes that carry no conviction. One of the humanities' major liabilities has been an unfortunate number of academic Casper Milquetoasts, who have taken refuge in scholastic nooks. When they timidly appear before a class or a meeting of their colleagues they come as a dismal proof of the failure of the humanities, for they are held up as examples of what happens by long exposure to this discipline. But they are the failures, the men who themselves proceeded no farther in the humanities than the bare externals. In Rabelais's phrase, they have long since become squint-minded, and as they peep out at life through a little hole they get no glimpse of the illumination they should have received from humanistic learning.

Lord Chesterfield, in one of the letters to his son, observed that because his countrymen had always believed that one Englishman could whip three Frenchmen, it had come about that actually one Englishman could whip *two* Frenchmen. If the professors of the humanities were good-enough humanists to believe that they could hold their own against any three other subjects, perhaps then they might stand against the two that have usurped their once proud place.

But we need not make too great a lamentation over the onslaught of the Philistines and the weakness of Israel. The humanities are by no means as dead as their critics would make it appear. Like the church, they have periods of decline, but they are so fundamental to thinking society—to humanity—that they must survive if civilization is to endure. Although the outcry against traditional learning is sometimes brassy and blatant, as noisier or more spectacular subjects clamor for public attention, an intelligent minority will continue to realize the importance of the older disciplines. In a passage defending the new poetry, in the Preface to *Lyrical Ballads,* Wordsworth wisely comments that "the human mind is capable of being excited without the application of gross and violent stimulants; and he must have a very faint perception of its beauty and dignity who does not know this, and who does not further know that one being is elevated above another in proportion as he possesses this capability." We do not look to the humanities for "gross and violent stimulants," but they provide intellectual nourishment that gives a few men the strength and power to rise above the common ruck of mediocrity. . . .

Even in the confusion of values at the moment we are waking to the danger facing our heritage of individualism that the democracies still cherish. We are realizing with a new vividness that intelligent individualism depends upon the development of a well-rounded thinking personality, not upon a training that makes mere technicians in a mechanized society. To literature, which mirrors our past, to history, and to philosophy we must look for aid in the cultivation of the individual's highest aesthetic, emotional, and intellectual powers. Man does not live by technical skill alone. If his technical training enables him to make a living in an eight-hour-a-day job, he still has at least eight waking hours to spend in other pursuits. Since the number of sensory, animal pleasures that he can enjoy is limited, in his hours of leisure he must ultimately fall back on his own inherent resources. If education does not fail it must provide stimulation for these inner resources. The fundamental basis of man's effective association with his own kind lies in the knowledge and wisdom which the humanities provide.

Although some disillusioned historians deny that men learn from history, or that we profit from the past experience of the race, wiser scholars know that the traditional past not only has been a great steadying force in civilization but that it has also been the source of new intellectual life. In emphasizing the utility and vitality of the historical disciplines, Ortega y Gasset comments that "the past is in truth the live, active force that sustains our today. There is no *actio in distans*. The past is not yonder, at the date when it happened, but here, in me." [2] In our brashness and inexperience we sometimes talk about the dragging weight of tradition that hampers progress, but before making this criticism we should first ask ourselves where our vaunted progress leads us.

During the last two years political events have focused attention upon the founders of the nation, the makers of the Constitution. And although

2. *Ibid.*, p. 316.

not everyone believes that these men provided an infallible prescription of government to be followed literally today, we have gained a new respect for the intelligence, integrity, and even the wisdom of the leaders who, in 1787, laid the foundations of a powerful and democratic state. Students have marveled that frontier colonies should have produced men of the intellectual breadth of the makers of the federal Constitution. These men were not sent from heaven in an hour of need to work a miracle. The statesmen who molded opinion in that critical period were gentlemen with all the background that their social station connoted. They had been educated in the humanistic tradition, and they had the wisdom of the ancients to guide them in the task of making a new nation.

The retreat of the humanities, which began in an era of materialistic "progress" and continued until it was almost a rout, is about over. Some of the new gods have already fallen; others are proving deaf to the supplications of a panic-stricken world. Thoughtful men are once more turning for aid to the disciplines which provide intellectual and emotional moorings, which teach a way of life that has symmetry and proportion. As we grow more aware of the crassness of our materialism, we are coming to realize the folly of a civilization worshiping only pragmatic techniques or tangible things. Chastened and humble, we are beginning to turn to the traditional learning that helped give wisdom to the men of 1787. And if the democracy of individualism survives, the humanities will again become a dominant force in our cultural life. Or perhaps one might better say that if the humanities survive and become a vigorous force, an intelligent democracy may once more rule in the world.

*Suggestions for Study*

1. In writing a précis of a long article, such as this one, it is better, until you have a good deal of practice, to make a précis of each paragraph first. From these paragraph précis you can trace the author's main line of thought and make an intelligent précis of the whole article. Try to make a final précis of 500 words or less.

2. What are the humanities? In what sense have they retreated? Does the author believe the retreat permanent?

3. What subjects supplanted the humanities in recent times? How did they do this? How did they appeal to students?

4. According to the author, who is to blame for the loss of prestige which the humanities have suffered?

5. What does he mean by *vulgar* errors? What errors about the humanities have gained currency in popular thinking?

6. What does he mean by "a jargon has enabled the little pedagogical fish to talk like big whales"?

7. By the standards of the marketplace, what utility do the humanities have?

8. Explain the meanings of the following words: irrelevant, heresy, votaries, mortality, obscurantist, apologist, blatant, automaton, brashness, crassness, millennium, scapegoat.

## Science and Human Values [3]

### HOWARD E. JENSEN

Human civilization is the cumulative product of man's age-old faith that the universe he inhabits is intelligible and rational. It embodies principles of unity and order that his mind can comprehend and his will can employ in adding to the comfort of his body and the delight of his soul. All the material and spiritual achievements of humanity bear testimony to the validity of this confidence. Wherever it fades, the human mind lapses into lethargy and the will into impotence. Civilizations collapse when it perishes, and are reborn when it revives.

But this faith was itself a slow and hard-won achievement. For the gift of intelligence did not come to man like the latest mechanical gadget, accompanied by detailed instructions for its use. For untold centuries he looked out upon the universe in awed wonder, with no method of exploring its nature but his groping curiosity. His conception of his world was consequently vague and confused, and his control over it wavering and uncertain. With no effective intellectual method of winnowing the true from the false, he made many mistakes, and his knowledge consisted of a few grains of fact buried amidst vast accumulations of error. Myths, legends, magical formulae, empirical rules of thumb, these were his only intellectual store. Yet for hundreds of thousands of years they sufficed for the development of the rudimentary economic techniques of hunting, fishing, herding, agriculture, and industry, together with social and political organization, and even morality, religion, and the fine arts. Only four or five thousand years ago, in ancient Egypt and Babylonia, did there appear the first intimations of those methods of critical thought and investigation through which man was able at last to attain his vast intellectual achievements in philosophy and science. And therewith he acquired an increasing confidence in himself, and a growing faith that the world of nature constitutes, in part if not in whole, an intelligible order which his mind can comprehend and his will can command.

But for centuries after these first beginnings, man's methods of inquiry into the world about him were crude and bunglesome. Not until three

3. From the *Scientific Monthly*, September, 1941. Reprinted by permission of the author and the publishers.

hundred years ago can his most effective intellectual tools for investigating physical nature, the scientific method, be said to have been definitely constituted, and only since the dawn of the nineteenth century can they be said to have been intensively developed and employed.

Indeed, for a millennium and a half, from the collapse of the classical civilization of Greece until the dawn of the Italian Renaissance, the western world merely marked time in so far as the further development of scientific method was concerned. Men of the Middle Ages, however intellectually active they may have been in the fields of philosophy and theology, paid little attention to the scientific phase of the Greek tradition, and made little significant positive contribution to it. But the intellectual upheavals of the Renaissance and the technical problems created by the rise of capitalism and nationalism joined theory to practice, and wedded observation and experiment with imagination and reason into that harmonious union which provided the scientific movement with a new dynamic.

Into this new movement Francis Bacon threw himself with such vigor and enthusiasm that he has often been called the father of inductive science. He was, however, rather its chief apostle, its leading interpreter and propagandist. The proper method of science, he said, is the wise interrogation of nature, and this consists in formulating problems so that they may be answered by a simple yes or no, and in devising experiments to produce the facts that constitute the answer. But for several generations the new method succeeded in imposing its program on astronomy and physics alone. Not until the close of the eighteenth century was it applied to chemistry, and not until the beginning of the nineteenth to biology. Finally, under the inspiration chiefly of John Stuart Mill in England and Auguste Comte in France, the idea became widespread that the methods which had won such notable successes in the study of the physical world might be applied to man and his institutions, to give him a control over human relations comparable to that already won over the physical and the physiological. The psychologist began to move out of the library of the philosopher into the laboratory of the scientist, and the economist, political scientist, and lastly, the sociologist moved out of the study where they had previously sought to explain social conditions, and entered the world of practical affairs which they now sought to investigate and describe as first-hand observers.

The scientific movement was accompanied by the greatest outburst of buoyancy and optimism that the human spirit had ever known. Bacon had insisted that the purpose of the new knowledge was exclusively to mitigate the sufferings and increase the happiness of mankind. And for nearly three centuries the triumphs of western civilization in mechanical invention, in medical improvement, in economic, political, and social organization, seemed to prove him right. Populations increased, cities grew, wealth accumulated, death rates fell, the span of life lengthened, standards of living rose, museums and art galleries were founded, schools and universities flourished. Forecasting the course of the future from the time of the French Revolution, Condorcet declared that "from the observation of the progress which the sciences and civilization have hitherto made . . . we shall find the strongest reasons to believe . . . that nature has fixed no limit to our hopes." Only the destruction of the earth itself can put an end to the infinite perfectibility of man and his institutions.[1] And throughout the century following, publicists and men of affairs, with now and then a rare exception, united in this hymn to progress. Herbert Spencer wrote:[2]

Progress therefore is not an accident, but a necessity. . . . The modifications mankind have undergone, and are still undergoing, result from a law underlying the whole organic creation. . . . As surely as the tree becomes bulky when it stands alone, and slender if one of a group; . . . so surely must the human faculties be molded into completeness for the social state; so surely must evil and immorality disappear; so surely must man become perfect.

In 1898 Alfred Russell Wallace described the hundred years just drawing to a close as "The Wonderful Century," and in 1919, F. S. Marvin referred to the period between the Napoleonic era and the close of World War I as "The Century of Hope." Even as late as 1920, Paul Haworth brought his study of the United States since the Civil War to a close with a chapter entitled "A Golden Age in History," while only twelve years ago, Herbert Hoover, in his campaign for the presidency, expressed his conviction that we are on our way to abolish poverty from the land, and to place two cars in every garage and two chickens in every pot.

Although it has long been apparent to thoughtful minds that science contains little promise of fulfilling the hopes it had raised, it is only within the last decade that the common man has come fully to realize the extent to which his hopes have been betrayed. For the ultimate problems of our civilization are social and moral, and science, while it has placed new and powerful instruments in the hands of men, has done nothing to clarify the moral and social purposes which these instruments are to serve. Consequently the instruments, which in the hands of men of social

1. *Outlines of an Historical View of the Progress of the Human Mind*, p. 319, London: J. Johnson, 1795.
2. *Social Statics*, p. 80. New York: D. Appleton and Company, 1865.

intelligence and good will might have realized our hopes, are now being employed by the strongest and most ruthless to destroy them.

The betrayal of man's higher spiritual values by the machines he has himself created is nowhere more poignantly portrayed than in the motto of the British Broadcasting Company, "Nation shall speak peace to nation," promulgated in a world in which the radio has become man's most efficient instrument of speaking lies and war. It was the radio that laid down the barrage of propaganda that prepared the way for the ruthless aggression practiced upon China, Ethiopia, Spain, Albania, Austria, Czecho-Slovakia, Poland, Lithuania, Latvia, Estonia, Finland, Denmark, Norway, Luxembourg, Belgium, and Holland. These sixteen peoples, nearly one fourth of all the independent nations of the world, have, within less than half a decade, passed under the yokes of conquerors made diabolically efficient by the contributions of physics and chemistry to the arts of destruction. In the economic field science has enormously increased our capacity to produce, but it has also made our opportunity to consume more insecure. It has concentrated wealth and economic power into the hands of a few, driven a wedge between the farmer and his land, the craftsman and his tools, and made both dependent, not upon their own industry and thrift, but upon the vagaries of the market and the price system. Viewing the results in these two fields alone, economics and international politics, what hope remains that applied science will promote the higher values of man's spirit?

To this indictment the scientist has two replies: first, that if the findings of science are bent to such nefarious ends, the responsibility does not rest upon the scientist, but upon the practical men of affairs, the statesmen, the politicians, the captains of industry and finance. But this is only to plead guilty to the charge of Launcelot Hogben. "The education of the scientist and technician," he says, "leaves them indifferent to the social consequences of their own activities." [3] We may justly paraphrase a question raised by Charles and Mary Beard in another connection, Are they to regard themselves as the members of a privileged gild, entitled to go their own way without reference to the fate of society? [4] Rare indeed among scientists is the social conscience of the Swedish chemist, Alfred Nobel, who shrank back in horror from the uses of human destruction to which his invention of dynamite had been put, and who devoted a considerable part of his life and fortune to the promotion of international peace, that the product of his genius might not continue to wreak havoc with mankind. Equally rare among inventors is the social conscience of

3. *The Retreat from Reason*, p. 3. London: Watts and Company, 1936.
4. *America in Midpassage*, Vol. II, p. 869. New York: The Macmillan Company, 1939.

the Rust brothers, of Memphis, Tennessee, who have refused to sell their mechanical cotton picker, but only license it for use, in order that its commercialization may not bring idleness and starvation to millions of farm laborers of the South, and who plan to use their profits to create a fund to relocate in industry the workers whom their invention may displace.

The second reply of the scientist to the indictment that science has been destructive of the higher human values is that science as such is morally neutral. It has no concern with value. It is interested in quantities, not qualities. It studies only what is, not what ought to be. It can tell us only what is true, not what is right or good or wise or beautiful or holy. For knowledge of these things we should turn, not to the scientist, but to the philosopher.

Even the social scientists have of recent years made common cause with the natural scientists in washing their hands of all concern with human values. The economist, the political scientist, the sociologist, we are told, must study a social situation as the astronomer studies a nebula or the biologist an organism, to describe what exists, and to predict, if he can, what must exist tomorrow, but that is all. He may study suicide, divorce, crime, poverty, unemployment, strikes, lynchings, war, but whether these things are good or bad he does not know. Any interest in their ethical implications, or any concern about human welfare, is scientifically taboo. He is a social technician solely. He can teach us efficiency in attaining our ends, but not wisdom in choosing them. He tries to learn, for example, how depressions are caused and how they may be prevented, but whether we should have bigger and better depressions or smaller and fewer, is a question of social ethics or social welfare, and he does not know. Lest this appear to be caricature, let us note a recent statement of a former president of the American Sociological Society:

That there has been any recent, catastrophic breakdown in the social order is not immediately evident. There has been, to be sure, a marked increase in unemployment and economic distress: the percentage of the population that is unable to secure unassisted the minimum means necessary to continued existence is large and increasing. But this does not in any real sense represent a breakdown in the system; on the contrary it may equally well be taken as representing the culmination and flowering of the traditional social and economic order.[5]

Under the pressure of this trend in sociology at least, if not also in economics, political science, and history, it is as much as a young man's academic future is worth to show an interest in the ethical or welfare

5. Quoted from *Social Forces*, 13 : 203, December, 1934.

aspects of social problems, and many an intelligent young graduate student is frightened away from research upon problems of the most pressing human concern for fear of the effect upon his future prospects of appointment and promotion.

We might for the present accept this defense of the scientist, that science is concerned with what is, not with what ought to be, and that for knowledge of human values we must turn not to him, but to the philosopher, if the scientist were in fact such a humble person as this answer implies. For it reduces the scientist to the role of a mere servant of the philosopher, providing the means whereby we can realize the human values which the philosopher validates and clarifies. But the scientist is rarely so self-effacing. He is usually quite convinced that scientific knowledge is alone entitled to respect, and, emerging from his laboratory, he thrusts aside the work of the philosophers as worthless, and proceeds to formulate a view of human life and destiny in harmony with his own professional bias. Thus, R. K. Duncan, a former professor of industrial chemistry in the University of Kansas, has written:

> We believe—we must believe, in this day—that everything in God's universe of worlds and stars is made of atoms, in quantities x, y, or z respectively. Men and women, mice and elephants, the red belts of Jupiter and the rings of Saturn are one and all but ever shifting, ever varying swarms of atoms. Every mechanical work of earth, air, and water, every criminal act, every human deed of love and valor: what is it all, pray, but the relation of one swarm of atoms to another? . . .
>
> Now, whether we call the atoms God's little servants or the devil's agents, one thing is sure—that every action of every thing, living or dead, within this bourne of time and space, is the action of one swarm of atoms on another, for without them there is but empty void.[6]

Here we have it clearly and baldly put: our human values, our acts of love and valor, our aspiration for goodness and beauty, are one with the belts of Jupiter and the rings of Saturn, atoms dancing in an empty void!

In such a world, man's belief that his choices are in any sense real, that he can engage in creative activity of any kind or contribute towards the realization of his ideals, that by taking thought and expending effort he can in any significant way modify the course of events, develop his personality, or conserve and enhance the world of values—all these are vain illusions. As Dr. John H. Bradley has expressed it:

> The desire to get somewhere is deeply rooted in the human heart. Man wants ends for his struggles, hopes, and fears, where he fancies he will find peace. But nature has an entirely different point of view. . . . She has imposed

6. Quoted from Max C. Otto, *Things and Ideals,* p. 182f. New York: Henry Holt and Company, 1924.

a cyclic pattern upon the universe, whereunder all things are charged to go on for ever, but never to arrive.[7]

In such a world man should never "waste time looking for a purpose where probably there is none," but "let it pass." [8]

Thus the scientific movement, beginning with the assertion that it has no concern with human values, often ends by heaping contempt upon philosophy, which has. For the natural scientist, working in his laboratory with the basic conceptions of matter and mechanism and quantity, is all too prone to think of the entire universe outside the laboratory in these terms, and to assert, as do the writers already quoted, that all reality is material reality, that all causation is mechanistic causation, and that all knowledge is quantitative knowledge. And, since the human values, truth, beauty, goodness, holiness, can not be weighed or measured, it follows that we can have no valid knowledge about them, and that they can be nothing more than illusions born of our desires. As Joseph Wood Krutch has expressed it, either the light of science is somehow deceptive, or all the things we cherish are unsubstantial, all the values we pursue and all the principles we cling to are but shadows, and the universe, emotionally and spiritually, is a vast emptiness.[9]

This shattering of confidence in spiritual values is the most damaging blow that science could strike mankind. It has centered attention upon the tangible and the ponderable, exalted material possessions as the measure of human worth, and substituted comfort, excitement, and entertainment for truth, goodness, and beauty, as the supreme values of life. This concern of modern man with material things has left a void in his soul, and, shut up between the darkness of the birth from which he came and the darkness of the grave to which he goes, he can only fill the void with an increasing volume of material possessions and an increasing intensity of sensuous satisfactions. It has made of life a system of tensions, a continuous succession of strains which is never followed by relaxation.

But these facts, disconcerting as they are, provide no basis for a fundamentalist tirade against science as such. The structure of modern science stands as the greatest achievement of man's intelligence; the technological inventions which it has made possible remain as the greatest accomplishment of his hands. But a science which assumes that its basic concepts of materialism and mechanism and quantity exhaust the possibilities of dependable knowledge has ceased to be science, and degenerated into a dogma which has betrayed civilization. For if we can discover no depend-

7. *Scientific Monthly*, 30 : 457, May, 1930.
8. C. C. Furnas, *Scientific Monthly*, 31 : 50, July, 1930.
9. *Atlantic Monthly*, 149 : 162–72, February, 1927, and 151 : 372, March, 1928.

able knowledge of the good life which the intelligence must recognize as valid and the will as obligatory, our civilization can not survive the forces which science has let loose within it. For unless the principles of moral and social obligation can be recognized as binding upon the impulses of every individual and the interests of every group because they are rationally valid, there remains no way of settling the conflicts that rage between individuals, economic classes, political parties, religious sects, nations, and races, but by the appeal to force and violence. "Let them fight it out," say those who have lost their faith in the capacity of intelligence to discover rational principles of social order. But they have not been able to fight it out in ten thousand generations, though they have destroyed innumerable civilizations in the attempt. And they can not fight it out in ten thousand generations to come, though still more civilizations perish. For though a nation can by force set its house in order, it can not by force establish order within its house. And though a nation can by war force another nation into submission, it can not by war force another nation into harmony with itself. Order and harmony come by agreements mediated by reason, not by treaties imposed by arms. When interests are repressed by force, they remain as occasions for new conflict; only when they are adjudicated by reason are they set permanently at rest.

But never in the history of Western civilization has confidence in a moral order based upon reason been weaker; never have moral principles been more cynically flouted, never have fraud and falsehood been more brazenly flaunted, never has force been more ruthlessly wielded. Never could less reliance be placed in the solemn treaties of nations or the pledged word of statesmen. For what can we expect of a civilization nourished intellectually on the bouillon cubes of science without the vitamins of value but that it should suffer from moral rickets?

One may, of course, be reminded of Malachi's despairing cry, ringing down twenty-five centuries of time from ancient Judea, "Why do we deal treacherously every man against his brother, profaning the covenant of our fathers?" He may be reminded, moreover, of Aristotle's cynical advice to the tyrant in the Fifth Book of his *Politics,* of the political immoralism of Machiavelli's *Prince,* or of Thomas Hobbes' observation that man is unto man a wolf and that his natural state is a war of each against all. The answer to this is fourfold.

First, these are the laments of prophets and the observations of scholars, not the confessed policy of statesmen. Not until the rise of the contemporary dictators have the responsible heads of states while still in power publicly acknowledged their use of fraud and violence as regular instruments of political policy, as Mussolini, and especially Hitler, have done in their official publications.

Second, the areas of social life still under the sway of the ordinary human decencies have been so wide that heretofore the dictator has been compelled by public opinion at home and abroad strictly to follow Machiavelli's advice to his Prince that, though he need be neither honest nor generous nor just, he must always appear to be so.

Third, while it is true that deception and violence have always stood in the background of human affairs, they have most of the time remained there, to be brought into action only in moments of extraordinary crisis, but the modern dictators have made the crisis perpetual. Bismarck considered war the extension of diplomacy, but it has taken a Hitler to make diplomacy an extension of war.

Fourth, although deceit and cunning and violence have never been absent from history, not until they became armed with the resources of modern science and technology could they on a scale so ruthless and colossal destroy all the human values which decent men prize. It is high time for all who call themselves scientists, whether physical or social, to make common cause with philosophy and the humanities in the defense of human values, and in the competence of scholarship and research to find a rational basis for them in human experience which all men must accept. For let there be no mistake about it, in the midst of the passionate social conflicts that rage about us, if scholarship and research are unable or unwilling to determine the ends of economics and politics by reason, economics and politics will determine the ends of scholarship and research by force.

Dictatorship is the legitimate fruit of our loss of faith in reason to discover dependable knowledge of human values. For if there are no universal principles of moral obligation which the minds of all men must recognize and the will of all men obey, one man's opinion of what is good and bad, right and just, is as valid as another's, and the only guides to human conduct that remain are the biological impulses of individuals and the vested interests of groups. But such an unrestrained conflict of impulses and interests must reduce the individual life to madness and the social life to chaos. So in the theory and program of nationalism the interests of the state have been made supreme over all other interests in conflict. When the interests of individuals and groups clash, it is recognized that all lesser interests must yield to the common good. It is recognized that there can be stability and harmony within the state only in the proportion that principles of equity and justice are available to serve as a basis on which the conflict can be resolved, not by might, but by agreement. But nationalism recognizes no such general principles of the rational good, binding upon it in a conflict within the family of nations. Here the nation becomes the final judge of its own interests; it is under no obligation to consider the consequences of its policies upon other nations, and as a last resort, there is no other alternative than the appeal to war. In that event, the highest moral obligation of the citizen is to die for his country, right or wrong.

But the dictator sees no grounds for applying one set of principles to conflicts between nations, and another to conflicts within them. If self-interest is supreme, and reason is degraded to serve the ends of expediency in the one case, it is equally so in the other. Neither within the nation nor without it can the reason discover principles which the will is bound to respect. Consequently, the human values, truth, goodness, beauty, holiness, justice, honor, right, are what the self-interest of the dictatorship pronounces them to be. The minister in his pulpit, the editor at his desk, the teacher in his classroom, the philosopher in his study, the scientist in his laboratory, all alike must prove and proclaim whatever the dictatorship requires; they must disprove and denounce whatever the dictatorship commands. As the Nazi courts have recently decreed, if an official commits a punishable act out of religious or other social motives, "these motives will be regarded not as attenuating circumstances, but as proof that he is involved in relationships which he values more highly than those which connect him with his superiors and with the state." [10]

The tragedy is that the greatest single intellectual influence in establishing this rule of unreason has been the dogma of natural science, that the only rationally valid knowledge is knowledge of things in their material and quantitative relationships, and that all alleged knowledge of human values is mere opinion, born of self-interest and desire. If science is to realize its earlier promise, and to contribute to the enrichment of human experience and the mitigation of its ills, it must abandon this dogma and lend its influence to the re-establishment of confidence in the competence of the human mind to discover rational and intelligible principles of unity and order, not only in the realm of physical nature, but also in the realm of the human spirit.

The knowledge most desperately needed is knowledge concerning the principles of social organization and the ends of social action. No social science is adequate to this task that is descriptive only, that confines itself to exploring what is and predicting what will be. For human nature and human society are vastly richer and more complex in their potentialities than in their accomplishments. An adequate social science will of course

10. *Information Service*, p. 3. New York, April 20, 1940.

begin with a careful collection of facts about how men carry on their common life together as families and communities, as economic classes and political parties and religious sects, as nations and races, but it will not stop there. It will pass on from this concrete knowledge of social actualities to the consideration of social possibilities. It will endeavor to work out all the logical possibilities of human association that rigorous analysis can disclose. It will formulate logically, in advance of the facts, the meaning and value which social life might contain if it were rationally ordered. If science is to contribute to human welfare, it must consider logical knowledge of the possibilities of social life as of equal importance with factual knowledge of its nature. For unless social policies are based upon fact they will not work; and unless they are grounded in logical principle they will not endure. A science which is adequate to our needs therefore will explore, both factually and logically, with a view to discovering both the actualities and possibilities of human existence, the five great fields of social relationships where civilized man now stands frustrated and defeated.

It will explore, first, the relations of men to one another as persons, in the family, the community, and other face-to-face groups, where the extent of their frustration and defeat is measured by the statistics of suicide, mental and nervous collapse, divorce, delinquency, criminality, and general personal maladjustment.

It will explore, second, the relations of men to one another as producers, or the problems of economics, where the extent of their frustration and defeat is measured by the statistics of unemployment, poverty, bankruptcy, business failure, and recurrent depressions.

It will explore, third, the relations of men to one another as citizens, or the problems of politics, where their frustration and defeat is measured in terms of political corruption, machine domination, and the general failure of our democracy heretofore positively to promote the common welfare which the Constitution of the United States places high among the primary purposes of government as stated in its Preamble, instead of giving its chief attention to the incidental and secondary rights of property which in the Constitution itself are tucked away in the due process clause of the Fourteenth Amendment as a sort of after-thought.

It will explore, fourth, the relations of men to one another as organized states, where their frustration and defeat stand disclosed in international anarchy, in the dread that stalks the lands, the horror that rains from the sky, the terror that lurks in the sea, and the fear that rides the ether.

It will explore, fifth, the relations of men to one another as biological varieties, or the problems of race, where the measure of their frustration and defeat is revealed in the obscenities and cruelties of race prejudice, in riots, lynchings, pogroms, and concentration camps.

It is a grim task, but beyond it there lies a great hope, the hope that by means of a social science that has become intelligent enough to extend its scope from social facts to social values, from a consideration of what is to what might be and ought to be, we may formulate a rationally valid conception of the general social welfare, and develop a social organization adequate to mediate between the conflicting interests of human groups.

This is an old hope. Ever since the Greek philosophers began to reflect about man's life and destiny, it has been the unwavering conviction of the clearest intellects and the choicest spirits that the human mind is a competent instrument in clarifying the ends of our existence, and the human will is an active agent in attaining them. If this hope be false, no civilization can endure, and there remains nothing out of the wrecks of time for which decent men should care to live.

But there is no reason to believe that the hope is false. It is often said that man is not a reasonable creature, but it may be remarked that if this is really so, only by reason can the fact be known. And reasoners who employ reason to prove the incompetence of reason are interesting objects of study. As Irwin Edman has said, "Reason may indeed become a fetish, but so may distrust of it." [11]

But that a major part of our behavior wells up out of biological impulses or socially acquired interests of which we are unconscious or only dimly aware, constitutes a quite different problem. Here the daily experience of every civilized man bears witness to the competence of intelligence to produce harmony and order out of the clash of impulse and desire. Every day we bring the ends which we impulsively desire under the control of larger ends which we rationally recognize as desirable. Every day in the common decencies of life we adjust the claims of our personal and group interests to the interests of other persons and groups freely and gladly, because we rationally recognize the allegiance we owe as human beings to a life that is wider than our own. But as individuals and groups forge their way to economic and political power the rational control of intelligence weakens, the sensitive sympathy of the heart withers, and the ruthless energy of the will abounds. From the destruction which this ruthlessness is now wreaking in our contemporary life, there can be no doubt but that the continuance of our civilization depends upon our ability to make this conception of the general social welfare as the only rational good so clear and convincing to man's intellect that in these wider areas of life it will compel the allegiance of his will.

11. *Four Ways of Philosophy*, New York: Henry Holt and Company, 1937.

Can we accomplish this result before our civilization is destroyed by the conflicts that now rage within it? We can not tell. If the odds against it seem heavy, we must remember that it has always been so. Life has always been fraught with risk and adventure, and the future with uncertainty. But if our present efforts fail, it is not unlikely that the same human nature which has pressed on through the repeated failures of vanished civilizations will persevere through future ages until it reaches whatever success its own capacities, the resources of physical nature, and the limits of time will permit. For within the processes of social development, from the dawn of man until now, there has been operating the irresistible human impulse to be, to know, and to do.

Our thought, then, ends in neither complacent optimism nor enervating despair. The outcome is doubtful enough that none of us dares be laggard, but hopeful enough to challenge us to the task with zest and high courage.

## Suggestions for Study

1. For how long have scientists intensively used the scientific method? Who is often called the "father of inductive science"?

2. Was the rapid growth of science accompanied by an optimistic or a pessimistic outlook on life? To what degree have expectations been fulfilled? What has produced this situation?

3. What two replies have scientists given when indicted on the count of not promoting human values?

4. In what way does the scientific movement often "heap contempt upon philosophy"? In what way is it mechanistic?

5. What has science often set up as the goal and main concern of man?

6. Can force establish world peace? On what only can peace hope to rest?

7. How can science make a real contribution to human welfare?

8. Answering the above questions should give you some of the more important considerations in this article. When you are certain that you have identified and understood each important concept, write a précis which will reproduce in short compass the thought of the article.

9. What similarities of point of view do you find between Mr. Jensen and Mr. Wright?

10. Define the following words from the article: empirical, diabolically, validate, tangible, sensuous, dogma, fetish, rational.

# PARTS OF THE COMPOSITION

## I
## THE WORD

### A. The Dictionary

THE appropriate place to begin the study of the word is in the dictionary, for here we learn the meanings, the spellings, and the levels of usage of our vocabulary. No student should attempt to proceed far with college work without possessing a good dictionary; however, without advice he is sometimes unable to tell a good dictionary from a poor one. Briefly, a good dictionary is one which is written accurately and scientifically; which provides adequate guides to pronunciation, derivation, meaning, parts of speech, and levels of usage; which furnishes synonyms and antonyms for important words; and which contains enough proper names, biographical data, and geographical information to make it useful as a reference work to aid the student with his general and assigned reading.

Dictionaries vary in size and value from the large unabridged works to those small enough to be carried in the pocket. For use in college work, the student should not buy one smaller than the desk variety described below; smaller ones are often inaccurate, unreliable, and incomplete; sometimes, because of poor proofreading, the words are even misspelled.

**The Unabridged Dictionaries.** The common unabridged dictionaries are *Webster's New International,* Funk and Wagnalls' *New Standard Dictionary, The New Century Dictionary, The New English Dictionary,* and *The Dictionary of American English.*

The culmination of these dictionaries is *The New English Dictionary* (also called the *Oxford English Dictionary*), an enormous work that was in progress for over seventy years before its completion in 1928. A corps of over 2,000 workers aided in its preparation. Under the direction of some of the ablest lexicographers of the time, these workers undertook to trace the biography of every English word for the last eight hundred years—when the word first appeared in surviving records and when it was dropped from use, or if it is in good repute still, what changes it has undergone. To illustrate the ways in which these words were used, the workers made some five million selections from every sort of book and document; and of these, more than two million illustrations were used. The result is a dictionary of many volumes, containing over 400,000 words, with a complete history of each word to date. Manifestly, this is not a dictionary to consult for ordinary purposes; but for anyone who wishes to know the status of any word at any given time it is indispensable. A recent American counterpart of this work, *The Dictionary of American English,* has been issued to define those words which have gained currency primarily in this country.

The purpose of an unabridged dictionary is to provide complete information and final authority on the spelling, pronunciation, etymology, meanings, and usage of words. Necessarily these dictionaries are too large to carry about and too expensive for the average college student to own. However, they can be found in the college library, and there they should be consulted frequently. Whenever a question about a word cannot be answered by reference to a small dictionary, you should consult the unabridged works, which represent the last court of appeal for the English language.

**The Abridged Dictionaries.** An abridged dictionary is one that omits a great deal of material which is of use to a specialist or information which must be available somewhere, but which is not used commonly enough to warrant its appearing in a smaller, less expensive work. This does not mean that an abridged dictionary is unreliable or, for ordinary use, incomplete. Actually, a good abridged dictionary is more practical, judged by day-to-day use, than an unabridged work. Its purpose is to provide a practical vocabulary, with the more common meanings of words and with correct but not exhaustive etymologies.

The commonly used abridged dictionaries are *Webster's Collegiate Dictionary,* Funk and Wagnalls' *College Standard Dictionary, The Winston Dictionary, Advanced Edition,* and the *Concise Oxford Dictionary.* Every student should, in his freshman year, buy one of these dictionaries and use it throughout his four years in college. It should be kept in a handy place and referred to frequently. Smaller works, ranging from small desk dictionaries to the pocket varieties, are to be recommended only for very poor spellers who need a small word-book to carry with them. The purpose of the pocket dictionary is not so much to give the meanings of words as to give correct spellings.

Since the most commonly used size is the desk dictionary, a brief description is given here. It consists of three parts: an introduction, the dictionary proper (alphabetical list of words), and the special features.

*The introduction.* All dictionaries have an introduction to explain to the reader the terminology used and to show him how to use the book most effectively. Here is found (a) a *guide to pronunciation,* in which is given the key to the diacritical marks; (b) an *example of a typical vocabulary entry,* with a careful explanation of every part; and (c) a *list of abbreviations used,* which should be studied by the student until he is familiar with the more common abbreviations, such as *OF., Lat., ML., MHG., AS., OE., ME., Mil., Naut., Gr.* This is probably the most important and useful part of the introduction. A short article on "Orthography" and "Rules for Spelling" is sometimes included in the introduction also.

*The dictionary proper.* This part, which contains an alphabetical list of the most important words in the English language, packs a great deal of material into a very small space. A typical entry in *Webster's Collegiate Dictionary* reads:

> **cal′lous** (kăl′ŭs), *adj.* [L. *callosus,* fr. *callum, callus,* callous skin.] 1. Having a callus; hardened; indurated. 2. Hardened in sensibility, feeling, etc.; unfeeling.—**Syn.** *Horny;* pachydermatous, thick-skinned.—**Ant.** Soft, delicate; sensitive.—**cal′lous·ly,** adv.—**cal′lous·ness,** *n.—v.t. & i.* To make or become callous.

The word which is to be defined appears first, followed by the pronunciation (if there are two possible pronunciations, the preferred one is usually given first); the part of speech (adj.); then in brackets the etymology of the word (Latin from *callum, callus,* "callous skin"). After the derivation of the word has been properly discussed, the definition or definitions follow. (The primary meaning of *callous* is *hardened;* from this there has developed a secondary meaning, *hardened in sensibility* or *unfeeling.*) In the definitions, quotations are often cited from English authors to illustrate the usage. Abbreviations commonly appear here, referring to a special meaning that the word has, for example, in commercial language (Com.—commercial). Next the synonyms and antonyms are listed. Antonyms, words which have the opposite meaning from that of the word listed, are frequently as useful as synonyms in giving clues to exact usage.

Next after the antonyms are usually found the formations of the other parts of speech derived from the word in question, especially those which are in any way irregular. Thus, from *callous* we have the adverb *callously* and the noun *callousness;* also a verb which can be used both transitively and intransitively and which means "to make or become callous." If the word belongs to a level of diction other than standard, the status of the word is indicated by *colloq., slang,* etc.

All this information is compressed into an extremely small space. The key which one must have to make effective use of an entry is a *knowledge of the abbreviations used* in the dictionary. Without such knowledge, much of the information becomes so much gibberish. Look in the front of your dictionary for the table of abbreviations.

*The special features.* Besides the introduction and the main body of the dictionary, there is a third section—the special features—with which the student should be familiar. The special features included in *Webster's Collegiate Dictionary,* Fifth Edition, are as follows:

Abbreviations Used in Writing and Printing
Arbitrary Signs and Symbols
Pronouncing Gazetteer
Pronouncing Biographical Dictionary
Pronouncing Vocabulary of Common English Christian Names
Foreign Words and Phrases
Vocabulary of Rhymes
Colleges and Universities in the United States and Canada
Punctuation, Compounds, Capitals, etc.
Preparation of Copy for the Press

Actually a good desk dictionary is a small encyclopedia. It is the most practical, generally useful, and valuable textbook which any student can possess.

**The Thesaurus.** Although all unabridged English dictionaries list some of the more common synonyms and antonyms, no attempt is made to do more than touch upon this important phase of vocabulary building. A thoroughgoing treatment is reserved for the thesaurus, which is a storehouse [fr. L. *thesaurus,* from Gr. *thēsauros,* treasure] of synonyms and antonyms. The best-known and most easily accessible thesauri are: *Roget's Thesaurus of English Words and Phrases* (now printed in a cheap edition), *The Roget Dictionary of Synonyms and Antonyms* (ed. C. O. Sylvester Mawson), Crabb's *Dictionary of Synonyms,* Smith's *Synonyms Discriminated,* March's *Thesaurus Dictionary of the English Language,* and *Webster's Dictionary of Synonyms* (a new, comprehensive work which, because of its alphabetical arrangement, is easy to use). The best of these are the Roget volumes and the Webster dictionary. A special sort of work is Fowler's *Dictionary of Modern English Usage,* which discusses shades of meaning of many words and also many other matters of usage that will interest serious students.

*Using the Thesaurus for synonyms.* A synonym is a word which has approximately the same meaning as another word. Very few pairs of exact synonyms exist; if two words mean exactly the same thing, one of them is likely to be discarded and forgotten. Therefore, a person who wishes to be precise in the use of words must discriminate carefully among synonyms, as one can readily understand if he opens *Roget's Thesaurus* to the seventy-nine synonyms of the verb *think.*

When one studies words which mean approximately the same thing, he should try to become aware of differences, of similarities, of the hundreds of very slight but nevertheless existing shades of coloring that are to be found in every word. For example, the verb *to eat* is a general word which has as synonyms *taste, nibble, dally with, gulp, bolt,* and *stuff.* In deciding which of these words to select for a particular purpose, one should examine the level of diction which has been used thus far in the paper and should consider the character of the person who is eating. A society matron or a college Dean of Women would scarcely *bolt* food at a formal sorority banquet, nor would a hungry athlete *nibble* his double steak smothered in mushrooms. In choosing a synonym of the verb *walk,* one can choose from *plod, trudge, tread, stride, saunter, meander, hike, tramp, stroll, march, mince, ramble, prowl, hobble,* and *sneak.* Looking over this list, one realizes how general is the meaning of *walk* and how much care should be taken in selecting a suitable synonym. Some of the words suggest leisurely movement (saunter, meander, stroll); others, furtive movement (sneak, prowl). Still others are suggestive of people's personalities: an effeminate person *minces,* a military man *marches,* a conceited individual *struts.* Thus the writer narrows the choice to one word which gives the meaning that he wants.

NOTE. The thesaurus does not usurp the place of the general English dictionary; the two must be used together for the best results. Some students, when using a thesaurus, run their fingers along the imposing list of synonyms until they find the one that they have heard used before or one that they can spell, and then without further thought of its precise meaning, jot it down on paper. Each synonym should be checked with the dictionary to make sure that the shade of meaning is the one wanted.

Do not use a word because it is big, and do not use a new word just for the sake of using it. Do not use an unnecessary word. Above all, never use a word whose meaning you have not carefully checked.

Do not use polysyllabic words in colloquial speech or friendly letters, or slang expressions in a formal paper. The synonym must be of approximately the same level of diction as that of the rest of the paper.

*Using the Thesaurus for antonyms.* An antonym is a word which has the opposite meaning from that of another word. In the enlarging of one's vocabulary, antonyms function by what psychologists call "the power of

**bluff** (blŭf), *v. t.* **1.** In poker, to deter (one) from betting by a show of assurance. **2.** To deter, dissuade, or frighten by a pretense of strength or resources; also, to deceive; fool. — *v. i.* To bluff, or try to bluff, a person; to deceive. — *n.* Act of bluffing; one who bluffs.

**blu'ing, blue'ing** (blōō'ĭng; 114), *n.* A preparation of indigo or the like used in laundering.

**blu'ish,** *adj.* Somewhat blue. — **blu'ish·ness,** *n.*

**blun'der** (blŭn'dẽr), *v. i.* [ME. *blunderen, blondren,* to stir, confuse, blunder.] **1.** To move confusedly or clumsily; to flounder and stumble. **2.** To make a serious error or commit a fault, through ignorance, stupidity, overconfidence, or confusion. — *v. t.* **1.** To utter awkwardly, stupidly, or confusedly; — usually with *out.* **2.** To mismanage; bungle. — *n.* A gross error or mistake. — **Syn.** See ERROR. — **blun'der·er,** *n.* — **blun'der·ing·ly,** *adv.*

**blun'der·buss** (-bŭs), *n.* [Corrupt. fr. D. *donderbus* thunder box, gun.] **1.** An obsolete short firearm with a large bore and, usually, a flaring muzzle, capable of holding a number of balls. **2.** A stupid blunderer.

Blunderbuss.

**blunge** (blŭnj), *v. t.;* BLUNGED (blŭnjd); BLUNG'ING (blŭn'jĭng). [Cf. *plunge* and *blend.*] To blend; to beat up or mix in water, as clay to form slip.

**blung'er** (blŭn'jẽr), *n.* One that blunges; specif.: **a** A wooden implement for blunging clay. **b** A vat with mechanical stirrers.

**blunt** (blŭnt), *adj.* [Early ME.] **1.** Insensitive; obtuse in feeling or perception. **2.** Dull in understanding; not acute. **3.** Having a thick edge or point; dull; not sharp or keen. **4.** Abrupt in address; tactlessly curt or frank. **Syn. Blunt, dull, obtuse, stupid.** As associated with sensibility or perception, **blunt** implies a certain (sometimes temporary) callousness or lack of nice perception. **Dull** implies a heavy, sluggish habit of mind, or a lack of vividness and intensity; **obtuse,** lack of sensitiveness, and even a certain impenetrability to emotions or ideas. **Stupid** denotes excessive dullness, when the faculties are, as it were, benumbed. In reference to pointed or edged tools, *blunt* and *dull* (opposed to *sharp, keen*) are sometimes interchanged. In present usage, however, *blunt* appears to be more commonly used of instruments or tools so made that a cross section near the edge subtends a relatively large angle; *dull,* of a tool or instrument whose edge or point has lost its sharpness by use. See BLUFF. — **Ant.** Sensitive, responsive; acute, keen. — *v. t. & i.* **1.** To make or become blunt. **2.** To impair in force, keenness, or susceptibility. — **blunt'ly,** *adv.* — **blunt'ness,** *n.*

**blur** (blûr), *v. t.;* BLURRED (blûrd); BLUR'RING. **1.** To obscure, soil, or blemish by smearing; to smudge; hence, to sully. **2.** To make dim or indistinct to the sight; as, haze *blurred* the horizon; also, to dim; to cloud; as, tears *blurred* her vision. — *v. i.* To become blurred; to make blurs. — **Syn.** Spot, blot, stain; obscure, darken. — *n.* **1.** A smear or stain which obscures without effacing. **2.** A blot or cloud, as upon one's name. **3.** Something obscurely or dimly seen, understood, etc. — **blur'ry,** *adj.*

**blurb** (blûrb), *n.* [Coined by Gelett Burgess.] *Colloq.* A fulsome commendation, esp. in advertising.

**blurt** (blûrt), *v. t.* To utter suddenly and unadvisedly or impulsively; as, to *blurt* out a secret. — **blurt,** *n.*

**blush** (blŭsh), *v. i.;* BLUSHED (blŭsht) or BLUSHT; BLUSH'ING. [ME. *bluschen,* fr. AS. *blyscan* to shine, be red, *ãblysian* to blush, fr. *blysa* torch, flame.] **1.** To become red, esp. in the cheeks or face, as from shame, modesty, or confusion; to flush. **2.** To grow, or be, red or rosy. **3.** To feel shame; — often with *at* or *for.* — *v. t.* **1.** To redden. **2.** To express by blushing. — *n.* **1.** A glance; look; — now only in *at* or *on* (*the*) *first blush.* **2.** A suffusion of the cheeks in blushing. **3.** A red or rosy tint. — *adj.* Ruddy; of the color of a blush. — **blush'er,** *n.* — **blush'ful,** *adj.* — **blush'ing·ly,** *adv.*

By permission. From Webster's Collegiate Dictionary
Fifth Edition
Copyright, 1936, 1941, by G. & C. Merriam Co.

**V.** CONVERGE, concur; come together, unite, meet, fall in with; close with, close in upon; center *or* centre, center round, center in; enter in; pour in.

CONCENTRATE, bring into a focus; gather together, unite.

**Adj.** CONVERGING &c. *v.*; convergent, confluent, concurrent; centripetal; asymptotic *or* asymptotical; confluxible [*rare*].

ify; branch off, glance off, file off; fly off, fly off at a tangent; spread. scatter. disperse &c. 73; deviate &c. 279; part &c. (*separate*) 44.

**Adj.** DIVERGING &c. *v.*; divergent, divaricate, radiant, radial, centrifugal, aberrant; broadcast.

**Adv.** broadcast; *passim* [*L.*].

---

**292.** [TERMINAL MOTION AT.] **Arrival.** — **N.** ARRIVAL, advent; landing; debarkation, disembarkation.

RECEPTION, welcome; *vin d'honneur* [*F.*].

DESTINATION, bourn *or* bourne, goal; landing -place,— stage; bunder *or* bandar [*Pers. & India*]; resting place; harbor, haven, port; terminus, terminal; halting -place, — ground; home, journey's end; anchorage &c. (*refuge*) 666; completion &c. 729.

RETURN, recursion [*obs.*], remigration, reëntry.

MEETING, joining, rencounter, encounter, rejoining.

**V.** ARRIVE; get to, come to; come; reach, attain; come up, — with, — to; overtake; make, fetch; come from, hail from; complete &c. 729; join, rejoin.

visit, pitch one's tent; sit down &c. (*be located*) 184; get to one's journey's end; be in at the death; come —, get- -back, — home; return; come in &c. (*ingress*) 294; make one's appearance &c. (*appear*) 446; drop in; detrain; outspan, offsaddle [*both S. Africa*].

LIGHT, alight, dismount.

LAND, make land, cast anchor, put in, put into; go ashore, debark, disbark [*rare*], disembark

MEET; encounter, rencounter [*rare*], come in contact; come to hand; come at, come across; hit; come —, light —, pop [*colloq.*] —, bounce [*colloq.*] —, plump [*colloq.*] —, burst —, pitch- upon.

**Adj.** ARRIVING &c. *v.*; homeward bound, terminal.

**Adv.** HERE, hither.

**Int.** WELCOME! hail! all hail! good-day! good-morrow! come in and rest your bonnet on a chair! [*Southern U. S.*], *bienvenu!* [*F.*].

\*\*\* "Journeys end in lovers meeting, Every wise man's son doth know" [*Twelfth Night*].

110

**293.** [INITIAL MOTION FROM.] **Departure.** — **N.** DEPARTURE, decession [*rare*], decampment; embarkation; outset, start, headway, inspan [*S. Africa*], debouchment, debouch *or* débouché [*F.*]; removal; exit &c. (*egress*) 295; congé [*F.*], exodus, hegira, flight.

LEAVE-TAKING, valediction, adieu, farewell, good-by *or* good-bye, Godspeed, stirrup cup; valedictorian.

STARTING POINT, starting post; point —, place- of -departure, — embarkation; port of embarkation.

**V.** DEPART; go, go away, part [*archaic*], take one's departure, set out; set —, march —, put —, start —, be —, move —, get —, whip —, pack —, go —, take oneself- off; start, boun [*archaic*], issue, march out, debouch; go forth, sally forth; sally, set forward; be gone.

leave a place, quit, vacate, evacuate, abandon; go off the stage, make one's exit; retire, withdraw, remove; "use your legs" [*Merchant of Venice*]; vamose *or* vamoose [*slang, U. S.*], mizzle [*slang*], skip [*slang*], cut [*colloq. or slang*], go one's way, go along, go from home; take flight, take wing; spring, fly, flit, wing one's flight; fly away, whip away; strike tents, decamp; break camp, break away, break ground [*naut.*], walk one's chalks [*slang*], cut one's stick *or* cut stick [*slang*], cut and run [*colloq.*]; take leave; say —, bid- good-by &c. *n.*; disappear &c. 449; abscond &c. (*avoid*) 623; entrain; saddle, bridle, harness up, hitch up [*colloq.*], inspan [*S. Africa*]; "speed the parting guest" [*Pope*].

EMBARK; go on board, go aboard; set sail; put to sea, go to sea; sail, take ship; hoist the blue Peter; get under way, weigh anchor.

**Adj.** DEPARTING &c. *v.*; valedictory; outward bound.

---

A page from *Roget's Thesaurus,* reproduced by permission of the Thomas Y. Crowell Co.

association," for when we see the word *love,* it is relatively simple to call to mind its opposite, *hate.* A great many meanings cannot exist without a conception of their opposites. For example, the word *light* has no meaning to the person who does not understand what is meant by *dark; long* and *short* and *fat* and *thin* are relative terms, depending altogether on the understanding one has of each of them. Antonyms, therefore, are sometimes as useful as synonyms in determining the meaning of a word. In actual writing they are especially valuable in contrasts and comparisons. Of course, the warning which was given about the selection of synonyms applies also to the selection of antonyms.

### Exercise

Distinguish among the following synonyms by using each word in a sentence in such a way that the shades of meaning are shown clearly.

1. pay, compensate, recompense, requite, reimburse, indemnify
2. proud, arrogant, presumptuous, haughty, supercilious, insolent, insulting
3. sin, vice, crime
4. impostor, mountebank, charlatan
5. good, serviceable, fit, excellent, sound, reliable
6. marriage, matrimony, wedlock, wedding
7. martial, warlike, military
8. old, ancient, antique, venerable, antiquated, archaic, obsolete
9. instrument, implement, tool, utensil, machine, apparatus, agent
10. ominous, portentous, sinister
11. interest, excite, entertain, engage, occupy, hold
12. rebellion, revolution, revolt, insurrection, mutiny
13. story, tale, anecdote
14. tear, rip, rend, cleave, split, rive
15. lessen, decrease, impair, weaken
16. irony, sarcasm, satire
17. walk, traverse, perambulate, meander, amble
18. flit, flutter, flicker, hover
19. talk, speak, converse
20. exceed, excel, surpass, transcend, outdo

(See *Workbook,* Exercises 1, 2, 3, and 4.)

## *Featherbeds and Parnassus* [1]

### CAROL HOVIOUS

Probably something of the same spirit that impels small boys to tie tin cans to puppy-dogs' tails prompted me to this experiment on my college Freshmen. Certain it is that I tortured them unmercifully, stretching their

1. Reprinted by permission of the author and of the *English Journal,* College Edition (now *College English*).

tender minds upon the ruthless rack of knowledge and subsequently cracking open their pates to see what had happened. I looked upon myself, of course, as a scientist in search of truth; campus legend, I am told, has not been so kind.

It all came about as the result of a wager. I was sitting one day in the Union with a member of the history department of the university where I peddled English. Over our coffee we fell to ringing changes on that favorite pedagogical lament—the low estate of incoming Freshmen. My companion brought his fist down upon the table with a belligerent thump.

"I tell you," he exploded, "these Freshmen can't think! All they can do with an idea is ogle it!" He puffed his pipe reflectively for a moment and then added with a sidewise swipe at me, "Or maybe it isn't that they're fundamentally incapable of handling an idea, but that the English department hasn't equipped them with words to express it."

"Oh, come now," I protested defensively, rubbing the tender heel of my wounded professional pride.

"Listen," he interrupted, wagging a bony finger knowingly at me, "I'm willing to lay you 10 to 1 that at least—hm-m—at least 90 per cent of your Freshmen will not know the meaning of so common a word as—as—oh, well, say 'prodigal.'"

I had—or thought I had—no illusions about the verbal capacity of college Freshmen. But still—90 per cent! That was a bit steep; particularly since "prodigal" was such an ordinary word. It was not an academic word; one ran across it every day in magazines, in newspapers, in common speech.

"Done!" I answered, already savoring my triumph and already preparing the crushing little speech with which I should rebuke him for his impertinent reflections upon the purveyors of English, once I had good evidence at hand.

Since my bet had gone statistical, I was taking no chances with my evidence. I was getting it in irrefutable, incontrovertible black and white. The next day I wrote the word "prodigal" on the board and asked each of my fifty Freshmen to jot down on a slip of paper the best definition he could muster.

To make a sad story short, my historical friend won—by a generous margin of 6 per cent! He confessed then that he had already tried the experiment for himself with similar results, adding that to collect his bet was almost as heartless as to take candy from the baby. However, he collected it.

I went out to grieve and salt my wounds. Only two of my flock of fifty

Freshmen had defined "prodigal" with reasonable accuracy as "wasteful." The other forty-eight miserable black sheep had gone variously astray, but their vagaries were of two general sorts. About one third of the miscreants confused "prodigal" with "prodigy" and hence informed me that the word meant "exceptional," "gifted," "a smart kid."

And would that the other two thirds had never heard the story of the prodigal son! With his ill-advised squanderings and wanderings in mind, they assured me that prodigal meant "one who returns after absence," "sort of hitchhiker a long time ago," "one who has strayed away," "a good-for-nothing," "worthless," "wayward," "a mild form of sinner."

When, dismayed, I sought to bring them back to sanity by asking them what such an expression as "the prodigal hand of nature" would mean, they only looked at me with blank faces.

The next day, possessed of a sort of horrible curiosity to discover if I could what other monsters of misconception lurked in the minds of my innocents, I led them to a second and more dreadful slaughtering. Picking a dozen or so words at random from current magazines in order to have a fairly representative list, I asked each student to state briefly what the word meant to him, and then, as a check, to use the word in a sentence.

I reaped a whirlwind of ignorance for my folly. In view of the fact that my fifty Freshmen were something better than the average, I determined on one last try which should give them every opportunity to show what they knew. I selected words from their own text in Freshman English; I warned them far enough in advance so that they could check over any unfamiliar words; and, finally, I did not ask them to formulate their own definitions or to write illustrative sentences—I asked only that they select the correct definition from the list I furnished them. The results of this test were, if possible, even more shocking than those of my earlier probings.

Sobered and saddened by these researches into the ignorance of my own students, I sought consolation by inducing my colleagues to try the test on their students—on the principle, I suppose, that misery loves fellow sufferers. The results were always the same; the more papers I scored and tabulated—and there were hundreds before my courage failed—the sorrier became the spectacle of the Freshman mind.

As I worked over the test papers, the errors of definition began gradually to sort themselves into certain general categories which I have labeled "dogberrian," "tangential," "etymological," and "orthographical." The orthographical confusions such as "assent" for "ascent" and "principle" for "principal" we may dismiss summarily, since they form a relatively small and innocuous group. Such confusions as these are, I suppose, inevitable as long as the English language continues to have homonyms and the human mind continues fallible.

The student who falls afoul of the dogberrian vice is in much worse case than his brother who sins orthographically. It is one thing to confuse "principle" and "principal" and quite another to blur the distinction between "odious" and "odorous," as did Mrs. Malaprop in her famous "comparisons are odorous." Mrs. Malaprop, of course, traces her lineage directly to Shakespeare's loquacious old constable, Dogberry, in *Much Ado about Nothing*. The basis of the "malapropism" is an auditory or visual confusion of words: "odious" and "odorous" both look and sound somewhat alike; so do "prodigy" and "prodigal." But what is merely amusing in Mrs. Malaprop becomes maddening in a college student. Shakespeare and Sheridan amused themselves and delighted their audiences by this simple device because it manifested itself in illiterate people of whom one expected nothing better. But the dogberrian disposition of college students is at once exasperating and terrifying to the professor who must address them seriously upon serious subjects which they are supposed to comprehend.

Typical dogberrian confusions are: "impetuous" with "impetus," "precipitous" with "precipice," "imminent" with "eminent," "veracity" with "voracity," and "utilitarian" with "Unitarian."

Tangential errors spring from a partial understanding of a word and are mostly context derived; that is, meanings inferred—erroneously—by a student from reading a word in a given context and subsequently attaching that meaning to the word permanently. Thus, Freshmen who told me that "prodigal" meant "a wanderer," or "a sinner," or "a hitchhiker" had in mind the tangential meanings of the word in the story of the prodigal son. To be sure, the young man in the biblical legend was a wanderer and a mild form of sinner, but he was not therefore called "prodigal." Probably the student came to associate wandering and sinning with prodigality because the emphasis in the story is more upon the young scapegrace's peregrinations than upon his wasteful dissipation of his patrimony.

Thus, it will be seen that a tangential definition comes close to the real meaning of a word, yet misses it, flies off at a "tangent" from it. To define "avidity" as "speed" is to miss the central meaning of the word —"greed"—and to emphasize a tangential meaning which is subsidiary. To define "recumbent" as "still" is likewise to skirt the truth, to come close to the real meaning and yet to miss it.

The student who defined "scrupulous" as "criminal" fell doubly upon evil days, for his thinking was at once dogberrian and tangential. In the first place, with malapropian ineptness he confused "scrupulous" with its opposite, "unscrupulous." In the second place he attached to "unscrupulous" the tangential meaning "criminal," rather than the exact meaning, "unprincipled."

The most ludicrous boners, however, were not malapropian or tangential, but philological. Students who have had too light a draft from the Pierian Spring become giddy and fall headlong into the most amazing abysses. Some of these falls from grace result from "little Latin and less Greek." If *homo* is Latin for "man," why should not "homogeneous" mean "pertaining to man"? The student is mildly outraged to discover that his little Latin will not unlock the secret meaning of every word. Occasionally the student is even betrayed by his own language and defines "salutary" as "one who salutes."

I am now about to offer an explanation for this amazing chaos in the minds of our college students. This explanation I realize is purely hypothetical. It is likely to be very unpopular with certain of our educationalists. Nevertheless, it is my best explanation, and I submit it.

Let us dismiss first of all the pseudoetymological errors. They come from a little learning, but even a little learning is not to be too lightly despised in these parlous times. They are to be regretted, but still forgiven. They are the ludicrous result of well-meaning Latinists who, intent upon salvaging Latin from the dead, have cried out insistently that Latin survives in the living speech. The Latinist may be forgiven much, for he has suffered much, but it might be wished that he preach his doctrine with a little caution.

More serious, however, is the malapropism. It is, I am convinced, an unwanted and unexpected child of the "configuration method" of teaching reading. No doubt the configurationists, who have flourished mightily in the last years, would disown the child I make so bold to lay upon their doorstep; whether they admit the parentage or not, the child has its father's eyes.

The configuration-taught child, it will be recalled, learns by wholes. He walks without bothering to creep or crawl; he builds glittering castles without any unpleasant digging in the basement; he reads right pop out of the box without any tedious fiddling with mere letters and their sounds.

All this is very gratifying to papas and mamas who adore being dazzled by their offspring. And no one can deny that children learn to read much more rapidly by this method. The theory is that having learned to read

whole words, the child gradually, by some vague and subterranean process, learns to recognize letters and their sounds.

Aye, but there's the rub! For the child learns no such thing. Many a
bewildered college student has come to me with groans and tears and
begged me to teach him "how to sound out words the way mother does."
And I—well, I give him a primer and let him sweat a bit over phonetics, for without a groundwork in phonetics he cannot spell nor can
he sound out new and unfamiliar words. It is this reading of words by
their shape that leads him to confuse such similars as "impetus" and
"impetuous."

The attachment of tangential instead of exact meanings to words, like
the malapropism, is a Dead Sea apple of an unwise pedagogy. It is the
result of substituting a guess for the dictionary. The student is not to be
blamed too harshly for this practice; he had been encouraged in it. Modern educational theory preaches that a child's pleasure in a book is chilled
by the frigid breath of the dictionary. One enthusiast opined—in print—
that it made no difference if the child who heard *Lady of the Lake* read
aloud thought it was about a "staggit eve." If the child caught the emotional lift of the poem, that was enough.

In short, a child need not know what a book is about. It is enough
that his imagination should soar upward on "wings of book" without
any scholarly ballast. If only he will read widely and rapidly, he will by
some inexplicable magic become a full man.

Such rhapsodists seem to overlook the cold fact that one cannot enjoy
what one does not understand. They overlook, too, the fact that children
are not altogether fools. Students learn early that a few round-eyed
"oh's" and beatific "ah's" judiciously placed will do more to bring home
an "A" than any amount of grubbing. So with their tongues in their
cheeks they turn sycophant and settle back to a life of intellectual
ease. They are pleased, of course, because they can be lazy with impunity
—but they are also secretly contemptuous of the system that lets them
get by with it.

Although the exigencies of space prevent an adequate elaboration of
the point, I should like to suggest in passing that the schools are not
primarily to blame for this unfortunate situation. After all, the schools
merely pander to the public taste. One needs but to scan the current
magazines to discover that we as a people are characterized by a desire
to get something for nothing—to acquire personal charm by perfume
instead of discipline, big salaries by techniques instead of hard work,
musical proficiency by charts instead of practice. The schools with their

modern "get-smart-quick" schemes are merely following the trend of the times.

The evil effects of this laxness are everywhere evident, but to me, specifically, as an English teacher, painfully so in my students' inability to deal with words. Without words they walk in a world of textbooks they cannot read, professors they cannot understand, misty ideas they cannot express. Words are the bright coin with which they buy their sheepskins, and they are paupers.

That students need not always remain in this intellectual workhouse I have tried to indicate by analyzing the sources of their verbal—and therefore ideational—incompetence. If we know that they are betrayed by our methods of teaching words by wholes and our airy disregard of the dictionary, we have at least a signpost pointing the road to rehabilitation.

But one thing is certain—there is no royal road to learning; there are no escalators up Parnassus. Every student must mount under his own power. If we carry him around on a featherbed all the days of his youth we have only ourselves to blame if he is not in trim for the stiff climb up Parnassus.

### Suggestions for Study

1. What rhetorical value does the introductory anecdote have?
2. Explain what is meant by dogberrian, tangential, etymological, and orthographical.
3. State the reasons for the students' making such blunders with words.
4. On whom can the blame be laid?
5. Is this lack of vocabulary serious for college students engaged in the mastery of intellectual subjects?
6. What suggestions are offered for remedying the situation?
7. How is the title of the article derived?
8. Define the following words used in the article: purveyors, irrefutable, incontrovertible, homonyms, fallible, orthographical, odious, odorous, loquacious, auditory, illiterate, impetuous, precipitous, imminent, veracity, utilitarian, context, scapegrace, peregrinations, patrimony, avidity, subsidiary, recumbent, scrupulous, ineptness, philological, Pierian Spring, homogeneous, salutary, etymological, parlous, salvage, subterranean, opined, sycophant, impunity, rehabilitation, Parnassus.
9. Using the tone employed by the author of the essay, write a paper on the same subject from your own point of view.

## B. Spelling

Spelling is primarily a problem of the grade school and high school. At least it should be mastered there. The student who has entered college without the ability to spell is laboring under a handicap which only he can remedy. The ability to spell comes gradually as a result of extensive reading and the forming of correct habits. Rules exist, but for most rules there are exceptions, so that on the whole the easiest way to learn to spell is to assimilate a few words each day. The following rules have been set down for the purpose of pointing the way to good spelling. They should be learned and applied, but the student must also use his dictionary conscientiously in order to impress upon his mind images of the words as they should appear, and thus make correct spelling a habit which cannot easily be broken.

**7a** **Rule for ie and ei.** To spell words like *believe* and *receive,* a help is to remember the jingle

> *i* before *e* except after *c*,
> or if sounded like *a*
> as in *neighbor* and *weigh*.

1. *i* before *e:* believe, relieve, achieve, siege, field, thief, grief, retrieve, mischief.

2. except after *c:* receipt, deceive, perceive, ceiling.

3. or if sounded like *a* as in *neighbor* and *weigh:* neigh, heinous, sleigh.

4. Exceptions: seize, weird.

**7b** **Rules Governing Prefixes** [2]   *letter other than a vowel*
  1. *If a prefix ends in a consonant (dis, con),*
  (a) the initial consonant of the word is doubled [3]
    (1) if the final consonant of the prefix is the same as the initial consonant of the word: *dis* and *satisfy, mis* and *spell, over* and *rate, under* and *rate, un* and *necessary, dis* and *solve*.
    (2) if the final consonant of the prefix is not the same as the initial consonant of the word, but is assimilated: *a(d)* and *similation*—assimilation, *a(d)* and *cede*—accede, *i(n)* and *legible*—illegible, *co(n)* and *mission*—commission, *o(b)* and *currence*—occurrence, *i(n)* and *mediate*—immediate, *o(b)* and *ponent*—opponent, *co(n)* and *rupt*—corrupt.
  (b) the initial consonant of the word is not doubled if the final consonant of the prefix is different from, and not assimilated with, the initial consonant of the word: *with* and *stand, over* and *take, per* and *spiration, con* and *ference*.

2. A prefix is a syllable combined or united with the beginning of a word to modify its meaning.

3. Actually, as a perusal of the rules which apply here will show, frequently it is not that the initial consonant is doubled, but that an apparent doubling occurs because of identical letters at the end of the prefix and the beginning of the stem.

2. *If a prefix ends in a vowel (a, re, de)*, no change takes place, whether the word begins with a consonant or a vowel: *peri* and *meter, de* and *scribe, a* and *rise, pro* and *ceed, pro* and *scription, re* and *engage, re* and *iterate, re* and *commend, de* and *cision, de* and *ride*.

### 7c Rules Governing Suffixes [4]

1. *If a suffix begins with a consonant,*

   (a) a word ending in any letter except *y* undergoes no change; the two are simply written together: *appease* and *ment, fate* and *ful, lone* and *some, lone* and *ly.*

   (b) a word ending in *y* changes *y* to *i: busy* and *ness*—business, *lazy* and *ness*—laziness.

2. *If a suffix begins with a vowel,*

   (a) a word of one syllable or a word accented on the last syllable that ends in one consonant preceded by one vowel will double the consonant: *drop* and *ed*—dropped, *occur* and *ed*—occurred, *plod* and *ed*—plodded, *whip* and *ing*—whipping, *equip* and *ing*—equipping, *run* and *ing*—running;

   (b) but if the word has more than one syllable, and if the accent is on some syllable other than the last, the final consonant does not double: *offer* and *ing*—offering, *enter* and *ing*—entering, *benefit* and *ed*—benefited.

   (c) In adding a suffix which begins with a vowel, drop final *e*. In adding a suffix which begins with a consonant, retain final *e: guide* and *ance*—guidance, *please* and *ure*—pleasure, *entire* and *ly*—entirely, *grace* and *less*—graceless, *dine* and *ing*—dining.

   (Both parts of the rule have many exceptions. Before a suffix beginning with a vowel, *e* is often retained in order to retain the soft sound of *c* or *g*, as in *peaceable, changeable, noticeable, singeing, serviceable.* Other exceptions to the first part of the rule are *dyeing, acreage, shoeing, hoeing.* Before a suffix beginning with a consonant, *e* is dropped in *duly, truly, wholly, ninth, awful, argument, acknowledgment, judgment.*)

### 7d Rules Governing the Spelling of the Plurals of Nouns

1. Nouns which do not end in *s* or an *s sound (s, z, x, sh, ch)* regularly form the plural by adding *s* to the singular form: *hats, stores.*

2. Nouns which end in *s* or an *s sound (s, z, x, sh, ch)* form the plural by adding *es* to the singular form: *churches, glasses.*

3. Nouns ending in *y* form their plurals in two ways:

   (a) If a consonant or *qu* precedes the *y*, the *y* is changed to *i* and *es* added: *lady—ladies, soliloquy—soliloquies.*

4. A suffix is an abstract element at the end of a word serving a derivative, formative, or inflectional function, such as *ly* in *manly, ness* in *sweetness, ed* in *hated.*

(b) If a vowel precedes the *y*, *s* is added to the singular form: *dray—drays, day—days*.

4. Nouns ending in *o* are divided into two major groups: those with a vowel before the *o*, and those with a consonant before the *o*.

(a) If a vowel precedes the *o*, the plural is formed by adding *s* to the singular form: *embryos, radios*.

(b) If a consonant precedes the *o*, the plural form usually ends in *es*: *heroes, potatoes*. There are many exceptions, however. All musical terms, for instance, end in *s—altos, banjos, sopranos, solos*—as well as many nonmusical terms—*curios, octavos*. Some words, moreover, have both endings: *cargos, cargoes; mottos, mottoes; zeros, zeroes*.

5. Most nouns ending in *f* form the plural by changing the *f* to *v* and adding *es*: *leaf—leaves* (exceptions are *roof, chief,* and others).

6. Letters, figures, symbols, or words out of their normal context form their plurals by adding *'s*:

Letters—The *A's* are legible in this MS.

Symbols—You have used two *5's* too many here.

Words—The *and's* and *so's* are far too numerous in your paper.

7. Compound nouns form their plurals by adding *s* to the part of the compound which carries the meaning of the word; this part of the compound may be the first or the second element: *bookstores, steamboats, mothers-in-law, attorneys-general, passers-by*. Compounds with *ful* add *s* to the latter element: *spoonfuls, cupfuls*.

8. Words which have been borrowed from foreign languages usually retain the plural form of their own language.

(a) Latin and Greek: *curriculum, curricula; stratum, strata; stimulus, stimuli; alumnus, alumni; alumna, alumnae; larva, larvae; crisis, crises; thesis, theses; appendix, appendices; phenomenon, phenomena; automaton, automata*.

(b) French: *beau, beaux; tableau, tableaux; madame, mesdames*.

(c) Hebrew: *cherub, cherubim; seraph, seraphim*.

**Words Frequently Misspelled.** From various studies of the writing of college freshmen it has been shown that the words listed below are most often misspelled. Altogether, these amount to fewer than four hundred. If you should learn three a day, you could master the whole list in a semester. Since most misspelled words are found in this list, it seems worth while to learn both the spellings and the meanings of the whole list.

absence
accessible
accidentally
accommodates
accompanied
accustomed
achieved
acquainted
across
advice
aisle
alley
all right
amateur
analyze
anxious
appearance
appetite
approach
appropriate
argument
arrangement
arrival
ascend
assistant
association
athletic
attendance
bachelor
balloon
beginning
believe
benefited
business
cafeteria
candidate
captain
carburetor
category
cede
cemetery
certain
changeable
changing
characteristic
climbed
committee
comparative

competent
competition
completely
concentration
concise
confident
connoisseur
consider
consistent
controlled
convenience
coolly
corroborate
courteous
criticism
crystal
decide
decision
definite
definition
describe
description
desirable
despair
desperate
determine
develop
development
different
dilemma
disappeared
disappointed
disastrous
discipline
discriminate
dissatisfied
dissipation
divine
division
dormitories
ecstasy
efficiency
eliminated
embarrass
emphasize
environment
equipped
especially

essential
exaggerated
exceed
excellent
exercise
exhilaration
existence
expense
experience
familiar
fascination
February
fiery
finally
financial
foreign
forty
friend
fundamental
generally
government
grammar
grievance
grievous
guard
height
heroes
hindrance
holiday
humorous
hungry
hurriedly
immediately
incidentally
increase
independent
indispensable
inimitable
inoculate
insistent
intelligence
interesting
interfere
interpret
irrelevant
irresistible
irritable
judgment

knowledge
laboratory
leisure
license
literally
literature
livelihood
loneliness
losing
magazine
maintenance
marriage
mathematics
meant
merely
miniature
misspelled
momentous
murmur
mysterious
necessary
newsstand
nickel
ninety
noticeable
occasion
occurred
occurrence
omitted
operate
opinion
opportunity
optimistic
organization
original
oscillate
panicky
parallel
paralyzed
particularly
perform
permanent
permission
permissible
perseverance
persistent
persuade
physically

| | | | |
|---|---|---|---|
| physiology | recede | sheriff | tragedy |
| picnicking | receive | shining | tranquillity |
| playwright | recognize | siege | transferred |
| pleasant | recommend | similar | truly |
| plebeian | referred | sincerely | twelfth |
| possess | relieve | sophomore | tyrannize |
| possible | religious | source | unconscious |
| practically | repetition | specimen | university |
| prairie | representative | strength | unnecessary |
| predictable | restaurant | stretched | unusual |
| prejudiced | rhetoric | studying | usually |
| preparation | rhythmical | succeed | vacillate |
| privilege | ridiculous | successful | vacuum |
| probably | sacrifice | suddenness | valuable |
| procedure | sacrilegious | supersede | varied |
| proceed | scarcely | superintendent | vegetable |
| professional | scene | surely | vengeance |
| professor | schedule | surprise | villain |
| prominent | secretary | surround | weird |
| pronunciation | seize | synonym | writing |
| propeller | separate | tariff | yeast |
| psychology | sergeant | technical | zoology |
| pursuing | severely | temperament | |
| really | shepherd | tendency | |

With the words in the following list, the trouble is not so much that the student misspells the word as that he uses the wrong word—that is, he uses one word in each group when he should use another. It is important with these to know the meaning of each word and to associate the spelling and meaning when writing the words. Those starred in the list are discussed on pages 194–198.

| | | |
|---|---|---|
| *accept, except | descent, decent | planning, planing |
| *affect, effect | desert, dessert | *preceding, proceeding |
| *allusion, illusion | device, devise | presence, presents |
| *already, all ready | dining, dinning | *principal, principle |
| altar, alter | discussed, disgust | prophecy, prophesy |
| *altogether, all together | eighth, eight | quiet, quite |
| ascent, assent | formerly, formally | *stationary, stationery |
| breathe, breath | fourth, forth | *there, their, they're |
| *capital, capitol | genius, genus | too, two, to |
| carrying, caring | hoping, hopping | until, till |
| choose, chose, chosen | *its, it's | vicious, viscous |
| clothes, cloths | *latter, later | whether, weather |
| coarse, course | led, lead | whose, who's |
| *compliment, complement | *loose, lose | woman, women |
| conscious, conscience, | pastime, past time | write, rite, right |
| conscientious | piece, peace | |

(See *Workbook*, Exercise 5.)

## C. Levels of Usage

Words, like people, exist on social levels which usually are fairly well defined; literary words like *efficacious* and *delineation* would be uncomfortably out of place in colloquial conversation in company with expressions like *auto* and *phone*. Conversely, expressions such as *high-toned* (stylish), *daffy,* and *groggy* would be immediately ostracized in formal writing. But, like the levels of society, levels of diction overlap, and words are constantly shifting from one level to another. Relative usefulness and color may raise a word from slang to standard speech. Great public interest in a technical process may bring a word from the jargon of scientists and engineers to the vocabulary of common intercourse. On the other hand, because of slipshod treatment expressions may degenerate from good, meaningful usage and become unacceptable or forgotten.

Thus, it is evident that a writer should have some knowledge of the social acceptability of words; he must know when to use a word as well as when not to. Such a knowledge involves the levels of usage. There are six such levels: (1) Common; (2) Literary; (3) Technical; (4) Colloquial; (5) Slang; (6) Illiterate.

### LEVELS OF DICTION

| LITERARY | COMMON DICTION | TECHNICAL |
|---|---|---|
| abortive invidious quintessence insensible | tree, day, night, house, building, weaken, straighten beautiful, energetic, finished | heliotropic palimpsest orthodontic pulmonary |
| COLLOQUIAL<br>flabbergasted, harum-scarum, blues, phone, auto |||
| SLANG<br>swell (adj.), stand the gaff, gadget, screwball, boyfriend |||
| ILLITERATE<br>ain't, youse, furriner, it don't, irregardless, those kind of |||

NOTE: The student should remember that this diagram represents the levels of usage of large groups of words, but that individual words are constantly shifting from one level to another, leaving the main structure, however, relatively constant.

**The Common Level.** This is the most extensive of all the levels of diction because here belong the words used and understood by everybody. Words such as *hat, coat, table, day, night, chair, see, feel,* and *know* are parts of the active vocabulary of all people to whom the English language is a native tongue. They are used by children as well as adults, and constitute not only the first words which an English-speaking person learns but also the linguistic stock which serves him best in all ordinary affairs throughout his life.

While the common level of speech is recruiting unceasingly among words of other levels, it avoids terminology which is too formal or literary to be compatible with easy conversation, or too technical to be readily understood, or too lacking in dignity to be useful in serious communication. It prefers a short word to a long one, the homely Anglo-Saxon expression to its more elegant synonym of Latin derivation. With a good vocabulary of words in common usage one can always make himself understood in a direct, forceful manner. Beauty and variety of expression, and sometimes exactness of expression, however, frequently require that a person have a command of all levels of diction except the illiterate. Cultivated taste and a sense of consistency in the use of language are guides which a person who desires to be educated should seek to possess.

**The Literary Level.** Words and expressions which are employed in formal writing but which are not commonly employed in ordinary speech belong to the literary level of diction. Most of these words are of Latin or Greek derivation. A literary sentence, "A large proportion of current slang is vulgar," may be reduced to a colloquial level by taking out the Latin derivatives: "A lot of everyday slang is coarse."

Ordinarily a person's passive vocabulary (*i.e.,* the words that he recognizes and understands in his reading, but which are not in his daily speech) comes under this heading. Literary diction is admirable and effective when it is used in ordinary speech by one thoroughly at home with it and to whom it comes as naturally as common diction does to most of us; but the person who uses literary diction for ordinary communication for the purpose of producing an effect of culture lays himself open to ridicule. In formal writing and in public addresses, however, literary diction is usually to be preferred because it is more accurate and more subtle than our common stock of words.

**The Technical Level.** Technical words and phrases are those which are limited to the vocabulary of particular professions or branches of knowledge. In standard dictionaries technical words are marked by an abbreviation of the particular branch of knowledge to which they belong. Some examples are *ceiling, strut* (aviation), *gamete* (zoology), *isotope* (chemistry), *stoma* (botany). Words such as these should be avoided in everyday writing if they have synonyms in common usage. They belong properly in special treatises and are understood by a limited number of people.

**The Colloquial Level.** *Colloquial* means conversational. The colloquial level of diction, therefore, is the level of informal oral communication. Of course, the conversational vocabularies of different kinds of people differ. Words used in conversation by educated people may not be understood by people of the illiterate class. However, the term *colloquial,* as used by the dictionaries, refers to the conversational vocabulary of fairly well-educated people.

8 The fact that a word is marked *Colloq.* by a dictionary does not mean that it is not a useful or legitimate word. It means merely that it is useful at a certain time and place and not at all times or places. *A colloquialism is out of place in formal writing, business letters, and most written exercises in college,* just as sport dress is out of place at a formal party. A generation or so ago, the distinction between written English and colloquial English was much more marked than it is now. Today a commencement speaker, a Phi Beta Kappa orator, and even the President of the United States are likely to make use of racy, pungent expressions taken from the conversation of common men. This, in most respects, is an admirable tendency. We speak much more often than we write; spoken English is the source of our language, and a strict cleavage between the diction of normal intercourse and that of public pronouncements can be only detrimental to literature and oratory. On the other hand, the person whose vocabulary is composed exclusively of colloquialisms is unable to achieve, upon demand, the accuracy of expression that is the characteristic of literary diction, the precision tool of communication.

A few of the more common colloquial expressions are in the list which follows. Obviously, all such expressions cannot be given here; but a study of this list will help you distinguish between words on the literary and the colloquial levels, and may lead you to question some of the words you use and to look up in a good dictionary any about which you have a doubt. When you find such a word marked *colloq.* in your dictionary, form the habit of substituting for it a word on the literary level.

*Ad* for *advertisement.*
*Auto* for *automobile.*
*Back of, back up* for *support:* Let's *support* the team (not *get back of* or *back up*).
*Balance* for *remainder:* Do the *remainder* (not *balance*) of these problems.
*Boost* for *lift, raise, advertise:* He is *advertising* (not *boosting*) our products.
*Brainy* for *intelligent:* He is an *intelligent* (not *brainy*) announcer.

*Combine* (as noun) for *combination of persons or organizations.*

*Considerable* (as noun) for *a great deal:* He paid *a great deal* (not *considerable*) for the dog.

*Cut* for *refuse to recognize* or *absent oneself from class.*

*Date* for *appointment:* I have an *appointment* (not *date*) at 11 today.

*Enthuse* (as verb) for *be enthusiastic about.*

*Fine* for *very fit* and in any adverbial sense.

*Fix* for *repair, arrange: Repair* (not *fix*) this pen.

*Funny* for *strange, odd, queer:* He was an *odd* (not *funny*) character.

*Have got* for *have, possess, must,* or *ought:* I *have* (not *have got*) two pencils.

*Jell* for *crystallize* or *solidify:* Leave the liquid to *solidify* (not *jell*) overnight.

*Kibitz, kibitzer* for *offering,* or *one who offers, gratuitous advice.*

*Lots of* for *many, much: Many* (not *lots of*) people are superstitious.

*Lovely* for *very pleasing:* This is a *very pleasing* (not *lovely*) view.

*No good* for *worthless, not good:* He is a *worthless* (not *no good*) manager.

*Out loud* for *aloud:* The class laughed *aloud* (not *out loud*).

*Outside of* for *except* or *besides:* I knew no one there *except* (not *outside of*) the family.

*Over with* for *finished, done, ended:* My work was *done* (not *over with*) at 4 o'clock.

*Plenty* (as adverb) for *quite, abundantly:* The blanket is *quite* (not *plenty*) soaked.

*Plug* for *advertise* or *advertisement:* He is *advertising* (not *plugging*) Hokums.

*Proposition* for *undertaking:* That is a dangerous *undertaking* (not *proposition*).

*Quite* for *rather. Quite* means *wholly, entirely.*

*Regular* for *entire, thorough:* He is a *thorough* (not *regular*) scoundrel.

*Run* for *manage, conduct:* He *manages* (not *runs*) a small factory.

*Scrappy* for *aggressive:* He made an *aggressive* (not *scrappy*) campaign.

*Shape* for *condition:* The car is in good *condition* (not *shape*).

*Show up* for *appear, arrive:* She *arrived* (not *showed up*) at the half.

*Size up* for *estimate, form a judgment about:* We *estimated* (not *sized up*) the crowd as about 2,000.

*Socialite* for *one socially prominent.*

*Thumb* for *request a ride of a passing motorist.*

*Terrible* for *tremendous, excessive,* etc.: He had a *painful* (not *terrible*) jolt.

*Try and* for *try to: Try to* (not *try and*) locate KDXY.

*Ugly* for *unpleasant, disagreeable:* That was an *unpleasant* (not *ugly*) situation.

9 **The Slang Level.** *Slang words and expressions* (marked *slang* in dictionaries, or else not listed) *are distinctly undesirable in formal writing.* Some students think that such words if placed in quotation marks are permissible, but this practice should not be encouraged. If a slang word is used in serious writing, it should be because it is the only expression which provides the shade of meaning and color which is de-

sired; it is, for the purpose in hand, a respectable word and should not be put in quotation marks.

The first charge that can be brought against slang is that it is ephemeral. Slang words are here today and gone tomorrow. Campus slang, for example, not only differs with geographical areas, but changes almost from one generation of students to the next. The person who writes or speaks with a serious purpose should desire to use language which will last at least throughout his lifetime.

The vagueness of many slang terms is another reason for their being inappropriate in careful writing. In recent years the word *swell* has become very popular as the lazy man's method of indicating any shade of commendation: a swell party, a swell guy, a swell view, a swell dinner, a swell compliment, a swell movie. *Swell* is applied so generally that it means almost nothing. But the language of an educated man should be exact. The person who depends on such general terminology not only does not express himself clearly, but is actually doing an injury to his mental processes. To a large extent the ability to think in terms of accurate distinctions depends on possessing in one's vocabulary the words which express such distinctions. To fail to acquire or to forget sharp, incisive diction is to deprive one's mind of indispensable tools of thought.

Finally, the connotations of slang are not suited to serious expression. With regard to the user, slang connotes extreme informality if not vulgarity; with regard to the occasion, casualness and lack of importance. An attempt to use slang to connote dignity and significance is doomed almost inevitably to failure.

This condemnation of slang in serious writing does not mean that slang expressions are without value to the English language. On the contrary, they play an important part in its development. A great many of our best words have come up to common diction from the level of slang. In general, such words have received their promotion for one or both of the following reasons: they expressed meanings for which there were no words in respectable diction, or they provided a vigorous figure of speech. Slang which creates metaphors is especially likely to achieve permanence —that is, if the comparison implied in the metaphor remains a part of general experience. When we call an ineffective person a *flat tire,* or a girl who is unable to attract men a *wallflower,* we employ graphic metaphors. Similarly, such terms as *snake in the grass* and *dud* create definite pictures. Words belonging in this group are the result of the free play of imagination, of originality among the English-speaking peoples. It is rather words like *lousy, swell, terrific, awful,* which are merely the generalizations of foggy minds, that have no legitimate place in good writing or speaking.

NOTE. Do not use slang expressions in papers that you write for college classes unless the special effect of such words is desired for a particular purpose, such as dialogue. In conversation with intimates and in friendly letters to people who are well known to you, slang may be used sparingly, but only when it adds specifically to the meaning. Such expressions as "The soph drag last night was tops, but I finally got the number of that dumb bunny I had in tow" are not to be countenanced.

In the following list are a few samples of slang. Much slang, as was said above, is so ephemeral that it disappears before it has time to be listed in a dictionary. Most of the terms which follow, however, have been in use for some time, and some of them may eventually be accepted in good usage; but the standing of all of them is questionable at present. The purpose of listing them here is to direct your attention to what slang is and to make you curious enough to look in a good dictionary for the standing of many words you and your friends use. By doing this, you may be able to add many words to this list.

*Allergic* for *irritated by:* Jim is *irritated* by (not *allergic to*) Bill's jokes.
*Awful, awfully* for *extreme, extremely:* That was an *extremely* (not *awfully*) funny caricature.
*Be on the beam* for *perform well:* Bill *recited well* (not *was on the beam*) this morning.
*Broke* for *lacking funds:* I *have no money* (not *am broke*) today.
*Bust, busted* for *strike with violence, be ruined financially, be dismissed from college.*
*Cheesecake* for *a photograph displaying feminine shapeliness.*
*Corny* for *stale, trite:* The program was *full of stale jokes* (not *was corny*).
*Crack down* for *bring pressure to enforce obedience:* The police *enforced the laws against* (not *cracked down on*) gambling.
*Crack up* for *collapse, break down:* Sara *collapsed* (not *had a crack up*) as a result of overwork.
*Cut out* for *cease:* Stop (not *cut out*) that noise.
*Dead pan* for *expressionless countenance.*
*Jalopy* for *dilapidated automobile* or *airplane.*
*Jive* for *swing music.*
*Panic* (as verb) for *impress an audience greatly.*
*Party* for *one person*, except as a legal term: I never met the *man* (not *party*).
*Put across, put over* for *complete, accomplish:* We *completed* (not *put across*) the campaign.
*Rib* for *make fun of* or *tease.*
*Screwball* for *eccentric, crazy.*
*Shellacking* for *drubbing, total defeat.*
*Smear* for *smother, rout.*

*Soap opera* for *radio serial.*
*Tops* for *most excellent:* John is *the best* (not *tops*) in his class.

**The Illiterate Level.** Here belong terms that occur commonly in the speech of those who have little or no education, and who therefore habitually violate grammatical rules and correct usages. Some of these expressions—*He don't talk like no furriner. I hain't seed him lately*—are unlikely to enter the speech of college students. Others, such as the double negative, *done* for *did, ain't, irregardless, seldom ever* for *rarely,* may persist into a student's college years, or longer, if he does not become aware of them and make a positive effort to eliminate them from his speech and writing.

These usages are classed in most dictionaries as *barbarisms, dialectal expressions, provincialisms,* and *illiteracies.* A barbarism is a word that was in good repute but has been corrupted through misuse, such as *disremember, unbeknownst,* light *complected.* A dialectal expression is one peculiar to a certain class, group, or race of people. A provincialism is a word or usage which is limited to a certain section of the country, as *tote* in the South, *calculate* for *think* in New England, and *sick to my stomach* in some sections of the Midwest.

Since illiteracies in speech or writing at once mark a person as uneducated, it is important that a college student watch his own language and be on his guard against using them. Form the habit of attending to the speech of cultured people, and when you hear a cultured person using a word with which you are unfamiliar, look it up in a dictionary and add it to your own vocabulary. Listen to the speech of other students, and if you hear one using a term that you suspect is incorrect, check upon it likewise by going to the dictionary. Look up terms you use yourself to see if they are marked as slang, colloquial, dialectal, or illiterate. In this way you establish an awareness of correct speech, and your own speech and writing will begin to improve. Such an attitude is not to become snobbish, but to make good use of the talents entrusted to you.

(See *Workbook,* Exercise 6.)

## D. The Right Choice of Words

Avoiding slang, colloquialisms, provincialisms, and other substandard words is the negative side of word selection. The positive side involves a conscious effort to build a good vocabulary by making the right choice of words. It has been long accepted that to be correct in formal communication, a word must be in national use—not a provincial or dialectal word; in current use—not obsolescent; and in reputable use—in favor with good writers and speakers. One who applies the test of national, current, and reputable use in selecting words is assured of being understood wherever the language is spoken. But there is more to the right choice of words than this test implies. A writer who aspires to something more than merely being understood must have a higher aim even than correctness.

Assiduous and extended attention to the way words are used by the best writers is necessary for a mastery of language. But this is a long process, and the results accrue slowly. Even a novice, however, can begin to make progress in the right use of words by heeding a few suggestions. First, a student who wishes to achieve a style above mediocrity will not be content with the first word that comes into his mind, but with the aid of the dictionary and thesaurus, he will search for the word that carries the exact shade of meaning he wishes to express. Second, he will learn to have such respect for words that he will never employ them loosely, taking several times the number he needs to express his meaning well. Third, he will prefer specific and concrete words to general and abstract ones. And fourth, for any writing except pure exposition he will choose words for their power of suggestion and will employ those that are richest in overtones of meaning. The first of these suggestions does not need expansion; the others are discussed more fully in the next few pages.

## I. ECONOMY OF DICTION

As in business dealings some people are misers and others spendthrifts, so in writing some miserly authors, because they are too sparing with their words, possess a crabbed and awkward style, and some lavish writers apparently have an inexhaustible supply of words. The first puzzle us with incoherent fragments, and the second confuse us with an unnecessary wealth of modifiers and synonyms.

These are the two extremes; the problem confronting one who wants to write effectively is to steer between them so that he will not give offense on either score. Most students, whatever they may say about their minds becoming blank as soon as they sit down to write a paper, err by using too many words. The reasons are that they do not discriminate carefully among words and that they think two or three words, however vague in meaning, are to be preferred to one that is precise. In short, they have not learned to use economy in diction. How are these faults, which are variously known as *Wordiness, Redundancy* (usually defined as the repetition of single words), *Circumlocution* (talking around a thing instead of coming to grips with it directly), and *Pleonasm* (the use of two words for the same grammatical function: "My Uncle Joe, *he* visited us yesterday"), to be remedied?

**10** The answer is, by precision. When each word in a sentence bears the precise meaning which the author wants, that sentence is correct, no matter how many words have been used; but *if some words have vague, hazy meanings, or can just as well be omitted, the writer is guilty of wordiness and inexactness.* For example, in the sentence "Now, I'd like to tell you about my case," just what does *case* mean? Is it a medical case (patient), a case of merchandise, a problem, or an experience? Again, the sentence "The white, shimmering orb of reflected light rose above the dark and unilluminated clouds" means simply "The moon rose above the dark clouds." Such diction serves to obscure the meaning, instead of making the sentence intelligible.

But economy and precision are very abstract terms to a student about to write a paper for a class in English composition. "What specifically can I do to avoid wordiness in my sentences?" asks the college freshman. The answer is in the following rules:

**10a** Do not use too many simple sentences. Such usage necessitates repetition of the subject and often of the verb. "John was a savage boy. He was always disobedient and revengeful. In addition he was cruel to his friends. For these reasons he had earned a bad reputation among his schoolmates." These short sentences can be thus economically telescoped: "John was a savage boy, always disobedient and revengeful, and, in addition, cruel to his friends. For these reasons he had earned a bad reputation among his schoolmates."

**10b** Do not begin sentences unnecessarily with *it, it was, there is, there are,* or other impersonal expressions. The sentence "There are many reasons which are given in defense of the superintendent's action" may be amputated to read, "Many reasons are given in defense of the superintendent's action."

**10c** Do not use vague, stereotyped expressions which make sentences more wordy and at the same time add to their ineffectiveness. The overuse of terms like *case, instance, factor, proposition, beg to reply, wish to state, along the line of, asset, the professional world, the business world, a new angle on, element, in the field of, development* is a sign of laziness. Sir Arthur Quiller-Couch, in *The Art of Writing,* labeled this kind of language *jargon* because many of the terms included in it are derived from the terminology of particular professions or occupations, but, when extended to general use, have lost their significance. Jargon is a crutch for the person with limited vocabulary, or the lazy person, or the person whose mind is too dull to perceive its lack of accuracy; and the fact that jargon is very widely used is proof only that many such persons exist.

Mention has been made already of the meaninglessness of *case*. Some people think that by substituting *instance* for *case* they have somehow achieved better diction, but *instance* has very little more meaning. Note how the following sentences are improved by eliminating both of these words:

> Let me tell you of a case where a student corrected his instructor. (Let me tell you of a student's correcting his instructor; *or* Let me tell you about a student who corrected his instructor.)
>
> In the case of Richard Roe, the circumstances are different. (For Richard Roe the circumstances are different.)
>
> In case you want help, call me. (If you want help, call me.)

Do not try to find synonyms for *case* and *instance,* because words which have no meaning cannot have synonyms; revise the sentence in such a way as to communicate the meaning directly. *Factor* has been used so indiscriminately that its legitimate meaning has been blurred. "Health is an important factor in education" means no more than "Health is important in education." *Proposition* has a good meaning as "something which is proposed," but is out of place in "Getting the water out of the cellar was a difficult proposition." *In the field of* and *along the line of* are generally deadwood. "He is succeeding in the field of medicine" should be "He is succeeding in medicine." "He is good in the line of scholarship" is awkward when compared with "He is a good scholar." Why should one say "He is an asset to the business world" when "He is a good businessman" is shorter and more direct?

It is unnecessary to cite more examples. Economy and accuracy of diction are hard to master, but they pay well in effectiveness. Unfortunately, indiscriminate diction of the kind which has been discussed can be heard everywhere, even among college professors, as the alert student will discover; but, regardless of the rank of persons who use jargon, the incisive thinker will not want his communication blurred and his mental processes atrophied by habitual use of weak terminology.[5]

**10d**  Do not use unnecessary phrases or clauses, as in the following examples:

> My classmate wrote me that he would be here *at no great date in the future* (soon).
>
> My automobile operates *with a high degree of efficiency* (efficiently).
>
> One of the noblest qualities *which John possesses is unselfishness.* (One of John's noblest qualities is unselfishness.)

5. See also the discussion of jargon under "The Business Letter."

At last the day dawned *in the east.* (Did it ever dawn in the west?)

The books that he held were oblong *in shape.* (How else could they be oblong?)

**10e**    Do not repeat expressions that are already etymologically present in a word which has been used. This error is largely due to ignorance of the meaning of words.

He returned *back to his home.* (The prefix *re* means *back.*)

Endorse this check *on the back.* (*Endorse* means *on the back.*)

Some day I am going to write *my* autobiography. (An autobiography is the life history of oneself.)

**10f**    Do not sprinkle a sentence with modifiers which add nothing to the meaning, as in the following sentences:

*Strict* accuracy requires that the *important* essentials be listed first.

*Successful* achievement is necessary if a *joint* partnership is to enjoy *abundant* wealth.

Her face was *just too* lovely; it was so *very* perfect that I thought she was *absolutely* the *most* unique girl at the party.

**10g**    Do not use ornamental phraseology, especially high-flown synonyms, for decorative purposes. Percy Marks, novelist and author of *The Craft of Writing,* places the use of such synonyms next to the excessive use of modifiers as the most frequently occurring fault of affected writers. Many students think that words which are in daily use are not fit to express lofty ideas and universal truths. Literature (with a capital L) means to them something concocted in unusual, exotic, and grandiose diction. A versatile author does command a larger vocabulary than most of his readers, but his diction is likely to be more accurate rather than more ornamental. Consider the dignity and also the simplicity of the following incident as related in the King James translation of the nineteenth chapter of I Kings:

And he arose, and did eat and drink, and went . . . unto Horeb the mount of God. And he came thither unto a cave, and lodged there; and, behold, the word of the Lord came to him, and he said unto him, "What doest thou here, Elijah?"

And he said, "I have been very jealous for the Lord God of hosts: for the children of Israel have forsaken thy covenant, thrown down thine altars, and slain thy prophets with the sword; and I, even I only, am left; and they seek my life, to take it away."

And he said, "Go forth, and stand upon the mount before the Lord."

And, behold, the Lord passed by, and a great and strong wind rent the mountains, and brake in pieces the rocks before the Lord; but the Lord was not in the wind: and after the wind an earthquake; but the Lord was not in the earthquake: and after the earthquake a fire; but the Lord was not in the fire: and after the fire a still small voice. And it was so, when Elijah heard it, that he wrapped his face in his mantle, and went out, and stood in the entering in of the cave.

The injunction against excessive ornamentation does not imply that only those words which are understood by uneducated people are permissible in good writing, or that student papers should be reduced to words of one syllable. Far from it. A good writer certainly should be given the freedom of the whole great treasure house which is the English language; but he knows that the *right* word brings with it its own weight, dignity, and beauty—qualities which cannot be achieved in any other way. Do not be satisfied with your present vocabulary: expand it; add new words every day—but do not use new words for the sake of making a show of them, and by all means possess an accurate understanding of them.

(See *Workbook,* Exercise 7.)

## 2. SPECIFIC AND CONCRETE WORDS

Words have one purpose only—to transmit images and ideas from one mind to another. Obviously, the more exact a word is, the better chance it has to transmit the precise image or idea in the mind of its user. A writer, therefore, who has in his own mind a clear, unblurred image or idea and who cares at all about transmitting it without distortion to someone else will seek the most specific terms he can find for his communication. He will also prefer concrete words to abstract ones, because abstract words lack the power that concrete words have to transmit exact images.

A general word, as the term implies, is one that refers to a whole group, class, or kind of objects or conditions. Since it includes many words in its meaning, it can transmit only a generalized or vague and indistinct image or idea. The general word *tree,* for example, refers to any one of a large class of woody plants ranging in size from a large shrub to the giant redwoods of California, and in shape from the slim poplar to the spreading banyan. The general word *laugh* refers to a way of showing mirth by certain facial expressions and guttural sounds, whereas the specific words *giggle, snicker, titter, chuckle,* and *guffaw* express a more precise sort of expression and sound. Likewise *cry* indicates a general state of unhappiness; *weep, sob, whine, whimper, howl, wail,* and *blubber* particularize the method of crying and transmit a more accurate image of the sort of unhappiness expressed. A general word, then, gives only a vague idea and indicates little concerning the particular characteristics of the object, act, or quality named; a specific word stands for a precise meaning which is different from all other meanings within the general class to which it belongs.

Abstract words are those which refer to qualities apart from any objects, as *blackness, honesty, loyalty, patriotism*. Concrete words, on the other hand, refer to things that can be perceived by the senses, as *rock, coffee, thunder, velvet, perfume*. Any reference that arouses a sensory image (*i.e.*, an artificially stimulated experience of the senses: seeing, hearing, tasting, feeling, smelling) will have a more powerful appeal than one that does not. Most of the knowledge that has particular meaning for us was arrived at through sensory experience; moral precepts, for instance, are likely to remain ineffective until their truth is demonstrated by specific experiences in actual life. Some examples may serve to make all this more clear.

In a scientific work, *The Variation of Animals and Plants under Domestication,* Charles Darwin wrote: "In scientific investigations it is permitted to invent any hypothesis, and if it explains various large and independent classes of facts, it rises to the rank of a well-grounded theory. The undulations of ether and even its existence are hypothetical, yet every one now admits the undulatory theory of light." In another part of the same work he wrote: "Savages set the highest value . . . on dogs; even half-tamed animals are highly useful to them. The Indians of North America cross half-wild dogs with wolves, and thus render them wilder than before, but bolder." Which of the passages is easier to comprehend? Which gives the clearer image? You may of course understand the first quotation, but it exists for you as an idea only after you are used to abstract terminology. The second quotation carries no difficulty even for the immature mind. What makes the difference? A superficial analysis shows that the first is made up almost wholly of abstract terms, the second of concrete ones.

Cicero, in his book *On the Nature of the Gods,* says: "Man's mind meditating on the celestial phenomena has come to the realization that Gods exist; and from this realization arose piety among men; this in turn gave rise to the idea of justice and the other virtues—all of which are the sources of a happy life." Now this is understandable to one who is used to dealing with abstract ideas, but to reach others, the more specific and concrete terms of the Psalms and Gospels are needed.

In *The Gilded Age,* Mark Twain and Charles Dudley Warner describe a room in these specific and concrete terms:

> A dreary old haircloth sofa against the wall; a few damaged chairs; the small table the lamp stood on; the crippled stove—these things constituted the furniture of the room. There was no carpet on the floor; on the wall

were occasional square-shaped interruptions of the general tint of the
plaster which betrayed that there used to be pictures in the house—but
there were none now. There were no mantel ornaments, unless one might
bring himself to regard as an ornament the clock which never came
within fifteen strokes of striking the right time, and whose hands always
hitched together at twenty-two minutes past anything and traveled in
company the rest of the way home.

The effectiveness of this passage, with such specific touches as *haircloth*
sofa, unfaded parts of the wall where pictures had hung, and the hitching
together of the clock hands, becomes apparent by comparing it with such
a general statement as the following:

> The furniture of the room comprised only the barest necessities. The
> floor was bare, no pictures were on the wall, and the mantel also was
> bare, except for a clock that was useless for telling the time.

A few short examples may complete these illustrations:

General: My brother was injured yesterday while playing in a game.
Specific: My brother broke his right ankle yesterday while playing left
halfback against Oklahoma.

General: The woman went into the store to make a purchase.
Specific: Mrs. Trout went into Finn's hardware store to buy a paring knife.

General and abstract: Good citizenship means being loyal and patriotic.
Specific and concrete: A good citizen is one who supports and obeys his
country's laws and institutions, who votes at election time, and who
is willing to fight for his country and if need be die for it in time of
war.

The great value to a writer who employs specific and concrete terms
is that his readers not only understand what he has to say, but cannot
misunderstand it. The words "a red pencil, three inches long, sharpened
at one end, containing a soft black lead, and with an eraser worn to the
metal cap" will evoke the same image in the mind of everyone who
reads them, but the words "a virtuous and handsome man with a high
code of honor" will not. What does the writer mean by virtue? What
is a handsome man? What constitutes a high code of honor? All these
need further explanation before writer and reader can be in complete
accord.

General and abstract words have their place in language, of course, or
they would not exist. Too many specific words may confuse a reader by
focusing his attention too much on details. Topic sentences of paragraphs
and summarizing sentences are often general. But a writer who aspires
to exactness will use general and abstract words frugally. The student

who forms the habit of replacing a general word with one more specific and an abstract word whenever possible with a concrete one will find himself better understood, and he will soon discover the added value of having his ideas and images become clearer to himself.

(See *Workbook,* Exercise 8.)

## Co-operation versus Competition

### JOHN RUSKIN

We can hardly arrive at a more absolute type of impurity than the mud or slime of a damp, overtrodden path in the outskirts of a manufacturing town. I do not say mud of the road, because that is mixed with animal refuse; but take merely an ounce or two of the blackest slime of a beaten footpath on a rainy day near a large manufacturing town.

That slime we shall find in most cases composed of clay (or brick dust, which is burnt clay) mixed with soot, a little sand, and water. All these elements are at helpless war with each other, and destroy reciprocally each other's nature and power, competing and fighting for place at every tread of your foot—sand squeezing out clay, and clay squeezing out water, and soot meddling everywhere and defiling the whole. Let us suppose that this ounce of mud is left in perfect rest, and that its elements gather together, like to like, so that their atoms may get into the closest relations possible.

Let the clay begin. Ridding itself of all foreign substance, it gradually becomes a white earth, already very beautiful; and fit, with help of congealing fire, to be made into finest porcelain, and painted on, and be kept in kings' palaces. But such artificial consistence is not its best. Leave it still quiet to follow its own instinct of unity, and it becomes not only white, but clear; not only clear, but hard; not only clear and hard, but so set that it can deal with light in a wonderful way, and gather out of it the loveliest blue rays only, refusing the rest. We call it then a sapphire.

Such being the consummation of the clay, we give similar permission of quiet to the sand. It also becomes, first, a white earth, then proceeds to grow clear and hard, and at last arranges itself in mysterious, infinitely fine, parallel lines, which have the power of reflecting not merely the blue rays, but the blue, green, purple, and red rays in the greatest beauty in which they can be seen through any fired material whatsoever. We call it then an opal.

In next order, the soot sets to work; it cannot make itself white at first, but, instead of being discouraged, tries harder and harder, and comes out clear at last, and the hardest thing in the world; and for the blackness that it had, obtains in exchange the power of reflecting all the rays of the sun at once in the vividest blaze that any solid thing can shoot. We call it then a diamond.

Last of all the water purifies or unites itself, contented enough if it only reach the form of a dewdrop; but if we insist on its proceeding to a more perfect consistence, it crystallizes into the shape of a star.

And for the ounce of slime which we had by political economy of competition, we have by political economy of co-operation, a sapphire, an opal, and a diamond, set in the midst of a star of snow.—*Modern Painters.*

*Suggestions for Study*

1. From the last paragraph of this selection, list the general words which the author wrote the article to clarify. Then list the specific words in the same paragraph which he used in making the clarification.
2. Having noted the important general and specific words, analyze each paragraph in turn for concreteness of diction. For example, in the first paragraph, which is more specific, *impurity* or *mud? type* or *slime?*
3. Do specific or general words predominate in the selection as a whole?
4. Explain Ruskin's purpose in this selection, and state his thesis.

## Basic English for Science [6]

### TOM BURNS HABER

The following letter (evidently not written to be posted) I found in the English notebook of one of my students in Freshman Composition:

To THE AUTHORS OF *A Botany Textbook:*

As a student in the botany course which is given at our university, I have become familiar with your textbook and workbook which are used in connection with the course. I wish to inform you that I am having a great deal of difficulty with botany, and I believe your books are largely responsible.

The purpose of botany, I believe, is to acquaint the student with the different types of plant life and to help him understand the growth and structure of plants. In my estimation *A Botany Textbook* defeats that purpose. The average student is lost in the maze of difficult and highly technical language of your text and in the complexity of the demonstrations and problems in your workbook. For example, in describing the beginning of a leaf you state that "development of a leaf begins with the proliferation of a primordium"—without any previous hint of what a primordium is!

As a result of your heavy treatment of the subject, botany is dreaded

6. From the *Scientific Monthly,* LXII (March, 1946), 258–262. Reprinted by permission of the author and of the *Scientific Monthly.*

and disliked by the majority of students on this campus. Many have failed the course because of this dislike—for which your boring textbook is largely responsible. You have, in the eyes of many students, attached a stigma to the useful science of botany.

The evident sincerity of this letter, I hope it will be agreed, entitles it to a fair hearing. What college freshman has not at some time or another felt a similar protest rising within him as he tried to advance through the maze of language between him and the subject he was studying? The writer of the above letter may pass her course in botany and give the lie to her fears. She may even go on to like botany. But what a pity that she must arrive in spite of the language in which her textbooks are written. Much has been said on the teachers' side of the difficulty instructors of physics, of botany, and of chemistry have in getting their students interested in these branches of science. Perhaps the main reason lies not in the students' dislike for the subject itself but for the language in which the subject is presented to them.

Too many college texts in science are burdened with an unnecessarily heavy style. The use of essential scientific words makes for economy; certainly the author is not expected to eschew them to the point of repeating long definitions. But why cannot he use "growth" instead of his beloved "proliferation"? "Chain of events" instead of "series of concatenations"? "Scaling off" instead of "desquamation"? It would seem that some authors of secondary science texts think that unless they write in the style of Herbert Spencer's definition of evolution, they cannot impress their readers with the importance of their subjects; as if what is stated simply cannot be worth learning. Clear exposition is a craft which scientific writers ought to regard as highly as the validity of their ideas. Generally speaking, they seem not to be aware of its existence; or, if they are, acknowledge it by keeping as far as possible from it—after the example of Professor Longbore, who used to open his science lectures each quarter with this warning, the only intelligible sentence in his discourses: "I do not intend to make clear to you in twelve weeks what it took me fifty years to learn."

The style of Professor Longbore and his ilk is probably the result of a passive rather that an active state of mind. As one turns the pages of a ponderously written text in college zoology, for example, he begins to wonder whether the author may not have drifted into his style merely by following the course of least resistance. A polysyllabic style is a lazy style. It is easy to master the learned jargon of any science, and mastery of the jargon is too often mistaken by publishers' readers for mastery of the subject. "Easy writing makes cursed hard reading," observed Dick

Sheridan; and although laborious writing is not guaranteed *per se* to make easy reading, it has a good chance to, if the writer knows what he wants to say and tries hard enough to say it. My point is that it is downright hard work to express scientific concepts in a clear, mature style. And yet texts written for college students ought to be worth that much effort.

For some writers, no doubt, there is a fascination in the weighty language of which my student complained. Thus the trap is baited and set for the author's complete undoing: he lets words take the place of thought. He has seen these splendid terms so often; they were right to him in the books he read. Are they not as good in his own? He does not stop to ask what the words really mean, how he expects his reader to interpret them. If by any chance a conscientious student narrows his eyes and carefully examines this lingo, the result is usually a feeling of dismay like that expressed in the letter at the beginning of this article.

Is there, for example, any reason why a book in psychology should be written in this style?——

> The apperception of self-motivation is a psychological fact. A concomitant phenomenon is the consciousness that the origin of this motivation is internal and not external.

Is not this what the writer *means?*——

> The mind is conscious that it is self-moving; and at the same time, that the motion comes from within itself.

The last sentence above is written in Basic English. This simplified English ought to have an especial appeal to scientific writers because its discovery was analogous to the procedure of the scientist seeking basic principles in the natural world. The originators of Basic English, sifting the thousands of words in our language, isolated 850 indispensable terms by which the meanings of the others could be expressed. For science an additional list of 100 words is provided.

The methods by which the Basic word list was determined can be tested by anyone who takes a dictionary in his hand. He will find in reading definitions that certain words keep returning time after time—usually little words such as *go, get, make, be, thing, name, true, good,* together with necessary conjunctions and prepositions. These words and others of their kind *are* the basic vocabulary of our language. They make a restricted common ground on which it is possible for writer and reader to meet with the least possible chance for confusion or mistake. In its inductive origin, as well as in its purposes, Basic English is scientific English.

It is not urged here that all writers of college texts in science adopt at once the Basic English vocabulary. The Spartan simplicity of Basic, though it is the handmaiden of truth, does not always serve other ideals as faithfully. Variety and subtlety, for example, are not main properties of Basic. These virtues and other qualities of a pleasing style ought not to be lacking from the books our science students read. Nevertheless Basic English could have a tonic effect upon these books. It could dispel much foggy thinking, which is the real cause of bad writing. If an author *thought* in Basic first, he would not write "heliotropic inclination toward the illuminating source." He would see that the meaning of his first word is repeated needlessly in the five that follow and might decide that his whole phrase could be put thus: "turning in the direction of the light" —which is good science and good Basic. No one can compose in Basic without having in his mind a pretty clear idea of what he wants to say. There are no superfluous terms in Basic to get between him and his manuscript. He will often be reminded that between his idea *A* and the words *B* that represent it there ought to be the same relation as between an object *a* held before a mirror and its reflection *b*. A true reflection requires a good mirror. Basic English has the makings of a good mirror because its vocabulary is level and impersonal—a plane reflector. Even though the scientific writer makes use of a larger vocabulary, if he keeps firmly in mind Basic equivalents as he composes his sentences, his writing will gain clearness, whatever words he finally chooses. And his readers —his students or his peers—will call him blessed.

But there is another field of scientific writing where the need for Basic English is far more pressing. I mean the scientific books and magazines printed in this country and Great Britain. A great many foreigners before World War II were coming into English via Basic. Now as an international language Basic is gaining steadily in general esteem everywhere. Public interest in it was greatly stimulated by Winston Churchill's ardent approval of Basic in his address at Harvard University, September 6, 1943. No artificial language can meet the stern needs of an international tongue as Basic English can. First, it has behind it the compelling prestige of the Anglo-Saxon tradition; it "looks" like English and it *is* English, the vital heart and core of the language of Shakespeare and Jefferson. Basic is easy for the non-English speaker to learn. A few weeks' steady effort under skilled direction can make an intelligent foreigner at home in written and spoken Basic. The demand for books in Basic, both here and abroad, is on the upswing. It is one sign of the world-hunger for unity and commonalty among the peoples of our shrinking planet.

In satisfying this hunger the place of science is nothing less than strategic. It remains for science to recognize some of the practical aspects of its position. Science, as an international agency, must create or adopt an international tongue. The scientist today is faced with the problems faced by English traders 500 years ago as they carried their goods and their language into the Seven Seas. Through necessity, between them and their brown-, black-, and yellow-skinned customers, a species of international language slowly developed. The barbarous pidgin ("merchant") English of the Far East is a natural phenomenon brought into being by the needs of men groping toward each other's minds. These needs are a hundred times more imperative today. The very existence of the race may depend upon our finding right answers to them. Science, like trade, now has the earth as its province. More fortunate than trade, science does not have to await the development of a crude, mass-made English. A scientifically evolved speech is at hand; in the words of Mr. Churchill, "a very carefully wrought plan for an international language, capable of very wide transactions."

It is a truism to say that the great impetus felt by scientific research during the past five years will continue and accelerate. Parallel with this step-up of activity in the ranks of the scientists is a keen public concern about what they are doing. Jet-propelled aircraft and atomic bombs have drawn the fearful attention of everyone to the laboratory of the technician. This public interest cannot be written off as mere curiosity. We are hearing it said on all sides: Why, if the scientist is so expert in devising the machines of death and destruction, why cannot he turn his talents as effectively to the service of humanity? This protest is admittedly naïve: Burbank and Edison were scientists. But the protest still stands. Its ultimate meaning is that everyone the world over wants to know what the scientist is about.

Modern science has therefore a vast new social responsibility which it cannot ignore. The day of unadulterated "pure" research is about over. Even though the scientist may not, like Terence, agree that "Everyman's business is my business," Everyman is telling the world and himself that "the scientist's business is my business." And Everyman pays the taxes and makes the grants that keep the scientist going. Everyman is a Chinese farmer, a Chicago businessman, a French taxi driver, a Greek fisherman, a Russian fur dealer. All these are invading the hitherto sacred confines of the technician's laboratory. And they have a right to do so.

In practical terms this means that the findings of the technician must be put on paper. Books must be written, articles contributed to scientific and lay journals. At present the chances are twenty to one that the native tongue of our hypothetical scientist will be English. Why should he not address himself to his world-wide audience in a truly international language—Basic English?

Basic is surprisingly easy for the English user to learn. With a little experience a copy writer can translate a full-English draft into Basic about as rapidly as he can compose. It is most desirable, of course, that the scientific writer prepare his own Basic version of his books and articles. Thus the thoughts of such authorities as Sir James Jeans, J. B. S. Haldane, Walter S. Landis, and Sir Arthur Stanley Eddington could go directly to the minds of men all over the earth without the warped meanings and false emphases that lurk in translations.

In facilitating this direct communication between the writing scientist and his universal reader, the American and British scientific journals have a place of unique importance. Their large circulation is a token of the immense service they can render to science and to humanity. By the use of complete articles in Basic English and by special Basic editions and supplements, they can directly interpret the findings of modern science to a circle of readers that in a very true sense is world-wide. In so doing they will be assuming their share in the large responsibilities borne by science in the world today. . . .

*Suggestions for Study*

1. Why do many authors resort to excessively heavy diction?
2. Why do many readers admire such wording?
3. What is Basic English?
4. What purposes does it have?
5. What virtues are lacking in a style employing only Basic?
6. Study your own textbooks for examples of unnecessarily difficult passages. Copy several of these, and then state the same idea in simple, clear wording.
7. Employing the resources of your library, investigate more fully the subject of Basic, its nature, uses, and limitations.
8. Define the following words from this article: eschew, validity, ilk, analogous, truism, hypothetical, facilitating.

# I Can't Quite Hear You, Doctor [7]

## JOSEPH A. BRANDT

For sixteen years I was the publisher of the scholarship of three of our great universities. Frequently, in the books I published, I was called

7. From *Harper's Magazine*, CXCII (March, 1946), No. 1150. Reprinted by permission of the author and *Harper's Magazine*.

upon to accept without question scientific conclusions which I and millions of my fellow men did not, and could not, understand.

Of course, there are certain areas of pure scientific exploration where
it would be ridiculous to try to reduce the terminology to such simple
terms that the student of the social sciences or of the humanities, or the
ordinary literate man or woman, could understand. But it is equally true
that all science is not pure mystery. At some stage, it must coincide with
the needs and the comprehension of mankind.

Yet so impenetrable is the language in which most scientists speak
that not only does the layman fail to understand it, but other scientists
often are puzzled by it. A zoologist once complained to me that he was
at a loss to understand the terms used by a colleague of his, a physical
scientist. A few days later I had occasion to bring up this question,
obliquely, with the physical scientist himself. I was delighted as well as
amused to find that he, too, felt that science was becoming so specialized
that it was impossible for him to keep abreast of the other disciplines—
and the science he mentioned as having the vocabulary most incompre-
hensible to him was zoology!

It is difficult to tell which controls scholarship today, the scholar or
the monstrous terminology which he has created. Terminologitis has
swept, like an uncontrollable forest fire, from the pure sciences into the
social sciences and even into the humanities. One of the most significant
books published thus far in this century is one I had the privilege of
publishing a number of years ago. Its field was social science. Its subject
concerned every thinking American. My colleagues were as excited as I
when the manuscript arrived, and as downcast after we had examined it.
Who, we wondered, would be able to read it? Because of my sincere
admiration for the content of the manuscript, I suggested to the author
that he substitute lucidity for terminology. By return mail the author
wrote me a blistering letter accusing me of wanting to commit intellectual mayhem. So the manuscript was published as written and found
as its audience mainly the specialists in the man's own field. It was little
satisfaction to us to have an acerbic reviewer, who wanted the author's
message shouted from the housetops, suggest that the publishers bring
out another edition—"in English"!

Why this insistence upon unintelligibility? I think the explanation lies
in the fact that the scholar, by the very nature of his training, is taught
to think of his work as something impersonal to everybody but himself,
whose future career is at stake. He must be "objective." He must be
colorless, lest he prove objectionable to the more conservative of the elder

statesmen who will pass ultimately upon the quality of his work and determine whether he can be admitted to the greater glory of doctorhood. Rarely, during his training, is he taught to think of an audience. So, when he turns writer, it is small wonder that he writes for no audience; or, if he is aware of readers, he thinks of them either as members of his own cult, or else as people he must impress—or whom he instinctively fears. And, since his associations are almost exclusively with fellow scholars, he rarely is aware of the painful longing, among people beyond the academic pale, for some insight into the comforting realm of certainty which the scholar rules.

Many have been the long and apparently fruitless sessions that I as a publisher have been compelled to have with physical scientists in particular, as I argued that science, as a social instrument, should be concerned with the ultimate ends to which its discoveries would be used.

Why, I used to ask these men, do the scientists not only leave to the inventor and the business man the task of applying what they discover for the benefit of man, but also maintain an attitude of such studied unconcern as to how it is applied? The great Bell or Du Pont laboratories are truly governed by as impeccable a sense of scientific truth as any university scientific body; but science in the commercial laboratory is shaping the destiny of man, and shaping it consciously. Why, I would ask, does the academician not assume a responsibility to people as well as to learning? The usual reply to this question was that *pure* research should be an end in itself. True scientific triumph lay in pushing a search to its conclusion—in the form of an answer satisfactory to the scientist himself. He was under only one obligation: to satisfy himself intellectually.

The result of this deliberate aloofness has been a curious state of affairs. In our American society the engineer has served as butler at the feast which the inventors supplied from the fertile fields of scientific research. The scientists, particularly the physical scientists, have been a sterile priesthood in the society served by the butlers. Although their intellectual achievements have been the most brilliant in the history of man, knowledge of these has been confined among the priesthood. No public relations council has explained to the rest of us the ultimate meaning of their discoveries. The scientists have maintained their own societies, published their own magazines; they have been a world apart, regally oblivious to the feudal society below them.

For the truth is that, in the period of the most widespread education in the history of mankind, we have established a twentieth-century feudalism. The difference between it and medieval feudalism is that it is intel-

lectual rather than economic. In the period of medieval feudalism, the
gulf between the lord of the manor and the villein or the serf tied to
the land was both intellectual and economic; but the principal characteristic of that gulf was economic. It is true, of course, that the serf had
no intellectual freedom. But it is equally true today that the average citizen cannot speak intelligently about, or criticize constructively, the scientific age. The gulf between him and those who understand it is too great.
And yet, as he has just discovered, he is tied to it inescapably, and the
penalty for forgetting that fact is the same as in the Middle Ages—death.

Envious of the exploits of science, American higher education as a
whole has sought to emulate the Brahmins, the physical scientists. It has
tried to reduce unpredictable and immeasurable man to a science. Social
study becomes social science. The humanities struggle in a maze, ignored,
shunned, and even suspected. Economics becomes statistics. Humane history becomes a social science, the science of footnotes. Home economics
is elevated to the level of philosophy, is given a curriculum all its own,
and becomes domestic science.

There is scarcely any limit to the catalogue of this dangerous academic
absurdity. At a certain university, when the faculty was confronted with
a candidate for the degree of Doctor of Philosophy whose entire work
for this degree was a statistical operation—adding and subtracting certain
classified types of man-hours—it hurriedly instituted the degree of Doctor
of Education. But the faculty was not trying to protect society against
uneducated educators. It was acting for the less worthy purpose of protecting an academic monopoly.

The Big Three—engineering, law, and medicine—have been less imita-
tive of scientism, but they have basked too long in the respect which
the American instinctively pays to the so-called professions, and have
paid too little attention to broadening their students as human beings.
The engineering curriculum (which for almost all engineering students
comprises the complete time they spend in a college or university) seldom
contains any subjects having to do with society. Law and medicine have
established prerequisite undergraduate training programs, but these in
the main do little to prepare the future lawyer or doctor to assume a place
of leadership in society except on the simple plane of professionalism.
This absence of training in social thinking on the part of doctors is
visibly placing the profession more and more in the unenviable position
of being at war with the society it serves. The argument of most doctors
against "socialized" medicine is not a social argument.

The higher learning in our country, despite brilliant exceptions, seems to have become a form of self-worship, a series of rites performed by a priesthood which has left its congregation to be served, so far as discernible leadership is concerned, solely by the politician. This is unfortunate because the politician, however skillful he may be in the management of human affairs, is as much lost in a world of scientism—thanks to the isolating policy of science—as is the humblest precinct captain.

The people have been long-suffering with their politicians, largely, I suspect, because they speak the people's own language, are their own kind, do things which people can see and experience. Huey Long left good roads and magnificent buildings for the people he deceived. They could ride along the roads, their children could go to their new state university, and they could look in wonderment at the magnificence of their state capitol. The politician, because he sees people in their homes and knows their wants, realizes how thin is the thread by which democracy clings to the star of destiny. He knows that the children of democracy are still, despite our relatively high standard of living, the children of poverty, and that the average man's abiding fear, even as American democracy enters the atomic age, is still of the breadline.

Despite their imperfections, the politicians have been far more scientific socially than the scientists, however pure they may be. Government somehow has moved along, and the citizen has felt some sense and certainty about it. When he votes, he votes with the realization that the parties and candidates have "educated" him to the issues.

The educator, on the other hand, and particularly the scientific educator, has had no such liaison with the people—as he discovered to his dismay after Hiroshima. Not until science had brought about an immediate possibility of the end of the world did it realize that socially it had been going nowhere at all. It was going nowhere because society was as unaware of it in all of its implications as an amoeba is of the niceties of a Tschaikovsky symphony.

Unless people understand, they cannot be led, except it be by the whip of fear. And frequently, when society does not understand, it destroys. How else can one explain the wanton destruction of the priceless Japanese cyclotrons? We ourselves are willing to destroy the science of another country if it frightens us.

Does this mean anything to the educator, the scientist? Yes. It means that the life of academic quietism is over. The man of learning, however ill-equipped he may be, must learn to become a man of action, a politician, a man of the people, speaking for people, leading people. Certainly, in my brief experience as a university administrator I never found any educator who was at all bashful about becoming an academic politician. The academician loves politics. The only trouble with him has been that he either fears people outside his academic world or is contemptuous of them.

The atomic bomb destroyed something more than Hiroshima and Nagasaki. It blew up the ivory tower. Ultimately, this may be the greatest gain we made by the conquest of the atom. Even when the physical scientists began their work on the atom bomb, they suddenly realized they had taken in their hands the fate of society, of a society which they had not prepared for the ultimate triumph of their scientism. Leaders among them, like Professor Harold C. Urey of Chicago, have gone to the people, to tell them about the fate which may be in store for us. And they are using simple, everyday language, such as the eloquent statement of Mr. Urey to *The New Yorker:* "I've dropped everything to try to carry the message of the bomb's power to the people, because, if we can't control this thing, there won't be any science worthy of the name in the future. I know the bomb can destroy everything we hold valuable and I get a sense of fear that disturbs me in my work. I feel better if I try to do something about it."

Perhaps the academic eclipse is over, an eclipse which Daniel Coit Gilman never intended when he established the modern American type of university at Johns Hopkins. We cannot expect all scholars to realize that the citadel which protected them from the people is gone. But we know now that the men most responsible for the kind of world in which we live are determined to reunite themselves with the people, and if possible to lead them.

This is pleasing to one who spent sixteen years trying to persuade scholars, scientists especially, to translate the translatable things they were doing. In far too many instances the scientist-scholar would reply, "Oh, I couldn't think of doing anything popular. Why, it would ruin me in the profession."

In all fairness, let me say that this attitude is not limited to scientism alone. I found it in all the academic disciplines. There was a fear, an unreasonable fear, of consequences among colleagues which constituted an unconscious condemnation of the entire academic profession.

Sometimes the youngsters were ready to go ahead but were held back by their older colleagues. I remember one young historian who had written a delightful and almost readable dissertation which, with some concessions to intelligibility, would have reached a large audience. The modifications I suggested to him had nothing to do with erudition or scholarship. They were concerned simply with pruning a too-lush thesis which had been designed to satisfy the vanity of a Ph.D. jury. With these modifications, the university, through its press, could have afforded to publish the dissertation and even pay the author royalties. But if the author, as I explained to him, insisted upon publishing a document designed for no audience, he would have to reimburse the university for the inevitable loss it would sustain.

The young scholar agreed heartily with my suggestions. "There's one thing I want to do, however," he said. "I think I should talk this over with the professor who directed my doctorial work."

"Well," I replied, "I know what the answer will be. I think you should keep in mind, however, that either you have been trained to be an independent thinker or you haven't been. Why should a single professor veto a real service which you can perform for the people?"

Nevertheless, the young man did consult the professor. My memorandum might be all right, the professor said. He didn't quarrel with it as a "commercial" proposition—I had written my memorandum from the point of view of a non-commercial institution, remember—but the young historian had better publish his dissertation just as he had written it. And the reason?

"You may want a job in another university some day," the professor told the young man. "You'll have to show some departmental chairman that you know how to do research. You may not get a job if you don't publish the thesis as you wrote it."

It is on that narrow plane, on that viciously anti-social plane, that we have been conducting the business of higher education. President Gilman's type of new university has degenerated through the years to become merely a super-employment service in the interest of scholars but not in the interest of society.

A young botanist I know had been doing fundamental research which he was translating for the benefit of the garden clubs of his state. Several magazines of general circulation asked him to write about his work, which he did and most successfully. It occurred to him that perhaps in view of this interest, he ought to write a book for the people. On his vacation, he went back to the university from which his doctorate had been awarded, to talk the matter over with the professor who had directed his work.

"Great heavens, man, why do you want to waste time writing for the layman?" the professor demanded indignantly. "You've got such a fine start with those papers you've been doing for the scientific journals. Keep on with that. Forget about the garden clubs."

On the other hand, I well remember the day, during the height of the dust storms in Oklahoma, when Paul B. Sears, then chairman of the Botany Department at the University of Oklahoma, walked into my office and without preliminaries said, "Joe, how would you like to publish a book called *Deserts on the March?*"

Paul Sears had seen what man was doing to nature. As an undergraduate he had been shocked at the frightful waste caused by the Ohio River floods. However, he pursued the normal research which is expected of any faculty man if he is to have pay and promotion. He had brought this research to the point where he knew that he had to do something for society. In Oklahoma we were cowed by the calamity of witnessing millions of tons of precious earth being swept daily into the atmosphere. The only hope that the Chambers of Commerce could hold out was rain. Professor Sears knew that the answer lay not alone with nature but with man, who has to live in harmony with nature or perish, as the physical scientists have themselves since discovered.

So he wrote *Deserts on the March,* one of the most brilliant and beautifully written books in the field of science in our time. Paul Sears knew the people, he liked them, and he associated with them. And he knew how to write for them. Because the book depended upon an Anglo-Saxon style rather than scientific terminology to carry its message, some of Mr. Sears' colleagues dismissed it with the remark, "It isn't science, it's literature."

Finally, I asked one of these scientific critics the question: "Well, what is literature if it isn't the record of life as we live it? And isn't science a part of life?"

The people read the book and took it to heart. Something was done about the Dust Bowl. Perhaps Mr. Sears had discharged a scholar's obligation to the people by writing so clearly, so forcefully, that they could understand and take action. But he did not stop at this point. He had a total sense of society. Everyone was involved in the destruction of the land—farmers, bankers, utility magnates. So Paul Sears turned politician.

He met with bankers. They had lent money on farms and still carried at full value the amount of their loans. Sears, who had inspected much of the land being devastated, could tell a banker that a loan still valued at $4,000 was now worth only $400—and why this was so. He met with farmers and repeated the message which the agricultural experts should have been giving, in language which persuaded them. Even so, there were far too many farmers who said boastingly, "Why, I've worn out three farms already."

The utility people are powerful in the Middle Western states and rather skeptical of scholars. Sears went into the lions' den. He told them what was happening, how it could be stopped, and what would happen if destruction of the land was not halted. Who, he asked, would buy the electricity?

Sears was a one-man crusade. Oklahoma and America are richer today because *one* scholar knew that science, scholarship, and the people must prosper together—or die together.

The lesson is one that all members of the scientific and scholarly priesthood may well take to heart. I suggest that, as they prepare to leave their feudal citadel, they begin by purchasing a dictionary of the English language.

### Suggestions for Study

1. According to the author, what are the causes of unintelligibility among writers in specialized fields, such as science and the social sciences? (Note the specific reasons given in the fifth paragraph.) What causes the unintelligibility in scholarly writing?

2. Contrast the ideas in paragraphs 7 and 8 with those expressed in Abraham Flexner's article, "The Usefulness of Useless Knowledge." How would you reconcile the opinions?

3. What is Dr. Brandt's chief charge against higher education in general? How do the various professional schools contribute to the conditions he attacks?

4. What is the abiding fear of the average man? Who has been the only one to realize this among those who serve the public?

5. What does the author think may have been the greatest gain we made by the conquest of the atom?

6. According to the author, on what narrow, viciously anti-social plane has the business of higher education been conducted? If you can locate three doctoral dissertations, examine them to see if you think he is fair and accurate in his statements.

7. What is the author's definition of literature?

8. What general principle did Paul Sears put into practice?

9. What specific suggestion does the author make to scholars? What is the point of the suggestion?

10. Consider the whole article carefully; if necessary write a précis of it; then write a thesis sentence for it.

### 3. IMAGINATIVE WORDS

**Connotation.** The connotation of a word is its suggested or implied meaning, an overtone which has become attached to the word because of repeated use in the same context. It is complementary to denotation, the literal meaning of the word as given by the dictionary. *Steed* denotes *horse;* but it connotes *knights in armor, tournaments, chivalry,* and *dress parades.* Names of colors are rich in connotative power: *red,* for example, denotes a kind of visual experience; it connotes *blood, revolution, Communism, anger, frenzy, danger. Green* connotes *coolness, freshness, inexperience, youth, the outdoors.* Connotations appeal to the imagination. They arouse associations by stimulating half-forgotten recollections of previous experiences with the things that words denote. Certain words have greater connotative power than others because they denote things which are directly connected with the more powerful and permanent emotions. *House* denotes a moderate-sized structure with four walls and a roof, and for most people connotes very little more; but *home* is rich in connotation because it is associated with the family and family life.

Anyone who can use a dictionary can become proficient in the denotations of words, but to use language in such a way as to realize its connotative overtones requires imagination and critical reading. Not only must the writer respond keenly to the meanings of words, but he must also be familiar with what words mean to other people. Particularly if he is a person of powerful and original imagination, he must check his own feelings about language against a knowledge of what language implies commonly among his readers, or he will not be able to communicate with them accurately. The poets of the last two decades have used a language of peculiarly rich connotative power, replete with suggested meanings; but they have appealed to a limited audience because the connotations of their words are often so oblique as to be outside the common experience of many people.

The connotations of words are harder to manage than denotations because they change rapidly. Denotations change also, as has been pointed out, but the connotations of a word, being so much more subtle, can change completely in a few months. Depending upon the current amount of public sympathy with the worker's point of view in industry, the term *labor organizer* can imply a popular hero or a public menace. At present there seems to be an attempt on foot to supplant *capitalist* with *industrialist* because of the unfavorable connotations which cluster about the former term, just as *capitalist* once supplanted *rich man.* In the 1920's *collegiate* connoted long fur coats, hot jazz, horn-rimmed glasses, and a flask on every hip; the word has nearly passed out of the present college student's vocabulary. The connotations of words, therefore, cannot be studied and learned once for all, as one learns the multiplication table. The person who wishes to use the language of his contemporaries as effectively as possible must be forever a learner, alert to every syllable he reads or hears.[8]

Although most student writers can hardly be expected to achieve thorough mastery of connotative diction, they can learn to be aware of connotations which are not in the spirit of the context. The connotations of slang, for example, are such that in a business letter or a formal address slang is as out of place as a pun in a prayer. The language of the editorial column, consisting of words which are chosen to arouse patriotic or civic emotion, is not appropriate for the research paper. An undignified word cannot rest peaceably in a dignified sentence, but confuses and misdirects the trend of the whole communication. A cold, lifeless word set in glowing poetic terminology is an intruder which must be cast out lest it deaden the effect of the passage. "On that memorable night in August the gale trumpeted past the steeple of Weatherby Church and the rain, rather than falling steadily with a rhythmic tattoo, flung itself with sudden slops against the windows." Here, *slops* is out of place. It is a vigorous word, and would perform notably elsewhere, but its connotations are not those of steeples and church windows. In the following sentence, which you may remember from reading *Macbeth,* select the words and phrases which you think are most suitable because of their connotations:

> (Any old day; tomorrow, and tomorrow, and tomorrow; day after day after day; throughout the whole future) creeps in this (daily chore; business of living; petty pace) from day to day to (the last syllable of recorded time; the bell ending the last round; the blast from the trumpet of Gabriel); and (all the days in the past; all our yesterdays; the innings that have been played) have lighted fools the way to (dirty, wormy, unlovely, dusty) death.

If you do not remember the terms Shakespeare chose, look up the passage in Act V of *Macbeth.* A comparison of Shakespeare's language with the other terminology suggested here may show the effectiveness of words chosen for connotations which fit the context.

**Figures of Speech.** The person who uses language imaginatively frequently has recourse to figures of speech, stated or implied comparisons between one set of experiences and another, or between an abstract idea and a sensory image. Figures of speech, if they are original and yet within the scope of common experience, add color and concreteness to writing. Following are the most common types.

a. *Simile.* A simile is a direct comparison between objects, experiences,

8. See also the discussion of connotation under "Reading," pp. 70–71 ff.

or ideas of different classes; it is usually introduced by *like, as, as if,* or *as when.*

> Horatius stood *like a sturdy oak.*
> His smile was *as cold as ice water.*

b. *Metaphor.* A metaphor implies a similarity rather than stating it directly. It says that a thing *is* something else rather than that it is *like* something else. "He sped through the opposing team like a bullet" is a simile; "He was a human bullet that afternoon as he shot through the opposing team" is a metaphor.

> Methought I heard a voice cry, "Sleep no more!
> Macbeth does *murder* sleep,"—the innocent sleep,
> Sleep that *knits up the ravel'd sleeve of care,*
> *The death of each day's life, sore labor's bath,*
> *Balm of hurt minds, great nature's second course,*
> *Chief nourisher in life's feast,* . . .

c. *Hyperbole.* A deliberate overstatement, not for the sake of misleading someone but for the sake of emphasis, is called hyperbole.

> Our neighbors cannot come to dinner; they say they have a *thousand* things to do.
> The terrace *bakes* in the mid-afternoon sun.

d. *Litotes.* A deliberate understatement for the sake of ironic emphasis is called litotes.

> That *wasn't a bad meal* for thirty-five cents.
> He is a person *of no little importance* in his home town.

e. *Personification.* Personification is the attribution of human qualities or characteristics to an inanimate object or an abstraction.

> The sun *showed his fiery face.*
> The moon *looked down* upon the quiet scene.
> O *Death,* where is thy sting?

When properly adjusted to the context, an original metaphor or simile may enliven an otherwise dull sentence. If figures of speech are to appear natural, however, a writer must exercise care in writing them. The best figurative language is that which is suggested spontaneously by observation of the common elements of life. It results from the play of imagination on experience. If a person sets out deliberately to invent figurative language, his writing will very likely show evidences of his laborious efforts. On the other hand, a spontaneous figure of speech should not be immune from a critical examination simply because it is spontaneous.

The three dangers of figurative language are (1) the mixed figure error, (2) overstraining, which produces insincere writing, and (3) trite-ness. A mixed figure is one which is improperly adjusted to its context or to another figure of speech with the same reference. The classic example is "I smell a rat; I see it floating in the air; but we shall nip it in the bud." Others: "All students who come to college have a spark of originality, which their instructors should water and make grow"; "Your contribution will seem like a drop in the bucket in this large bundle of red tape." It scarcely needs pointing out that such mixed figures are evidences of a muddled mind rather than an imaginative one.

Instances of overstraining are the forcing of ornate modifiers and of figures of speech in passages that deal with simple and commonplace matters, and are therefore better related by good, honest, common words. Imaginative words have high value in the right place, but in the wrong place they are merely tawdry.

11    *Trite expressions, or clichés, are those that have been used so frequently that they have lost all their connotative force and have become threadbare.* They are the staple of those who lack imagination or who are too lazy to think of fresh, new expressions and figures of speech. In an article following this section, "The Cliché Expert Takes the Stand," Mr. Frank Sullivan satirizes those who employ such terms.

A list of trite expressions would run to many pages and still be incomplete. The following examples, however, will serve to illustrate what is meant: alluding to a person as being strong as an ox, weak as a kitten, pale as a ghost, or white as a sheet; to a girl as a member of the fair sex, a raving beauty, a blushing bride, or as entering upon the sea of matrimony; to someone as reclining in the arms of Morpheus, being hungry as a bear, making a Herculean effort, falling with a sickening thud, beating a hasty retreat, burning the midnight oil, or being sadder but wiser. Certain quotations and proverbs have become equally colorless from overuse: the exception proves the rule, great minds run in the same channels, it never rains but it pours, variety is the spice of life, ignorance is bliss, and many others. The one who first coined such expressions probably had a highly imaginative mind, but the one who continues to repeat them long after they have ceased to stimulate a mental image exemplifies, if not weakmindedness, at least a mind that has ceased to grow.

**Euphemisms.** A writer who aspires to use language imaginatively will avoid euphemisms—pale synonyms or circumlocutions for common terms which allude usually to something unpleasant. Although euphemisms often become clichés, they are unlike clichés in that the latter are the product of a lazy mind, whereas euphemisms are the product of a timid mind. Reporters on small-town newspapers, for instance, fill their stories of births, marriages, and deaths with such words as *the grim reaper,* a man's *passing, Hymen, Cupid, the stork,* and *a little stranger being ushered into the world.* To the euphemist addict, *sweat* becomes *perspire, spit* becomes *expectorate, a drunken man* is *intoxicated,* no one ever *tells a lie* but *misrepresents the facts,* the *poor* are the *underprivileged,* an *undertaker* is a *mortician,* and *boarders* are *paying guests.* The irony connected with the use of euphemisms is that they soon fall into disrepute and become more objectionable than the common word they try to displace. Thus their connotations become bad, and the one who employs them will find his work lacking in appeal.

Words do not need to be new, exotic, or different to have the power to stimulate the imagination and to have rich connotations. Such words as *friend, brother, rose, girl, dog,* and a thousand others we use every day, never grow old or shopworn. The writer who uses them without affectation, who deals sparingly in ornamentation and flowery verbiage, and who avoids trite expressions and euphemisms will find that his writing will take on the imaginative appeal for which he is seeking.

(See *Workbook,* Exercise 9.)

## *The Cliché Expert Takes the Stand* [9]

### FRANK SULLIVAN

Question—Mr. Arbuthnot, you are an expert in the use of the cliché, are you not?

Answer—Yes, sir, I am a certified public cliché expert.

Q.—In that case would you be good enough to answer a few questions on the use and application of the cliché in ordinary speech and writing?

A.—I should be only too glad to do so.

Q.—Your occupation?

A.—Well, after burning the midnight oil at an institution of higher learning, I was for a time a tiller of the soil. Then I went down to the sea in ships for a while, and later, at various times, I have been a guardian of the law, a gentleman of the Fourth Estate, a poet at heart, a bon vivant and raconteur, a prominent clubman, an eminent—

Q.—Just what is your occupation at the moment, Mr. Arbuthnot?

A.—At the moment I am an unidentified man of about forty, shabbily clad.

9. Reprinted by permission of the author and the *New Yorker.*

Q.—How do you cliché experts reveal yourselves, Mr. Arbuthnot?

A.—In our true colors, of course.

Q.—And you expect to live to . . . A.—A ripe old age.

Q.—What do you shuffle off? A.—This mortal coil.

Q.—What do you thank? A.—My lucky stars.

Q.—What kind of retreats do you like? A.—Hasty retreats.

Q.—What do you do to hasty retreats? A.—I beat them.

Q.—Regarding dogs, what kind of dog are you? A.—A gay dog.

Q.—And how do you work? A.—Like a dog.

Q.—And you lead? A.—A dog's life.

Q.—So much for dogs. Now, Mr. Arbuthnot, when you are naked, you are . . . A.—Stark naked.

Q.—In what kind of daylight? A.—Broad daylight.

Q.—What kind of outsider are you? A.—I'm a rank outsider.

Q.—How right are you? A.—I am dead right.

Q.—What kind of meals do you like? A.—Square meals.

Q.—What do you do to them? A.—Ample justice.

Q.—What is it you do to your way? A.—I wend my way.

Q.—And your horizon? A.—I broaden my horizon.

Q.—When you buy things, you buy them for . . . A.—A song.

Q.—You are as sober as . . . A.—A judge.

Q.—And when you are drunk?

A.—I have lots of leeway there. I can be drunk as a coot, or a lord, or an owl, or a fool——

Q.—Very good, Mr. Arbuthnot. Now, how about the fate of Europe?

A.—It is hanging in the balance, of course.

Q.—What happens to landscapes? A.—Landscapes are dotted.

Q.—What kind of precision are you cliché-users partial to?

A.—Clocklike precision.

Q.—And what kind of order? A.—Apple-pie order.

Q.—When you watch a parade, you watch it from . . .

A.—A point of vantage.

Q.—And you shroud things . . . A.—In the mists of antiquity.

Q.—What kind of threats do you make? A.—Veiled threats.

Q.—And what kind of secrets do you betray? A.—Dark secrets.

Q.—How about ignorance? A.—Ignorance is always abysmal.

Q.—When you travel, what do you combine?

A.—I combine business with pleasure.

Q.—And you are destined . . . A.—To go far.

Q.—Thank you, Mr. Arbuthnot. What time is it? A.—High time.

Q.—How do you point?

A.—I point with pride, I view with alarm, and I yield to no man.

Q.—What do you pursue? A.—The even tenor of my way.

Q.—Ever pursue the odd tenor of your way?

A.—Oh, no, I would lose my standing as a cliché expert if I did that.

Q.—As for information, you are . . . A.—A mine of information.

Q.—What kind of mine? A.—A veritable mine.

Q.—What do you throw? A.—I throw caution.

Q.—Where? A.—To the winds.

## Suggestions for Study

1. Examine the papers you have written so far in your composition course. Are you dependent on clichés, like those in this selection, for instruments of communication?

2. Make a list of clichés that you hear during one day, and note who uses them—another student, an instructor, and so on.

## Emotional Meanings [10]

### ROBERT H. THOULESS

When we use a word in speech and writing, its most obvious purpose is to point to some thing, or relation, or property. This is the word's "meaning." We see a small four-footed animal on the road and call it a "dog," indicating that it is a member of the class of four-footed animals we call dogs. The word "dog" as we have used it there has a plain, straightforward, "objective" meaning. We have in no way gone beyond the requirements of exact scientific description.

Let us suppose also that one grandparent of the dog was a collie, another was an Irish terrier, another a fox terrier, and the fourth a bull-dog. We can express these facts equally scientifically and objectively by saying that he is a dog of mixed breed. Still we have in no way gone beyond the requirements of exact scientific description.

Suppose, however, that we had called that same animal a "mongrel." The matter is more complicated. We have used a word which objectively means the same as "dog of mixed breed," but which also arouses in our hearers an emotional attitude of disapproval towards that particular dog. A word, therefore, can not only indicate an object, but can also suggest an emotional attitude towards it. Such suggestion of an emotional attitude does go beyond exact and scientific discussion because our approvals and

10. From *How To Think Straight* by Robert H. Thouless. (Copyright, 1932, 1939, by Simon and Schuster). Reprinted by permission of Simon and Schuster and Hodder and Stoughton, the English publisher.

disapprovals are individual—they belong to ourselves and not to the objects we approve or disapprove of. An animal which to the mind of its master is a faithful and noble dog of mixed ancestry may be a "mongrel" to his neighbor whose chickens are chased by it.

Similarly, a Negro may be indicated objectively as a "colored man" or with strong emotional disapproval and contempt as a "nigger." The use of the latter word debases any discussion in which it is used below the level of impartial and objective argument.

Once we are on the look-out for this difference between "objective" and "emotional" meanings, we shall notice that words which carry more or less strong suggestions of emotional attitudes are very common and are ordinarily used in the discussion of such controversial questions as those of politics, morals, and religion. This is one reason why such controversies cannot yet be settled.

There is a well-known saying that the word "firm" can be declined as follows: I am *firm,* thou art *obstinate,* he is *pig-headed.* That is a simple illustration of what is meant. "Firm," "obstinate," and "pig-headed" all have the same objective meaning—that is, following one's own course of action and refusing to be influenced by other people's opinions. They have, however, different emotional meanings; "firm" has an emotional meaning of strong approval, "obstinate" of mild disapproval, "pig-headed" of strong disapproval.

In much the same way when, during the war, our thought was dominated by emotion, our newspapers contrasted the *spirit* of our heroic boys with the mentality of the *Huns,* and the *unquenchable heroism* of our troops with the enemy's *ponderous foolhardiness.* Now, with the more objective attitude which has been brought by the lapse of time, we can look back and see that a *spirit* and a *mentality* are objectively the same thing, only the one word has an emotional meaning of approval, the other of disapproval. We can see too that a soldier going forward under shellfire to probable death is doing the same thing whether he is a German or one of our own countrymen, and that to distinguish between them by applying the word *foolhardiness* to the action of the one and *heroism* to that of the other is to distort reality by using words to make an emotional distinction between two actions which are objectively identical.

Such thinking in war-time may do much harm by leading humane people to condone cruelty. When the ordinarily liberal-minded Swinburne wrote a poem during the Boer War on the death of a British officer who had been blamed for the bad condition of the camps in which the Boer women and children were interned, he said:

Nor heed we more than he what liars dare say
Of mercy's holiest duties left undone
Towards *whelps* and *dams* of *murderous* foes, whom none
Save we had spared or feared to starve and slay.

*Whelps* and *dams* clearly mean in objective fact *children* and *wives* with the added meaning of the emotional attitude adopted towards the females and young of wild beasts, while *murderous* means no more in objective fact than that our foes killed us when they could (as we also killed them), with the added emotional meaning of an attitude towards them which is our attitude to those who are guilty of murder.

The use of emotionally toned words is not, of course, always to be condemned. They are always harmful when we are trying to think clearly on a disputable point of fact. In poetry, on the other hand, they have a perfectly proper place, because in poetry (as in some kinds of prose) the arousing of suitable emotions is an important part of the purpose for which the words are used.

In *The Eve of St. Agnes,* Keats has written:

Full on this casement shone the wintry moon,
And threw warm gules on Madeline's fair breast.

These are beautiful lines. Let us notice how much of their beauty follows from the proper choice of emotionally colored words and how completely it is lost if these words are replaced by neutral ones. The words with strikingly emotional meanings are *casement, gules, Madeline, fair,* and *breast. Casement* means simply a kind of window with emotional and romantic associations. *Gules* is the heraldic name for red, with the suggestion of romance which accompanies all heraldry. *Madeline* is simply a girl's name, but one calling out favorable emotions absent from a relatively plain and straightforward name. *Fair* simply means, in objective fact, that her skin was white or uncolored—a necessary condition for the colors of the window to show—but also *fair* implies warm emotional preference for an uncolored skin rather than one which is yellow, purple, black, or any of the other colors which skin might be. *Breast* has also similar emotional meanings, and the aim of scientific description might have been equally well attained if it had been replaced by such a neutral word as *chest.*

Let us now try the experiment of keeping these two lines in a metrical form, but replacing all the emotionally colored words by neutral ones, while making as few other changes as possible. We may write:

Full on this window shone the wintry moon,
Making red marks on Jane's uncolored chest.

No one will doubt that all of its poetic value has been knocked out of the passage by these changes. Yet the lines still mean the same in external fact; they still have the same objective meaning. It is only the emotional meaning which has been destroyed.

Now if Keats had been writing a scientific description for a textbook on physics instead of a poem, it would have been necessary for him to have used some such coldly objective terms as those into which we have just translated his lines. Such emotionally charged phrases as *warm gules* and *fair breast* would only have obscured the facts to which the scientist exactly but unbeautifully refers when he speaks of "the selective transmission of homogeneous light by pigmented glass."

The purpose of the present essay is to deal with the kind of problem in which cold and scientific thinking is required. Most of the practical problems of life are of this order. The fact that I shall abuse the use of emotional thinking in connection with such problems as tariffs, prohibition, social ownership, and war does not mean that there is no place for emotional thinking. Poetry, romantic prose, and emotional oratory are all of inestimable value, but their place is not where responsible decisions must be made. The common (almost universal) use of emotional words in political thinking is as much out of place as would be a chemical or statistical formula in the middle of a poem. Real democracy will come only when the solution of national and international problems is carried out by scientific methods of thought, purged of all irrelevant emotion. Into the action which follows decision we can put all the emotion which we have refused to allow in our thinking. Let us think calmly and scientifically about war, and then actively oppose it with all the passion of which we are capable.

The growth of the exact thinking of modern science has been very largely the result of its getting rid of all terms suggesting emotional attitudes and using only those which unemotionally indicate objective facts. It was not always so. The old alchemists called gold and silver "noble" metals, and thought that this emotionally colored word indicated something belonging to the metals themselves from which their properties could be deduced. Other metals were called "base." Although these terms have survived as convenient labels for the modern chemist they carry none of their old emotional significance.

In popular biological discussions, on the other hand, such words are still used with their full emotional meaning, as when the "nobility" of man is contrasted with his alleged "base" origin. In this respect, popular biological discussion differs from that of the textbook and the laboratory, in which are used terms almost as devoid of emotional meaning as those of physics or chemistry.

Psychology is still younger in the ranks of the sciences, and the clearing away from it of emotional words has not gone very far. "Passion," "emotion," "sex" are all terms of our science which carry strong emotional meanings, so that it is difficult to discuss a controversial matter in psychology without using words which rouse strong emotions and confuse all issues. A beginning is being made. "Intelligence" was a subject on which it was difficult to think clearly because it carried so much emotional meaning. Now Professor Spearman has replaced it by what he calls "g" (or the "general factor"), which is a conception derived from the statistical analysis of a large collection of figures, and yet which is in its essence all that was really scientific in the old conception of intelligence. Some day a psychological genius will give us $X$ or $Z$ to replace the old emotional conception of sex, and we shall be able to discuss psychoanalysis as objectively as a mathematical physicist can discuss the quantum theory.

When we turn to politics and international questions, we are still further from straight scientific thinking. Such words as "Bolshevik," "reactionary," "revolutionary," "constitutional," "national honor," etc., are all words used in national and international political thinking which carry more of emotional than of any other meaning. So long as such words are the ordinary terms of rival politicians, how can we hope to think straight in national and international affairs? If a chemist doing an experiment depended on such thought processes as a nation uses in selecting its rulers or in deciding on peace or war with other nations, he would blow up his laboratory. This, however, would be a trivial disaster in comparison with what may result from emotional thinking in politics. Better have a hundred chemical laboratories blown up than the whole of civilization!

We must look forward to and try to help on the day when the thinking about political and international affairs will be as unemotional and as scientific as that about the properties of numbers or the atomic weights of elements. The spirit of impartial investigation of facts unswayed by irrelevant emotions has given us great advances in the sciences. Its triumphs will be even greater when it is applied to the most important affairs of life. We look forward to the day when we shall be able to discuss and settle such questions as Tariffs, Prohibition, Public vs. Private Ownership, and Disarmament treaties as successfully as physicists have discussed and settled Einstein's theory of relativity.

Let us try to study a few more examples of the use of words with emotional meanings taken from various sources. Accounts of wars are rich sources of such material, so we are not surprised to find in a book on the French Commune the statement that large numbers of the regular troops were *assassinated* during the street fighting by the communards, while a much larger number of the latter were *summarily executed* by the regulars. In order to reduce this to a statement of objective fact it is clear that the one word "killed" should be used in place both of *assassinated* and *summarily executed*. We have already noticed how such a choice of words with the same objective but opposite emotional meaning can be used to make us feel sympathetic to one and hostile to the other of two sides in warfare. During the conflicts between Red and White forces in Russia and in China, our newspapers told us of the *atrocities* of the Bolsheviks and of the *wise severity* of the White commanders. Examination of the details (often possible only long afterwards) shows that the objective facts of an *atrocity* and of *wise severity* are much the same, and that they are not the kind of objective facts which will call out an emotion of approval in a humane person.

A similar choice of words will be noticed in political discussion. A fluent and forcible speech delivered by one of our own party is *eloquent*, a similar speech by one of the opposite party is *rhodomontade*; again two words with the same objective meaning but with the opposite emotional meanings of approval and strong disapproval. The practical proposals of the opposition, moreover, are *panaceas*—a highly emotional word calling out the strongly disapproving emotions which we feel for those quack patent medicines which make extravagant claims. Those who show enthusiasm in support of proposals with which a speaker disagrees are *extremists*; while those showing similar enthusiasm on his own side are called *staunch*. If a politician wishes to attack some new proposal he has a battery of these and other words with emotional meanings at his disposal. He speaks of "this suggested *panacea* supported only by the *rhodomontade of extremists*"; and the proposal is at once discredited in the minds of the majority of people, who like to think of themselves as moderate, distrustful of panaceas, and uninfluenced by windy eloquence. Also we may notice that it has been discredited without the expenditure of any real thought, for of real objective argument there is none, only the manipulation of words calling out emotion.

It is not, however, only in warfare and politics that such words are used in order to influence opinion more easily than can be done by words embodying real thought. Art criticism is also a good source for this kind of material. Ruskin said of Whistler's Nocturnes: "I have heard and seen much of *Cockney impudence* before now, but never expected to hear a *coxcomb* ask two hundred guineas for *flinging a pot of paint in the public's face."* As in earlier passages, I have italicized the words or phrases with strongly emotional meanings. Stripped of these and reduced to a statement of objective fact, the passage would have to be paraphrased in some such way as follows: "I have heard and seen much of the behavior of Londoners before now, but never expected to hear a painter ask two hundred guineas for painting a picture which seemed to me to have no meaning." Plainly not much is left of Ruskin's criticism after this operation has been performed on it.

As a last example, we may take a part of an attack made by a newspaper on a novel. This runs: "Its *vicious plea* for the acknowledgment and *condonation* of *sexual perversity,* and the grounds on which it is based, loosen the very *sheet-anchor of conduct."* This passage calls out such strong emotions of abhorrence that most readers will be content to condemn the novel without further inquiry. Yet the effect is gained entirely by the choice of words with emotional meanings. It happens to deal with a subject on which emotions are strong, so a dispassionate examination is all the more necessary. We note that a *plea* is simply an argument, plus a suggestion of repugnance for the kind of argument used; that *condonation* is tolerance plus an emotional suggestion that such toleration is indefensible; that *sexual* means something in the life of love of which we disapprove, and that a *perversity* is an unusualness plus an emotional suggestion of abhorrence. The loosening of a *sheet-anchor* is a metaphor implying change and suggesting to a landsman the emotion of fear, while *conduct* is simply behavior of which we approve.

So reduced to its bare bones of statement of objective fact (ignoring for a moment the special difficulties raised by the word *vicious*) the passage becomes: "Its argument for the acknowledgment and tolerance of unusualness in the life of love, and the grounds on which it is based, change the principles of behavior." This clearly is an important statement if it is true, but is not enough in itself to condemn the book, because undoubtedly our principles of behavior do need changing from time to time. We can only decide intelligently whether or not they need changing in the particular case under discussion, when we have made a dispassionate statement of what the proposed changes are and why they are defended. As in all other cases, discussion of the question with emotionally charged words obscures the problem and makes a sensible decision difficult or impossible.

The word *vicious* has some special difficulties of its own. It arouses emotions of disapproval, but there is no word with the same objective meaning which would not. If we call the book bad, corrupt, or evil, the

same emotions would be aroused. So we cannot perform the simple operation of replacing *vicious* by an emotionally neutral word with the same
objective meaning. Can we then leave it out altogether, on the ground
that it has no objective meaning, but that it is used merely to arouse
emotion?

Here we are up against a problem about which there has been much
dispute. Some people consider that all such words as "good," "bad,"
"beautiful," "ugly," only indicate one's own emotional reactions towards
actions or things and in no sense properties of the actions or things themselves. But when we see a man steal a penny from a child and we call his
action "bad," we are in fact saying something meaningful about the
action itself and not merely about our own feelings. As to what that
something is we may leave the philosophers to dispute; it may only be
that the man's action has subtracted from the total amount of human
happiness. So to say a book is *vicious* is not the same kind of thing as
contrasting the *assassination* of regular troops by communards with the
*summary execution* of the communards by regular soldiers. The statement that the book is vicious has a meaning which is not merely emotional, although, of course, the statement may not be true.

On the other hand, it is clearly not quite the same kind of meaning as
a simple statement of outside fact such as "This is a book." Whether the
book is good or bad is a real question, but it is a question peculiarly
difficult to decide. Our own statement one way or the other is likely to
be nothing but a reflection of our own personal prejudices and to have,
therefore, no sort of scientific exactness. At the same time, such words
certainly arouse strong emotions and should, therefore, be used sparingly
in honest argument. The use of words implying moral judgments in the
course of argument is very generally an attempt to distort the hearers'
view of the truth by arousing emotions.

If we are trying to decide a simple question of fact, such words should
be left out, because it is easier to settle one question at a time. If a man is
accused of poisoning his wife, the prosecuting attorney should not say,
"This *scoundrel* who hounded his wife to her grave." The question to be
decided is whether the man did poison his wife. If he did, he is a "scoundrel" undoubtedly, but calling him a scoundrel does not help to decide
the question of fact. On the contrary, it makes a correct decision more
difficult by rousing emotions of hatred for the accused in the minds of the
jury. Another obvious objection to the use of the word "scoundrel" before
the man is convicted, which puts it in the ranks of "crooked thinking," is
that it "begs the question" or assumes what is to be proved. The man is

only a scoundrel if he is guilty, and yet the word has been used in the course of an argument to prove that he is guilty.

These two objections can be urged against the word "vicious" in the condemnation of a book quoted above. It calls up strong emotions, making a just decision of the nature of the book difficult, and it assumes exactly what the article professes to prove—that the book is a bad one.

The aim of this essay has been to distinguish one kind of crooked thinking, in the hope that those who recognize how their opinions can be twisted away from the truth by the use of words with emotional meanings may be able to recognize this source of error and to guard themselves against it. Those of its readers who have found anything new to them in the ideas of this essay should not, I suggest, be content simply to read the essay, but should try to do some practical work on its subject-matter. If you were studying botany, you would not be content merely to read books on botany. If you were, that would not carry you far in botanical knowledge. Instead you would gather plants from the hedges and weeds from your garden, dissecting them, examining them with a microscope or magnifying glass, and drawing them in your note-book. Psychology too should be studied by practical methods. Emotional thinking (like most of the other kinds of crooked thinking) is as common as a weed. It is to be found in the leading articles of newspapers, in the words of people carrying on discussions on political, religious, or moral questions, and in the speeches made by public men when these deal with controversial matters. In order to understand it, we should collect specimens by putting them down on paper and then we should dissect them.

The practical exercise which I recommend is one which I have already performed on some passages in which truth seemed to be obscured by emotional thinking. I suggest that readers should copy out controversial passages from newspapers, books, or speeches which contain emotionally colored words. Then they should underline all the emotional words, afterwards rewriting the passages with the emotional words replaced by neutral ones. Examine the passage then in its new form in which it merely states objective facts without indicating the writer's emotional attitude towards them, and see whether it is still good evidence for the proposition it is trying to prove. If it is, the passage is a piece of straight thinking in which emotionally colored words have been introduced merely as an ornament. If not, it is crooked thinking, because the conclusion depends not on the objective meaning of the passage but on the emotions roused by the words.

When we condemn such a use of emotional words in writings and speeches, we must remember that this is a symptom of a more deep-seated evil—their prevalence in our own private, unexpressed thinking. Many of our highly-colored political speakers whose speeches stir us as we are stirred by romantic poetry show themselves unable to think calmly and objectively on any subject. They have so accustomed themselves to think in emotionally toned words that they can no longer think in any other way. They should have been poets or professional orators, but certainly not statesmen.

It really does not matter much if we sometimes use emotional words. We all do when we are trying to produce conviction. What does matter is that we should not lose the power to think without them. So a more important exercise than any we can perform on written material is one we can perform on our own minds. When we catch ourselves thinking in emotional phraseology, let us form a habit of translating our thoughts into emotionally neutral words. Thus we can guard ourselves from ever being so enslaved by emotional words and phrases that they prevent us from thinking objectively when we need to do so—that is, whenever we have to come to a decision on any debatable matter.

## Suggestions for Study

1. List five words with an explanation of their objective and emotional meanings.

2. From current newspapers or magazines select ten examples of emotional meanings intended to make us feel hostile or sympathetic toward one side or another of a discussion.

3. Under what conditions is the use of emotional meanings permissible? Substitute in a line or two of poetry an objective word for each emotional one, and analyze the result.

4. What problem does the psychologist face in using the terms of his science?

5. Under what conditions is the use of emotional meanings harmful?

6. State the thesis sentence of the article.

7. What relation does this discussion bear to that of Mr. Haber in "Basic English for Science"? What is its relation to the following article "On Word Magic" by Mr. Gardiner?

8. Define the following words from the article: controversial, humane, condone, homogeneous, dispassionate, prevalence.

## On Word Magic [11]

### A. G. GARDINER

I see that a discussion has arisen in the *Spectator* on the "Canadian Boat Song." It appeared in *Blackwood's* nearly a century ago, and ever since its authorship has been the subject of recurrent controversy. The author may have been "Christopher North," or his brother, Tom Wilson, or Galt, or the Ettrick Shepherd, or the Earl of Eglinton, or none of these. We shall never know. It is one of those pleasant mysteries of the past, like the authorship of the Junius Letters (if, indeed, that can be called a mystery), which can never be exhausted because they can never be solved. I am not going to offer an opinion; for I have none, and I refer to the subject only to illustrate the magic of a word. The poem lives by virtue of the famous stanza:

> From the lone shieling of the misty island
>   Mountains divide us, and the waste of seas—
> Yet still the blood is strong, the heart is Highland,
>   And we in dreams behold the Hebrides.

It would be an insensible heart that did not feel the surge of this strong music. The yearning of the exile for the motherland had never been uttered with more poignant beauty, though Stevenson came near the same note of tender anguish in the lines written in far Samoa and ending:

> Be it granted me to behold you again, in dying,
>   Hills of home, and to hear again the call,
> Hear about the graves of the martyrs the peewees crying—
>   And hear no more at all.

But for energy and masculine emotion the unknown author takes the palm. The verse is like a great wave of the sea, rolling in to the mother shore, gathering impetus and grandeur as it goes, culminating in the note of vision and scattering itself triumphantly in the splendor of that word "Hebrides."

It is a beautiful illustration of the magic of a word used in its perfect setting. It gathers up the emotion of the theme into one chord of fulfilment and flings open the casement of the mind to far horizons. It is not the only instance in which the name has been used with extraordinary effect. Wordsworth's "Solitary Reaper" has many beautiful lines, but the peculiar glory of the poem dwells in the couplet in which, searching for

11. From *Leaves in the Wind* by A. G. Gardiner, published and copyrighted by E. P. Dutton & Co., Inc., New York.

parallels for the song of the Highland girl that fills "the vale profound," he hears in imagination the cuckoo's call

> Breaking the silence of the seas
> Among the farthest Hebrides.

Wordsworth, like Homer and Milton, and all who touch the sublime in poetry, had the power of transmuting a proper name to a strange and significant beauty. The most memorable example, perhaps, is in the closing lines of the poem to Dorothy Wordsworth:

> But an old age serene and bright,
> And lovely as a Lapland night
> Shall lead thee to thy grave.

"Lapland" is an intrinsically beautiful word, but it is its setting in this case that makes it shine, pure and austere, like a star in the heavens of poetry. And the miraculous word need not be intrinsically beautiful. Darien is not, yet it is that word in which perhaps the greatest of all sonnets finds its breathless, astonished close:

> Silent—upon a peak—in Darien.

And the truth is that the magic of words is not in the words themselves, but in the distinction, delicacy, surprise of their use. Take the great line which Shakespeare puts into the mouth of Antony—

> I am dying, Egypt, dying.

It is the only occasion in the play in which he makes Antony speak of Cleopatra by her territorial name, and there is no warrant for the usage in Plutarch. It is a stroke of sheer word magic. It summons up with a sudden magnificence all the mystery and splendor incarnated in the woman for whom he has gambled away the world and all the earthly glories that are fading into the darkness of death. The whole tragedy seems to flame to its culmination in this word that suddenly lifts the action from the human plane to the scale of cosmic drama.

Words of course have an individuality, a perfume of their own, but just as the flame in the heart of the diamond has to be revealed by the craftsman, so the true magic of a beautiful word only discloses itself at the touch of the master. "Quiet" is an ordinary enough word, and few are more frequently on our lips. Yet what wonderful effects Wordsworth, Coleridge, and Keats extract from it:

> It is a beauteous evening, calm and free;
> The holy time is quiet as a nun,
> Breathless with adoration.

The whole passage is a symphony of the sunset, but it is that ordinary word "quiet" which breathes like a benediction through the cadence, filling the mind with the sense of an illimitable peace. And so with Coleridge's "singeth a quiet tune," or Keats':

> Full of sweet dreams and health and quiet breathing.

Or when, "half in love with easeful Death," he

> Called him soft names in many a mused rhyme
> To take into the air my quiet breath.

And again:

> Far from the fiery noon and eve's one star
> Sat grey-hair'd Saturn, quiet as a stone.

There have been greater poets than Keats, but none who has had so sure an instinct for the precious word as he had. Byron had none of this magician touch. Shelley got his effects by the glow and fervor of his spirit; Swinburne by the sheer torrent of his song, and Browning by the energy of his thought. Tennyson was much more of the artificer in words than these, but he had not the secret of the word magic of Shakespeare, Wordsworth, or Keats. Compare the use of adjectives in two things like Shelley's "Ode to the Skylark" and Keats' "Ode to the Nightingale," and the difference is startling. Both are incomparable, but in the one case it is the hurry of the song, the flood of rapture that delights us; in the other each separate line holds us with its jeweled word. *"Embalmed* darkness." *"Verdurous* glooms." "Now more than ever seems it *rich* to die." "Cooled a long age in the *deep-delved* earth." *"Darkling* I listen." "She stood in tears amid the *alien* corn." "Oh, for a beaker full of the *warm south."* "With beaded bubbles *winking* at the brim." "No *hungry* generations tread thee down." And so on. Such a casket of jewels can be found in no other poet that has used our tongue. If Keats' vocabulary had a defect it was a certain overripeness, a languorous beauty that, like the touch of his hand, spoke of death. It lacked the fresh, happy, sunlit spirit of Shakespeare's sovereign word.

Word magic belongs to poetry. In prose it is an intrusion. That was the view of Coleridge. It was because, among its other qualities, Southey's writing was so free from the shock of the dazzling word that Coleridge held it to be the perfect example of pure prose. The modulations are so just, the note so unaffected, the current so clear and untroubled that you read on without pausing once to think "What a brilliant writer this fellow is." And that is the true triumph of the art. It is an art which addresses itself to the mind, and not the emotions, and word magic does not belong to its true armory.

## Suggestions for Study

1. What "place words" does the author think especially magical?

2. Since he gives no scientific proof that he is correct in attributing magic to these words, what does he assume concerning his reader? Has he a right to make such an assumption?

3. What does he say is necessary to bring out the "perfume of their own" which words possess? What instances does he give to illustrate his statement?

4. Where would word magic be employed? Why would it be out of place in much prose?

5. Define the following words from the article: recurrent, poignant, transmute, intrinsically, incarnated, benediction, cadence, modulations.

### 4. GLOSSARY OF FAULTY DICTION

## 12            a. Faulty usage

*Allow.* A provincialism for *declare, maintain, assume;* it really means *permit:* I assume you are right (not: *allow*).

*Alternative.* Do not use *alternative* when a selection is to be made among three or more things. An alternative offers two things from which a choice must be made.

My alternative was to attend college or go to work.

I was given a choice: to play the piano, the trumpet, or the cello.

*Any place, no place.* Illiterate for *anywhere, nowhere.*

I have nowhere to go this evening (not: *no place*).

*As.* 1. Do not use *as* in a negative comparison: It is as clear as it was yesterday, but not *so* cold.

2. Do not use *as* in substitution for *that* or *whether*: I don't believe *that* I can go today.

*As per.* Mixing English and Latin in the same phrase is unacceptable. *According to* is preferred: Let us proceed *according to* schedule.

*At.* Not to be used in conjunction with *where*: Where is he? (not: Where is he *at?*)

*But.* Illogical after *no doubt* and *no other*. In this sort of expression *but* has a negative function which is unnecessary after the negative in *no doubt* or *no other*.

There is no doubt that Jerry was elected.

It was no other than Henry.

*Claim.* Not a synonym for *maintain*. It means *to demand because of having a right to something*.

I maintain that he is right.

I claim my inheritance.

*Data.* A plural noun: *These* data *are* correct.

*Different than.* See *Than.*

*Due to.* An adjective construction, not to be used as a compound preposition introducing an adverbial prepositional phrase.

The mishap was due to carelessness.

Mary was elected because of her popularity.

*Etc.* An abbreviation for *et cetera,* which means *and other things.* Therefore to say *and etc.* is redundant. In formal writing *and so forth* or *and the like* is preferred to *etc.*

*Expect.* Improperly used as a synonym for *suspect, think,* or *suppose.* It means *to look forward to* or *to anticipate with confidence.*

I suppose that this is the house.

I expect to be in town next week.

*Hardly, scarcely.* Each is a negative, not to be used in addition to another negative.

He could not find his way in the fog.

He could hardly (or, scarcely) find his way in the fog.

*Help but.* Illogical when used after the adverb *not,* which expresses fully a negative idea and so renders the negative *but* unnecessary: I can not help thinking that you are correct.

*Inferior than.* See *Than.*

*Irregardless.* An incorrect form. Always use *regardless.*

*Kind, sort.* When singular, these nouns should always be modified by singular adjectives: *This* kind of glove is sold everywhere.

*Kind of, sort of.* Incorrect for *rather, somewhat:* He looked rather puzzled (never: He looked *sort of* puzzled).

*Majority.* An incorrect substitute for *most of.* It refers to numbers.

He had most of the money.

The majority of the people voted wisely.

*More so.* Illogical as a substitute for a preceding adjective.

Incorrect: He was slow, but she was more so (more so slow?).

Correct: He was slow, but she was slower.

*Nice.* Improper in the sense of *pleasant* or *agreeable.* It means *delicate, fastidious, subtle.*

Our violinist has a nice ear for music.

He provided us a very pleasant entertainment.

*No other.* See *But.*

*No place.* See *Any place.*

*Of.* 1. Illiterate when following *off:* Keep off the porch (not: *off of*).

2. Illiterate after *could* or *should:* We could have gone (not: could *of*).

*Preferable than.* See *Than.*

*Proven.* Archaic and dialectal for *proved:* His ability has been proved.

*Real.* An adjective, not to be used in an adverbial sense: Our parents visit us very frequently (not: *real* frequently).

*Remember.* A transitive verb, not to be followed by *of:* William remembered his friends (not: *of* his friends).

*Scarcely.* See *Hardly.*

*So.* 1. Improper in the sense of *very* or *exceedingly:* I was very tired (not: *so* tired).

2. Improper for *so that:* I drove rapidly so that I could arrive on time (not: *so* I could arrive on time).

3. Frequently improper for introducing the second independent clause of a compound sentence; subordinating the first clause is often a better construction: Because he told the truth, he was not punished (not: He told the truth; so he was not punished).

*Sort, sort of.* See *Kind* and *Kind of.*

*Such.* Incorrect as an intensive: It was such a hot day that we went swimming (not: It was *such* a hot day).

*Superior than.* See *Than.*

*Sure.* An adjective, not to be used in place of *surely.*

That was surely record time.

His aim was sure.

*Suspicion.* A noun, not to be used for the verb *to suspect.*

He suspected that we would lose the game.

His suspicions were confirmed.

*Taste of. Of* is unnecessary after *taste:* He tasted his food.

*Tend to.* When *tend* is transitive, *to* is omitted; when intransitive, *to* is used.

Transitive: We willingly tend the sick.

Intransitive: We usually tend to our business.

*Than.* 1. A conjunction, often used to introduce an elliptical clause and so to be followed by the nominative case: He is taller than *I* (elliptical for: He is taller than I am tall).

2. *Than* is to be used after adjectives and adverbs in the comparative degree and so should not be used after such positive forms as *different, superior, inferior,* and *preferable.*

Larry is stronger than I.

He is different *from* me in every respect.

Their methods are superior *to* those of the Russians but inferior *to* ours.

His style of play is preferable *to* mine.

*Very.* When a participle is used as a true adjective preceding a noun, it can be modified by *very,* but when it is part of a participial phrase, it should be modified by *very much.*

Bill was a very tired man last night.

Bill, very much rested after his sleep, greeted us gaily.

*Want.* To be followed by an infinitive, not a clause: I want you to come (not: I want *that* you should come).

## b. Words often confused

*Accept, except. Accept* means *to receive; except,* as a verb, means *to omit* or *leave out.*

My friends willingly accepted our proposal.

The executive officer excepted no one from his directive.

*Affect, effect. Affect* means *to influence; effect,* as a verb, means *to accomplish* or *bring about. Affect* is never a noun (except in a very technical usage in psychology); *effect* as a noun means *result.*

The war greatly affected their lives.

The prisoners effected their escape.

The effect upon the group was remarkable.

*Aggravate, irritate. Aggravate* means *to make worse; irritate* means *to anger* or *annoy.*

The pranks of the children irritated me.

My headache was aggravated by their noise.

*All ready, already. Already,* an adverb, means *previously* or *by this time; all ready,* a phrase, means *completely ready.*

The suitcases were all ready to be carried away.

The train had already left.

*All right, alright.* The correct form is *all right.*

*Allusion, illusion.* An *allusion* is an indirect reference; an *illusion* is a false impression or misconception.

Pope's allusions to Horace are well known.

He was misled by illusions of grandeur.

*All together, altogether. All together* means *in one group; altogether,* an adverb, means *entirely.*

The group stood all together to have its photograph taken.

John is altogether honest and dependable.

*Among, between. Between* applies to two objects, *among* to more than two.

A rivalry exists between my brother and sister.

The rivalry is keen among the men at the club.

*Apt, likely, liable. Apt* and *likely* are often used synonymously, although *apt* means *inclined* or *having an inborn disposition to,* whereas *likely* means *probable. Liable* means *responsible* or *exposed to certain unfortunate consequences.*

An impulsive man is apt to become angry.

Our team seems likely to win tomorrow.

The boys are liable to blow up the house with their experiments.

*Can, may. Can* means *to be able to; may* means *to have permission.*

Can he lift that trunk?

May we return next Sunday?

*Capital, capitol. Capital* refers to the city which is the seat of the government; *capitol* refers to the building in which the legislative body meets.

Washington is the capital of the United States.

The legislative chamber is a beautiful room in the capitol in Lansing.

*Censor, censure. Censor* means *to examine material with the intention of barring its publication if it is objectionable; censure* means *to criticize adversely.*

His letters were severely censored.

The committee censured his actions but praised his attitude.

*Climactic, climatic. Climactic* pertains to climax, *climatic* to climate.

The play reaches its climactic scene in the third act.

Climatic conditions favored the growth of palm trees.

*Complement, compliment. Complement* means *to supply what is needed to fill out or complete a thing; compliment* means *to praise.*

The students' work in the laboratory complements their class work.

The instructor complimented the class upon its work.

*Continual, continuous. Continual* means *occurring in rapid succession* or *at intervals; continuous* means *occurring without a break.*

Continual interruptions prevented me from finishing my work.

A continuous murmur filled the auditorium.

*Disinterested, uninterested. Disinterested* means *impartial* or *free from selfish interest; uninterested* means *lacking interest.*

Henry will make an admirably disinterested judge of our dispute.

He was uninterested in the spectacle before him.

*Effect.* See *Affect.*

*Except.* See *Accept.*

*Farther, further.* Although sometimes used synonymously, *farther* ordinarily refers to space or distance, *further* to time, quantity, or degree.

It is farther to the beach than I thought.

The committee is making a further study of the problem.

*Fewer, less. Fewer* means *a smaller number; less* means *a smaller amount.*

We have heard fewer concerts this year.

We have earned less money this year.

*Hanged, hung. Hanged* is used of capital punishment; *hung* is proper in other connections.

The criminal was hanged by the neck until dead.

The branches hung low over the water.

*Illusion.* See *allusion.*

*Imply, infer. Imply* means *to hint; infer* means *to deduce* or *draw a conclusion from facts.*

The dean implied that we were wrong.

We inferred from the dean's comments that he believed us wrong.

*Incidents, incidence. Incidents* are *events* or *occurrences; incidence* is a technical word used in economics and physics.

Do not use such incidents in your narrative.

The instructor demonstrated the angle of incidence.

*In regard to, as regards. In regard to* is a compound preposition, meaning *about* or *concerning; regards,* in the expression *as regards,* is a transitive verb.

The pastor came in regard to reroofing the church.

I agree with him as regards this matter.

*Irritate.* See *Aggravate.*

*Its, it's. Its* is a possessive pronoun meaning *of it; it's* is a contraction meaning *it is.*

Everyone recognized its power.

It's warmer today.

*Later, latter. Later* is the comparative degree of *late; latter* means *the second of two things which have been mentioned.*

Bill arrived later than we did.

We can go by bus or train; the latter seems preferable.

*Lay, lie. Lay* (principal parts: *lay, laid, laid*) is a transitive verb meaning *to put* or *place; lie* (principal parts: *lie, lay, lain*) is an intransitive verb meaning *to put yourself down* or *to be in a horizontal position.*

I laid the papers on your desk.

I cannot lie in bed late tomorrow morning.

*Leave, let. Leave* means *to go away from* or *allow to remain; let* means *to permit.*

Leave the manuscript on my desk.

Let him go home now.

*Less.* See *Fewer.*

*Liable.* See *Apt.*

*Likely.* See *Apt.*

*Like, as. Like* is a preposition; it should not be used in place of *as* or *as if* to link clauses.

The coach looks as if he is tired.

My brother looks like me.

*Loose, lose. Loose* means *to set free; lose* means *to misplace* or *fail to win.*

He found he was unable to loose the bonds that held him.

The students all hope that we shall not lose the game.

*Luxuriant, luxurious. Luxuriant* pertains to *abundant growth, luxurious* to *luxury.*

The foliage of the vines was luxuriant.

As long as he had money, he led a luxurious life.

*May.* See *Can.*

*Most, almost. Most,* generally an adjective, means *nearly all* or *the greatest; almost,* an adverb, means *nearly.*

Most men agree on that subject.

Almost all men will agree on that subject.

*Principal, principle. Principal,* as a noun, means *a leader, the executive officer of a school* or in finance *the sum from which interest is derived;* as an adjective it means *chief. Principle,* always a noun, means *a basic law.*

That high school has an energetic principal.

He draws two per cent interest on his principal.

Fairbanks is our principal player.

The scientists were unable to grasp the principle of operation.

*Precede, proceed. Precede* means *to go before in time or in order of rank; proceed* means *to advance* or *continue a movement which is already started.*

Bill preceded me to the game.

He then proceeded from the baseball game to the tennis match.

*Set, sit. Set* (principal parts: *set, set, set*) means *to put* or *place; sit* (principal parts: *sit, sat, sat*) means *to put oneself,* as in taking a seat. *Set* is ordinarily transitive, *sit* intransitive.

Maria sets the chair on the lawn.

Tom quickly sits in the chair.

*Specie, species. Specie* means *money in the form of coins; species,* which has the same form for singular and plural, means *a class* or *kind.*

The government resumed specie payments.

Wilton has recognized a new species of beetles.

*Stationary, stationery. Stationary,* usually an adjective, means *fixed* or *not changing; stationery,* a noun, means *writing materials,* such as pens, pencils, paper, and ink.

We bolted the desk to the floor to make it stationary.

A new shop selling stationery has been opened near the campus.

*Stimulant, stimulus.* Although synonymous in medical usage, elsewhere *stimulant* refers to *a physical goad, stimulus* to *a mental goad.*

A cup of fresh coffee is a stimulant.

Hope is a stimulus to labor.

*Than, then. Than* is a conjunction following the comparative degree of adjectives and adverbs; *then* is an adverb expressing time.

My salary is less than yours.

We shall then be near the summit.

*Their, there, they're. Their* is the possessive case of *they; there* is an expletive or an adverb; *they're* is a contraction of *they are.*

Their work is done.

There are ten people in the room.

He sat there thinking.

The children brought their lunches.

They're all coming to the dance tonight.

*Uninterested.* See *Disinterested.*

(See *Workbook,* Exercises 10, 11, and 12.)

# II
## THE SENTENCE

### *Preview*

IN order to communicate effectively one must learn to use language correctly. Even the person who has always heard perfect English spoken by those with whom he has associated, and who can usually distinguish a correct from an incorrect form merely by deciding what sounds right, needs to learn grammar. For all of us, the study of grammar, the systematic description of the ways of the English language, is necessary before we can be sure that what we speak or write is correct. Grammar, then, is not a discipline to be studied for its own sake, nor is it a device invented by teachers to make their subject hard. It is a set of tools for shaping one's language into a correct and logically sound medium of expression.

**The Sentence.** The basic grammatical unit for expressing complete ideas is the sentence. A sentence always has two indispensable parts, a subject and a predicate.

The subject is that about which something is said. It may be a single word or a group of words, as the italicized parts of the following examples indicate.

*Newsboys* yell.
*The excited newsboys* yell.
*The raucous newsboys, pushing and shoving amid the crowds,* yell.

When several words form a subject, the whole group is called the *complete subject;* and the specific thing or person spoken of—in the preceding examples, *newsboys*—which the other elements of the subject merely serve to describe more fully, is called the *simple subject.*

The *predicate* is what is said of the subject. The *simple predicate* is the one word or group of words (the verb) which states in the simplest terms the action or state of being which is indicated with regard to the subject. The *complete predicate* includes the simple predicate with all its modifiers and completers. When two elements of equivalent value are linked to form the subject or the predicate, the term *compound subject* or *compound predicate* is used to describe them.

In the following sentences the subject and predicate are separated by a vertical line, and the simple subject and the simple predicate are italicized.

    a. *Men* | *walk*.
    b. The old *men* | *walk* slowly in the sun.
    c. Two old *men,* watery eyed and scraggly bearded, their frail bodies bent with age, | *walk* slowly and painfully along the parched path in the blistering August sun.
    d. *They* | *will have been gone* an hour.
    e. The *boys* and *girls* | *had gone* on a picnic.
    f. *Swimming* | *is* good exercise.
    g. *To go* or *to stay* | *was* the problem.
    h. *He* | *caught* the ball and *dashed* off down the field.

In the sentence "The captain called the squad together," there is no difficulty in determining that *captain* is the subject, and that the word which states what the captain did is *called,* the simple predicate. But the difficulty increases somewhat in inverted sentences—sentences in which the parts of speech are out of their normal order. A simple example of this sort is "Down fell Humpty-Dumpty." Having discovered that the simple predicate, or verb, is *fell,* you ask who or what fell. Surely not *down;* and if not, then it must have been Humpty-Dumpty. Would it be any harder to determine who fell if the sentence read, "Down from the high stone wall which encircled the court of the king fell that silly-looking, egg-shaped Humpty-Dumpty"?

More difficult still is the problem of finding the subject and predicate when they are separated by modifiers. An example of this sort is the sentence, "A list of rules has been posted." Having noted that *has been posted* is the simple predicate, you ask what has been posted. If you answer without thinking, you are likely to say *rules,* since it is the rules which seem important. But then you notice that *of rules* serves to describe *list. List,* then, you decide, rightly, is the subject, not *rules.* The matter is clearer in the sentence "A list of eligible players has been posted"; for the idea of a group of football players impaled on a wall somewhere appeals to your sense of the absurd, and you would smile at anyone who in that sentence supposed *players* to be the subject.

In many sentences much longer modifying elements separate•the subject from the predicate.

> Pushing up out of a mist of clouds and fog, the highest peak in the mountain chain, glistening with snow on its summit, from the airplane appeared as a craggy island in a desolate waste of ocean.

An analysis of this sentence shows that *appeared* is the simple predicate. By following the usual procedure of asking who or what appeared, you discover that it was not *mist, clouds, fog, chain, snow,* or *summit;* it was *peak. Peak,* then, is the simple subject.

**Words.** A sentence is constructed by arranging words in such a way that they express an idea. The meaning of any sentence can be changed by rearranging the words in their relationship to one another. In accordance with their functions in a sentence, therefore, words are classified into *parts of speech.* To provide a bird's-eye survey of these classes before taking them up in detail one by one, they are listed below. The definitions are designed merely to introduce briefly the terminology rather than to achieve scholarly completeness and accuracy.

1. A *noun* is the name of somebody or something: *man, chair, city.*

2. A *pronoun* is a word used in place of a noun: *he, who, that, us.*

3. An *adjective* is a word which qualifies or limits a noun or pronoun: *good, hot, dusty, forty.*

4. An *adverb* is a word which explains, qualifies, or limits a verb, adjective, or another adverb: *enthusiastically, lightly, solemnly.*

5. A *verb* expresses action or being: *eat, shoot, become.*

6. A *conjunction* is a connecting word which, as a rule, joins elements which are alike: *and, but, because.*

7. A *preposition* is a word which relates a substantive (a noun or its equivalent) to another word in the sentence: *in, from, by, for.*

8. An *interjection* is a word which is used for emphasis only and is not essential to an understanding of the sentence: *Oh! Alas!*

9. *Verbals* are not, strictly speaking, separate parts of speech, but are of sufficient importance and difficulty to be treated as such. They are de-

rived from verbs, but are used as other parts of speech. There are three kinds. (1) Participles are derived from verbs, but are used as adjectives: *Growing* boys are clumsy. *Bent* twigs become crooked trees. (2) Gerunds are derived from verbs, but are used as nouns: *Seeing* a movie is a form of relaxation. I like *swimming*. (3) Infinitives are derived from verbs, but are used as nouns, adjectives, and adverbs: *To know* her is *to love* her. I have no money *to spend*. He came *to meet* his daughter.

**Phrases.** Words are the simplest of the elements which make up a sentence, and, as has been indicated, every word can be classified as a part of speech. Words, however, can act collectively within a sentence as well as individually, and when acting collectively function as single parts of speech. Word groups are classified, on the basis of formation, according to whether they contain a subject and a predicate. A phrase is composed of two or more related words without a subject and a predicate and having in a sentence the force of a single part of speech.

If one can determine the part of speech which is represented by a single word, he should have little or no difficulty applying his knowledge to phrases. In the sentence "The spotted dog alarmed the neighbors," the noun *dog* is qualified by the adjective *spotted*. But if the sentence should read, "The dog with brown spots alarmed the neighbors," does not the word group *with brown spots* qualify the noun *dog* in exactly the same manner? *With brown spots* must, then, be an adjective construction, since by definition an adjective is an element which qualifies or modifies a noun or a pronoun. Or, suppose we add another element to the sentence: "The dog with brown spots alarmed the neighbors *by barking*"; *by barking* indicates the manner in which the alarming was accomplished— it modifies the verb *alarmed*. Therefore, it must be an adverbial construction, since words that modify verbs are adverbs. Other examples are:

(As adjective) That pen *on the desk* leaks.
               He owns the house *with the shutters*.
(As adverb)   They fished *in the inlet*.
               The coach ended his scolding *with a chuckle*.

Note that the phrases mentioned above are composed of a preposition (*with, by, on, in*) and a substantive plus whatever modifiers are attached to the substantive. The substantive is called the object of the preposition, and the whole phrase is called, *according to its formation,* a prepositional phrase. According to its *use,* it is an adjective or an adverbial phrase. The student should not be disturbed, therefore, when he hears phrases classified in two ways; he should merely remember that one classification applies to the form of the phrase and the other to the way it is used in a sentence.[1]

**Clauses.** The largest group inside the sentence is the clause, which is defined as a group of words containing a subject and a predicate. Clauses are of two types: *independent* (often called *main* or *principal*) and *dependent* (often called *subordinate*).

Independent clauses are capable of standing alone; that is, if the rest of the sentence were omitted, an independent clause would make good sense by itself. In the sentence "He walked to town, because his car had broken down," the independent clause is the part of the sentence preceding the comma—*He walked to town*. Read by itself, this group of words provides a complete meaning. For the sake of accuracy, we should note here that the term *clause* applies only to an element inside a sentence. A single, complete expression, beginning with a capital letter and ending with a period, question mark, or exclamation point, is not referred to as a clause, since it is not *part* of a sentence, but *is* a sentence.

> Independent clause: *He fell* because he did not see the ditch.
> Sentence: He threw the ball with all his strength.

A dependent clause is one which cannot stand alone, but depends on the rest of the sentence for its meaning. Being a clause, it is composed of a complete subject and predicate, but it is joined to the independent clause by means of a linking word. The sentence "He came because he was called" contains the dependent clause *because he was called;* it cannot make complete sense when read alone, it contains a subject and predicate, and these are joined to the independent clause by a linking word, *because*.

The sign of a dependent clause is the linking word, which is always (a) a relative pronoun—who, whom, whose, which, what, that; (b) a relative adverb—where, when, whence, while, since, before, after, as, till, until, how, why; or (c) a subordinating conjunction—although, though, because, since, if, unless, provided, whereas.

> NOTE. The linking word is dropped occasionally, and thus is not present as a means of identifying the dependent clause; but when it is omitted, there should be no more difficulty in supplying it than there is in supplying, say, the subject of an imperative sentence. Examples of such omission are the following: He said [that] he would go. He brought me the book [which] I required.

A second instance of the omission of the linking word occurs when a partial

---

1. Besides prepositional phrases, there are participial, infinitive, and gerund phrases; but these, because of their difficulty, are reserved for discussion later. Gerund phrases and some infinitive phrases are, by function, nouns.

inversion of the subject and predicate of the dependent clause makes the linking word unnecessary, as in the sentence "Had it happened that way, I should have known it," where *had it happened* stands for *if it had happened*.

Like phrases, dependent clauses are used as single parts of speech—as nouns, adjectives, and adverbs.

1. A noun clause is a dependent clause which is used in the place of a noun or a pronoun. The sentence "Our hardships were more than we could bear" has the noun *hardships* as subject; but in its place can be substituted a clause: "What we suffered was more than we could bear." The clause *what we suffered* is therefore a noun clause, as it is used in place of the noun as subject of the verb.

2. An adjective clause is a dependent clause which is used as an adjective. The sentence "The tall man is my brother" contains the adjective *tall;* the idea may also be expressed as "The man who is tall is my brother." The clause *who is tall,* because it is used like an adjective, is called an adjective clause.

3. An adverb clause is a dependent clause which is used as an adverb. The sentence "He left hurriedly" contains the adverb *hurriedly,* for which an adverb clause might be substituted thus: "He left *as if he were in a hurry."*

Having completed this brief survey of the principal instruments of communication, we can proceed to a more intensive examination of English grammar.

## Grammar

### WILLIAM COBBETT

Without understanding [the grammar of your own language] you can never hope to become fit for anything beyond [menial labor]. It is true that we do (God knows!) but too often see men have great wealth, high titles, and boundless power heaped upon them, who can hardly write ten lines together correctly; but, remember, it is not *merit* that has been the cause of their advancement; the cause has been, in almost every such case, the subserviency of the party to the will of some government, and the baseness of some nation who have quietly submitted to be governed by brazen fools. Do not you imagine that you will have luck of this sort; do not you hope to be rewarded and honored for that ignorance which shall prove a scourge to your country, and which will earn you the curses of the children yet unborn. Rely you upon your merit, and upon nothing else. Without a knowledge of grammar, it is impossible for you to write correctly, and it is by mere accident if you speak correctly; and pray bear in mind that all well-informed persons judge of a man's mind (until they have other means of judging) by his writing or speaking. The labor necessary to acquire this knowledge is, indeed, not trifling: grammar is not, like arithmetic, a science consisting of several distinct departments, some of which may be dispensed with; it is a whole, and the whole must be learned, or no part is learned. The subject is abstruse; it demands much reflection and much patience; but when once the task is performed, it is performed *for life,* and in every day of that life it will be found to be, in a greater or less degree, a source of pleasure or of profit or of both together. And what is the labor? It consists of no bodily exertion; it exposes the student to no cold, no hunger, no sufferings of any sort. The study need subtract from the hours of no business, nor, indeed, from the hours of necessary exercise; the hours usually spent on the tea and coffee slops and in the mere gossip which accompany them, those wasted hours of only *one year,* employed in the study of English grammar, would make you a correct speaker and writer for the rest of your life. You want no school, no room to study in, no expenses, and no troublesome circumstances of any sort. I learned grammar when I was a private soldier on the pay of sixpence a day. The edge of my berth, or that of the guard bed, was my seat to study in; my knapsack was my writing table; and the task did not demand anything like a year of my life. I had no money to purchase candle or oil; in winter time it was rarely that I could get any evening light but that of *the fire,* and only my *turn* even of that. And if I, under such circumstances, and without parent or friend to advise or encourage me, accomplished this undertaking, what excuse can there be for *any youth,* however poor, however pressed with business, or however circumstanced as to room or other conveniences? To buy a pen or a sheet of paper I was compelled to forego some portion of food, though in a state of half starvation; I had no moment of time that I could call my own; and I had to read and to write amidst the talking, laughing, singing, whistling, and brawling of at least half a score of the most thoughtless of men, and that, too, in the hours of their freedom from all control. Think not lightly of the *farthing* that I had to give, now and then, for ink, pen, or paper! That farthing was, alas! a *great sum* to me! I was as tall as I am now; I had great health and great exercise. The whole of the money, not expended for us at market, was *twopence a week* for each man. I remember, and well I may! that upon one occasion I, after all absolutely necessary expenses, had on a Friday made shift to have a halfpenny in reserve, which I had destined for the purchase of a red herring in the morning; but, when I pulled my clothes off at night, so hungry then as to be hardly able to endure life, I found that I had *lost my halfpenny!* I buried my head under the miserable sheet and rug, and cried like a child! And again I say, if I, under circumstances like these, could encounter and overcome this task, is there, can there be, in the whole world a youth to find an excuse for the nonperformance? What youth, who shall read this, will not be ashamed to say that he is not able to find time and opportunity for this most essential of all the branches of book learning?

## Suggestions for Study

1. Why does Cobbett believe a knowledge of grammar is necessary?
2. Although the study of grammar requires labor, why is not the learning of it arduous?
3. What equipment is needed to learn grammar? What surroundings?
4. From a rhetorical point of view, why does Cobbett include the personal illustration that occupies the last half of the article?
5. Define the following words from the selection: subserviency, brazen, dispensed, abstruse, forego, farthing.

## A. Parts of Speech

### I. THE NOUN

A noun is a word which is used as the name of a person, place, or thing. The examination of such nouns as *Thomas Jefferson, house,* and *loyalty,* however, reveals that all nouns are not alike. They are divided into two main groups: proper nouns and common nouns.

PROPER NOUNS are the names of particular people *(Abraham Lincoln),* places *(Central Park, Nevada),* or things *(White House, Charter Oak).*

COMMON NOUNS, more general in meaning, refer to all members of a common group of objects. Here belong the majority of our everyday nouns: *woman* (a proper noun would be *Mrs. Smith*), *horse* (proper noun, *Man O' War*), and *city* (proper noun, *Cleveland*). Common nouns are of three kinds:

*Concrete nouns*—names of objects that can be perceived by the senses: *book, paper, wool, stone.*

*Abstract nouns*—names of things which cannot be perceived by the senses: *loyalty, patriotism, wisdom.*

*Collective nouns*—names applied to entire groups considered as single units: *family, army, legislature.*

(See *Workbook,* Exercise 13.)

## 2. THE PRONOUN

A pronoun is a word used in place of a noun. For example, in the sentence "Bring the vase; it belongs on this table," using the pronoun *it* enables one to avoid an awkward repetition of the noun *vase*. The noun for which a pronoun is substituted is known as the *antecedent* of the pronoun. For several reasons, it is important to know the classes of pronouns and the pronouns that belong to each class. The following section, therefore, is important enough to be learned with care.

PERSONAL PRONOUNS express distinctions concerning person and so take a variety of forms. Examine the following, and if you do not already know them, learn them now.

|  | *Nominative* | *Possessive* | *Objective* |
|---|---|---|---|
|  |  | SINGULAR |  |
| 1st person | I | my, mine | me |
| 2nd person | you | your, yours | you |
| 3rd person | he, she, it | his, her, hers, its | him, her, it |
|  |  | PLURAL |  |
| 1st person | we | our, ours | us |
| 2nd person | you | your, yours | you |
| 3rd person | they | their, theirs | them |

RELATIVE PRONOUNS connect adjective clauses to their antecedents. They have the dual function of introducing the clause and of playing a part in it as subject, object, or the like. In the sentence "I knew the man who was speaking," *who* is a relative pronoun introducing the adjective clause *who was speaking* and also acting as subject in that clause. For a full discussion of adjective clauses, see pages 203 and 229.

The man *who* bought the house is here.
The book *which* I found is expensive.
The movie *that* we saw was very poor.

INTERROGATIVE PRONOUNS are used in asking questions: *who? which? what? Who* is at the door? With *whom* are you going? *Which* is your car? *Whose* is this? *What* did you say? He asked *who* his friend was.

The relative and interrogative pronoun *who* has three forms: the nominative *who,* the possessive *whose,* and the objective *whom.*

DEMONSTRATIVE PRONOUNS are used to point out or identify: *this, that, these, those. This* is my hat; *that* is yours. *These* belong to me, *those* to you.

REFLEXIVE PRONOUNS refer to the subject of the sentence and are formed by adding *self* or *selves* to personal pronouns: *myself, yourself, oneself, ourselves, themselves,* and the like.

> He likes *himself*.
> We bought *ourselves* a book.
> I gave *myself* a present.

INTENSIVE PRONOUNS, which have the same forms as the reflexive, are used to emphasize nouns or pronouns.

> John *himself* was not able to be there.
> I *myself* chopped down the tree.
> They relied on Jane *herself* to be there.

INDEFINITE PRONOUNS are a special group employed with a general antecedent, usually unexpressed: *little, other, such, none, several, certain, much, one, each, some, few, all, both, enough, everyone, either, neither, many*.

> *Everybody* likes Jane.
> *Some* brought their books.
> *Little* is known of him.
> *Many* were absent, but *few* will be missed.

A second kind of indefinite pronoun, the compound indefinite, embraces such words as *whoever, whomever, whichever,* and *whatever*. Although not a compound word, *what* is usually included with these others, as it functions in the same manner.

> I know *what* you want.
> He appoints *whoever* is most likely to succeed.
> We shall send *whomever* you recommend.
> *Whatever* you recommend will be accepted.
> *Whichever* suits you will likewise suit us.

(See *Workbook,* Exercise 14.)

### 3. THE VERB

A verb is a word which asserts something. By expressing action (He *ran* swiftly) or state of being (He *is* tall), it tells what a subject *does* or *is*. Sometimes, to gain additional shades of meaning, the verb requires helping or *auxiliary* words, such as the various forms of *be, have, do, may, can, shall, ought to,* and *must*.

| | |
|---|---|
| He will run. | He is running. |
| He must run. | He may run. |
| He has run. | He did run. |
| He could run. | He should run. |

MOOD. Most verbs make a simple statement of fact and are therefore in the *indicative* mood: He *told* my uncle. The world *is* in chaos. I *did tell* him. He *is going*.

If, however, a verb expresses a command or entreaty, it is said to be in the *imperative* mood: *Get* into uniform. *Come* to the park. *Bring* me some ice cream.

A third mood, called the *subjunctive,* expresses unreality, uncertainty, or doubt. A first group of verbs in the subjunctive expresses unreality, that is, an idea contrary to actual fact.

> I wish Bill *were* here.
> If I *were* president, I would declare a holiday.
> If the sun *were* to rise in the west, we would be surprised.
> *Had* he *been* more careful, this would not have happened.

Another group of verbs in the subjunctive expresses doubt or uncertainty:

> If that *be* the case, we had better stop.
> If the book *were* to be a best seller, his fortune would be made.

A third group follows such verbs of command as *desire, order, recommend, beg, vote, entreat,* and the like.

> I vote that he *be allowed* to join.
> The committee recommended that he *be honored.*
> We desire that he *be admitted.*

VOICE. Verbs expressing action are also classified as *active* or *passive.* A verb is said to be active if its subject performs the action of the verb, but passive if its subject is acted upon or receives the action. "The tower gave us landing instructions" contains an active verb; "Landing instructions were given us by the tower," a passive verb.

Active: All the farmers in the community plant their crops at the same time.
Passive: Crops are planted at the same time by all the farmers in the community.

Active: Economists do not know the causes of the depression.
Passive: The causes of the depression are not known.

TENSE. Tense expresses the time when the action of the verb takes place.

The *present tense* ordinarily expresses an action happening in the present: I *wonder* why the stars *are* so bright. But it may also state a universal truth (*In a vacuum a pound of lead falls at the same rate as a pound of feathers*) or occasionally a future meaning (*I am going to a movie tonight*).

The *past tense* refers to simple past time.

> The guide *pointed* out the most interesting sights.
> Our friends *entered* several contests.

The *future tense,* expressed by the auxiliaries *shall* and *will,* denotes future time. Generally, *shall* accompanies the first person singular and plural (*I shall go. We shall* go) and *will* the second and third persons (*He will go. You will go*).

The *present perfect tense,* identified by the auxiliary *have (has),* refers to an action completed at the present time: He *has eaten* his lunch. The verb means that the lunch was eaten in the past, but that the action was completed by the present time.

> The fish *have* all *left* the river.
> He *has finished* his assignment.

The *past perfect tense,* identified by the auxiliary *had,* denotes an action completed in the past.

> The dinner *had been eaten* by the time I arrived.
> They *had locked* the door behind us.

The *future perfect tense,* less commonly used in English, signifies an action to be completed some time in the future.

> John *will have eaten* his lunch before we arrive.
> The game *will have been completed* by five o'clock.

The foregoing discussion has pertained only to the regular verb forms, but two others—the progressive and the emphatic—are recognized in English. The progressive (*I am walking home*) denotes that an action is in progress or continuing over a period of time. The emphatic (*I did walk home*) usually gives special emphasis to the verb, but in questions or negations the emphasis is lacking: *Did* you walk? I *did* not walk.

**Examples of Conjugation.** Conjugation is the special term used for the inflection of the verb. A complete conjugation consists of all the persons, numbers, tenses, and moods, both active and passive voice, but a verb may be conjugated in any mood and tense. For example, if a student were asked to conjugate the present tense, active voice, indicative mood of *to sing,* he would write,

| | |
|---|---|
| I sing | we sing |
| you sing | you sing |
| he sings | they sing |

THE SYNOPSIS OF A VERB is a condensed statement of the forms which are asked for. For example, if you were asked to write a synopsis of the verb *to see* in the third person singular, indicative mood, active voice, you would write:

| | |
|---|---|
| Present | He sees |
| Past | He saw |
| Future | He will see |
| Present Perfect | He has seen |
| Past Perfect | He had seen |
| Future Perfect | He will have seen |

A synopsis of the verb *to find,* third person plural, subjunctive mood, passive voice is:

| | |
|---|---|
| Present | They be found |
| Past | They were found |
| Present Perfect | They have been found |
| Past Perfect | They had been found |

NOTE. In making a synopsis remember that intransitive verbs have no passive voice.

THE COMPLETE CONJUGATION OF THE VERB. As indicated in the preceding section, English verbs are conjugated to show forms for the different persons, numbers, voices, moods, and tenses. Because the verb *to be* plays such an important part as an auxiliary in the conjugation of verbs, the student should learn the following paradigms:

### to be

| *Present infinitive* | *Past* | *Past participle* |
|---|---|---|
| be | was | been |

### INDICATIVE MOOD

| *Present tense* | | *Present perfect tense* | |
|---|---|---|---|
| I am | We are | I have been | We have been |
| You are | You are | You have been | You have been |
| He is | They are | He has been | They have been |

| *Past tense* | | *Past perfect tense* | |
|---|---|---|---|
| I was | We were | I had been | We had been |
| You were | You were | You had been | You had been |
| He was | They were | He had been | They had been |

| *Future tense* | | *Future perfect tense* | |
|---|---|---|---|
| I shall be | We shall be | I shall have been | We shall have been |
| You will be | You will be | You will have been | You will have been |
| He will be | They will be | He will have been | They will have been |

## SUBJUNCTIVE MOOD

| *Present tense* | | *Present perfect tense* | |
|---|---|---|---|
| I be | We be | I have been | We have been |
| You be | You be | You have been | You have been |
| He be | They be | He have been | They have been |

| *Past tense* | | *Past perfect tense* | |
|---|---|---|---|
| I were | We were | I had been | We had been |
| You were | You were | You had been | You had been |
| He were | They were | He had been | They had been |

## IMPERATIVE MOOD

| *Singular* | *Plural* |
|---|---|
| Be | Be |

## VERBALS

| *Participles* | *Gerunds* | *Infinitives* |
|---|---|---|
| Present: Being | Present: Being | Present: To be |
| Past: Been | Perfect: Having been | Perfect: To have been |
| Perfect: Having been | | |

Besides these primary moods of the verb are many other modal forms, which furnish additional shades of meaning. That is, in English one may say not only *I plan,* but such other variants as *I am planning, I do plan, I may plan, I can plan, I must plan,* and *I ought to plan,* all forms of the verb "to plan."

(See *Workbook,* Exercise 15.)

### 4. THE ADJECTIVE

An adjective is a word which modifies a noun or other substantive (that is, a part of speech used like a noun). In its function of describing or limiting a noun, it usually answers the questions *what kind? how many?* In the sentence "The green fields were beautiful," *green* tells what kinds of fields and is therefore an adjective. In the sentence "Five birds flew swiftly by," *five* tells how many birds and is likewise an adjective.

Occasionally a noun is employed like an adjective, as in the sentence "He studied his *history* lesson," but such nouns are easily identified because they are perfectly regular in describing other nouns and so meet all the usual tests of adjectives.

The definite and indefinite articles are also adjectives. *The* is the definite article, *a* or *an* the indefinite. *A* is generally used before a consonant (*a cart*) or an aspirated *h* (*a history*), *an* before a word beginning with a vowel (*an eel*) or a silent *h* (*an hour*).

(See *Workbook*, Exercise 16.)

## 5. THE ADVERB

An adverb is a word which modifies a verb, adjective, or other adverb.

He speaks French *fluently*. (*Fluently* modifies the verb.)
She was a *very* beautiful girl. (*Very* modifies the adjective *beautiful*.)
You drive *too* recklessly. (*Too* modifies the adverb *recklessly*.)

Most adverbs will answer one of four questions concerning the word which they modify: *how? when? where?* or *how much?*

1. Expressing manner in answer to the question *how?*

He walked *rapidly* to school.
My brother examined the evidence *carefully*.

2. Expressing time in answer to the question *when?*

*Yesterday* we played the Northern team.
He will be here *soon*.

3. Expressing place in answer to the question *where?*

We found the money *here*.
Why don't you go *home?*

4. Expressing degree in answer to the questions *how much?* or *how little?*

My friends were *very* serious.
The tire was *almost* flat.

It should be borne in mind that the part of speech derives from its function. Hence in such a sentence as "Jeanne hurried home," *home,* although normally a noun, is here an adverb because it tells where Jeanne hurried. Nouns are frequently used as adverbs.

The class met *Saturday*.
The pole is ten *feet* high.

(See *Workbook*, Exercise 16.)

## 6. THE VERBALS

A verbal is a word derived from a verb but used as another part of speech. The three kinds of verbals are participles, gerunds, and infinitives.

THE PARTICIPLE. Verbals used as adjectives are called participles. They answer the question *what kind?* concerning nouns and pronouns just as the simple adjectives do, but differ from simple adjectives in expressing action or condition of being, as verbs do.

> The *swirling* snow blocked the roads.
> The *pelting* rain fell in torrents.
> The team, *beaten* last week, won today.
> *Singing* loudly, he merrily strode up the street.
> *Having been asked* twice, Mason agreed to run.

As these sentences illustrate, participles like verbs have different forms according to their tense and voice:

### to believe

|  | Active voice | Passive voice |
|---|---|---|
| Present | believing | being believed |
| Past | (none) | believed |
| Perfect | having believed | having been believed |

THE GERUND. Verbals ending in *ing* and used as nouns are known as gerunds. They differ from nouns in expressing action or state of being.

> *Walking* is good exercise.
> Many of my friends enjoy *singing*.
> *Resting* occasionally is a good habit.
> After *walking* for an hour we rested.
> He demonstrated his great strength by *lifting* a huge weight.

Although the majority of gerunds are in the present tense, active voice, they may be found in as many as four different forms:

### to like

|  | Active | Passive |
|---|---|---|
| Present | liking | being liked |
| Perfect | having liked | having been liked |

Participles, like other adjectives, are modified by adverbs; gerunds, like other noun forms, are modified by adjectives.

Participle: *Driving recklessly,* he endangered our lives.
Gerund: His *reckless driving* endangered our lives.

Yet, inasmuch as the gerund is derived from a verb, it may also be modified by an adverb.

> *Driving recklessly* endangers life.
> *Eating rapidly* invites indigestion.

THE INFINITIVE. An infinitive is the first principal part of a verb, usually is introduced by *to,* and is used as a noun, an adjective, or an adverb.

As a noun: *To see* is *to believe.*
I like *to swim.*
As an adjective: The best book *to buy* is not expensive.
We have no apples *to sell.*
As an adverb: *To find* peace, he went to the woods.
The assignment is easy *to understand.*

The infinitive may have as many as four forms:

**to see**

| | Active | Passive |
|---|---|---|
| Present | to see (progressive—to be seeing) | to be seen |
| Perfect | to have seen (progressive—to have been seeing) | to have been seen |

Like verbs, the infinitives are modified by adverbs.

*To read diligently* takes time.
*To drive carefully* is wise.

(See *Workbook,* Exercise 17.)

### 7. THE PREPOSITION, THE CONJUNCTION, AND THE INTERJECTION

THE PREPOSITION. A preposition is a connecting word which shows the relation of a noun, pronoun, or other substantive to some other word in the sentence. For example, in the sentence "We walked to town," *to* is a a preposition which connects the noun *town* to the verb *walked* and thereby creates a construction to tell where we walked. *Town* is called the object of the preposition, and this combination of a preposition and its object is termed a *prepositional phrase.*

Prepositions may be simple (*to, for, at, through, by, up,* and the like) or compound (*in spite of, instead of, in regard to, on account of, because of, out of, according to, as to*).

He walked *in* the rain.
They opened the door *with* a key.
The game was halted *because of* darkness.
We went *in spite of* the weather.

THE CONJUNCTION. A conjunction is a connective which joins words or groups of words in a sentence.

Words: John *and* I came home together.
Groups of words: He felt ashamed *when* the error was marked.

Conjunctions belong to two general classes: co-ordinating and subordinating.

1. *Co-ordinating conjunctions.* Co-ordinating conjunctions join elements of equal rank: *and, but, or, nor, for, neither, either.*

He went to the game, *but* Jeanne stayed at home.
Bill *or* Tom is going.
Slowly *and* carefully he drew the line.

2. *Subordinating conjunctions.* Subordinating conjunctions join groups of words (clauses) of unequal rank. Common subordinating conjunctions are *unless, because, since, as, as if, before, when, while, after, wherever, so that, that, whereas, if, although, though, even if, even though, in order that, inasmuch as, no matter what, in spite of the fact that, notwithstanding that.*

I have not seen him *since* he left.
She will not go *unless* you do too.
Fishing is best *when* the lake is calm.
*In order that* he may come, I shall pay his fee.
I shall not attend *even though* they offer to pay me.

3. *Transitional words.* A third group of connectives, only loosely to be considered conjunctions, is the transitional words (or transitional adverbs), which are used to supplement and reinforce the co-ordinating and subordinating conjunctions in carrying meaning from one group of words to another. These transitional words include *however, nevertheless, furthermore, accordingly, meanwhile, hence, therefore, likewise, indeed, moreover, namely, consequently, thus, similarly, yet, still,* and the like. The transitional phrases are similar in function: *in fact, that is, for example, in addition, on the other hand, as a result, on the contrary, in other words, for this reason, for instance, of course,* and so on.

THE INTERJECTION. An interjection is an exclamatory word or phrase introduced parenthetically into the sentence for emphasis or to indicate feeling on the part of the speaker. It has no grammatical connection with the rest of the sentence, and, accordingly, is set off by commas, or more emphatically by an exclamation mark.

*Oh,* you can't believe that.
He was, *alas,* my friend.
*Ouch!* that hurt.
*Help!* I'm drowning.

(See *Workbook,* Exercise 18.)

## B. The Formation of a Sentence

A sentence is a group of words, comprising a subject and a predicate, which expresses a single, complete thought. It always begins with a capital letter and ends with a period, a question mark, or an exclamation point. It may make a statement of fact, ask a question, give a command, or make an exclamation.

A *declarative sentence* is one which states something as a fact. A period is used to close it.

Autumn has come.
The marvels of science are not always unmixed blessings, as the development of poison gas will witness.

An *interrogative sentence* is one which asks a question. It is punctuated at the close by a question mark.

Where do the wild geese go in autumn?
When did he say he would come?

An *imperative sentence* is one which makes a request or gives a command. It is closed by a period. The subject is often omitted, since such a sentence is always addressed to someone or something, and who or what is addressed is clear without being mentioned.

Please bring note paper to class.
Leave margins in your manuscript.
You take the south court this morning.

An *exclamatory sentence* is one which expresses strong feeling or emotion, as of pity, fear, surprise, delight, disgust, or horror. It is usually punctuated at the close by an exclamation point, though in long sentences, where the feeling or emotion is largely submerged and only the arrangement of words indicates that the sentence is exclamatory, a period may be used.

What a bargain that turned out to be!
How beautiful those leaves are!

To understand a sentence more thoroughly, study the following pages carefully for illustrations of how the parts of speech are combined to form sentences.

## I. MAJOR SENTENCE UNITS

THE SUBJECT. Every sentence makes a statement about some object, person, or idea, called the subject of the sentence. The subject is a noun, pronoun, or other substantive, such as a gerund or infinitive; ordinarily it precedes the verb: The *barn* burned. Our *horse* was saved. Occasionally, however, the word order is reversed: Blue were her *eyes;* but that does not alter the fact that the sentence makes a statement about *eyes,* which is accordingly the subject. Likewise, if a sentence begins with the indefinite word *there,* known as an *expletive* (*There are twenty men here*), the subject (*men*) will follow the verb but again is easily identified as subject, for it is about men that the sentence makes an assertion.

Notice that when the verb is in the imperative mood, the subject is clearly implied but is not directly stated: Come here. Bring me the book. The subject of each of these sentences is of course *you,* a word which is clearly understood but only implied.

Four parts of speech studied thus far may be used as subject.

> Noun: The *book* is very long.
> Pronoun: *You* must visit me soon.
> Gerund: *Whistling* can be an art.
> Infinitive: *To paint* well demands long practice.

Although the sentences given thus far have had but one subject, many sentences do have two or more subjects, often called *compound* subjects.

> *Tom* and *Bill* were there.
> *Whistling* and *singing* are pleasant to hear.

The term *complete subject* is sometimes employed to designate the subject and all its modifiers, but the word *subject* here and hereafter is used in the sense of the simple subject, just that word or those words about which the sentence makes its assertion.

THE PREDICATE. Having chosen a subject for his sentence, a writer next selects a word or group of words to state what action is performed by the subject (*The teacher rang the bell*) or what condition exists regarding the subject (*The child is pretty*). The element which fulfills this function in the sentence is called the predicate. The verb is accordingly the most important element in the predicate and is often known as the *simple predicate*: The batter *hit* the ball. The term *complete predicate* designates the verb and any modifiers or completers of the verb: The plane *rose quickly into the air.*

The verb is the only part of speech which can constitute a predicate;

verbals, which are merely derived from verbs and do not express a complete action, cannot form a simple predicate by themselves.

Predicates, like subjects, may be compound.

> The boys *talked* and *sang* late into the night.
> The engineer *rang* the bell and *blew* the whistle as he neared the crossing.

The use of different types of verbs necessitates the use of different types of complete predicates. One type of verb is known as the *intransitive verb,* which has two subdivisions. The first, containing the intransitive verbs with complete predication, embraces those verbs which make complete meaning by themselves in the predicate or when followed by modifiers.

> The girl *smiled.*
> The dog *ran* swiftly down the road.

The second group involves the use of the subjective complement.

THE SUBJECTIVE COMPLEMENT. Those intransitive verbs known as linking verbs require a noun form or an adjective form to follow in order that their meaning will be completed. The term *subjective complement* (a general term embracing the specific terms *predicate noun* and *predicate adjective*) designates this element which follows the linking verb to fill out the meaning of the sentence. The linking verb is just a link or coupling to connect the subject and its complement. The commonest linking verb is *be;* others, such as *become, seem,* and *appear,* are very frequently linking in their function; still others, such as *taste, feel, look,* and *grow,* are occasionally linking.

> The principal crop *was* potatoes.
> The defendant *is* guilty.
> The defendant *seems* guilty.
> The peaches *tasted* good.

In each of these sentences the word following the verb completes the meaning of the subject. *Potatoes* is identified with *crop,* the adjective *guilty* tells what kind of *defendant* is referred to, and *good* tells what kind of peaches.

The subjective complement is composed of either the noun forms—noun, pronoun, gerund, infinitive—or the adjective forms—adjective, participle.

> Noun: The speaker is a *professor.*
> Pronoun: It is *I.* (Notice the nominative case after a linking verb.)
> Gerund: His pastime is *walking.*
> Infinitive: To see is *to believe.*

Adjective: He seems *angry*.
Participle: The weather seems *threatening*.

Inasmuch as verbals are derived from verbs, they too share the quality of being intransitive and so taking a subjective complement.

Participle: Jack, *being* tired, went to bed.
Gerund: *Being* president is a great responsibility.
Infinitive: *To be* ready at all times is our code.

THE DIRECT OBJECT. The second main type of verb is the *transitive verb*. Its function is to carry an action from the subject to another word following the verb and known as the direct object (the word *transitive* is derived from a Latin word meaning "to go across").

The driver *saw* the truck.
I *gave* the cake to a tramp.
The farmer *raised* a good crop.

In these sentences the three direct objects are *truck, cake,* and *crop.* The direct object is similar to the subjective complement only in that it will answer the question *what?* following the verb.

Subjective complement: He is—*what?*—president.
Direct object: She baked—*what?*—a cake.

The two forms differ in other respects. A noun subjective complement is identical in meaning with the subject (*he* and *president*), but a direct object is in no way identical with the subject (*she* and *cake*).

The parts of speech which can act as direct objects are the nouns, pronouns, gerunds, and infinitives.

Noun: The new law soon produced many *strikes*.
Pronoun: We saw *him* after the movie.
Gerund: The government began *seizing* the plants.
Infinitive: Labor began *to plan* a new campaign.

Any verbal derived from a transitive verb may also take a direct object.

After a participle: The boss, denouncing their *policy,* made a bitter speech.
After a gerund: Sending a *letter* will not solve the problem.
After an infinitive: To make a *hit* is not easy in this game.

The distinction of active and passive voice pertains only to transitive verbs, as intransitive verbs are not capable of forming the passive voice.

Active voice: Feller *threw* many fast balls in that game.
Passive voice: Many fast balls *were thrown* by Feller in that game.

ADDING MODIFIERS. The simple sentence constructed thus far contains a subject (what one is talking about), a simple predicate (which tells what the subject *does* or *is*), and any needed completing forms such as a subjective complement (which supplements the subject) or a direct object (which receives an action from the verb). To give a more complete thought, one may next add to these basic units any desired adjectives or adverbs. The adjectives will describe or limit nouns, pronouns, or gerunds; the adverbs will qualify the meaning of the verbs, verbals, adjectives, or other adverbs.

In addition, a skillful writer will also frequently add prepositional phrases. These phrases, consisting of a preposition and its object, act precisely as simple adjectives or adverbs do. That is, a writer may describe a barn by using a simple adjective such as *red,* but if he chooses, he may also use an adjective prepositional phrase such as *with a red roof.* Prepositional phrases are thus either adjective or adverb in use.

Adjective prepositional phrases:

> The man *with the tall hat* is related to me.
> The dog *with the long tail* is a greyhound.
> This house *of mine* is in poor condition.

Adverbial prepositional phrases:

> *During the night* he left *for New York.*
> We shall play our match *on Saturday.*
> He defeated his opponent *with great ease.*

With these few tools a writer is able to construct many sentences of apparent complexity. For example, let us analyze the sentence "Budge served the ball over the net with blinding speed and completely bewildered his nervous opponent." The subject is *Budge;* the predicate is compound, consisting of the verbs *served* and *bewildered;* ball is the direct object of *served, opponent* the direct object of *bewildered;* the verb *served* is qualified by two adverbial prepositional phrases—*with blinding speed* tells how the ball was served, *over the net* tells where; *blinding* is a participle modifying *speed, completely* is an adverb modifying *bewildered,* and the two adjectives *his* and *nervous* describe the noun *opponent. And* is the conjunction linking the two parts of the compound predicate.

Such lengthy descriptions of a sentence, however, are somewhat clumsy. Many students will welcome in substitution the pictorial method of representing a sentence known as the diagram. It is a device to show quickly the relationship of the parts of a sentence. The first step in making a diagram is to draw a straight line intersected at right angles by a short vertical line to indicate the division of the subject from the predicate, both of which are written on the line: subject | predicate. If the sentence contains a direct object, that term is added on the line just to the right of the verb and separated from the verb by another vertical line but not projecting below the line: subject | predicate | direct object. If

the sentence contains a subjective complement rather than a direct object, the line to the right of the verb slants toward the subject: subject | predicate \ subjective complement. The simple construction

"Budge served the ball" is diagramed this way: Budge | served | ball.

Any modifier of these units is placed on a slanting line below the word modified:

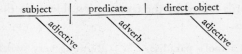

The sentence "Quickly Budge served a hard ball" is diagramed like this:

A prepositional phrase is placed below the word it modifies and is represented by a slanting line on which the preposition is written, followed by a horizontal line on which the object of the preposition is placed: \_. The sentence "Budge served the ball over the net with great speed" is diagramed like this:

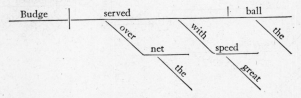

If the subject, predicate, or direct object is compound, a brace is used to describe this fact: ———< . The sentence "Budge served the ball and bewildered his opponent" takes this form:

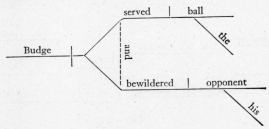

A participle is described like the prepositional phrase but with a loop at the juncture of the two lines ( ), and the gerund by a jagged line set on a stilt ( ). An infinitive, when used as an adjective or adverb, is placed below the word it modifies by the same device used for the prepositional phrase but with a loop over the *to* to distinguish it from a preposition ( ); when used as a noun, the infinitive is set on a stilt ( ). Conjunctions are placed on a dotted line running between the words joined by the conjunction. Here are diagrams of some sample sentences.

Traveling is a fool's paradise.

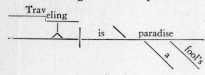

Running very swiftly, he slipped on the ice.

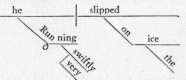

Tiring suddenly, he ceased running and sprawled on the grass.

This morning Tom and Bob accompanied us to get eggs.

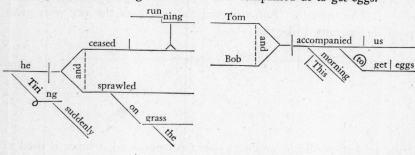

To buy costumes is difficult and taxes one's ingenuity.

Trying to buy costumes discouraged me.

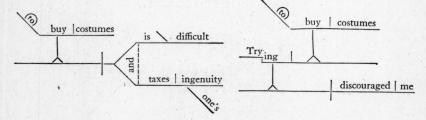

What do you want?

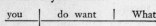

Why did you come?

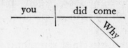

Bring the basket to me.

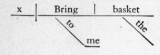

There are ten men in the room.

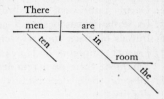

## Sentences for Diagraming

1. The box contained twenty matches.
2. Send the remittance to our office.
3. Thayer is the treasurer.
4. A discount will be granted under those conditions.
5. The mayor, planning a safety campaign, sought the aid of the traffic bureau.
6. The campaign began last month and proved a huge success.
7. Reducing fatalities was the aim of the campaign.
8. During the month fifty lives were spared by the careful motorists.
9. A new highway was built to relieve traffic congestion.
10. The highway had four lanes and no intersections.
11. The engineers promoted safety by banking the corners scientifically.
12. To prevent excessive speeds, the police enforced a speed limit.
13. Guessing the next move, my opponent maneuvered his men on the board to avoid a trap.
14. Soon I made an error of judgment and lost the game.
15. Pushing into the wilderness, we soon lost sight of civilization.
16. For six days we did not come to a single human habitation.
17. On the seventh day a trapper appeared and courteously shared his food with us in his rude shack.
18. His fare was venison, cooked well.
19. To keep our directions more easily, we followed the river for fifty miles.
20. Hungry and cold, we emerged from the forest near the Canadian border.
21. These botanists, loving flowers well, studied them assiduously.
22. In the mountain valleys they found many new species hidden from the casual eye.
23. These specimens they took home.
24. Other botanists have known flowers well but have not loved their beauty.
25. Planting seeds by mid-summer will yield abundant harvest.
26. By picking the flowers each day, you will increase the production of each plant.
27. To frighten us, the pirates hoisted a black flag.

28. We replied by sending a volley across their bow.
29. The fight soon began and lasted into the night.
30. Battling with desperation, we drove them to their ship and escaped with our lives.
31. The little child ran along the road begging money from us.
32. We could not resist the childish appeal.
33. Soon we passed an ancient temple built by the Romans.
34. Deeply impressed, we admired its remarkable state of preservation.
35. Its statuary was beautiful and hardly touched by time.
36. Initials of many tourists were written around the base of each column.
37. Former emperors had occasionally taken marble slabs from the walls to ornament their own temples.
38. Despite these desecrations the temple retained its original grace and dignity.
39. Here was the huge ruin of a mighty stadium.
40. The Coliseum is still an inspiring sight for the tourists.

(See *Workbook,* Exercise 19.)

### 2. MINOR SENTENCE UNITS

The sentence elements just considered constitute the most frequently used parts of the simple sentence, but several others are often employed to express particular shades of meaning.

INDIRECT OBJECT. A writer frequently states *to whom* or *for whom* an action was performed without using the prepositions *to* or *for*. This construction, possible only after certain verbs, is called the indirect object. The sentence "She sent a letter to her mother" is perfectly correct, but the same meaning is conveyed by an indirect object, "She sent her *mother* a letter." In this sentence the preposition *to* is implied rather than stated, a characteristic always true of the indirect object.

> My mother baked *us* a cake.
> Hilda gave *Bob* a lecture on temperance.
> The secretary read *us* a letter from Washington.

APPOSITIVE. The appositive, usually a noun, further identifies or points out another substantive and ordinarily is placed immediately after the word with which it is in apposition: My new car, a convertible *coupe,* runs very well. The appositive, *coupe,* here gives additional information about the noun *car.*

> He is my brother *Tom.*
> Bobbie, a very swift *dog,* chased the rabbit.

NOMINATIVE OF ADDRESS. A noun or pronoun used in addressing a person and having no grammatical connection with the rest of the sentence is known as a nominative of address.

> Where were you this afternoon, *George?*
> I was told, *Doctor,* that Jim is feeling very well.

OBJECTIVE COMPLEMENT. Sometimes after such verbs as *elect, choose, make, appoint, call, name, nominate,* and the like, a noun or pronoun is needed to supplement or fill out the meaning of the direct object. This construction, known as the objective complement, follows the direct object.

> The governor appointed him *head* of the Commission.
> We call John the best-dressed *man* on the campus.
> The society elected Bill *vice-president.*

Notice that the term *to be* is implied between the direct object and the objective complement: The governor appointed him (to be) head.

NOMINATIVE ABSOLUTE. A nominative absolute consists of a noun or pronoun modified by a participle and lacking any grammatical connection with the rest of the sentence.

> *The storm having subsided,* we left the shelter.
> *The wheels of the plane having touched the ground,* we sighed with relief.

This construction, which in the hands of unskillful writers often proves awkward and cumbersome, should be used warily by the novice.

OBJECTIVE INFINITIVE. Used as the direct object of a verb, the objective infinitive is composed of a noun or pronoun in the objective case, acting as the subject of an infinitive. The sign of the infinitive *to* may be either stated or implied.

> We wanted *her to have* an education.
> Our friends advised *us to accept* the offer.
> We saw *Bill win* the high hurdles.
> I heard *the car roar* past.

DIAGRAMING THE MINOR SENTENCE UNITS.

*The indirect object.* As the indirect object is essentially an implied prepositional phrase, it is diagramed like the prepositional phrase but with an *x* on the slanting line.

They gave him a costly gift.

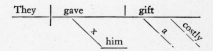

*The appositive.* Place the appositive in parentheses beside the word with which it is in apposition.

My brother Dick visited us.

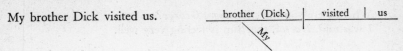

*The nominative of address.* Having no grammatical connection with the rest of the sentence, the nominative of address is set off by itself on a separate line.

Have you heard the news, John?

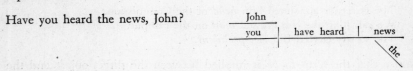

*The objective complement.* Place the objective complement just to the left of the direct object and separated from the verb by a slanting line.

The voters elected him governor.

*The nominative absolute.* As the nominative absolute is grammatically unconnected with the rest of the sentence, place the noun form on a separate line with the participle modifying it.

The car having gone, we walked to town.

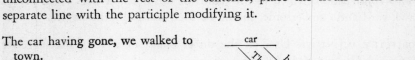

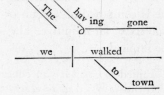

*The objective infinitive.* Place the entire objective infinitive construction on a stilt with a vertical line between the direct object and the infinitive.

He asked me to play the piano.

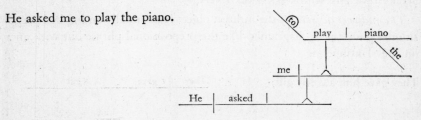

## Sentences for Diagraming

1. The committee awarded me a bronze medal.
2. Jones, chairman of the committee, congratulated every contestant.
3. The ceremony having ended, the audience went home quickly.
4. Bill, why did you go to the convention?
5. The board asked me to go and paid my expenses.
6. Then the committee on nominations elected me secretary of the association.
7. They also wanted me to be treasurer but did not insist.
8. The committee knowing my desires, my name was not mentioned again.
9. The railroad reserved me a lower berth.
10. Making the reservation fortunately was not difficult.
11. The ticket agent, a friend of mine, got me the reservation without delay.
12. I wish to go by plane on the next trip.
13. Saving a few hours in that way, I can transact more business.
14. The different breeds having been timed, the greyhound proved to be the fastest dog.
15. Running for short distances, the greyhound can defeat the race horse.
16. Over long distances the horse, being larger and stronger, has superior speed and stamina.
17. Many people believe the jackrabbit to be the fastest animal.
18. In a straight course the greyhound can overtake the jackrabbit swiftly.
19. The cheetah, a jungle animal trained to hunt, can probably exceed the swiftest greyhound in speed.
20. The cheetah, a native of Asia and Africa, is a member of the cat family.
21. Built for quick dashes, it can catch the antelope.
22. Hunting silently like a cat and running swiftly like a dog, it is a deadly killer.
23. To the instructor I spoke hesitantly about my ideals and dreams.
24. In his old age, shorn of his strength, the veteran athlete did not lose courage.
25. From the workers in the fields sounds of merriment could be heard.
26. Keats, a youthful genius, was a target for hostile criticism.
27. My father bought me a beautiful red dress.
28. Slender and graceful, he appeared a prince in disguise.
29. Clear and true were the notes of the carillon.
30. All men of good will should lend their aid to the cause.
31. Wishing to have company, she forced me to go with her.
32. The notes of the bugle having sounded, the first rank began its charge.
33. We asked Jim to provide the entertainment.
34. The manuscript, carelessly written, was returned to its author.
35. The editor granted me more time to complete the manuscript.
36. The salesman tried selling an expensive product.
37. Making no sales, he soon became weary.
38. Taking him from his former position, they made him a district manager.
39. The promotion gave him a larger salary and pleased him immensely.
40. The rumor spreading this morning is a libel on our candidate.

(See *Workbook,* Exercise 20.)

## 3. CLAUSES

In the sentences constructed thus far, you have observed but one subject and one predicate, although either might have been compound. In
such a sentence, however, as "The professor said that the book costs a
great deal," you notice that the complete thought involves the use of two
separate sets of subject and predicate: *professor said* and *book costs.* To
understand such sentences involves a knowledge of clauses and their relation to the four kinds of sentences: simple, compound, complex, and
compound-complex.

THE SIMPLE SENTENCE. Sentences studied thus far have all been simple sentences; that is, they have contained only one independent clause. A clause
is that part of a sentence which contains a subject and predicate; if independent, it contains a main idea and frequently makes complete sense by
itself without the assistance of any other clause. If dependent, however,
it does not make complete sense by itself, for it contains a subordinate
idea, present in the sentence only to lend meaning to a main idea. For
example, "No trains were running" is an independent clause, containing
a main idea and, as it happens, making complete sense by itself; "because
the trainmen were on strike" is a dependent clause, as it makes only part
of a statement and is present in the sentence only to contribute meaning
to another idea. The sentence "No trains were running because the
trainmen were on strike" therefore contains one independent and one
dependent clause. Returning to our original statement, we can now repeat
that a simple sentence contains but one independent clause.

THE COMPOUND SENTENCE. A sentence which is composed of two or more
independent clauses is a compound sentence. It expresses two or more
closely linked ideas of equal importance. Ordinarily the co-ordinating
conjunctions—*and, but, or, nor, for*—are either stated or implied as links
between independent clauses.

> The signals were flashed, *and* the train pulled out.
> The men went to the game, *but* the women preferred to stay at home.
> All nations must agree to the terms, *or* war will break out.
> Art is long; life is short. (*But* is implied.)
> Platinum is a catalyst; that is, it promotes a reaction without itself being
> affected.

THE COMPLEX SENTENCE. A sentence composed of an independent clause
with one or more dependent clauses is called a complex sentence. These
dependent clauses function in the sentence in the same manner as several
parts of speech already studied. One type of dependent clause is known

as a noun clause, as it can be used in almost any capacity in a sentence that a noun can; a second type, the adjective clause, modifies noun forms just as the simple adjectives do; a third type, the adverbial clause, is employed like the simple adverb. Each of the dependent clauses is linked to the independent clause by a subordinating conjunction or relative pronoun.

*The noun clause.* Easily the most common subordinating conjunction used to introduce a noun clause is *that,* although occasionally others, such as *why, who,* and *what* and the compound indefinite pronouns *whoever, whomever, whichever, whatever,* are employed. Remembering that the noun clause is used like the simple noun, study the following examples of the common uses of the noun clause.

As subject: *That he writes poorly* is not to his credit.
As direct object: We know *that he walks home each night.*
      I know *who he is.*
      We found *what the answer is.*
As subjective complement: The fact is *that we have few students.*
As object of a preposition: I shall give it to *whoever needs it.*
As delayed subject: It is clear *that our team will lose.*
As appositive: The fact *that the world is round* was clearly shown.

*The adjective clause.* The adjective clauses—sometimes called relative clauses—are introduced almost always by one of three relative pronouns —*who, which,* and *that.* These pronouns not only introduce the dependent clause but also play a part in the clause as subject, object, or the like. This latter function is imposed upon them by virtue of the fact that they are basically pronouns and substitute in the dependent clause for the word which the clause modifies. For example, the sentence "The man who is wearing the straw hat is my father" contains the adjective clause *who is wearing the straw hat,* which serves to tell what man is referred to, just as a simple adjective would do. The relative pronoun *who* not only links the clauses but also acts as subject of the dependent clause.

She bought a dress *which fits her perfectly.*
Anyone *who is discriminating* will like the play.
The chair *in which I sat* is an antique.
The boat *that I bought* is not worth much money.

*The adverbial clause.* Adverbial clauses, which function in the sentence in the same manner as the simple adverbs, are introduced by many different subordinating conjunctions, such as *although, because, as, as if, if, while, when, where, so that, whereas, though, even if, in order that, before, after, unless,* and *since.* Here are some of the common uses of the adverbial clauses.

Time: I left *before my family returned.*
Place: They found the money *where the pirates had buried it.*
Comparison: He sings better *than he whistles.*
Condition: He could have won *if he had expended more effort.*
Cause: *Because he was too tall,* he was refused admittance.
Result: We were *so* tired *that we didn't stop to eat.*
Purpose: We have come *in order that we may get our grades.*

THE COMPOUND-COMPLEX SENTENCE. If a sentence contains two or more independent and one or more dependent clauses, it is said to be a compound-complex sentence. A few examples should serve to clarify this type without further discussion.

He is a native of Holland, where he lived until he was sixteen, but he now refers to America as home.
Although a strike was called, labor took a conciliatory policy, and the government did not have to intervene.

### DIAGRAMING CLAUSES

*The compound sentence.* Place the co-ordinating conjunction on a dotted line between the two independent clauses.

The vase was dropped, but no damage was done.

Buy this radio, or I shall sell it to Joe.

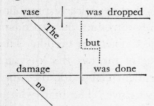

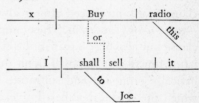

*The complex sentence.*

*Noun clause.* Place the noun clause on a separate line raised on a stilt above the point in the independent clause where it functions. Place the subordinating conjunction above the noun clause.

That he speaks well is obvious.

Bill says that he will come.

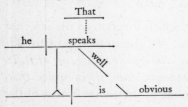

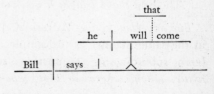

The Major converses with whoever is present.

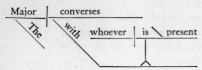

It is certain that he will be elected.

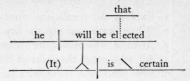

*Adjective clause.* Place the adjective clause on a separate line from the independent clause, and link the adjective clause to the independent clause by a dotted line from the relative pronoun to the word which the clause modifies.

She bought a dress which fits her.

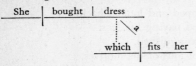

The man whom I know is very tall.

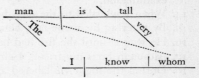

The car in which we rode is a coupe.

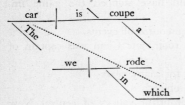

The chair in which I sat is an antique.

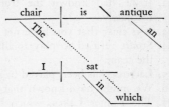

*Adverbial clause.* Place the adverbial clause on a separate line below the line of the independent clause, with the subordinating conjunction on a dotted line from the dependent clause to the word modified in the independent clause.

Because he will not wait, he will lose his money.

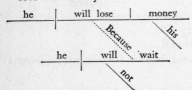

He ran more swiftly than I did.

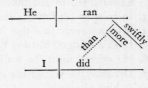

## Sentences for Diagraming

1. Explain our reasons to whoever asks.
2. Where have you put the book that was on the table?
3. Anyone who reads the newspapers can follow current events.
4. All who enter these doors must expect labor and hardship.
5. Few who take these tests can pass them.
6. The territory in which we landed was inhabited by cannibals.
7. The sonnets of Wordsworth which are found in this book are beautiful.
8. The airplane from which we leaped crashed in the swamp.
9. If she had realized her mistake, she could have rectified it.
10. The tyranny which has enslaved our people must be ended.
11. Bill decided to leave school, but Tom preferred to continue his studies.
12. Having graded the papers, the professor strode from the classroom.
13. Because he had studied diligently, the student was not dreading the examination.
14. When I whistled to the dog, he stopped and looked back.
15. By entering his name late, he avoided paying his fees.
16. He waited until the fire had been extinguished.
17. Although he is my friend, I am suspicious of his motives.
18. During the night we labored assiduously to complete the job.
19. Shylock asserted that Antonio owed him a pound of flesh.
20. I have never seen anyone who could equal John's record.
21. Send me the latest news that reaches you from Brazil.
22. If he had known the truth, he would have stopped the game immediately.
23. It is clear that you have not followed the course of events.
24. Stuart refused to play football, but his roommate Clem was captain of the team.
25. Lacrosse has been played by the Indians for many years.
26. We might have known that you would object.
27. The Finger Lakes, which lie in the beautiful valleys of central New York, attract many tourists each year.
28. The executive who should have sent me the memorandum is now holding a conference.
29. We enjoy a long walk while the dew is on the grass.
30. One of my classmates once inserted several blank pages between the covers of his term paper.
31. If you exercise frequently, you probably have good health.
32. Because the sentence was answered incorrectly, the answer was heavily underscored in red ink.
33. In spite of his father's influence, he did not retain his position.
34. My roommate said that he wanted to borrow my tuxedo.
35. I am a midget, but my brothers are very tall.
36. He waited until the walks had been cleared.
37. Defiantly he waved the club over his head, but his friends merely looked at him pityingly.
38. Walking home through the drifting snow was very enjoyable.

39. When he called last night, I told him that I had decided to go home.
40. With great care he packed his parachute.
41. One pastime of the idle is collecting shells.
42. I see no reason for believing this doctrine.
43. The rumor is that a break in market prices is imminent.
44. The broker that whispered the rumor to me has commanded great respect in the past.
45. The regulation that all sales must be cash may avert a sharp decline.
46. Stripping fertile top soil from millions of acres was the result of carelessness.
47. To catch trout, drop your line in a running stream.
48. All summer we have been looking for a house to rent.
49. The printer should have been enraged by the manuscript, which was covered with blots and emendations.
50. The minstrel boy slung the harp over his shoulder and went to the wars.
51. Feeling tired, Jack dropped the oars and drifted with the current.
52. After trying in vain to attract our attention, the little dog trotted away.
53. After Joe was elected to office, his manner became insufferable.
54. The rumor that we pay our athletes is utterly false.
55. Every athlete who plays on our teams is primarily a scholar.
56. We do not even provide jobs for those who play football for us.
57. We believe that students should come to college to study.
58. Football should be played for the sport which it gives to the competitors.
59. Rattling along the road in his ancient Ford, Tom was enjoying himself thoroughly.
60. Borne up by the waves, the cask approached the shore.
61. Being frightened by a large dog, the tramp raced for the nearest tree.
62. Whoever buys a dog should give it excellent care.
63. If a dog receives attention, it will probably be happy and healthy.
64. Our landlord would not rent an apartment to anyone who had a baby or a dog.
65. A shortage of supplies has hampered our work this year, but that shortage may soon be a thing of the past.
66. Bring your textbook to class when you come tomorrow.
67. The plane in which we traveled was built by Lockheed.
68. This new plane will fly faster than previous planes.
69. It is possible that both our candidates will be elected.
70. Discuss this matter with the friends whom you trust.
71. When you write, mention the name of the pilot with whom we rode.
72. Upon request he resigned his position, but he refused to stop fighting for his ideals.
73. That he fought well cannot be disputed.
74. The sergeant under whom we drilled was a severe taskmaster.
75. He could talk faster than I can.
76. Although he was highly satisfied with our progress, he kept drilling us every day.
77. One day he asked me to drill the squad.

78. Because I had never given commands, I refused.
79. He then made me platoon leader and forced me to take command.
80. The loyal fans gave him a new car in appreciation of his services.
81. Bowed with grief, he slowly left the room.
82. Soon gaining control of himself, he returned with a jaunty air.
83. The conditions under which we conducted the experiment were not ideal.
84. Proving our contention was not easy.
85. Scientists who had not studied our evidence were highly skeptical.
86. Despite all the criticism our theory has lasted extremely well.
87. We hope that soon it will be a scientific law.
88. Gaily whistling as he walked, the postman neared the house.
89. The novel which we read contains a stimulating theme.
90. The narrative is told very well, but the characterization is very weak.
91. After reading a book, a student should make a short summary of its contents.
92. It is good practice to write a paragraph every day.
93. To write fluently, one must write frequently.
94. Even though you do not have genius, you still may learn to write clearly.
95. By taking us through a dense wood, the guide confused us.
96. We could not find our way home.
97. The tolerance that comes from experience will deepen your character.
98. The hasty conclusion at which you have arrived does not do credit to your intelligence.
99. By walking every day, I maintain good health.
100. The diagrams which you have been making illustrate your ability to analyze a sentence and also demonstrate that you will understand the basic structure of any sentence which you write.

(See *Workbook,* Exercises 21, 22, 23, and 24.)

## C. Grammatical Correctness

You have now studied the parts of speech and their combination into sentences. You will find, however, that if you are not careful in forming sentences, you may make many errors in grammar and so give your reader an erroneous impression of what you wish to say to him. Study the following pages carefully so that you may avoid making such mistakes.

### 1. NOUNS

Nouns ordinarily occasion a writer little difficulty, yet certain matters pertaining to number, gender, and case may prove troublesome.

PLURALS. For the rules governing the formation of plurals, see pages 140–141.

GENDER. The genders distinguished in modern English are:

*Masculine*—a member of the male sex: *uncle, brother, boy, gander, buck, Patrick.*

*Feminine*—a member of the female sex: *hen, sister, lady, Patricia.*

*Neuter*—an object that is without sex: *stone, city, hamlet, table.*

*Common*—a noun which may be either masculine or feminine: *reader, parent, child, cousin, butterfly.*

The distinction between masculine and feminine gender in English is made in the following ways:

1. by use of different words: *buck—doe; rooster—hen.*
2. by use of a suffix, of which the more common are
   (a) those added to the masculine to form the feminine: (1) *ess—waiter, waitress; host, hostess; count, countess;* and (2) *ix—aviator, aviatrix; executor, executrix.*
   (b) those added to the feminine to form the masculine: *widow—widower.*
3. by placing a word indicating the sex before or after the word to make a compound noun: *manservant—maidservant; billy-* or *he-goat—nanny-* or *she-goat; foreman—forewoman; landlord—landlady.*
4. by changing the *us* to *a* in Latin words: *alumnus—alumna; Julius—Julia.*

POSSESSIVE CASE. The failure to use a possessive case where needed and the failure to form the possessive properly are among the most frequent errors made on student papers. The possessive case, as the name implies, is almost always used to denote possession or ownership of a person or thing.

If you are to form the possessives correctly, follow these rules:

**13**
1. To form the possessive singular add *'s*:[1] *boy's, man's, Jones's, witness's.*
2. To form the possessive plural:
   (a) If the noun ends in *s*, add simply the apostrophe ('): *hunters', students', wives'.*
   (b) If the noun does not end in *s*, add *'s*: *fishermen's, children's, men's, mice's.*

NOTE. Compound words add the inflection (according to the above rules) to the last element: *son-in-law's, King of England's.*

If two or more nouns are to be considered as one group, the possessive case ending is given only to the last one: *John and Bill's place* (John and Bill being the owners). If, however, they refer separately to the noun upon which

1. See p. 280 for exceptions.

they depend, the possessive case endings are added to all the nouns: *He is now beyond an enemy's or a friend's hand* (two hands—one belongs to an enemy, one to a friend).

Usually possession is not attributed to inanimate objects. Do not, for instance, say *the barn's color,* but rather *the color of the barn.* (Exceptions to this rule are words relating to time and money: *dollar's worth, month's pay,* in which an old form is retained in modern usage.)

(See *Workbook,* Exercise 25.)

### 2. PRONOUNS

The pronoun requires special care in usage, for it is much more troublesome than the noun. The paragraphs which follow indicate the matters which need closest attention in the use of pronouns.

14 ANTECEDENT. *A pronoun must always have a definite, particular antecedent* (unless the pronoun is such an indefinite as *little, anyone, everybody*). By definition a pronoun is a word used in place of a noun, so that the same noun will not have to be repeated over and over again. Therefore, a reader must be perfectly sure for what noun each pronoun is substituting.

Do not use a pronoun when the antecedent is only implied: I have always liked chemistry and so decided to become one. What is the antecedent of the pronoun *one?* Restate the sentence: I have always liked chemistry and so decided to become a chemist. The personal pronoun *they* in particular demands care in use, for many students think erroneously that it can be used without an antecedent.

> Faulty: They often have accidents at that crossing.
> Correct: Careless drivers often have accidents at that crossing.

The pronoun *which* should likewise never be used unless it refers to a definite, particular antecedent. The sentence "In that race he was defeated, which troubled him greatly" tries to make the pronoun *which* substitute for a whole clause or for the verb *was defeated,* but a pronoun logically cannot substitute for a whole clause or for a verb. The sentence should read "His defeat in that race troubled him greatly" or "In that race he met a defeat which troubled him greatly."

Never cause a reader to guess what word is the antecedent of a pronoun. If you write "She took the dresses from the hangers and laid them on the bed," your reader has no way of knowing whether the dresses or the hangers were laid on the bed. Repeat the antecedent, or completely revise your sentence to avoid such ambiguity: She laid the dresses on the bed after removing them from the hangers.

**15** AGREEMENT. *A pronoun must always agree with its antecedent in person, number, and gender.* If a pronoun does not meet this requirement, a reader cannot be sure that he understands to which antecedent the pronoun is referring. If you write "Whenever a play was given, people enjoyed seeing them very much," a reader distrusts his judgment which tells him that *them* is substituting for the noun *play;* a plural pronoun does not adequately replace a singular noun. Write "Whenever a play was given, people enjoyed seeing it very much."

Observe that most indefinite pronouns are singular in number and so are followed by a singular pronoun.

> *Everyone* in the room drank *his* tea without comment.
> If *either* does *his* task well, we shall succeed.
> *One* must believe much that *he* hears.
> If *anyone* is going, *he* should start immediately.

A few indefinite pronouns, however, logically are plurals and so demand plural pronouns.

> *Many* will take *their* bathing suits.
> *Some* have been taking pictures with *their* cameras.
> *Few* take *their* work seriously.
> *Both* lost *their* cars in the flood.

An accepted convention is to use a masculine pronoun to refer to a group composed of both sexes.

> Each student in the class brought *his* own paper.
> Each person in the audience expressed *himself* freely.

CASE. As most pronouns have different forms for the nominative and objective cases, be sure that you have employed the proper case.

**16** *If a pronoun is used as subject or subjective complement, it should be in the nominative case (I, he, we, she, they, who, whoever).*

*If a pronoun is used as direct object, object of a preposition, or indirect object of a verb, it should be in the objective case (me, him, us, her, them, whom, whomever).*

*Nominative case*

> Subject: *Who* is there?
> *I* know it.
> *He* will tell.
> We must tell *whoever* is present.

(Observe in the latter sentence that *whoever* is nominative because it is the subject of the noun clause *whoever is present.* The fact that the whole clause is a direct object of the verb *must tell* has no bearing on the case of the pronoun in the dependent clause.)

> Subjective complement: It is *he*.
> It seems to be *he*.

## Objective case

> Direct object: I know *him*.
> *Whom* do you know?
> The man *whom* you elected is honest.
> Invite to the party *whomever* you like.
> Object of a preposition: He told it to *me*.
> To *whom* did you tell the story?
> Indirect object: I gave *him* the car.
> Buy *her* some candy.

**17** POSSESSIVE PRONOUNS. *The possessive case of personal, relative, and interrogatory pronouns never requires an apostrophe—yours, his, hers, ours, theirs, whose, its.* If you write "It's a warm day," the sentence means "It is a warm day"; the possessive pronoun *its* is properly used in the sentence "The dog lost *its* bone." Similarly, "Who's there?" means "Who is there?" but the sentence "Whose hat is this?" contains a true possessive form.

**18** INTENSIVE PRONOUNS. *An intensive pronoun must either stand next to its antecedent or refer to the subject of the same sentence.* Never write such a sentence as "He called for Henry and myself." The sentence should read: "He called for Henry and me." The following sentences illustrate the correct use of the intensive pronoun.

> John *himself* was not able to be there.
> John was not able to be there *himself*.
> I *myself* chopped down the tree.
> They nominated John *himself* for the office.

(See *Workbook*, Exercises 26 and 27.)

### 3. VERBS

**19** AGREEMENT. *A verb must agree with its subject in person and number.* If the subject is in the first person, the verb must be in the first person; if the subject is in the third person, the verb must be in the third person.

> *I eat* cereal every morning.          *I don't* wish to go.
> *He eats* cereal every morning.         *He doesn't* wish to go.

Also if the subject is singular, the verb must be singular; if plural, the verb should also be plural.

> The *subject is* difficult for me.
> These *subjects are* difficult for me.
> This *student works* hard.
> These *students work* hard.
> There *is* only one *way* of doing the job.
> There *are* fourteen *pages* in this manuscript.

Notice that if the subject is compound, the verb will have to be plural to agree.

> *Bill* and his *wife are* here now.
> *Tom* and *Willie are going* home.

The following five rules contain some minor but none the less often-times puzzling matters of agreement for beginning writers. Examine them closely.

1. *When correlatives are used as subject, that division of the subject closest to the verb determines the agreement of the verb.*

> Either Don or *I am* at fault.
> Neither the teacher nor the *students know* the answer.
> The gentlemen or the *lady pays* the bill.
> The judge or the *lawyer is* guilty.
> The judge or the *lawyers are* guilty.

2. *A singular subject will always require a singular verb even though plural modifiers of the subject intervene between it and the predicate.*

> *Eileen,* together with her uncle and two brothers, *is coming.*
> The *officer,* accompanied by several deputies, *is arriving.*
> An innocent *man* as well as those who were guilty *was punished.*

3. *Collective nouns usually take singular verbs.*

> The *army is marching* now.
> Our *family is waiting* at the station.

4. *Sums of money and measurements are regularly singular.*

> *Twenty dollars is* my highest bid.
> *Nine hundred miles is* a long drive.

5. *Literary titles are singular.*

> *Grapes of Wrath is* a realistic novel.
> *The Women was* an interesting play.

20  THE INCOMPLETE SENTENCE. *Every sentence must contain a complete subject and predicate.* The commonest errors of this sort are occasioned by forgetfulness to add a verb or by a mistaken belief by the

writer that a participle can be substituted for a verb without damage to meaning.

Faulty: The man that I know.
Correct: The man that I know is very pleasant.
Faulty: The old man believing himself dead.
Correct: The old man believed himself dead.

The exceptions to this rule are few and in general should be avoided by students until they have demonstrated to the instructor that they know how to use a complete sentence.

The following, however, are some legitimate uses of the incomplete sentence.

In transitional sentences: Now for the second cause.
To go a step further.
Next, to consider another argument.
In questions and answers when the meaning is clear from the context:
We had reached the end of the trail. What now?
Who says this? My brother.
In exclamatory words and phrases: What a wonderful view!
Here at last!
How peaceful!
In conversation: "Bob was there."
"With Mary?"
"No. With Clara."

TROUBLESOME VERB FORMS. As many verbs have irregularities in their conjugation, *exercise care in using the past tense and the past participle.* Here is a list of particularly troublesome verb forms:

| | | | | | |
|---|---|---|---|---|---|
| arise | arose | arisen | feed | fed | fed |
| bind | bound | bound | fling | flung | flung |
| bite | bit | bitten | fly | flew | flown |
| blow | blew | blown | give | gave | given |
| break | broke | broken | grind | ground | ground |
| bring | brought | brought | know | knew | known |
| build | built | built | lay | laid | laid |
| burst | burst | burst | lead | led | led |
| choose | chose | chosen | lend | lent | lent |
| cling | clung | clung | lie | lay | lain |
| come | came | come | meet | met | met |
| dive | dived | dived | rend | rent | rent |
| do | did | done | ring | rang | rung |
| draw | drew | drawn | seek | sought | sought |
| drink | drank | drunk | send | sent | sent |
| drive | drove | driven | set | set | set |
| eat | ate | eaten | shed | shed | shed |
| fall | fell | fallen | shoot | shot | shot |

| | | | | | |
|---|---|---|---|---|---|
| shrink | shrank | shrunk | sting | stung | stung |
| sing | sang | sung | swear | swore | sworn |
| sink | sank | sunk | swell | swelled | swollen (swelled) |
| slay | slew | slain | swim | swam | swum |
| sling | slung | slung | take | took | taken |
| slink | slunk | slunk | tear | tore | torn |
| spring | sprang | sprung | think | thought | thought |
| steal | stole | stolen | | | |

(See *Workbook,* Exercises 28, 29, 30, and 31.)

#### 4. ADJECTIVES AND ADVERBS

**21**   *Adjectives modify nouns or pronouns; adverbs modify verbs, adjectives, or other adverbs.* Do not therefore interchange adjectives with adverbs.

> Faulty: He worked *good*.
> Correct: He worked *well*.
> Faulty: He played third base *poor*.
> Correct: He played third base *poorly*.

**22**   *An adjective, not an adverb, normally follows a linking verb.* These verbs do not promote any action in the sentence but simply describe a state of being concerning the subject and so necessitate the use of adjectives in the subjective complement.

> The church is *tall*. (The tall church)
> The man is *strong*. (The strong man)
> The man became *strong*.
> The man feels *strong*.
> The driver seems *tired*. (The tired driver)

An adverb is used following a verb when one wishes to describe not the subject but the verb.

> Adjective: The cereal tastes *good*.
> Adverb: He tasted the cereal *carefully*.

> Adjective: John felt *bad* about his error in the third inning.
> Adverb: John felt the sharp edge *cautiously*.

> Adjective: The morning air smells *good*.
> Adverb: He smells the morning air *vigorously*.

> Adjective: The hills look *beautiful*.
> Adverb: He looks at the hills *closely*.

**23**   *The comparative degree of adjectives and adverbs is used to compare two objects, the superlative to compare more than two.*

The carpenter wore an *older* hat than the blacksmith did.
The carpenter wore the *oldest* hat I have ever seen.
She is the *taller* of the two.
She is the *tallest* of the group.

24    *The comparative and superlative degrees of adjectives of one syllable are formed by adding* er *and* est *to the positive degree; those of three or more syllables, by adding* more *or* most, less *or* least *to the positive form.* Most adjectives of two syllables take *more-most* for the comparative and superlative, but there are many exceptions to this rule. Consult your dictionary when you are in doubt.

He is *stronger* than I.
He is the *tallest* man in the room.
She is *more beautiful* than Hedy.
He is the *most extraordinary* athlete in the college.

Although a few adverbs take the *er* and *est* endings in the comparative and superlative, *in general, most adverbs form their comparative and superlative by the addition of more-most, less-least.*

He runs *more swiftly* than his brother.
She answers *more spontaneously* than her brother does.
I came home *sooner* than I had expected.

25    *Some adjectives and adverbs by their very nature cannot be compared at all*—square, round, dead, unique, fatally, entirely, quite, the cardinal numbers (one, two, three), and the ordinals (first, second, third). There are no degrees of squareness or roundness; a figure is round, or it is not. A person is dead or alive; no degrees intervene. A unique object is the only one of its kind.

The following irregularities in comparison require attentive study.

| | Positive | Comparative | Superlative |
|---|---|---|---|
| Adjectives: | bad | worse | worst |
| | good, well | better | best |
| | little | less (lesser) | least |
| | many (much) | more | most |
| | late | later, latter | latest, last |
| | old | elder (older) | eldest (oldest) |
| Adverbs: | well | better | best |
| | little | less | least |
| | ill (badly) | worse | worst |
| | far | farther (further) | farthest (furthest) |
| | many, much | more | most |

(See *Workbook*, Exercise 32.)

## 5. VERBALS

**26** DANGLING VERBALS. *Never allow a verbal to dangle*. Every participial phrase, every adjective and adverbial infinitive phrase, and every prepositional gerund phrase must refer unmistakably to the correct noun or pronoun present in the sentence. If such a reference is not clearly made, the verbal is said to dangle. This rule is required by the same logic that prescribes a subject for every predicate; the reader must know who is executing any action referred to in the sentence. Verbals are even trickier than verbs, for they often try to associate themselves with the wrong noun and so produce ludicrous meanings, as in the first faulty sentence below.

Dangling participle: *Having walked* a mile, the lake came into view.
Correction: Having walked a mile, we came in sight of the lake.

Dangling infinitive: *To play* every day, good health is necessary.
Correction: To play every day, one must be in good health.

Dangling gerund: After *noting* the weather, the game was called.
Correction: After noting the weather, the umpire called the game.

Observe that each of the faulty sentences was easily corrected by the writer's placing, immediately after the verbal phrase, that noun or pronoun which executes the action of the verbal. If that formula is followed consistently, those verbal phrases which begin sentences should not occasion any trouble.

(See *Workbook,* Exercise 32.)

# D. Good Sentences

You have now studied the parts of speech, their combination into sentences, and those constructions which may occasion trouble grammatically in the formation of a sentence. To construct a good sentence, however, demands that a writer ask himself two further questions: are the sentence elements put together in the best manner possible to achieve absolute clarity of thought, and is the style of expression as excellent as possible?

### I. CLARITY

PROPER ARRANGEMENT OF SENTENCE ELEMENTS. A first principle in securing clarity is to assure yourself that each sentence element is in its proper place. Pay particular attention to the placement of adjectives, adverbs, correlative conjunctions, phrases, and clauses, and to the avoidance of improper splitting of constructions which logically belong together.

**27** *Adjectives. Place each adjective in the sentence so that it will always modify the word which you intend it to modify.* Although less likely to cause error than the adverb, the adjective seems to take Puckish delight in getting its user into trouble. Such constructions as the following are most likely to cause difficulty.

> Faulty: I found a red woman's pocketbook this morning.
> Clear: I found a woman's red pocketbook this morning.

> Faulty: He collects old men's suits for repair.
> Clear: He collects men's old suits for repair.

**28** *Adverbs. Place such adverbs as* only, merely, hardly, almost, even, not, never, *and* ever *next to the words they modify.* Note, for instance, how a change of position changes the meaning of the following sentences.

> Only I went to the picnic.
> I only went to the picnic.
> I went only to the picnic.

> He merely tried to learn the rules.
> He tried merely to learn the rules.
> He tried to learn merely the rules.

Although all these examples are logical, each has a different meaning. A writer, therefore, should be careful to place each word so that the sentence says exactly what he means it to say.

**29** *Correlative conjunctions. The correlative conjunctions (*not only— but also, neither—nor, either—or, both—and*) should always be followed by those similar or parallel parts of speech which are co-ordinate.* If one correlative, for instance, is followed by a predicate, the other should be followed by a predicate. If one is followed by a subjective complement, the other should be followed by a subjective complement.

> Faulty: He neither feared man nor beast.
> Clear: He feared *neither* man *nor* beast.

> Faulty: This should not only be considered by students but by citizens as well.
> Clear: This should be considered *not only* by students *but* by citizens as well.

**30** *Phrases and clauses. Place phrases or clauses next to the words they modify, or at least so near that whatever element they are intended to modify will always be easily apparent.*

Faulty: We visited the house where Emerson lived *last summer*.
Clear: Last summer we visited the house where Emerson lived.

Faulty: "His wife was successfully operated upon for appendicitis at the Good Samaritan Hospital *which suddenly attacked her Monday at her home on Mozart Avenue*."—Cincinnati *Times-Star*.[2]
Clear: At the Good Samaritan Hospital his wife was successfully operated upon for appendicitis, which suddenly attacked her Monday at her home on Mozart Avenue.

Faulty: "I number among my friends an actress who retired to rear four children, *two schoolteachers, and the proprietor of a small grocery store*."—Reader's *Digest*.[2]
Clear: I number among my friends two schoolteachers, the proprietor of a small grocery store, and an actress who retired to rear four children.

Faulty: "The price of tickets will be $1.00, *which may be obtained at the door*."—Invitation to a Phi Beta Kappa banquet.[2]
Clear: Tickets, which may be obtained at the door, will cost $1.00.

**31** *Squinting modifiers. Never place a modifier in the sentence in such a way that it may refer to either of two elements.* As such modifiers seem to look both ways, they are called squinting modifiers. To avoid them, rearrange the sentence or add any needed punctuation.

Faulty: He asked me *when the match was over* to go to his room.
Clear: He asked me to go to his room when the match was over.
or When the match was over, he asked me to go to his room.

Faulty: He wrote that if he could not collect *within a week* he would turn the matter over to a lawyer.
Clear: He wrote that if he could not collect, within a week he would turn the matter over to a lawyer.
or He wrote that if he could not collect within a week, he would turn the matter over to a lawyer.

**32** *Split constructions. Do not insert a word, phrase, or clause between words which normally belong together.* Although such split constructions are not invariably incorrect, ordinarily they are awkward and give the reader added difficulty in grasping the meaning of the sentence.

a. *Split verb phrases.* Although simple adverbs and short adverbial phrases may be inserted between the auxiliary and the main verb ("The ship was *hardly* moving"), the insertion of longer phrases and clauses produces confusion.

2. These examples are reproduced from the *New Yorker*, which makes a point of collecting and commenting humorously upon various sorts of errors in writing.

Faulty: He is, *or so his sister told me,* going.
Clear: He is going, or so his sister told me.

Faulty: He was *so far as the eye could see* hardly moving.
Clear: So far as the eye could see, he was hardly moving.

b. *Split co-ordinate elements.* Keep co-ordinate elements together.

Faulty: *As it was rainy,* the match was postponed, *as the courts were wet.*
Clear: As it was rainy and the courts were wet, the match was postponed.

Faulty: *If he asks us,* I shall accept *if you will go.*
Clear: If he asks us and if you will go, I shall accept.

c. *Split comparisons.* In such sentences as "He is as tall, if not taller than John," the omission of the word *as* after *tall,* occasioned by the splitting of the comparison, produces an incorrect construction that is awkward and not always clear. Improve such sentences by writing "He is as tall as John, if not taller," or "He is as tall as or even taller than John."

d. *Split infinitive.* Do not insert a word or short phrase between the particle *to* and the verb proper unless such an insertion adds to the clearness and effectiveness of the sentence, and do not insert a long phrase or clause under any circumstances. Such sentences as these are indefensible:

Football players find it hard *to,* day after day, week after week, for nearly three months, *go* out for practice.
It is hard *to,* while you wait for your girl to get ready, *be* relaxed and at ease.

Even splitting the infinitive by the use of a single word often produces awkwardness; "He seemed always to be hungry" is a better phrasing than "He seemed to always be hungry." Only occasionally is a split infinitive so apt that to avoid it would be an act of mere pedantry: "They have promised to more than double the output of trucks."

CONSISTENCY. Consistency means maintaining one point of view throughout a sentence. *When a writer commits himself to one subject, voice, mood, tense, and number in his sentence, he keeps to his selection without needless and confusing shifting.*

33

a. *Subject.* Never make a shift in the subject between clauses merely to avoid repeating that subject.

Faulty: We climbed to the top of the hill, and the city lay stretched out below us.
Clear: We climbed to the top of the hill and saw the city stretched out below us.

Faulty: As you come to a break in the hedge, a glimpse of the river greets you.

Better: As you come to a break in the hedge, you catch a glimpse of the river.

b. *Voice.* Under ordinary circumstances voice is not shifted between consecutive clauses. If the active voice is chosen for the first clause, the active voice is used for the subsequent clause, unless some particular point of emphasis is desired.

Faulty: They went to Portage Lake, and a good time was had.

Better: They went to Portage Lake and had a good time.

Faulty: We stayed on deck all day, and the water was scanned for flying fish.

Clear: We stayed on deck all day and scanned the water for flying fish.

c. *Mood.* Do not waver unnecessarily from one mood to another. If you have chosen the indicative mood, keep to that and do not shift needlessly to the imperative.

Faulty: Take a knife and cut the limb off square without damaging the bark. I use a sharp knife for this. Next, I cut the bark all round about two inches from the end of the stick. Now beat the bark with your knife.

Clear: Take a knife and cut the limb off square without damaging the bark. Use a sharp knife to make the task easier. Next, cut the bark all round about two inches from the end of the stick, and beat the bark with your knife.

d. *Tense.* When you have selected a dominant tense within a sentence or between sentences, keep to that tense.

Consistency requires that when a writer begins an article in the present or the past tense, he keep to that tense. Yet changes are common in the work of inexperienced writers. Perhaps the chief reason for this is lack of awareness of the point of view in time. There are two principal ways to relate something: (1) as if the events or ideas are unrolling before the writer as he composes, and (2) as if the events occurred at some past time, and the writer is merely recalling them as he writes. In the first of these ways the writer is a spectator, and he uses the present tense; in the second way he considers the past from his vantage point in the present, and he uses the past tense. Now if the writer does not remain aware of the point of view from which he is noting the action, he may make unwarranted shifts in tense without realizing that he is doing so. One way to avoid such shifts is to dramatize one's own position in relation to the ideas or events being recounted. If the events belong to the past, but the writer wishes to write of them as if he were present, he should imagine himself transported to that past time and himself to be moving amid the scenes he describes. If they belong to the present, he should think of them as actually passing before him and his describing them as they happen. If they belong to the past and he wishes to treat them as having already happened, he should think of himself as occupying a position in the present and contemplating the past as a historian, not as an observer.

In the following excerpts the first two are examples of the correct use of tense, and the final excerpts illustrate the wrong shifting of tenses.

*Past events described from the vantage point of the present—the usual way:*

The day broke—the day which was to decide the fate of India. At sunrise the army of the Nabob, pouring through many openings of the camp, began to move towards the grove where the English lay. Forty thousand infantry, armed with firelocks, pikes, swords, bows and arrows, covered the plain. They were accompanied by fifty pieces of ordnance of the largest size, each tugged by a long team of white oxen, and each pushed on from behind by an elephant. Some smaller guns, under the direction of a few French auxiliaries, were perhaps more formidable. The cavalry were fifteen thousand, drawn, not from the effeminate population of Bengal, but from the bolder race which inhabits the northern provinces; and the practiced eye of Clive could perceive that both the men and the horses were more powerful than those of the Carnatic. The force which he had to oppose to this great multitude consisted of only three thousand men. . . .

The battle commenced with a cannonade in which the artillery of the Nabob did scarcely any execution, while the few fieldpieces of the English produced great effect. Several of the most distinguished officers in Surajah Dowlah's service fell. Disorder began to spread through his ranks. His own terror increased every moment. One of the conspirators urged on him the expediency of retreating. The insidious advice, agreeing as it did with what his own terrors suggested, was readily received. He ordered his army to fall back, and this order decided his fate. Clive snatched the moment, and ordered his troops to advance. The confused and dispirited multitude gave way before the onset of disciplined valor. . . . . In an hour the forces of Surajah Dowlah were dispersed, never to reassemble.—T. B. Macaulay, "Lord Clive."

*Past events described as if the writer were present:*

It is Sunday morning, January 8, 1815. Dawn is still a half hour away. Suddenly from the British lines a rocket flares—the signal of attack. In two solid columns the British approach our ramparts, bristling with infantry and artillery, behind which General Jackson has a force of four thousand. Our men are well protected, but the British must advance with bare bosoms upon the storm of bullets, balls, and shells which our guns pour forth. The slaughter is awful. Every bullet reaches a mark. Two hundred men are cut down by one discharge of a thirty-two pounder, loaded to the muzzle with musketballs and poured into the head of a column at a distance of but a few yards. General Jackson walks slowly along his ranks, saying to his men, "Stand to your guns! Don't waste your ammunition! See that every shot tells! Let's finish this business today!" Two hours of this inferno pass, and the attacks stop. The smoke lifts. The enemy has disappeared. The ground is so covered with dying and dead that for a quarter of a mile in front of our lines one may walk upon their bodies. Far away in the distance the remnant of the army may be seen in disorderly retreat.—Adapted from a description of the battle of New Orleans in an old history text.

*Tenses shifted wrongly:*

(1) We took seats, while the guides explained the origin, history, lighting, and natural air conditioning of the caverns, and then told us that the lights will be turned off for a few seconds to leave us in total darkness. The lights are off, and in the distance we hear a voice singing the hymn, "Rock of Ages." Then the lights were gradually turned on. At last we came to a place which looked like a large room. It is called the Green Lake Room because it contains a small lake of green water.

(2) Strong pieces of bull's-eye glass were set in the upper part of the diving bell so as to admit light. Casks filled with air and loaded down with lead are lowered to the men in the bell. When the casks are lowered, the bungholes are facing downward. The casks having arrived at the bottom, the men inside the bell took hoses made of leather and sucked out the air.

e. *Number.* The shifts of number that produce confusion have already been considered in this book in the section devoted to grammatical errors. These shifts consist in the failure of pronouns to agree with antecedents and predicates to agree with subjects.

Unnecessary shifts, it is worth observing, are confusing not only within the sentence but between neighboring sentences as well.

SUBORDINATION AND CO-ORDINATION. To gain clarity, a skillful writer estimates for his reader the relative importance of the ideas in his paper. Under ordinary circumstances he places the ideas of major importance in independent clauses and relegates ideas of lesser importance to dependent clauses, verbal phrases, or prepositional phrases. He has, of course, no abstract standard with which to determine the relative importance of ideas, but simply uses his good judgment according to what he is trying to emphasize in the paragraph which he is writing. In general, he employs a compound sentence to stress two or more rather equivalent ideas, and a complex sentence to stress one main idea which is

modified by one or more lesser or contributing ideas. The best general
rule in this situation is: *Do not place subordinate ideas in inde-*
**34** *pendent clauses nor major ideas in dependent clauses or phrases.*

*Proper subordination.* Minor ideas belong in dependent clauses and
phrases, for dependent constructions are present ordinarily in the sentence not for their own sake but only insofar as they contribute meaning
to ideas of greater importance. Beginning students, however, tend to
violate this rule primarily through excessive co-ordination, which elevates
minor ideas into independent clauses or separate simple sentences, and
also through upside-down subordination, which completely reverses the
proper emphasis by throwing the major idea into the dependent clause.

a. *Excessive co-ordination.* You are very likely to be guilty of excessive
co-ordination if you find yourself employing a series of short simple sentences or of compound sentences. An inexperienced speaker or writer
commonly expresses himself just by adding one idea to another without
thought of proper subordinations, but a mature writer knows that he
must overcome this fault if transmission of his ideas is to be clear.

> Faulty: I bought a house, and it needed painting.
> Clear: The house which I bought needed painting.

> Faulty: I went to the game, and Williams hit a home run.
> Clear: In the course of the game which I attended, Williams hit a home
> run.

> Faulty: I looked over my opponent, and I saw he was a man of great
> strength.
> Clear: As I looked over my opponent, I saw he was a man of great
> strength.

b. *Upside-down subordination.* Upside-down subordination is particularly perplexing to a reader in that it tries to force upon him a false
evaluation of the importance of two concepts and requires him to revalue
both if he is to understand the sentence properly.

> Faulty: He exerted a great burst of speed, forging ahead in the last few
> yards to win.
> Clear: Exerting a great burst of speed, he forged ahead in the last few
> yards to win.

> Faulty: Congress passed the bill, which caused widespread panic through-
> out the country.
> Clear: The bill which Congress passed caused widespread panic through-
> out the country.

*Proper co-ordination.* Proper co-ordination results from balancing ideas
of equal importance, usually through the aid of the co-ordinating con-

junctions *and, but, or, nor,* and *for.* In the sentence "Near the close of the baseball season Detroit will be playing its games at home, but Boston will be on the road," the writer has employed proper co-ordination to impress two concepts equally upon the reader.

The beginning student of writing must guard against first his constant urge to write all sentences as simple or compound, and secondly his desire to string together unrelated ideas under the guise of their being co-ordinate clauses of one sentence. The latter tendency results in the error of the *run-together sentence.* Remember: as all parts of a sentence should be units of only one thought, *never huddle together into one sentence several unrelated thoughts.*

**35**

> Faulty: He was a good doctor, and the means of getting around was by horse and buggy.
> Clear: He was a good doctor, but he was known as such only within a very limited area. Because he lived when the sole means of transportation was the buggy, he could not go so far as the modern doctor who drives a car.

> Faulty: Coming around the bend in a rowboat was an old man, we called to him, he was rowing at a good clip, and he came in close to shore.
> Clear: Coming around the bend in a rowboat was an old man, rowing at a good clip. When we called to him, he came in close to shore.

**36**

*Parallelism.* One of the best means to co-ordinate sentence elements clearly is parallelism. That is, *any elements in the sentence which are co-ordinate in value or position should be phrased in similar form.* In the sentence "For exercise I swim, box, and a game of tennis is always welcome," the last element is actually co-ordinate with *swim* and *box,* but its being phrased without parallel structure prevents a reader from seeing that relationship. The sentence should read: "For exercise I swim, box, and play tennis."

> Faulty: He is a writer, a painter, and also plays a musical instrument well.
> Clear: He is a writer, painter, and musician.

> Faulty: He skated with ease, grace, and had plenty of speed too.
> Clear: He skated with ease, grace, and exceptional speed.

> Faulty: The governor said that he favored the labor bill, opposed the extension of the vote, and the bonus was a question on which he had not made up his mind.
> Clear: The governor said that he favored the labor bill, opposed the extension of the vote, but had not yet made up his mind on the bonus.

**37** LOGICAL CONSTRUCTIONS. *For a sentence to be clear, all its parts must show both a logical and a grammatical relationship.* Jumbled and mixed constructions are the result of carelessness, hurry in composition, and lack of proper revision. It was probably not a college freshman who wrote in an advertisement, "Do not go elsewhere to be cheated; come to our store," but sentences as ludicrous mar many freshman papers.

a. *Do not omit any part of a sentence necessary to complete an expression of any sort.*

> Faulty: I like Sally better than her cousin.
> Clear: I like Sally better than her cousin does. (or)
> I like Sally better than I like her cousin.

> Faulty: The wages of a factory worker are higher than a teacher.
> Clear: The wages of a factory worker are higher than those of a teacher.

b. *Do not make one word do more than its share of the work in a sentence.*

> Faulty: Take his track career allowed him to visit many places.
> Clear: Take his track career; it enabled him to visit many places.

> Faulty: When he was only thirteen went to sea as an apprentice.
> Clear: When he was only thirteen, he went to sea as an apprentice.

c. *Do not fail to complete one statement before beginning another.*

> Faulty: Anyone who has a chance to go to college, most people would envy him.
> Clear: Most people would envy anyone who has a chance to go to college.

> Faulty: A tattered old coat through which his bare skin could be seen hung on a peg behind the door.
> Clear: A tattered old coat, through which his bare skin showed when he wore it, hung on a peg behind the door.

PROPER TRANSITIONS. If a reader is to grasp an author's thought quickly and clearly, he must be assisted from clause to clause and from sentence to sentence by exact transitional words and conjunctions.

**38** *Always use the proper co-ordinating conjunction to link co-ordinate clauses.*

> Faulty: Bill tried out for the swimming team, *and* I took up tennis.
> Clear: Bill tried out for the swimming team, *but* I took up tennis.

> Faulty: I went to class *while* Joe decided to stay in bed.
> Clear: I went to class, *but* Joe decided to stay in bed.
> (*While* means *during the time that:* "She knitted while I read.")

**39** *Always indicate clearly the relation of a dependent clause to an independent clause by the use of the proper subordinating conjunction.*

Faulty: Jane was pleased *when* she won the scholarship cup.
Clear: Jane was pleased *that* she won the scholarship cup.

Faulty: Think *when* you act.
Clear: Think *before* you act.

Faulty: *While* grandmother is well, she could hardly stand the excitement.
Clear: *Although* grandmother is well, she could hardly stand the excitement.

**40** *Always use the proper transitional word to indicate the relationship of thought between sentences.*

Faulty: We walked slowly forward all night. In the morning, *however,* our legs were tired.
Clear: We walked slowly forward all night. In the morning, *therefore,* our legs were tired.

Faulty: As we neared the field, the sophomores showed themselves eager to fight. The freshmen, *in addition,* were unwilling to begin the battle.
Clear: As we neared the field, the sophomores showed themselves eager to fight. The freshmen, *however,* were unwilling to begin the battle.

(See *Workbook,* Exercises 33, 34, 35, 36, and 37.)

### 2. STYLE

Up to this time we have discussed various means for building a clear, accurate sentence, devoid of grammatical blunders. The average freshman should feel proud of his work if he has been able to write papers employing the principles discussed thus far. But most freshmen will not be satisfied until they have mastered certain other matters. These are points relative to a good style. The experienced writer states his idea not only correctly and clearly but gracefully as well. His writing accordingly becomes more pleasant to read and takes on added authority for his audience. From experience you know that you are more likely to listen attentively to a speaker who talks delightfully than you are to one who may have even more to say but says it boringly. It is difficult to analyze and present all the attributes of a good style, for each skilled writer finds devices which suit him best, but here are a few considerations for your attention.

EMPHASIS. Amateurish writers resort to underscoring or to other mechanical devices in order to draw attention to what they wish to emphasize, but such devices serve in the end only to irritate and drive away possible readers. The best writing gains its effects by such an arrangement of the words that the words emphasize themselves. We have already seen, for example, that the idea in an independent clause gets an emphasis for the good reader which the idea in the dependent clause lacks. Here are four other points to bear in mind for securing emphasis.

a. *Loose and periodic sentences.* The average beginner writes almost entirely in what are termed *loose* sentences, as those we habitually use in speech. In such sentences the important thought contained in the subject, predicate, and other vital elements is presented near the beginning of the sentence; less important ideas, which could be omitted without materially affecting the main thought of the sentence, are added toward the close of the sentence. Simple sentences beginning with the subject and predicate, almost all compound sentences, and all complex sentences in which the independent clause is placed first are loose in their structure.

> The sun had set, leaving a splendor of color in the sky beyond the mountains.
> He went because he had promised to go.
> We liked the idea, which we had never heard expressed before in that way.

Loose sentences are by no means to be avoided entirely, as they are often exceedingly graceful, but with the exception of those employing a striking parallelism they are ordinarily not emphatic. Emphasis comes from arranging details out of their usual order. By placing the subordinate phrases or clauses toward the beginning of the sentence and withholding the major concepts until the end, one achieves a *periodic* sentence which emphasizes these major ideas. The periodic sentence, since it is not the more natural one for a student to write, will call for greater attention and practice from him.

> As the plane neared the end of the runway, all eyes were riveted upon it.
> By inching his way toward the door, he avoided attracting attention.
> With a tremendous effort he leaped the chasm.

b. *Inversion.* The normal word order of sentence elements is subject-predicate-object. Any inversion of this order is likely to throw emphasis on the element not in its normal position. Thus the statement "The dancers swirled round and round the hall" can be made more emphatic by reversing the order, "Round and round the hall swirled the dancers." If judiciously used, inversions can be very effective.

c. *Position.* The emphatic positions in the sentence are at the beginning and ending. To preserve the force of the sentence beginning, a good writer is careful not to start his sentences frequently with such weak expressions as *there is, there are, it is, I think,* and *it seems to me.* If such expressions as the latter must be used, they should be tucked into the sentence near the beginning: "The entire discussion, *it seems to me,* is out of order."

Also, as a general rule, the transitional words, such as *however, moreover, therefore, for example,* and the like, should not begin the sentence but should be placed within the sentence near the beginning.

> His place, *therefore,* was with his troops.
> It follows, *moreover,* that one should accept his advice.
> His advice, *to be sure,* was not of the best.

The close of a sentence is also an emphatic position. By reserving his most important idea for that position, a writer frequently can get advantage of *climax* to lend added emphasis. The rule of climax requires that the least important idea of a series be placed first, the next important next, and so on to the last, which should be the most important.

> Faulty: The book was extremely boring, long, and poorly bound.
> Emphatic: The book was poorly bound, long, and extremely boring.

> Faulty: During the summer he learned how to swim so well that he saved a boy from drowning, and he learned how to cook over an open fire.
> Emphatic: During the summer he learned how to cook over an open fire, and he learned how to swim so well that he saved a boy from drowning.

d. *Repetition.* Good writers quite properly guard against the injudicious repetition of words and phrases; yet they know that a careful use of repetitions can secure needed emphasis for important ideas. Such statements as Lincoln's "of the people, by the people, for the people," and Lowell's words about Garfield, "The soil out of which such men as he are made is good to be born on, good to live on, good to die for and to be buried in," gain emphasis by repetition. Note, for instance, the increasing effectiveness of the repetitions in the following quotation from St. Paul's letter to the Corinthians:

> Though I speak with the tongues of men and of angels, and have not charity, I am become as sounding brass, or a tinkling cymbal. And though I have the gift of prophecy, and understand all mysteries, and all knowledge; and though I have all faith, so that I could remove mountains, and have not charity, I am nothing. And though I bestow all my goods to feed the poor, and though I give my body to be burned, and have not charity, it profiteth me nothing. Charity suffereth long, and is kind; charity envieth not; charity vaunteth not itself, is not puffed up, . . . thinketh no

evil; rejoiceth not in iniquity, but rejoiceth in the truth; beareth all things, believeth all things, hopeth all things, endureth all things. Charity never faileth: but whether there be prophecies, they shall fail; whether there be tongues, they shall cease; whether there be knowledge, it shall vanish away. . . . When I was a child, I spake as a child, I understood as a child, I thought as a child; but when I became a man, I put away childish things. For now we see through a glass, darkly; but then face to face: now I know in part; but then shall I know even as also I am known. And now abideth faith, hope, charity, these three; but the greatest of these is charity.

The foregoing passage illustrates two kinds of repetition: the repetition of a single word till it becomes strikingly effective, and the repetition of sentence forms—both highly effective when skillfully employed. The second of these types of repetition is best employed in the balanced sentence, as in the following examples:

> Othello and Desdemona were different in almost every way. He was black; she was white. He was old; she was young. He was acquainted only with war and what pertained to it; she was an excellent needle-woman and musician, and knew nothing of war.
>
> Ended are the long summer days of fun and play; at hand are the short autumn days of study and work.

VARIETY. To write pleasingly, good authors employ a happy variation of sentence beginnings and sentence types. Monotony results from the elementary-school type of writing, which features a series of simple sentences, each beginning with the subject and predicate: I have a ball. The ball is red. I like to play ball.

Many variations will occur to students who have studied the text carefully to this point. First are the variations arising from blending the four major types of sentence—simple, compound, complex, and compound-complex. Beginning writers should strive particularly to employ more complex sentences, as the simple and compound types come all too readily to most writers.

Secondly, a judicious mixture of loose and periodic sentences will produce variety. Once again let it be observed that the beginning writer should strive for a more frequent use of periodic sentences, as they come less naturally to mind than do the loose constructions. Through the use of periodic sentences to vary the sentence beginnings from the subject-predicate pattern, skillful writers can often produce a pleasing variety while using only simple sentences. The frequent use at the beginning of sentences of dependent verbal phrases, which are not used sufficiently by most students, will promote the same end.

Thirdly, a student of grammar knows that he has several types of constructions, all playing the same part in the sentence, from which he may select at will. Among adjective constructions he knows of the simple adjective, the adjective prepositional phrase, the participial phrase, and the adjective clause. He may, therefore, write "The spired church," "The church with a spire," "The church having a spire," or "The church which has a spire," any one of which may express his meaning. Simple adverbs, adverbial prepositional phrases, and adverbial clauses may likewise offer a choice: "He disappeared speedily into the wood," "With a new burst of speed he disappeared into the wood," or "As he exhibited a new burst of speed, he disappeared into the wood."

These three suggestions do not by any means exhaust the possible ways of securing variety. A student should analyze any passage of good prose to see additional means. He should also remember that after the first draft of his own manuscript is done, he should study the structure of his own sentences to see that he has not written them all according to one monotonous pattern.

CONCISENESS. Stating an idea without the use of unnecessary words or phrases is as much an attribute of good style as emphasis and variety are. As the principles concerning conciseness have already been discussed in the section of this book on the word (see pages 151–155), they need not be repeated here.

(See *Workbook*, Exercises 38, 39, 40, and 41.)

## E. Punctuation

To write sentences which express the exact meaning we intend to convey, we must know and practice certain accepted rules of punctuation. In oral speech, tone of voice, manner of stress, and pauses help convey our meaning; in writing, it is necessary to substitute for these aids some device familiar enough to the average reader to suggest where pauses are intended and what tone and stress are needed. The substitute on which writers must chiefly rely is punctuation.

Since the purpose of punctuation is to help make a writer's meaning clear to a reader, it is obvious that the writer must not use some private system of punctuation which he alone knows, but must use a system which is as familiar to his reader as to himself. While usage in matters of punctuation is not everywhere and at all times uniform, some fundamental rules are accepted, and in general adhered to, wherever English is written. These rules have not been arrived at arbitrarily; they have evolved from experiments of writers to make their work comprehensible to every reader. Not to know them is to frustrate one's attempt to write so that a reader will have full comprehension of what one intends. To know them is to feel a double sense of satisfaction: that in writing we shall convey to a reader more exactly what we mean, and in reading we shall understand more precisely what the author had in mind. The rules are logical and scientific, and they are therefore reasonably easy to learn and use.

**The Comma.** According to studies of errors made in writing, three fourths of all errors of punctuation are in the use of the comma. If a knowledge and use of the rules applying to the comma will reduce errors in punctuation to such an extent as these studies indicate, it is evident that close attention should be given to a mastery of the rules which follow.

41  *A comma is used to separate independent clauses which are linked by the co-ordinating conjunctions* and, but, for, or, neither, *and* nor.

> It was a lazy October day, and in the still air not a leaf was stirring.
> This is completely different from the original version, nor has it anything to do with the *Clair de lune.*
> He sat in the shade all afternoon, for the day was too hot to work.
> Let not your heart be troubled, neither let it be afraid.

42  *A comma is used to separate each item when three or more co-ordinate elements form a series without linking words between all the elements.*

> Fields, wooded hills, roads, and lakes lay below us.
> For breakfast we had orange juice, coffee, and poached egg on toast.
> He was one who was aggressive without being offensive, who was calm without being phlegmatic, and who was friendly without being obsequious.

NOTE. According to this rule, when an *and* is used between the last two elements only, it does not take the place of a comma. If a linking word is used between all the elements—*He came and saw and conquered*—it replaces the comma, unless one desires to give special emphasis to each element. But on the ground of consistency, and to avoid ambiguity in some instances, when the linking word appears between the last two elements only, the comma is used between these elements as well as between those where the linking word is omitted. In newspapers and most magazines, where space is so precious that it must be conserved even at the risk of occasional ambiguities, the comma is omitted before the linking word, as it is in many other instances where good style would require it. (Note, for instance, the ambiguity of the following sentence, taken from a newspaper account of a talk to a luncheon club. "He stressed the three objectives of Civitan: the prevention of disease, the prevention of crime and good citizenship.") But in works where the style is more important than the saving of some minuscule bit of space, the comma is put in. Note how confusing the following newspaper sentence would be to anyone not acquainted with the names of various railroads: "This ruling involved the Atchison, Topeka and Santa Fe, Chicago, Rock Island and Pacific, Baltimore and Ohio and Pennsylvania systems."

An exception, however, does occur in the names of companies, no comma being used before the word which links the last two names: Smith, Barney and Company; Bell, Taft, Jones & Company.

**43**  *A comma is used to separate consecutive adjectives which modify the same noun when the adjectives have a co-ordinate relationship.* In other words, if each adjective in the series modifies the noun in about the same degree as all the others in the series, a comma is used to separate them; but if the final adjective is so closely related to the noun that the two might virtually make a hyphenated word, no comma is used in the series. Some examples may perhaps make this clearer. All of the following sentences are punctuated correctly.

> The gaudy, showy binding detracted from the appearance of the book.
> His sharp, bright, bitter epigrams appealed to his readers.
> He wore a tattered old straw hat.
> He was a prominent public official.

NOTE. A test for deciding when to use the comma between adjectives in a series is to supply an *and* between the words. If the sentence sounds well with the *and,* use commas when the *and* is omitted; if it does not sound well with the *and,* omit the commas. Thus one might say "The gaudy and showy binding," but not "An old and straw hat."

Observe that the final adjective is not separated from the noun by a comma.

**44**  *A comma is used to separate elements which might be misread if the comma were omitted.*

> As we ate, the dog came running up the beach.
> Abruptly the car stopped, throwing her forward.
> While we were watching, the coach, a stockily built man, came over to us.
> As we approached, the gate was on our left.

No ambiguity would result if one were to write "As I approached he held out his hand," since we do not say *As I approached he;* but if the sentence were "As I approached John held out his hand," the reader would not realize until he had reached *held* that *John* is the subject of *held* rather than the object of *approached.* A moment's confusion would therefore have resulted; and to save the reader even momentary confusion, the comma is inserted.

**45**  *Commas are used to set off nonrestrictive clauses and phrases.*
(a) A nonrestrictive clause is a *dependent* clause which is not required to identify or limit the element it modifies, but merely gives

added information about it. Such a clause could be omitted without altering the meaning of the main clause. Consider the following examples.

> My blue tie, which John is wearing, was a birthday present.
> (The speaker has but one blue tie. The clause *which John is wearing* merely points out its present whereabouts.)
> Conrad Aiken, who is considered one of America's leading poets, lived for many years in England.
> (There is only one American poet named Conrad Aiken. The fact that he is considered one of America's leading poets has nothing to do with his residence in England. The dependent clause, therefore, merely adds some information about him, and it is nonrestrictive.)
> My only brother, who served in the Italian campaign, is an engineer.
> (*Only* shows that the speaker has but one brother. The dependent clause, therefore, is not needed to identify which brother, nor can it limit *brother* further. "My only brother is an engineer" is completely understandable alone; "who served in the Italian campaign" merely adds this extra information about him.)

NOTE. The matter of determining whether a clause is nonrestrictive is one of logic, not grammar. If the element modified by the dependent clause is something the reader readily identifies, as *Conrad Aiken, Niagara Falls, Boston, only brother,* the modifying clause is always nonrestrictive. But if the element which is modified is a common noun and is not limited by some such word as *only,* a reader cannot know, without other information, whether the dependent clause is nonrestrictive; and the punctuation is essential to give him this information. In the sentence "My blue tie, which John is wearing, was a birthday present," the setting off of the dependent clause by commas tells the reader that the writer has but one blue tie, for if he had more than one, the modifying clause would be necessary to point out which was the birthday present; in other words, it would restrict the tie which was a birthday present to the one John is wearing, and the commas would be omitted.

(b) Exactly the same rules that apply to nonrestrictive clauses apply to nonrestrictive phrases. Note, for instance, the following examples.

> My brother John, now living in Wheeling, is going to be married.
> (It is most improbable that the writer has more than one brother named John. Since the name sufficiently identifies which brother is going to be married, the phrase about where he lives is merely added information; it is therefore nonrestrictive and requires commas to set it off.)
> Bring along several husky boys, such as Tom or Bill.
> The Grand Canyon, in northern Arizona, is one of nature's marvels.

(c) Most appositives are nonrestrictive and should therefore be set off by commas. An appositive is a word that *stands next to another* in order to explain or characterize it and that is an equivalent of the word it explains.

The rose, the queen of flowers, is my favorite.

My father, Robert Browning Jones, was named for the poet.

Phi Beta Kappa, an honorary scholarship society, was founded at William and Mary College.

Note, however, that with proper names when through long usage the appositive has come to be considered part of the name, no commas are used—Charles the Bold, Alexander the Great, Richard the Lionhearted.

NOTE. It is highly important to bear in mind that nonrestrictive elements and parenthetic elements interrupt the main statement, and it is as important to mark the end of the interruption as the beginning. This rule is so often violated by careless writers that it is worth special emphasis: *When any nonrestrictive or parenthetic element comes elsewhere than at the beginning or*

**46** *end of a sentence, two commas—one at the beginning and one at the end of the interrupter—must be used.*

**47** *Commas are used to set off parenthetic elements,* such as (a) items of address and geographical names, (b) dates, (c) references, (d) words used in direct address, (e) introductory expressions and those used to mark transitions, (f) absolute phrases, (g) mild interjections, and (h) a title after a proper name.

(a) Commas are used to separate items in an address, and geographical names. It should be noted especially that they set off the name of a city after a street address and the name of a state after a city, a comma coming after these elements as well as before.

Stephen Foster was born in Pittsburgh, Pennsylvania, in 1826.

She lives at 222 West Congress Street, Tucson, Arizona, but she is now in San Diego, California.

St. Louis, Missouri, and Memphis, Tennessee, are towns on the Mississippi River.

(b) Commas are used to separate dates. When a year is given after a month, a comma should be used after the year as well as before.

Stephen Foster was born on July 4, 1826, in Pittsburgh.

Stephen Foster was born in July, 1826.

At 11 a.m., November 11, 1918, the first World War officially ended.

(c) Commas are used to separate the items in a reference, and a comma is placed after the last item in a reference which is followed by other elements.

In *Hamlet,* II, ii, 255, you will find the reference you ask about.

In *Paradise Lost,* III, 30–40, Milton refers to his blindness.

(d) Commas are used to set off words used in direct address.

Is it true, John, that you have been to New Orleans?

Tell me, Sue, what you and Jane talked about.

(e) .Commas are used to set off introductory expressions and those used to mark transitions. (For the use of the comma after *namely* and *e.g.,* see the last two examples under rule 65e.)

> Well, I should not believe that if I were you.
> I hold, in the second place, that the principle is unworkable.
> The restrictive clause, on the other hand, limits the main clause.
> Yes, I told him I would go.
> It is true, nevertheless, that this principle will not work.
> You must, however, follow the advice of others in this matter.

(f) Commas are used to set off absolute phrases.

> That being true, nothing remains to be said.
> We had to hurry, John wishing to start at once.

(g) A comma is generally used instead of an exclamation point to set off a mild interjection.

> Alas, I had to give up the idea.
> Ah, that is something I mustn't tell.
> I knew him, oh, ages ago.

(h) Commas are used to set off a title after a proper name.

> In the car were Stith Gordon, professor of history, and Samuel James, president, of Miller College.
> Defeated were Warren, senator from Ohio, and Billings, representative from Indiana.

NOTE. When the title comes before the name, it is not separated from the name by a comma: Professor Stith Gordon and President Samuel James, of Miller College, were in the car. Senator Warren, of Ohio, and Representative Billings, of Indiana, were defeated.

**48** *A comma is used to set off introductory participial, infinitive, and prepositional gerund phrases.*

> In order to succeed, you must work harder.
> After winning the election, Brown was jubilant.
> Driving very rapidly, he arrived just in time.

**49** *A comma is used to separate a long introductory adverbial clause from the rest of the sentence;* but if it is not an introductory clause, the rules for restrictive and nonrestrictive clauses apply as in any other dependent clause.

> As I was coming down town this morning, I met a friend I had not seen for many years.
> As soon as we received the storm warnings, we started towards the harbor.

While we were on our way to class this morning, we made our plans for the Christmas vacation.

**50** *A comma is used to separate a short direct quotation from the statement which precedes it or follows it.*

He was saying as I came up, "Nobody on the peninsula had a boat."
He called out, "Don't touch that; the power is on."
"Take that road to the left," he said, pointing across the valley.

NOTE. When the statement is long or formal, a colon is used to separate the quotation from the rest of the sentence.

If the quotation is given indirectly, no comma separates it from the rest of the sentence: He said that nobody on the peninsula had a boat.

When the comma and quotation mark come at the same point, the comma comes first and then the quotation mark: "I am going tomorrow," he said, "and I shall be gone a week."

**51** A comma is used (a) after the salutation in an informal—but not a formal—letter: *Dear Jim, Dearest,* and the like; (b) after the complimentary close of a letter: *Yours very truly, Sincerely yours, Yours ever,* and the like; and (c) after a parenthesis when it would be used if the statement in parenthesis were omitted: "He returned my book (Wolfe's *Look Homeward, Angel*), which he said he had enjoyed reading."

*Wrong Uses of the Comma.* Perhaps as important as knowing when to use a comma is knowing when not to use one. A safe course is never to use a comma unless there is a rule for its use.

**52** *Do not use a comma to separate elements of a sentence which have a close grammatical relationship,* such as (1) subject and verb, (2) verb and object, (3) adjective and noun, (4) preposition and object, (5) conjunction and the clause which follows it, (6) relative pronoun and the clause which follows it, (7) an intensive pronoun and its antecedent, (8) two co-ordinate words or phrases connected by *and* or *or,* and (9) correlatives.

NOTE. This rule, of course, refers to these elements when no interrupter intervenes. When an interrupter comes between any of these elements it is set off by *two* commas or dashes or parentheses; thus the commas *set off the interrupter* rather than separate the elements listed under this rule.

In the following examples of wrong usage, the incorrectly inserted commas are enclosed in brackets.

(Between subject and verb)   The poem about the man with the hoe[,] was written by Edwin Markham.
The vacation to which she had looked forward all year[,] proved to be a disappointment.

| (Between verb and object) | He told her[,] that he would come Thursday.<br>She said[,] that she would meet him at 3 o'clock.<br>This device will do[,] what the manufacturer promises. |
| (Between adjective and noun) | She walked down the grassy, winding[,] path.<br>White, fleecy[,]clouds were in the sky. |
| (Between preposition and object) | John has worked in turn at[,] a furniture factory, an oil station, and an automobile plant.<br>His experience with[,] boys at camp, boys scouts, and a boating club[,] helped him obtain the job. |

Note. The first and last elements in a series are not separated from preceding or succeeding elements of a sentence unless the series as a whole is nonrestrictive: Pies, cakes, and pastries[,] were excluded from the menu.

| (Between conjunction and clause) | He intended to go yesterday, but[,] he could not leave until today.<br>The speech was long and uninteresting, and[,] the audience was restless and noisy. |

Note. The comma comes *before* the conjunction which joins co-ordinate clauses, not after.

| (Between relative pronoun and clause) | They were visited last week by their uncle after whom[,] their oldest son is named.<br>They were given a Siamese kitten which[,] they did not want. |
| (Between intensive pronoun and antecedent) | He would give the message only to the manager[,] himself.<br>She was wearing a dress she[,] herself[,] had made. |
| (Between two co-ordinate words or phrases) | Every game was played in the rain[,] or in the snow.<br>The morning for work[,] and the afternoon for play[,] was his motto. |
| (Between correlatives) | He was *as* tall[,] *as* his brother.<br>He was *both* willing to aid us[,] *and* ready to do so.<br>*Neither* the manager of the firm[,] *nor* the secretary was in.<br>The applicant must be *either* a junior[,] *or* a senior. |

**53** *Do not use a comma to set off restrictive clauses and phrases.* A restrictive clause or phrase is one that is needed to identify or limit the element it modifies. If it is omitted, the main clause does not make logical sense or takes on a meaning that the writer did not intend. The dependent element, therefore, is so closely identified with the element it modifies that it is not separated by commas.

My blue tie which John is wearing was a birthday present.

(The speaker has more than one blue tie. The one which was a birthday present is distinguished from the others by its being pointed out as the one John is now wearing.)

A bird is nesting in the oak tree which is just outside my bedroom.

(There are many oak trees in the world, some of which no doubt have birds nesting in them. The speaker restricts his statement to the tree just outside his bedroom.)

The statement that democracy has failed in Europe remains to be proved.

(There are many statements which remain to be proved. The speaker is restricting his statement to the one *that democracy has failed in Europe*.)

The bird nesting over my east window is a robin.

He picked up the book lying on the desk.

**54**  *Comma splice. Do not use a comma, but a semicolon or period, between independent clauses when the co-ordinating conjunction is lacking.* This error is called the *comma splice* or, sometimes, *comma fault*. All the following examples are correct, but if the semicolon or period were replaced by a comma, the result would be a comma splice error.

I heard him out; however, I did not heed him.

He was thoroughly wet; moreover he was chilled to the bone.

We shall listen to all the arguments; then we shall decide.

The north bank was wooded; the south bank was grassy.

The cat was away. The mice were playing.

**The Semicolon.** The semicolon has a function in punctuation about midway between that of the comma and the period. At times it substitutes for the comma, at other times for the period. But when it replaces a comma or period, there must be a logical basis for the substitution; it must not be used indiscriminately, according to the mere whim of a writer. The few rules discussed below should give a student an intelligent conception of the uses of the semicolon. When one knows and can use these rules correctly, he is well along towards the mastery of some of the more complex principles of punctuation.

**55**  *Use a semicolon to separate the co-ordinate clauses of a compound sentence when they are not linked by a co-ordinating conjunction.* Two occasions arise here for the use of the semicolon: (a) when there is no linking word between the clauses and (b) when the word joining the clauses is a conjunctive adverb.

(a) Sometimes the relationship between the clauses of a compound sentence is so apparent that a linking word is not required to show the relationship. When this is true, the clauses are separated by a semicolon.

> We must not let our emotions sway us; we must consider the facts calmly and objectively.
>
> He did not join the air corps; he joined the artillery.
>
> Suddenly around right end dashed Tatum; he grabbed the ball without breaking his stride; down the field he sprinted and across the last stripe for a touchdown.

NOTE. In applying this rule it is as important to remember that the clauses must have a close and logical relationship as to remember to use the semicolon rather than the comma to separate them. If they are not component elements of one complete thought, parts of a single picture, a period should separate them:

> We must not let our emotions sway us. The rumors we have heard may not be true.
>
> He had all the symptoms of a cold. The next day he went swimming.

(b) A semicolon is used to separate co-ordinate clauses when a conjunctive adverb, unaccompanied by a co-ordinating conjunction, joins the clauses. The most common conjunctive adverbs are *therefore, nevertheless, however, moreover, consequently, so, also, thus, hence, then, still, accordingly, besides, furthermore, likewise,* and *otherwise.* When you use one of these words between independent clauses, put a semicolon before it.

> We used a new method of cultivation; therefore the yield was greater.
>
> I warned him that the bridge was out and the road otherwise dangerous; nevertheless he went ahead.
>
> The team had to make the long trip by bus without a pause for practice on the way; moreover several players could not play because of injuries.

NOTE. Modern practice is to omit the comma after the conjunctive adverb except when it is necessary to avoid misreading. In such a sentence as "I plan to go this week; however, the transportation must be considered," a reader might suppose *however* to be a simple adverb and expect it to modify some word in the second clause till he had read to the end of the clause. To save him from this error, the comma is used after *however.* There would be no danger of such misreading in the three examples given above; therefore the comma is omitted after the conjunctive adverb.

**56** *The second main use of the semicolon is to separate elements which ordinarily would be separated by a comma, but which because of complicated internal punctuation are separated by the semicolon for the sake of clarity.*

(a) In a compound-complex sentence when some of the dependent clauses are nonrestrictive, a semicolon marks the main divisions, even when the linking words are simple conjunctions. Since the nonrestrictive modifiers are separated by commas, the semicolon is needed to mark the main divisions.

> On our trip we went to the Grand Canyon by Route 66, which skirts the Ozarks, bisects the oil fields of Oklahoma, and cuts through northwestern Texas; and from the Grand Canyon we turned south, going to Phoenix and Tucson, Arizona, and on to Nogales, Mexico; but there we turned back towards home, taking the Bankhead Highway as far as the Mississippi.

(b) In complex sentences containing several dependent clauses which have internal punctuation, the semicolon is generally used to mark the main divisions.

> I hold that democracy, in spite of its inefficiencies, the slowness with which it achieves results, and the danger of demagoguery inherent in it, is the best form of government; that the modicum of freedom we possess, though it has been bought with suffering and misery and torture and death, is worth what it cost; and that this form of government is worth living for, fighting for, and if need be dying for.

NOTE. The semicolon must not be used to separate the dependent clause nearest the main clause from the latter: for example, *I hold; that democracy* etc. It separates only elements which are co-ordinate, not those which are of different value, as main and dependent clauses.

(c) In simple sentences containing a complicated series, or elements having internal punctuation, the semicolon is generally used to separate the main divisions.

> We must get butter, bread, coffee, and eggs at the grocery store; bacon, sausage, and lamb chops at the meat market; soap and toothpaste at the drug store; and some waxed paper at the dime store.

*Wrong Uses of the Semicolon.* As was said of the comma, it is as important not to use semicolons in the wrong place as it is to use them

57   in the right place. *Do not use the semicolon (1) to set off dependent sentence elements, such as nonrestrictive clauses, verbal or prepositional phrases, or other elements which are not co-ordinate, (2) to follow the salutation in a letter, (3) to precede a direct quotation.* After the salutation in a letter, use the comma if the letter is informal, the colon if it is formal; before a direct quotation, use a comma if the quoted passage is short or if the style is informal, a colon if the passage is long. If there is a rule for using the semicolon, use it; if there is none, do not use it.

NOTE. One bit of information about the use of the semicolon *after* a quoted passage may be given here, though it will be considered again under quotations: When a quotation is interrupted to add a directive expression, such as "he said," a comma always precedes the directive expression; and after the directive expression, the semicolon is used if it would be used normally in the quotation at the place where the interruption comes.

"He couldn't decide whether to play golf or go fishing," Jane said; "finally, however, he agreed to go with Jean to the golf course."

**The Colon.** The colon is a mark of introduction or anticipation, and in general it denotes formality. In very long and complicated sentences wherein the elements separated by semicolons are not the chief divisions, it is sometimes used to mark the main divisions; but students in the apprentice stage of writing should probably avoid writing sentences of this sort. For ordinary composition, it will suffice to know the following rules.

**58** *The colon is used to introduce a long or formal direct quotation.*

An entry in his diary is his best epitaph: "Well, I have had a happy life. I do not know that anybody whom I have seen close has had a happier."

In his essay "The Function of Criticism," Matthew Arnold says: "It is of the last importance that English criticism should clearly discern what rule for its course . . . it ought to take. The rule may be summed up in one word—*disinterestedness.* And how is criticism to show disinterestedness? By keeping aloof from what is called 'the practical view of things'; by resolutely following the law of its own nature, which is to be a free play of the mind on all the subjects which it touches."

**59** *The colon is used to introduce a number of examples or a list of any sort.*

He has played a number of minor Shakespearean roles: Bardolph, the disreputable associate of Prince Hal; Shallow, the country justice; Dogberry, the ignorant law officer; and Sir Andrew Aguecheek, the drunken companion of Sir Toby Belch.

The team met eight opponents in seven weeks: Northern, Central, Southeastern, Western, Tech, St. Joseph's, Northeastern, and Bascombe.

**60** *The colon is used between independent clauses when the second amplifies the first, or when the second gives a concrete illustration of a general statement in the first.*

In time, however, one of his favorite contentions was justified: that in the long run, the majority of those who apply themselves to a matter will arrive at the right opinion, no matter how vociferous and professedly expert the opposition.

Bridges in one of his sonnets says that the very names of things beloved are dear to us: the name of the one to whom he addressed the poem seemed to him the loveliest of all names.

**61** *The colon by common acceptance is used in the following specific instances:*

(a) after the salutation in a formal or business letter—

Dear Sir:
Dear Mr. Jones:
Dear Professor Garrison:
Dear Madam:

(b) between the hour and minute when time is expressed in figures—12:15 o'clock; 2:30 p.m.

(c) between chapter and verse in reference to the Bible—*Genesis* 9:10.

(d) between the place of publication and the name of the publisher in bibliographical references—New York: F. S. Crofts & Co.

NOTE. Do not capitalize the first word after a colon unless it is the beginning of a quotation or the beginning of an independent sentence.

Do not use the colon to introduce an indirect statement, nor to introduce an informal list: Bring with you slacks, a warm sweater, and walking shoes.

**The Period.** Every college student knows, of course, that a period is used at the end of a declarative or imperative sentence, and at the end of certain legitimate fragmentary sentences (see page 240). What every college student does not *do,* however, is to use this knowledge always in his writing. As was discussed in the chapter on the fragmentary sentence, the period is often employed illegitimately to cut off phrases and dependent clauses. Such use is called the *period fault;* and it is considered a major error in writing, because it indicates that those who commit it lack a knowledge of the most rudimentary principle of composition —what a sentence is.

**62** *The period has but two uses: to mark the end of a declarative or imperative sentence and to mark an abbreviation.* Concerning the first use enough has been said, except to add the caution to be certain that it is a *sentence* (or a *legitimate* fragmentary sentence) at the end of which you place a period. Concerning the second usage, little more need be said. Some of the abbreviations most frequently used are *viz., e.g., Mr., Mrs., Dr., Ph.D., LL.D., A.B., M.A.,* A.M., P.M., B.C., *p.* or *pp., etc.* The following matters relating to abbreviations should be kept in mind:

When a period is used after an abbreviation, it is followed, except at the end of a sentence, by whatever mark of punctuation would normally be used there.

Washington, D.C., is the capital.
Breakfast is served at 8 a.m.; lunch is served at 12:30 p.m.; dinner is served at 6:30 p.m.

When the abbreviation comes at the end of a sentence, one period serves two purposes—to mark the abbreviation and to end the sentence.

Formerly a period was used after Roman numerals, but this is no longer done. One now writes "Henry VII was the first Tudor king."

Do not use a period after your own title of an essay, poem, or story.

Do not use a period after contractions in which the omission occurs within the word and is marked by an apostrophe, as in *hasn't, doesn't, weren't*.

**63**    **The Question Mark.** *The question mark is used after every direct question*: "Who goes there?" "What are you doing?" "When can you come to see me?" It is not used, however, after an indirect question: "He asked what you are doing." "I am writing to ask when you can come to see me."

In a series, a question mark may follow each question if special emphasis is desired. When used thus, it takes the place of the comma; and each element begins with a small letter: "Where is my text? my pen? my notebook?" If it is not desired to emphasize each question in the series, use a comma except at the end of the sentence.

The question mark, in parenthesis, is used to indicate doubt concerning the authenticity of some fact: "Nathaniel Bacon, the Virginia patriot, was born in 1642(?)." "Among Shakespeare's friends were Marlowe(?), Jonson, Drayton, and John Fletcher." It should not be used, however, to call attention to the fact that one is making a joke or is being ironical: "Ben, you know, is the most studious(?) member of the family." Such usage shows bad taste, since it seems to imply that the reader is not intelligent enough to see that one is joking or is being ironical. If the reader is not well enough acquainted with the matter under discussion to catch the writer's intention, the sentence should be changed; if he is acquainted with it, the question mark is unnecessary.

**64**    **The Exclamation Point.** *The exclamation point is used at the end of an exclamatory sentence, and after words which express strong emotion or feeling.*

> What a world for men of good will to live in!
> Look out! You'll fall!
> What! I don't believe it.

What was said of the question mark as a means of labeling irony or humor applies also to the exclamation point. Such usage is considered bad taste and is to be avoided. In fact, the excessive use of the exclamation point anywhere is considered poor taste. The constant resort to exclamation points indicates lack of ability to gain effects by normal means, and shows the writer to be shallow and flighty, and his statements probably untrustworthy.

**65a** **The Dash.** *The dash is used when a sentence is abruptly broken off and something entirely different added.*

The game will be—by the way, are you going to the game?
It says in this story—but I can't tell you all that now.

**65b** *The dash is used in writing conversation to show that a speech was not finished.* When this is done, no period follows the dash, though a question mark or exclamation point is used if it would be required in the completed sentence.

"The result will be——"
"I don't care what the result will be."
"But let me tell you what——"
"No, my mind is made up."
"Isn't that a stubborn——?"
"Not stubborn—firm."

**65c** *The dash is used to show hesitation or confusion on the part of a speaker.* This use is generally restricted to reporting conversation.

Where is the—er—the—tidying up you promised to do?
"I say I—would you—I'm sorry, but I left my money in my other coat pocket—will you buy the tickets?" he stammered.

**65d** *The dash is used to indicate the omission of words or letters.*

Little acorns—great oaks, you know.
Have you read Poe's poem entitled "To F——s S. O——d"?

**65e** *The dash is used before a statement which summarizes a preceding series, which is an emphatic repetition of the preceding statement, or which is introduced by* namely, e.g., *and the like.*

The professional patriot, the constant flag-waver, the agitator who would pass laws to compel men to go through forms of appearing patriotic— all these are abhorred by those whose sense of patriotism lies too deep for words and trivial outward forms.

All his books are written in a learned language—in a language which nobody hears from his mother or his nurse.—Thomas Macaulay

Every rule in composition suggests three acts on your part—namely, learn it, use it, check your writing to see if you have observed its use correctly.

Some pairs of words are bothersome to students—e.g., affect and effect, loose and lose, sit and set.

**65f**    *The dash is used to designate an ironical contrast.*

My opponent loudly affirms that he is for labor—and hobnobs with lobby-ists for large corporations; he says he is against alcohol—and keeps a bar in his house; he claims he is a friend of education—and votes to cut school appropriations.

**65g**    *The most common use of the dash is to set off (a) appositives which have internal punctuation or which are emphatic and (b) other modifying expressions which have internal punctuation or which have a very loose connection with the sentence in which they stand.* In this usage there are always two dashes—one at the beginning of the modifying expression and one at the end—unless the second dash coincides with a period or semicolon, when it is absorbed by the period or semicolon. The following examples, from Macaulay's essays, show these uses.

Compared with the labor of reading through these volumes, all other labor—the labor of thieves on the treadmill, of children in factories, of negroes in sugar plantations—is an agreeable occupation.

They have in consequence been thrown in the shade by writers who . . . understood far better the art of producing effect—by Livy and Quintus Curtius.

In an evil day, though with great pomp and solemnity—we quote the language of Bacon—was the ill-starred alliance stricken between the old philosophy and the new faith.

In the temper of Bacon—we speak of Bacon the philosopher, not of Bacon the lawyer and politician—there was a singular union of audacity and sobriety.

NOTE. In modern practice, commas are rarely used in connection with dashes, although some stylebooks suggest the use of commas as well as dashes when a comma would normally be used if the dash were omitted. It is correct, however, to use dashes only, and since this is the simpler and the more common modern practice, it is recommended.

In printing, three dashes of varying length are used: the *en* dash between inclusive figures (1776–1789) and between elements which normally require a hyphen but which contain two or more words in one or both of the elements (the New Haven–New York run); the *em dash,* which is the normal dash used in most instances; and the *2-em dash* when a sentence is not finished. In manuscript which is typewritten, the best practice is to use a hyphen to designate the en dash, two hyphens to designate the normal dash, and four hyphens to designate the 2-em dash—without space before or after the hyphens; in handwriting, the different kinds of dash cannot be so clearly distinguished, but except for the en dash, the length should be at least a quarter of an inch to distinguish it from the hyphen.

The dash is a valuable mark of punctuation when it is used correctly. Needless to say, the indiscriminate use of the dash in the place of commas and periods, frequently affected by the more flighty high-school students, is to be avoided.

**Parentheses.** Parentheses—sometimes called *curves*—have four uses.

**66a** *Parentheses are used to enclose matter only indirectly related to the main thought of the sentence*—matter which is irrelevant or purely explanatory, and which is more formal and less essential to the meaning than that for which dashes are used. This rule applies particularly to examples, illustrations, definitions, and references when these are short (if they are long, it is better to give the information in a footnote).

> The conjunctive adverb (see page 266) is used to link independent clauses.
> At 3:30 a.m. (the time agreed upon at the conference the evening before) the attack on the fort began.
> No one play could deal with a war in its entirety (even in Hardy's *Dynasts,* perhaps the most ambitious play ever written, the conflict is centralized in the characters of Napoleon, Wellington, and Nelson); therefore the playwright presents some phase of the greater conflict in the lesser conflicts that form his plot.—Milton Marx, *The Enjoyment of Drama.*
> Yet for all their seeming lack of structure, the plays of Chekhov contain (or perhaps a better word would be conceal) the highest artistry.—*Ibid.*

**66b** *Parentheses are used in personal letters and informal writing to enclose an aside which the reader is likely to know but may for the moment not recall.*

> My Uncle John Simpson (my mother's brother) came to see us last week.

**66c** *Parentheses are used to enclose figures or letters which mark items in an enumeration.* (For an example see rule 47 under "The Comma.")

**66d** *Parentheses are used to enclose signs, figures, and words when accuracy is essential.* Except in legal documents or when accuracy is extremely vital, it is no longer considered necessary to use this rule, however.

> The check should be made out for the exact amount ($19.98).
> I am sending you fifty dollars ($50) to pay the rent for one month.

NOTE. *Before* a parenthesis within a sentence no punctuation mark is used. *After* a parenthesis within a sentence no mark is used unless it would be required if the parenthesis were removed; then whatever mark would be required normally, follows the parenthesis. *Within* a parenthesis inside a sentence, the punctuation is the same as if the matter were a separate sentence, except that when it is a complete sentence no capital is used at the beginning and no period at the end—though a question mark or an exclamation point is used if one is required. Parentheses may, of course, enclose a separate sentence, in which case the ordinary rules for using the capital and period apply.

Parentheses should never be used to emphasize a word (italics are used for that), to indicate a title (italics or quotation marks, according to the sort of title, are used for that), or to cancel a passage (see note, page 17). Avoid using parentheses for other than the legitimate purposes discussed in this section; if there is any question about their correctness, it is better to rewrite the sentence so as to avoid using them than to use them incorrectly.

**67a** **Brackets.** *The chief use of brackets is to enclose something—a correction, an addition, an explanation, or some comment—which a writer interpolates in matter he is quoting.*

> "In the collection are letters by E[dward]. L[ear]., Thomas Woolner, and [Edward] Fitzgerald."
>
> "It [the acknowledgment of Henry VIII as head of the church] was the first step in a policy by which the Church was to be laid prostrate at the foot of the throne."—J. R. Green.
>
> "In 1630 [a typographical error for 1603] James came to the throne."
>
> "The song [Jesus, Lover of My Soul] has become a treasury of spiritual wealth."—J. B. Reeves.
>
> In applying for the job, he wrote, "I am very good in atheletics [*sic*], and I can teach mathmatics [*sic*]."

NOTE. The term *sic,* Latin for *thus,* is inserted to show that a misspelling or some other error, as of a date, appeared in the original and is not an error by the one quoting.

**67b** *Brackets are used when it is necessary to place a parenthesis within a parenthesis;* but in general, such complicated usages should be avoided.

> At 3:30 a.m. (the time agreed upon at the conference the evening before [see the correspondence by Captain Williams, Letter X]) the attack on the fort began.

**67c** *Brackets are generally used to enclose stage directions in plays, although usage varies here.*

> MRS. ANNERLY [*sipping her coffee*]. I don't wonder.

In the use of other punctuation marks with brackets, the same rules apply as with parentheses.

**68** **Quotation Marks.** *The main function of quotation marks is to enclose matter quoted from any source. A subsidiary function is to enclose words used in a special manner and to enclose certain titles. In the*

United States, and for the most part in Great Britain, double quotation marks are commonly used except for a quotation within a quotation; hence in this section *quotation marks* will refer to double marks unless single marks are mentioned specifically.

**68a** *Quotation marks should enclose every direct quotation which a writer uses,* whether a word or several pages, except that in lengthy quotations they may be omitted if some other means is employed to call attention to the passage as a quotation. A summary of the ideas of another is not so enclosed. There is no such thing as a halfway quotation: if the direct words of another are used, they should appear exactly as in the original and should be enclosed by quotation marks; if the source is not quoted exactly, do not use quotation marks, but state that the ideas in general are those of whatever source you are using. Indirect discourse is never enclosed in quotation marks.

**68b** *Use quotation marks to enclose the title of (a) a chapter in a book, (b) an individual poem or essay or story in a volume, and (c) any item from a book or magazine;* for the title of the book itself or magazine, use italics. Usage in this respect varies, nearly all newspapers and most magazines, for instance, making no distinction between titles of whole volumes and single items in them. The reason for this is that it would take time to change from ordinary type to italics or that many lino-type machines are not equipped to print italics; and since it is more essential with most newspapers and popular magazines to save expense than to maintain a perfect style, fine distinctions in style are normally not striven for in them. Those who are careful to observe the best rules of style, however, make the distinction noted in this rule. Fortunately for students, it takes no more time or effort in longhand or typescript to be exact in applying this rule than to lump all titles in one class; and since this rule is observed in all masters' and doctoral theses, in all formal papers, in all books that have pretensions to good style, and in the best magazines, it is highly recommended that students use the rule as stated.

> Read the poems "Emerson" and "Lands End" in the volume *More People* by Edgar Lee Masters.
> For information about the development of frequency modulation in radio, see "Revolution in Radio" in *Fortune,* October, 1939.

NOTE. Do not enclose a title of your own manuscript in quotation marks, unless it is a quotation. Even when your title is a quotation, it need not be quoted. Such titles as *Look Homeward, Angel* and *Gone with the Wind,* for instance, are taken from the works of other authors and are used without quotation marks.

**68c** *Use quotation marks to enclose words used in a special manner, or words coined for some special, limited use.*

> They were in close association with "bounty-jumpers," men who deserted as soon as the bounty was received and enlisted elsewhere under other names.—J. S. Bassett, *A Short History of the United States.*
>
> If thousands were squandered on the subsidization of newspapers, were they not "loyal" newspapers? If unheard-of prices were paid in the furnishing of the State House, were not the purchases made of "Union men"?—C. G. Bowers, *The Tragic Era.*

NOTE. Authorities differ widely on the question of using quotation marks to enclose slang expressions, colloquialisms, newly coined technical terms, and the like. Good taste would indicate that the introduction of slang and colloquialisms in formal, dignified style is out of place. On the other hand to report a conversation between college students, carpenters, or oil-field workers in formal, grammatically correct sentences would, to say the least, give an air of unreality to the conversation. The best rule to adopt in this matter is to avoid using slang or colloquial expressions in formal writing, but, if it becomes essential to use such a term, to designate it by the use of quotation marks; and when reporting conversation or writing informally to use such expressions when it is natural to do so, and to omit the quotation marks. As to newly coined technical terms, if it is reasonably certain that readers in general will be unfamiliar with the terms, use quotation marks to suggest that their status in the language is tentative.

Rules for punctuating sentences containing direct quotations are in general standardized. Any concerning which usage varies are omitted in the discussion which follows.

**69a** (a) Directive expressions or words introducing or explaining something which is quoted may come at the beginning or the end of the quotation, or they may interrupt it.

When the introductory expression precedes the quotation, use a comma if the quotation is short, and a colon if the quotation is long or if it is introduced in a formal manner.

> He called out, "What are you doing with my driver?"
> He said hesitantly, "I don't see how I can do that."
> Stephen Leacock, in his essay "American Humour," says: "It is perhaps not difficult to understand why so few writers have attempted a painstaking and scientific analysis of what is humorous. There appears to be a sort of intellectual indignity involved in the serious study of the comic."

When the explanatory expression interrupts the quotation, a comma precedes it; and a comma follows it if no punctuation mark or a comma would be employed were the interrupter omitted, and a semicolon or period if one were normally required in the absence of an interrupter.

"It is not," she interrupted, "my habit to change my mind so quickly."

"That is my idea," she declared; "therefore I won't have you stealing it."

"It is a fine day," John called. "Are you going to the game?"

When the explanatory expression comes after the quotation, a comma precedes it unless the quotation itself ends with a question mark or an exclamation point, in which instance the comma is omitted.

"Well, that settles the matter," she said.

"What are you going to do about it?" she inquired.

"What a beautiful car!" she exclaimed.

**69b** (b) A comma and a period always precede the closing quotation marks. A semicolon and a colon always come after the closing quotation marks. A question mark and an exclamation point come before the quotation marks if the quotation itself is a question or an exclamation, and after the quotation marks if the quotation itself is not interrogative or exclamatory but forms a part of an interrogative or exclamatory sentence.

He called out, "I shall not take a minute."

"That isn't the point," he said.

Yesterday we studied Milton's "Lycidas"; today we shall read Shelley's "Adonais."

In this essay, F. A. Woods defines "oily words": they are words which "are difficult to handle," which "slip through the fingers like the long thin fish of three letters of a cross-word puzzle."

"What a wonderful day!" she exclaimed.

"Are you coming?" he asked.

Have you ever heard her say, "I don't play bridge"?

Do you know the song "Did You Ever See a Dream Walking"?

How charming of her to say, "You may wear my hat"!

Note. When a question mark or exclamation point ends a quotation, no other punctuation mark is used. (Note the last four sentences above.)

When a question is asked about a quoted question, the question mark which would normally follow the quoted expression is omitted, and the final question mark does duty for both questions.

**69c** The following general rules always apply in the use of quotation marks.

(a) Do not use the comma to set off quotations built into a sentence.

He said that his car would "do eighty miles an hour" and he was "going to let it out."

This folder refers to Chicago as "The American Venice, where beautiful streets wind along twenty-five miles of lake front."

(b) In a single quotation of several sentences without an interpolation, use quotation marks at the beginning and end only, not for each sentence:

> He said, "I don't believe that man's statement. I have evidence of my own to disprove it. I think he was just guessing."

When the remarks of several different speakers are reported in one sentence, however, each person's remarks are enclosed by quotation marks.

> John was the first to get back from the game, and everyone shouted questions at once: "Who won?" "What was the score?" "What did Jim do?" "Was there much passing?"

(c) When quoting several paragraphs, use quotation marks at the beginning of each new paragraph, but at the end of only the final paragraph. The purpose of this rule is to indicate to a reader at the beginning of each paragraph that the quotation continues, and at the end of each paragraph that it is not yet ended.

If the quotation is very long, however, consisting of a long paragraph or several paragraphs, it is better to omit the quotation marks and to indicate the quotation by indenting about two inches on each margin when writing in longhand; and to indent and single space the lines in typescript.

(d) When quoting a fragment, do not begin the quotation with a capital letter unless the quoted passage began with a capital.

> He said "the machinations of a corrupt political machine" would have to stop.

(e) Do not use quotation marks for proverbs and phrases which are the common knowledge of everyone.

> He said the devil would find no mischief for his hands to do.
> He was honest not because he believed that honesty is the best policy, but because honesty was inherent in his make-up.

(f) Do not use quotation marks to label your own humor or irony. What was said of using the question mark or the exclamation point for this purpose applies as well to the use of quotation marks.

(g) Do not use quotation marks for statements which are not quoted from someone else, but are quotations in form only.

> He said to himself: I believe I am going to win this race.
> She thought, Shall I wear my new hat to the game?

(h) The usage concerning quotations within quotations is to place a quotation within a quotation in single quotation marks; then if a quotation is given within this quotation, to use double quotation marks again; and so alternate the double and single quotation marks with all matter quoted.

> In his letter, John wrote: "I have been following the example of my instructor, who said, 'When I decide to write something, I first sit down and read Wordsworth's "Ode to Duty" to give myself impetus to finish'; but I find it doesn't work for me."

(i) In writing dialogue, put each speech in a separate paragraph and enclose it in quotation marks.

> "I doubt our being able to do so much," said Morland.
>
> "You croaking fellow!" cried Thorpe, "we shall be able to do ten times more. Kingsweston! aye, and Blaize Castle too, and anything else we can hear of; but here is your sister says she will not go."
>
> "Blaize Castle!" cried Catherine; "what is that?"
>
> "The finest place in England; worth going fifty miles at any time to see."
>
> "What, is it really a castle, an old castle?"
>
> "The oldest in the kingdom."
>
> "But is it like what one reads of?"
>
> "Exactly: the very same."
>
> "But now, really, are there towers and long galleries?"
>
> "By dozens."
>
> "Then I should like to see it; but I cannot, I cannot go."
>
> "Not go! my beloved creature, what do you mean?"
>
> "I cannot go, because" (looking down as she spoke, fearful of Isabella's smile) "I expect Miss Tilney and her brother to call on me to take a country walk. They promised to come at twelve, only it rained; but now, as it is so fine, I dare say they will be here soon."
>
> "Not they, indeed," cried Thorpe; "for, as we turned into Broad Street, I saw them. Does he not drive a phaeton with bright chestnuts?"
>
> "I do not know, indeed."
>
> "Yes, I know he does; I saw him. You are talking of the man you danced with last night, are you not?"
>
> "Yes."
>
> "Well, I saw him at that moment turn up Lansdown Road, driving a smart-looking girl."—Jane Austen, *Northanger Abbey*.

NOTE. In using quotation marks, always be careful to put them at the end of a quotation as well as at the beginning. Omitting the final quotation mark is a common error in the manuscripts of students. It is the result solely of carelessness, and is inexcusable. There is no such thing as one quotation mark: use a pair—one at the beginning and one at the end of a quotation—or none.

**70** **The Apostrophe.** *The apostrophe has three uses:* (1) *to form the possessive of nouns and indefinite pronouns,* (2) *to denote the omission of letters or figures,* and (3) *to form the plural of figures, letters, signs, and words to which special allusion is made.*

**70a** *Always use an apostrophe to designate the possessive case of nouns and indefinite pronouns.* Next to the incorrect use of the comma, the greatest number of errors in punctuation results from the omission of the apostrophe. The reason for most of these errors is carelessness. Watch possessives, and form the habit of inserting an apostrophe to denote a possessive, as in earlier years you formed the habit of dotting your *i's* and crossing your *t's*. And be certain that the apostrophe is placed properly. The rules about the position of the apostrophe are very definite.

(a) To form the possessive of a noun or indefinite pronoun, singular or plural, which does not end in a sibilant sound (*s, x, z*), add an apostrophe and an *s: dog's leash, horse's bridle, man's hat, men's hats, children's hats, William's hat, Marivaux's plays* (*x* silent), *one's hat.*

(b) To form the possessive of a plural noun or indefinite pronoun ending in *s, x,* or *z,* add only an apostrophe: *dogs' leashes, horses' bridles, girls' hats, the Smiths' dinner party, the Thomases' house, The Beaux' Stratagem, others' ills.*

(c) To form the possessive of a singular noun ending in a sibilant sound (*s, x, z*), add an apostrophe and an *s* except in one case: if the noun has two or more syllables, if the last syllable is not accented and is preceded by a sibilant sound, add only the apostrophe: *Burns's poems, Jones's store, the fox's tail, Liz's idea, Moses' law, Ulysses' voyage, Jesus' sake, conscience' sake* (the *ce* is a sibilant sound).

NOTE. The reason for the exception here is to prevent the disagreeable sound of too many sibilants in succession. The *s* when added to form the possessive is pronounced as a syllable. Such combinations of sound as *for Jesus-es sake, Moses-es law, for goodness-es sake* are not pleasant to the ear, hence the omission of the *s* to form the possessive of these words.

When forming the possessive of a word ending in *s,* be especially careful to place the apostrophe *after* the *s* which is a part of the word. Never write *Keat's* for John Keats, the poet, for instance. The *s* here is a part of his name, and it is as incorrect to write *Keat's* as *Ji'ms* for *Jim's.*

(d) To denote joint possession, add the apostrophe or apostrophe and *s* after the second noun only: *Harrold and Templeman's Victorian prose collection, the Watfords and Tuckers' annual picnic.*

(e) To form the possessive of compound nouns and indefinite pronouns add the apostrophe or apostrophe and *s* after the last element of the compound: *her daughter-in-law's opinion, the menservants' opinions, everyone else's opinion.*

(f) Do not use an apostrophe to form the possessive of a personal pronoun—*his, hers, its, theirs, yours*—or the relative pronoun *whose.* These pronouns, since they retain the inflectional ending of an old genitive case, have the idea of possession inherent in them; hence no sign is necessary to denote the possessive.

NOTE. Two of these pronouns require special attention. *It's* is a contraction for *it is,* and is correct in such a sentence as "He thinks it's too far to go." *Who's* is incorrect as the possessive of *who,* but is a contraction of *who is.* Each of the following is correct: Who's going with me? It's his who's there first. Whose shoes are these?

**70b** *The apostrophe is used to denote the omission of letters or figures.*

He *hasn't* been here today.
They *weren't* anxious to go.
The class of '25 had its reunion this year.
Meet me at two *o'clock.*
"Good *mo'nin',*" he drawled; *"I'm goin'* back to my *ol'* home."

NOTE. When using the apostrophe to denote the omission of a letter, be careful to put it where the letter is omitted. Careless students frequently put the apostrophe before the *n* in such contractions as *haven't, shouldn't,* etc. This is as bad as leaving it out entirely, perhaps worse, for such misusage indicates that they know an apostrophe is necessary, but they aren't interested enough to place it where it should go.

**70c** *The apostrophe is used to designate plurals of figures, letters, signs, and words to which special allusion is made.*

If there are no *6's* left in this type, use *9's* turned upside down.
Your *T's* and *F's* are too much alike, and your *v's* and *u's.*
Use *+'s* and *—'s* to denote whether the sentences are correct or not.
When *and's* and *the's* are used in titles, they should not be capitalized.

**71** **The Hyphen.** *A hyphen is used* (1) *to mark the division of a word which comes at the end of a line, and* (2) *to designate certain compound words or phrases.*

**71a** When it is necessary to divide a word between two lines, always place a hyphen at the end of the first line, never at the beginning of the second. Divide the word only between syllables (if you are not certain where to divide, consult a dictionary).

(a) Never divide words of one syllable. This applies to words ending in *ed* but pronounced as one syllable—*e.g., called, spelled, bowled*—as well as to words like *brought, which,* and *world.*

(b) In general avoid dividing words of more than one syllable, but if a considerable space remains to be filled at the end of a line, divide according to the following rules. Note the pronunciation, and do not divide words so that the different parts sound unnatural, as would be true in such divisions as *comp-arisons, und-erscoring, syllab-le, foll-owing.* When a consonant is doubled and stands between two vowels, divide between the consonants—*expres-sion, stab-bing, run-ning.* Divide between two vowels when each is sounded—*zo-ology, co-operate, sci-ence.* Divide between the body of a word and a prefix or a suffix—*dis-appear, con-struct, lead-ing, habit-able.* When a consonant stands between two vowels, usually the division is made between the first vowel and the consonant—*ame-nable, la-borer.* When two or more consonants stand between vowels, the division is usually made between the consonants—*sym-bolic, conten-tious;* but there are frequent exceptions to this rule, and it is well to con-sult a dictionary when you have to divide such a word. Do not divide a digraph or trigraph (two or three letters representing a single sound, as *eau* in *beautiful,* or *ph* in *diphthong*).

**71b** In forming compound words, it is usually better to consult a dictionary until one is familiar with a certain usage, for there is wide variance in the use of hyphens in compounds. *Bedroom,* for in-stance, is written as one word, *dining room* as two words, and *drawing-room* as one word with a hyphen; *trade-mark* is hyphenated, *trade name* is written as two words. A few general rules, however, apply to the use of the hyphen in forming compounds.

(a) Use a hyphen between a prefix ending with a vowel and a root word beginning with the same vowel (sometimes two dots—called a diaeresis—are placed over the second vowel to indicate that it is to be sounded separately) to avoid mispronouncing the word: *co-operate, pre-eminent, re-elect, re-enforce.*

(b) Use a hyphen when a compound word would be confused with one spelled similarly but having a different meaning—*re-create, recreate; re-form, reform.*

(c) Use a hyphen between a prefix and a proper name—*post-Aristo-telian, pro-Nazi, anti-Fascist, pre-Hoover.*

(d) Use a hyphen in compounds formed of a noun or verb and a preposition—*set-to, head-on, house-to-house, passer-by.*

(e) Use a hyphen in compound numerals between twenty-one and ninety-nine, whether these are used singly or with larger figures—*thirty-three, one thousand and sixty-seven.*

**71c** When two or more words precede a noun and have the force of a single adjective, it is the preferred usage to insert a hyphen be-tween them—*a long-established custom, an up-to-date method, a well-known author.* This usage, however, does not apply when one of the words is an adverb which ends in *ly—a highly paid executive;* nor when the words come after the noun.

Use a hyphen in writing out a fraction which is used as a single adjective before a noun, but not with a fraction which consists of an adjective plus a noun—*a five-eighths-inch bolt, a one-fourth share, two thirds of a mile, three fourths of a pie.*

**72** **The Ellipsis Mark.** *The ellipsis mark consists of three periods with a space between each, and it is used to denote an omission from a passage which is being quoted.* If the omitted passage comes at the end of a sentence a period is added, making four periods.

> In his essay "Hebraism and Hellenism" Matthew Arnold says: "The final aim of both Hellenism and Hebraism . . . is no doubt the same: man's perfection. . . . The very language which they both . . . use . . . is often identical. Even when their language indicates by variation . . . the different courses of thought which are uppermost in each discipline . . . the unity of the final end and aim is still apparent. To employ the actual words of that discipline with which we ourselves are . . . most familiar . . . that final end and aim is 'that we might be partakers of the divine nature.' "

Among contemporary writers of fiction particularly, the ellipsis mark is sometimes used to denote a brief passage of time, or in the stream-of-consciousness type of writing to denote the gliding of the mind from one fragment of thought to another.

**73** **The Caret.** *The caret is an inverted v-shaped mark ($\wedge$) which is put at the bottom of a line between two words where something has been omitted.* The omitted word or passage is then written above the line where the omission occurred. If the caret comes near the end of a line and the omitted passage is somewhat long, it is better to begin the omitted passage near the beginning of the left margin than to carry it over to the following line.

>          where
> We were standing $\wedge$ we could see the magician well.
>         and the ease with which they were caught by Williams
> We were so busy watching the beautiful passes of Johnson $\wedge$ that we had not observed the great work which Howard and Owens were doing in the line.

In the final revision of a manuscript, it is legitimate to add an omission in this way rather than recopy the whole page; but if there are many omissions, it is always better to rewrite the paper. To mark the addition, use the caret, not some private mark, and place the caret at the bottom of the line, not above it.

(See *Workbook,* Exercises 42 and 43.)

## *F. Mechanics*

Rules concerning capitalization, italics, abbreviations, and the representation of numbers have evolved from practices which literate writers and printers have found to be economical and effective, rather than from fundamental laws of language. Some have been developed gradually from ancient practices, and others established arbitrarily in more modern times. The result is that all do not have the same degree of acceptance, and it is easy to find variations in usage regarding them. In the discussion which follows, however, matters over which much controversy exists are omitted, and the rules given are generally accepted by good writers everywhere.

**74**     **Capitals.** The tendency today is to use as few capitals as possible; hence a good practice is not to use a capital unless a rule exists for its use. In contemporary practice, *capitals are used primarily* (1) *to mark the first word of a sentence, the first word of a direct quotation, and the first word of a line of poetry,* (2) *to designate proper nouns and proper adjectives, and* (3) *to mark the important words of titles and for certain other specific purposes.*

**74a**     The rule that a capital should mark the first word of a sentence carries the implication that capitalizing some internal part of a sentence, unless of course it begins with a proper noun or adjective, is incorrect; and also that capitalizing a fragment which is not meant as an independent unit of thought is incorrect. Sometimes, however, single words or phrases which may be used legitimately instead of complete sentences are capitalized, as in the following examples:

> On the mark!

> "Ready?"
> "Yes."

Furthermore, the rule to begin each direct quotation with a capital implies that an indirect quotation should not be capitalized:

> He asked, "Are you ready to go?"
> He asked if we were ready to go.

As to the use of capitals to mark the first words of lines of poetry, the rule must be followed scrupulously when the poem being quoted followed this practice; but some recent writers capitalize first words of those lines only which begin a sentence, and in these instances, the usage of the author should be followed:

This is the land of lost content,
    I see it shining plain,
The happy highways where I went
    And cannot come again.
                        —A. E. Housman

Once Wonder dwelt here, child-wise and joyous, watching
    through the five windows, through the open door;
  saw all the pageant of life pass by, nor heeded
the spiders, dim in the cornice, the sharp-toothed beetles under the floor.
                        —Horace Shipp

NOTE. Two matters of usage when something is being quoted as an integral part of a writer's own sentence should be noted. (1) When only part of a sentence is being quoted directly, do not capitalize the first word, as in the following examples:

> The caretaker asked us to "row along the inlet as far as the Dahlman cabin, and in the event of anything suspicious, shout"; but we saw nothing.
>
> After hearing those old crones gossiping, I felt as Lear did when he requested "an ounce of civet, good apothecary, to sweeten my imagination."

(2) When quoting more than one line of poetry and not following the poet's own line arrangement, retain the capitals as in the original:

> When I confessed that I could not understand her, she looked at me quizzically and said I should remember Pope's words, "And yet believe me, good as well as ill, Woman's at best a contradiction still."

**74b** The rule to capitalize all proper nouns and proper adjectives will give no trouble to those who without hesitation can identify proper nouns and adjectives. Included here, of course, are the names and initials of individuals; nicknames and titles used as part of the name (Blondy Johnson, Alexander the Great); names referring to the Deity and to deities of all religions and times, and pronouns referring to God; names of months, days of the week, holidays, and holy days (October, Tuesday, Epiphany, Fourth of July); names of organizations, political parties, religious bodies (Boy Scouts, the Democratic or Republican Party, the Catholic Church, the Methodist Church); names of places, geographical sections, political divisions (Lake Erie, Portage Lake, Carson City, the Missouri River, Pike's Peak, the Second Precinct, the First Ward, the Southwest); names of specific historical events, specific laws, departments of government (the signing of Magna Charta, the Bill of Rights, the Patent Office, the Department of State); names of divisions of a college or university (the Department of Chemistry, the College of Arts and Sciences, the School of Business Administration); titles prefixed to the names of individuals and abbreviations after a name (General John J.

Pershing; Professor Harry Smith, A.B., A.M., Ph.D.; the Reverend James Thorne; Father O'Flynn; Charles Tennyson, Esq., C.M.G.); names of specific buildings, ships, trains, airplanes (the Empire State Building, the *America,* the *Spirit of St. Louis*); and personifications (Tell me, Fancy, sweetest child). Of the words in these classes, few will present difficulties if one bears in mind the rule that a specific person or thing is a proper noun, and adjectives derived from these are proper adjectives and should be capitalized, and that a reference to any one of a class of persons or things does not require a capital. Some special stumbling blocks among these are discussed below.

(a) The words *father, mother, brother, sister,* and the like should be capitalized if used in direct address or if not preceded by a possessive pronoun:

> I must tell you, Sister, of my new roommate.
> Let's ask your mother if we may go.
> Where is Father this morning?

(b) In the use of such particles as *d', de, von, van, le,* and *della* in proper names, usage in this country varies; and the only safe way is to take careful note of how an individual writes his name and extend him the courtesy of following his example. The same is true of the abbreviations *jr.* and *sr.* after a name, for despite categorical statements in some texts that these should or should not be capitalized, a careful check indicates that usage is almost exactly divided in this matter.

(c) In the capitalization of the generic term which follows a proper name, usage varies; but except in newspapers and periodicals which affect a newspaper style, the best practice is to capitalize the generic term, thus: the Ohio River, the San Francisco Peaks, Central Park, the Atlantic Ocean.

(d) Note that a section of the country is capitalized, but a direction of the compass is not, thus: Birds which spent the winter in the South are beginning to fly north.

(e) In referring to a specific department in a college, use capitals, but do not capitalize a subject unless it is derived from a proper noun.

> I am majoring in mathematics; hence I know best the instructors in the Department of Mathematics. But as I am minoring in French and physics, I know several instructors in those departments too.

(f) The words *honorable* and *reverend* are not really titles but are complimentary adjectives; hence when used they should be followed by the first name, the initials, or the appropriate title. When used in the body of a sentence they should be capitalized and should be preceded by *the:* the Honorable James A. Hill, the Reverend Dr. Jones.

(g) Titles and places should not be capitalized when they are generic in reference, even when one refers to a specific person or thing:

> I saw the professor coming from the library just now.
> I saw Professor Pugh in the Smith Library just now.
> He was on the way to the theater.
> He was going to the Majestic Theater.
> He graduated from high school but did not attend college.
> He graduated from Beaumont High School and then entered Albion College.
> He served as dean for several years.
> There is Dean Williams of the School of Business Administration.

(h) Capitalize derivatives of proper nouns which are used as proper adjectives: an Elizabethan play, Mexican music, an Indian arrowhead, a Spanish course, a Papal decree, a Western habit.

**74c** In addition to the rules of capitalization as noted in the foregoing sections, there are several special rules which should be observed.

(a) Capitalize the first word and all other words except articles, conjunctions, and prepositions of titles of books, magazines, newspapers, articles, stories, poems, musical compositions, and chapters or subdivisions of books and periodicals.

> You will find that article in the Book Review Section of this week's *New York Times.*
> *An Enquiry into the Nature of Certain Nineteenth Century Pamphlets,* though actually concerned with bibliography, is a brilliant piece of detective work.
> Aunt Jane reads every page of the *Atlantic Monthly.*

NOTE. The best modern practice is not to capitalize an article which begins the title of a newspaper or magazine unless it is the first word of a sentence, but to capitalize such an article in the title of a book: the Kansas City *Star* (newspaper), the *New Yorker* (magazine), *The Enjoyment of Drama* (book), *A Short History of the English People* (book).

(b) Capitalize the first and last words of a salutation, and the first word of the complimentary close of a letter: Dear Sir, My dear Sir, Dear Mr. Birch, Yours truly, Yours very sincerely.

(c) Capitalize the words *Whereas* and *Resolved* in formal resolutions, and the first word following either of these.

(d) Capitalize *I* and *O* (but not *oh* unless it comes at the beginning of a sentence), and the abbreviations *A.D.* and *B.C.* (In printing the latter are generally set in small capitals: A.D., B.C.)

**74d** (e) In addition to the rules already stated, the following *don'ts* concerning capitalization should be observed.

Do not capitalize for emphasis.

Do not capitalize the names of the seasons: spring, autumn.

Do not capitalize (1) the names of college classes—freshman, sophomore, etc.—unless the class is referred to as a specific organization, or (2) the name of a member of a college class.

Do not capitalize prefixes to proper names: ex-President Hoover, anti-Nazi, pre-Revolutionary.

Do not capitalize *earth, sun, moon* (but capitalize the names of other planets, stars, and constellations).

Observe contemporary usage in the matter of capitalizing words which were once proper nouns but which through usage are in the process of becoming common nouns. When in doubt about such a word, do not trust your own judgment, but consult a dictionary. Note, however, that many such words have already become common nouns and should not be capitalized, as *macadam, boycott, bowdlerize, venetian blinds, leghorn hat, scotch plaid,* and many others.

**Italics.** To designate in manuscript that something is to be printed in italics, underline once. The most common uses of italics are as follows:

**75a** *To emphasize a word.* This usage, however, is generally avoided by good writers, and it should be employed with great discretion.

**75b** *To refer to a word or letter taken out of its context.*

> Always dot your *i*'s and cross your *t*'s.
> Do not write *and* and *the* slantwise across the line.
> The word *thane* referred to one of superior rank.

**75c** *To designate a foreign word not yet anglicized.*

> Do you like potatoes *au gratin?*

The abbreviations *ibid., c., loc. cit., q.v.,* and the like, which are commonly used in footnotes, refer to Latin words, and should therefore be italicized. Such commonly used abbreviations as *etc., i.e.,* and *e.g.,* although from Latin words, are now anglicized and need not be italicized.

**75d** *To indicate titles of books, pamphlets, newspapers, magazines, dramas, and musical compositions.* Note that the titles of books and magazines are italicized, and parts of these, as chapters in a book and articles in a magazine, are designated by the use of quotation marks (see page 275).

Note. In designating the titles of magazines, the best contemporary practice is not to italicize an article which comes at the beginning of the title, and in the titles of newspapers not to italicize the article or the name of the city. The following are correct: I read a good article this week in the *Survey Graphic*. I saw that in the Boston *Transcript*.

**75e** To designate the names of ships and airplanes: the *Queen Mary*, the *Winnie Mae*.

**75f** To mark the word *Resolved* in formal resolutions.

**Abbreviations.** Both courtesy and intelligence suggest to a writer the removal of every possible obstacle between himself and a reader. *Since*

**76** *abbreviations are likely to be such obstacles, all abbreviations except a very few which are accepted universally are to be avoided in ordinary writing.* Even many abbreviations which the average reader will have little trouble recognizing are avoided in ordinary writing by careful writers.

**76a** Among abbreviations to be avoided, as indicating questionable taste on the part of a writer, are the following:

(a) Names of states, countries, and cities—even in informal letters and in addresses on envelopes.

(b) Names of months and days of the week.

(c) Given names, as *Chas.* for *Charles, Jno.* for *John, Jas.* for *James,* and *Wm.* for *William.*

(d) *Etc.* for *and so forth* or *and the like.*

NOTE. When *etc.* is used, as in footnotes or lists, observe that it is the abbreviation for *et cetera,* meaning *and others,* and that the *t* precedes the *c.*

(e) *Co.* for *company,* except in lists, footnotes, or other places where abbreviations in general are permissible.

(f) Words such as *avenue, boulevard, court, street,* and *building* in addresses.

**76b** It is correct to use the following abbreviations:

(a) *Mr., Mrs., Messrs., Dr.,* and *St. (Saint)* in connection with proper names, whether initials or first names are included. Such abbreviations as *Rev., Hon., Prof., Gen., Col., Capt.,* and *Lieut.,* are allowed when they precede the full name—surname and given name; when only the surname is used, however, these should be written out.

(b) *Esq., A.B., A.M., Ph.D., LL.D., Sr., Jr.,* and the like when used after proper names. All titles, whether those which precede or follow names, should be written in full unless they are used in connection with a proper name. The following, for instance, are correct:

Prof. John Williams, A.B., Ph.D., will lecture here tonight.

Professor Williams, who has the degree of Doctor of Philosophy, will lecture.

The Hon. Joseph Green will speak at assembly tomorrow.

Charles Tennyson, Esq., is a grandson of Alfred, Lord Tennyson.

In England *Esquire* is a complimentary title used when writing to someone not of the nobility but above the class of artisan.

(c) The sign $ for *dollars, B.C.* and *A.D., a.m.* and *p.m.*, and *No.* (for number) when used with numerals. In formal writing, however, these abbreviations except *B.C.* and *A.D.* should be avoided.

(d) Such abbreviations as *e.g. (exempli gratia,* for example), *ibid. (ibidem,* in the same place), *i.e. (id est,* that is), and *viz. (videlicet,* namely) in footnotes and bibliographies; and abbreviations of many kinds in indexes, statistical tables, lists, and so on, provided an explanation of all abbreviations is attached.

NOTE. A period should always follow an abbreviation, but no period follows a contraction, such as *can't, don't.*

**Numbers.** For the representation of numbers, the following rules are in general use.

**77a** Use figures for dates, house numbers, telephone numbers, page numbers of books, decimals, and hours of the day when *a.m.* or *p.m.* is used.

The first public museum in America was opened in Charleston, South Carolina, on January 12, 1773.

He lives at 1447 Devon Avenue.

Call me at Argyle 2-3926.

You will find that quotation on page 637 of your poetry text.

That was a .32 caliber revolver.

The *Mercury* arrives at Chicago at 4:45 p.m.

**77b** Write out round numbers and numbers under a hundred when only one or two are given; but for numbers requiring more than one or two words, for several numbers close together or complicated sets of numbers, or in quoting statistics, use figures.

**77c** Write out a fraction unless it follows a whole number, and spell out a number used as part of a compound adjective.

A vote indicates that two thirds of the class will go on the picnic.

The sizes I require are as follows: shoes, 8½; collar, 16¼; and hat, 7¼.

He bought a ten-dollar hat.

**77d** Write out a number at the beginning of a sentence.

**77e** When writing figures for dollars, do not use a decimal point and two zeros for cents when the amount is in even dollars, but write $15, $68, $125.

**77f**    Except in legal papers or where great accuracy is essential, do not write out a number and then repeat it in figures in parentheses. In ordinary writing, use one or the other method, not both.

**77g**    When a number has more than three figures, set off figures in groups of three by commas, except street numbers and years, which should be written without punctuation.

**77h**    Designate volume and chapter numbers and the main divisions of outlines by roman numerals: Vol. III, ch. x.

**77i**    In writing out compound numerals from twenty-one to ninety-nine, use hyphens: The river is eighty-seven yards wide here.

NOTE. The convention of indicating a decimal point by *and* in mathematics sometimes leads a writer to omit the *and* in writing out such numbers as six hundred and sixty-seven, on the assumption that *and* here is incorrect. The use of this *and* in mathematics, however, is special and technical, and has nothing to do with representing numbers in ordinary writing. The *and,* therefore, should be kept in such instances.

(See *Workbook,* Exercises 44 and 45.)

## *My America*[3]

### JOHN BUCHAN (LORD TWEEDSMUIR)

I first discovered America through books. Not the tales of Indians and the Wild West which entranced my boyhood; those seemed to belong to no particular quarter of the globe, but to an indefinable land of romance, and I was not cognizant of any nation behind them. But when I became interested in literature, I came strongly under the spell of New England. Its culture seemed to me to include what was best in Europe's, winnowed and clarified. Perhaps it was especially fitted to attract youth, for it was not too difficult or too recondite, but followed the "main march of the human affections," and it had the morning freshness of a young people. Its cheerfulness atoned for its occasional bleakness and anemia. Lowell was the kind of critic I wanted, learned, rational, never freakish, always intelligible. Emerson's gnomic wisdom was a sound manual for adolescence, and of Thoreau I became—and for long remained—an ardent disciple. To a Scot of my upbringing there was something congenial in the simplicity, the mild austerity, and the girded discipline of the New England tradition. I felt that it had been derived from the same sources as our own.

3. From *Pilgrim's Way* (published in England under the title of *Memory Hold the Door*) by John Buchan (Lord Tweedsmuir). (Copyright 1940 by the Houghton Mifflin Company). Reprinted by permission of the Houghton Mifflin Company, Lady Tweedsmuir, and Hodder and Stoughton, the English publisher.

Then, while I was at Oxford, I read Colonel Henderson's *Stonewall Jackson* and became a student of the American Civil War. I cannot say what especially attracted me to that campaign: partly, no doubt, the romance of it, the chivalry and the supreme heroism; partly its extraordinary technical interest, both military and political; but chiefly, I think, because I fell in love with the protagonists. I had found the kind of man that I could whole-heartedly admire. Since those days my study of the Civil War has continued, I have visited most of its battlefields, I have followed the trail of its great marches, I have read widely in its literature; indeed, my memory has become so stored with its details that I have often found myself able to tell the descendants of its leaders facts about their forbears of which they had never heard.

My interest soon extended from the soldiers to the civilians, and I acquired a new admiration for Abraham Lincoln. Then it was enlarged to include the rest of America's history—the first settlements, the crossing of the Appalachians, the Revolution, the building of the West. Soon America, instead of being the unstoried land which it appears to most English travelers, became for me the home of a long tradition and studded with sacred places. I dare to say that no American was ever more thrilled by the prospect of seeing Westminster Abbey and the Tower, Winchester and Oxford, than I was by the thought of Valley Forge and the Shenandoah and the Wilderness.

I came first into the United States by way of Canada—a good way to enter, for English eyes are already habituated to the shagginess of the landscape and can begin to realize its beauties. My first reflection was that no one had told me how lovely the country was. I mean *lovely,* not vast and magnificent. I am not thinking of the Grand Canyon and the Yosemite and the Pacific coast, but of the ordinary rural landscape. There is much of the land which I have not seen, but in the East and the South and the Northwest I have collected a gallery of delectable pictures. I think of the farms which are clearings in the Vermont and New Hampshire hills, the flowery summer meadows, the lush cow-pastures with an occasional stump to remind one that it is old forest land, the quiet lakes and the singing streams, the friendly accessible mountains; the little country towns of Massachusetts and Connecticut with their village greens and elms and two-century-old churches and court houses; the secret glens of the Adirondacks and the mountain meadows of the Blue Ridge; the long-settled champaign of Maryland and Pennsylvania; Virginian manors more Old-England perhaps than anything we have at home; the exquisite links with the past like much of Boston and Charleston and all of Annapolis; the sunburnt aromatic ranges of Montana and Wyoming; the Pacific shores where from snow mountains fishable streams descend through some of the noblest timber on earth to an enchanted sea.

It is a country most of which I feel to be in a special sense "habitable," designed for homes, adapted to human uses, a friendly land. I like, too, the way in which the nomenclature reflects its history, its racial varieties, its odd cultural mixtures, the grandiose and the homespun rubbing shoulders. That is how places should be named. I have no objection to Mechanicsville and Higginsville and Utica and Syracuse. They are a legitimate part of the record. And behind are the hoar-ancient memorials of the first dwellers, names like symphonies—Susquehanna, Ticonderoga, Shenandoah, Wyoming.

"Ah, my cabbages!" Henry Adams wrote, "when will you ever fathom the American? Never in your sweet lives." He proceeds in his genial way to make epigrams about his own New Englanders: "Improvised Europeans we were and—Lord God!—how thin!"—"Thank God I never was cheerful. I come from the happy stock of the Mathers, who, as you remember, passed sweet mornings reflecting on the goodness of God and the damnation of infants." Where an Adams scrupled to tread it is not for a stranger to rush in. But I would humbly suggest a correction to one reading which, I think, has the authority of Robert Louis Stevenson. America is, no doubt, a vast country, though it can be comfortably put inside Canada. But it is not in every part a country of wide horizons. Dwellers on the Blue Ridge, on the prairies, and on the western ranges may indeed live habitually with huge spaces of land and sky, but most of America, and some of its most famous parts, is pockety, snug and cozy, a sanctuary rather than a watch-tower. To people so domiciled its vastness must be like the mathematician's space-time, a concept apprehended by the mind and not a percept of the eye. "The largeness of Nature and of this nation were monstrous without a corresponding largeness and generosity of the spirit of the citizen." That is one of Walt Whitman's best-known sayings, but let us remember that the bigness of their country is for most Americans something to be learned and imaginatively understood, and not a natural deduction from cohabiting with physical immensities.

Racially they are the most variegated people on earth. The preponderance of the Anglo-Saxon stock disappeared in the Civil War. Look today at any list of names in a society or a profession and you will find that, except in the navy, the bulk are from the continent of Europe. In his day Matthew Arnold thought that the chief source of the strength of the American people lay in their homogeneity and the absence of sharply defined classes, which made revolution unthinkable. Other observers, like Henry James, have deplored the lack of such homogeneity and wished for their country the "close and complete consciousness of the Scots." (I pause to note that I cannot imagine a more nightmare conception. What would happen to the world if a hundred and thirty million Scotsmen, with their tight, compact nationalism, were living in the same country?) I am inclined to query the alleged absence of classes, for I have never been in any part of the United States where class distinctions did not hold. There is an easy friendliness of manner which conceals a strong class pride, and the basis of that pride is not always, or oftenest, plutocratic. Apart from the social snobbery of the big cities, there seems to be everywhere an innocent love of grades and distinctions which is enough to make a communist weep. I have known places in the South where there was a magnificent aristocratic egalitarianism. Inside a charmed circle all were equal. The village postmistress, having had the right kind of great-great-grandmother, was an honored member of society, while the immigrant millionaire, who had built himself a palace, might as well have been dead. And this is true not only of the New England F.F.M.'s and the Virginian F.F.V.'s, the districts with long traditions, but of the raw little townships in the Middle West. They, too, have their "best" people who had ancestors, though the family tree may only have sprouted for two generations.

No country can show such a wide range of type and character, and I am so constituted that in nearly all I find something to interest and attract me. This is more than a temperamental bias, for I am very ready to give reasons for my liking. I am as much alive as anyone to the weak and ugly things in American life: areas, both urban and rural, where the human economy has gone rotten; the melting-pot which does not always melt; the eternal colored problem; a constitutional machine which I cannot think adequately represents the efficient good sense of the American peoples; a brand of journalism which fatigues with its ruthless snappiness and uses a speech so disintegrated that it is incapable of expressing any serious thought or emotion; the imbecile patter of high-pressure salesmanship; an academic jargon, used chiefly by psychologists and sociologists, which is hideous and almost meaningless. Honest Americans do not deny these blemishes; indeed they are apt to exaggerate them, for they are by far the sternest critics of their own country. For myself, I would make a double plea in extenuation. These are defects from which today no nation is exempt, for they are the fruits of a mechanical civilization, which perhaps are more patent in America, since everything there is on a large scale. Again, you can set an achievement very much the same in kind against nearly every failure. If her historic apparatus of government is cranky, she is capable of meeting the "instant need of things" with brilliant improvisations. Against economic plague-spots she can set great experiments in charity; against journalistic baby-talk a standard of popular writing in her best papers which is a model of idiom and perspicuity; against catchpenny trade methods many solidly founded, perfectly organized commercial enterprises; against the jargon of the half-educated professor much noble English prose in the great tradition. That is why it is so foolish to generalize about America. You no sooner construct a rule than it is shattered by the exceptions.

As I have said, I have a liking for almost every kind of American (except the kind who decry their country). I have even a sneaking fondness for George Babbitt, which I fancy is shared by his creator. But there are two types which I value especially, and which I have never met elsewhere in quite the same form. One is the pioneer. No doubt the physical frontier of the United States is now closed, but the pioneer still lives, though the day of the covered wagon is over. I have met him in the New England hills, where he is grave, sardonic, deliberate in speech; in the South, where he has a ready smile and a soft, caressing way of talking; in the ranges of the West, the cowpuncher with his gentle voice and his clear, friendly eyes which have not been dulled by reading print —the real thing, far removed from the vulgarities of film and fiction. At his best, I think, I have found him as a newcomer in Canada where he is pushing north into districts like the Peace River, pioneering in the old sense. By what signs is he to be known? Principally by the fact that he is wholly secure, that he possesses his soul, that he is the true philosopher. He is one of the few aristocrats left in the world. He has a right sense of the values of life, because his cosmos embraces both nature and man. I think he is the most steadfast human being now alive.

The other type is at the opposite end of the social scale, the creature of a complex society who at the same time is not dominated by it, but, while reaping its benefits, stands a little aloof. In the older countries culture, as a rule, leaves some irregularity like an excrescence in a shapely tree-trunk, some irrational bias, some petulance or prejudice. You have to go to America, I think, for the wholly civilized man who has not lost his natural vigor or agreeable idiosyncrasies, but who sees life in its true proportions and has a fine balance of mind and spirit. It is a character hard to define, but anyone with a wide American acquaintance will know what I mean. They are people in whom education has not stunted any natural growth or fostered any abnormality. They are Greek in their justness of outlook, but Northern in their gusto. Their eyes are shrewd and candid, but always friendly. As examples I would cite, among friends who are dead, the names of Robert Bacon, Walter Page, Newton Baker, and Dwight Morrow.

But I am less concerned with special types than with the American people as a whole. Let me try to set down certain qualities which seem to me to flourish more lustily in the United States than elsewhere. Again, let me repeat, I speak of America only as I know it; an observer with a different experience might not agree with my conclusions.

First I would select what, for want of a better word, I should call homeliness. It is significant that the ordinary dwelling, though it be only a shack in the woods, is called not a house, but a home. This means that the family, the ultimate social unit, is given its proper status as the foundation of society. Even among the richer classes I seem to find a certain pleasing domesticity. English people of the same rank are separated by layers of servants from the basic work of the household, and know very little about it. In America the kitchen is not too far away from the drawing-room, and it is recognized, as Heraclitus said, that the gods may dwell there. But I am thinking chiefly of the ordinary folk, especially those of narrow means. It is often said that Americans are a nomad race, and it is true that they are very ready to shift their camp; but the camp, however bare, is always a home.[1] The cohesion of the family is close, even when its members are scattered. This is due partly to the tradition of the first settlers, a handful in an unknown land; partly to the history of the frontier, where the hearth-fire burnt brighter when all around was cold and darkness. The later immigrants from Europe, feeling at last secure, were able for the first time to establish a family base, and they cherished it zealously. This ardent domesticity has had its bad effects on American literature, inducing a sentimentality which makes a too crude frontal attack on the emotions, and which has produced as a reaction a not less sentimental "toughness." But as a social cement it is beyond price. There have been many to laugh at the dullness and pettiness of the "small town." From what I know of small-town life elsewhere, I suspect obtuseness in the satirists.

Second, I would choose the sincere and widespread friendliness of the people. Americans are interested in the human race, and in each other. Deriving doubtless from the old frontier days, there is a general helpfulness which I have not found in the same degree elsewhere. A homesteader

---

1. In the Civil War homesickness was so serious a malady that the "printed forms for medical reports contained an entry for nostalgia precisely as for pneumonia."—Douglas Freeman, *The South to Posterity*, p. 4.

in Dakota will accompany a traveler for miles to set him on the right road. The neighbors will rally round one of their number in distress with the loyalty of a Highland clan. This friendliness is not a self-conscious duty so much as an instinct. A squatter in a cabin will share his scanty provender and never dream that he is doing anything unusual.

American hospitality, long as I have enjoyed it, still leaves me breathless. The lavishness with which a busy man will give up precious time to entertain a stranger to whom he is in no way bound remains for me one of the wonders of the world. No doubt this friendliness, since it is an established custom, has its fake side. The endless brotherhoods and sodalities into which people brigade themselves encourage a geniality which is more a mannerism than an index of character, a tiresome, noisy, back-slapping heartiness. But that is the exception, not the rule. Americans like company, but though they are gregarious they do not lose themselves in the crowd. Waves of mass emotion may sweep the country, but they are transient things and do not submerge for long the stubborn rock of individualism. That is to say, people can be led, but they will not be driven. Their love of human companionship is based not on self-distrust, but on a genuine liking for their kind. With them the sense of a common humanity is a warm and constant instinct and not a doctrine of the schools or a slogan of the hustings.

Lastly—and this may seem a paradox—I maintain that they are fundamentally modest. Their interest in others is a proof of it; the Aristotelian Magnificent Man was interested in nobody but himself. As a nation they are said to be sensitive to criticism; that surely is modesty, for the truly arrogant care nothing for the opinion of other people. Above all they can laugh at themselves, which is not possible for the immodest. They are their own shrewdest and most ribald critics. It is charged against them that they are inclined to boast unduly about those achievements and about the greatness of their country, but a smug glorying in them is found only in the American of the caricaturist. They rejoice in showing their marvels to a visitor with the gusto of children exhibiting their toys to a stranger, an innocent desire, without any unfriendly gloating, to make others partakers in their satisfaction. If now and then they are guilty of bombast, it is surely a venial fault. The excited American talks of his land very much, I suspect, as the Elizabethans in their cups talked of England. The foreigner who strayed into the Mermaid Tavern must often have listened to heroics which upset his temper.

The native genius, in humor, and in many of the public and private relations of life, is for overstatement, a high-colored, imaginative, paradoxical extravagance. The British gift is for understatement. Both are legitimate figures of speech. They serve the same purpose, for they call attention to a fact by startling the hearer, since manifestly they are not the plain truth. Personally I delight in both mannerisms and would not for the world have their possessors reject them. They serve the same purpose in another and a subtler sense, for they can be used to bring novel and terrible things within the pale of homely experience. I remember on the Western Front in 1918 that two divisions, British and American, aligned side by side, suffered a heavy shelling. An American sergeant described it in racy and imaginative speech which would have been appropriate to the Day of Judgment. A British sergeant merely observed that "Kaiser 'ad been a bit 'asty." Each had a twinkle in his eye; each in his national idiom was making frightfulness endurable by domesticating it.

The United States is the richest, and, both actually and potentially, the most powerful state on the globe. She has much, I believe, to give to the world; indeed, to her hands is chiefly entrusted the shaping of the future. If democracy in the broadest and truest sense is to survive, it will be mainly because of her guardianship. For, with all her imperfections, she has a clearer view than any other people of the democratic fundamentals.

She starts from the right basis, for she combines a firm grip on the past with a quick sense of present needs and a bold outlook on the future. This she owes to her history; the combination of the British tradition with the necessities of a new land; the New England township and the Virginian manor *plus* the frontier. Much of that tradition was relinquished as irrelevant to her needs, but much remains: a talent for law which is not incompatible with a lawless practice; respect for a certain type of excellence in character which has made her great men uncommonly like our own; a disposition to compromise, but only after a good deal of arguing; an intense dislike of dictation. To these instincts the long frontier struggles added courage in the face of novelties, adaptability, enterprise, a doggedness which was never lumpish, but alert and expectant.

That is the historic basis of America's democracy, and today she is the chief exponent of a creed which I believe on the whole to be the best in this imperfect world. She is the chief exponent for two reasons. The first is her size; she exhibits its technique in large type, so that he who runs may read. More important, she exhibits it in its most intelligible form, so that its constituents are obvious. Democracy has become with many an unpleasing parrot-cry, and . . . it is well to be clear what it means. It is primarily a spiritual testament, from which certain political and economic orders naturally follow. But the essence is the testament: the orders may change while the testament stands. This testament, this ideal of citizenship, she owes to no one teacher. There was a time when I fervently admired Alexander Hamilton and could not away with Jefferson; the latter only began to interest me, I think, after I had seen the University of Virginia, which he created. But I deprecate partisanship in those ultimate matters. The democratic testament derives from Hamilton as well as from Jefferson.

It has two main characteristics. The first is that the ordinary man believes in himself and in his ability, along with his fellows, to govern his country. It is when a people loses its self-confidence that it surrenders its soul to a dictator or an oligarchy. In Mr. Walter Lippmann's tremendous metaphor, it welcomes manacles to prevent its hands shaking. The second is the belief, which is fundamental also in Christianity, of the worth of every human soul—the worth, not the equality. This is partly an honest emotion, and partly a reasoned principle—that something may be made out of anybody, and that there is something likeable about everybody if you look for it—or, in canonical words, that ultimately there is nothing common or unclean.

The democratic testament is one lesson that America has to teach the world. A second is a new reading of nationalism. Some day and somehow the peoples must discover a way to brigade themselves for peace. Now, there are on the globe only two proven large-scale organizations of social units, the United States and the British Empire. The latter is not for export, and could not be duplicated; its strength depends upon a thousand-year-old monarchy and a store of unformulated traditions. But the United States was the conscious work of men's hands, and a task which has once been performed can be performed again. She is the supreme example of a federation in being, a federation which recognizes the rights and individuality of the parts, but accepts the overriding interests of the whole. To achieve this compromise she fought a desperate war. If the world is ever to have prosperity and peace, there must be some kind of federation—I will not say of democracies, but of states which accept the reign of Law. In such a task she seems to me to be the predestined leader. Vigorous as her patriotism is, she has escaped the jealous, barricadoed nationalism of the Old World. Disraeli, so often a prophet in spite of himself, in 1863, at a critical moment of the Civil War, spoke memorable words:

There is a grave misapprehension, both in the ranks of Her Majesty's Government and of Her Majesty's Opposition, as to what constitutes the true meaning of the American democracy. The American democracy is not made up of the scum of the great industrial cities of the United States, nor of an exhausted middle class that speculates in stocks and calls that progress. The American democracy is made up of something far more stable, that may ultimately decide the fate of the two Americas and of "Europe."

For forty years I have regarded America not only with a student's interest in a fascinating problem, but with the affection of one to whom she has become almost a second motherland. Among her citizens I count many of my closest friends; I have known all her presidents, save one, since Theodore Roosevelt, and all her ambassadors to the Court of Saint James's since John Hay; for five years I have been her neighbor in Canada. But I am not blind to the grave problems which confront her. Democracy, after all, is a negative thing. It provides a fair field for the Good Life, but it is not in itself the Good Life. In these days when lovers of freedom may have to fight for their cause, the hope is that the ideal of the Good Life, in which alone freedom has any meaning, will acquire a stronger potency. It is the task of civilization to raise every citizen above want, but in so doing to permit a free development and avoid the slavery of the beehive and the antheap. A humane economic policy must not be allowed to diminish the stature of man's spirit. It is because I believe that in the American people the two impulses are of equal strength that I see her in the vanguard of that slow upward trend, undulant or spiral, which today is our modest definition of progress. Her major prophet is still Whitman. "Everything comes out of the dirt—everything; everything comes out of the people, everyday people, the people as you find them and leave them; people, people, just people!"

It is only out of the dirt that things grow.

*Suggestions for Study*

1. What is the tone of the article? Would the tone appeal most to Americans, to Englishmen, or to both equally?

2. Cite several instances to show that the author was writing for British readers in order to dispel erroneous ideas about America.

3. The author was a Scot, a novelist, and a statesman who traveled extensively in the United States. Do you think his observations accurate and just? Consider closely the list of "weak and ugly things in American life": are his statements here true and apt? Be prepared to discuss these weaknesses and to write a paper concerning them. Note also all the virtues which he lists. Did he miss any important ones? Is he correct in attributing these virtues to Americans?

4. Do you know any people who exemplify his two outstanding American types—the pioneer and the truly cultured man? If so, write a character sketch

of one of them (for instructions on writing a character sketch, see section in this book under Biography).

5. Name the three characteristics which Lord Tweedsmuir says are special with the American people. Do you agree with him? If you know the people of any foreign country well try to enumerate characteristics of them that will distinguish them as well as Lord Tweedsmuir does.

6. What does he mean by the statement that democracy is a negative state which "provides a fair field for the Good Life, but is not in itself the Good Life"? What does he mean by "the Good Life"?

7. Discuss the level of diction which he employs, his use of general and concrete words, and the kind of sentences he favors.

8. Analyze any three paragraphs in the article which you consider to be especially well written, and note down all the stylistic devices used in them, such as parallelism, loose and periodic sentences, transitional words and phrases, variation of sentence types and of sentence beginnings, repetition for emphasis, and the like.

9. Define the following words in the article: recondite, winnowed, gnomic, austerity, protagonist, aromatic, nomenclature, sanctuary, homogeneity, plutocratic, egalitarianism, extenuation, obtuseness, sodalities, gregarious, ribald, testament, deprecate.

## I Chose America [4]

### PERCY WAXMAN

It was not to escape tyranny or poverty that I became an American citizen. I was born in Australia, educated there in the traditional British manner. Up to my twenty-third year even the idea of renouncing allegiance to the Empire would have seemed sacrilege.

Then one day the opportunity came to take a trip around the world. I went first to the United States. After a brief stay in San Francisco I eagerly set out for Chicago, which I had been led by tourist literature to believe was a cross between Paris and Paradise. I arrived there on an April morning—and in the midst of a raging, subzero blizzard. That Arctic wilderness did not seem enticing to one who had never before seen snow. A train for New York was leaving in ten minutes; so I dashed aboard.

I immediately found myself confronted by an embarrassing situation. I had left the West Coast with only enough money to last until I reached Chicago, where I could use my letter of credit, for I had been warned that carrying money around America was highly hazardous. So after paying for ticket and berth to New York I was left with exactly 75 cents.

4. From the *Reader's Digest*, XXXVII (December, 1940), 77-80. Reprinted by permission of the author and The *Reader's Digest* Association, Inc.

It was a 28-hour run to New York, and I had the hollow prospect of going all that time without food.

I asked the porter to tell the dining-car conductor of my situation and find out if I might not open an account with him based on my letter of credit. A few minutes later a middle-aged man stopped where I was sitting.

"I overheard the porter telling the conductor that you were in need of money," he said, "and I thought I'd see if I could help out."

Considerably embarrassed, I sputtered forth the reasons for my predicament, and that man, a complete stranger, loaned me $10. When I asked him to come to the bank with me as soon as we reached New York he said:

"Oh, I get off at Cleveland. Here's my card. You can send me the money when you get settled."

The fact that the man had *sought me out* to render me a kindness impressed me tremendously. I concluded that a country where such things happen to a stranger was a country well-worth knowing. One year after this incident I returned to the United States to stay.

I have made my home here for over thirty years. During my first years in New York I took no steps to become naturalized. One day I received notice to serve on a jury. Not being a citizen, I ignored it. A few days later I was served with a summons to appear at City Hall. There I presented myself to a gentleman of the old dyed-mustache school of Tammany statesmen who menacingly demanded to know why I had paid no attention to the previous notice. Somewhat smartalecky I asked: "What is the penalty for a British subject serving on an American jury?"

"Oh, that's it, is it?" he remarked with Irish fervor and across the face of my summons wrote "Alien" in big red letters, as if he wished to impress me with the full significance of that sinister designation.

On my way home I thought over this experience. At first with amusement, then more seriously. Here I was, living and working in America, enjoying its privileges but not sharing full responsibilities. I decided to be an alien no longer. And now after having been a citizen for almost twenty-five years I can honestly say that the longer I live here the better I like it. My love for America has nothing to do with that brand of patriotism which a cynical friend defined as "self-interest multiplied by population."

It has often been said that Americans are dollar-chasers. But it has been my experience that one of the characteristics of Americans is the casualness with which they regard money. No people are more generous or extravagant. After having lived in many different parts of the world, I can honestly say that if I were friendless, unemployed, and penniless I would rather take my chances asking for help on the corner of an American street than anywhere else on earth.

I can say these things openly where a born American might hesitate. The fact that I am naturalized gives me a sort of detached privilege to speak freely without seeming to talk about myself.

American hospitality is proverbial. Was there ever anything to compare with the open-hearted reception accorded a foreign visitor? Nothing is too good for him. No one bothers to inquire who his ancestors were. In spite of their reputed smartness, Americans are more liable to be swindled by foreigners than foreigners are by Americans.

As for sportsmanship, no people are more ready to give the competing foreigner a break. I have been a spectator several times during Davis Cup matches here and abroad. There is no comparison between the sportsmanlike attitude of the Forest Hills crowd and foreign spectators. At Wimbledon there is, to be sure, a certain aloof politeness toward American players but at Auteuil I have witnessed vociferous demonstrations against non-French contestants that made me wonder at what moment diplomatic relations would be broken off.

This is the only country I know where unsatisfactory performers in the theater are not loudly booed. And where else but in America could the following have occurred:

Some years ago a famous English vaudeville performer came to this country with tremendous advance publicity. New York's Palace Theater was packed the day he made his debut. But his material, so popular in England, failed to click with the American audience. After his third number the actor, tears streaming down his cheeks, stepped in front of the curtain and said: "Ladies and gentlemen, I am doing my best to entertain you, but apparently you do not like what I am offering. I am sincerely sorry." That audience, the so-called hardboiled New Yorkers, touched by such manifest sincerity, cheered him and from then on his act was a triumph.

These incidents may seem unimportant but it is the trivial happenings, the spontaneous daily incidents that reveal a nation's character. And the character of America is something of which to be proud. In the maintenance of American ideals we who are naturalized have our part to play in gratitude for benefits received. We must do more than wave flags and sing *God Bless America*. We who *chose* America must remember that if the privileges we enjoy are worth living for, they are also worth dying for.

I sometimes think that we who *chose* to be Americans and had to make some effort to achieve citizenship have the greatest appreciation of the true significance of our American heritage. In my own particular circle of friends I belong to the minority group who have read the Bill of Rights, have a nodding acquaintance with the Constitution, and don't have to fake along with "Da de da da de da" when *The Star-Spangled Banner* is being sung. Born Americans have more of a take-it-for-granted attitude than the naturalized, perhaps because most of the latter become Americans to escape unhappy conditions in their native land.

On the pedestal of the Statue of Liberty are inscribed the following words written by Emma Lazarus:

> Give me your tired, your poor,
> Your huddled masses yearning to breathe free,
> The wretched refuse of your teeming shore,
> Send these, the homeless, the tempest-tossed to me,
> I lift my lamp beside the golden door.

As one of the 38,000,000 of "wretched refuse" (a rather unhappy phrase I think, Miss Lazarus) who have settled here in the past hundred years, I believe that every American should kneel daily and thank God for the privilege of living in the United States. And if this expression of gratitude applies to those *born* here it is at this fateful hour 50 times more applicable to naturalized Americans.

To me the name America symbolizes an idea and connotes a way of life. And the more I study its history the more significant becomes its genesis and the more far-reaching its destiny. It has become a trite saying that America is the land of opportunity. But it is too often forgotten that the opportunity sought by its original settlers had a spiritual, not a material, basis. This momentous fact has had an overwhelming influence in shaping the destiny of the United States. Despite temporary checks to our economic progress, America can never fail so long as we preserve a free educational system, freedom of opportunity, a jealous regard for individual rights, and a constantly lessening sense of class distinction.

This matter of class distinction has always seemed to me one of the most important factors in the preservation of American ideals, a factor which distinguishes this country from all lands where hereditary privilege or a titular aristocracy exists.

In America we have a fervent loyalty to a way of life, to a kind of society that presents definite promises to the most humble of its citizens. In this free atmosphere is an electric sparkle that spells hope for every legitimate ambition. And a minimum of class distinction is our guarantee of maximum opportunity for each individual in each generation.

*Suggestions for Study*

1. What incident impelled the author to become a citizen?
2. List several American qualities which he finds noteworthy.
3. Of what may the naturalized citizen have greater awareness than the native American?
4. What ideals does the author deem necessary for the preservation of the country?

## Is the U. S. Fit to Lead the World? [5]

### BRUCE HUTCHISON

If a Roman citizen of the fifth century A.D. could visit Washington these days he would quickly conclude that the old show was still playing, and that this is where he came in.

Superficially the parallel between the capital of the United States and the capital of the Roman Empire just before the Fall is rather terrifying— the centralized bureaucracy reeling under its own weight, the new and insoluble problems which seem to arise out of every solution, the deepening class struggle, the intoxication of luxury, even the attempt to provide bread and circuses through the Roman technique of piling up debt.

As an American professor of history reminded me, the Emperor Caligula appointed his favorite horse as Roman consul; and viewed with hindsight, the professor said, some of the appointments in Washington today are of the same order.

If Washington were the American nation, then obviously the nation would be falling to pieces; and if this nation were falling to pieces it would be impossible, in our time at least, to put the shattered fragments of the world together. But Washington is not the U. S. nation and the nation is not falling to pieces.

On the contrary, it is just beginning to find its full strength and to use it for the first time. On the use of its strength the immediate future of human civilization will largely hang.

If we look beyond the outer layer of confusion, we are witnessing in Washington today one of the most hopeful political movements in the history of our species. But it is just beginning, and it can go on the rocks before it is even fully launched.

The civilization we know, the kind of civilization in which all men may live as men and not as slaves, was invented in Greece, travelled to Rome, was blotted out there by the Empire, went underground in the

5. From *Maclean's Magazine*, LIX (1946), No. 5. Reprinted by permission of the author and *Maclean's Magazine*, Toronto, Canada.

darkness of the Middle Ages, was rediscovered in England, and immigrated to the American colonies. The home of civilization in Europe has been torn to pieces. Its leadership has been inherited by the United States. The torch first lighted in Athens is now in the hands of the American people. This is the most obvious and perhaps the most important political fact of our times.

Obvious, yes, and easy to write down as an abstract truth. But for the American people to translate the fact into dynamic reality is by far the most difficult task they have ever faced, and the third great challenge of their history as a people. They met their first challenge under Washington, when they won their independence. They met their second challenge under Lincoln, when they saved the Union in a fratricidal war. Their third challenge, which is nothing less than the moral leadership of the free world, they began to meet under Roosevelt and must now meet under Truman and his successors.

By comparison the Revolution and the Civil War were simple processes which all men could understand, and yet, complex and unique as the new task appears today, it is essentially a continuation of the first two, an attempt to complete the destiny which began when the first settlers landed in New England. It is, in short, the extension to the world at large of those truths the Founding Fathers held to be self-evident, the rights of all men to life, liberty, and the pursuit of happiness.

The chaos in Washington today, the spectacle of two wings of Government at war with one another, the effort of the President to dominate the Congress and the Congress to dominate the President, the baffling shift and change of foreign policy, the day-to-day improvisations, and the private bewilderment of men who must, in public, appear to know exactly where they are going and why—all this, in my opinion, is not, as it appears on the surface, evidence of a process of disintegration and weakness. It is evidence of new growth and strength. We are watching the most powerful nation ever devised by men writhing in an agony of construction, and not in the spasm of decay. We are watching the American people adjusting their political system, their economic system, and, above all, their inner minds to the kind of world which their own genius unwittingly played a large part in inventing.

The United States was founded by men who sought to escape the world, and from Washington's Farewell Address down to the isolationist speeches of both presidential candidates in the election of 1940 the central theory of American politics—that the United States' only essential business and paramount concern lay within its own boundaries—always triumphed over every threat to repeal it. But it is one of history's great ironies that the American people themselves, by creating the atom bomb in the year 1945, finally destroyed the theory overnight.

The sovereign question of our time is whether the opposite theory—that the world must achieve unity with freedom or be dissolved in atoms—will work. It cannot work without the leadership of the United States, which alone has the qualifications for this task, the qualifications of military power, industrial technique, and, more important, of political ideas.

It has the qualifications, but will they be used? And to what ends?

These questions are raised at a most difficult and inopportune moment. They arrive and clamor for an answer when the nation is engaged in a deep social revolution within itself, when none of the great problems emerging from the depression has been solved, when the minds of the people are inevitably concentrated on the bread-and-butter controversies at home. They come at a familiar moment, like that following the Civil War and World War I, when peace brings a sudden letdown, a human yearning for the futile dream which President Harding called normalcy. And they come at a moment when the accepted leader of the people, like Lincoln and Wilson before him, is struck down before his work is done and power is passed to lesser, untried hands.

Whether the spiritual collapse of Johnson's time, after Lincoln, and Harding's, after Wilson, is to recur, we should know before the year is out, and no people anywhere can escape the results either way. The swirling chaos of Washington is the consequence of the attempt of the American people, more by instinct than by reason, to avoid such a collapse, and this time to complete the work which history has laid upon them.

The internal convulsions in the United States, the political struggle, the class struggle, and the struggle to complete Roosevelt's New Deal, should not obscure the progress which has been made in the larger process of American leadership in the world. The responsibilities which the United States has accepted throughout the world in the last year, and almost without division, will be judged in history as the most sudden, complete, and astounding change of policy ever undertaken by a great nation in such a period.

The United States, which managed to remain largely outside the world for 170 years, has entered the world, and entered it more deeply than most Americans yet realize. That much is clear. But on what terms and for what purpose, and with what principles of conduct? Those are the great remaining questions, and the answer to them has not yet been given.

The United States can lead the free world, for a time anyway, on its own terms; and two choices are before it.

It can follow the example of other newly rich empires of the past, which entered the world only to dominate it and fatten on its resources. Or it can enter the world to serve it and save it, serving and saving itself in the process.

Let no one underestimate the strength of those Americans who would follow the first course. Isolationism in a new form, the theory of self-protection by an extension of American military power beyond the perimeter of the nation, is not dead and has powerful advocates in high places.

On the other hand, imperialism—and this kind of self-protection is nothing more than the imperialism which is condensed in other nations —has always been rejected by the American people after every brief adventure in it. Moreover, the United States is the first dominant world power in history which, because of its own resources, has no need to control or enslave any other nation, which requires no foreign territory, resources, or labor. History, in fact, has never presented before such a clear opportunity for the physically greatest world power to become also its greatest moral power.

For when we consider the principles which the United States will attempt to establish throughout the world we perceive that the political problem is far less important than the moral problem. Assuming, first, that the United States maintains its position of leadership in the world, and second, that this leadership is used for the benefit of the world and not to establish an American empire of the old sort, there still remains the question of American morality. This will finally overshadow every other question, because the paramount issue of humanity in our time is a moral and not a political or economic issue.

The issue is, simply, whether men can develop a moral sense strong enough to control the weapons which they have invented. Their civilization will survive or perish as this issue is decided. Since the American people were the chief developers of these weapons and the complex industrial processes which make them possible, and as the United States is for the present the most powerful nation in the world and the accepted leader of the free world, we must examine primarily the morality of the American people.

What, in brief, does American civilization actually stand for in the lives of ordinary men?

You might have answered that question without hesitation when the Republic was founded. It stood, over and above all purely economic and selfish ambitions, for the freedom of individual man under God. Its freedom and its whole concept of government were built on the cardinal assumption that "all men are created equal, that they are endowed by their Creator with certain unalienable Rights." Democracy in England came out of the religious beliefs of the Puritan Revolution, and it was on those beliefs that it was established in the United States. The principles of American democracy, as it began, were inseparable from a deep religious conviction, from a faith in God, and from an individual life of virtue.

The most dangerous thing that has happened to American life in the last several generations, and probably the most profound thing, is the attack on these original ideals. Life and liberty so far remain as sacred in the United States as when they were written into the Declaration, or at least as safe as it is practical to expect at this moment of history. But the pursuit of happiness has been distorted beyond the recognition of the Founding Fathers.

The American people are the first who have ever had the chance of general prosperity, of ample goods for everybody. In the past such an opportunity has been confined to a few small areas of the world and to a few privileged classes which enslaved the remainder of the population. The American people possessed half a continent, replete with nearly all the essential resources, at the moment when invention made it possible to convert these resources into goods. By this unique combination they have built the highest standard of living ever known, and this they have called the pursuit of happiness.

The Founding Fathers, who coined this phrase, would not recognize it in its modern interpretation, for the highest standard of living has not produced the highest standard of happiness. Many poorer nations are far happier; and by all the indices of American life—by its literature, by its crime, by its divorce rate and the breakdown of home life, by its desperate efforts to escape the reality of its life through a huge and shallow industry of entertainment, by the restlessness and discontent which sends it hurtling over its highways away from home—we can see that the pursuit of happiness has not succeeded.

Happiness, it is platitudinous but still true to say, comes from within, and the American people are far from attaining it—much farther, I think, than the Canadian people or the relatively poor people of Britain. The reason, surely, is that the central idea which made the nation, the deep religious belief and inner faith, has been wearing thin. Instead of seeking happiness within, the American people have been dazzled and almost overwhelmed by their physical success, by their ability to create, as no one before them, the paraphernalia of outer happiness, the glittering, thin satisfactions of unexampled luxury, which threaten to drug them.

The dynamism which built a nation out of a few struggling farmers and backwoodsmen was not a belief in things but in men. Today the chief drive of American life and politics is to create more things in the belief that they will create better men. The philosophy, preached by every political party, every successful politician, by business and by labor, holds that if enough goods are produced and distributed all the problems of human life will be cured. The national income figure, of which the early Americans had never heard, is being glorified into the index of national character, the supreme measurement of success. As every man knows, by the test of his own life, it is a false index and a totally inaccurate measurement.

At the moment there is no cessation of this futile pursuit. Where their ancestors sought happiness in their own souls, happiness is now sought in two cars in every garage. The search for truth becomes for millions a search for a new kind of bathtub, rather like the one Caligula used in Rome just before the unwashed barbarians arrived. The gods currently worshipped closely resemble the Roman deities, which were then created by the Senate and are now created by Hollywood.

Is this to be the philosophy, the habit of thought, and way of life which America is going to export to the world? Are the great ideals of American life to be merely incidentals, shipped as an afterthought with cargoes of machinery and gadgets?

Such exports have been already and have penetrated many parts of the world, and nowhere more than Canada. We, more than any other people, because we are so close to the source of supply, have been affected by the same theories and daily habits. The rest of the world is hungry for them, and the American standard of living appears to be humanity's ideal of salvation, the answer to every riddle, the secret to life everlasting.

There is no final answer to anything here. The standard of living is only the first beginning of a true standard of life. Prosperity is useful only if it creates a climate in which the happiness of the mind and spirit can grow, but generally in all past civilizations this happiness has withered just about the time prosperity began to appear.

The riddle of American civilization, therefore, is not to be found in the current controversies of politics, either domestic or international. It lies in the life of the ordinary American. The riddle is whether the first people who ever have had the chance of almost unlimited wealth can control and use it for happiness and the growth of the mind, or whether, like so many lesser peoples in the past, they will be corrupted and ruined by it.

In short, can the United States stand prosperity?

This is no longer an American question. It is a universal question, because the techniques and the mental habits of America are now spreading throughout the world and because the free world cannot survive without American leadership. As was said earlier in this report from Washington, the frenzy and convulsion there are the struggle of the American people to catch up with history and take their destined part in the business of the world. But when this struggle has succeeded, as I believe it will certainly succeed, the other and deeper problem will remain.

If, in this American century, a tolerable and viable world civilization is to be built for the first time, if civilization as we know it is to continue at all, then it will have to be built on the original ideals of Americans as inherited from Britain and not on the ideals of mere abundance which threaten to become dominant. The world can have prosperity and a decent physical life for all people if it has the brains to use and share its resources, but this alone will give it neither permanent prosperity nor permanent peace. Civilization cannot be built to last on the theory of two cars in every garage, for such a civilization will be no better than a Hollywood scenic set with the glitter of chorus girls in front of it and nothing behind it.

The final question which remains in your mind as you watch the fabulous spectacle of Washington is not whether the American people can solve the political and economic problems of the world but whether they can solve the problem of their own life, the problem of maintaining the old integrity of that life against the disease of luxury which has invariably sapped and destroyed all groups of men who enjoyed luxury in the long past.

If this problem is not met and solved, all the political and economic solutions will finally collapse. We can put the question in old and familiar terms—and no language has ever been more true—by asking how it will benefit America, or any of us, if it gains the whole world and loses its own soul.

We shall find no answer in Washington. We shall find it in the millions of unknown homes of the United States, among the obscure and forgotten men and women who make up this new and extraordinary experiment in human community and who, today, almost without realizing it, are the hope of the world. Knowing them, I think it is still a sound and reasonable hope. But we must be patient, and in observing the physical miracles wrought by this people, the political and economic struggle, we must never lose sight of the deeper process which is at work beneath them, a process in which we are all intimately involved, none so deeply as we ourselves in Canada.

*Suggestions for Study*

1. Does the author believe that appearances of chaos in Washington are a true indication of the condition of the United States?

2. Now that America has entered into world affairs, what choice confronts it? What paramount issue faces not just Americans but all mankind? Why must America concern itself especially with this issue?

3. What did American civilization once mean for the common man? What seems to have been substituted in modern times for these original ideals? With their economic wealth have Americans become happier than the rest of the world? How is this a reflection of their ideals? How is the American attitude affecting the rest of the world?

4. On what does America's hope for the future rest? Does the author view the future hopefully?

5. Choose any well-written paragraph in the article, and study it closely for matters of style—variety, emphasis, and the like.

6. Define the following words from the article: platitudinous, dynamism, imperialism, cardinal, fratricidal, viable.

## *Background for Peace* [6]

Years ago Wisconsin's stubby, pragmatic *bon vivant,* Philosopher Max Otto, stood on the bank of the upper Mississippi one Sunday sunset to ask himself again what force it was that prevented the technology of the modern world from being used to the greater happiness of the plain man. Afternoon darkened into evening; the shining silver of the river blurred in the darkness; lights began to appear in the village.

Modern man's strength is greater than his knowledge or his will, thought this aging Midwestern professor. "The vast economic material body of the world lacks a mind to match it, and is not animated by a commensurate moral spirit. This backwardness is the tragic inadequacy of our time. It is the basic problem which the agencies of aspiration and intelligence have to solve."

Each American had now to develop a spirit comparable to his achievements, to recreate the spirit that had made his achievements possible. To preserve and strengthen his precarious new position in the world, he had to understand what had brought him to that position, what were the spiritual springs that made him an American. Whether he knew it or not, or liked his new role, each dweller in the United States had become a leading citizen of the world and one on whose conduct the hopes of the world rested.

The world had changed in its feeling about the United States. Once

6. From *Time,* March 22, 1943. Copyright Time Inc., 1943. Reprinted by permission of *Time.*

American technology was a storehouse of learning that Europe hired, as United States engineers built dams and railroads in Russia, automobiles and cracking plants in Germany, developed oil in England, piped the fields of Rumania. But through the years of war and prewar depression the rest of the world changed in its view of what it wanted from the United States. It no longer wanted only the wealth that United States industry could produce. It no longer wanted American builders only to imitate on foreign soil the kind of machinery that was indigenous to the United States. It wanted the essential secret of United States enterprise, the quality within it that brought forth on the continent a new nation, a new birth of liberty, and with them a new wealth beyond the richest visions of the old. Thus the 132,000,000 Americans, honest and dishonest, good, bad, and humanly both, had become the only people of the earth's two billion who could save the hopes of the world in the simple struggle to save their own.

The United States was unchanged. Isolationists, interventionists, Democrats, New Dealers, Republicans, keeping the same beliefs, the same politics, the same internal squabbles, . . . the same newspapers, the same columnists, radio commentators, movie stars, had unwittingly grown in stature as the earth grew smaller. The United States was still the land of plenty: it was the land of faith that government of the people, by the people, and for the people should never perish from the earth. It was the land where millions sang without selfconsciousness that their eyes had seen the glory of the coming of the Lord. It was the land where all men are created equal and endowed by their Creator with the inalienable rights of life, liberty, and the pursuit of happiness. It was the land where farmers exchanged notions on the best ways to cultivate crops and where manufacturers visited each other's plants to learn the latest production wrinkles. It was the land where its most bitterly hated politician had truly stated the creed of democratic government: "With malice toward none, with charity for all, with firmness in the right as God gives us to see the right. . . ."

Out of range of the headlines, like reconnaissance planes soaring high above anti-aircraft guns, the philosophers and religious teachers struggled with the task of organizing these underlying concepts so that the modern mind and modern morality might equal the modern world's physical strength.

*How could the United States, based on a belief in equality, accept its power without aggressively forcing its faith on others?* "Treat human beings according to what they may become," said Cleveland-born philosopher William Ernest Hocking, "with the best available aid, and our own."

*What religion could man worship to fill the aching heart that all the glory of the good material things of life had left empty?* "There is no sure shield against the tyranny of this ruinous passion for possession," said Britain's gentle, eloquent, 77-year-old teacher W. Macniele Dixon, "save a transference of our affections from possession to admiration, from immoderate craving for wealth and power to an intense longing for beauty and excellence."

*How could man rediscover this religion?* "Democracy must go down to the tomb and arise," said Kansas' William Allen White. "Men . . . slowly are giving up old ideas, old prejudices, slowly are coming to the realization that it is necessary in politics, in society, in economic organization, to preserve the dignity of man, the dignity of all men. . . . This belief in the dignity of man as an individual was a latent faith in men's hearts even while they basked in a civilization they did not intelligently appreciate or quite believe in—a faith that in due time should remake the world. . . .

"Regeneration is no theological formula. It is a function of spiritual progress—a part of the evolutionary spiritual growth of the race. That repentance is needed now for rebirth . . . to lessen its load of sin. Sin is only unneighborly conduct. Democracy's rebirth will be hard, most ungodly hard. But enslavement would be harder. We have no other alternative. We must conquer by heroic self-denial or be conquered by ruthless force. World democracy, rich and proud and pharisaical, is the camel before the gate of the needle's eye. He must go through. He must bend low, even to the dust. He must slip off his load and his proud trappings of purse and power. To be saved for 'a new Heaven and a new Earth' the diverse people of democratic civilization must think in new terms—new terms as citizens, new terms as nations, new terms as a modern, remade world, in a new day and time."

Democracy is going down to the tomb. The need for world fellowship, bred in terror, is furnishing a binder to hold men together. The belief in the dignity of man, of all men, is in itself a primary protection against the perfidies of the war of nerves, a check against the regimentation of domestic life, a guarantee against life's waste in war. It is the bond between the drawings of the engineer and the unformed hope of the man in the street; it is the force that overcomes the bickerings of allies, the conflicts of national prestige; it is the measure of United States responsibility for shaping the future. It is inescapable. Says Russell Davenport: "Cain never received an answer to his outraged question, 'Am I my brother's keeper?' But the answer is: 'You are.'"

The world that carried the hopes and the work of millions as it wheeled in its circle of the sun carried the burden of war and the misery that flowed from its worship of false gods. From Pearl Harbor to Warsaw the life of the times whispered the agony of that worship. If the new terms of the new world were not to be wild echoes of the past or the wild grasping for a new turbulence, they could begin with the truth. If democracy reborn is based on belief in the dignity of man, that dignity carries with it the positive affirmation that all men are brothers and that their death and their sinful unneighborliness is a part of the denial of their brotherhood. If the unharnessed power of the Yangtze flowing for thousands of years past the unseeing Chinese can light the lamps of China, the power of an equally familiar but unseen idea can provide the new terms of the remade world.

To have human value, to get down to the ordinary business of ordinary life, to fill the routines of plowing and planting and the humdrum tasks of every day with a spirit that will make them conscious efforts to create a better destiny, the ideas must result in programs, and the programs must be fulfilled by living, sweating, striving, imperfect, and hopeful people. The ideas and ideals strong enough to rebuild the old world and remake the new cannot be the special province of planners and experts. They must be general enough to cross frontiers and local enough to give meaning to the village carpenter's place in the world. . . .

The world that carried war around the sun carried the millions of minds that must serve as the connective tissue between the thoughts of the philosophers, the vast practical programs and the toilers who alone could bring them about. Through good weather and bad, in sickness, defeat, in agony of spirit, and against the dull weight of ignorance and fear, the soul of each man must be nourished to undertake of his own free will works which in their total are bigger than the slave-built wall of China and in their daily demands as warming as the building of a home. Coercion cannot order the materials; bombast cannot inspire the efforts; the fear of death cannot release the imagination's shortcuts or bring about the emotions' quick ability to generate for a time their superhuman strength.

If some stimulus is to be broadly effective, then the ideal of the coming human fraternity, "the truth that the world, like the human self, has its own unity in a living purpose," cannot reside only in the distant words of philosophers. Such truths and ideals must be the equipment of millions of humble leaders close to the task. Americans are too close to their destiny to rely only on a few far-away leaders. They must find near at hand those who can formulate the causes, interpret principle in definite acts, nourish their spirit by giving them tasks to work on in the direction of their hopes.

The strength of America, thus released, would fulfill the moral purpose of its founders, or the institutions they created would end. The new world after the war still needed its Founding Fathers: businessmen, teachers, engineers, soldiers, had become teachers and builders to the world. The responsibilities the new world had placed upon Americans could be tasks grudgingly assumed or an adventure cheerfully undertaken. In the crucial importance of that task they could say, "Let us raise a standard to which the wise and honest can repair," certain again that the wise and honest were numbered in the millions throughout the spinning earth.

And in that adventure, for the first time in 100 years, Americans could repeat, in the words of their poet:

> *Passage to more than India!* . . .
> *Away O soul!* . . .
> *Sail forth—steer for the deep waters only.*

### Suggestions for Study

1. State in your own words the "tragic inadequacy" of our times, as expressed by Professor Otto.

2. What does the rest of the world now seek from America in addition to our secrets of machine design, production, and the like?

3. Summarize in a few sentences the ideals for human action stated by philosophers Hocking, Dixon, and White. Before beginning to write, however, be sure that you understand their fundamental agreement of opinion.

4. Although such ideals are formulated by philosophers, who must put them into practice?

5. What special responsibility has been placed upon Americans? What crucial choice must they make?

6. State the thesis of this article.

7. Study the sentence variety in paragraphs three and four, and be prepared to explain the devices used by the author to secure his effect. Do loose or periodic sentences predominate in paragraph three?

What device is used in paragraph five to provide coherence and emphasis? From this paragraph select any five words which have a particularly strong and favorable connotation for Americans.

Make a thorough study of any paragraph in the article for stylistic devices and diction.

8. Define the following words from the article: animated, commensurate, precarious, pragmatic, *bon vivant,* regeneration, pharisaical, perfidies.

# Credo [7]

## THOMAS WOLFE

I believe that we are lost here in America, but I believe we shall be found. And this belief, which mounts now to the catharsis of knowledge and conviction, is for me—and I think for all of us—not only our own hope, but America's everlasting, living dream. I think the life which we have fashioned in America, and which has fashioned us—the forms we made, the cells that grew, the honeycomb that was created—was self-destructive in its nature, and must be destroyed. I think these forms are dying, and must die, just as I know that America and the people in it are deathless, undiscovered, and immortal, and must live.

I think the true discovery of America is before us. I think the true fulfillment of our spirit, of our people, of our mighty and immortal land, is yet to come. I think the true discovery of our own democracy is still before us. And I think that all these things are certain as the morning, as inevitable as noon. I think I speak for most men living when I say that our America is Here, is Now, and beckons on before us, and that this glorious assurance is not only our living hope, but our dream to be accomplished.

I think the enemy is here before us, too. But I think we know the forms and faces of the enemy, and in the knowledge that we know him, and shall meet him, and eventually must conquer him is also our living hope. I think the enemy is here before us with a thousand faces, but I think we know that all his faces wear one mask. I think the enemy is single selfishness and compulsive greed. I think the enemy is blind, but has the brutal power of his blind grab. I do not think the enemy was born yesterday, or that he grew to manhood forty years ago, or that he suffered sickness and collapse in 1929, or that we began without the enemy, and that our vision faltered, that we lost the way, and suddenly were in his camp. I think the enemy is old as Time, and evil as Hell, and that he has been here with us from the beginning. I think he stole our earth from us, destroyed our wealth, and ravaged and despoiled our land. I think he took our people and enslaved them, that he polluted the fountains of our life, took unto himself the rarest treasures of our possession, took our bread and left us with a crust, and, not content, for the nature of the enemy is insatiate— tried finally to take from us the crust.

I think the enemy comes to us with the face of innocence and says to us: "I am your friend."

7. From *You Can't Go Home Again,* by Thomas Wolfe (copyright, 1940). Reprinted by permission of Harper & Brothers, the publishers.

I think the enemy deceives us with false words and lying phrases, saying:

"See, I am one of you—I am one of your children, your son, your brother, and your friend. Behold how sleek and fat I have become—and all because I am just one of you, and your friend. Behold how rich and powerful I am—and all because I am one of you—shaped in your way of life, of thinking, of accomplishment. What I am, I am because I am one of you, your humble brother and your friend. Behold," cries Enemy, "the man I am, the man I have become, the thing I have accomplished—and reflect. Will you destroy this thing? I assure you that it is the most precious thing you have. It is yourselves, the projection of each of you, the triumph of your individual lives, the thing that is rooted in your blood, and native to your stock, and inherent in the traditions of America. It is the thing that all of you may hope to be," says Enemy, "for"—humbly— "am I not just one of you? Am I not just your brother and your son? Am I not the living image of what each of you may hope to be, would wish to be, would desire for his own son? Would you destroy this glorious incarnation of your own heroic self? If you do, then," says Enemy, "you destroy yourselves—you kill the thing that is most gloriously American, and in so killing, kill yourselves."

He lies! And now we know he lies! He is not gloriously, or in any other way, ourselves. He is not our friend, our son, our brother. And he is not American! For, although he has a thousand familiar and convenient faces, his own true face is old as Hell.

Look about you and see what he has done.

### Suggestions for Study

1. Does Thomas Wolfe believe in a static America, content with its customs and institutions, or a dynamic America, willing and able to change to meet the future? Does he have faith in our people?

2. What true discovery does he envision lying ahead of us and forming our dream of the future?

3. What is our arch enemy? What is meant by its appearing before us "with a thousand faces"?

4. Were the Founding Fathers confronted by the enemy, or is it of modern origin?

5. What guise does it assume in deceiving us? What ideal of life does it demand that we follow blindly? What more fitting ideal does Wolfe suggest we follow?

6. Study the author's style with particular attention to his use of loose and periodic sentences and of parallelism.

7. Define the following words from the selection: catharsis, compulsive, insatiate, sleek, incarnation.

*Suggestions for Writing*

1. The preceding selections all deal with the attitudes of various writers towards the United States. All of them except Lord Tweedsmuir's and Wolfe's articles were written during or after World War II, and these were written just as the war began in Europe. One is by an Englishman, one by a Canadian, one by an Australian who became a citizen of the United States, and two are by Americans. Now that some time has elapsed since the close of the war, write a paper in which you discuss what views in the various articles are justified at this time; or write a paper in which you consider the shades of difference indicated in the articles towards America.

2. Write a paper commenting upon Clemenceau's statement that "America is the only nation in history which miraculously has gone directly from barbarism to degeneration without the usual interval of civilization."

3. Write an essay showing the fundamental likeness of Mr. Hutchison's reasoning to that of philosophers Otto, Hocking, Dixon, and White as quoted in "Background for Peace."

4. Discuss what favorable characteristics you have observed in the American people as a whole. If you have been in another country or have known well a number of people from another country, see if you can write a pleasing paper on the country or the more favorable characteristics of the people.

5. Consider the American people as a whole from another critical position. What less desirable traits of the American people have you observed? What seems to cause these inadequacies? Do our peoples now lack some of those ideals which Mr. Hutchison mentioned as characteristic of the common folk of Revolutionary times?

6. From your reading of these selections you have encountered some of the problems which America is facing. Others you have thought about yourself. Write a paper presenting an analysis of one of these major problems with which the country is confronted.

# III

# THE PARAGRAPH

## A. Definition

THE paragraph is used in writing or printing to mark transitions in thought or to designate steps in the development of an idea so that a reader may follow more easily and clearly what an author is saying. Except for certain special uses to be noted later, a paragraph may be defined as a unit of the whole composition in which one single, main idea is developed by means of supporting details. Although it is in itself a complete, logical unit of thought, it is also part of the total idea as expressed in the whole composition. Paragraphs may thus be likened to the innings of a baseball game: each inning is a unit in itself, with its own procedures, rules, and limits; yet each bears a distinct relation to the other innings and is a part of the entire game. A paragraph, likewise, has it own characteristics, structure, and limits; yet it has a close relation to neighboring paragraphs and is a logical element of the whole composition.

**Length.** The paragraph is variable in length. It may range from a few words to hundreds of words, depending on the effect desired and on the writer's skill. The paragraphs in the body of a student's paper should contain, perhaps, from seventy to a hundred words, but that is only a rough estimate. If they are but two or three sentences in length, they are probably too choppy; if they are several hundred words in length, they probably contain too much material and should be divided into smaller units. The theory is that if the paragraphs are too choppy, the reader has difficulty in grasping the main idea amid so many small units. If they are too long, he cannot readily find the key ideas. But this simple theory is complicated by the kind of reader for whom the composition is intended. An experienced reader, thoroughly at home among books, can deal with a long paragraph, but an inexperienced reader or one with a low level of intelligence can cope with small units only.

78 **The Topic Sentence.** *Almost all good paragraphs are built around a central idea,* which sometimes is not directly stated but which more often appears in what is known as the topic sentence. A paragraph is then fundamentally a main idea amplified by supporting details. Writing a paragraph is really not much different from conducting a conversation. Talking over a baseball game, for example, a player might remark, "We sure lost that game because of the umpires." That would be his topic sentence. He would then elaborate with the supporting detail. "When Joe hit that infield ball and was called out at first for the third out, we were robbed. Mike was across the plate with the tying run." His friends would chime in with additional instances to explain the original statement. A paragraph would thereby be constructed verbally. If the game were reported in the papers, the incident might appear as follows:

> The real cause of losing the game was the poor umpiring. In the third inning, with Mike Jones on third and two out, Haines hit an infield ball which he seemingly beat out for a hit. He was, however, called out, and although Jones crossed the plate with the tying run, the tally did not count. Again in the ninth inning Thomas hit a terrific line drive over the left-field fence which was called foul, even though it was several feet in fair territory. Such poor umpiring is a disgrace to the league and an unfair handicap to the players.

In this manner the paragraph is the expansion of one idea.

There is no rigid rule about where in a paragraph to put the topic sentence. Ordinarily it is the first, second, or third sentence. A reader accordingly knows from the beginning what a paragraph concerns and is better able to follow the development of the ideas. In the following paragraphs, the topic sentence comes at the beginning: in the first selection, it opens the paragraph; in the second, it comes as the second sentence:

> The student who repairs to them sees in the list of classes and of professors a fair picture of the world of knowledge. Whatever he needs to know there is some one ready to teach him, some one competent to discipline him in the way of learning; whatever his special bent, let him but be able and diligent, and in due time he shall find distinction and a career. Among his professors, he sees men whose names are known and revered throughout the civilized world; and their living example infects him with a noble ambition, and a love for the spirit of work.—T. H. Huxley, "A Liberal Education."

> Choose your hypothesis; I have chosen mine. I can find no warranty for believing in the distinct creation of a score of successive species of crocodiles in the course of countless ages of time. Science gives no countenance to such a wild fancy; nor can even the perverse ingenuity of a commentator pretend to discover this sense, in the simple words in which the writer of Genesis records the proceedings of the fifth and sixth days of the Creation.—T. H. Huxley, "On a Piece of Chalk."

Many times, however, an author who is sure that his readers follow him, places his topic sentence at the end of the paragraph. This is sometimes an advantage, since he can thus prepare a reader to accept a startling idea, or approach the main idea gradually in order to put emphasis upon it, or provide a reader with facts necessary to understand the topic idea. The following paragraph is an example of this method:

> It was apparently his principal endeavor to avoid all harshness and severity of diction; he is therefore sometimes verbose in his transitions and connections, and sometimes descends too much to the language of conversation; yet if his language had been less idiomatical, it might have lost somewhat of its genuine Anglicism. What he attempted, he performed; he is never feeble, and he did not wish to be energetic; he is never rapid, and he never stagnates. His sentences have neither studied amplitude, nor affected brevity; his periods, though not diligently rounded, are voluble and easy. Whoever wishes to attain an English style, familiar but not coarse, and elegant but not ostentatious, must give his days and nights to the volumes of Addison.—Samuel Johnson, "The Life of Addison."

When special emphasis is required, an author sometimes places the topic sentence at both the beginning and the end of the paragraph. The following paragraph gains increased emphasis by the use of "genteel" in the opening lines and of "vulgar" in the last line:

But whatever we might do or leave undone, we were not genteel, and it was uncomfortable to be continually reminded that, though we should boast that we were the Great West till we were black in the face, it did not bring us an inch nearer to the world's West-End. That sacred enclosure of respectability was tabooed to us. The Holy Alliance did not inscribe us on its visiting list. The Old World of wigs and orders and liveries would shop with us, but we must ring at the area-bell, and not venture to awaken the more august clamors of the knocker. Our manners, it must be granted, had none of those graces that stamp the caste of Vere de Vere, in whatever museum of British antiquities they may be hidden. In short, we were vulgar.—J. R. Lowell, "On a Certain Condescension in Foreigners."

**78a**  A general rule, however, is to place the topic sentence where it will be most readily noted, so that the reader can understand the paragraph quickly and easily.

**Transitional and Narrative Paragraphs.** To the preceding remarks, one must add two exceptions: the *transitional paragraph* and the *narrative paragraph*. Each of these has its own particular purpose and hence its own particular structure. The transitional paragraph is intended to make a bridge between large sections of a composition. It enables a reader to note when a writer leaves one point and begins consideration of the next. The following paragraph forms a transition in Edmund Burke's *Speech on Conciliation with America:*

These, Sir, are my reasons for not entertaining that high opinion of untried force by which many gentlemen, for whose sentiments in other particulars I have great respect, seem to be so greatly captivated. But there is still behind a third consideration concerning this object, which serves to determine my opinion on the sort of policy which ought to be pursued in the management of America, even more than its population and its commerce—I mean its *temper and character.*

The narrative paragraph also has a specific purpose: to carry forward a story. Therefore it cannot be governed by our already formulated principle of a topic sentence supported by explanation or proof. The narrative moves forward progressively, and therefore the paragraphs in it must aid that movement. The use of long paragraphs, that is, the grouping of material into large units, aids the flow of a story; the use of short paragraphs puts emphasis upon bits, such as exciting action or vivid description or sharp dialogue. The writer therefore judges the length of a paragraph by the purpose which he has in mind. Observe how the following long paragraph forwards the action:

In about six weeks from the time when the *Pilgrim* sailed, we had all the hides which she left us cured and stowed away; and having cleared up the ground and emptied the vats, and set everything in order, had nothing more to do, until she should come down again, but to supply ourselves with wood. Instead of going twice a week for this purpose, we determined to give one whole week to getting wood, and then we should have enough to last us half through the summer. Accordingly we started off every morning, after an early breakfast, with our hatchets in hand, and cut wood until the sun was over the point—which was our mark for noon, as there was not a watch on the beach—and then came back to dinner, and after dinner started off again with our hand-cart and ropes, and carted and "backed" it down until sunset. This we kept up for a week, until we had collected several cords—enough to last us for six or eight weeks—when we "knocked off" altogether, much to my joy; for, though I liked straying in the woods and cutting very well, yet the backing the wood for so great a distance, over an uneven country, was, without exception, the hardest work I had ever done. I usually had to kneel down, and contrive to heave the load, which was well strapped together, upon my back, and then rise up and start off with it, up the hills and down the vales, sometimes through thickets—the rough points sticking into the skin and tearing the clothes, so that at the end of the week I had hardly a whole shirt to my back.—Dana, *Two Years before the Mast.*

In the following selection the short paragraphs emphasize those details which the author desires to stand out:

The sun was nearly setting, and Gerard, who had now for some time been hoping in vain to find an inn by the way, was very ill at ease. To make matters worse, black clouds gathered over the sky.

Gerard quickened his pace almost to a run.

It was in vain: down came the rain in torrents, drenched the bewildered traveler, and seemed to extinguish the very sun; for his rays already fading could not cope with this new assailant. Gerard trudged on, dark and wet and in an unknown region. "Fool! to leave Margaret," said he.

Presently the darkness thickened.

He was entering a great wood. Huge branches shot across the narrow road, and the benighted stranger groped his way in what seemed an interminable and inky cave with a rugged floor, on which he stumbled and stumbled as he went.

On, and on, and on, with shivering limbs, and empty stomach, and fainting heart, till the wolves rose from their lairs and bayed all round the wood.

His hair bristled; but he grasped his cudgel, and prepared to sell his life dear.

There was no wind; and his excited ear heard light feet patter at times over the newly fallen leaves, and low branches rustled with creatures gliding swiftly past them.—Reade, *The Cloister and the Hearth.*

A special use of the paragraph is in writing dialogue. Here the rule is to make a separate paragraph of each speech and the directive element or explanatory matter that goes with it, as in the following example:

"Kate," said Eli, "fear not; Richart and I will give him glamour for glamour. We will write him a letter, and send it to Rome by a sure hand with money, and bid him home on the instant."

Cornelis and Sybrandt exchanged a gloomy look.

"Ah, good father! And meantime?"

"Well, meantime?"

"Dear father, dear mother, what can we do to pleasure the absent, but be kind to his poor lass; and her own trouble afore her?"

"'Tis well!' said Eli; "but I am older than thou." Then he turned gravely to Margaret: "Wilt answer me a question, my pretty mistress?"

"If I may, sir," faltered Margaret.

"What are these marriage lines Gerard speaks of in the letter?"

"Our marriage lines, sir. His and mine. Know you not we are betrothed?"

"Before witnesses?"

"Ay, sure. My poor father and Martin Wittenhaagen."

"This is the first I ever heard of it. How came they in his hands? They should be in yours."

"Alas, sir, the more is my grief; but I ne'er doubted him: and he said it was a comfort to him to have them in his bosom."

"Y'are a very foolish lass."—Reade, *The Cloister and the Hearth*.

An exception to the foregoing is found when the quotation is relatively unimportant or through its brevity is contained within another sentence: "I rushed up the stairs and called out, 'Hello! Who's there?' as I flung open the door and burst into the room."

For instructions on the punctuation of the narrative paragraph, see p. 279.

## B. Unity, Coherence, and Emphasis

**Unity.** Whenever a whole composition or a paragraph follows but one progression of thought, which it expands fully and completely to the reader's satisfaction, it is said to have unity. But whenever it rambles from the subject, it violates this principle. *Thus one observes the unity of a paragraph by keeping strictly to the topic idea.* All ideas, no matter how attractive in themselves, which do not develop the topic idea directly are withheld. By such restraint the unity of the whole composition is also assured. It follows that if each paragraph develops but one idea, and if each topic sentence pertains directly to the main idea of the whole composition, unity of the whole will be attained.

**79**

A comparison of the following selections will illustrate what is meant by a lack of unity in a paragraph:

The novel *Mr. Midshipman Easy* was written by Captain Marryat. It is one of the best sea stories of the nineteenth century. Jack Easy, son of a crackbrained philosopher, went to sea on the vessels of the British navy, in the service of which he landed in a thousand scrapes. The atmosphere and the way in which the story is told are reminiscent of the novels by Smollett, which were written in the previous century. Smollett was one of a group of four—Fielding, Richardson, and Sterne were the others—who were responsible for giving the novel a strong start in English literature. Fielding was especially successful in handling the novel, for the plot of his famous work *Tom Jones* is often referred to as one of the finest plots ever created.

Smollett was one of the group of four—Fielding, Richardson, and Sterne were the others—who were responsible for giving the novel a great impetus in English literature. Before their time, to be sure, the novel had been in existence. In Elizabethan times, for example, Lyly wrote his *Euphues,* Lodge his *Rosalynde,* and Sidney his *Arcadia,* each of which featured a plot. In the seventeenth century Bunyan made his religious allegory, *Pilgrim's Progress,* in narrative form. Defoe in the early eighteenth century wrote exciting stories of adventure in *Robinson Crusoe* and many other novels, and of course Swift's severe satire, *Gulliver's Travels,* is a good story. But Smollett and his fellows in the mid-eighteenth century were the first to bring the English novel to full flower with a careful balancing of story and character.

The first of these two paragraphs obviously violates unity by beginning with an account of Marryat's novel, shifting in the middle to a discussion of Smollett, and ending by praising Fielding. Three unrelated ideas are bound into one paragraph. The second paragraph, on the other hand, uses numerous details to support but one proposition, the contribution of Smollett and three other novelists to English literature. It expands one idea without rambling and therefore offers a good example of paragraph unity.

**80** **Coherence.** *A writer must also make his paragraphs coherent—that is, arrange his ideas in a clear, logical order.* He must avoid jumps in thought and gaps between sentences. If inexperienced, he might begin a paper thus: "The rain was falling fast outside. Tom was reading the latest novel. He knew that if he did not get downtown soon, he would miss his appointment." But the ideas are so widely separated here that a reader must fill in the gaps for himself in order to fashion a continuous narrative.

Such weak writing may be avoided in several ways. The first is to present the ideas in a logical order. Perhaps the best device by which to secure such unity and coherence is the outline. Imagine for a moment that you are writing a report on how to make a workable budget plan for the family. As an automobile is usually a large item of expense in the average family, you decide that at least one paragraph of the report should be devoted to the place of the automobile in the budget plan. Hence for one paragraph your topic sentence might be: "It is advisable to carry an account book in the dash compartment of your automobile." You may then expand this suggestion by indicating the best method for keeping such an account. The little outline for your paragraph might develop into the following form:

1. It is advisable to carry an account book in the dash compartment of your automobile.
   a. To record gas expenditure
      (1) The date of purchase
      (2) The amount of gas purchased
      (3) The cost
      (4) The mileage on the car at the time of the purchase
   b. To record oil and other lubrication expenditures
      (1) The date of purchase
      (2) The amount purchased
      (3) The cost
      (4) The mileage on the car
   c. To record miscellaneous expenditures
      (1) Insurance costs
      (2) Tires
      (3) Automobile club fees
      (4) Repairs

Your paragraph could then be put together very quickly somewhat as follows:

It is well to assist your keeping of an accurate budget by carrying an account book in the dash compartment of your automobile. There each item of cost for your automobile can be listed at the time that the expenditure is made. In one column of the book you can place the amount spent for gas, noting for your convenience such details as the date of the entry, the amount of gas purchased, its cost, and the mileage recorded on the speedometer at the time of the purchase. Likewise in another column may well be kept the expenditures for oil and other lubricants, with again a listing of the date of purchase, the amount, the cost, and the mileage on the car. In a third column can be put the miscellaneous expenditures, such as those for insurance, tires, automobile club fees, and repairs. In this way you will be able to compute easily at the end of each month the operating cost of your automobile and be able to make allowances for that cost in your budget.

It is apparent that such an outline keeps one to his topic sentence and prevents him from discussing any subject but the pertinent one. Of course, an outline as elaborate as this is rarely written out for one paragraph by an experienced writer, for he has trained himself to set up an equally orderly scheme in his own mind; but an inexperienced writer may well use such a method.

Here are a few other examples to illustrate further what is meant by the skeleton outline for the paragraph:

1. In buying a summer suit, look for certain specific qualities.
   a. Coolness
   b. The quality of the tailoring
   c. The ability to hold a press
   d. The suitability of the color

2. The new textbook is more attractive in appearance than the old one.
   a. The cover design is striking.
   b. The paper is of a high quality.
   c. The margins are wide.
   d. The type is large and clear.
   e. The illustrations are beautifully executed.

3. Shakespeare perhaps gained much from both his parents.
   a. From his father
      (1) The love of a good jest
      (2) An interest in practical affairs
      (3) A desire for landed property
   b. From his mother
      (1) A gentle nature
      (2) A love of the manners and traditions of the past
      (3) A tolerance towards Catholics

Even after the writer has organized his ideas in a logical manner, he will find that certain gaps remain which need filling to promote ease and coherence. Several specific devices are used to close such gaps. First are transitional words and expressions, which link closely associated ideas. The following list classifies a few of these to show their use in the sentence:

To carry forward the same progression of thought from one sentence to the next:
   *also, besides, especially, finally, for example, furthermore, in addition, indeed, in fact, in other words, likewise, moreover, namely, next, similarly, that is, then.*
To show how one statement is the result of the preceding statement:
   *accordingly, as a result, consequently, for this reason, hence, inevitably, so, therefore, thus.*
To present a contrast between ideas:
   *however, nevertheless, on the contrary, on the other hand, still, yet.*

To illustrate the value of transitional words, the following paragraph is shown first without such words, then with them. Note in the first how disconnected the ideas seem, but in the second how the addition of a few transitional expressions promotes smoothness and meaning:

> In the summer all the snow above the snow line does not melt. The exact position of this line is not fixed. The line is lower in cold latitudes and higher in warm latitudes. Temperature appears to be important in determining its position. Other conditions enter, for a low snow line may sometimes be found in a warm climate.

> In the summer all the snow above the snow line does not melt. The exact position of this line, however, is not fixed. Ordinarily the line is lower in cold latitudes and higher in warm latitudes. Therefore, temperature appears to be important in determining its position. Yet other conditions occasionally enter, for a low snow line may sometimes be found in a warm climate.

**80a** Transitional expressions ease the task of reading not only by showing the connection between ideas inside the paragraph, but also by serving as links between paragraphs. The use of such expressions, for instance, as *in addition to this fact, as a consequence, as stated above, despite the fact that, most important of all, on the whole, secondly, these circumstances being true,* obviates sudden jumps, and aids the reader in seeing the structure of the whole paper. He needs these guideposts if he is to grasp the argument of the paper fully and quickly.

There are several other ways by which to secure coherence in the paragraph. One is to avoid shifts of subject, voice, and tense in consecutive clauses (see pages 246–249). Another is to repeat important constructions in consecutive sentences. This repetition may be effected by selecting the outstanding word or idea from one sentence to inaugurate the following sentence (as in this very sentence the word "repeat" has been taken from the preceding sentence to act in its noun form as subject); or it may be effected by using pronouns to refer frequently to the important word in the paragraph, as "The individual is important. He must not be fettered, or he will lose his forcefulness. He must be given freedom to exercise his initiative and assistance in the completion of his enterprises." Perhaps the most successful of all devices for securing coherence, however, is parallelism, a device which may at first seem to the inexperienced writer stilted and unnatural, but which he quickly finds that he can master to good effect. Parallelism is the repetition in consecutive words, phrases, clauses, or sentences of identical or similar word order and form to express ideas which are nearly equal in importance. Parallelism of single words of like part of speech is found in a sentence like this: "Our candidate is honest, brave, and resolute." Parallel phrases are exemplified here: "From the villages of New England, from the plantations of the South, and from the dense forests of the frontier came delegates to the convention." The following are parallel clauses: "The prisoner declared that he had no criminal record, that he was ignorant of the charges brought against him, and that on the night in question he was at home asleep." Parallel sentences, most important of the group for binding together a paragraph, are seen here: "Whenever Antony was gloomy, Cleopatra was gay. Whenever he was merry, she was sad." Parallelism thus not only indicates to the reader which ideas balance but also promotes an orderly arrangement of topics. Study carefully the parallelism in the following famous paragraph from Lincoln's Gettysburg Address. The parallelism exists both within and between sentences:

> But, in a larger sense, we cannot dedicate—we cannot consecrate—we cannot hallow—this ground. The brave men, living and dead, who struggled here, have consecrated it far above our poor power to add or detract. The world will little note nor long remember what we say here, but it can never forget what they did here. It is for us, the living, rather, to be dedicated here to the unfinished work which they who fought here have thus far so nobly advanced. It is rather for us to be here dedicated to the great task remaining before us—that from these honored dead we take increased devotion to that cause for which they gave the last full measure of devotion; that we here highly resolve that these dead shall not have died in vain; that this nation, under God, shall have a new birth of freedom; and that government of the people, by the people, for the people, shall not perish from the earth.

81 **Emphasis.** *Emphasis is secured in the paragraph by essentially the same means as in the sentence: the first and the last are the important positions.* For that reason the topic sentence normally should be located in one of these two positions, according to the principles already formulated. Special emphasis is gained by putting the topic sentence in both positions. Inside the paragraph other devices such as the frequent use of transitional expressions and of parallelism will promote emphasis by breaking the monotony of excessively regular sentence structure.

### Exercises

1. Using parallelism of structure, develop one of the following topic sentences into a paragraph of approximately 125 words.

For several reasons he is my favorite radio announcer.
The Senator's speech was very dull.
The rents on houses and apartments are rising rapidly.
The successful politician must follow several principles.
The new plan is a glorious success.
Hockey is a rougher sport than basketball.

The countryside looked beautiful in the autumn haze.

The building showed signs of aging.

Our new refrigerator is better than any we have owned before.

The members of a college faculty are divided into various ranks according to length of service and achievement.

2. Using as many transitional words and phrases as you can, develop one of the following topic sentences into a paragraph of approximately 125 words; underline each transitional expression.

A porch is pleasant to own in the summer time.

The circus clowns worked one trick to perfection.

The cost of maintenance of an automobile is about five cents a mile.

The styles for women's hats show little change this year.

He plays a few tunes over and over on his trombone.

We often cooked our meals outdoors, but seldom could I eat what we cooked.

The mania for owning a large stadium has proved costly to many universities.

The school was organized on a democratic principle.

The initial impression of the instructor is often erroneous.

The reunion was highly successful.

A man should be very particular about the color of his necktie.

The new factory will be immense.

The towns in that locality are slowly dying.

In some ways the diesel engine is more economical than the steam engine.

3. The following paragraphs are lacking in unity. Strike out the passages which are extraneous.

(a) Jacques was extremely limited in his interests. So far as anyone knew, he cared for only one thing—the steam locomotive. Perhaps he had never been introduced to any other subject, but no one knew about that, for he spoke but seldom and had no intimates. Only to his engines did he speak in a kindly tone of voice. And he was never known to show affection for any engine but the steam engine. Diesels he snorted at in disgust, even though the diesel locomotive is one of the smoothest and most economical performers in the business. Just within the last few years the railroads, particularly those of the West, have installed diesel locomotives, not only for passenger traffic but for freight hauls as well. But Jacques hated them. All he knew and all he wanted to know was the old iron horse.

(b) Several years ago an unusual competition arose among the leading colleges of America. These institutions, mostly private, were not particularly concerned about getting enough students to meet their quotas, but they were concerned about getting students of a high quality to set good standards on their campuses. Each institution, therefore, set up a series of scholarships to be awarded to select students, and each institution sent out representatives in the spring to visit the leading preparatory and high schools all over America. Inducements were not being offered to athletes, as most of these universities were sincere in their attempt to curb the evils known to accompany such practices. Some colleges have been known to put eleven hired men on the football field in the fall, men who could not meet the scholastic requirements but who were given special considerations because of their athletic ability. The feeling which such action aroused on the campus was not altogether desirable. These institutions in question, however, gave no inducements to high-school athletes, but sought men who were excellent students and who had well-rounded personalities. So from Washington to Florida, from Maine to California, their representatives toured the country each spring.

4. Each of the following paragraphs lacks coherence. Insert conjunctions and transitional expressions to make them stylistically acceptable.

(a) He was a small man; he was tiny. He was by no means insignificant. The magnetism of his personality drew instant attention. His every movement was quick and alert. The smile never left his face. He was an optimist, made to look on the better side of things and to take the bad with the good. He did not have a deep character. His quickness was superficial. Prolonged concentration was out of the question for him. Where deep thinking and planning were demanded, he was wanting. What could be accomplished by force of personality, by quick action, by good will and readiness to help, that he would accomplish.

(b) He is completely at home in the woods. He had helped his father cut a way into the wilderness and build a home. He had gone into the lumber camps with ax and saw. He pushed his way forward into the wilderness of the West. He blazed trails for settlers to follow. He grumbles that the homesteaders have come within fifty miles of his retreat. He is being driven on to new lands. The woods are his home; the luxuries of a soft bed and a cozy armchair he has never known and never misses. Where there is a wilderness retreat, there he will be happy.

## The Author's Account of Himself

### WASHINGTON IRVING

(1) I was always fond of visiting new scenes, and observing strange characters and manners. (2) Even when a mere child I began my travels, and made many tours of discovery into foreign parts and unknown regions of my native city, to the frequent alarm of my parents, and the emolument of the town-crier. (3) As I grew into boyhood, I extended the range of my observations. (4) My holiday afternoons were spent in rambles about the surrounding country. (5) I made myself familiar with all its places famous in history or fable. (6) I knew every spot where a murder or robbery had been committed, or a ghost seen. (7) I visited the neighboring villages, and added greatly to my stock of knowledge by noting their habits and customs, and conversing with their sages and great men. (8) I even journeyed one long summer's day to the summit of the most distant hill, whence I stretched my eye over many a mile of *terra incognita,* and was astonished to find how vast a globe I inhabited.

(9) This rambling propensity strengthened with my years. (10) Books of voyages and travels became my passion, and, in devouring their contents, I neglected the regular exercises of the school. (11) How wistfully would I wander about the pierheads in fine weather, and watch the parting ships, bound to distant climes; with what longing eyes would I gaze after their lessening sails, and waft myself in imagination to the ends of the earth!

(12) Further reading and thinking, though they brought this vague inclination into more reasonable bounds, only served to make it more decided. (13) I visited various parts of my own country; and had I been merely a lover of fine scenery, I should have felt little desire to seek elsewhere its gratification, for on no country have the charms of nature been more prodigally lavished. (14) Her mighty lakes, like oceans of liquid silver; her mountains, with their bright aërial tints; her valleys, teeming with wild fertility; her tremendous cataracts, thundering in their solitudes; her boundless plains, waving with spontaneous verdure; her broad deep rivers, rolling in solemn silence to the ocean; her trackless forests, where vegetation puts forth all its magnificence; her skies, kindling with the magic of summer clouds and glorious sunshine—no, never need an American look beyond his own country for the sublime and beautiful of natural scenery.

(15) But Europe held forth the charms of storied and poetical association. (16) There were to be seen the masterpieces of art, the refinements of highly cultivated society, the quaint peculiarities of ancient and local custom. (17) My native country was full of youthful promise: Europe was rich in the accumulated treasures of age. (18) Her very ruins told the history of times gone by, and every moldering stone was a chronicle. (19) I longed to wander over the scenes of renowned achievement—to tread, as it were, in the footsteps of antiquity—to loiter about the ruined castle —to meditate on the falling tower—to escape, in short, from the commonplace realities of the present, and lose myself among the shadowy grandeurs of the past.

(20) I had, beside all this, an earnest desire to see the great men of the earth. (21) We have, it is true, our great men in America: not a city but has an ample share of them. (22) I have mingled among them in my time, and been almost withered by the shade into which they cast me; for there is nothing so baleful to a small man as the shade of a great one, particularly the great man of a city. (23) But I was anxious to see the great men of Europe; for I had read in the works of various philosophers, that all animals degenerated in America, and man among the number. (24) A great man of Europe, thought I, must therefore be as

superior to a great man of America as a peak of the Alps to a highland of the Hudson; and in this idea I was confirmed by observing the comparative importance and swelling magnitude of many English travelers among us, who, I was assured, were very little people in their own country. (25) I will visit this land of wonders, thought I, and see the gigantic race from which I am degenerated.

(26) It has been either my good or evil lot to have my roving passion gratified. (27) I have wandered through different countries, and witnessed many of the shifting scenes of life. (28) I cannot say that I have studied them with the eye of a philosopher, but rather with the sauntering gaze with which humble lovers of the picturesque stroll from the window of one print shop to another, caught sometimes by the delineations of beauty, sometimes by the distortions of caricature, and sometimes by the loveliness of landscape. (29) As it is the fashion for modern tourists to travel pencil in hand, and bring home their portfolios filled with sketches, I am disposed to get up a few for the entertainment of my friends. (30) When, however, I look over the hints and memorandums I have taken down for the purpose, my heart almost fails me at finding how my idle humor has led me aside from the great objects studied by every regular traveler who would make a book. (31) I fear I shall give equal disappointment with an unlucky landscape painter, who had traveled on the continent, but, following the bent of his vagrant inclination, had sketched in nooks, and corners, and by-places. (32) His sketchbook was accordingly crowded with cottages, and landscapes, and obscure ruins; but he had neglected to paint St. Peter's, or the Coliseum; the cascade of Terni, or the bay of Naples; and had not a single glacier or volcano in his whole collection.

## Suggestions for Study

1. What is the thesis sentence of this article? The purpose? Where is the thesis stated?

2. What is the topic sentence of paragraph one? What transition is to be found in sentence two? In sentence three? What device binds together sentences five, six, seven, and eight?

3. What is the topic sentence of paragraph two? What words link paragraph two to paragraph one? What device aids clarity and binds together the independent clauses of sentence eleven?

4. What is the topic sentence of paragraph three? Does the opening sentence contain a link to carry the thought from paragraph two? What is the effect of the list of items in paragraph three?

5. Does paragraph four attach itself clearly to paragraph three in any way as a development of the main idea of paragraph three? Does it have a topic

idea of its own? What device do you find in sentence nineteen to promote concreteness, clarity, and emphasis?

6. What transitional words carry the thought from paragraph four to paragraph five? What is the topic sentence of paragraph five? What pronoun binds sentence twenty-three to sentence twenty-two? What word sets off the contrast beginning in sentence twenty-three? What is the transitional word in sentence twenty-four? What transitional expression follows the semicolon in sentence twenty-four? In sentence twenty-five, what is the linking word?

7. What links paragraph six with the preceding paragraphs? What is the purpose of paragraph six? Point out the parallelism in this paragraph. What end does it serve? What transitions are to be found in sentences thirty and thirty-two? What is the topic idea of this paragraph?

8. Define the following words from the article: emolument, propensity, wistfully, gratification, verdure, moldering, chronicle, baleful, picturesque, vagrant, cascade.

## C. Paragraph Development

The student who has learned the principles of structure already noted has gone far toward mastering the paragraph. At times, however, he may be uncertain as to how he shall amplify his topic sentence to make it fully understood; or, as he revises his writing, he may feel that some of his topic sentences need clarifying or proving. A study of the methods of paragraph development may extricate him from this dilemma, or at least make him more aware of the capabilities of the paragraph and the ways in which material can be presented interestingly.

82 Note first, however, that the test of all good writing is the author's ability to transmit his thoughts to a reader. If he does not present his ideas clearly, or if he deals with his subject so lackadaisically that questions remain in the reader's mind, he is not successful. Consequently, the best method for amplifying the idea in the topic sentence is to consider what the reader would like to know concerning that statement. Suppose, for instance, the topic sentence, "Students should work their way through college." Upon the examination of this sentence, a reader might have many questions: What kind of students, those with high marks or all students? What kind of work is meant, full-time work or just enough to provide pocket money? Should it be hard physical labor that might tax the student's energies? What benefits are derived from working? The writer who considers such questions and tries to answer them will be the most certain to write successfully. The good paragraph is one which leaves the reader satisfied.

**Development by Detail.** The two most useful methods of development are those of detail and illustration. The other methods are really but extensions of these two basic types. Development by detail consists in citing facts, figures, short examples, or some sort of concrete details in support of the topic sentence. Only by having instances which he can readily understand or visualize can a reader know exactly what is meant by the statement in the topic sentence or understand exactly why the topic sentence is true. The first of the following paragraphs begins with the general statement that Byron retired to Newstead to hold a few weeks of farewell revelry before departing on a trip; if a reader is to understand Byron's character fully at this period in his life, he must know the exact nature of these revels. With this requirement in mind the author carefully inserted a set of details to show precisely what Byron and his friends did at Newstead. In the second paragraph the author is trying to show one way in which an amateur with a camera can take satisfactory pictures. It is obviously not sufficient to tell a novice to take detailed pictures; he must be shown what detail in photography means, before such can be achieved.

Meanwhile Byron had again retired to Newstead, where he invited some choice spirits to hold a few weeks of farewell revel. Matthews, one of these, gives an account of the place, and the time they spent there—entering the mansion between a bear and a wolf, amid a salvo of pistol shots; sitting up to all hours, talking politics, philosophy, poetry; hearing stories of the dead lords, and the ghost of the Black Brother; drinking their wine out of the skull cup which the owner had made out of the cranium of some old monk dug up in the garden; breakfasting at two, then reading, fencing, riding, cricketing, sailing on the lake, and playing with the bear or teasing the wolf. The party broke up without having made themselves responsible for any of the orgies of which Childe Harold raves, and which Dallas in good earnest accepts as veracious, when the poet and his friend Hobhouse started for Falmouth on their way *"outre mer."*—John Nichol, *Byron.*

The real film *raconteur* will turn his camera on the detailed rather than the general. His film will not show "a woods," but rather a tall, stately tree with sunlight shafting through the leaves; a cluster of violets at the base of a rotted stump; a ripple on the brook and the water bubbling over into a quiet pool disturbed only by leaves falling quietly on the surface of the water; a butterfly nervously hovering above a flower; the tiny handprints made by a raccoon the night before; a squirrel, undecided whether to run or stay, peering around the trunk of a tree. Our cameraman will not see "a field." Instead, he will photograph the way the tall grass ripples in the wind; the grouse scuttling out of the hedge; the tattered scarecrow with sparrows teetering impertinently on the broomstick arms.—Robert W. Wagner, "Man with Camera." [1]

**Development by Illustration.** The second important method of development clarifies a topic sentence by illustrating its meaning—that is, by pre-

1. From the *News Letter,* XI (1946), No. 6 (an organ of the Ohio State University). Reprinted by permission of the author.

senting an incident, an anecdote, or a broad example containing the truth embraced by the topic sentence. Instead of choosing numerous concrete details as in the previous means of development, a writer selects one or possibly two broad situations which support his topic statement. The illustration, if sufficiently extensive, need not be confined just to one paragraph for its statement, but may, for the reader's convenience, spill over into two or more paragraphs.

Sometimes, but rarely, one may be caught making the same speech twice over, and yet be held blameless. Thus, a certain lecturer, after performing in an inland city, where dwells a *Littératrice* of note, was invited to meet her and others over the social teacup. She pleasantly referred to his many wanderings in his new occupation. "Yes," he replied, "I am like the Huma, the bird that never lights, being always in the cars, as he is always on the wing."—Years elapsed. The lecturer visited the same place once more for the same purpose. Another social cup after the lecture, and a second meeting with the distinguished lady. "You are constantly going from place to place," she said.—"Yes," he answered, "I am like the Huma,"—and finished the sentence as before.

What horrors, when it flashed over him that he had made this fine speech, word for word, twice over! Yet it was not true, as the lady might perhaps have fairly inferred, that he had embellished his conversation with the Huma daily during that whole interval of years. On the contrary, he had never once thought of the odious fowl until the recurrence of precisely the same circumstances brought up precisely the same idea. He ought to have been proud of the accuracy of his mental adjustments.
—Holmes, *The Autocrat of the Breakfast-Table.*

He who cultivates an interest in and an understanding of people—in the little things they do, the characteristic ways in which they act—will find that human beings are made up of particulars, not generalities. Realizing this, Ray Milland, for example, in preparation for his characterization of an alcoholic in *The Lost Weekend,* spent hours watching drunks at bars. He carefully noted how the heavy drinker typically hunches over his liquor as if to protect it. He studied the way an alcoholic walks, how he talks, how the facial muscles immobilized with the effect of the alcohol, how the hand that lifted the shot-glass quivered. The problem was to translate these small but significant human actions into film images.—Robert W. Wagner, "Man with Camera." [2]

**Development by Comparison** is used to clarify the idea contained in the topic sentence by likening it to another idea supposedly better known to the reader. The following paragraphs will show how clear and specific the topic sentence can be made by comparison:

As having their own way is one of the greatest comforts of life to old people, I think their friends should endeavor to accommodate them in

2. From the *News Letter,* XI (1946), No. 6. Reprinted by permission of the author.

that, as well as in anything else. When they have long lived in a house, it becomes natural to them; they are almost as closely connected with it, as the tortoise with his shell; they die, if you tear them out of it; old folks and old trees, if you remove them, it is ten to one that you kill them; so let our good old sister be no more importuned on that head.—Franklin, from a letter to Mrs. Jane Mecom, April 19, 1757.

But it will be said that I am forgetting the beauty, and the human interest, which appertain to classical studies. To this I reply that it is only a very strong man who can appreciate the charms of a landscape as he is toiling up a steep hill along a bad road. What with shortwindedness, stones, ruts, and a pervading sense of the wisdom of rest and be thankful, most of us have little enough sense of the beautiful under these circumstances. The ordinary schoolboy is precisely in this case. He finds Parnassus uncommonly steep, and there is no chance of his having much time or inclination to look about him till he gets to the top. And nine times out of ten he does not get to the top.—T. H. Huxley, "A Liberal Education: and Where to Find It."

**Development by Contrast** is the converse of the preceding method. Instead of amplifying the thesis idea by showing its likeness to another idea, the writer amplifies it by showing how it differs from another idea. As a light background sets off a dark object, so does one idea set off an unlike idea:

Man is timid and apologetic; he is no longer upright; he dares not say "I think," "I am," but quotes some saint or sage. He is ashamed before the blade of grass or the blowing rose. These roses under my window make no reference to former roses or to better ones; they are for what they are; they exist with God today. There is no time to them. There is simply the rose; it is perfect in every moment of its existence. Before a leaf bud has burst, its whole life acts; in the full-blown flower there is no more; in the leafless root there is no less. Its nature is satisfied and it satisfies nature in all moments alike. But man postpones or remembers; he does not live in the present, but with reverted eye laments the past, or, heedless of the riches that surround him, stands on tiptoe to foresee the future. He cannot be happy and strong until he too lives with nature in the present, above time.—Emerson, "Self-Reliance."

It is true that Lord Byron's high notions of rank were in his boyish days so little disguised or softened down as to draw upon him, at times, the ridicule of his companions; and it was at Dulwich, I think, that from his frequent boast of the superiority of an old English barony over all the later creations of the peerage, he got the nickname among the boys, of "the Old English baron." But it is a mistake to suppose that, either at school or afterwards, he was at all guided in the selection of his friends by aristocratic sympathies. On the contrary, like most very proud persons, he chose his intimates in general from a rank beneath his own, and those boys whom he ranked as *friends* at school were mostly of this description; while the chief charm that recommended to him his younger favorites was their inferiority to himself in age and strength, which enabled him to indulge his generous pride by taking upon himself, when necessary, the office of their protector.—Moore, *Notices of the Life of Lord Byron.*

**Development by Cause and Effect** consists in stating the causes which have produced a certain effect, or the reasons supporting a certain conclusion.

The calamities of this disgraceful rout did not cease with the loss of a few hundred soldiers on the field of battle; for it brought upon the provinces all the miseries of an Indian war. Those among the tribes who had thus far stood neutral, wavering between the French and English, now hesitated no longer. Many of them had been disgusted by the contemptuous behavior of Braddock. All had learned to despise the courage of the English, and to regard their own prowess with unbounded complacency. It is not in Indian nature to stand quiet in the midst of war; and the defeat of Braddock was a signal for the western savages to snatch their tomahawks and assail the English settlements with one accord, murdering and pillaging with ruthless fury, and turning the frontier of Pennsylvania and Virginia into one wide scene of havoc and desolation. —Parkman, *The Conspiracy of Pontiac.*

Of all the dispositions and habits which lead to political prosperity, religion and morality are indispensable supports. In vain would that man claim the tribute of patriotism, who should labor to subvert these great pillars of human happiness, these firmest props of the duties of men and citizens. The mere politician, equally with the pious man, ought to respect and to cherish them. A volume could not trace all their connections with private and public felicity. Let it simply be asked, Where is the security for property, for reputation, for life, if the sense of religious obligation *desert* the oaths which are the instruments of investigation in courts of justice? And let us with caution indulge the supposition that morality can be maintained without religion. Whatever may be conceded to the influence of refined education on minds of peculiar structure, reason and experience both forbid us to expect that national morality can prevail in exclusion of religious principle.—Washington, *Farewell Address.*

**Development by Elimination** consists in eliminating from the reader's consideration what the writer does not mean, in order that what he does mean will stand out more clearly. This device is especially suitable in defining or in giving clear-cut distinctions or descriptions.

I think the authors of that noble instrument intended to include *all* men, but they did not intend to declare all men equal *in all respects.* They did not mean to say all were equal in color, size, intellect, moral developments, or social capacity. They defined with tolerable distinctness in what respects they did consider all men created equal—equal with "certain inalienable rights, among which are life, liberty, and the pursuit of happiness." This they said, and this they meant. They did not mean to assert the obvious untruth that all were then actually enjoying that equality, nor yet that they were about to confer it immediately upon them. In fact, they had no power to confer such a boon. They meant simply to declare the right, so that enforcement of it might follow as fast as circumstances should permit.—Lincoln, Speech at Springfield, Illinois, June 26, 1857.

If then a practical end must be assigned to a University course, I say it is that of training good members of society. Its art is the art of social life, and its end is fitness for the world. It neither confines its views to particular professions on the one hand, nor creates heroes or inspires genius on the other. Works indeed of genius fall under no art; heroic minds come under no rule; a University is not a birthplace of poets or of immortal authors, of founders of schools, leaders of colonies, or conquerors of nations. It does not promise a generation of Aristotles or Newtons, of Napoleons or Washingtons, of Raphaels or Shakespeares, though such miracles of nature it has before now contained within its precincts. Nor is it content on the other hand with forming the critic or the experimentalist, the economist or the engineer, though such too it includes within its scope. But a University training is the great ordinary means to a great but ordinary end; it aims at raising the intellectual tone of society, at cultivating the public mind, at purifying the national taste, at supplying true principles to popular enthusiasm and fixed aims to popular aspiration, at giving enlargement and sobriety to the ideas of the age, at facilitating the exercise of political power, and refining the intercourse of private life. —Newman, "The Aim of a University Course."

**Development by Questions.** In this type of development the thought of the paragraph is carried forward by a series of aptly proposed questions. If used sparingly, this device will promote a pleasing variation in sentence structure and paragraph construction.

Do we call this the land of the free? What is it to be free from King George and continue the slaves of King Prejudice? What is it to be born free and not to live free? What is the value of any political freedom, but as a means to moral freedom? Is it a freedom to be slaves, or a freedom to be free, of which we boast? We are a nation of politicians, concerned about the outmost defenses only of freedom. It is our children's children who may perchance be really free. We tax ourselves unjustly. There is a part of us which is not represented. It is taxation without representation. We quarter troops, we quarter fools and cattle of all sorts upon ourselves. We quarter our gross bodies on our poor souls, till the former eat up all the latter's substance.—Thoreau, "Life without Principle."

**Development by a Combination of Methods.** Although attention has been centered thus far on the development of the paragraph by a single method, the student should not suppose that only one means can be used in each paragraph. Most paragraphs, in fact, are a combination of several methods. The following paragraphs illustrate the combination of methods. The first employs cause and effect as its general device, but also comparison, detail, and a slight amount of contrast and elimination to establish the cause and effect. The second uses comparison, detail, and questions.

Still, we do not think that the blame of Burns's failure lies chiefly with the world. The world, it seems to us, treated him with more, rather than with less kindness than it usually shows to such men. It has ever, we fear, shown but small favor to its teachers: hunger and nakedness, perils and reviling, the prison, the cross, the poison-chalice have in most times and countries been the marketprice it has offered for wisdom, the welcome with which it has greeted those who have come to enlighten and purify it. Homer and Socrates, and the Christian Apostles, belong to old days; but the world's martyrology was not completed with these. Roger Bacon and Galileo languish in priestly dungeons; Tasso pines in the cell of a madhouse; Camoens dies begging on the streets of Lisbon. So neglected, so "persecuted they the Prophets," not in Judea only, but in all places where men have been. We reckon that every poet of Burns's order is, or should be, a prophet and teacher to his age; that he has no right to expect great kindness from it, but rather is bound to do it great kindness; that Burns, in particular, experienced fully the usual proportion of the world's goodness; and that the blame of his failure, as we have said, lies not chiefly with the world.—Carlyle, "Burns."

Commerce has enriched thousands, it has been the cause of the spread of knowledge and of science, but has it added one particle of happiness or of moral improvement? Has it given us a truer insight into our duties, or tended to revive and sustain in us the better feelings of our nature? No! no! when I consider what the consequences have been, when I consider that whole districts of men, who would otherwise have slumbered on in comparatively happy ignorance, are now little less than brutes in their lives, and something worse than brutes in their instincts, I could almost wish that the manufacturing districts were swallowed up as Sodom and Gomorrah.—Coleridge, *Additional Table Talk.*

### Exercises

1. Identify the topic sentence and the most important means of development in each paragraph:

(a) Modern geography, modern history, modern literature, the English language as a language; the whole circle of the sciences, physical, moral, and social, are even more completely ignored in the higher than in the lower schools. Up till within a few years back, a boy might have passed through any one of the great public schools with the greatest distinction and credit, and might never so much as have heard of one of the subjects I have just mentioned. He might never have heard that the earth goes round the sun; that England underwent a great revolution in 1688, and France another in 1789; that there once lived certain notable men called Chaucer, Shakespeare, Milton,

Voltaire, Goethe, Schiller. The first might be a German and the last an Englishman for anything he could tell you to the contrary. And as for science, the
only idea the word would suggest to his mind would be dexterity in boxing.
—T. H. Huxley, "A Liberal Education."

(b) A tree is an underground creature, with its tail in the air. All intelligence is in its roots. All the senses it has are in its roots. Think what sagacity
it shows in its search after food and drink! Somehow or other, the rootlets,
which are its tentacles, find out that there is a brook at a moderate distance
from the trunk of the tree, and they make for it with all their might. They
find every crack in the rocks where there are a few grains of the nourishing
substance they care for, and insinuate themselves into its deepest recesses.
When spring and summer come, they let their tails grow, and delight in
whisking them about in the wind, or letting them be whisked about by it;
for these tails are poor passive things, with very little will of their own, and
bend in whatever direction the wind chooses to make them. The leaves make
a deal of noise whispering. I have sometimes thought I could understand
them, as they talk with each other, and that they seemed to think they made
the wind as they wagged forward and back. Remember what I say. The next
time you see a tree waving in the wind, recollect that it is the tail of a great
underground, many-armed, polypuslike creature, which is as proud of its
caudal appendage, especially in summertime, as a peacock of his gorgeous
expanse of plumage.—Holmes, *Over the Teacups.*

(c) The civilities we everywhere receive give us the strongest impressions of
the French politeness. It seems to be a point settled here universally, that
strangers are to be treated with respect; and one has just the same deference
shown one here by being a stranger, as in England by being a lady. The
customhouse officers at Port St. Denis, as we entered Paris, were about to
seize two dozen of excellent Bordeaux wine given us at Boulogne, and which
we brought with us; but, as soon as they found we were strangers, it was immediately remitted on that account. At the Church of Notre Dame, where we
went to see a magnificent illumination, with figures, &c., for the deceased
Dauphiness, we found an immense crowd, who were kept out by guards; but,
the officer being told that we were strangers from England, he immediately
admitted us, accompanied and showed us everything. Why don't we practice
this urbanity to Frenchmen? Why should they be allowed to outdo us in anything?—Franklin, a letter to Mary Stevenson.

(d) Women are more quick-sighted than men; they are less disposed to
confide in persons upon a first acquaintance; they are more suspicious as to
motives; they are less liable to be deceived by professions and protestations;
they watch words with a more scrutinizing ear, and looks with a keener eye;
and, making due allowance for their prejudices in particular cases, their
opinions and remonstrances, with regard to matters of this sort, ought not to
be set at naught without great deliberation. Louvet, one of the Brissotins who
fled for their lives in the time of Robespierre, . . . relates that being on his
way to Paris from the vicinity of Bordeaux, and having no regular passport,
fell lame, but finally crept on to a miserable pot-house in a small town in the
Limosin. The landlord questioned him with regard to who and what he was,
and whence he came, and was satisfied with his answers. But the landlady,

who had looked sharply at him on his arrival, whispered to a little boy, who ran away and quickly returned with the mayor of the town. Louvet soon discovered that there was no danger in the mayor, who could not decipher his forged passport, and who, being well plied with wine, wanted to hear no more of the matter. The landlady, perceiving this, slipped out and brought a couple of aldermen, who asked to see the passport. "Oh yes, but drink first." Then there was a laughing story to tell over again at the request of the half-drunken mayor; then a laughing and more drinking; the passport in Louvet's hand, but never opened, and while another toast was drinking, the passport slid back quietly into the pocket, the woman looking furious all the while. At last, the mayor, the aldermen, and the landlord, all nearly drunk, shook hands with Louvet, wished him a good journey, and swore he was a true *sans culotte;* but he says that the "sharp-sighted woman, who was to be deceived by none of his stories or professions, saw him get off with deep and manifest disappointment and chagrin." I have thought of this many times since, when I have had occasion to witness the quick-sightedness and penetration of women.—William Cobbett, *Advice to Young Men*.

(e) Thus began that memorable war which, kindling among the forests of America, scattered its fires over the kingdoms of Europe, and the sultry empire of the Great Mogul; the war made glorious by the heroic death of Wolfe, the victories of Frederic, and the exploits of Clive; the war which controlled the destinies of America, and was first in the chain of events which led on to her Revolution with all its vast and undeveloped consequences. On the old battleground of Europe, the contest bore the same familiar features of violence and horror which had marked the strife of former generations—fields ploughed by the cannon ball, and walls shattered by the exploding mine, sacked towns and blazing suburbs, the lamentations of women, and the license of a maddened soldiery. But in America, war assumed a new and striking aspect. A wilderness was its sublime arena. Army met army under the shadows of primeval woods; their cannon resounded over wastes unknown to civilized man. And before the hostile powers could join in battle, endless forests must be traversed, and morasses passed, and everywhere the ax of the pioneer must hew a path for the bayonet of the soldier.—Parkman, *Conspiracy of Pontiac*.

(f) It is well said, in every sense, that a man's religion is the chief fact with regard to him. . . . By religion I do not mean here the church creed which he professes, the articles of faith which he will sign and, in words or otherwise, assert; not this wholly, in many cases not this at all. We see men of all kinds of professed creeds attain to almost all degrees of worth or worthlessness under each or any of them. This is not what I call religion, this profession and assertion; which is often only a profession and assertion from the outworks of the man, from the mere argumentative region of him, if even so deep as that. But the thing a man does practically believe (and this is often enough *without* asserting it even to himself, much less to others); the thing a man does practically lay to heart, and know for certain, concerning his vital relations to this mysterious Universe, and his duty and destiny there, that is in all cases the primary thing for him, and creatively determines all the rest. That is his *religion;* or, it may be, his mere skepticism and *no-religion;* the manner it is in which he feels himself to be spiritually related to the Unseen World or No-World; and I say, if you tell me what that is, you tell me to a very great extent what the man is, what the kind of things he will do is.—Carlyle, *Heroes and Hero-Worship.*

(g) The definition of good prose is—proper words in their proper places;—of good verse—the most proper words in their proper places. The propriety is in either case relative. The words in prose ought to express the intended meaning, and no more; if they attract attention to themselves, it is, in general, a fault. In the very best styles, as Southey's, you read page after page, understanding the author perfectly, without once taking notice of the medium of communication;—it is as if he had been speaking to you all the while. But in verse you must do more;—there the words, the *media,* must be beautiful, and ought to attract your notice—yet not so much and so perpetually as to destroy the unity which ought to result from the whole poem. This is the general rule, but, of course, subject to some modifications, according to the different kinds of prose or verse.—Coleridge, *Table Talk.*

(h) The title *wise* is, for the most part, falsely applied. How can one be a wise man, if he does not know any better how to live than other men?—if he is only more cunning and intellectually subtle? Does Wisdom work in a tread-mill? or does she teach how to succeed *by her example?* Is there any such thing as wisdom not applied to life? Is she merely the miller who grinds the finest logic? It is pertinent to ask if Plato got his *living* in a better way or more successfully than his contemporaries—or did he succumb to the difficulties of life like other men? Did he seem to prevail over some of them merely by indifference, or by assuming grand airs? or find it easier to live, because his aunt remembered him in her will? The ways in which most men get their living, that is, live, are mere makeshifts, and a shirking of the real business of life—chiefly because they do not know, but partly because they do not mean, any better.—Thoreau, "Life without Principle."

(i) He [Man] *was* invariably sensible of the existence of gods, and went about all his speculations or works holding this as an acknowledged fact, making his best efforts in their service. *Now* he is capable of going through life with hardly any positive idea on this subject—doubting, fearing, suspecting, analyzing—doing everything, in fact, *but* believing; hardly ever getting quite up to that point which hitherto was wont to be the starting point for all generations. And human work has accordingly hardly any reference to spiritual beings, but is done either from a patriotic or personal interest—either to benefit mankind, or reach some selfish end, not (I speak of human work in the broad sense) to please the gods.—Ruskin, *Modern Painters.*

(j) Even participles that are perfectly grammatical may be unintentionally jocular, like the one in a sentence about a Revolutionary ancestor of one of our University presidents: "Having lost an arm in firing a salute, he took up law." It would seem that the loss of an arm, preferably in firing a salute, is a prerequisite to the study of law or that one-armed men make better lawyers. The woman who sat "with legs crossed and playing a wind instrument" must have had in those members a means of economic as well as physical support. A forester's sentence is not without humor: "The actual discharge of the pump was found by obtaining the mean of five complete strokes caught in a pail and measured to the nearest cubic centimeter."—E. S. McCartney.[3]

2. Select a topic sentence from the following list, and develop it twice, using in each paragraph a different method of development:

The draft revealed many interesting facts about the physical development of American young men.

A car benefits by occasional trips on the open road.

Reduction of gasoline consumption is necessary in a war crisis.

The radio commentator has a vast influence over public opinion.

The catcher is the key man on the baseball team.

The principle of the stereopticon is simple.

The cheapest car is not always the best purchase.

The wayside cabin is proving more useful to tourists than is the hotel.

A ten-dollar pipe seems to have little advantage over a three-dollar pipe for the average smoker.

The radio has been a valuable aid in giving the American public cultural interests.

The lack of good radio reception has stimulated victrola sales in the backwoods sections of America.

The New Deal had made the United States alphabet-conscious.

Small portable motors, developing less than one horsepower, have proved to be popular because of their variety of uses.

An outboard motor for fishing trips has several drawbacks.

Radio reception in certain parts of the country is very poor.

3. The following topic sentences are designed to be developed by a wide variety of means. Select one and develop it by the means most appropriate to its content.

Motorists differ widely in their estimates of the best gasoline.

The harbor was shaped like a gigantic letter C.

In some ways we have not advanced beyond the ancient Greeks.

I ran across an unusual idea the other day.

Our transportation system is considerably better than that of even ten years ago.

He has perfectly atrocious table manners.

The pleasantest companions for a trip are these.

Do not think the best courses are always the easiest courses.

The greatness of Washington and Lincoln was brought out in time of crisis.

Jackson is the most popular man on the campus.

University life is in several ways unlike that of the business world.

The fraternities are a good influence on campus life.

It is necessary to conserve the wild life of this forest.

After the car gathers speed, drive with care.

The city is laid out on the plan of a wagon wheel.

The amateur golfer gets into all sorts of trouble.

3. From "Some Participles I Have Met." Reprinted by permission of the author and of the *Michigan Alumnus Quarterly Review*.

He has no skill in the kitchen beyond that required to boil water.
Seventy-five years ago family life was different.
Textbooks cost too much.
The introduction to a composition can be made interesting.

## D. Introduction and Conclusion

Even for the experienced writer two sections of the composition are especially difficult: the introduction and the conclusion. The one must generate momentum for the reader; the other must check the momentum. The introduction in particular is likely to cause trouble because the writer has not yet warmed to his subject and his thoughts will not flow easily. Nevertheless, some few principles and some examples of introductions and conclusions may help to make the writing of these sections of the paper somewhat easier.

**The Introduction.** The introduction is not just a preliminary flourish which the writer makes before settling down to the task of presenting his

**83** subject. *It has a definite function: to attract the attention of the reader, and to put him in possession of whatever is needed to make an intelligent approach to the body of the material.*

**83a** *Attracting attention.* If the reader has a previously acquired interest in the subject matter, his attention can best be caught by an immediate statement of the thesis or of the problem which the thesis will ultimately solve. Such a beginning is also forceful. Francis Bacon begins an essay with his thesis sentence in this manner: "Houses are built to live in, and not to look on; therefore let use be preferred before uniformity, except where both may be had." Poe illustrates how the problem on which one is writing may be stated in the opening paragraph:

> The natural scenery of America has often been contrasted in its general features, as well as in detail, with the landscape of the Old World—more especially in Europe—and not deeper has been the enthusiasm, than wide the dissension, of the supporters of each region. The discussion is one not likely to be soon closed, for although much has been said on both sides, a word more yet remains to be said.—"The Elk."

If, however, the reader has no special interest in the subject, his attention must be attracted. A little story or anecdote will often catch his interest. For example, Stevenson begins thus his essay "The English Admirals":

> There is one story of the wars of Rome which I have always very much envied for England. Germanicus was going down at the head of the legions into a dangerous river—on the opposite bank the woods were full

of Germans—when there flew out seven great eagles which seemed to marshal the Romans on their way; they did not pause or waver, but disappeared into the forest where the enemy lay concealed. "Forward!" cried Germanicus, with a fine rhetorical inspiration, "Forward! and follow the Roman birds." It would be a very heavy spirit that did not give a leap at such a signal, and a very timorous one that continued to have any doubt of success.

An attractive question, an apt saying, an unusual or startling statement may turn the trick, provided that the writer is not being so forced and unnatural that the introduction does not fit the body of the paper. Mark Twain begins a humorous sally against chambermaids with this opening exclamation: "Against all chambermaids, of whatsoever age or nationality, I launch the curse of bachelordom!" Reinhold Niebuhr stimulates attention with this catching statement: "The political situation and problem of America in world affairs can be put in one sentence: America is at once the most powerful and politically the most ignorant of modern nations." (The *Atlantic Monthly,* January, 1932.) Robert M. Gay begins an article this way: "Some dogs are christened in jest, some in earnest, and some with malice aforethought, but the Boojum was christened by inspiration." (The *Atlantic Monthly,* January, 1932.)

**83b**    *Providing necessary information.* The other function of the introduction is to provide whatever knowledge is needed for comprehension of the body of the article. It must tell what the paper is to be about, a necessity which requires the immediate statement of the problem to be discussed or of the thesis. The problem may be stated first if the writer feels that he wishes to withhold the thesis until certain facts, essential for its comprehension, have been discussed. But from the outset the nature of the material to follow must be clearly indicated. To make doubly sure that the reader will follow the discussion, the writer can not only state the thesis but briefly outline the paper by stating the major points to be considered.

Sometimes an author wishes to explain why he is writing his paper and so makes an introductory statement of purpose. Josiah Royce begins *The Spirit of Modern Philosophy* in this way:

> In the following course of lectures I shall try to suggest, in a fashion suited to the general student, something about the men, the problems, and the issues that seem to me most interesting in a limited but highly representative portion of the history of modern philosophy. I undertake this work with a keen sense of the limitations of my time and my powers. I plead as excuse only my desire to interest some of my fellow students in the great concerns of philosophy.[4]

4. Used by permission of the publishers, Houghton Mifflin Co.

Notice how the author has limited his subject and makes no pretence at covering the whole of modern philosophy. To limit the subject to any one point of discussion is very acceptable in the introduction so that the reader is not led to expect more than he gets. Josiah Royce also establishes a fine tone in his introduction by making no claims to universal knowledge. The reader immediately feels more confidence in him. A skillful writer may also find it useful to bring out at the beginning in what way he is qualified to write on his subject, to establish himself as an authority or to explain how he happens to be writing. Stevenson says in the first paragraph of his article on the Japanese reformer, Yoshida-Torajiro:

> I wish to say that I am not, rightly speaking, the author of the present paper: I tell the story on the authority of an intelligent Japanese gentleman, Mr. Taiso Masaki, who told it me with an emotion that does honor to his heart; and though I have taken some pains, and sent my notes to him to be corrected, this can be no more than an imperfect outline.

The importance of the topic may also be established at the start in order that the reader's interest may be quickened. This introduction is particularly fitting where the reader is not well acquainted with the subject matter. John Nichol begins a chapter on the ancestry of Byron in this way:

> Byron's life was passed under the fierce light that beats upon an intellectual throne. He succeeded in making himself—what he wished to be —the most notorious personality in the world of letters of our century. Almost every one who came in contact with him has left on record various impressions of intimacy or interview. . . . All concur in the admission that Byron was as proud of his race as of his verse, and that in unexampled measure the good and evil of his nature were inherited and inborn. His genealogy is, therefore, a matter of no idle antiquarianism.—*Byron.*

The introduction is also a good place in which to define any terms with which the reader may be unacquainted or which need to be sharply defined for purposes of discussion. Argument is dependent on an accurate knowledge of the implications of the terms used. Here is Poe's beginning to "The Rationale of Verse":

> The word "Verse" is here used not in its strict or primitive sense, but as the term most convenient for expressing generally and without pedantry all that is involved in the consideration of rhythm, rhyme, meter, and versification.

84 **The Conclusion.** The student must begin by ridding himself of the idea that a short composition must have a special concluding paragraph. In a short composition which contains in all probability an obvious

set of ideas and a clear organization, to use a whole paragraph for summary is a waste of words, and to indulge in an emotional appeal to arouse the reader's feelings is absurd. Such conclusions as the latter are useful only on special occasions, as possibly in Fourth-of-July addresses. Usually all that a paper needs is a final sentence, perhaps a restatement of the thesis, introduced by a transitional expression such as "in the end," "finally," "therefore," "after all," "in the last analysis."

In long papers with complex material the conclusion is usually a summary. It re-emphasizes the thesis idea or restates the major points very briefly so that they stand out sharply and their relationships are made clear. Henry Fielding ends his essay "On the Knowledge of the Characters of Men" with this conclusion:

> Thus I have endeavored to show the several methods by which we can purpose to get any insight into the characters of those with whom we converse, and by which we may frustrate all the cunning and designs of hypocrisy. These methods I have shown to be threefold, viz., by the marks which nature hath imprinted on the countenance, by their behavior to ourselves, and by their behavior to others. On the first of these I have not much insisted, as liable to some uncertainty; and as the latter seem abundantly sufficient to secure us, with proper caution, against the subtle devices of hypocrisy, though she be the most cunning as well as malicious of all the vices which have ever corrupted the nature of man.
>
> But, however useless this treatise may be to instruct, I hope it will be at least effectual to alarm my reader; and sure no honest, undesigning man can ever be too much on his guard against the hypocrite, or too industrious to expose and expel him out of society.

He thus summarizes his major points and brings out the importance of his subject once again for the reader.

### Exercises

1. From selections given in any part of this textbook, select five introductory and five concluding paragraphs, and be ready to state the method used in each.

2. Write a composition. After the completion of it, underline topic sentences once, transitional words and phrases twice, and list in the margin of the paper the means of development used in any three paragraphs.

# Scholars, Poor and Simple [5]

DOUGLAS BUSH

## I

I once heard from a Cambridge don a pleasant anecdote of A. E. Housman. Housman and three advanced students of Latin regularly met in a large lecture room where they pored over textual problems in that astrological poem of Manilius which students of poetry neglect. Before the end of the hour the room would begin to fill with undergraduates and all the unoccupied old ladies of Cambridge, and when the hour was up the four devotees of truth, Housman at the head flashing fires of scorn, had to elbow their way out through the crowd assembled to hear a lecture by the charming Quiller-Couch.

The picture might be taken as an allegory of the relations between scholars, especially literary scholars, and the public. They are always being derided or damned because they write with painful dullness for other scholars, instead of displaying their wares in artistic fashion for the general reader. The usual reason, spontaneously supplied by journalists and others, is that scholars are out of touch with contemporary literature and the contemporary mind, that they have no vital ideas even about the past, and that if they had they could not write anyhow. The more charitable admit that scholars now and then may have ideas, but in the shape of frozen assets. So the literary world is divided into two very unequal groups, the academic scholars who play solemn, futile games by themselves and the large body of intelligent writers who produce all the books that matter, review them, go on lecture tours to spiritualize academic communities, and, in a word, carry on the great task of forming our minds and tastes. If the scholars who teach in our universities and colleges are of any value to the geniuses who for a while are in their charge, it is mainly in a negative way; they represent something to be revolted against.

Such complaints are of course not unwarranted, and indeed are often made by scholars themselves. Volumes of research do get published from which even specialists derive small nourishment. Learned journals, however valuable for those who know enough to be able to use them, would not be chosen for one's desert island, unless for tinder. A scholar who has had a surfeit of research, his own or other people's, is sometimes seized with a revulsion against his austere ideals and limitations. He

5. Reprinted by permission of the author and of the *Atlantic Monthly*.

knows in his heart that literature was meant to provide a truce from cares, not to add to them, and he vows that he will henceforth be a human being and write for other human beings. He will cease to be a digger and delver and become a man of letters. By way of clearing his brain and exercising a fresh set of muscles for the great enterprise, the scholar reads or rereads a number of successful popular books. . . . And then he vows that he would rather be damned with Housman than saved with "Q" (not that "Q" hasn't his virtues), that it is better to be a burrowing mole than the crawling scourge that smites the leaf (to borrow an elegant eighteenth-century phrase for a caterpillar).

For the scholar is a less noxious kind of parasite than the popularizer. At his worst the scholar, like John Earle's plodding student, brings to his task nothing but patience and a body, and he does no harm to his subject and his few readers. The popular writer, at his worst, brings nothing but impatience and a temperament, and he often gives a distorted picture of his subject to a multitude of readers. One pernicious thing about popular books on literary figures is that they enable people to feel that they have read a great author's works without the trouble of doing it. Of the thousands who read *Ariel,* how many were moved to read Shelley? Perhaps it would have been odd if they had been.

Of course, it may be granted once for all, we do have popular or semi-popular biographies, mostly written by academic scholars, which are as far from shallow inadequacy as from dullness. But our concern here is with the great mass of average productions. In the last nine years there have been four biographies, English and American, of Sir Philip Sidney, no one knows why; the Elizabethan scholar still turns to the sober and standard *Life* by Principal Wallace. There is an unceasing stream of books about the Brownings, about Byron, about all the legendary figures, and, since publishers continue to print them, one must assume that they sell.

The thirst for literary cocktails seems to be maintained by two motives, neither of which is the desire for a help toward appreciating the works of Sidney or the Brownings or Byron. In the first place, people can escape from humdrum life or excessively realistic fiction by reading about the romantic embodiment of Elizabethan chivalry or the wedded lovers or the noble rake; their cultural inferiors find similar solace in contemplating Clark Gable and Ronald Colman. Secondly, for the last twenty years or so America, as Sherwood Anderson once remarked, has been on a culture jag, and the itch for self-improvement inspires or afflicts all classes of society. Instead of leading a natural life in the state to which God has called them, people still want to rise to power by way of the Harvard

Classics, or to keep up with their children and be sure of the difference between Sir James Jeans and James Joyce, or to hold their own in conversation; or they may have an entirely pure and earnest desire to give their souls a shampoo.

Though sentimental or romantic "human interest" is perhaps the surest ground of popular appeal, our self-consciously candid age has nourished a strong rival. The author who wants a popular audience has won half the battle if he, or she, chooses a subject with an aura or halo of scandal. The splenetic Carlyle declared that the biographies of men of letters were the wretchedest chapters in our history, except perhaps the Newgate Calendar. But that was the croak of a Victorian Calvinist. The modern biographer may slight facts and ideas, yet he rightly prides himself on the frankness which the modern reader so abundantly craves. While Judy O'Grady holds her breath over *True Confessions,* the colonel's lady reads a biography or, what is even more rewarding, an undraped autobiography. Think how Wordsworth's stock has gone up since the discovery that he had a natural daughter. And Byron's, though always high, rose higher when the business of Mrs. Leigh was aired. Who would write or read about Rossetti if it were not for Elizabeth Siddal? Who would write or read about Poe if it were not for alcohol, the child wife, and the platonic seraglio?

The great authors who have worn the white flower of a blameless life —happily few!—are at a discount. One often wishes that Tennyson might be found to have been the father of, say, Lillie Langtry. And there is always the hope of unearthing an intrigue between Longfellow and one, or preferably both, of the Miss Carys. Alfred Austin might take rank as a poet if only he could be caught out on the tiles. If scandal or pathology is lacking, one's subject can be made a text for the exposure of an earlier generation's puritanical hypocrisy. The popular writer's notion of the Victorian age in England and America reminds one of Mr. Shaw's speech in a mock trial: "Does the court think that an upright and intelligent jury is to be influenced by such a thing as evidence?" Then something can always be done with a title. The laborious and artless scholar would put forth a drab tome, *Jane Austen: Her Life and a Study of Her Works, with Some Unpublished Letters.* The knowing popular author would have a gayly colored volume called *The Spinster of Steventon,* or, better, *That Georgian Wench.* The authors of a book on the heroines of English fiction contrived to season their learning with unexpected anatomical detail. One wonders how soon scholars may be introducing a touch of sentiment or a strain of salacious gossip into the *Publications of the Modern Language Association,* so that the five thousand subscribers will be tearing off the austere wrappers with eager excitement.

Certainly the scholar who thinks of seeking a wider field of usefulness, as clergymen say or used to say, soon learns some fundamental lessons about the treatment of literature. Great authors are to be viewed as persons, in themselves and in their relations with others. Reference may be made to their works, since after all they were writers, but there must be no serious discussion of their ideas or their art. General readers, like many undergraduates, do not want to think or to be spurred on to read original texts; they insist upon unexacting entertainment as the prime function of their mentors. Any publisher shies violently at the thought of a philosophic, critical, non-biographical book. "People must be amuthed," as Dickens's asthmatic circus proprietor said. This is satisfactory all round. The popular author has little new light to shed, since his book is normally a smartened abridgement of older and solider works (the modern psychological approach saves a good deal of time and trouble), and readers are kept at home enjoying the pleasant sensation of improving their minds with things that count. Of course both parties might be much worse employed. Sometimes they are. Several years ago the highly intellectual critic and poet, Mr. Herbert Read, published a long essay called *In Defence of Shelley;* the defence consisted mainly in the proof that Shelley was a homosexual narcissist. A scholar who had something to say about Shelley's poetry would look in vain for a hospitable editor or publisher—unless there happened to be a centenary, and even then he would have to chatter about Harriet. I remember an essayist who said he tried to get by an editor with a piece beginning, "It is now a hundred and thirty-three years since the death of Cowper," but this seductive chronological gambit did not succeed.

## II

Many popular books are deservedly successful because the writers are not too many jumps ahead of their readers to have lost the common touch. The case of Mr. Will Durant illustrates the advantages of conducting one's education in public. What many thousands of people welcomed as *The Story of Philosophy* some regarded rather as a lively handbook of night-school liberalism. After omitting the mediæval scholastics from that work, since they included no great central personality, Mr. Durant later admitted Thomas Aquinas to his list of the world's ten greatest thinkers, a decision which, though reluctant, must have gratified the anxious spirit of Saint Thomas. The considerable advance in learning and wisdom represented by Mr. Durant's *The Life of Greece*

(1939) was accompanied, one may guess, by a drop in sales. If Mr. Durant has gone forward as a popularizer, Professor E. T. Bell has gone backward. Professor Bell, having produced a good popular book, *Men of Mathematics,* on a subject he understood, evidently fancied himself as a philosopher and universal doctor and undertook, in *Man and His Lifebelts,* to expose some of the fallacious creeds mankind has lived by. The chief result was an exposure of the obtuseness and dogmatic ignorance which so often go with what complacently regards itself as hardheaded scientific rationalism. As a soldier in the liberation war of humanity, Professor Bell fights side by side with Mr. E. Haldeman-Julius. And since Spurius Lartius and Herminius need a Horatius, he may be found in the prolific Harry Elmer Barnes.

In popular historical writing the vigorous merits of Mr. James Truslow Adams have been amply and justly rewarded. From *Building the British Empire* the reader who knows nothing beforehand will learn a good deal, at least about the procession of events. About the fundamental causes of those events, economic, political, religious, and the like, he will not learn much; but the sufficient answer to that is that he doesn't want to.

In the field of cultural history probably no theme attracts popular writers more than the Italian Renaissance, and most books about it may be roughly described as Cecil De Mille mixtures of Burckhardt and Baedeker. Burckhardt's work is a classic of artistic scholarship, but there can be few competent scholars today who accept his theory of the Renaissance. Popular writers, however, continue with undiminished zest to serve the good old Italian dishes, with the prescribed romantic sauce and spicy scandal about the Borgias. Mr. Ralph Roeder's title, *Man of the Renaissance,* suggests an exceedingly difficult and complex problem, but Mr. Roeder simplified it for popular consumption by writing biographical essays on four men—Savonarola, Machiavelli, Castiglione, and Aretino. And even in the treatment of these four the proportion of ideas to personal and political chronicle is decidedly small. It is doubtless a minor matter in a book on the Renaissance that Latin quotations should be commonly either misspelled or mistranslated. To quote a random example, *ita omnes qui bene sentiunt uno ore loquantur* is rendered "So that all who feel rightly pray an hour a day!"

The dean of popularizers is Mr. Van Loon, who knows all there is to know but is a plain man who does not put on airs about it. When an individual sets up as a two-legged Chautauqua it would be both mean and foolish to speak of particular errors. Yet one has hardly got into *The Arts* before one meets a particularly notorious fallacy which has long been buried—which was in fact killed in the eighteenth century, though later revived by popular historians—namely, that the fall of Constantinople in 1453 inaugurated the Greek renaissance by driving Greek scholars to western Europe. Mr. Van Loon's manner of writing raises a more general question. He believes that art is and should be popular, and his cultural salad is sprinkled with the evidently appetizing sauce of journalese. One may seriously ask, are people led by vulgarity to an appreciation of art that is not vulgar?

If these names tell us what the public wants, we have still further proof in the fact that eminent highbrows occasionally stoop to conquer. There is the conspicuous example of Mr. Santayana, who has always been suspect among philosophers because he is a stylist, and has been neglected by the general reader because he is a philosopher; but as soon as he wrote a sort of novel he became the theme of clubs and dinner tables. Mr. Van Wyck Brooks's earlier writings won him a notable place among the intellectual, but he enjoyed little popular fame until, in the *Flowering of New England,* he concealed ideas, very skillfully, behind a mass of personal detail and local color.

### III

It is clear that the scholar who wishes to propagate truth among the many, who wishes, in short, for sales, must concentrate on narrative, people, anecdotage. If he cannot hope to emulate Professor Phelps as a mighty hunter of literary lions, he can at least cultivate that engaging gentleman's habit of liking almost everything in print. General readers (and reviewers) are not disposed to be critical, to complain of the absence of ideas or the presence of mistaken ones. If our ambitious scholar is determined to touch ideas, he must suppress his instinct for evidence and learn to generalize freely and spaciously. Scholars are notoriously timid in that respect. They think truth has to be sought for and, when found, demonstrated. Popular writers, on the contrary, are endowed with the imaginative insight and intuition which render caution and research superfluous. Holding the history of civilization in the hollow of their hand, they can sum up in one compelling phrase the complex character of antiquity or the Middle Ages or the Renaissance or any period whatever. Why, it may be said, should a churlish reader not be content with such writers' broad artistic interpretations, based as they commonly are on the solid researches of a generation or two ago?

Well, if a book has any excuse for existing, apart from the writer's desire to write, it ought to contain some new facts or ideas along with its new phrases, and the informed and intelligent reader is not prepared to put his hand in the author's and be led on in childlike faith. He wants to be able to check the author's sources and inferences. "Oh," says a foe of pedantry, "you are surely not pleading for footnotes!" It always puzzles a scholar to observe that, while the general reader readily digests the most inadequate or erroneous idea or fact if it appears in regular type, his sensitive stomach turns at an authentic fact or reference in small type, so that footnotes almost automatically exclude a book from general circulation. People who don't want to read footnotes don't need to; there are others who do. Miss Lowell's *John Keats* would have been less amorphous if she had not put her footnotes into the text. If Lytton Strachey had been obliged to give footnote references for his *Elizabeth and Essex,* that theatrical romance could hardly have been written; nor, for that matter, could some of his nineteenth-century satires. Even the *Queen Elizabeth* of such an authoritative historian as J. E. Neale gained popular success at the cost of scholarly usefulness; but one need not condemn Mr. Neale for preferring fame and fleshpots. The name of Elizabeth, by the way, recalls a book on that annual theme, Mary Queen of Scots, a book based on deep study, in which Mary, undoubtedly an original woman, was described as firing a sackbut; surely so remarkable a feat might have warranted a note.

The world expects scholars to get their reward in the discovery of truth, and it may be hoped the world is right, since they get nothing else. They toil for years, they scorn delights and live laborious days, and when they have written a book they are lucky if they can get it published. If they do they usually have to pay for it, though the professorial salary does not allow for subsidies to publishers. Sometimes a scholar has the superlative good fortune to get a book published for nothing. Sometimes the work of many years cannot get published at all. It is by no means a sufficient explanation to say that scholars can't write; many a scholar writes well, but if he objects to the cheaper arts of salesmanship the world will have none of him. The popular middleman, however, spends a few months in a public library, dashes off a book in time for the Christmas lists, and receives handsome royalties. The scholar meekly accepts the way of the world, but he does wonder now and then why the swift-footed gentlemen of letters do not more often pause to take account of scholars' findings. In the scholar's creed, truth has its rights on the lowest as well as the highest levels, and nothing is too insignificant to be verified. But "What is truth?" says your man of letters, and does not stay for an answer; at least he does not stay long enough to consult a bibliography. Whatever his radical instincts, the man of letters is a conservative in one respect; he does hold fast to ideas and "facts" that scholars have abandoned.

While the scholar can at best hope for little more than toleration from the world of letters—unless he happens to be a Mr. Lowes, and there is only one of him—it is a different story when a member of the literary set produces a book about books. Mr. Burton Rascoe's *Titans of Literature* received an immediate chorus of acclaim from his numerous friends. Some of the author's pages, in an academic book, would have been damned as barren pedantry; in his, they were impressive learning. But more than that, this was the kind of big, vital book that the professors simply couldn't write. No doubt, to their loss, professors' literary loves and hates are less intense and erratic than Mr. Rascoe's, and there certainly is something about exact knowledge which checks naïve superlatives and schoolboy capers—which, in the journalistic creed, is so much the worse for knowledge. Mr. Rascoe would probably subscribe to Mr. Ezra Pound's boast, "I am still *impetuus juventus*"—an exquisite bit of Latinity which proclaims more clearly than his copious invectives that Mr. Pound abhors grammarians. *Titans of Literature,* incidentally, reminds me of one of the quaintest items I have met in a long study of reviewing columns. Mr. Rascoe was mildly rebuked by the normally truculent Mr. Ernest Boyd for presuming to demolish Milton when Milton had already been disposed of; see an earlier essay by Mr. Boyd. From both studies of Milton the curious scholar may learn many things. If I hear a murmur that Mr. Boyd's terrific *Literary Blasphemies* are *vieux jeu,* it may be said in the first place that they were scarcely novel when they were printed; and, secondly, they deserve notice here because they constituted a signal recognition of great literature on the part of one of the superior magazines which for many years has had no room for criticism of dead authors and next to none for living ones.

Probably the scholar should not be left standing here in a state of partial paralysis, yet what elixir will supple his joints and rejuvenate his mind? How can the lamb hope to lie down with the lions? Throughout the history of culture, learning and literature have generally gone hand in hand, but the spread of democratic literacy changed all that. Nowadays, especially perhaps in the United States, the scholar and the popular author bite their thumbs at each other. The latter's want of learning, as Witwoud said of his friend Petulant, is his happiness; it gives him the more opportunities to show his natural parts. The scholar, it seems, has no natural parts. This cleavage is bad for both, and for the public. But the fault is not, as common opinion goes, merely on one side. At any rate, when we scholars venture out of our Platonic cave to take a peep or a jaundiced squint at the bright world of real letters, we feel quite unqualified to live there, even if we were wanted. And our chilly cells with their card indexes may appear, to eyes dazzled by the literary scene and the literary racket, to possess a sort of plain and enduring charm. They imply a mode of life which doubtless lacks the intensities of creative effort and the intellectual excitement of publishers' teas, yet which in its own way gives its peculiar votaries a no less satisfying illusion of being near the center of things.

## Suggestions for Study

1. Compare the paragraph length with that of the following article. How is this a reflection of the intended reading group?
2. State the purpose of parts, I, II, and III respectively.
3. What device does the author use in the opening paragraph to attract attention? In the concluding paragraph, how does he bring the article to a close?
4. In paragraph two, what adaptation is made to the reading group? What tone is the writer using in this paragraph?
5. In Part I, find an example of development by each of the following means: cause and effect, contrast, elimination, illustration, detail.
6. In Part II, what is the major method of development?
7. Answer the following questions concerning Part III:
   (a) What is the difference between the scholar's and the popularizer's creed in reference to facts and generalities?
   (b) What should a book contain to justify its existence?
   (c) With what attitude should a reader accept the facts to be found in a book?
   (d) What is a sackbut?
   (e) In the author's estimation, can the scholar write well?
   (f) Why does the scholar not feel at home in the domain of popularized letters?
8. Define the following words from the article: don, devotees, allegory, vital, unwarranted, surfeit, austere, noxious, pernicious, embodiment, solace, aura, splenetic, gambit, fallacious, obtuseness, prolific, notorious, fallacy, propagate, emulate, amorphous, bibliography, erratic, truculent, elixir, votaries.

# You Know Me, Allergy [6]

### WEARE HOLBROOK

During the late summer and early autumn, hay fever sufferers usually have things pretty much their own way—so much, in fact, that the term "sufferers" is almost a misnomer. It is my opinion that most of them really enjoy their affliction; they look forward to the first sneeze as eagerly as a child looks forward to Christmas. And why not? For it identifies them as Very Special People who must be coddled and sheltered and sympathized with until the sneezing season is over.

6. Reprinted by permission of the New York *Herald Tribune*.

They surround themselves with filter screens, fans, atomizers, inhalators, and a thousand and one concoctions designed to cure hay fever. Or they take extended trips to the mountains and the seashore, while the rest of us stay at home and breathe pollen. But do they ever get cured? They do not. If the truth were known, they don't want to get cured. That would take all the fun out of life.

It is generally conceded that hay, *per se,* has no more to do with hay fever than with the Hay diet or the Hay-Pauncefote treaties. Ragweed is the real villain in the garden plot. But "ragweed fever" sounds too inelegant to be accepted in the best circles; so, hay it is—with or without a nonny-nonny. Furthermore, it usually calls for the possessive pronoun. You seldom hear anyone speak of "my dandruff" or "my whooping cough." But the systematic sneezer always refers fondly to "my hay fever." Long association has endeared it to him, and he would feel quite lost without it.

Well, all I can say is that the hay feverites had better make the most of the sympathy and attention they get this season. From now on they're going to have competition. The rest of us are going allergic.

Until recently I thought an allergy was a poetical form—a sort of cross between an allegory and an elegy. Or perhaps it would be more exact to say that I didn't think at all. My knowledge of this subject is still rather limited, but I have read enough to know that the hay fever gang has no monopoly on the allergy racket. No, sir; anyone can muscle in.

An allergy is simply an involuntary phobia, and practically everybody in the world is allergic—which is something to think about on rainy Monday mornings. People who get hives from strawberries, or strawberries from hives, are allergic. So are the unfortunates who get eczema from sumac leaves, warts from toads, and moths from fur coats.

I had an uncle who was very allergic. (We didn't call it allergic in those days, of course; we just pretended not to notice.) He used to come out in spots whenever he ate lobster. And his vest was even more allergic. It came out in spots whenever he ate anything.

Many allergies are seasonal, like hay fever, although they have no relation to dust or pollen in the air. My Cousin Agnes, for example, is allergic to horsehair sofas—but only in warm weather. In the winter time she can sit on one all day long in perfect comfort. But when she puts on a light summer frock and sits on a horsehair sofa, she breaks out in a rash.

We are all familiar—but I trust not *too* familiar—with people who grow pale at the sight of an oyster on the half-shell, or become nauseated by a whiff of boiled cabbage, or shudder violently at contact with suede leather. There are some sensitive souls who can literally be knocked down with a feather.

One night not long ago, a prominent barfly of my acquaintance, while undressing in the dark, as was his custom, accidentally put his hand on a plush pincushion that was lying on the bureau. The shock immediately gave him an attack of galloping allergy. Screaming, he leaped out of the room, ran down the hall, and fell into a syncope. He has never been the same since, and we are all very pleased about it.

Such phenomena are fairly common. The unafflicted majority assumes that the victims are born "peculiar," and can't help being that way. I maintain, however, that they *can* help being that way if they want to. They just don't want to, that's all.

Acting on this theory, I have investigated my own case and discovered several clearly defined allergies. There is spinach, for instance. A hay fever addict will tell you that it isn't the goldenrod that upsets him; it's the pollen on the goldenrod. That's my situation exactly. I don't mind the spinach itself; the sand in the spinach is what gets me. There may be some truth in the maxim that we dig our graves with our teeth, but I don't see why we have to be so literal about it.

Tapioca pudding is another delicacy to which I am definitely allergic. After one helping of this apparently innocuous dessert I have sharp pains in the neck, and am not responsible for my behavior for the rest of the day. This is due, no doubt, to the shock of chewing, or trying to chew, tapioca. The jaws come crashing together with nothing to break the force of the impact; the vibration travels up the jawbone to the base of the brain, and in no time at all I am as batty as a bassoon player. No more tapioca for me, if you please.

The experts say that an allergist's reaction toward the object of his aversion is often the result of inhaling invisible particles of that object, which are floating in the air. This may account for the strange stupor that comes over me whenever I go to the opera; I inhale the tiny particles of plush that infest the atmosphere, and before you can say "Gotterdammerung" I am sound asleep.

Another distressing phobia that often embarrasses me in public is "prodigal's paralysis." When I am dining at a restaurant with a group of friends and the waiter puts the check on the table, I find it physically impossible to reach out and pick it up. The other members of the party may scramble for it with mock belligerence, crying, "Drop that, you son-of-a-gun!" "Let me take it!" "No, this is on me!" But although longing to join in their good-natured rivalry, somehow I can neither move nor speak. For rigor mortis sets in as soon as I hear the waiter tear the check from his book, and continues until after the check has been paid.

It is my belief that the tearing of the check sprays tiny particles of paper into the air and I breathe them in, causing an allergy—for I notice the same symptoms in a milder degree when I read a new book with uncut pages. As there is never a paper-knife handy, I always have to use the edge of a cardboard match-book cover—with the result that after half an hour of sawing and nibbling I say, "Oh, to hell with it!" and read a newspaper instead. And that, of course, is not the proper attitude to take toward literature.

They say that scientists are hard at work immunizing allergists and turning them into normal people again. They can make dozens of tiny scratches in your skin, put a solution of a different substance in each scratch, and eventually desensitize you against your particular phobia, whatever it happens to be.

No doubt this is highly beneficial to the human race as a whole. But as far as I'm concerned, "allergy" is just another way of spelling "alibi," and no scientists are going to scratch my skin. I know a good thing when I've got it. And I've got it.

*Suggestions for Study*

1. Contrast this informal essay with the formal essay by Professor Bush. What difference do you observe in general purpose? in the type of reader for whom it is meant? How does that affect the paragraph length? Which paragraph length do you think is more easily read? Which paragraph length is more suitable for presenting a complex subject which requires considerable explanation of major points? Why?

2. Analyze the article for structure. What are its two main divisions of subject matter? What is the major means of paragraph development in each division?

3. What levels of diction does the author employ?

4. State the thesis. Where is it placed in the article?

5. Define the following words from the article: misnomer, affliction, coddled, inhalator, *per se,* allegory, elegy, phobia, syncope, maxim, innocuous, aversion, belligerence.

## *Topics for Writing*

The following list is given merely to suggest topics on which a student may write. The individual items are not meant to serve as titles.

I. Concerning college life
   The failure of high school to prepare me for college
   What my goal is in college

The value of good grades
Are the classical languages worth studying?
Are any foreign languages worth studying?
How much rhetoric should students be required to take?
Should all students be required to take literature courses?
The ideal college instructor
Common faults of college instructors
What constitutes a good college course?
Are daily quizzes desirable?
Should mid-semester examinations be abolished?
Are final examinations justified?
Should examinations be essay-type or objective?
Is the honor system desirable during examinations?
Can fraternities justify their existence?
What qualities should a fraternity look for in freshmen whom it might
    wish to pledge?
Is it worth while to belong to a fraternity?
Should initiates to a fraternity be hazed?
Should freshmen have to undergo hazing of any sort?
Are freshman caps justifiable?
What is the proper dress to wear to class?
Should girls wear slacks on campus?
The value of intramural sports
How essential is a winning football team to an institution?
Should coaches be appointed on long-term contracts?
Methods of playing various sports well
Should students pay large sums to "name" bands for college dances?
Should colleges be coeducational?
Preparing for examinations
Proper methods of studying
Dormitory life
Possible jobs for college students
Should all college students work their way through college?
Are marking systems fair?
How should marks in college be compiled?
Should attendance at class be required?
Should the student council punish students for infractions of the rules
    of the institution?
Campus politics
Do intercollegiate athletics actually promote good sportsmanship?
Do some sports encourage fair play more than others?
What architecture is best adapted to collegiate buildings?
What code of morals is prevalent for students on campus?
What vacations are essential during the college year?
Are college entrance requirements too high?
What type of news should appear in the college newspaper?
Should the newspaper be strictly censored?
Should football teams play postseason games?

Is it desirable that athletic teams go on long trips?
Are athletes good scholars?
Should athletic scholarships be given by the college?
Does the library staff co-operate with students?
What makes a good textbook?
Should students keep their textbooks after finishing a course?
What situations need attention in your institution?

II. Concerning reading
What constitutes a good novel?
Are book clubs worth joining?
The value of poetry
What is necessary to gain a large circulation for a magazine?
A magazine that I like
Types of poetry
What the average American reads
A consideration of comic strips
The different editorial policies of various newspapers
The difference between the tabloids and other types of newspapers
What constitutes good sport writing for a newspaper?

III. Concerning politics and government
The salaries of public officials
The control of strikes
Should the term of office of the President be limited to two terms?
Government control of broadcasting
Is the sales tax a fair method of taxation?
What are the most desirable forms of taxation?
Are there inadequacies in our present income-tax system?
What are the virtues of a unicameral legislature?
What qualifications should a congressman have?
How can good men be induced to enter politics?
Should automobile insurance be required by law?
Should gasoline taxes be used for purposes other than highway maintenance?
Should the government operate the railroads?
What limits should be imposed upon freedom of speech?
Is socialized medicine advisable?
For what does each of our political parties stand?
Is our party system desirable?
Should the electoral college be abolished?
Should the legal voting age be lowered to eighteen?
How to reduce international animosity
Methods of curbing child delinquency
Programs of law enforcement
The value of patriotic symbols such as the flag

IV. Concerning the definition of difficult terms
A liberal education            Religion
Superstition                   Immortality

Progress
Rights of man
Propaganda
Heroism
Liberalism
Good morals
Reds
Patriotism
Agnosticism
"All men are created equal"

Evolution
Introverts
Cowardice
Democracy
Radicalism
Respectability
Genius
Hypocrisy
Cheating

V. Concerning miscellaneous topics
The curtailment of radio advertising
Recent marvels of surgery
Diesel *versus* steam locomotives
How old should one be before marrying?
The case against suicide
Philately
Interior decorating problems
The scientific method
Operas in English
The values of classical music
What is jazz music?
Should capital punishment be abolished?
Fads in clothing styles
Movies or the legitimate stage?
The evils of gambling
Drug addiction in America
How to train a dog
Should women smoke?
Why I attend church
Methods of preventing seasickness and airsickness
Air travel as opposed to train travel
Is flying safe?
Love at first sight
Simplified spelling
Women as business executives
What is a high standard of living?
Causes of war
Superhighways
Desirability of billboards along the highways
Applying for a job
Is compulsory military training desirable?
Planning a new home
The latest devices to aid the housewife

# THE WHOLE COMPOSITION

## I

## BASIC PRINCIPLES AND ORGANIZATION

THE goal of a student in composition is the acquiring of such mastery of skills and techniques as will enable him to organize a series of related ideas into a unified and coherent whole, and to write a manuscript of some scope that will show evidence of this mastery. The preceding sections of this text have dealt with parts of the composition: words, sentences, paragraphs. How these parts combine in the best way to form essays, articles, stories, biographies, letters, and the like is the purpose of the remaining sections of the text.

**Three Basic Principles: Unity, Coherence, Emphasis.** Three time-honored principles which form the basis of clear and correct writing are those of unity, coherence, and emphasis; and these apply to the total unit no less than to such parts as the sentence and the paragraph. Despite fads and varying styles and new methods, the primary aim of writing still is to convey ideas from one mind to another; and as aids in accomplishing this aim, these principles are of paramount importance.

*Unity* is the principle of oneness: oneness of theme, of purpose, of tone. To possess unity, a composition must have one aim, one recognizable point of view, and definite limits. Any matter which does not contribute to a unified total effect, which is not part of the writer's aim as stated in his specific purpose, must be rigidly excluded, however interesting it may be in itself. Thus a student who knows what is meant by the principle of unity, and applies it in his writing, will avoid long, rambling introductions before he comes to the main point under discussion; he will likewise avoid lingering, trailing conclusions after he has finished what he had to say; and along the way he will avoid detours, however alluring the by-roads, and will stick to the main route as charted in the statement of his specific purpose and in his thesis sentence. A composition will have unity if a writer chooses one main idea to develop, begins without preamble with a consideration of this idea, and when he has finished with the development of his main idea, stops. It is the lackadaisical approach to a subject, without plan or chart, that makes for lack of unity in writing.

*Coherence* is the principle of order and arrangement applied to composition. It means a steady progress towards a definite goal. It involves the arrangement of ideas in a clear order, so that first things come first, co-ordinate ideas are clearly indicated by their position as being co-ordinate, subordinate details are given their proper place and clearly shown to be subordinate, and related ideas are grouped according to a definite pattern. The pattern may be that of a natural order, an order according to time, an order according to proximity and position, or an order of increasing importance; but whatever the pattern chosen, it should be followed throughout the composition without any deviation, and it should be fixed clearly in the writer's mind from his first sentence to his last in any given piece of writing. Observing the principle of coherence will save a writer from backing up to develop some point that belonged elsewhere, but which he forgot to take up at the proper place, from shifting his point of view unnecessarily, from putting the cart before the horse, and from other practices which scatterbrained writers all too frequently fall into.

*Emphasis* is the principle of placing stress on the most important ideas in a composition, and making this stress obvious to a reader. It involves ordering ideas in such a way that the importance of a certain point or idea will stand out clearly. In short papers two or three points at most should be emphasized, and even in long papers it is best to limit the number of points on which one lays stress. The two chief ways of showing emphasis are by position and by proportion. As in the sentence and the paragraph, the most emphatic positions in the whole composition are at the beginning and the end. Whatever stands first or last in an article is likely to attract special notice. In arranging his ideas, therefore, a writer should develop a plan whereby ideas he wishes to stand out will come at the beginning or the end of a composition. Another way of securing emphasis is to give more space to an idea the writer deems important, since it is true that the devotion of considerable space to some idea will indicate that the writer considers it more important than an idea to which he gives little space. This method is called emphasis by proportion.

# THE OUTLINE

The best method of insuring the principles of unity, coherence, and emphasis in a piece of writing is to construct an outline before beginning to write the article. Making the outline is the last step in planning the composition, and how to do this will be considered next. In considering the outline, however, bear in mind that it belongs to the general process of planning, which also includes selecting a subject, determining the specific purpose, writing the thesis sentence, and selecting a title. (For these matters, review pages 22–27.)

The outline serves as an aid to both reader and writer. It enables the reader to preserve in skeleton form the important points in a work which he is perusing. It enables the writer to organize his thoughts before he puts them on paper. Such an organization is essential if the presentation is to be coherent.

**The Mechanical Form of the Outline.** The purpose of the outline is to present the structure of the whole work at a glance. Therefore, certain purely mechanical features must be observed.

First, a consistent system of notation must be used. Perhaps the most usual system employs Roman numerals to indicate main points, and in descending order of importance, capital letters, Arabic numerals, small letters, Arabic numerals in parentheses (1), and small letters in parentheses (a). Second, each subdivision should be clearly indented. Third, divisions of equal importance should be placed immediately under each other. Fourth, it is well to capitalize the first word in each point. The outline thus takes this form:

I.
  A.
  B.
    1.
    2.
II. etc.

Such a form indicates that *I* and *II* are of relatively equal importance—that is, they are co-ordinate. *A* and *B* in turn are of less importance than *I* and *II* but are also co-ordinate, and *1* and *2* are of even less importance but again are equal to each other. The outline thus serves to indicate clearly the relative importance of various topics.

**The Composition of the Outline.** The major principle of the outline is division. If that is remembered, making an outline will be less difficult.

It means, first of all, that each major point is a subdivision of the thesis of the paper; if an outline has four main headings, the thesis, therefore, has four parts. Also point *I* has two parts if *A* and *B* are listed under it. Never try to make an outline by adding *A* and *B* to *I* as additional thoughts; *A* and *B* can only be parts of *I,* not additions to it.

The principle of division means secondly that the outline must have at least two main points, and that each section which is divided must have at least two parts. It is obviously impossible to divide anything into fewer than two parts. Suppose, for example, that you are making an outline for a paper on roofs. The first main point is "Fireproof roofs"; however, as slate is the only kind of fireproof roof which occurs to you, you make an outline this way:

    I. Fireproof roofs
       A. Slate
    II. . . .

Such outlining procedure is illogical, for if slate is the only kind of fireproof roof, slate is not a subdivision of the main point; it *is* the main point. The error can be corrected this way: I. Fireproof roofing: slate. Of course, many times one can find other subdivisions by a more careful analysis of the topic. Here, for example, tile and metal would readily occur as additional types of fireproof roofing.

A few cautions must be made concerning the division. First, be sure that no two co-ordinate points contain material in common. Suppose your outline on roofs takes the following form:

    I. Shingle roofs
    II. Slate roofs
    III. Durable roofs

You notice immediately that points two and three overlap. Slate roofs are durable roofs. Between points *I* and *II,* however, the division is clear and the outline correct.

The cure for overlapping of points lies in establishing a *basis of classification.* In classifying roofs, decide whether you wish to consider them according to cost or durability or composition or some other basis; then adhere strictly to that one method. Your outline might take any one of the three following forms:

| I. Shingle | I. Roofs with short life | I. Expensive roofs |
|------------|--------------------------|--------------------|
| II. Slate | II. Durable roofs | II. Medium-priced roofs |
| III. Thatch | | III. Inexpensive roofs |
| IV. Tile | | |

Select, therefore, the most suitable basis for classifying co-ordinate points, and do not shift carelessly to any other basis; otherwise overlapping will result.

Knowing that an outline employs division founded on one basis of classification, you will be able to see that the introduction and conclusion to a paper should not be numbered. It would be possible to classify on the basis of structure, employing Introduction, Body, and Conclusion as the main points, but that is unnecessary. The basis of classification should be content, not structure. Roman numerals should be reserved to signify the main points in the body of the paper, that is, the points which subdivide the thesis directly. Being on a different basis of classification, the introductory and concluding material cannot be numbered co-ordinately with them. The following form can be used:

Introduction: . . .
    A. . . .
    B. . . .
  I. . . .
 II. . . .
Conclusion: . . .
    A. . . .
    B. . . .

Note that the terms "Introduction" and "Conclusion," because they are general terms, must never be left in the outline without a statement of the material included in them. After the colon following the word "Introduction" might well go the thesis or the general problem to be solved in the paper, two statements commonly found in introductory paragraphs. The subpoints, as *A* and *B,* would state any divisions of the main topic that might appear in the introduction. The form of the outline accordingly becomes logical. Roman numerals indicate the main divisions of the thesis, and the words "Introduction" and "Conclusion," which are on a different basis of classification and hence not numbered, state the material preceding or following the body of the paper.

A few other general considerations remain. Have only a few main headings or overlapping will result. Secondly, as a general practice, leave no heading undivided which is designated by a Roman numeral, as such topics are so important as to require further explanation by division. Thirdly, do not encumber the outline with excessive detail or with examples or illustrations, although, of course, you should organize fully all essential material.

**The Topic Outline.** Although there are many types of outlines, two are in common use: the topic and the sentence. The topic outline expresses each point by means of a phrase or a catchword. Because each point is brief, the topic outline is useful in organizing material, for the topics can be shifted around readily and their relationship quickly perceived. Its brevity, however, may make it obscure at a later date or to some other person.

It is important therefore in using the topic outline to state the points as carefully as possible. Do not try to make a topic by cutting the subject from a sentence, by omitting part of the verb, or by omitting articles. Restate the point entirely. Thus, if you wish to convey the idea that "Material is needed for the work to continue," do not express the point as "Material needed for work to continue," nor as "Need material for work to continue"; restate it concisely as "The urgent need for material." Such wording gives brevity and clarity.

Take particular care to use parallel structure for co-ordinate headings, for it will enable you to organize your ideas more logically. The Roman numerals, which designate co-ordinate points, should be parallel; *A* and *B* under *I,* which are also co-ordinate, should be parallel, and so on. The latter two points, however, are not co-ordinate with *A* and *B* under *II* and therefore need not be parallel with them. Notice how defective is the following outline:

How to Prune a Fruit Tree

I. Proper time of year
  A. Late fall
    1. To prevent "bleeding"
    2. Insects
  B. etc.

The writer of this outline cannot be sure that heading 2 under *A* is logical. What does "insects" mean? If the point were stated "To guard against insects," the writer could be sure that it was properly classified. Time spent on wording of the outline will be time saved in writing the paper.

Placing a thesis sentence at the top of the outline is an excellent practice. Such a sentence will keep the writer's thinking directed on the problem at hand.

*Example of a topic outline*

Thesis: College English should increase a student's ability to understand and use the English language.
  I. His ability to read
    A. To comprehend the printed page ·
    B. To understand the qualities of good writing
  II. His ability to express himself
    A. In speech
      1. By instruction in correct forms

  2. By practice
   a. In informal recitation
   b. In oral recitation
 B. In writing
  1. By drill on mechanical details
  2. By the study of correct models
  3. By practice in writing
III. His ability to think clearly
 A. To construct a logical train of thought
  1. By the study of instructions in the text
  2. By the study of his instructor's comments
   a. Oral
    (1) In class
    (2) In conference
   b. Written: comments on assigned papers
 B. To be intelligently critical of the ideas of others

**The Sentence Outline.** The sentence outline is made up of complete sentences rather than phrases or catchwords. For purposes of suggesting your organization to someone else or of keeping a plan of organization lucid in your own mind over a long period of time, it is superior to the topic outline. The same principles govern it that have just been applied to the topic outline.

*Example of a sentence outline*

Thesis: College English should increase a student's ability to understand and use the English language.
 I. College English should increase his ability to read.
  A. It should give him power to comprehend the thought of the printed page.
  B. It should give him an understanding of the qualities of good literature.
 II. It should increase his power of expression.
  A. It should improve his habits of speech.
   1. It should teach him what good speech is.
   2. It should give him mastery of it by constant practice.
    a. It should provide instruction through informal recitation.
    b. It should provide instruction through formal talks.
  B. It should improve his written expression.
   1. It should provide benefits by drill on mechanical details.
   2. It should provide benefits by the study of correct models.
   3. It should provide benefits by constant practice in writing.
 III. It should increase his ability to think clearly.
  A. It should enable him to construct a logical train of thought.
   1. The textbook should offer instructions on logical presentation.
   2. The instructor should offer comments on logical presentation.
    a. The instructor should offer oral comments.
     (1) These comments should be given in class.
     (2) These comments should also be given in conference.

b. The instructor should give written criticism in his comments on
assigned papers which the student submits.

B. It should enable him to be intelligently critical of the ideas of others.

## Exercises

### A

Immediately following are three lists of words. Without adding or subtracting words from any list, rearrange the words according to their proper
classification and importance into a topic outline form with correct outline
numbering.

Example: Large blackboards  
    Good classrooms  
    Poor classrooms  
    Hot  
    Ill-lighted  
    Good illumination  
    Good ventilation

I. Poor classrooms  
  A. Hot  
  B. Ill-lighted  
II. Good classrooms  
  A. Large blackboards  
  B. Good illumination  
  C. Good ventilation

1. Winter sports  
  Tennis  
  Skating  
  Summer sports  
  Boating  
  Hockey  
  Fall sports  

  Swimming  
  Football  
  Cross-country running  
  Tobogganing  
  Soccer  
  Skiing  
  Golf

2. Social studies  
  History  
  Economics  
  English  
  Corporation finance  
  German  
  Foreign languages  

  American literature  
  American history  
  Money and banking  
  Shakespeare  
  French  
  Spanish  
  Modern European history

3. Denotation  
  Sentence structure  
  Uses of the objective case  
  Grammar  
  Noun  
  Direct object  
  Complex sentence  
  Types of sentences  
  Compound sentence  
  The word  
  Levels of usage  
  Parts of speech  
  Preposition  
  Economy of wording  

  Indirect object  
  Colloquialisms  
  Opening prepositional phrases  
  Variety in sentence beginnings  
  Opening gerund phrases  
  Adjective  
  Adverb  
  Opening participial phrases  
  Object of a preposition  
  Verb  
  Pronoun  
  Slang  
  Simple sentence

## B

Each of the following outlines is defective in some way. Revise each in such a way as to make it conform to the principles in the preceding chapter. The first three outlines are to be topic outlines; the fourth is to be a sentence outline.

1. Thesis: The reformers were responsible for many useful changes.

    I. In eating and drinking
        A. They wanted people to drink water
        B. Coarse, wholesome foods
    II. In education
        A. They protested against dull routine
        B. Against corporal punishment
    III. They advocated reforms in the position of women
        A. Educating them
        B. Equal political rights

2. Thesis: The three types of epic poetry are the heroic, the literary, and the mock.

    I. The heroic epic
        A. Gives account of great struggle of nations
        B. Great national ideals stressed
    II. The second type of epic is the literary epic
        A. It also depicts great national struggles
        B. An imitation of the heroic epic by a literary artist
    III. The mock epic
        A. Written to apply epic grandeur to a minor theme
        B. To mimic the epic

3. Thesis: English poetry contains several types of basic feet.

    I. The four common types
        A. The iambic foot
            1. It is composed of two syllables
            2. The accent on the second
        B. The trochaic foot also has two syllables
            1. It has an accent on the first
        C. The anapestic foot has three syllables
            1. The accent on the third syllable
        D. The dactylic foot
            1. Possessing three syllables
            2. Accenting the first syllable
    II. There are two uncommon feet
        A. The spondaic foot
            1. Two syllables
            2. Both syllables accented
        B. The second is the pyrrhic foot
            1. The syllables are two
            2. Neither accented

4. Thesis: A course in composition is valuable to every college student.

    I. The objections to college composition are based on a misunderstanding of its aims.

        A. It does not aim to produce professional writers.

            1. It could not if it would.

                a. Most composition teachers are not trained for such a function.

                b. Composition teachers realize that such a purpose would be foolish.

        B. It does not put emphasis on style rather than on content.

            1. Style and content are considered inseparable.

            2. Content should determine style.

    II. College composition does not teach an impracticable kind of English.

        A. Modern textbooks stress current usage.

        B. Many colleges try to employ teachers who are themselves writers.

    III. The composition course helps the student in his other courses.

        A. It trains him in the techniques of reading.

        B. It trains him to express what he knows.

            1. In written reports.

            2. Examinations.

            3. Recitation.

        C. It helps the student to write better term papers.

        D. It helps the student to write better reports on outside reading.

    IV. The composition course broadens the student's interests.

        A. It makes him more broadminded.

        B. It introduces him to subject matter he is not familiar with.

            1. Through readings.

            2. He writes on diversified topics.

        C. He becomes familiar with many new words.

    V. A composition course trains the student to be more critical of the language he hears.

        A. He is less susceptible to propaganda.

            1. He is discriminating about words.

            2. He is not overpowered by gorgeous, vague terminology.

            3. He acquires an admiration for specific words.

    VI. The composition course helps a student after he graduates.

        A. It equips him with the means of communicating with people of culture and importance.

        B. The writing of a formal letter does not frighten him.

        C. It provides him with the means of becoming an appreciative reader.

## C

From each of the following paragraphs, select the topic sentence and write it down. Then below the topic sentence, write a topic outline of the material in the paragraph.

1. One of the first English dictionaries was that by Henry Cockeram, printed in 1623. It had three parts: the first contained difficult words with an explanation of their meaning; the second contained easy words translated into

hard words; the third was a key to classical and mythological terms to be found in the best reading of the day.

2. One of the most important dictionaries was that written by Samuel Johnson in the middle of the eighteenth century. His dictionary was inadequate in that it contained inexact quotations, it revealed his personal prejudices (such as his dislike of the Scots), and it sometimes defined words in language too difficult to be readily comprehended. But it had many desirable features that stamp it as a great dictionary. Johnson studied a great many writings to get accurate definitions, he made more exact the specific meanings of many words, he entered more words than previous lexicographers had, and he gave fuller information about each word. His dictionary stands as a great work for its time.

3. Perhaps the greatest of modern dictionaries is the Oxford English Dictionary. It contains over 400,000 words, and has nearly 2,000,000 illustrations to show their meanings in the writings of standard authors. But it is great in other ways than size. It is complete in furnishing information about every word used in the language for the last eight hundred years. It is scholarly, for each word is traced through its various changes of meaning, and the time of its entrance into or exit from the language is stated. It is also scholarly in its use of fresh quotations for study to derive exact meanings.

4. The Transcendentalist movement in America produced many reforms. Some of the reformers wished to stay in the world and make their changes from within. They thought that through the agency of the churches and schools society could be bettered. Others, however, withdrew in despair from the world and turned to the life of the country. A few, like Thoreau, were solitary hermits, but many congregated in ideal communities. Fruitlands and Brook Farm and the Oneida Community were communities formed by the Transcendentalists in the search for perfect human societies.

5. The results of the Transcendental reforms were both bad and good. All kinds of cranks and reformers associated themselves with the movement to exploit absurd ideas. But through the agency of many intelligent men and women, the movement contributed to such matters as the extension and modernization of education, the establishment of equal rights for women, and the abolition of slavery.

6. The contrast between Benjamin Franklin and Jonathan Edwards, two of the leading figures of eighteenth-century America, is interesting in showing two sides of an unusual century. Franklin was in sympathy with the age, but Edwards struggled against it, trying desperately to change the dominant trend. Franklin was looking ahead toward the modern, secular point of view, whereas Edwards was seeking to restore the older Calvinist religion to its former leading position as the guide of both religious and secular thinking. Franklin was correspondingly a man of the world, interested in practical invention, much traveled, statesmanlike, and practical; Edwards was unworldly, mystical, interested in things eternal, and exhorting mankind to look ahead to the next world.

7. The Shakespearean theater had certain advantages over that of today. The absence of elaborate stage settings led to speedy presentation. The absence of these settings also resulted in closer concentration upon the drama itself. To

follow the action, the spectators had to listen very intently to the spoken word, and they were compelled to build mental pictures of the scene in which the action took place, pictures derived from listening to the poetic descriptions given in the dramas. The audience, therefore, centered its attention upon essentials and was not distracted from the drama itself.

8. James Burbage had quite a problem in selecting a place for a theater in Elizabethan London. He had to find a spot which was outside the jurisdiction of the city authorities, for they were puritanical and hated the drama. But at the same time he had to be near the center of activity so that people could attend his performances and so that he could make a profit from his venture. The solution was found in the plots of land once owned by different monasteries. The monasteries situated in London had been from olden time free from molestation by city authorities, and when Henry VIII had abolished them as monasteries, he had not removed their special privilege. So by building his theater upon one of these plots, Burbage solved his problem.

9. Dean Martin has distinguished for us the educator from the propagandist. The propagandist, he says, tries to induce people to act contrary to their best interests. He closes their minds in order to convert people to a cause, sell them a product, and the like; his goals he seeks at any cost by means of superficial arguments, the loss of intellectual honesty, and the use of slippery phraseology. The educator, on the other hand, has as his goal the creation of a well-rounded personality. He endeavors to open the minds of his students and advocates their learning by the scientific method of personal examination. The student is taught to consider such learning as experimental, and to hold his conclusions tentatively as he seeks further evidence. The propagandist, therefore, seeks to close the human mind and use people against their best interests; the educator seeks to open the human mind and to build men.

10. Professor Lane Cooper has defined the reading which he believes a technical man, such as an engineer, should do. He states that the engineer should read all those books which have stood the test of time and are loosely referred to as "classics." The Bible and the works of Homer, Dante, Shakespeare, and Milton fall into this classification. The engineer should also not be afraid to reread such works many times, for rereading promotes that understanding which enables one to be a better man and a better citizen of his country. Lastly, the engineer should read widely in such books.

## D

1. Write down the names of a dozen or so members of your high-school graduating class. Arrange these people in classifications on the basis of what they are doing at the present time. Make a topic outline which will represent these classifications. Arrange subordinate divisions which will state the particular occupation of each person.

2. Convert the topic outline made for Exercise 1 into a complete sentence outline.

3. Ask eight or ten students their opinions as to the best way to prepare for final examinations. Organize and outline their opinions.

4. Read the editorial opinions of several newspapers in your college library

concerning some recent event of national importance. Make an outline which would serve as a guide for a paper on "The Stand Certain Newspapers Are Taking on . . ."

5. Make an outline for a paper on types of music (or books, pictures, girls, boys, neckties, and so forth) which you like and which you do not like, with your reasons.

6. Classify the instruments in a symphony orchestra, those in a college band, the players on an athletic team, the members of a newspaper staff, or the student organizations on your campus, in at least three different ways. Make an outline of each method of organization.

## The Conditions of Art

### JOHN RUSKIN

Beautiful art can only be produced by people who have beautiful things around them, and leisure to look at them; and unless you provide some elements of beauty for your workmen to be surrounded by, you will find that no elements of beauty can be invented by them.

I was struck forcibly by the bearing of this great fact upon our modern efforts at ornamentation, in an afternoon walk last week, in the suburbs of one of our large manufacturing towns. I was thinking of the difference in the effect in the designer's mind, between the scene which I then came upon, and the scene which would have presented itself to the eyes of any designer of the middle ages when he left his workshop. Just outside the town I came upon an old English cottage, or mansion, I hardly know which to call it, set close under the hill, and beside the river, perhaps built somewhere in the Charleses' time, with mullioned windows and a low arched porch; round which, in the little triangular garden, one can imagine the family as they used to sit in old summertimes, the ripple of the river heard faintly through the sweet-brier hedge, and the sheep on the far-off wolds shining in the evening sunlight. There, uninhabited for many and many a year, it had been left in unregarded havoc of ruin; the garden gate still swung loose to its latch; the garden, blighted utterly into a field of ashes, not even a weed taking root there; the roof torn into shapeless rents; the shutters hanging about the windows in rags of rotten wood; before its gate, the stream which had gladdened it now soaking slowly by, black as ebony, and thick with curdling scum; the bank above it trodden into unctuous sooty slime; far in front of it, between it and the old hills, the furnaces of the city foaming forth perpetual plague of sulphurous darkness; the volumes of their storm clouds coiling low over a waste of grassless fields, fenced from each other not by hedges but by slabs of square stone, like gravestones, riveted together with iron.

That was the scene for the designer's contemplation in his afternoon walk at Rochdale. Now fancy what was the scene which presented itself, in his afternoon walk, to a designer of the Gothic school of Pisa—Nino Pisano, or any of his men.

On each side of a bright river he saw rise a line of brighter palaces, arched and pillared, and inlaid with deep red porphyry, and with serpentine; along the quays before their gates were riding troops of knights, noble in face and form, dazzling in crest and shield; horse and man one labyrinth of quaint color and gleaming light—the purple, and silver, and scarlet fringes flowing over the strong limbs and clashing mail, like sea waves over rocks at sunset. Opening on each side from the river were gardens, courts, and cloisters; long successions of white pillars among wreaths of vine; leaping of fountains through buds of pomegranate and orange; and still along the garden paths, and under and through the crimson of the pomegranate shadows, moving slowly, groups of the fairest women that Italy ever saw—fairest because purest and thoughtfulest; trained in all high knowledge, as in all courteous art—in dance, in song, in sweet wit, in lofty learning, in loftier courage, in loftiest love—able alike to cheer, to enchant, or save, the souls of men. Above all this scenery of perfect human life, rose dome and belltower burning with white alabaster and gold: beyond dome and belltower the slopes of mighty hills hoary with olive; far in the north, above a purple sea of peaks of solemn Apennine, the clear, sharp-cloven Carrara mountains sent up their steadfast flames of marble summit into amber sky; the great sea itself, scoring with expanse of light, stretching from their feet to the Gorgonian isles; and over all these, ever present, near or far—seen through the leaves of vine, or imaged with all its march of clouds in the Arno's stream, or set with its depth of blue close against the golden hair and burning cheek of lady and knight—that untroubled and sacred sky, which was to all men, in those days of innocent faith, indeed the unquestioned abode of spirits, as the earth was of men; and which opened straight through its gates of cloud and veils of dew into the awfulness of the eternal world—a heaven in which every cloud that passed was literally the chariot of an angel, and every ray of its Evening and Morning streamed from the throne of God.

What think you of that for a school of design?

I do not bring this contrast before you as a ground of hopelessness in our task; neither do I look for any possible renovation of the Republic of Pisa, at Bradford, in the nineteenth century; but I put it before you in order that you may be aware precisely of the kind of difficulty you have to meet, and may then consider with yourselves how far you can meet it. To men surrounded by the depressing and monotonous circumstances of English manufacturing life, depend upon it, design is simply impossible. This is the most distinct of all the experiences I have had in dealing with the modern workman. He is intelligent and ingenious in the highest degree—subtle in touch and keen in sight; but he is, generally speaking, wholly destitute of designing power. And if you want to give him the power, you must give him the materials, and put him in the circumstances for it. Design is not the offspring of idle fancy; it is the studied result of accumulative observation and delightful habit. Without observation and experience, no design—without peace and pleasurableness in occupation, no design—and all the lecturings and teachings and prizes and principles of art in the world are of no use, so long as you don't surround your men with happy influences and beautiful things. It is impossible for them to have right ideas about color, unless they see the lovely colors of nature unspoiled; impossible for them to supply beautiful incident and action in their ornament, unless they see beautiful incident and action in the world about them. Inform their minds, refine their habits, and you form and refine their designs; but keep them illiterate, uncomfortable, and in the midst of unbeautiful things, and whatever they do will still be spurious, vulgar, and valueless.—*The Two Paths,* Lecture 3.

## Suggestions for Study

1. In what two parts of the article do you find the thesis stated? Formulate that thesis in your own words.

2. What means of paragraph development is used in paragraphs two and four? State the topic sentence of each paragraph. What means is used for the presentation of the composition as a whole?

3. In Ruskin's estimation, is the modern craftsman lacking in intelligence and artistic ability? What then does he lack?

4. Make an outline of this selection. Limit the number of main headings which you employ; preferably do not use more than two here. State the thesis before you begin to outline, then consider what parts of the composition are subdivisions of the thesis, and what parts serve only to introduce or summarize it. Do not use numerals for the latter parts, as they are the thesis itself, not parts of it.

5. Define the following words from the selection: mullioned, ebony, unctuous, porphyry, serpentine, pomegranate, alabaster, amber, renovation, destitute, accumulative, spurious.

# Types of Industrial Organization [1]

## WILLARD L. THORP

There are a number of different ways in which business enterprises may be organized. The most important are: individual ownership, the partnership, the corporation, and the co-operative society. The business-man must operate through one or another of these forms of organization.

More establishments of the United States are operated by individuals than in any other way. The figures for 1919 for manufacturing concerns are as follows:

|  | Number of Establishments | Per Cent |
|---|---|---|
| Individuals | 138,112 | 47.6 |
| Corporations | 91,517 | 31.5 |
| All others | 60,476 | 20.8 |
| Total | 290,105 | 100.0 |

These figures without further interpretation do not give an accurate picture. They must be supplemented by the following:

|  | Number of Employees | Per Cent |
|---|---|---|
| Individuals | 623,469 | 4.0 |
| Corporations | 7,875,132 | 86.0 |
| All others | 597,771 | 10.0 |
| Total | 9,096,372 | 100.0 |

From these two tables it appears that although corporations number less than one third of the establishments, they employ more than six sevenths of the wage earners. Furthermore, they produce more than seven eights of the total value of all products. This situation is also found in the mining industries. But in agriculture, and, until recently, in retail trade, the corporate form of organization has made little headway.

Nearly one half of the manufacturing concerns in the country and the bulk of agricultural and mercantile enterprises are operated by individuals. These enterprises start usually without formality or legal permission. One person assumes all responsibility. In some cases, he may be required to obtain a license, as in restaurants, or pass examinations, as with doctors and lawyers.

In such a concern, control is concentrated in the hands of one person.

1. From *Economic Institutions,* by Willard L. Thorp. Reprinted by permission of The Macmillan Company, publishers.

This saves much red tape and routine, and is desirable where the business is one which cannot be systematized. The fact that the business rests on one individual, however, limits it in many respects. The most direct limitation is in the amount of money which a single person can borrow. It should be noted that, in case of failure, the individual is liable not only for the amount he has put into the business but to the extent of all his assets.

Individually-owned concerns are seldom long-lived. Beginning and ending their existence is an easy matter. Retail stores sometimes change hands several times in one year. The owner may sell out, the store may go bankrupt, or, more happily, it may grow into a corporation or partnership.

When one man finds that he cannot satisfy his business ambitions alone, one way out is to take one or more partners into his business. Each partner invests a certain sum, not necessarily equal in amount, and a contract is signed, which is legally binding. This definitely states the purposes of the organization and the rights and duties of the partners.

Although the exact nature of the partnership may vary according to the conditions of the contract, certain advantages are common to all. A partnership puts at the disposal of the business a larger amount of capital than any one partner could advance alone. Each partner is liable for the entire debt of the firm. If the firm runs heavily into debt, the creditors may collect all that is owed from any of the partners. Obviously, such a condition necessitates the greatest care in selecting partners, and prevents the formation of partnerships with many members.

Since each partnership is based upon a contract between several persons, it automatically ends when one member withdraws or dies. If the business is to continue a new partnership must be formed. Partnerships are found chiefly in mercantile undertakings, small manufacturing concerns, and in the professions, especially the law.

In recent years, a new form of business organization has greatly overshadowed all others. Upon request of a prescribed number of individuals and the passing of certain formalities, a state government creates a corporation. This corporation is legally an individual, behaving in the eyes of the law as if it were a person. It may commit a crime, may be sued for damages, and the like. The capital, or money with which it begins business, is supplied by persons who receive shares, commonly called stock, in exchange for a sum invested. The possession of these shares gives them a proportion of the total ownership in accordance with the relative amount of stock each owns. The owners of shares elect directors who guide and operate the business. The policies of the corporation are determined by this board of directors. They presumably keep in close touch with the business, though generally engaging competent individuals to make and carry out decisions of minor importance.

The corporation differs vitally from the forms of business organization already discussed. In the first place, it is permanent. Its charter may run for a limited time but can usually be easily renewed. Ownership may be transferred from one person to another; even though all the original incorporators die, the corporation still lives. In the second place, the liability of each individual is limited. Quite different from the individual enterprise, or partnership, he may lose only what the share of stock has cost him. Beyond that he is not liable, no matter how much his corporation owes. One of the few exceptions to this rule is a national bank, in which each stockholder is liable for an additional sum equal to his original investment. In the third place, there is no limit to the amount of capital such a concern may obtain, if it can persuade persons to invest. It may issue stock and thereby gather capital from thousands of stockholders. This may all be done, however, without losing centralized control, vested in the directors.

The corporate form also has certain disadvantages. In the first place, it is difficult to fix responsibility. There are many persons partly responsible for anything that may be done. No one individual feels that concentrated responsibility which exists in the case of a single owner or a partner. In the second place, ownership is almost wholly separated from management. The firm is actually run by managers or engineers under salary. The owners are far away, many of them having no knowledge of the business, and little interest beyond the scale of dividend payments. In the eyes of the law, an act by the manager, such as entering an unlawful combination, is punished by fining the corporation. The distant stockholders bear the burden for acts, the responsibility for which is certainly far from theirs. In the third place, this "absentee ownership of capital" leaves the chief responsibility in the hands of a small group. There can be concentration of control in very few hands, despite widespread ownership. The corporation is operated in accordance with the mandates of the holders of a majority of the stock. The small stockholders, who may be many, have really no control. In the fourth place, any corporation is an impersonal organization. Loyalty or co-operation between employer and employed is difficult to stimulate. Perhaps the prejudice which so many persons feel against corporations is caused by their impersonality.

Incorporation may be used as a method whereby an energetic promoter can obtain money from individuals without pledging himself that they will receive any return. In many corporations the stockholder has no intelligent understanding of the real activity of the enterprise of which he is part owner. On the other hand, he feels no responsibility since no one thinks of identifying him as one of the owners of the U.S. Steel Corporation unless he has a very large block of the stock. At the beginning of 1925 the U.S. Steel Corporation had 96,285 stockholders, the Pennsylvania Railroad 145,174, and the American Telephone and Telegraph Company 345,133. These figures represent large increases over the prewar distribution of holdings. . . .

Co-operative societies are organizations formed by a group of producers or consumers for joint economic action. The most important types are societies for co-operative handling and marketing of products, societies for co-operative buying, and societies for co-operative credit.

The societies for co-operative handling and marketing of products are, in many cases, well known. In 1925 the United States Department of Agriculture reported that there were 10,803 such societies, grouped as follows:

| *Industries* | *Number of Societies* |
|---|---|
| Grain | 3,338 |
| Dairy products | 2,197 |
| Livestock | 1,770 |
| Fruits and vegetables | 1,237 |
| Cotton and cotton products | 121 |
| Tobacco | 24 |
| All others | 2,116 |
| Total | 10,803 |

The estimated membership of these organizations is 2,450,000 farmers. These organizations are engaged in providing elevators and storehouses, shipping, advertising, and the actual marketing of products. The farmer is generally far from market, unacquainted with market conditions, and unable to sell his product to his best advantage. By organizing co-operative societies, he is able to reduce the expense of selling his crop, as well as to do it more conveniently.

The United States Department of Agriculture reports 1,217 societies among farmers for co-operative purchasing. These include general purchasing associations, co-operative stores, lumber yards, fuel yards, and the like. Their purpose is two-fold: they save by purchasing in large quantities; and they avoid the necessity of paying a profit to middlemen. They must meet the costs of their enterprise, but they can keep the profits in their own pockets.

The co-operative credit societies most often take the form of building and loan associations. There were 10,000 such organizations in the United

States in 1923, with a membership of nearly seven million persons. Their assets were $3,342,000,000.

The co-operative movement has not made so rapid an advance in this country as in Europe. The lack of experience among the members and their failure to select competent managers have hindered their expansion. Recent legislation has encouraged the formation of co-operative organizations, and the Department of Agriculture openly supports the movement.

## Suggestions for Study

1. Of what rhetorical use is the enumeration, in the introduction, of the major points of the article?
2. What statistics indicate the strength of the corporations?
3. State the advantages and limitations of individual concerns.
4. State the differences between the individual concern and the partnership.
5. What major risk is involved in forming a partnership?
6. In what way does the law regard a corporation?
7. How are shares important in a corporate organization? Who determines the policies of the corporation?
8. State three major differences between the corporation and the two preceding types.
9. State four disadvantages of the corporation.
10. Define a co-operative society.
11. For what reader is this selection written?
12. Make an outline to show in diagrammatic form the analysis of this subject.
13. Define the following words from this selection: mercantile, prescribed, liability, vested, dividend, mandates, competent.

## The Importance of Dust [2]

### ALFRED RUSSEL WALLACE

The majority of persons, if asked what were the uses of dust, would reply that they did not know it had any, but they were sure it was a great nuisance. It is true that dust, in our towns and in our houses, is often not only a nuisance but a serious source of disease: while in many countries it produces ophthalmia, often resulting in total blindness. Dust, however, as it is usually perceived by us, is, like dirt, only matter in the wrong place, and whatever injurious or disagreeable effects it produces are largely due to our own dealings with nature. So soon as we dispense with horse-power and adopt purely mechanical means of traction and conveyance, we can almost wholly abolish disease-bearing dust from our streets, and

2. From *The Wonderful Century* (New York, 1898), by A. R. Wallace. Reprinted by permission of the publishers, Dodd, Mead & Company, Inc.

ultimately from all our highways; while another kind of dust, that caused by the imperfect combustion of coal, may be got rid of with equal facility so soon as we consider pure air, sunlight, and natural beauty to be of more importance to the population as a whole than are the prejudices of the vested interests of those who produce the smoke.

But though we can thus minimize the dangers and the inconveniences arising from the grosser forms of dust, we cannot wholly abolish it; and it is, indeed, fortunate we cannot do so, since it has now been discovered that it is to the presence of dust we owe much of the beauty, and perhaps even the very habitability of the earth we live upon. Few of the fairy tales of science are more marvelous than these recent discoveries as to the varied effects and important uses of dust in the economy of nature.

The question why the sky and the deep ocean are both blue did much concern the earlier physicists. It was thought to be the natural color of pure air and water, so pale as not to be visible when small quantities were seen, and only exhibiting its true tint when we looked through great depths of atmosphere or of organic water. But this theory did not explain the familiar facts of the gorgeous tints seen at sunset and sunrise, not only in the atmosphere and on the clouds near the horizon, but also in equally resplendent hues when the invisible sun shines upon Alpine peaks and snowfields. A true theory should explain all these colors, which comprise almost every tint of the rainbow.

The explanation was found through experiments on the visibility or non-visibility of air, which were made by the late Professor Tyndall about the year 1868. Everyone has seen the floating dust in a sunbeam when sunshine enters a partially darkened room; but it is not generally known that if there was absolutely no dust in the air the path of the sunbeam would be totally black and invisible, while if only very little dust was present in very minute particles the air would be as blue as the summer sky.

This was proved by passing a ray of electric light lengthways through a long glass cylinder filled with air of varying degrees of purity as regards dust. In the air of an ordinary room, however clean and well ventilated, the interior of the cylinder appears brilliantly illuminated. But if the cylinder is exhausted and then filled with air which is passed slowly through a fine gauze of intensely heated platinum wire, so as to burn up all the floating dust particles, which are mainly organic, the light will pass through the cylinder without illuminating the interior, which, viewed laterally, will appear as if filled with a dense black cloud. If, now, more air is passed into the cylinder through the heated gauze, but so rapidly that the dust particles are not wholly consumed, a slight blue haze will begin to appear, which will gradually become a pure blue, equal to that of a summer sky. If more and more dust particles are allowed to enter, the blue becomes paler, and gradually changes to the colorless illumination of the ordinary air.

The explanation of these phenomena is that the number of dust particles in ordinary air is so great that they reflect abundance of light of all wavelengths, and thus cause the interior of the vessel containing them to appear illuminated with white light. The air which is passed slowly over white-hot platinum has had the dust particles destroyed, thus showing that they were almost wholly of organic origin, which is also indicated by their extreme lightness, causing them to float permanently in the atmosphere. The dust being thus got rid of, and pure air being entirely transparent, there is nothing in the cylinder to reflect the light, which is sent through its center in a beam of parallel rays so that none of it strikes against the sides; hence the inside of the cylinder appears absolutely dark. But when the larger dust particles are wholly or partially burnt, so that only the very smallest fragments remain, a blue light appears, because these are so minute as to reflect chiefly the more refrangible rays, which are of shorter wavelength—those at the blue end of the spectrum—and which are thus scattered in all directions, while the red and yellow rays pass straight on as before.

We have seen that the air near the earth's surface is full of rather coarse particles which reflect all the rays, and which therefore produce no one color. But higher up the particles necessarily become smaller and smaller, since the comparatively rare atmosphere will support only the very smallest and lightest. These exist throughout a great thickness of air, perhaps from one mile to ten miles high or even more, and blue or violet rays being reflected from the innumerable particles in this great mass of air, which is nearly uniform in all parts of the world as regards the presence of minute dust particles, produce the constant and nearly uniform tint we call sky-blue. A certain amount of white or yellow light is no doubt reflected from the coarser dust in the lower atmosphere, and slightly dilutes the blue and renders it not quite so deep and pure as it otherwise would be. This is shown by the increasing depth of the sky-color when seen from the tops of lofty mountains, while from the still greater heights attained in balloons the sky appears of a blue-black color, the blue reflected from the comparatively small amount of dust particles being seen against the intense black of stellar space. It is for the same reason that the "Italian skies" are of so rich a blue, because the Mediterranean Sea on one side and the snowy Alps on the other do not furnish so large a quantity of atmospheric dust in the lower strata of air as in less favorably situated

countries, thus leaving the blue reflected by the more uniformly distributed fine dust of the higher strata undiluted. But these Mediterranean
skies are surpassed by those of the central Pacific ocean, where, owing
to the small area of land, the lower atmosphere is more free from coarse
dust than in any other part of the world.

If we look at the sky on a perfectly fine summer's day, we shall find
that the blue color is the most pure and intense overhead, and when looking high up in a direction opposite to the sun. Near the horizon it is
always less bright, while in the region immediately around the sun it is
more or less yellow. The reason of this is that near the horizon we look
through a very great thickness of the lower atmosphere, which is full of
the larger dust particles reflecting white light, and this dilutes the pure
blue of the higher atmosphere seen beyond. And in the vicinity of the
sun a good deal of the blue light is reflected back into space by the finer
dust, thus giving a yellowish tinge to that which reaches us reflected
chiefly from the coarse dust of the lower atmosphere. At sunset and sunrise, however, this last effect is greatly intensified, owing to the great
thickness of the strata of air through which the light reaches us. The
enormous amount of this dust is well shown by the fact that, then only,
we can look full at the sun, even when the whole sky is free from clouds
and there is no apparent mist. But the sun's rays then reach us after having passed, first, through an enormous thickness of the higher strata of
the air, the minute dust of which reflects most of the blue rays away from
us, leaving the complementary yellow light to pass on. Then, the somewhat coarser dust reflects the green rays, leaving a more orange colored
light to pass on; and finally some of the yellow is reflected, leaving almost
pure red. But owing to the constant presence of air currents, arranging
both the dust and vapor in strata of varying extent and density, and of
high or low clouds, which both absorb and reflect the light in varying
degrees, we see produced all those wondrous combinations of tints and
those gorgeous ever-changing colors, which are a constant source of admiration and delight to all who have the advantage of uninterrupted
view to the west, and who are accustomed to watch for these not unfre-
quent exhibitions of nature's kaleidoscopic color-painting. With every
change in the altitude of the sun the display changes its character; and
most of all when it has sunk below the horizon, and, owing to the more
favorable angles, a larger quantity of the colored light is reflected toward
us. Especially is this the case when there is a certain amount of cloud.
The clouds, so long as the sun is above the horizon, intercept much of
the light and color; but, when the great luminary has passed away from
our direct vision, his light shines more directly on the under sides of all

the clouds and air strata of different densities; a new and more brilliant light flushes the western sky, and a display of gorgeous ever-changing tints occurs which are at once the delight of the beholder and the despair of the artist. And all this unsurpassable glory we owe to—dust!

A remarkable confirmation of this theory was given during the two or three years after the great eruption of Krakatoa, near Java. The volcanic débris was shot up from the crater many miles high, and the heavier portion of it fell upon the sea for several hundred miles around, and was found to be mainly composed of very thin flakes of volcanic glass. Much of this was of course ground to impalpable dust by the violence of the discharge, and was carried up to a height of many miles. Here it was caught by the return currents of air continually flowing northward and southward above the equatorial zone; and since, when these currents reach the temperate zone, where the surface rotation of the earth is less rapid, they continually flow eastward, the fine dust was thus carried at a great altitude completely around the earth. Its effects were traced some months after the eruption in the appearance of brilliant sunset glows of an exceptional character, often flushing with crimson the whole western half of the visible sky. These glows continued in diminishing splendor for about three years; they were seen all over the temperate zone; and it was calculated that, before they finally disappeared, some of this fine dust must have traveled three times round the globe.

The same principle is thought to explain the exquisite blue color of the deep seas and oceans and of many lakes and springs. Absolutely pure water, like pure air, is colorless, but all seas and lakes, however clear and translucent, contain abundance of very finely divided matter, organic or inorganic, which, as in the atmosphere, reflects the blue rays in such quantity as to overpower the white or colored light reflected from the fewer and more rapidly sinking particles of larger size. The oceanic dust is derived from many sources. Minute organisms are constantly dying near the surface, and their skeletons, or fragments of them, fall slowly to the bottom. The mud brought down by rivers, though it cannot be traced on the ocean floor more than about 150 miles from land, yet no doubt furnishes many particles of organic matter which are carried by surface currents to enormous distances and are ultimately dissolved before they reach the bottom. A more important source of finely divided matter is to be found in volcanic dust which, as in the case of Krakatoa, may remain for years in the atmosphere, but which must ultimately fall upon the surface of the earth and ocean. This can be traced in all the deep-sea oozes. Finally there is meteoric dust, which is continually falling to the surface of the earth, but in such minute quantities and in such a finely-divided state that it can be detected only in the oozes of the deepest oceans, where both inorganic and organic débris is almost absent.

The blue of the ocean varies in different parts from a pure blue somewhat lighter than that of the sky, as seen about the northern tropic in the Atlantic, to a deep indigo tint, as seen in the north temperate portions of the same ocean: owing, probably, to differences in the nature, quantity, and distribution of the solid matter which causes the color. The Mediterranean, and the deeper Swiss lakes, are also a blue of various tints, due also to the presence of suspended matter, which Professor Tyndall thought might be so fine that it would require ages of quiet subsidence to reach the bottom. All the evidence goes to show, therefore, that the exquisite blue tints of sky and ocean, as well as all the sunset hues of sky and cloud, of mountain peak and Alpine snows, are due to the finer particles of that very dust which, in its coarser forms, we find so annoying and even dangerous.

But if this production of color and beauty were the only useful function of dust, some persons might be disposed to dispense with it in order to escape its less agreeable effects. It has, however, been recently discovered that dust has another part to play in nature; a part so important that it is doubtful whether we could even live without it. To the presence of dust in the higher atmosphere we owe the formation of mists, clouds, and gentle beneficial rains, instead of water spouts and destructive torrents.

It is barely twenty years ago since the discovery was made, first in France by Coulier and Mascart, but more thoroughly worked out by Mr. John Aitken in 1880. He found that if a jet of steam is admitted into two large glass receivers—one filled with ordinary air, the other with air which has been filtered through cotton wool so as to keep back all particles of solid matter—the first will be instantly filled with condensed vapor in the usual cloudy form, while the other vessel will remain quite transparent. Another experiment was made, more nearly reproducing what occurs in nature. Some water was placed in the two vessels prepared as before. When the water had evaporated sufficiently to saturate the air the vessels were slightly cooled; a dense cloud was at once formed in the one while the other remained quite clear. These experiments, and many others, show that the mere cooling of vapor in air will not condense it into mist clouds or rain, unless *particles of solid matter* are present to form *nuclei* upon which condensation can begin. The density of the cloud is proportionate to the number of the particles; hence the fact that the steam issuing from the safety-valve or the chimney of a locomotive forms a dense white cloud, shows that the air is really full of dust particles, most of which are microscopic but none the less serving as centers of condensation for the vapor. Hence, if there were no dust in the air, escaping steam would remain invisible; there would be no cloud in the sky; and the vapor in the atmosphere, constantly accumulating through evaporation from seas and oceans and from the earth's surface, would have to find some other means of returning to its source.

One of these modes would be the deposition of dew, which is itself an illustration of the principle that vapor requires solid or liquid surfaces to condense upon; dew forms most readily and abundantly on grass, on account of the numerous centers of condensation this affords. Dew, however, is now formed only on clear cold nights after warm or moist days. The air near the surface is warm and contains much vapor, though below the point of saturation. But the innumerable points and extensive surfaces of grass radiate heat quickly, and becoming cool, lower the temperature of the adjacent air, which then reaches saturation point and condenses the contained atmosphere on the grass. Hence, if the atmosphere at the earth's surface became supersaturated with aqueous vapor, dew would be continuously deposited, especially on every form of vegetation, the result being that everything, including our clothing, would be constantly dripping wet. If there were absolutely no particles of solid matter in the upper atmosphere, all the moisture would be returned to the earth in the form of dense mists, and frequent and copious dews, which in forests would form torrents of rain by the rapid condensation on the leaves. But if we suppose that solid particles were occasionally carried higher up through violent winds or tornadoes, then on those occasions the supersaturated atmosphere would condense rapidly upon them, and while falling would gather almost all the moisture in the atmosphere in that locality, resulting in masses or sheets of water, which would be so ruinously destructive by the mere weight and impetus of their fall that it is doubtful whether they would not render the earth almost wholly uninhabitable.

The chief mode of discharging the atmospheric vapor in the absence of dust would, however, be by contact with the higher slopes of all mountain ranges. Atmospheric vapor, being lighter than air, would accumulate in enormous quantities in the upper strata of the atmosphere, which would be always supersaturated and ready to condense upon any solid or liquid surfaces. But the quantity of land comprised in the upper half of all the mountains of the world is a very small fraction of the total surface of the globe, and this would lead to very disastrous results. The air in contact with the higher mountain slopes would rapidly discharge its water, which would run down the mountain sides in torrents. This condensation on every side of the mountains would leave a partial vacuum which would set up currents from every direction to restore the equilibrium, thus bringing in more supersaturated air to suffer condensation and add its supply of water, again increasing the indraught of more air. The result would be that winds would be constantly blowing toward every mountain range from all directions, keeping up the condensation and discharging, day and night and from one year's end to another, an amount of water equal to that which falls during the heaviest tropical rains. All of the rain that now falls over the whole surface of the earth and ocean, with the exception of a few desert areas, would then fall only on rather high mountains or steep isolated hills, tearing down their sides in huge torrents, cutting deep ravines, and rendering all growth of vegetation impossible. The mountains would therefore be so devastated as to be uninhabitable, and would be equally incapable of supporting either vegetable or animal life.

But this constant condensation on the mountains would probably check the deposit on the lowlands in the form of dew, because the continual updraught toward the higher slopes would withdraw almost the whole of the vapor as it arose from the oceans, and other water surfaces, and thus leave the lower strata over the plains almost or quite dry. And if this were the case there would be no vegetation, and therefore no animal life, on the plains and lowlands, which would thus be all arid deserts cut through by the great rivers formed by the meeting together of the innumerable torrents from the mountains.

Now, although it may not be possible to determine with perfect accuracy what would happen under the supposed condition of the atmosphere, it is certain that the total absence of dust would so fundamentally change the meteorology of our globe as, not improbably, to render it uninhabitable by man, and equally unsuitable for the larger portion of its existing animal and vegetable life.

Let us now briefly summarize what we owe to the universality of dust, and especially to that most finely divided portion of it which is constantly present in the atmosphere up to the height of many miles. First of all it gives us the pure blue of the sky, one of the most exquisitely beautiful colors in nature. It gives us also the glories of the sunset and the sunrise, and all those brilliant hues seen in high mountain regions. Half the beauty of the world would vanish with the absence of dust. But, what is far more important than the color of sky and beauty of sunset, dust gives us also diffused daylight, or skylight, that most equable, and soothing, and useful, of all illuminating agencies. Without dust the sky would appear absolutely black, and stars would be visible even at noonday. The sky itself would therefore give us no light. We should have bright glaring sunlight or intensely dark shadows, with hardly any half-tones. From this cause alone the world would be so totally different from what it is that all vegetable and animal life would probably have developed into very different forms, and even our own organization would have been modified in order that we might enjoy life in a world of such harsh and violent contrasts.

In our houses we should have little light except when the sun shone directly into them, and even then every spot out of its direct rays would be completely dark, except for light reflected from the walls. It would be necessary to have windows all around and the walls all white; and on the north side of every house a high white wall would have to be built to reflect the light and prevent that side from being in total darkness. Even then we should have to live in a perpetual glare, or shut out the sun altogether and use artificial light as being a far superior article.

Much more important would be the effects of a dust-free atmosphere in banishing clouds, or mist, or the "gentle rain of heaven," and in giving us in their place perpetual sunshine, desert lowlands, and mountains devastated by unceasing floods and raging torrents, so as, apparently, to render all life on the earth impossible.

There are a few other phenomena, apparently due to the same general causes, which may here be referred to. Everyone must have noticed the difference in the atmospheric effects and general character of the light in spring and autumn, at times when the days are of the same length, and consequently when the sun has the same altitude at corresponding hours. In spring we have a bluer sky and greater transparency of the atmosphere; in autumn, even on very fine days, there is always a kind of yellowish haze, resulting in a want of clearness in the air and purity of color in the sky. These phenomena are quite intelligible when we consider that during winter less dust is formed, and more is brought down to the earth by rain and snow, resulting in the transparent atmosphere of spring, while exactly opposite conditions during summer bring about the mellow autumnal light. Again, the well-known beneficial effects of rain on vegetation, as compared with any amount of artificial watering, though, no doubt, largely due to the minute quantity of ammonia which the rain brings down with it from the air, must yet be partly derived from the organic or mineral particles which serve as the nuclei of every raindrop, and which, being so minute, are the more readily dissolved in the soil and appropriated as nourishment by the roots of plants.

It will be observed that all these beneficial effects of dust are due to its presence in such quantities as are produced by natural causes, since both gentle showers as well as ample rains and deep blue skies are present throughout the vast equatorial forest districts, where dust-forming agencies seem to be at a minimum. But in all densely-populated countries there is an enormous artificial production of dust—from our ploughed fields, from our roads and streets, where dust is continually formed by the iron-shod hoofs of innumerable horses, but chiefly from our enormous combustion of fuel pouring into the air volumes of smoke charged with unconsumed particles of carbon. This superabundance of dust, probably many times greater than that which would be produced under the more natural conditions which prevailed when our country was more thinly populated, must almost certainly produce some effect on our climate; and the particular effect it seems calculated to produce is the increase of cloud and fog, but not necessarily any increase of rain. Rain depends on the supply of aqueous vapor by evaporation; on temperature, which determines the dew point; and on changes in barometric pressure, which determine the winds. There is probably always and everywhere enough atmospheric dust to serve as centers of condensation at considerable altitudes, and thus to initiate rainfall when the other conditions are favorable; but the presence of increased quantities of dust at the lower levels must lead to the formation of denser clouds, although the minute water vesicles cannot descend as rain, because, as they pass down into warmer and dryer strata of air, they are again evaporated.

Now, there is much evidence to show that there has been a considerable increase in the amount of cloud, and consequent decrease in the amount of sunshine, in all parts of our country. It is an undoubted fact that in the Middle Ages England was a wine-producing country, and this implies more sunshine than we have now. Sunshine has a double effect, in heating the surface soil and thus causing more rapid growth, besides its direct effect in ripening the fruit. This is well seen in Canada, where, notwithstanding a six months' winter of extreme severity, vines are grown as bushes in the open ground, and produce fruit equal to that of our ordinary greenhouses. Some years back one of our gardening periodicals obtained from gardeners of forty or fifty years' experience a body of facts clearly indicating a comparatively recent change of climate. It was stated that in many parts of the country, especially in the north, fruits were formerly grown successfully and of good quality in gardens where they cannot be grown now; and this occurred in places sufficiently removed from manufacturing centers to be unaffected by any direct deleterious influence of smoke. But an increase of cloud, and consequent diminution of sunshine, would produce just such a result; and this increase is almost certain to have occurred owing to the enormously increased amount of dust thrown into the atmosphere as our country has become more densely populated, and especially owing to the vast increase of our smoke-producing manufactories. It seems highly probable, therefore, that to increase the wealth of our capitalist-manufacturers we are allowing the climate of our whole country to be greatly deteriorated in a way which diminishes both its productiveness and its beauty, thus injuriously affecting the enjoyment and the health of the whole population, since sunshine is itself an essential condition of healthy life. When this fact is thoroughly realized we shall surely put a stop to such a reckless and wholly unnecessary production of injurious smoke and dust.

In conclusion, we find that the much-abused and all-pervading dust, which, when too freely produced, deteriorates our climate and brings us dirt, discomfort, and even disease, is, nevertheless, under natural conditions, an essential portion of the economy of nature. It gives us much of the beauty of natural scenery, as due to varying atmospheric effects of sky, and cloud, and sunset tints, and thus renders life more enjoyable; while, as an essential condition of diffused daylight and of moderate rainfalls combined with a dry atmosphere, it appears to be absolutely necessary for our existence upon the earth, perhaps even for the very development of terrestrial as opposed to aquatic life. The overwhelming importance of the small things, and even of the despised things, of our world has never, perhaps, been so strikingly brought home to us as in these recent investigations into the widespread and far-reaching beneficial influences of Atmospheric Dust.

## Suggestions for Study

Read this article attentively, and make an outline of it. As a necessary first step, state the thesis sentence; it is repeated three times in the course of the reading, once near the beginning, once in the middle, and once at the end. It contains in its statement the major divisions of subject matter. This division of the subject is further clarified for you by a transitional paragraph about midway in the article, which tells you again that dust has a two-fold importance. Having chosen the main points, then carefully select the co-ordinate minor subdivisions of them, using the topic sentences of the successive paragraphs to guide you. Do not clutter up your outline with needless details and illustrative explanations.

Be able to answer such questions as the following:

1. What does the opening paragraph indicate concerning the reader for whom this article is intended? What adaptation is made to this reader?

2. If no dust were present in the air, what would be the appearance of the path of a sunbeam? How was this result proved? What is the reason for this phenomenon?

3. How can the blueness of the sky be explained? Why is the sky bluer when seen from the top of a mountain?

4. What accounts for the beauty of the sunset?

5. Is the blueness of water determined by the same forces that determine the blueness of the air? What are the sources of the minute particles in the water?

6. What is the practical use of dust as differentiated from the aesthetic contribution of dust?

7. How does dust affect condensation and rainfall? Were no dust present in the air, where would the rainfall concentrate?

8. Why is the air clear and blue in the spring, but mellow and hazy in the autumn?

9. In what way has the growth of manufacturing affected the climate in England?

10. Who was Alfred Wallace?

11. Define the following words from this article: opthalmic, combustion, organic, laterally, transparent, luminary, translucent, subsidence, accumulate, saturate, aqueous, meteorology, equatorial, deleterious, diminution, deteriorate, aquatic.

## Insects and Men [3]

### JAMES E. BOYLE

The world's history needs to be rewritten once more. It has already been told in terms of politics, economics, geography, climate, sea power, war, race, sex, and of great men and heroes. It should next be written in terms of insects. This is not the age of man; this is the age of insects. What the yellow fever mosquito, for instance, or the cattle tick, or the tsetse fly has done to the human race is still largely unrecorded.

France has erected in the Midi three battle monuments to commemorate her victory over a single plant louse. This little insect, the Phylloxera, was swiftly and surely destroying the grape industry of that grape-famous country. This bug, an American immigrant, was finally defeated by means of help from the United States. Roots of our wild grapevines, immune to this little plant louse, were taken to France, and French grapevines grafted on them. Since the insects attacked only the root, this meant defeat and death to this pest.

There are estimated to be over four million kinds of insects in the world, and all of them are of significance to mankind. Most of them are frankly and openly either our friends or our enemies; few are neutral. They are all our competitors—we are all bidders for the world's limited food supply. Who shall finally inherit this earth, man or bug, will depend

3. From the *Atlantic Monthly,* CXLIV (October, 1929), 529. Reprinted by permission of Mrs. James E. Boyle and of the *Atlantic Monthly.*

in the last analysis on which creature is more efficient in securing his daily ration.

When we remember the bug's appetite for food, particularly for the green and growing plant, and the bug's capacity to reproduce and multiply, we begin to feel uncertain about our own future survival. Consider, for instance, that little tiny green bug, the cabbage aphid. Under favorable conditions, there are thirty generations of these bugs in one year. Under somewhat unfavorable conditions in New York State, from a single pair will come twelve generations in one summer. Twelve or thirteen days are needed for one generation. The mother aphid who lays her eggs the first of April becomes the progenitor of twelve generations by the middle of August. She produces forty-one young in one generation. Therefore, by the middle of August, if all the mother-aphid descendants should live, there would be alive at one time some five hundred and sixty-four quadrillion aphids! Or to state it more exactly, we should have the astronomical number 564,087,257,509,154,652 aphids. A minute calculation of the weight of these aphids by Professor Glenn Herrick shows that they would weigh eight hundred and twenty-two million tons—that is, almost exactly eight times the weight of all the human inhabitants of this globe.

This shows rather strikingly what one mother aphid can do in four and one-half months, if she has plenty of food and no enemies. In a warmer climate, such as Texas, she would do much better than this. In this connection we must also remember the size of the insect's appetite—especially when it is in the larva stage. Familiar examples of the larva are the maggots—children of the common housefly—and the unsightly caterpillars, grubworms, tomato worms, tobacco worms, and so on, children of the butterflies and moths which play like fairies in the sunlight or moonlight. In fact, most of our common ugly worms are the larvae of these dainty winged creatures. For many of our insects go through the complete metamorphosis—the egg, the larva, the pupa, and the adult stage. The larva stage is devoted to growth, the sole business of a larva being to eat and grow.

We can get some idea of the appetite of the larva when we note the food consumption of the caterpillar of the common Polyphemus moth. When this worm is fully grown, that is, in about fifty-six days, he has actually consumed 86,000 times his original weight. This is rather a terrifying fact, on the face of it, but we are able to reflect that thus far, at least, we have held our own against these greedy competitors for our food. That is the situation; the balance has been maintained thus far, between man and bug, so that the bug has not yet deprived his human competitors of too much of their food supply except in those few cases of insect plagues. Obviously, it would be very easy to disturb this "balance of nature."

Will man or bug inherit the earth? If it is a question of the survival of the fittest, then the argument is all in favor of the bug. The cockroach, for instance, was here a million years before man came; therefore, he will likely be here a million years after man has joined the dinosaur and the dodo. The cockroach came with the coal age. He is versatile enough to adjust himself to his environment. Living first in Asia, he traveled by ship to Holland, and later became at home all over Europe. While he prefers the warm climate, he is found in numbers among the Laplanders of the far north. He even destroys in some years great quantities of the dried fish put away for the winter by these northern settlers. More famous, however, are the cockroaches of Brazil. One traveler reports spending some time in a private home on the Upper Paraguay. Here were a dozen children, each with his eyelashes more or less eaten off by cockroaches. The eyelashes were bitten off irregularly, and in some places quite close to the eyelid. Since Brazilian children naturally have the beautiful drooping lashes of the Latin race, their appearance as defaced by the cockroaches was indeed strange. These same cockroaches also bite off bits of the toenails. Apparently they confine their depredations to children.

As the cockroach has migrated all over the world, so, too, many other insects are doing. Man's scientific means of insect control, which is his main argument in favor of ultimate survival, is offset by the modern means of travel which the insect now uses. Sailing ships have given place to steamships; horse carts to automobiles; and finally comes the airplane. When Lindbergh finished his 46,000-mile flight in 1928, touching three continents and dozens of countries, think of the scores of new insects he picked up and brought back to the United States! One female insect— even one insect egg—is enough to start a new insect pest in the United States which may have most serious economic consequences. Polyembryony, they term it, when one female insect lays a single egg which hatches out into a large number of maggots.

Whence came our present insect pests? Most of them came from foreign countries. The cotton boll weevil is from Mexico; she came, the theory is, in the egg state, in a dirty cotton mattress of a Mexican laborer. The corn borer is from Europe, the gypsy moth from Japan, the cottony scale from Australia; the Mediterranean fruit fly was landed in Florida by some bootleggers from the West Indies; and so on. And far more serious, they come here without their natural enemies. In this way the balance is disturbed, the disturbance being wholly in favor of the insect. An insect in his home land is often so harmless and obscure that his presence is not even noted. This is because his natural enemies keep him in his place. But transplant this little bug to America, give him plenty of rich food and no enemies, and he will show what the biological laws of reproduction mean, and what the mathematical formula of geometric progression looks like when put into practice.

We have had many examples of this kind. The best one is perhaps the white fluted or cottony scale which once threatened the complete, speedy, and absolute extinction of the orange- and lemon-growing industry of California. The adult female of this beautiful and dangerous insect has a body which is scalelike and dark orange-red in color.

It was in the seventies when this insect came by ship from Australia to California, and made its first appearance on some acacia trees in Menlo Park. The insect attacked apple trees, fig, quince, pomegranate, roses, and it soon developed a preference for orange and lemon trees. The trees attacked were ruined. Since this insect left all its enemies behind in Australia, it had a free field for action, until the counterattack by man himself began. Few jobs ever done by the United States Department of Agriculture in the field of entomology or elsewhere have been so spectacular and so immediately beneficial as was this fight on the cottony scale. Victory was secured by the introduction from Australia of a particular ladybug whose diet is this cottony scale, and whose appetite is for this insect only.

But to win this battle was not the work of one year, for it was not so simple as it looks in retrospect. First of all, the Department sent two men to California to study the life history of the scales. These entomologists spent one year in this study and came to the correct conclusion that the insect was a native of Australia, but was not a pest there because natural enemies were keeping it down. One of the more seasoned bug hunters of the Department was accordingly sent to Australia to spy out these insects, and to collect specimens of its enemies. This entomologist, Mr. Albert Koebele, was a skilled collector. He found a small fly laying its eggs on the cottony scale; these eggs hatched and the little maggots devoured the scale. But this was not the final solution. He also found a little ladybug, small, reddish-brown, with a voracious appetite for this one insect. His next job was to transport a number of these ladybugs alive from Australia to California, a very difficult feat, for ladybugs do not have the habit of crossing the equator and going on ten-thousand-mile voyages.

Koebele selected a large number of the ladybugs. He put them in tin boxes, with food. These he placed in the ice box of the steamer at Sydney. Upon arrival in California they were found to be alive and well. A test was immediately made in Los Angeles to determine whether or not the scientist had correctly reasoned out his problem. An infested orange tree was surrounded with a tent of gauze. It was a glorious triumph for the scientist. The Australian ladybugs fell upon the American cottony scales with avidity; indeed, their appetites seemed whetted by the long sea voyage. The results more than justified the most sanguine expectations. It was the "most perfect experiment ever made by the Department," said the Chief of the Bureau of Entomology.

There are distinct and peculiar reasons why this experiment was such an unqualified success. First, there is the rate of increase of the ladybugs. Each female lays on the average three hundred eggs, and each of these eggs hatches into a hungry larva. If we assume that one half of these larvae produce female bugs, and maximum reproduction goes on for the summer, a simple calculation shows that in five months a single ladybug becomes the ancestor of seventy-five billions of other ladybugs, each capable of destroying many cottony scales. The ladybug breeds twice as fast as the cottony scale. The ladybug feeds upon the eggs of the cottony scale. And this particular type of ladybug has no enemies of its own, although our American ladybugs have many parasite enemies. Finally there is the very important military advantage in favor of the ladybug in its attack on the scale—the ladybug is a quick mover, while the scale is still. For these reasons the ladybug is almost a perfect remedy for the fluted cottony scale. There have been no failures in its introduction into any of the different countries to which it has been carried. No other insect tried in international work has had such perfect success. California's greatest agricultural industry was thus saved from complete destruction and one of our greatest and most delicious health foods rescued to us by introducing from a foreign country one small insect which restored the "balance of nature."

Next to this achievement stands our success in saving the dominating industry of the Hawaiian Islands—cane sugar—from annihilation at the hands of another Australian insect. In this case it was the cane-leaf hopper. Its depredations ran up into many millions of dollars. The rise and decline of this insect may be sharply pictured by the statistics of sugar production on one big plantation:

| | | |
|---|---|---|
| 1904 | . . . . . | 10,954 tons |
| 1905 | . . . . . | 1,620 " |
| 1906 | . . . . . | 826 " |
| 1907 | . . . . . | 11,630 " |

This diminuendo and crescendo marks the fight put on by the Department of Agriculture. The entomologist sent to Australia succeeded, finally, in finding and carrying to Hawaii the parasite which is the natural enemy of the cane-leaf hopper. The parasite multiplied rapidly. His rise marked the decline of the leaf hopper. *C'est la guerre!* There is no pity, no mercy, in this war. Like the battle of Kipling's mongoose and the cobra, it ends only when one of the combatants is dead. When Chief L. O. Howard of the Bureau of Entomology visited Hawaii in 1915 he pronounced the situation with regard to the sugarcane-leaf hopper as "almost perfect."

These two brilliant successes in overcoming our insect enemies had one undesirable effect, and that was, they created a sense of false security in the minds of the general public. The feeling became general that for our defense in the war against the insect hordes we may look with confidence to the highly proficient professional entomologists in the Department of Agriculture and in the State colleges and experiment stations. The fact remains that in only a few conspicuous cases have we won the battle against the bug. With most of the harmful insects in the United States, either the bug has definitely won the war or the fighting is still going on. We have already surrendered to the chestnut blight, and these noble and useful trees are fast becoming extinct. Congress last year spent ten million dollars in the corn-borer campaign, and the total effect was to mitigate very slightly the ravages of this insect pest. Scientists on the job report that the slow westward march of the corn borer will not stop with Ohio and Michigan, but will inevitably continue until the whole corn belt is covered. We shall have to sign a truce with this bug and give him perpetual tribute in the form of a few million or a few hundred million bushels of corn a year. This pest has never been stopped yet in any country.

In this manner we have learned to live with the Hessian fly, who came over from Europe with the mercenary troops of the British army during the Revolutionary War. We have already paid him tribute to the extent of hundreds of millions of bushels of wheat, and shall keep on doing so indefinitely.

The Mediterranean fruit fly, one of the most dangerous insects known in the citrus industry, was discovered in Florida early in 1929. In a few months it had traveled westward as far as Dallas, Texas. It now definitely threatens the citrus industry of California.

The cotton boll weevil arrived at Brownsville, Texas, in 1892 from Mexico. By the year 1924 it had traversed the cotton belt and reached Virginia. Its original home is the plateau region of Central America and Mexico. Its only food is the cotton plant. This insect has definitely established himself in every cotton state except California. He is with us as a permanent boarder. The fight will continue against him, as against the corn borer, not to exterminate him, but to keep him within bounds. It would take several pages just to list the harmful insects now definitely and permanently established in the United States, all of which are in real competition for our food supply, and all of which are capable of rapid reproduction.

We multiply our scientific means of overcoming these harmful insects. But as fast as one bug is destroyed we discover two new ones to take his place. Hence our worst pests today are bugs which our grandfathers never heard of. We may venture the prophecy, therefore, that our grandchildren will be struggling with new and more harmful insects than we now know. Even at the present moment entomologists estimate that we are acquainted with only one kind of insect out of eight or ten actually in existence.

The biological methods of fighting insects—those which maintain the balance of nature—are far the most effective. By this we mean the work done by the birds, by insects themselves, and by those most tiny of all insects, the predacious parasites.

First of all, we ought to encourage the birds to come, and we ought to protect them in every way. This may involve getting rid of a large portion of the cats, particularly those night prowlers which destroy birds on their nests. The nuthatch, or the downy woodpecker which works up and down the limbs of trees in the wintertime, inspecting each nook and cranny with meticulous care, destroys the eggs of insects. We can calculate how large a quantity of insects would come from the eggs destroyed in a single day by a single bird if the eggs were left to hatch. Studies made of the food of birds show that from three hundred to five hundred insects are sometimes found in the stomach of one bird. Insects constitute 65 per cent of the food of the downy woodpecker, 95 per cent of the food of the house wren, and 96 per cent of the food of the flycatcher. Birds have their own peculiar habits in catching insects. The phoebe, the flycatcher, and swallows live upon flying insects; robins and meadowlarks feed upon ground insects and grubs; cuckoos, orioles, warblers, and vireos catch leaf-eating insects; titmice, creepers, woodpeckers, nuthatches, and chickadees explore tree trunks and limbs for small insects and insect eggs.

It is when we turn to our insect friends, however, that we find the most efficacious means of fighting our insect enemies. Shakespeare makes Touchstone say, "I will kill thee a hundred and fifty ways." But when it comes to various and sundry methods of killing, the insects have Touchstone beaten. In our boyhood days we became familiar with the thread-waisted wasp, known as mud dauber. This wasp is not merely a skilled engineer and mechanic, but she also has uncanny skill in the use of anaesthetics. At any rate, she lays by a stock of food for her unhatched larvae, the food consisting of tender, juicy spiders put to sleep by an injection of the wasp's powerful narcotic in exactly the right nerve center. The relation of the spider to the fly is so well known that it has become a proverb; but the relation of certain flies to the spider is not appreciated. There is a group of hunchbacked, small-headed flies which feed entirely on spiders. These carnivorous flies in the maggot or larva stage live within the bodies of the spiders or in their egg cases.

Some insects attack others openly, as do the dragonflies and the praying mantis. The praying mantis is the only bug with a religious name—*Mantis religiosa*—and he gets this name because he folds his hands as if in prayer. At such moments he is ready to prey on the first insect that comes within his clutches.

Some insects catch other insects in snares, like the spider web, or in pits of ingenious construction, like the ant lion's trap. These predacious insects, as they are called, account for a great many victims. But the great majority of insect-eating insects, when young, live within the bodies of their victims and eat their way out, or within their eggs. These are the true parasites; they are the farmer's real friends. It is not an uncommon thing, especially in vineyards, to find a feeble caterpillar with its back covered with little white oblong bodies, which the casual observer usually takes for its own eggs. These are the cocoons of a little fly parasite known as the braconid parasite. Its larvae eat and grow within the body of the caterpillar. Just before the caterpillar dies, they leave it and spin their silken cocoons upon its back.

Most of the caterpillars you see are already marked for an untimely death, for they have a sort of glorified form of tuberculosis. Within their own bodies are the maggots of these parasites, which must eat their way out.

One of the most interesting of these small braconid flies is called the aphidius, and she deposits her egg within the body of that troublesome plant louse, the aphid. The aphid is then doomed to a death more horrible than that of tuberculosis; the parasite in emerging from his host cuts a very regular circular lid in the top of his host's abdomen. You can sometimes catch the mother aphidius in the act of depositing her eggs; she selects the plant louse, and stands with her head toward it. Bending her abdomen under her thorax, she darts her ovipositor forward into the body of the aphis. The dreadful end of the aphis is then a matter of a few days.

The tachinid fly, which looks like a housefly, is an enemy of many insects. Some tachinids lay their eggs on the back of the caterpillar so that the maggot can bore in and live a life of ease and gluttony as long as the caterpillar can carry on. When life departs from the caterpillar, the maggot is ready to do likewise. Other tachinid flies deposit eggs on leaves of plants infested with caterpillars. The caterpillar devours the egg with the leaf, but without chewing or injuring the egg. In due season the egg hatches, and the maggot sets up housekeeping within his host. He feeds upon the body of the caterpillar till he destroys it. Still other flies have other means of attacking the nonresisting caterpillar; some deposit living maggots on the leaves, and these maggots attach themselves firmly to the first caterpillar that comes along, and complete their growth within the body of the luckless caterpillar; other flies deposit living maggots within the body of the caterpillar, which is, of course, then marked for death.

Predacious parasites have even more refined ways of killing. Some of the small flies, the parasitic Hymenoptera, lay their eggs within the eggs of other insects. Here the tiny parasites come to maturity. Dr. Grace Griswold has succeeded in finding parasite eggs within the parasite eggs within the insect eggs.

> Great fleas have little fleas upon their backs to bite 'em,
> And little fleas have lesser fleas, and so *ad infinitum*.

Our scientific and practical progress in entomology during the last fifty years has been enormous. To two people much of this success is due—Professor John Henry Comstock of Cornell, and his wife, Anna Botsford Comstock. Almost exactly fifty years ago (1879–1881) Professor Comstock was in charge of the work in entomology of the United States Department of Agriculture. He had three and a half workers under him. Forty years later there were 545 workers in the Bureau of Entomology. Another outstanding piece of pioneering done by Professor Comstock was the establishment of the first insectary in the world. Indeed, he coined the word himself, applying it to a building on the Cornell campus erected in the early eighties. "There should be a place," he said, "where living plants can be kept with insects upon them, and all the conditions of growth of both plants and insects should be under control." So a building, named an insectary, was erected. After many years this building gave place to a modern structure. Breeding cages are used for insects. Subterranean insects are observed by means of root cages—boxes with glass sides. Now there are many such insectaries scattered over the world.

*Suggestions for Study*

1. In outlining this selection, mark off that portion of the beginning which can properly be called introductory. Then, concerning the body of the article, answer these general questions:

What is the problem being discussed, and is it a serious one?
Have we had any successes in solving it in the past?
Has our fight in general been successful or unsuccessful?
By what means shall we continue our fight in the future? From your con-

sideration of these essential questions you should be able to frame the main points of your outline.

2. Define the following words from the article: depredation, diminuendo, crescendo, mercenary, predacious, efficacious.

# II

# THE FOUR FORMS OF WRITING

PROSE in general is divided into four main categories: exposition, argumentation, description, and narration. The principal aim of exposition is to inform through explanation, definition, analysis, and interpretation; of argumentation, to persuade, often with a view to stimulating a reader to action; of description, to present a picture; of narration, to relate a story, usually with the idea of entertaining a reader. In actual practice, these forms are often mixed. Thus in an expository article, passages of considerable extent may be devoted to description or narration; and in narration, much expository matter may be inserted. In each piece of writing, however, one form will be dominant; and a writer should know clearly what his chief aim is in each piece of writing—whether it is to inform, to persuade, to present a picture, or to tell a story—so that, for instance, if his intention is to explain how to make a camp, he will not change his purpose, and end by telling a story of a camping trip on which he has gone. A somewhat detailed discussion of each of these forms follows.

## A. Exposition

At every turn an educated person is called on to define, explain, or interpret something. Even if he would, he cannot escape answering questions that seek information: How is that made? What does the term mean? What are the facts of this matter? What are the aims of this book or that organization? In answering such questions, he makes use of exposition.

Exposition, then, is that form of discourse which aims primarily at explaining or interpreting facts and ideas. By telling what something is, how it is made, or how it functions, exposition tries to make a concept clear. Of course, if a reader is to gain a perfect understanding of what is being explained, you as a writer must have an unblurred and undistorted idea in your mind, and you must be logical in organizing your thoughts. Exposition is addressed to the intellect rather than to the emotions. It does not seek primarily to persuade or amuse, although actually, of course, it may do both or either in addition to informing. If you will bear this primary purpose in mind, you will often save yourself from violating the principle of unity in your expositions.

DEFINITION. The first method of exposition, and perhaps the most important, is definition. It is useful in making essential terms clear and thus obviating any misconceptions. The mastery of it gives in addition an awareness of the exact significance of words and offers training in the important skill of making distinctions.

Some definitions can be made very simply and yet be completely clear. Verbs, adjectives, and adverbs, for example, can ordinarily be defined just by a synonym, as *to expedite* means *to hasten*. These definitions will cause little trouble if you are careful to define a word by another which is the same part of speech—an adjective by another adjective, an adverb by another adverb, and so on.

> *To frown* is *to scowl.*
> *Martial* means *warlike.*
> *Often* means *frequently.*

Other words, however, nouns in particular, cannot be defined so easily. These need more extended consideration.

INTENSIVE DEFINITION. You can best define the meaning of a noun by placing it in a certain classification and then distinguishing it from all the other terms in the same classification. To examine this procedure, consider first not the expository composition devoted to definition, but the intensive, logical definition of the kind found in the dictionary. This latter kind contains the essentials of any type of definition; it also offers the clearest illustration because of its limited scope.

*Classification.* By classification is meant the inclusion of a term in the general group to which it belongs by its characteristics. To begin the definition of the word "barometer," you might classify it as an instrument. The first part of the definition would read: "The barometer is an instrument." In like fashion, a bicycle is classified as a vehicle, a manse as a residence, and filtration as a process. The reader is thereby given his first clue as to the meaning of the word. How ably he is assisted by the classification is perhaps best illustrated by the consideration of a word that may be unfamiliar to most people. What is a "nepman"? Does the word refer to a person or a thing? If it refers to a person as the suffix of the word would seem to indicate, what kind of person is meant? These questions are immediately answered by the classification. A nepman is "one who engages in private trade." The first limits are thus imposed upon the word.

*Differentiation*. Very obviously, however, the explanation is not completed by the classification of the word. To say merely that a barometer is an instrument is not to distinguish it from other instruments. The second part of the definition, that known as the differentiation, has as its purpose the explanation of how the term differs from all other terms in the same classification. *Webster's New International Dictionary* differentiates the barometer from all other instruments in this manner: a barometer is an instrument "for determining the pressure of the atmosphere and hence for judging of the probable changes of weather, for ascertaining the height of any ascent, etc." Thus the limitations of the word are clearly marked. A bicycle is "a light vehicle having two wheels one behind the other. It has a steering handle, and a saddle seat or seats, and is propelled by the feet acting upon treadles connected with cranks or levers." A manse is "the residence of an ecclesiastic." Filtration is the process of separating a fluid from the solids suspended in it by straining them out. A nepman is "one who engages in private trade as permitted by the Nep [the New Economic Policy]. *Russia*." The technique of definition, therefore, consists in making a classification and following it with a sharp differentiation.

*Precautions*. To employ this technique to advantage, use clear, simple terms that will be understood by the reader. Samuel Johnson's often-quoted definition of a network as "anything reticulated or decussated with interstices between the intersections" is of scant assistance to most readers. Even in the definition of the manse, as given above, the word "ecclesiastic" might occasion difficulty for some readers. A simplified explanation might substitute "a member of the clergy," or, more loosely, "a minister."

Second, do not employ any derivative of the word being defined. The statement that filtration is the process of filtering or that division is the process of dividing tells nothing.

Third, do not make the definition too inclusive or too restrictive. It should never be so broad that it embraces more than the one word, and never so narrow that it fails to give a complete explanation. For example, if a revolver is defined as a portable firearm, the definition is too inclusive because rifles, shotguns, and other portable firearms could be contained in it equally well. On the other hand, if rhetoric is defined as the art of writing well, the definition is too narrow, for rhetoric also includes the art of speaking well. The explanation must, therefore, be of just the right scope. Of some assistance in securing such precision is a careful limitation of the classification. The definition of a revolver can be made through the use of the term "weapon" as the classifying word, but the definition is greatly simplified by the use of a more specific term, "firearm." This latter word includes weapons which discharge a shot by explosion and has in addition specific reference to small arms. Thus, the more the classification can be restricted without damaging the meaning, the more effective will be the explanation.

Fourth, make a real classification. The most common error in definition is the use of "is when" and "is where" in place of a classification: filtration is when a liquid is separated from the solids suspended in it; a nepman is where a Russian engages in private trade according to the regulations of the New Economic Policy. Obviously, filtration is not a "when," nor is a nepman a "where."

EXTENSIVE DEFINITION. The extensive definition is simply a broader application of the technique of the intensive definition. As a grown plant is the expansion of the parts found in a seed, so is an extensive definition the amplification of the elements found in an intensive definition. The value of such amplification is that some definitions can be made more significant by fuller treatment. The explanations of the barometer, the bicycle, and the nepman, for example, seem to call for amplification. This can come through discussion of either the classification or the differentiation. The reader desires more knowledge of the differentiae of the barometer and the bicycle, but he might be curious about private trade in Russia and so demand more about the classification of the nepman.

Extensive definitions can be of two kinds. Some can be made absolutely comprehensive—the treatment of the barometer, for example—but others can never reach such perfection, and so make no pretense at completeness. No definition of abstract terms—such as romanticism or democracy—can be completely satisfying. Each reader has certain conceptions of the term which he would like to see added, and few readers would agree on certain inclusions.

The means of expansion for the extensive definition are those studied in connection with the development of the topic sentence of the paragraph: detail, illustration, comparison or contrast, division, elimination, and cause and effect. The definition of the revolver or bicycle would lend itself to development by detail, as the parts and operation of these would be enumerated. A more general term, however, such as patriotism, is more suitable for illustration; the writer can draw freely upon history or fiction for examples of patriotic deeds. Comparison or contrast is valuable to explain an unfamiliar term by linking it with a term known to the reader. Comparison aids particularly in establishing the classification; contrast aids in marking the differentiae. For example, if you were attempting to explain an automobile to a South Sea islander, the classification might be created by comparing the automobile to a vehicle of the islanders, some kind of cart. The differentiae could be shown by the contrast of the automobile and the cart.

Division is useful for developing a subject that is capable of being reduced to its component parts. The best definition of narrative poetry, for example, would probably divide this subject into the metrical tale, popular and literary ballads, the metrical romance, the mock epic, the literary epic, and the heroic epic. Elimination is also useful, for it rules out of consideration those members of a classification group which are not meant. An explanation of the Elizabethan meaning of the word "humour" might begin by the elimination of the modern meaning of that term, or the definition of democracy could be made through the elimination of other forms of government, such as the monarchy, the aristocracy, the theocracy, and the communalistic society. Having established these limitations to the term democracy, you could then proceed to more positive assertions. Cause and effect, as used in relation to definition, is a statement of the origin and growth of the meaning of a word. To take a simple example, the word "familiar" assumes fresh meaning when it is seen in reference to the word from which it stems, the word *familiaris* meaning "belonging to the *familia* or household." In this way the meaning of certain words may be clarified and given added significance.

Definition then merits close study and further use by most writers. Every discussion involving a possible ambiguity of meaning should begin by a definition of terms. Otherwise reader and writer will not progress along the same paths. Moreover, definition is valuable for placing one on guard against inexactness of usage in the writing of others and in offering training in logical analysis.

### Exercises

1. Define each of the following words by means of an intensive definition; underline the classification term of each word:

haberdasher, orphan, pen, lake, bookplate, installment, inventory, Mocha, pun, saxophone, sauerkraut, coloratura, hydrogen, lagniappe, pier, plane, plaid, equilibrium, index, palanquin, corbel, bellows, saw, target, filigree, micrometer, metronome, aisle, blockhouse, phonograph, philology, unicorn, whirlpool, zombi, yard.

2. Ascertain the error in each of the following definitions, and then write a correct definition:

A memoir is a history or narrative.
A propitiator is one who propitiates.

Proximity is a close propinquity in time.
Pseudonymous is using a pseudonym.
Theism is a religious belief.
A sacristy is a room in a church.
Caliph is the title of the former spiritual rulers of Turkey.
A didapper is a dabchick.
An entr'acte is when one takes an intermission between two acts of a play.
A pastiche is a pasticcio.

3. Define one of the following words first by means of an intensive definition, and then by means of an extensive definition of a paragraph in length:

sonnet, thermodynamics, thermometer, carburetor, hemstitch, innuendo, nebula, snaffle, mashie, lob, monarchy, lyric, transept, frieze, galley, carbine,
diamond, element, paragraph, cathedral.

4. By means of a careful intensive definition, distinguish between the meanings of the words in any five of the following groups:

mansion, dwelling, cottage
pork, ham, bacon
mare, filly, colt
river, stream, creek
mountain, hill
ocean, sea, lake
tree, shrub
mist, vapor, cloud
sloop, dinghy, schooner
star, planet
book, volume
periscope, telescope, microscope
acquaintance, friend
mashie, brassie, putter
orchestra, band
hamlet, town, village, city
street, highway, boulevard
delusion, allusion
sarcasm, irony
earnings, winnings
arrogance, insolence, superciliousness, haughtiness
event, occurrence
pity, sympathy, compassion, commiseration, condolence
contemplation, anticipation
condonement, excuse, pardon
interrogation, question
discrimination, promiscuousness
litigation, jurisdiction

5. Write an extensive definition of one of the following words:

romance, heroism, democracy, patriotism, citizenship, honor, virtue, folly, understanding, Nazism, Americanism, religion, atheism, agnosticism, criticism, home, charity, friendship, progress, culture, education, socialism, communism, literature.

## Donjon [1]

The strongest part of a strong castle of the European Middle Ages. It was usually a tower more or less completely separated from the other works and defenses, but always capable of prolonged defense after the rest of the castle had been mastered by the assailants. The earlier donjons were usually round towers, but in the fourteenth century and later they were often square or of irregular outline. Originally, the apartments of the lord of the castle and his family were in the donjon, but this ceased when the desire became manifest for much more spacious and comfortable rooms, and when, at the same time, the entire circuit of the walls became an organized whole, capable of defense, every part in harmony with and assisting every other. From both these causes, the peculiar importance of the donjon disappears as early as 1350, although there still remains an exceptionally strong tower or group of towers which can be called by that name.

### Suggestions for Study

1. State the intensive definition. Distinguish the classification and the differentiation.

2. Trace the changes in meaning of the word *donjon*. Why is such a word history often necessary in definition?

## Bathtub [1]

### W. P. GERHARD

A receptacle of sufficient size and of proper shape to enable a person to immerse the body in water, for washing and bathing purposes, and, in modern buildings, a stationary plumbing fixture, generally provided with waste and overflow pipes, hot and cold water supply pipes, plug and chain or waste valve, and single or combination bibbs. . . . The fixture is either set on the floor, or raised from it on legs, or sunk into the floor.

Examples of fine monolithic Roman bathtubs cut out of large blocks of granite or marble are on exhibition in some of the museums of Europe. Similar marble baths of great splendor were constructed for the French kings. It was usual to place in the tub a linen sheet, as the sides

1. From the *Dictionary of Architecture and Building,* by Russell Sturgis, *et al.* Reprinted by permission of The Macmillan Company, publishers.

were cold, and this custom has remained in France up to the present day. Marble tubs being costly and cold, bathing tubs were subsequently made of wood and of sheet metal. Some curious varieties, like the "sofa" baths . . . were designed by the French furniture makers of the past centuries. A "mechanical" bathtub, the invention of a certain French count, is mentioned, in which the water was constantly kept in motion to imitate the effect of a river or surf bath. A similar device, called a *"Wellen"* or *"Schaukel-bad"* has attained some popularity in Germany at the present day. Another curious out-of-date form of bathtub, the so-called "slipper bath," consisted of a tub in the shape of a shoe, and partly covered, in which the bather sat erect with his feet in the toe of the slipper. The object of the covering was to prevent the spilling of water, to protect the bather, and to enable a person to take a long soaking bath, as required by some medical practitioners. In some of the towns of Provence in the south of France slipper baths may be found at this day. In England, the modern tub baths are sometimes designated as "slipper baths." . . . The modern bathtub, as used in private houses, is manufactured of wood lined with zinc or with copper; of heavy copper; of cast iron or sheet iron, painted, galvanized, or enameled; or porcelain or stoneware, and, quite recently, of glass. In the older patterns the long sides are tapering in plan and also from the top toward the bottom; all recent tubs have parallel sides which make the tub more roomy. The head end of the tub is semicircular in plan and commonly sloped; sometimes both ends are sloped and built symmetrical. The length of tubs varies from 4 feet to 6 feet 6 inches; the width varies from 22 inches to 32 inches; according to the inside depth the bath is called either a shallow or a deep tub.

Special forms of tubs, for bathing only parts of the body, are the sitz bath . . ., the foot bath, the bidet, and the cleansing tubs arranged in modern swimming baths for bathers to take a thorough ablution with soap and warm water before they are permitted to enter the swimming pool.

*Suggestions for Study*

1. State the intensive definition of a bathtub. Distinguish the classification and the differentiation. Name several other items from which the bathtub is differentiated.
2. List several different types of bathtubs. Why was it necessary for the author to discuss these in his definition?
3. Make a topic outline of this definition.
4. Define the following words from this selection: immerse, bibbs, monolithic, practitioners, galvanized, ablution.

## Radicalism and Conservatism [2]

### ARTHUR M. SCHLESINGER

What do the terms "conservative" and "radical" mean? Popular usage has tended to rob these expressions of exact meaning and to convert them into epithets of opprobrium and adulation which are used as the bias or interest of the person may dictate. The conservative, having mapped out the confines of truth to his own satisfaction, judges the depravity and errors of the radical by the extent of his departure from the boundaries thus established. Likewise the radical, from his vantage-point of truth, measures the knavery and infirmities of his opponents by the distance they have yet to travel to reach his goal. Neither conservative nor radical regards the other with judicial calm or "sweet reasonableness." Neither is willing to admit that the other has a useful function to perform in the progress of society. Each regards the other with deep feeling as the enemy of everything that is fundamentally good in government and society.

In seeking a workable definition of these terms, the philosophic insight of Thomas Jefferson is a beacon light to the inquirer. When Jefferson withdrew from active political life at the close of his presidency in 1809, he left behind him the heat and smoke of partisan strife and retired to a contemplative life on his Virginia estate, where his fellow-countrymen learned to revere him as the "Sage of Monticello." The voluminous correspondence of these twilight years of his life is full of instruction for the student of history and politics. His tremendous curiosity caused him to find an unfailing source of speculation in the proclivity of mankind to separate into contrasting schools of opinion. In one luminous passage, representative of the bent of his thought, he declared: "Men, according to their constitutions, and the circumstances in which they are placed, differ honestly in opinion. Some are Whigs, Liberals, Democrats, call them what you please. Others are Tories, Serviles, Aristocrats, etc. The latter fear the people, and wish to transfer all power to the higher classes of society; the former consider the people as the safest depository of power in the last resort; they cherish them, therefore, and wish to leave in them all the powers to the exercise of which they are competent."

In this passage Jefferson does not use the expressions "conservative" and "radical"—indeed, those words had no place in the American political vocabulary until Civil War times—but his penetrating analysis throws a flood of light on the significance of those terms nevertheless. The Tory

2. From *New Viewpoints in American History,* by A. M. Schlesinger. Reprinted by permission of The Macmillan Company, publishers.

who fears the people and the Whig who trusts them are equivalent to our own categories of "conservative" and "radical." Thus Jefferson finds the vital distinction between the two schools of opinion in their respective attitudes toward popular government.

But before accepting Jefferson's classification as correct, what shall we do with the common notion that the conservative is a person who opposes change and that the ear-mark of the radical is his liking for innovation? This does not seem to be a fundamental distinction. If a difference of opinion concerning the need of change were the basic difference between the two, then Americans who advocate a limitation of the suffrage to male property-owners may properly be regarded as radicals, for they advocate an alteration in the established order; and French patriots of today opposing the re-establishment of the Orleanist monarchy are to be classed as conservatives, for they would keep things unchanged. Few people would be willing to follow the logic of their premises to such conclusions. On the other hand, it cannot be denied that history has generally shown the radical in the role of an active proponent of change and has cast the conservative for the part of the stalwart defender of things as they are. Is such evidence to be dismissed as a coincidence oft-repeated, or has there been behind the actions of both radical and conservative some self-interested purpose which has determined their respective attitudes toward the established order?

The very question perhaps suggests the answer. Broadly speaking, all history has been an intermittent contest on the part of the more numerous section of society to wrest power and privilege from the minority which had hitherto possessed it. The group which at any period favored broader popular rights and liberties was therefore likely to find itself as a contender for the new and untried, leaving to its antagonists the comfortable repute of being the conservators of the *status quo* and the foes of change. But, though the historical conditions influenced the character of the contest, such conditions were, after all, merely the stage setting of the struggle. Advocacy of change should, under such circumstances, be regarded merely as the means employed to attain an end and, in no sense, as an end in itself. Recurring now to Jefferson's definition, the goal sought by each group—whether it be in the direction of greater or less democracy—would appear to constitute the real difference between the two.

## Suggestions for Study

1. In what light do conservatives and radicals commonly regard each other?
2. State Jefferson's distinction between the Whigs and the Tories.

3. Does the term "conservative" find an adequate counterpart in Jefferson's term "Tory"?

4. Is it advisable to base the distinction between the conservative and the radical just on their opposition to or liking for change?

5. Using your own words, frame an intensive definition of each of the two terms "conservative" and "radical."

6. Define the following words used in the article: opprobrium, adulation, depravity, knavery, infirmities, partisan, proclivity, luminous, depository, innovation, suffrage, intermittent, advocacy.

## A Gentleman

### JOHN HENRY NEWMAN

It is almost a definition of a gentleman to say he is one who never inflicts pain. This description is both refined and, as far as it goes, accurate. He is mainly occupied in merely removing the obstacles which hinder the free and unembarrassed action of those about him; and he concurs with their movements rather than takes the initiative himself. His benefits may be considered as parallel to what are called comforts or conveniences in arrangements of a personal nature: like an easy chair or a good fire, which do their part in dispelling cold and fatigue, though nature provides both means of rest and animal heat without them. The true gentleman in like manner carefully avoids whatever may cause a jar or a jolt in the minds of those with whom he is cast—all clashing of opinion, or collision of feeling, all restraint, or suspicion, or gloom, or resentment; his great concern being to make every one at their ease and at home. He has his eyes on all his company; he is tender towards the bashful, gentle towards the distant, and merciful towards the absurd; he can recollect to whom he is speaking; he guards against unseasonable allusions, or topics which may irritate; he is seldom prominent in conversation, and never wearisome. He makes light of favors while he does them, and seems to be receiving when he is conferring. He never speaks of himself except when compelled, never defends himself by a mere retort, he has no ears for slander or gossip, is scrupulous in imputing motives to those who interfere with him, and interprets everything for the best. He is never mean or little in his disputes, never takes unfair advantage, never mistakes personalities or sharp sayings for arguments, or insinuates evil which he dare not say out. From a long-sighted prudence, he observes the maxim of the ancient sage, that we should ever conduct ourselves towards our enemy as if he were one day to be our friend. He has too much good sense to be affronted at insults, he is too well employed to remember injuries, and too indolent to bear malice. He is patient, forbearing, and resigned, on philosophical principles; he submits to pain, because it is inevitable, to bereavement, because it is irreparable, and to death, because it is his destiny. If he engages in controversy of any kind, his disciplined intellect preserves him from the blundering discourtesy of better, perhaps, but less educated minds; who, like blunt weapons, tear and hack instead of cutting clean, who mistake the point in argument, waste their strength on trifles, misconceive their adversary, and leave the question more involved than they find it. He may be right or wrong in his opinion, but he is too clear-headed to be unjust; he is as simple as he is forcible, and as brief as he is decisive. Nowhere shall we find greater candor, consideration, indulgence: he throws himself into the minds of his opponents, he accounts for their mistakes. He knows the weakness of human reason as well as its strength, its province and its limits. If he be an unbeliever, he will be too profound and large-minded to ridicule religion or to act against it; he is too wise to be a dogmatist or fanatic in his infidelity. He respects piety and devotion; he even supports institutions as venerable, beautiful, or useful, to which he does not assent; he honors the ministers of religion, and it contents him to decline its mysteries without assailing or denouncing them. He is a friend of religious toleration, and that, not only because his philosophy has taught him to look on all forms of faith with an impartial eye, but also from the gentleness and effeminacy of feeling, which is the attendant on civilization.

Not that he may not hold a religion too, in his own way, even when he is not a Christian. In that case his religion is one of imagination and sentiment; it is the embodiment of those ideas of the sublime, majestic, and beautiful, without which there can be no large philosophy. Sometimes he acknowledges the being of God, sometimes he invests an unknown principle or quality with the attributes of perfection. And this deduction of his reason, or creation of his fancy, he makes the occasion of such excellent thoughts, and the starting point of so varied and systematic a teaching, that he even seems like a disciple of Christianity itself. From the very accuracy and steadiness of his logical powers, he is able to see what sentiments are consistent in those who hold any religious doctrine at all, and he appears to others to feel and to hold a whole circle of theological truths, which exist in his mind no otherwise than as a number of deductions.

Such are some of the lineaments of the ethical character, which the cultivated intellect will form, apart from religious principle. They are seen within the pale of the Church and without it, in holy men, and in profligate; they form the *beau idéal* of the world; they partly assist and partly distort the development of the Catholic. They may subserve the education of a St. Francis de Sales or a Cardinal Pope; they may be the limits of the contemplation of a Shaftesbury or a Gibbon. Basil and Julian were fellow students at the schools of Athens; and one became the Saint and Doctor of the Church, the other her scoffing and relentless foe.— *Idea of a University*, Discourse 8.

## Suggestions for Study

1. State five or six general propositions to embrace the attributes of the gentleman, as given in the first paragraph.

2. What is the classification term in the essay, and from whom is the gentleman being differentiated?

3. Give an intensive definition of a gentleman, as defined in this article.

4. Define the following words from the article: concur, unseasonable, scrupulous, insinuate, affronted, bereavement, irreparable, misconceive, lineaments, pale, profligate, subserve.

**The Process.** The expository form known as *the process* is devoted to explaining how to make or do something. Processes are very frequently written, for such manuals as cookbooks, textbooks on rhetoric or engineering or accounting, pamphlets on the care of automobiles or refrigerators or typewriters, are all processes.

*General principles.* Be simple and clear. That is the cardinal principle for writing a process. Such advice demands, of course, that the reader be constantly kept in mind, for if he is immature or has little technical knowledge, the explanation must proceed slowly and employ elementary terminology, but if he is more advanced, then the process may move forward swiftly. Nevertheless, it is perhaps better for the composition to err on the side of being too simple than of being too advanced. It is also well to define at the outset any terms likely to occasion difficulty, and to hold technical terminology to a minimum. Of course, technical terminology is often required by the subject matter, but if you wish to be understood, use popular phraseology wherever you can.

A good process also never takes too much for granted. If you possess a thorough command of a subject, you often assume that certain essentials of that subject are common knowledge and hence fail to mention or explain them, much to the reader's bewilderment. If an explanation of how to play football failed to mention the system of four downs, the reader would lack so vital a piece of information that his comprehension of the game would be slow indeed. And, of course, one of the stock complaints of students against their teachers is that the subject matter is presented so rapidly or with so little consideration of the actual knowledge possessed by students that learning is difficult. One of the qualities of a good teacher is an understanding of the problems of the beginner; the same might be said of the writer of the process.

*Specific considerations.* Generally speaking, there are two kinds of processes—simple and complex. The simple process is an elementary explanation such as directing a stranger to a particular city street, explaining how to make a dish of junket, how to milk a cow, or how to buy a savings bond. The method used in the explanation is chronological; that is, the process is followed step by step from the beginning as if one were actually performing it. If the process requires the use of several pieces of equipment or ingredients, as in a laboratory experiment or a cooking recipe, these had better be listed before the chronological relation is begun. Also, in your zeal to tell the reader what to do, do not forget to tell him how to do it. In an explanation of how to drive a car, it is not enough to tell a novice to shift gears from low to high after the car is started; he must be told how to perform that act. The simple process is then but a matter of arranging all the necessary steps carefully in chronological order before the account is begun, and thereafter presenting these with constant attention to how each step is managed.

The second type of process is complex, involving the explanation of a complicated procedure: how to repair a typewriter, how to clean a watch, how to build a radio. Obviously more skill must be exercised here than in the simple process. The best advice is to proceed from the general to the particular. That is, at the beginning of the account, give the reader a general view of what he is to do, its purpose, the materials employed, the relationship of these materials in the process, and any points of special difficulty in the performance. The efficacy of such a procedure is realized when one thinks of such an example as that of the French soldiers during the first World War, who were praised for the intelligent manner in which they carried out assignments; part of their success undoubtedly lay in the procedure of their superiors who considered them not as automatons but as human beings, and accordingly outlined to them the general plan of each battle. In seeing how their individual assignments fitted into the general action, the soldiers were able to perform them more successfully. Thus a reader needs to be oriented somewhat before he is plunged into a mass of details. Suppose that you are explaining how to print handbills or the like, a process which is relatively simple for an experienced printer but difficult for a beginner. Assuming that a novice has access to suitable equipment, you might begin by identifying several of the materials for him, such as the type and its frame, the composing stick, the galley, and so on, with a brief word as to their relationship in the process. The discussion of the details, which would come next, can usually be handled best by dividing the subject into convenient units. A first unit of this subject might be on the different kinds of type, their identification by the point system and perhaps the differences between them as they appear on the printed page. The following unit might be on the method of composition, with explanation of such topics as the arrangement of type cases, the use of the composing stick, the problem of making the lines fall evenly on the margins, and the transference of the type to the galley. A final section could explain how to lock up the galleys for printing. In this way, a complex subject can be reduced to its parts and so made intelligible to the learner. The steps in the explanation are, therefore, a brief, general description of the process, a statement of the equipment needed, and a division of the subject into logical units for detailed presentation.

You will undoubtedly find it advisable to avoid trying the complex process until you have mastered the technique of the simple process. Then address your article to a reader who has little or no knowledge of the subject. In making the explanation clear to him, do not be afraid to use diagrams or charts, for they will give him a pictorial representation and avoid many complicated descriptions. As a final word, do not be too dull. A touch of humor or of human interest will do much toward making the process both instructive and appealing.

### Exercise

Write a process explaining how to do one of the following:

| | |
|---|---|
| Drive a car | Make a dress |
| Operate a bookstore (or other store) | Play jazz |
| Write a composition | Write an advertisement |
| Play golf (or other game) | Plant a garden |
| Build a bookcase (or other article of furniture) | Make pottery |
| Change a tire | Tie knots |
| Operate a machine (of any type) | Sail a boat |
| Get a job | Watch a football game |
| Typewrite | Conduct a track meet |
| Paint a picture | Decorate a room |
| Model a statue | Study |
| Give a party | Build an outdoor fireplace |
| Knit | Make camp for the night |
| Engrave | Build a fire |
| Take photographs | Make a telescope |
| Read a newspaper | Drill a well |
| Break in a horse | Lay a concrete walk |
| | Pledge a freshman to a fraternity |

Cure a cold

Teach an animal tricks

Serve a meal

Sell a car (or other product)

Write a song lyric

Play a musical instrument

Form a band

Choose an apartment

Solder

Perform a laboratory experiment

Paint a house

Climb a mountain

Ride a horse

Give first aid to someone

## How to Write a Book [3]

### HAROLD NICOLSON

In Sloane Square the other day I met a friend who had just been demobilized. I asked him what he meant to do now. "Well," he answered, "as a matter of fact, I was thinking of writing a book. Tell me, since you know about these things, how does one write a book?"

I gazed across that ungainly Square towards the bright façade of Peter Jones. "Many years ago," I said, a trifle sententiously perhaps, "I asked Somerset Maugham how one wrote a play. He gave me excellent advice."

"And what was that advice?" my friend asked me.

"He said, 'Well, you get an idea; and then you write a p-p-p-play about it.'"

"Yes, I see," my friend murmured, and thereat we went our different ways across pavements glistening in September rain.

I realized, as I walked, that I had not been helpful. I realized that having written books myself, I should have asked the man to luncheon and explained at length to him how the thing is done. I realized that on that afternoon of all afternoons I should have been in a mood of philanthropic helpfulness, since on that very morning I had typed the last words of the final chapter of a book on which I had been engaged for two years. I should have been filled with a mood of achievement and lassitude, of melancholy and delight, such as assailed Gibbon on the night of June 27, 1787, when he paced his acacia walk having just blotted the last words of the *Decline and Fall*.

I should have been more communicative and less selfish. I should have told him that the first essential is to know what one wishes to say; that the second essential is to decide to whom one wishes to say it. Once one has chosen the theme and selected the audience, then the book more or less should write itself. But would that have been helpful to a young officer recently demobilized? And how, after all, does one really write a book?

3. From the *Atlantic Monthly*, CLXXVII (January, 1946), p. 111. Reprinted by permission of the author and the *Atlantic Monthly*.

I am not thinking, of course, about creative writing. I am well aware that the poets and the novelists do not, as Aristotle observed, "create what they create by taking thought; but owing rather to natural temperament and in a mood of ecstasy." I am thinking rather of those who, being gifted with average industry and certain powers of narrative, wish to record in written form either their own experiences or the experiences of others.

The creative writers stand in a class apart. They possess a special gift, such as that which enables a painter to paint or a pianist to play; they are driven by some inner daemon who afflicts them with strange spasms of intuition interspersed with long blanks of discouragement. Their days and nights are disturbed by the conflict between their sense of power and their consciousness of powerlessness; they "learn in suffering what they teach in song."

The ordinary writer, the man who "thinks of writing a book," lives in a more equable climate, and remains unaffected by the typhoons and the doldrums of genius; he can, with ordinary skill and attention, navigate his little ship through quiet seas. If he has a good story to tell, whether it be firsthand or secondhand, his task is almost mechanical. It is as if he were building a house. He must start with some idea of the size and proportions of the house he wants to build; he must have some conception of the relation between surfaces and decoration; he must remain constantly aware of the purposes for which the house is intended; and thereafter he must assemble his material in the right order and fit it neatly and efficiently into place.

If he starts with the intention of building a bungalow and then determines that he will turn it into a hotel, the resultant effect is likely to be confused. If he begins in lath and plaster and later decides to try a little brickwork, the ultimate impression will not be orderly. Yet with ordinary sense and prevision he should be able to avoid such discrepancies. And there are, I suppose, certain suggestions which one can make to him which may save undue wastage of energy and time.

The man who sets out to "write a book" about his own experiences may imagine that the problem of proportion, the actual plan, will be determined by the chronological sequence. This is an incorrect assumption. Only those who possess an acute sense of audience realize that those passages of time which interest them personally are not necessarily the passages which will interest their readers.

Most adults, for instance, have a nostalgic affection for their own childhood which is rarely communicable to those whose associations have been different. Many autobiographical writers tend to dwell lovingly and at length on passages of time which for them are illumined by an experience which they are too reticent to relate; their readers, being ignorant of the significant event, fail to be warmed by the required glow of reminiscence.

It often occurs, moreover, that a man who is recounting his own adventures is unduly interested in the mood of anticipation which surrounded him before the adventures began; he will thus tend to devote disproportionate space to his prelude, to "the journey out," without realizing that the reader is becoming impatient. The purely chronological method, moreover, unless it is firmly controlled, is apt too accurately to reflect the intermittences of actual life.

It is seldom that adventure moves in a continuous curve from prelude, through climax, to solution; there is liable to occur a suspension or, what is worse, a repetition of climax. That in itself may prove an interesting theme; but it requires skill and management on the part of the writer to convince the reader that these gaps and repetitions are due to competence rather than to incompetence.

The man who writes the narrative of his own experiences should thus realize that time is measured, not by the amount of seconds it absorbs, but by the intensity of experience it contains; and that unless he can communicate to his readers an intensity of experience similar to his own, he will find that the chronological method complicates his proportions, instead of simplifying them.

On the other hand, the man who writes the story of other men's experiences (the man, that is, who writes biography or history) is less exposed to such subjective dislocations; for him the time-sequence does in fact constitute a useful blueprint. His task is to arrange and to interpret a vast mass of material in such a manner as to provide a true and lucid narrative; and as such his difficulty is almost wholly one of preparation and arrangement. The beginner who decides to write a history or a biography should realize that his main difficulty will not be the actual writing of the narrative but the previous absorption and arrangement of his material.

I recommend, for what it is worth, the following procedure. The intending biographer or historian should first purchase a very large and, if possible, loose-leaved notebook. He should then acquire the most detailed standard work upon his subject. He should then devote much time and trouble to summarizing in his notebook the facts and comments contained in the standard work. If he does this carefully, legibly, and methodically, if he above all leaves himself a large amount of space for subsequent additions, he will then after much toil have before him the main outlines of the narrative to which he wishes to give his personal interpretation.

Thereafter he will read all available works or documents bearing on his subject, and will insert in his notebook all the additional material he acquires. He must have the energy and the patience to write out these references in full, so that in the end his notebook contains, correctly arranged, far more material than he can possibly use. He can then discard all works of reference and use his notebook as the sole quarry from which to build his house.

Had I said all this to my demobilized friend in Sloane Square should I have encouraged or discouraged him? There are other things I might have said. I might have warned him of the dark days when his book would grow stale to him as the sound of his own voice. I might have warned him that there would come moments when his material, however carefully arranged, would become disorganized and flap round him in confusion like a colony of rooks. I might have warned him that there would come a time when he would hate his characters and his narrative with a wearied loathing. And I could have told him that the morning would come when he would write the last word of the last chapter and walk elatedly thereafter upon pavements glistening in September rain.

*Suggestions for Study*

1. How much of this article can properly be called introduction? Why is such an introduction a necessary part of the presentation?

2. To what reader are these remarks addressed? What kind of book does the author presume that the reader wishes to write?

3. What is the "chronological sequence" of organizing materials? What dangers are inherent in its use? To what sort of writing is it well adapted?

4. Summarize the author's advice both to the writer of autobiography and to the writer of history or biography.

5. Define the following words from this article: philanthropic, lassitude, intuition, interspersed, nostalgic, reticent.

## How to Detect Propaganda [4]

If American citizens are to have clear understanding of present-day conditions and what to do about them, they must be able to recognize propaganda, to analyze it, and to appraise it.

But what is propaganda?

As generally understood, *propaganda is expression of opinion or action by individuals or groups deliberately designed to influence opinions or actions of other individuals or groups with reference to predetermined ends.* Thus propaganda differs from scientific analysis. The propagandist

4. From *Propaganda Analysis,* November, 1937. The devices for propaganda analysis were worked out at Teachers College, Columbia University, and were made available to the Institute for Propaganda Analysis by Professor Clyde R. Miller, by whose permission the article is here reprinted.

is trying to "put something across," good or bad, whereas the scientist is trying to discover truth and fact. Often the propagandist does not want careful scrutiny and criticism; he wants to bring about a specific action. Because the action may be socially beneficial or socially harmful to millions of people, it is necessary to focus upon the propagandist and his activities the searchlight of scientific scrutiny. Socially desirable propaganda will not suffer from such examination, but the opposite type will be detected and revealed for what it is.

We are fooled by propaganda chiefly because we don't recognize it when we see it. It may be fun to be fooled but, as the cigarette ads used to say, it is more fun to know. We can more easily recognize propaganda when we see it if we are familiar with the seven common propaganda devices. These are:

1. The Name Calling Device
2. The Glittering Generalities Device
3. The Transfer Device
4. The Testimonial Device
5. The Plain Folks Device
6. The Card Stacking Device
7. The Band Wagon Device

Why are we fooled by these devices? Because they appeal to our emotions rather than to our reason. They make us believe and do something we would not believe or do if we thought about it calmly, dispassionately. In examining these devices, note that they work most effectively at those times when we are too lazy to think for ourselves; also, they tie into emotions which sway us to be "for" or "against" nations, races, religions, ideals, economic and political policies and practices, and so on through automobiles, cigarettes, radios, toothpastes, presidents, and wars. With our emotions stirred, it may be fun to be fooled by these propaganda devices, but it is more fun and infinitely more to our own interests to know how they work.

Lincoln must have had in mind citizens who could balance their emotions with intelligence when he made his remark: ". . . but you can't fool all of the people all of the time."

## Name Calling

"Name Calling" is a device to make us form a judgment without examining the evidence on which it should be based. Here the propagandist appeals to our hate and fear. He does this by giving "bad names" to those individuals, groups, nations, races, policies, practices, beliefs, and ideals which he would have us condemn and reject. For centuries the name "heretic" was bad. Thousands were oppressed, tortured, or put to death as heretics. Anybody who dissented from popular or group belief or practice was in danger of being called a heretic. In the light of today's knowledge, some heresies were bad and some were good. Many of the pioneers of modern science were called heretics; witness the cases of Copernicus, Galileo, Bruno. Today's bad names include: Fascist, demagogue, dictator, Red, financial oligarchy, Communist, muckraker, alien, outside agitator, economic royalist, Utopian, rabble-rouser, troublemaker, Tory, Constitution wrecker.

"Al" Smith called Roosevelt a Communist by implication when he said in his Liberty League speech, "There can be only one capital, Washington or Moscow." When "Al" Smith was running for the presidency, many called him a tool of the Pope, saying in effect, "We must choose between Washington and Rome." That implied that Mr. Smith, if elected President, would take his orders from the Pope. Likewise Mr. Justice Hugo Black has been associated with a bad name, Ku Klux Klan. In these cases some propagandists have tried to make us form judgments without examining essential evidence and implications. "Al Smith is a Catholic. He must never be President." "Roosevelt is a Red. Defeat his program." "Hugo Black is or was a Klansman. Take him out of the Supreme Court."

Use of "bad names" without presentation of their essential meaning, without all their pertinent implications, comprises perhaps the most common of all propaganda devices. Those who want to *maintain* the status quo apply bad names to those who would change it. For example, the Hearst press applies bad names to Communists and Socialists. Those who want to *change* the status quo apply bad names to those who would maintain it. For example, the *Daily Worker* and the *American Guardian* apply bad names to conservative Republicans and Democrats.

## GLITTERING GENERALITIES

"Glittering Generalities" is a device by which the propagandist identifies his program with virtue by use of "virtue words." Here he appeals to our emotions of love, generosity, and brotherhood. He uses words like truth, freedom, honor, liberty, social justice, public service, the right to work, loyalty, progress, democracy, the American way, Constitution defender. These words suggest shining ideals. All persons of good will believe in these ideals. Hence the propagandist, by identifying his individual group, nation, race, policy, practice, or belief with such ideals, seeks to win us to his cause. As Name Calling is a device to make us form a judgment to *reject and condemn,* without examining the evidence, Glittering Generalities is a device to make us *accept and approve,* without examining the evidence.

For example, use of the phrases, "the right to work" and "social justice," may be a device to make us accept programs for meeting the labor-capital problem which, if we examined them critically, we would not accept at all.

In the Name Calling and Glittering Generalities devices, words are used to stir up our emotions and to befog our thinking. In one device "bad words" are used to make us mad; in the other "good words" are used to make us glad.

The propagandist is most effective in use of these devices when his words make us create devils to fight or gods to adore. By his use of the "bad words," we personify as a "devil" some nation, race, group, individual, policy, practice, or ideal; we are made fighting mad to destroy it. By use of "good words," we personify as a godlike idol some nation, race, group, etc. Words which are "bad" to some are "good" to others, or may be made so. Thus, to some the New Deal is "a prophecy of social salvation" while to others it is "an omen of social disaster."

From consideration of names, "bad" and "good," we pass to institutions and symbols, also "bad" and "good." We see these in the next device.

### TRANSFER

"Transfer" is a device by which the propagandist carries over the authority, sanction, and prestige of something we respect and revere to something he would have us accept. For example, most of us respect and revere our church and our nation. If the propagandist succeeds in getting church or nation to approve a campaign in behalf of some program, he thereby transfers its authority, sanction, and prestige to that program. Thus we may accept something which otherwise we might reject.

In the Transfer device, symbols are constantly used. The cross represents the Christian Church. The flag represents the nation. Cartoons like Uncle Sam represent a consensus of public opinion. Those symbols stir emotions. At their very sight, with the speed of light, is aroused the whole complex of feelings we have with respect to church or nation. A cartoonist by having Uncle Sam disapprove a budget for unemployment relief would have us feel that the whole United States disapproves relief costs. By drawing an Uncle Sam who approves the same budget, the cartoonist would have us feel that the American people approve it. Thus, the Transfer device is used both for and against causes and ideas.

## Testimonial

The "Testimonial" is a device to make us accept anything from a patent medicine or a cigarette to a program of national policy. In this device the propagandist makes use of testimonials. "When I feel tired, I smoke a Camel and get the grandest 'lift.'" "We believe the John L. Lewis plan of labor organization is splendid; C.I.O. should be supported." This device works in reverse also; counter-testimonials may be employed. Seldom are these used against commercial products like patent medicines and cigarettes, but they are constantly employed in social, economic, and political issues. "We believe that the John L. Lewis plan of labor organization is bad; C.I.O. should not be supported."

## Plain Folks

"Plain Folks" is a device used by politicians, labor leaders, business men, and even by ministers and educators to win our confidence by appearing to be people like ourselves—"just plain folks among the neighbors." In election years especially do candidates show their devotion to little children and the common, homey things of life. They have front porch campaigns. For the newspaper men they raid the kitchen cupboard, finding there some of the good wife's apple pie. They go to country picnics; they attend service at the old frame church; they pitch hay and go fishing; they show their belief in home and mother. In short, they would win our votes by showing that they're just as common as the rest of us—"just plain folks," —and, therefore, wise and good. Business men often are "plain folks" with the factory hands. Even distillers use the device. "It's our family's whiskey, neighbor; and neighbor, it's your price."

## Card Stacking

"Card Stacking" is a device in which the propagandist employs all the arts of deception to win our support for himself, his group, nation, race, policy, practice, belief, or ideal. He stacks the cards against the truth. He uses under-emphasis and over-emphasis to dodge issues and evade facts. He resorts to lies, censorship, and distortion. He omits facts. He offers false testimony. He creates a smokescreen of clamor by raising a new issue when he wants an embarrassing matter forgotten. He draws a red herring across the trail to confuse and divert those in quest of facts he does not want revealed. He makes the unreal appear real and the real appear unreal. He lets half-truth masquerade as truth. By the Card Stacking device, a mediocre candidate, through the "build-up," is made to appear an intellectual titan; an ordinary prize fighter a probable world champion; a worthless patent medicine a beneficent cure. By means of this device propagandists would convince us that a ruthless war of aggression is a crusade for righteousness. . . . Card Stacking employs sham, hypocrisy, effrontery.

## THE BAND WAGON

The "Band Wagon" is a device to make us follow the crowd, to accept the propagandist's program en masse. Here his theme is: "Everybody's doing it." His techniques range from those of medicine show to dramatic spectacle. He hires a hall, fills a great stadium, marches a million men in parade. He employs symbols, colors, music, movement, all the dramatic arts. He appeals to the desire, common to most of us, to "follow the crowd." Because he wants us to "follow the crowd" in masses, he directs his appeal to groups held together by common ties of nationality, religion, race, environment, sex, vocation. Thus propagandists campaigning for or against a program will appeal to us as Catholics, Protestants, or Jews; as members of the Nordic race or as Negroes; as farmers or as school teachers; as housewives or as miners. All the artifices of flattery are used to harness the fears and hatreds, prejudices, and biases, convictions and ideals common to the group; thus emotion is made to push and pull the group on to the Band Wagon. In newspaper articles and in the spoken word this device is also found. "Don't throw your vote away. Vote for our candidate. He's sure to win." Nearly every candidate wins in every election—before the votes are in.

## PROPAGANDA AND EMOTION

Observe that in all these devices our emotion is the stuff with which propagandists work. Without it they are helpless; with it, harnessing it to their purposes, they can make us glow with pride or burn with hatred, they can make us zealots in behalf of the program they espouse. As we said at the beginning, propaganda as generally understood is expression of opinion or action by individuals or groups with reference to predetermined ends. Without the appeal to our emotion—to our fears and to our courage, to our selfishness and unselfishness, to our loves and to our hates—propagandists would influence few opinions and few actions.

To say this is not to condemn emotion, an essential part of life, or to assert that all predetermined ends of propagandists are "bad." What we mean is that the intelligent citizen does not want propagandists to utilize his emotions, even to the attainment of "good" ends, without knowing what is going on. He does not want to be "used" in the attainment of ends he may later consider "bad." He does not want to be gullible. He does not want to be fooled. He does not want to be duped, even in a "good" cause. He wants to know the facts and among these is included the fact of the utilization of his emotions.[1]

Keeping in mind the seven common propaganda devices, turn to today's newspapers and almost immediately you can spot examples of them all. At election time or during any campaign, Plain Folks and Band Wagon are common. Card Stacking is hardest to detect because it is adroitly executed or because we lack the information necessary to nail the lie. A little practice with the daily newspapers in detecting these propaganda devices soon enables us to detect them elsewhere—in radio, news-reel, books, magazines, and in expression of labor unions, business groups, churches, schools, political parties.

*Suggestions for Study*

1. Distinguish the aims of the propagandist from those of the scientist.
2. Why do the devices of the propagandist deceive us?
3. Be prepared to define each of the seven devices of the propagandist. State an example of each drawn from your own experience or reading.
4. Compare this investigation of propaganda with the study made by R. H. Thouless in his article "Emotional Meanings."
5. The usual process organizes its material in a chronological sequence, following regularly from the first act to be performed to the last act. Why is an alternation of this plan necessitated by this subject?
6. Define the following words from this article: dispassionately, heretic, sanction, titan, effrontery, espouse, gullible.

# Be Your Own Weatherman [5]

## CARL WARDEN

Rainbow at night is the shepherd's delight. . . . Red sky at morning is a sailor's sure warning. . . . The higher the clouds, the finer the weather. . . .

For centuries, sayings such as these have been part of the folklore of the sky. Modern science has proved the truth of many of these beliefs concerning clouds and winds as weather prophets. By understanding a few simple facts about the whys and wherefores of changes that take place

1. For better understanding of the relationship between propaganda and emotion see Chapter One of *Folkways* by William Graham Sumner. This shows why most of us tend to feel, believe, and act in traditional patterns. See also *The Mind in the Making* by James Harvey Robinson. This reveals the nature of the mind and suggests how to analyze propaganda appealing to traditional thought patterns.

5. From *Popular Science Monthly*, CXXXVI (March, 1940), 65. Reprinted by permission of *Popular Science Monthly*.

over your head, you can foresee, with reasonable accuracy, the coming of storms and rapid shifts in temperature. You don't have to know anything about aneroid barometers or wind gauges. It doesn't make any difference if you can't tell an isobar from an iceberg. With two eyes as your only equipment, you can read the weather from the sky.

Take the clouds, for instance. Divided into four general types—nimbus, cirrus, stratus, and cumulus—they form one of the most important sources of clews to weather. Nimbus clouds are the thick banks, sometimes with ragged edges, from which rain or snow is falling. Cirrus clouds, consisting of ice crystals, are the thin, feathery wisps that glide across the sky at high altitudes. Stratus clouds, as the name implies, collect in layers and often thicken into an unbroken, leaden mass without form or structure, while the fluffy, cottonlike billows that appear during clear weather are the familiar cumulus variety.

Other important clouds are either variations or combinations of these four basic types. Cirro-cumulus, for example, the sailor's "mackerel sky," a good-weather cloud, is a combination of cirrus and cumulus. Cumulo-nimbus, combining cumulus and nimbus, is the awesome "thunderhead" that occurs in spring and summer. Rising like huge mounds of white smoke from the dark base of a gigantic fire, they tower up to tremendous heights and often hold millions of gallons of rain. When the prefix "alto" or "fracto" is included in the name of a cloud, remember that the former merely means high, and the latter broken. Alto-stratus clouds, therefore, are high stratus, and fracto-cumulus are wind-broken cumulus.

In general, the cumulus and the cirrus clouds are classified as fair-weather types, while the stratus and nimbus are associated with rain or snow. Rain generally falls from the gray nimbus clouds, but it may also occur with cumulo-nimbus and sometimes with strato-cumulus. In winter, alto-stratus clouds may produce snow, but only on rare occasions will rain fall from them.

However, a better guide to weather changes is found in the sequence of the clouds—since, as bad weather approaches your locality, the clouds normally form in a definite order. First to appear after a period of good weather are the cirrus clouds. Blown along at speeds that sometimes exceed 200 miles an hour, and at heights as great as 50,000 feet, they often precede the center of an approaching storm by several days. If the wind is blowing thin cirrus wisps from the northwest or the west and the sky is a bright blue, look for fair weather to continue for twenty-four hours or more; but if the cirrus clouds are developing into a translucent blanket, rain or snow generally follows.

Trailing cirrus in this parade of the clouds is the stratus variety, the commonest of all. When these clouds form their gray cover over the sky, it is usually a sure indication that a storm is on its way toward you. Eventually, unless the wind shifts into the west, they normally thicken to form nimbus or rain clouds.

As the storm center progresses and passes over you, the nimbus formation will break up and the skies will clear. The next morning probably will be cloudless. Soon, however, the fourth basic type, cumulus clouds, will begin to form against the bright, blue sky to complete one cycle of the clouds from fair weather through rain or snow and back to fair weather again.

Cirrus, stratus, nimbus, cumulus—knowing this normal sequence of the clouds gives you a good start in learning to predict the weather. For if you see stratus clouds forming, you know that nimbus or rain clouds are generally next in line. And when nimbus clouds begin to break up, and you sight cumulus puffs through the holes the wind has torn, it's a good bet that clear weather is on the way. However, there are exceptions to every rule, and if you see huge mounds of cumulus clouds lying close to the horizon in the direction from which the wind is blowing, expect a storm within a comparatively short time.

But clouds can serve the amateur weather forecaster in other ways. They may give you tips about what the temperature will be. For example, if clouds disappear from the sky at nightfall, the temperature probably will drop during the night. And if thin cirrus clouds, nicknamed "mare's-tails," are blowing across the sky from the north, fair and warmer weather is on the way.

The clouds can also serve as a weather vane to tell you the direction of the winds, which form another important factor in weather prediction. To use them for this purpose, always look at them in relation to some object on the ground—a church steeple, a tall tree, or the corner of a building. Observe those flying directly overhead, for perspective may fool you if you concentrate on the clouds near the horizon. And if cloud movements are very slow, support your head firmly against a solid object to make sure that it is the *clouds* that are moving in a certain direction, and not your own eyes.

In general, north and west winds are associated with fair weather, and south and east winds with rain and squalls. An enduring southeast wind, particularly on the east coast, is a sure sign of rain. But the shifting of the wind from one direction to another is the important point for a weather forecaster. For when gentle westerly winds begin to swing around into the south and east, it is a fairly reliable indication that a storm center is on the way. Conversely, a shift in the opposite direction is a good sign, for if the wind is blowing from almost any direction and then shifts into the west, the approach of a period of good weather is practically an assured fact.

But why does the shifting of the wind have a bearing on weather changes? To understand that, first glance at the weather map . . . issued daily by the U.S. Weather Bureau and . . . mailed to anyone for a nominal sum. You will notice certain areas marked "high" and others marked "low." As the Bureau points out in its weather-map explanation pamphlet, "lows" indicate areas where the atmospheric pressure, or weight of the air, is low because of warm, rising currents of air. These "lows" mark the center of general storms, which may cover an area as wide as 1,000 miles. "Highs," on the other hand, indicate areas of high atmospheric pressure and are generally the centers of fair weather. The arrows on the map, which fly *with* the wind—not into it—and show its direction at various observation stations, demonstrate the shifting of the wind.

In the northern hemisphere, winds blow in a general counterclockwise direction toward and around the center of a "low," and clockwise around a "high." Moreover, these pressure centers move across the United States roughly from west to east, traveling at an average rate of about 500 miles a day in summer and over 700 miles a day in winter, the "lows" normally preceded by warmer temperatures and the "highs" by colder, though not invariably.

Therefore, the wind in your locality is likely to shift into the south or east as a "low," or storm center, approaches you from the west. And when the storm has passed, and a period of good weather is on its way, the wind will tend to shift into the west or northwest.

Generally, rain is most prevalent in the southeast section of these circular storm centers. A daily weather map will tell you pretty accurately whether your locality lies in this southeast sector, but you can establish the fact roughly without this printed aid by applying a law worked out by Buys Ballot, a famous Dutch meteorologist: When you stand with your back to the prevailing wind, atmospheric pressure will generally be lower toward your left and higher toward your right. That means that if a "low" is approaching and you are standing with your back to a southwest wind, the center of the "low," or storm area, will be toward your left, and you will therefore be in the "low's" southeast sector where rain is more prevalent.

Numberless variations on this sequence of clouds, winds, and temperatures are possible, of course, but figuring them out forms part of the duties of the professional and much of the fun of the amateur weather forecaster. The official weather experts have the advantage of long years of scientific training, plus a host of valuable meteorological instruments, such as barometers, wet- and dry-bulb thermometers, automatic weather balloons, and theodolites. But from accurate observations of the clouds, in addition to wind directions and temperature changes, you can sometimes make a better prediction for your immediate locality than the U.S. Weather Bureau, although their batting average over a long period and over wider areas is bound to be better.

As you become more and more proficient in your forecasting, buy a small pocket notebook and keep an accurate day-to-day log of your observations. Make notes on the cloud formations, the temperature, the direction of the wind, and the amount of rain, snow, and hail. After a period of a year or so, your log will provide you with a complete history of the weather in your locality and, by allowing you to compare present conditions with past performances, will help you to read weather clews more accurately.

Don't expect to gain fame as a weather prophet the first week you make predictions. For, in addition to a good working knowledge of the whys and wherefores of weather, you must learn to make accurate observations and then draw the correct conclusions from this evidence you find in the sky. That takes practice—but so does everything else. Good luck to you as a weather forecaster!

*Suggestions for Study*

1. Define each of the four types of clouds. What two are fair-weather clouds? What two are rain or snow clouds?
2. In what three ways do clouds aid in forecasting the weather?
3. How do shifting winds affect weather?
4. How does the author attract the reader's attention at the beginning of the article? What does the introduction tell you concerning the intended reader for the article? Is the article adapted well to this reader?
5. State the general divisions of subject matter. Does this plan of organization promote ease of comprehension?
6. What person (first, second, third) is used for the point of view in this process? How does the author keep this point of view from becoming monotonous through excessive use?
7. Define the following words from the article: isobar, translucent, conversely, prevalent, barometer.

# Skiing [6]

### STRAND MIKKELSEN

If all the people in New York, Boston, Philadelphia, Cleveland, Detroit, Chicago, St. Louis, and San Francisco went skiing at once, their number would be no greater than the huge army of enthusiasts who actually indulge in the sport. Throughout the world, more than 16,000,000 persons last winter strapped on skis and ran, slid, and leaped from hills on these seven-league wooden shoes.

Each season the sport gains new converts. Although it is only twenty-five years old in this country, there now are 200,000 skiers in the United States, organized in hundreds of clubs. Even in countries where you would least expect it, skiing is in high favor. In Japan, for example, there are at least 100,000 skiers, and Italy has double that number.

Reasons for the great and growing popularity of skiing are not far to seek. Personally, I know of nothing more thrilling and exhilarating, and I have tried and enjoyed several other sports, including skating, running, and soccer. Among winter sports, skiing is king. For pleasure, it compares with snowshoeing as apple pie does with bread-and-butter. It beats skating because it is far less restricted as to place and time. In skiing the whole snow-covered world is your playground, and in the right kind of country, you can enjoy months of the sport each season.

The best thing about skiing is that it is easy to learn and, once mastered, offers infinite variety. There is no chance of its getting monotonous. I have been skiing for eighteen years—since I was a boy of eight, in fact—and I never yet saw two ski hills that were alike, nor one that was the same on different days. Every new landscape, every new snow tests the powers of the skier in another way. The fun is always as fresh as the snow itself and lasts as long.

As far as I know, skiing is the simplest sport to learn—provided you get the right start. Naturally, everyone who wants to ski would like to jump and experience the thrill of flying through the air with a white world beneath him. But in skiing you cannot begin by jumping any more than you can run before you walk. The great mistake of young skiers in this country is that they try to jump before being able to walk and slide on skis.

The first essential is to have the right equipment. Get good skis, and be sure that, when upended, they stand as high as you can reach. In other words, if you, for instance, are five feet ten inches tall and you can reach

6. From *Popular Science Monthly*, CXVIII (January, 1931), 38. Reprinted by permission of *Popular Science Monthly*.

one foot above your head, your skis should be six feet ten inches long. Then buy a pair of good ski boots.

The most important item, however, is the fastenings, which should be strong and heavy and correctly fit the boots. Remember this, for not having proper bindings will set you back in skiing, and you never can learn to jump with poor bindings. One of the main reasons for the prowess of Norwegian, Swedish, and Swiss ski runners is that, no matter how young they were when they began, their ski-wise parents provided them with good fastenings from their very start in the sport.

Assuming that you have the proper outfit, you now are ready to learn walking or sliding on level ground. Here we go! Lunge forward on one foot, keeping the weight well on the front ski. Before the skis stop, lunge forward again and slide on the other ski, transferring your weight. The chief points to remember are: Never lift the skis from the ground, and *keep sliding*.

Propel your skis with easy, dipping motions of the legs and manage your weight with corresponding balancing motions of the arms. The action somewhat resembles skating, except that the feet are not turned sideways to make a forward push, but are kept in a straight line.

The next thing to master is sliding downhill. This is where the fun begins. I can give you only one rule for sliding, but that one is important: Don't bend either the body or the knees, but keep perfectly straight. The rest is a matter of practice and achieving form. No two skiers ride downhill in the same way; neither do they jump in the same fashion. Start with low hills that have level slopes. Then take steeper hills. After those, try hills with bumps. All this is easy, and should take no longer than two or three weeks.

As a majority of ski runners make curves on level ground with the momentum attained by sliding downhill, you now are ready to try your hand at curves. There are several kinds of turns, but the principal types are the Christiania swing and the Telemark swing. The Christiania is the easiest.

Move the left foot forward so that the heel of the left foot is even with the toe of the right, and keep your body weight on the left ski. Steer to the left with your weight, and make the right ski follow by a slight dipping motion of the knees to produce the necessary slide, holding the arms out straight to maintain balance. Continue again with the left ski, twisting the body to keep the weight on the left foot, but holding back a little for the sake of balance. Repeat these steps until the curve is achieved. In making the turn to the right, it is necessary to reverse the process.

The Telemark is the prettiest and most popular of the curves, and expert skiers often use it as a finish to a perfect ski jump. In this curve you turn to the left by pushing the *right* ski two feet ahead of the left. Then stretch the arms out straight. Bend the left knee way down and the right knee a little, meanwhile twisting the right ankle to the left and leaning in toward the left until the swing is completed. Here, as you see, the right ski is the steering ski.

If the Telemark is made to the right, the entire action is, of course, reversed. But since with most people the right leg is stronger than the left, the curve usually is executed to the left. I make the Telemark both ways, but something tells me that it will take you quite a little while to do this.

Sliding downhill is great fun and almost anyone can do it in some fashion, but going uphill is not so easy. The main thing in hill climbing is to make a quick study of each hill as you come to it. Carefully observe its shape and the character of the upgrade, and map out a little campaign as to how to reach the top.

If the hill is low and of gentle slope, walk straight up with the aid of your two poles. All skiers use two poles, except the Lapps, that strange race of Mongolian people who inhabit the northern parts of Norway, Sweden, and Finland. They are the only skiers who never use more than one pole. The reason is that they utilize it as a weapon in their frequent fights with the wolves that attack their reindeer herds. In such a battle, a second pole would be a severe handicap.

To climb steep hills, you must resort to side-stepping, half-side-stepping, and herringboning. In side-stepping you simply turn your profile to the hill and walk sideways. It is used in tramping the ski hill below the take-off. In the half-side-step, you push one ski forward diagonally, at the same time making sure to bring up the heel of the ski in such a way that the ski in its new position is parallel to but ahead of the other ski. Then lift up the lower ski to take its place beside the other.

The half-side-step is the least fatiguing and most useful of all hill-climbing steps. The herringbone, used to climb steep, short, narrow trails and to negotiate hilltops quickly, is much more difficult and a considerable strain on the leg muscles. Face straight up the hill. Keep the feet apart and turn your toes out as far as convenient. Then walk uphill Charlie Chaplin fashion.

The next trick to learn is the kick-turn. This is almost indispensable in hill climbing, and especially useful in reversing your position on steep slopes. Let us suppose you want to make a kick-turn to the right. Lift the right foot as high as you can, twist it to the right, and bring it down with the ski in a horizontal position, so that it clears the toe of the left ski. Now, shifting your weight to the right and lifting the left foot, turn it and then bring it down beside the right. The kick-turn is used only on steep hills, or when going over a fence.

As for braking, snow-plowing is the easiest method, especially if you have no poles. It is best to try the snow-plow when not under too much speed. Straddle the legs wide apart, force the heels out, and bring the points of the skis as close together as possible. The skis, in this position, will be forced half sideways instead of end on through the snow. To make the snow-plow still more effective for braking, edge the skis by making yourself knock-kneed. When under great speed, snow-plowing is better as a preventive than as an actual means of stopping, because when you are coming down very fast all your strength may not be sufficient to hold the skis apart. Stemming is half snow-plowing. To stem, simply run one ski straight ahead and force the other partly sideways through the snow.

Just a few words about handling the poles. On level ground, they may be used effectively in two ways. One is to propel yourself by alternate downward punches of the left and right pole, using your arms much in the same way as when climbing a steep stairway with the aid of two banisters. The other method somewhat resembles rowing. Hold the poles behind you, swing both forward simultaneously, punch the spikes into the ground, and literally pull yourself through between the poles.

When you have mastered all the foregoing, you are ready for the dessert of the meal—jumping. Most people are under the impression that ski-jumping is dangerous, but this is not true so long as the skier does not overreach himself. I started in my native Norway when I was eight years old, and never had an accident until 1924, when I was twenty. The track was icy and on the take-off, just as I was about to make the leap, I fell backwards with my legs up in the air and landed 110 feet downhill at a speed of forty miles an hour. I tried hard to get back on my feet, but in vain. I landed on my arm and broke it in two places.

The only other accident I suffered occurred last year. In February, 1929, I won the national amateur ski championship at Brattleboro, Vt., jumping 141 and 131 feet. In October, I went to Norway, to "show my medals" to my mother. And just like a soldier who goes through a war unscathed and, on coming home, breaks his neck by slipping on a banana peel, I fell while practicing one morning on a very low hill near our house. I sprained my arm so badly that I was laid up for five weeks. My mother's good care and massage treatment, however, put me back in condition, and I was able to compete again in the national meet at Canton, S.D., in February, 1930, when I lost the championship to Caspar Oimon by one foot.

I have told of these personal experiences to show the low average of accidents in skiing. Two comparatively minor injuries in eighteen years certainly indicate that this thrilling sport is far from dangerous.

In learning to jump, start on a low hill, but one with a slope of sufficient length to prevent you from striking level ground. We never hit the level in ski-jumping, because if we did the shock might be injurious or even fatal. It simply would be like jumping off a building. Instead, we always land on the lower end of the slope and slide down to level surface, usually ending the jump with a graceful curve or swing.

During the rundown, always slide naturally. This is one of the main secrets of good form. Your attitude should be easy and steady, with the upper part of the body leaning a little forward. Never retard your speed. Keep your arms at your side, bend your knees slightly, and preferably keep them together. The skis must be kept *close together*.

As you approach the take-off, gradually increase the bending forward of your body and the bending of your knees. Throw the weight of your body more and more forward, the skis *always close together*. When you reach the edge of the take-off, straighten the knees and body vigorously and throw your body forward. Don't try to thrust your arms backward.

In the air, you must hold your body erect with an increasing lean forward according to the steepness of the landing slope. Your skis must be close together, parallel and in the same plane. Move the arms in an easy, winglike, flying motion. After your skis leave the take-off, they should gradually point more and more downward until parallel with the landing slope at the point of landing. During the last part of the flight, fix your eyes on the spot where you will make contact with the hill so as to prepare yourself for a steady landing.

The landing must be elastic, springlike, and firm without stiffness. Your body still should be balanced correctly and the skis must still be together. When you land, bend your knees. The knee of the foremost leg should be bent slightly, and the knee of the rear leg more so. If the hill has a comparatively flat landing slope, or if the snow is in poor condition, the foremost foot should be particularly far advanced.

This is the common jump. Only two types are recognized as good form —the common jump and the jackknife. The jackknife is executed in the same manner as the common jump, except that, in the air, the body is bent forward from the hips. You gain the upright position as soon after the landing as possible.

Many skiers have jumped distances of more than 200 feet, but the achievement of such feats does not class them as great ski-jumpers. The outstanding ski-jumper is he who, in competition and under any set of circumstances, has jumped farther than any other proficient competitor.

*Suggestions for Study*

1. Describe the equipment needed. Is it good rhetorical practice in a process to begin with a statement of equipment? What does such a method accomplish?

2. Divide this complicated process into the small processes that make it up. Do you see any plan or order in the sequence of these processes?

3. Select two or three instances in which comparisons have been used to facilitate the explanation. Why are comparisons useful in processes?

4. Do any passages serve to relieve the continuous flow of instructions? Are there any bits of humor in the article?

5. What sort of reader does the author have in mind for this paper? Is he an experienced skier? If so, would the introduction be suitably adapted to him? What rhetorical function does this introduction have?

6. How complete a process is this? Are any instructions omitted that the reader might find useful?

7. Define the following words from the process: negotiate, diagonally, indispensable, elastic, proficient.

**Mechanisms and Organizations.** A common and important type of exposition concerns mechanisms and organizations, that is, how mechanisms operate, how organizations function, how scientific experiments have been performed, how laws of nature operate, how natural phenomena like volcanic explosions or disastrous storms happened. In these explanations you must, of course, remember that you are not giving instructions to be followed by a reader (as in the process) but are promoting understanding of an operation of some sort.

The starting point for such description is a general statement of what the mechanism purports to do, what it looks like, what its important parts are, and what the relationship of the parts is. In this way the reader builds a general plan in his mind into which he can fit the later details. For example, if you wish to tell of the operation of an oil well, the first step would be to explain that the oil pressure in the rock far below the surface is so great that it forces the oil to the surface through pipes and thence to the separators and the field storage tanks. The equipment consists generally then of a pipe sunk anywhere from a few hundred feet to two and one-half miles into the earth, a system of valves at the top of the pipe to regulate the flow of oil, a conduit line to the separators, and a further conduit to the field storage tanks. The reader can accordingly see the basic principle upon which the mechanism works and the relationship of the primary parts.

Having established a general picture of the operation, you can then explain the details. Observe, however, that you cannot describe every detail in the mechanism, unless the details are very few in number. A writer endeavoring to explain the operation of an automobile by such methods would become hopelessly involved. The methods of arranging the details are two: either they can follow a chronological sequence, or they can follow from an important or striking part of the mechanism. The chronological method would probably be better to describe bringing oil to the surface. You might begin with the situation of the oil underground, imprisoned in a trap or pocket of the rock, with some explanation of the geologic formation of these traps. The oil would then be traced as it is forced from the trap through the pipe. The tubing and the casing around it would be described, and the system of valves at the top of the pipe explained in relation to its function of regulating the flow of oil. The account would continue to the separators where the crude oil is removed for piping to the storage tanks, and where the by-products are handled. This is the chronological method.

On the other hand, in describing the drilling of the well, you might begin with the derrick as the most conspicuous and striking feature of the scene, even though chronological order would call for following the transmission of power from the operating machines to the turntable which revolves the rotary drill so often used in modern well-digging. But whatever procedure is employed, be sure to observe an orderly progression adapted to the reader's ability.

All the general principles stated in connection with the process must again be observed here. The reader and his knowledge of the subject matter need to be carefully ascertained, and the purpose must be analyzed in terms of the reader. For example, a paper on the oil fields might be on many different subjects: on the location of oil to interest financiers, on a new drilling rig to interest the drillers, on the operation of wells to instruct engineering students, or on methods of determining the location of oil to instruct geology students. The reader and the purpose must, therefore, be closely analyzed.

Thus far the illustrations have dealt exclusively with writing the mechanism, but the principles for describing other operations are the same. An account of the United States Senate would introduce first a brief sketch of the Senate and its place in the national government. The details of the operation of the Senate could then be given through such a device as following the passage of a bill from the time it is introduced until it becomes law.

The tendency of unskilled writers is to make the account of the mechanism or organization very dull. It is perhaps better to be dull and accurate than lively and inaccurate, but better still is to be lively and accurate. The introduction of diagrams or charts may help to ease the task of describing with the written word and so add interest to the writing. Bits of humor, vivid diction, analogies, and human interest may also make the paper pleasant as well as instructive.

### Exercise

Explain the production or operation of a mechanism or organization suggested by one of the following general subjects:

Steel mills
Farm equipment
Road making
Cotton gins
Radio construction
Automobile construction
Sports equipment
Electrical apparatus, as the dynamo
or transformer
Stock exchanges
Clearing houses
Dress designs
Shoes
Bookmaking
Paper
Cotton thread
Plastics
Photography
Glass
Metals or alloys, such as steel, copper,
aluminum
Mines, as coal or copper mines
Locomotives
Newspapers
Telegraphy
Streamlining
Airplanes

Dictionaries
Filing systems, such as the Library of
Congress system
Musical instruments
Summer camps
City government
Typewriters
Tobacco products
Plumbing systems
Pumps
Lumbering
Geologic formations
Timepieces
Explosives
Permanent waves
Marketing a popular song
Presentation of a radio program
Church services
Traffic control
Lens grinding
City planning
Blueprints
House construction
Interior decoration
Lawmaking
Smoke elimination
Optical work

## Under Mobile River [7]

### R. G. SKERRETT

Mobile, Alabama, on the much-traveled old Spanish Trail, has built, at a cost of $4,000,000, a different type of subaqueous tunnel for the convenience of automotive traffic. The tunnel will shorten the east and west route by 7½ miles, and will materially reduce heavy traffic congestion.

7. From the *Scientific American*, CLXIII (September, 1940), 135. Reprinted by permission of the *Scientific American*.

Mobile is at the mouth of Mobile River and at the head of Mobile Bay at a point 30 miles inland and north of the Gulf of Mexico. The city is Alabama's historic and only seaport. It is on the west bank of the stream, opposite Blakely Island.

Work on the Bankhead Tunnel, as the river underpass is called, was started in July of last year. It links Mobile with Blakely Island and connects with a 10½-mile causeway extending eastward from the island and spanning several narrow water gaps.

The underwater sections of the tunnel were built at a local shipyard, launched one by one, towed to a nearby slip on the west side of Blakely Island, and there brought to a stage of near completion before being moved to and sunk in a deep trench dug in the river bed. Five of the seven sections are each 298 feet long, and the two other sections are each 225 feet long. The under-river structure has a total length of 2,000 feet; and near each shoreward end there is a transition section which connects with a rectangular or box-like section of the tunnel. At the Mobile end, an open ramp approach extends downward from the street level to the portal of the western section. On Blakely Island, the steel box section runs right up to the ground surface, and is equipped with a steel gate which may be closed, in time of hurricanes, against water piled up on the island. The Bankhead Tunnel has a total length of nearly 3,390 feet between grade levels, and its roadway is 21 feet wide for two traffic lanes—eastbound and westbound.

The Bankhead Tunnel is similar in principle to the Detroit Tunnel, built in 1930, but differs in a number of particulars which represent engineering advances. Each tubular section of the under-river divisions is made up of an inner steel cylinder 30 feet in diameter surrounded by an octagonal steel tube that has a minimum diameter of 34 feet. The two concentric tubes were tied together by equidistant radial ribs, and the spaces between the two tubes filled with concrete before the tubes were finally sunk in the trench and covered. The inner tube of each section is lined with reinforced concrete not less than 18 inches thick. The top of the tunnel, in mid-channel, is about 46 feet below the level of mean low water.

Each end of each tube was sealed temporarily with a watertight steel bulkhead before launching; and concrete was poured into the intertubular space to a height of 10 feet to give each section stability when it was first launched. Steelwork was put together by welding; and, before launching, each tube was coated with soapy water and subjected to internal air pressure—any leak promptly blew tell-tale bubbles.

At Blakely Island, openings were cut in the top plates of each inner tube to give temporary access to the inside of a section so workmen could place the concrete lining, the conduits for power, lighting, and telephone circuits, the roadway slabs, and the ventilating duct beneath the mid-section roadway for a distance of 400 feet. That done, the access hatchways were sealed, and the sections, starting at Blakely Island, were floated to the trench and sunk.

At the trench, the last of the concrete was poured into the spaces between the inner and outer shells until a section lost its buoyancy. It was held suspended in a sling and lowered deliberately. Succeeding sections were brought together by pulling the newly laid section, with ratchet turnbuckles, snugly against one already installed. A projecting ring on one fitted into an annular recess filled with a rubberized gasket on the other. Divers did this work. Later, the joint was covered on the outside with concrete poured underwater. Finally, when bulkheads were cut away, adjacent inner tubes were tied together by a welded ring of steel.

One ventilation building, on Blakely Island, is equipped with exhaust fans only which suck vitiated air into ports on both sides of the roadway level for 400 feet in the mid-section of the river part. No fresh air is blown into the tunnel, but the action of the fans at the low point is counted upon to draw fresh air inward and downward from both portals and maintain proper circulation. This arrangement is based upon experimental work of the U.S. Bureau of Mines. An unusual feature of the illumination is that, while lights are arranged to give proper illumination at all points in the tunnel, special additional lights are installed near each portal. These latter lights burn only during the day, their purpose being to make the transition more gradual for the eyes of the driver as he enters from the strong outside sunlight.

## Suggestions for Study

1. What is the function of the first four paragraphs?
2. Describe the construction of each tube. What are the different layers that compose each?
3. What ingenious device was used to test for air leakage?
4. Describe the method of laying the tube.
5. What new feature characterizes the ventilation system?
6. Describe the reader for whom the author was writing. How much technical knowledge does he have? Cite specific points to illustrate your answer.
7. What plan does the author use to organize his material? Make a topic outline of the article.
8. Define the following words from the selection: subaqueous, slip, ramp, tubular, equidistant, radial, bulkhead, stability, conduits, ratchet, turnbuckles, annular, gaskets, vitiated.

## Earthquakes [8]

### REV. JOSEPH LYNCH, S.J.

A story is told of a night watchman who was watching an astronomer making some observations through a large telescope. Suddenly, in the region of the sky towards which the telescope was pointing, a star fell—a shooting star. The watchman whistled in amazement and exclaimed to the astronomer, "Gee, Mister, that was some shot!"

Our watchman gave the astronomer credit for far more than he was able to do, and in the study of earthquakes we seismologists too are often given credit for far more than we are able to do. People have often expressed surprise that we are able to record an earthquake here that is occurring thousands of miles away. The fact is, we don't record it—the earthquake is obliging enough to record itself for us. It does not require the talent of a Sherlock Holmes to find the name of a friend who has called to see us during our absence, if the caller has been thoughtful enough to leave his visiting card under our door. So it does not require the talent of a Sherlock Holmes to find out what earthquake is visiting the earth if the quake is obliging enough to leave its visiting card under our seismic observatory door—which is what every earthquake does. True, sometimes it is difficult to make out the writing on the card, but most quakes write their names sufficiently legibly for us to make them out. We have to supply the pen and ink and even the card, but the quake does the rest. On Monday, January 15, at 3:43 A.M. New York time, a violent earthquake visited northeastern India, and some ten minutes later its visiting card was under our observatory door.

But what is the signature of a quake and how does it write its name?

Before discussing the signature of a quake let us see what an earthquake is. An earthquake may be described as a sudden slipping of a portion of the earth's crust—a readjustment of the crust to a change of forces. A landslide is a readjustment of the crust on a small scale. A snowslide on a sloping roof is an example on a still smaller scale. When the underneath part of the snow melts, the snow begins to slide down the roof, and blocks of it fall with a thud to the ground. The force holding the snow to the roof, causing it to stick to the roof, is lessened considerably and the slipping is a readjustment to this change of force—the snow moves until it finds a force which will hold it in place. A slight readjustment of the earth's crust is going on nearly all the time at Niagara. From

8. From the *Scientific American*, CL (May, 1934), 246. Reprinted by permission of the author and the *Scientific American*.

time to time huge boulders of rock fall into the water. The softer rocks underlying the overhead rock become washed away by the spray of the falls. The supporting force is thus removed from under this overhead rock, and boulders of it fall in readjustment. The rock readjusts itself to the forces present.

An earthquake is such a readjustment to changes of pressure, but a readjustment on a much larger scale. It is a readjustment taking place deep in the earth's crust, down to the depth of a hundred miles or so. The changes of pressure on such earth blocks may be due to a multiplicity of causes—erosion and deposition; tidal forces; centrifugal force (indicated by the fact that earthquakes are more or less confined to the equatorial belt); and numerous others beyond the scope of this short article. Briefly then, an earthquake is a sudden movement of a portion of the earth's crust.

This sudden movement causes the whole earth to quiver. This quiver travels through the earth as ripples through a pond, only much faster. It is not very noticeable, but it has been noticed on the surface of mercury levels and still ponds. But, while not noticeable as a rule by our unaided senses, it may be made noticeable by a seismograph, the microscope of the geophysicist.

The seismograph is the fountain pen used by the earthquake to write its signature. Its essential part is a delicately supported pendulum, something like a clock pendulum, the tip of the pendulum being equivalently the penpoint. When the earthquake occurred in India the whole earth quivered and, as the quiver passed through the ground under our delicately suspended pendulum, it made our pendulum quiver, and this quivering was traced out by the pen on our paper record underneath it, giving us the signature of the quake.

We said the pendulum quivered—actually, the pendulum did not quiver. The observatory and the paper record and everything in contact with the earth quivered under the pendulum while the latter alone remained still. Hence, relative to the paper, we say the pendulum quivered, just as we say the sun rises when really it is the earth that is in motion and not the sun. Because it stays still while ground and observatory move underneath it, the pendulum is able to trace out for us the motion of the ground and to give us the signature of the earthquake. The pendulum stays still, while all around it quivers, because of its inertia—literally laziness. It will not respond to the earth's quiver for the same reason that none of us care to respond to the alarm clock in the morning. All bodies possess this inertia or laziness of motion. If a careless chauffeur starts a car suddenly, the passengers are thrown backward. Actually, they do not move, but refuse to move; they do not respond to the quick motion of the car because of their inertia, and are left behind—that is, stay still—while the car moves forward; hence they are equivalently thrown backward in the car. Similarly, if the chauffeur jams on the brakes suddenly, the passengers are thrown forward. Because of their inertia they refuse to have their motion stopped; so they continue forward while the car stops—hence they lurch forward in the car. We show this inertia in a personal way: we hate to go to bed, but once there we hate to get up. When the earth moves suddenly, then, under a delicately suspended pendulum, the pendulum lurches backward or forward, depending on the motion of the ground. We say it lurches—actually it stays still while the ground underneath it lurches.

This slight motion of the pendulum can be magnified in many ways: mechanically by a system of levers, electrically by winding a coil round the pendulum and setting the latter up between the poles of a strong magnet—the slight motion of the coil across the magnetic field generates a current which can be magnified in many ways. The most sensitive seismographs we have at Fordham University magnify the motion of the ground about 2,000 times. This magnified motion is recorded on paper by attaching a pen to the pendulum or its lever system. To lessen friction and increase magnification, on the more sensitive instruments the motion is recorded on photographic paper by a beam of light reflected from a mirror attached to the pendulum in place of a pen. Such a seismograph set up anywhere on the globe will be set in motion by the quivering of the earth due to an earthquake and will faithfully record the latter's signature.

But how can we tell the signature of one quake from that of another? Just as we have the Christian name and the surname or family name in any signature, so we have, as it were, a Christian name and family name in every quake signature. The quiver that is sent out through the earth from every quake is a double quiver. The first pushes or compresses the earth ahead of it and is called a compressional quiver and travels five miles a second. The second quiver is a twist quiver, twisting or shaking the earth from side to side as it travels. It travels more slowly than the first, averaging only three miles a second. The farther an observatory is from the scene of a quake the longer will be the interval between the arrival of these two quivers, and the more drawn out will be the signature of the quake.

We recognize the signature of the quake from this double signature. If it is a long drawn out signature it is a distant quake. If the two names —that is, if the two quivers—are recorded close together it is a close quake, the exact distance being told at once by measuring carefully just how far apart the two quivers are on our record, which is kept moving at a constant rate under our pendulum, the time being marked on it automatically every second by the clock.

These two quivers or waves are due to the elasticity of the earth. The "push wave" is due to the elasticity of volume of the earth, the "shake wave" to its elasticity of shape. We have something similar in the case of a lightning bolt—an earthquake in the sky if you wish. We have two distinct waves sent out—a lightning wave which we see, and a thunder wave which we hear. The lightning wave travels much faster than the thunder wave; hence we always see the lightning before we hear the thunder. In fact we can estimate the distance of the lightning bolt by the number of seconds that elapse between the arrival of the lightning and the arrival of the thunder—each second putting the bolt a fifth of a mile away. In a similar way we can estimate the distance of an earthquake from a seismograph by measuring the number of seconds that elapse between the arrival of the "push wave" or primary wave and the arrival of the "shake wave" or secondary wave. A set of tables has been compiled giving the distance of the quake for each time interval in seconds. In addition to the push and shake waves, a third wave, a combination of the two, travels around the outside of the earth and arrives much later. It is not necessary for the computation of the quake's distance, but it acts as a useful check since its speed is likewise known.

I can imagine your saying that this explains how we can tell the distance of a quake from its signature, but it does not tell us just where the quake is. The long-drawn-out signature of the Indian quake could tell us it was a quake 7,600 miles away, but could not tell us whether it were in India or Chile because both are about 7,600 miles away. How can we tell the direction from the signature? If we had only one seismograph we could not tell the direction, but we have a whole family of seismographs, and the quake obligingly writes its name under each one. Three seismographs of any one type are required if we are to be able to tell not only the distance but also the direction of the quake from its signature. One seismograph is set so as to respond only to motions from the north or south, another seismograph is set so as to respond only to motions from the east or west, and a third seismograph has the weight of its pendulum suspended by a coiled spring so as to respond only to an upward push or a downward pull of the ground. It tells us whether the ground is first pushed up or pulled down under it as a result of the quake. If we piece together all three motions, the first two tell us whether the quake is, say, from the northeast or the southwest. The third or vertical instrument tells us whether the ground was being pushed from the north-east or pulled from the south-west.

Hence with three instruments we can tell both distance and direction. Moreover, we have the addresses of nearly all quakes that are likely to call at any time, and if we have the distance and probable direction of a quake that has called we can usually say, "That is that South Mexican quake calling again," or "That is that Aleutian Island quake calling again." Both of these were frequent callers during the past year; nine calling from the Aleutian Islands and six from South Mexico.

Often, of course, the signature of the quake is a poor one—very illegible. Legible enough to tell us the distance but not the direction. In that case we consult two other stations and, knowing the distance of the quake from three stations, we draw three circles on our globe with the three stations as centers and the three distances as radii. The three circles can intersect only in one point, and that point is the scene of the quake.

We said we had a whole family of seismographs—at Fordham University we have eight in operation. Three of these are very sensitive and magnify about 2,000 times. For a very large quake, however, they are sometimes too sensitive and magnify the motion too much. So we have a pair of less sensitive instruments to give us the signatures of the larger quakes. Then again we sometimes have little baby quakes that are felt only locally. They are not only much feebler than the larger quakes but they quiver more rapidly—the baby takes shorter and quicker steps than its parents, and we have to have a more rapidly quivering pendulum to be able to write down these quick baby steps. We have two so-called short-period seismographs for near and baby quakes.

With regard to the frequency of quakes: During the past ten months nearly 300 quakes called on us—more than one a day. Of these, about 50 left signatures sufficiently legible for us to recognize and locate definitely. Few of these did any serious damage until the last Indian quake, which destroyed about 5,000 people.

But of what practical use is an earthquake observatory? The new seismology, or the scientific study of earthquakes, since its birth around 1895, has busied itself mainly with four lines of investigation: What can seismology tell us about the nature of the earth's interior; how can seismology be used in prospecting for oil, coal, and such materials; how can we construct buildings that will withstand earthquake shocks; and, lastly, how can we foretell when an earthquake is due in any given locality?

Much progress has been made along all four lines. We have now a fairly accurate picture of the internal structure of the earth. Seismology has, as it were, let down its camera into the interior of the earth and photographed it for us, and we find it to be a solid sphere with a dense core probably of nickel or iron, starting about halfway down like the core of a baseball. For many years the interior of the earth was thought to be liquid, but a liquid core does not fit in with the findings of seismology. The existence of the core is deduced from the fact that earthquake waves are refracted or bent as they pass through the earth, much as light waves are refracted as they pass through glass or water. From the amount of refraction we can argue to the depth of the refracting surface. The twist or shake or secondary wave is due to the elasticity of shape and can exist only in a medium which has a shape of its own; namely, a solid. Since the twist wave passes through the core, we conclude that the core is solid, since only a solid can transmit a twist wave.

With regard to the prediction of earthquakes, seismology has not yet reached the stage where we can foretell quakes, but investigations in this direction which are being carried out in Japan give hope that the time is not far distant when such prediction will be possible. It has been noticed that in earthquake regions the earth shows evidence of tilt or gradual rising for some years before the quake occurs, much as the inner tube of a tire or the bladder of a football rises gradually through a tear in the cover before finally bursting. The tilt of the ground is being carefully observed and measured, and it is hoped that it will finally give the clue to the forecasting of earthquakes.

Seismology has been used successfully in prospecting for oil and coal. An artificial earthquake is set up in the ground to be prospected by setting off an explosive in the ground, portable seismographs being set up at known distances from the center of this artificial quake. The time of the arrival of the earthquake waves from the artificial quake is carefully observed on these instruments, and this time gives a clue to the structure of the ground through which the waves have passed.

In the matter of building, much has been accomplished. The data on seismology given to the engineers have enabled the latter to revise the building codes in California and Japan considerably, and these codes offer a basis for safer construction in other earthquake regions. According to the late Professor Suyehiro, even in the violent Japanese earthquake, buildings which had been designed to resist a horizontal force of one-tenth of their weight successfully withstood the shock. The increased building cost necessary to provide this resistance to earthquake shock has been carefully figured and is ridiculously small—about fifteen per cent. Quakes can, with a little forethought and a little extra trouble in building construction, be effectively provided against.

Seismology has also shed light on earthquake insurance. The late Dr.

Freeman has shown that earthquake risk has in the past been enormously exaggerated. Even in the most disastrous quakes, the actual damage has always been confined to a comparatively small area, and careful analysis reveals the assuring fact that the actual loss seldom exceeds five per cent of the structural value. Were the full facts made clear, both to the public and to the insurance companies, each would be better served; premiums would be reduced, helping the insured, and insurance would be more generally taken out, helping the companies.

In conclusion we might say that earthquakes are nature's safety-valve, wisely arranged by Divine Providence for our greater protection. They come for the most part in uninhabited regions, but if at times they cause sorrow and hardship, perhaps those beautiful lines of Father Tabb will come to our aid in viewing them in the light of blessings in disguise:

> My life is but a weaving between my God and me.
> I offer Him the threads, He weaveth steadily.
> Full oft He weaveth sorrow and I in foolish pride
> Forget He sees the upper and I the under side.

## Suggestions for Study

1. Define an earthquake. What are some causes of earthquakes?
2. Explain the principle of operation of the seismograph. What is inertia?
3. What are the three kinds of quake waves? What are their relative speeds?
4. How do these waves enable the seismologist to determine the location of the quakes? What further aids are there in determining locations?
5. Of what use is the work done is seismology?
6. How can seismology determine the internal structure of the earth?
7. What methods are being used in the endeavor to predict quakes?
8. With what added cost can buildings be made shock-proof?
9. State the rhetorical function of the opening anecdote of the article.
10. Define the reader. Cite six or seven points of adaptation to this reader. What means are used to make the mechanism of interest?
11. What are the three major divisions of the explanation?
12. Define the following words from the article: seismologist, legibly, erosion, centrifugal, geophysicist, compressional, elasticity, illegible, refraction, portable.

## Maestro of the Atom [9]

### LORING A. SCHULER

One night, eleven years ago, a young associate professor named Ernest Lawrence sat in the University of California Library, plowing through reports of experiments in physics. Mostly they were routine, but one caught his eye.

The experimenter had hitched together two long vacuum tubes, and the speed of the electrified particles had been measurably stepped up as they jumped from one tube to the other. Why, Lawrence thought to himself, only two tubes? If the fellow had hitched up ten, wouldn't he have got the impelling force of a million volts?—enough, perhaps, to smash atoms? But ten tubes in a straight line would be impossibly long. Why not, instead, a circular vacuum chamber, with two half-round, shallow copper boxes, shaped like the halves of a pill box cut down through the middle, as electrodes? Oscillating electric current would shift rapidly from one box to the other; a magnet would straddle the chamber, at right angles. If his theory was correct, the same small voltage, used over and over again, would give charged particles a series of electric pushes, while the magnet would keep them going round and round in a compact spiral, something like the spiral on a phonograph record. And thus the hopelessly long device Lawrence had first thought of could be made practicable after all. The particles would go faster and faster, until perhaps they would pile up the speed needed to crack atoms.

That was the birth of the cyclotron, for which the same Ernest Orlando Lawrence has been awarded the great Nobel Prize in physics as the world's number one atom smasher.

Today, with two huge cyclotrons that he has built at Berkeley—vastly bigger and infinitely more complicated than what he dreamed of that night in the library—he is helping to solve some of the most fundamental and mysterious problems of science.

And, in the unpredictable manner of scientific discovery, what started out to be abstract research is turning out to have such practical value that today medical doctors, chemists, biologists, botanists, entomologists, and a great many other scientific gentlemen are all thumbing rides on the cyclotron because it promises to take them to places they have never

9. From the *Scientific American*, CLXIII (August, 1940), 68. Reprinted by permission of the *Scientific American*.

Although written before the atomic bomb experiments, in which Dr. Lawrence played an important part, this article is important in the light it throws on early experiments in this work.

been able to reach before. A powerful ray is under experimental use as a hopeful weapon against cancer. Artificially irradiated substances, with properties like those of radium, are being created for the study of growth and the treatment of various ailments, while in the field of agriculture plants are being made to tell how they absorb nourishment and make starch and sugar.

These are measurable gains in life and health and wealth. But there is much more, Lawrence knows, to be found beyond the frontiers that he has already explored; so now he is getting ready to build another atom smasher, twenty times as big as his biggest, with which he confidently expects to be able to reveal Nature's secret source of energy, tap enormous new supplies of power for industry, and transmute the elements by this modern alchemy.

For twenty-five centuries, men of science believed there was a basic, indivisible particle of matter, the atom, out of which all things were made. Then, only a generation ago, evidence piled up to prove that each atom was like a tiny universe, with a nucleus at the place of the sun, and electrons whirling round it much as Venus and Earth and Mars and Jupiter and the rest of the planets whirl around the sun. All the electrons were identical.

Furthermore, it was discovered that there were as many kinds of atoms as there were basic substances—hydrogen and oxygen and sulphur and zinc and tin and copper and silver and gold and radium, and so on to the number of 92 in all, which were called elements. What made each one different from the others in chemical properties was the number of electron planets that each individual atom had spinning around its nucleus sun. Hydrogen, for example, had one electron; oxygen had eight; copper had 29; tin had 50; gold had 79; radium had 88; and uranium, heaviest of all, had 92. The elements are known in science by those "atomic numbers."

But strangely enough the electrons, which are charged with negative electricity, could be removed without essentially changing the character of the atom. It would still be an atom of gold or iron, for example. So, the researchers said, there must be something in the nucleus, with its positive electric charge, that we don't know about, and inquisitively they turned experimental guns against the little sun that was the center of each atom universe. Did the nucleus, too, have smaller parts? They found that it did, and named those parts protons and neutrons, and said that here at last were the elemental building blocks out of which everything in the world was made. Meat and potatoes, gold and iron, oil and water —all substances were made of the same protons, neutrons, and electrons, arranged in different patterns. That statement still stands, though Lawrence may find something else when he has built his bigger cyclotron.

But, it may be asked, how did the scientists themselves discover all this about particles which they could not see? Mostly by the painstaking accumulation of evidence. They could take photographs of the tracks of particles in motion, showing streaks like tiny comets; and they could "hear" two particles collide in a vacuum when the effect of their collision was amplified and converted to sound.

It is easy enough to strip the electrons from an atom. The ancients did it, though they didn't know it, in that first electrical experiment of rubbing amber with a piece of cloth. But smashing a nucleus is quite a different matter. More than 2,000,000 atoms could lie in a straight line across the dot over the letter $i$. And each nucleus occupies no more space in its atom universe than a fly in a cathedral. The protons and the neutrons are held together by forces of enormous strength. Here is the storehouse of atomic power. To separate the particles, so that the power could be released, would take prodigious energy. That was why Ernest Lawrence, back in 1929, was yearning for a million volts.

Scientists were pretty well agreed that only an atom could be used to smash another atom. If one lot of atoms, they figured, could be made into high-powered, high-speed bullets and fired at another lot of atoms, those that were hit might be smashed. The problem was how to get the necessary power and speed. A couple of German physicists built an elaborate apparatus to harness the lightning; they might have had something if they could have manufactured thunderstorms at will.

The virtue of Lawrence's idea was its comparative simplicity. Along in the spring after that night when he made his first sketch in the library, he got around to making a model of the device, exactly following his original specifications. It was only six inches in diameter—a couple of D-shaped shallow copper boxes, mounted between circular pieces of glass and sealed with red sealing wax. But when the air was pumped out and a borrowed magnet was held at right angles to it and the current was turned on, particles actually did spiral round and round at increasing speed. The thing worked.

Later, he built another one, a little bigger, and that worked, too, with even higher velocity. Still, he wasn't smashing any atoms, but he was speeding up electrified particles to greater and greater velocities.

For this he needed a magnet of tremendous size, and, though magnets like that don't grow on trees, he was lucky enough to find one that had been junked in California when the Chinese government failed to pay for a radio broadcasting outfit of which it was a part. It weighed 74 tons.

There were exciting days and nights in the dusty old radiation laboratory at Berkeley while the first working cyclotron was being built. Discouragements when it wouldn't perform according to schedule; cheers when the difficulties were overcome. Parts melted off under the terrific heat that was generated, and were replaced by water-cooled contrivances. Lawrence was everywhere, driving his small crew of helpers, working like a madman himself, taxing even his own great ingenuity to devise ways of getting results without spending money.

But it worked! It really did smash atoms. It did more than Lawrence or anyone else had expected it would. Weirdly, it performed unexpected transmutations. Sodium, with an atomic number of 11, became magnesium, 12, by capturing a neutron out of a heavy-hydrogen nucleus that was shot at it. Aluminum, 13, became phosphorus, 15, by swallowing an electrified particle of helium. Nitrogen, 7, dropped a helium nucleus and became boron, 5, when it was bombarded with neutrons. There were even more complicated changes, and as time went on the laboratory workers found that they could make five different substances out of any element that they put under fire in the cyclotron—they could add or subtract one number or two, producing absolutely different elements, or they could make a variation of the original material.

Other things happened, too. After being bombarded by the cyclotron's fast-flying particles, all the lighter elements, at least, developed the curious power of throwing off rays, which only radium and its immediate family can do in nature. They were, in scientific terminology, "radioactive."

That calls for some explanation, which for the sake of clarity must start with the operation of the machine itself.

Into the very center of the cyclotron, between the two semicircular, hollow copper boxes, is admitted a stream of atoms of hydrogen or heavy-water hydrogen or helium. A tungsten filament ionizes them—that is, strips off the electrons, leaving the nuclei as naked positive charges. They are caught up by the alternating 80,000-volt electric field from the cyclotron's powerhouse. But as they start off in a straight line, the powerful electro-magnet swings them into an arc. Then when they dash across the gap between the two D-shaped boxes, the quickly reversed voltage picks them up and kicks them on again.

A hundred or more times this happens. Round and round the ions spiral in ever-widening circles, picking up speed at each half turn while the voltage reverses some 20,000,000 times a second. It is the principle of the old rope swing—with the original 80,000 volts magnified by each hundred half circles of acceleration to 8,000,000 volts. And by the time they reach the outer edge of the copper boxes the particles are traveling at a speed of 18,000 miles a second, which is 35,000 times faster than a rifle bullet.

At the exit, a target is set up, smeared with sodium or phosphorus or some other element. The speeding ions strike the quiet atoms in the target, and, though the aim is inexact, two quadrillions—2,000,000,000,-000,000—of bullets every second, concentrating on a target of two square inches, are bound to make some direct hits.

When an atom is "smashed," the protons and neutrons in its nucleus are rearranged. Here, for example, is an atom of boron. A physicist would draw the picture of its nucleus as a circle, with ten little spheres inside, five of them representing protons and five of them neutrons. The atom is hit in the cyclotron by a charged particle of heavy-water hydrogen, known as a deuteron, which may be drawn as a circle containing two little spheres, one a proton and one a neutron. The boron and the deuteron combine. There are now six protons and six neutrons, which make carbon. One substance has been transmuted into another. The new hot carbon throws off one neutron at once, in its effort to regain stability, just as boiling water throws off steam in an effort to get cool. But it still has an excess of energy, and some time later it will throw off still another particle. That is radioactivity.

Some elements expel these excess particles almost immediately. Others let them stay for a while, and then toss them out, perhaps in a minute or an hour or a matter of years. Nature abhors instability, and each atom tries to regain the stability that it lost when new particles crowded into its family circle.

The cyclotron makes radioactive substances easily, and from many elements. The doctors pounced upon it quickly when that was discovered. Radium is very rare and very costly. It can be dangerous as well as beneficient. The artificial radioactive substances have a shorter active life than radium, which is an advantage because they can be used internally with less danger. And besides they cost a great deal less—a day's bombardment of a common salt produces radioactive salt that for a day or two will do the work of several hundred thousand dollars' worth of radium.

Twenty departments of the University of California are now demanding radioactive products from the cyclotron for their own studies. Biologists are using them to study growth and metabolism. Botanists are having fertilizers irradiated, so that they can find out how growing plants use these "labeled atoms." With radioactive carbon they are learning how plants combine carbon dioxide, water, and sunshine to make starch and sugar. In insect research, sodium is traced through the pests. In industry, radioactive hydrogen is helping to perfect petroleum refining, and radio-active salt can be used instead of radium and X-rays to find defects in battleship armor.

There's more and yet more. Beryllium atoms under bombardment give up neutrons in such great quantities that a healing ray, something like the X-ray or the gamma ray of radium, has become known. The doctors have already used this neutron ray with fair success to halt the wild growth of cancer cells in animals, and some of them believe it offers the most powerful weapon against human cancer that has yet been found.

Because of the medical value of both the neutron ray and the radio-active substances, a new cyclotron, with a magnet weighing 220 tons, was built on the Berkeley campus last year, and thirty-five other cyclo-trons have been built in other states and other nations.

Lawrence's next cyclotron will be tagged for fundamental research, to unfold the secrets of atomic power and transmutation. Its construction will take three years, and will cost $1,400,000 of which $1,150,000 have already been given by the Rockefeller Foundation. Its magnet will weigh 4900 tons. It will generate 100,000,000 electron volts, perhaps much more. It will be built high in the Berkeley hills, and its operators will huddle in an underground control room, 150 feet away, when the machine is running.

So powerful an engine of atomic disintegration is dangerous as well as useful. Even the present big cyclotron—one twentieth the size of the one to come—is treated with respect by scientists. Five-foot-thick walls of lead and water protect them from flying neutrons.

When the cyclotron is running, nothing moves except the atoms whirl-ing in the vacuum chamber, and you couldn't see them even if you were at the heart of the machine. If you should stick your hand into the deuteron beam which is sometimes released as a spectacular stream of bluish-lavender light you would be burned as if you had fooled with a blow torch.

Will industry eventually be able to harness atomic power? There are two ways in which this might conceivably come about. Both have been sufficiently proved to take them out of the class of pure theory; neither is at all near to the stage of practicability now.

The first is energy produced by fission, or splitting, of an atom. Within the past year, atoms of uranium 235, an isotope, or variety, of the heaviest of all elements, have been split by neutron bombardment, which divides them into types of other lighter elements, with the release of immense energies. On paper, the splitting of a uranium atom produces 50,000,000 times the energy release resulting from the burning of an atom of carbon in coal, though researchers quickly reduce this ratio to 17,000 because of scarcity and other factors. The released energy from uranium manifests itself as heat, and if enough could be had steam could be produced to run factories.

The trick will be to bring about what is called "chain reaction." This seems possible because when uranium 235 splits, excess neutrons come out, and these, in theory, will attack other atoms and start a chain disintegration with a ceaseless and increasing flow of heat.

So much for theory. On the basis of facts now known, coal isn't likely soon to be supplanted by uranium. Only uranium 235 will split and very little of this has been purified; an increase in consumption would boost the price out of sight; and, last but not least, uranium has a disconcerting high-explosive quality. . . .

The other theoretical method of squeezing power from the atom is by annihilation. Two electrons will disintegrate into a wave of energy when they collide. From this, physicists reason that a far greater emission of energy would result if they could make the heavier protons and neutrons kill themselves off in the same way.

Lawrence has written: "A simple calculation according to the relativity theory shows that a glass of water, if completely destroyed and converted into useful energy, would yield more than a billion kilowatt hours, enough energy to supply a city with light and power for quite a time."

The released energy, if it could be produced at will, would be in the form of heat, which could then be used to make steam, to turn generators, to make electricity for the use of industry.

Lawrence also says: "When we can produce atomic projectiles of 100 to 200 million volts, we shall be able to unloose new energy in light and heat. We shall have new riches perhaps more important than those we have already found. Radium gives off enough energy to raise its own weight of water to boiling temperature every hour, and it continues to do this for thousands of years. There is reason to hope that we shall find the means of releasing the vast store of energy in the nucleus of commoner substances. Indeed, this is more than a hope; it is already a likely possibility."

Coworkers in the laboratory call Lawrence the "Maestro." He is a big man, tall and broad of shoulders; with eyes that are always busy behind his low-set spectacles, and a big, wide, tooth-filled laugh. He plays a good hard game of tennis; has a cruising boat on San Francisco Bay that he won't take out unless there is rough water to make things exciting. Most of all he's curious and generous and honest, sharing each triumph of achievement with associates who love to work with him.

At 38, he is in the top flight of great physicists, and, as one friend wired him on the day the Nobel award was announced: "Dear Ernest, Your career is showing promise."

## Suggestions for Study

1. What services for the reader are performed by the opening paragraphs?
2. Where is the general principle of operation of the cyclotron explained?
3. What does the explanation of the construction of the atom tell you concerning the reader for whom the article is intended? What rhetorical device does the author use in making that explanation? Cite other words or passages that enable you to determine the reading group.
4. Explain the effect on the nucleus of smashing an atom. What is radioactivity?
5. Why did the author begin his explanation with the original, primitive cyclotron rather than with the cyclotron now under construction?
6. Define the following words from the article: electrode, transmute, alchemy, stability, metabolism, fission, emission.

## The Struggle for Existence [10]

### HENSHAW WARD

This chapter is the first step in describing evolution. It is a description of the fundamental fact—never understood a century ago—that the life of every plant and animal is a struggle in a fierce competition for a chance to exist and propagate. If nature had caused all her creatures to live by a policy of "give the weak ones a chance," there never would have been any development of such adaptations as were described in the previous chapter.

Early in every man's life there comes a time when he hears the story of the blacksmith who offered to shoe a farmer's horse for some grains of wheat—thus: one grain for the first nail, two for the second, four for the third, and so on. Of course the farmer was pleased with such a price. The driving of the fifth nail cost him only sixteen grains, and the total wages for putting on the first shoe were only two hundred fifty-five grains. The farmer kept tally: two hundred fifty-six grains for the ninth nail, five hundred twelve for the tenth, one thousand twenty-four for the eleventh. He was amused, and the more so because his wheat was small; it took five hundred of the grains to fill a cubic inch, and a million of them to make a bushel. The last nail of the second shoe cost him not much over a quart. He lighted his pipe and smoked contentedly, reflect-

10. Chapter 6 from *Evolution for John Doe,* by Henshaw Ward (copyright, 1925). Reprinted by special permission of the publishers, The Bobbs-Merrill Company.

ing that he was paying hardly anything for the labor and nothing for the material.

The trouble began while the third shoe was going on; the twentieth nail cost 524,288 grains—half a bushel; the twenty-first a bushel, the twenty-second two bushels, the twenty-third more than four bushels; the total for the third shoe amounted to sixteen bushels. The thirty-first nail cost over a thousand bushels; the total price for the job was 4,256 bushels.

When we tell this story to children, we are amused at their skepticism and pleased with our effort to show them the difference between adding two and multiplying by two. We do not realize that we need the lesson for ourselves when we consider successive generations of animals. The rate of increase is not found by *adding* to their number each time, but by multiplying. Most animals tend to increase by a factor larger than two, and it does not require a long stretch of years to include thirty-two generations. Even a seasoned mathematician is rather startled when he figures the number of descendants that one pair may produce in no long while.

The largest and most slow-breeding kind can furnish amazement if we grant them a few centuries. Suppose that the average pair of elephants produces only four children that live to have grandchildren, and suppose that there are only three generations in each century, and suppose that the parents die as soon as they have brought up their last child. Under these conditions one pair will have sixteen great-grandchildren in the world after a century, one hundred twenty-eight descendants after two centuries, and one thousand twenty-four after three centuries. The rate of increase may seem as insignificant as it did to the guileless farmer. But in five hundred years there will be sixty-six thousand descendants; in six hundred years there will be over half a million, and after another century over four million. Now the numbers roll up. In the thirty-second generation of descendants there will be eight billion five hundred million —that is, five times the human population of the globe. After seven more centuries of increase there would not be standing room for the elephants if they were packed closely on every acre of land surface from pole to pole. Does seventeen centuries seem a long while? It is not the thousandth part of the centuries during which elephants have been breeding on our earth.

There is no trick in this reckoning; the figures do not lie; they give a conservative estimate of the way elephants actually would have increased if they had had a chance. We know as a matter of history that a few horses, left by the Spanish conquerors of Mexico to run wild, must have increased on our western plains for a century or more at a rate that doubled their numbers in each generation.

As soon as we deal with smaller and more short-lived animals, the normal rate of increase is prodigious. In 1860 a few rabbits were carefully conveyed to Australia and tenderly nourished there with the hope that a few of them might be able to live and propagate. Never was a hope more abundantly fulfilled. So rapidly did they multiply that within twenty years they were a pest; rabbit-drives had to be organized, and such heaps of the animals were slaughtered that it was difficult to dispose of the carcasses. A fence of wire mesh was run clear across the continent in order to head off this prairie-fire of life.

Any animal that bears several young in one litter and breeds several times a year can soon make a counting-machine weary. In two years of the World War the rats multiplied enormously along the battle line— amid all the destruction of artillery and poison gas, in spite of the utmost efforts to hold them in check. Against the unremitting warfare of man, rats have always increased wherever there is food. One estimate of their fecundity in England is that, even if ninety-five per cent of them died without breeding, they could quadruple their numbers in a year. If they had food and room, and were not opposed, their skins could make a carpet for the earth in a few decades.

Some similar computation would be true of any animal that is normally adapted to hold its own in the world. It is fitted to increase in swarms, and ever multiplying swarms; and whenever it has opportunity, it infallibly lives up to the predictions about its fertility, actually does propagate in overwhelming numbers. The English sparrow was brought to our shores in 1851 and promptly set to work producing every season several large broods. Within twenty years it had become more numerous than any native bird. The point of this story is not that a certain sparrow is an undesirable citizen, but that any bird in a favorable environment will unfailingly produce astounding numbers in a few years. A very moderate estimate will show that a pair of blackbirds could easily become ten millions in ten years, and that many ordinary birds could have two billions of descendants in fifteen years—would unquestionably have that many in favorable surroundings. When the Ohio Valley was being settled, the pigeons used to be seen in such numbers that we gasp as we read the naturalist Wilson's account of what he saw in Kentucky. "They were flying with great steadiness and rapidity, at a height beyond gunshot, in several deep strata. From right to left, as far as the eye could reach, the breadth of this vast procession extended, seeming everywhere equally crowded. It was then half past one. About four o'clock in the afternoon the living torrent above my head seemed as numerous and extensive as ever." Wilson reckoned that in this one "torrent" there were two-billion pigeons; and this was "only one of several aggregates known to exist in various parts of the United States." Yet these pigeons hatched *only two eggs at a time.*

Every form of plant or animal life has some similar ability to multiply its numbers. Until we hear that statement repeated, and repeatedly emphasized with examples, we cannot have any conception of the prolific power of all life. For even observant people have very little opportunity to realize the abounding vitality of all animate nature. And most of us are not observant. I, for example, hardly see one rat a year, hardly know an English sparrow by sight, am much impressed by the way my trees and shrubs tend to die. I always see, year after year, the same number of crows or buzzards or woodchucks. What do I know about the power of life to multiply? . . .

It is easy enough to see why an animalcule does not continue its rate of increase—there is not space for it in the universe. It is clear why no fish has packed the ocean full and why elephants are not standing five hundred thick on every acre of land. The reproduction of every species —even if it were the only one in the world—is limited by the supply of food. And since there are half a million species of animals, each of which would like to fill the earth and would be quite able to do so, there must be a severe pressure upon every species by all the other species that are tending to swell in numbers and to occupy the same territory. Such a pressure must cause intense rivalry; it must restrict, must strongly check, the increase of each individual. This check upon the increase of numbers causes the "Struggle for Existence."

As soon as we hear that ominous phrase, we naturally begin to think of warfare, of bloody design. Indeed the literature of evolution is dotted with hints of this sort, and of late years the story-writers have given us many pictures of the world of nature as a battle-ground where all feet are swift to shed blood, a cruel place where venom and claw make way with enemies, where "nature is red of tooth and fang," where life is a "gruesome cockpit." This horrible notion [1] is so generally held that it has been used to justify human warfare. The German Bernhardi actually argued as crudely as this: "Wherever we look in nature, we find that war is a fundamental law of evolution. This great verity, which has been rec-

---

1. William J. Long in his *Mother Nature* has done good service by denouncing this notion as "an appalling and degrading superstition" (though his own notion is not one that many naturalists endorse). The ideas of "cruelty" and "terror" are not to be found in Darwin. Long's book is only an amplifying of the description that Darwin gives as a summary at the close of Chapter III of the *Origin of Species*: "When we reflect on this struggle, we may console ourselves with the full belief that the war of nature is not incessant, that no fear is felt, that death is generally prompt, and that the vigorous, the healthy, and the happy survive and multiply."

ognized in past ages, has been convincingly demonstrated in modern times by Charles Darwin."

In the main all such ideas are false. To compare the struggle of nature with human warfare is absurd. Because we human beings are cruel to one another, because *we* plunge into ruthless wholesale killing, because *we* have tortured and enslaved and exterminated one another in our struggles for *domination,* we cannot assume that the struggle for existence is similar. Only a gorilla has a right to such an argument. Before any one can have a true view of evolution, he must thoroughly purge his mind of this common and deep-seated error. Before we go on in this chapter to picture the struggle for existence as it is, we must take time to see what it is not.

It is not what our sentimental human minds would suppose. If we conceive it as cruel, as fierce-minded, as warlike, we are making the old mistake of having the great sun of nature revolve around our little mental sphere. Nature is not bitter with human hate. Nor, on the other hand, is nature sweet with human sentimentality. Nature is as different from a man as the starry heavens are from their reflection in a pool. "Nature" is simply a name for The Way Things Are. In this great scheme of things we cannot detect any plotting of altruism nor any exercise of cruelty, neither sympathy nor jealousy. To our poor senses nature may seem like a loving mother, or like a stern inexorable stepmother; but the beauty and the harshness alike are flimsy imaginings; they are not nature.

The struggle for existence does not invite men to go to war nor certify that might makes right nor discourage charity. It is not hideous, but partakes of the beauty of all truth. It contains no cruelty unless all facts are cruel.

In the whole long history of false reasoning there is no funnier chapter than the record of how man has sentimentalized the struggle for existence. He has shuddered at the fierceness of the tiger while digesting the beefsteak of a slaughtered cow. He has written poetry about "the pious robin"; yet for every kill of a tiger a robin will slay his hundreds. The only relentless and unreasonable slaughterer on earth is man. No wonder that man, who exterminates moose and bison while he tolerates the marriage of idiots, is quite unable to comprehend the wisdom and purity of the struggle for existence that is decreed by nature.

The struggle for existence is a contest in which there is no motive of cruelty, no lust for power over others, no desire to do harm to another creature. It is an effort by every creature to do his best, his utmost, to live and have young. Every force of his being is animated by these two elemental instincts: (1) he must live according to the law that nature has planted in him, and (2) he must obey the primal commandment to be

462 THE WHOLE COMPOSITION

fruitful. Every act in the natural struggle for existence is entirely innocent and wholesome.

In another way the struggle is unlike what we might assume. It is not
a universal combat in which every creature's weapons are turned against
other creatures. In a great variety of ways animals and plants are useful
to each other, confer benefits on others in the course of seeking their
own welfare—as when birds remove caterpillars from leaves. Success in
the struggle often comes from avoiding competition—as when the sage-
brush grows on the desert where other plants cannot live.

In another and more important way the struggle differs from what we
have so far dwelt on. It is to a large extent not a set of duels between individuals; the contest is often impersonal, unfelt, unsuspected. Perhaps an
illustration from human life will be useful here: if an actor or an author
pleases the public, his work may be highly paid for, and the income of
some other actors or authors be reduced. Stevenson says that a successful
author—who may be a shrinking, affectionate person—stabs other authors
with his pen as surely as if he used a dagger. So impersonal and unsuspected may the struggle for existence be at times in human affairs. Much
more is it true that the unreasoning lives of a large part of the animal
kingdom may be passed without any consciousness of rivalry, in peaceful
success. Success need not depend on the ability to kill. All through the
millions of years of the geologic ages the armored fighters have perished;
today one of the most prolific animals is the least offensive—the rabbit.
The rats and beetles have not conquered in the strife by slaughter. Some
of the most successful animals are those that organize a society, like the
ants and bees, in whose colonies there is no individualism but only a
ceaseless, unstinted labor for the whole group.

But the struggle, for all kinds alike, is none the less fierce and unremitting because it is indirect and unknown. It is pitiless. If a communistic
society of bees cannot find nectar in competition with other societies, it
will fail to leave offspring as surely as the lonely pair of eagles that fail
to strike enough victims in their wide domain of sixty square miles. When
any kind of organism cannot produce enough seed, or suck enough water
from the ground, or resist a plague of fungus, or withstand a change of
climate, it dies. There is no more tragedy about this for the individual
than there is about the most successful life, for every individual, weak or
strong, must die. The only difference is that, in the long run, the weak
leave few offspring; the earth is peopled by those who leave most offspring. "Reproduce or perish" is the eternal necessity. In this struggle to
propagate, the mushroom feeds upon decaying matter, the condor wheels
its lonely flight above the mountains, the fish feels its sightless way in

caves and ocean depths, the mosquito swarms beyond the arctic circle, the snow-plant spreads its abundant red upon the ice-fields of cold heights, the beaver builds his dam. High and low, everywhere under the whole heavens, in every cranny of space, with every imaginable adaptation, the urge of life compels every individual to seek out a living and have young.

Though we can learn very little about the adjustments in nature, we can guess at them to some extent by what we see when man disturbs any balance. As soon as the dry valleys of California were set to orchards about fifty years ago, the cottony cushion scale multiplied upon them at such a rate that destruction was in sight. The orchards were rescued [2] by studying nature's adjustments in Australia, the home of the scale. It was found that there the scale was kept in bounds by ladybird beetles; some of these were imported, bred and turned into the orchards; they promptly and completely played their expected part in the struggle for orchards. The canteloupes were saved from a pest by a similar army of ladybirds brought by the bushel from the high Sierras. Man's best, and often the only, way of coping with the multitudes of nature is to employ the troops of nature, as in fighting the gypsy moth, the Hessian fly, and the grain aphis. We are in a perpetual contest with the hordes of life that swarm against our interests.

Some such gross examples are about all that man can learn of the interplay of forces that work in the struggle for existence. If we look at any landscape, we see that all forms of life are fitted into a mosaic where each can thrive to a certain extent, thus far and no farther. Each is, in the ordinary course of the seasons, checked from dominating over others. Grass and spruce trees and violets and robins exist in abundance, and now one and now another may fluctuate somewhat in its numbers; but as the decades pass, the balance only swings to and fro about a center. Each plant and animal is severely restrained by the whole competition. Year after year we look upon the same peaceful assemblage, hear the same songs, see the same bright blossoms, exclaim with the same satisfaction at the restful peace of it all.

But there is no peace. In any landscape each leaf and beak and fin is tirelessly at work to keep up its numbers. Every plant bears seeds in prodigious quantity; every animal's body is a factory of countless eggs or sperms. With all the power of every mother's being there is effort to rear young. Every pair of individuals is doing its best to leave descendants that would spread over the whole region. With what result? Only this: that next year, and ten years hence, and fifty, and a hundred, there will probably be the same number of descendants. All this ceaseless power is some-

2. Elizabeth A. Ward, "Mustering Nature's Mercenaries," *Forum*, October, 1915.

how held in check by the competition of powers. Of all the seeds that are formed by a plant with such lavish extravagance only a few sprout. "There is a British starfish which produces at least two hundred millions of eggs, *and yet it is not what one would call a common animal.*"[3] There is something fearsome about such tremendous possibilities that accomplish no more than just to keep the numbers of this starfish from decreasing. Many of the lower animals hatch a thousand eggs to insure one offspring. And only a small fraction of the young can grow up. The rearing of all the offspring with such intense devotion has only one result, that when the years have passed and the parents have died, there are two other members of the species to take their places.

Here is a fact to which the ordinary citizen never gives a thought. The pretty scene that he surveys from a porch or a canoe is a cemetery for the young that never mature. We need not weep their fate, but we observe the fact. This is the struggle for existence.

*Suggestions for Study*

1. Is the potential rate of increase of animals a matter of addition or multiplication?

2. Have there been instances when animals did increase in keeping with their potential rate of propagation?

3. Why do not all animals increase according to their potential rate?

4. Can the struggle for existence in nature be used properly as a justification for human warfare? Explain.

5. Is nature cruel, kindly, or neither?

6. Do creatures invariably kill off one another, or are there instances in which they are useful to each other?

7. Is it accurate to say that success in the struggle for existence depends upon the ability to kill?

8. Even with a tremendous potential power to increase their kind, what is the net result of the striving of creatures to reproduce?

9. Analyze carefully the reader addressed by Mr. Ward in this article, and cite several ways in which he adapted his writing to that reader.

10. Outline the article so that you will be well aware of the divisions of the subject matter. Then observe how each major unit of subject matter slowly and clearly advances the thought for the intended reader's easy assimilation.

11. Return to Professor Boyle's article "Insects and Men," and reread it with the knowledge which you now have of the struggle for existence.

12. Define the following words used in the article: propagate, prolific, inexorable, unstinted, prodigious.

**Analysis.** Another highly important type of exposition is analysis. It is the resolution of a subject into its parts to see of what it is made. The

3. J. A. Thomson, *The System of Animate Nature.*

small boy who takes apart a watch to discover what makes it tick is employing a rudimentary form of analysis. On a higher plane, a chemist analyzes a solution to determine its ingredients, an engineer analyzes a river bed and the river banks to decide if a new bridge would be practicable, a major-league manager analyzes his team to learn who is deserving of an increase in salary, an architect analyzes the needs of a family and the characteristics of a community before he designs a new dwelling. Analysis is therefore a common and important procedure.

*Formal analysis.* The first kind of analysis—often called formal analysis —is an exhaustive, impersonal division of a subject until every aspect of it has been considered. The method is essentially scientific, as it accounts for all known evidence. It may constitute a *partition,* that is, the analysis of an individual person or object, or a *classification,* the analysis of a group of people or objects.

To observe the method used in formal analysis, let us consider a classification of rocks.[11] The primary division of this subject—and remember that analysis is division—produces three main parts: sedimentary, igneous, and metamorphic rocks. Each of these parts is capable of further division. The sedimentary rocks, when analyzed, prove to be of two kinds: the major rock masses of conglomerate, sandstone, shale, and limestone, and the minor rock deposits of coal, iron ore, rock salt, gypsum, and chert or flint. For each of these minor parts further divisions are demanded. The conglomerates, for example, are typical conglomerates, breccia, and arkose; shale is laminated shale or mudstone. Thus an outline of this analysis would take the following form:

I. Sedimentary rocks
   A. Major rock masses
      1. Conglomerate
         a. Typical conglomerate
         b. Breccia
         c. Arkose
      2. Shale
         a. Laminated shale
         b. Mudstone
      3. Sandstone
         a. Even-grained varieties
         b. Hybrid varieties
            (1) Verging on conglomerate
            (2) Verging on shale

11. The classification used here is that of *A Textbook of Geology,* Part I, by Louis V. Pirsson, revised by William Agar *et al.,* third edition.

                4. Limestone
                    a. Chalk
                    b. Coquina
                    c. Dolomite
        B. Minor rock deposits
            1. Coal
            2. Iron ore
            3. Rock salt
            4. Gypsum
            5. Chert
    II. Igneous rocks
    III. Metamorphic rocks

Actually, of course, this outline stops short of a complete treatment of the subject as the points under *I.B.* are not divided, nor are the main points *II* and *III,* but the method shown will illustrate how an analysis of these points could be made in order to render this a truly formal analysis. The type of paper written from such an analysis has therefore the intent of presenting an impersonal, complete report.

*Informal analysis.* Also in common use is the informal analysis. It differs in purpose from the formal analysis in that it tries to be not complete but selective. Just as in definition certain words were noted to be so general as not to admit of complete delineation, so in analysis certain topics do not admit of complete division. The analysis of a contemporary world problem, for example, cannot be exhaustive, for no one and no group has all the facts needed to make the formal analysis. It takes many years before the causes of a war can be fully ascertained and a complete analysis made of them. Thus many of the articles appearing in our modern news magazines and journals on contemporary affairs are informal analysis. They endeavor to present certain aspects of their subject which seem of primary importance without making a pretense of completeness. The term "informal" describes their method in so far as the judgment of the writer is exercised when a selection is made. In addition, the writer is given greater freedom of presentation. In keeping with his subject, his writing may be as satirical, humorous, or serious as he wishes. The formal analysis, on the other hand, makes a more impersonal presentation.

The following brief illustration may perhaps depict the method of the informal analysis. An educator, requested to write an article for a publication read by high-school teachers, chose as his subject the qualities of a good teacher. If he had filled a volume with his observations, it is doubtful if he could have exhausted this subject, but with only a few hundred words at his disposal, he was severely limited. He therefore chose four points which he believed to embody the chief characteristics of the good teacher: a cheerful devotion to the tasks facing the teacher, a knowledge of subject matter, skill in classroom presentation, and an understanding, pleasant personality. Such points, for example, as the relation of the teacher to the community or to the high-school faculty were disregarded, and all the skill of the educator was thrown into presenting the four divisions of the subject as clearly, forcefully, and entertainingly as possible.

*Precautions.* A first precaution is to realize clearly the problem being analyzed and the persons for whom the analysis is being made. If the general subject is the playgrounds in a certain city, the exact problem in that extensive topic must be ascertained. An analysis might be made of the need for new playgrounds, of the expense involved in the upkeep of existing playgrounds, of the benefits of the existing playgrounds, of the supervision to be found on them, or of many similar problems. So first determine exactly what you are analyzing. Having made a selection, then decide to whom you are addressing your remarks. A report to the Chamber of Commerce would demand one technique, a talk to the Rotary Club another, and a letter to the newspaper still a third. The reader, purpose, thesis, and principle of unity thus deserve careful attention.

As the division of the subject is begun, *a basis of classification* must be formulated immediately. For example, the buildings on a campus might be classified according to their style of architecture; some might be Gothic, others colonial, and others Georgian. Style of architecture would thus be the basis of classification. It is apparent, however, that many other bases of classification would be available for an analysis of the buildings: beauty of appearance, suitability for classroom purposes, age, cost of erection or maintenance, function, and so on. The precaution is that only one such basis should be established for the main points of the outline. Only in the subpoints can a different basis be used. For example, the table of classification of igneous rocks in *A Textbook of Geology* by L. V. Pirsson employs texture of the rock as the basis of classification. The main division thus employs such headings as granular, glassy, and fragmental and thereby includes all igneous rocks in the classification. To insert any other basis would break the classification and introduce confusion by the overlapping of points. The insertion of such a heading as "granite" would shift the basis of classification to mineral composition and so remove granite from its proper position as a subdivision of "granular." However, in the subdivisions a new basis may sometimes be established, although such a shift is not necessary in all analyses. In the classification of igneous rocks, the mineral composition is made the basis of the subpoints; granular is divided into granite, diorite, gabbro, dolerite, and peridotite. The basis must be closely adhered to, however, once it has been chosen in the subdivision.

One basis of classification must be formulated for all co-ordinate points.

As another precaution, each heading must have at least two subpoints if it is to be divided at all. Analysis is division. Thus it is as impossible to divide any topic into less than two parts as it is to cut an apple into fewer than two pieces. If in the above outline, "granite" had seemed to be the only type of granular rock, the classification would *not* read:

    I. Granular
        A. Granite
    II. Granular and porphyritic, etc.

Such an arrangement would be logically impossible because granite would be the equivalent of the main heading "granular" and so would not be a part of that heading. No division would take place, and the form should read:

    I. Granular: granite
    II. Granular and porphyritic, etc.

Actually, of course, in this classification, there were types of granular rocks other than granite, and a fuller division could be made. Such is usually true of any main heading.

From this discussion it follows that the sum of the subdivisions must equal the main heading. When added to one another, granite, diorite, gabbro, dolerite, and peridotite constitute exactly the class of granular igneous rocks. So in a complete analysis the sum of the minor points equals the main point. Arithmetically this process would read:

    I. 4
        A. 1
        B. 1
        C. 1
        D. 1

By observing the principle of division and by employing but one basis of classification for co-ordinate points, you should be able to construct a satisfactory analysis. For other principles, refer to the section in this textbook on outlining.

### Exercises

1. Criticize and reconstruct the following outlines.
    a. Thesis: All kinds of people play golf.
        I. Duffers
            A. Those who are beginners
            B. Those who have played long but who play poorly

II. Experts
  A. Amateurs who play well
  B. Professionals
III. People of all ages
  A. Young people
  B. Old people
IV. Men
  A. Office workers
  B. Manual workers
V. Women

b. Thesis: A good room is essential for effective studying.
  I. Proper lighting
    A. Large windows
    B. A good desk lamp
  II. Good ventilation
    A. Plenty of fresh air
  III. Comfort
    A. A large desk
    B. A comfortable chair
    C. Convenient bookcases
    D. Quiet
  IV. Good technique of study
    A. A well-planned program of study hours
    B. The ability to read well
    C. The ability to outline well
    D. Skill in taking notes

c. Thesis: Certain economies are possible under a large-scale operation of business.
  I. The economy in producing goods
    A. Purchasing in large quantities
    B. Specializing through the use of large plants
    C. Making use of by-products
  II. The economy in marketing goods
    A. Shipment in large quantities
    B. Maintenance of selling agencies
    C. Loss of contact between producer and consumer
  III. The economy in administering the plant
    A. Comparatively low fixed charges
    B. Comparatively low office charges
    C. Comparatively low cost of advertising because of large volume
    D. Piling up of financial reserves in case of emergency
  IV. The economy in regulating industrial finance
    A. Availability of lower rates of interest on loans

2. For the same limited aspect of one of the following general subjects, construct two outlines to illustrate the analysis of the subject upon two different bases of classification:

teachers, colleges, trees, automobiles, the engineering profession, radios, rhetoric, lyrical poetry, railroading, insects, types of architecture, bridges, shoes, furniture, doctors, orchestras, clocks, cameras, houses, hobbies, operas, paintings, golf clubs, schools, food, the errors in your compositions of this year.

3. Write an article which makes an analysis of a limited aspect of one of the following subjects:
college students, magazines, newspapers, sports, guns, pumps, oil, oceans, lakes, mountains, airplanes, balloons, ships, harbors, canals, swamps, diseases, scientists, rivers, dogs, watches, any industry, a zoo, brushes, Congress.

## The Business Type [12]

### JAMES TRUSLOW ADAMS

First let us analyze the businessman himself. Is there such a thing as a business "type"? Thinking of all the variations among those one knows, much as one thinks of one's varied French friends, one may think it impossible to classify them under one head; but just as, contrasting one's French friends with English or Russian, a French type does emerge, so contrasting a man who is in business all his life with those engaged in other pursuits, a business type does also take form. Apart from initial tastes and nature, a man is bound to be molded by the aims, ideas, ideals, and whole nature of the career to which he devotes practically his entire energies and time. It is obvious that a poet or musician will react to the facts of existence differently from the way a steel manufacturer, an admiral, a high ecclesiastic, a politician, or a Supreme Court judge would do. All of them naturally have to provide themselves with a living, but the fundamental facts that regulate their reactions to the world about them are different.

For a businessman that fundamental fact is, and is bound to be, *profit*. Having made money, the businessman may be, as he often is, more generous and careless with it than an aristocrat or a churchman; but that does not alter the fact that the main function of his work, his main preoccupation, and the point from which he views everything connected with his work is that of a profit. For one thing, all men, whether they be poets, soldiers, diplomats, or department-store owners, crave, as we have said, success and recognition in their chosen field. The hallmark of success in business is the extent of profit a man gets out of it. An artist may find no public for his wares, but, if he is doing great work, he will be supported by the opinion of his peers. A doctor may struggle in a country village with nothing but a pittance, but he has the satisfaction of a noble work

12. From *Our Business Civilization* (New York, 1929), by James Truslow Adams. Reprinted by permission of Albert & Charles Boni, Inc., publishers.

nobly done. A man like Asquith may spend his whole life in the service of his country and yet retire as prime minister with the income of a bank clerk. But a man who spends his life in business and ends no wealthier than he began is voted a failure by all his fellows, even though he may have personal qualities that endear him to his friends.

This fundamental preoccupation with making a profit has been much emphasized by the shift of business from the individual to the corporate form. A man may do what he likes with his own, and if he chooses to be quixotic he can be; but in the new triple relationship of workmen, executives, and stockholders in the modern corporation there has ceased to be personality anywhere. The American is a great believer in the magical power of words. The bare facts of business are now being covered over by the new American gospel of "service"; but when we analyze this, does it not merely come down to the obvious facts that the businessman performs a highly useful function in society and that, so far as he can, he should see that the public gets its full money's worth? The fundamental need of profit remains. The professional classes—doctors, artists, scholars, scientists, and others—may, as they often do, work for little or nothing at all, but, except in the rarest of personal instances, the businessman is precluded from doing so. What stockbroker, manufacturing company, railway, or electric light corporation, with all their talk about service, would ever consider running their business at a voluntary loss in order to render greater service or tide the public over a crisis? It cannot be done. It is profit first, and then, perhaps, as much service as is compatible with profit.

· Now this primary and essential preoccupation with making a profit naturally tends to color a businessman's view of his entire world, and is what, in my opinion, mainly differentiates business from the professions. Nor do I speak as an impractical intellectual. Of the last thirty years I have spent about one half in business and half in professional work, and I realize the great difference, having paid my monthly bills, between concentrating primarily on the work rather than the profit.

Moreover, dealing inevitably with material things and with the satisfying of the world's material wants, the businessman tends to locate happiness in *them* rather than in the intellectual and spiritual unless he constantly refreshes his spirit away from business during his leisure. When the pressure of business on his time, or his concentration on it, becomes so great as to preclude his reasonable use of leisure for the development of his whole human personality, he is apt to become a complete materialist even if, as is now frequently not the case, he ever had it in him to become anything else. He may live in a palace, ride in the most luxurious

cars, and fill his rooms with old masters and the costliest manuscripts
which his wealth can draw from under the hammer at Christie's, but if
he cares more for riches, luxury, and power than for a humanely rounded
life he is not civilized but what the Greeks properly called a "barbarian."

Aside from narrowness of interests, the businessman, from the nature
of his major occupation, is apt to have short views and to distrust all
others. It was once said, as superlative praise, of the late J. P. Morgan, one
of the most public-spirited and far-sighted businessmen we have had, that
he "thought in ten-year periods." Most businessmen think—and do well
to do so as businessmen—in one- or two-year periods; the businessman
cares nothing for the tendency of what he is doing. This has been emphasized in the American businessman by the vast extent of the natural
resources with which he has had to deal and the recuperative powers of
an active people in a half-settled continent. If, as he did in the northern
Mississippi Valley, he can make his personal profit by ripping the forests
off the face of half a dozen states in a decade, he is content to let those
who come later look after themselves.

Nor is he any more solicitous about the social results of his activities.
Obviously, what interests the businessman as a businessman is a free hand
to gather wealth as quickly as may be, combined with a guarantee that
society shall protect him in that wealth once he has gathered it. He may
steal the water resources of a dozen states but, once they are stolen, he is
a defender of the Constitution and the sanctity of contract. It is not hard
to understand why the United States is the most radical country in the
world in its business methods and the most conservative in its political!

Preoccupation with profit, again, tends to make a businessman, as businessman, blind to the aesthetic quality in life. A beautiful bit of scenery,
such as Montauk Point, is for him merely a good site for a real-estate
development; a waterfall is merely waterpower. America's most successful
businessman, Mr. Ford, while rolling up millions by the hundreds in
profits, was content to turn out what was, perhaps, the ugliest car on the
market. It was only when his profits were threatened that he turned to
the consideration of beauty, and he would not have done so had it not
promised profit. No sane businessman in charge of a large business would
do so. It is much the same with the cultivation of the businessman's mind.
Time is money, and anything which takes time and does not give business
results is waste. But if you tell him that if he shows an interest in Keats
he can probably land Smith's account—Smith being a queer, moony guy
—or that if he will go to hear the "Rheingold" he can make a hit with
that chap he has long been after, the effect will be magical. Innumerable

advertisements of books on teaching of foreign languages will easily illustrate what I mean.

These and other qualities of the businessman are his qualities *as* a businessman. They are qualities that are bred in him by his occupation. Plenty of businessmen are much more than businessmen and outside of their offices and business hours have other qualities and other interests. But there is this to be said. Society at large, including the businessman himself, owes its opportunity for a fully rounded life mainly to those who have not been businessmen. What will be the effect on all of us of the growing dominance of the business type and of the hold which the businessman and business ideals have attained upon our civilization?

*Suggestions for Study*

1. What is the aim of the businessman? By what is he tested as a success or failure?
2. What distinguishes business from the professions?
3. What qualification does the author have to be writing on this subject?
4. In what does the businessman seek to find happiness? What is narrow about this conception?
5. Why will he be nothing more than a "barbarian" if he puts his trust in riches, luxury, and power?
6. What is the second great weakness of the business type?
7. What weakness in the business type explains why the United States is radical in business methods and conservative in politics?
8. What attitude does the business type take toward the aesthetic quality in life? What will serve to stimulate his interest in the aesthetic?
9. Is this analysis a partition or a classification? Is it a formal or an informal analysis?
10. Define the following words from the analysis: ecclesiastic, crave, pittance, quixotic, precluded, compatible, differentiate, humanely, recuperative, solicitous, sanctity, preoccupation.

## *You Are One of These* [13]

### VERGIL D. REED

Few things are more firmly imbedded in our minds than our mental image of the typical American—our picture of ourselves: We are a young people. Most of us live in a growing city, or on a farm in a growing state. Most of us work in a factory or on a farm. We are of the melting pot, partaking of all the races and nationalities; likely as not, our parents were born in Europe. These are some generally held impressions.

But not one of these statements is true! The average age of Americans

13. From the *Nation's Business* (June, 1946), and the *Reader's Digest* (July, 1946). Reprinted by permission of the author and the *Reader's Digest*.

today is 30; it used to be 16—another way of saying we are rapidly getting to be a nation in which old folk predominate. Most of our cities are not growing, and most of our states are losing population. Twice as many persons are employed in the service industries—trade, transportation, communications—as in factories or on farms. And we are getting to be as American as corn on the cob or ham and eggs. Half the babies born in the United States in 1915 had one parent at least who was foreign born. Now nine out of ten babies have two American-born parents.

Census figures tell us a great deal more than the mere size of New York and Walla Walla. Carefully studied, they reveal themselves to be packed with drama—the drama of a changing America. To begin with, our country will not continue to grow as it did formerly. By 1980 we probably shall have reached our peak population, about 150,000,000. From then on, population figures will remain stationary or show a slight decline. This is quite natural in a maturing industrial nation and does not mean that our standard of living need decline.

But while the population is growing more slowly than in past decades, the number of *families* is increasing faster than ever. In the ten years between the last two censuses, population increased only 7.2 percent while the number of families increased 16.6 percent. That meant, of course, that the size of the average family was decreasing (from 4.1 persons to 3.8 persons). This increase in the number of families is more important to many industries than the increase in population, for the sale of refrigerators, kitchen ranges, automobiles, and many other things depends upon the number of families rather than the number of individuals. It is the increase in the number of families that intensifies our present headache, the housing shortage.

We start founding families a little earlier than we used to. The average age of the bridegroom in 1940 was 24.3 years; in 1890, 26.1. The 1940 bride was 21.6 years old; her grandmother married at 22. The war years, for which statistics are not yet available, undoubtedly brought the age of first marriage even lower.

Our birth rate, taking the long view, is declining; it fell from 25 births per thousand persons in 1915 to a low of 16.6 in 1933. But there is a great wave, or hump, on this long-term downward curve. The birth rate rose to 17.6 in 1940 and to 21.5, its wartime peak, in 1943. The decline has started again, and the baby boom will be over in 1947. When these babies reach childbearing age, their babies will cause another, but smaller wave, and it, too, will slide down the declining trend. Each generation, that wave will recur on smaller scale until it finally disappears.

In 1947 the babies born in 1941 will begin to flood our schools. We will find ourselves short of schoolrooms and teachers. That seven-year wave will later on pass through each grade, through elementary and high schools and into the colleges. Aside from the war wave, the fact that far more young people are going through high school and college than in the past will add to the troubles of school officials.

After the seven-year wave passes, many school boards and superintendents will be surprised at the sudden drop in enrollments—and the vacant space left. Manufacturers and retailers of children's goods will be in for similar surprises, unless they know the nature of this "bonus," which will not occur again for a generation. The baby boom will have passed.

Speaking of babies, there are 106 boys born for every hundred girls, and this approximate figure prevails the world over. However, males continue to die off faster than females all through life, in peace as well as in war. So the ladies finally prevail by a considerable margin.

There will be no shortage of husbands, except among the elders. When Miss America reaches her 20th birthday her chances of marrying within the year are 15.5 out of 100, and her normal chances of ever marrying are 92 out of 100. Eleven out of every 12 persons reaching the age of 15 will eventually marry.

America is aging. Almost a fourth of our people are over 45 already. Between 1930 and 1940 those over 65 rose about 35 percent. There will be three times as many people over 65 years of age in 1980 as there were in 1930.

From birth rates to taxes this increasing proportion of elders will influence our future. People are living longer. The old do not bear children. This cuts the birth rate further and decreases the proportion of the young. There will be more old people to be supported by fewer young ones. This will raise taxes to provide old-age pensions, social-security benefits, institutions, and medical care. For better or for worse, there will be enough voting elders "to do something about it."

The increase in the aged will have many other effects, too.

An unusually large proportion of our people is *now* in the employable range of 20 to 59 years of age. More jobs have to be found *now*. But because fewer persons are approaching 20 and more persons are passing 59, this large wave of extra workers will ultimately decrease.

Industry's own retirement, benefit, and employe-relations plans will be greatly affected and undoubtedly liberalized. Elders will have more leisure time, and more assured incomes with which to enjoy it. Conservatism in politics will probably increase. Many changes in tastes, preferences, and needs for goods and services will develop. Geriatrics, the study and treatment of the ailments of old age, will be a promising field of medicine for our future doctors.

Recreation and amusement will have to take account of the habits and preferences of the elders. Many will move to warmer climates or spend their winters there. There will be more travel, both at home and abroad.

The rate of growth of our urban population has been slowing up since 1910. Large cities have practically ceased to grow within their corporate limits, with few and temporary exceptions. Their suburban areas, however, are growing rapidly and will continue to grow. Half of us now live in 140 metropolitan districts made up of cities of over 50,000 population and adjoining townships. Industry is already beginning to decentralize, with more but smaller factories outside the big cities.

As decentralization continues there will be more and better shopping centers in the suburbs; suburban land values will increase while urban values decrease, or increase at much slower rates.

The proportion of our population on farms was standing still before the war at 23.1 percent. Every basic trend is against a back-to-the-farm movement. Better methods, better seeds, mechanization, and the wider use of fertilizers make possible vast increases in production on fewer acres and with fewer workers. The standard of living of those who remain on farms will increase if these better methods and means are used. The number of farms is decreasing, their size increasing.

The proportion of our labor force employed in trade, transportation, and the service "industries" has been increasing for more than a hundred years. These fields, excluding government, accounted for 45.8 percent of our civilian employed persons in 1940. Manufacturing employed 23.4 percent, while agriculture, forestry, and fisheries combined accounted for only 18.8 percent.

Two definite mass migrations have taken place in recent years: the "Grapes of Wrath" depression migration in the '30's, and the late war-boom migration. The West Coast states were big gainers in population, along with Florida. A solid tier of states, from North Dakota to Oklahoma, were the big losers. Substantial increases in Maryland and Virginia really represent the growth of Washington, which has spilled over its own boundaries.

This pattern of migration is a long and basic one. For example, there is no reason to look for a net reverse migration from the West Coast. New factories, more favorable freight rates, climate, and future trade with the Orient are among the factors favoring further growth there. By 1950 the population of the Pacific states will probably exceed its war peak by a considerable margin. The West and Southeast will continue to gain, largely at the expense of the North and Northeast.

During the war years the number of women in rural-farm areas decreased 11.3 percent but increased in cities. Of this female migration cityward, 665,000 were between 14 and 24 years of age. These younger women have acquired new wants, tastes, and standards which will greatly affect their future outlook on life.

Our long-run prospects are excellent. These people—of whom you are one—have what it takes. What we do with it is up to us.

*Suggestions for Study*

1. What percentage of babies are born of two American-born parents?
2. At about what figure will our population stop increasing, and about when shall we reach that figure?
3. How has the number of families increased in ratio to the number of individuals?
4. Do young people marry, on an average, at an earlier age than their grandparents did?
5. Explain how the wave of births in 1941–1947 will create problems in our school systems.
6. Explain what is meant by "America is aging."
7. Is the general trend toward living in large cities or in suburban areas? Is there a back-to-the-farm movement?
8. What sections of the country are growing?
9. Make an outline of this analysis to indicate clearly into what divisions the subject of population has been broken.

## *When You Drive Fast* [14]

### CURTIS BILLINGS

In the whole realm of automobile safety—about which not too much is known—there is nothing so confused and confusing as the relation of speed to accidents. Most people will agree (because they feel it in their bones) that as speeds go up accidents become more severe, but few motorists realize *how* great is the effect of an increased rate of travel on an accident involving a car; and almost nobody understands why it is that accidents are *more* likely to occur at high speed.

In fact many would be quick to dispute this latter point. They themselves have driven cars or have ridden in cars traveling up to 80 or 90 miles an hour without an accident, without, indeed, any particular feeling of discomfort or danger. It is not easy for them to see why such rates in

14. From *Harper's Magazine*, CLXXIII (June, 1936), 173. Reprinted by permission of the author.

themselves are hazardous, and it is difficult to demonstrate that they are. The physical laws involved are complicated, and explanations of them must be somewhat technical; but with speeds ever increasing and the death rates from automobile accidents leaping higher correspondingly, it would seem vital for the American motorist to understand the forces he must deal with when he pushes his accelerator down.

Physicists in their laboratories sometimes roll marbles down inclined planes to demonstrate the tremendous increase in the energy of a moving body as its speed goes up. In this way they show beyond dispute that as the speed of a moving object is doubled, its energy (or destructive force) increases four times; as its speed is tripled, its energy increases nine times; and as its speed is quadrupled, its ability to destroy itself and whatever it strikes is increased sixteen times. In other words, the energy of a moving body increases as the square of its speed.

That this bit of theoretical knowledge, which teachers spout so glibly, has a direct bearing on motor vehicle accidents can be shown from the records. E. Raymond Cato, chief of the California Highway Patrol, recently said that in his State a fatality seldom occurs to passengers of cars going less than 20 miles an hour, that, on the other hand, the majority of slain motorists were riding in automobiles traveling in excess of 45. Michigan records show that if you are going to have an accident there your chances of killing someone are five times as great if you are traveling over 50 miles an hour as they are at a rate under 20. Numerous States and cities have reduced automobile deaths promptly by lowering average driving speeds; and, obversely, they have experienced sharp and sudden increases in fatalities when they relaxed their control of speed.

It is, however, one thing to adduce data to prove that accidents grow worse as speeds go up; it is quite another to show how and why accidents are *more likely* to occur at high speed. The latter is the more difficult task, but the lesson to be learned is even more valuable to the driver.

R. A. Moyer, associate professor of highway engineering at Iowa State College, made a four-year research of the action of automobiles on highways, paying particular attention to the effects of variations in speed. His study illuminates this whole problem. He distinguishes three important types of accidents which seldom occur at low speeds and shows why they occur at high speeds. In all three accidents the driver loses control of his car: in the first case he loses control because of speed and surface roughness; in the second case because of speed plus unwise or inadequate braking; in the third case because of speed at curves. The accident in any of the cases may be one in which the car collides with another machine or strikes a tree or bridgehead or runs off the road and turns over, or does any of the hundred and one things that cars do when they are out of control. Inasmuch as the speeds are high, the accidents are usually frightfully severe.

Surface roughness is a greater factor than one would ordinarily suppose. Who has not driven over a rutted dirt road pitted with hub-deep holes? Nothing happened and the car was in no particular danger of turning over or bouncing into the ditch. But one was driving at a very low rate of speed, probably in second or low gear. At high speed it would be impossible to drive on such a road. One of the smoothest surfaces in the world, that at Daytona Beach, Florida, was too rough to meet the requirements of the world's fastest driver, Sir Malcolm Campbell. For it was a surface roughness quite imperceptible to the eye that caused Sir Malcolm to leave Daytona and go to the perfectly level salt flats of Utah, there to make his world record of more than 300 miles an hour. A waviness in the beach bed at Daytona measuring only two inches to the hundred feet was sufficient at the rates Sir Malcolm traveled to send his six-ton racing car soaring through the air.

The only contact between a car and the highway is through the tires. As one drives along a level road the tires make a uniform contact with the surface. But as waves or other aberrations appear the contact varies. In the instant after leaving the crest of a bump, however small, the tires *tend* to leave the pavement and this reduces the area of the tire that is pressing against the road. As the speed of the car goes up, this tendency increases until the tire actually does leave the surface.

A car need not be traveling at an extremely high rate to "take off." Forty-five miles an hour is sufficient if the rise on the surface measures only four inches in forty feet. The take-off amounts to a veritable flight if the speed is 70 or 80 miles an hour when the car shoots over such a bump. While rises of this height are common enough on old pavements and on unpaved surfaces, they are rather rare, fortunately, on new pavements. They are especially numerous of course in localities where the subgrade is poor, as near bridges and culverts, and where frost has caused the pavement to heave and settle. The weight of the car has nothing to do with the tendency to take off: one is as likely to do it in a Cadillac as in a Ford. Speed and the steepness of the rise or bump are the only factors.

On curves it is easy to see why this sudden reduction of the friction between the tire and the roadway may cause the driver to lose control of his machine. The thing that keeps a speeding car on a curve (when centrifugal force is always trying to impel it off in a straight line) is the sidethrust friction between the tires and the road. This friction must continue or the car will go into a skid. If on a perfectly dry pavement there is a bump on the surface which momentary inattention or a defect in vision induces the driver to overlook, the all-important friction will be reduced and in that instant centrifugal force will get its chance at the car. By cool, quick work the driver may avert a crash, but if he cannot, the car may slide off the curve and land bottom-side up along the fence line—as many do.

The same thing can occur on the straightaway. Even here one occasionally turns and sometimes sharply, as when one passes a vehicle and cuts back into line before an oncoming machine gets too close. In such a maneuver the same forces are brought into play as on a curve. When one is traveling straight ahead, a bump over which the wheels of only one side of the car pass may throw the vehicle sideways with such force that control is lost. Or, indeed, when the whole car takes off evenly, a strong cross wind catching it in midair can wrench control away from the driver.

Professor Moyer says that surface roughness on the speedway at Indianapolis (which looked so smooth to the spectators) probably was the outstanding circumstance in the series of accidents which took the lives of 27 drivers and mechanics there. "The variations in the surfaces of many miles of our main highways are so great that 70 or 80 miles an hour are impossible with safety," he declares.

Of all driving operations the one which causes the most skidding is the improper use of brakes or the use of improper brakes at high speed. When a car skids it is out of control. If one is skillful and the highway is wide and if other cars are not near by, one can sometimes manipulate the car out of the skid and back into control; but too often the driver does not know how to do this or cannot act fast enough to regain command of his vehicle.

Tests show that if there is 40 per cent more braking power on one side of the car than on the other, an attempt at a sudden stop at the rate of 40 miles an hour can and usually will pull the machine out of its lane of traffic and into the adjacent lane. If the greater power is on the left side, this means swerving the car suddenly into the lane of oncoming traffic; if it is on the right side, it means forcing the car onto the shoulder of the highway or perhaps into a bridgehead, guardrail, or ditch. Automobiles have been observed to skid end for end on dry pavements when all the braking force was delivered on one wheel.

But are brakes as faulty as this common enough to warrant special notice? In conducting his researches Professor Moyer tested the brakes of 2,134 cars taken at random. Of these 31 per cent had brakes which had at least 40 per cent more braking power on one side than on the other. The brakes on fully half of the cars in use were found to be inadequate. One can appreciate how much more hazardous such brakes are as speeds increase beyond the forty-mile-an-hour mark. The swerving can be so violent that control of the vehicle is utterly lost. And such swerving always occurs in dangerous situations—situations which called for the emergency stop.

So much for the dangers involved in the use of improper brakes. Now let us consider the *improper use* of brakes and how this causes and accentuates skids. At the outset I might say that at low speeds on ordinary pavements there is scarcely such a thing as the improper use of brakes: braking can be improper only at speeds which are too high for conditions.

First it is necessary to explain how brakes act. When a motorist decides to stop he must depend largely upon the friction which can be developed at two points on his car. The first of these is between the brake bands and the drums, the second between the tires and the road. It may seem odd, but the actual stopping of the car is brought about at the weaker of the two points, *i.e.* the one with the less friction, because it is at this point where the slippage occurs which takes up the car's energy. Thus when a car is traveling on a dry abrasive surface, the coefficient of friction or gripping power of the tires on the road surface is generally greater than that developed by the brakes. Under these conditions the slippage at the brakes will provide the friction necessary to stop the car. If the brakes exert a stronger drag on the car than that provided by the tires and the road, they will lock the wheels, causing the tires to slide, thus bringing the car to a stop. There are numerous conditions which affect the gripping power of the tires on the highway. First, no two types of road surfaces exert the same power. Loose dirt or mud or ice or snow may cover the surface and reduce drastically the available friction. Second, tires are important. Even though variations between them are not so great as between road surfaces, new tires with good treads have a higher coefficient of friction on ordinary pavements than old ones which have been worn smooth. The third and most important condition is the speed at which the car is traveling; for on paved roads the all-important friction between tire and surface decreases as the speed increases so that when one needs the most friction one has the least. At very high speeds on wet surfaces even comparatively weak brakes will have more friction than can be developed between the tire and the road, and applying them will lock the wheels and throw the car inevitably into a skid.

We all know that when a machine begins to skid on ice the most dangerous thing for the driver to do is to put on the brakes. Doing so will only make the skid worse because the driver loses what benefit he had from the turning of the wheels. The same thing is true at high speeds on perfectly dry pavements. When, under these conditions, a car begins to skid or when it becomes so unmanageable that it is difficult to steer it and you think it is going to skid, jamming on the brakes may lock one or more wheels at once, sending the car into a skid from which it is impossible to save it.

It would be well to point out to the reader at this point that there is a very great difference between skidding at low speeds and at high. If you are driving on ice at a necessarily low rate and your car begins to skid you can frequently turn the front wheels in the same direction in which the rear wheels are sliding and resume control. But if you are traveling at a high rate on a curve and strike an unlooked-for patch of ice, mud, or even water, or, if at this rate on a dry pavement you apply the brakes, the car will go into a skid *within your reaction time* or, in other words, quicker than you can think. The instruction to turn the wheels with the skid is of no use whatever. The car has skidded off the road and perhaps turned over so quickly that you simply do not know what happened. It can occur in a tiny fraction of a second, and the average person requires at least three-quarters of a second to react to such a situation. By the time he is able to react he is wrecked. One must remember then that the proper control of a car on a slippery pavement or on a curve at high speed is not a braking problem, but a problem of steering combined with the skillful use of the throttle.

Professor Moyer says that motor-car manufacturers have a problem in developing brakes which are adequate for the high driving speeds of today. What is urgently needed, he says, is a braking system in which the wheels cannot be locked, a system which will deliver maximum braking resistance at each wheel for each type of road surface, and which will provide stopping forces equally balanced right and left for both front and rear wheels.

We have seen that high speeds make accidents more likely to occur on highways of even moderate roughness and that emergency stops by the use of brakes are ever so much more hazardous at high speeds than at low. Now why is a driver apt to lose control of his car on curves while traveling at a high rate of speed, and what can he do about it?

A car on a curve is, as we have seen, the object of attention of two opposing forces, and the outcome of their tug-of-war is of utmost importance to the passengers. These forces are centrifugal force on the one hand and side-thrust friction between the tires and the road on the other, aided by the pull of gravity if the curve is banked. Although few drivers realize it, when taking a curve at a high rate the wheels are always out of line with the direction of travel and so the car really slips or slides round the curve at an angle. This is true of any car which takes a curve at a rate higher than that for which it was banked, but it is especially evident in a racing car taking a curve at maximum speed. This "slip angle" may be so large that the rear end of the car is several feet farther out on the curve than the front end. The greater the speed the greater the slip angle must be, because the friction required to hold the car on the road increases as the square of the speed. Thus at 40 miles an hour the amount of friction needed to hold a car on a curve is not twice but four times the amount needed at 20 miles an hour. Increasing the slip angle will provide the friction up to a certain point, but above that point the car will go into a skid or turn over or otherwise pass out of the control of the driver. The slippage at 80 miles an hour even on a comparatively gentle highway curve is so great that the most skillful driver will have difficulty in steering.

Accidents on curves are usually the result of entering the curve too fast. This is true both on racing courses and on public highways. It is the prime error, and the motorist all too frequently makes it. He is lured on by a fast, quiet automobile, a highway that looks smooth and wide, and utter ignorance of the forces that go to work on his vehicle when he attempts to turn. I shall not go into a discussion of radial acceleration but shall merely point out with all the emphasis that I can give to words that a fast driver must slow down on entering a curve unless he is content to risk his life and the life of everybody riding with him at every twist of the highway.

Despite the fact that the outcome of an automobile race depends largely on the speed with which the drivers can take the turns and despite the fact that racing drivers are extremely expert daredevils, they all slow down to enter a curve. The braking action in slowing down throws the rear end of the car out on the curve to provide the wide slip angle they need. Slowing down also enables a driver to turn his steering wheel from its position on the straightaway, or tangent, to the new angle required by the curve.

Almost every driver has had the harrowing experience of attempting to take a curve so fast that he found it impossible to make the necessary adjustment in his steering angle. He turned the wheel either too far or not far enough and wove unsteadily back and forth across the highway with the car almost out of control. While this may rightfully be termed reckless driving, Professor Moyer says that the fault does not lie entirely with the driver. If highway engineers were to design *transition* curves such as are universally used by the railroads, much of the danger of driving on curves would be removed. Instead of consisting of an arc of a circle connecting two tangents or straightaways, which requires the driver to make a sudden large adjustment in his steering angle, the transition curve is made up of arcs of gradually increasing curvature as one approaches the center of the curve. Thus as the driver enters the curve it is necessary for him to turn the steering wheel only slightly. As he continues on the curve he gradually keeps on turning the wheel until he reaches the circular arc itself. He has come to this circular arc very gradually and leaves it by the same gentle gradations.

This improvement would give a driver on a curve two or three times the margin of safety that he now has. In other words, if a curve is such that a racing driver can barely drive round it safely at 60 miles an hour, and the average motorist cannot manage it safely above 40—and there are many such curves—building transitions into the curve would enable the motorist to take it at 60 as safely as he now can at 40. The device would not impel faster driving or even encourage it; it would simply spare the lives of a lot of people who unwittingly attempt to enter curves too fast.

Banking a curve so that gravity will be utilized to offset centrifugal force is a great help to motorists, but they must remember that curves are not banked for high rates of speed and that gravity remains constant for all speeds while centrifugal force increases as the square of the speed. Just because a curve is banked the motorist must not attempt to maintain any rate he chooses—if he wants to live.

The danger of encountering snow, ice, or mud on a curve (or water on some types of pavements) is so apparent that it scarcely needs mention. A driver is entirely dependent on the frictional resistance of the tires on the road, and if this resistance is reduced suddenly his car will go into a skid.

It is seen then that accidents on curves are far more likely to occur at high speed. For the driver who wants to be safe on our present highway curves there is one thing to do: reduce speed, particularly when entering the curve.

This discussion of the dangers of fast driving would be incomplete without mention of one other aspect of it: how high speed affects the accelerating power of an automobile and why one must allow a far greater distance for passing a car going 60 miles an hour than one going 30, even though one's machine is capable of such a high rate as 90. Accidents resulting from the exercise of poor judgment in passing cars when a third car is approaching from the opposite direction are particularly serious because they occur at high rates and frequently take the form of head-on collisions.

Professor Moyer says that a 1934 Ford V-8 or a car of like accelerating ability requires 600 feet to pass a car which is traveling 30 miles an hour. (This assumes that the overtaking car is following the other at a safe distance before starting to pass and that it will not cut back into line until a safe clear distance between it and the passed car is available.) More than twice this distance, or 1,350 feet, is required to pass a car traveling at 60 miles an hour. To pass one going 80 miles an hour, 1,875 feet are needed. The reason for this great increase in necessary distance is that the ability of an automobile to accelerate decreases as its speed goes up. It is far easier for your car to accelerate from 30 to 40 miles an hour than from 60 to 70 miles an hour because in the former instance it has more reserve power.

If an automobile is approaching from the opposite direction as you decide to pass another machine on the road, how much clear distance must you have between your car and the one which is approaching? If it is coming at 40 miles an hour and you are trailing a car traveling at 30, the required clear distance is 1,050 feet. But if you are trailing a car traveling at 60 and the approaching automobile is coming at the same rate, to pass safely you will need no less than 2,300 feet, or almost half a mile. Since it is impossible to judge speeds accurately, a safe rule to follow is this: do not attempt to pass a car which is moving at 40 miles an hour or more unless there is a clear distance between your car and an approaching car of one-half to three-quarters of a mile. When in the slightest doubt wait until the approaching car has gone by. Other rules which grow out of this discussion are as follows:

1. Drive slowly over rough surfaces. At high rates of speed beware of even small bumps and rises on the pavement.

2. Keep your brakes equalized and never apply them if the car begins to zigzag on a curve or to skid.

3. Slow down *before* entering a curve.

4. Remember, the higher the speed the worse the accident. Fatal accidents are most common at speeds above 45 miles an hour.

It is a question whether the American motoring public taken as a whole will ever learn how to handle an automobile safely at speeds above 50 miles an hour. Can the thirty million drivers in the country be capable of the precision of control that such rates demand? Surely they cannot be unless they comprehend the physical laws that they are up against when they sit behind the wheel—laws which are inviolable, which no traffic judge, however lenient, can set aside.

*Suggestions for Study*

1. Why did the author find it desirable to begin his article with the materials found in the opening paragraph?

2. State the three major reasons for accidents at high speeds.

3. What does friction have to do with the control of a car on a rough road?

4. Why should brakes have a uniform braking force? In what ways are brakes the causes of accidents?

5. What is a "slip angle"? What cautions govern safe driving on curves?

6. For what reason does the author make a summary at the end of the article?

7. To what group of people is the author addressing his remarks? How much technical knowledge is required for an understanding of the content?

8. State in one sentence the idea that Mr. Billings is trying to convey in this article.

9. State the three major parts into which the author has analyzed his subject. Summarize briefly his discussion of each point. Then construct a sentence outline of the article in order that the full division of the subject will be apparent.

10. Define the following words from the article: obversely, centrifugal, manipulate, accentuate, abrasive, radial, inviolable, lenient.

## Humor and America [15]

### MAX EASTMAN

Once I called on a famous psychologist in Europe, and in the course of a not too psychological conversation received some advice.

"I want you to go home," he said, "and write a book on America, and I will tell you what to call it. *Misgeburt*—what is that word in English? No, not *monster*. *Miscarriage*—that's it. The *Miscarriage of American Culture*—that shall be the title of your next book, and you will tell the truth about the whole awful catastrophe."

We laughed, somewhat unsymmetrically, at this jest and I asked:

"What makes you hate America so?"

"Hate it?" he said. "I don't hate America, I regret it. I regret that Columbus ever made the mistake of discovering it!"

It happens that I am as a patriot rather slow to boil. I think of myself instinctively as a citizen of the world and have the habit of discussing the defects and merits of my native land—except for its plumbing conveniences, about which I brook no two opinions—in a mood of cool appraisal. Therefore this violence of idea, in a great authority on the manner in which violent ideas are formed, stimulated rather than incensed me. America *has* failed to shine in most branches of human

15. From *Scribner's Magazine*, C (July, 1936), 9. Reprinted by permission of the author.

culture which transcend the mood of the matter-of-fact. We are a hard-surfaced folk, or have been. Our serious culture is like one of those modernist plays enacted on a bare stage with no backdrop and no scenery —and withal a sentimental play. We have used our brains well, but not our imaginations, not our emotional perceptions. We lack "depth"— whatever depth is—and we lack fineness.

I recognize all these facts and sense a validity in the viewpoint of the old-world critic. And yet as I left his study I settled back with a very comfortable feeling into being an American, and being a part of the process of creating an American culture. My feeling was not only comfortable, but also a little gleeful, a little on the laughing side. It was as though I had said to the old man: "It is just as well you don't understand our system—wait till the homestretch and we'll show you."

The basic thing historically is that America was born late, and spent her youth with grown-up brothers and sisters. She is precocious—or she is "old-wise," to translate a better German term. I mean in so far as she is wise at all, and not like all other countries full of dead men and clods. Our earliest heroes—Franklin, Jefferson, Washington, Tom Paine—were disbelievers in the legends in which all other early heroes lived and breathed. They were heroes of the matter-of-fact, and of will and resolution based upon a knowledge of it. A lot of religious and cultural top hamper that came over with us on the ships, and then the long and pious effort of our second-rate geniuses to imitate it, has obscured this fact. Where other "national minds" were born in an atmosphere of imaginative belief, ours was born in an atmosphere of skeptical common sense. It was born with the industrial revolution and with modern science.

"Poets," said Benjamin Franklin, in a poem almost bad enough to prove it, "are the mere *wastepaper* of mankind."

This does not mean that we are standing still at a goal. It means that we are moving in a different direction. We started in fact and are moving toward imagination; other cultures have moved the other way. I have no assurance where we shall come out. It may be impossible to work this process backward. But if it is not, then those other more imaginative cultures will fade out and die. For facts *are* facts, and once they are known you cannot with inward dignity deny them. I think and hope that American poets will find a way to unleash the imagination, and cultivate subtleties of feeling, without losing that inestimably precious sense of hard fact which is instinctive with us and not a thing that we have slowly had to learn. Nothing could be more interesting than to try to do this. No national mission, or adventure, could be more exciting.

That is why I felt comfortable in returning to my own nest of Americanness, after agreeing with so much that the great man in Europe said Why I felt like laughing is not so easy to tell. It may be that I was retreating into the fastnesses of our own cultural territory. I was running up the flag on our sole impregnable fortress. For America *has* unleashed imagination and cultivated feelings in the one realm where, held down by that harsh sense of fact, she instinctively could—the realm of humor. "You may laugh at our crudity and make jokes about Columbus, but we could make a better joke and laugh with more imagination." That is perhaps what I was saying to the old man. That is what I want to say here.

It is no accident that Mark Twain and Abraham Lincoln—both men in whom humor took the place of ideological anchorings—became and have remained in the world's eyes the representative Americans. Their headstrong sensibleness, their steadfast confrontation of fact, and their adjustment through humorous emotion to the predicament in which facts, steadfastly confronted, place the wishful heart of man, is the keynote of our culture if we have one.

There was hardly a bolder and lonelier thing a man could do in Lincoln's place than crash through military discipline with acts of human mercy. There, if anywhere, he needed the support of angels or ideas. "Well, I don't believe shooting will do him any good," he would say to the indignant military. Or: "I put it to you to decide for yourself; if God Almighty gives you a cowardly pair of legs, how can you help their running away with you?" And in this acceptance with a quizzical playful emotion of life's ultimate predicament, his mind would find rest, his will the requisite support. It is not a trivial or incidental thing to be as humorous as Lincoln was.

"I'm quite sure," said Mark Twain, "that . . . I have no race prejudices, and I think I have no color prejudices nor caste prejudices nor creed prejudices. Indeed, I know it. I can stand any society. All that I care to know is that a man is a human being—that is enough for me; he can't be any worse."

In that, it seems to me, you have the whole temper and equilibrium of Mark Twain's mind, the ruthless vision—out of those hawk's eyes—and the laughter. You cannot separate the two as solemn critics do, and arrive at something called "Mark Twain's philosophy." Facts are awful, but you can be honest if you laugh—that was his "philosophy."

I am not saying that these attitudes are final, but just the opposite, that they are the starting point of a distinctively American culture, and that nothing is final. In order to see them so, however, it is necessary to disregard most of what has been done by the historians, for they call American culture everything that developed on this continent. I can find roots running back, but I think American culture as a distinct entity began not so very early in the nineteenth century. And it has its natural beginning, just as all national cultures have, in a mythology—a mythology which has been described, rather unfortunately, as the "tall talk" of the western frontier. If you want to see how much more it is than that, you should read a few pages of Lowell Thomas's sapless collection of "Tall Stories," and compare it with a page of Constance Rourke's chapter on "The Gamecock of the Wilderness" in her book about *American Humor*. I spare you the sample from Lowell Thomas, but here is a page from Constance Rourke's rich book. She is describing the legends which grew up around the historic figure of Davy Crockett.

The story of his life in one of the almanacs began by picturing him as a baby giant planted in a rock bed as soon as he was born and watered with wild buffalo's milk. Another declared that as a boy he tied together the tails of two buffaloes and carried home five tiger cubs in his cap. In another he wrung the tail off a comet, and announced that he could "travel so all lightnin' fast that I've been known to strike fire agin the wind." . . . On one of his adventures he was barred by an "Injun rock so 'tarnal high, so all flinty hard, that it will turn off a common streak of lightnin' and make it point downward and look as flat as a cow's tail." Once he escaped up Niagara Falls on an alligator. "The alligator walked up the great hill of water as slick as a wild cat up a white oak."

In the end he became a demigod, and spoke in his own person:

One January morning it was so all screwen cold that the forest trees were stiff and they couldn't shake, and the very daybreak froze fast as it was trying to dawn. The tinder box in my cabin would no more ketch fire than a sunk raft at the bottom of the sea. Well, seein' daylight war so far behind time I thought creation war in a fair way for freezen fast: so, thinks I, I must strike a little fire from my fingers, light my pipe, an' travel out a few leagues, and see about it. Then I brought my knuckles together like two thunderclouds, but the sparks froze up afore I could begin to collect 'em, so out I walked, whistlin' "Fire in the mountains!" as I went along in three double quick time. Well, arter I had walked about twenty miles up the Peak O'Day and Daybreak Hill I soon discovered what war the matter. The airth had actually friz fast on her axes, and couldn't turn round; the sun had got jammed between two cakes o' ice under the wheels, an' thar he had been shinin' an' workin' to get loose till he friz fast in his cold sweat. C-r-e-a-t-i-o-n! thought I, this ar the toughest sort of suspension, an' it mustn't be endured. Somethin' must be done, or human creation is done for. It war then so anteluvian an' premature cold that my upper and lower teeth an' tongue war all collapsed together as tight as a friz oyster; but I took a fresh twenty-pound bear off my back that I'd picked up on my road, and beat the animal agin the ice till the hot ile began to walk out on him at all sides. I then took an' held him over the airth's axes an' squeezed him till I'd thawed 'em loose, poured about a ton on't over the sun's face, give the airth's cog-wheel one kick backward till I got the sun loose—whistled "Push along, keep movin'!" an' in about fifteen seconds the airth gave a grunt, an' began movin'. The sun walked up beautiful, salutin' me with sich a wind o' gratitude that it made me sneeze. I lit my pipe by the blaze o' his top-knot, shouldered my bear, an' walked home, introducin' people to the fresh daylight with a piece of sunrise in my pocket.

Is it any wonder that this childlike and savage imaginative explosion, crashing in on the refined habits of English literary humor of the genteel tradition, gave rise to the idea that exaggeration is the sole thing at which Americans laugh? Expressing, as Miss Rourke says, "an exhilarated and possessive consciousness of a new earth and even of the wide universe," these legendary heroes found no room to exist in British drawing rooms of the Victorian era. They were indeed too big for that. But among their own companions—and the companions of Davy Crockett are Theseus and Hercules, Thor and Baldur—these American heroes are not distinguished by size but by humor. All mythical heroes have been exaggerations, but they have been serious ones. America came too late for that. Her demigods were born in laughter; they are consciously preposterous; they are cockalorum demigods. That is the natively American thing—not that her primitive humor is exaggerative, but that her primitive exaggerations were humorous.

I am not very strong in history—it is one of the things I have put off writing until I should have time to read up on it. But it seems to consist of riding some idea through a morass of facts that would bog you down and drown you if you were not mounted. And I should like to propose a brief history of American literature, of American imaginative culture, in which the idea would be that it is only about one hundred years of age, and is not to be regarded as a gradual deposit of calcium in the backbone and vision in the eyes of nice, white-handed New England teachers and preachers, mastering a graceful penmanship and learning to write almost as well as the English poets, but as a rough, laughing growth springing up out of the struggles of the pioneers, and having its background in a humorous mythology, in legendary heroes taken as a joke.

If imagination is what we failed of in our belated infancy, it is in this humorous mythology rather than our sober poets that we began vigorously to have it. And it is in the humorists, rather than the poets, that, up to recent times at least, this vigor of imagination flourished. This was what made them something of a sensation in the world. They did of course exaggerate. Imaginative humor runs out automatically into exaggeration. How could you play laughing havoc with the qualities of things, and not pile them up into quantities that also overwhelm the mind? The two things go together like size and shape—the inordinate quantity and the preposterous image. Ring Lardner said that "if the penalty for selling honest old beer to minors was a $100 fine why two to fourteen years in a meat grinder would be mild for a guy that sells white pop on the theory that it is a drink." As a modification of the penal code that is indeed extreme, but it is also—is it not—fantastic? And the fantasy, not the extremeness, is what makes Ring Lardner's hand unmistakable in the writing of it.

At high noon the wind was blowing a 2 inch gale backwards and neither scow would move, so the starter postponed it till along came a breath of fresh air, which was a ¼ to 2″. Then away went the two sloops like a snail with paralysis.

They were in Brock's inner office, the walls of which were adorned with autographed pictures of six or seven of the more celebrated musical comedy stars, and a too-perfect likeness of Brock's wife, whom he had evidently married in a dense fog.

She smiled and Rita noticed her teeth for the first time. Most of the visible ones were of gold, and the work had evidently been done by a dentist for whom three members of a foursome were waiting.
"Does she think," said Stu, "that just because she comes from the golden State she has to run around with a mouthful of nuggets?"

That is the way Ring Lardner exaggerates. And here is Mark Twain:

"Kings" and "kingdoms" were as thick in Britain as they had been in little Palestine in Joshua's time, when people had to sleep with their knees pulled up because they couldn't stretch out without a passport.

I own millions and millions of feet of affluent silver leads in Nevada—in fact the entire undercrust of that country nearly, and if Congress would move that State off my property so that I could get at it, I would be wealthy yet.

Twenty-four years ago, I was strangely handsome. . . . In San Francisco, in the rainy season I was often mistaken for fair weather.

Pa's got a few buck-shot in him, but he don't mind it 'cause he don't weigh much anyway.

You can find all the exaggerations you want in Baron Munchausen, but you cannot find a phrase to match those in any writer of English before Mark Twain. Even Lord Byron's wit was not lighted with these exploits of poetic humor. In Charles Dickens you could search all day for a phrase to print on the page with them. "Mark Twain can be quoted in single sentences," says Stephen Leacock, "Dickens mostly in pages." But all vigorously imaginative minds can be quoted in sentences—all of the tribe of Shakespeare. And American humorists, casual and unsustained as their flights are, belong to the tribe of Shakespeare. It is as though that revival of an Elizabethan gleam and range of vision which we call the romantic movement, and which occurred in poetry in England at the beginning of the nineteenth century, occurred a half century later in the United States and in humor instead of poetry.

Comic imagination, then, or what I prefer to call poetic humor, would stand not only at the beginning but close to the center of my briefer history of America's imaginative culture. Another feature of my history would be our humor troubadours. For America has not only a comic mythology; she has had her minstrelsy of laughter too, her jesting tramps or gleemen, who got about by making people smile instead of singing to them. Artemus Ward was the prince of this tribe, a travelling printer who could write "copy," and subsequently a platform entertainer. And he brought something from his Eastern home that was not to be found at all in that loud humor of the pioneers. It was not exactly what we call a "dry New England wit," and I am not sure but he got it out of his own bosom rather than out of some abstraction called New England. It was what underlies that dry wit in a laughter-loving rather than a caustic mind—a taste for pure absurdities. Artemus Ward liked to speak out before the public the kind of "foolishness" that is indulged at home. Phrases like "of the same similarness," or "Why is this thus? What is the cause of this thusness?" acquired a delicious drollness on his lips. He made people laugh by saying things that made absolutely no sense, or which there was absolutely no sense in saying.

I was born in the state of Maine of parents.

One of the peculiarities of my lecture is that it contains so many things that haven't anything to do with it.

He used to have with him when lecturing on the Mormons a panorama representing what he saw in Utah. In his picture the lion on Brigham Young's gate had a ridiculously elongated tail. He would point to it and say: "Yonder lion, you will observe has a tail. It will be continued a few evenings longer." It appears that his British audience could hardly hold their joy when he pointed to one of the Nevada mountains and said in a modestly informing tone: "The highest part of that mountain is the top."

It is of course impossible to revive the alluring plausibility which his presence could impart to such a statement, how he could make the whole mortal being of a listener move with breathless playful expectation to this simple fall. We merely know that it was true. When it came to making humor humorous—and it very often does—Artemus Ward seems to have had no equal among men. No man on the platform was ever more successful or more loved.

I think the unique quality of his humor can be conveyed, after a fashion, by saying that his jokes were almost always blunt. If they had a point, he would slur it in the utterance so that you could hardly catch the gleam. And frequently they had no point. And frequently they would seem to lose their point, or forget all about it, and go wandering off in search of some ludicrous situation or image.

"Does this railroad company allow passengers to give it advice, if they do so in a respectful manner?"
The conductor replied in gruff tones that he guessed so.
"Well, it occurred to me that it would be well to detach the cowcatcher from the front of the engine and hitch it to the rear of the train, for you see we are not liable to overtake a cow, but what's to prevent a cow from strolling into this car and biting a passenger?"

Artemus Ward was not perhaps more gifted than other American humorists, but his gift was more unusual. He was, like Poe among our poets, a prodigy. And like Poe he was so recognized in Europe as well as in America. After his first London lecture in 1866, *Punch,* in an editorial ovation, advised "funny men on or off the stage to hear Artemus Ward 'speak his piece' at the Egyptian Hall, and then, in so far as in them lies, to go and do likewise.

"To be sure Artemus Ward's delivery of fun is 'un-English.' But there are a good many things English one would like to see un-Englished. Gagging, gross, overdone low comedy is one of them. Snobbishness is another. The two go hand in hand. One of the best of many good points of Artemus Ward's piece is that it is quite free from all trace of either of these English institutions."

Those who think that British humor is a very subtle fluid whose quiet stream has been disturbed by the coarse, loud guffaws of the Americans, may learn something from these lines. The fact is that Artemus Ward so surprised London with the possibility of a gentle grace and mental quietness in platform humor, that all English society was excited about it. Even the heavy-sitting queen was lifted by the general wave of enthusiasm.

"The most delightful fooling," she said, "that it has ever been our good fortune to hear. During his extraordinary prologue the audience fairly laughed till they could laugh no more, for the strange, quaint, quiet, gentlemanly humor of the lecturer was irresistible."

"Never was an American in London so beloved," said Moncure D. Conway, and Charles Reade nicknamed him "Artemus the delicious." "His jokes," said the *London Times,* "are of the true transatlantic type to which no nation beyond the limits of the States can offer any parallel."

It would be easy, with such a lead, to exaggerate Artemus Ward's Americanness. In his love for pure absurdity, he must take his place with Lewis Carroll as an event in world literature rather than an American event. Chesterton has said that the Victorians "discovered nonsense," and it is true that they were first in the pure love of it. But their nonsense derives some sense from the fact that it was designed for the entertainment of children. Their pointless jokes have always that point. That serious thought sustains many a true lady and gentleman in the indignity of enjoying them. It gives moreover a flavor of condescension, almost a baby-talk flavor, to some of their finest foolishness. Artemus Ward's delicious absurdities were for grown-up minds. He loved nonsense with a manly and mature love.

Unfortunately for the world, he died in the midst of those lectures in London, when he had barely become conscious of his powers. No literary monument exists to perpetuate his rare spirit. Only in the testimony of those who heard him, and in collected fragments—here too like the poetry of Edgar Allan Poe—is the original quality of his mind to be perceived. But almost as Poe stands at the source of a tendency toward "pure poetry," or poetry as an art and not a preachment, so Artemus Ward stands at the source of a tendency toward pure humor—toward the cultivation of absurdity so exquisitely that it is treasured without condescension for its own sake.

It is the blending of these two strains—the primitive vigor of imagination and the mature enjoyment of nonsense—that gives its distinct flavor to American humor. Both Mark Twain and Josh Billings were aware of this flavor, and tried to identify it by isolating the word "humor" for the purpose. Mark Twain said that the art of telling a "humorous," as opposed to a "comic," or a "witty" story, "was created in America and has remained at home." And Josh Billings apologized for the failings of this art by explaining that "Americans haven't had time yet to bile down their humor and git the wit out ov it."

Josh Billings was a crude character in comparison to Mark Twain—a "cracker-box philosopher," and on some subjects rather more of a cracker-box than a philosopher. But he possessed these two gifts, the comic vision and the liberated taste for foolishness, in a degree that enabled him to create a new artistic form. He would appear in our brief and reckless history as the father of imagism. For he was the first man in English literature to set down on his page, quite like a French painter reared in the tradition of art for art's sake, a series of tiny highly polished verbal pictures, and leave them there for what they might be worth.

The crane is neither flesh, beast, nor fowl, but a sad mixtur ov all theze things.

He mopes along the brinks of kreeks and wet places, looking for sumthing he haz lost.

He haz a long bill, long wings, long legs, and iz long all over.

When he flies thru the air, he is az graceful az a windmill broke loose from its fastenings.

The gote is a koarse wollen sheep.

They have a good appetite, and a sanguine digestion.

A maskuline gote will fite ennything, from an elephant down to his shadder on a ded wall.

They strike from their but-end, instead ov the shoulder, and are as liable to hit as a hammer is a nail-hed.

They kan klime ennything but a greast pole, and know the way up a rock, az natral az a woodbine. . . .

The Duk iz a kind ov short-legged hen.

They kan sale on the water as eazy as a grease spot.

Duks hav a broad bill which enables them tew eat their food without enny spoon.

Thare ain't any room on the outside of a duk for enny more feathers.

The duk don't kro like a rooster, but quaks like a duk.

There is little in New England poetry up to that date as graphic as some of this Poughkeepsie auctioneer's metaphors—nothing quite comparable to his statement that goats "know the way up a rock as natural as a woodbine," which is Homeric. Our history would make much of the originality of Josh Billings, and also of his crudity—for our whole history would be of something crude.

We should also devote a considerable and animated section to the great American art of laughing at oneself—that "humor of discomfiture written in the first person," which Leacock again says "absolutely distinguishes" Mark Twain from Dickens. It was not original with us, nor with anyone in history. But with us, I think, it first became a humorous convention. It first seemed the natural and appointed way to engage a reader in the joys of ridicule. One of the most interesting processes in cultural history, and most indisputable, has been the steady playing down of cruelty, and playing up of sympathy, in laughter. And this tendency of American humor stands at the height of that curious, and seemingly almost Christian, development. When you have taken upon your own person a defect or misfortune with which you propose to invite laughter, you are surely not inviting sneers. That is what Constance Rourke means, perhaps, by attributing to American humor as a whole a quality of "tenderness." A more complete and universal understanding of the mood of play would probably describe it better.

We hold ourselves up to laughter because we believe in laughter. We understand it, and know how to distinguish it from snarling and showing of teeth. We believe in being humorous. We believe in it more with our souls than most civilized folk. And this, if my hypothesis about our general culture is correct, is because we have had the energy and the abounding spirits of a young nation, and yet our childhood fell in a day of skepticism instead of animal faith. We have made more of humor because deprived in infancy of serious childish fancies.

Such in outline would be my chapter on humor as the origin and almost the central stem of America's distinctly own imaginative culture. It would go on to tell, of course, how this native tree of laughter, rooted in a humorous mythology, grew to its height in Mark Twain and his contemporaries, and then about the time of his death suddenly burgeoned out all over the sky and with a violent hilarity, and a certain thinning of the life sap, blossomed. We might call our chapter *The Root, Stem, and Petals of American Humor*. It would not agree with the prevailing opinion that this recent phenomenon, this still continuing shower of arrantly hilarious laughter, known variously as The Newer Nonsense, the Larger Lunacy, the Higher Goofyism—or "Humor Gone Nuts," as Donald Ogden Stewart calls it—is an essentially new departure. It is the natural bloom of the tree. It was all foretold and predestined in the riotous mythology of the pioneers and in Artemus Ward's consecration of absurd nonsense—two things which might almost exonerate Columbus for his little mistake, a natural one after all when sailing west for India, in discovering America.

That would not be the whole of our history. It would say much of Edgar Allan Poe, stifled in this cold climate of fact because he lacked the gift of laughter. And it would say more of Walt Whitman, so like Mark Twain in his passion for democracy and fact, and yet unlike him as another world because instead of humor he relied on mystical belief. And with these strands to weave, it would say something about the future—about what might be done by a mind, trained in fact and true to it, equipped as such a mind must be with humor, and yet not ill at ease in deeps of feeling and among fervent ventures of imagination, not ill at ease among revolutionary ideas, not condemned to make a final resting place of fact and laughter.

*Suggestions for Study*

1. How much of this article may be regarded as introductory? What rhetorical function is performed by that introduction? State the major idea contained in it.

2. In what does the author find consolation amid the jibes at America?

3. In what way are Mark Twain and Lincoln representative Americans?

4. What is the English conception of American humor?

5. State the three qualities of American humor which Eastman presents.

6. Characterize Artemus Ward.

7. What basis of classification does the author use in his main points? Is there any shift in his subpoints?

8. Is this a formal or an informal analysis? Why?

9. Define the reading group, the purposes, and the thesis of this article. Then make an outline of it.

10. Define the following words from the article: unsymmetrically, appraisal, incensed, impregnable, ideological, entity, morass, troubadours, caustic, elongated, plausibility, prologue, perpetuate, animated, burgeoned, exonerate.

## B. Argumentation

The aim of argumentation is to convince a reader of the truth of a conclusion. It may try to stimulate an audience which is but lukewarm in its acceptance of an idea or which has yet been unable to make up its mind at all; more difficult to accomplish, it may also try actually to reverse the judgment of an audience which shows an aggressive hostility to a measure. An engineer's report to a city manager on the feasibility of establishing new water mains is an example of addressing an undecided reading group; in Shakespeare's *Julius Caesar* the speech of Mark Antony in defense of Caesar is an example of changing the mind of a hostile audience.

The general problem, then, is to present a set of facts in such a manner psychologically that they will insinuate themselves into a reader's mind and cause him to act as you desire. The first step, of course, in achieving that aim is the collection of pertinent facts, complete enough so that you will not have overlooked any important consideration. But before you begin to write your paper, you must subject these facts to a logical analysis, for the arguments which you are preparing are very slippery and your reasoning can easily go awry. Such an analysis should begin with a scrutiny of the thesis which you are defending, usually termed a *proposition* in argument. Next it must examine the major *issues* which you must prove to win your point. Once the proposition and issues are decided upon, you are in a position to construct an outline and write your argumentative paper.

THE PROPOSITION. The first step in argument is the definition of the proposition. By a proposition is meant the point which is being argued. Every word in the proposition must be clearly defined before any logical arguing can be done. For example, a discussion of the proposition, "Poetry is a type of reading which most students dislike," could never reach any satisfactory conclusions. The terms are too vague. Poetry embraces a wide variety of materials; some people might enjoy lyrics but dislike epics; others might like ballads but dislike ballades. The term "poetry" would quickly turn out to be too general to suffice in a logical argument without careful definition. The proposition also contains another troublesome word—"most." If a more specific word such as "majority" were substituted, a poll of students might be undertaken to establish the proposition. But what kind of students? Grade-school pupils are students. Thus every word in the proposition must be closely scrutinized for ambiguity or looseness.

THE ISSUES. The next step in the argument, once the point has been clearly defined, is to formulate the specific issues which must be settled in the course of the discussion. In order to be convinced, a reader must have certain questions concerning the proposition answered to his satisfaction. For example, suppose that a salesman is trying to sell a house to a prospective buyer. He praises the beauty of the location, the attractiveness of the grounds surrounding the house, the pleasing appearance of the exterior, the satisfactory arrangement of rooms, and so on. The buyer courteously listens to the eloquent plea but asks one question: What does the house cost? That to him is a major issue. If it is answered to his satisfaction, then he is willing to be convinced on other issues. But if the price is too high, then all the other pleading has no effect on him.

The salesman might proceed in the following manner in preparing his argument. First, he might list all the questions that need to be answered in order to make the sale. These would be purely temporary:

What will it cost?
How can it be financed?
What will be the tax rate?
What kind of furnace has it, and how much will fuel cost?
Is it cool in summer and warm in winter?
Will the grounds afford space for children to play?
Is there room for a garden?
Are the neighbors congenial?
Is the community a desirable one?

Many such questions would occur to him. He could then condense these to a few in number so that he could answer them effectively. One question would deal with the cost and financing of the house; a second with the upkeep; a third with the condition of the house and grounds; and a fourth with the community. The revised list would then read:

What will it cost, and how can it be financed?
What will be the cost of upkeep?
What is the condition of the house and grounds for comfort, convenience, and attractiveness?
What is the nature of the community?

By analyzing these issues, the salesman can convince his customer, but by the neglect of almost any one, he may lose the sale. Thus it is in any argument.

THE METHODS OF REASONING. For the construction of a logical argument revolving round a definite proposition and comprehensive issues, two methods of reasoning may be employed: *inductive* and *deductive*. The former is a derivation of a conclusion from the observation of a group of facts; the latter is a derivation of a conclusion by the application of a general principle to an isolated fact.

*Inductive reasoning*. A student walking across the campus in spring notices that the girls are wearing their new spring attire. One girl after another passes him, dressed in brightly colored sweaters, peasant skirts, and saddle shoes. After some time, the student concludes: the spring fashions for college women demand brightly colored sweaters, peasant skirts, and saddle shoes. He is reasoning inductively. From a set of facts which he has observed, he has drawn a conclusion. This method of reasoning has been made more famous as the scientific method. Laboratory technique to establish a hypothesis, theory, or law from the observation of a multitude of facts is inductive.

*Causes of error in inductive reasoning*. In employing inductive reasoning, be careful to avoid certain causes of error. A first cause is faulty observation. A color-blind student might well come to the wrong conclusion about the colors of the spring attire. Those pseudo scientists who believe that a hair when placed in water will metamorphose into a snake are guilty of the same mistake. Perhaps the most universal errors of this kind were the beliefs that the world is flat and that the sun revolves about the earth. It is essential to guard against superficial observation.

A second cause of error is the derivation of a conclusion too hastily. Most of us tend to state a conclusion without having accumulated enough evidence. One or two girls dressed in a particular manner would not present enough evidence for one to derive a satisfactory conclusion concerning the fashions; only the observation of a great many girls can lead to a tenable conclusion. Students at classification time often err in enrolling for courses because of this logical error. They accept the word of a classmate that a particular course is easy, only to find later to their dismay that it is very difficult for them. They fail to accumulate sufficient evidence. A second human tendency is to state a conclusion without having accumulated pertinent facts. If fifty girls who care nothing for their manner of dress should troop across the campus, one might conclude hastily that no new spring fashions had been created. The conclusion would be unwarranted only because the facts were not representative. This error is the one which all pre-election and other straw polls endeavor to avoid. The famous poll conducted by the *Literary Digest* magazine which predicted the easy victory of Alfred Landon over Franklin Roosevelt erred because its sampling of the voting public was not a representative sampling; the facts were not pertinent.

A third cause of error lies in the source of the facts. Some facts we can amass ourselves; others we can gather only at second hand. Thus a reliance upon inaccurate sources of information can produce error. The source must first be checked for its timeliness. In wartime, facts concerning the imports and exports of European nations are nearly useless if they are much more than a month old. Likewise, an argument concerning present policy toward Japan would err if the writer employed for his information on Japan solely the writings of Lafcadio Hearn dated forty years ago. The timeliness of the facts must therefore be ascertained. The latest material, of course, is not always the best. On the character of Shakespeare, for example, one would rather accept the testimony of a contemporary who knew him well than to accept the conjectures of a later critic or biographer.

The source of information must also be checked for its authority. If we are to accept a man's word as fact, we must first ask, what authority has he for making this statement? A general rule is *never accept as fact the testimony of a man when he is speaking outside his special study*. For example, when Bill Jones who operates a machine in a local factory states that the machines in that factory are unsafe for use, he may well be believed, with certain reservations. But when the same Bill Jones declares that the last ruling of the Supreme Court was erroneous, his word is subject to error. Or when Professor Calkins of the mathematics department speaks on the teaching of mathematics, his words carry weight; when he speaks on the teaching of history, his authority is immediately diminished. Or when Senator Sorghum advises on his special study of taxation, he is more significant than when he expresses an opinion on international trade agreements. Having ascertained a man's authority, you may next ask, did he actually say this? If his remark has been repeated at second, third, or fourth hand, it has probably been altered materially. A girl involved in an accident while swimming escaped unscathed; soon after, her parents received the crushing news that she was drowned. Such is the fallacy of hearsay evidence. Each recipient of the evidence is very likely to interpret it to suit his own liking or to be sensational. Next we may ask: is the authority prejudiced? The testimony of those who are in a perfect position to speak authoritatively is often worthless because of their bias. The shopkeeper who is paying tribute to gangsters for "protection" will not speak truly to the police because he fears for the lives of his wife and children. The Jew persecuted in Germany would scarcely be able to write accurately of conditions in that country. Many times, the bias is purely unintentional. The United States is full of people who affirm sincerely that the locality in which they live is the most beautiful in the land. Thus it behooves one to determine whether a prejudice exists, and to make due allowance for it.

A fourth cause of error is the derivation of an unwarranted conclusion from accurate facts. Error is likely to occur in any statement of cause and effect. One common assumption is that because two events happen in close proximity, the one causes the other. On a sullen day a small patch of blue appears in the sky; the sun shines through it; soon the whole sky has cleared up. Therefore, the sun cleared away the cloud masses. Such a conclusion is unwarranted. Because the clouds were clearing up, the sun was able to shine through them. People often reason rather superstitiously in this manner. Last Thursday I was going to take out insurance on my automobile, but I forgot; on Friday, I was in an accident and my car was smashed beyond repair. Therefore, the failure to take out the policy occasioned the accident. Political reasoning often follows similar channels. President Hoover was in office when the depression of 1929 broke; therefore he was responsible for it and must be defeated at the polls. President Roosevelt and the New Dealers were in office during the 1930's; therefore they are responsible for all the ills of that decade. This is often called *post hoc propter hoc* reasoning, in which a purely time sequence is mistaken for a cause and effect sequence.

Sometimes, too, an effect is attributed to a cause which is too slight to have produced it. This fallacy is frequently responsible for the dismissal of athletic coaches. When a team falls into a losing streak, the coach is usually blamed. A football coach is but one man; on the field are eleven men who do the actual playing, and on the bench are perhaps sixty more. Yet the coach alone is held responsible for the games which are lost.

The apparent cause and effect may also be invalid through the operation of a more powerful yet hidden cause. For example, if the nephew of a prominent governmental official were appointed to an important post, the usual comment would be, "Well, he's the nephew, you know; he has the pull that the rest of us lack." But if the nephew had passed a civil service examination with the highest possible grade, his appointment would be on sheer merit and the obvious cause would be entirely inoperative.

These errors—faulty observation, insufficient evidence, faulty sources, and the illogical derivation of cause and effect—will suffice to show how careful you must be in the pursuance of inductive argument. If you fall into errors such as these, your argument may prove fallacious.

*Deductive reasoning.* Instead of proceeding from particulars to a generalization, deductive reasoning proceeds from a generalization to the particular. A statement which is assumed to be true is made as a general classification; a particular fact is then classified under that generalization, and a conclusion is drawn as a consequence. Reduced to its logical elements, this process is known as the syllogism, the three parts of which are called the major premise, the minor premise, and the conclusion. Here is a typical syllogism:

Major premise: All students in this class are over seventeen years of age.
Minor premise: Bill is a student in this class.
Conclusion:    Bill is over seventeen years of age.

A general classification of students is made in the major premise; a particular student is placed in this group by means of the minor premise; the conclusion is then drawn that as long as the student belongs in this classification, its characteristics belong to him as well as to the other members of the group.

It will be clear that the generalization to be found in the major premise is the result of inductive reasoning. From the examination of many individual instances, certain general laws of the world have been derived. That is the inductive process. But once these laws have been established, they can be used to interpret any number of individual instances that come within their scope. That is the deductive process.

*Causes of error in deductive reasoning.* Every member of the syllogism must be accurately stated if the conclusion is to be true. First be sure that the major premise is sound, for obviously, if it is faulty, no true conclusion can be drawn.

All radios cost more than thirty dollars.
This is a radio.
Therefore, it costs more than thirty dollars.

The fact that some radios cost as little as ten dollars invalidates the major premise and hence the conclusion also. Especially dangerous are unwarranted generalizations, such as "All the good fellows on campus are fraternity members" or "All the great industrialists in the world are Americans."

The minor premise must also be true. For example, a chemist might fall into error by reasoning this way:

> Sodium sulphate when added to barium chloride produces a barium sulphate precipitate.
> This is sodium sulphate.
> Therefore, when added to barium chloride, it will produce a barium sulphate precipitate.

Failing to get the desired precipitate, he analyzes the supposed sodium sulphate and finds it to be another compound. The classification of the minor premise was inaccurate and the conclusion therefore erroneous.

The conclusions must also arise logically from the premises. Error may first come from a failure to make a classification in the minor premise.

> Outdoor sports provide good exercise.
> Basketball provides good exercise.
> Therefore, basketball is an outdoor sport.

There is, of course, no classification in this syllogism. Error may also come from the use of more than three terms in the syllogism. In the proper syllogism, two terms are given in the major premise (as *Conscientious students* study their *lessons*), an additional term is added in the minor premise (*John* is a conscientious student), but the conclusion adds no new term (Therefore, *John* studies his *lessons*). If a fourth term is given in the conclusion, error will result, as in the following:

> Iced drinks are cooling in summer.
> This grape juice is an iced drink.
> Therefore, it should be pleasing.

> Patriotic deeds are greatly in demand.
> John's deed was patriotic.
> Therefore, John is much in demand.

APPLICATION OF REASONING TO THE WRITING OF ARGUMENT. The two major processes of reasoning which have just been considered have a direct application to the writing of argument. If the argument is presented inductively, a statement at the beginning of the paper establishes the subject which is being discussed, the facts are then presented, and the conclusion is finally drawn from these facts. This method is especially desirable for persuading a hostile reader. If the argument is well presented, he finds that he cannot escape the conclusion which follows from the facts.

Deduction is no less useful but calls for more practice. If the writer can present a sound generalization in his paper and have the minor premise correctly classified under it, then the reader must accept the conclusion which follows logically from the premises. Suppose that the president of a state university is arguing before the budget committee of the state legislature that his institution needs a new physics building. His aim is to get the committee by its vote to appropriate the necessary funds. He must establish therefore as his major premise what the general principle of voting is as applied to this situation. He decides that this generalization should read: All needs of a state institution should be met by your appropriation of necessary funds. If he deemed it necessary, he might then establish more fully this concept of the legislator's duty. Having fortified the major premise, he might frame the minor premise: Our need of a physics building is a need of a state institution. His task would clearly be to prove the minor premise. To make the proof, he might again have recourse to the syllogism: Physicists can carry on modern research only with proper equipment and building facilities; we have on our campus a whole department of physicists; therefore, they can carry on modern research only with proper equipment and building facilities. Poor buildings and equipment are detrimental to the work of both students and faculty; our present physics building is poor; therefore, it is detrimental to the work of both students and faculty. Through such a process of reasoning the minor premise might well be proved. Therefore, the legislators would logically have to accept the conclusion:

> All needs of a state institution should be met by your appropriation of necessary funds.
> Our need of a physics building is a need of a state institution.
> Therefore, our need of a physics building should be met by your appropriation of necessary funds.

Although this argument has been conducted by deductive reasoning in general, inductive reasoning may be employed at any point to support the truth of any major or minor premise. Thus the two are not exclusive but may be used in conjunction with each other.

FINAL PRECAUTIONS. As you may mislead both the reader and yourself in the course of an argument—and we are assuming here that you wish to be scientifically accurate, and not to resort to propagandist devices intended to mislead the reader—you must guard against certain human weaknesses that may destroy the force of your logic. Some of these precautions have been stated already, but others are of such importance that they need to be mentioned also.

*Analogy.* Reasoning is sometimes conducted by means of analogy. That is, a writer argues that because two objects are alike in one respect, they must be alike in other respects. Suppose that you were arguing that college freshmen should not be subjected to a close discipline in grammar and sentence structure, but should spend their time in mastering various subjects so that they would have something to say in their papers. You might offer an analogy. If a man cannot handle an ax, you would not spend hour after hour teaching him how to grasp it and swing it and make a clean cut; on the contrary, you would give him a few words of instruction as you led him to the woodpile, and then you would let him start chopping wood. Soon by trial and error and by experience, he would chop well because once he saw his goal and what he had to do to achieve it, he would quickly find the means. So, you argue, it is in rhetoric. Give the student a goal that he can see and a mastery of content so that he can achieve it, and he will find the suitable means of expression. That argument sounds very good; indeed argument by analogy is one of the most persuasive means of reasoning—to the unwary. Actually, analogy carries no proof. The best it can do is to indicate that *perhaps* some point may be true. In the analogy given above, there is no essential similarity between the two processes; they are both learning processes, but the one is a relatively simple physical process, whereas the other is a very difficult mental process. It may be true that rhetoric students should be given such leeway, but the analogy does not prove that proposition. A writer should therefore use analogy only with the intent of clarifying. It is an excellent means whereby a difficult point may be explained. Lincoln once spoke of his administration during the Civil War as being similar to a tight-rope walker crossing Niagara Falls on a tight wire. No one would think for a moment of interfering with that performer for fear that he should fall. In like manner no one should interfere with the administration of the government which was passing through equally perilous times. Thus Lincoln made clear what he meant—but he proved nothing.

*Rationalizing.* Justifying an action by a *post facto* chain of reasoning is called "rationalizing." A man wishes to play golf when he knows he should attend to his business; at the links he meets a man whose good will may help him in his business. He then convinces himself that his decision to play golf was an excellent business stroke. Akin to this is "wishful thinking." We should like to have easy victories and quick success in time of war; hence we interpret each action of the enemy as a sign of weakness. The skilled logician, however, does not blind himself to essential facts, but he analyzes basic motives and facts to arrive at truthful conclusions.

*The argument against the man.* An old trick of the propagandists which one must guard against in his own thinking is the direction of the argument against a man rather than against the cause which he advocates. To discredit socialism or communism, one does not attack, let us say, Mr. Thomas or Mr. Browder. Nor to praise the New Deal, does one praise the character of Mr. Roosevelt. An argument concerns the issues of a question and not the men involved.

*The argument to the people.* The appeal to the emotions rather than to the intellect is known as the argument to the people. It is extremely pleasing to all of us and hence very dangerous. Through its force a generalization is accepted without being sufficiently examined. Many times have bad leaders of nations struck up the band, waved the flag, shouted about the nation's honor, and so marched the people off to war without their stopping to consider whether the war was well justified. Such emotionalism is, to be sure, often used by writers to further a worthy cause, but you must be very careful to distinguish in your own mind between the moment when you are indulging in emotionalism and the moment when you are on the solid ground of fact and logic.

*The red herring.* A remark which is drawn across the main path of the argument and so turns it into by-paths is known as a red herring. During the course of an argument to prove that the university needs a new stadium, it might come to light that forty years ago old President Whitebeard declared that the university had no need for a stadium of large proportions. The argument might well be switched off into a discussion of the president and his statement, the whole discussion being quite beside the point, as conditions have changed materially in the forty-year period. Thus the writer must keep to the main issues and not be led into by-paths by a red herring.

*Ignoring the issues.* Once an argument has been started, the main issues must be fully analyzed. Many arguments founder because only minor issues are settled or because the ground of the argument is shifted. Comparing football scores to indicate the relative strength of teams often fails as a true basis. Just because Yale defeated Princeton, and Princeton defeated Cornell, one cannot argue that Yale will necessarily defeat Cornell. The scores are but one issue. One must analyze further the size of the scores, the weather conditions during the games, the physical conditions of the teams, the heaviness of the respective schedules, and many other factors before any logical argument can be made.

Many people shift so rapidly from one point to the next that none is settled completely. A student talking to his adviser expressed difficulty in securing a good mark in chemistry. Suspecting that poor reading was a major cause of the boy's trouble, the adviser placed an English book before him and asked him to read a passage and tell exactly what it said. The student was unable to do so. The adviser counseled him thereupon to adopt sounder methods of reading, but the student, shifting the ground, urged that reading from an English book has little in common with reading from a chemistry book. The instructor produced a chemistry book, and the experiment was repeated with a similar result. The student again shifted the ground by declaring that he could not read with the instructor watching him but that in his own room he had no difficulty in mastering the chemistry text, and that his trouble was caused by the chemistry instructor's dislike for him. Thus the discussion would have ended in an argument against the man had the adviser allowed it to continue far along that path. Each issue must therefore be adhered to and completely settled before the argument proceeds to the next.

The argument must proceed in carefully planned steps from a clear and definite proposition. In the course of the argument no rash generalizations may be indulged in, no facts may be disregarded, and the writer must be very sure when he is being intellectually logical and when he is being emotional.

### Exercises

1. State a proposition and the subsequent issues for one of the following general subjects:
Rationing of goods, the tariff, my home town as a place favorable for business establishments, the national debt, honor systems in college, required freshman courses, fraternities, crop control, proration of oil, a platform of a political party, drivers' licenses, income taxes, radio advertising, surrealism, All-American football teams, hitch-hiking, divorces, speed limits, admission to college.

2. An enthymeme is an abbreviated syllogism. Construct the syllogism contained in each of the following enthymemes:
Because we have been playing tennis lately, we are physically fit.
I got less than eight hours' sleep last night and therefore feel very tired.
Golf playing will be difficult today because of the strong wind.
Because the morale of our team is high today, we are likely to win.
Calculus, as it is a mathematics course, is difficult for me.

3. Examine each of the following statements for any possible error in reasoning:
The people in the Middle West are friendlier than those anywhere else in America.
My teacher, I am sure, must have been good, or she would not have been in the school.
Students who work must watch their pennies and cannot spend money foolishly for such things as fraternities.

The population of a city cannot be placed successfully upon an honor system; therefore, no better results will come from placing their children on an honor system in school.

I know that she plays the piano beautifully; her mother has told me so many times.

Chadwick has no right to be on the committee to study conditions in the colleges of the state. He has never been to college.

He no sooner sold his stocks than their price fell twenty points; whereupon he bought in again. He must have been responsible for engineering a coup so that he could sell profitably.

You have no right to bring a lie detector to work on this case; it's un-American.

Joe forgot to tap the plate as he came to bat; so, of course, he struck out.

Jumbo is so big that he can beat anyone in wrestling.

No one will ever pole vault over sixteen feet.

Her new pillow causes her hay fever; she never had hay fever until she purchased it.

He must be the best doctor in town. He cured Bill's sore throat very quickly.

I'm not going to vote for any political party that Josephson belongs to.

Of course Jack is intelligent; he graduated from the University last month.

Smoke Tabasco cigarettes. Rudolpho Weatherbanks, the famous movie actor, says they are the best.

Lightning automobiles are the finest on the market. Just last year a stock model won the Guadalupe Mountain hill-climbing test.

In this crisis, vote again for our party; don't change horses in the middle of the stream.

Si Maglie, who runs a shop on 33rd street, says that there is no racketeering going on in that district.

College professors should not be used in a governmental brain trust. They are all just theorists.

4. In each of the following statements, accept the major premise as true. Then examine the reasoning for accuracy as it proceeds from that premise. If you are in doubt about the accuracy of any reasoning, reduce it to its syllogistic form:

(a) A legal principle which has been evolved in our history is that any enterprise which engages in interstate commerce should be subject to regulation by the federal government. The operators of long-distance moving vans are protesting against federal regulation, but as they are engaged in interstate commerce, they should be so regulated.

(b) It has been shown that engineers in modern locomotives are seldom responsible for accidents in which their trains are involved. It is clear, therefore, that engineer Casey was not responsible for the accident in which his train was involved at Centerville last night.

(c) A controversial question for many years has been the socialized control of medicine. Certainly governmental support of individuals is likely to undermine their initiative and so produce inefficiency. Socialized medicine, of course, involves the governmental support of doctors, and so must fail by undermining the doctors' initiative and producing medical inefficiency.

(d) The radio industry since its inception has guarded against taking sides in debatable political or social arguments. It has been right in taking this stand, for any industry which affects large masses of people should avoid the attempt to sway the populace on controversial issues.

(e) The national debt which a country bears is not necessarily an economic evil. During the depression the United States added materially to its debt by spending freely for relief works. The conclusion which we see, therefore, is that the country has not erred in establishing relief works.

(f) Educational institutions of higher learning, if they are to be of value, should teach only those students who are capable of mastering advanced and complex subject matter. The State University was quite within its province therefore in rejecting those applicants who showed inability to master their high-school subjects.

(g) Our forefathers decided long ago that no American citizen of a certain age and fitness should be denied the right to vote. Sweeney is no American citizen and therefore must be denied the right to vote.

(h) Any instrument which produces greater ease and speed of writing is likely at the same time to encourage haste and slovenliness of rhetoric. In the hands of even an inexperienced operator, the modern typewriter increases the speed of writing nearly fifty per cent, and with an experienced operator, it increases the speed several hundred per cent. Writing with a typewriter thus has the danger of producing writing which is careless and inexact.

(i) It is better to raise public money directly by taxation than to try to float bond issues and so add to the public debt. The recent increase in taxation is therefore commendable.

(j) I think that my poor vision is attributable to a cramp of the eye muscles, for such a cramp often produces poor vision.

(k) The United States should maintain the freedom of the worker to strike whenever conditions imposed upon him become too severe. The recent strikes because of low wages and poor working conditions were therefore justified.

(l) The average adult in the United States has a mentality of fourteen years of age. Bert Robinson, who is an adult, has therefore a mental age of fourteen years.

(m) The telephone company customarily cuts off the service of any customer who does not pay his bill. Jack had his service cut off last week, and so we may assume that he did not pay his bill.

(n) The physical education department of a university should have as its duty the maintenance of good health among the undergraduates. The physical education department of the State University is accordingly obligated to give free health inspection to all students.

(o) The word "propaganda" has taken on a bad connotation, but actually propaganda which is skillful often aids a worthy cause. The propaganda which we are issuing is highly skillful and therefore is aiding a worthy cause.

Every college student, whether he wishes to be or not, should be deeply interested in such problems as whether another war is probable and what will result if one comes, and in what steps are being taken to prevent another war.

We have therefore made a selection of articles relating to these matters and have grouped them here. Not every one is an argument, except by implication. The articles by Dr. Urey and Mr. Shalett provide facts and information necessary for a realization of the importance of the issue; their arguments are implicit, for the purpose of the authors in relating the facts they do could hardly be missed. The other articles discuss the implications arising from these facts and offer various suggestions for solving the perplexing problems facing the statesmen and citizens of the world. We suggest that you study the whole group of articles, separately and as a unit, supplementing them by other readings on the same topic in current periodicals, and then write an argument of your own based on all this information and your own thinking on these matters.

## I'm A Frightened Man [16]

### HAROLD C. UREY
#### (as told to Michael Amrine)

I write this to frighten you.

I am a frightened man, myself. All the scientists I know are frightened —frightened for their lives—and frightened for *your* life.

For the past few weeks we have been in Washington giving our advice —when we are asked—concerning the potentialities of the atomic bomb. In so doing, we have naturally learned a good deal about the potentialities of politics. What we learn has increased our fears.

I say to you—and I wish I could say it face to face—that we who have lived for years in the shadow of the atomic bomb are well acquainted with fear, and it is a fear you should share if we are intelligently to meet our problems. We were dealing with unknowns in the structure of matter. Now, in thinking about world control, mankind is dealing with new and unknown factors in the structure of international civilization. Here political leaders must pioneer as scientists have pioneered. At present they are extremely reluctant to do so, partially because they have not lived daily with this subject as atomic scientists have done for years. It is hard for

16. From *Collier's*, CXVII (January 5, 1946), No. 1. Reprinted by permission of Harold C. Urey and Michael Amrine.

Mr. Amrine, thinking that young writers might like a glimpse behind the scenes in order to learn something of how professional writers work, adds the following information about the writing of the article: "It was rewritten completely at least four times. I was working for the London *Herald*—Washington office—when I met the atomic scientists and became aware that they had a message to convey which was as yet unrealized by the public. I decided to write an article to convey exactly what they were trying to say, but to put it in popular language. I wrote a long version of it one weekend and then began going over it inch by inch with various scientists. It was done over a three-weeks period, and each time I went to scientists' headquarters there were new ones there, and we sort of had to start over. . . . The scientists were very busy—a very hectic period—and we could not easily get together. One night at midnight I got a call that they had time to talk. . . . Finally I had an evening session with Doctor Urey and it was finished."

anyone who did not live through it to comprehend the suspense of that atomic arms race.

As soon as it appeared that scientists would accomplish this mission, we lived in fear that Germany might capture the secret before we did. We knew enough to know this would mean the end of our countries as we loved them—the obliteration of London, Washington, New York, Detroit, or Los Alamos and Oak Ridge. That terrible fear was heightened whenever we read newspaper reports of "mysterious explosions" along the French Coast, or commando raids on "research stations" which we later learned to have been V-2 laboratories. My point is this: a few years from now that fear may come home to you. By that time you will no longer feel so relaxed and carefree—happy that the war is over. A few years from now, *you* may be wondering what is going on behind the locked doors of laboratories all over the world, just as we once wondered, night and day. Then you will understand our suspense and know why we were frightened—but then it may be too late.

Now, in Washington, we have learned a new fear: we are afraid of what politicians and diplomats may do with the atomic bomb.

Perhaps you are thinking this scientist is not going to talk about science —he is going to talk about politics. He has no right to do that. What does he know about politics?

I know this: I hear people talking about the possible use of the atomic bomb in war.

As a scientist, I tell you: *there must never be another war.*

As to how to avoid war, you do not want any detailed opinions on a World Government or the machinery which might be set up by the Big Three or the Security Council of the United Nations. A scientist is not fitted to do the job of the diplomats and the politicians. We are now seeing world diplomats rising to new levels of statesmanship in their understanding and leadership in atomic problems.

But there are certain aspects of this thing which are both technical and political—for example, the question of international inspection. In addition, we scientists can speak as citizens. As citizens we are people who have had more time than the rest of you to think about the political possibilities of the bomb. We do not begin to know all the answers. But by this time, we know the questions.

Our stay in Washington has shown me that, despite all the reams of material which have been written about this, a dangerous proportion of politicians apparently does not know or understand *the questions.*

For example, they keep asking us, "Won't there be some defense against the atomic bomb?"

I have never heard—and you have never heard—any scientist say there is any scientific defense against the atomic bomb.

In the world as we know it there is no conceivable barrier which could keep any possible plane from somehow getting through from one country to another. Furthermore, the mere presence of the bomb cannot be detected by any "magical" means, and it is of such a size that it could fairly easily be smuggled in pieces from one country and assembled in another to await explosion at the touch of a distant radio control.

I do not know that it would even be necessary to knock out 40 or 50 cities with 40 or 50 bombs. In a country possessing excellent news communications, is it not possible that when a few cities are atomically destroyed, panic might empty the remaining cities and thus destroy the power of that country to resist?

You may say that bombing failed to reduce the will-to-resist of the British or even of the German people. But the atomic bomb is entirely different from other bombs.

Ordinary bombs do damage in a relatively small area. Relatively few persons are killed by any single bomb of the older type. If an ordinary bomb, even a block-buster, explodes in a city block, that block is horribly shattered, but unless the bomb lands near a theater or public meetingplace, relatively few persons die. The bomb may kill, say, 500 persons, and wound others. Ambulances rush to the scene. Rescue crews dig through the rubble. Wounded are sped to a hospital. Survivors thank their lucky stars and may continue to hope the next bomb will also miss them.

But in an atomic explosion, thousands die within a fraction of a second. In the immediate area, there is nothing left standing. There are no walls. They are vanished into dust and smoke. There are no wounded. There are not even bodies. At the center, a fire many times hotter than any fire we have known has pulverized buildings and human beings into nothingness.

The report of the U. S. Strategic Bombing Survey showed that in Germany incendiaries did *eight times the damage done by high explosives*. A single atomic bomb has the effect not only of 20,000 tons of TNT, but in addition starts a fire of hurricane intensity. Through the blitz, London saved itself with an army of volunteer fire fighters. In the war of the future there would be precious few fire fighters left. For the majority of wounded, there would be no hope of hospitals. The heart of a great city like London, representing centuries of human struggle and art and sacrifice, would simply vanish in a flash of fire and light. As atomic bombs are further developed, the will to fight will not lengthen the life of an attacked city five minutes. If such a bomb fell on London, there would be no London. There would be few Londoners.

A British scientist, Dr. M. L. Oliphant, has publicly stated that much bigger atomic bombs may soon be achieved. The Hiroshima bomb was equal to 20,000 tons of TNT. He thinks bombs of the future will be equal to a million or two million tons of TNT.

Against this the only imaginable "scientific defense" would not actually be a defense, but a retreat. I refer to the dispersion of cities. America has 200 cities with populations of more than 50,000—altogether we have a population of more than 50 million living in cities. To move them in a fantastic flight from the consequence of our evil genius would be an incredibly large project, larger even than the mass migrations of peoples of Europe since the rise of Hitler. No one can scientifically estimate such a project in terms of money—but some one has made a guess at $250,000,000,000.

Because America is such an industrialized country, with such large populations concentrated into exposed cities, *the effect of the atomic bomb will be to weaken America's military position*. Military strength will be measured in an interim stage not by industrial strength or naval strength or the strength of air power, but by the amount of urban concentration. In this interim period England's position, for example, will be all but hopeless.

An atomic arms race would soon reach a saturation point. If we are determined to make them, we can have a stockpile of 10,000 atomic bombs. So could other great powers. As soon as opposing nations have enough bombs to ruin each other's cities, you will actually have an armaments race which ends in a tie. The side which shoots first will win.

Such thinking leads scientists to say this bomb must not be used again for any purpose, not even "to enforce international justice." Suppose a small nation should begin mistreating its neighbor, in defiance of international law, treaties, or common decency. Regardless of how guilty the *rulers* of that nation might be, do you think it would be right for the great powers or an international police force to strike that nation a blow which would kill tens of thousands of innocents and cripple the culture and economy of that small nation for generations?

Intelligent men say No! Mankind's solution does not lie in overwhelming force, any more than the safety of individual persons in a large city lies in their knowledge of jiu-jitsu, or their ability to throw hand grenades. The safety of countries in the future, like our personal safety in cities, must rest on the *law and conscience of man,* backed by a vigilant world patrol, and the intelligent use of light arms.

Yet the scientists in Washington hear people talking of the possibility of another war. They read statements of generals and admirals which imply there could be another war. Let us do some more thinking about *that next war which must never be.*

Two outstanding things to remember about the bomb are:

1. It is much more powerful than anything previously known.

2. It could be a weapon of complete surprise—and probably will be.

Military men, who proverbially "prepare for the last war," frequently think of the bomb in terms of air power, as dropped from an airplane. It is much more apt to be used as a warhead in a V-2 rocket travelling faster than sound.

As England knows, with present knowledge it is impossible to devise means of intercepting V-2s. The V-2 and the atomic bomb, militarily speaking, are made for each other—the V-2 at present cannot land on a precision point, but it can land in a general area. The atomic bomb is a weapon which needs only to go off in the general area to demolish its target.

But remember that if we continue to think of a world of force instead of law, still more likely is the use of an improved model of the atomic bomb as a mine. Some Congressmen are slow to grasp this thought: such an atomic bomb exploded at Washington's Union Station would blast the marble of the Capitol into powder finer than flour.

We might not even know who had set that bomb. We might have been in a diplomatic crisis with one nation while yet another aggressor had planted the actual bombs. So we could have something new in the world, indeed—an Anonymous War. This could be the ultimate blindness brought to a world which would not open its eyes to the possibilities of a new age.

Many of us thought the possibilities would be so apparent that when humanity saw what science had done they would see immediately that here was the end of war; that this must be the end of war forever and ever. When we went into this project we hoped that we would find and prove that it could not be done. When it seemed possible we worked to get it before Japan or Germany. We thought the democracies would use it wisely to end the war to end all wars.

One idea was to drop the bomb on some vacant territory in Japan just to show that we had it. That might very well have ended the war. After all, Japan did surrender with an Army intact, proving that it is possible to knock out a nation psychologically. I am certain one bomb would have knocked out Japan if its political leaders had been in a position to listen to their nuclear physicists. Apparently the Japanese did not listen, any more than some of our leaders have listened to America's physicists. Jap slowness of comprehension cost them dearly. At Hiroshima, men were killed. At Nagasaki they committed suicide. Further slowness of comprehension will mean further and more terrible mass suicide.

Several of us have listened to men who studied the damage at Hiroshima and Nagasaki. They confirm our belief that ending this menace—this menace to New Orleans or London or Paris—is the most important thing in the world today. As the scientists see it—and they are remarkably near unanimity—there is only one answer: *World Control.*

Slowly we are losing our original illusions. There is no secret. There is no defense. The bomb is essentially cheap—compared with the cost of other weapons and their comparative effectiveness, the bomb is the cheapest war weapon in the world.

When you are talking about World Control you are, in a sense, talking politics. Most scientists, I think, prefer to view their present interest as "social awareness." It is as if a bacteriologist had discovered a dread disease which might lead to a disastrous epidemic. He would not be a "politician" if he asked that the city health commission take measures to deal with a plague. He would merely be demonstrating common decency and social awareness of what his discovery meant to human lives. So in this case the discoverers plead for a commission.

In the past most attempts to set up an international agency for world cooperation have broken up over one main issue: National Sovereignty.

The desire for national sovereignty, the right of a nation to do as it pleases, was of course behind the "veto power" given in the Security Council of the UNO, a veto power which in practice renders the present Council unable to cope with our problem.

It does not require a political mind to see that the idea of world control of the atomic bomb conflicts with the concept of national sovereignty.

Sovereignty to a nation is comparable to the freedom you have in the privacy of your home. Naturally nations, like individual persons, enjoy national sovereignty because it means freedom to do what they like without other nations poking their noses into their private business.

We are all glad to live in a country where no member of a gestapo has a right to come into your front room and ask to be shown through the house. But if you knew that a certain plague was abroad in the world and a health inspector came to visit you I believe you would welcome him.

To avoid what is potentially the worst plague which ever threatened mankind, we must learn to get along with less freedom for the sake of not having our heads blown off.

For years I have been a marked man—along with hundreds of other scientists. We have been watched and controlled most carefully. If an international police and inspection force is set up, it will mean still more control for all of us. But I assure you scientists will welcome these restrictions to guarantee there would never be another atomic bomb exploded anywhere.

The world has become much smaller and much more explosive.

Now we are all crowded together into a single house. Beneath the floor of our house there is a time bomb ticking away, as I write this . . . as you read this. Nations are crowded into a very small space as considered by the standards of the supersonic rocket and the atomic age. The explosion of an atomic war would smash our house of civilization—smash it beyond human comprehension. Those who even think of an atomic arms race, those who boast of battleships and air power, those who speak of using national force to maintain peace, simply do not understand this crowded house of fear.

They do not think of what the situation may be a few years from now.

Picture two men facing each other with loaded machine guns. Each is afraid the other man will shoot. Each knows whoever shoots first will win. There is no doubt of that. They do not worry about technical excellence, about getting a bigger or better gun. Whoever shoots first will win.

What of national sovereignty—the national sovereignty we would not give up at San Francisco? What about freedom to do as you please?

If we have that, what can we say about Freedom From Fear?

In Washington I hear endless echoes of old rivalries and jealousies between Allies. There is evidence of a new nationalism based, as always, on fear. Smaller nations are enfolded by the larger powers, whether swallowed whole or merely "protected" or huddled together through fear. If you—the people—let things drift, we will perhaps see a world divided into two great spheres of interest, east and west, afraid of each other, *afraid of one unguarded word*. Freedom From Fear?

We will eat fear, sleep fear, live in fear, and die in fear.

Because atomic energy is the basic energy of this world there is little point in seeking scientific defenses against this weapon or against its dreadful development in radio-active poisons.

We are at last face to face with the powers which, philosophically speaking, are supreme in our universe. There never will be a Maginot Line against the limitless powers of the universe as developed by the limitless imagination of Man.

Our "defense" is Control.

First, as proposed in the Anglo-American communique, a free exchange of scientific information. In the case of splitting the atom, which is based on principles well-known and widely discussed before the war, that does not involve giving much away. Those principles were not secret but were the common property of all free men who cared to study the world we live in.

We might fully restore scientific freedom through a world organization of scientists, with special attention to nuclear physicists.

There is one very fortunate fact in all this. You cannot become a competent nuclear physicist, able to supervise the splitting of the atom or constructing an atomic bomb plant, without a great deal of study. That study must be made in company with established physicists and use of the established instruments, such as the cyclotron. You cannot become a nuclear physicist capable of real work in the field merely by studying alone in a library, any more than you can become a Jesuit without a certain number of years spent in company with Jesuit scholars. This, and the fact that scientists are among the most international-minded of men, may well be the most important factor in our survival.

Most scientists think wars and national boundaries are a menace to the true creative spirit by which science must live, they hate war and they are terrified of atomic war—because they know its possibilities.

Then recall that secrecy in this project was accomplished only by almost superhuman effort and planning. If the world were pledged to freedom and not to secrecy, the hidden production of atomic power would be difficult indeed.

If the powers renounce atomic war and agree to international control, scientists of all nations will take that pledge seriously and will report any sudden disappearance of a number of nuclear physicists. As our problem is fully comprehended, I think we may hope realistically for a patriotism not to one country but to the human race, and it is that patriotism which would appear should an aggressor, through his warlords, seek to interest a group of nuclear physicists in secretly betraying an international agreement against production of atomic bombs. This, to me, is a very real hope, for I have had the privilege of knowing scientists from many countries. I know we all speak the same language. We will be bound together more strongly than ever with a common fear and a common pledge and a common hope.

Another hopeful fact is that at present the production of these bombs requires large industrial plants. It requires various substances which are comparatively rare and which an inspection force of engineers and scientists could, I think, watch with comparative ease. The sheer size of these plants, with their need for huge supplies and for specialized materials and gadgets, will help world control. I do not believe it is beyond the ingenuity of man to establish an international commission to check these things and guarantee peace of mind to the world. We have done what seemed many times more difficult.

I have been told the question of an inspection force, which seems to have been left "up in the air" by the Truman-Atlee-King communique, was purposely not decided because of technical doubts. I could understand *political* doubts based on fear of the public's reactions against foreigners and strangers, roving through all the countries of the world. But most scientists, I think, believe that the *technical* difficulties of inspection are not insurmountable. I believe we will see much more discussion of technical inspection, and while the scientists discuss it I hope mankind will continue to work towards an acceptance of the political implications.

Now let us think about Russia. If you realize, as scientists do, that Russian science includes some of the best brains in the world today, I think you will understand, first, the Russian leaders must naturally be frightened of the possibilities of this power, and secondly, that it will not be long before they also are masters of it. As to their attitude, let us consider how we would feel if they had this terrible weapon and we had not, if *they* were the ones who had temporarily gotten a lead which *we* knew *we* could overcome.

I can foresee an eventual meeting of the leaders of the great powers in company with their scientists. I know that scientific advisors would reflect the good faith of their leaders. Scientists will have no trouble understanding each other. When they meet I think their recommendations will be almost unanimous. I think further that they could succeed—if they are asked—in conveying this urgent message of fear—and hope.

No country knows the devastation of war better than Russia. None has lost more in men and material. Russians understood this war, and they will understand atomic war. No one who understands atomic war wants anything but peace.

This is indeed The Year Atom Bomb One. It has opened most ominously. We must waste no time if we plan to be alive in A.B. 5 or A.B. 10.

We must support those of our political leaders who realize that a revolution has happened. We must listen carefully to those leaders who give us their best thought on what to do about that revolution. We must deal with those leaders who still think what was good enough in other ages must certainly be good enough for the Atomic Age. As mankind slowly comprehends, our problems will slowly become more simple. But the most fearful factor of all is Time.

Years ago a modern prophet said our civilization is a race between education and catastrophe.

That "race" was once a figure of speech.

Today it is *the fact of facts*.

Now in that race between education and catastrophe, atomic power has given catastrophe a fearful lead. Atomic war could unleash forces of evil so strong no power of good could stop them. Make no mistake. Other civilizations have died because they would not learn their lessons in time. Remember that if Hitler had beaten us to this weapon—as he beat us to the V-2—America today would be a slave province in a fascist World State. Today we are not so much in competition with other countries—humanity is in competition with itself. Think! Because we would not face the obvious, mankind allowed fascism to blast Europe. Now if we still refuse to learn the lesson of co-operation it will be not Europe, but the world, which will lie in ruins.

What we would not learn from Hitler we must learn from Hiroshima!

Other issues wait. Other problems will stand delay. But the main race between man's powers for evil and his powers for good—that race is close to a decision. The bomb is fused. The time is short.

You must think fast. You must think straight.

*Suggestions for Study*

1. Do scientists know of any defense against the atomic bomb?

2. Is it reasonable to expect that atomic bombing may reduce the will-to-resist of a whole people?

3. In what ways would an atomic-bomb attack differ from an attack of the conventional kind?

4. Does the heavy industrial concentration of the United States strengthen or weaken its defense against the atomic bomb?

5. Why is the V-2 rocket ideally suited for carrying an atomic-bomb warhead?

6. Do the bulk of scientists welcome the idea of the control of the bomb and of the scientists at work on it?

7. Do scientists feel confident that international inspection of bomb facilities would prove successful?

8. Who is Dr. Urey? Is his opinion worth heeding on this subject?

9. Examine the argument carefully to separate facts from opinions. Cite several examples of each.

10. What propositions are the authors defending in this article? What do they consider the significant issues in the discussion?

# The Deadliest War [17]

### SIDNEY SHALETT

Suppose that on the morning of December 5, 1958—just two days and three years short of the 20th anniversary of Pearl Harbor—a man named Smith dies in a New York hospital after a short, violent illness, during which he becomes delirious with pneumonia, breaks out with ugly sores, and coughs up blood. In the post-mortem, doctors diagnose his ailment as plague—the "Black Death" of the fourteenth century. They are puzzled, because there hadn't been even an isolated case of plague in the United States for fifteen years.

Suppose, also, that this incident coincides with another apparently unrelated event in a fast-moving international situation: The envoys of the new Axis have just flown home after unsatisfactory meetings with our Secretary of State. Some observers are warning that war may come any moment in the form of a cataclysmic, robot-atomic bomb attack; others are saying this is nonsense, for the United Nations security inspection has functioned so well that no nation is believed to have produced atomic material for war purposes.

Later that day, another man dies of plague in New York, and alarmed doctors all over the city begin reporting cases which they suddenly realize have all the symptoms of "Black Death." Six men die of it the next day, and deaths are reported in Miami, San Francisco, Corpus Christi, and Detroit.

Suddenly the nation seems in the grip of a strange, unbelievable series of epidemics. What Pittsburgh health authorities had thought an ordinary food-poisoning wave is diagnosed as an epidemic of dread and rare botulism. Workers at the $10,000,000,000 underground laboratories and arsenals in the New Mexican desert—the first of the plants which the United States had placed beneath the earth in the national program of conversion for the Atomic Age—begin dropping from cholera, tularemia, psittacosis, and glanders (the last highly puzzling because it usually affects horses, not humans). In the Texas cow country, rinderpest breaks out among the cattle—the first such cases on the North American continent.

If all this should happen—in 1958—it would mean that the third World War had begun. Contrary to prophecies of the military experts, the first blow would have been struck not with the atom bomb but with BW—biological warfare.

17. From *Collier's*, CXVII (June 15, 1946), No. 24. Copyright, 1946, by The Crowell-Collier Publishing Company. Reprinted by permission of the author and The Crowell-Collier Publishing Company.

This is, perhaps, farfetched. But it is possible, on the basis of scientific knowledge, not twelve years hence, but today. What defense is possible?

First, martial law is declared. Federal, state, and county health officers are placed under orders of the Surgeon General of the Department of Common Defense. Armed guards are set up at our water and milk supplies, but in many places it is too late; the saboteurs already have done their work.

Even while the military doctors are busy rounding up the civilian population for dozens of inoculations and issuing the masks and protective clothing that make the wearers look like men from Mars, the enemy planes, balloons, and rockets come, spraying mists of germs over our cities. These are combined, of course, with poison-gas attacks and bombings, for now the enemy is playing for keeps. Our air defenses are functioning and not all the enemy planes get through, but those that do, strafe our coastal installations with bullets that are infected with poison germs. Even the bomb fragments are tainted. If a bullet or a fragment even scratches a man, he is likely to die from disease.

The creeping horror is enhanced by the discovery, on the third day, that vectors—disease-bearing mosquitoes, lice, ticks, rats—have been turned loose in the country by saboteurs.

The enemy doesn't need the atomic bomb. When his troops swarm ashore on both coasts on the seventh day, they find American troops vomiting in the beach defenses, the civilians in the towns too weak to defend their homes. Their beachheads are secured.

The foregoing is an imaginative picture of what might happen to America if there is a third World War. Fortunately, it may remain fiction because in World War II, American scientists, working in the strictest secrecy, learned so much about germ warfare that, if we remain alert, any enemy thinking about attacking us with BW is likely to stop and consider what he would get in return.

BW is a comparatively slow thing which does not destroy the victim immediately. It gives him a chance to strike back if he is ready. And the United States is ready. Just as it has done with poison gas, this country, in order to be able to defend itself against possible BW attack and also to be able to retaliate in kind, has discovered perhaps more than any potential enemy nation about the defensive and, of necessity, the offensive phases of biological warfare. If the United States were attacked with biological agents, it would be able to take steps not only to protect itself, but to strike back with terrible vengeance.

Biological warfare is officially defined as "the employment of bacteria, fungi, viruses, rickettsiae (certain organisms, usually lice- or tick-borne), and toxic agents derived from living organisms to produce death or disease in man, animals, or growing plants." Some authorities, particularly high-placed civilian officials, view germ warfare as a horrible and inhumane thing, which this country should use only in self-defense. Others, including many in the medical field, question the effectiveness of such a weapon and think the United States, if it stays scientifically alert, will be able to detect and control such attacks.

Still another school of thought, of which Major General Alden H. Waitt, Chief of Chemical Warfare Service, is an articulate spokesman, believes that BW can be employed with tremendous effectiveness and that it is unintelligent and inconsistent not to use germs, poison gas, and any other weapons that will hasten the end of a war. They hoot at the theory that germs and poison gas are inhumane while atom bombs, incendiaries, bayonets, and the like aren't.

Most authorities, civilian and military, are in agreement, however, that BW is a very real and significant menace; that it is something which any small "have-not" nation could cook up clandestinely, using university laboratories and even breweries and distilleries as secret factories, and that the United States cannot afford not to stay ahead of the world in this field of research.

Biological warfare experiments, which this country undertook in co-operation with Britain and Canada, were conducted during the war in an atmosphere of great secrecy. There probably were fewer inadvertent "leaks" about germs than about atomic bombs, as it was a smaller project and easier to "button up."

Military and naval authorities never have announced a list of the diseases in which they were dabbling. The Germans and Japanese, who were concocting their own biological agents, have a pretty good idea of what the obvious research channels would be, and any competent scientist can figure out the obvious goals. Lately, the Army has adopted a realistic attitude—one which benefits scientific research—by approving publication in scientific journals of a series of reports by its BW scientists, and these reports name a number of the diseases.

These are some of the identified or obvious diseases, and you can take your pick as to what to expect if germs are ever used against us:

*Botulism.* A form of food poisoning which can be, one authority says, "1,000 times more deadly than phosgene or mustard gas." It is spread by a spore, which breeds in rotten meat, spoiled olives, manure. In 12 to 24 hours after a man absorbs the toxin, paralysis sets in which in 60 to 70 per cent of cases causes death.

*Brucellosis.* Commonly known as undulant or Malta fever. It is transmitted by infected milk and disables man through recurring and protracted waves of severe fever.

*Psittacosis.* The dread "parrot disease" which, when transmitted to humans, causes fever, pneumonia, often fatal.

*Tularemia.* The so-called "rabbit fever," also severely disabling and, in 5 to 10 per cent of natural cases, fatal to man.

*Cholera.* The often lethal disease which hits man abruptly, causing great weakness, profuse diarrhea, cramps and vomiting, and shrinks the victim to the appearance of a mummy.

*Plague.* Man's age-old curse, spread by infected fleas and lice on rats and other rodents. In the fourteenth century it is believed to have killed 25,000,000 persons.

*Encephalitis.* The highly infective virus disease of the nervous system—miscalled "sleeping sickness"—which strikes the brain, causing death or permanent disability.

*Anthrax.* A disease spread by spores so hardy they can withstand boiling for several hours. It usually affects cattle and sheep, with 75 to 100 per cent fatality, but also occurs in man, causing malignant, discolored pustules, pneumonia, or intestinal disorders.

*Glanders.* A rare and often fatal animal disease, usually affecting horses but sometimes occurring in man; extremely hard to control.

*Rinderpest.* A cattle disease capable, if uncontrolled, of wiping out a nation's entire beef supply.

*Foot-and-Mouth Disease.* A cattle disease that has been responsible for destruction of thousands of animals in the United States.

These are only a few of the possibilities. The respiratory diseases—pneumonia, influenza, cerebrospinal meningitis, etc.—and typhoid, tetanus, and staphylococcic food poisoning must be considered, either by themselves or in combination with other infections, which would greatly confuse diagnosis and treatment. For instance, a BW agent designed for offensive use conceivably might combine typhoid, botulism, pneumonia, and three or four other diseases—not a pretty prospect, nor an easy one for doctors to diagnose and counter.

All of the country's leading authorities on the theory of biological warfare emphasize that the United States studied offensive uses of BW purely as a means of better understanding defensive measures. Not all of them, however, agree that it is wise to shun the offensive possibilities.

From these experts, the following picture shapes up:

Infectious disease is "a perfectly natural and common thing." It is the common cause of death, and, in the old days, authorities say, used to kill more men in war than bullets did. Of the infectious diseases, the respiratory group is the worst.

In considering offensive use of disease by artificial means, it is elementary, therefore, that scientists would select the most virulent strains of the most damaging agents, and would attempt to enhance their virulence by what might be called "unnatural mixtures." This can be done. The laboratory men can increase the staying quality of a disease. Typhoid, for instance, which usually is contracted through food or water, can be given both extra staying and spreading quality by dissemination through artificial mist; this way, you don't have to eat or drink the germ—you only have to breathe it. The dread anaerobe which normally spreads botulism through food can be made more deadly if conveyed through an open wound or the lungs; therefore, why not put it on a bullet or spread it by mist?

Scientifically, the problem has been: How to mix agents which ordinarily do not mix, how to enhance their stability, and then how to graduate production of such poisons from the test tube to the 500-gallon tank? Militarily, the offensive problem is: How to spread such agents by mists, bombs, shells, or otherwise, and how to protect your own troops, by inoculation, protective clothing, or otherwise, against "backfire" from your own germs?

Defensively, the medical and military scientists have tackled it from a different standpoint—immunity. Most infectious diseases produce some sort of immunity, but it is a relative thing which generally can be broken down by rare germs or complex mixtures.

A scientist would presume that the enemy, in attacking us biologically, would not choose a simple agent to which most persons are ordinarily resistant.

All BW agents, a leading authority points out, are not necessarily horrible or fatal. They do not all produce agony or quick death. In conducting biological warfare, therefore, a nation theoretically could tailor its tactics to fit its purpose. It could, if it wished, select an agent which would disable a population temporarily, such as dysentery, or the staphylococcic agents which produce the type of poisoning commonly miscalled "ptomaine." In this event, an invading army might find the defending soldiers and civilian population physically too weak to resist but not in danger of dying.

Or the BW strategists could select diseases producing more protracted but nonfatal results. Undulant fever, for which no good vaccine is known to exist, would be a good example.

Finally, if truly vicious and positive results were desired, one could attack with the "killers"—both epidemic and nonepidemic. Cholera, plague, botulism, psittacosis, glanders, anthrax would provide such weapons.

Despite its horrendous new implications, biological warfare is by no means a twentieth-century innovation. Back in Biblical times they were poisoning wells, which is a form of BW. George W. Merck, who served as Director of War Research Service, the first agency created to spur our investigation of the potentialities of germ warfare, points out in his report to former Secretary of War Stimson that there was "incontrovertible evidence that German agents here in 1915 used bacteria cultures—glanders—to infect horses and cattle being shipped to the Allies."

In this war, postoccupational Intelligence reports show definitely that the Japanese were well along in BW research. We constantly were worrying about possible Japanese attempts to cause epidemics in this country by sending over germs in their paper balloons.

In mid-December, 1943, the Office of Strategic Services reported to the Joint Chiefs of Staff that the Germans were believed to be considering attacking the British Isles with rocket-borne BW agents. That report got the Allies into bacteriological research with both feet.

By June, 1944, the War Department was running the whole show. Chemical Warfare Service, with support of the Army Surgeon General's Office, was the kingpin, although Navy and civilian personnel were close partners. Research contracts on twenty-five "problems" were soon in full swing. . . .

Paradoxically enough, as usually is the case when man dabbles in new ways of increasing the horrors of war, civilization already has benefited—and stands to benefit more—from some of the discoveries of BW. In the animal field, a new method of large-scale production of a vaccine that absolutely controls rinderpest—the costly cattle plague—will alone pay for the whole deal. Valuable knowledge also was acquired on control of diseases of fowls.

In the plant field, through learning how to wipe out an enemy's growing food supplies, we discovered some valuable weed killers.

In the human field, we have a highly effective botulinus toxoid, and have advanced our knowledge of cures for anthrax, brucellosis, psittacosis, tularemia, and other diseases. Science will benefit greatly by new knowledge in diagnosis and treatment of these cases, and by advancement of knowledge for large-scale production of biologicals which can be used for good or evil.

As Admiral McIntire says, "Out of all this horror will come good. . . ."

What is the potential strategic importance of BW as an offensive weapon? Some authorities think it limitless. As one pointed out, you can brew concoctions with germs "1,000 times more deadly" than poison gases; you can't see them, smell them, taste them, or detect them, except by cultures, and, by the time you get suspicious and make a culture, half your population might be dead. Even General Waitt, the Chief of Chemical Warfare Service, a zealous advocate of the efficacy of poison gas since the last war, concedes that BW's potentialities are "far greater" than those of the "orthodox" poison gases.

General Waitt has firm opinions on BW. "I believe it to be a practical form of warfare which has great potentialities," he says. "Our nation cannot afford to neglect it.

"It is so futile," he continues, with obvious impatience, "to talk about the horrors of gas and biological warfare, and then condone atomic warfare. It is neither consistent nor intelligent.

"I am entirely out of sympathy with talk about the humanity or inhumanity of a weapon. The thing that really is inhumane is war. Furthermore, if you can outlaw a weapon, you can outlaw war."

Vice-Admiral Ross T. McIntire, Surgeon General of the Navy, agrees with General Waitt on BW's importance, but he is less pessimistic about the possibilities of defense against it. Rear Admiral Harold W. Smith, Chief of the Research Division under Admiral McIntire's Bureau of Medicine & Surgery, feels that BW is such an uncontrollable weapon, offering hazards, to the invader as well as the invaded, that it would be used by an enemy only as "a weapon of desperation."

Also, Admiral Smith points out, an enemy hardly could use it in his own country as a weapon against an invader, because the danger of epidemic to his own population is too great.

The cost of BW research in this war, it is estimated, was under fifty million dollars. BW, compared with the cost of other weapons—the two-billion-dollar atomic bomb, for example—is relatively inexpensive.

That, also, is the great danger of BW in the hands of a poor, have-not nation, which could not afford an atomic bomb project.

## Suggestions for Study

1. Is biological warfare possible today?
2. How would the attack function?
3. The atomic-bomb attack could be primarily a devastating surprise. Will biological warfare act that quickly? Would the two supplement each other?
4. Has our nation experimented extensively in biological warfare?
5. Does this type of warfare seem more deadly than poison-gas attacks?
6. Is this article dominantly expository or argumentative?

## Science and Our Future [18]

### E. U. CONDON

The war's destruction far exceeds that of any catastrophe yet known. The war ended with the application of a new weapon that is a thousand times more frightful than the weapons which produced most of the war's frightfulness. And already we have responsible statements from scientists who effected this development that bombs a thousand times more powerful than those already used are capable of being made in the near future. There are men living who know how to make a single bomb whose destructiveness is equal to a million ten-ton blockbusters. One such bomb, dropped on Washington or any other major city, may be expected to wipe out its population, to destroy its buildings utterly, and to render the site uninhabitable due to poisoning by radioactive materials.

In the face of this situation, people react essentially in one of two ways. One group says: "It's just another weapon. Mankind learned to adapt to the long bow, and the cross bow, and the B-29. We have always had wars." An extreme expression of this kind is found in a speech delivered in Philadelphia last December by Prof. Leslie A. White, of the Anthropology Department of the University of Michigan, who said: "As for the extermination of the human race as a consequence of hurling atomic thunderbolts, this too may be admitted as a possibility, and all we can say is that if it is to come, it will come." This is indeed a rather coldly hopeless, fatalistic expression. Prof. White further says: "Extravagant expressions of horror will not alter the course of events."

There is a certain rhetorical trick here in that, in our language, "extravagant" connotes exaggeratedly inaccurate, and thus emotionally detracts from the serious warnings which responsible physicists are trying to give us. I would agree that expressions of horror *alone* will not alter the course of events. But I insist that if we look at what civilization has suffered in World War II, even before the atom bomb, and couple it with the picture of a war with plentiful use of the old-fashioned "one-hoss shay" atom bombs, and further with the picture of a war with both sides equipped with the really potent 1950 models—then no expression of horror of which our hearts are capable can be exaggerated or extravagant. We need not, and should not, fatalistically await death, reading papers to an academic society meeting in a museum in Philadelphia.

The second kind of people react differently. We say: "This is the end."

18. From *Science*, CIII (April 5, 1946), 415. Reprinted by the permission of the author and *Science*, the journal of the American Association for the Advancement of Science. This is from an address to winners of certain scholarships in science.

Mankind has brought down suffering and death on its head, spiritual values have been destroyed, hatreds have been nourished and developed into great social cancers by war, war fears, and war suspicions and divisions among men.

This has been going on since the beginning of time and will surely destroy us all if we let it continue. This second kind of people say simply that this must stop. We say there is such a thing as progress toward a higher level of development. With all the stumbling and fumbling, we see an upward trend throughout human history. We read the lesson of history to be that men can go forward together, and that men can progress to new freedoms and new areas of social adjustment.

We see that man's growing mastery over the forces of nature also serves to amplify the magnitude of the social crises which confront him. Centuries ago, wars were local affairs; however terrible, they affected only relatively small sectors of civilization. But the last two major wars were world wars in a true sense. Their damage literally affected everyone. We face a situation in which a future world war, employing atom bombs, rockets guided by radio, and many other marvels of man's perverted ingenuity, will achieve a destructiveness thousands of times greater than ever achieved before. The magnitude of the crisis is such that we must soberly think of the choice as being between drifting into a war which will lead to the destruction of civilization, leaving a remnant of stunned, confused, poverty-stricken, frightened men and women amid the ruins, or a wholesome healthy development of a united mankind, using its intelligence cooperatively for the good of all.

I beg of you, cast in your lot with the persons of the second kind—those who believe there is a possibility that men throughout the world can live in freedom and justice, in love and good will, that they can devote their full energies to constructive application of the rational thinking to call science to the arts of peace. In asking you to join with us, I make no promise of certain security. I only promise hope and tell you that the other way leads to certain doom. If we try to establish the brotherhood of man on earth, we may fail, but if we do not even try, we shall surely fail—and what an unbearable load of guilt our consciences will then have to carry! . . .

## Suggestions for Study

1. Delineate two representative reactions of people to the atomic-bomb situation.

2. Summarize Mr. Condon's answer to these people. Is his tone reasonable and in keeping with his factual data, or does he indulge himself in suggestions not in keeping with the facts?

3. State his thesis idea. Is he in general agreement with Dr. Urey?

4. Bear in mind his general statement of an intellectual position as you turn to the following articles which give more specific suggestions on forming a "brotherhood of man on earth."

## Where There Is No Vision—[19]

### STANLEY HIGH

"Our goal," says Secretary of State James F. Byrnes, "is permanent peace."

"Under the Providence of God," says a recent church document, "the people of the earth have been given an opportunity to establish a warless world."

America, says Walter Lippmann, is called to exercise a "mediating, stabilizing influence" and so fulfill its current destiny as "peacemaker among the powers."

I submit that "permanent peace" is *not* our foremost goal; that "a warless world" is *not* the immediate opportunity which the Providence of God has visited upon the people; that to be "peacemaker among the powers" is *not* sufficient destiny for America.

I submit that "peace," as democracy's Cause, is as self-defeating now as it was at Munich; that its postwar pursuit already threatens us with a succession of Munichs; that unless democratic nations discover, declare, and prepare to defend some greater objective the United Nations will go the way of the League of Nations, the evils we fought the war to destroy will be reborn, and our world, like the world of Munich, will face disaster.

"Government," said Alexander Hamilton, "ought to contain an active principle." Peace is neither active nor a principle. Webster defines it as the "state or situation of being free from war." It is not necessarily a good situation. It can be intolerably evil. From the Bill of Particulars in the Declaration of Independence down to the Atlantic Charter, the history of the modern struggle for freedom proves that peace can be even more intolerably evil than war.

Whether peace is good or evil depends entirely upon the kind of principles which produce and maintain it: whether they are good or evil. To put peace before principle is to put the consequence before the cause and to bring both in jeopardy.

Not peace but only a *good* peace is worth aiming for. Not peace but those principles out of which a *good* peace can be fashioned offer a sufficient purpose for the world's free peoples.

19. From the *Reader's Digest*, XLIX (July, 1946), No. 291. Reprinted by permission of the *Reader's Digest* and the author.

We have tried it the other way.

The issue between ourselves and Hitler was not "peace." Hitler wanted peace. He promised his people a thousand years of it. But he wanted a peace produced by the extension and establishment of his evil principles.

The democracies were grist for his mill. They had no comparably passionate beliefs. More, even, than physically, they were morally disarmed.

In our country, professors had taught that property, not freedom, was the motive of the American Revolution; that American democracy, after 150 years, was little better than the sum total of all the things that were wrong with it; that our way of life was hardly worthy of export. Preachers had declared that they would "never bless another war." Church bodies had "renounced the war system" and even resolved for "the resignation of our clergy from the office of chaplain in our Army and Navy."

"Peace" was the democratic Cause; "peacemaker" the role of democratic statesmen; "the consolidation of peace" the aim of democratic policy. Nothing could have been better suited to Axis purposes.

There were at least seven occasions when the democracies, if principles instead of peace had been their foremost aim, could probably have prevented the war. In September, 1931, the Japanese seized Manchuria. That was a moral, far more than a military, challenge. If the democracies had honored their sworn commitment to resist aggression—joined, as they would have been, by Soviet Russia—they would have achieved more than the rescue of China. They would have restored their own souls. They would have learned how to act effectively together to support their principles. They would have posted a momentous warning to all subsequent aggressors that they could be counted on to act that way.

They did not honor their commitment. They bartered it for "peace." It was a costly trade. It hastened the decline of the moral stamina of democracy, and prepared the way for further sacrifice of principle.

On March 16, 1935, Hitler repudiated the disarmament clauses of the Versailles Treaty. On October 3, 1935, Mussolini invaded Ethiopia. On March 7, 1936, Hitler marched into the Rhineland. In July, 1937, the Japanese renewed their aggression against China. On March 12, 1938, the Nazis seized Austria. On September 19, 1938, they sent their ultimatum to Czechoslovakia.

Each of these succeeding crises violated principles which democratic nations were morally bound to defend. They did not defend them. They kept the "peace."

Thereafter, the retreat from conviction to concession became a rout. Three times Neville Chamberlain, the British Prime Minister, flew to

Germany. "If at first you don't concede," ran a cynical rhyme, "fly, fly again." In triumph, he finally brought back from Munich "peace in our time."

Winston Churchill said: "Britain and France had to choose between war and dishonor. They chose dishonor. They will have war."

One watches the present, postwar drama unfold its melancholy scenes with the feeling: "This is where I came in." The setting is different. The characters have changed. The situation is ominously familiar.

On his return from London after the first meeting of the United Nations Security Council, Senator Arthur H. Vandenberg said: "I missed an uplifting and sustained zeal for a great, crusading moral cause."

The Senator's criticism was not leveled at the Russians. Their zeal for what, to them, is "a great, crusading moral cause" threatened the first of the Security Council meetings and almost disrupted the second. This despite the fact that the international Communist organization appears "peace-minded." The loudest crying "peace" press in the world—and the press which is most aggressively embattled against the assertion of democratic principles more important than peace—is, without doubt, the Communist. Pro-Communists who picketed Winston Churchill's recent speeches in New York City carried peace banners strongly reminiscent of the time when the Party line called for a peace-at-any-price with Hitler: "We Want Peace; Churchill Wants War." "No More Blood, Sweat, and Tears."

The issue between democracy and Communism is not peace—but what kind of peace. Communists do not want just any kind of peace. Quite plainly, they want a peace based upon the extension and establishment of their kind of principles. It is their passionate belief that this purpose is more important than peace and its only guarantee.

That belief is their right. If it is also a peril, the responsibility is ours as much as the Communists'. The great words of the Atlantic Charter, like the great words of the League of Nations Covenant, were presumed to be a declaration of principles which, to the democracies, were more important than peace:

"No aggrandizement." "No territorial changes that do not accord with the freely expressed wishes of the peoples concerned." "The right of all peoples to choose the form of government under which they shall live." "To all nations the means of dwelling in safety within their own borders . . . that all men in all lands may live out their lives in freedom from fear and want."

These were principles of a *good* peace. We have not adequately supported them. We have bartered them for "peace." It is proving a costly trade.

The Communists—who put principles first—can hardly be blamed if they exploit the fact that we are, thus, morally disarming; if they strive to keep us "peace-minded"; if they press us to make way for their principles by the sacrifice, for "peace," of our own.

There is no longer much argument among us as to the machinery and procedures necessary for the better world order. We agree that the U.N. is indispensable; that the relations between nations must, increasingly, be regulated not by treaty but by law; that, gradually, absolute national sovereignty must be modified.

Our uncertainty is not mechanical but moral. If the U.N. is weak, that is not because of faulty machinery but because its builders and operators have not decisively determined the moral nature of the product which the machine is expected to create. The modifying of national sovereignty is not likely to take place until it has been decisively determined whose moral values that modification will promote.

There may be little immediate prospect of unanimity among the nations on these moral issues. That fact is less ominous than the likelihood that democratic nations will fail to assert and support their own agreement.

"Throughout Europe," said an American correspondent in a recent broadcast from Paris, "timid democrats are whimpering their fears of Communism. A century and a half ago, democracy was a splendid danger everywhere. Why is it no longer a danger to anyone but itself?"

Why? Because democracy has lost its sense of mission and democrats their missionary zeal. The evangelical, crusading convictions which made democracy "a splendid danger" have gone out of it. Democrats are "timid" and "whimpering" because of their own moral and spiritual uncertainty.

In Philadelphia, on the way to his first inaugural, Lincoln said: "Our great principle is that sentiment in the Declaration of Independence which gave liberty not alone to the people of this country but hope to the world for all future time; which gave promise that the weights would be lifted from the shoulders of all men. I would rather be assassinated on this spot than surrender it."

We are no longer sure that *that* is our faith; or that *that* faith is what we have to offer the world; or that it is still the world's best hope. Because we are not sure, the world is not sure of us and the prospect of a better world is dimmed.

To dispel that uncertainty will not require any new commitments from democratic nations. It will require, first, renewed determination to practice, within their own borders, the principles to which they are already committed. It will require, second, the renewed conviction that the advance of the democratic idea can only be accomplished by persuasion and contagion; that to attempt to advance it by power politics or by direct or indirect coercion is to deny the democratic idea and defeat it.

It is not by much preaching or high pressure that democracy has won its way in the world, but by the force of example. It has offered more, and, better than any competing faith, it has made its offer good.

With the power at their disposal, democratic nations doubtless could "tell the world." Their opportunity is to "show the world." To win their way against today's aggressive competition, they must even more conclusively prove their faith with their works—toward dependent peoples, toward minority and underprivileged groups, and in every situation where, for lifting the standard and quality of human life, democrats profess to have the answer. The validating of democracy, like that of every other missionary faith, begins at home.

Thus, from an increasingly unassailable position, democratic nations can assert their principles for the world and insist upon the free and unhampered opportunity of every people to choose and to live by those principles.

Such assertion and insistence—based upon added proof that these nations proposed to practice what they preach—would not wreck the United Nations' mechanism. It would make that mechanism a moral force. It would probably make it—so deep is the desire for a better world order—an irresistible moral force.

"Oh, for an Isaiah or a St. Paul," said President Truman recently, "to reawaken this sick world to its moral responsibilities."

An Isaiah or a St. Paul may be slow appearing. The world will hardly wait. The world's freedom-loving people need not wait. They can initiate their own revival—knowing that the strength of democracy and its advance depend upon the person-by-person rediscovery of what democracy has to offer and the community-by-community determination to make that offer good.

The American Revolution, wrote John Adams, "was effected before the war commenced. The Revolution was in the minds and hearts of the people."

Concluding his report to the U.S. Senate on the London meeting of the United Nations, Senator Vandenberg said: "You may tell me that I speak of the millennium. I reply in the words of Holy Writ: 'Where there is no vision, the people perish.'"

It is not lack of political or economic or diplomatic implements that makes the future threatening. It is the democratic lack—beginning with the daily practices of freedom-loving peoples—of an implemented Vision.

### Suggestions for Study

1. What definition of peace does the author accept in this discussion? Does he think peace in this sense is our aim?
2. What mistakes did the Allies make in seeking a false peace between 1931 and 1938?
3. What kind of peace does the author think the Russians want? Are they willing to crusade for it?
4. What have we lacked in seeking a good peace? What two things are needed to dispel this uncertainty? How best can democracy spread around the world?
5. State the proposition Mr. High is defending.
6. How does his argument support that of Sir Norman Angell in the discussion of the United Nations' Charter? How does his discussion agree with that of Mr. King-Hall?

## World Government or World Destruction? [20]

### STEPHEN KING-HALL

The dropping of atomic bombs on Hiroshima and Nagasaki was a fearful business, but it may be that never in all the long history of human slaughter have lives been lost to greater purpose. For now it is evident that every human being has a stake in the conduct not only of national affairs but of world affairs.

You are a unit of *humanity,* linked to all your fellow human beings, irrespective of race, creed, or color, by bonds which have been fused unbreakably in the diabolical heat of those explosions. The atomic bomb has made political and economic nationalism meaningless, and so has abolished large-scale national war.

Yet the fact that large-scale national or "total" war is obsolete, along with the nation-state, is still not fully realized. It is said that to every means of offense a defense can be provided. This is still true, but what must be understood is that the defense against the atomic bomb is unlikely to be found in the material sphere. It is no use having better bombs or more of them; it is no use going underground and thinking in terms of the old-fashioned war of 1939–45, which is now as out of date as the Battle of Hastings. The only defense against atomic bombs is the creation

20. From the *National News-Letter* (of England), (August 16, 1945) and the *Reader's Digest,* XLVII (November, 1945), No. 283. Reprinted by permission of the *Reader's Digest* and of the author.

of a world in which no one has the slightest desire to drop atomic bombs on anyone else.

Today, for instance, we Britons know that the U.S.A. possesses atomic bombs and also the planes to carry them over London between sunset and dawn. Yet, we do not go about our business in the shadow of the valley of death. We are hardly conscious of the fact that we are potentially at the absolute mercy of the Americans. Can we honestly say that we should feel quite so comfortable if we heard that General Franco had a bagful of atomic bombs?

Look at it from another angle. It is a fair assumption that at least three great powers, the U.S.A., Great Britain, and Russia, will soon be able to make atomic bombs; they will be joined by France, Sweden, and others. The manufacture of atomic bombs will become easier. What then? It is impossible to imagine that the masses will tolerate a situation in which every time the papers report a ruffle on the waters of international politics people will say, "Suppose they send over 100 atomic bombs tonight!"

No country will ever again dare issue an ultimatum to another with a time limit of even six hours, because the reply in five hours might be a shower of atomic bombs. It is obvious that the national sovereign state, in its political and economic manifestations (as opposed to its very necessary and useful cultural existence) finds itself in a dilemma. The only way out is the creation as rapidly as possible of a world state. There is *no* other way out, except to get out of this world via a series of terrific explosions.

The emergence of a world state as a consequence of natural evolution would probably not have come for another century or two. The League of Nations was a successor of many similar attempts, yet the nations could not bring themselves to bend their proud necks under the relatively light yoke of the Covenant. Twenty-five years later, at San Francisco, an even feebler attempt to rationalize national sovereignty for the good of all men was adopted in an atmosphere of cynicism. All this humbug is blown away in an instant by two bombs and a few young men in a couple of B-29 planes.

Yes or No? Life or Death? Get together or blow yourselves to hell? Those are the brutal questions put by the mighty ultra-microscopic atom released by the brain of man from the natural bonds of its balanced existence.

Consider the problem in greater detail. Of what use now are battleships, aircraft carriers, cruisers, submarines? The tank, the flame-thrower join on the scrap heap the myriads of batteries of guns, great and small. The vast and ponderous apparatus of combined operations, such as were being prepared for the invasion of Japan, are junk. Arguments for and against conscription are meaningless. For the atomic bomb enables its user to strike suddenly and with devastating effect at the whole of the enemy's civil population. Whoever uses it first does not necessarily win the war, because the atomic-bombers of nation A may be on their way to bomb nation B while their own homeland is being turned into a crematorium.

The statesmen of the Great Powers now find themselves obliged to grapple with the postwar problems of Europe, the Middle East, and the Far East at a moment when the atomic bomb has blown the normal standards of power politics to smithereens.

If we attempt to grapple with these tremendous matters with the thought that they are only more complex reproductions of problems which have plagued us since 1914, we shall fail. If we are so mistaken as to imagine that we can overcome the world's troubles inside the framework of and with the tools provided by the United Nations' Charter, Bretton Woods, and the Foreign Secretaries' Conference in London, we shall deceive ourselves. I say this for two reasons:

First, because our present-day problems are *not* reproductions of old ones. They are in principle a new kind of problem. They are not merely national problems with world implications. They are indisputably *world problems* and *humanity problems.*

Secondly, because the organizations and instruments mentioned above are based on the assumption that *national sovereign rights* are the foundations on which we must build. These organizations are like monkeys hanging head down from their national tails. We must have organizations which are like men sitting on their tails with their heads together.

If we are to solve these problems we must not be afraid to admit that world government is no longer merely a vision held by a few idealists. *World government has now become a hard-boiled, practical, and urgent necessity.*

If it is to be created quickly enough to avoid disaster, men in government must be bold in action. It is not enough, now, to have consultations at irregular intervals. The heads of states—using the machinery of the United Nations Security Council if nothing better is available—must meet regularly and become in effect a world executive committee. "Security" has almost overnight assumed a far more comprehensive meaning than was attached to it when the Council was established at San Francisco. This World Council must issue decisions and see that they are carried out.

We need not despair of human ability being capable of extracting a real peace and a new world from these seething difficulties. The mere fact that, through the workings of men's minds, events have occurred which have brought the world face to face with the greatest crisis in its history also shows that we are capable of thinking out the answer and taking appropriate action. It can be done. It must be done.

*Suggestions for Study*

1. Why does the author declare that the atomic bomb has made political and economic nationalism meaningless?

2. What is the only possible defense against the atomic bomb?

3. Is the United Nations' Charter sufficient in itself to solve the situation? Why?

4. What proposition does Mr. King-Hall argue for here? Is his proposal opposed to, in accord with, or an extension of Dr. Urey's thesis in "I'm a Frightened Man"?

## U.N. or World State? [21]

### U.N.—We Have It. Now Let's Use It!

#### SIR NORMAN ANGELL

Let us be clear as to what it is we want. We do not want merely "peace." We could have had "peace" by sheer submission to Hitler or a Japanese conqueror who, as long as we humbly obeyed all the commands of our alien masters, would doubtless have left us alone. They would also have given us a world government if we had been willing to accept a totalitarian police State. But we rejected both peace and world government on those terms. We want those things to be compatible with the political freedoms for which we thought we were fighting in two world wars. We want, not alone peace, but security for the right to live our own way of life in our own land, free of foreign subjugation.

The United Nations proposes to achieve this by applying the principle of collective defense to its members. Aggression against any member of the Organization shall be resisted by the power of the whole, so that a member shall not be helpless to defend his rights against the violence of a stronger neighbor. This is the first job of any society, national or international. It is no good endowing a man with rights and freedoms if the first gangster that comes along can bump him off with impunity. So, in the words of the Charter, the Organization undertakes to defend its members by "such action by sea, air, or land forces as may be necessary."

21. From the *Rotarian*, LXVIII (June, 1946), p. 12. Reprinted by permission of the *Rotarian* and of the authors.

This is an attempt, in the light of the experience of two world wars, to make collective power a means of deterring aggression, preventing war, not merely a means by which we win wars after we have drifted into them.

At the close of the First World War Lloyd George, when asked how it could have been prevented, remarked that if Germany had known before she started upon her policy of aggression that she would have to meet the whole power of the United States, the British Empire and Commonwealth, as well as that of France and Russia, she would never have followed that policy, and there would have been no war. It was doubtless in part this truth which prompted Clemenceau, when he asked for an Anglo-American guaranty of French security after World War I. He warned both Wilson and Lloyd George in these terms: "If you now, in 1919, tell Germany that you will defend France in the future, you won't have to do it, because Germany won't attack. But if you don't say this, and if your action is in doubt, you will have to do it finally because Germany will gamble on your neutrality." Germany did gamble on that neutrality, and both Britain and the United States did have to fight, proving Clemenceau a true prophet.

It is true that the Great Powers can veto any action against themselves. Any constitution will break down if the chief parties to it decide to challenge it. But despite the veto the Iran issue has proved that the U. N. can be used to check the drift to aggression by even the greatest power. Russia, the greatest military power in the world, attempted to ride roughshod over one of the weakest, and yet was checked despite the fact that the giant "walked out." Even though the same crisis may reappear—as it probably will—in other forms, the action of the Security Council and its voting constituted *a warning to a possible aggressor how power would shape up against him if he continued aggressive policies.*

There have always been those who argue that the whole principle of collective security is wrong; that it won't work, because, runs the argument, you cannot enforce law against a State, coerce a whole people. The enforcement of law, say these critics, is only possible against individuals; and very commonly the example of the American Constitution and the arguments of the Federalists are cited to condemn any attempt to coerce a State. Federal law is only enforceable against individuals, and Federal authority must operate within the confines of the States, members of the Federation.

There is a confusion here. Our first job is not the enforcement of laws in the ordinary sense: it is defense of nations against aggression, war. That we believe it possible to deter aggression against us by our power, to prevent attack by being strong, is proved by the fact that every nation takes precisely that measure to defend itself. A nation's army is not a means of coercing another nation, it is a means of making it impossible for that other to coerce us; not a means of imposing our laws upon him, but of making it impossible for him to impose his laws upon us. And the argument behind the U. N. is that that defense will be most effective if it is collective, defense by many nations combined against the attacker.

The principle of collective security, as distinct from the creation of a superstate, is not new in American foreign policy. Under the Monroe Doctrine the United States in effect said: "An attack on any American republic is an attack on us." It was a purely defensive measure. By helping others to defend themselves, the United States promoted its own security. The principle worked. Later the plan developed into something more mutual and reciprocal: the Pan American Union as we now know it. But the point is that if Monroe, instead of proceeding along this line, had attempted to create a federal government or superstate for the whole hemisphere, including turbulent and unstable countries that had not yet acquired their sea legs in the difficult navigation of democracy, the thing would probably either have proved a complete failure or have ended in a Washington dictatorship as the only alternative to chaos.

Just as the collective principle has been successfully applied to the Western Hemisphere without the creation of a superstate, so has it been applied to the nations of the British Commonwealth. In two world wars Canada, Australia, New Zealand, and South Africa have joined with Britain in resisting aggression. Yet the Dominions have always opposed the creation of a superstate in London, even in the form of Imperial Federation. There is still no government of the Commonwealth. There is a government of Canada (which happens to be a Federation) and of Australia (which happens to be another), and so with the other Dominions. But there is no government of the Commonwealth as a whole, and it is more than likely that if Britain had insisted upon the creation of a federal government in London, the Dominions would have gone out of the Commonwealth—which they are entitled to do under the statute now governing their relationship with each other.

Now, it may well be that mankind will at long last come to a federal form of world government, in which the sovereignty and independence of each nation will be merged into the supreme sovereignty of the world authority. But the question is not where world government will end, but where it will begin. If we were dealing with a world inhabited by people of broadly similar outlook, with the same scale of moral values, accustomed pretty much to the same broad principles of law and morality, experience in free government, a federal government for mankind could, perhaps, be established and be made to work.

The difficulty in peacemaking never has been to find the ideal plan; the difficulty has been to secure agreement to it by a vast variety of people and many nations of fundamentally different outlook. The trouble with far-reaching schemes of federal government for the whole world at this moment is that they run the risk of making the best the enemy of the better. By insisting upon a very far-reaching and "entangling" form of world government we run the risk of its final rejection. (Recall how very near we came at San Francisco to getting rejection even of the relatively noncommittal Charter.) And if that happened, we should be further from our goal than ever. The fact that in the early stages of the discussion of any plan there is considerable support for it, is by no means conclusive.

The American people, after being for some time quite favorable to the idea of a League of Nations, on second thought rejected it utterly. If it had merely been a matter of the 1920 election, it would be possible to argue that they were just confused and would have been willing to participate in the League if their minds had not been turned to domestic issues. But the rejection of Wilson was followed by nearly two decades of the intensest kind of isolationism, resulting in the Johnson Act and the Neutrality Act. These decisions, remember, were taken by the most educated, the most civilized, the most peace-loving people in the world. We should have to secure assent to world government by many nations, far less educated, with far less political experience. A federal form of world government would have been immensely more entangling than the League or the U. N.

Does anyone suggest that a people which had rejected Wilson's League as too much of a good thing would have accepted a form of world authority in which Japan (then a member of the Grand Alliance), China, the States of Latin America, India, would have had a preponderant influence? Whatever we may say about the story of America's rejection of Wilson, we can at least say that the rejection would have been still more emphatic if he had proposed, instead of a world league in which America still remained master in her own house, a world government having authority to act on American soil.

Let us keep in mind the immense difficulties of acceptance encountered not merely by Wilson a quarter of a century ago, but also at San Francisco as late as last year.

I suggest that the course of wisdom is not, having planted the U. N. after much pain and travail, to tear it all up and try to plant something else, but to see whether we can start it growing in the direction which we want—the direction, it may well be, of a true world government, with functions and powers we might refuse before we see the institution at work, but agree to when successful working had given us confidence.

This growth has in fact already begun, if only we would encourage it. Any competent handling of the atomic bomb will involve giving to an international commission under the aegis of the United Nations powers of inspection, control over individuals. That is the thin end of the federal wedge, and we should drive it home where opportunity presented.

We may, by such a process of developing the United Nations, find we have in fact a world government which we could never have created if we had at the beginning collided head on with the fears, hesitations, and prejudices of nationalism, isolationism, and traditional ways of thought.

## World State—Anything Less Will Fail

### OWEN J. ROBERTS

In the United Nations (U. N.) Charter is a provision which dooms it to failure. Article 2 states: "The Organization is based on the principle of the sovereign equality of all its members."

That means—and was intended to mean—that no member nation or all the other member nations can, of right, limit or control the action of a single member, though that action be plainly contrary to the purpose of the Charter.

Despite the high-sounding phrases of the Charter, no nation signing it gives up one whit of its national independence. Each can continue to do as it pleases, and, as of old, the only way for other nations to prevent its action is by war.

But, you might say, is not the United States—to take my own country—bound to follow the principles laid down in the Charter? Must it not comply with other nations' demands made pursuant to the Charter? The answer is "No."

The U. S. Senate ratified the Charter as a treaty. Under our Constitution a later treaty—or indeed a mere law passed by Congress—may nullify the treaty and break its binding force on this country. The same applies to other nations. We had the Kellogg-Briand treaty by which nations pledged themselves never to resort to war to settle disputes. Did it save us from a war with Germany, with Japan, or with Italy?

Remember, further, that every nation a member of the U. N. remains free to make treaties with any of the other members. For example, the United States can make a trade treaty with Latin-American countries shutting out every nation of Europe from dealing with Latin America or with us. What would Europe do? Latin America is a natural market of Europe. She is close in space, her trade routes are shorter, and her whole tradition is European. Europe would fight, of course, and the U. N.'s Charter could do nothing about it.

If some of the member nations of the Security Council thought our treaty created a threat of war, the Council could take action to make us behave, if we, the United States, consented, but not otherwise. This is because any one of the Big Five can veto any action proposed against it. Suppose we do veto? What is the alternative? A war against us by the aggrieved nations or submission to our will.

Such things can happen under the Charter. They are happening now. Russia has made a treaty by which she is walling off Rumania and Bulgaria from the rest of the world. England wants to wall off Greece. Can this result in anything but war—or supine submission to the more powerful nations by those less strong?

As an instrument to prevent international dissensions, to curb national greed, to remove the causes of war, the Charter is a mere rope of sand!

No international organization can effectively control conduct between nations until it has the two requisites of any government: the power to make law and the power to enforce it. The United Nations Charter creates a General Assembly in which each nation has one vote. But it can pass no law affecting the action of any nation; it cannot even make a recommendation to the Security Council about a threat unless the Council requests it.

Nor does the United Nations have real police power. There is no international police force, and there never will be—unless each nation sends troops to put down an aggressor. The U. N. will have only such troops as each nation will provide. In America the Congress will decide whether American boys will be sent to suppress aggression by Rumania or Bulgaria or some other nation.

If the United Nations won't work, what will?

History teaches that there are only two ways of securing peace. One is by conquest. This is the Hitler way. Had he accomplished his purpose we should have had an orderly and peaceful world. Germany would have imposed her rule on men unable to resist. That peace would have endured until some group became strong enough successfully to rebel. But for you and me it would have been a peace of slavery.

The other way, the only sure way to secure enduring peace, is by the institution of government—government by consent and agreement of individual men—not agreement of nations.

Internal peace has always resulted from the reign of law; and law means a rule of conduct made by the representatives of the citizens, the legislature, and enforced by their other representatives, the courts and police.

A system of law may be purely local, it may be State-wide to embrace the common concerns of a larger group, or it may be national to cover the still broader common interests of the people of all the States composing the nation. These Governments have developed from the local plane to higher planes as necessity has arisen to deal with common interests of broader groups.

What is needed now is extension of this development to the next higher plane—the international level. Creation of such a higher instrument of government involves the surrender of nothing by the citizen of Sussex, the Ukraine, or Fukien, any more than the citizen of Virginia surrendered anything when that State became one of the United States. Rather, American, Englishman, Russian, and Chinese will have created something new from which each will derive vast benefits—as the Virginian did when the United States was created.

The foreign relations of all the people of all the States, the armies for their common defense, the commerce between them and with other nations, were all provided for and regulated out of a common treasury by a Government that represents every citizen of every State in the Union. And domestic affairs peculiarly of local concern were left to be dealt with by the States without interference by the Federal Government. Instead of surrendering power, citizens granted appropriate powers to their own creature, the Federal union. That Government operated only in those fields in which they authorized it to act—all other powers remained in their States, counties, cities, and townships.

Now, what would the citizens of the various countries of the world gain by a world government? Like the citizen of an American State, they would gain an agency to represent them on matters of common interest. To illustrate: Is the United States competent to regulate the conduct of a Chinese? Of course not! But the American and the Chinese have certain common interests and problems in this world, however diverse may be their domestic habits and institutions. The only known means of resolving these problems peacefully is a system of laws made by a common agency representing both Americans and Chinese. Only such laws can ameliorate and arbitrate conflicting interests, and only the government which makes those laws should possess the armed forces needed to enforce them. Such enforcement would not be war but law enforcement, for the laws would not be addressed to the nations, but to individuals owing allegiance and obedience to the higher government as well as, in local affairs, to their own nations.

In international government the United Nations is where national government in America was under the Articles of Confederation. After declaring their independence from Great Britain, the colonies drew up these Articles, which were nothing but a treaty between independent States. They failed miserably because each delegate spoke for his State—not for his people. All the jealousies and clashes of interest between these independent States emerged in Congress, but Congress had no power to legislate for or against the people of those States; it had to deal with the sovereign States. When these sovereignties did not like an act of Congress, they did not comply with it. So the Articles were torn up and a real Federal union of the people was created.

Today the postwar agitation for peace is spurred by a nervous feeling over the atomic bomb. There are those in the United States who contend it is unthinkable even to permit anyone else to know the secret of it. You hear talk in the streets: "Shall we let Russia know about it?" "Shall we let England know the whole story, or shall we hide it ourselves for public defense?"

Under a world government, production methods of even so monstrous a thing as the atomic bomb would not need to be a secret. Let's look again at a parallel in the State-nation relationship in my country. What has the United States done about morphine—which in some ways is just as bad as the atomic bomb? What has the United States done about firearms in interstate commerce? If the people of Massachusetts have developed and manufactured such things, is it all right for them but not Pennsylvania to have them? No. We have passed a Federal law to regulate the manufacture and sale of such products. We haven't gone to war with Tennessee because some of its residents make moonshine or with other States because opium is sold within their borders. No. We have sought out and prosecuted the moonshiners and the opium peddlers.

Every citizen of New York, Pennsylvania, or Tennessee has a right to know about the atomic bomb. So has every citizen of Sussex, the Ukraine, or Fukien. But there should be government of those citizens to regulate the bomb under law upon moral principles, because otherwise nothing will save us from destruction by it.

Science, with its awesome bomb, is miles ahead of our progress in government. Are we so devoid of imagination, so incapable of invention, so destitute of resources, that we cannot build an equally powerful force for peace—a federation of man?

There is only one answer to this question. If we want the best in our time, if we want to endow our sons and grandsons with a durable peace in which to pursue their destinies, then we must lift the torch to a union that will have a single foreign policy, one secretary of state, free exchange, a universal currency—a union which will have one army, one navy, one air force, one atomic bomb.

## Suggestions for Study

*Concerning the argument in favor of continuing the United Nations:*

1. Define the term *peace* as used in this article.
2. In what way does the United Nations propose to achieve peace?
3. Does Mr. Angell believe that the threat of collective power will deter any nation envisioning aggressive war?
4. Cite one reason for German aggression that produced the first World War.
5. Does Mr. Angell conceive the United Nations' immediate task as one of law enforcement in the usual sense? Explain his concept.
6. Is he opposed to a world government?
7. Why does he think a world government is not feasible at the moment?
8. State the proposition which he is defending.
9. List the significant issues involved in his presentation.
10. Define the following words from his argument: alien, compatible, impunity, coerce, reciprocal, statute, alien, noncommittal, travail, aegis.

*Concerning the argument in favor of a world state:*

1. Need the United States comply with the demands of other nations made pursuant to the United Nations' Charter?
2. In Mr. Roberts's estimation, is that a weakness in the Charter? If so, in your estimation is that weakness so serious as to nullify Mr. Angell's conception of the aim of the United Nations?
3. What two controls must any government have? Does the United Nations have these controls?
4. Name the two methods of securing peace. Can a government exist by the consent and agreement of nations or only of individuals?
5. Would the citizens of the world surrender anything of value in joining a world state? What would they gain?
6. Could the production plans of the atomic bomb be safely entrusted to all the world under a world government plan?
7. State Mr. Roberts's proposition and significant issues.
8. Consult reference works in the library for information concerning the qualifications of the two authors to write upon this subject.
9. Make a decision on the relative merits of each argument. Weigh Mr. Angell's defense of the United Nations with Mr. Roberts's attack on it, and then the doubts of Mr. Angell on the immediate feasibility of a world state with the plea for it made by Mr. Roberts.
10. Construct an argument of your own on this same subject, using not

just the ideas presented in these two articles but also the results of your other reading and thought on this subject.

## Suggestions for Writing

1. Write a composition presenting an inductive argument suggested by one of the following statements or sets of statistics:

(a) Recent figures on education in the United States were:

    1. College graduates: 2,380,000
       Those with some college work: 4,600,000
       Per cent of population: 9
    2. High-school graduates: 6,400,000
       Per cent of population: 8
    3. Those with some high school training: 15,130,000
       Those with grammar-school training or less: 49,590,000
       Per cent of population: 78
    4. Illiterate: 4,100,000
       Per cent of population: 5

(b) A governmental bureau published a survey revealing the mental age of the average radio listener as fourteen years.

(c) In the same general period of years, the employees of a street railway company prepared a report that the minimum wage on which they could live decently was $1900 a year; but the average wage for clergymen was $735 a year, for country schoolteachers in the Middle Atlantic states was $870 a year, for village teachers was $1244 a year, for instructors, assistant professors, associate professors, and full professors on university faculties was $2958, for railway freight conductors was $3570 and for railway freight engineers was $4700.

(d) In 1929, the United States was paying 11 pensions as a result of the War of 1812, 849 as a result of the war with Mexico, 272,906 as a result of the Civil War. The total payments for pensions resulting from the Revolutionary War was $70,000,000; for the War of 1812 was $46,198,000; for the Mexican War was $59,073,000; for the Civil War was $7,244,677,000. To 1929, the cost of the World War I to the United States was $37,573,960.

(e) In 1910, 45.8 per cent of the total population was urban (that is, was found in urban centers with 2,500 population and higher) and 54.2 per cent was rural; in 1930, 56.2 per cent was urban, and 43.8 per cent was rural.

(f) The number of horses, colts, and mules on farms decreased from 26,500,000 in 1915 to 15,182,000 in 1939; the period from 1930 to 1940 showed an increase of 746,000 tractors. In 1935 the WPA estimated that the tractor, motortruck, and automobile saved the labor in agriculture of 345,000 persons for one year.

(g) In 1939 automobile registration dropped slightly to 29,425,000 vehicles, but gasoline consumption increased 4.8 per cent to 20,600,000,000 gallons. Deaths as a result of automobile accidents increased to 31,500 for the year.

(h) Industrial output for 1939 was 23 per cent higher than that of 1938. Unemployment was reduced by an estimated 1,000,000, but another 8,000,000 were left unemployed; factory employment increased by 8 per cent, and factory wages by approximately 16 per cent. Labor strikes and disputes in 1939 lost nearly 18,000,000 man days of labor, a sum about twice the loss in 1938.

2. Write a composition based on deductive principles; choose any aspect of one of the following subjects:

The persuasion of a high-school student to attend your college.

The improvement of one of your college courses.

The statement by Dr. Compton in favor of governmental support of research work: "There is a peculiarity of pure research, inherent in its nature, which gives a logical basis for this conclusion."

The addition of a new course to the curriculum.

The appropriation of funds to build a municipal golf course.

The adoption of daylight saving time in your home town.

The adoption or abolition of parking meters in the city.

The selection of movies shown in the local theater.

The rigorous enforcement of the state speed limit.

The establishment of a new factory in your home town.

Night baseball games.

Changes in requirements for graduation.

Reduction in prices of athletic contests.

The machine as an aid or detriment to industrial employment.

Changes in tuition for resident and out-of-state students.

A centralized school in your rural district.

Teachers' salaries in rural schools.

Industrial strikes.

Socialized medicine.

The study of foreign language.

3. After reading the various articles on the atomic bomb and the postwar organization of world government, read the latest articles on the same subjects in current periodicals to bring yourself up to date on these problems. (Since these matters form the basis of much international thinking, and since statesmen are busy trying to settle such problems, it is probable that new issues will be uppermost by the time you make this study.) After you have completed your reading, write an argument on some matter connected with this subject. The intervening time may enable you to argue better whether Sir Norman Angell or ex-Justice Roberts is more correct, for instance, or whether the views of scientists on the atomic bomb are justified in the light of subsequent events.

## C. Description

The purpose of description is to reproduce for the reader a clear, vivid impression of a scene, a person, a sensation, an emotion, or other image which exists in the writer's own consciousness. Obviously, no one can transmit a clear, vivid impression of something which is blurred or distorted in his own mind. The first requisite of good description, therefore, is to perceive clearly and accurately what one wishes to describe. The second is to find words that will reproduce the image as faithfully as language can do it. The third is to utilize certain techniques which insure logical development. These are consistency of point of view, transmission of the dominant impression, and the choice and arrangement of details.

**Accurate Observation.** Ability to observe accurately, to take in details readily, to catalogue impressions correctly and quickly comes of attention and practice. Because most people are content with general or hazy impressions, their senses grow dull through disuse. Yet the senses respond amazingly to demands upon them. The cotton buyer merely by feeling a sample of cotton can tell the length of the staple. The cattle judge can tell at a glance the weight of a steer. The good conductor can detect a sour note amid the sounds of a hundred-piece orchestra. Long and continual practice, however, is necessary to reach such adeptness. Back of the vivid images in the work of great writers is long effort. The comment of de Maupassant [22] is pertinent in this connection, as he relates what he learned as a novice from his master Flaubert:

> Talent is long patience. It is a question of looking long enough and with enough attention at everything you want to express to discover a facet of it that no one else has seen and expressed. There is in everything something of the unexplored, because we are accustomed to using eyes only in the light of what has been expressed before about whatever we observe. The least thing contains a bit of the unknown. Let us find it. To describe a flaming fire and a tree on a plain, let's stand looking at this fire and this tree until, so far as we are concerned, they no longer resemble any other tree or any other fire.
> That is the way you become original.
> Besides, having stated this truth, that in the whole world there are not two grains of sand, two flies, two hands, or two noses exactly alike, he [Flaubert] used to make me express in a few sentences a being or an object in such a way as clearly to individualize it, to make it distinct from all other objects of the same race or the same species.
> "When you pass by a grocer seated in his doorway," he used to tell me, "before a janitor smoking his pipe, before a cab-parking station, show me that grocer and that janitor, their posture, their whole physical appearance, containing also, indicated by the skill of the depiction, their whole moral nature, so that I cannot confuse them with any other janitor; and with a single word make me see how a cab horse is different from the fifty others who follow or precede him."
> ... Whatever you wish to say, there is only one word to express it, one verb to animate it, one adjective to qualify it. So you must keep looking for this word, this verb, this adjective until you have found them, and never be satisfied with an approximation.

De Maupassant states the goal: to isolate and animate an object in such a way as to distinguish it from all others. Ability to do this comes only of

22. In the introduction to his *Pierre et Jean*. The whole of this introduction is worth close study.

practice. From what de Maupassant says, it is clear that his own skill at depiction was an acquisition, not an endowment. Inability of the novice to equal the skill of a great writer in making a scene or sensation come to life is no cause for discouragement. The remedy is to start practicing, it doesn't matter at what. Begin with buildings and landscapes, with dogs or faces or flowers, with postures or tones. Note exact shades of color, precise shapes and contours, arrangement of objects in a room. In all this, effort and persistency are the virtues to cultivate; the results will accrue.

**Choice of Words.** Selecting the exact word to convey an idea is important to good writing of any sort; it is a necessity in writing good description. A painter with a few strokes of his brush can suggest the appearance of a skyscraper, or he can mix his paints to reproduce the precise shade of color in a dress or landscape. An orchestra performing Beethoven's *Sixth Symphony* can give a remarkable approximation of the rolling of thunder and the pouring of rain. What the painter or musician does by means of brush or instrument, the writer must accomplish with words. Since the best he can do will not reproduce an image with absolute fidelity, he must use the utmost care in selecting words that give exact impressions if he expects a reader to have even a fair approximation of what is in his own mind. One of the best means of reproducing an image faithfully is to use specific and concrete words rather than general or abstract ones.

*Run* is a general word; *dash, scramble, scurry, jog* are specific words. "Hearing the siren, Bill ran to the window" gives a more vivid picture than "went to the window" would give, but "Bill dashed to the window" gives a still more accurate picture of the action. "Frightened by the stranger, the little dog scrambled under the steps" evokes a more vivid picture of the dog's way of going than would "ran under the steps." "He was dressed in a slovenly fashion" is too general a statement to give a vivid, clear image of the man; but "His grease-spotted suit was baggy at the knees and elbows, and his collar and cuffs were gray with sweat stains and grime" projects a picture that is sharp and accurate and therefore forceful. Specific and concrete words force the reader to see, hear, smell, taste, touch, and because the senses are the most powerful stimulators of the imagination, the reader's natural indolence is overcome, and he becomes interested enough to participate in making the picture come to life.

Another gain in using specific and concrete words is that they are more suggestive than general and abstract terms. They connote as well as denote. *Scramble,* for instance, connotes a lack of dignity, an overtone of meaning which adds much to the image of the frightened dog. *Grease-spotted* and *sweat stains* mean not only carelessness in dress (slovenliness), but also physical repulsiveness. Attention to these overtones of connotation enables the writer of description to say a great deal with a few words. It imparts to a passage a richness of familiar experience. Notice the connotative power of the concrete terminology in the following selection from Thomas Wolfe's *Look Homeward, Angel*. The author does little other than give the names of things; yet the senses, particularly the sense of smell, are excited in an extraordinary way.

He remembered yet the East India House at the Fair, the sandalwood, the turbans, and the robes, the cool interior and the smell of India tea; and he had felt now the nostalgic thrill of dew-wet mornings in Spring, the cherry scent, the cool clarion earth, the wet loaminess of the garden, the pungent breakfast smells, and the floating snow of blossoms. He knew the inchoate sharp excitement of hot dandelions in young Spring grass at noon; the smell of cellars, cobwebs, and built-on secret earth; in July, of watermelons bedded in sweet hay, inside a farmer's covered wagon; of canteloupe and crated peaches; and the scent of orange-rind, bitter-sweet, before a fire of coals. He knew the good male smell of his father's sitting-room; of the smooth worn leather sofa, with the gaping horsehair rent; of the blistered varnished wood upon the hearth; of the heated calf-skin bindings; of the flat moist plug of apple tobacco, stuck with a red flag; of wood smoke and burnt leaves in October; of the brown tired autumn earth; of honeysuckle at night; of warm nasturtiums; of a clean ruddy farmer who comes weekly with printed butter, eggs, and milk; of fat limp underdone bacon and of coffee; of a bakery oven in the wind; of large deep-hued stringbeans smoking hot and seasoned well with salt and butter; of a room of old pine boards in which books and carpets have been stored, long-closed; of Concord grapes in their long white baskets.

Yes, and the exciting smell of chalk and varnished desks; the smell of heavy bread sandwiches of cold fried meat and butter; the smell of new leather in a saddler's shop, or of a warm leather chair; of honey and of unground coffee; of barreled sweet-pickles and cheese and all the fragrant compost of the grocer's; the smell of stored apples in the cellar, and of orchard-apple smells, of pressed-cider pulp; of pears ripening on a sunny shelf, and of ripe cherries stewing with sugar on hot stoves before preserving; the smell of whittled wood, of all young lumber, of sawdust and shavings; of peaches stuck with cloves and pickled in brandy; of pine sap, and green pine needles; of a horse's pared hoof; of chestnuts roasting, of bowls of nuts and raisins; of hot cracklin, and of young roast pork; of butter and cinnamon melting on hot candied yams.

Yes, and of the rank slow river, and of tomatoes rotten on the vine; the smell of rain-wet plums and boiling quinces; of rotten lily-pads; and of foul weeds rotting in green marsh scum; and the exquisite smell of the South, clean but funky, like a big woman; of soaking trees and the earth after heavy rain.[23]

23. From *Look Homeward, Angel*, by Thomas Wolfe (copyright, 1929, by Charles Scribner's Sons). Reprinted by permission of Charles Scribner's Sons, the publishers.

In addition to choosing specific and concrete words, a young writer should learn to use modifying words with discretion and to be chary in the use of figures of speech. Many students, when attempting to write effective description, are conscious only of the power of modifying words, adjectives and adverbs, and consequently overburden their style with them. A good rule to follow is never to use a combination of noun and adjective when a more specific noun can be found which will do the work of both. The same rule applies to verbs and adverbs. Superfluous modifiers, even when used with the best of intentions, weaken one's style.

Figures of speech are among the most useful instruments for the writer of description, but they, also, should be used with discretion. Overornamentation of style is like the wearing of an excessive amount of jewelry. Too many similes, especially, are a mark of awkward elaboration. If figurative language is desired, try to use more metaphors than similes. "The ruby burned on the jet black dress" is stronger than "The ruby looked like a coal of fire on the jet black dress." Figures of speech which are too obviously attempts at ornamentation rather than instruments for the clarifying of meaning give a writer's style an amateurish effect. Figurative language is good if it adds clearness, if it brings concrete experience to a meaning which would otherwise be abstract, but if it confuses, or repeats unnecessarily a perfectly clear meaning, it is an encumbrance which should be omitted.

**Point of View.** The arrangement of details is as important in a written description as composition in a painting. Since the writer cannot hope that his description will be read and assimilated in a glance, his first problem is to direct the perception of the reader by means of an organization of details in such a way that images will be stimulated in an orderly fashion. A chaotic scrambling of images will defeat his purpose. Accordingly, he assumes a point of view with regard to his material.

The physical point of view will determine the order in which images will be presented and the scale in which they will be drawn. The painter, wishing to determine where he will set up his easel in order to get the best view of a landscape, shifts his position and travels up and down the countryside. When he has finally settled himself and started his picture, he will not paint one portion of the landscape from one point of view and another portion from another. This would bring about meaningless distortion. The perspective, in which objects appear smaller or larger depending on their distance from the observer, would become hopelessly confused. Similarly, the writer of description establishes himself and his reader in a certain physical relation to the scene and presents the details as they would appear to the reader if the scene were actually before him. The position which is taken is explained in the opening sentence, if possible, and is not changed unless the reader is clearly warned of what is happening. The writer will not give a pilot's-eye view of a wheat field, and then shift without notice to the scene as it appears to a farmer riding a combine harvester.

If the writer observes the normal processes of perception, he will notice that the eye transmits to the brain certain parts of a scene before others. Large masses are perceived before small, bright colors before dull, distinct differences of light and shade before subtle. If the scene is extensive, a dominant central figure or mass is perceived before subordinate details. To take in a panorama, the eye may travel from right to left, left to right, or up and down. The written description, therefore, should be organized carefully so that the images will be created in a normal sequence. A farmhouse and barn sitting in the middle of a bleak prairie should certainly receive attention before the rooster strutting in the barnlot. The general characteristics of a milling horde of Christmas shoppers should be presented before the reader is asked to single out Mary Smith, who is buying a necktie from a tired-eyed clerk. It is also important that the principle of perspective be kept in mind. If a lumberjack clearing the top from a redwood tree is being described from the point of view of a person on the ground, it would be ridiculous to mention that the hands of his wristwatch point to a quarter to twelve.

A shifting point of view is permissible if the reader is kept informed as to the movements which are being made. A description of the Palisades of the Hudson as seen from the deck of a river steamer would necessitate the reader's knowledge that the boat is moving at a certain speed. Changes of time, also, should be indicated clearly, as when a body of water is described first at sunset and then at dusk.

A consistent mental point of view, moreover, is as important as the physical. A view through a glass-bottomed boat of a tropical ocean bed may impress an ordinary tourist only with color, luxuriance, and strangeness. He may be somewhat frightened, even, when some odd-shaped creature swims beneath him. But the same scene from the mental point of view of a marine biologist reveals hundreds of fascinating species of plants and animals. A little red schoolhouse on a country road may look like scores of others to a passing motorist, but to the man who learned his three R's there and perhaps courted his first sweetheart behind his geography book, the building is invested with sentiment and beauty. An adult who goes to a circus sees the bored, set expressions of the performers, the tarnished costumes, and the wash strung between the wagons behind the main tent; but the child sees only glamorous people wearing wonderful clothes, animals that have been captured at the risk of the lives of daring men in far corners of the earth, and clowns who do things that are side-splittingly funny. The atmosphere, tone, and mood of the description depend on the mental point of view which the writer assumes.

**Dominant Impression.** Dominant impression is closely related to point of view and can be determined only when the point of view is established. It is that feature or quality of whatever is being described which the writer emphasizes in such a way that it dominates the whole. The dominant impression which the reader of *David Copperfield* receives of Uriah Heep is his hypocritical " 'umbleness." In his description of the House of Usher on a "dull, dark, and soundless day in the autumn of the year," Poe establishes a feeling of gloom which pervades the whole story. The person who visits the Abraham Lincoln Memorial in Washington at dusk comes away remembering best the quietness and dignity of the huge statue of Lincoln.

The writer should study the subject of his description to determine what should receive the greatest emphasis. Is it to be some physical aspect, a mood, or an interpretation? Whatever it is, it will serve to co-ordinate the parts of the description and give meaning to it. Without a dominant impression, a description may be truthful enough, but it will be flat. It will lack the emphasis and point which will make the difference between the reader's remembering something important from the description or his leaving it with a recollection of only scattered fragments.

A good way to illustrate the principle of dominant impression is to think back to some scene which was familiar to you when you were a child. Do you remember distinctly all the details, or is it not true that some feature remains clear whereas nearly everything else has faded? And is it not true that some feeling about that scene recurs whenever you recollect it? This is dominant impression in retrospect. The artist in description focuses attention on the most important element in his subject and subordinates other information in order that the reader will receive just such an impression as has been noted with regard to the experience of childhood. Notice how Washington Irving, in the physical description of Ichabod Crane in "The Legend of Sleepy Hollow," makes every detail contribute to an impression of ungainly angularity.

> The cognomen of Crane was not inapplicable to his person. He was tall but exceedingly lank, with narrow shoulders, long arms and legs, hands that dangled a mile out of his sleeves, feet that might have served for shovels, and his whole frame most loosely hung together. His head was

small and flat at top, with huge ears, large green glassy eyes, and a long snipe nose; so that it looked like a weathercock perched upon his spindle neck, to tell which way the wind blew. To see him striding along the profile of a hill, with his clothes bagging and fluttering about him, one might have mistaken him for the genius of famine descending upon the earth, or some scarecrow eloped from a cornfield.

It is true that this description is a caricature rather than an exact portrait. No man ever had "hands that dangled a mile out of his sleeves" or "feet that might have served as shovels." The writer, knowing that his story was grotesque, wanted to create a character which would fit the atmosphere. But one can usually observe a principle best when it is exaggerated.

**Choice of Details.** As dominant impression is dependent on point of view, so the choice of details is dependent on the dominant impression. In a way, the dominant impression acts in description as the thesis sentence acts in exposition; it serves as the central core which the details amplify. The details exist for the sake of supporting the main idea. No image is allowed to impinge upon the reader's mind which does not contribute to the unity of the whole impression.

Unity demands that the writer choose carefully the details which he introduces into his description. Intelligent selection is a basic principle in all art. The painter who portrays a log cabin would never think of drawing each log minutely or making an arresting detail of every shingle. Having determined the general effect he wants to produce, he scans his subject for those parts which will contribute and rejects those which are irrelevant. The writer of description, also, presents only the significant portions of his subject. He knows that it is impossible for him to tell everything which the closest scrutiny discloses; furthermore, point of view and perspective automatically eliminate a great deal. The literary artist who produces a pen portrait of Abraham Lincoln selects details which create an image of a very tall, gaunt, stooped, kindly, sadly-humorous man. The number of buttons on his coat or the glint of light from his watch chain would hardly be included.

In the following paragraphs Dickens characterizes Mr. and Mrs. Tibbs in different ways. Little is said about Mrs. Tibbs herself, but the description of her house implies so much about the one who runs it that the reader constructs a definite image of her. All we are told about Mr. Tibbs pertains to his size, legs, long face, and habit of speaking, but, again, we know Mr. Tibbs pretty well as the result. Details have been chosen very effectively.

Mrs. Tibbs was, beyond all dispute, the most tidy, fidgety, thrifty little personage that ever inhaled the smoke of London; and the house of Mrs. Tibbs was, decidedly, the neatest in all Great Coram Street. The area and the area steps, and the street door and the street door steps, and the brass handle and the doorplate, and the knocker, and the fanlight were all as clean and bright as indefatigable whitewashing and hearthstoning and scrubbing and rubbing could make them. The wonder was that the brass doorplate, with the interesting inscription "Mrs. Tibbs," had never caught fire from constant friction, so perseveringly was it polished. There were meat-safe-looking blinds in the parlor windows, blue and gold curtains in the drawing-room, and spring-roller blinds, as Mrs. Tibbs was wont in the pride of her heart to boast, "all the way up." The bell lamp in the passage looked as clear as a soap bubble; you could see yourself in all the tables, and French-polish yourself on any one of the chairs. The banisters were beeswaxed; and the very stair wires made your eyes wink, they were so glittering.

Mrs. Tibbs was somewhat short of stature, and Mr. Tibbs was by no means a large man. He had, moreover, very short legs, but by way of indemnification, his face was peculiarly long. He was to his wife what the o is in 90—he was of some importance *with* her—he was nothing without her. Mrs. Tibbs was always talking. Mr. Tibbs rarely spoke; but if it were at any time possible to put in a word when he should have said nothing at all, he had that talent. Mrs. Tibbs detested long stories, and Mr. Tibbs had one, the conclusion of which had never been heard by his most intimate friends. It always began, "I recollect when I was in the volunteer corps in eighteen hundred and six,"—but, as he spoke very slowly and softly, and his better half very quickly and loudly, he rarely got beyond the introductory sentence. He was a melancholy specimen of the storyteller. He was the Wandering Jew of Joe Millerism.—*Sketches by Boz.*

Descriptive writing is rare apart from one of the other forms of discourse. A writer has little occasion to describe something unless he is explaining it, arguing about it, or using it in a story. The most common use of description is in narration. Practice in writing description is useful, however, especially in its emphasis on the choice of words and on a logical arrangement of images. The examples which follow, most of them taken from narratives, illustrate some of the more common uses of description.

*Sense Impressions*

## On Observing Colors

### JOHN RUSKIN

If you want to color beautifully, color as best pleases yourself at *quiet times,* not so as to catch the eye, nor to look as if it were clever or difficult to color in that way, but so that the color may be pleasant to you when you are happy or thoughtful. Look much at the morning and evening sky, and much at simple flowers—dog-roses, wood hyacinths, violets, poppies, thistles, heather, and such like—as Nature arranges them in the woods and fields. If ever any scientific person tells you that two colors are "discordant," make a note of the two colors and put them together whenever you can. I have actually heard people say that blue and green were discordant; the two colors which Nature seems to intend never to be separated, and never to be felt in either of them in its full beauty without the other!—a peacock's neck, or a blue sky through green leaves, or a blue wave with green lights through it being precisely the loveliest things, next to clouds at sunrise, in this colored world of ours. If you have a good eye for colors, you will soon find out how constantly Nature puts purple and green together, purple and scarlet, green and blue, yellow and neutral gray, and the like; and how she strikes these color concords for general tones, and then works into them with innumerable subordinate ones; and you will gradually come to like what she does, and find out new and beautiful chords of color in her work every day. If you *enjoy* them, depend upon it you will paint them to a certain point right: or, at least, if you do not enjoy them, you are certain to paint them wrong. If color does not give you *intense* pleasure, let it alone; depend upon it, you are only tormenting the eyes and senses of people who feel color, whenever you touch it; and that is unkind and improper.—*Elements of Drawing*.

## Water

### JOHN RUSKIN

Of all inorganic substances, acting in their own proper nature, and without assistance or combination, water is the most wonderful. If we think of it as the source of all the changefulness and beauty which we have seen in clouds; then as the instrument by which the earth we have contemplated was modeled into symmetry, and its crags chiseled into grace; then as, in the form of snow, it robes the mountains it has made with that transcendent light which we could not have conceived if we had not seen; then as it exists in the foam of the torrent—in the iris which spans it, in the morning mist which rises from it, in the deep crystalline pools which mirror its hanging shore, in the broad lake and glancing river; finally, in that which is to all human minds the best emblem of unwearied, unconquerable power, the wild, various, fantastic, tameless unity of the sea; what shall we compare to this mighty, this universal element, for glory and for beauty? or how shall we follow its eternal changefulness of feeling? It is like trying to paint a soul. . . .

To paint the actual play of hue on the reflective surface, or to give the forms and fury of water when it begins to show itself—to give the flashing and rocketlike velocity of a noble cataract, or the precision and grace of the sea wave, so exquisitely modeled, though so mockingly transient—so mountainous in its form, yet so cloudlike in its motion—with its variety and delicacy of color, when every ripple and wreath has some peculiar passage of reflection upon itself alone, and the radiating and scintillating sunbeams are mixed with the dim hues of transparent depth and dark rock below—to do this perfectly is beyond the power of man; to do it even partially has been granted to but one or two, even of those few who have dared to attempt it. . . .

The fact is that there is hardly a roadside pond or pool which has not as much landscape *in* it as above it. It is not the brown, muddy, dull thing we suppose it to be; it has a heart like ourselves, and in the bottom of that there are the boughs of the tall trees, and the blades of the shaking grass, and all manner of hues, of variable, pleasant light out of the sky; nay, the ugly gutter that stagnates over the drain bars in the heart of the foul city is not altogether base; down in that, if you will look deep enough, you may see the dark, serious blue of far-off sky, and the passing of pure clouds. It is at your own will that you see in that despised stream either the refuse of the street or the image of the sky—so it is with almost all other things that we unkindly despise.—*Modern Painters,* I, 5, 1.

## Christmas Tree [24]

### HERMAN SMITH

I have seen many a Christmas tree . . . in far places on land and sea and at home, but never such a tree as that of my childhood. There it stood, tall and straight and green, a noble young hemlock filling the air with fragrance. Its lacy branches were aglitter with wax candles of every hue, each in a holder that ended with a gold or silver star, each with its halo of rainbowed light, such as must have surrounded that small and sacred head on the first Christmas in the Bethlehem stable.

No modern tree with silvered or gilded boughs, no tree of ostrich plumes hung with pearls, no tree hung with jeweled flowers and ablaze with electric lights in varicolored forms, can ever equal the tree that was disclosed to our gaze on Christmas Eves. Strings of popcorn and cranberries, oranges and crimson apples, gilded nuts, cornucopias of isinglass filled with anise and caraway drops, gold and silver stars, and suspended

24. From *Stina, the Story of a Cook,* by Herman Smith (copyright, 1942, by Herman Smith). Reprinted by permission of M. Barrows and Company, Inc., the publishers.

over its spear-crowned tip was a fat wax angel with shining quivering wings.

## Water Hyacinths [25]

### HARNETT T. KANE

The Captain frowned and pointed. "Maybe you wouldn't believe it, but that's our worst trouble." His finger was directed at a narrow line of fragile green and lavender flowers on each side of the canal, that bobbed lightly as we passed—water hyacinths, "orchids of the bayou." Somewhere behind us, on the route, one or two had crept into the scene almost unnoticed, and now they were thickening and widening as we went, reaching toward the center of the channel. A few yards forward was a circular mat of the plants, a floating garden of tight-packed, waxlike leaves. From the glistening bulbous centers protruded upthrust blossoms, pale bunches of delicate, perfumeless bloom. I managed to reach below the rail and catch a handful. They were easily crushed, more water than green cells. Below each plant extended light, colorless strings of roots, for several feet. The flowers faded quickly; in a few minutes they were limp on the wet deck. It was hard for me to realize that I held in my hand a major threat to navigation over most of South Louisiana.

This beauty is in heavy over-production and must literally be plowed under. Wherever there are bayous, the hyacinths intrude, an ever-invading, advancing army—a fragile subversive. Lakes, bays, small waterways and large ones are entered and overgrown almost in a season. Unless something is done, within the next few years they will be impassable. The matted leaves can cover a spread of water so completely that it seems like land. The man with the paddle finds passage impossible; even a heavy motorboat can be stopped by this flowered barrier, its propeller hopelessly enmeshed. The wise pilot does not attempt to penetrate a waterway so blanketed.

## Rain in Mexico [26]

### GERTRUDE DIAMANT

While we argued the rain came, the thunderous drumming incontinent downpour which may last ten minutes or the whole afternoon. This is the spring of Mexico, the rainy season that ends the long golden monotony of the dry months. But it is no pleasant spring of burgeoning trees

25. From *The Bayous of Louisiana,* by Harnett T. Kane (copyright, 1943, by Harnett T. Kane). Reprinted by permission of William Morrow & Company, Inc., the publishers.

26. From *The Days of Ofelia,* by Gertrude Diamant (copyright, 1942, by Gertrude Diamant). Reprinted by permission of Houghton Mifflin Company, the publishers.

and greening lawns. It is not a season for a poet, but one for priests and a primitive religion; for the rains come with elemental force, scourging the earth wrathfully each day.

If you must be caught in the rain, be caught in the market place. It is like seeing the approach of doom. The peddlers wait until the last minute under the livid sky, and their cries sound far away and faint against the roll of thunder. Then the first drops fall, and there is a frantic rout, a folding of tents, dumping of vegetables, and scurrying away, and in the next minute nothing but the empty streets awash like a ship in a storm, and desolate as if humanity had never been there.

Or watch the rain from under a tree on the Reforma, where you will be thoroughly drenched but unable to move, because the rain is an impenetrable wall around you. It thunders down in white spears, with a roar of wind in which the palm trees flail like straws; and blots out the world, and there is only a solitary charro on horseback, a black silhouette against the rain. He sits under his poncho, becalmed, and you think the rain must have beaten horse and rider to death. But then the white spears thin out, the air grows lighter and the rain darker, the sun appears, and the charro rides away, his wet poncho shining.

I liked the rainy season better than the dry, because I like weather better than climate. The dry season is a golden vacuum; but the rainy season has change, which is weather. And while climate may create a race, weather creates the temper and sensibility of the individual. Most mornings were still clear, with a blue sky more brilliant than ever. But there were some that were dull and pleasantly clouded with premonition of the rain. And the skies that came before and after each day's cloudburst were, so to speak, not of this earth.

Perhaps it is the rarefied atmosphere that gives the clouds their solidity, their depth and effulgence of color. They rise from the mountains in the early afternoon and fill the sky, inexhaustible as chaos, sweeping the earth with a splendor of shafted light. Slowly the hot white masses and purple depths begin to lose color. A livid gray suffuses and melts them, and then the rain rips from a sky grown hard and opaque as metal.

## The Merry-Go-Round [27]

### STEPHEN CRANE

Within the Merry-Go-Round there was a whirling circle of ornamental lions, giraffes, camels, ponies, goats, glittering with varnish and metal

27. From "The Pace of Youth" in *Men, Women, and Boats*. Reprinted by permission of Alfred A. Knopf, Inc.

that caught swift reflections from windows high above them. With stiff wooden legs, they swept on in a never-ending race, while a great orchestrion clamored in wild speed. The summer sunlight sprinkled its gold upon the garnet canopies carried by the tireless racers and upon all the devices of decoration that made Stimson's machine magnificent and famous. A host of laughing children bestrode the animals, bending forward like charging cavalrymen, and shaking reins and whooping in glee. At intervals they leaned out perilously to clutch at iron rings that were tendered to them by a long wooden arm. At the intense moment before the swift grab for the rings one could see their little nervous bodies quiver with eagerness; the laughter rang shrill and excited. Down in the long rows of benches, crowds of people sat watching the game, while occasionally a father might arise and go near to shout encouragement, cautionary commands, or applause at his flying offspring. Frequently mothers called out: "Be careful, Georgie!" The orchestrion bellowed and thundered on its platform, filling the ears with its long monotonous song. Over in a corner, a man in a white apron and behind a counter roared above the tumult: "Popcorn! Popcorn!"

## Sounds in Late Summer

### RICHARD JEFFERIES

The loudest sound in the wood was the humming in the trees; there was no wind, no sunshine; a summer day, still and shadowy, under large clouds high up. To this low humming the sense of hearing soon became accustomed, and it served but to render the silence deeper. In time, as I sat waiting and listening, there came the faintest far-off song of a bird away in the trees—the merest thin upstroke of sound, slight in structure, the echo of the strong spring singing. This was the summer repetition, dying away. A willow-wren still remembered his love, and whispered about it to the silent fir tops, as in after days we turn over the pages of letters, withered as leaves, and sigh. So gentle, so low, so tender a song the willow-wren sang that it could scarce be known as the voice of a bird, but was like that of some yet more delicate creature with the heart of a woman. . . .

Next morning the August sun shone, and the wood was all a-hum with insects. The wasps were working at the pine boughs high overhead; the bees by dozens were crowding to the bramble flowers; swarming on them, they seemed so delighted; bumble-bees went wandering among the ferns in the copse and in the ditches . . . and calling at every purple heath-blossom, at the purple knap-weeds, purple thistles, and broad handfuls of yellow-weed flowers. Wasplike flies barred with yellow suspended themselves in the air between the pine-trunks like hawks hovering, and suddenly shot themselves a yard forward or to one side, as if the rapid vibration of their wings while hovering had accumulated force which drove them as if discharged from a crossbow. The sun had set all things in motion.

There was a hum under the oak by the hedge, a hum in the pine wood, a humming among the heath and the dry grass which heat had browned. The air was alive and merry with sound, so that the day seemed quite different and twice as pleasant.—From "The Pine Wood," in *The Open Air*.

## Early Morning [28]

### SIEGFRIED SASSOON

I can almost re-smell the early autumn air, while the musical cry of hounds goes swinging round the covert, and the voices of the hunt-servants are heard with "Tallyo bike" and other cub-scaring exhortations, varied by saddle-rappings and rebukes of "Ware rabbit" to members of the young entry. An indignant cock-pheasant whirrs upward from the undergrowth and skims away across a stubble field. A hound lollops past me and plunges through the brambly hedge into the wood, while I wonder how long it will take me to learn all their names.

## Making Tortillas [29]

### GERTRUDE DIAMANT

Sleep was only a small moment before the sun sprang up from the mountains, and I heard the women making tortillas—the steady slap-slap as they tossed the dough between their palms.

It is the sound of Mexico, as the blue of the sky is its color. And the cold of the mountain night is still in the air when it begins. I would rise and draw the curtains, and see the sun low and clear on the level white buildings. From the huts came a haze of smoke and the morning noises—chopping of wood, water splashing, and the pigs squealing; and Ofelia's little sister singing shrilly over and over, "To heaven, to heaven let me go, to receive the blessed crown, the blessed crown." And through it all the insistent slap-slap of tortilla-making, a rhythmic sound like part

28. From *The Weald of Youth* by Siegfried Sassoon (copyright, 1932, by Siegfried Sassoon). Reprinted by permission of The Viking Press, Inc.

29. From *The Days of Ofelia,* by Gertrude Diamant (copyright, 1942, by Gertrude Diamant). Reprinted by permission of Houghton Mifflin Company, the publishers.

of a ceremonial, and one seems to hear far off the accompanying beat of feet in some primitive dance.

I could see the women working in the smoky huts where the night still lingered, their hands twinkling in the obscure light, their faces bronze and shadowy as if emerging from a dark canvas. Outside the men were washing, dousing their heads in the dirty water in the barrels; and then, drying their faces, they went into the huts to eat. They squatted on the dirt floor, and took many tortillas at a time, and folded them and downed them with black coffee.

## The Wind [30]

### R. C. HUTCHINSON

Chiefly the change was for my skin and lungs. This was a lane where the wind would meet you in both directions, and had rubbed my face with a harshness no more disagreeable than your own dog's tongue. It was a cold wind still, but the harshness had all gone; it was a parting instead of a slapping wind, quietened by the sun which showed now and again between the high fast convoy of white clouds. It bore damp odors, as the autumn wind had, but of a homelier kind; not of the high bogs and salty, mountain mists, but of water trickling through stone and moss, of valley ferns and faintly, with the farmstead smells from Randall's Gift, of cowslip and hyacinth. This richness of sensation, born of moss and stippled cloud with the quick green light on Nelden, possessed me by degrees as the bus's exhaust was brushed away.

## Apples

### JOHN BURROUGHS

Is there any other fruit that has so much facial expression as the apple? . . . The swaar has one look, the rambo another, the spy another. The youth recognizes the seek-no-further, buried beneath a dozen other varie-ties, the moment he catches a glance of its eye, or the bonny-cheeked Newtown pippin, or the gentle but sharp-nosed gilliflower. He goes to the great bin in the cellar and sinks his shafts here and there in the garnered wealth of the orchards, mining for his favorites, sometimes com-ing plump upon them, sometimes catching a glimpse of them to the right or left, or uncovering them as keystones in an arch made up of many varieties.

---

30. From *Interim,* by R. C. Hutchinson (copyright, 1945, by R. C. Hutchinson), Rine-hart & Company, Inc. Reprinted by permission of the author.

In the dark he can usually tell them by the sense of touch. There is not only the size and shape, but there is the texture and polish. Some apples are coarse-grained and some are fine; some are thin-skinned and some are thick. One variety is quick and vigorous beneath the touch, another gentle and yielding. The pinnock has a thick skin with a spongy lining; a bruise in it becomes like a piece of cork. The tallow apple has an unctuous feel, as its name suggests. It sheds water like a duck. What apple is that with a fat curved stem that blends so prettily with its own flesh—the wine-apple? Some varieties impress me as masculine—weather-stained, freckled, lasting, and rugged; others are indeed lady apples, fair, delicate, shining, mild-flavored, white-meated, like the egg-drop and the lady-finger. The practiced hand knows each kind by the touch.—*Winter Sunshine,* published by Houghton Mifflin Company.

## Christmas Breakfast [31]

### HERMAN SMITH

What a gay breakfast table was ours on Christmas morning, with all of us, my brothers with their wives and broods, cousins, uncles, and aunts, crowded about the table extended to its full length, with a smaller one for the children. How we ate of Stina's homemade sausage, eggs fried in rosemary butter, apple pancakes dripping with buckwheat honey, and winding up with her *tarte à la crème avec les mirabelles,* a tart made of raised sweet dough, filled with thick cream, dotted with yellow plums, dusted with sugar and cinnamon, and baked. With all of this there were endless cups of coffee from what must have been the grandmother of all the coffee pots on earth. Even I was allowed to have *café au lait,* and I drank it proudly from a cup decorated with a wreath of roses and the words "For a Good Boy" in letters of gold luster around the brim. Beside me sat my elephant sagely nodding his head, and in the pocket of my jacket the last battered banana awaited some moment of hunger later in the day.

My sisters flew from kitchen to dining room replenishing plates and cups, and over all beamed Stina in her red woolen hood. . . .

31. From *Stina, the Story of a Cook,* by Herman Smith (copyright, 1942, by Herman Smith). Reprinted by permission of M. Barrows & Company, Inc., the publishers.

## Dinner At Cousin Lil's [32]

### HERMAN SMITH

My sisters, in the best and stiffest of Victorian tradition, did not admire Cousin Lil. In shocked confidence they whispered that she not only used too much powder and perfume, but that she actually painted—a thing no lady of impeccable reputation might dare to do. But of all my more distant relatives I liked Cousin Lil the most. She was big and generous and gay, full of jokes and laughter and broad-minded far beyond her time. . . .

What a thrill it was to turn into Uncle Fred's unbarred gateway and to see the low rambling farmhouse, rosy welcoming light streaming through its windows, with Cousin Lil's Amazonian figure framed in the open doorway. She wore a red merino dress. Her booming welcome rose above the whistling of the wind. When I was far enough unwound, warming up beside the shining kitchen range, she gave me a resounding and highly perfumed smack.

But other and more enticing smells greeted our half-frozen noses as they emerged into that grateful scented warmth, when Cousin Lil from time to time lifted a pot cover or opened the oven door. I could not wait for the formality of the others in presenting their gifts, but promptly offered my own. Never, said Cousin Lil, in all her born days had she seen such a valentine, such fat and dimpled cupids, such lifelike doves, so many bleeding hearts. Why, you could almost smell the red roses and the violets, and she didn't know but what she'd have it framed. She exclaimed equally over the oysters, her enthusiasm and praise completely thawing the Victorian ice from my sisters' hearts. . . .

The table was spread in the low-ceilinged dining room which had a latticed wall paper of red and blue morning glories. A lamp with a pink china shade painted with bluebirds and butterflies hung from chains by which it could be raised or lowered at will. Its roseate glow disclosed in the center of Aunt Mary's best white damask cloth a gigantic five-layered fresh coconut birthday cake, towering high on the cake-stand. . . .

In addition to that miraculous combination which comprised her famous potato soup and the oysters brought from our home, which were enough for the lustiest of appetites, there were platters of crisp fried chicken with a garnish of crescent-shaped turnovers filled with spicy country sausage. Accompanying them were feathery potatoes mashed

32. From *Stina, the Story of a Cook*, by Herman Smith (copyright, 1942, by Herman Smith). Reprinted by permission of M. Barrows & Company, Inc., the publishers.

with green onion tops and beaten eggs, with little indented lakes of sweet butter on the top. There were flat yellow bowls of cole slaw made with tart apples and sour cream. There were hot biscuits, "rizen" rolls and homemade bread, tomatoes stewed with corn, and homegrown celery crunchy and sweet.

Around the table in leaf-shaped dishes of pressed glass moved a procession of jams, jellies, pickles, and preserves—their reds, yellows, greens, purples, and golden browns flashing back from the iridescent prisms of the hanging lamp. Flanking the cake were glass compotes, one holding strawberries, the other peaches, grown and canned on the farm.

*Places*

## Mexico City [33]

### GERTRUDE DIAMANT

An American city may be an ugly hodge-podge. It may have its slums close to rich sections, and its unemployed idle in the shade of busy factories. But all its contradictions are part of one age, part of its industrial growth. But Mexico City is different. For all the shining new cars that rush so wildly through the streets, and the modern hotels proudly advertising "Stean [sic] Heat," and the skyscrapers built on special foundations on the swampy ground, the modernism of the city is only the thinnest veneer over all its past. It is still a village, part of the primitive countryside around it and the primitive Indian life. It is still the colonial city of the Spaniards, and the romantic nineteenth-century city of Porfirio Díaz; it is only superficially of this century and the things of this century. It is like a fresco in which there is no perspective to make things recede in time and space. Everything is of the present, jumbled together. One remembers the words of Bernal Díaz del Castillo, who was one of the soldiers who followed Cortés, and who in his old age sat down to write "the true history of the conquest," very indignant over the lies that had been told about it. ". . . For in a manner of speaking all that I tell happened only yesterday." He wrote that four centuries ago, and one still feels that all that has happened in Mexico was only yesterday.

I think the markets have not changed much. When the Spaniards had come to the city, by perilous marches over the mountains from the seacoast, and after they had met Montezuma with great ceremony and received lodgings in the palace, they sallied forth like good tourists to see

33. From *The Days of Ofelia*, by Gertrude Diamant (copyright, 1942, by Gertrude Diamant). Reprinted by permission of Houghton Mifflin Company, the publishers.

the market. And it must have been very much like those that tourists see today.

"And when we had come to the Grand Plaza, as we had never beheld such a thing, we were astonished at the multitude of people and the abundance of merchandise, and the order and arrangement that there was in everything. And I will mention first the vendors of gold and silver and precious stones, and feathers and robes and embroidered things.[1] Then there were other vendors who sold cloth and ropes of hennequen, and sandals, which are the shoes that they wear, and everything was in one part of the Plaza in its appropriate place. Let us go and talk of those who sold beans and herbs and other vegetables. Let us go to those who sold chickens and rabbits and hares and other things of the sort. Let us speak of those who sold pottery made in a thousand different ways from big basins to little pitchers, which were by themselves apart, and also of those who sold honey and sweetmeats, and wood and firewood and resinous pine strips."

The list gets so long that he adds rather testily: "What more do you want me to say?" Naturally he could not mention the ugly lithograph calendars (made in Japan) which are now sold in the markets and which Mexicans buy for their gorgeous color, though they may be unable to read the days of the month; or the glittering pins with false stones (made in the United States), which Mexicans prefer to their own silverwork. The resinous pine strips that he mentions are still used for a quick fuel; and because they are so much used, together with charcoal, the land around Mexico City has been denuded of its forests. But now the Government is talking of using its newly recovered oil for making gas, which is still a luxury in Mexico. And the little pitchers that were by themselves apart, are still the chief kitchenware. They are made of mud and sell for a centavo. One need stand on the streets only three minutes to see a cargador pass with a huge pile of them on his back.

But the Spaniards seem to have suffered the usual tourist difficulties, for as Bernal Díaz says, "the Plaza was so big and full of people it was impossible to see everything in one day." And so they left the market and went to see the great temple, ascending the hundred and fourteen steps with the aid of two priests, whom Montezuma sent to help them so that they should not get tired.

"And as we climbed to the top of the grand temple, we came to a platform covered with stones, where they placed the sad Indians for sacrifice. . . ."

1. All these things, however, have since moved into the tourist stores, where they command a better price.

Then Montezuma took Cortés by the hand and told him to look at the great city and all its environs, and it was very easy to see everything. . . . And they saw the three great highways leading into the city, and all the canals and the great lake of Texcoco crowded with canoes coming and going. The highways are still the same, but few of the canals are left now, and those near the city are muddied with pestilential drainage waters. And the great lake of Texcoco is dry, a tiny Sahara from which dense yellow clouds of dust rise in the rainy season to envelop the city. And all the glory of Tenochtitlan, the city that Cortés gazed on from the temple, is gone too. It withstood the siege of the Spaniards and their Indian allies for sixty-five days—a siege by land and water, for Cortés ordered ships built and launched them on the lake, and from them discharged the big guns on the city. And whatever the fighting did not destroy, the Spaniards destroyed when they entered the city again. . . .

The great Indian city is gone, but the sad Indians remain. One is curious to know whether Bernal Díaz found all the Indians sad, or only those who were about to be sacrificed, in which case it is very understandable. But it is certain that the Indians of today are sad. It may be racial, or it may be a sadness that comes from the conditions of their life. In the four centuries following the conquest nothing was added to the life of the Indians, everything was taken away. The Indians lived, and still live, under the most primitive conditions—a degraded form of the primitive because it is not a cultural stage, but a total deprivation of all that human beings should have. Only since the Revolution have the Indians been counted as part of the population of Mexico, and they are, whether pure-blooded or mixed, a good three fifths of it. But the work of the Revolution can better their lives only slowly, but that is its chief task, and it is the future of Mexico. The sad Indians had the first word, and they will probably have the last.

And they come to the city as though it were only a big village, and they never take the streets seriously, but sit down to rest or eat their tortillas in front of the modern buildings. Groups of campesinos come in their white smocks and white trousers, sandaled or barefoot, with leather bags slung over their shoulders, on pilgrimage to the Virgin of Guadalupe or to see about their lands. And they gape up at the big buildings, or look into the store windows where there are displays of modern farm machinery, or stand listening to a gramophone bawling American jazz. I think it is this constant reminder of the primitive in a modern setting that gives Mexico its quality of excitement. And it makes for comedy too.

I remember one day in the Alameda. It is a park in the center of town, bosky and well-treed like all the parks of the city, but cluttered with bad statues. At the end near the Palace of Fine Arts, the Inquisition used to burn its victims. Later it became a fashionable promenade. Now it is a pleasant place to read the paper, to have your shoes shined, to pass the siesta hours while you wait for the city to come to life again. I was reading the paper near one of the statues—a whipped-cream female nude— when the sound of suppressed laughter made me look up. A man and a woman, barefoot and very ragged . . ., were looking at the statue, nudging each other, laughing with their hands to their mouths, finding it indescribably funny. It was the most forthright piece of art criticism I have ever seen, and I enjoyed that statue with them, as I have enjoyed few works of art. Later a campesino came to have his picture taken. There are photographers in the Alameda who give you a donkey to sit on, or a sarape to drape over your shoulder, or a big oleograph of the Cathedral of Guadalupe for a background. This photographer happened to have a huge bull fiddle, and the campesino posed himself with it, and everyone stopped to watch in utter solemnity. Only the gringa laughed and went off in disgrace, but with a feeling that the day had been well spent.

## *Farmhouse Cellar* [34]

### HERMAN SMITH

A farmhouse cellar is not to be confused with what is known as a basement. Our cellar was of stone and extended under practically the entire house. Its floor was of red brick, and its walls were freshly whitewashed every spring. There was a special room under the west wing for the apples, pears, turnips, carrots, cabbages, parsnips, and beets, which were to supply us with food while we waited for spring.

In shallow trenches—made of boards and filled with sand—celery, endive, chicory, and leeks made rows of summery green in the dim light which filtered through the little frosted windows set high in the walls. In summer, in that cellar I could see and smell the lilies-of-the-valley which grew and bloomed all around the foundation of our house. But to a small and ever hungry boy the winter sights and smells were best.

In the cupboards of whitewashed pine, tier on tier, stood the result of the summer labor of my sisters—for canning was the one work which Stina was willing to share with them. Every known kind of jelly, pickle, conserve, and jam, with preserved cherries, peaches, pears, plums, raspberries, strawberries, gooseberries, and blackberries from our own trees

34. From *Stina, the Story of a Cook*, by Herman Smith (copyright, 1942, by Herman Smith). Reprinted by permission of M. Barrows & Company, Inc., the publishers.

and vines, stood in shining jars. There were gallon jars of huckleberries, purple black and sweet, from our marshes along the creek. . . . Great stone jars as large as small barrels held cucumbers pickled with dill, sauerkraut and grape leaves, and cuts of home-corned beef, tangy with garlic, bay leaves, and peppercorns. . . .

Also in our cellar, resting on a platform of oak beams, were small barrels of homemade wine of various kinds, and of cider, often drawn upon by Stina for use in dishes in which to her, as to all supercooks, the use of wine is imperative.

## The Furnished Room [35]

### O. HENRY

The guest reclined, inert, upon a chair, while the room, confused in speech as though it were an apartment in Babel, tried to discourse to him of its divers tenantry.

A polychromatic rug like some brilliant-flowered, rectangular, tropical islet lay surrounded by a billowy sea of soiled matting. Upon the gay-papered wall were those pictures that pursue the homeless one from house to house—The Huguenot Lovers, The First Quarrel, The Wedding Breakfast, Psyche at the Fountain. The mantel's chastely severe outline was ingloriously veiled behind some pert drapery drawn rakishly askew like the sashes of the Amazonian ballet. Upon it was some desolate flotsam cast aside by the room's marooned when a lucky sail had borne them to a fresh port—a trifling vase or two, pictures of actresses, a medicine bottle, some stray cards out of a deck.

One by one, as the characters of a cryptograph become explicit, the little signs left by the furnished room's procession of guests developed a significance. The threadbare space in the rug in front of the dresser told that lovely woman had marched in the throng. The tiny fingerprints on the wall spoke of little prisoners trying to feel their way to sun and air. A splattered stain, raying like the shadow of a bursting bomb, witnessed where a hurled glass or bottle had splintered with its contents against the wall. Across the pier glass had been scrawled with a diamond in staggering letters the name "Marie." It seemed that the succession of dwellers in the furnished room had turned in fury—perhaps tempted beyond forbearance by its garish coldness—and wreaked upon it their passions. The furniture was chipped and bruised; the couch, distorted by bursting springs, seemed a horrible monster that had been slain during

35. From The Four Million, by O. Henry (copyright 1905, 1933, by Doubleday, Doran & Company, Inc.). Reprinted by permission of Doubleday, Doran & Company, Inc.

the stress of some grotesque convulsion. Some more potent upheaval had cloven a great slice from the marble mantel. Each plank in the floor owned its particular cant and shriek as from a separate and individual agony. It seemed incredible that all this malice and injury had been wrought upon the room by those who had called it for a time their home; and yet it may have been the cheated home instinct surviving blindly, the resentful rage at false household gods that had kindled their wrath. A hut that is our own we can sweep and adorn and cherish.—"The Furnished Room."

*Persons*

## Captain Ahab

### HERMAN MELVILLE

There seemed no sign of common bodily illness about him nor of the recovery from any. He looked like a man cut away from the stake, when the fire has overrunningly wasted all the limbs without consuming them, or taking away one particle from their compacted aged robustness. His whole high, broad form seemed made of solid bronze and shaped in an unalterable mold, like Cellini's cast of Perseus. Threading its way out from among his grey hairs and continuing right down one side of his tawny scorched face and neck, till it disappeared in his clothing, you saw a slender rodlike mark, lividly whitish. It resembled that perpendicular seam sometimes made in the straight, lofty trunk of a great tree, when the upper lightning tearingly darts down it. . . .

So powerfully did the whole grim aspect of Ahab affect me, and the livid brand which streaked it, that for the first few moments I hardly noted that not a little of this overbearing grimness was owing to the barbaric white leg upon which he partly stood. It had previously come to me that this ivory leg had at sea been fashioned from the polished bone of the sperm whale's jaw. "Aye, he was dismasted off Japan," said the old Gay-Head Indian once; "but like his dismasted craft, he shipped another mast without coming home for it. He has a quiver of 'em."

I was struck with the singular posture he maintained. Upon each side of the *Pequod's* quarterdeck and pretty close to the mizzen shrouds, there was an auger hole, bored about half an inch or so into the plank. His bone leg steadied in that hole, one arm elevated, and holding by a shroud, Captain Ahab stood erect, looking straight out beyond the ship's ever-pitching prow. There was an infinity of firmest fortitude, a determinate, unsurrenderable willfulness, in the fixed and fearless, forward dedication of that glance. Not a word he spoke; nor did his officers say aught to him, though by all their minutest gestures and expressions they plainly showed the uneasy, if not painful, consciousness of being under a troubled master eye. And not only that, but moody, stricken Ahab stood before them with an apparently eternal anguish in his face, in all the nameless, regal, overbearing dignity of some mighty woe.—*Moby Dick*.

## Eustacia Vye

### THOMAS HARDY

Eustacia Vye was the raw material of a divinity. On Olympus she would have done well with a little preparation. She had the passions and instincts which make a model goddess, that is, those which make not quite a model woman. Had it been possible for the earth and mankind to be entirely in her grasp for a while, had she handled the distaff, the spindle, and the shears at her own free will, few in the world would have noticed the change of government. There would have been the same inequality of lot, the same heaping up of favors here, of contumely there, the same generosity before justice, the same perpetual dilemmas, the same captious alternation of caresses and blows that we endure now.

She was in person full-limbed, and somewhat heavy; without ruddiness, as without pallor; and soft to the touch as a cloud. To see her hair was to fancy that a whole winter did not contain darkness enough to form its shadow; it closed over her forehead like nightfall extinguishing the western glow.

Her nerves extended into those tresses, and her temper could always be softened by stroking them down. When her hair was brushed, she would instantly sink into stillness and look like the Sphinx. If in passing under one of the Egdon banks, any of the thick skeins were caught, as they sometimes were, by a prickly tuft of the large *Ulex Europœus*—which will act as a sort of hairbrush—she would go back a few steps and pass against it a second time.

She had Pagan eyes, full of nocturnal mysteries. Their light, as it came and went, and came again, was partially hampered by their oppressive lids and lashes; and of these the under lid was much fuller than it usually is with English women. This enabled her to indulge in reverie without seeming to do so: she might have been believed capable of sleeping without closing them up. Assuming that the souls of men and women were visible essences, you could fancy the color of Eustacia's soul to be flame-like. The sparks from it that rose into her dark pupils gave the same impression.

The mouth seemed formed less to speak than to quiver, less to quiver than to kiss. Some might have added, less to kiss than to curl. Viewed sideways, the closing line of her lips formed, with almost geometric precision, the curve so well known in the arts of design as the cima-recta, or ogee. The sight of such a flexible bend as that on grim Egdon was quite an apparition. It was felt at once that that mouth did not come over from Sleswig with a band of Saxon pirates whose lips met like the two halves of a muffin. One had fancied that such lip curves were mostly lurking underground in the South as fragments of forgotten marbles. So fine were the lines of her lips that, though full, each corner of her mouth was as clearly cut as the point of a spear. This keenness of corner was only blunted when she was given over to sudden fits of gloom, one of the phases of the night side of sentiment which she knew too well for her years.

Her presence brought memories of such things as Bourbon roses, rubies, and tropical midnights; her moods recalled lotus-eaters and the march in "Athalie"; her motions, the ebb and flow of the sea; her voice, the viola. In a dim light, and with a slight rearrangement of her hair, her general figure might have stood for that of either of the higher female deities. The new moon behind her head, an old helmet upon it, a diadem of accidental dewdrops round her brow, would have been adjuncts sufficient to strike the note of Artemis, Athena, or Hera respectively, with as close an approximation to the antique as that which passes muster on many respected canvases.—*The Return of the Native.*

## Stina [36]

### HERMAN SMITH

I can see her now—small, almost elfin—with the brightest, blackest, wisest eyes I have ever seen. Her face was crisscrossed with innumerable wrinkles which broke into sunbursts when she smiled. A despot she was —not always amiable—but a cook whom I know now to have been deserving of the *cordon bleu*. She slept in a small, cold, immaculate chamber not far from mine, but all her waking hours were spent in the kitchen which was her pride. . . .

In winter she wore a full-gathered skirt of dark-brown wool, a waist buttoned to the brooch of tiny, gold-clasped hands at her throat. A voluminous apron of blue, white-sprigged calico was tied about her waist. Upon her head, which was only slightly gray, she wore a little knitted

36. From *Stina, the Story of a Cook,* by Herman Smith (copyright, 1942, by Herman Smith). Reprinted by permission of M. Barrows & Company, Inc.

hood of dark red wool; and often in the morning before the kitchen was warmed up, she wore a sleeveless, knitted woolen vest of the same dark red.

Sharp-eyed, sometimes sharp-tongued—though never to me—she concocted the most heavenly dishes with the ease and pride of the artist, for she was a genius in that most intimate of all the arts—the art of cookery.

*Changing Point of View*

## A Road in England [37]

### R. C. HUTCHINSON

A road's excellence lies in its power to yield the unexpected; and this lane concealed its riches until you were right upon them. It took you for half a mile as straight and respectably as the lanes of Lincolnshire; you thought you could see ahead how it would curve to manage the rising ground. Then, when it had bent a little, it dodged abruptly to avoid a house that stood in its way and became immediately the high road of a village. I do not know if it has a name, this place; "yonder over edge" was how I had heard it called, as if the world ended there; it was a rhombic green, shaved close by goats and fenced with beeches, on which a dozen cottages stood at independent angles like children at the beginning of a party. Instead of taking the obvious course, the lane suddenly wheeled right again and squeezed between two granaries. You were in a beechwood now, where the breeze was oddly stilled and the day seemed to have strode forward into evening. And now, as the road dipped sharply, the fence of brush gave place to rock; you smelt and heard the flow of water over rock before you found it running beside you. For perhaps twelve minutes, at our pace, the lane tried to edge away from the beck; but the wall of rock, now sloped to carry little oaks, now moistly bare and vertical, would nudge it in again; until, squeezed hard by the narrowing gorge, it boldly turned to step across the beck, rose in one leap upon a gentle slope it found there, and broke away and up to the freedom of Pitchnose Fell. Again you had made landfall on a foreign soil. The smell of moss and the stream's rustle fell away; all the rock you saw was the giant boulders that lay dry amidst the broom. Like small beasts born prisoner, we had been content with a prospect stretching to forty feet on either hand, with the gush and trickle of white water through hanging ferns, fragmented light on the marriage of cliff and green. We

37. From *Interim*, by R. C. Hutchinson (copyright, 1945, by R. C. Hutchinson), Rinehart & Company, Inc. Reprinted by permission of the author.

emerged in a land whose only boundary was the sky and the sky-toned hills, where the eye's convenient mark was the thrust of Skiddaw twenty miles away.

The wind here was fresh, but duller-edged than you would hope for in this season, for the sun had been clear all day to tame it. Strangely, it did not seem to blow from any quarter, and it stirred the bracken hardly at all; you felt its motion rather as the movement of the crowd about you watching a procession, a constant, not unfriendly pressure on all your sides. And the light was strange: pale and constant like summer evening's light reflected from a calm sea. I had thought this country had no new colors to show me; I knew the whole range of its grays, the bracken's luster, and the mournful shades of peat and dying heather. And now they came as if the eyes I used were subtler than my own, tones more translucent, more sensitively joined. About the level of the road a film of mist spread flat to the nearer hills. I saw it not as a cloud but rather as if a watered brush had been drawn across my view. Within this band the colors of moor and hill were paled, so that they seemed not Nature's but a romantic painter's reverie; and all the shades below and above, to where the sky held constant sympathy, were changed and softened to keep it in communion. Our chatter faded there; we walked beside the road and our shoes on the resilient turf were almost silent. From very far we heard an engine whistle as it scuttled into the Redknock tunnel. But that was another world, and this we saw, fastened in stillness, was a new creation for ourselves.

## A Steamboat Landing at a Small Town

MARK TWAIN

Once a day a cheap gaudy packet arrived upward from St. Louis, and another downward from Keokuk. Before these events, the day was glorious with expectancy; after them, the day was a dead and empty thing. Not only the boys but the whole village felt this. After all these years I can picture that old time to myself now, just as it was then: the white town drowsing in the sunshine of a summer's morning; the streets empty, or pretty nearly so; one or two clerks sitting in front of the Water Street stores, with their splint-bottomed chairs tilted back against the wall, chins on breasts, hats slouched over their faces, asleep—with shingle-shavings enough around to show what broke them down; a sow and a litter of pigs loafing along the sidewalk, doing a good business in watermelon rinds and seeds; two or three lonely little freight piles scattered about the "levee"; a pile of "skids" on the slope of the stone-paved wharf, and the fragrant town drunkard asleep in the shadow of them; two or three wood flats at the head of the wharf, but nobody to listen to the peaceful lapping of the wavelets against them; the great Mississippi, the majestic, the magnificent Mississippi, rolling its mile-wide tide along, shining in the sun; the dense forest away on the other side; the "point" above the town and the "point" below, bounding the river-glimpse and turning it into a sort of sea, and withal a very still and brilliant and lonely one. Presently a film of dark smoke appears above one of those remote "points"; instantly a negro drayman, famous for his quick eye and prodigious voice, lifts up the cry, "S-t-e-a-m-boat a-comin'!" and the scene changes! The town drunkard stirs, the clerks wake up, a furious clatter of drays follows, every house and store pours out a human contribution, and all in a twinkling the dead town is alive and moving. Drays, carts, men, boys, all go hurrying from many quarters to a common center, the wharf. Assembled there, the people fasten their eyes upon the coming boat, as upon a wonder they are seeing for the first time. And the boat *is* rather a handsome sight too. She is long and sharp and trim and pretty; she has two tall fancy-topped chimneys, with a gilded device of some kind swung between them; a fanciful pilot-house, all glass and "gingerbread," perched on top of the "texas" deck behind them; the paddle boxes are gorgeous with a picture or with gilded rays above the boat's name; the boiler deck, the hurricane deck, and the texas deck are fenced and ornamented with clean white railings; there is a flag gallantly flying from the jack staff; the furnace doors are open and the fires glaring bravely; the upper decks are black with passengers; the captain stands by the big bell, calm, imposing, the envy of all; great volumes of the blackest smoke are rolling and tumbling out of the chimneys—a husbanded grandeur created with a bit of pitch pine just before arriving at a town; the crew are grouped on the forecastle; the broad stage is run far out over the port bow, and an envied deckhand stands picturesquely on the end of it with a coil of rope in his hand; the pent steam is screaming through the gauge cocks; the captain lifts his hand, a bell rings, the wheels stop; then they turn back, churning the water to a foam, and the steamer is at rest. Then such a scramble as there is to get aboard, and to get ashore, and to take in freight, and to discharge freight, all at one and the same time; and such a yelling and cursing as the mates facilitate it all with! Ten minutes later the steamer is under way again, with no flag on the jack staff and no black smoke issuing from the chimneys. After ten more minutes the town is dead again and the town drunkard asleep by the skids once more.—*Life on the Mississippi.*

*Suggestions for Study*

1. Study the selections under "Sense Impressions" and for each selection state which sense is chiefly appealed to. If the selection appeals to more than one sense, list the senses appealed to, beginning with the sense to which the greatest appeal is made.

2. State the dominant impression which each selection gives.

3. State the specific purpose for each of the selections by Ruskin.

4. For each of the selections beginning with "Christmas Tree" through "The Furnished Room," give the exact setting and the position of the speaker in that setting.

5. If you were an artist, which of the selections could you illustrate most faithfully? Which would be more difficult to illustrate? State the reasons for your opinion.

6. Study the three selections under "Persons": What is the dominant impression in each? Compare the descriptions of actual physical features of the three. Of each, state whether the author was trying to transmit an impression of the whole character or a photograph of the exterior appearance.

7. Of the selections under "Changing Point of View," state concerning each whether the changing point of view is one of place or time or both.

8. Answer the following specific questions on the selections:

"On Observing Colors": (a) In what mood should the artist be when he is trying to color? Would the same hold true for one trying to transmit a picture by words instead of by brush? (b) According to Ruskin, what is the most beautiful thing in the world? the next most beautiful? (c) What advice does he give about putting colors together?

"Water": (a) How many different forms in which water may be observed does he mention? (b) To whom is the selection addressed primarily? Does it have value for those who depict through words? Explain your answer.

"Christmas Tree": (a) What date would you give to this Christmas tree? Why? (b) Mark any words in the selection which you could not define and look them up in a dictionary. Does this make the focus more sharp? (c) What do you deduce about the author from this selection?

"Water Hyacinths": (a) Could you draw a water hyacinth from the author's description? (b) What exact information about the water hyacinth does the selection give? (c) Do the flowers have an odor? (d) Why did the captain frown when he pointed to them?

"Rain in Mexico": (a) What does the author mean by the rainy season's not being for the poet but for the priest? (b) State in your own words what takes place as the rain approaches. (c) What distinction does the author make between climate and weather? (d) Look up the following words: incontinent, burgeoning, livid, charro, poncho, rarefied, effulgence.

"The Merry-Go-Round": (a) List the words that denote movement. (b) List all the sounds mentioned in the selection.

"Sounds in Late Summer": (a) What is the chief difference between the two scenes in the selection? (b) What differences in the sounds does the author note between the two scenes? (c) Try to find a single word that will best give the impression on the listener in each scene.

"Early Morning": (a) What is the occasion for this bit of description? (b) Explain the meaning of the last clause in the first sentence. (c) What adjectives and verbs seem well chosen to give an accurate impression with the fewest words?

"Making Tortillas": (a) List separately all the sounds and sights mentioned in the selection. (b) What is the dominant impression?

"The Wind": (a) What is the time of year? (b) What senses are appealed to? Which dominates? Which is next? (c) Try to locate the setting—general and specific.

"Apples": (a) Does the author's use of fantasy in any way vivify the description? (b) Which paragraph gives you the best impression? Which sense is appealed to in each?

"Christmas Breakfast": (a) What special privilege was given the author at Christmas breakfast? (b) Who were present? (c) Who assumed the duties of waiting table? (d) Consider the selection very carefully, then tell which of the senses is appealed to most.

"Dinner at Cousin Lil's": (a) Why did the author's sisters disapprove of Lil? (b) What date would you assign to the occasion? (c) Describe Cousin Lil—physical appearance and character. (d) What was the time of year and what the specific occasion for the dinner?

"Mexico City": (a) What contrast exists between Mexico City and an American city? (b) What changes have taken place in Mexico City in 400 years? What conditions persist? (c) According to the author, what gives Mexico its quality of excitement? (d) Who was the gringa? Why did she go away from the park in disgrace?

"Farmhouse Cellar": (a) In which season did the author most enjoy the cellar? (b) Describe the cellar in your own words. (c) List the contents of the cellar.

"The Furnished Room": (a) List the principal words which give the selection its dominant tone. (b) What specific clues indicated some of the past tenants of the room? (c) To what does the author attribute the treatment of the room by its tenants? (d) Which is important—physical or mental point of view?

"Captain Ahab": (a) In what order are the details of Ahab's appearance presented? (b) Is the omission of details of facial features bad? (c) What three figures of speech in the first paragraph dominate the description?

"Eustacia Vye": (a) Why do the last three sentences return to the idea of the first paragraph? (b) Are the reference to the Sphinx and the adjective *Pagan* in tone with the rest of the description? Why does he use the latter word instead of "peculiar"? (c) What hint does the description of Eustacia's hair give to her character? What other hints are present in the selection? (d) In the last paragraph, what do the attributes of her presence, moods, and voice have in common?

"Stina": (a) List the attributes of Stina as given in the selection. (b) Does her physical description and what the author says of her character harmonize?

"A Road in England": (a) In what does a road's excellence lie? (b) What was the shape of the village? What was it called? (c) List the main views a traveler along the road would have. (d) Make a list of words in the selection which are unfamiliar to you and look them up. Does knowing the words bring the picture into sharper focus? (e) List the terms that indicate a changing point of view.

"A Steamboat Landing": (a) Are the images produced by the description general or specific? (b) What point of view does the author assume in his description? Where would he have to be to see all that he describes? Is the changing point of view one of place, time, or tone?

## Suggestions for Writing

1. Observe one of your college buildings from a distance of a block or two. Make a list of details in the order that they would appear in a description of the building from that point of view. State the dominant impression. Then approach to within twenty paces of the main entrance and make another list. Is the dominant impression the same?

2. Write a description of the classroom to which you go for freshman composition. Assume the point of view of yourself as you sit in your accustomed seat.

3. Using one of the topics suggested below, write a description of five hundred words or more. State at the top of your paper your point of view and dominant impression.

A familiar landmark on your campus
A country store
A third-rate movie house
A modern filling station
A favorite picture
A piece of antique furniture
A room in a historic house
A blizzard
A room in a broadcasting station
The community Christmas tree
A streamlined train
The house you would like to live in
A favorite camping spot
A stage setting for a play or opera
Backstage in a theater
A hotel or theater doorman
Some notable person in your home town
The janitor of a college building

4. Write a description in which the point of view changes or which involves the passing of time. Suggestions:

A trip up an elevator in a department store
The characteristic countryside seen by a motorist in some part of the country
The banks of a river as seen from a canoe
An airplane passenger's view of the country below
The crowd before and after a football game
The appearance of your room before and after your friends come in to investigate a box from home

5. Write a description which includes a wide sweep of vision—a panorama, in other words. Suggestions:

The audience which comes to witness free movies in a small town

A tourist camp

An airport

A city as seen from the top of a tall building

A crowd gathered to witness the departure of a steamship

The crowd at a professional baseball game

An automobile dump

A large industrial plant

6. Write a description which emphasizes the experiences of one sense only. Suggestions:

A "hamburger joint"

What a ball game sounds like to a person outside the fence

The noise of a carnival

The locker room of the gymnasium

A night in a Pullman berth

A roller coaster ride

The bodily sensations experienced when one is frightened while following a dark path at night

How to distinguish different kinds of cloth by the sense of touch

Riding in a rumble seat

7. Describe the auditory sensations you experience when listening to a certain piece of music in terms of images involving the other senses. If the piece of music tells a story, that can be part of your description, but do not be content with the story only. What pictures or other sensations does the music create?

## D. The Narrative

Narration deals with material in which the passing of time is a fundamental element. Exposition, argumentation, and description may make use of narration; for example, the explanation of a process certainly involves the passing of time as the writer takes up one step of the process and then another. But narration, properly speaking, places emphasis on the *result* of a sequence of events, whereas the explanation of a process puts emphasis on the *manner* in which the events take place. A narrative is a story, and a story, even of the simplest variety, leads to something. The reader or auditor wants to know what happens next. Thus, when telling about changing a tire, a person can be motivated by at least two entirely different purposes and thereby produce different effects. He may intend to explain the process, and consequently he tells how the jack works, describes the best kind of wrench to use on the lugs, cautions the reader against injuring the valve stem, and so forth. Or he may put the experience in the form of a story. Doing so, he encourages the reader to wonder whether he was successful in getting the old tire off and the spare tire on. He takes up the steps in chronological order, each step being related to the one which precedes it and the one which follows. The various processes are important, not necessarily because of what the reader can advantageously learn from them, but because of the interest which they arouse with regard to a final result. A conflict emerges between the man and the situation. A climax is reached either when the spare tire is safely on and the car speeds away, or when the would-be mechanic throws down his wrench and calls a garage.

**The Technique of the Narrative.** If, then, the chief aim of the narrative is to focus the attention of the reader on a sequence of events and keep him interested in what is going to happen next, the technique of the narrative is the proper arranging of characters and incidents to the end that this aim may be achieved. Possibilities of variation are infinite. A novel by Dickens usually begins with the early childhood of the hero or heroine and proceeds, by straight chronology, through the stages in his development until he is a mature adult. A modern murder mystery may begin with a corpse lying cold and stiff on the hearthrug, and then, with the aid of a master detective, reconstruct the steps leading to the crime. A moving picture or radio play may start at a point near the end of a chain of events and, by a system of "cut-backs," fill in scenes from the past. But whatever the method of handling the story may be, every narrative has three basic parts: the *initial situation,* the *action,* and the *conclusion.* This has been recognized since the time of Aristotle, who spoke of the beginning, middle, and end. To this ancient analysis of the parts of a narrative, we may add three characteristic qualities of a good story: *unity, suspense,* and the *illusion of reality*.

**The Initial Situation.** The initial situation should contain the germ of everything which comes afterward. There are two versions of the story of Little Red Riding Hood: in one the heroine is gobbled up by the wolf who has ensconced himself in the grandmother's bed; in the other, at the latest possible moment, some brothers of Little Red Riding Hood arrive in the nick of time to chop the wolf to pieces with their axes. The second version may serve as more wholesome entertainment for children than the first, since it is the wicked old wolf, rather than the innocent heroine, who meets a violent end. The first version, however, is the more artistic, because everything in the story develops logically from the initial situation, which contains no mention of watchful guardians in the form of brothers. The initial situation, then, does more than simply start the ball rolling. It states the nature of the ball, provides it with motive power, and limits the direction in which it will be allowed to roll. Thus, the initial situation can hardly be written in complete form until the author has in mind what he intends to produce as action and conclusion.

*Conflict.* The opening parts of the narrative, of course, present the setting and the important characters; but, more important, the basis for the conflict, which is waged in the action and resolved in the conclusion, is arranged. Obviously, there are as many different kinds of conflict as there are possibilities for stories, but the writer should be clear in his mind as to the exact conflict with which he is dealing. Without conflict there can be no suspense, and without suspense the narrative loses force. Furthermore, unless the writer understands the kind of conflict which is inherent in the situation he has arranged, his story will be crude. The struggle of one army against another, of one business against another, of a pursuit flyer against an enemy bomber, or of a prize fighter against his opponent is a fairly easy kind of conflict to imagine and to keep in control. The more subtle kinds of struggle require more penetration and greater care. Such is true in a narrative containing a contest between a man and his conscience, between the two parts of a split personality, between a man and his environment, man and machines, or man and the universe. In a very slight narrative, such as the anecdote, the conflict is often merely between expectation and reality.

*Tone.* The initial situation is also important in setting the tone of the narrative. By tone is meant the emotional atmosphere which envelops the story and permeates the reader. Is it to be the long-winded, colloquial, tall story of the Western settler, like Mark Twain's "Celebrated Jumping Frog"; or the whimsical, slightly scandalous sort of thing associated with Thorne Smith? The tone should be set in the opening words of the narrative. A story which begins, "Once upon a time, in a beautiful palace, there lived . . ." acquires a definite tone immediately, just as the one which starts with "Jack Roper zoomed his pursuit plane sharply upward, just in time to catch a glimpse of the bomber sliding into a cloudbank."

*Point of view.* Another important element in the technique of the story which is set by the initial situation is the point of view. Most stories are told in the third person. That is, the author assumes a Godlike position, from which he can see and hear anything at any time and in any place. The "once upon a time, there was . . ." story is of this order. The virtue of this point of view is its great flexibility. Once the reader agrees (which he readily will, since this convention is so old that it is easier to accept it than to question it) to allow the author to assume this Godlike position, the author is at liberty to reveal any information he chooses.

regardless of the physical difficulties in the way of his being in possession of it. He may shift in one sentence from an occurrence at the beginning of the sequence of incidents to one at the end; he may even lift off the top of a character's head, so to speak, and show the reader the thoughts being formed inside. Very frequently, the third-person narrator, while retaining his right to make a shift when he so desires, emphasizes the point of view of one of his characters, as Dickens does in *Oliver Twist*.

The use of the first person in narration has the effect, in many instances, of increasing the illusion of reality. The autobiography is sometimes preferred to the biography because it is likely to give a more authentic account of actual experiences. Similarly, the narrative told in the first person establishes an intimate narrator-to-reader contact. The story of Robinson Crusoe, told by the castaway himself, is probably more effective than it would be if Defoe had thrust himself between the actor and the reader as the storyteller. The superb authenticity of Huckleberry Finn's experiences on the Mississippi is due in part to the fact that Huck is allowed to tell his story in his own way. Perhaps this is one reason for the superiority of that book over *Tom Sawyer*.

Nevertheless, serious difficulties confront the writer who uses the first person. A few readers find the first-person technique unbearable because of what seems to be egotism on the part of the narrator. A more important disadvantage is that, since the story is limited to what the narrator can hear and see as a flesh-and-blood person, the author sometimes finds it hard to avoid unnatural and unconvincing maneuvering in order to acquaint the reader with some essential detail. In *Moby Dick*, after describing the sinking of the *Pequod* and the death of her crew, Herman Melville was forced to rescue one sailor, the person who tells the story.

A third method appears occasionally, using the point of view of a first-person narrator who is not personally implicated in the events of the story, and can therefore give objectivity and elasticity to the narrative along with the much-desired authenticity. Joseph Conrad's use of such a character, Marlowe, furnishes a good example. Marlowe is an inquisitive and philosophical observer. He gathers up from numerous sources the details of a series of events which have happened to someone who has attracted his attention, and then relates them in a more or less carefully documented yarn. The inherent difficulties in the use of the point of view of the first person, however, are shown when even Conrad is forced occasionally to introduce scenes and conversations which Marlowe had no means of knowing about.

### Exercise

Following are the opening paragraphs of two well-known stories. With regard to each of them, (1) enumerate four possible sequences of events which can progress naturally from the initial situation, (2) describe the tone which has been set, and (3) state the point of view.

1. The "Red Death" had long devastated the country. No pestilence had ever been so fatal, or so hideous. Blood was its avatar and its seal—the redness and the horror of blood. There were sharp pains, and sudden dizziness, and then profuse bleeding at the pores, with dissolution. The scarlet stains upon the body, and especially upon the face, of the victim were the pest ban which shut him out from the aid and from the sympathy of his fellow men. And the whole seizure, progress, and termination of the disease were the incidents of half an hour.

But the Prince Prospero was happy and dauntless and sagacious. When his dominions were half depopulated, he summoned to his presence a thousand hale and light-hearted friends from among the knights and dames of his court, and with these retired to the deep seclusion of one of his castellated abbeys. This was an extensive and magnificent structure, the creation of the Prince's own eccentric yet august taste. A strong and lofty wall girdled it in. This wall had gates of iron. The courtiers, having entered, brought furnaces and massy hammers, and welded the bolts. They resolved to leave means neither of ingress nor egress to the sudden impulses of despair or of frenzy from within. The abbey was amply provisioned. With such precautions the courtiers might bid defiance to contagion. The external world could take care of itself. In the mean time it was folly to grieve, or to think. The Prince had provided all the appliances of pleasure. There were buffoons, there were improvisatori, there were ballet-dancers, there were musicians, there was Beauty, there was wine. All these and security were within. Without was the "Red Death."—Edgar Allan Poe, "The Masque of the Red Death."

2. As Mr. John Oakhurst, gambler, stepped into the main street of Poker Flat on the morning of the 23d of November, 1850, he was conscious of a change in its moral atmosphere since the preceding night. Two or three men, conversing earnestly together, ceased as he approached, and exchanged significant glances. There was a Sabbath lull in the air, which, in a settlement unused to Sabbath influences, looked ominous.

Mr. Oakhurst's calm, handsome face betrayed small concern in these indications. Whether he was conscious of any predisposing cause, was another question. "I reckon they're after somebody," he reflected; "likely it's me." He returned to his pocket the handkerchief with which he had been whipping away the red dust of Poker Flat from his neat boots, and quietly discharged his mind of any further conjecture.

In point of fact, Poker Flat was "after somebody." It had lately suffered the loss of several thousand dollars, two valuable horses, and a prominent citizen. It was experiencing a spasm of virtuous reaction, quite as lawless and ungovernable as any of the acts that had provoked it. A secret committee had determined to rid the town of all improper persons. This was done permanently in regard of two men who were then hanging from the boughs of a sycamore in the gulch, and temporarily in the banishment of certain other objectionable characters. I regret to say that some of these were ladies. It is but due to the sex, however, to state that their impropriety was professional, and it was only in such easily established standards of evil that Poker Flat ventured to sit in judgment.

Mr. Oakhurst was right in supposing that he was included in this category. A few of the committee had urged hanging him as a possible example, and a sure method of reimbursing themselves from his pockets of the sums he had won from them. "It's agin justice," said Jim Wheeler, "to let this yer young man from Roaring Camp—an entire stranger—carry away our money." But a crude sentiment of equity residing in the breasts of those who had been fortunate enough to win from Mr. Oakhurst overruled this narrower local prejudice.

Mr. Oakhurst received his sentence with philosophic calmness, none the less coolly that he was aware of the hesitation of his judges. He was too much of a gambler not to accept fate. With him life was at best an uncertain game, and he recognized the usual percentage in favor of the dealer.

A body of armed men accompanied the deported wickedness of Poker Flat to the outskirts of the settlement. Besides Mr. Oakhurst, who was known to be a coolly desperate man, and for whose intimidation the armed escort was intended, the expatriated party consisted of a young woman familiarly known as "The Duchess"; another, who had won the title of "Mother Shipton"; and "Uncle Billy," a suspected sluice-robber and confirmed drunkard. The cavalcade provoked no comments from the spectators, nor was any word uttered by the escort. Only when the gulch which marked the uttermost limit of Poker Flat was reached, the leader spoke briefly and to the point. The exiles were forbidden to return at the peril of their lives.—Bret Harte, "The Outcasts of Poker Flat."

**Action.** When one says that a narrative has three parts, initial situation, action, and conclusion, he must remember that it is frequently hard, sometimes impossible, to state that a particular part begins precisely here and ends there. Children's stories and most fiction written for adults until fairly recent times follow a conventional pattern in which the initial situation (containing the germ of the action and establishing the tone and point of view), action, and conclusion are easily distinguishable. Many modern storywriters, however, believe that a better procedure is to start with action, making use of a technique which gradually brings to light the elements which commonly constitute the initial situation. The purpose of a technique of this kind is to establish an illusion of reality and create suspense as quickly as possible by plunging the reader into an interesting conversation or an exciting incident, the complete meaning of which will not be clear until he reads further.

*Suspense.* Regardless of whether the action of a narrative represents a solid mid-section or is extended in the manner just mentioned, the main problem is to create and maintain suspense. The familiar formula of the English writer, Wilkie Collins, "Make 'em laugh, make 'em cry, make 'em wait," is good in any place or age. Whether a person is composing scenarios for "to be continued" Saturday night movie thrillers or preparing an anecdote for an after-dinner speech, the success of his product rests largely on his skill in dosing out to his audience, minute by minute, exactly the right proportions of information. Even when the reader or the audience knows what the end of the story is going to be (as in a narrative which begins, "Let me tell you how I caught my first big fish"), curiosity can be aroused concerning other elements.

The length of a narrative depends, of course, on how much material is to be covered; but, from the point of view of technique, the narrative should be as long as suspense can be maintained without sacrificing unity —exactly no longer and no shorter. If the action is drawn out to the extent that the reader loses his grasp on the whole narrative and becomes involved in incidents which are only loosely related to the whole, unity is lost, and the narrative should be pruned down. However, most student narratives are not developed enough. When the student is told that he should make more of his material, he complains that he cannot do so without padding; but judicious padding is an essential part of any art. It becomes objectionable only when it is not related to the main issue or when it deadens suspense rather than enhances it.

Consider, for example, the excerpt, "The Duel in the Long Shrubbery," from Robert Louis Stevenson's novel, *The Master of Ballantrae*.[38]

Mr. Henry laid down his cards. He rose to his feet very softly, and seemed all the while like a person in deep thought. "You coward!" he said gently, as if to himself. And then, with neither hurry nor any particular violence, he struck the Master in the mouth.

The Master sprang to his feet like one transfigured; I had never seen the man so beautiful. "A blow!" he cried. "I would not take a blow from God Almighty."

"Lower your voice," said Mr. Henry. "Do you wish my father to interfere for you again?"

"Gentlemen, gentlemen," I cried, and sought to come between them.

The Master caught me by the shoulder, held me at arm's length, and still addressing his brother: "Do you know what this means?" said he.

"It was the most deliberate act of my life," says Mr. Henry.

"I must have blood, I must have blood for this," says the Master.

"Please God it shall be yours," said Mr. Henry; and he went to the wall and took down a pair of swords that hung there with others, naked. These he presented to the Master by the points. "Mackellar shall see us play fair," said Mr. Henry. "I think it very needful."

38. From *The Master of Ballantrae*, by Robert Louis Stevenson, Charles Scribner's Sons. Used by permission of the publishers.

"You need insult me no more," said the Master, taking one of the swords at random. "I have hated you all my life."

"My father is but newly gone to bed," said Mr. Henry. "We must go somewhere forth of the house."

"There is an excellent place in the long shrubbery," said the Master.

"Gentlemen," said I, "shame upon you both! Sons of the same mother, would you turn against the life she gave you?"

"Even so, Mackellar," said Mr. Henry, with the same perfect quietude of manner he had shown throughout.

"It is what I will prevent," said I.

And now here is a blot upon my life. At these words of mine, the Master turned his blade against my bosom; I saw the light run along the steel; and I threw up my arms and fell to my knees before him on the floor. "No, no," I cried, like a baby.

"We shall have no more trouble with him," said the Master. "It is a good thing to have a coward in the house."

"We must have light," said Mr. Henry, as though there had been no interruption.

"This trembler can bring a pair of candles," said the Master.

To my shame be it said, I was still so blinded with the flashing of that bare sword that I volunteered to bring a lantern.

"We do not need a l-l-lantern," says the Master, mocking me. "There is no breath of air. Come, get to your feet, take a pair of lights, and go before. I am close behind with this—" making the blade glitter as he spoke.

I took up the candlesticks and went before them, steps that I would give my hand to recall; but a coward is a slave at the best; and even as I went, my teeth smote each other in my mouth. It was as he had said, there was no breath stirring: a windless stricture of frost had bound the air; and as we went forth in the shine of the candles, the blackness was like a roof over our heads. Never a word was said; there was never a sound but the creaking of our steps along the frozen path. The cold of the night fell about me like a bucket of water; I shook as I went with more than terror; but my companions, bareheaded like myself and fresh from the warm hall, appeared not even conscious of the change.

"Here is the place," said the Master. "Set down the candles."

I did as he bade me, and presently the flames went up as steadily as in a chamber in the midst of the frosted trees, and I beheld these two brothers take their places.

"The light is something in my eyes," said the Master.

"I will give you every advantage," replied Mr. Henry, shifting his ground, "for I think you are about to die." He spoke rather sadly than otherwise, yet there was a ring in his voice.

"Henry Durie," said the Master, "two words before I begin. You are a fencer, you can hold a foil; you little know what a change it makes to hold a sword! And by that I know you are to fall. But see how strong is my situation! If you fall, I shift out of this country to where my money is before me. If I fall, where are you? My father, your wife who is in love with me—as you very well know—your child even who prefers me to yourself: how will these avenge me! Had you thought of that, dear Henry?" He looked at his brother with a smile; then made a fencing-room salute.

Never a word said Mr. Henry, but saluted too, and the swords rang together.

I am no judge of the play, my head besides was gone with cold and fear and horror; but it seems that Mr. Henry took and kept the upper hand from the first engagement, crowding in upon his foe with a contained and glowing fury. Nearer and nearer he crept upon the man till, of a sudden, the Master leaped back with a little sobbing oath; and I believe the movement brought the light once more against his eyes. To it they went again, on the fresh ground; but now methought closer, Mr. Henry pressing more outrageously, the Master beyond doubt with shaken confidence. For it is beyond doubt he now recognized himself for lost, and had some taste of the cold agony of fear; or he had never attempted the foul stroke. I cannot say I followed it, my untrained eye was never quick enough to seize details, but it appears he caught his brother's blade with his left hand, a practice not permitted. Certainly Mr. Henry only saved himself by leaping on one side; as certainly the Master, lunging in the air, stumbled on his knee, and before he could move, the sword was through his body.

I cried out with a stifled scream, and ran in; but the body was already fallen to the ground, where it writhed a moment like a trodden worm, and then lay motionless.

"Look at his left hand," said Mr. Henry.

"It is all bloody," said I.

"On the inside?" said he.

"It is cut on the inside," said I.

"I thought so," said he, and turned his back.

I opened the man's clothes; the heart was quite still, it gave not a flutter.

"God forgive us, Mr. Henry!" said I. "He is dead."

"Dead?" he repeated, a little stupidly; and then with a rising tone, "Dead? dead?" says he, and suddenly cast his bloody sword upon the ground.

Almost any reader would agree that this is an absorbing incident. When asked to give a reason for its being such, he might say, "Well, it tells about a duel, and violent action is always interesting." This is true enough, but a person with an eye for good storytelling technique will discover that an extraordinarily fine use of suspense enabled Stevenson to make the most of his subject matter. Notice how skillfully and unobtrusively he interposes obstacle after obstacle between his initial situation (the difficulty over cards and the blow) and his conclusion (the death of the Master). The opening sentences act swiftly and briefly to arouse curiosity. Is there actually going to be a duel, and if so, who is going to be killed? But no sooner has Mr. Henry insulted the Master than Mackellar interrupts and tries to pacify the brothers. He is swept aside, and the action proceeds as the challenge is confirmed and the swords are taken from the wall. An inexperienced writer would now have the brothers fall to at once—but not Stevenson. The situation is too good to finish it so quickly. So there is dialogue concerning the best place for the duel; but again, when the men have decided to fight in the long shrubbery, the action is delayed by Mackellar's protest. Mackellar is cowed by the sight of the Master's sword, and the way is left clear for advancing the action, only to be blocked for another moment by the question of lights. At last, the men leave the house. Mackellar's description of the cold, dark night follows, not only for the sake of providing a stage setting for the approaching climax, but also to prolong the suspense. Having at last arrived at the dueling ground, the Master, with his complaint about the light, is made use of to present another obstacle; again, his speech to Mr. Henry adds another moment or two to the timing of the climax. Finally, the duel itself, while not described in great detail, is told at sufficient length to keep the reader waiting through another good-sized paragraph. The thrusting of Mr. Henry's sword through the body of the Master is postponed to the latest possible moment. The important thing is that the timing is so good, and the choice of obstructions to place in the path of the action is so interesting, that the reader is pleased, rather than annoyed, at being delayed. Really, the climax carries more weight and importance because the path to it has been prepared so carefully.

*Characterization.* Having read this episode from *The Master of Ballantrae,* ask yourself whether you are pleased at the outcome. Which man did you favor to win? Undoubtedly Mr. Henry. Why? Examine the selection again. From the beginning, Mr. Henry acts and speaks like a sober, quiet, responsible person who has been provoked beyond endurance; while the Master shows himself a braggart and a bully, possibly a coward. His first words are, "A blow! I would not take a blow from God Almighty"—rash words, to say the least. He threatens poor Mackellar with his sword, insists on having the advantage of the light before he will fight, and taunts his brother with his having won for himself the affections of Mr. Henry's wife and child. We have no physical description of either of the brothers; not once does the author step in to tell us what to think of either one (except as his mouthpiece, Mackellar, gives us one or two hints); yet our sympathies are focused from the beginning.

This, of course, is important. It would be unfortunate if the reader sympathized with the wrong person, and the writer should be on his guard to see that this does not happen. Manufacturers of comic strips for newspapers depend almost entirely on the physical appearance of their characters to elicit sympathy or antagonism. A square jaw for a man and eyes large as turkey eggs for a woman are undeniable essentials among "good" people of the comic strip world. A beard or even the most immature mustache seldom mars the physiognomy of a hero unless he is in disguise. To give him a foreign accent would be fatal. The writer of fiction can, of course, make use of these conventions also; but, if his purpose is at all serious, he will depend much less on physical description than on the impression formed on the reader by what the character says and does. The modern reader is likely to object seriously if the author, obviously and artificially, interposes himself and his views between the reader and the story. If, therefore, you wish to give the impression that a character is honorable, make him act honorably and speak honorably; do not pin a label on him: "This is an honorable man."

*Foreshadowing.* Turning again to the episode from *The Master of Ballantrae,* let us take note of one more thing, the foreshadowing of events. What is the effect of Mr. Henry's exclamation, "You coward!" and of his later remark, "Mackellar shall see us play fair. I think it very needful"? Do not both speeches drop a hint that the Master may resort to trickery or foul play, and does not the Master's act, grasping his opponent's sword in his left hand, verify that suspicion? In other words, the climax of the episode is foreshadowed by these bits tucked away in the earlier part so that they are almost overlooked.

The knack of clever foreshadowing is also an important part of the storyteller's technique. It is frequently an essential element in the action, heightening the force of the conclusion and emphasizing the quality of inevitability which is necessary if the illusion of reality is to be maintained. Heavily underscored foreshadowing which discloses too much, or which is too obviously the voice of the author speaking from behind the scenes, is bad. It insults the intelligence of the reader, who feels that the author is treating him as a child when he says, in effect, "Look out, reader! Remember that Desperate Joe has a knife in his boot. He's the kind of person who would stick Honest James in the back if he cared to. Be prepared for what is coming." However, the observant reader takes satisfaction in recognizing a hint dropped unobtrusively, and is pleased with himself when the conclusion bears out his suspicions. Remember, a complete surprise is seldom pleasant; it is more likely to be overwhelming or bewildering. On the other hand, half-formed suspicions or anticipations may be made sources of pleasure when they are wholly or partially verified.

**Conclusion.** If a narrative is adequately planned, the writing of the conclusion should be a comparatively easy task; yet both critics and the reading public are likely to find fault with the conclusion of a story more quickly than with the other parts. A story should build up to the conclusion with all the cumulative power which suspense and the illusion of reality can generate, and if the conclusion, when it is reached, is un satisfactory, a great deal of time has been wasted. It is well, therefore, to consider the virtues of a good conclusion. These are clearness, inevitability, and the quality of being aesthetically satisfying.

*Clearness.* A person who has planned his narrative in his head before he has put much of it on paper, and who is possibly familiar with it to the point of boredom, should be quite sure that he has not omitted some small detail without which the conclusion lacks meaning. Clearness is doubly necessary at that point of the story at which the reader's emotions have reached the highest pitch, and where an interruption is comparable to the intensely irritating moments moviegoers used to experience when the operator had to shut off his machine in order to change reels. The conclusion should by all means be brief, but not so brief as to be cryptic. It is possible to say or imply a great deal with a few words and still be as lucid as if pages had been covered.

*Inevitability.* In the section on the initial situation it was said that the beginning of a story should contain the seed of all that develops later. The conclusion, therefore, should seem to be the natural result of forces which were set in motion in the initial situation and came into conflict during the action. It is at this point that experience with life and insight into human nature is of utmost importance to the writer. He is concerned with a character or characters upon whom certain influences have been brought to bear. What will be the effect of these influences? The interplay of character and character, or character and environment, or character and circumstances, is a fascinating study, and the results are to a certain extent unpredictable. However, no matter what he experiences, a character remains himself; and it is necessary that the storyteller understand that essential nature of a character which may suffer superficial alterations, but which remains fundamentally the same.

Tim McCarty, who after many years of successfully picking pockets was sent to prison, is released and becomes a trusted clerk in a jeweler's store. Is he going to be steadfastly honest, or is he merely waiting his chance to make the greatest haul of his career? The answer to the question involves a knowledge of just who Tim McCarty really is, the fundamental traits of character with respect to which his actions or occupations are symptoms or results. If the writer who uses Tim as a character wishes to make him turn out an honest man, he will have to indicate that when Tim was a pickpocket, he considered his occupation a regrettable but necessary evil; or he will have to show that Tim has undergone a recognizable and understandable change, *one which the conditions of Tim's own nature make possible.* Having chosen his characters, the writer must live with them, study them, and be true to them.

Nothing will destroy the illusion of reality more effectively than what appears to be a manipulated plot—a sequence of incidents which seem to have their origin more truly in the writer's laboratory than in his observation of probable situations from life. Roman dramatists, having succeeded in getting their plots snarled hopelessly, sometimes in the last act introduced a god who, with his supernatural power, would clear up everything and make possible a happy ending. Folk tales and fairy stories frequently make use of a pixie or fairy godmother or guardian angel who appears unexpectedly in the nick of time to set right what otherwise would be a calamity. The same technique might be used in the story of Tim, the pickpocket-jeweler. Tim has lived a life of crime and has been hardened further by his time in prison. He gets his job in the jeweler's store and makes plans for burglary on a large scale. But, just as he is throwing the last sterling spoon in his bag before making off with his loot, he hears, from the church across the street, the organ playing and the choir singing (it is Christmas Eve, of course), and he is so affected that he puts everything back in the glass cases and runs across the street through the softly falling snow to pray at the altar.

The reader would have a perfect right to be disgusted with Tim and Tim's author, because the story has certainly been manipulated beyond the limits of credibility. Is this the first time in his life that Tim has heard church music? Certainly not. Then why should he succumb to it now? We have been given no opportunity to note anything in Tim's nature which would respond in such a way, and therefore we condemn the author for either failing to give us necessary information about Tim or deliberately falsifying the story for the sake of a "happy" ending.

"But," someone might reply, "it is not at all impossible for something which responds to Christmas Eve and religious music to have been buried so deeply in Tim's character that it has never been noticeable. After all, human nature is the most unpredictable thing we know." True enough; but an artistic story should have a probable development rather than just any possible development. Since a story is a composition, something which is composed, there must be a logical relationship among the parts. Every artist follows a pattern of some kind, and the pattern of the artist in narration is derived from probable experience. If a storyteller wishes us to recognize a certain element as being a legitimate part of his pattern, the least he can do is to acquaint us with its presence.

Before leaving the discussion of inevitability in a narrative, we should take some note of the "trick" or "snap" ending which has been used effectively by such authors as O. Henry and Leonard Merrick. This type of ending, by giving a quick twist to the sequence of events in the story, leaves the reader pleasantly surprised. In an O. Henry story, "Soapy," a bum, concludes that because cold weather is coming he should do whatever is necessary to be sentenced to a nice, warm jail. But after committing several offenses and remaining strangely immune to the penalties of the law, he passes a church and, reminded of home and mother, decides to get a job and become a decent citizen. At that moment he feels the firm hand of a policeman on his shoulder, and he is given ninety days for vagrancy. This is an unanticipated ending; but notice that the materials for this ending were inherent in the story from the beginning, and that the surprise is not due to the introduction of a new element. Thus, a "trick" ending may be used legitimately if it does not contradict the rest of the story and does not introduce new elements.

*Aesthetic satisfaction.* A worker derives a certain kind of satisfaction from contemplating any finished creation that turns out well, whether it is a brick wall, a chocolate cake, or a story. Hence a writer is sure to feel a sense of satisfaction over a story that is well integrated and well timed and that develops with increasing intensity and dramatic emphasis. There is, however, a still higher satisfaction for the writer of narrative, what we may call aesthetic satisfaction, that comes from writing—or reading—a story which evidences a complete understanding by the author of his characters and of the influences to which they are subjected, and the end of which is a logical and necessary product of the sort of character which the actors possess.

Certain periodicals which cater primarily to readers of limited mental attainments will use no story that does not "end happily," regardless of prior tendencies or of the aesthetic demands of the story. Intolerance of such an untrue attitude towards life has led some artistic rebels to go to the other extreme and make every story they write end unhappily, even when the characters and actions in the story do not inevitably demand such an ending. The attitude of both the artistic rebels and those directing the policy of the popular periodicals is of course wrong. Aesthetic satisfaction results for the writer—and also for the intelligent reader—when the end is a natural and inevitable consequence of the sort of character possessed by the actors in the story and of the influences exerted on them; it fails when a writer so manipulates the final action that he reaches a conclusion which is not an inevitable outgrowth of character and influences working on it. A happy ending may be as satisfying artistically as an unhappy one, or the opposite may be true. What is necessary is that the reader must feel that he has experienced through the story events and actions and a result essentially true to life—not what is possible, but what is probable.

An exception to this general rule is farce and fantasy. Farce is like caricature in drawing: it exaggerates actions and peculiarities of character and holds up the actors to good-natured ridicule. The reader accepts this situation and surrenders his normal critical faculties to the author in order to enjoy the exaggerated depiction of actions and characters. Even in farce, however, there must be a basis of reality, for as a caricature fails in its purpose if the artist exaggerates to such an extent that no one can identify his subject, so farce that departs from normal human actions so far that a reader loses all sense of probability will fail to satisfy any save the most immature minds.

Fantasy likewise deals with the improbable, but in a more imaginative, delicate, and whimsical way than does farce. In fantasy, the writer assumes a reader who, like himself, is interested in the purely imaginative and who, as in farce, is willing to surrender his everyday notions of reality and follow the author into an imaginative world of fancy. Yet successful creators of fantasy are careful to use basic elements of character, actions, and scenes that are familiar enough to the reader to make the supernatural or purely imaginative elements which they introduce seem plausible.

In the examples of narrative at the end of this section, Mark Twain's yarn about the blue jay and Thurber's "You Can Look It Up" are farces; "Laura" and "Brandy for Breakfast" are fantasies which make use of basically realistic situations, characters, and conversation; and the others represent attempts, with varying success, to deal with situations that are true to life. As you read the farces and fantasies, note your own reactions, and see whether you surrender willingly to the authors' guidance and allow them to lead you into a world of unreality where birds talk, ghosts appear and tell stories, someone who dies returns to play jokes on a person she dislikes, and a tough manager of a baseball club uses a midget in a crucial baseball game. And as you read the other stories, analyze them to see if an author resorts to any manipulation of plot or character to secure an end contrary to the one you expected, to see if sentiment plays too great a part in any, and to see in which is present every element to make the story true to life and the end inevitable.

## TYPES OF NARRATION

Narrative ranges from such simple forms as the fable, the parable, the anecdote, and the incident to long novels. For the freshman composition course, it seems sufficient to differentiate two types—the short informal narrative which of course has a plan and is well built structurally but which lacks a carefully designed plot, and the carefully plotted narrative which we call a short story.

**Simple Narrative.** Simple, informal narration is perhaps the most common form of writing which the average person does. Everyone who writes a friendly letter is very likely to write narrative, for it is a natural impulse to report events one has witnessed or experiences in which one has participated. Yet few writers make the most of their chances to recreate events and experiences so vividly that these live for their readers. To do this requires a writer to plan the structure of his narrative so that (1) it has a carefully considered beginning, middle, and end, (2) the details are selected and arranged with care, and (3) the whole piece conveys to the reader a dominant impression. The simple narrative usually lacks the sort of suspense which is associated with the short story, though suspense in some degree is a part of nearly all good narrative; and it lacks a well-developed plot. There is usually a steady progression of events of somewhat equal intensity, each following the others in some normal manner, usually chronological, but all so fitted together as to give a single dominant effect.

Such writing may range from a report of a single incident to a number which together form one unified event or experience. The incident relates a single occurrence. When we speak of the incidents of a day's fishing or a trip to the city or country, we mean the individual small happenings which may be interesting or even important in themselves, but which do not constitute for us the chief interest of the day or the trip. If one of these should be lifted out of the day's happenings and related without reference to the other events of the day, it would constitute the most simple form of narrative writing. In the examples which follow this section, for example, the narrative of the car's hitting the turtle is inserted as a separate chapter by John Steinbeck in his *Grapes of Wrath*. Although it has a purpose in the whole novel, it could be omitted without detracting from the story. The incident, then, is a single action, event, or occurrence, of probably minor general significance, but possessing some inherent interest in character, local color, peculiarity of action, or the like, that makes it worth relating.

If several incidents are joined or a succession of actions are depicted, all of which relate to the same scheme but do not arouse high suspense and progress to a climax, the resulting piece of writing is usually termed a sketch. In the sketch, the narrative, if graphed, would appear as a relatively even plateau instead of climbing in a series of foothills and peaks as in the short story. This unemphatic structure tends to give the sketch an impromptu effect. That does not mean, of course, that informal writing of this sort is carelessly done, but that the organization appears informal because suspense is of secondary importance or may be absent altogether.

The writer of the simple narrative is less interested in creating suspense than in depicting character, portraying local color, recreating an experience or action. While he describes events as they take place, selecting of course only those that relate to his theme or that help to create the dominant impression he expects to convey, his tempo remains substantially the same throughout the narrative. He is thus perhaps nearer the informal essayist than the short story writer. The inexperienced writer needs to exercise great care, however, lest his narrative become merely a string of generalized statements which lack internal relationship and give no dominant impression—except one that the author is a lazy, careless person who was merely bent on filling some pages with dull and pointless matter. Like all good composition, the simple narrative has unity—unity of tone and unity of purpose. There must be a thesis sentence, a specific purpose; and all the parts of the narrative must contribute to the creation of a dominant impression. The mere piecing together of incidents that happened to one person does not in itself produce unity.

## Finding a Room [39]

### GERTRUDE DIAMANT

The street behaved just like a river. It rambled through empty lots and circled a field of corn, and then it disappeared. There was a high white wall where it disappeared, but not a sign or a person to tell me where the street had gone. Presently a boy on a bicycle came by, and seeing me standing in perplexity, he waved and called: "Follow the wall." I followed it, and there was the street again.

I was looking for Atoyac number 82, where the morning paper said there was a furnished apartment—cheap, comfortable, decent, ideal for an American. And I was in that part of Mexico City where all the streets bear the names of rivers. Already I had crossed the Tiber, the Rhine, and the River Po, old favorites familiar from high-school days. But what of the River Atoyac? Nobody knew where it was, and nobody seemed to have heard of it. The sun was high and the sidewalk burned my feet,

39. From *The Days of Ofelia*, by Gertrude Diamant (copyright, 1942, by Gertrude Diamant). Reprinted by permission of Houghton Mifflin Company, the publishers.

and I wandered on, hoping that the street would not disappear again. For I was carrying the two big valises which I had brought with me to Mexico, and which now contained all that I owned in the world.

It was a way of burning my bridges behind me. I was tired of living in boarding-houses (those beautiful old colonial mansions of the guide-books) with their damp dark rooms, slippery floors, and dreadful furniture. I had vowed never to enter another old colonial mansion, but to leave them all to their decaying splendors and to the Spartan Mexicans. And if there was no place in the city with an easy-chair and a comfortable bed and dry and sunny, then I would go back to the States. But I did not want to go back, either. There are three hundred thousand Otomí Indians in Mexico, and I had tested a mere one hundred. I must test another two hundred at least to prove—but no, it is not scientific to know in advance what one is going to prove.

I put my valises down, flexed my arms, and looked around. There were houses now, but not a sign to tell me if I had come to the River Atoyac. To know where you are in Mexico City, you must look at the corner houses; and with luck you will see a tiny plaque which bears the name of the street. But usually it isn't there at all, and the Mexicans have a sweet reasonableness when they cannot enlighten you. "Pues . . . you see, señorita, the signs are missing which should bear the names of the streets. So I cannot tell you, señorita, forgive me." It was Sunday and the stores were closed and the street deserted. I left my valises standing and walked until I came to where a man was sitting on the curb. He looked up from under a wide sombrero. "No, señorita," he said, "really I cannot tell you. I have little time here." "Time!" I thought scornfully. "What time do you need to tell me the name of a street?" And then I remembered my still meager Spanish. It is an idiom meaning that one has only just come to a place. "But if you ask the señor at the little stand over there," he went on, "possibly he can tell you. He has much time here." So I crossed to the little stand.

"Atoyac!" mused the man of much time. "Atoyac!" He smiled engagingly. "Forgive me, señorita, but I am unable to say. I do not concentrate on the names of the streets. However, if you should wish for the Street of the River of the Plata"—he pointed with an exquisite grace—"it is over there, señorita, just two blocks over there." "Thank you," I said, "I do not wish for the Street of the River of the Plata." And I went back and gathered my valises and wandered on. There were empty lots again and many blocks where the houses were still being built. Soon I would come to the city limits. I could see fields of corn and beyond them the mountains, splendidly luminous in the afternoon light. But at the last corner before the fields began I came to a house that miraculously bore the number 82. Five little girls sat on the doorstep.

"Is there a furnished apartment here?"

They chorused raggedly, pointing. "Arriba . . . upstairs." And I saw that they all had the same shade of brown-green eyes. Then they rose in a body and we all went up.

### Suggestions for Study

1. Analyze the structure of this selection to determine how much is beginning, middle, and end.

2. Write a thesis sentence for the piece. What is its dominant impression?

3. List the separate incidents which make up the episode.

4. These are the opening paragraphs of *The Days of Ofelia*. How much do we learn about the speaker from this selection? Try your hand at writing a brief character sketch of her, basing your conclusions on the style and mental point of view as well as on the descriptive details.

5. Write a sequel to this episode, telling what you think occurred when the author arrived upstairs; then procure a copy of the book and compare your account with the author's.

## Adventure of a Turtle [40]

### JOHN STEINBECK

The sun lay on the grass and warmed it, and in the shade under the grass the insects moved, ants and ant lions to set traps for them, grasshoppers to jump into the air and flick their yellow wings for a second, sow bugs like little armadillos, plodding restlessly on many tender feet. And over the grass at the roadside a land turtle crawled, turning aside for nothing, dragging his high-domed shell over the grass. His hard legs and yellow-nailed feet threshed slowly through the grass, not really walking, but boosting and dragging his shell along. The barley beards slid off his shell, and the clover burrs fell on him and rolled to the ground. His horny beak was partly open, and his fierce, humorous eyes, under brows like fingernails, stared straight ahead. He came over the grass leaving a beaten trail behind him, and the hill, which was the highway embankment, reared up ahead of him. For a moment he stopped, his head held high. He blinked and looked up and down. At last he started to climb the embankment. Front clawed feet reached forward but did not touch. The hind feet kicked his shell along, and it scraped on the grass, and on the gravel. As the embankment grew steeper and steeper, the more frantic

---

40. From *The Grapes of Wrath*, by John Steinbeck (copyright, 1939, by John Steinbeck). Reprinted by permission of The Viking Press, Inc.

were the efforts of the land turtle. Pushing hind legs strained and slipped, boosting the shell along, and the horny head protruded as far as the neck could stretch. Little by little the shell slid up the embankment until at last a parapet cut straight across its line of march, the shoulder of the road, a concrete wall four inches high. As though they worked independently the hind legs pushed the shell against the wall. The head upraised and peered over the wall to the broad smooth plain of cement. Now the hands, braced on top of the wall, strained and lifted, and the shell came slowly up and rested its front end on the wall. For a moment the turtle rested. A red ant ran into the shell, into the soft skin inside the shell, and suddenly head and legs snapped in, and the armored tail clamped in sideways. The red ant was crushed between body and legs. And one head of wild oats was clamped into the shell by a front leg. For a long moment the turtle lay still, and then the neck crept out and the old humorous frowning eyes looked about and the legs and tail came out. The back legs went to work, straining like elephant legs, and the shell tipped to an angle so that the front legs could not reach the level cement plain. But higher and higher the hind legs boosted it, until at last the center of balance was reached, the front tipped down, the front legs scratched at the pavement, and it was up. But the head of wild oats was held by its stem around the front legs.

Now the going was easy, and all the legs worked, and the shell boosted along, waggling from side to side. A sedan driven by a forty-year old woman approached. She saw the turtle and swung to the right, off the highway, the wheels screamed and a cloud of dust boiled up. Two wheels lifted for a moment and then settled. The car skidded back onto the road, and went on, but more slowly. The turtle had jerked into its shell, but now it hurried on, for the highway was burning hot.

And now a light truck approached, and as it came near, the driver saw the turtle and swerved to hit it. His front wheel struck the edge of the shell, flipped the turtle like a tiddly-wink, spun it like a coin, and rolled it off the highway. The truck went back to its course along the right side. Lying on its back, the turtle was tight in its shell for a long time. But at last its legs waved in the air, reaching for something to pull it over. Its front foot caught a piece of quartz and little by little the shell pulled over and flopped upright. The wild oat head fell out and three of the spearhead seeds stuck in the ground. And as the turtle crawled on down the embankment, its shell dragged dirt over the seeds. The turtle entered a dust road and jerked itself along, drawing a wavy shallow trench in the dust with its shell. The old humorous eyes looked ahead, and the horny beak opened a little. His yellow toe nails slipped a fraction in the dust.

## Suggestions for Study

1. Note especially the adjectives and verbs. Are there too many of either? See how many words could be omitted in the first paragraph without appreciably changing a reader's understanding of the events.
2. What is the point of including the incident of the head of wild oats?
3. Note that the author does not presume to attribute the ability to think to the turtle. Does the depiction of action alone interest you in the turtle? If you answer yes, list the details that aid in this.
4. Is the author successful in giving the point of view of both a human observer and the turtle? How is this done?
5. Are the details arranged in an effective sequence? Would the omission of the incident of the first driver detract in any way from the sketch?

## Baker's Blue-Jay Yarn

### MARK TWAIN

Animals talk to each other, of course. There can be no question about that; but I suppose there are very few people who can understand them. I never knew but one man who could. I knew he could, however, because he told me so himself. He was a middle-aged, simple-hearted miner who had lived in a lonely corner of California, among the woods and mountains, a good many years, and had studied the ways of his only neighbors, the beasts and the birds, until he believed he could accurately translate any remark which they made. This was Jim Baker. According to Jim Baker, some animals have only a limited education, and use only very simple words, and scarcely ever a comparison or a flowery figure; whereas, certain other animals have a large vocabulary, a fine command of language and a ready and fluent delivery; consequently these latter talk a great deal; they like it; they are conscious of their talent, and they enjoy "showing off." Baker said, that after long and careful observation, he had come to the conclusion that the blue-jays were the best talkers he had found among birds and beasts. Said he:

"There's more *to* a blue-jay than any other creature. He has got more moods, and more different kinds of feelings than other creatures; and mind you, whatever a blue-jay feels, he can put into language. And no mere commonplace language, either, but rattling, out-and-out book-talk —and bristling with metaphor, too—just bristling! And as for command of language—why *you* never see a blue-jay get stuck for a word. No man ever did. They just boil out of him! And another thing: I've noticed a good deal, and there's no bird, or cow, or anything that uses as good grammar as a blue-jay. You may say a cat uses good grammar. Well, a cat does—but you let a cat get excited, once; you let a cat get to pulling fur with another cat on a shed, nights, and you'll hear grammar that will give you the lockjaw. Ignorant people think it's the *noise* which fighting cats make that is so aggravating, but it ain't so; it's the sickening grammar they use. Now I've never heard a jay use bad grammar but very seldom; and when they do, they are as ashamed as a human; they shut right down and leave.

"You may call a jay a bird. Well, so he is, in a measure—because he's got feathers on him, and don't belong to no church, perhaps; but otherwise he is just as much a human as you be. And I'll tell you for why. A jay's gifts, and instincts, and feelings, and interests, cover the whole ground. A jay hasn't got any more principle than a Congressman. A jay will lie, a jay will steal, a jay will deceive, a jay will betray; and four times out of five, a jay will go back on his solemnest promise. The sacredness of an obligation is a thing which you can't cram into no blue-jay's head. Now on top of all this, there's another thing: a jay can out-swear any gentleman in the mines. You think a cat can swear. Well, a cat can; but you give a blue-jay a subject that calls for his reserve-powers, and where is your cat? Don't talk to *me*—I know too much about this thing. And there's yet another thing: in the one little particular of scolding— just good, clean, out-and-out scolding—a blue-jay can lay over anything, human or divine. Yes, sir, a jay is everything that a man is. A jay can cry, a jay can laugh, a jay can feel shame, a jay can reason and plan and discuss, a jay likes gossip and scandal, a jay has got a sense of humor, a jay knows when he is an ass just as well as you do—maybe better. If a jay ain't human, he better take in his sign, that's all. Now I'm going to tell you a perfectly true fact about some blue-jays.

"When I first begun to understand jay language correctly, there was a little incident happened here. Seven years ago, the last man in this region but me, moved away. There stands his house—been empty ever since; a log house, with a plank roof—just one big room, and no more; no ceiling —nothing between the rafters and the floor. Well, one Sunday morning I was sitting out here in front of my cabin, with my cat, taking the sun, and looking at the blue hills, and listening to the leaves rustling so lonely in the trees, and thinking of the home away yonder in the States, that I hadn't heard from in thirteen years, when a blue-jay lit on that house, with an acorn in his mouth, and says, 'Hello, I reckon I've struck something.' When he spoke, the acorn dropped out of his mouth and rolled down the roof, of course, but he didn't care; his mind was all on the thing he had struck. It was a knothole in the roof. He cocked his head to one side, shut one eye and put the other one to the hole, like a 'possum looking down a jug; then he glanced up with his bright eyes, gave a wink or two with his wings—which signifies gratification, you understand,—and says, 'It looks like a hole, it's located like a hole,—blamed if I don't believe it *is* a hole!'

"Then he cocked his head down and took another look; he glances up perfectly joyful, this time; winks his wings and his tail both, and says, 'O, no, this ain't no fat thing, I reckon! If I ain't in luck!—why, it's a perfectly elegant hole!' So he flew down and got that acorn, and fetched it up and dropped it in, and was just tilting his head back, with the heavenliest smile on his face, when all of a sudden he was paralyzed into a listening attitude and that smile faded gradually out of his countenance like a breath off'n a razor, and the queerest look of surprise took its place. Then he says, 'Why, I didn't hear it fall!' He cocked his eye at the hole again, and took a long look; raised up and shook his head; stepped around to the other side of the hole and took another look from that side; shook his head again. He studied a while, then he just went into the *de-* tails—walked round and round the hole and spied into it from every point of the compass. No use. Now he took a thinking attitude on the comb of the roof and scratched the back of his head with his right foot a minute, and finally says, 'Well, it's too many for *me,* that's certain; must be a mighty long hole; however, I ain't got no time to fool around here, I got to 'tend to business; I reckon it's all right—chance it, anyway.'

"So he flew off and fetched another acorn and dropped it in, and tried to flirt his eye to the hole quick enough to see what become of it, but he was too late. He held his eye there as much as a minute; then he raised up and sighed, and says, 'Consound it, I don't seem to understand this thing, no way; however, I'll tackle her again.' He fetched another acorn, and done his level best to see what become of it, but he couldn't. He says, 'Well, *I* never struck no such a hole as this, before; I'm of the opinion it's a totally new kind of a hole.' Then he begun to get mad. He held in for a spell, walking up and down the comb of the roof and shaking his head and muttering to himself; but his feelings got the upper hand of him, presently, and he broke loose and cussed himself black in the face. I never see a bird take on so about a little thing. When he got through he walks to the hole and looks in again for half a minute; then he says, 'Well, you're a long hole, and a deep hole, and a mighty singular hole altogether —but I've started in to fill you, and I'm d—d if I *don't* fill you, if it takes a hundred years!'

"And with that, away he went. You never see a bird work so since you was born. He laid into his work like a nigger, and the way he hove acorns into that hole for about two hours and a half was one of the most exciting and astonishing spectacles I ever struck. He never stopped to take a look any more—he just hove 'em in and went for more. Well, at last he could hardly flop his wings, he was so tuckered out. He comes a-drooping down, once more, sweating like an ice-pitcher, drops his acorn in and says, '*Now* I guess I've got the bulge on you by this time!' So he bent down for a look. If you'll believe me, when his head come up again he was just pale with rage. He says, 'I've shoveled acorns enough in there to keep the family thirty years, and if I can see a sign of one of 'em I wish I may land in a museum with a belly full of sawdust in two minutes!'

"He just had strength enough to crawl up on the comb and lean his back agin the chimbly, and then he collected his impressions and begun to free his mind. I see in a second that what I had mistook for profanity in the mines was only just the rudiments, as you may say.

"Another jay was going by, and heard him doing his devotions, and stops to inquire what was up. The sufferer told him the whole circumstance, and says, 'Now yonder's the hole, and if you don't believe me, go and look for yourself.' So this fellow went and looked, and comes back and says, 'How many did you say you put in there?' 'Not any less than two tons,' says the sufferer. The other jay went and looked again. He couldn't seem to make it out, so he raised a yell, and three more jays come. They all examined the hole, they all made the sufferer tell it over again, then they all discussed it, and got off as many leather-headed opinions about it as an average crowd of humans could have done.

"They called in more jays; then more and more, till pretty soon this whole region 'peared to have a blue flush about it. There must have been five thousand of them; and such another jawing and disputing and ripping and cussing, you never heard. Every jay in the whole lot put his eye to the hole and delivered a more chuckle-headed opinion about the mystery than the jay that went there before him. They examined the house all over, too. The door was standing half open, and at last one old jay happened to go and light on it and look in. Of course that knocked the mystery galley-west in a second. There lay the acorns, scattered all over the floor. He flopped his wings and raised a whoop. 'Come here!' he says, 'Come here, everybody; hang'd if this fool hasn't been trying to fill up a house with acorns!' They all came a-swooping down like a blue cloud, and as each fellow lit on the door and took a glance, the whole absurdity of the contract that that first jay had tackled hit him home and he fell over backwards suffocating with laughter, and the next jay took his place and done the same.

"Well, sir, they roosted around here on the house-top and the trees for an hour, and guffawed over that thing like human beings. It ain't any use to tell me a blue-jay hasn't got a sense of humor, because I know better. And memory, too. They brought jays here from all over the United States to look down that hole, every summer for three years. Other birds too. And they could all see the point except an owl that come from Nova Scotia to visit the Yo Semite, and he took this thing in on his way back. He said he couldn't see anything funny in it. But then he was a good deal disappointed about Yo Semite, too."—*A Tramp Abroad*.

*Suggestions for Study*

1. This belongs to a special *genre* of American literature known as the "tall tale." Does it gain in effectiveness by being attributed to Jim Baker?
2. What sort of person is Jim Baker? Describe him in your own words as you conceive him from the narrative.
3. What words would you use to describe the jay who tried to fill the hole? What quality does he have in common with the owl?
4. If you assume this to be a fable, in the manner of Aesop, what "moral" would you write for it?
5. Do the opening sentences help to make the story seem plausible? If the first paragraph were omitted, would the story be as interesting?

## *The Dinner Party* [41]

### MONA GARDNER

The country is India. A large dinner party is being given in an up-country station by a colonial official and his wife. The guests are army officers and government attachés and their wives, and an American naturalist.

At one side of the long table a spirited discussion springs up between a young girl and a colonel. The girl insists women have long outgrown the jumping-on-a-chair-at-sight-of-a-mouse era, that they are not as fluttery as their grandmothers. The colonel says they are, explaining that women haven't the actual nerve control of men. The other men at the table agree with him.

"A woman's unfailing reaction in any crisis," the colonel says, "is to scream. And while a man may feel like it, yet he has that ounce more of control than a woman has. And that last ounce is what counts!"

The American scientist does not join in the argument, but sits watching the faces of the other guests. As he looks, he sees a strange expression

41. From the *Saturday Review of Literature* (January 31, 1942). Reprinted by permission of the author and the *Saturday Review of Literature*.

come over the face of the hostess. She is staring straight ahead, the muscles of her face contracting slightly. With a small gesture she summons the native boy standing behind her chair. She whispers to him. The boy's eyes widen: he turns quickly and leaves the room. No one else sees this, nor the boy when he puts a bowl of milk on the verandah outside the glass doors.

The American comes to with a start. In India, milk in a bowl means only one thing. It is bait for a snake. He realizes there is a cobra in the room.

He looks up at the rafters—the likeliest place—and sees they are bare. Three corners of the room, which he can see by shifting only slightly, are empty. In the fourth corner a group of servants stand, waiting until the next course can be served. The American realizes there is only one place left—under the table.

His first impulse is to jump back and warn the others. But he knows the commotion will frighten the cobra and it will strike. He speaks quickly, the quality of his voice so arresting that it sobers everyone.

"I want to know just what control everyone at this table has. I will count three hundred—that's five minutes—and not one of you is to move a single muscle. The persons who move will forfeit 50 rupees. Now! Ready!"

The twenty people sit like stone images while he counts. He is saying ". . . two-hundred and eighty . . ." when, out of the corner of his eye, he sees the cobra emerge and make for the bowl of milk. Four or five screams ring out as he jumps to slam shut the verandah doors.

"You certainly were right, Colonel!" the host says. "A man has just shown us an example of real control."

"Just a minute," the American says, turning to his hostess; "there's one thing I'd like to know. Mrs. Wynnes, how did you know that cobra was in the room?"

A faint smile lit up the woman's face as she replies: "Because it was lying across my foot."

## Suggestions for Study

1. This is not an original story. In sending it to the publisher, Miss Gardner explained that she had heard it many years before and was sending it to be reprinted in the hope of learning who the author was. This accounts for her telling the story in the present tense and as briefly as possible. Does this increase the effectiveness of the narrative, or would it be better if told in the past tense and if more details were added?

2. What part does the bowl of milk play?

3. What is the purpose of the argument at the start of the narrative?

4. Is the end a surprise? Qualify your answer. Would this be different if the original author were telling the story?

## The Evening Service [42]

### R. C. HUTCHINSON [43]

Yes, I know now it was three nights that Eadell spent with us. I remember for some reason that he came on a Friday, and he was with Bernard and me when we went to Dubbledale on the Sunday evening. . . .

The road goes through Isaiah's Drinkle, and the Ordnance surveyors, with their egregious breadth of mind, have colored it as second-class. I found it first when we traversed it in convoy, cursing its awkward dips and turns and the cottages which leaned across it at the sharpest corners: a tedious twenty minutes of clouding dust and jacitation and incessant change of gears. A scrabble of wide ruts was left on the verge where our quads had been slackly steered, here and there the banks were breached; but the dust had settled, the reek and rattle were long absorbed in the sanitary tides of wind. Curious, the diverse records that the same pair of eyes will make. I had noted the route carefully, matching ground to map, on the chance that I might have to pick it up by night. So the aspects were familiar, the very shape of the buildings had stayed on my mind's plate as solid pointers for a doubtful fork or obscure turn. But those pictures were like passport photographs in their likeness to what I saw this evening. A white cottage, which had merely shown itself more trim than its neighbors, was revealed now as a Georgian manor in perfect miniature. The granary beside Wisk Fall was no longer a rectangle of stone but a work of faultless grace in the fit of height to length, in the pitch of its stone roof, an artist's narrowing of the muscular steps which rose to the attic door. I had remarked a little bridge to have in mind that the road went over the Toin there; I had never seen how sensitively its parapets were curved. And the half-wit urchins who had darted in front of our wheels had grown through a month or two into fair and smiling images of God. . . .

At Drinkle we left the road and took the bridle path which is said to save you nearly half a mile; it does, perhaps in terms of distance. It may

42. From *Interim,* by R. C. Hutchinson (copyright, 1945, by R. C. Hutchinson), Rinehart & Company, Inc. Reprinted by permission of the author.

43. The excerpt here reprinted is from chapter 11 of the novel. Father Eadell, a Jesuit priest, is visiting an old college friend, Bernard Quindle, a medical missionary in China, whom the war had forced home to England. Quindle, an Anglican, takes a service occasionally when the vicar is away. The two old collegemates are on intimate terms despite their theological differences. The scene is Cumberland in northern England. The narrator, who purports to be the author, is a soldier stationed near the Quindle home.

have been habit which sent Bernard that way; it was a deviltry (or I am astigmatic to human foible) which made him leave the bridle for a cut of his own over Wirrup Crag. He had led us all the way, at least a pace ahead on the flat; the shackles of rheumatism seemed to have no power against the ferocious energy with which he walked. I had run a steady second, with Eadell panting a pace or two behind, short legs and tiny feet moving like a barber's scissors to carry his vast bulk forward. And they had argued almost incessantly about the teaching of August Comte. . . .

The path had become a chute of boulders, and I was dripping with sweat when Bernard, as one who boards the 8:45 at Woking, took a handful of briar and hoisted himself on to a shelf of rock. I followed, and by the time I had landed there he was thirty feet higher, plowing like a bulldozer through the gorse towards the naked scree. Eadell came after us, but his dialectic powers were stifled at last. . . .

By way of a knife's-edge bridge of rock we reached the southern shoulder-blade of Wirrup and rounded it crabwise, clinging and sliding on the scree. From the other side you looked straight down into St. Bridget's tarn, shaped almost as perfectly as a church's font, and saw to your right the ladder of Seven Tarns reaching down to Clouden Mere. The wind was mettlesome here, cold with the coming nightfall, pleasant to our hot faces. In these few minutes the light had dropped in tone, and the birds' voices quieted. Towards the Clucker range the mist had formed to snowy hills with green lakes in between, and on the greening sky a shoal of narrow clouds had gathered to build up a floating landscape with its own soft hills and plateau and lake. So real that land seemed, and so ethereal the misted country beneath, the eye lost power to mark reality; I felt the strip of land we walked on was a vessel slumbering in unknown seas, that the seas would presently engulf it. The wind pouring in my ears strengthened this feeling of detachment; unreasonably, it increased our stillness and repose. We found Bernard waiting where a sheep-track started; he was standing against the wind as a sailor does and smelling it with an epicure's nose. He asked, as we came level, "Did you bust a boot-lace or something?" He gave Eadell the coat he had been carrying. "Here, lad, you'd better put this on now." And presently, as we began the descent, he stopped again. "I find it almost intolerable," he said, gathering in his eyes the tarns and the Clucker hills with the clouds' grace and opalescence, "to have all this when men are being burnt and torn to bits." We slithered downwards on shallow turf, scattering the amazed sheep, came into gorse again and rejoined the bridle.

Dubbledale clings to the steep side of Cleat Rigg; its alleyways and gardens are put where nature allows them, the farms spread in the easier slopes above. Its one cartworthy street goes below it, sharing a narrow gully with a racing beck. Except for a pair of brawling dogs the street was lifeless when we came there; in the retreating light the houses looked to have shut as flowers do; fresh from the hills, we were like discoverers of a place long lost from human sight. A slab of stone took us over the beck; a flight of steps wedged narrowly between two cottages brought us up to the level of the lowest roofs. There were lights in the window here; on one side you saw a child being undressed for bed, from the other you got the smell of ham cooking. The church, still high above us, was a pattern of black and silver planes in the horizontal light of the falling day. . . .

At the sexton's cottage we were greeted by a tough, small woman, with a man's muscles in hand and arm. Chidroach was in bed with the bronchitty, she told us. She had the misfortune of a diagonal squint; she seemed to be gazing alternately at the top of the Church and down into the village. No, the church boiler had not been attended to since yesterday forenoon, she said, with sibylline relish, neither were the lamps dressed; a flock of sheep astray had chewed up a number of the prayerbooks, and the organist had broken her leg. Would Chidroach like to see Dr. Quindle? Well, to say truth, Chidroach was in a powerful humor, not caring for the fiery poultice which had been slapped on his chest by Mr. Partiquer the vet; and had sworn to break the nose of the next doctor who came inside the house.

I sigh even now when I think of Eadell's sufferings. Bernard, I suppose, would have left him out of the evening's labor; but the sexton's wife had gathered from his peculiar clothes that he was some kind of servant; it was he whom she commanded to clear up what the sheep had left in the chancel, he who caught the thong of her sarcasm when we tried to reanimate the stove. Having the will of a man and the strength of two, she held the sex in small esteem. "Well, you can help so long as you don't get in my way!" When Eadell staggered into the boiler house with a bucket he'd filled from the wrong coke-stack she seized it roughly from his hands, took it back, and emptied it. Heroically, in the semi-darkness, he put a shovel-full on the fire as it began to blaze. "If you want to put the fire out," she said, "you may as well use water."

"You know, Mrs. Chidroach," Bernard said, "my friend here is one of the most learned men in England." She snorted. "You," she said, with her eyes swivelling from heaven to hell, but apparently meaning me, "you'd better do the lamps. Unless you're a college lad as well."

That picture has stayed clearer than so many more important ones: the bald, distinguished Eadell, half-paralyzed with exhaustion and mirth, trying to nourish the Protestant boiler; Mrs. Chidroach on his one side, like a tigress ready to spring; on the other Bernard pincered between embarrassment and his palate for the absurd, muttering, "Leave it to me, lad, for heaven's sake leave it! Go and ring the bell if it won't ruin your conscience. For heaven's sake leave this to me." And a little afterwards Eadell, with the sly face of Naaman in the house of Rimmon, tugging awkwardly at the Protestant bell.

Of the service I remember little, for I had been detailed to play the organ and was wholly occupied by the anxieties of that employment. Only when Bernard began his sermon had I time to relax and to let my eyes wander about the miniature church; to see, among its infinite small beauties, the tablet commemorating "Master Edward Hake who, in his Forty-Ninth Year, at God's Call, was Trampled by the Nearside Horse of the London Coach and Entered into Rest." With its light from four small lamps in the nave and one in the chancel the building had a Josef Israels quality: pillars and hammer-beams emerged from a suspended lake of darkness, the faces of children shyly herded in the rearmost pews were flakes of paleness in the shadow; only within an armspread of the lamps were features deeply etched. There, encompassed by a trio of plump dalesmen's wives, an ox-jowled youth in the weekly anguish of collar and tie stared far ahead with his fine, Cumbrian eyes. An Australian corporal sat bolt upright like one on horseback, and as if to point the anchylosis of his face the squat couple who shared his pew had faces like butter soaking into toast. In the second pew a very small, hunched woman with a widow's bonnet sat by herself. I suppose she had passed her ninetieth year, but she did not look as if age had brought her face to this nobility: the deep and regular creasing in her forehead and the margins of her eyes, the way the shrunk, almost transparent flesh was stretched upon its frame, seemed rather the achievement of a deliberate artist than any overripeness in her body's evolution. I turned my head a little to get a sidelong view of Bernard, who stood on the lower chancel step with his knuckles wedged between chest and chin. He was smiling faintly, in the way of one recounting an adventure he has undergone some time before. He spoke as he always did, slowly, as if he would give way to anyone who wished to take the company's ear; and I noticed that a Derbyshire inflexion which one sometimes heard very faintly in his voice was near to its surface now. . . .

A farmer who had said all the wrong responses was now stertorously asleep; his anemic daughter still gazed with bovine fascination at the boa in the adjoining pew. But the corporal's face was of one who sees from a train window some patch of country he once found pleasure in; and on the mouth of the sexton's wife, who had dumped her little body in a rearward corner, I saw with astonishment the daybreak of a smile. It was a company which reminded me of provincial auction rooms, outmoded pieces gathered from old attics, the erroneous ardor of cottage dressmakers brought dreadfully to public view. But the measured light enclosed them in its old pattern; it found even a point of gallantry in the white of an old man's head above the dullness of his coat, in a girl's red scarf against the shadowed stone. And the voice, now hesitant, now eager, made us a circle no less intimate than any which formed in the Orchilly dining-room. Perhaps my emotions were warmed by the closeness of the air, the heat which grew from our breathing, and from the odorous lamps. I know that I felt myself in the very weft of these strangers, and discovered pride in feeling so, and would have kept this plot of time for ever lingering. . . .

At some point Eadell had stolen back into the church. I had not seen him come; I noticed suddenly the shape of his head far back in the darkness by the door. I smiled to him. But it was the pollard farm lad nearer to me who caught and answered my smile. The speaker's voice fell quieter still; it was no more public than the voice he used across the Orchilly table; but in the stillness it had won, the chiselled words were like small fires that leap in a darkened countryside. Eyes which had strolled about the pews came back to rest upon his face; I had the sense of dreams in which the surge and conquest depend upon your utter stillness. From that tranquillity my own eyes turned to search for Eadell again. But the place he had sat in was empty; like a shadow at nightfall he had slipped away.

I should not find again the cottage we went to afterwards. I reached it in the moving disc of light from someone's lamp; we seemed to go up and down many steps and across the yard of a public-house. In the little, crowded room we reached, the people who had been only clothes and faces turned into individuals. The old woman from the front pew became a gay and rather flirtatious creature; the man who had slept through half the sermon was volubly persuading me to try his home-brewed beer. Yet I do not think of that evening as falling into separate parts. The smiles, the squeezing of elbows which I took part in, now were rather a flowering of what had gone before; and this Bernard who was talking to a child with his mouth full while he bandaged her arm, who scolded the Australian corporal for the size of his feet, was in every part identical with the one who had stood on the chancel step and mastered us with his quietness. An unusual meal we had, some standing and some at the table. I ate about a quartern of Grasmere cheese, while a man in a corduroy suit told me how his uncle had died of it. The woman I took to be our hostess gave me pink blancmange in a breakfast cup, and directly afterwards I had to take potato broth from a milk-jug, using a gravy spoon.

It was not, I think, a healthy room to sleep in, as a little boy was trying to do in a truckle bed behind the sofa; for from beneath the surface-odors of onion and hot linen there rose at intervals the indubitable smell of sewage. Nor had it any kind of comfort. Edging my way between the sewing machine and a laden piano, sitting on the arm of a broken chair and then leaning against the mangle, I thought I saw a clue to the many small infirmities discovered here; for of ten or twelve in the room there were few who did not suffer from deafness, or the pallor of some pulmonary disorder, or a nervous twitch. Yet as I saw them now, encompassed by the flow of Bernard's laughter, they were radiant with content; and I have found no group of people more generous to one who, with my total ignorance of beasts and grain, must have seemed to them not far removed from dementia. I remember the charm of a squirrel-like man who told me in hoarse whispers, continuously smiling, about the intestinal problems of a certain Mrs. Richardson; and the lovely, childlike eyes of a gaunt spinster who repeated many times, breathing chutney into my face, "But Government can't raise dead men any road, no matter what tax they put on t' brewing, no more than sow in farrow can skippit through daisy-chain." I was sorry when we had to go.

## Suggestions for Study

1. In your own words give a brief character sketch of the three friends who make the trip.
2. What is the purpose of the trip?
3. What do you gather about the speaker as a result of the change he has undergone towards the scenery?
4. Is the character of Mrs. Chidroach overdrawn?
5. The author is handling a situation that contains inherent elements of sentimentality (this is especially true in the book itself in which part of Bernard's sermon—omitted here because although it has a place in the entire book, it is not an essential part of this sketch—is given). How does he keep the story from crossing the borderline into sentimentality?

## Suggestions for Writing

1. All parents are fond of relating amusing or frightening things which happened to their children when they were small. Write one such incident which you have heard told about you.
2. Isolate some happening which occurred during a camping trip, hitch-hiking expedition, or other journey, from the rest of the trip and relate it in such a way that it will stand as an independent unit. If introductory material is needed, remember to make it as brief as possible.

3. Read carefully an incident in the Bible. Try to understand the full meaning of the occurrence for each of the people concerned. Reconstruct and amplify the incident, using modern English instead of Biblical English. If you wish, choose the point of view of one of the characters and tell the story in the first person.

4. Write an account of some historical incident from the point of view of an unimportant witness. (For example, the signing of the Magna Carta as told by a retainer of one of the barons; the assassination of Lincoln as told by an actor other than John Wilkes Booth; a visit by Walt Whitman to a Washington hospital, as told by a wounded soldier.)

5. Scan the newspapers for a brief story which you can rewrite as an incident. Do not try to rewrite something which has been given a big headline; look for short articles on the inside pages—even in the "want ad" and "personals" columns.

6. Write an episode which actually occurred or which you imagine as occurring in some place with which you are familiar but which is likely to be unfamiliar to your readers. Put enough information into it to give your readers a good idea of the place and of those participating in the action.

7. Write a sketch of the most exciting (or humorous or embarrassing or happy) event in your own life. Use all your skill to make it interesting to a reader.

8. Write a sketch which makes use of some interesting custom or recurring event in your home town or neighborhood.

9. Take a day of college life and see if, by selecting and arranging the details in such a way as to secure unity, you can make an interesting narrative.

10. By means of a narrative sketch, make a character study of an individual so that the person lives for the reader by what he says and does rather than by direct description.

**The Short Story.** By drawing on experience or observation or by the exercise of a moderate imagination, any student, with some care and practice, should be able to write interesting simple narrative. To write good short stories, however, demands mature skills; for in addition to the requirements for simple narrative, the short story must have plot, intensity and compression of style, and mounting suspense. The chief difference, in fact, between simple narrative and the short story lies in the greater intensity of struggle in the latter and in the dramatic arrangement of details in such a way as to create growing suspense.

A short story must have plot—a situation involving conflict and struggle and reaching some aesthetically satisfactory conclusion. Starting from an equilibrium, the action goes through a series of oscillations of growing intensity until another state of equilibrium, different from that at the start, is reached. To have conflict there must be opposing forces: hero–villain, protagonist–antagonist. The hero or protagonist should be animate—a person or animal—but the antagonist may be either animate or inanimate, and if inanimate, it may be some objective force like a mountain or desert, or be subjective. (In the examples at the end of this section, the antagonist in "The Color of Mama Josefina's Life" is objective—the drab village; in "The Coward" it is subjective—the protagonist's cowardly fears.) The conflict, however, need not be obvious at a glance—as it is in "Brandy for Breakfast" and "That Greek Dog"; some of the best short-story writers suggest the conflict so adroitly and subtly that it may not be at once apparent to a casual reader wherein the conflict lies.

Other elements which need attention by the short-story writer are setting, characters, and atmosphere. It is not necessary to lay the setting of a story in some distant, romantic spot; an intense drama may occur anywhere, as O. Henry demonstrated in his story, "A Municipal Report." But it is important to have the setting clearly in mind, and it and the action in harmony. It is possible, of course, to write a story without a specific setting, but frequently the setting can be used advantageously; and since the short story must move at a much swifter pace than a novel, the writer must take account of every element that will aid him.

Since short stories generally depend more on plot and incident than on character, the characters need not be so carefully drawn as in the novel. Yet they must be well enough depicted and differentiated so that what they do matters to a reader. And, as was said earlier in this chapter, their character and actions must be in harmony: no one in the story must perform an action which is out of keeping with his character.

Because of the brevity of the short story, every use possible should be made of atmosphere, or tone. Poe, who was adept in the use of atmosphere, is not, however, the best guide for the modern short-story writer; for the novice who parodies him may overdo the matter. It is better to suggest the atmosphere by a word here and a phrase there, or to create the desired effect through conversation or obliquely by the association of ideas in the reader's mind. Yet the short-story writer must be intensely aware of the atmosphere he wishes to establish, and must be constantly alert to insinuate this atmosphere into the story.

For the successful development of a short story, the incidents must be so arranged that each grows naturally out of the preceding incident and leads inevitably to the next one. Thus throughout the action there is a growing intensity until the climax is reached. This is usually followed in the modern short story by a swift conclusion. In this regard, the chief care of the novice must be to see that each incident actually furthers the action and increases the interest of the reader. If it does not do this, it has no part in the story and must be omitted.

One other characteristic of the short story is compression. The situation having been defined and the line of action determined, everything which does not pertain directly to the matter in hand is cut away. Incidents which in a novel would occupy a chapter are condensed to a page. Seldom is an attempt made to portray a character completely; that phase of the character which is pertinent to the story is stated concisely, but the rest is omitted. Unless for some reason the writer of the short story is striving consciously for another effect, the technique of his medium demands swift, absorbing movement.

Finally, the short story possesses unity of effect. Probably more frequently than not a story writer starts with something he has observed, an anecdote, or a newspaper clipping—in other words, the nucleus of the story itself rather than the effect which he wants the story to produce. Nevertheless, even if a story does not produce a unified emotional effect, it possesses a singleness of purpose which may serve quite as well. If the story has as its core a theme—a comparison, contrast, or philosophical judgment—the theme is supported by the full weight of the narrative. The energy of the story is not dissipated upon other ideas. The force which is directed upon the reader is united.

The short stories which follow are included here for study and analysis; therefore they vary in quality purposely. In analyzing them, keep in mind the statements of the preceding section.

## A Coward

### GUY DE MAUPASSANT

He was known in society as "the handsome Signoles." His name was Viscount Gontran Joseph de Signoles.

An orphan and the possessor of a sufficient fortune, he cut a dash, as they say. He had style and presence, sufficient fluency of speech to make people think him clever, a certain natural grace, an air of nobility and pride, a gallant mustache and a gentle eye, which the women like.

He was in great demand in the salons, much sought after by fair dancers; and he aroused in his own sex that smiling animosity which they always feel for men of an energetic figure. He had been suspected of several love affairs well adapted to cause a young bachelor to be much esteemed. He passed a happy, unconcerned life, in a comfort of mind which was most complete. He was known to be a skillful fencer, and with the pistol even more adept.

"If I ever fight a duel," he would say, "I shall choose the pistol. With that weapon I am sure of killing my man."

Now, one evening, when he had accompanied to the theater two young lady friends of his, whose husbands also were of the party, he invited them, after the play, to take an ice at Tortoni's. They had been at the café but a few moments, when he noticed that a man sitting at a table near by was staring persistently at one of his fair neighbors. She seemed annoyed and uneasy, and lowered her eyes. At last she said to her husband:

"That man is staring me out of countenance. I don't know him; do you?"

The husband, who had noticed nothing, raised his eyes, and answered: "No, not at all."

The young woman continued, half smiling, half vexed:

"It is very unpleasant; that man is spoiling my ice."

The husband shrugged his shoulders:

"Pshaw! don't pay any attention to him. If we had to bother our heads about all the impertinent fellows we meet, we should never have done."

But the viscount had risen abruptly. He could not suffer that stranger to spoil an ice which he had offered. It was to him that the affront was paid, since it was through him and for him that his friends had entered the café, so that the affair was his concern, and his alone.

He walked towards the man and said to him:

"You have a way of looking at those ladies, monsieur, that I cannot tolerate. I beg you to be so kind as to stare less persistently."

The other retorted:

"You may go to the devil!"

"Take care, monsieur," said the viscount, with clenched teeth; "you will force me to pass bounds."

The gentleman answered but one word, a foul word, that rang from one end of the café to the other, and caused every guest to give a sudden start, as if moved by a hidden spring. Those whose backs were turned wheeled round; all the others raised their heads; three waiters whirled about on their heels like tops; the two women at the desk gave a jump, then turned completely round, like automata obedient to the same crank.

Profound silence ensued. Suddenly a sharp sound cracked in the air. The viscount had slapped his adversary. Every one rose to interfere. Cards were exchanged between the two.

When the viscount had returned to his apartment he paced the floor for several minutes, with great, quick strides. He was too much agitated to reflect. A single thought hovered over his mind—"a duel"—without arousing any emotion whatsoever. He had done what he should have done; he had shown himself to be what he ought to be. His conduct would be discussed and approved; people would congratulate him. He said aloud, speaking as one speaks when one's thoughts are in great confusion:

"What a brute the fellow was!"

Then he sat down and began to consider. He must find seconds, in the morning. Whom should he choose? He thought over those of his acquaintances who were the most highly esteemed and the best-known. He decided at last upon the Marquis de la Tour-Noire and the Colonel Bourdin—a great noble and a soldier—excellent! Their names would sound well in the papers. He discovered that he was thirsty, and he drank three glasses of water in rapid succession; then he resumed his pacing of the floor. He felt full of energy. If he blustered a little, seemed determined to carry the thing through, demanded rigorous and dangerous conditions, insisted upon a serious duel, very serious and terrible, his adversary would probably back down and apologize.

He picked up the card, which he had drawn from his pocket and tossed on the table, and read it again, as he had read it in a glance at the café, and again in the cab, by the glimmer of every street-lamp, on his way home. "Georges Lamil, 51 Rue Moncey." Nothing more.

He examined these assembled letters, which seemed to him mysterious, full of vague meaning. Georges Lamil! Who was this man? What was his business? Why had he stared at that lady in such a way? Was it not disgusting that a stranger, an unknown, should cause such a change in one's life, because it had pleased him to fasten his eyes insolently upon a lady?

And the viscount again exclaimed aloud:

"What a brute!"

Then he stood perfectly still, thinking, his eyes still glued to the card. There arose within him a fierce anger against that bit of paper—a malevolent sort of rage, blended with a strange feeling of discomfort. What a stupid business! He took a penknife that lay open to his hand, and stuck it through the middle of the printed name, as if he were stabbing someone. So he must fight! Should he choose swords, or pistols?—for he deemed himself the insulted party. He ran less risk with the sword; but with the pistol he had a chance of making his opponent withdraw. A duel with swords is rarely fatal, mutual prudence preventing the combatants from engaging near enough to each other for a point to enter very deep. With the pistol his life was seriously endangered; but he might in that way come out of the affair with all the honors, and without coming to a meeting.

"I must be firm," he said. "He will be afraid."

The sound of his voice made him tremble, and he looked about him.

He felt extremely nervous. He drank another glass of water, then began to undress for bed.

As soon as he was in bed he blew out the light and shut his eyes.

He thought:

"I have all day tomorrow to arrange my affairs. I must sleep now, so that I may be calm."

He was very warm under the bedclothes, but he could not manage to doze off. He twisted and turned, lay on his back five minutes, then changed to the left side, then rolled over on his right.

He was still thirsty. He got up again, to drink. Then a disquieting thought occurred to him:

"Can it be that I am afraid?"

Why did his heart begin to beat wildly at every familiar sound in the room? When the clock was about to strike, the faint whirring of the spring making ready made him jump; and then he had to keep his mouth open for several seconds to breathe, the oppression was so great.

He commenced to argue with himself concerning the possibility of this thing:

"Am I afraid?"

No, of course he was not afraid, as he had determined to carry the thing through, as his mind was fully made up to fight, and not to tremble. But he felt so profoundly troubled that he asked himself the question:

"Is it possible to be afraid in spite of one's self?"

And that doubt, that disquietude, that dread took possession of him; if some force stronger than his will, a dominating, irresistible power should conquer him, what would happen? Yes, what could happen? He certainly would go to the ground, inasmuch as he had made up his mind to go there. But suppose his hand should tremble? Suppose he should faint? And he thought of his position, of his reputation, of his name.

And suddenly a strange fancy seized him to get up, in order to look in the mirror. He relit his candle. When he saw the reflection of his face in the polished glass, he could hardly recognize himself, and it seemed to him that he had never seen this man before. His eyes appeared enormous; and he was certainly pale—yes, very pale.

He remained standing in front of the mirror. He put out his tongue as if to test the state of his health, and of a sudden this thought burst into his mind like a bullet:

"The day after tomorrow, at this time, I may be dead."

And his heart began to beat furiously again.

"The day after tomorrow, at this time, I may be dead. This person in front of me, this I, whom I am looking at in this mirror, will be no more! What! I am standing here, looking at myself, conscious that I am a living man; and in twenty-four hours I shall be lying on that bed, dead, with my eyes closed, cold, lifeless, gone!"

He turned towards the bed, and he distinctly saw himself lying on his back, between the very sheets that he had just left. He had the hollow cheeks that dead bodies have, and that slackness of the hands that will never stir more.

Thereupon he conceived a fear of his bed, and, in order to avoid looking at it, passed into his smoking-room. He mechanically took a cigar, lighted it, and began to pace the floor anew. He was cold; he walked to the bell cord to wake his valet; but he stopped, with his hand halfway to the cord.

"That fellow will see that I am afraid."

And he did not ring, but made the fire himself. His hands trembled slightly, with a nervous shudder, when they touched anything. His brain was in a whirl; his troubled thoughts became fugitive, sudden, melancholy; a sort of intoxication seized on his spirit as if he had been drunk.

And ceaselessly he asked himself:

"What am I going to do? What will become of me?"

His whole body quivered, shaken by jerky tremblings. He got up, went to the window, and drew aside the curtains. The day was breaking, a summer's day. The rosy sky made rosy the city, the roofs, and the walls. A great burst of light, like a caress from the rising sun, enveloped the awaking world; and with that glimmer, a sudden, enlivening, brutal hope seized on the heart of the viscount. How insane he was to have allowed himself to be so struck down by terror, even before anything was decided, before his seconds had met those of Georges Lamil, before he knew whether he was really to fight!

He made his toilet, dressed himself, and left the house with a firm step.

As he walked, he said to himself again and again:

"I must be firm, very firm. I must prove that I am not afraid."

His seconds, the marquis and the colonel, placed themselves at his disposal, and after warmly shaking his hand, discussed the conditions.

The colonel asked:

"Do you desire a serious duel?"

"Very serious," the viscount replied.

"You insist upon pistols?"

"Yes."

"Do you leave us at liberty to make the other arrangements?"

The viscount articulated with a dry, jerky voice:

"Twenty paces, firing at the word, lifting the arm instead of lowering it. Shots to be exchanged until someone is badly wounded."

"Those are excellent conditions," said the colonel, in a tone of satisfaction. "You are a good shot; the chances are all in your favor."

And they separated. The viscount returned home to wait for them. His agitation, which had been temporarily allayed, increased from moment to moment. He felt along his arms and legs, in his chest, a sort of shudder, an incessant vibration; he could not keep still, either sitting or standing. He had only a trace of moisture in his mouth, and he moved his tongue noisily every second, as if to unglue it from his palate.

He tried to breakfast, but he could not eat. Thereupon it occurred to him to drink to renew his courage, and he ordered a small decanter of rum, from which he gulped down six little glasses, one after another. A warmth, like that caused by a burn, invaded his whole frame, followed as soon by a giddiness of the soul.

"I have found the way," he thought; "now it is all right."

But in an hour he had emptied the decanter, and his agitation became intolerable. He was conscious of a frantic longing to throw himself on the floor, to cry, to bite. Evening fell.

A ring at the bell caused him such a feeling of suffocation that he had not the strength to rise and receive his seconds.

He did not dare even to talk to them any longer—to say: "How do you do?" to utter a single word, for fear that they would divine everything from the trembling of his voice.

"Everything is arranged according to the conditions that you fixed," said the colonel. "At first, your adversary claimed the privileges of the insulted party, but he gave way almost immediately and assented to everything. His seconds are two military men."

The viscount said:

"Thank you."

The marquis added:

"Excuse us if we stay but a moment, but we still have a thousand things to attend to. We must have a good doctor, as the duel is not to stop until somebody is severely wounded; and you know there's no trifling with bullets. We must arrange about the place, too—near a house to which the wounded man may be taken if necessary, etc.; in short, we still have two or three hours' work before us."

The viscount succeeded in articulating a second time:

"Thank you."

The colonel asked:

"You are all right? quite calm?"

"Yes, quite calm, thanks."

The two men withdrew.

When he was alone once more it seemed to him that he was going mad. His servant having lighted the lamps, he seated himself at his table to write some letters. After tracing at the top of a page: "This is my Will," he rose with a jump and walked away, feeling incapable of putting two ideas together, of forming any resolution, of deciding any question whatsoever.

So he was really going to fight! It was no longer possible for him to avoid it. What on earth was taking place in him? He wanted to fight; his purpose and determination to do so were firmly fixed; and yet he knew full well that, despite all the effort of his mind and all the tension of his will, he would be unable to retain even the strength necessary to take him to the place of meeting. He tried to fancy the combat, his own attitude, and the bearing of his adversary.

From time to time his teeth chattered with a little dry noise. He tried to read, and took up Chateauvillard's dueling code. Then he asked himself:

"Has my opponent frequented the shooting galleries? Is he well known? What's his class? How can I find out?"

He remembered Baron de Vaux's book on pistol shooters, and he looked it through from end to end. Georges Lamil's name was not mentioned. But if the fellow were not a good shot, he would not have assented so readily to that dangerous weapon and those fatal conditions! As he passed a table, he opened the case by Gastinne Renette, took out one of the pistols, then stood as if he were about to fire, and raised his arm. But he was trembling from head to foot, and the barrel shook in all directions.

Then he said to himself:

"It is impossible. I cannot fight like this!"

He regarded the little hole, black and deep, at the end of the barrel, the hole that spits out death; he thought of the dishonor, of the whispered comments at the clubs, of the laughter in the salons, of the disdain of the women, of the allusions in the newspapers, of the insults which cowards would throw in his face.

He continued to gaze at the weapon, and as he raised the hammer, he saw the priming glitter beneath it like a little red flame. The pistol had been left loaded, by chance, by oversight. And he experienced a confused, inexplicable joy thereat.

If he did not display in the other's presence the calm and noble bearing suited to the occasion, he would be lost forever. He would be disgraced, branded with the sign of infamy, hunted from society! And that calm and bold bearing he could not command—he knew it, he felt it. And yet he was really brave, because he wanted to fight! He was brave, because—. The thought that grazed his mind was never completed; opening his mouth wide, he suddenly thrust the barrel of the pistol into the very bottom of his throat and pressed upon the trigger.

When his valet ran in, alarmed by the report, he found him on his back, dead. The blood had spattered the white paper on the table, and made a great red stain under the four words:

"This is my Will."

### Suggestions for Study

1. Name the protagonist and the antagonist in this story.
2. What is the point of view in this story? What limitations are placed on the writer by this point of view?
3. Can you guess, after an examination of this story, what is meant by the "stream of consciousness" technique in writing fiction?
4. Make a diagram of the action. Does the diagram indicate a series of climaxes which rise steadily toward a grand climax, or does the action proceed irregularly?
5. Make a list of a dozen or so specific details which indicate to the reader that Signoles is a coward. Does the author tell you directly, at any point other than in the title, that Signoles is a coward?
6. At what places in the story might a less skilled writer than De Maupassant have impeded the action by introducing extraneous material?
7. Most readers of De Maupassant's stories comment on the irony which appears in nearly every one of them. Is "A Coward" an ironical story in any sense?
8. Explain the play on the word "will" in the last sentence of the story.
9. Is this a story of plot or of character?
10. State the author's specific purpose in the story.
11. What essential difference is there between the conflict in this story and in "Brandy for Breakfast"?
12. Explain the meaning of the following words: affront, malevolent, articulate, marquis, viscount, decanter.

## Foot in It [44]

### JAMES GOULD COZZENS

There were three steps down from the street door. Then the store extended, narrow and low between the book-packed walls, sixty or seventy feet to a little cubbyhole of an office where a large sallow man worked

44. Reprinted by permission of the author and of *Redbook Magazine*. Copyright 1935 by McCall Corporation.

under a shaded desklamp. He had heard the street door open, and he
looked that way a moment, peering intently through his spectacles. Seeing
only a thin, stiffly erect gentleman with a small cropped white mustache,
standing hesitant before the table with the sign *"Any Book 50 Cents,"*
he returned to the folded copy of a religious weekly on the desk in front
of him. He looked at the obituary column again, pulled a pad toward him
and made a note. When he had finished, he saw, upon looking up again,
that the gentleman with the white mustache had come all the way down
the store.

"Yes sir?" he said, pushing the papers aside. "What can I do for you?"

The gentleman with the white mustache stared at him keenly. "I am
addressing the proprietor, Mr. Joreth?" he said.

"Yes sir. You are."

"Quite so. My name is Ingalls—Colonel Ingalls."

"I'm glad to know you, Colonel. What can I—"

"I see that the name does not mean anything to you."

Mr. Joreth took off his spectacles, looked searchingly. "Why, no sir. I
am afraid not. *Ingalls.* No. I don't know anyone by that name."

Colonel Ingalls thrust his stick under his arm and drew an envelope
from his inner pocket. He took a sheet of paper from it, unfolded the
sheet, scowled at it a moment, and tossed it onto the desk. "Perhaps," he
said, "this will refresh your memory."

Mr. Joreth pulled his nose a moment, looked harder at Colonel Ingalls,
replaced his spectacles. "Oh," he said, "a bill. Yes. You must excuse me.
I do much of my business by mail with people I've never met personally.
'The Reverend Doctor Godfrey Ingalls, Saint John's Rectory.' Ah, yes,
yes—"

"The late Doctor Ingalls was my brother. This bill is obviously an
error. He would never have ordered, received, or wished to read any of
these works. Naturally, no such volumes were found among his effects."

"Hm," said Mr. Joreth. "Yes, I see." He read down the itemized list,
coughed, as though in embarrassment.

"I see. Now, let me check my records a moment." He dragged down
a vast battered folio from the shelf before him. "*G, H, I—*" he muttered.
"*Ingalls.* Ah, now—"

"There is no necessity for that," said Colonel Ingalls. "It is, of course,
a mistake. A strange one, it seems to me. I advise you strongly to be more
careful. If you choose to debase yourself by surreptitiously selling works
of the sort, that is your business. But—"

Mr. Joreth nodded several times, leaned back. "Well, Colonel," he said,
"you're entitled to your opinion. I don't sit in judgment on the tastes of

my customers. Now, in this case, there seems unquestionably to have been an order for the books noted from the source indicated. On the fifteenth of last May I filled the order. Presumably they arrived. What became of them, then, is no affair of mine; but in view of your imputation, I might point out that such literature is likely to be kept in a private place and read privately. For eight successive months I sent a statement. I have never received payment. Of course, I was unaware that the customer was, didn't you say, deceased. Hence my reference to legal action on this last. I'm very sorry to have—"

"You unmitigated scoundrel!" roared Colonel Ingalls. "Do you really mean definitely to maintain that Doctor Ingalls purchased such books? Let me tell you—"

Mr. Joreth said: "My dear sir, one moment, if you please! Are you in a position to be so positive? I imply nothing about the purchaser. I mean to maintain nothing, except that I furnished goods, for which I am entitled to payment. I am a poor man. When people do not pay me, what can I do but—"

"Why, you infamous—"

Mr. Joreth held up his hand. "Please, please!" he protested. "I think you are taking a most unjust and unjustified attitude, Colonel. This account has run a long while. I've taken no action. I am well aware of the unpleasantness which would be caused for many customers if a bill for books of this sort was made public. The circumstances aren't by any means unique, my dear sir; a list of my confidential customers would no doubt surprise you."

Colonel Ingalls said carefully: "Be good enough to show me my brother's original order."

"Ah," said Mr. Joreth. He pursed his lips. "That's unfair of you, Colonel. You are quite able to see that I wouldn't have it. It would be the utmost imprudence for me to keep on file anything which could cause so much trouble. I have the carbon of an invoice, which is legally sufficient, under the circumstances, I think. You see my position."

"Clearly," said Colonel Ingalls. "It is the position of a dirty knave and a blackguard, and I shall give myself the satisfaction of thrashing you." He whipped the stick from under his arm. Mr. Joreth slid agilely from his seat, caught the telephone off the desk, kicking a chair into the Colonel's path.

"Operator," he said, "I want a policeman." Then he jerked open a drawer, plucked a revolver from it. "Now, my good sir," he said, his back against the wall, "we shall soon see. I have put up with a great deal of abuse from you, but there are limits. To a degree I understand your provocation, though it doesn't excuse your conduct. If you choose to take yourself out of here at once and send me a check for the amount due me, we will say no more. If you prefer to wait for the arrival of an officer—"

Colonel Ingalls held the stick tight in his hand. "I think I will wait for the officer," he said with surprising composure. "I was too hasty. In view of your list of so-called customers, which you think would surprise me, there are doubtless other people to be considered—"

The stick in his hand leaped, sudden and slashing, catching Mr. Joreth over the wrist. The revolver flew free, clattered along the floor, and Colonel Ingalls kicked it behind him. "It isn't the sort of thing the relatives of a clergyman would like to have made public, is it? When you read of the death of one, what is to keep you from sending a bill? Very often they must pay and shut up. A most ingenious scheme, sir."

Mr. Joreth clasped his wrist, wincing. "I am at loss to understand this nonsense," he said. "How dare you—"

"Indeed?" said Colonel Ingalls. "Ordinarily, I might be at loss myself, sir; but in this case, I think you put your foot in it, sir! I happen to be certain that my late brother ordered no books from you, that he did not keep them in private or read them in private. It was doubtless not mentioned in the obituary, but for fifteen years previous to his death, Doctor Ingalls had the misfortune to be totally blind. . . . There, sir, is the policeman you sent for."

*Suggestions for Study*

1. This narrative is what in recent years has come to be called a short short story. On the basis of this story can you draw some conclusions concerning some of the problems which this type of writing places before the writer?
2. Is this a story of character, plot, or situation?
3. Are the elements of the story realistic or romantic?
4. On what element does the story chiefly depend for its interest?

## The Happiest Man on Earth [45]

### ALBERT MALTZ

Jesse felt ready to weep. He had been sitting in the shanty waiting for Tom to appear, grateful for the chance to rest his injured foot, quietly, joyously anticipating the moment when Tom would say, "Why, of course, Jesse, you can start whenever you're ready!"

For two weeks he had been pushing himself, from Kansas City, Missouri, to Tulsa, Oklahoma, through nights of rain and a week of scorch-

45. From *Harper's Magazine*, CLXXVII (June, 1938), 74. Reprinted by permission of the author.

ing sun, without sleep or a decent meal, sustained by the vision of that one moment. And then Tom had come into the office. He had come in quickly, holding a sheaf of papers in his hand; he had glanced at Jesse only casually, it was true—but long enough. He had not known him. He had turned away. . . . And Tom Brackett was his brother-in-law.

Was it his clothes? Jesse knew he looked terrible. He had tried to spruce up at a drinking fountain in the park, but even that had gone badly; in his excitement he had cut himself shaving, an ugly gash down the side of his cheek. And nothing could get the red gumbo dust out of his suit even though he had slapped himself till both arms were worn out. . . . Or was it just that he *had* changed so much?

True, they hadn't seen each other for five years; but Tom looked five years older, that was all. He was still Tom. God! was *he* so different?

Brackett finished his telephone call. He leaned back in his swivel chair and glanced over at Jesse with small, clear blue eyes that were suspicious and unfriendly. He was a heavy, paunchy man of forty-five, auburn-haired, rather dour-looking; his face was meaty, his features pronounced and forceful, his nose somewhat bulbous and reddish-hued at the tip. He looked like a solid, decent, capable businessman who was commander of his local branch of the American Legion—which he was. He surveyed Jesse with cold indifference, manifestly unwilling to spend time on him. Even the way he chewed his toothpick seemed contemptuous to Jesse.

"Yes?" Brackett said suddenly. "What do you want?"

His voice was decent enough, Jesse admitted. He had expected it to be worse. He moved up to the wooden counter that partitioned the shanty. He thrust a hand nervously through his tangled hair.

"I guess you don't recognize me, Tom," he said falteringly, "I'm Jesse Fulton."

"Huh?" Brackett said. That was all.

"Yes, I am, and Ella sends you her love."

Brackett rose and walked over to the counter until they were face to face. He surveyed Fulton incredulously, trying to measure the resemblance to his brother-in-law as he remembered him. This man was tall, about thirty. That fitted! He had straight good features and a lank erect body. That was right too. But the face was too gaunt, the body too spiny under the baggy clothes, for him to be sure. His brother-in-law had been a solid, strong young man with muscle and beef to him. It was like looking at a faded, badly taken photograph and trying to recognize the subject: the resemblance was there but the difference was tremendous. He searched the eyes. They at least seemed definitely familiar, gray, with a curiously shy but decent look in them. He had liked that about Fulton.

Jesse stood quiet. Inside he was seething. Brackett was like a man examining a piece of broken-down horseflesh; there was a look of pure pity in his eyes. It made Jesse furious. He knew he wasn't as far gone as all that.

"Yes, I believe you are," Brackett said finally, "but you sure have changed."

"By God, it's five years, ain't it?" Jesse said resentfully. "You only saw me a couple of times anyway." Then, to himself, with his lips locked together, in mingled vehemence and shame, What if I have changed? Don't everybody? I ain't no corpse.

"You was solid-looking," Brackett continued softly, in the same tone of incredulous wonder. "You lost weight, I guess?"

Jesse kept silent. He needed Brackett too much to risk antagonizing him. But it was only by deliberate effort that he could keep from boiling over. The pause lengthened, became painful. Brackett flushed. "Jiminy Christmas, excuse me," he burst out in apology. He jerked the counter up. "Come in. Take a seat. Good God, boy"—he grasped Jesse's hand and shook it—"I *am* glad to see you; don't think anything else! You just looked so peaked."

"It's all right," Jesse murmured. He sat down, thrusting his hand through his curly, tangled hair.

"Why are you limping?"

"I stepped on a stone; it jagged a hole through my shoe." Jesse pulled his feet back under the chair. He was ashamed of his shoes. They had come from the relief originally, and two weeks on the road had about finished them. All morning, with a kind of delicious, foolish solemnity, he had been vowing to himself that before anything else, before even a suit of clothes, he was going to buy himself a brand-new strong pair of shoes.

Brackett kept his eyes off Jesse's feet. He knew what was bothering the boy and it filled his heart with pity. The whole thing was appalling. He had never seen anyone who looked more down and out. His sister had been writing to him every week, but she hadn't told him they were as badly off as this.

"Well now, listen," Brackett began, "tell me things. How's Ella?"

"Oh, she's pretty good," Jesse replied absently. He had a soft, pleasing, rather shy voice that went with his soft gray eyes. He was worrying over how to get started.

"And the kids?"

"Oh, they're fine. . . . Well, you know," Jesse added, becoming more attentive, "the young one has to wear a brace. He can't run around, you know. But he's smart. He draws pictures and he does things, you know."

"Yes," Brackett said. "That's good." He hesitated. There was a moment's silence. Jesse fidgeted in his chair. Now that the time had arrived, he felt awkward. Brackett leaned forward and put his hand on Jesse's knee. "Ella didn't tell me things were so bad for you, Jesse. I might have helped."

"Well, goodness," Jesse returned softly, "you been having your own troubles, ain't you?"

"Yes." Brackett leaned back. His ruddy face became mournful and darkly bitter. "You know I lost my hardware shop?"

"Well sure, of course," Jesse answered, surprised. "You wrote us. That's what I mean."

"I forgot," Brackett said. "I keep on being surprised over it myself. Not that it was worth much," he added bitterly. "It was running downhill for three years. I guess I just wanted it because it was mine." He laughed pointlessly, without mirth. "Well, tell me about yourself," he asked. "What happened to the job you had?"

Jesse burst out abruptly, with agitation, "Let it wait, Tom, I got something on my mind."

"It ain't you and Ella?" Brackett interrupted anxiously.

"Why no!" Jesse sat back. "Why however did you come to think that? Why Ella and me—" He stopped, laughing. "Why, Tom, I'm just crazy about Ella. Why she's just wonderful. She's just my whole life, Tom."

"Excuse me. Forget it." Brackett chuckled uncomfortably, turned away. The naked intensity of the youth's burst of love had upset him. It made him wish savagely that he could do something for them. They were both too decent to have had it so hard. Ella was like this boy too, shy and a little soft.

"Tom, listen," Jesse said, "I come here on purpose." He thrust his hand through his hair. "I want you to help me."

"Damn it, boy," Brackett groaned. He had been expecting this. "I can't much. I only get thirty-five a week and I'm damn grateful for it."

"Sure, I know," Jesse emphasized excitedly. He was feeling once again the wild, delicious agitation that had possessed him in the early hours of the morning. "I know you can't help us with money! But we met a man who works for you! He was in our city! He said you could give me a job!"

"Who said?"

"Oh, why didn't you tell me?" Jesse burst out reproachfully. "Why as soon as I heard it I started out. For two weeks now I been pushing ahead like crazy."

Brackett groaned aloud. "You come walking from Kansas City in two weeks so I could give you a job?"

"Sure, Tom, of course. What else could I do?"

"God Almighty, there ain't no jobs, Jesse! It's slack season. And you don't know this oil business. It's special. I got my Legion friends here but they couldn't do nothing now. Don't you think I'd ask for you as soon as there was a chance?"

Jesse felt stunned. The hope of the last two weeks seemed rolling up into a ball of agony in his stomach. Then, frantically, he cried, "But listen, this man said *you* could hire! He *told* me! He drives trucks for you! He said you *always* need men!"

"Oh! . . . You mean *my* department?" Brackett said in a low voice.

"*Yes,* Tom. That's it!"

"Oh no, you don't want to work in my department," Brackett told him in the same low voice. "You don't know what it is."

"Yes, I do," Jesse insisted. "He told me all about it, Tom. You're a dispatcher, ain't you? You send the dynamite trucks out?"

"Who was the man, Jesse?"

"Everett, Everett, I think."

"Egbert? Man about my size?" Brackett asked slowly.

"Yes, Egbert. He wasn't a phony, was he?"

Brackett laughed. For the second time his laughter was curiously without mirth. "No, he wasn't a phony." Then, in a changed voice: "Jiminy, boy, you should have asked me before you trekked all the way down here."

"Oh, I didn't want to," Jesse explained with naïve cunning. "I knew you'd say no. He told me it was risky work, Tom. But I don't care."

Brackett locked his fingers together. His solid, meaty face became very hard. "I'm going to say no anyway, Jesse."

Jesse cried out. It had not occurred to him that Brackett would not agree. It had seemed as though reaching Tulsa were the only problem he had to face. "Oh no," he begged, "you can't. Ain't there any jobs, Tom?"

"Sure, there's jobs. There's even Egbert's job if you want it."

"He's quit?"

"He's dead!"

"Oh!"

"On the job, Jesse. Last night if you want to know."

"Oh!" . . . Then, "I don't care!"

"Now you listen to me," Brackett said. "I'll tell you a few things that you should have asked before you started out. It ain't dynamite you drive.

They don't use anything as safe as dynamite in drilling oil wells. They wish they could, but they can't. It's nitroglycerin! Soup!"

"But I know," Jesse told him reassuringly. "He advised me, Tom. You don't have to think I don't know."

"Shut up a minute," Brackett ordered angrily. "Listen! You just have to *look* at this soup, see? You just *cough* loud and it blows! You know how they transport it? In a can that's shaped like this, see, like a fan? That's to give room for compartments, because each compartment has to be lined with rubber. That's the only way you can even *think* of handling it."

"Listen, Tom—"

"Now wait a minute, Jesse. For God's sake just put your mind to this. I know you had your heart set on a job, but you've got to understand. This stuff goes only in special trucks! At night! They got to follow a special route! They can't go through any city! If they lay over, it's got to be in a special garage! Don't you see what that means? Don't that tell you how dangerous it is?"

"I'll drive careful," Jesse said. "I know how to handle a truck. I'll drive slow."

Brackett groaned. "Do you think Egbert didn't drive careful or know how to handle a truck?"

"Tom," Jesse said earnestly, "you can't scare me. I got my mind fixed on only one thing: Egbert said he was getting a dollar a mile. He was making five to six hundred dollars a month for half a month's work, he said. Can I get the same?"

"Sure, you can get the same," Brackett told him savagely. "A dollar a mile. It's easy. But why do you think the company has to pay so much? It's easy—until you run over a stone that your headlights didn't pick out, like Egbert did. Or get a blowout! Or get something in your eye, so the wheel twists and you jar the truck! Or any other God damn thing that nobody ever knows! We can't ask Egbert what happened to him. There's no truck to give any evidence. There's no corpse. There's nothing! Maybe tomorrow somebody'll find a piece of twisted steel way off in a cornfield. But we never find the driver. Not even a fingernail. All we know is that he don't come in on schedule. Then we wait for the police to call us. You know what happened last night? Something went wrong on a bridge. Maybe Egbert was nervous. Maybe he brushed the side with his fender. Only there's no bridge any more. No truck. No Egbert. Do you understand now? That's what you get for your God damn dollar a mile!"

There was a moment of silence. Jesse sat twisting his long thin hands. His mouth was sagging open, his face was agonized. Then he shut his eyes and spoke softly. "I don't care about that, Tom. You told me. Now you got to be good to me and give me the job."

Brackett slapped the palm of his hand down on his desk. "No!"

"Listen, Tom," Jesse said softly, "you just don't understand." He opened his eyes. They were filled with tears. They made Brackett turn away. "Just look at me, Tom. Don't that tell you enough? What did you think of me when you first saw me? You thought: 'Why don't that bum go away and stop panhandling?' Didn't you, Tom? Tom, I just can't live like this any more. I got to be able to walk down the street with my head up."

"You're crazy," Brackett muttered. "Every year there's one out of five drivers gets killed. That's the average. What's worth that?"

"Is my life worth anything now? We're just starving at home, Tom. They ain't put us back on relief yet."

"Then you should have told me," Brackett exclaimed harshly. "It's your own damn fault. A man has no right to have false pride when his family ain't eating. I'll borrow some money and we'll telegraph it to Ella. Then you go home and get back on relief."

"And then what?"

"And then wait, God damn it! You're no old man. You got no right to throw your life away. Sometime you'll get a job."

"No!" Jesse jumped up. "No. I believed that too. But I don't now," he cried passionately. "I ain't getting a job no more than you're getting your hardware store back. I lost my skill, Tom. Linotyping is skilled work. I'm rusty now. I've been six years on relief. The only work I've had is pick and shovel. When I got that job this spring I was supposed to be an A-1 man. But I wasn't. And they got new machines now. As soon as the slack started they let me out."

"So what?" Brackett said harshly. "Ain't there other jobs?"

"How do I know?" Jesse replied. "There ain't been one for six years. I'd even be afraid to take one now. It's been too hard waiting so many weeks to get back on relief."

"Well you got to have some courage," Brackett shouted. "You've got to keep up hope."

"I got all the courage you want," Jesse retorted vehemently, "but no, I ain't got no hope. The hope has dried up in me in six years' waiting. You're the only hope I got."

"You're crazy," Brackett muttered. "I won't do it. For God's sake think of Ella for a minute."

"Don't you *know* I'm thinking about her?" Jesse asked softly. He plucked at Brackett's sleeve. "That's what decided me, Tom." His voice became muted into a hushed, pained whisper. "The night Egbert was at our house I looked at Ella like I'd seen her for the first time. *She ain't pretty any more,* Tom!" Brackett jerked his head and moved away. Jesse followed him, taking a deep, sobbing breath. "Don't that tell you, Tom? Ella was like a little doll or something, you remember. I couldn't walk down the street without somebody turning to look at her. She ain't twenty-nine yet, Tom, and she ain't pretty no more."

Brackett sat down with his shoulders hunched up wearily. He gripped his hands together and sat leaning forward, staring at the floor.

Jesse stood over him, his gaunt face flushed with emotion, almost unpleasant in its look of pleading and bitter humility. "I ain't done right for Ella, Tom. Ella deserved better. This is the only chance I see in my whole life to do something for her. I've just been a failure."

"Don't talk nonsense," Brackett commented without rancor. "You ain't a failure. No more than me. There's millions of men in the identical situation. It's just the depression, or the recession, or the God damn New Deal, or . . . !" He swore and lapsed into silence.

"Oh no," Jesse corrected him in a knowing, sorrowful tone, "those things maybe excuse other men. But not me. It was up to me to do better. This is my own fault!"

"Oh, beans!" Brackett said. "It's more sun spots than it's you!"

Jesse's face turned an unhealthy mottled red. It looked swollen. "Well I don't care," he cried wildly. "I don't care! You got to give me this! I got to lift my head up. I went through one stretch of hell but I can't go through another. You want me to keep looking at my little boy's legs and tell myself if I had a job he wouldn't be like that? Every time he walks he says to me, 'I got soft bones from the rickets and you give it to me because you didn't feed me right.' Jesus Christ, Tom, you think I'm going to sit there and watch him like that another six years?"

Brackett leaped to his feet. "So what if you do?" he shouted. "You say you're thinking about Ella. How's she going to like it when you get killed?"

"Maybe I won't," Jesse pleaded. "I've got to have some luck sometime."

"That's what they all think," Brackett replied scornfully. "When you take this job your luck is a question mark. The only thing certain is that sooner or later you get killed."

"Okay then," Jesse shouted back. "Then I do! But meanwhile I got something, don't I? I can buy a pair of shoes. Look at me! I can buy a suit that don't say 'Relief' by the way it fits. I can smoke cigarettes. I can buy some candy for the kids. I can eat some myself. Yes, by God, I want to eat some candy. I want a glass of beer once a day. I want Ella dressed up. I want her to eat meat three times a week, four times maybe. I want to take my family to the movies."

Brackett sat down. "Oh, shut up," he said wearily.

"No," Jesse told him softly, passionately, "you can't get rid of me. Listen, Tom," he pleaded, "I got it all figured out. On six hundred a month look how much I can save! If I last only three months, look how much it is—a thousand dollars—more! And maybe I'll last longer. Maybe a couple of years. I can fix Ella up for life!"

"You said it," Brackett interposed. "I suppose you think she'll enjoy living when you're on a job like that?"

"I got it all figured out," Jesse answered excitedly. "She don't know, see? I tell her I make only forty. You put the rest in a bank account for her, Tom."

"Oh, shut up," Brackett said. "You think you'll be happy? Every minute, waking and sleeping, you'll be wondering if tomorrow you'll be dead. And the worst days will be your days off, when you're not driving. They have to give you every other day free to get your nerve back. And you lay around the house eating your heart out. That's how happy you'll be."

Jesse laughed. "I'll be happy! Don't you worry, I'll be so happy, I'll be singing. Lord God, Tom, I'm going to feel *proud* of myself for the first time in seven years."

"Oh, shut up, shut up," Brackett said.

The little shanty became silent. After a moment Jesse whispered: "You got to, Tom. You got to. You got to."

Again there was silence. Brackett raised both hands to his head, pressing the palms against his temples.

"Tom, Tom—" Jesse said.

Brackett sighed. "Oh, God damn it," he said finally, "all right, I'll take you on, God help me." His voice was low, hoarse, infinitely weary. "If you're ready to drive tonight, you can drive tonight."

Jesse didn't answer. He couldn't. Brackett looked up. The tears were running down Jesse's face. He was swallowing and trying to speak, but only making an absurd, gasping noise.

"I'll send a wire to Ella," Brackett said in the same hoarse, weary voice. "I'll tell her you got a job, and you'll send her fare in a couple of days. You'll have some money then—that is, if you last the week out, you jackass!"

Jesse only nodded. His heart felt so close to bursting that he pressed both hands against it, as though to hold it locked within his breast.

"Come back here at six o'clock," Brackett said. "Here's some money. Eat a good meal."

"Thanks," Jesse whispered.

"Wait a minute," Brackett said. "Here's my address." He wrote it on a piece of paper. "Take any car going that way. Ask the conductor where to get off. Take a bath and get some sleep."

"Thanks," Jesse said. "Thanks, Tom."

"Oh, get out of here," Brackett said.

"Tom."

"What?"

"I just—" Jesse stopped. Brackett saw his face. The eyes were still glistening with tears, but the gaunt face was shining now with a kind of fierce radiance.

Brackett turned away. "I'm busy," he said.

Jesse went out. The wet film blinded him but the whole world seemed to have turned golden. He limped slowly, with the blood pounding in his temples and a wild, incommunicable joy in his heart. "I'm the happiest man in the world," he whispered to himself. "I'm the happiest man on the whole earth."

Brackett sat watching till finally Jesse turned the corner of the alley and disappeared. Then he hunched himself over, with his head in his hands. His heart was beating painfully, like something old and clogged. He listened to it as it beat. He sat in desperate tranquillity, gripping his head in his hands.

*Suggestions for Study*

1. What constitutes the conflict in this story? Name the protagonist and the antagonist.

2. What would you say is the purpose of this story? What would you expect other stories by the same author to be like?

3. Upon what elements in the story do you base your opinion of Tom Brackett? Does your opinion of him remain fixed from the moment he is introduced, or does it change? If it changes, point out the factors which cause the change.

4. Is the point of view completely consistent throughout the story?

5. Do the things that Jesse wants to buy with his money seem trivial (shoes, clothes, candy, cigarettes, beer, meat four times a week)? What do these things indicate concerning Jesse's psychology?

6. Is Jesse's desire to earn money at the risk of his life made believable? Give your reasons.

7. Is this story basically one of plot or of character?

8. Are the elements of the story realistic or romantic?

9. Is sentiment held sufficiently in restraint? If so, how does the author achieve this?

## Brandy for Breakfast [46]

### LAURENCE W. MEYNELL

Towards the end of October a well-knit figure, with a pleasant air of vagabondage about it, was climbing the slopes of the Long Mynd.

"If you are on one of your insane walking tours, do come over our way," Hilary had written. "You will find Overley full of rather noisy people, but we shall all be delighted to see your serious old face." And a postscript had been added in an only too familiar scrawl, "Especially me—Anne."

Anne and Hilary and Overley House, a great, rambling thing, full of places where your head bumped and your feet stumbled, and quite completely full of an atmosphere in which your heart rejoiced—all excellent reasons (thought Roger Ascham) why a man should leave his chambers in Lincoln's Inn and set his face to that part of England which lies on the west of the Severn.

Shropshire was new country for Roger to walk in. When he had been to Overley before, it had been by train; and he was increasingly glad of his new approach there. He was as fit and youthful a forty as you could find (in spite of Hilary's rude remarks about his "serious old face"), and his long, athletic legs had brought him ahead of his schedule.

All day long he had been walking on the bare hills, those slopes as old as England that carry across them the very first tracks made by human feet on English soil. All day long he had had the sheep-nibbled, springy turf under him, and such names as Squilver, Stedment, Stiperstones, and Stent for companions. By nine o'clock at night he reached as lonely a wayside inn as even that bare countryside could show, where—for all the loneliness of the place—was a jewel of a woman who fried him such a plate of ham and eggs as he had never hoped to taste.

Roger ate his meal in the bar at an oaken table that was old when Trafalgar was fought, and afterwards he sat on there, sipping a pint of excellent beer and studying his map. Three other men were in the bar, of the dark and wiry sort that have been in these hills since time was.

They were uncommunicative at first, but thawed a little after a round of drinks, and Roger listened delightedly to the broad, unhurried dialect. Two of them were old and one was young, but they had all come out of the same mold and, in a way, were much alike.

The inn had only one drawback—it could not put him up; on the other hand, the Fates had provided a glorious full moon, and Roger had no

46. From the *Story Teller* (1936). Reprinted by permission of the author.

doubts about what he would do. There was a hamlet some six miles ahead where he felt certain a bed of some sort could be obtained, and he intended to push on there in the moonlight as rapidly as was reasonably possible.

It seemed to him that the map offered a choice of two ways: the high-road; and, what was at least a mile shorter, a track up the hill and over the side. Wisely he sought local confirmation concerning his route.

"Road 'll tak' 'ee straight theare, sir," he was assured.

"Follow 'un aäl the way and 'ee's bound to come to 'un."

Roger nodded. "But can't I cut up over the hill?" he asked. There was a moment's silence.

"Up the Old Traäck?" someone queried.

"Yes, if that's what it's called."

Again there was that momentary silence, and for the first time it struck Roger that there was something odd about it. One of the old men broke it to say, "Anyone can go on the Old Traäck as 'as got a mind to. But maybe the road's the better way in the moonlight."

Roger folded his map up and laughed at rustic reasoning. If there was one time when the track was better than the road, he argued, it must be by moonlight when it could be seen easily.

He drained the last drop of his beer, set his tankard down noisily, and with a cheery "Good night" to everybody went out into the darkness.

"Good night, sir." Three men answered him, and not one of them looked at him as they did so; nor, after he had left, did they look for a minute or two directly at each other. Roger was swinging along the road, and in the nature of things he could not hear the remarks that followed his departure.

The moon was rising rapidly, and there was no difficulty in seeing where the track led off the road. Roger turned up it whistling and tackled the long climb with a light heart. It was a track first made no one knew when and since trodden by countless generations of feet and almost equally countless generations of wheels. As Roger climbed, the country-side fell away from him on either side, bare and beautiful under the silver moonlight. Far away on the right, perhaps a mile away, a single light moved unevenly along the valley road, and its presence there seemed to Roger somehow friendly and reassuring. When the first crest of the hill was gained he saw, quite unexpectedly, a big farmhouse and its buildings lying amid trees on the left. The straight roofs of the house and the rounded tops of the barns glinted in the moonlight, but there was little light, and the pine trees behind rose dark and stiff and almost sinister. "A lonely place," Roger thought as he swung along, and on the instant, as though to contradict his verdict, a figure came out of the dark shadow of the wayside trees and joined him.

Thinking it over afterwards, Roger found it hard to say whether he overtook the other man or was overtaken by him. His attention had been on the house, and all he could say was that at one moment he was alone and at the next he had a companion.

The man gave him "good evening" in a low, musical voice, and Roger willingly fell in step beside him, glad of his company.

"You're out late on the hill road, mister," the man said, and Roger countered with, "Well, you're pretty late yourself, you know."

The man laughed quietly. "Suppose I am," he agreed. "Us chaps have to be about latish at times. There's a tuthree things to do."

Roger wondered whether he were a gamekeeper or poacher perhaps, and did not mind either way. In either event he was company.

They walked in silence for a while, Roger abating his quick, nervous gait to the countryman's unhurried pace, characteristic of his sort the world over. He was a well-made man with a fine pair of shoulders on him, and he looked well in his corduroys of the old country fashion and design.

"Fine night." Roger ventured at last to break the silence which was growing a little oppressive.

"Ay, good for any harvesting or plough work to be done extra-like."

"You wouldn't plough by moonlight surely?" Roger asked.

The other laughed his agreeable laugh again. "I've had to before now," he said.

"I suppose you work hereabouts?"

The man jerked his head backwards. "Up to Ladywood," he said.

"Is that the big farm I've just passed?"

"That's it. Mr. Lang's. This is all Ladywood land we're on now."

"Pretty good land, I suppose."

"It's been better," the man said cryptically, and Roger was debating this utterance, and wondering why every man is so prone to glorify the past, when the track dipped suddenly and ran by the side of a dark wood. The air was damper in the hollow, and Roger said abruptly:

"I never did like pine trees much. Why they can't plant good English oak, I don't know."

They had come to the end of the wood now, and the countryman stopped and rested his hand on a gate. "That's the Lady Wood," he said. "Gives its name to the farm, I reckon."

The upright trees, absolutely still in that windless air, looked dark and mysterious in the moonlight, almost as though there were secrets in the unexplored blackness of the wood which they were guarding and would not yield.

"There's a deal of folk don't care about coming past here o' night time," the man said suddenly, and instantly Roger's ears were pricked. He was blessed (or cursed, he could never himself be sure which) with an insatiably curious mind and was always avid to hear any new thing.

"Why's that?" he asked.

"Tales—well, one tale in particular, I reckon."

Silence. Roger broke it with an encouraging extension of his cigarette case. "Have a cigarette?"

"No, thank you, mister. I've never had no use for them things. One time o' day I used to smoke a bit o' baccy in a pipe, but that's all."

"And the story?" Roger prompted. "The tale that makes people afraid to come along here?"

"I'll tell it you if you've a mind to hear it; seeing as we've happened on each other, 'companions in the way' as the Bible says. Only it's ghosts, of course, and I reckon you're a book-learned man and maybe you don't believe in such things and aren't interested in 'em."

"I'm interested in everything," Roger said, and it was very nearly true.

The countryman hesitated a minute as though wondering how to start his tale; one hard, muscled hand rested on top of the five-barred gate; one side of him was in shadow, the other silvered by the moonlight; his eyes were fixed on the dark mystery of the wood.

"It's about old days now," he said, "though not really old in a manner of speaking. Michaelmas, eighteen-eighty-eight, it all began, the way the old chaps always tell the tale. In they days there was always a Michaelmas Mop Fair at Wenlock. Wenches used to go to be hired out for servants and chaps for work on the farms. Stood in two rows they always did, chaps in the front and wenches at the back, and each one wearing summat to show what his work was. Then the farmers 'ud come and look 'em over and pick out a likely one, and they'd strike a bargain, master and man, for a year or three years maybe, and the money was fixed and the 'ulowances and everything; and the farmer always had to pay a shilling there and then earnest money. That was a right way of striking a bargain to my mind. Master could see man and man master, and each gave his word and stuck to it. None of this writing and notices and cards and such.

"The chap this tale is about stood there Michaelmas, eighteen-eighty-eight, in the Market Square at Wenlock with a whip in his hand to show he was a horseman. Twenty-four years old he was, and knew his work. Born the other side of the Clee at Hope Bowdler, a sleepy sort of place some reckon it; well, I daresay we are sleepy these parts, sleepy still as far as that goes. But I'll warrant he didn't feel sleepy that particular morning standing in Wenlock Square with all the noise of the fair round him, and chaps hollering and the auctioneer calling out the bids for the beasts and all the wenches about him.

"Good-looking chap they reckon he was, ought to have gone for a soldier, some say, time the 'cruiting sargent with his red sash came round and stood all beer, and then maybe he wouldn't have got into his trouble. But that's as may be. I reckon things work out to an appointed end, and if it hadn't been trouble here, it would have been trouble the other side of the world somewhere, in lands he didn't know. There was a girl or two looked at this chap in Wenlock, seemingly; I reckon he must have looked a good one to wed with, but if he me't have smiled at one or two, there was nothing more, him being married for two years and happy.

"When the farmers came out of the Arms all the argufying and bargain-making started, louder than selling the beasts. And the outcome of it was this chap, Dale his name was, engaged himself to Ladywood Farm to serve his master faithful and well for three years as horseman. Fifteen shillings a week and a cottage found, and extra money harvest time, and a bit of meal every now and again to help him keep a pig if he'd a mind to. Mr. Lang the farmer was. There was Langs at Ladywood then, of course, and always have been, pretty well.

"This Lang, Harry Lang *his* name was, he was a man about fifty, very quick-tempered and must have what he wanted; but if he did make his men work, he worked alongside them with his coat off. A great man for getting the most out of everything, fly into a temper he would if your headlands were a foot too wide when you were ploughing. But if you worked well he gave you credit for it; he was that sort. Ted Dale understood that sort of man, and if ever they lost tempers with one another and got to widdershins he stood up to him. The horseman's cottage was in the next valley then, Well Cottage it was called. It's been pulled down since they days. A little bit of a place it was, two up and two down, and a pigsty; but a man can make his bit of heaven where's he's a mind to, so be as he's got the woman he loves and it's his home.

"Ted Dale served his three years and was happy there, and time they was up they struck another bargain, master and man, in the big stable at Ladywood Farm.

"'You stay along o' me another three years, Dale,' Mr. Lang said, 'and I'll raise you two shillings a week.' And they shook hands on it there and then, and Mr. Lang called for a girl to bring out some homebrewed from the cellar to make a bargain of it. Mr. Lang wasn't married, then, being a widower; his wife died in childbirth and the baby died too, a little after.

So Ladywood had been without a mistress for a good number of years, which didn't seem right in a farmhouse somehow, but there it was.

"Of course, they days there *was* ploughing to do; all this country was under corn then, and the old men today'll tell you the same. A man had to mind his horses then, or they'd never have stood up to the work. But this chap Dale he loved his cattle, and there was always a prize or two came Ladywood way, Wenlock or Ludlow show times.

"When Dale had been at Well Cottage four years, Mr. Lang got married again. Took everyone by surprise because no one had seen any walking-out or courting or such; and no wonder, for he didn't marry a Shropshire woman, but brought a lady straight from London, wed and all in order before he got here, and put her in at Ladywood as mistress straight away.

"Of course, there was a do after she came; they cleared the big barn and there was a supper and music and dancing and such like. And some speeches like they always make. And Mr. Lang stood up and said he'd got himself a wife as every man ought to do, and he had brought her to Lady-wood to look after it for him, and he reckoned to be a farmer's wife was as good a thing as any woman, lady or no, could wish for. And when he'd done Mrs. Lang got up, a slim slip of a woman, quality-bred, as 'ad never done a day at the washtub in her life, and thanked everybody nice and proper and said she was sure she was going to be happy at Ladywood. She looked that lissom and bright-colored, like a bit of china, I'll warrant there was above a man or two there would have changed places willingly with Harry Lang.

"They days there wasn't much in the way of funning these parts; time Mayday sports was over there was nothing till Harvest Home; and then only the Mummers at Christmastime to break the winter. So a do like this wedding-feast got talked of a good deal, and everyone was saying what a proper lady Mr. Lang had brought home with him. But laborers didn't have much to do with the big house, and this chap Ted Dale didn't see his master's wife again for a tuthree months; only, times, he thought of her looking so small and dainty and so different from the heavy, yeavy things as filled his life.

"Harvest Home he saw her and she spoke to him; quick, bright words she had like the chirrup of a bird. And Christmastime, when all went to all to wish happiness, he saw her again, standing in the firelight of the big kitchen and laughing and looking like a fairy.

"There was more ploughing than ever that next spring. Corn looked to rise in price, and Mr. Lang dearly loved a bargain and was mad to grow all he could. He worked man and beast hard. They days there was no hours and agreements and Acts of Parliament about us chaps; it was up by starlight and back to bed by starlight and work all in between. And yet never enough to satisfy him. He was like that, desperate after a thing as he'd set his mind on, and everything else he'd reckon waste of time and sinful.

"April time one of Ted Dale's children went ill and one day, as was too wet to plough and he was at home mending gear, Mrs. Lang came from the farm with a basket of comforts. First he knowed about it, the bit of a hovel where he sat working was darkened, and he looked up to see her in the doorway.

"'Can I come in?' she says. And a bit of April sun came out at that second, and she looked gold and glorious all at once like she me't be a shining angel.

"That was the first time as Ted Dale ever saw her alone, and there was only two more times in his life—three in all. Strange, I always reckon that. Yet I suppose it's like these clever artists who can paint a picture with half-a-dozen quick strokes and you see the thing plain and vivid enough to make you cry out. I reckon God can do the same with us humans when He's a mind to.

"Ted Dale bid her come her ways in, and stood up a bit awkward, what with his hair tousled and sleeves rolled up and the shirt open on his chest. But I suppose the sun and the wind put a color on a man, especially one who's got a great pair of shoulder and a happy smile, as a woman likes to see above niceties of dress.

"Ten minutes and more she talked to him and never offered to go. You me't almost have thought as she was glad of someone to talk to.

"Ted talked it all over with his wife that evening. Pleasant and good, they both reckoned, it was of her to come, and charitable.

"'That's the sort of woman we want at the farmhouse,' Mary said. But, night-time, when he lay awake in the dark and Mary sleeping safe beside him, all Ted could remember was the moment when he looked up and saw her shining in the doorway, and caught his breath the instant as he had seen a vision.

"July was half done and hay harvest almost finished before he saw her again. A hot day it was, with no wind and the hum of the insects so steady on those lonely fields as would lull a man to sleep. Ted Dale was walking through the Long Meadow Coppy, which was the shortest way from the farmhouse to the far hayfield, where there was still a load or two to carry. They days the coppy was thicker than it is now, all a mass of lush and undergrowth, and so still in the midst of it a man me't be alone in all the world, only times a yaffle would startle you by its noise, or a dog-fox run across the ride. Suddenly he saw her sitting on a log in the clearing. He was on her before he could give any warning of his coming, and she looked up quickly and gave a little cry as she was frightened, and he could see that her eyes were streaming wet with tears. Very awkward and uncomfortable he felt in his corduroys although she made to smile when she saw him, but she would have him sit beside her on the log and no refusal.

"She wasn't the lady at the big house, but just a dear human heart fighting with itself and desperate unhappy.

" 'Oh,' she says beating her little, white hands on the back of the log, 'I'm so lonely, Dale. Lonely, lonely, lonely. I thought Ladywood was lovely when I came to it, but I tell you it's a prison, a prison.'

"Then she told him—yet, in a way, it wasn't telling *him,* but just *telling,* just easing her heart of what it must say to someone—she told him of what it had been like in London where she lived and the menservants and parties and theaters and bright lights and all such which was like a dream to Ted Dale. Then Harry Lang had set eyes on her and, never mind her three elder sisters, he wanted her desperate bad. Would have her too, yea-word or nay-word from her parents. And her parents were dead set against him. Pride puffed up their hearts, maybe, as it has puffed up many others to their unhappiness. They wanted a London man with money for their prettiest girl, and here was a farmer from the middle of Shropshire swearing he must have her, and angry at any delay. The end of it was he was forbidden the house, and she was told plain she must forget him and look elsewhere.

"But at twenty-one it is hard to look elsewhere when there's a man pouring out such passionate love to you as most women never hear in their lives.

" 'You've got to live your own life, my dear,' Harry Lang said (and by that he meant live *his*), 'and never mind about your parents.'

"And she listened to him; with his kisses hot on hers and his arms aching to hold her closer yet, she listened; what woman wouldn't? And one night between one hour and the next she slipped out of the big London house into the gaslit streets with a lie on her lips and wonder in her heart and all life an adventure before her.

"Harry Lang had all ready, and next day they were wed at a registrar's, and he brought her to Ladywood, and she had never seen or heard of her family since.

"But Harry Lang the farmer was different from Harry Lang the lover. Beasts in the stockyard and women in the kitchen, that's what he liked to see. That was the way he reckoned life should be, and he didn't set up to understand any other. It wasn't so much the work—though that was bad enough—as the loneliness that she got to hate. All this countryside is lonely; they days it stood lonelier still, and Ladywood the loneliest of it all. Times a month will go without you see anyone outside the household; and should a stranger chance to come it sets all the parish talking. It was very different from London and the menservants and the traffic in the lighted streets.

" 'Oh,' she cried, 'I hate Ladywood now. It's like a cage. I feel like a bird trapped in it all the time. It's like a cage I tell you.'

"Ted Dale understood that. He could never abear to see any caged or chained thing and had always a mind to set all free as he saw. It always seemed terrible to him to see the sunlight and not to be able to be in it. He forgot she was his master's wife; in a way, the manner of her speaking to him had made him forget it.

" 'Now, dear heart,' he told her, 'don't 'ee take on so. There's up and down in life, 'tis the way of things, and 'twill all come smooth in the end.'

"Oh, but she didn't want it smooth in the end; in the end she would be old and stiff-limbed and not mind whether 'twas spring or autumn, and now she was young and warm-blooded and was lonely, lonely, lonely. And she went into a fit of weeping there and then, like a child that had broken its toy. And angry, too, against him, mad angry, for trying to fob her off with old saws that parsons use.

"And suddenly, in the midst of it, she jumped up and stood against him, and they looked at each other. 'Ah,' she said, and her voice had gone very quiet like it me't be a little stream running alongside a meadow. 'Ah, I liked you, Ted Dale, the very first time I saw you.' And quick as a fly-catcher she darted down and kissed him full on his lips, and then she was up and running down the ride to the house before he could move.

"Time he did move and got to the Long Meadow, Mr. Lang was hollering from across the field at him why had he been so long and perhaps he reckoned hay harvest would wait for him and all such. And Ted Dale never answered a word; not a thing could he see in the bright sunlight, neither Harry Lang, nor the cocks of hay, nor the red and blue wagon, nor his own great horses, nor anything in the whole hayfield save only a little elfish face against him and two lips on his.

"That was the second time of his seeing her alone, and it lasted him through the end of hay harvest, right through corn harvest (and there *was* a corn harvest those times) to the beginning of the back-end. A time or two when he was at the buildings he might catch a glimpse of her in the farmhouse talking to a maid, or among the bright flowers in the garden or some such, but never to speak to. But not a day went by when he didn't think on her.

"Folks used to read the Bible a deal those times, even rough laboring chaps would have it in their cottages. 'My soul is troubled and grievously afflicted,' Ted Dale would read, or may be, 'Beauty hath lifted up mine eyes and made me afraid.' And times he'd turn to the love song where it says, 'A cluster of grapes my beloved is to me in the vineyards of Engaddi.' And all the while he was thinking of one thing. Sinful he knew it was, because Mary was his lawful wedded wife for better or worse, through rough and smooth as long as they both lived, and he loved her.

"But this other woman had got into his blood. She haunted him like she was a ghost, so light and delicate and like a bit of china, and yet her lips so soft and warm and yes-saying on his that time in Long Meadow Coppy. Aye, and once he read, 'A man shall dream and have an image set in his heart,' and he let the Book slip and sat staring over it like he was struck.

"Well, that was a poor way for a man to be in, but he had his work of course to keep him busy. Time harvest was done and all raught in, there was winter ploughing to start, and October was always a rare month these parts for working. There was a day the end of that October as this chap Dale was sent to plough this very field here by the Lady Wood. Grass it's been long since, but they days it was plough and always had bin. Mr. Lang was away to Ludlow to buy beasts, and Ted Dale was to plough Spinner's Piece as they call it. There'd been a touch of frost in the night and there was a mist everywhere like a white curtain and the sun certain to come through by noonday. Proper October weather it was. Captain and Brownie he was ploughing with, and it was music to him to hear their harness jingle as he took them down the lane to work.

"Mr. Lang was set on having the Piece ploughed as soon as me't be, and Dale stuck at it steady all morning with the mist clearing all the time and the rooks waddling after him like aldermen in the furrows and the steam standing up off his horses in the still air.

"Noon day was gone and he was just getting to the end of a furrow when summat made him look up and there across the headland looking at him over the hedge top she was. Neither said a word for a minute, and he could only think of those words, 'A man shall dream and have an image set in his heart' because just at that moment he had been thinking of her clear and vivid and here was his image set over against him.

"Then she said, 'Busy?' And slipped off her horse and tied him to this very gate stump here. She had taken a horse from Ladywood stables and ridden out to see him. Ted Dale was struck silly at first.

" 'I was just a-goöing to have my middays,' he said.

" 'I reckoned you would be,' she made answer, 'and I thought I'd come and have mine with you. Mr. Lang's away to market and I'm tired of having meals alone.'

" 'Well, I must finish the furrow first,' Ted said, and she laughed out loud at him, such a noise it sounded in these still fields all bright and silvery.

" 'No you must *not*,' she says. 'You can finish that after.' And for the first time in his life Ted left his horses standing in the middle of a furrow; no shade or headland nibbling nor nothing. Just left them there and followed her into the Lady Wood.

"She made him sit down very close to her. 'Ah Ted,' she says, 'we ought to have seen one another before this. You've been avoiding me.' And, 'Oh Ted, I can't stand it any more, no one to talk to and nothing to do and loneliness all day long.' And she slid her arm on his, which was hot and sweaty from plough-work, and she said, 'Ted Dale, you've got wonderful powerful arms, a man's arms . . .'

"Well, that was the way of it. There'll be plenty ready to blame, but the world's made of men and women; and, times, all promises, all honor, all happiness counts nothing beside a mad hour's pleasure.

"And then, in the middle of it, when neither had been listening to aught but the other's whispers, a twig snapped, and Harry Lang stood there looking at them like a man mazed.

"Halfway to Ludlow he chanced to meet the man whose beasts he wanted to buy, and they struck a bargain there and then in a wayside inn and no need to go to market at all. And Harry Lang was so pleased at saving half-a-day he drove straight back to Ladywood to kiss his wife in high humor; but on the way he thought he'd turn aside for ten minutes to see how Dale was getting on with the Spinner's Piece. And by the roadside to his amazement he saw Bluebell, the Ladywood hacking mare, tied to a gatepost. 'What the devil's this?' he thought to himself. And when he made his way into the Wood what it turned out to be was his wife in the arms of his ploughman.

"He was that struck he couldn't do naught but stare at first; it was almost funny to see him.

"He had his shotgun with him which he always took wherever he went in case there might be a rabbit or a rook as he walked up the hedgeside. And Ted Dale thought, 'He'll shoot me certain sure.' And he made to push the woman away from him in case she got shot too.

"But Lang had his courage. He was that angry at someone daring to take what was his it wouldn't be good enough just to shoot him; he must prove himself the better man. He handled his gun, but only to put it down on the ground.

" 'My God, Dale,' he says, very quiet and white all the time, 'you're going to remember this.' And he took off his market-going coat and put it down very neatly beside him.

"Then they went to it, master and man—or man and man, I should say, with the woman looking on.

"Dale had the years of the other man, but Harry Lang was like a mad person; if you hit him he didna' feel it; you could have burnt him with a bare flame and he'd not have known.

"It was naked fists, and ugly, naked anger, and blood enough soon in all conscience; and the woman forgotten you me't say, sobbing and crying in the background.

"And then in the silence of that quiet place and sending all the rooks like a handful of black stones into the sky, a noise like it was the end of the world.

"And so it was the end of the world for one of the men. The woman had picked up the gun, and from not ten yards off, no, not five either, had taken aim at one of them and fired, and the fighting stopped at once. Maybe she hit the one she aimed at, maybe the twisting and turning of their bodies defeated her—who knows? Only she; and it was too late to say. She and her husband stared at one another over the dead body of her lover, and gradually the echoes died away in the Lady Wood and the rooks settled again in the furrows, and silence came back to the place.

"Aye, that was the way of it, mister; love and anger and a dead man all in an hour as you me't say.

"And then the two of them that remained, man and woman, in the bright sunshine and the air. What to do, was what they asked themselves. Run into Ludlow town calling, 'I've shot my lover, I've shot him'? Aye, some would; but I'll not blame the woman, whoever does. Life's sweet, mister, very sweet when spring comes and Shropshire orchards are white with blossom. I'll not blame the woman. No one but those three had heard the shot; no one but them knew aught of the happening.

"There was, aye there still is, a pool in the Lady Wood, a deepish bit of water, and dark such as you get in woods. Harry Lang carried his ploughman to it and tipped him in. He made ripples like a stone would, and then the ripples ceased and all was still.

"Harry Lang put his wife on Bluebell and made her ride home beside him and never a word was said about Dale between them.

"Next day Lang asked, 'Where's Dale?' And nobody knew, and Mary all in a state at Well Cottage because he hadn't been back all night.

" 'He's gone off then,' Lang said, and gave out his tale, how he had been to see Dale at work and reprimanded him and they had quarreled. ('He struck me. Look at the marks.') And he warned him he would have him up before the Bench for assault, and he must have taken fright and gone.

"It made a bit of a stir at the time, but it soon quietened down, and folks believed what the farmer said. They days one ploughman more or less didn't matter a lot; there was always a tuthree more.

"Ah, well, it's an old tale and over now. But two things Harry Lang couldn't stop: he couldn't stop Ted Dale coming back o' nights to finish his furrow; and he couldn't stop his wife going down to the Lady Wood when she'd a mind to and sitting there staring. Time after time he forbade her and was angry about it, but go she would, nay-word or no; and he daresen't speak too much about it before the maids and such-like, for someone me't ask: why shouldn't she go to the Lady Wood if so she'd a mind?

"She'd go there and sit very still, listening. Not by the pool she wouldn't sit, as a rule, but just out of sight of it, inside the wood. And as she listened times she thought she would hear horses as it me't be ploughing, and a man's voice very rich and musical (which she always had noticed about it) calling very faint and ghostly, 'Gee, *ay,* Captain,' or maybe, 'Co-oop, Brownie,' and quick as a flycatcher she would dart to the side of the wood and there was nothing but an empty, lonely field.

"But she went to the Lady Wood once too often. Christmastime she went, towards dusk one day. A proper mournful, dead sort of a place it would seem, with drippings falling *pat pat pat* from the bare branches and all the dead leaves beneath. That time she never came back, and folks would have it that the pool must be dragged.

"They found her, of course; maybe in the dark she had slipped in by mistake; maybe she thought she heard something calling her from the bottom of the black water. For there was still something else there. They found it when they were dragging, far gone, of course, but enough to see it was a man; and some said enough to tell there was a gunshot wound all down one side—well, look, mister . . ."

The man turned so that the side of him that had been in shadow should have been silvered by the moonlight, and yet it was not silvered but dark and ugly. "Look, mister," he said in his low, musical voice, and Roger took one look and tried to scream and fainted.

A milk float passes along that lonely road soon after six in the morning. Its driver found Roger Ascham; recognized by his clothes that he was one of the mad gentlemen who walk, and brought him to the next farm down the road. Here warmth, a glass of hot milk and kindliness did their work. And Roger, who was a determined person, left again on foot by half-past seven. He walked quickly, without a single glance behind him. If a stranger had stepped out of the roadside to talk to him, he would have screamed with terror. By nine o'clock precisely he stood in the porch of Overley.

A typical Overley breakfast was in progress, noisy, hilarious, prodigious.

"Roger!" Anne shrieked. "Darling Roger, where on earth have you come from at this hour?"

"What'll you have, Roger?" Hilary's deep voice asked from the sideboard. "There's bacon, kidney, or the odd egg."

"I'll have," said Roger, with the greatest clarity and decision, "a double brandy-and-soda, thank you."

## Suggestions for Study

1. What purpose is served by the description of Overley House in the third paragraph?

2. Why did the author not start the story with Roger trudging along the Old Track in the moonlight, thus eliminating the scene at the inn?

3. Why is emphasis laid on the age of the Shropshire countryside?

4. Of what significance is it that the ploughman says "Good evening" in a "musical" voice? Does the quality of his voice figure later in the story?

5. What elements of foreshadowing occur in the first part of the dialogue between Roger and the ploughman?

6. Examine the structure of the ploughman's story. Is the story skillfully told? Is any advantage gained by having the story told in dialect by a country person?

7. Is Harry Lang a thoroughly unlikable person? Is it beyond comprehension that Mrs. Lang was willing to marry him?

8. Why is it that the reader is left somewhat in doubt as to which man Mrs. Lang intended to shoot?

9. Does the story provide a possible natural explanation for Roger's experience?

10. Was the author's main aim to develop character or to build an interesting plot?

11. As the author develops the story, does it seem at all plausible?

12. This is an example of a story within a frame. Is there an advantage in this so far as this type of story is concerned?

## Laura [47]

### BY SAKI (H. H. MUNRO)

"You are not really dying, are you?" asked Amanda.

"I have the doctor's permission to live till Tuesday," said Laura.

"But today is Saturday; this is serious!" gasped Amanda.

"I don't know about it being serious; it is certainly Saturday," said Laura.

"Death is always serious," said Amanda.

"I never said I was going to die. I am presumably going to leave off being Laura, but I shall go on being something. An animal of some kind, I suppose. You see, when one hasn't been very good in the life one has just lived, one reincarnates in some lower organism. And I haven't been very good, when one comes to think of it. I've been petty and mean and vindictive and all that sort of thing when circumstances have seemed to warrant it."

"Circumstances never warrant that sort of thing," said Amanda hastily.

"If you don't mind my saying so," observed Laura, "Egbert is a circumstance that would warrant any amount of that sort of thing. You're married to him—that's different; you've sworn to love, honour, and endure him: I haven't."

"I don't see what's wrong with Egbert," protested Amanda.

"Oh, I dare say the wrongness has been on my part," admitted Laura dispassionately; "he has merely been the extenuating circumstance. He made a thin, peevish kind of fuss, for instance, when I took the collie puppies from the farm out for a run the other day."

"They chased his young broods of speckled Sussex and drove two sitting hens off their nests, besides running all over the flower beds. You know how devoted he is to his poultry and garden."

"Anyhow, he needn't have gone on about it for the entire evening and then have said, 'Let's say no more about it' just when I was beginning to enjoy the discussion. That's where one of my petty vindictive revenges came in," added Laura with an unrepentant chuckle; "I turned the entire family of speckled Sussex into his seedling shed the day after the puppy episode."

"How could you?" exclaimed Amanda.

"It came quite easy," said Laura; "two of the hens pretended to be laying at the time, but I was firm."

47. From *The Short Stories of Saki* (H. H. Munro) (copyright, 1930, by The Viking Press, Inc., N. Y.). Reprinted by permission of the Viking Press, Inc. and John Lane The Bodley Head, the English publisher.

"And we thought it was an accident!"

"You see," resumed Laura, "I really *have* some grounds for supposing that my next incarnation will be in a lower organism. I shall be an animal of some kind. On the other hand, I haven't been a bad sort in my way, so I think I may count on being a nice animal, something elegant and lively, with a love of fun. An otter, perhaps."

"I can't imagine you as an otter," said Amanda.

"Well, I don't suppose you can imagine me as an angel, if it comes to that," said Laura.

Amanda was silent. She couldn't.

"Personally I think an otter life would be rather enjoyable," continued Laura; "salmon to eat all the year round, and the satisfaction of being able to fetch the trout in their own homes without having to wait for hours till they condescend to rise to the fly you've been dangling before them; and an elegant svelte figure—"

"Think of the otter hounds," interposed Amanda; "how dreadful to be hunted and harried and finally worried to death!"

"Rather fun with half the neighborhood looking on, and anyhow not worse than this Saturday-to-Tuesday business of dying by inches; and then I should go on into something else. If I had been a moderately good otter I suppose I should get back into human shape of some sort; probably something rather primitive—a little brown, unclothed Nubian boy, I should think."

"I wish you would be serious," sighed Amanda; "you really ought to be if you're only going to live till Tuesday."

As a matter of fact Laura died on Monday.

"So dreadfully upsetting," Amanda complained to her uncle-in-law, Sir Lulworth Quayne. "I've asked quite a lot of people down for golf and fishing, and the rhododendrons are just looking their best."

"Laura always was inconsiderate," said Sir Lulworth; "she was born during Goodwood week, with an Ambassador staying in the house who hated babies."

"She had the maddest kind of ideas," said Amanda; "do you know if there was any insanity in her family?"

"Insanity? No, I never heard of any. Her father lives in West Kensington, but I believe he's sane on all other subjects."

"She had an idea that she was going to be reincarnated as an otter," said Amanda.

"One meets with those ideas of reincarnation so frequently, even in the West," said Sir Lulworth, "that one can hardly set them down as being mad. And Laura was such an unaccountable person in this life that I should not like to lay down definite rules as to what she might be doing in an after state."

"You think she really might have passed into some animal form?" asked Amanda. She was one of those who shape their opinions rather readily from the standpoint of those around them.

Just then Egbert entered the breakfast-room, wearing an air of bereavement that Laura's demise would have been insufficient, in itself, to account for.

"Four of my speckled Sussex have been killed," he exclaimed; "the very four that were to go to the show on Friday. One of them was dragged away and eaten right in the middle of that new carnation bed that I've been to such trouble and expense over. My best flower bed and my best fowls singled out for destruction; it almost seems as if the brute that did the deed had special knowledge how to be as devastating as possible in a short space of time."

"Was it a fox, do you think?" asked Amanda.

"Sounds more like a polecat," said Sir Lulworth.

"No," said Egbert, "there were marks of webbed feet all over the place, and we followed the tracks down to the stream at the bottom of the garden; evidently an otter."

Amanda looked quickly and furtively across at Sir Lulworth.

Egbert was too agitated to eat any breakfast, and went out to superintend the strengthening of the poultry yard defences.

"I think she might at least have waited till the funeral was over," said Amanda in a scandalized voice.

"It's her own funeral, you know," said Sir Lulworth; "it's a nice point in etiquette how far one ought to show respect to one's own mortal remains."

Disregard for mortuary convention was carried to further lengths next day; during the absence of the family at the funeral ceremony the remaining survivors of the speckled Sussex were massacred. The marauder's line of retreat seemed to have embraced most of the flower beds on the lawn, but the strawberry beds in the lower garden had also suffered.

"I shall get the otter hounds to come here at the earliest possible moment," said Egbert savagely.

"On no account! You can't dream of such a thing!" exclaimed Amanda. "I mean, it wouldn't do, so soon after a funeral in the house."

"It's a case of necessity," said Egbert; "once an otter takes to that sort of thing it won't stop."

"Perhaps it will go elsewhere now that there are no more fowls left," suggested Amanda.

"One would think you wanted to shield the beast," said Egbert.

"There's been so little water in the stream lately," objected Amanda; "it seems hardly sporting to hunt an animal when it has so little chance of taking refuge anywhere."

"Good gracious!" fumed Egbert, "I'm not thinking about sport. I want to have the animal killed as soon as possible."

Even Amanda's opposition weakened when, during church time on the following Sunday, the otter made its way into the house, raided half a salmon from the larder and worried it into scaly fragments on the Persian rug in Egbert's studio.

"We shall have it hiding under our beds and biting pieces out of our feet before long," said Egbert, and from what Amanda knew of this particular otter she felt that the possibility was not a remote one.

On the evening preceding the day fixed for the hunt Amanda spent a solitary hour walking by the banks of the stream, making what she imagined to be hound noises. It was charitably supposed by those who overheard her performance that she was practising for farmyard imitations at the forthcoming village entertainment.

It was her friend and neighbor, Aurora Burret, who brought her news of the day's sport.

"Pity you weren't out; we had quite a good day. We found at once, in the pool just below your garden."

"Did you—kill?" asked Amanda.

"Rather. A fine she-otter. Your husband got rather badly bitten in trying to 'tail it.' Poor beast, I felt quite sorry for it, it had such a human look in its eyes when it was killed. You'll call me silly, but do you know who the look reminded me of? My dear woman, what is the matter?"

When Amanda had recovered to a certain extent from her attack of nervous prostration Egbert took her to the Nile Valley to recuperate. Change of scene speedily brought about the desired recovery of health and mental balance. The escapades of an adventurous otter in search of a variation of diet were viewed in their proper light. Amanda's normally placid temperament reasserted itself. Even a hurricane of shouted curses, coming from her husband's dressing-room, in her husband's voice, but hardly in his usual vocabulary, failed to disturb her serenity as she made a leisurely toilet one evening in a Cairo hotel.

"What is the matter? What has happened?" she asked in amused curiosity.

"The little beast has thrown all my clean shirts into the bath! Wait till I catch you, you little—"

"What little beast?" asked Amanda, suppressing a desire to laugh;

Egbert's language was so hopelessly inadequate to express his outraged feelings.

"A little beast of a naked brown Nubian boy," spluttered Egbert.

And now Amanda is seriously ill.

### Suggestions for Study

1. From a rational point of view this story is completely implausible. As a reader, do you resent the author's imposing on you or do you accept the situation? What gives it the air of verisimilitude?

2. What are the most humorous elements of the story to you?

3. Who are the only ones in the story who know the truth? What elements in the character of each—merely hinted at—make them willing to accept the irrational as true?

4. Could anything be omitted without damage to the story? Would the story be better if the author had quoted authorities to make the idea of reincarnation more plausible?

5. Is Laura's estimate of her own character correct, or is she really bad?

## You Could Look It Up [48]

### JAMES THURBER

It all begun when we dropped down to C'lumbus, Ohio, from Pittsburgh to play a exhibition game on our way out to St. Louis. It was gettin' on into September, and though we'd been leadin' the league by six, seven games most of the season, we was now in first place by a margin you could 'a' got it into the eye of a thimble, bein' only a half a game ahead of St. Louis. Our slump had given the boys the leapin' jumps, and they was like a bunch a old ladies at a lawn fete with a thunderstorm comin' up, runnin' around snarlin' at each other, eatin' bad and sleepin' worse, and battin' for a team average of maybe .186. Half the time nobody'd speak to nobody else, without it was to bawl 'em out.

Squawks Magrew was managin' the boys at the time, and he was darn near crazy. They called him "Squawks" 'cause when things was goin' bad he lost his voice, or perty near lost it, and squealed at you like a little girl you stepped on her doll or somethin'. He yelled at everybody and wouldn't listen to nobody, without maybe it was me. I'd been trainin' the boys for ten year, and he'd take more lip from me than from anybody else. He knowed I was smarter'n him, anyways, like you're goin' to hear.

This was thirty, thirty-one year ago; you could look it up, 'cause it was the same year C'lumbus decided to call itself the Arch City, on account

48. From the *Saturday Evening Post*, CCXIII (April 5, 1941), No. 40 (copyright by James Thurber). Reprinted by permission of the author and the *Saturday Evening Post*.

of a lot of iron arches with electric-light bulbs into 'em which stretched acrost High Street. Thomas Albert Edison sent 'em a telegram, and they was speeches and maybe even President Taft opened the celebration by pushin' a button. It was a great week for the Buckeye capital, which was why they got us out there for this exhibition game.

Well, we just lose a double-header to Pittsburgh, 11 to 5 and 7 to 3, so we snarled all the way to C'lumbus, where we put up at the Chittaden Hotel, still snarlin'. Everybody was tetchy, and when Billy Klinger took a sock at Whitey Cott at breakfast, Whitey throwed marmalade all over his face.

"Blind each other, whatta I care?" says Magrew. "You can't see nothin' anyways."

C'lumbus win the exhibition game, 3 to 2, whilst Magrew set in the dugout, mutterin' and cursin' like a fourteen-year-old Scotty. He bad-mouthed everybody on the ball club and he bad-mouthed everybody offa the ball club, includin' the Wright brothers, who, he claimed, had yet to build a airship big enough for any of our boys to hit it with a ball bat.

"I wisht I was dead," he says to me. "I wisht I was in heaven with the angels."

I told him to pull hisself together, 'cause he was drivin' the boys crazy, the way he was goin' on, sulkin' and bad-mouthin' and whinin'. I was older'n he was and smarter'n he was, and he knowed it. I was ten times smarter'n he was about this Pearl du Monville, first time I ever laid eyes on the little guy, which was one of the saddest days of my life.

Now, most people name of Pearl is girls, but this Pearl du Monville was a man, if you could call a fella a man who was only thirty-four, thirty-five inches high. Pearl du Monville was a midget. He was part French and part Hungarian, and maybe even part Bulgarian or somethin'. I can see him now, a sneer on his little pushed-in pan, swingin' a bamboo cane and smokin' a big cigar. He had a gray suit with a big black check into it, and he had a gray felt hat with one of them rainbow-colored hatbands onto it, like the young fellas wore in them days. He talked like he was talkin' into a tin can, but he didn't have no foreign accent. He might 'a' been fifteen or he might 'a' been a hundred, you couldn't tell. Pearl du Monville.

After the game with C'lumbus, Magrew headed straight for the Chittaden bar—the train for St. Louis wasn't goin' for three, four hours—and there he set, drinkin' rye and talkin' to this bartender.

"How I pity me, brother," Magrew was tellin' this bartender. "How I pity me." That was alwuz his favorite tune. So he was settin' there, tellin' this bartender how heartbreakin' it was to be manager of a bunch a blindfolded circus clowns, when up pops this Pearl du Monville outa no-wheres.

It give Magrew the leapin' jumps. He thought at first maybe the D.T.'s had come back on him; he claimed he'd had 'em once, and little guys had popped up all around him, wearin' red, white, and blue hats.

"Go on, now!" Magrew yells. "Get away from me!"

But the midget clumb up on a chair acrost the table from Magrew and says, "I seen that game today, Junior, and you ain't got no ball club. What you got there, Junior," he says, "is a side show."

"Whatta ya mean, 'Junior'?" says Magrew, touchin' the little guy to satisfy hisself he was real.

"Don't pay him no attention, mister," says the bartender. "Pearl calls everybody 'Junior,' 'cause it alwuz turns out he's a year older'n anybody else."

"Yeh?" says Magrew. "How old is he?"

"How old are you, Junior?" says the midget.

"Who, me? I'm fifty-three," says Magrew.

"Well, I'm fifty-four," says the midget.

Magrew grins and asts him what he'll have, and that was the beginnin' of their beautiful friendship, if you don't care what you say.

Pearl du Monville stood up on his chair and waved his cane around and pretended like he was ballyhooin' for a circus. "Right this way, folks!" he yells. "Come on in and see the greatest collection of freaks in the world! See the armless pitchers, see the eyeless batters, see the infielders with five thumbs!" and on and on like that, feedin' Magrew gall and handin' him a laugh at the same time, you might say.

You could hear him and Pearl du Monville hootin' and hollerin' and singin' way up to the fourth floor of the Chittaden, where the boys was packin' up. When it come time to go to the station, you can imagine how disgusted we was when we crowded into the doorway of that bar and seen them two singin' and goin' on.

"Well, well, well," says Magrew, lookin' up and spottin' us. "Look who's here. . . . Clowns, this is Pearl du Monville, a monseer of the old, old school. . . . Don't shake hands with 'em, Pearl, 'cause their fingers is made of chalk and would bust right off in your paws," he says, and he starts guffawin' and Pearl starts titterin' and we stand there givin' 'em the iron eye, it bein' the lowest ebb a ball-club manager'd got hisself down to since the national pastime was started.

Then the midget begun givin' us the ballyhoo. "Come on in!" he says, wavin' his cane. "See the legless base runners, see the outfielders with the butter fingers, see the southpaw with the arm of a little chee-ild!"

Then him and Magrew begun to hoop and holler and nudge each other till you'd of thought this little guy was the funniest guy than even Charlie Chaplin. The fellas filed outa the bar without a word and went on up to the Union Depot, leavin' me to handle Magrew and his new-found crony.

Well, I got 'em outa there finely. I had to take the little guy along, 'cause Magrew had a holt onto him like a vise and I couldn't pry him loose.

"He's comin' along as masket," says Magrew, holdin' the midget in the crouch of his arm like a football. And come along he did, hollerin' and protestin' and beatin' at Magrew with his little fists.

"Cut it out, will ya, Junior?" the little guy kept whinin'. "Come on, leave a man loose, will ya, Junior?"

But Junior kept a holt onto him and begun yellin', "See the guys with the glass arm, see the guys with the cast-iron brains, see the fielders with the feet on their wrists!"

So it goes, right through the whole Union Depot, with people starin' and catcallin', and he don't put the midget down till he gets him through the gates.

"How'm I goin' to go along without no toothbrush?" the midget asts. "What'm I goin' to do without no other suit?" he says.

"Doc here," says Magrew, meanin' me—"doc here will look after you like you was his own son, won't you, doc?"

I give him the iron eye, and he finely got on the train and prob'ly went to sleep with his clothes on.

This left me alone with the midget. "Lookit," I says to him. "Why don't you go on home now? Come mornin', Magrew'll forget all about you. He'll prob'ly think you was somethin' he seen in a nightmare maybe. And he ain't goin' to laugh so easy in the mornin', neither," I says. "So why don't you go on home?"

"Nix," he says to me. "Skiddoo," he says, "twenty-three for you," and he tosses his cane up into the vestibule of the coach and clam'ers on up after it like a cat. So that's the way Pearl du Monville come to go to St. Louis with the ball club.

I seen 'em first at breakfast the next day, settin' opposite each other; the midget playin' "Turkey in the Straw" on a harmonium and Magrew starin' at his eggs and bacon like they was a uncooked bird with its feathers still on.

"Remember where you found this?" I says, jerkin' my thumb at the midget. "Or maybe you think they come with breakfast on these trains," I says, bein' a good hand at turnin' a sharp remark in them days.

The midget puts down the harmonium and turns on me. "Sneeze," he says; "your brains is dusty." Then he snaps a couple drops of water at me from a tumbler. "Drown," he says, tryin' to make his voice deep.

Now, both them cracks is Civil War cracks, but you'd of thought they was brand new and the funniest than any crack Magrew'd ever heard in his whole life. He started hoopin' and hollerin', and the midget started hoopin' and hollerin', so I walked on away and set down with Bugs Courtney and Hank Metters, payin' no attention to this weak-minded Damon and Phidias acrost the aisle.

Well, sir, the first game with St. Louis was rained out, and there we was facin' a double-header next day. Like maybe I told you, we lose the last three double-headers we play, makin' maybe twenty-five errors in the six games, which is all right for the intimates of a school for the blind, but is disgraceful for the world's champions. It was too wet to go to the zoo, and Magrew wouldn't let us go to the movies, 'cause they flickered so bad in them days. So we just set around, stewin' and frettin'.

One of the newspaper boys come over to take a pitture of Billy Klinger and Whitey Cott shakin' hands—this reporter'd heard about the fight— and whilst they was standin' there, toe to toe, shakin' hands, Billy give a back lunge and a jerk, and throwed Whitey over his shoulder into a corner of the room, like a sack a salt. Whitey come back at him with a chair, and Bethlehem broke loose in that there room. The camera was tromped to pieces like a berry basket. When we finely got 'em pulled apart, I heard a laugh, and there was Magrew and the midget standin' in the door and givin' us the iron eye.

"Wrasslers," says Magrew, cold-like, "that's what I got for a ball club, Mr. Du Monville, wrasslers—and not very good wrasslers at that, you ast me."

"A man can't be good at everythin'," says Pearl, "but he oughta be good at somethin'."

This sets Magrew guffawin' again, and away they go, the midget taggin' along by his side like a hound dog and handin' him a fast line of so-called comic cracks.

When we went out to face that battlin' St. Louis club in a double-header the next afternoon, the boys was jumpy as tin toys with keys in their back. We lose the first game, 7 to 2, and are trailin', 4 to 0, when the second game ain't but ten minutes old. Magrew set there like a stone statue, speakin' to nobody. Then, in their half a the fourth, somebody singled to center and knocked in two more runs for St. Louis.

That made Magrew squawk. "I wisht one thing," he says. "I wisht I was manager of a old ladies' sewin' circus 'stead of a ball club."

"You are, Junior, you are," says a familyer and disagreeable voice.

It was that Pearl du Monville again, poppin' up outa nowheres, swingin' his bamboo cane and smokin' a cigar that's three sizes too big for his face. By this time we'd finely got the other side out, and Hank Metters slithered a bat acrost the ground, and the midget had to jump to keep both his ankles from bein' broke.

I thought Magrew'd bust a blood vessel. "You hurt Pearl and I'll break your neck!" he yelled.

Hank muttered somethin' and went on up to the plate and struck out.

We managed to get a couple runs acrost in our half a the sixth, but they come back with three more in their half a the seventh, and this was too much for Magrew.

"Come on, Pearl," he says. "We're gettin' outa here."

"Where you think you're goin'?" I ast him.

"To the lawyer's again," he says cryptly.

"I didn't know you'd been to the lawyer's once, yet," I says.

"Which that goes to show how much you don't know," he says.

With that, they was gone, and I didn't see 'em the rest of the day, nor know what they was up to, which was a God's blessin'. We lose the night-cap, 9 to 3, and that puts us into second place plenty, and as low in our mind as a ball club can get.

The next day was a horrible day, like anybody that lived through it can tell you. Practice was just over and the St. Louis club was takin' the field, when I hears this strange sound from the stands. It sounds like the nervous whickerin' a horse gives when he smells somethin' funny on the wind. It was the fans ketchin' sight of Pearl du Monville, like you have prob'ly guessed. The midget had popped up onto the field all dressed up in a minacher club uniform, sox, cap, little letters sewed onto his chest, and all. He was swingin' a kid's bat and the only thing kept him from lookin' like a real ballplayer seen through the wrong end of a microscope was this cigar he was smokin'.

Bugs Courtney reached over and jerked it outa his mouth and throwed it away. "You're wearin' that suit on the playin' field," he says to him, severe as a judge. "You go insultin' it and I'll take you out to the zoo and feed you to the bears."

Pearl just blowed some smoke at him which he still has in his mouth.

Whilst Whitey was foulin' off four or five prior to strikin' out, I went on over to Magrew. "If I was as comic as you," I says, "I'd laugh myself to death," I says. "Is that any way to treat the uniform, makin' a mockery out of it?"

"It might surprise you to know I ain't makin' no mockery outa the uniform," says Magrew. "Pearl du Monville here has been made a bone-of-fida member of this so-called ball club. I fixed it up with the front office by long-distance phone."

"Yeh?" I says. "I can just hear Mr. Dillworth or Bart Jenkins agreein' to hire a midget for the ball club. I can just hear 'em." Mr. Dillworth was the owner of the club and Bart Jenkins was the secretary, and they never stood for no monkey business. "May I be so bold as to inquire," I says, "just what you told 'em?"

"I told 'em," he says, "I wanted to sign up a guy they ain't no pitcher in the league can strike him out."

"Uh-huh," I says, "and did you tell 'em what size of a man he is?"

"Never mind about that," he says. "I got papers on me, made out legal and proper, constitutin' one Pearl du Monville a bone-of-fida member of this former ball club. Maybe that'll shame them big babies into gettin' in there and swingin', knowin' I can replace any one of 'em with a midget, if I have a mind to. A St. Louis lawyer I seen twice tells me it's all legal and proper."

"A St. Louis lawyer would," I says, "seein' nothin' could make him happier than havin' you makin' a mockery outa this one-time baseball outfit," I says.

Well, sir, it'll all be there in the papers of thirty, thirty-one year ago, and you could look it up. The game went along without no scorin' for seven innings, and since they ain't nothin' much to watch but guys poppin' up or strikin' out, the fans pay most of their attention to the goin's-on of Pearl du Monville. He's out there in front a the dugout, turnin' handsprings, balancin' his bat on his chin, walkin' a imaginary line, and so on. The fans clapped and laughed at him, and he ate it up.

So it went up to the last a the eighth, nothin' to nothin', not more'n seven, eight hits all told, and no errors on neither side. Our pitcher gets the first two men out easy in the eighth. Then up come a fella name of Porter or Billings, or some such name, and he lammed one up against the tobacco sign for three bases. The next guy up slapped the first ball out into left for a base hit, and in come the fella from third for the only run of the ball game so far. The crowd yelled, the look a death come onto Magrew's face again, and even the midget quit his tomfoolin'. Their next man fouled out back a third, and we come up for our last bats like a bunch a schoolgirls steppin' into a pool of cold water. I was lower in my mind than I'd been since the day in Nineteen-four when Chesbro throwed the wild pitch in the ninth inning with a man on third and lost the pennant for the Highlanders. I knowed something just as bad was goin' to happen, which shows I'm a clairvoyun. or was then.

When Gordy Mills hit out to second, I just closed my eyes. I opened 'em up again to see Dutch Muller standin' on second, dustin' off his pants, him havin' got his first hit in maybe twenty times to the plate. Next up was Harry Loesing, battin' for our pitcher, and he got a base on balls, walkin' on a fourth one you could 'a' combed your hair with.

Then up come Whitey Cott, our lead-off man. He crotches down in what was prob'ly the most fearsome stanch in organized ball, but all he can do is pop out to short. That brung up Billy Klinger, with two down and a man on first and second. Billy took a cut at one you could 'a' knocked a plug hat offa this here Carnera with it, but then he gets sense enough to wait 'em out, and finely he walks, too, fillin' the bases.

Yes, sir, there you are; the tyin' run on third and the winnin' run on second, first a the ninth, two men down, and Hank Metters comin' to the bat. Hank was built like a Pope-Hartford and he couldn't run no faster'n President Taft, but he had five home runs to his credit for the season, and that wasn't bad in them days. Hank was still hittin' better'n anybody else on the ball club, and it was mighty heartenin', seein' him stridin' up towards the plate. But he never got there.

"Wait a minute!" yells Magrew, jumpin' to his feet. "I'm sendin' in a pinch hitter!" he yells.

You could 'a' heard a bomb drop. When a ball-club manager says he's sendin' in a pinch hitter for the best batter on the club, you know and I know and everybody knows he's lost his holt.

"They're goin' to be sendin' the funny wagon for you, if you don't watch out," I says, grabbin' a holt of his arm.

But he pulled away and run out towards the plate, yellin', "Du Monville battin' for Metters!"

All the fellas begun squawlin' at once, except Hank, and he just stood there starin' at Magrew like he'd gone crazy and was claimin' to be Ty Cobb's grandma or somethin'. Their pitcher stood out there with his hands on his hips and a disagreeable look on his face, and the plate umpire told Magrew to go on and get a batter up. Magrew told him again Du Monville was battin' for Metters, and the St. Louis manager finely got the idea. It brung him outa his dugout, howlin' and bawlin' like he'd lost a female dog and her seven pups.

Magrew pushed the midget towards the plate and he says to him, he says, "Just stand up there and hold that bat on your shoulder. They ain't a man in the world can throw three strikes in there 'fore he throws four balls!" he says.

"I get it, Junior!" says the midget. "He'll walk me and force in the tyin' run!" And he starts on up to the plate as cocky as if he was Willie Keeler.

I don't need to tell you Bethlehem broke loose on that there ball field. The fans got onto their hind legs, yellin' and whistlin', and everybody on the field begun wavin' their arms and hollerin' and shovin'. The plate umpire stalked over to Magrew like a traffic cop, waggin' his jaw and pointin' his finger, and the St. Louis manager kept yellin' like his house was on fire. When Pearl got up to the plate and stood there, the pitcher slammed his glove down onto the ground and started stompin' on it, and they ain't nobody can blame him. He's just walked two normal-sized human bein's, and now here's a guy up to the plate they ain't more'n twenty inches between his knees and his shoulders.

The plate umpire called in the field umpire, and they talked a while, like a couple doctors seein' the bucolic plague or somethin' for the first time. Then the plate umpire come over to Magrew with his arms folded acrost his chest, and he told him to go on and get a batter up, or he'd forfeit the game to St. Louis. He pulled out his watch, but somebody batted it outa his hand in the scufflin', and I thought there'd be a free-for-all, with everybody yellin' and shovin' except Pearl du Monville, who stood up at the plate with his little bat on his shoulder, not movin' a muscle.

Then Magrew played his ace. I seen him pull some papers outa his pocket and show 'em to the plate umpire. The umpire begun lookin' at 'em like they was bills for somethin' he not only never bought it, he never even heard of it. The other umpire studied 'em like they was a death warren, and all this time the St. Louis manager and the fans and the players is yellin' and hollerin'.

Well, sir, they fought about him bein' a midget, and they fought about him usin' a kid's bat, and they fought about where'd he been all season. They was eight or nine rule books brung out and everybody was thumbin' through 'em, tryin' to find out what it says about midgets, but it don't say nothin' about midgets, 'cause this was somethin' never'd come up in the history of the game before, and nobody'd ever dreamed about it, even when they has nightmares. Maybe you can't send no midgets in to bat nowadays, 'cause the old game's changed a lot, mostly for the worst, but you could then, it turned out.

The plate umpire finely decided the contrack papers was all legal and proper, like Magrew said, so he waved the St. Louis players back to their places and he pointed his finger at their manager and told him to quit hollerin' and get on back in the dugout. The manager says the game is percedin' under protest, and the umpire bawls, "Play ball!" over 'n' above the yellin' and booin', him havin' a voice like a hog-caller.

The St. Louis pitcher picked up his glove and beat at it with his fist six or eight times, and then got set on the mound and studied the situation.

The fans realized he was really goin' to pitch to the midget, and they went crazy, hoopin' and hollerin' louder'n ever, and throwin' pop bottles and hats and cushions down onto the field. It took five, ten minutes to get the fans quieted down again, whilst our fellas that was on base set down on the bags and waited. And Pearl du Monville kept standin' up there with the bat on his shoulder, like he'd been told to.

So the pitcher starts studyin' the setup again, and you got to admit it was the strangest setup in a ball game since the players cut off their beards and begun wearin' gloves. I wisht I could call the pitcher's name—it wasn't old Barney Pelty nor Nig Jack Powell nor Harry Howell. He was a big right-hander, but I can't call his name. You could look it up. Even in a crotchin' position, the ketcher towers over the midget like the Washington Monument.

The plate umpire tries standin' on his tiptoes, then he tries crotchin' down, and he finely gets hisself into a stanch nobody'd ever seen on a ball field before, kinda squattin' down on his hanches.

Well, the pitcher is sore as a old buggy horse in fly time. He slams in the first pitch, hard and wild, and maybe two foot higher 'n the midget's head.

"Ball one!" hollers the umpire over 'n' above the racket, 'cause everybody is yellin' worsten ever.

The ketcher goes on out towards the mound and talks to the pitcher and hands him the ball. This time the big right-hander tries a undershoot, and it comes in a little closer, maybe no higher'n a foot, foot and a half above Pearl's head. It would 'a' been a strike with a human bein' in there, but the umpire's got to call it, and he does.

"Ball two!" he bellers.

The ketcher walks on out to the mound again, and the whole infield comes over and gives advice to the pitcher about what they'd do in a case like this, with two balls and no strikes on a batter that oughta be in a bottle of alcohol 'stead of up there at the plate in a big-league game between the teams that is fightin' for first place.

For the third pitch, the pitcher stands there flat-footed and tosses up the ball like he's playin' ketch with a little girl.

Pearl stands there motionless as a hitchin' post, and the ball comes in big and slow and high—high for Pearl, that is, it bein' about on a level with his eyes, or a little higher'n a grown man's knees.

They ain't nothin' else for the umpire to do, so he calls, "Ball three!"

Everybody is onto their feet, hoopin' and hollerin', as the pitcher sets to throw ball four. The St. Louis manager is makin' signs and faces like he was a contorturer, and the infield is givin' the pitcher some more advice about what to do this time. Our boys who was on base stick right onto the bag, runnin' no risk of bein' nipped for the last out.

Well, the pitcher decides to give him a toss again, seein' he come closer with that than with a fast ball. They ain't nobody ever seen a slower ball throwed. It come in big as a balloon and slower'n any ball ever throwed before in the major leagues. It come right in over the plate in front of Pearl's chest, lookin' prob'ly big as a full moon to Pearl. They ain't never been a minute like the minute that followed since the United States was founded by the Pilgrim grandfathers.

Pearl du Monville took a cut at that ball, and he hit it! Magrew give a groan like a poleaxed steer as the ball rolls out in front a the plate into fair territory.

"Fair ball!" yells the umpire, and the midget starts runnin' for first, still carryin' that little bat, and makin' maybe ninety foot an hour. Bethlehem breaks loose on that ball field and in them stands. They ain't never been nothin' like it since creation was begun.

The ball's rollin' slow, on down towards third, goin' maybe eight, ten foot. The infield comes in fast and our boys break from their bases like hares in a brush fire. Everybody is standin' up, yellin' and hollerin', and Magrew is tearin' his hair outa his head, and the midget is scamperin' for first with all the speed of one of them little dashhounds carryin' a satchel in his mouth.

The ketcher gets to the ball first, but he boots it on out past the pitcher's box, the pitcher fallin' on his face tryin' to stop it, the shortstop sprawlin' after it full length and zaggin' it on over towards the second baseman, whilst Muller is scorin' with the tyin' run and Loesing is roundin' third with the winnin' run. Ty Cobb could 'a' made a three-bagger outa that bunt, with everybody fallin' over theirself tryin' to pick the ball up. But Pearl is still maybe fifteen, twenty feet from the bag, toddlin' like a baby and yeepin' like a trapped rabbit, when the second baseman finely gets a holt of that ball and slams it over to first. The first baseman ketches it and stomps on the bag, the base umpire waves Pearl out, and there goes your old ball game, the craziest ball game ever played in the history of the organized world.

Their players start runnin' in, and then I see Magrew. He starts after Pearl, runnin' faster'n any man ever run before. Pearl sees him comin' and runs behind the base umpire's legs and gets a holt onto 'em. Magrew comes up, pantin' and roarin', and him and the midget plays ring-around-a-rosy with the umpire, who keeps shovin' at Magrew with one hand and tryin' to slap the midget loose from his legs with the other.

Finely Magrew ketches the midget, who is still yeepin' like a stuck sheep. He gets holt of that little guy by both his ankles and starts whirlin' him round and round his head like Magrew was a hammer thrower and Pearl was the hammer. Nobody can stop him without gettin' their head knocked off, so everybody just stands there and yells. Then Magrew lets the midget fly. He flies on out towards second, high and fast, like a human home run, headed for the soap sign in center field.

Their shortstop tries to get to him, but he can't make it, and I knowed the little fella was goin' to bust to pieces like a dollar watch on a asphalt street when he hit the ground. But it so happens their center fielder is just crossin' second, and he starts runnin' back, tryin' to get under the midget, who had took to spiralin' like a football 'stead of turnin' head over foot, which give him more speed and more distance.

I know you never seen a midget ketched, and you prob'ly never even seen one throwed. To ketch a midget that's been throwed by a heavy-muscled man and is flyin' through the air, you got to run under him and with him and pull your hands and arms back and down when you ketch him, to break the compact of his body, or you'll bust him in two like a matchstick. I seen Bill Lange and Willie Keeler and Tris Speaker make some wonderful ketches in my day, but I never seen nothin' like that center fielder. He goes back and back and still further back and he pulls that midget down outa the air like he was liftin' a sleepin' baby from a cradle. They wasn't a bruise onto him, only his face was the color of cat's meat and he ain't got no air in his chest. In his excitement, the base umpire, who was runnin' back with the center fielder when he ketched Pearl, yells, "Out!" and that give hysteries to the Bethlehem which was ragin' like Niagry on that ball field.

Everybody was hoopin' and hollerin' and yellin' and runnin', with the fans swarmin' onto the field, and the cops tryin' to keep order, and some guys laughin' and some of the women fans cryin', and six or eight of us holdin' onto Magrew to keep him from gettin' at that midget and finishin' him off. Some of the fans picks up the St. Louis pitcher and the center fielder, and starts carryin' 'em around on their shoulders, and they was the craziest goin's-on knowed to the history of organized ball on this side of the 'Lantic Ocean.

I seen Pearl du Monville strugglin' in the arms of a lady fan with a ample bosom, who was laughin' and cryin' at the same time, and him beatin' at her with his little fists and bawlin' and yellin'. He clawed his way loose finely and disappeared in the forest of legs which made that ball field look like it was Coney Island on a hot summer's day.

That was the last I ever seen of Pearl du Monville. I never seen hide nor hair of him from that day to this, and neither did nobody else. He just vanished into the thin of the air, as the fella says. He was ketched for the final out of the ball game and that was the end of him, just like it was the end of the ball game, you might say, and also the end of our losin' streak, like I'm goin' to tell you.

That night we piled onto a train for Chicago, but we wasn't snarlin' and snappin' any more. No, sir, the ice was finely broke and a new spirit come into that ball club. The old zip come back with the disappearance of Pearl du Monville out back a second base. We got to laughin' and talkin' and kiddin' together, and 'fore long Magrew was laughin' with us. He got a human look onto his pan again, and he quit whinin' and complainin' and wishtin' he was in heaven with the angels.

Well, sir, we wiped up that Chicago series, winnin' all four games, and makin' seventeen hits in one of 'em. Funny thing was, St. Louis was so shook up by that last game with us, they never did hit their stride again. Their center fielder took to misjudgin' everything that come his way, and the rest a the fellas followed suit, the way a club'll do when one guy blows up.

'Fore we left Chicago, I and some of the fellas went out and bought a pair of them little baby shoes, which we had 'em golded over and give 'em to Magrew for a souvenir, and he took it all in good spirit. Whitey Cott and Billy Klinger made up and was fast friends again, and we hit our home lot like a ton of dynamite, and they was nothin' could stop us from then on.

I don't recollect things as clear as I did thirty, forty year ago. I can't read no fine print no more, and the only person I got to check with on the golden days of the national pastime, as the fella says, is my friend, old Milt Kline, over in Springfield, and his mind ain't as strong as it once was.

He gets Rube Waddell mixed up with Rube Marquard, for one thing, and anybody does that oughta be put away where he won't bother nobody. So I can't tell you the exact margin we win the pennant by. Maybe it was two and a half games, or maybe it was three and a half. But it'll all be there in the newspapers and record books of thirty, thirty-one year ago and, like I was sayin', you could look it up.

## Suggestions for Study

1. This story is of course implausible. It belongs to the same *genre* as Mark Twain's "Baker's Blue-Jay Yarn." As you read it, do you have any intense desire to question the plausibility of the incidents? On what elements does the author depend to give it the illusion of plausibility?

2. Who is the protagonist and who the antagonist? Or is the conflict between forces rather than persons? If you say the latter, name them.

3. What is the author's purpose in giving the story the title he does?

4. Give a character sketch of the narrator. Would the story gain or lose in interest if it were narrated by a sophisticated sports writer or by the author, assuming an omniscient point of view and writing in good English?

5. Are the characters well delineated, or are they simply pegs on which to hang the action?

6. Are there any elements of the story that could be omitted without in any way detracting from it?

7. What is the purpose of the last two paragraphs? Would the story be better if they were omitted?

## The Virtuoso [49]

### MARGARET MACPHERSON

So the teacher asks me, "What is a virtuoso?"

When I says, "It's an auctioneer that don't sell nothing," all the kids laugh like mad. Okeydoke. Okeydoke. Let 'em laugh. But I'm not so dumb as they think. That auctioneer, Mr. Steinmetz, that came to sell Gran up, he was a virtuoso. I heard old Mr. McCutcheon, the millionaire, say so.

Came in a big shiny car, this auctioneer did. Pearl pin in his tie. And his clothes—*boy!* Not flashy, mind, but quiet and rich. I have heard tell that he was a Jew. I dunno. He had gentle brown eyes and his face was —well, it was thin and—and fine. Know what I mean? *Fine.*

He came in very brisk and said, "Now, Mrs. Stepnowski, let us appraise the stuff."

So Gran dried her eyes and started showing him her bits of things. Well, she ain't got much.

"Any treasures?" he says, looking round at our shabby furniture which so many kids has kicked. So she shows him the pictures of Uncle Jan that's a marine somewheres in the Pacific, and Uncle Steve that's fighting in Germany, and my dad that was killed in North Africa. I'm a bit like my dad, but Gran says boys are not as good as they used to be. (Aw, shucks, I guess they never were!) She's brought me up ever since my ma died, when I was a baby.

Then she showed him that group picture that always makes me so mad. Y'see, Gramp ain't *in* it! It's a group of the Truck Farmers' Delegation to Washington in 1912, taken on the steps of the White House. But Gramp got so drunk he was unmanageable, and he never went with the Delegation, although he's supposed to be one of them.

"He's not in it," says Gran, showing it to the auctioneer, proud, "but

49. From *Tomorrow,* V (March, 1946), No. 7. Reprinted by permission of the author and *Tomorrow,* a magazine published by the Creative Age Press.

he shoulda been. He ain't there, but it's the only picture I got of him."

The auctioneer turned away and blew his nose hard. Then he says, patient, "By treasures, I mean antiques. Any *antiques,* Mrs. Stepnowski? You see, if you had a few good things, we could sell them and save the farm. I want to save the farm for those soldier sons of yours coming back."

But we ain't got no antiques. Polacks don't have 'em.

Y'see, down our way, society is divided into three classes—the Old Families, the Summer People, and the Polacks. Well, the old families *has* antiques. The summer people goes around to all the sales, buying 'em. But us Polacks is just working truck farmers, and we ain't got nothing much.

Well, soon it's time for the sale. A crowd of folks has come. The auctioneer gets up into his little pulpit that his assistant has set up in our kitchen, and looks around at the people. He nods to old Mr. McCutcheon, the millionaire; and to Mrs. Chumley, a rich old dame that Gran was kitchen-maid to about three thousand years ago; and a few others he seems to know. All our neighbors was there, too, and farmers from miles around.

I could hear some of the summer people whispering.

"It's Steinmetz himself," they says, excited. "That means there must be some finds. He only comes when there's something special."

Gran is sitting sideways, up at the front. Before the folks came, he arranged her, like as if she was having her photo taken.

"I want to get a 'Whistler's Mother' effect," he says to me, putting his head on one side and looking at her. "You know 'Whistler's Mother,' boy?"

So I whistle "The Whistler's Mother-in-Law" real good, but it seems it's not the same thing. Well, there she sits, sideways, with her white hair combed back, and her hands in her lap. (Hard old hands, she's got, all callouses and cuts; but she can be that gentle you'd think it was a butterfly touching you.)

So there they are: Gran in front, him in his pulpit, and the folks all spread around. He raps with a little hammer.

"Now, ladies and gentlemen," he says, "who's going to bid for this old woman's little treasures?"

Seems to me that was a bad way to start. Making 'em feel like they hadn't ought to buy her stuff.

He looks around and he points to an old, old blackened box by the hearth.

"Hold up that old case," he says to his assistant. "Who'll give a dollar for the old box? Come, it's worth that, if only for kindling. Well, someone start me at fifty cents."

The crowd looked mad. They hadn't come all that way to buy kindling. He leans forward and looks around at them, solemn. You'da thought it was the priest talking, not a salesman.

"This," he says, "is no ordinary box. See that photo of the marine on the wall? That's her son, Jan, now in the Solomons. This box was his cradle, twenty-five years ago. One dollar? Thank you, sir."

I could see Gran's hands clutching each other, nervous-like.

"Yes, she's had three boys in the service," he goes on quiet and serious, "and each one of them had this old box for his first bed. Two dollars? Three? Four, Mrs. Chumley? Thank you, ma'am." And he makes a deep bow to this rich old dame.

"Thank *you,* for inviting me to come." And she bows back at him like a queen.

"Holy *Crow!*" says a red-haired farmer next to me.

"Yes," says Mr. Steinmetz, and his voice was so sad it made you feel all weepy inside, like—like the sound of a fiddle makes you, playing in the night. "Yes, this old box has seen a lot of service. Her second son, the one that was killed in North Africa, used it as a sled when he was a kid. He used to pull the groceries home from the store in it. He was a fine lad. Too bad she had to lose him." A lady near me got out her handkerchief and wiped her eyes.

"Five Dollars," she says, blowing her nose.

"I know," says Mr. Steinmetz, apologetic, "that most of you are looking for antiques. Sorry, Mr. McCutcheon, sir, to keep you waiting, but we'll soon dispose of this."

The old millionaire looked real ashamed of himself for waiting for antiques, and he spluttered out—"Ten!"

"Twelve," says Mrs. Chumley, prompt.

"Holy *Crow!*" says the red-headed Polack next to me.

Mr. Steinmetz reached down and took the box from his assistant and turned it over in his hands, holding it gentle, like it was something sacred.

"When her fourth child was born," he said, "her husband put rockers on it. That was a little girl. They had to rock her nearly all the time, she cried so much. She was a sickly baby, and they couldn't afford doctors. See the marks on the linoleum over there?" The folks stared at the worn patch like they was hypnotized. "That's where they used to rock her. Maybe you've seen her little grave in Southold Churchyard" . . . He paused. . . . "Any advance on twelve?"

A rich farmer from Cutchogue shouted "Twenty dollars!"

Mr. McCutcheon said "Thirty."

Mrs. Chumley said "Forty."

A thin voice at the back said "Forty-five."

Mr. Steinmetz said, "I'm not taking any half-bids now. Make it fifty? Thank you, sir."

I looked at Gran. She had closed her eyes.

The auctioneer turned the box around, thoughtful.

"See," he said, "it's all shiny on this side. I guess she must have sat at this side whilst she rocked them to sleep. Many's the Polish lullaby this old box has heard. Still," he seemed to pull himself out of a dream, "we mustn't waste time on it. I know you're waiting for antiques."

He glances at Mr. McCutcheon again, and Mr. McCutcheon swallows hard and says "One hundred!"

"Two hundred," says Mrs. Chumley prompt.

"Two-fifty," says the thin voice from the back.

"No half-bids," says Mr. Steinmetz. "Make it three hundred?"

"Okay."

"Holy *Crow!*" says Redhead, next to me.

The summer people were crowding forward now, and the local Polacks had moved back and were just watching with their eyes and mouths wide open. Everybody was listening, quiet, like as if they was in church.

"Seems tragic she has to be sold up," Mr. Steinmetz went on, his voice soft and yonderly, "especially as there's practically nothing to sell. But the war's beaten her as completely as if she were an enemy. Her boys could have applied for deferment, but they didn't. They couldn't foresee that their father'd be killed the way he was—coming out of the bar and stepping in front of a speeding truck without even seeing it. Then she got rheumatic fever, and whilst she was in hospital the farm got ahead of her. Well, let's get done with this item. Any advance?"

"Five hundred," says Mrs. Chumley in a choky voice. Lots of the folks had their handkerchiefs out and was wiping their eyes.

"One thousand," said Mr. McCutcheon very loud, as much as to say nobody could be more sorry than *him*.

I tell you, I never seen nothing like it. I been to sales before. Mostly, the auctioneer is a noisy guy with a line of wisecracks. "Patter," they call it. Mr. Steinmetz was quiet. He was like—he was like one of them chari- oteers in the olden days that could handle a team of maybe twenty horses all at one time. He'd speak gentle, and everybody was held, although there was no reins. And then he'd give 'em a little flick, and the bidding was off —gallop-a-gallop-a-gallop. I don't remember all his words, but he spoke about America and human brotherhood and good neighbors. He said what a good neighbor Gran had always been. (Well, she has. She'd give you the boots off her feet.) He made them rich folks want to give all they could afford and *more* than they could afford. When they started bidding in thousands it seemed like a dream. You ever counted a thousand? Boy, that's a lot of money! They went up to four thousand, and then he put the box down as gentle as if there was a baby still in it.

"Well, ladies and gentlemen," he says, "you've been very patient and very generous, and I won't waste any more time. The box that has cradled three American soldiers is going at four thousand. Going once! Going twice—"

"Five!" roars Mr. McCutcheon, glaring at Mrs. Chumley.

"Six," says she, very sweet.

"Ten!" shrieks Mr. McCutcheon.

Just then I noticed that Gran was swaying. She was pressing her hands very tight together, and she'd turned a nasty gray color. I just got to her by the time she fell to the floor.

Mr. Steinmetz and me picked her up and carried her into the back bedroom.

"She couldn't have timed it better if she was Helen Hayes herself," he says, just like he was *pleased* to see an old woman faint! "Put some cold water on her head. I'm going back before the effect wears off." And he ran out of the room.

When the crowd had gone he come back and sat on the bed beside her. She was very white, but she'd come to, and her eyes was open.

"There, that's better," he says in that gentle voice of his. "You're going to be all right. No more to worry about. See, here's a little gift for you." And he went and pulled the old box into the room.

"You didn't sell it?" she says, quavery.

"No." He blew his nose. "The folks figured you'd probably like to keep it, so they handed it back."

She got up, shaky-like, and went over to it.

"Why, mister," she says, "it's full of paper!"

"Yes," he says, "everyone felt they'd like to make you a present of their highest bid, so we made a collection of their checks and bills. There's nearly twenty thousand dollars there, ma'am, so if you feel all right we'd better go and bank it."

"But," Gran put up her hand, all trembly, and pushed back a wisp of white hair out of her eyes, "that box never was no cradle, mister. My kids never had no cradle. I used to carry them in a shawl on my back. That's an old whisky case. And the side of it got shiny from my old man toting it home from the saloon every month for over forty years."

"I know," he said. "But we'll just keep that to ourselves."

"You know me, mister?" she said then. "You knew me before this sale?"

"Do you remember," he said, dreamy-like, "about thirty-five years ago, a little boy rushing into your yard with a lot of other boys after him yelling *Kike! Kike!* And you drove them off, and wiped his face and held him while he cried his eyes out against your skirts? And gave him a cookie and let him out the back way?"

Gran put her hand up to her head.

"I musta forgot that," she said.

"I," said Mr. Steinmetz, "sort of remembered it."

When we went out to his car to take the money to the bank, old Mr. McCutcheon came up and held out his hand to him.

"Steinmetz," he says, "you're a virtuoso."

See?

## Suggestions for Study

1. Is this story any more plausible than "Laura"? On what does the author depend to make it appear plausible? (Name all the elements.)

2. Does it gain in effect by being told by a boy who does not understand so fully as the reader is supposed to do the dramatic elements of the story?

3. Does the story gain from the first two and last three paragraphs?

4. Does the author succeed in keeping the story from sentimentality? If you say no, show where it breaks down; if you say yes, show how this is accomplished.

5. What sort of person was Gramp? Is there any effort on the part of the auctioneer to hide his character?

6. Is there any evidence that those who bid on the "cradle" realized that they were imposed on?

7. What do you think was the principal aim of the author in the story?

8. Which is more important, plot or character?

## The Color of Mama Josefina's Life [50]

### MARY MAIN

Everyone in the pueblo knew Mama Josefina, for she was not a woman one could easily ignore. She was so large and so very noisy. She was more grossly fat than any woman so active had a right to be; and she was noisier, Don Gumesindo said, than the bullfrogs down by the *laguna*. But, of course, Don Gumesindo owned the other *almacén* and was prejudiced.

50. From *Tomorrow*, V (May, 1946), No. 9. Reprinted by permission of the author and *Tomorrow*, a magazine published by the Creative Age Press.

Mama Josefina was a source of amazement, envy, and righteous indignation to every other woman in the pueblo; she had been ever since the death of her husband when, instead of allowing her aunt Rosa's idle son to take charge of the *almacén,* as her aunt so charitably suggested, she herself sold the olive oil, pajama jackets, sugar, gingham, wine, and rosaries with which the shop was stocked; and bought and sold again and made a profit, too! Although, as her aunt Rosa's idle son had said to his friend, Don Gumesindo, her *almacén* was no more than a tin shed, it had the good fortune to be so placed that everyone on entering or leaving the pueblo must pass it. Don Gumesindo's own *almacén* was an ostentatious concrete building; as it also stood on the only street in the pueblo, one might have supposed it to be equally advantageously situated.

Not only had Mama Josefina taken over her husband's business but, before the grass was green above his grave, she had cast aside her widow's weeds, crying that since she had not loved him alive she saw no reason to mourn him dead; and she blossomed once more wearing the gaudy prints she favored.

To women who were mourning half their lives, this was profoundly shocking. But there was worse to follow.

Mama Josefina had an only child, a little girl named Celia. When Celia was ten years old, Mama Josefina sent her to a convent school in Buenos Aires and, when she was graduated, to college in that city. Mama Josefina had seen her daughter only half a dozen times in the past ten years. That was a wickedness impossible to condone; even her friends, and she had staunch ones, shook their heads dubiously while those who openly said they were not her friends, cried, "But what barbarity! Casting out her only child! What lack of all maternal feeling!" over this, Mama Josefina's most lamentable eccentricity.

And now Celia was twenty and she was returning to visit her mother, and the whole pueblo was agog to see what sort of daughter she had become.

Mama Josefina had been in a fever of activity ever since she had heard from Celia. She had painted the walls of her *almacén* white, and the roof red—it was made of corrugated iron and had never seen a lick of paint before. She sent for a length of silk, strawberry-colored roses sprawling on an olive green background, and made it into the shapeless sort of sack she called a dress. Her vast, waddling figure could be seen at any hour steaming down the center of the road, her rope-soled *alpargatas* shuffling in the dust till she raised a cloud as thick as a passing troop of horse, followed by such a trail of urchins, loafers, and mongrels as might follow any circus from the city.

On the day of Celia's arrival every soul in the pueblo was at the station; this was usual, for the passing of the train from Buenos Aires—it stopped only on request—was the highlight of the week; but this day everyone was on tiptoe with expectancy.

Mama Josefina held the center of the stage, her purpling face, beaded with sweat, contorted into one beatific grin, her gold tooth flashing, her voice hoarse with emotion. Behind her the waiting crowd, the women in rusty shawls and faded gowns, the men in wide cotton *bombachas* and striped pajama jackets, the scantily clad, inquisitive-eyed children, appeared colorless and unreal, as if painted cloudily against the backdrop of a scene.

Celia had looked forward to her return with some misgiving, the cause of which she would not permit herself to acknowledge. She prepared for her reunion with her mother with as much care as she dressed to keep a date with Fernandito; indeed it was possible that she might be seeing Fernandito, for his uncle had an *estancia* not far from her home, and this link had been the first step in their friendship. But it was not of Fernandito she was thinking; it was of her mother.

Strange to be so unfamiliar with one's own mother! It was wrong, thought Celia, who had strong convictions as to right and wrong. It had been she who had insisted on this visit; her mother had not encouraged her return. Not that Mama Josefina did not love her daughter; Celia could not doubt her mother's love. Mama Josefina's love was as solid and dependable as the earth under your feet. Celia's fears were of another nature.

As the engine heralded their arrival with a piercing hoot of triumph, Celia took one last anxious look at herself in her mirror. She had that cool and unruffled air which some women seem able to maintain through fire and flood, and eighteen hours of dusty travel had in no way disturbed her.

As the train jolted to a standstill, Celia jumped down the steps with her arms held out to greet her mother.

Mama Josefina let out a bellow of joy and flung herself upon her daughter, and Celia found herself enveloped in an aura of garlic, sweat, and the tangy, vinegary smell of the *almacén*. Involuntarily she drew back, but almost before Mama Josefina could be aware of her recoil, she embraced her mother with added tenderness.

Then Mama Josefina turned, her arm still about her daughter, the tears coursing down her quivering cheeks, and cried in her hoarse, stentorian tones, "This is my daughter, people! Is she not beautiful? And brains! She has more in that pretty little headpiece than there are in all the flea-infected noddles in this hovel! Make way there, you louts! Make way for my daughter! You there, Gumesindo with the belly, carry the lady's valise instead of standing with your eyes goggling as if you had swallowed a chicken bone! Make way there!"

Celia was scarlet with mortification. She could not look her old acquaintance in the eye. Someone at the back of the crowd sniggered, for Don Gumesindo had, without thinking, obediently gathered up the valise. Don Gumesindo scowled but he did not let go of the valise, because Celia was so exceptionally pretty.

Mama Josefina had her daughter firmly by the elbow and was propelling her up the center of the road, followed by every man, woman, child, and cur in the place. Still pink in the face and with the tears pricking her eyelids, Celia gazed at the scenes of her childhood with growing despondency. It was more dreary and sordid than ever she remembered: the mudbrick houses unrelieved by paint; the scrawny chickens scratching in the dust; the mangy, mean-eyed mongrels; the flies and the dust, the penetrating, omnipresent dust.

"I am so happy to see you, Mama, I must weep!" Celia lied bravely.

"Weep then," said her mother, "for tears relieve the heart."

That evening the *almacén* was crowded; everyone suddenly wanted to buy a kilo of maté or a liter of wine and see at closer quarters this prodigy from the city. Celia had to endure all their impertinent stares, suggestive allusions, crude jokes and laughter while she helped her mother behind the counter. It seemed as if Mama Josefina was not conscious of her suffering but egged them on by talking loudly of her daughter's charms. Yet, when Celia was not looking, her mother observed her shrewdly and with sympathy, and when Don Gumesindo appeared in the doorway and stood there in a new mauve-striped pajama jacket, chewing on a toothpick while he stared at Celia in greedy silence, Mama Josefina sent him scuttling by shouting jocosely, "What, is your own wine so sour that you drink here, fat Gumesindo? Ask your wife for some from the barrel she keeps for the young Florindo. I saw him ride by and wondered why he did not stop to quench his thirst. But then, he does not have to pay cash for the wine your wife gives him!" She let out a guffaw of laughter, for Don Gumesindo was gone. Don Gumesindo's wife, Mama Josefina knew, was well able to defend herself.

When the noise was at its height, Celia went out into the back yard to breathe the cool air; the stench of stale wine nauseated her. The sun had set and left a rim of crimson on the dark horizon; above her head the stars began to twinkle; the kindly shadows hid the dust and dirt. Celia sighed, thinking lovingly of her mother and of her own fastidious shrinking with dismay.

Down the darkening road a youth came riding; he was not more than sixteen, yet he had an air of quiet serenity that blended with the wide, still world around.

"*Buenas noches,*" he said unsmilingly. "I come in search of the señorita Celia Olivera."

"I am Celia Olivera," Celia answered, her heart beating violently.

"I have a letter for you," he said, riding right up to her but without dismounting, for it was more natural for him to remain in the saddle. "I am to await an answer."

"Oh . . ." said Celia, feeling that fierce constriction of the heart which word from Fernandito always brought her. She took the letter to the bedroom to read.

It was in the bold, flowing hand that was so characteristic of Fernandito. He was at his uncle's house, he wrote; might he come in his car tomorrow and take her and her mother to visit his uncle? His uncle was most anxious to make her acquaintance.

Celia's heart sank. She knew of Fernandito's uncle, an elegant old man with a reputation for wit. She could well imagine how such wit could be used against her mother! How they would laugh! Celia burned with the fierce defensive loyalty of youth.

She sat down and wrote the answer at great speed. She was sorry but she and her mother were too busy to receive or pay visits. Indeed, on consideration, she thought their friendship had gone far enough and had better cease.

She ran out and gave the letter, the ink scarcely dry, to the boy who had waited there motionless as a statue.

"Remain with God," he said gravely, turning his horse's head.

"Go with God," Celia whispered as he rode away. But the farewell was not for the messenger.

Celia's was a quiet and docile nature that hid a stubborn will. She was proving more stubborn than her mother; Mama Josefina said Celia must return to work in the city, and Celia said her place was at her mother's side. Celia might not have argued with such determination had she not been shamed to find how shocked she was by her mother's vulgarity and the squalor of her surroundings; if she had wanted to stay she might have been persuaded to go. It was wrong, Celia decided, to be unhappy in your home, to be embarrassed by your mother. What was good enough for Mama should certainly be good enough for her; she must get used to this environment and prepare to devote her life to the care of her mother.

"But in the name of all the saints, child, do you think I spent that money on your education to see you spend your days measuring out wine or watching Gumesindo lest he diddle you? Your place is in the city. I can see you there," Mama Josefina clasped her hands over her stomach, "seated behind the teacher's desk. . . . Or up on the platform presenting prizes to your pupils. . . . I did not have you educated that you might choke your mind with dust and flies! And I tell you, girl, it has cost no small amount. . . . Though, bless you, I would not begrudge it if it cost my life!"

"But, Mama, it is not right that you should spend your life slaving here," Celia cried, "while I live in luxury! You are getting old and I should be here to look after you. . . ."

"Old!" Mama Josefina fairly screeched with rage. "I'll have you know, my girl, I'm as good a woman as any and better than some of these puling things the men bring home these days as brides. Old! If there were a man in this pueblo with a thought beyond his stomach or an idea above the bottom of his glass, you'd see how old I am! Old!"

"All the same, Mama, you need me here."

"And who do you think you'll find to marry in this mudhole? Tell me that!"

"I do not intend to marry," Celia said, her voice trembling for all her self-control. "I will stay and help you in the business."

"Mother of God, have mercy on my soul!" Mama Josefina cried, flinging up her hands to heaven. "Now for sure I shall be ruined! Well, since you must help, go and tell that Hipolito he can pay his debt in kind. I want two cows with calf, fat and sleek. You can drive them home yourself."

Mama Josefina stood in the doorway watching Celia walking down the road. It was obvious that the girl was unhappy for all her determined cheerfulness. Mama Josefina's heart bled for her. The young, she thought, if they have no troubles of their own, must fabricate them! As if a girl like Celia could be happy in a hole like this! She gave one scornful glance up and down the empty road and waddled angrily back into her shop.

Celia was unhappy, but it was not only her surroundings that made her so. It was a week since she had sent Fernandito that ungracious note, and she had had no word from him. Undoubtedly he was furious, for Fernandito had a temper that flared up like dry straw. And he had every right to be! She would never hear from him again, of that she could be sure, she told herself miserably.

The thick, warm dust had seeped into her high-heeled shoes so that walking was painful, and she had to stop every so often and balance on one leg while she emptied the other shoe. Soon she would be wearing the rope-soled *alpargatas* as all the other women did; soon her clothes would take on the hue and smell of dust. If Fernandito should one day pass through the pueblo she would be indistinguishable from the rest! Only Mama Josefina had survived the dust!

Of course, Celia thought, as if she had discovered a bright new idea, Mama wears those gaudy clothes, Mama talks loudly and behaves in an eccentric fashion in revolt against the dust. Mama will not allow the dust to bury her in oblivion. Mama, thought Celia with deep feeling, is wonderful! And she sighed and mused about Fernandito, and her misery returned.

Hipolito, she found, had no intention of paying his debt at all. He told her so in no uncertain language, but Celia was not her mother's daughter for nothing, and she browbeat him into promising to have the cows driven into a corral so that next morning she might take her pick. She was frankly relieved that she did not have to drive the animals home that evening.

The shadows were long when she turned home, and a faint breeze had sprung up, cooling to her moist brow. The countryside was beautiful at this hour, beautiful in the remote, austere fashion of the pampas.

The lamp was twinkling in the *almacén;* two hounds came rushing forth at her approach, but above their barking she could hear her mother's raucous voice. Mama Josefina was singing and, not knowing Mama Josefina, one might have supposed her drunk. The song she sang was no drawing-room ditty, and she bellowed it forth with huge Rabelaisian gusto as if she smacked her lips over each word. Suddenly a man's voice broke in with the chorus.

At this sound Celia stopped abruptly and then began to run toward the *almacén.* She burst through the curtain that hung across the door and stood on the threshold, gaping.

Mama Josefina was perched on her own counter; beside her sat Fernandito and between them lay an open tin of anchovies and a bottle of wine. Fernandito had one hand on Mama Josefina's shoulder and in the other he held a toothpick with which he speared at the anchovies. They were both singing lustily.

"Celia!" Fernandito cried when he saw her. "Why did you not tell me Mama Josefina was your mama? She is an old friend of mine. I used to come stealing her anchovies when I was a kid, didn't I, Mama Josefina, love?" He slid off the counter and came across to Celia, his brown eyes looking into hers and laughing in a way he had. "You know your letter made me so mad I swore I would never see you again! And then I had the good sense to come and tell Mama Josefina all my troubles. It was as simple as that. Mama Josefina says all girls write that sort of letter once to the man they really love!"

He said this with so disarming a grin that Celia found it impossible to be angry; besides, she was all at once so very happy. Mama Josefina got off the counter with a thud that shook the building and came waddling over and put an arm round each of them, looking from one to the other with her gold tooth flashing.

"This silly boy was always after my pickles and anchovies. Not a sweet tooth like other boys. He likes things with a nip in them!" She chuckled deeply, "But why did you tell me nothing about this handsome young fellow, girl? That to me is suspicious! The foolish things that girls are; if there are not enough troubles in the world already they must go inventing more!"

"You explain to her the way you did to me, Mama Josefina," Fernandito said, putting his arm affectionately around the old woman's waist. "Then she will see sense."

"Oh, well . . ." Mama Josefina hesitated coyly.

"Go on," Fernandito urged her gently.

"Well, it is like this, daughter," the old woman began awkwardly as if the words were drawn from the bottom of her heart. "I hate this place! I hate this pueblo and this life where nothing happens from one year to the next! Most I hate the dust! It takes all the color out of you. It takes all the juice out of you. Pah, the dust, I spit on it! But I know I am too old to escape from it, too old and too ignorant! Oh, you think I do not see myself with your young eyes? A fat, smelly old woman! No, don't interrupt! It is true. I am dirty and I stink and I know no other way of life. I cannot escape. . . ." She swung round and faced her daughter dramatically, her old body held painfully erect, and spoke with suppressed and tragic rage. "I fight the dust! I will not let it take the color from my life. I will not let it take you! Only through you can I escape! I can live, thinking of your freedom. Thinking of you I can feel myself young and lovely and full of life! Thinking of you I can forget the dust! But if you remain here, Celia," she turned her massive head away and her voice trembled, "if you stay here, if I have to watch you lose your youth, watch the color fade from your cheek and the light from your eye, see you shuffling through the dust in *alpargatas* . . . I could not bear it! I could fight no more. The dust would bury me . . ."

There was a moment of silence and then Celia put her arm about her mother's waist. "Forgive me, Mama. Now I understand. I will go back." She felt Fernandito's hand laid over hers, and her mother gave a convulsive sob, flung her arms about her, and embraced her enthusiastically.

"That's my girl!" she cried tearfully. "That's my Celia! Now come and eat some anchovy before this greedy boy guzzles the lot!" She wiped her nose with the back of her hand. "And now we will sing and enjoy ourselves, and you can hold hands all you like behind my back. . . . Eh, you think I don't know what goes on! You think I have as much fat on my brains as I have on my body!" She guffawed with laughter and nudged them both knowingly. "Come on, sing and enjoy life!"

### Suggestions for Study

1. This story has in reality two antagonists. Name them and show how each is overcome.
2. Is the method of bringing the story to a conclusion plausible? What elements of foreshadowing does the author insert in order to make the last incident plausible?
3. Do the differences between Mama Josefina and Celia seem too incongruous?
4. Whose story is this really—Mama Josefina's or Celia's?

## Railroad Harvest [51]

### GEOFFREY HOUSEHOLD

We, the French,—said Maître Braillard, stretching his feet under the table and swallowing a draught of the acid white wine which was all the café had to offer,—are ever ready to accept tradition. I speak to you as a lawyer and perhaps I exaggerate. But in my opinion the worst that the occupation did to us was to destroy our sense of continuity with the past.

This wine is revolting, but will do while we wait for better. There will —said Braillard, with as keen satisfaction as if he himself would taste by the palate of a descendant—there will be good wine again for our children.

It is customary—he went on—to prophesy that the revolution we are undoubtedly about to suffer will be more drastic than our revolution one hundred and fifty years ago. I do not believe it. We wish to order our lives by the law. We accept immediately the law. It is only when we know not what the law is that we become a little difficult.

*Tiens!* I will tell you a story. It has a slight piggery, but we are after dinner—if indeed we may dignify by the name the small portions of antique horse and salad that we have just consumed.

Do you know the municipality of Saint-Valery-sur-Marne? No? I am not surprised. Saint-Valery is ten kilometers from the fortifications, and

51. From the *Atlantic Monthly*, CLXXVII (January, 1946), 48 (copyright, 1946, by Geoffrey Household). Reprinted by permission of the author and the *Atlantic Monthly*.

remarkable only for its ugliness and its extensive railroad yard. If you travel round Paris from the Gare du Nord to the Quai d'Orsay, your train will inevitably pass through Saint-Valery. But why should you be in it? You will of course spend some hours in Paris, and will pick up your train again at the Quai d'Orsay.

Saint-Valery has a black canal, and some small industries without any permanence, built of cement and corrugated iron. There is no architecture. There are only hoardings, and houses of the most melancholy. It is quite evident that one is compelled to inhabit Saint-Valery: one does not choose it.

In the middle of this tasteless wilderness are the railroad tracks, and in the middle of the tracks is a little tower of dirty brick. The tower is old. I do not know how old, nor what it was for; it might have been the base of a round dovecot. But now the interior has been rearranged—you understand—for the convenience of the railway men.

It stood, this tower, upon a triangle of blackened gravel between the canal sidings and the main loopline round Paris. In spite of this little-promising situation, the brickwork was covered by a resplendent vine. There was no other green thing within three hundred meters; not even a dandelion could live in such a waste of steel and cinders. But the vine was older than the railroad, and its roots were far down in good French soil. It was well nourished by the iron that filtered in solution through the gravel, and had no doubt, some other excellent sources of fertility.

In this August of 1945 the vine was superb. It rejoiced in its liberation. The walls and parapet of the tower were jeweled with bunches as long as my forearm. The grapes were of that indescribable tint which is purple, yet not quite purple. All the station staff of Saint-Valery were agreed that it needed but twenty-four more August hours for fifty bunches to be at their perfection.

Mme. Delage, who was the wife of the stationmaster and impatient for good morsels as befitted an admirable housekeeper who was tormented by the impossibility of a decent table, was the first to lose her self-restraint. One had not yet decided upon the ultimate destiny of the grapes; one had perhaps deliberately avoided so delicate a subject. Mme. Delage, however, had set her heart upon a bunch, already and indubitably ripe, which hung on the south wall immediately above the window of the tower.

I knew her well. She had a black mustache, and her rotundities, though massive, were more square than round. She had no reason to hope for those attentions which traditionally await the wives of stationmasters. She wore high-heeled shoes, as was proper for the consort of an important functionary, but they did not become her ankles. She resembled, I thought, a hippopotamus on skates. Nevertheless M. Delage was a model husband. She had fine brown eyes, one must admit, and then he was very afraid of her.

At six in the morning Mme. Delage, with a basket and a pair of scissors, waited before the door of the tower. I say she waited, for the tower was occupied and she could only reach her chosen bunch through the window from the inside. After a while she permitted herself to hammer on the door.

This intemperate gesture being without effect, she approached Lulu, who was waiting on the track, and climbed upon her footplate and blew her whistle loudly. It was Charles Cortal, the driver, who had christened his locomotive Lulu. He loved little else but Lulu and all humanity, for he was a communist. But humanity is too large to love with enthusiasm. His true affection was for Lulu.

Charles Cortal launched himself in a fury from the tower.

"Madame!" he cried. "It is forbidden by the regulations of the company to climb upon a locomotive!"

"It is also forbidden," Madame replied, "to leave a locomotive unattended."

I was not present, you understand, but I can imagine what Cortal retorted. I have had dealings with him. He answered, with a beautiful selection of obscenities, that there were times when locomotives had to be left, above all when his cretinous fireman had gone to pour a coffee into his filthy guts, and that if he had known Madame so urgently required the tower he would have made other arrangements.

To this Madame replied, with the exasperating calm in which she was accustomed to address the angry proletariat, that he knew very well she desired only to gather a bunch of grapes.

"Then gather them, *nom de Dieu!*" shouted Charles Cortal. "But without disturbing me!"

"One can reach the grapes only from the inside," answered Madame.

She was, you will agree, in the wrong. And to Cortal she exhibited plainly, immediately, the shocking inhumanity and acquisitiveness of the bourgeoisie. He therefore demanded why Madame should gather grapes which had been the property of the company's drivers and firemen as long as the Third Republic existed. Then Madame began to tell him what she thought of this right he had so brilliantly invented. And Cortal said that for one old cow she made more noise than a whole veterinary surgeon's back yard.

And *patati, patata!* And before anyone knew of the quarrel, Mme.

Delage was off to swear a *procès-verbal* against Cortal for insult and con-tumely, and Cortal had gone to complain to the local secretary of the union.

Meanwhile Lulu remained where she was as a protest. M. Delage and the signalmen might say what they liked, but not a driver would move her. The loop line was blocked, and on the telephone from Paris were jolly things to be heard.

After a hasty breakfast, M. Delage placed upon his head the gold-braided hat of office and visited the Café de la Gare, where Charles Cortal was expressing his opinions over a glass of very bad *eau de vie*. Before them all he accused Cortal of sabotaging the transport system of France. Cortal, without hesitating an instant, called him a collaborator, a Pétain-iste, and a pro-Boche. After that there was no more to be said.

M. Delage was a man of duty. It was his business to see that trains ran, and he saw that they did run, even during the occupation. He did not understand the Resistance; he was paid, he said, by the company. All the same, he looked the other way when it was required of him, and he kept his mouth closed. I would never call him a collaborator, but he was narrow.

At midday arrived from Paris the general secretary of the union. He was a reasonable man. True, he had the hungry and *farouche* appearance of a revolutionary of the most murderous; but it was expressly cultivated. In manner he was tactful as a director of funerals. Though his sympa-thies were naturally with Cortal, he was determined to restore discipline at Saint-Valery.

After he had most wholly failed with the drivers and firemen, he took it upon himself to make Delage laugh at this petty affair—as between men of the world, you understand. But Delage was in no laughing mood; there was, he said, a question of principle involved. He pulled out the railroad regulations and made the secretary read the powers of the stationmaster: how he was responsible to the company for all property, movable and im-movable, in or upon the station and the yards, and in the event of any attempt upon such property might call upon the civil power—and so on. Delage was prepared to admit that he might have no right to eat the grapes. A court of law, he said, would settle that. But as to his right or that of his wife, acting as his agent, to pick the said grapes at maturity there could be no doubt at all.

The secretary was inclined to agree, but, to excuse Cortal, he suggested that an overworked and honest driver, disturbed in a moment of tran-quillity, might permit himself expressions which—

"Monsieur," said Delage gravely, "she waited a reasonable time."

"But, Monsieur, consider the impropriety!"

"Monsieur accuses my wife of impropriety?"

"Of no such thing, I assure you. I wished to say that Madame with her delicate susceptibilities would not have desired to gather grapes had she been aware—"

"Madame is above such petty considerations. And then, I repeat, she waited a reasonable time."

"Monsieur would be good enough to define a reasonable time?" asked the secretary, who was beginning to forget his tact.

"Ah, *par exemple!* Let us say five minutes!"

"It is in the regulations, perhaps?"

"It is in the regulations that a driver shall not leave his locomotive unattended."

"When France mourns for so many missing sons," said the secretary sharply, "one cannot manage labor by red tape, especially at 5.00 A.M."

"It was six, Monsieur."

"In any case, Monsieur, it was a suspiciously early hour that Madame chose to sneak her grapes."

"Monsieur, I forbid any criticism of my wife!"

To which the secretary, at last under the infectious influence of the vine and angry as lesser men, replied by a pleasantry in the poorest taste. And then M. Delage slapped his face.

They were separated by the chief clerks of the Grande Vitesse and the Petite Vitesse. Those two were invaluable. They were calm, you see. They voted for the Catholic center and had all that was necessary to their convenience upon the station. They had thus no conceivable right to the grapes.

It was quite otherwise with the shunters. They disagreed entirely with the claim that Charles Cortal had put forward for the drivers and firemen. The shunters had an excellent case in all respects; two of them had even pruned the vine.

The solidarity of the working class vanished altogether when the shunter, Hippolyte Charvet, took it upon himself to remove Lulu while she still had steam. He made a speech from the footplate explaining that the act he was about to perform must not be interpreted as having any bearing upon the future of France, and had nothing to do with the dispute between the stationmaster and the locomotive engineers. In that argument the engineers were right, and Delage, the so-called stationmaster, was a fascist who would shortly receive his deserts. No, comrades, he removed the locomotive merely because in its present position it kept the afternoon sun from the shunters' grapes.

He thereupon returned Lulu to the sheds. I think he is still in the hospital. Charles Cortal did not even permit the oiling of Lulu by any but himself.

To hear the arguments, you would have thought that every man remembered exactly what had happened before the war. Even Cortal's claim, which he had obviously invented merely because he was angry, was taken seriously. But nobody in fact remembered any tradition at all. For five years the Boche RTO in charge of the yards and his Boche staff had eaten the grapes themselves and allowed no one else to approach them. That alone was certain.

*Eh bien,* I will now give you the intelligence summary for Saint-Valery at nightfall. M. Delage was prostrated, partly by answering telephone calls from Paris and partly because he feared to be shot as pro-Boche. Mme. Delage was at her lawyer's for the third time. The drivers and firemen were on strike. Charles Cortal was summonsed for the attempted murder of Hippolyte Charvet. The shunters had a peaceful picket round the vine. Grande Vitesse was occupied in composing an apology for the union secretary, who had not the least wish in the world to fight a duel, and Petite Vitesse was doing the same for Delage. And Saint-Valery yards were just as idle as when all the employees used to pretend they heard an air-raid warning.

The next day it was hot. But how hot! Only to think of it gives me a thirst even for this wine. We descended, a horde of officials, upon Saint-Valery. I was among them, being the union's attorney. There was the undersecretary of the Ministry; there were two big men of the Resistance; there were all the union officials and the company officials. There were even some soldiers. In these days one can never have a row between civilians without soldiers' desiring to be present.

First of all we held a quite informal conference at the station. We arrived at the facts. And then we protested that the whole affair was ridiculous. The Resistance men laughed. That started us off. A complainant had only to mention the tower for us to giggle like boys, all of us and uncontrollably. On a hot day one laughs easily. One's companions are themselves comical. They mop their faces. The poor railway men of Saint-Valery were more furious than ever.

It was Charles Cortal who imposed more gravity upon us. He mounted on a barrow and addressed the union officials.

"We," he bellowed, "we, the drivers and firemen, we were the heart of the Resistance in Saint-Valery. A month after the liberation we were thanked. And now, a year after the liberation, observe how they allow us to be mucked about by insults from a son of pig of a collaborator! Comrades, one steals our birthright!"

And then he called Delage by the names of various animals, and commented, without any regard for zoology, upon his probable descent from others.

This wiped the smiles off the faces of the company officials; they were about to be nationalized, and it would do no good to their salaries to have the reputation of capitalist tyrants.

Mme. Delage had dressed herself like a pretty countrywoman, but in surprisingly good taste. She chose her moment to direct a few words to the General Manager. Everybody listened.

She was going, she said quietly, in the freshness of the dawn to cull a bunch of grapes.

Our chivalry leaped to our hearts. She had a fine voice, and she made one see French Womanhood, all pure and laborious, going about its simple tasks at sunrise.

She had been insulted, she sighed, but that was nothing. There were gentlemen in plenty to defend a Frenchwoman in distress. No, it was not for herself that she asked justice, but for her husband.

Delage was in his best cap and uniform, looking handsome and pale and very much the old soldier. Of course she touched that string too. His service in the last war. Wounded for France. Twice mentioned. And now to be called a collaborator!

She picked up Delage's hand and kissed it passionately.

"That is what I think of him!" she cried. "And I, will anyone dare to say that I, Susanne Hélène Delage, am a collaborator?"

That wiped the smiles off the union officials too. Lack of discipline, inability to appreciate the plight of the country, incitement to rebellion against the government—those were the accusations they saw coming.

It was time to treat the affair with all the dignity of public men. One whispered. One formed lobbies. One admitted the need of subcommittees. And at last we constituted ourselves into a commission and decided to sit in the upstairs hall of the Café de la Gare. We summoned all witnesses and representatives to accompany us.

There was a yell from Charles Cortal.

"And leave these camels here to steal our grapes while we are away?" he asked. "These thieving sons of mackerels?"

Two of the shunters were still, unobtrusively, picketing the tower. A third was inside. We formally ejected them. Grande Vitesse and Petite Vitesse were called upon to stand guard.

"And if one wishes to enter?" asked Grande Vitesse timidly.

"It cannot be permitted," the General Manager ordered. "One can find everything necessary on the station."

"That I forbid absolutely!" shouted Delage.

"*Eh bien,* one will be instructed to make whatever arrangements one can," said the General Manager in his most conciliatory manner.

I cannot say that the commission was a success. The hall had not been used for a long time. We could not expand in an atmosphere which reeked of mice and the ancient smoke of locomotives. And then—we could not create tradition where none existed.

We suggested that the grapes be given to a hospital. Not one of the railway men agreed. They said that next year and for all the years we liked they would send enough grapes to hospitals to resurrect the dead; but this year it was unthinkable. There had been insults. There was a question of principle to be decided—though heaven alone knows what cursed principle it was.

So we offered a third to the drivers and firemen, a third to the shunters, and a third to the stationmaster. No takers! Each wanted a half, and the other half to be divided.

The property of the company, then? Delage, being legally-minded, agreed to this, but the engineers and shunters would not have it. They explained with superfluous precision their right to the grapes, and demanded whether a company which had, in the immortal phrase, neither soul to be saved nor backside to be kicked could in any way be held responsible for the vine's luxuriance.

It was, I think, one of the big men from the Resistance who at last proposed that we should analyze the problem more closely by counting the bunches to be divided. He was used to the open air and desired an excuse to return to it. He was very bored by the commission.

The suggestion was ridiculous, but really we could think of nothing useful to do. So Grande Vitesse and Petite Vitesse were put to counting bunches, while we, the others, broke into groups, according to age and political inclination, up and down the yard. The heat was abominable. I sympathized with Eve. One heard the tempter merely by looking at those grapes. They were magnificent, and the last twenty-four hours had brought them to perfection.

Between the shunters and the drivers the military were compelled to take a little promenade. As for us, the visitors, we argued courteously and from an academic point of view; but it was not difficult to see that strong words would be used if we permitted ourselves to take the affair seriously. The Resistance man had already described Mme. Delage to the General Manager in terms for which I had to persuade him to apologize.

No one noticed the man with the wheelbarrow. He arrived unobtrusively. He was so much a part of France that one did not question his right to be in the railroad yard. He was a little old peasant, bent by labor in the fields, and with the long, gray mustache of an ancient Gaul. He was wheeling a barrow with a ladder on it.

He stopped at the tower and looked benevolently at Grande Vitesse, who was on the roof counting bunches, and at Petite Vitesse, who was performing the feats of an acrobat through the window. He knew at once that their intentions were honest—they understood each other, those children of old France.

"They are just right, my grapes!" said the ancient, rubbing his hands. "Ah, how I know you! You have not changed in the war."

And he patted the trunk of the vine as if to congratulate it upon so punctual a response to the season.

He was quite unaffected by the crowd. I doubt if he even noticed us. Or perhaps he thought that we had come to watch. He had the face of a man who enjoys all the protection of his conscience and the law. I hastened to his side before everyone could speak at once.

"Is it your vine?" I asked him.

He sat down on the wheelbarrow and drew from his vast pocket a portfolio. The documents were imposing. They dated from the time of Napoleon III. Paper like that is not made nowadays. And he read them aloud, on and on—that the said Sieur Henri Duval sold to the railroad company the property as set forth in the accompanying schedule with all buildings and land and produce growing thereon with the exception of the said vine, and the said Sieur Henri Duval should have access at all times for the purpose of cultivating the said vine and the fruit of the said vine should belong to him and his heirs and assigns, and the said railroad company on their part—

"I am François Duval, *voyez-vous,*" he declared, "son of Henri Duval, and I have here my birth certificate and copy of the will of Henri Duval."

"But the grapes are his!" grumbled Charles Cortal, who, you will remember, was a communist and did not believe in private property. "Why worry about the damned documents? He can just as well leave them for us in the tower."

He shrugged his shoulders and strolled off to prepare Lulu for the road. We returned to Paris.

*Suggestions for Study*

1. What was the primary aim of the author in this story: to analyze the French character by means of a story, to satirize labor squabbles, to satirize

government intervention in labor disputes, to create several French types, or to write a story for the sake of plot?

2. Is the way the story ended implicit in the narrative from the start, or does the author drag in old Duval in order to bring the story to an end?

3. The author of this story also wrote the popular novel *Rogue Male*. If you have read that novel or have time to do so, compare its style and intent with this story. Would you believe the same man wrote both? Explain your answer.

4. Is this a realistic or romantic story? Is it a story of character, plot, situation, or atmosphere primarily?

5. Does the story gain or lose by being written in the idiom of the Frenchman who tells the story and by the inclusion of a few French words?

6. What is the tone? the point of view of the author?

## *That Greek Dog* [52]

### MAC KINLAY KANTOR

He received . . . praise that will never die, and with it the grandest of all sepulchers, not that in which his mortal bones are laid, but a home in the minds of men.—THUCYDIDES (more or less).

In those first years after the first World War, Bill Barbilis could still get into his uniform; he was ornate and handsome when he wore it. Bill's left sleeve, reading down from the shoulder, had patches and patterns of color to catch any eye. At the top there was an arc—bent stripes of scarlet, yellow, and purple; next came a single red chevron with the apex pointing up; and at the cuff were three gold chevrons pointing the other way.

On his right cuff was another gold chevron, only slightly corroded. And we must not forget those triple chevrons on an olive-drab field which grew halfway up the sleeve.

People militarily sophisticated, there in Mahaska Falls, could recognize immediately that Mr. Basilio Barbilis had been a sergeant, that he had served with the Forty-second Division, that he had been once wounded, that he had sojourned overseas for at least eighteen months, and that he had been discharged with honor.

His khaki blouse, however, was worn only on days of patriotic importance. The coat he donned at other times was white—white, that is, until cherry sirup and caramel speckled it. Mr. Barbilis was owner, manager, and staff of the Sugar Bowl.

He had a soda fountain with the most glittering spigots in town. He had a bank of candy cases, a machine for toasting sandwiches, ten small

52. From the *Saturday Evening Post*, CCXIV (August 9, 1941), No. 6 (copyright, 1941, by Curtis Publishing Company). Reprinted by permission of the author.

tables complete with steel-backed chairs, and a ceiling festooned with leaves of gilt and bronze paper.

Beginning in 1920, he had also a peculiar dog. Bill's living quarters were in the rear of the Sugar Bowl, and the dog came bleating and shivering to the Barbilis door one March night. The dog was no larger than a quart of ice cream and, Bill said, just as cold.

My medical office and apartment were directly over the Sugar Bowl. I made the foundling's acquaintance the next day, when I stopped in for a cup of chocolate. Bill had the dog bedded in a candy carton behind the fountain; he was heating milk when I came in, and wouldn't fix my chocolate until his new pet was fed.

Bill swore that it was a puppy. I wasn't so certain. It looked something like a mud turtle wearing furs.

"I think he is hunting dog," said Bill, with pride. "He was cold last night, but not so cold now. Look, I make him nice warm bed. I got my old pajamas for him to lie on."

He waited upon the sniffling little beast with more tender consideration than ever he showed to any customer. Some people say that Greeks are mercenary. I don't know. That puppy wasn't paying board.

The dog grew up, burly and quizzical. Bill named him Duboko. It sounded like that; I don't know how to spell the name correctly, nor did anyone else in Mahaska Falls.

The word, Bill said, was slang. It meant "tough" or "hard-boiled." This animal had the face of a clown and the body of a hyena. Growing up, his downy coat changing to wire and bristles, Duboko resembled a fat Hamburg steak with onions which had been left too long on the griddle.

At an early age Duboko began to manifest a violent interest in community assemblage of any kind or color. This trait may have been fostered by his master, who was proud to be a Moose, an Odd Fellow, a Woodman, and an upstanding member of the Mahaska Falls Commercial League.

When we needed the services of a bugler in our newly formed American Legion post and no bona fide bugler would volunteer, Bill Barbilis agreed to purchase the best brass instrument available and to practice in the bleak and cindery space behind his store. Since my office was upstairs, I found no great satisfaction in Bill's musical enterprise. It happened that Duboko also lent his voice in support—a Greek chorus, so to speak, complete with strophe and antistrophe.

Nevertheless, I could register no complaint, since with other members of the Legion I had voted to retain Bill as our bugler. I could not even kick Duboko downstairs with my one good leg when I discovered him in my reception room lunching off my mail.

Indeed, most people found it hard to punish Duboko. He had the ingratiating, hopeful confidence of an immigrant just off the boat and assured that he had found the Promised Land. He boasted beady eyes, lubberly crooked paws, an immense mouth formed of black rubber, and pearly and enormous fangs which he was fond of exhibiting in a kind of senseless leer. He smelled, too. This characteristic I called sharply to the attention of his master, with the result that Duboko was laundered weekly in Bill's uncertain little bathtub, the process being marked by vocal lament which might have arisen from the gloomiest passage of the *Antigone.*

Mahaska Falls soon became aware of the creature, in a general municipal sense, and learned that it had him to reckon with. Duboko attended every gathering at which six or more people were in congregation. No fire, picnic, memorial service, Rotary conclave, or public chicken-pie supper went ungraced by his presence.

If, as sometimes happened on a crowded Saturday night, a pedestrian was brushed by a car, Duboko was on the scene with a speed to put the insurance-company representatives to shame. If there was a lodge meeting which he did not visit and from which he was not noisily ejected, I never heard of it. At Commercial League dinners he lay pensive with his head beneath the chair of Bill Barbilis. But, suffering fewer inhibitions than his master, he also visited funerals, and even the marriage of Miss Glaydys Stumpf.

Old Charles P. Stumpf owned the sieve factory. He was the richest man in town; the nuptials of his daughter exuded an especial aura of social magnificence. It is a matter of historical record that Duboko sampled the creamed chicken before any of the guests did; he was banished only after the striped and rented trousers of two ushers had undergone renting in quite another sense of the word. Grieved, Duboko forswore the Stumpfs after that; he refused to attend a reception for the bride and bridegroom when they returned from the Wisconsin Dells two weeks later.

There was one other place in town where Duboko was decidedly *persona non grata.* This was a business house, a rival establishment of the Sugar Bowl, owned and operated by Earl and John Klugge. The All-American Kandy Kitchen, they called it.

The Brothers Klugge held forth at a corner location a block distant from the Sugar Bowl. Here lounged and tittered ill-favored representatives of the town's citizenry; dice rattled on a soiled mat at the cigar counter; it was whispered that refreshment other than soda could be purchased by the chosen.

The business career of Earl and John Klugge did not flourish, no matter what inducement they offered their customers. Loudly they declared that their failure to enrich themselves was due solely to the presence in our community of a Greek—a black-haired, dark-skinned Mediterranean who thought nothing of resorting to the most unfair business practices, such as serving good fudge sundaes, for instance, to anyone who would buy them.

One fine afternoon people along the main street were troubled at observing Duboko limp rapidly westward, fairly wreathed in howls. Bill called me down to examine the dog. Duboko was only bruised, although at first I feared that his ribs were mashed on one side. Possibly someone had thrown a heavy chair at him. Bill journeyed to the Clive Street corner with fire in his eye. But no one could be found who would admit to seeing an attack on Duboko; no one would even say for a certainty that Duboko had issued from the doorway of the All-American Kandy Kitchen, although circumstantial evidence seemed to suggest it.

Friends dissuaded Bill Barbilis from invading the precinct of his enemies, and at length he was placated by pleasant fiction about a kicking horse in the market square.

We all observed, however, that Duboko did not call at the Kandy Kitchen again, not even on rare nights when the dice rattled loudly and when the whoops and catcalls of customers caused girls to pass by, like pretty Levites, on the other side.

There might have been a different tale to tell if this assault had come later, when Duboko was fully grown. His frame stretched and extended steadily for a year; it became almost as mighty as the earnest Americanism of his master. He was never vicious. He was never known to bite a child. But frequently his defensive attitude was that of a mother cat who fancies her kitten in danger; Duboko's hypothetical kitten was his right to be present when good fellows—or bad—got together.

Pool halls knew him; so did the Epworth League. At football games an extra linesman was appointed for the sole purpose of discouraging Duboko's athletic ardor. Through some occult sense, he could become aware of an approaching festivity before even the vanguard assembled. Musicians of our brass band never lugged their instruments to the old bandstand in Courthouse Park without finding Duboko there before them, lounging in an attitude of expectancy. It was Wednesday night, it was eight o'clock, it was July; the veriest dullard might know at what hour and place the band would begin its attack on the *Light Cavalry Overture*.

Duboko's taste in music was catholic and extensive. He made a fortuitous appearance at a spring musicale, presented by the high-school orchestra and glee clubs, before an audience which sat in the righteous hush of people grimly determined to serve the arts, if only for a night.

The boys' glee club was rendering selections from *Carmen*—in English, of course—and dramatically they announced the appearance of the bull. The line goes, "Now the beast enters, wild and enraged," or something like that; Duboko chose this moment to lope grandly down the center aisle on castanetting toenails. He sprang to the platform. . . . Mahaska Falls wiped away more tears than did Mérimée's heroine.

In his adult stage, Duboko weighed forty pounds. His color suggested peanut brittle drenched with chocolate; I have heard people swear that his ears were four feet long, but that is an exaggeration. Often those ears hung like limp brown drawers dangling from a clothesline; again they were braced rigidly atop his skull.

Mastiff he was, and also German shepherd, with a noticeable influence of English bull, bloodhound, and great Dane. Far and wide he was known as "that Greek dog," and not alone because he operated out of the Sugar Bowl and under the aegis of Bill Barbilis. Duboko looked like a Greek.

He had Greek eyes, Greek eyebrows, and a grinning Greek mouth. Old Mayor Wingate proclaimed in his cups that, in fact, he had heard Duboko bark in Greek; he was willing to demonstrate, if anyone would only catch Duboko by sprinkling a little Attic salt on his tail.

That Greek dog seldom slept at night; he preferred to accompany the town's watchman on his rounds, or to sit in the window of the Sugar Bowl along with cardboard ladies who brandished aloft their cardboard sodas. Sometimes, when I had been called out in the middle of the night and came back from seeing a patient, I would stop and peer through the window and exchange a few signals with Duboko.

"Yes," he seemed to say, "I'm here. Bill forgot and locked me in. I don't mind, unless, of course, there's a fire. See you at Legion meeting tomorrow night, if not at the County Medical Association luncheon tomorrow noon."

At this time there was a new arrival in the Sugar Bowl household—Bill's own father, recruited all the way from Greece, now that Bill's mother was dead.

Spiros Barbilis was slight, silver-headed, round-shouldered, with drooping mustachios which always seemed oozing with black dye. Bill put up another cot in the back room and bought another chiffonier from the secondhand store. He and Duboko escorted the old man up and down Main Street throughout the better part of one forenoon.

"I want you to meet friend of mine," Bill said. "He is my father, but he don't speak no English. I want him to meet all my good friends here in Mahaska Falls, because he will live here always."

Old Mr. Barbilis grew deft at helping Bill with the Sugar Bowl. He carried trays and managed tables, grinning inveterately, wearing an apron stiff with starch. But he failed to learn much English except "hello" and "good-by" and a few cuss words; I think that he was lonely for the land he had left, which certainly Bill was not.

One night—it was two o'clock in the morning—I came back to climb my stairs, stepping carefully from my car to the icy sidewalk in front of the Sugar Bowl. I moved gingerly, because I had left one foot in the Toul sector when a dressing station was shelled; I did not like icy sidewalks.

This night I put my face close to the show window to greet Duboko, to meet those sly and mournful eyes which, on a bitter night, would certainly be waiting there instead of shining in a drifted alley where the watchman prowled.

Two pairs of solemn eyes confronted me when I looked in. Old Mr. Barbilis sat there, too—in his night clothes, but blanketed with an overcoat—he and Duboko, wrapped together among the jars of colored candy and the tinted cardboard girls. They stared out, aloof and dignified in the darkness, musing on a thousand lives that slept near by. I enjoy imagining that they both loved the street, even in its midnight desertion, though doubtless Duboko loved it the more.

In 1923 we were treated to a mystifying phenomenon. There had never been a riot in Mahaska Falls, nor any conflict between racial and religious groups. Actually we had no racial or religious groups; we were all Americans, or thought we were. But, suddenly and amazingly, fiery crosses flared in the darkness of our pasture lands.

I was invited to attend a meeting and did so eagerly, wondering if I might explore this outlandish nonsense in a single evening. When my car stopped at a cornfield gate and ghostly figures came to admit me, I heard voice after voice whispering bashfully, "Hello, doc," "Evening, doc. Glad you came." I was shocked at recognizing the voices. I had known the fathers and grandfathers of these youths—hard-working farmers they were, who found a long-sought freedom on the American prairies, and never fumed about the presence of the hard-working Catholics, Jews, and black men who were also members of that pioneer community.

There was one public meeting in the town itself. They never tried to hold another; there was too much objection; the voice of Bill Barbilis rang beneath the stars.

A speaker with a pimply face stood illuminated by the flare of gasoline torches on a makeshift rostrum, and dramatically he spread a dollar bill between his hands. "Here," he cried, "is the flag of the Jews!"

Bill Barbilis spoke sharply from the crowd: "Be careful, mister. There is United States seal on that bill."

In discomfiture, the speaker put away his bank note. He ignored Bill as long as he could. He set his own private eagles to screaming, and he talked of battles won, and he wept for the mothers of American boys who lay in France. He said that patriotic 100-per-cent Americans must honor and protect those mothers.

Bill Barbilis climbed to the fender of a car. "Sure," he agreed clearly, "we got to take care of those mothers! Also, other mothers we got to take care of—Catholic mothers, Greek mothers, Jew mothers. We got the mothers of Company C, One Hundred Sixty-eighth Infantry. We got to take care of them. How about Jimmy Clancy? He was Catholic. He got killed in the Lorraine sector. Hyman Levinsky, he got killed the same day. Mr. Speaker, you don't know him because you do not come from Mahaska Falls. We had Buzz Griffin, colored boy used to shine shoes. He go to Chicago and enlist, and he is wounded in the Ninety-second Division!"

It was asking too much for any public speaker to contend against opposition of that sort; and the crowd thought so, too, and Duboko made a joyful noise. The out-of-town organizers withdrew. Fiery crosses blazed less frequently, and the flash of white robes frightened fewer cattle week by week.

Seeds had been sown, however, and now a kind of poison ivy grew within our midnight. Bill Barbilis and Duboko came up to my office one morning, the latter looking annoyed, the former holding a soiled sheet of paper in his hand. "Look what I got, doc."

The message was printed crudely in red ink:

We don't want you here any more. This town is only for 100 per cent law-abiding white Americans. Get out of town! Anti-Greek League.

It had been shoved under the front door of the Sugar Bowl sometime during the previous night.

"Bill," I told him, "don't worry about it. You know the source, probably; at least you can guess."

"Nobody is going to run me out of town," said Bill. "This is my town, and I am American citizen, and I am bugler in American Legion. I bring my old father here from Greece to be American, too, and now he has first papers." His voice trembled slightly.

"Here. Throw it in the wastepaper basket and forget about it."

There was sweat on his forehead. He wiped his face, and then he was able to laugh. "Doc, I guess you are right. Doc, I guess I am a fool."

He threw the paper away and squared his shoulders and went downstairs. I rescued a rubber glove from Duboko and threw Duboko into the hall, where he licked disinfectant from his jaws and leered at me through the screen.

A second threatening letter was shoved under Bill's door, but after that old Mr. Spiros Barbilis and Duboko did sentry duty, and pedestrians could see them entrenched behind the window. So the third warning came by mail; it told Bill that he was being given twenty-four hours to get out of town for good.

I was a little perturbed when I found Bill loading an Army .45 behind his soda fountain.

"They come around here," he said, "and I blow hell out of them."

He laughed when he said it, but I didn't like the brightness of his eyes, nor the steady, thrice-assured activity of his big clean fingers.

On Friday morning Bill came up to my office again; his face was distressed. But my fears, so far as the Anti-Greeks were concerned, were groundless.

"Do you die," he asked, "when you catch a crisis of pneumonia?"

It was one of his numerous cousins, in Sioux Falls. There had been a long-distance telephone call; the cousin was very ill, and the family wanted Bill to come. Bill left promptly in his battered, rakish roadster.

Late that night I was awakened by a clatter of cream cans under my window. I glanced at the illuminated dial of my watch, and lay wondering why the milkman had appeared some two hours before his habit. I was about to drop off to sleep when sounds of a scuffle in the alley and a roar from Duboko in the Barbilis quarters took me to the window in one leap.

There were four white figures down there in the alley yard; they dragged a fifth man—nightshirted, gagged, struggling—along with them. I yelled, and pawed around for my glasses, spurred to action by the reverberating hysterics of Duboko. I got the glasses on just before those men dragged old Mr. Barbilis into their car. The car's license plates were plastered thick with mud; at once I knew what had happened.

It was customary for the milkman to clank his bottles and cans on approaching the rear door of the Sugar Bowl; Bill or his father would get out of bed and fetch the milk to the refrigerator, for there were numerous cream-hungry cats along that alley. It was a clinking summons of this sort which had lured the lonely Mr. Barbilis from his bed.

He had gone out sleepily, probably wondering, as I had wondered, why the milkman had come so early. The sound of milk bottles lulled Duboko for a moment.

Then the muffled agony of that struggle, when the visitors clapped a pillow over the old man's face, had been enough to set Duboko bellowing.

But he was shut in; all that he could do was to threaten and curse and hurl himself against the screen. I grabbed for my foot—not the one that God gave me, but the one bought by Uncle Sam—and of course I kicked it under the bed far out of reach.

My car was parked at the opposite end of the building, out in front. I paused only to tear the telephone receiver from its hook and cry to a surprised Central that she must turn on the red light which summoned the night watchman; that someone was kidnaping old Mr. Barbilis.

The kidnapers' car roared eastward down the alley while I was bawling to the operator. And then another sound—the wrench of a heavy body sundering the metal screening. There was only empty silence as I stumbled down the stairway in my pajamas, bouncing on one foot and holding to the stair rails.

I fell into my car and turned on the headlights. The eastern block before me stretched deserted in the pale glow of single bulbs on each electric-light post. But as my car rushed into that deserted block, a small brown shape sped bulletlike across the next intersection. It was Duboko.

I swung right at the corner, and Duboko was not far ahead of me now. Down the dark, empty tunnel of Clive Street the red taillight of another car diminished rapidly. It hitched away to the left; that would mean that Mr. Barbilis was being carried along the road that crossed the city dump.

Slowing down, I howled at Duboko when I came abreast of him. It seemed that he was a Barbilis, an Americanized Greek, like them, and that he must be outraged at this occurrence, and eager to effect a rescue.

But he only slobbered up at me, and labored along on his four driving legs, with spume flying behind. I stepped on the gas again and almost struck the dog, for he would not turn out of the road. I skidded through heavy dust on the dump lane, with filmier dust still billowing back from the kidnapers' car.

For their purpose, the selection of the dump had a strategic excuse as well as a symbolic one. At the nearest boundary of the area there was a big steel gate and barbed-wire fence; you had to get out and open that gate to go through. But if you wished to vanish into the region of river timber and country roads beyond, you could drive across the wasteland without opening the gate again. I suppose that the kidnapers guessed who their pursuer was; they knew of my physical incapacity. They had shut the gate carefully behind them, and I could not go through it without getting out of my car.

But I could see them in the glare of my headlight—four white figures, sheeted and hooded.

Already they had tied Spiros Barbilis to the middle of a fence panel. They had straps, and a whip, and everything else they needed. One man was tying the feet of old Spiros to restrain his kicks; two stood ready to proceed with the flogging; and the fourth blank, hideous, white-hooded creature moved toward the gate to restrain me from interfering. That was the situation when Duboko arrived.

I ponder now the various wickednesses Duboko committed throughout his notorious career. Then for comfort I turn to the words of a Greek— him who preached the most famous funeral oration chanted among the ancients—the words of a man who was Greek in his blood and his pride, and yet who might have honored Duboko eagerly when the dog came seeking, as it were, a kind of sentimental Attican naturalization.

"For even when life's previous record showed faults and failures," said Pericles, with the voice of Thucydides, to the citizens of the fifth century, "it is just to weigh the last brave hour of devotion against them all."

Though it was not an hour by any means. No more than ten minutes had elapsed since old Mr. Barbilis was dragged from his back yard. The militant action of Duboko, now beginning, did not occupy more than a few minutes more, at the most. It makes me wonder how long men fought at Marathon, since Pheidippides died before he could tell.

And not even a heavy screen might long contain Duboko; it is no wonder that a barbed-wire fence was as reeds before his charge.

He struck the first white figure somewhere above the knees. There was a snarl and a shriek, and then Duboko was springing toward the next man.

I didn't see what happened then. I was getting out of the car and hopping toward the gate. My bare foot came down on broken glass, and that halted me for a moment. The noise of the encounter, too, seemed to build an actual, visible barrier before my eyes.

Our little world was one turmoil of flapping, torn white robes—a whirling insanity of sheets and flesh and outcry, with Duboko revolving at the hub. One of the men dodged out of the melee, and stumbled back, brandishing a club which he had snatched from the rubble close at hand.

I threw a bottle, and I like to think that that discouraged him; I remember how he pranced and swore.

Mr. Barbilis managed to get the swathing off his head and the gag out of his mouth. His frail voice sang minor encouragement, and he struggled to unfasten his strapped hands from the fence.

The conflict was moving now—moving toward the kidnapers' car. First one man staggered away, fleeing; then another who limped badly. It was an unequal struggle at best. No four members of the Anti-Greek League, however young and brawny, could justly be matched against a four-footed warrior who used his jaws as the original Lacedaemonians must have used their daggers, and who fought with the right on his side, which Lacedaemonians did not always do.

Four of the combatants were scrambling into their car; the fifth was still afoot and reluctant to abandon the contest. By that time I had been able to get through the gate, and both Mr. Barbilis and I pleaded with Duboko to give up a war he had won. But this he would not do; he challenged still, and tried to fight the car; and so, as they drove away, they ran him down.

It was ten A.M. before Bill Barbilis returned from Sioux Falls. I had ample opportunity to impound Bill's .45 automatic before he came.

His father broke the news to him. I found Bill sobbing with his head on the fountain. I tried to soothe him, in English, and so did Spiros Barbilis, in Greek; but the trouble was that Duboko could no longer speak his own brand of language from the little bier where he rested.

Then Bill went wild, hunting for his pistol and not being able to find it; all the time, his father eagerly and shrilly informed Bill of the identifications he had made when his assailants' gowns were ripped away. Of course, too, there was the evidence of bites and abrasions.

Earl Klugge was limping as he moved about his All-American Kandy Kitchen, and John Klugge smelled of arnica and iodine. A day or two passed before the identity of the other kidnapers leaked out. They were hangers-on at the All-American; they didn't hang on there any longer.

I should have enjoyed seeing what took place, down there at the Clive Street corner. I was only halfway down the block when Bill threw Earl and John Klugge through their own plateglass window.

A little crowd of men gathered, with our Mayor Wingate among them. There was no talk of damages or of punitive measures to be meted out to Bill Barbilis. I don't know just what train the Klugge brothers left on. But their restaurant was locked by noon, and the windows boarded up.

A military funeral and interment took place that afternoon behind the Sugar Bowl. There was no flag, though I think Bill would have liked to display one. But the crowd of mourners would have done credit to Athens in the age when her dead heroes were burned; all the time that Bill was blowing Taps on his bugle, I had a queer feeling that the ghosts of Pericles and Thucydides were somewhere around.

## Suggestions for Study

1. What was the specific purpose of the author of this story—to arouse interest in dumb animals, to show the difficulties of returned soldiers in establishing themselves in business, to denounce intolerance, or to portray an interesting animal character?

2. Who are the protagonist and the antagonist in the story?

3. Does the story gain or lose in interest by being told by the doctor? Do you think it would have been better if told directly by the author, using the omniscient point of view? Does the method chosen handicap the author in any way? If so, in what way?

4. Is the plot overdrawn at any point? Be ready to defend your answer.

5. Do any of the characters come to life, or are they merely types to carry the plot? Which characters seem to you best realized as living, animate beings?

6. Is there anything symbolical in having Duboko a mongrel?

7. Is the denouement esthetically satisfactory? Would it have been a more satisfactory ending to have Duboko drive off the kidnapers and thereafter become the town hero?

8. When you have finished the story, what do you know about the narrator? Can you think of a good plot for a story in which he is the protagonist?

9. Are there any elements of this story which are still timely after the second World War?

10. What is the point of making Mahaska Falls the setting of the story? Would any small town in the United States do as well? (In this connection, if you do not know the story, go to the library and read O. Henry's "A Municipal Report.")

## Suggestions for Writing

1. A good way to gain practice by one who has never written a short story is to rewrite one, using a different point of view from that of the original,—for instance, "The Color of Mama Josefina's Life" by Celia, "You Could Look It Up" by the midget, and so on.

2. Write a realistic story of a high-school girl or boy who is determined to go to college, and whose antagonist is poverty and environment, or whose antagonist is ignorant relatives.

3. Write a story in which through dialogue and incident you depict the character of a certain community or section. Develop a plot, but let this be secondary to your aim of characterization.

4. Write a story in which some crisis brings out some theretofore unsuspected trait in the character of the protagonist. (You need not follow "The Coward" in finding a bad trait; how some shy lad becomes a hero is one possibility, how a colorless girl becomes the belle of the J-Hop is another.)

5. Write a story in which conflict with objective forces drives the protagonist to his utmost endurance in order to win.

6. By means of dialogue alone, develop a story of conflict between persons of divergent character, and bring the story to a conclusion which is esthetically satisfactory.

7. Make an informal outline of three plots which you think might make good short stories and submit these to your instructor for comment and counsel.

# III
# BLENDING THE FOUR FORMS OF WRITING

## A. The Research Paper

THIS section deals with a kind of writing which can be of great value to you while in college. Many instructors lay considerable emphasis on "term papers," and grade heavily on them as indexes of your ability to judge and to organize. They presume that having passed a freshman composition course, you know how to handle such assignments.

"Term paper," "investigative theme," "source paper," and "research paper" are all names for the same thing: a paper of some length, mainly expository, which involves the organizing of material according to the methods used by experienced scholars. These methods pertain to analyzing the topic, finding sources of information, gathering the material, and writing a report which shows clearly the authenticity of the information and the extent of the research done. A glance at professional journals in the library or on the desks of such people as physicians, lawyers, teachers, and engineers, will show that the research paper is not merely a contrivance to plague undergraduates. It is the standard method of communication in any field of activity where the organizing of accurate information is important.

The research paper is considerably different from the ordinary written assignment. It is longer. More time is put into its preparation. It contains such items as footnotes and a bibliography. It involves extensive library work. Finally, it is not original, in the sense of being drawn from the writer's imagination or casual observation. But although originality in one sense has no place in the research paper, in a different sense it is just as important as in any other writing. What you do with the material is essentially original. Most of the time you will be using information unearthed by a number of other people; but inasmuch as you are reorganizing this information, bringing together facts and opinions from various authorities on the basis of your own plan, there is room for a great deal of originality.

One more general consideration. The research paper need not be dry as dust, a dull mosaic of quotations. If you are interested in the topic which you have chosen, there is no reason why you should not write as entertainingly as in any other assignment.

**Choosing a Topic.** If the instructor does not assign a topic for the research paper, you face the problem of choosing one for yourself. In doing so, remember that much of the success of the paper will depend on the care and thought which is given to this initial task. If the choice is good, the paper may almost seem to write itself, but a bad topic can plunge you into hopeless confusion. Here are some of the questions which should be asked concerning a topic.

1. *Is it interesting?* Even the dullest student can find so many things that are interesting that it is foolish to labor with something which does not intrigue him in the least. By leaving the choice of topic until the last minute and then picking one aimlessly, you are setting up more hurdles than the rules require. Do you have a hobby? Do you have an occupational interest? Has some character or happening in history ever aroused your curiosity? Are you curious about the roots of some present national problem? Would you like to know more about some of the discoveries of science? Make a list of six or eight general fields of information which you already know something about or would like to investigate. Then proceed to ask the next question about each of them.

2. *Is it too big?* Many students, to their sorrow, fail to ask this question. Looking over the list of things which you find interesting, you will probably discover that it represents general topics rather than specific. For example, suppose you once read Kingsley's novel *Westward Ho!* and found the description of Elizabethan naval battles thrilling. Later, while rummaging for interesting topics, you remembered this experience and wrote down, "The Spanish Armada." Now, this is a good start, but it is no more than that. What about the Spanish Armada? Just where are you going to begin, and how much ground can you reasonably expect to cover? Try splitting the general topic into smaller ones and then whittling them to finer points.

One of the divisions of this subject might be "Why the Spanish Armada Was Built." But, upon analyzing the topic still further, you might conclude that as there were so many reasons for the Spanish king's building his huge fleet, it would be wise to bring the topic to a still finer point.

Then you decide on "Economic Reasons for the Building of the Spanish Armada," or "Religious Reasons," or "Diplomatic Reasons."

Probably the ability to see clearly the difficulties involved in a topic comes with experience. But surely it is apparent that no one can write, within the limits of two or three thousand words, a discussion of "The Automobile Industry" which says much that the ordinary person does not know already. If you have "The Automobile Industry" on a list of interesting topics, see if you can conveniently handle some aspect of it. Perhaps "The Development of the Gasoline Engine" occurs to you. Better yet would be "The V-8 Engine."

A good topic is worded in such a way that it provides an exact description of the subject of the paper. "The United Nations" and "Chinese Art" are the vaguest of labels, providing almost nothing to guide either the reader or the writer of a paper. But "The Early Development of the United Nations" and "The Use of Nature Subjects in Chinese Art" are much better. The reader knows what to expect, and the writer knows what he wants to accomplish. It is really *knowing what you want to do* and *limiting your ambitions to what it is possible for you to do* which will prevent your selecting a topic which is too large.

3. *Is it trivial?* Doubtless students find it harder to avoid topics which are too big than to escape the charge of triviality. Nevertheless, ask yourself whether or not you are assembling a body of information which matters particularly. It is said that doctoral dissertations have been written on the best methods of peeling potatoes, but most people would agree that such an exercise is a waste of time. Remember that while you are learning the technique of writing a research paper, you can also be adding to your stock of the kind of information which it will be more difficult to acquire after you are out of college.

4. *Is it within the range of your present ability?* Be ambitious, of course, to accomplish something bigger than you ever have before, but be discreet also. You will be thwarted if you launch into terminology and techniques which you are not prepared to understand. Given time, you might remedy the deficiency, but the few weeks allotted to the research paper in the composition course will be full enough without adding problems unnecessarily. Do not try to discuss Einstein's work without being well grounded in mathematical theory. Do not try to settle the tariff problem. Above all, do not depend on a large vocabulary of high-sounding words to cover up a lack of mastery of the topic. Experience has probably taught your instructor how to distinguish between the pose of knowing and real knowledge.

5. *If it is a controversial topic, are you prepared to treat it objectively?* The person who has strong convictions regarding his topic should be careful. A research paper is not like a debate speech, an oration, or an editorial. These types of communication often appeal to the emotions as well as present facts. The research paper, however, should be strictly scientific. The purpose of the writer is to discover and present the truth, using emotional coloring only to make the paper interesting, not to persuade the reader that a particular point of view is right. Do not choose a topic like "The Superiority of Christianity over Buddhism." Besides the topic's being much too big, the wording of it suggests that you have already made up your mind about it and that you are going to test both religions by a set of values which is acceptable only to the Christian. However, the student who is really capable of working without bias on a subject concerned with comparative religion might compare Christian and Buddhist ideas and practices with regard to two or three points. But he should be sure that he presents no more than objective facts; in other words, that he informs his reader rather than preaches to him.

6. *Is it possible to obtain the necessary material in your locality?* Some students seem to have the idea that all libraries of any size contain approximately the same books. Actually, libraries are as different as people. A normal college library, for instance, is likely to be best equipped with books, bulletins, and magazines dealing with education. A state technical college library will be admirably stocked with material on agriculture, engineering, and home economics, but may be deficient in books of philosophy, history, and literature. Even the libraries of large universities differ considerably because of donations of money for special purposes, and because of efforts by scholars on the faculty to collect books for their own use.

If you cannot gain access to the stacks (bookshelves) of the local library, consult the card catalogue and talk with one of the librarians concerning available material for a topic which you are considering. This preliminary survey should not take more than two or three hours, if proper use has been made of the library attendants. Of course, there are other ways of getting material. The Library of Congress, certain university libraries, federal and state bureaus, state technical schools, and even certain industries will lend books and send free bulletins. But do not depend too much on such methods of getting material because they are frequently slow and sometimes costly. If your local library cannot provide you with enough material, choosing another topic would be wise.

## Exercise in Choosing a Topic for a Research Paper

Consider each of the following topics carefully. If a topic is good, write "G" in the blank at the left. If it is bad, write the appropriate number, or numbers, corresponding to the questions in the preceding discussion.

_____ Horse Racing

_____ Alcohol, the Ruin of Modern Youth

_____ The Functions of the Thyroid and Endocrine Glands

_____ The Greatness of the Poet Shelley

_____ The Causes of Earthquakes

_____ Refrigeration

_____ How an Electric Refrigerator Works

_____ Boulder Dam

_____ How Books Are Bound

_____ Some Reasons for and against the Use of the Platoon System in City Schools

_____ How the Medieval Church Made Use of Drama

_____ How to Make a Bed

_____ Platonism in the Thought of the English Humanists

_____ Methods of Surfacing Country Roads

_____ The Use of Light Filters in Photography

_____ Some Great Books I Have Read

_____ Is Bernard Shaw's Characterization of Joan of Arc Historically Accurate?

_____ The Importance of Antarctica to Future Civilization

_____ The Extent of the Oil Industry in Michigan

_____ The Siege and Capture of Detroit during the War of 1812

_____ Can the Deaf-Mute Learn to Talk?

_____ How to Dig Bait

_____ The Heroic Game of Football

_____ The Status of Religion in Nazi Germany

**The Use of the Library.** *The card catalogue.* Only the student who enjoys very special privileges is admitted into certain parts of the college library. Probably the only rooms in which there are shelves of printed material to which you have personal access are the reference room and the periodical room. The efficient use of the resources of these rooms will be discussed a little later. We are concerned first with the great body of the library collection which, for practical reasons, is shelved in rooms where perhaps only the library staff and the faculty may enter. But although the student never has the opportunity to rummage through these shelves and discover at first hand what is there, the contents can be known to him by means of the card catalogue. This is contained in cases of small filing boxes and is

# BLENDING THE FOUR FORMS OF WRITING 703

usually found near the main desk of the library. Here, every book, bulletin, magazine,[1] or manuscript which the library possesses is indexed according to a system which anyone can understand. You will make so much use of the card catalogue while you are in college that you should familiarize yourself with it as early as possible.

If the library is adequately staffed and completely up to date, every item in it is represented by at least three cards in the catalogue. These cards are filed alphabetically according to author, title, and subject matter respectively. Thus, if you want E. K. Chambers's work on *The Medieval Stage,* you can find it by looking in the C's for the author's name, or in the M's for the title, or under a subject matter caption referring to the material in the book. If your topic is "Costuming in the Medieval Morality Play" and you have no idea who the chief authorities are on that subject, by looking under such captions as "stage," "medieval stage," "costume," you will probably discover cards for the book by E. K. Chambers. The use of the subject matter indexing will be of most value in the initial stages of finding what resources the library has to offer for your topic. A little ingenuity will have to be used in thinking of the probable catchword or phrase which the librarian has used to describe the information in which you are interested. If no caption "Spanish Armada" can be found, try "naval history," or "Spanish history."

Having discovered the general organization of the card catalogue, the student should achieve a clear understanding of what is on the cards themselves.

---

JK
146
.B368    Beard, Charles Austin, 1874—

       An economic interpretation of the Constitution of the United States, by Charles A. Beard . . . New York, The Macmillan Company, 1913.

       vii, 330 p. map. 22½ cm.

       1. U.S.—Constitutional History. 2. U.S.—Constitution. 3. U.S.—Economic Conditions. I. Title

       Library of Congress   JK146.B135     13–9314
       Copyright A 346373   [a35i²1]     342.73

---

At the top, in the left-hand corner, is the call number, the symbol which

1. Cards for magazines are often segregated in the catalogue under the caption "Periodicals."

indicates to the librarian where the book should be shelved.[2] On the first line is the author's name, last name first, and the dates of his birth and (if it has occurred) death. Next comes a transcription of the title page of the book, followed by the facts of publication (place, publisher, and date). The symbols on the next line indicate that there are seven pages of prefatory material (small Roman numerals), followed by three hundred and thirty pages of text. A map is included, and the book is twenty-two and a half centimeters high. This is followed by a list of three subject-matter classifications which apply to this book. The rest of the material at the bottom of the card is chiefly for the use of librarians.

*General book indexes.* Although you have been advised to limit the topic to something which can be handled with local resources only, you should know that there are means of compiling a fairly complete list of all the best works in that field of inquiry. By comparing the resources of the college library with such a list, a student can determine to what extent the information available to him is adequate. This task will immediately introduce you to the Reference Room, the best place to find concise information on books, people, institutions, industries, occupations, and statistics.

Several hours' browsing in the comparatively unattractive-looking books lining the walls should impress you with the fact that a large part of a college education can be obtained there. Take down from the shelves and thumb through the following reference works, keeping in mind the question of how they will be of help in supplementing the card catalogue in preparing a complete list of books for your topic.

*A. L. A. (American Library Association) Index.* Second edition, 1900. Supplements bring it up to 1925.
*American Catalogue of Books,* 1876–1910.
*Book Review Digest,* 1905———.
*Catalogue of United States Public Documents,* 1893———.
*Cumulative Book Index.* Annual supplement to the *United States Catalog.*

2. Most libraries adopt one of two systems, the Library of Congress system or the Dewey Decimal system. The Library of Congress uses letters to denote twenty divisions of all knowledge: A—General works and Polygraphy; B—Philosophy and Religion; C—History and Auxiliary Sciences; D—History and Topography of foreign countries; E and F—American History and Topography; G—Geography and Anthropology; H—Social Sciences; J—Political Sciences; K—Law; L—Education; M—Music; N—Fine Arts; P—Languages and Literature; Q—Sciences; R—Medicine; S—Agriculture, and Plant and Animal Husbandry; T—Technology; U—Military Science; V—Naval Science; and Z—Bibliography and Library Science.

The Dewey Decimal system divides knowledge into ten groups and designates the groups by numbers: 000—General works; 100—Philosophy; 200—Religion; 300—Sociology; 400—Philology; 500—Natural Sciences; 600—Useful Arts; 700—Fine Arts; 800—Literature; and 900—History. These groups are further subdivided to provide smaller classifications within the larger divisions. Unless the student has access to the library stacks, there is little need for him to learn these systems.

*English Catalogue of Books,* 1801———.
*United States Catalog.* To 1912.

*Periodical indexes.* Indexes to material printed in magazines, in large bound volumes, are usually placed on tables or shelves in the Periodical Room. The oldest work of this sort is *Poole's Index to Periodical Literature,* which was started in 1802 and was continued for one hundred and five years. It is an index to subjects, not authors, except when authors are treated as subjects.

The best index of twentieth-century magazines is the *Reader's Guide to Periodical Literature,* which covers the period from 1900 to the present. It is issued monthly, and the most recent issues will be found still in their paper covers. Older numbers are bound in volumes. Since the *Reader's Guide* lists articles under author, title, and subject, with numerous cross references, it is more convenient than *Poole's Index.* If you are looking for material on the Munich Conference, the most direct method is to find out the date of the conference and then look under "Munich" in all subsequent issues of the *Reader's Guide.* A page near the front of each number will provide a key to the symbols used in the entries.

The indexes mentioned above do not as a rule cover articles appearing in technical journals of limited circulation. If there is a special index, such as the *Industrial Arts Index* or the *Agricultural Index,* for the subject in which you are interested, by all means use it as well as the *Reader's Guide.*

Again, if a topic has been chosen which deals with information currently called "news," such as military events, Congressional activities, sports, or political campaigns, you should make the acquaintance of the *New York Times Index.* This is a complete index to articles printed in one of the best American newspapers, the New York *Times.* The *Index* has been issued quarterly since 1913. A similar index has been issued by *The Times* of London since 1886.

*Dictionaries and encyclopedias.* Nearly everyone is familiar with the more obvious uses of dictionaries and encyclopedias, but it is surprising how many students are unable to make full use of these common reference works. The dictionary has already been discussed in the section on "The Word"; now it might be well to discover the uses of these miscellaneous specialized dictionaries:

*Allen's Synonyms and Antonyms,* 1938.
*Century Cyclopedia of Names,* 1889–1913.
*Crabb's English Synonyms,* 1917.
Henderson, I. F., and W. D. Henderson, *Dictionary of Scientific Terms,* 1929.

A number of dictionaries have the special purpose of explaining allu-sions and tracing the origins of quotations. Some of these follow:

Apperson, G. L. *English Proverbs and Proverbial Phrases*, 1929.
Bartlett, John. *Familiar Quotations*, 1937.
Bartlett, John. *New and Complete Concordance . . . of Shakespeare*, 1894.
Benham, W. G. *Book of Quotations, Proverbs, and Household Words*, 1929.
Brewer, E. C. *Dictionary of Phrase and Fable*, 1931.
Cruden, Alexander. *Complete Concordance of the Old and New Testament*,
    1930.
Smith, W. G. *Oxford Dictionary of English Proverbs*, 1935.
Stevenson, B. E. *Home Book of Quotations*, 1934.

Since the days of Plutarch, people have been interested in concise biog-raphies of famous men and women. Modern scholarship has provided us with numerous biographical dictionaries, of which a few are listed below:

*American Men of Science*, 1933.
*Dictionary of American Biography*, 1928–1936. 20 vols. (Sometimes called the
    *DAB*.)
*Dictionary of National Biography*, 1885–1901. 63 vols. 7 supplementary vol-
    umes to 1927. (Sometimes called the *DNB*.)
*National Cyclopedia of American Biography*, 1892–1935. 24 vols.
*Who's Who*, 1849——.
*Who's Who in America*, 1899——.
*Who's Who in American Education*, 1928–1940.
*Who's Who in Engineering*, 1925.

You have probably used an encyclopedia before, but have you been aware that at the ends of the more important articles are excellent bibliog-raphies, which can lead you to the standard sources actually used by the people who wrote the articles? Have you made use of the index volume and the cross-references which suggest other articles in the encyclopedia itself that have a bearing on the topic you are looking up? These are aids which many students overlook. The following encyclopedias are the most authoritative:

*Encyclopaedia Britannica*, 14th edition, 1929.
*Encyclopedia Americana*, 2nd edition, 1940.
*Americana Annual*, 1922——. Annual supplement to the *Encyclopedia Amer-
    icana*.
*New International Encyclopedia*, 1922–1930.
*New International Year Book*, 1908——. Annual supplement to the *New
    International Encyclopedia*.

*Reference works in certain special subjects.* By the time you have sur-veyed the reference sources already listed, it may appear that all human knowledge has been so carefully and accurately recorded that there is nothing more to be done. This is a natural reaction, but do not allow it to destroy the critical attitude toward the books you use. As you use reference works, especially those which are listed on the next pages, ask these questions:

1. How reliable is the factual information in the book? Until you are able to judge of this from your own knowledge, it will be necessary to rely on the authority of the author. What can you find out about him? The title page of the book will perhaps tell what positions he has held and what his university degrees are; and by consulting biographical dictionaries and one of the *Who's Who* books, you can find other information about him, such as what other books he has written and what learned societies he belongs to. Be especially critical of statistical information when the source is not stated exactly.

2. How recent is the book? The copyright statement on the reverse of the title page will give the date of publication. If the book has been re-edited, are you sure that you are using the latest edition? Distinguish between an edition and a reprint. When an author re-edits his book, he goes over the former edition carefully, making corrections and perhaps adding new material. The new edition must be set up in fresh type. A reprint is simply a running off of more copies of the book from the old type. The new copies will be exactly like those of the first printing.

3. Does the book contain bibliographies which will lead to other sources of material? Always be on the lookout for such aids to your research. Eventually you should be aware even of footnotes for adding to your list of sources for your topic.

4. Does the book contain a good index, if the articles in it are not arranged alphabetically? If the articles are arranged alphabetically, are there adequate cross-references? If, for example, you are looking up the execution of Charles I of England, does the article on Charles I refer you to the article on the English Revolution?

5. What is the scope of the book? Is the book too general in its purpose to provide detailed information? An article on silos in an agricultural encyclopedia, for instance, should be more detailed and specific than the similar article in the *Britannica*.

## AGRICULTURE

Bailey, L. H. *Cyclopedia of American Agriculture*, 1907–1911.
U. S. Department of Agriculture. *Year Book of Agriculture*, 1894——.

## ARCHITECTURE

Fletcher, Sir Banister. *History of Architecture on the Comparative Method*, 1931.

Rathbun, S. H. *A Background to Architecture,* 1926.
Sturgis, Russell. *History of Architecture,* 1906–1915.

## ART

*American Annual of Photography,* 1887——.
*Art Index,* 1930——.
Bryan, Michael. *Bryan's Dictionary of Painters and Engravers,* 1905.
Carotti, G. *History of Art,* 1923.
Fielding, Mantle. *Dictionary of American Painters, Sculptors, and Engravers,* 1926.
Hiler, H., and M. Hiler. *Bibliography of Costume,* 1939.
Jervis, William P. *Encyclopedia of Ceramics,* 1902.
Johnson, A. P., and M. K. Sironen. *Manual of Furniture Arts and Crafts,* 1928.

## CHEMISTRY

American Chemical Society. *Chemical Abstracts,* 1907——.
Bolton, H. C. *Select Bibliography of Chemistry,* 1893–1904.
Thorpe, Sir Thomas. *A Dictionary of Applied Chemistry,* 1922–1927. Supplement, 1934–1936.

## CLASSICS

Peck, H. T. (ed.) *Harper's Dictionary of Classical Literature and Antiquities,* 1897.
Sandys, Sir John. *A Companion to Latin Studies,* 1925.
Smith, Sir William. *Classical Dictionary of Greek and Roman Biography,* 2 vols., 1890.
Whibley, Leonard. *A Companion to Greek Studies,* 1931.

## COMMERCE, ECONOMICS, STATISTICS, ETC.

Chisholm, G. C. *Handbook of Commercial Geography,* 1932.
Clark, V. S. *History of Manufactures in the United States,* 1929.
*Encyclopedia of the Social Sciences,* 1930–1935.
Schuyler, W. M. *The American Year Book,* 1916——.
*The Chicago Daily News Almanac and Yearbook,* 1901——.
United States Bureau of the Census. *Census,* 1790——.
United States Department of Commerce. *Commerce Yearbook,* 1922——.
United States Department of Commerce. *Statistical Abstract,* 1878——.
Whitaker, Joseph. *Almanack,* 1902——.
*World Almanac,* 1868——.

## CUSTOMS, FOLKLORE, AND HOLIDAYS

Brand, John. *Observations on the Popular Antiquities of Great Britain,* 1888–1890.
Chambers, Robert. *The Book of Days,* 1914.
Frazer, Sir James. *The Golden Bough,* 1925–1935.
Schauffler, R. H. *Our American Holidays,* 1907–1933.

## EDUCATION

*Education Index,* 1929———.
Marsh, C. S. *American Universities and Colleges,* 1940.
Monroe, Paul (ed.). *Cyclopedia of Education,* 1911–1913.

## GEOLOGY

*Bibliography of North American Geology,* 1931–1934.
United States Geological Survey. *Geological Atlas of the United States,* 1894.

## HISTORY

Adams, J. T. (ed.) *Dictionary of American History,* 1940.
*Cambridge Ancient History,* 1923–1939.
*Cambridge Medieval History,* 1911–1936.
*Cambridge Modern History,* 1934.
Dutcher, G. M. (ed.) *Guide to Historical Literature,* 1937.
Larned, J. N. *The New Larned History for Ready Reference,* 1922–1924.
*Pageant of America; a pictorial history of the United States,* 1925–1929.
Shepherd, W. R. *Historical Atlas,* 1929.
*Writings on American History,* 1904–1933.

## LITERATURE

*A. L. A. Booklist,* a guide to the best new books, 1905———.
*Cambridge History of American Literature,* 1931.
*Cambridge Bibliography of English Literature,* 1941.
*Cambridge History of English Literature,* 1933.
Firkins, Ina. *Index to Plays, 1800–1926.* Supplement, 1927–1934. 1935.
Firkins, Ina. *Index to Short Stories,* 1923. Supplements, 1929 and 1936.
Logasha, Hannah, and Winifred Ver Nooy. *An Index to One-Act Plays,* 1924–1932.
Manly, J. M., and Edith Rickert. *Contemporary American Literature.* Revised by Fred B. Millett, 1929.
Manly, J. M., and Edith Rickert. *Contemporary British Literature.* Revised by Fred B. Millett, 1935.
Modern Humanities Research Association. *Annual Bibliography of English Language and Literature,* 1920———.
Sharp, R. F. *Biographical Dictionary of Foreign Literature,* 1935.
Taylor, W. F. *A History of American Letters,* 1936.
*Who's Who among Living Authors of Older Nations,* 1928———.
*Who's Who among North American Authors,* 1921———.

## MEDICINE

*Quarterly Index Medicus,* 1927———.
Stedman, T. L. *Practical Medical Dictionary,* 1934.

## MUSIC

Grove, Sir George. *Grove's Dictionary of Music and Musicians,* 1928.
Kobbé, Gustav. *The Complete Opera Book,* 1935.

*The Oxford History of Music,* 1929–1934.
Thompson, O. (ed.) *The International Cyclopedia of Music and Musicians,* 1939.

## MYTHOLOGY

Bulfinch, Thomas. *The Age of Fable,* 1898.
Gayley, C. M. *The Classic Myths in English Literature and in Art,* 1911.
Gray, L. H. (ed.) *Mythology of All Races,* 1916–1932.

## PHILOSOPHY AND PSYCHOLOGY

Baldwin, J. M. *Dictionary of Philosophy and Psychology,* 1928.
*Psychological Abstracts,* 1927——.
*Psychological Index,* 1894——.
Rand, Benjamin. *Bibliography of Philosophy, Psychology, and Cognate Subjects,* 1905.
Rogers, A. K. *A Student's History of Philosophy,* 1932.
Townsend, H. G. *Philosophical Ideas in the United States,* 1934.

## PHYSICS

Glazebrook, Sir Richard (ed.). *A Dictionary of Applied Physics,* 1922–1935.

## RELIGION

*Catholic Encyclopedia,* 1907–1922.
Hastings, James (ed.). *Encyclopedia of Religion and Ethics,* 1911–1927.
*Jewish Encyclopedia,* 1901–1906.
Schaff, Phillip. *The New Schaff-Herzog Encyclopedia of Religious Knowledge,* 1908–1912.

## SOCIOLOGY

*A Bibliography of Social Surveys,* 1930.
*Encyclopedia of the Social Sciences,* 1930–1935.
*Social Science Abstracts,* 1929——.
*Social Work Year Book,* 1929——.

### Exercise in the Use of the Library

Find the answers to the following questions. Note also the reference works in which the answers were found.

1. How many persons were employed on farms in the United States on July 1, 1939?
2. Name three books on Shakespeare which appeared during 1939.
3. What is the cost of board and room for a year at the Connecticut College for Women?
4. How many portraits is Gilbert Stuart supposed to have painted?
5. What is the American Council on Education?
6. List five works on eighteenth-century European costume.
7. Approximately how many people who published poetry resided in Kansas in 1939?

8. What change in the minimum wage of employees engaged in interstate commerce took place October 24, 1939?
9. Who is the author of the following:

> "The World's as ugly, ay, as sin,—
> And almost as delightful."

10. What is the source of "A lover without indiscretion is no lover at all"?
11. How many motorcars were registered in the United States in 1939?
12. Why was Tom Paine nearly guillotined?
13. What was the origin of Santa Claus as the symbol of Christmas?
14. Did Van Wyck Brooks's *The Flowering of New England* receive generally favorable or unfavorable criticism when it was published?
15. Who was "Boss" Tweed?
16. What, so far as is known, was the first use in America of the word "schooner"?
17. Who was the United States Ambassador to Japan in 1938?
18. Who won the Big Ten championship in football in 1925?
19. What is the address of Herbert Hoover?
20. What was the name of Mrs. Franklin D. Roosevelt before she was married?
21. Why and how do the English celebrate the 5th of November?
22. What meanings has the word "apology" had in the history of the English language?
23. What is the "dying god" idea in folklore and religion?
24. Where was Winston Churchill, former Prime Minister of England, educated?

**Forms for Bibliography Cards.** A bibliography is a list of books, articles, and other sources of information compiled for purposes of investigating a topic. The work which has been done in the library should have acquainted you with the value of ready lists of source material. A periodical index alone saves a scholar months of labor. You will, however, need to compile your own bibliography for your research topic. Of course, you will make all the use you can of bibliographies in reference works, but probably no bibliography in a single reference work will be adequate for your purposes.

The preliminary bibliography which should be made before anything in particular is done in the way of taking notes constitutes a list of *all* sources of material which can be found bearing on the subject. It may be that when they are examined more closely, only a few of them will be useful. Some sources may turn out to be too general or too trivial, others may be too technical, and still others may overlap. However, there is no dependable way to know which are good and which are bad sources at the outset. Therefore, after you have settled, with the aid of your instructor, upon the topic for the paper, your first task will be to make a preliminary bibliography of everything which seems likely to contain useful material. Start with the card catalogue and then carefully exhaust the reference books and periodical indexes, trying to find, first of all, whole books on your topic, and afterwards listing the smaller items. Take down not only the titles of sources which you know are in the college library, but the titles of all sources which can be found. By so doing, you may discover that your library is inadequately supplied with material on your subject; if so, notify your instructor, who may advise you to change your topic.

The form which you will be required to use for recording your sources may seem to be very arbitrary, but without doubt you will soon discover valuable things about it. In the first place, get a supply of cards or pads of paper measuring three by five or four by six inches. Cards are more durable, but also bulkier than paper. The four by six size is preferable because it provides enough space for a good deal of writing without crowding, and since you will use cards for note-taking as well as bibliography, this is an important item to consider.

Put *only one* bibliographical item on a card. As bibliography cards accumulate, keep them filed alphabetically by author (or, if no author is given, by the first important word of the title). This method is infinitely preferable to the method of the ordinary careless or untrained student, who copies down all his titles on a sheet of paper, which ultimately becomes an illegible, scrawled mess as he makes notations concerning call numbers, location, and value. Bibliography cards neatly filed in a cardboard box or a heavy paper carrier which can be bought at a drug store provide ready access to any item. Changes can be made, cards can be thrown out, the notations can be jotted down without spoiling the appearance of the entire lot.

The entry on the bibliography card should be made carefully, because, when your paper is finished, you will copy the useful items from the preliminary bibliography cards on sheets of paper to be attached to the manuscript. You should not have to waste time searching again for the books and articles which have been used in order to get correct data. A good bibliography entry should contain enough information to identify that book or that article from all other books and articles. Take down the information in the following order:

1. Author's name, last name first.
2. Title of book, underlined; or title of article, in quotation marks. (Underlining in a manuscript or typescript is the equivalent of italicizing in print.) Be sure to copy the whole title accurately, including spelling and punctuation.

3. For a book: edition, if other than the first; place of publication; publisher; date of publication (if not given on the title page, see the last copyright date); number of volumes, if more than one.

For an article: title of periodical, encyclopedia, etc. in which the article appears, underlined; volume number, in Roman numerals; date of issue of the periodical, in parentheses; page numbers, in Arabic figures.

By following this form carefully with every entry, you will save time in the long run, although it may seem that so much attention to method slows you down temporarily. Uniformity of procedure always pays for itself in the end. Notice that the title of any item which is published separately (a book, magazine, encyclopedia, newspaper) is underlined; the title of an item which is published as a part of something larger (a chapter in a book, an essay in a collection, a poem in an anthology, an article in a magazine) is put in quotation marks. Also, volume numbers are differentiated from page numbers by the use of Roman numerals for the former and Arabic figures for the latter. When both volume and page appear in an entry, and there is no possibility of misunderstanding, the abbreviations *vol.* and *p.* or *pp.* may be omitted. Thus, XIV, 396 means volume fourteen, page three hundred and ninety-six.[3]

A bibliography card for Carl Van Doren's *Benjamin Franklin* would look like this:

Van Doren, Carl
*Benjamin Franklin*
New York: The Viking Press, 1938

Although the bibliography card should not be used for taking notes, there is no reason why you should not put on it certain memoranda for future use. The library call number in the upper left-hand corner will save future trips to the card catalogue. A notation to the effect that the book contains several excellent pictures of Franklin might be useful. If the activities of Franklin in the Constitutional Convention constitute an important part of the information necessary for the paper, you might state at the bottom of the card that material on that subject occurs on pages 742-756. Certainly it would be useful to indicate that the book contains an excellent bibliography.

The bibliography card shown above is very simple. Books that have been re-edited, translated, or otherwise prepared for the reader require more data. Also, the title page of Mr. Van Doren's book is brief compared with others. The following sample forms should provide models for nearly all the entries which you will have to make.

3. For other common abbreviations see the list on pages 727-8.

Entry for a book which is, in the main, a collection of material selected and edited, rather than written, by the persons whose names appear on the title page:

> Sanders, Gerald DeWitt, and John Herbert Nelson (eds.)
> *Chief Modern Poets of England and America*
> New York: The Macmillan Company, 1929

Entry for a book by two authors:

> Beard, Charles Austin, and Mrs. Mary Beard
> *The Rise of American Civilization*
> New York: The Macmillan Company, 1927

Entry for a book by more than three authors:

> Sizer, Theodore and others
> *Aspects of the Social History of America*
> Chapel Hill: The University of North Carolina Press, 1931.

Entry for a book which has been revised:

> Hanford, James Holly
> *A Milton Handbook*
> Revised edition
> New York: F. S. Crofts & Co., 1933

Entry for a work of more than one volume:

> Calvin, John
> *The Institutes of the Christian Religion*
> Tr. by Henry Beveridge
> Edinburgh: T. & T. Clark, 1895
> 2 vols.

Entry for a book which is part of a series:

> Chesterton, G. K.
> *Robert Browning*
> New York: The Macmillan Company, 1926
> ("English Men of Letters")

Entry for a University Bulletin:

> *The Articulation of High-School Studies with Freshman Courses in the University*
> A Series of Reports by the University Committees and Representatives of the Michigan High Schools. University of Michigan Official Publication, Vol. XXXVII, No. 42
> Ann Arbor, Michigan, 1936

Entry for an item in a collection of readings:

> Dunne, Finley Peter
> "On the Victorian Era" in Walter Blair, *Native American Humor*
> (*1800–1900*)
> New York: American Book Company, 1937

Entry for an article in an encyclopedia: [4]

> Pfeil, Stephen
> "Jurisprudence"
> *The Encyclopedia Americana.* 1940 Edition
> Vol. 16.

Entry for a magazine article:

> Lane, James
> "The Craze for Craziness"
> *Catholic World,* CXLIV (December, 1936), 306–9

**Note-taking and the Use of Sources.** By this time the point should be clear that the research paper is based upon wide reading in a number of different sources. The paper which is based altogether on one or two sources of information may be a good summary of the material contained therein, but it by no means qualifies as a research paper. To do so, it must weigh, evaluate, sift, and arrange facts and opinions from as many authorities as possible, taking into account time limits and inexperience. Probably the average number of sources used in good student research papers is somewhere between six and sixteen.

Since you will be using information from as many places as this, it will not be possible to write the paper while you are doing your reading. You must do your reading, take careful notes, and then write the paper from the notes. It is evident, therefore, that a good system of note-taking is indispensable. Notes which are illegible, fragmentary, or inaccurate are a waste of time, and if you take such notes you will pay heavily for your carelessness when the time comes to write the paper. If, when you are writing your paper, you find it necessary to scurry repeatedly to the library to take another look at your sources, your note-taking has been bad; but if you find that you need not examine any source a second time, your notes are good. It should hardly be necessary to say that recopying notes on a typewriter or in longhand is a waste of time. Do the job carefully the first time.

Before doing much reading, make a tentative outline of the classifica-

---

4. Name of publisher and place are generally omitted for the best-known encyclopedias. Edition and date are important, however.

tions into which you think your material should fall. This is not a formal outline; it is simply a temporary guide, and only a few divisions are necessary. Suppose your topic is "The Rise and Spread of Theatrical Activities in the United States before 1800." A little thinking about the topic will reveal several possible organizations, of which the following might be one:

1. Earliest beginnings
2. Spread of theatrical activity
3. Prominent people
4. Kinds of plays

This little outline may or may not approximate the main divisions in the final outline which will be attached to your paper, but it will suffice for the present.

For this topic, let us suppose that you have compiled a preliminary bibliography composed of twenty or twenty-five sources of information. Which should be read first? You will do well to select one of the more general works, since it will probably give a broad view of your subject, which is very desirable to help you to understand what you read later. Suppose you choose a recent history of American literature, P. H. Boynton's *Literature and American Life*. Looking up "theater" in the index, you are referred to pages 105–10. The first thing you read is a statement that a professional theater, like a professional orchestra and the opera, is likely to come late in the development of any society, because it is expensive and therefore dependent on the existence of large communities containing groups of prosperous people who have time and interest for these kinds of entertainment. This appears to be interesting and valuable background information. So you take a card, the same size as those used for the bibliography, and at the top, in the left-hand corner, write "Earliest beginnings," the caption in the tentative outline which best applies to this point. Then you write down the bit of information which you have just read.

The question immediately arises, should you take down the exact words of the author or summarize? Notes are taken *verbatim* when the material involved is important and is so exceptionally well stated that the inclusion of it, word for word, would be an asset to the paper; or when the point at issue is controversial and the exact statement of a recognized authority would carry weight; or when for some other reason the paper would be clearer and more authoritative because of a direct quotation. *Material quoted directly should always be put in quotation marks on the note card.*

This material from Boynton's book is fairly important, but it is rather obvious, and since no conceivable good can be derived from quoting it directly, you summarize it. Then, at the bottom of the card, you make a brief notation of the source. The card will look like this:

---

Early beginnings
Professional theater, like prof. orchestra and opera, comes late in development of any society. Is expensive; therefore dependent on large communities with prosperous people who have time and interest.
                    Boynton, *Lit. & Amer. Life,* 104

---

Notice that the source notation is as brief as it possibly can be and still be recognized.[5] It is positively necessary to cite a source for every note, including the page. *Leave nothing to your memory.* No matter how sure you may be that you will remember the source of some data, a page reference, or the name of an individual, write it down. It may be weeks before you make use of that information, and if your memory is like that of most people, it cannot be trusted for that length of time.

Reading on in Boynton, you find that, much to the indignation of some of the citizens of Boston, somebody suggested holding a dramatic entertainment in the Council Chamber in 1714. Using another card, you make the following entry:

---

Early beginnings                        1714
     Somebody suggested holding a dramatic entertainment in the Council Chamber of Boston in 1714. Some citizens indignant.
                    Boynton, *Lit. & Amer. Life,* 106

---

And so you continue through this book by Boynton and the other sources in the bibliography. *Only a single point from a single source is put on one card.* At the top of each card, in the left-hand corner, is an index caption corresponding to one of the topics in the preliminary outline. All cards having the same index caption are filed together, so that gradually you accumulate a box of notes carefully organized according to their contents.

Probably in certain sections of the notes you will find it useful to classify

5. If the bibliography contains only a few items, they can be numbered and the corresponding numbers placed on the note cards in place of the ordinary source notations. However, when a bibliography is of ordinary length, the numbering of sources is not advised.

the cards further in accordance with a subheading, which is placed in the upper right-hand corner. (See the second note from Boynton above.)

Do not be afraid of adding to the number of major index captions; only be sure that what you are adding is a major classification, rather than a subdivision of a classification which already exists. Thus, taking again the early American theater topic as an example, we find that the Revolutionary War played an important part in early American drama. In 1774 the Continental Congress closed all theaters, but a number of propaganda plays were written, and the war provided a patriotic *motif* for several plays written shortly afterward. However, the first of these points is logically a part of the "spread of activity" caption, and the second might well be included under "kinds of plays." Keeping your preliminary organization in good order will help enormously to keep the topic well defined in your mind.

In the same part of Boynton's history of American literature to which reference has been made, an interesting sidelight on colonial prejudice against the theater is given in the form of a quotation from Samuel Sewall. The Puritan judge, infuriated by the incident of 1714, wrote that, although the ancient Romans were fond of the theater, they were not "so far set upon them as to turn their Senate House into a playhouse. . . . Let not Christian Boston goe beyond heathen Rome in the practice of shameful vanities." This quotation from the old judge would certainly liven your discussion, and you should, by all means, have it in your notes. Try to get it from a source as near the original as possible, however. Never take a writer's word for something someone else said if you can get access to the original book or document. Some writers are careful with quotations; others are not. Professor Boynton says in a footnote that his source for the Sewall quotation is an article, "Letter-Book of Samuel Sewall," in the *Massachusetts Historical Society Collections,* sixth series, Vol. II, p. 30. If your library possesses this publication, look up the article in question and quote directly from it.[6] If you cannot get access to this article, then quote it through Boynton's book, stating in the source notation on your note card that Boynton (*Lit. & Amer. Life,* 106) quotes Samuel Sewall's statement as given in the article which we have just cited. Never, purposely, or otherwise, lead your reader to believe that you have read something which you haven't.

Perhaps, if you have been conscientious in making a bibliography and the list numbers fifteen or twenty items, some of them of considerable length, you have been frightened by the amount of careful reading which

---

6. Of course, even this is not the original source. The true original is Sewall's own manuscript, but only one copy of that is in existence, and you can hardly be expected to consult it.

will be necessary before you can start to write the paper. Your apprehension is a healthy sign, indicating that you are actually impressed by the importance of knowing the subject in sufficient detail; however, it is quite possible that the reading which has been mapped out will not be quite so arduous as at first appears.

The burden can be lightened in several ways. When you made out the preliminary bibliography, you listed *everything* you could find which seemed to have a bearing on the topic. Obviously, a brief examination of the sources listed will show that some of them are of no value. Perhaps a work is too old to be useful, or maybe it is a very general or trite treatment of material which is more adequately handled elsewhere. Having satisfied yourself that, for some reason or other, a work is not useful, discard it, making a notation on the bibliography card which corresponds to it that it is without value for such and such reasons.

Of those references which are of value, some will, of course, be of more value than others. Having taken detailed notes on the best sources, you can merely outline the others, being careful, however, to outline material on only one idea on a single note card; otherwise, your filing system will be disturbed. You will doubtless find much repetition of information among the sources. By exercising a little judgment, you can select the source which gives the information in the most useful manner and take good notes on it, omitting to take notes altogether on duplicated material or, if the point is an important one, indicating on a note card that this author agrees substantially with another on this point. Referring to the card on this material by the second author, in the same section of the note file, you can find the information in question. Understand that you are not being advised to read each of your sources of information on a single point before going on to another point. In general, read the source through and take the necessary notes on it before going on to another. But if you read what seem to be the most important and helpful sources first, the work with those of secondary importance can be simplified by the methods just mentioned.

Too much directly quoted material in a paper should be avoided, since it gives an appearance of laziness and unoriginality, but probably, in the process of note-taking, it would be better to quote too much than too little. Remember that it is of utmost importance that you copy the original exactly, even to the least comma, and enclose it in quotation marks. Even typographical errors, slips in spelling, and other mistakes should be copied as they stand, in which instance insert in brackets, after the word or statement in question, the term *sic* (Latin for "thus it is") to show that the author you are quoting, not you, made the mistake.

It is frequently helpful to be able to insert in a quotation some information of your own. This can be done without breaking the quotation marks around the whole by enclosing the inserted material in brackets. (Never use parentheses for this purpose.) "In the year [1374] Chaucer was provided with a house in London rent-free." Often, too, it is desirable to omit part of a quotation which is not pertinent to the point at issue. This can be done, without breaking the quotation marks, by indicating the omission by a series of three dots (exclusive of a period or other mark of punctuation if such appears immediately before the omission). "This act of Congress, which revoked previous legislation on this point, . . . was made a law in 1924." Of course, when you transfer quoted material from your notes to your paper, you must be scrupulously careful to copy it exactly as you have it.

**Evaluating Sources: Evidence.** Almost any topic chosen for a research paper will present, sooner or later, the problem of evaluating sources. Unless your paper is to be what has been called previously a "dull mosaic" of second-hand information, you must consider yourself at the apex of a pyramid of scholarship, choosing carefully and critically from the work which has preceded yours the truth about your subject. You are, if not the most competent, at least the most recent worker in your field of research, and your position is essentially that of any scholar who must make use of the observation of other people.[7]

In the first place, no author is so accurate as to deserve the halo of infallibility. All books are written by men and women, some more learned and accurate than others, but all human. Even dictionaries, considered by a great many people as unquestionable authorities, differ. Make use, therefore, of what scholars and authors can offer, but remain at the apex of the pyramid, looking upon what others have done with a critical, dispassionate eye. Even "monumental scholarship" can be biased or shortsighted.

Examine the book itself. When was it written? Have there been important happenings with respect to the subject since its publication? Was

7. A word might be said here about the difference between primary and secondary research. The scholars who bring to light the various layers of civilizations which cover the site of an ancient city, or the investigators in a laboratory who isolate and describe a new kind of bacteria, are pursuing primary research. They are making their own observations of actual phenomena. The literary scholar who, by examining letters, diaries, and written works of various kinds left by an author, brings to light new facts (or confirms old ones) concerning the life of that author, is also doing primary research. The student who writes a "research paper" is usually doing secondary research since it is unlikely that he can examine primary evidence. Although good primary research is an altogether necessary basis for good secondary research, both are important and valuable. The goal of most student papers, to clarify and organize material presented by other people, has also its uses and benefits.

it written at a time when this subject was especially dominated by prejudice? Take note of the purpose of the book or article. Is it written primarily to gain adherents to a cause or belief, or is it coolly scientific in its aims? Is it issued by an institution or industry as camouflaged advertising propaganda, or is it the effort of a detached investigator to determine facts? Beware of apparently trustworthy brochures and booklets sent, usually free of charge, by large corporations. If they were not designed as advertising, they would not be sent free of charge. Be critical, also, of popularized surveys of science, history, art, and religion. Some of them are accurate and, being easy to read, might serve well as an introduction to the topic. But in general they are overambitious and oversimplified.

Look at the documentation of the book (that is, the footnote and bibliography apparatus which shows sources of material). If the author has taken no pains to indicate the authenticity of his statements, he is at least open to the charge of carelessness. Read the preface or introduction. If the book represents a considerable amount of work, the author should somewhere acknowledge indebtedness to people who have helped him: librarians, owners of manuscripts, other scholars, authorities who have read and criticized his manuscript before publication. With respect to an article, notice the kind of periodical in which it is published. Periodicals which number their readers by the hundreds of thousands must cater to popular taste and the average mind. They may include well-known names in their tables of contents, but they cannot afford to present a widely unpopular opinion or publish an article which is above the heads of ordinary readers.

Take into account also the kind of evidence which is presented. Direct evidence is the testimony of an eyewitness, or proved historical data, or an accurate statistical survey. Indirect evidence consists chiefly of authoritative opinion. Thus, while tramping through the woods you may obtain direct testimony of your own eyes that a snake sheds its skin, but if you have never seen the phenomenon itself, you must depend on the word of other people who presumably know what they are talking about. Direct evidence in the library research which you are doing takes the form of what are called original, or primary, sources. If you are studying Shakespeare's conception of an ideal king in *Henry V,* the original source is the play itself. Secondary sources are the books and articles about the play. Many students, writing on such a problem, make the mistake of using secondary sources almost entirely. They seize upon such works eagerly because they provide ready-made opinions. If you are a person of independent mind, however, you will make a study of the primary source your first consideration. The exercise of your own ability to read accurately and reason validly with regard to the original text is more profitable, both as education and as research, than the absorption of second-hand judgments. Use secondary sources, of course, for what they can give you. Principally, they provide means of checking your own conclusions by comparing them with those of other people; but, so far as your library facilities will allow, form your own opinions first on the basis of primary sources.

An opinion concerning an author can be obtained best by reading his book, but you should learn as much as possible about him from other sources. The title page, or the page facing it, may provide a list of other books which he has written. (Do not be unduly impressed by quantity, however.) The paper dustcover which is on the book when it comes from the dealer frequently gives a considerable amount of information. Thus, we learn from the page preceding the title page of Carl Van Doren's *Benjamin Franklin* that the author has written an autobiography, four biographies of literary men, two novels, six books of literary history and criticism, and has edited three works, one of them the *Cambridge History of American Literature*. From the dust cover (which has been removed from the book if you use a library copy, but which the librarian can perhaps show you), we learn that he has been a teacher at Columbia University, literary editor of the *Nation* and *Century,* and editor-in-chief of the Literary Guild. We are also told that he worked on the Franklin book ten years. This certainly appears to be the record of a recognized scholar.

More often the facts concerning an author must be obtained from one or more of the reference works cited above. The various biographical dictionaries should be consulted. Bibliographies should be scanned for the author's name and the titles of other works. And, of course, the *Book Review Digest* is particularly valuable for its excerpts from reviews of the book in question.

Not only the likelihood of a scholar's competence in research, but also the soundness of his judgment and the probability of an unbiased mind should be weighed. If a recognized scholar in chemistry should suddenly publish a book of opinions concerning the League of Nations, what reason would there be for accepting his opinions at their face value any more than those of anyone else, except for the fact that the scholarly chemist has had more than ordinary training in the accurate observation of natural phenomena? It may be that his training is actually a detriment, because he has always worked with physical observations, whereas his new subject is one in which intangible, human phenomena are most important. Sometimes geographical and racial attachments must be considered. Political affiliations also should be examined critically. But business or professional attachments are most likely to cause prejudice or actual falsification of material. A large stockholder in a private utilities corporation would not be the person to give the most acceptable evidence on the desirability of government-owned power resources. The opinion of an editorial writer should be considered in the light of the editorial policy of his newspaper. The source of a man's bread and butter, social prestige, or professional rating almost invariably affects the objectivity of his judgment.

**The Outline.** As soon as you have taken the necessary notes for the paper, re-examine the preliminary organization of material which you made in the early stages of your reading. Perhaps you have changed it or added to it as you became more familiar with the subject. At any rate, if you followed directions, the cards in your note file are arranged according to a definite plan which should approximate the outline you must now make.

No matter how good the temporary outline has been, spend some time reading over your notes, evaluating the contents of the various divisions, and otherwise taking stock of your position before entering upon the final stages of the work. If one or two divisions of the notes contain nearly all your material, either the organization is at fault or the material is inadequate. Check the bibliography cards again for sources which might have been missed which may help to fill out the notes. Perhaps the thin sections in your notes represent topics which are really not as important as you originally expected. When you are satisfied that the notes are in good order and that the material is adequate, make a complete-sentence outline which will guide you from the beginning of the paper to the end.

**Footnotes and the Final Bibliography.** The writer of a research paper is morally obligated to give credit to the sources he has used. The method for doing so, the use of footnotes and a bibliography, is called documentation, and, as has been said before, proper documentation is one of the first signs of careful work which the critical reader looks for. (See p. 21.)

*Footnotes to acknowledge sources.* A footnote reference is necessary for every statement of fact or opinion which is not a matter of general knowledge and which is not derived from the writer's own original observation. The question of what constitutes general knowledge is sometimes debatable, but if there is any doubt in the writer's mind, it is better to include the footnote than to omit it. The date of the signing of the Declaration of Independence, certainly, is common knowledge, and no source need be given for it; but a statement concerning the number of passenger cars registered in New Jersey in 1940 must be documented. The fact that Abraham Lincoln was assassinated by John Wilkes Booth is common knowledge, but a statement to the effect that Booth was a member of a ring of conspirators who had carefully planned the assassination needs footnoting.

*Footnotes to acknowledge quotations.* All material which is quoted directly should be followed by a citation of source. Such material must either be put in quotation marks or be single-spaced and indented more deeply than the regular margin of the page. The reason now appears for being so scrupulously careful in using quotation marks for quoted material on the note cards. If the directions have been followed with regard to this matter, the writer should encounter no difficulty in knowing which of his notes represent his own summaries, which he can legitimately use without acknowledgment, and which are quoted from the sources.

*Footnotes to define terms.* Sometimes the terminology used in a treatment of a technical subject is familiar enough to a person trained in that subject, but is likely to be confusing to an ordinary reader. The footnote is a convenient place to present definitions of terms of this kind. Translations of foreign words and sentences can also be placed in footnotes.

*Footnotes to provide additional information.* The writer of a paper sometimes has material in his notes which is interesting and useful, but which, if presented in the body of his text, would be an unnecessary digression. Illustrations, anecdotes, and biographical data, for instance, can frequently be placed in a footnote when they would only serve to clutter the paper if used along with more important information.

*Form for footnotes.* Let it be understood that a footnote need not repeat any information which is included in the body of the paper. Occasionally, all the data necessary to identify a source of information or a quotation occurs in the text, thus: "The essay on 'Mark Twain' written by Stuart P. Sherman for the *Cambridge History of American Literature,* Vol. III, Chapter VIII, states that . . ." When this happens, no footnote is necessary. However, the constant inclusion of documentation in the text of the paper makes the style unreadable. If the sentence reads, "The essay on 'Mark Twain' written by Stuart P. Sherman for the *Cambridge History of American Literature* states that . . . ," a footnote should provide the volume and chapter but should not repeat what has already been stated in the sentence to which it refers.

The indication in the text that a footnote should be referred to at the bottom of the page is an Arabic number placed just *after* the portion to which the footnote corresponds and raised slightly above the line (thus, [3]). The numbering should be continuous throughout the whole paper or throughout chapters of it. The practice of beginning to number anew on each page can lead to confusion if the manuscript is copied or typed and the paging becomes different.

The text of a page should be separated from the footnotes by a ruled line extending from margin to margin. Below the line are all the foot-notes for that page, their numbers corresponding to numbers in the text. A little foresight will be required to estimate the amount of room which should be saved at the bottom of the page for footnotes. The notes should not be crowded. The principle of neatness applies to them as well as to any other part of the manuscript.

Manuscripts prepared for publication are generally not accompanied by a bibliography, and therefore the footnotes should include complete bibliographical data. Student papers, however, are always accompanied by a complete bibliography, and for that reason certain items which appear in the bibliography proper are omitted from the notes. The proper form for footnotes referring to books appears below:

1. Thurman W. Arnold, *The Folklore of Capitalism,* p. 123.
2. Arthur Young, *A Six Months' Tour through the North of England.* London, 1771, I, 222, as quoted in A. H. Johnson, *The Disappearance of the Small Landowner,* pp. 102–3.
3. Stuart P. Sherman, "Mark Twain," *Cambridge History of American Literature,* Vol. III, Chap. VIII.
4. Rudyard Kipling, "The Courting of Dinah Shadd," *Life's Handicap: Being Stories of My Own People,* pp. 117–45.
5. "North American Indians," *Encyclopaedia Britannica.* Eleventh Edition, Vol. XIV.

Forms for articles in magazines appear below:

1. Lindsay Rogers, "Crisis Government: 1936 Model," *The Southern Review,* I (Spring, 1936), 696 ff.
2. Fletcher Pratt, "Crime as a Profession," *American Mercury,* XL (1937), 214.
3. Anon., "Foreign News: Canada," *Time,* August 24, 1936, p. 24.

Forms for newspaper articles and bulletins appear below:

1. "Administration Planning New Expenditures," Chicago *Daily News,* Sept. 5, 1940.
2. Curriculum Commission for the National Council of Teachers of English, *An Experience Curriculum in English,* p. 114.

*Short forms for footnotes.* In a research paper of considerable length, the mechanical labor involved in composing footnotes is great. Fortunately, there is practically universal agreement concerning certain standardized short forms and abbreviations.

The first time a source is mentioned in a footnote, the citation should take the form of one of the examples given above; thereafter, future references to the same source can be shortened, if that is possible without rendering the footnote ambiguous. "W. P. Ker, *Epic and Romance: Essays on Medieval Literature*" can, after the first reference, become "Ker, *Epic and Romance.*" "Fletcher Pratt, 'Crime as a Profession,' *American Mercury,* XL (1937)" can become "Pratt, 'Crime as a Profession.'" However, no shortening of a reference is excusable if it can possibly result in confusion of one source with another.

Footnotes can be shortened even further by the use of three standardized abbreviations: *ibid.* (for *ibidem,* meaning "in the same place"), *op. cit.* (for *opere citato,* meaning "in the work cited"), and *loc. cit.* (for *loco citato,* meaning "in the place cited"). *Ibid.* (which, like the other two abbreviations, should always be underlined) is used to avoid repeating a citation when reference is made *consecutively* to the same source. It always duplicates the citation which immediately precedes it, or as much of it as is appropriate for the new citation. If *ibid.* stands alone, it is understood that the entire previous citation is being repeated; if it is qualified, as in *"Ibid.,* p. 23," it is understood that the previous citation is being repeated with the exception of the page number, the new page number being 23.

When one or more footnotes have intervened between a citation and a footnote which must repeat all or part of the citation, *ibid.* obviously will not do; another abbreviation, *op. cit.,* is used in these circumstances. *Op. cit.* can never stand alone, but must always appear in conjunction with the author's name or some other part of the original reference, in order to indicate just what work is being cited. Thus, "McKerrow, *op. cit.,* p. 193" would refer the reader to a book by McKerrow which has been cited previously, but between the citation of which and the present footnote something else has intervened.

*Loc. cit.* is used in place of *op. cit.* for references to a passage cited in a preceding footnote (see p. 727, note 10).

The uses of these abbreviations are easy to learn. Remember that they are not interchangeable. Each has a distinct meaning which cannot be violated. The following set of illustrations may serve to make their uses clearer:

1. Joseph Quincy Adams (ed.), *Chief Pre-Shakespearean Dramas,* pp. 9–24. [This specimen is a first footnote.]
2. *Ibid.* [Repeats footnote 1.]
3. *Ibid.,* p. 26. [Repeats footnotes 1 and 2 except for page number.]
4. John Dove, *Confutation of Atheism,* pp. 25–27. [Another first note.]
5. Adams, *op. cit.,* p. 28. [Refers to work cited in 1, 2, and 3.]

6. *Ibid.* [Repeats footnote 5.]

7. Dove, *op. cit.,* p. 28. [Refers to work cited in 4.]

8. John Wilson, "Shakespeare and the Strolling Players," *PMLA,* XXXVIII (1923), 178. [Another first note.]

9. Adams, *op. cit.,* p. 89. [Refers to work cited in 1, 2, 3, 5, and 6.]

10. Wilson, *loc. cit.* [Refers to the place cited in 8.]

*Bibliography forms.* A final bibliography, providing a complete list of all the sources actually used for reference, should be attached to the student research paper. It should be arranged alphabetically, by authors, last names first (or, if the author is not known, by the first important word in the title). If the bibliography is long, it may be well to place books and article in two separate lists.

The arrangement of the items in each entry in the final bibliography is the same as was used for the bibliography cards, except that the entry is written in a linear fashion instead of being spread out over several lines. Some punctuation is added, also. The following examples should provide adequate models:

Adams, Joseph Quincy (ed.). *Chief Pre-Shakespearean Dramas.* Boston: Houghton Mifflin Co., 1924.

Anon. *The Lottery. A Farce.* London: J. Watts, 1732.

"Chemical Costs," *Chemical and Metallurgical Engineering,* XXXIX (January, 1932), 1–8.

Evans, Michael. "Prohibition's Attempted Comeback," *Coronet,* X (September, 1941), 3–8.

Lardner, Ring. "Haircut." In Donald Davidson, *American Composition and Rhetoric.* New York: Charles Scribner's Sons, 1939.

"North American Indians," *Encyclopaedia Britannica.* Eleventh Edition. Vol. XIV.

Simms, W. Gilmore. *Charlemont; or, The Pride of the Village.* Chicago, New York, San Francisco: Belford, Clarke & Co., 1889. New and revised edition.

University of Chicago Press. *A Manual of Style.* Chicago, 1937. Tenth edition.

*Final form for the research paper.* Since the research paper is probably the longest and, in many ways, the most exacting written assignment required during the year, its final form should receive careful attention. If possible, it should be typed. Before it is turned in, it should be read carefully for errors, omissions, and misspelled words. When it is completed it should consist of the following parts, in order: title page, outline, text, bibliography.

## List of Common Abbreviations

bk. (pl., bks.), book

*c.* or *ca.,* about

cf., compare

chap. or ch. (pl., chaps. or chs.), chapter

col. (pl., cols.), column

ed., editor (pl., eds. or edd.), edited
by
fig. (pl., figs.), figure
*ibid.,* in the same place
*infra,* below
l. (pl., ll.), line
MS (pl., MSS), manuscript
*op. cit.,* in the work cited
*passim,* here and there

p. (pl., pp.), page
pp. 7 f., page 7 and the following
page
pp. 7 ff., page 7 and following pages
sec. (pl., secs.), section
*supra,* above
tr. or trans., translator; translated by
vol. (pl., vols.), volume
vs. (pl., vss.), verse

### Exercise in Bibliography Forms

Rewrite the following descriptions of printed material in such a way that they conform to the bibliographical usage explained in this text.

1. A book called The Handy Dictionary of Biography written by Charles Morris and published in 1905 in Philadelphia by the John Winston Company.
2. A book by H. G. Wells called The Shape of Things to Come, published by The Macmillan Company in New York in 1933.
3. A book published in New York by Albert and Charles Boni, Inc., in 1927. Title is The Bridge of San Luis Rey, and the author is Thornton Wilder.
4. A book by John Franklin Genung called A Guide to Biblical Literature, published in Boston by Ginn & Company in 1919.
5. A book called The Modern Reader's Bible edited by Richard G. Moulton, published in 1908 by The Macmillan Company in New York.
6. An article called Pardon My Harvard Accent published in the Atlantic Monthly in its September, 1941, issue, pages 318–29, volume CLXVIII.
7. An article in the magazine called Life entitled Vichy vs. France. The author is Richard de Rochemont. Volume eleven. Pages 66–73. September 1, 1941.
8. In James Whitcomb Riley's volume of poems entitled Child-Rhymes can be found a well-known poem entitled Little Orphant Annie. It appears on pages 23–8. The book was published in Indianapolis by the Bobbs-Merrill Company in 1888.
9. A newspaper story in the Chicago Daily Tribune for September 16, 1941, with the headline Manila Harbor Ravaged by $1,000,000 Fire.
10. The article in the Encyclopaedia Britannica, volume four of the fourteenth edition, on Bascule Bridges.

### Suggested Topics for Research Papers

1. The Methods of Color Photography
2. The Experiment with Army Universities in World War II
3. The Scientific Aspects of Hypnosis
4. The Importance of the Almanac in the History of American Journalism
5. The Conquering of Yellow Fever
6. Modern Tendencies in the Rules Governing College Football
7. The Conspiracy of Benedict Arnold
8. The Conspiracy of Aaron Burr

9. Methods of Rehabilitating Drouth Areas
10. The Efficiency of Federal Pure Food Laws
11. Desperados in American Folk Ballads
12, How Fur Coat Buyers Are Cheated
13. The Importance of Skeletal Traction in Surgery
14. The Sources of Income of —— College
15. The Public Transit Problems of the City of ——
16. The Literary Sources Used by Richard Wagner in his Ring operas
17. A Brief Description of Boulder Dam (or any other engineering project)
18. The Rise of the Committee for Industrial Organization
19. The Purposes and Plans of the Civil Aeronautics Authority
20. How Phonograph Records are Made
21. The Beginning of Methodism in America
22. The Theory of Impressionism in Nineteenth-Century Painting
23. Indemnities Imposed by the Versailles Treaty on Germany
24. The Importance of *Godey's Ladies' Book* in the Feminine Culture of the Nineteenth Century
25. A Definition of Melodrama
26. The Present Status of Prefabrication in the Construction of Houses
27. American Diplomatic Relations with Japan from the Beginning of the War with China until Pearl Harbor
28. The Organization of the National Broadcasting System
29. The Organization of the Confederate States of America

## Hank Monk and Horace Greeley [1]

### RICHARD G. LILLARD

For a third of a century Hank Monk [1] was one of the best-known stage drivers in the Far West. After he died his fame lived on vigorously for three decades more. As a driver and storyteller he no doubt had his equals, but as the center of a cycle of anecdotes and as a popular hero he surpassed in celebrity any of his compeers. His special prominence arose from a single event in 1859 which associated him briefly with Horace

---

1. From *American Literature*, XIV (May, 1942), p. 126. Reprinted by permission of the author, *American Literature*, and the Duke University Press. The footnotes which follow are those of the author of the article.

---

1. Henry Monk was born in Waddington, St. Lawrence County, N. Y., on March 24, 1826. He always had a great fancy for horses, and once drove eight horses abreast in Boston, during a civic celebration. He came to California in 1852 and began to drive stage between Sacramento and Auburn for the California Stage Company. Later he drove between Sacramento and Placerville. In 1857 and thereafter he drove stage for J. B. Crandall between Placerville and Genoa, Nevada. He continued the run when the line was bought, in turn, by Brady and Sundland, and Wells, Fargo, and Company. He drove Nevada stages for more than twenty years, notably between Virginia City and Carson City for "Billy" Wilson and between Carson City and Glenbrook for "Doc" Benton. He died of pneumonia in Carson City on February 28, 1883 (Gold Hill *News*, March 28, 1876, reprinted in Sacramento *Union*, April 1, 1876; J. A. Yerington, "Stories of Hank Monk," *Sunset*, XII, 24-28, Nov., 1903).

Greeley, who was regarded in the Western mining camps as a very great man. The story of their trip across the Sierra Nevadas, widely circulated within less than six months, became "the topic of the entire coast country,"[2] and popular writers gave it extensive distribution in the East. One can safely say that no other frontier story, true or untrue, has reached a larger audience and amused (or bored) more persons.

Two important contemporary writers who retold the Greeley story denied its truth. Albert Richardson claimed it was "apocryphal," although he did record that certain Californians had given Monk a gold watch in honor of his exploit.[3] Mark Twain, who came to despise the story, said in *Roughing It*, written in 1870–71, that the ride "never occurred" and thus the chief possible virtue of a "worn" and "flat" anecdote was gone.[4]

Evidence proves, however, that the incident actually took place. In his correspondence to the *Tribune*, reprinted the following year, Greeley himself narrated his exciting ride. It began at dawn on August 1 at an inn fifteen miles west of Genoa. The road went up the headwaters of Carson River, over Luther Pass, up Myer's Grade to Johnson Pass, and down the American River Canyon to Placerville.[5] Along a mere shelf,

with hardly a place to each mile where two meeting wagons can pass, the mail-stage was driven at the rate of ten miles an hour (in one instance eleven), or just as fast as four wild California horses, whom two men could scarcely harness, could draw it. Our driver was of course skillful; but had he met a wagon on suddenly rounding one of the sharp points or projections we were constantly passing, a fearful crash was unavoidable. Had his horses seen fit to run away (as they *did* run once, on the unhooking of a trace, but at a place where he had room to rein them out of the road on the upper side, and thus stop them) I know that he could not have held them, and we might have been pitched headlong down a precipice of a thousand feet, where all of the concern that could have been picked up afterward would not have been worth two bits per bushel. Yet at this break-neck speed we were driven for not less than four hours or forty miles, changing horses every ten or fifteen, and

2. Yerington, *op. cit.*, p. 26.

3. Albert Richardson, *Beyond the Mississippi* (Hartford, 1867), pp. 382-384. As a member of the staff of the New York *Tribune*, Richardson had good reason for minimizing a story that gave undignified treatment to the editor-in-chief.

4. Mark Twain, *Roughing It* (New York and London, 1913), I, 143.

5. Following is a table of distances from Sacramento to Carson City "via Placerville and Carson Valley Road." Figures indicate miles from Sacramento. Folsom, 22; Shingle Springs, 37; Mud Springs, 44; Diamond Springs, 45; Placerville, 48; Elk Horn House, 55; Sportsman's Hall, 60; Junction House, 64; South Fork Bridge, 67; Summit Hill, 69; Brockliss' Post, 75; Peavine Hill, 77; Silver Creek, 84; Valley South Fork, 87; Strawberry Valley, 91; Slippery Ford, 93; Boulder Hill, 94; Summit Sierra, 100; Lake Valley, 101; Marlett's Flat, 104; Hope Valley, 108; Woodford's, 112; Van Sickles', 129; Genoa Station, 131; Carson City, 145 (*The Sacramento Directory of 1861-1862*, pp. 165-166; *Guide to Degroot's Map of Nevada Territory*, San Francisco, 1862, p. 6).

raising a cloud of dust through which it was difficult at times to see anything. . . .

Greeley was glad to find himself in Placerville. It was "a balm for many bruises to know that [he was] at last in California." [6]

Eight years later in his *Recollections of a Busy Life*,[7] Greeley mentioned crossing the double summit on August 1, 1859, but omitted all details of his fast ride to Placerville, going on at once to discuss California forests and the Yosemite. His exclusion of a major travel experience is explained by what Joseph Goodman, editor of the Virginia City *Enterprise*, told Albert Bigelow Paine years afterward.

When I was going East in 1869 I happened to see Hank Monk just before I started. "Mr. Goodman," he said, "you tell Horace Greeley that I want to come East, and ask him to send me a pass." "All right, Hank," I said, "I will." It happened that when I got to New York City one of the first men I met was Greeley. "Mr. Greeley," I said, "I have a message for you from Hank Monk." Greeley bristled and glared at me. "That—rascal?" he said. "He has done me more injury than any other man in America." [8]

The "injury" was in the form of a short anecdote that contained undignified dialogue. The original version was no doubt very close to that in a letter from "Cornish" to the popular San Francisco *Golden Era*. "Cornish" told of crossing the Sierras with Hank Monk, "a young man of about twenty-five years . . . a perfect Jehu—a great 'whip,' " who recounted the trip.

Just before I left Strawberry, Mr. Greeley called me one side: "Driver," said he, "can you get me into Placerville this evening by 5 o'clock, because the committee expect me, and I do not wish to disappoint them; this is the last telegraph station, and *if you are not sure* I will send them a message; if there is anything I dislike in this world 'tis to be disappointed, so do not promise unless you are *certain*." "I'll get you there," says I, and off we went. I drove him to Dick's,[9] eleven miles, in fifty-three minutes. (This part of the road is almost indescribable—down hill and over huge boulders.) [10] Just before I got to Dick's I looked into the coach and there was Greeley, his bare head bobbing, sometimes on the back and then on the front seat, sometimes in the coach and then out, then on top and then in the bottom, holding on to whatever he could grab. Presently some one touched me on the back: "Driver," said a voice, *"I am not particular for an hour or two!"* "Horace," says I, *"keep your seat!* I told you I would get you there by 5 o'clock, and by G—, I'll do it, if the axles hold!" *And I did.* When I arrived at Sportsman's Hall

6. Horace Greeley, *An Overland Journey from New York to San Francisco in the Summer of 1859* (New York, 1860), pp. 280-282.

7. New York, 1868, pp. 379-380.

8. Albert B. Paine, *Mark Twain: A Biography* (New York and London, 1912), I, 303.

9. Perhaps Collins' Station. There is no Dick's on contemporary maps.

10. Interpolation by "Cornish."

there was the committee, with a carriage and six horses.—Mr. Greeley had become pretty familiar by this time. "Hank," says he, "when you get into Placerville call on me immediately. I wish to see you. Of course, I shall proceed from this point more rapidly than you." "All right!" said I, and away he went. I had a bully team, took a short cut, drove like the d—l, and was in a long time ahead. I was standing among the crowd when Greeley arrived. He called the proprietor of the hotel to him and said: "When Hank comes in, be sure and tell him I wish to see him." Says I, "Horace, I've been here an hour and a half!" "Young man," says he, "come with me;" and he took me up street and bought me the best suit of clothes he could find in Placerville.[11]

The story, for which this may be considered the original text, spread through the California and Nevada mining camps and along the Western stage routes with all the speed of "a good thing." If one can believe the evidence in *Roughing It,* in 1861, when Twain first came West, the Greeley story was one of the hazards of travel. In one chapter [12] Twain has the tale told identically four full times—by a driver near Julesburg on the Platte River, by a Denver man picked up at a Wyoming crossroads, by a soldier at Fort Bridger, and by a Mormon preacher eight hours out of Salt Lake City. A "poor wanderer" near Ragtown, Nevada, is not allowed to finish the anecdote and dies at once from the strain of holding it in. The version they tell introduces a hole in the roof. It keeps the trip on the true route, Carson to Placerville, but begins the conversation at Carson, however, and not at Strawberry. Twain's fellow travelers all tell what they announce as "a very laughable thing indeed, if you would like to listen to it," and then proceed without a pause.

Horace Greeley went over this road once. When he was leaving Carson City he told the driver, Hank Monk, that he had an engagement to lecture at Placerville and was very anxious to go through quick. Hank Monk cracked his whip and started off at an awful pace. The coach bounced up and down in such a terrific way that it jolted his head clean through the roof of the stage, and then he yelled at Hank Monk and begged him to go easier—said he warn't in as much of a hurry as he was awhile ago. But Hank Monk said, "Keep your seat, Horace, and I'll get you there on time!"—and you bet he did, what was left of him! [13]

In repeating this story four times in immediate succession, Twain was obviously satirizing the uncritical repetition of the anecdote in the West. *Roughing It* appeared in 1872. At least twice before Twain had publicly burlesqued the popularity of the story. In his lecture in Virginia City in

11. *Golden Era,* April 15, 1860, p. 5.

12. Twain, *op. cit.,* Chapter XX, "What Hank Said to Horace Greeley," pp. 137-143.

13. "The particulars of that drive as told by Mark Twain are not all correct" (Hank Monk, paraphrased in Gold Hill *News,* March 28, 1876).

1866 he repeated the story several times to miners already sick of it,[14] and afterwards in a lecture in San Francisco he "did the daring thing of repeating three times the worn-out story of Horace Greeley's ride with Hank Monk." The first time there was no laughter and the audience felt sorry for him. The second time, astonished, they pitied him. The third time he worked the story in they saw his intention and laughed themselves hysterical.[15]

Twain's cruel repetition was his own natural reaction to a painful experience. Even if his testimony in *Roughing It* be greatly discounted, he had heard too often what Hank said to Horace. Twain testifies that in six years he crossed the Sierras thirteen times by stage and listened to the story over four hundred and eighty times—as told by drivers, conductors, landlords, chance passengers, "Chinamen," and Indians. The same drivers would tell it two or three times in one afternoon. A traveler heard it flavored with cologne, tobacco, garlic, onions, grasshoppers, and whiskey. Says Twain, "I never have smelt any anecdote as often as I smelt that one; never have smelled any anecdote that smelt so variegated as that one." The traveler would think that the real wonder of the Pacific Coast was not the Yosemite or the giant Sequoias, or even Lake Tahoe, but only the trip Greeley had with Hank Monk.[16]

While in California and Nevada in 1863–64, Artemus Ward learned the story and both modified and extended it. As it appears in *Artemus Ward: His Travels* and the *Complete Works* [17] and the several reprints of portions of Artemus Ward, it is as hilarious as it is truly apocryphal.[18] It reverses Greeley's route, substituting the west-east one that Ward himself followed in his approach to Placerville. Late in the afternoon the stage company at Folsom, twenty-four miles west of Placerville, asked Hank Monk to get "this great man" to Placerville by seven in the evening. With abundant detail, Ward tells how Monk drove slow for a while, over roads that were in "an awful stage," as Greeley exhorted him to hurry. Then, still driving laconically, Monk whipped up his horses to a terrific speed, so that Greeley bounced "from one end of the coach to the other like an india-rubber ball" and eventually managed to get his head out of the window to ask, "Do-on't-on't-on't you-u-u-u think we-e-e-e

14. Virginia City *Union*, Nov. 12, 1866.
15. Paine, *op. cit.*, p. 303.
16. Twain, *op. cit.*, pp. 141-143.
17. Charles F. Browne, *Artemus Ward: His Travels* (New York, 1865); *The Complete Works of Charles F. Browne, Better Known as "Artemus Ward"* (London, n.d.).
18. Don C. Seitz in *Horace Greeley* (Indianapolis, 1926), p. 306, says, "Ward's narrative of the incident has never been contradicted." Seitz also recalls that in the early 1890's Monk drove the overland stage for the Wild West show run by Nate Saulsbury and Buffalo Bill. Monk died in 1883.

shall get there by seven if we do-on't-on't-on't go so fast?" Finally a frightful jolt forced Mr. Greeley's bald head through the roof. "Stop, you—maniac!" he roared, but Monk replied with the famous line, "Keep your seat, Horace!" Ward describes an elaborate delegation with a military company, a brass band, and a wagonload of beautiful girls that were assembled at Mud Springs to escort Greeley the remaining four miles to Placerville. Hank slowed down. "Is Mr. Greeley on board?" asked the chairman of the committee. "He was, a few miles back," said Hank, who looked down through the hole. "Yes, yes, I can see him! He is there!" But Hank would not stop. He cried, "I've got my orders!" and dashed on toward Placerville, Greeley's head ever and anon showing itself "like a wild apparition, above the coach-roof." Ward's fiction corresponds in one detail to "Cornish's" version: "There is a tradition that Mr. Greeley was very indignant for awhile; then he laughed, and finally presented Mr. Monk with a bran-new suit of clothes." Ward also states that Monk "is rather fond of relating a story that has made him famous all over the Pacific coast."

Ward's version of the anecdote was read before Congress. In the House of Representatives on March 29, 1866, Representative Hulburd of New York quoted a Greeley editorial that castigated some remarks of his on a loan bill and advised him and others to bring about immediate resumption of specie payments. Hulburd commented that Greeley was going a little too fast, that he was in as much of a hurry as once on the Pacific coast, and asked the Clerk to read an account of Greeley's ride with Hank Monk. The Clerk read it while the House laughed. Afterwards Representative Ingersoll of Illinois wanted to expunge the story from the records of the House. It was disgraceful to the body that it would waste "so much time in listening to such balderdash and nonsense." But the House took no parliamentary action and serious debate went on.[19]

A quantity of miscellaneous material testifies to the renown that the Greeley episode gave to Hank Monk. A special correspondent of the San Francisco *Alta,* "Traviata," told stories of Monk and called him "a celebrity on the *stage,* almost rivalling Charles Kean."[20] A correspondent of the New York *Tribune* who was riding from Glenbrook to Carson City

asked the driver if he had ever heard of Hank Monk, the famous whipster who had given Mr. Greeley such excellent advice about keeping his seat when the stage was in motion. I soon found I was talking to the man himself, and I involuntarily raised my hat to the modest hero. Hank is too shrewd a man

19. *The Congressional Globe, Containing the Debates and Proceedings of the First Session of the Thirty-ninth Congress,* pp. 1531-1532.
20. San Francisco *Alta,* Nov. 18. 1864.

to throw away the glory that his legend sheds upon him, and so encourages its repetition in detail. Aside from Hank Monk's facetious fame as Mr. Greeley's driver, he enjoys the universal reputation of being the most fearless and scientific, as well as the safest reinsman in this Western country.[21]

News items about Monk that appeared in Nevada papers were frequently reprinted in California papers.[22] Wild, incredible "reminiscences" by alleged "old-timers" came out in newspapers.[23] Monk's pranks and stories were frequently retold.[24] The story of the Greeley ride was retold or alluded to by numerous writers.[25]

C. C. Goodwin commemorated Monk's death with an eloquent obituary that began,

> The famous stage driver is dead. He has been on the down grade for some time. On Wednesday his foot lost its final hold on the brake and his coach could not be stopped until, battered and broken on a sharp turn, it went over into the canyon, black and deep, which we call death.[26]

A Carson City paper said:

> His friend Horace ought to do the fair thing by him and be on hand at the pearly gates with a blazing chariot and a spanking team of angels, send Hank spinning over the golden pavements at a speed that would remind the old Jehu of other days.[27]

Many persons treasured pictures of Monk. These showed his curly hair, long moustache, dark beard, straight glance, and keen eye. They were captioned "the noted Stage Driver of the Sierras." One such picture still

21. *Ibid.*, Sept. 21, 1871.

22. For example, *ibid.*, Feb. 23, 1878, and Aug. 10, 1881.

23. One from the New York *Sun* was reprinted in the San Jose *Pioneer*, April 6, 1878; one from the Leadville *Democrat*, in the San Francisco *Call*, March 5, 1885.

24. Virginia City *Enterprise*, reprinted in the San Francisco *Alta*, July 18, 1874; C. C. Goodwin, *As I Remember Them* (Salt Lake City, 1913); Wells Drury, *An Editor on the Comstock Lode* (New York, 1936); William Wright (Dan de Quille), *History of the Big Bonanza* (Hartford and San Francisco, 1876).

25. In addition to those mentioned in the text, by George H. and Captain William Banning, *Six Horses* (New York, 1930); Samuel Bowles, *Across the Continent* (Springfield, 1866); C. W. Haskins, *The Argonauts of California* . . . (New York, 1890); Harvey Rice, *Letters from the Pacific Slope* (New York, 1870); Frank Root, *Overland Stage to California* (Topeka, 1901); William Wright, *op. cit.*, Mark Twain claimed that the story was recounted by Ross Browne and Bayard Taylor, but it does not appear in any of their books on the West. Joaquin Miller made Hank Monk the hero of the "poetic" play, "Tally-Ho!" (in *Joaquin Miller's Poems*, San Francisco, 1910, VI, 123-167). In this murder melodrama Monk retells the incident as occurring on a tally-ho east bound over the Sierras. One twentieth-century error takes the locale of the ride from the Sierras and places it in the Virginia Range, on the steep Geiger Grade from Virginia City down toward Reno (Rufus Steele, "The University and Diversity of Nevada," *Sunset*, XXXII, 95, May, 1914; Max Miller, *Reno*, New York, 1941, p. 65).

26. Virginia City *Enterprise*, March 6, 1883.

27. Quoted in Yerington, *op. cit.*, p. 28.

hangs in the taproom of the brewery in Carson City. In 1903 the Nevada Exhibit at the Louisiana Purchase Exposition in St. Louis displayed Monk's watch and many other personal possessions and also the coach that Greeley rode in.[28]

The question rises, Why was the story of Monk and Greeley told with gusto so many thousands of times? There are several answers. (1) Its personages were important: the great New York editor who advocated the Pacific railroad and other popular causes, and the man of the people who was an acknowledged master of the profession of stage driving, in the days when a driver had all the personal prestige of a pilot on the Mississippi. (2) It was a local story, to be told to visitors and new arrivals from the East, and newcomers were abundant, especially on the Placerville road, which during bonanza days in Virginia City was one of the nation's leading thoroughfares. (3) It was a good story. It had brisk dialogue, action, and point. It invited detailed elaboration. It showed the native humiliating the greenhorn, the West outdoing the East. It turned on characterization. Its ending was droll. It dramatized speed, efficiency, keeping on schedule, daring, and uncanny skill. (4) To make its qualities all the more substantial, it was true.

First-hand evidence of what a veteran *raconteur* of the story thought of it appeared in the Chicago *Record* during March, 1897, in a feature story [29] by Carl Smith. Smith was in Carson City during the training period of James Corbett and "Bob" Fitzsimmons, prior to their championship prizefight on March 18. According to his account, Smith wished to hire a rig to follow one of the fighters along the road during a workout and went to a large livery stable owned by "Doc" Benton.[30] Smith asked Benton what the hire would cost, and Benton said he would have to see what time it was. He pulled a massive gold watch from his pocket and looked reflectively at it. Ignoring the question as to the price, he started talking about the watch. It had belonged to Hank Monk, who drove for him sixteen years. Some San Franciscans had given it to Monk, and Benton had inherited it. The watch was large, heavy, and elaborate. Inside the case was an inscription that asserted friendship and admiration for Hank

28. *Ibid.* One can wonder whether or not the authentic coach was exhibited. A. H. Hawley, who was proprietor of a trading post in Lake Valley, on the Upper Carson River, at the time Greeley crossed westward, wrote long ago that Greeley rode "in a miserable little old four horse team and small mud wagon instead of the high toned outfit that is so much talked about" ("Lake Tahoe—1883," MS in Bancroft Library, reprinted in *Nevada Historical Papers, 1913-1916,* Carson City, I, 177). Greeley's own account specifies four horses only.

29. Reprinted in Carson *Morning Appeal,* March 23, 1897.

30. James M. Benton, proprietor of Livery and Feed Stable, later Livery and Ice Dealers; listed in *Nevada Directories* from 1868-69 to 1925.

and quoted the line: "Keep your seat, Horace." Teasingly, Smith asked Benton what it meant, although he had already heard the story "repeatedly and tirelessly," thirty-two times, since his arrival a week or so before. Benton promptly started to repeat the story. Many times Smith interrupted him to ask irrelevant questions. How far away is Placerville? What was the exact speed? How much horse power was exerted? What was the exact gradient? How big a crowd did Mr. Greeley have at Placerville? Did Mr. Greeley have time to take a bath before appearing? Benton stared at Smith and then gazed at the watch in his hand.

Pshaw, friend, you don't seem to understand the point of the thing at all. It ain't the speed. It ain't the horses, it ain't the road, it ain't the crowd at the opera house—it is just Hank and Horace. There's the point of it, don't you see? In Hank and Horace. "Keep your seat, Horace," says Hank, "and I'll see you through."

After more interruptions from Smith, Benton made it clear that to him the story was the most vivid piece of literature on earth. It was a short drama of two strong wills in conflict on a careening stage in the rugged Sierras. The teller identified himself with the triumphant Westerner. He, too, uttered the classic impertinence:

Oh, pshaw! pshaw! . . . It wasn't so much the case of the ride, although that's something, nor speed, as I've said, though that was something, too. But it was Hank and Horace. Just imagine Hank looking down and saying: "Keep your seat, Horace! . . ."

## Suggestions for Study

Although a careful analysis of the variations of the Hank Monk story and its universality, this paper demonstrates that a research paper need not be dull. Study how the author has achieved a pleasing tone. Observe in particular his use of direct quotations and his method of relegating certain materials to footnotes. How do you know, however, that he has not allowed a desire to be amusing to interfere with the accuracy of his investigation? What do the footnotes tell you in this regard?

Study the different devices he has used in the footnotes to give needed information and yet to save space. Why does the second footnote contain *op. cit.*? Why would *ibid.* not suffice? Why is *ibid.* satisfactory in footnote 21?

Study the wide variety of references quoted in the footnotes as examples of the varied sort of references that can yield rich produce for a careful research man.

## "I Have Not Yet Begun to Fight" [1]

### CHARLES LEE LEWIS

The famous war cry of John Paul Jones is alleged to have been uttered at the climax of one of the most renowned ship duels in history. This was the battle off Flamborough Head, England, on September 23, 1779, between the British ship *Serapis* and the American vessel *Bonhomme Richard*. The battle had been in progress for an hour or more, the ships were lying alongside lashed together, and the crisis of the bloody contest seemed to be at hand. The gunner, the carpenter, and the master-at-arms, thinking that the *Richard* was sinking and that both John Paul Jones and his first lieutenant had been killed, rushed up on deck and called loudly to the British for quarter. Captain Pearson of the *Serapis,* hearing the cry, demanded of Jones to know if he had struck. His reply, according to popular histories and biographies, was, "I have not yet begun to fight!"

Jones might have settled this question at once and for all time, if he had set down in his official report his exact reply to the British captain; but such communications are usually stripped rather bare of personal and picturesque details of that kind. In his letter of October 3, 1779, to Franklin,[1] the only official report of the battle that he wrote, all that Jones states which bears upon the slogan is merely this: "The English Commodore asked me if I demanded quarter, and I having answered him in the most determined negative, they renewed the battle with double fury." It is necessary, therefore, to look elsewhere for the source of the exact language of the slogan.

Contemporary newspaper accounts, published in England, are of no particular value as evidence, except where they corroborate other statements; but some of them are extremely interesting as showing the widely varying versions of the war cry which have appeared in print. For example, the London *Evening Post* of September 30, 1779, gives this picturesque account: "In the engagement between the *Serapis* and Paul Jones, his vessel was so disabled, that the Captain of the *Serapis* called out to Jones to strike, else he would sink him. To which the latter replied, 'that he might if he could; for whenever the Devil was ready to take him, he would rather obey his summons, than strike to any one.' . . . The foregoing account is from the affidavits of seven seamen, who made their

---

1. From the *Mississippi Valley Historical Review* (September, 1942), p. 229. Reprinted by permission of the author, who has revised the article slightly for use here.

---

1. John Henry Sherburne, *Life and Character of the Chevalier John Paul Jones; A Captain in the Navy of the United States during Their Revolutionary War* (Washington, 1825), 120. The original letter is in the Library of Congress.

escape after the engagement, before the Mayor of Hull." [2] This account may be the source of a similar story in *Naval Heroes* by S. Putnam Waldo, 1823, which reads as follows: "The Captain of the *Serapis* said, 'I give you an opportunity to strike; if you do not, I will sink you at the next broadside.' The indignant Jones replied in a rage, 'Sink me if you can; if I must go to the Devil, I had rather strike to him than to you'." [3] In the London *Public Advertiser* of October 20, 1779, there is another highly embroidered account, which runs thus: "One of the men escaped from Paul Jones says that in the engagement with the *Serapis,* Jones, almost exhausted with fatigue, sat down upon a hen coop. The Lieutenant of Marines went up to him and said, 'For God's sake, Captain, strike!' Jones looked at him, paused a moment, then leaped up from his seat and said, 'No, I will sink, I will never strike'." [4] Of about the same purport are these lines from the well-known contemporary ballad:

> Our gunner, affrighted, unto Paul Jones he came,
> "Our ship is a-sinking, likewise in a flame";
> Paul Jones he replied, in the height of his pride,
> "If we can do no better, we'll sink alongside." [5]

It is true that some British prisoners, who had taken part in the battle, did escape at the close of the engagement. But the above accounts are not cited as reliable proof. They are referred to in passing only to show that immediately after the battle there were various and conflicting reports, and that the very best authority should be sought before the acceptance of any version whatsoever.

The official report of Captain Richard Pearson and his evidence afterwards are interesting. He wrote his report, of course, as a prisoner of war; it was headed, *"Pallas,* French frigate in Congress Service, Texel, 6 October, 1779."* The portion which bears directly upon the question is this: "At ten o'clock they called for quarter from the ship alongside, and said they had struck; hearing this, I called upon the Captain to know if they had struck; or if he asked for quarter; but no answer being made, after repeating my words two or three times, I called for the boarders, and ordered them to board, which they did; but the moment they were on board her, they discovered a superior number laying under cover with pikes in their hands ready to receive them, on which our people retreated

2. Quoted in Don C. Seitz, *Paul Jones: His Exploits in English Seas during 1778-1780: Contemporary Accounts Collected from English Newspapers* (New York, 1917), 55.
3. S. Putnam Waldo, *Biographical Sketches of Distinguished American Naval Heroes in the War of the Revolution* (Hartford, 1823), 120.
4. Quoted in Mrs. Reginald [Anna] de Koven, *The Life and Letters of John Paul Jones* (2 vols., New York, 1913), I, 461, n.
5. Burton Egbert Stevenson, ed., *Poems of American History* (Boston, 1908), 224.

instantly into our own ship, and returned to their guns again till half past ten." [6] But at the court-martial proceedings in 1780 Pearson made this additional statement: "I did not myself hear the reply; but one of my midshipmen, Mr. Hood, did hear it and soon reported it to me. It was to the effect that he was just beginning to fight." [7]

We have exactly the same words reported in a French pamphlet, called *Memoir du Combat.*[8] The author was Pierre Gerard, who is said to have been a French volunteer on the *Bonhomme Richard.* Augustus C. Buell, in a footnote in his *Life of Jones,* says that this Gerard was Jones's French orderly on the day of the battle, that he afterwards rose in the French naval service after the French Revolution, and that he was a lieutenant on the *Généreux,* one of the two French ships which escaped at the Battle of the Nile, and was second in command of the *Neptune* in the Battle of Trafalgar. Buell claims that the pamphlet is a rare one, and that it was first published at l'Orient in 1780, and a year later at Paris. According to him, Gerard wrote, "En ce moment, crie le capitaine anglais, 'Avez vous amené votre pavillon?' Auquel, férocement, et lachant un gros juron, a repondu le Commodore Jones—'Non! je vais à l'instant commencer le combat!'" [9]

Still another account, which gives practically the same language, is furnished by Dr. Benjamin Rush of Philadelphia. He was an intimate friend of John Adams, and was not only an author of medical treatises but also a careful observer of men. Among the diaries, letters, and pen portraits of his celebrated contemporaries, which have been published by his greatgrandson, Mr. Louis Biddle, is the following account of a conversation with John Paul Jones at a dinner, during which Jones declared, concerning the famous battle: "Towards the close of the battle while his deck was swimming in blood, the Captain of the *Serapis* called to him to

6. Pearson's report is printed in *The Naval Chronicle* (London), XXIV, 1810, p. 357; also in *The Remembrancer: or, Impartial Repository of Public Events for the Year 1780, Part I* (London), IX, 47.

7. Augustus C. Buell, *Paul Jones, Founder of the American Navy: A History* (2 vols., New York, 1900), I, 225. Buell is notably unreliable, however. Upon inquiring of the Public Record Office in London as to the accuracy of the above statement, the author received this reply: "I am directed to inform you that the Minutes of the Court-Martial held on 10 March 1780, for the trial of Captains Pearson and Piercy and the officers and men of the *Serapis* and *Countess of Scarborough,* have been examined, but no record of the statement said to have been made by Captain Pearson during the proceedings was found."

8. As far as the writer has been able to determine, no one but Buell has ever cited the *Memoir du Combat* as an authority. The pamphlet appears in no bibliographies relating to Jones; hence its present location or place and date of publication cannot be supplied with any certainty.

9. Buell, *Paul Jones,* I. 222, 224, 227.

strike. 'No, sir!' he said, 'I will not, we have had but a small fight yet.' " [10]

These three reports agree that the slogan was, in substance, "I am just beginning to fight." And they may have been the source of the slogan as it is now commonly worded, for only a slight change is needed to convert the former into the latter. But it should be remembered that scholars have shown that Buell's *Life of Jones* is thoroughly unreliable; the Gerard pamphlet is not listed in any of the John Paul Jones bibliographies, and hence it may have existed only in Buell's imagination.[11] As to the Rush account, the words therein recorded sound more like something quoted from memory than an exact transcription made at the time they were spoken. If, however, we had no further light on the slogan, we might be disposed to consider the words given above as a fairly correct approximation to what was spoken on that occasion, and there rest the case. But there is better and more definite evidence to be considered.

It is not commonly known that John Paul Jones himself has put on record the words that he used. They are to be found in the *Journal* which he prepared for Louis XVI in 1786. There is a well-authenticated French copy of the original *Journal* in the Library of Congress. It bears the following ponderous title: "Extrait du Journal de mes Campagnes, ou j'expose mes principaux Services et rapelle quelques circonstances de ce qui m'est arrivé deplus remarquable pendant le cours de la Révolution Américaine, particuliérement en Europe." Jones's account of the slogan, when translated into English, reads as follows: "The Captain, on hearing the gunner express his wishes to surrender, in consequence of his supposing that we were sinking, instantly addressed himself to me, and exclaimed, 'Do you ask for quarter? Do you ask for quarter?' I was so

10. *A Memorial Containing Travels through Life or Sundry Incidents in the Life of Dr. Benjamin Rush . . . Published privately for the benefit of his Descendants by Louis Alexander Biddle* (1905), 121.

11. In the preface (p. 11, n.) to his edition of *Fanning's Narrative; Being the Memoirs of Nathaniel Fanning, An Officer of the Revolutionary Navy, 1778-1783* (New York, 1912), John S. Barnes wrote, in reference to Buell's claim that he quoted from Fanning in his biography of Jones: "The editor informed Mr. Buell of his error regarding Fanning, to which he made no reply. His book is, however, so replete with pure fabrications that it can only be classed as an interesting romance through which runs but a slender thread of truth, and its title a misleading assumption unworthy to be called history."

When Buell was questioned by George Canby, a grandnephew of Betsy Ross, as to Buell's claim in his biography of Jones that the first American flag was made in Portsmouth, Buell replied in part on October 4, 1901: "The fact is that when compiling the matter for my history I never had any idea of being made a defendant in the premises or being called upon to prove anything by proffer of original documents." See de Koven, *John Paul Jones*, II, appendix D, 453.

At the United States Naval Academy Buell is considered so unreliable that his biography is placed on reserve in order that midshipmen may not be misinformed by reading it.

occupied, at this period, in serving the three pieces of cannon on the forecastle that I remained totally ignorant of what had occurred on deck; I replied, however, 'I do not dream of surrendering, but I am determined to make you strike!'" It is well known that Jones was a great lover of the picturesque phrase, and it seems almost inconceivable that, if he had used the more vigorous and expressive words, "I have not yet begun to fight," they would not have remained in his memory and been set down verbatim in this *Journal,* which was written only seven years after the battle in which they were used.

There is, furthermore, strange confirmation that he did use the substance of the language recorded in the *Journal.* A letter from Amsterdam, dated October 8, 1779, was printed in the London *Evening Post* of October 12, 1779, and contained these words: "Captain Pearson hearing all that was said, asked Jones if he had struck? (at this time the flag was shot away). 'No, sir,' says he, 'I have not as yet thought of it, but am determined to make you strike.'"[12] It is not at all improbable that the writer of this letter heard either in Amsterdam or Texel, both of which places Jones visited after the battle, the great hero himself describe the engagement and use those very words. At all events, their substantial identity is most striking.

In addition to this letter there is another corroborative account. On the *Bonhomme Richard* there was a midshipman by the name of Nathaniel Fanning, who during the engagement commanded the marines and sailors in the maintop. He kept a sort of diary, which he wrote out in the form of a continuous narrative in 1801 and published anonymously in 1806. After his death, it was published in 1808 under the title *Memoirs of the Life of Captain Nathaniel Fanning.* His version of the incident is as follows: "The enemy now demanded of us if we had struck, as they had heard the three poltroons halloo for quarter. 'If you have,' said they, 'why don't you haul down your pendant?', as they saw our ensign was gone. 'Ay, ay,' said Jones, 'we'll do that when we can fight no longer, but we shall see yours come down the first, for you must know that Yankees do not haul down their colors till they are fairly beaten.'"[13] This, as will be readily seen, is but an amplification of the words set down by Jones in his *Journal.* It is, of course, improbable that Fanning heard Jones speak the slogan, for he was in the tops at the time. But he is reported to have acted as Jones's secretary during a part of the cruise,

12. Quoted in Seitz, *Paul Jones,* 88.
13. Barnes, *Fanning's Narrative,* 45. The original edition (1806) of *Fanning's Narrative* is a rare item. There is a copy privately owned in Annapolis and one in the library of the New York Historical Society. The above quotation is from Barnes's edition.

and, besides, all the most minute happenings of that memorable day must have been the common knowledge of all the officers of the *Bonhomme Richard*. Thomas Wilson in his *Principal American Military and Naval Heroes* (1817) must have based his account on the Fanning narrative, for he says, "Jones replied that his colors would never descend, till he was fairly beaten." [14]

What, then, was the origin of the slogan as usually written? It has already been stated that there was some slight authority for the words, "I am just beginning to fight." These, slightly edited and made more emphatic, almost certainly were the foundation of the commonly accepted wording of the war cry. They appear to have been recorded for the first time in this final form in Sherburne's *Life of Jones* (1825). When Sherburne was preparing this biography, Richard Dale, who had been the first lieutenant on the *Bonhomme Richard*, furnished him with an account of the battle, in which he gives the slogan in the well-known words, "I have not yet begun to fight." [15] But at the time Dale gave Sherburne this information, the former was an old man. Dale died the following year at the age of seventy. To show that he failed to remember some of the most important details of the battle correctly, the following passage is cited: "The *Serapis* soon passed ahead of the *Bonhomme Richard*, and when he thought he had gained a distance sufficient to go down athwart the fore foot to rake us, found he had not enough distance, and that the *Bonhomme Richard* would be aboard him, put his helm alee, which brought the two ships on aline, and the *Bonhomme Richard*, having headway, ran her bows into the stern of the *Serapis*. We had remained in this position but a few minutes when we were again hailed by the *Serapis*, 'Has your ship struck?' To which Captain Jones answered, 'I have not yet begun to fight.'"

That is to say, he states very clearly (and this is Dale's language and not Sherburne's) that the slogan was spoken "a few minutes" after the ships fouled each other; but both Jones and Pearson in their official reports state that the action had been going on very much longer than that when the call for quarter was heard and the answer given. Pearson says definitely that the ships were lashed together at 8:30 and that the call for quarter was heard about 10:00 o'clock. Jones plainly implies in his report that a period of about one hour intervened.

May not this confusion have been caused by Dale's feeling that the words, "I have not yet begun to fight," which had by that time become

---

14. Thomas Wilson, *The Biography of the Principal American Military and Naval Heroes* (2 vols., New York, 1817), I, 126.

15. Sherburne, *Life and Character of the Chevalier John Paul Jones*, 127.

the accepted form, would have been more naturally spoken near the beginning of a close action than toward the end of a battle which had been continuing for an hour or more? That Dale's account may have been thus affected is made more credible by an examination of James Fenimore Cooper's narrative of this incident. In his *History of the United States Navy* Cooper writes as follows: "The wind being light, much time was consumed in these different manoeuvers, and near an hour had elapsed between the firing of the first guns, and the moment when the vessels got foul of each other in the manner just described. The English now thought it was the intention of the Americans to board them, and a few minutes passed in the uncertainty which such an expectation would create; but the positions of the vessels were not favorable for either party to pass into the opposing ship. There being at this moment a perfect cessation of the firing, Captain Pearson demanded, 'Have you struck your colors?' 'I have not yet begun to fight,' was the answer." [16] He goes on to relate that the ships then broke apart and were afterwards lashed together. One will note in this account, therefore, an even greater straining of the facts in order to make this apparently exaggerated slogan fit into the context. In other words, in his endeavor to place the war cry as near as he can to the beginning of the battle, Cooper has stated that the words were spoken even before the ships were lashed together. This is a gross error, which Maclay and other naval historians have passed along.[17] It is in such errors that the slogan, as now commonly known, will be found imbedded.

It seems unreasonable, therefore, to take as an authority the account of an old man near seventy years of age, written forty-six years after the battle, rather than the record of John Paul Jones himself, the author of the slogan, who wrote it down only seven years after the occasion of its utterance. It may be that Jones did not set down in his *Journal* the exact words that he spoke; but it seems certain that we have there the substance of his famous war cry, which is so markedly different from the popular slogan. There is no question but that the latter is more forceful, more

16. James Fenimore Cooper, *History of the Navy of the United States of America* (3rd edition, 2 vols. in 1, Philadelphia, 1847), I, 107.

17. Cf. Edgar S. Maclay, *A History of the United States Navy from 1775 to 1901* (3 vols., New York, 1901), I, 120. Very curiously, Alfred Thayer Mahan sidesteps the slogan. In his famous *Influence of Sea Power upon History* he makes no mention of Jones, although Jones's exploits are within the limits of the book's dates. In an article in *Scribner's Magazine* (New York), XXIV, 1898, p. 210, he recounts the battle in detail but mentions no battle cry as having been made by Jones. The only cry he refers to is that of the frightened gunner who called for quarter. Of this Mahan writes: "This cry Pearson heard, and called to know whether his opponent had struck. Receiving no answer, for Jones had hurled his boarding pistols at the clamorer's head, breaking his skull and silencing his yells, he ordered his men to board."

picturesque, and more inspiring; but that is not the point at issue. The simple question is, "Have we good and sufficient authority for believing that Jones said, 'I have not yet begun to fight'?" The answer is in the negative. John Paul Jones said, "I do not dream of surrendering, but I am determined to make you strike!"

## Suggestions for Study

In making your analysis of this research paper, study closely Professor Lewis's method of sifting the evidence concerning Jones's war cry. Does he find it more acceptable, for example, to go directly to the primary documents, such as Jones's manuscripts, contemporary diaries kept by those in the fight, and the like, or to rely upon secondary evidence, such as later transcripts by those not present at the combat? Is his method in general the better one for research scholars?

Also consider whether it would be possible to report a scientific investigation of this sort convincingly without footnotes. In giving your answer, consider the situation in the light of the article by Douglas Bush, "Scholars Poor and Simple," in this text. Also study the different kinds of footnotes used. For example, what is the full purpose of the first footnote? Note the different devices used in the footnoting. Why did the author insert the brackets in the fourth footnote? What do the three dots mean in the tenth footnote?

Pertaining to your own selection of a topic for research, observe how excellently the author of this investigation limited his topic. But also notice how many words were demanded from him to make even so limited a topic clear and persuasive in its presentation.

## B. The Feature Article

The term "feature article" comes from journalism, where it means a type of news story which aims to entertain as well as supply information. Since the feature article is a type of composition which everyone can engage in while in college and after,[1] it may well merit attention in a general course in writing.

The feature article is kin to the research paper, but it is less formal and usually more readable than the formal research paper. It is based, however, on careful investigation, though this need not be investigation in a library or records but may be by means of observation or interviews. Many articles, nevertheless, are based on library research, and these may differ from formal research papers only in being enlivened by narrative, anecdote, and the like.

Usually, the research paper is not directed at a large reading public.

1. Many college students actually pay part of their expenses by writing feature articles, and a great many people who have other occupations than writing supplement their incomes by writing features for newspapers and magazines.

The writer assumes that only a limited number of persons in a particular profession will be interested in the material. While he does his utmost to make his paper interesting and readable for those persons, he does not try to attract a large audience of laymen. The feature writer, on the other hand, is primarily interested in the general attractiveness of his product. If he is writing the history of his home town, he aims his article not only at those few individuals who are already engaged in antiquarian research in the locality, but also at all natives and residents who are literate enough to read a newspaper. He takes pains, therefore, to enliven his material with anecdotes, personal histories, and "background" information. Narration, description, and exposition are interwoven freely and easily. Appeal to popular interest takes its place along with accuracy in the dual category of virtues of the feature article.

**Finding Ideas for Feature Articles.** The student who has written a research paper already has material for at least one feature article, perhaps several. If, for some reason, this material is unsatisfactory, in the student's immediate vicinity there are actually hundreds of possible topics. As has been stated, the ordinary undergraduate research paper is limited to information derived from printed material, but the feature article can be written from experience or observation. Usually, both sources of information are drawn upon. The locality in which the student lives or in which he is going to school is one source of a topic. There is not a town or village whose early history could not be written interestingly and instructively. Peculiar features of the community, such as historic landmarks, buildings, industries, organizations, and institutions, are gold mines of ideas. Local people and their achievements suggest another classification of topics. Remember that the local resident who lives in the finest house or who has his name in the paper most frequently does not always live the most interesting life. The mail carrier, the bridge tender, the photographer, the bank messenger, the college janitor may be better subjects than the industrial magnate or the society leader. The subject matter of college courses is another rich field for the feature writer to explore. The work of glaciers, the assaying of gold, the character and personality of a figure in history, the story behind a poem, the real meaning of a treaty —these are only a handful of suggestions.

Inventions and discoveries, and the people connected with them, are popular topics. Professions, businesses, and trades offer an unlimited number of opportunities for profitable investigation and observation. Games, holidays, national customs, outdoor life, health, hobbies, and travel need only mentioning to suggest their possibilities for the feature writer.

**Making the Article Interesting.** Whatever the topic, the important consideration is to make the treatment of it interesting. An article on Frederick the Great might begin, for instance, by a reference to the great admiration in which Frederick was held by the Nazi leaders of Germany. The configuration of a certain hill or moraine well known to local residents may serve to introduce a discussion of the work of glaciers.

The beginning of the article is especially important in providing the proper contact with the reader—so important that many professional writers finish the body of the article first and then return to write the beginning. It must (1) catch the reader's eye and attract him to a reading of the article, (2) give the reader an idea of the content of the article and the point of view to be maintained, and (3) provide a point of contact with interests which the reader already holds. Since Americans are great readers of fiction, a beginning which makes use of a bit of narrative or dialogue is likely to be more effective than strict exposition. Description, a direct quotation, or merely a question may serve equally well, although the type last mentioned ("How many students know that . . .") is overworked by high-school writers. The opening (or *lead,* as it is called in newspaper parlance) which plunges the reader into a concrete situation about which he can build sensory images—in other words, one based on something which the reader can experience with pleasure or excitement—will serve the purpose of attracting attention and advertising the material which will follow.

It is essential, also, that the lead be integrated with the rest of the article so that the reader will not feel that he has been cheated with a showy display window that fronts a shabby store. The more striking the lead is, the more difficult it is to graduate the style and content of the article down to a level which can be maintained.

**The Feature Story Based on Library Research.** The student who has succeeded in writing an acceptable formal research paper should be sufficiently acquainted with the resources of the library and methods of using them to need no further instruction in using the library for purposes of the feature article. Every reference work on the shelves in the reading room can suggest topics and furnish information. Many professional feature writers make regular trips to public libraries merely to browse through the card catalogues. The suggestions for topics which an hour's time in the library can furnish are limited only by the imagination of the writer.

A never-failing source of material is anniversaries and holidays. Those which are more commonly known are frequently overworked, but less familiar anniversaries can always be used for interesting articles. Here are a very few:

January 27 (1880)—Edison patents the incandescent light.
February 7 (1893)—First long distance telephone operated between Boston and New York.
February 26 (1856)—Costa Rica declares war against a single man, a soldier of fortune named Walker.
March 30 (1842)—Ether first used as an anesthetic.
March 30 (1867)—Alaska purchased from Russia for $7,200,000.
April 2 (1792)—Birthday of the United States Mint.
May 10 (1501)—Amerigo Vespucci sails on second trip to America.
July 4 (1826)—Two presidents die: John Adams and Thomas Jefferson.
July 26 (1847)—First electrical locomotive exhibited and operated.
September 25 (1690)—First American newspaper issued.
October 8 (1891)—Great Chicago fire.
October 27 (1904)—New York subway opened to the public.
November 6 (1847)—First American Missionary church established in China.
December 1 (1863)—Patent granted for making artificial limbs.

Any fair-sized library will provide sufficient material for an article on such events. Remember that the mere retelling of the incident does not constitute a good feature article. The information must be made attractive to ordinary people, many of whom found history in the public school dull. Characters must be made to emerge with real human traits. The drama and irony of events must be emphasized; and, if possible, a link with some contemporary occurrence of wide interest must be contrived to make the material seem more than usually pertinent.

**The Feature Article Based on the Interview.** Using the library as a source of material for the feature article is essentially the same as using it for the research paper, but some suggestions should be made concerning the interview, which is a method widely used by feature writers. The article based on the interview has the twofold attraction of containing up-to-date information and presenting an individual who may be interesting to readers. Although the person interviewed is usually prominent in community life, in his profession, or in the news of the day, any person is, in some sense or other, interesting.

*Technique of interviewing.* As a rule, the best procedure to follow in getting an interview is to make an appointment by letter or telephone several days in advance. The interviewer should explain briefly his purpose and the kind of information he would like to have. Allowing a person time to gather his thoughts before being questioned is more courteous than plunging into his home or office unannounced; furthermore, the person is more likely to feel that he and the writer are collaborating on a piece of work. Although it is sometimes better to arrange to talk somewhere other than at the person's place of business in order to be free from distracting influences, the interview will perhaps be more colorful and informative if it takes place amid the operations which the writer will try to describe in his article.

It is extremely important that the writer make exact preparations before making his call. First, he should inform himself as to the personality, idiosyncrasies, hobbies, and achievements of the person he is about to question. No good feature writer will drop into his subject's office, sprawl on a chair, and begin, "Now, Mr. Brown, tell me all about your business." He will have prepared twenty or thirty questions, tactfully phrased, which will start the conversation and keep it going in the desired channels. The interview itself is conducted more like an informal conversation than the grilling of a witness on a stand. The interviewer has his questions well in mind and drops them in casually when the talk lags or departs from the desired path. Invariably courtesy, intelligent enthusiasm, and attentiveness mark the good interviewer.

*Writing the interview article.* The article may consist almost entirely of direct quotation, or it may make use of direct quotation as an embellishment for material which is partly quoted indirectly and partly derived from sources other than the interview. The second method of writing is usually the more effective. Most feature articles of this kind begin with a lead consisting of a description of the subject and his surroundings, and the opening words of the interview or the most striking sentence of the interview. Whatever the lead may be, the feature writer, like the short story writer, will not proceed far before giving his readers a sharply defined picture of the person under consideration. Whether the article is primarily about him, or whether he has been chosen as one of a class of people and his statements used to personalize an otherwise objective treatment of the information, the writer should keep in mind the principle that people are more interesting than things to readers.

## Fifty Ideas for Newspaper Features [2]

To sell these ideas to local papers, tie the idea in with local people, events, and places. For sale of the same idea to a state paper (a newspaper

---

2. Reprinted by permission of the *Writer's Digest,* 22 East Twelfth Street, Cincinnati, Ohio.

with a "State Edition" that is sold throughout the entire state) tie the idea in with prominent state people, places, and events. Pictures make the feature. Submit "glossy prints" about 5 x 7 inches.

1. "The Lord Is Where You Look." Any town of 250,000 or over will show, on careful investigation, many singular religious sects with their own leaders, their own curious ways, and peculiar meeting places. Normally we think of churchgoers traveling to a dignified stone building, in their Sunday best, sitting quietly through services, and nodding pleasantly to acquaintances. But there are millions of Americans whose churches have colorful names, and even more exciting services, manners, and customs.

2. Kite flying as a serious hobby; as a toy for boys; as an industry. Ben Franklin used a kite in his experiments. The weather departments use them, and there are kite flying clubs of young men who love the sport.

3. Unusual epitaphs in your community. Bob Ripley has revived interest in humorous tombstone lines. Write up not only the amusing ones in your city or state, but the dramatic ones that speak tragedy (murder, accident, fire, epidemics).

4. Origin of street and suburb names in your city. Do they reflect historical trends and fads? Were German names changed during World War I? Are there reminiscences of the Civil, Spanish-American, and World Wars? Are local heroes honored? Were the streets preplanned and prenamed before they were built (as in Salt Lake City)?

5. How successful has the police radio been in your community? Cite instances of thrilling captures of criminals by broadcasts to a squad car. Take the other side of the story, too. Have police broadcasts helped any bad men to escape?

6. How various students in college earn money performing odd chores to help pay their tuition or to help make money for their fraternities or other organizations. Part-time work in a drug store, restaurant, or typing, sweeping, grass-cutting, tutoring, garage duties.

7. Tribulations of a movie usher. Has to be a Beau Brummell, diplomat, Sherlock Holmes, night nurse, and encyclopedia, all in one. Interview some interesting ushers, learn their stories and ambitions. Be sure to mention notables who have at one time served as ushers—Tyrone Power is only one movie usher who has zoomed to the top.

8. Minerals, gems, soil strata in your community. Interview geologists, ask them about interesting items, historical facts, or new discoveries. Look into early mining in your section of the state; past gold rushes, lost gold mines, ghost towns, dignitaries of old who prospected and prospered.

9. Advent of the "gasoline buggy" in your town. What citizen owned

the first car; who operated the first garage, where the mechanics were known as "car doctors"? Early motorcades. Dip into old newspaper files and look for amusing headlines—especially those stressing the danger and the daring of the "Horseless Carriage."

10. Feminine Fliers in your city or in a nearby city. What are their reasons for flying? Have they had to hurdle family opposition or financial difficulties in order to follow their aviation ambitions?

11. If there is a penitentiary nearby, interview the man who pulls the switch for the electric chair in the death house. His emotions. His recollections of "last words," "last requests," "last suppers" of the doomed men. His observations of human courage and fears, as based upon his death house experiences. Was there an instance of a doomed man being pardoned at the last minute?

12. Early theaters in your vicinity. The first opera, play, or performance. The last. What great actors graced the stage? What great personages swelled the audiences? What romances culminated on that stage? What has become of the building?

13. Talking books for blind students. How sightless pupils get their lessons; how they amuse themselves; how they earn a living.

Are there any shut-in societies in your community? Are crippled and disabled persons encouraged to make a living through their skill and handiwork? How do they manage?

14. Adventures of a federal narcotic agent. The dangers and thrills in his work. Some characters he has met; "innocent" victims! dangerous and elusive criminals; his hairbreadth experiences in solving narcotic cases. Unsolved cases.

15. The National Guard of your state. Its duties and activities in peacetime; its activities in the defense program.

16. Interview a newsreel photographer. Make him the real "power behind the throne" or the backstage hero. Stress his risks and dangers in "getting that picture." His most humorous experience; his greatest danger; some of his hardships, black moments, his favorite stories, his favorite pictures, his favorite characters. Emphasize unsung hero angle.

17. Is there an unpublicized ventriloquist in your community? There were myriads of ventriloquists struggling to earn daily bread long before Chase and Sanborn discovered Charlie McCarthy.

18. Experiences of a local parachute jumper. Some of his narrow escapes from death. How he became interested in this thrilling profession; does he still get a thrill with each jump or is he nonchalant and used to it all? Does he have any pet superstitions, or lucky days?

19. Experiences of a dog-catcher. His full duties. (In most cities the dog

catcher is also the Deputy Sheriff and, therefore, is an important individual. Is the hard-heartedness conception of the dog-catcher untrue in this case? Is this particular dog-catcher fond of children?)

20. Local hero feature story about neighborhood personalities who have been awarded the Carnegie medal for bravery.

21. The bicycling craze. Begin with the current Hollywood fad of bicycling for slenderness and health and the latest bike models, with handlebar brakes and other up-to-date features.

22. Evolution of the barbering trade. Old-time tonsorial shops with *Police Gazette* on hand. Changes in methods, gossip, literature. Some tonsorial oldtimers in your community.

23. Anything interesting about typewriters in your communities? Who owned the first one in your town? What is the oldest model you can find? Development of the typewriter; some of its inventors; first stenographers were men.

24. Beauty parlor operators. How they happened to go into that work. Do they find it monotonous or exhilarating?

25. Unusual collection of old firearms. Does a local citizen or police department own pistols of historical or dramatic interest? Pistols once belonging to a notorious outlaw or pirate—or perhaps to a famous soldier?

26. A veteran music teacher who has maintained a studio for 20 years or more, and has, perhaps, been a famous artist at one time. His or her experiences in guiding the hands and musical tastes of many youngsters.

27. Interview an old-time druggist in your community. Oldest drug store in town. Ancient drugs, ones most in demand in old times; newest products and fads.

28. The fingerprinting of civilians, including schoolchildren. Individual reactions to it: objection, superstitions. How these clues have been used to trap culprits, to identify amnesia victims, find missing persons, and reconcile families. Look for dramatic stories and humorous incidents here.

29. There may be a good story in a local florist shop. How did the florist get interested in flowers? Has he or she discovered anything interesting and unusual about flowers? What types are most in demand during what seasons? Has the florist been able to trace romances through floral orders?

30. Interview a veteran veterinarian for an appealing article on the art of healing the diseases and injuries of domestic animals. How animal hospitals prolong animals' lives and cure injuries and diseases which formerly took a huge toll of pet life.

31. Experiences of a hypnotizer or a psychology professor who has hypnotized students in his experiments. Highlights of his career; inter-

esting points and experiences concerning hypnotism; how he has told a hypnotized person to perform a certain act and how, later when the hypnotic state has been dispelled, the person will perform that act without knowing why. Conclusions the hypnotizer has drawn from his experiences. How this has effected certain benefits, caught criminals? Psychoanalysts use hypnotism.

32. Unique experience of a pawnbroker. Out-of-the-ordinary articles which people have deposited with him as security on loans.

33. Interview with a woman physician. Her preparation and the highlights of her medical career.

34. The city's most enthusiastic and successful autograph collector. Some of his (or her) most distinguished signatures; the personal favorites of the collector, and the story behind them. Interesting experiences in securing, and the story behind them.

35. History of a fraternal organization in your city or campus. The leaders, past and present. Initiation fun and terrors. Build it around one main character.

36. A genealogical expert. How he or she collects data about different families. The demand for such work, the compensation? What are this genealogist's opinions of human vanity and man's interest in himself? Does he or she connect our increasing interest in genealogy with Oriental and Biblical ancestor-worship?

37. Interview an ant or insect specialist. What started the person in this work? What has he found most interesting in the life and habits of ants and similar insects? Has the student other vocations? You might make references to Henry David Thoreau and his life at *Walden*.

38. A professional rat exterminator. How the modern "Pied Piper" conducts a campaign to rid a city of rodents. Some of the biggest triumphs.

39. Experiences of a state highway patrolman. Exciting captures of dangerous desperadoes and close calls.

40. Interview a weather prophet of note. Ask him his methods of forecasting and their accuracy. How he first became interested in weather forecasting. Ask him his theories as to the important position of his profession in modern warfare; how weather forecasts have affected war.

41. Get a story about an ancient piano in your vicinity. Who was the first citizen to own one? Did the early pioneers of your section rebel against the use of pianos in Sunday School or church services? Are there any harpsichords, clavichords, and other forerunners of the piano nearby?

42. Interview with a Judge in a Juvenile Court. How he deals with cases of young lawbreakers. His theories.

43. The growth of a local humane society. Facts about the personality

and the life of the founder. Was there a personal reason for going into this charitable field? The task of finding homes for animals. Fate of animal pets in war.

44. Experiences of a theater cashier. Any holdups or humorous happenings? What types of movies are preferred by men, by women, by children?

45. A local bridge champion. What system does he use? To what does he ascribe his success?

46. Interesting article about razors, from the oldest in your community to a streamlined late-model electric razor. The advent of the safety razor; then the electric. Facts concerning beard. Interview someone in your town who has a full beard or a Van Dyke.

47. The history of hospitalization in your city. Pioneer hospitals and distinguished doctors of the past and present. Interesting experiences; unusual cases where patients have benefited from hospitalization.

48. Trace the history of military conscription throughout our American wars. (It really started in Biblical times.) But stress conscription in the Civil War. The age limits at various times during the War. Under the Draft Act passed by Congress in March, 1863, a drafted person could be exempted from service by hiring a substitute or by paying $300.

49. Thrills of a lifetime among local golfers. Some unique holes-in-one; how they perfected "trick" plays or characteristic shots; their superstitions, best memories.

50. Famous Indian fighters of your state. Some of Paleface's outstanding exploits, and close escapes from death.

### Sidewalk Fisherman [3]

#### MEYER BERGER

Sam Schultz has always been hydrophobic. Even as a kid, in a Central Park rowboat he would go white with fear of the water. When he grew up and friends invited him on fishing parties he'd always refuse, saying he had a tendency to seasickness. It took a vast economic disturbance, the depression, to throw him into grate-fishing when all his natural instincts were against it, but today he is probably the world's champion grate-fisherman, the man who can haul up coins from subway gratings with more efficiency than anybody else in the business. Grate-fishing was a primitive art when Sam became identified with it after losing his job as a truckman's helper seven years ago. It was just something that bums

3. From the New Yorker, XIV (July 23, 1938), No. 23. Reprinted by permission of the author and the New Yorker.

worked at for beer money. Sam has made it an exact science, and he earns a living by it.

Sam works with a few feet of light twine and a plummet of his own design—a piece of steel five inches long, an eighth of an inch thick, and about an inch and three-quarters wide, just right to lower through a grate slot. He lets it down endways until it gets to the bottom, and then lets it fall broadside on the coin. Sam will point out that his five-inch plummet thus covers a potential working area of almost ten inches. The flat side of the plummet is greased so that the coin sticks to it; all Sam has to do then is to haul away, and he's got the money. The bums of the grate-fishing industry use tiny weights for plummets and have to maneuver their lines a long time before they hit. "My way," Sam will tell you, "is pure headwoik."

Sam's second and equally important contribution toward uplift of the industry was an all-weather stickum to take the place of the chewing gum or taxicab-wheel grease which the bums use on their casting plummets. Chewing gum was all right in summer but it hardened at the first frost. Taxi grease worked into your pores, got under your fingernails, and made your hands untidy. It took months of experiment before Sam found the right thing—white petroleum jelly, or vaseline. A thin coat of this on the plummet will pull pennies, dimes, nickels, and even big money out of any subway grate, come frost or heat wave.

Sam buys the vaseline in the Liggett's drugstore on Times Square. The clerks there know him now and they plop the jar on the counter the minute he walks in. A single jar will last a month in winter and about three weeks in summer, if you husband it and don't oversmear, which is the general fault of amateurs. Runoff, because of heat, accounts for the extra summer waste, and so far Sam hasn't found a way around that. When you're after big money (quarters and halves), it is better to thicken the vaseline coating on your plummet, but not too much. Sam figures, for example, that proper bait for a silver dollar would be around a sixteenth of an inch. That's pure theory, because cartwheels are practically extinct in New York and he has never had a chance to work on one.

Sam may not look it now, but he was a machine gunner in the World War. Hunching over grates has rounded his shoulders and has taken something from his five feet, seven inches. He keeps his hat brim far down over his face, which is red from exposure. He got into that habit when he first took up grate-fishing. He was ashamed of his work and always afraid he might be recognized by the Brooklyn crowd who used to invite him around to pinochle and poker games when he was a truck-man's helper. Incidentally, he thinks that stuff about Times Square being the crossroads of the world is just a myth. He's fished the Square almost every night for seven years and hasn't seen one of his old acquaintances.

Sam's people were German-American. They died before he got through 6B in Public School 25 on First Avenue at Fifth Street. He wasn't much at school except in history and arithmetic, and most of that is gone now. He doesn't think, though, that he will ever forget the stuff about George Washington, Abraham Lincoln, and Captain John Smitz. The sturdy Captain sticks in his mind. "Captain Smitz," he will say, "was so tough a tommyhawk bounced off his neck and the Indians had to turn him loose."

Sam always liked horses, and when he got out of school in the middle of the sixth year he drove a wagon for a neighborhood fruit-and-vegetable man. That's how he came to get his first job as a truckman's helper when he lived in Harlem. He had to give that up when he was drafted into the Thirty-second Machine Gun Battalion and sent to Camp Meade. He liked machine-gunning. He recalls that it made a man feel like somebody to have a Lewis gun kicking against his shoulder. Sadness overtakes him now when he remembers how Spanish flu swept the camp in October of 1918, forty-eight hours before his outfit was scheduled to go to France. The quarantine held until the war ended.

When he got back to New York from Camp Meade, Sam looked around for another helper's job and finally landed one over in Brooklyn. He started at $12 a week and worked up to $26. That had been cut to $21 when the job was swept out from under him altogether by the depression. With that he lost all his Brooklyn interests, even his (up till then) unshaken faith in the Dodgers. He doesn't get to the ball games on Sundays as he used to, but if he could raise the price of a bleacher seat he supposes he might root for the Yanks. Sam thinks a man ought to be loyal to some team and he never liked the Giants anyway.

Grate-angling prickles with fine points that you'd never dream of if you hadn't put your mind to it as Sam has. He knows all the midtown gratings by heart and can tell you, within a few cents, what his yield has been in each one. He watches waste cans for discarded newspapers, and scans the lists of goings on in town to figure out the night's working schedule. If there is nothing happening at Madison Square Garden, for example, he will stick to Times Square, which is to the grate-angler what the Grand Banks are to a Gloucesterman. Sometimes he'll just play a hunch and go over to the East Side, now that the Kingfish has disappeared. The Kingfish was a giant Negro who would pound your ears right down to your ankles if you poached on his Lexington and Madison Avenue grates. No one seems to know what has happened to him this past month, but he hasn't been around. Rival fishermen hope it's nothing slight; Sam, in any case, is uneasy every time he works on the East Side. He figures that the Kingfish, who used to spend all his haul for gin, may merely be doing a short bit on the Island for assault or something and may get back any day. Sam, by the way, isn't a drinking man at all, though he will take a glass of beer on hot days.

The Garden is the best spot in town on fight nights, or when there's wrestling or hockey. Patrons of those sports are A-1 droppers. If you're a fast worker, like Sam, you can fish from fifty or sixty cents all the way up to a dollar on the Garden side of Eighth Avenue, from Forty-seventh Street north, on any night when there's a good fight card. Sam keeps away, though, during the Horse Show or when there is a Communist rally. He has come to learn that the Horse Show crowd either use their own cars or, when they pay off a taxi, simply don't drop any change. Communists, he'll advise you bitterly, are the lousiest droppers in the world. You can't count much on special events, either. Sam figured from what he'd read in the newspapers, for example, that the American Legion Convention would bring a big week of fishing. He worked like hell all through the thing, and at the end, what had he? Less than if those apple-knocking wise guys with their electric shockers had stayed home on the farm. The whole thing still puzzles him. Sam hates to see his carefully worked-up theories go to pieces. Things like the flop of the American Legion Convention make him lose confidence in his judgment.

Newspaper stands set up on subway gratings are highly favored spots, for obvious reasons. When Sam first figured that out, he had wild ideas about canvassing the stand people all along Broadway and Seventh and Eighth Avenues to move their positions from building fronts to the curb. He toyed with the project for a while, but could never quite bring himself to making the proposition. Some of the papersellers looked sour, and then, too, maybe it wouldn't have been honest. Sam is a stickler for honesty. He turned down an idea advanced by a Broadway chiseler who thought Sam might induce some kid to bump into people counting out change near the gratings. Sam just walked away from the fellow.

He has a working arrangement, however, with several of the busier newsstand owners. The man who operates the big stand on the northwest corner of Forty-second Street and Seventh Avenue drops on an average of $1.80 to $2 a month. Every time Sam comes by, the stand man indicates where coins have been dropped and Sam does his stuff. If the haul is small money he keeps all of it. On quarters, though, he gets only ten cents and on half-dollars only thirty cents. He thinks that's fair enough, and even if he didn't, what could he do? Let some other fisherman get the business? He had a trade argument one time with another stand owner, a woman, and before he knew it she had her own kid fishing for the drops.

Movie-house barkers will tip Sam off when people drop money, as they often do while fighting to buy tickets in a crowd. Some barkers, though, are apt to be snooty, especially the ones with fancy uniforms. Sometimes they snarl at Sam and tell him to scram. That always makes him curl up inside. Whenever it happens he tries to think of Camp Meade and the machine gun kicking away at his shoulder. One night a man dropped a twenty-dollar bill, wrapped around a half-dollar, through the grating in front of the Rialto. Sam got the flash from the barker but a subway porter beat him to the money—lifted one of the grates and got two dollars' reward for the job. Whenever Sam thinks of the incident he grows wistful. Even without the reward it was a swell chance to set a world record for grate-fishing.

Sam walks from ten to fifteen miles every night covering the grates, but never has foot trouble. The only time he ever had sore feet was a few years ago when he took a laborer's job up in Narrowsburg, New York, clearing out underbrush on the site of a Boy Scout camp. The ground was so soft and so alien to his feet that they slid all over the place and finally burst out in big blisters. He quit the sylvan quiet and was glad to get back to Times Square.

Sam usually works twelve hours a day, from five o'clock at night until daybreak. In addition to the general avenue runs he visits certain selected spots, in the manner of a trapper looking over his traps. After the early-evening rush the bus stop on the east side of the Times Building in the Square is nearly always good for twenty to thirty cents. The yield might be even better if some busybody hadn't wired boards under part of that grating. Sam doesn't know who's responsible, the *Times* people or the I.R.T. Another favored spot is the Lexington Avenue side of Grand Central Terminal in the morning and evening rush hours. Commuters use that entrance and they're very good droppers, especially on quarters; Sam can't say why. Loew's Lexington, between Fiftieth and Fifty-first, isn't bad either. At both places, of course, you've got to watch out for the Kingfish. The Waldorf is a continual disappointment—not nearly as good as Bickford's Restaurant at 582 Lexington Avenue or Foltis-Fischer's, next door to Bickford's. They're on the same side of the street as the Waldorf, one block further north.

No part of the garment center is worth working, and that goes, generally, for everything below Forty-second Street except the Hotel New Yorker. At that, the best bit of fishing Sam ever did was in front of the

Hotel York, on Seventh at Thirty-Sixth, but it was just one of those freak things. He fished up a fountain pen with a lot of people watching and someone thought it might be a good idea to hold a sidewalk auction. The bid went to $1.10, the highest single sum Sam has ever earned at grate-angling. He fished another pen—a two-minute job in front of the United Cigar store at Forty-second and Seventh—but that was a flat-rate assignment from the owner and paid only fifty cents. The pen was a gift, with initials on it, and the fellow was very grateful; couldn't get over Sam's skill.

Sam tried Brooklyn once, on a sudden inspiration, but came back disgusted. He didn't so much as make carfare and bait money there, although he surveyed every grate in the neighborhood of the Fulton Street department stores. The same goes for the Manhattan shopping district around Macy's, Saks, and Gimbels. Women drop less than men because their handbags are so big-jawed that change usually falls right back into them. He's never tried Queens, but feels instinctively it would be no better than Brooklyn.

Sam figures his fishing nets him an average of a dollar a day, or a little more. Some days, he says, you're lucky, and you may get as much as $1.65 or even $1.85. Lots of days, though, it's like going out for trout; you just don't have any luck at all. A few weeks ago, Sam hauled out only six cents in fourteen hours on the grates—a nickel in front of the Rialto and one cent from the Times island bus stop. He knew the recession was coming even before the papers began to notice it. Almost overnight Times Square was overrun with outsiders (any newcomer is an outsider to Sam) working the grates with disgustingly primitive equipment.

When the day's yield is a dollar or over, Sam feels justified in spending fifty cents for a room in the Seventh Avenue Mills Hotel. If it happens to be a little less, he puts up at the Vigilant, on Eighth Avenue near Twenty-eighth, where they charge only forty cents. He prefers the Mills because the guests are more genteel—not so apt to get boisterous. You don't get soap or towels with the rooms, so Sam carries his own, neatly wrapped in newspaper. He carries two suits of underwear, too; an extra pair of socks, a Gillette, and a stick of shaving soap. He bathes once a week in the Municipal Baths on Forty-first Street, at Ninth, when it's cold, but will go two or three times in hot weather. He feels a man loses his grip altogether if he doesn't clean up at least once a week.

Sam has no fancy tastes in food, although his work in the open air sharpens his appetite. When he finishes the early-morning run of the grates he has breakfast at the Manhattan, on Seventh Avenue near Forty-first. It's pretty nearly always the same—wheat cakes and coffee, for a dime. On good days he tries to get down to Beefsteak John's, at Third Avenue and Twenty-first, where they serve a stew, coffee, and bread for fifteen cents. If the day's haul warrants it, Sam may have a cut of coconut pie, the only dessert that ever tempts him. Sometimes, but not unless he has room money reserved, there's a late snack at the Manhattan and, because Sam's imagination doesn't seem to work where food's concerned, it's very likely to be wheats and java again. He has a good stomach— always did have—and never gets sick.

It's a mistake, unless you're out to bait Sam, to bring up the subject of stinkers. You wouldn't know about them, but stinkers are the parasites of the grate-fishing industry. When they sense that Sam is having a lucky night, they run on ahead and cut in on his grates. There's nothing you can do about it, either. Gratings are more or less public domain and anybody can fish them. What stirs Sam's gall, though, is the utter lack of ethics (he says "ettics") in the business—something he's tried to correct, but without much luck. "By me," he's apt to tell you with astonishing violence, "a stinker is rat poison—in spades."

Most grate-fishermen are antisocial. They don't so much as ask one another's names. Oh, once in a while one of them may look up from a grate and say "Hya, fisherman!" but you can't count on it. On chatty occasions they may ask about your luck, but that's more or less perfunctory, too. No oldtimer in the business will tell another fisherman how much he's made; certainly not *where* he made it. Sam does have a working arrangement with a young grate-angler who has been in and around the Square the past four years. He's a shy, shabby fellow who has an expression of constant bewilderment. Cabdrivers make him the butt of their unsubtle jokes (Shellshock is their name for him, because of that rabbity look), but he's rather handy with the plummet. Once a week he or Sam will ride down to Barclay Street on the B.-M.T. and buy a dozen flashlight batteries at a cut-rate hardware store. All grate-anglers use flashlights to show up what's at the grating bottoms. At the cut-rate stores the batteries are three cents apiece, against five cents for the same thing at Woolworth's; so Sam and Shellshock save a total of fourteen cents on the deal, even when you count in the carfare. There's always a chance, too, to fish carfare out of the downtown grates, but outside of William Street and maybe Church, financial-district fishing is lousy.

Three batteries make one fill for the flashlight and will last about three days. Sam always has three extra ones bulging his pockets, along with his portable toilet kit. Most grate-anglers are rather sloppy—carry their plummets in their pockets, grease and all. Sam is a neat fellow and packs his equipment in a Prince Albert tin. It took him quite a while to convince Shellshock that it wasn't nice to get his pockets all smeary, but he never has sold Shellshock the vaseline idea. Shellshock just wipes off his plummet after each performance and gets new grease from the wheels of the nearest cab.

People keep asking Sam if it's true that grating fishermen find valuable diamonds and things like that. He knows of but two cases. One time a traffic cop lost a diamond ring near Penn Station. This cop went home at the end of the day, rigged up a childish fishing outfit, and came back to fish. By that time, of course, the ring was gone. Sam doesn't know who got it. In the other case (Sam won't vouch for this, because it's only hearsay), the Kingfish was supposed to have done a job for a woman who lost a five-thousand-dollar bracelet on Lexington Avenue. The woman gave him a quarter, so the story goes, and the Kingfish would have busted her crumpet if she had been a man.

Right now Sam is doing some research on a pocket-battery outfit—something on the automobile-lighter principle—that will melt thin ice at the bottom of a grating. If he perfects this invention, he feels he can practically control the industry this winter. He hasn't thought the whole thing through yet, but he's the dogged type and will probably work it out all right.

## Suggestions for Study

1. What do you judge to have been the author's source of information for the material in this article? Study the article to see if you can detect more than one source.

2. Cite several instances of direct and indirect quotation that give insight into Sam's character. Why does the author use such words as "lousiest," "flop," and "apple-knocking"? Enumerate several other words of this sort that are not on a standard level of diction.

3. Is Sam honest? hard-working? intelligent? thrifty? neat? a lover of the rural countryside? a gourmand? List the words used to describe him.

4. Characterize the Kingfish and "Shellshock."

5. Trace the major divisions of the sketch to show its organization.

6. List each incident and comment that you think was inserted to attract and hold the reader rather than to give information.

7. Define the following words from the selection: hydrophobic, plummet, alien, canvassing, sylvan, recession, ethics, perfunctory.

## Enterprise and Old Iron [4]

### JOHN PATRIC

On a fertile plateau above the raging Snake River, near Jackson, Wyoming, Ora Grisamer owned a ranch. Until last year, he and his neighbors were virtually marooned there. Their only way across the turbulent Snake, 300 feet wide, was riskily by skiff or along a swaying footbridge sagging from a half-inch cable.

And now Ora Grisamer's tractor had broken down. There was no way to get it to a repair shop. Once there had been a ferry across the river—a scow pulled along a cable—but a flood had washed it away. Recently Grisamer had heard that a strange fellow named McCrary—a wizard mechanic—was camping in the canyon across the river. People said that Charles McCrary could make or repair anything—out of junk; that he had gathered around him the queerest caravan of old iron ever assembled west of the Missouri.

Grisamer hunted him up. In a clearing, he found the McCrary caravan, a bizarre collection of gadgetry on wheels, a traveling Valhalla of noble junk. There was a trailer as big as a box car, hitched to a mammoth but decrepit coal truck. The truck was loaded with a donkey engine, a ton of tools belonging to all trades and professions, and a mountainous assortment of cogs, ratchets, springs, and unclassified gear that McCrary had collected in his wanderings. Near by was the family jalopy and a smaller trailer where the family ate and slept. The family included Mrs. McCrary, four children, and a white goat. Strangest of all was a homemade contraption that McCrary proudly called his "drag-line" rig—another old truck on which was mounted a sort of power shovel whose bucket hung from pulleys at the end of a derrick.

Yes, McCrary would be glad to earn a few dollars by repairing Grisamer's tractor. The two men carried McCrary's tools over the narrow catwalk of the footbridge. "A wagon bridge would be worth $1,000 to me and my neighbors," said Grisamer, "but there's no use talking about it. Government engineers say that it would cost at least $10,000 to swing any kind of bridge across this river."

McCrary said nothing. But while he worked on the tractor, he did a little figuring in the back of his mind. Finally he said, "I'll build you a bridge for $1,250. And I'll guarantee it to hold three tons."

It sounded good to Grisamer. A bridge would make his farm more

---

4. From the *Christian Science Monitor*, December 21, 1940. Reprinted by permission of the *Christian Science Monitor*.

valuable. He knew his neighbors would chip in too. So that night by lamplight in a simple contract McCrary agreed for $1,250 to build—of second-hand steel and old cable—a suspension bridge eight feet wide, with railings, across the Snake. Grisamer agreed to advance $400 when actual construction began, and the remaining $850 when he could drive a three-ton load over the completed bridge.

McCrary walked home to his trailer camp, tingling with confidence. All his life he'd been making his own way, despite hard times, with supreme self-reliance, and never a penny from charity or relief. When his little repair shop in Missouri had burned in 1933, he started west with his family, in their old car, landing finally in Wyoming, where he made a living by reconditioning junked cars and selling them. Accumulating a stake, he leased an abandoned coal mine, operating it with machinery from the junk heaps, reconditioned by his expert hands. During a long winter he made his drag-line rig—also from junk—and with it got jobs clearing fields and building roads. Why shouldn't he likewise build a bridge from junk?

McCrary's only cash was the $6 he had charged Grisamer for repairing the tractor. But he did have his drag-line excavator. Its 900-pound bucket, made of old bridge girders cunningly welded together with a makeshift acetylene torch, would scoop up half a ton of gravel at a single bite. The rest of the machine consisted of such things as scrambled bits of gaspipe, a bicycle chain, a hay-rake seat, a locomotive coupling, and parts from automobiles and farm machines that McCrary had found on junk heaps. In cold cash, it had cost him only $3.50, mostly for bolts and screws. With this contraption he was going to dig the foundations of his bridge.

McCrary knew nothing of engineering; but he had a picture postcard of the Golden Gate Bridge: that would serve him in lieu of blueprints. He figured that his own towers, allowing for the droop in the cables, would have to be 30 feet high on Grisamer's side of the river and 40 feet on the lower Jackson side.

One morning he leveled off a shelf on the Jackson side, and set up his beloved drag-line rig. He climbed to the old hay-rake seat, started the engine, and dropped the bucket for the first load of dirt. Days later, two deep holes yawned darkly. McCrary could dig his pits no deeper; the bottom was solid rock. And now the once-rusty, bridge-steel bucket shone like a plowshare on a spring evening.

To find steel for the supporting towers of his bridge would have stymied a less ingenious fellow. But McCrary remembered a twisted heap of bridge ruins washed out in a flood of the Gros Ventre River. The mangled bridge still lay buried in the swirling river; wading out to his armpits, he cut off four girders with his acetylene torch. Then he dragged them through Jackson, one at a time, on a rude trailer made of two auto wheels and an axle. On the bank of the Snake River he laid them in approximate position near the holes he had dug.

Now for the cables! McCrary set out in his old truck for the oil fields, a several-hundred-mile trip, made none the easier by 17 flats. He knew that the long cables used in well drilling are discarded when they develop kinks. Oil men gave McCrary all the discarded cable he could haul away. Soon, at the bridge site, he had eight flawless pieces of cable, each about 400 feet long. He was ready to begin construction of the Jackson end of the bridge.

Erecting the steel uprights was a grueling job that required patience and precision. Aided only by his 13-year-old boy, Buster, McCrary picked up a pair of bridge towers with his drag-line rig, now transformed into a derrick, and lowered them into the hole already dug. With the $400 advanced by Grisamer, he bought a small cement mixer. He swapped an old automobile engine he had found in the dump, and then repaired, for a stationary gas engine to run his mixer. With this equipment he poured tons of concrete, reinforced by scrap iron, around the bases of the towers. Behind the towers he sank a 10-foot section of steel I-beam, and buried it in concrete under 100 tons of rock and earth. This was the shoreward anchorage for eight cables which were to be festooned across the river. He did not know it, but the cost of this extra anchorage, required by the nature of the soil, had thwarted past plans for building such a bridge.

Thus far, McCrary and his boy Buster had done all the work themselves. They would have continued alone, but two jobless wayfarers turned up and McCrary hired them at 40 cents an hour. Their wages would cut into his profit, but he knew what it was to be jobless. The quartet now began the task of stringing the eight suspension cables across the river. First they pulled a light cable to Grisamer's side and with that, tugging like demons, they dragged each of the heavy bridge cables through the foaming waters of the Snake.

After the cables had been drawn across, McCrary strung two of them on a temporary scaffolding. Then he devised a sort of cablecar that ran along them on pulleys, with the drag-line rig supplying motor power. On this cablecar, tools, cement, and cement mixer went across. But now came the herculean job of transporting the 7,000-pound tower to the farthest side of the river! Would the cablecar support it? The cables sagged perilously under the burden. McCrary's face was gray with strain. But the cables held fast; the tower reached the other side. Then the four bridge builders tipped it into holes already blasted for it.

But now McCrary had ominous visitors—two U.S. Forest Rangers. "You should have gotten a permit before you started this work," they said. McCrary hurried to Grisamer. "Have we got to stop work?" he asked.

"Not unless you want to, Mac," the farmer replied, "and I don't figure you will when you hear what they're saying uptown. They're saying, 'Grisamer's hired a little boy and a couple of tramps and a dumb mechanic, who never saw a suspension bridge in his life, to build him one with stuff from the town dump.'"

"That's so," McCrary grinned. "But she'll be a bridge. I'll show 'em!"

A few days later, as the concrete tower bases were slowly hardening, the county engineer came up to McCrary: "You fellows are undertaking something pretty serious here," he said. "The United States Forest Service has been to see me. May I see your blueprints?"

"Blueprints? What blueprints?"

"Your plans and specifications."

"Ain't got any."

"But, man, you must have something!"

From his pocket, McCrary pulled his postcard of the San Francisco Bridge. "I'm making it something like that," he said. "But"—apologetically—"not so big, of course." The engineer shook his head and turned to gaze at McCrary's bridge admiringly. "I don't see how you did it. But there she stands." After a careful inspection, the engineer passed judgment. "McCrary, if you'll make a few minor changes, I'll O.K. your bridge for a three-ton limit."

McCrary thanked the engineer and went back to work. Six more cables were strung and anchored in concrete. A solid plank floor was laid. Stout wooden handrails were fitted along the sides. County Commissioners, impressed by the job, agreed not only to improve the road approaches to the bridge but to pay the lumber bill also, thus saving McCrary $200. Whereupon, he promptly raised the wages of his two helpers from 40 to 50 cents an hour, with back pay from the beginning. Charlie McCrary wasn't in the bridge-building game for the purpose of getting rich!

At the opening of the bridge, just two months from the day McCrary started building it, no Government official cut any ribbons. But there was a ceremony just the same, with just a touch of sadness about it. Ora Grisamer, who had waited half his life for a bridge, passed on just before it was finished. But his tractor, driven by his daughter, headed the procession. Then came the two helpers and the McCrarys in the family jalopy, with the white goat bringing up the rear. The bridge was as steady as a cathedral under the tramping of a little cavalcade.

This story has an epilogue.

I visited Jackson last summer and found McCrary living in a real house, with his trailer rented to campers. Financially, things were a little easier with him; he owned two building lots, a bank book—and a new baby. I saw him slip a dollar into the collection plate the day he took me to church with his family. The drag-line rig was earning good money. It had moved houses, dug basements for new homes and stores. Already it was a Jackson legend, a fragment of the greater legend that is America.

The bridge, McCrary told me, had held up during the past winter even when there were—by careful reckoning—15 tons of wet snow on it. More than that, loads had gone across on the snow before the farmers found out how much it weighed.

I last saw Charlie McCrary sitting in the old hay-rake seat, digging a water-main ditch. As he swung his bucket to and fro, I saw him as a living symbol of American ingenuity and self-reliance.

## Suggestions for Study

1. How much do you know about McCrary's life before he started the bridge across the Snake? Where does this information occur in the article? Why does it not occur sooner?

2. What might have been some of the sources of information used by the writer of this article?

3. Does the writer make McCrary's accomplishment plausible or not?

4. Find half a dozen places in the article where information is given which helps you to form a mental picture of McCrary.

5. Explain the meaning of the following words: epilogue, bizarre, Valhalla, decrepit, turbulent, acetylene, stymied.

## Tracking Down a Murderer [5]

### J. LESLIE HOTSON

Ancient murderers arouse in some of us a deep detecting interest. To ferret them out and to turn the world's eye upon them gives a particular pleasure. The modern criminal, on the other hand, leaves us comparatively cold. We abandon him, with his large fortune and temporary mental aberration, to the sordid pillory of the headlines. Our preferred murderers are those far figures who, having drawn a cloak of centuries over their crime, are trying to slip unnoticed down the dark highway of history. Such we like to tap on the shoulder.

But "First catch your hare," says the oracle of the kitchen. And the

5. From the *Atlantic Monthly*, CXXXV (June, 1925), 733. Reprinted by permission of the author and of the *Atlantic Monthly*.

greatest initial obstacle to the exposing of lost murderers is of course the catching of them. Clues are clues only to those who have their eyes open. As a specimen of ancient hidden murder, I take the case of Nicholas Colfox. This man, we have just discovered, was a murderer denounced, under a cloak of poetry, by Geoffrey Chaucer. An obscure corner of history shows Colfox as the chief accomplice of Thomas Mowbray in the abduction and secret murder of Thomas, Duke of Gloucester, in 1397. This discovery has now for the first time opened our eyes to the damning finger which Chaucer points in his "Tale of the Cock and the Fox":

> A Colfox, full of sly iniquitee . . .
> Wayting his time on Chaunticleer to falle,
> As gladly doon thise homicydes alle,
> That in awayt liggen to mordre men.
> O false mordrer, lurking in thy den!

But the story we have to tell here is not the hunting of the Colfox. We shall come down two centuries, and relate the chase of the man who killed the dramatist Christopher Marlowe. And the beginning of the story lies in Bloomsbury.

You must know, first, that the houses in Bloomsbury are all alike—on the outside. Idiosyncrasy may find a place within door, but it is drab uniformity which orders the antique right-dress and the jaded eyes-front of the smoky exteriors. In a garret of one of these indistinguishable houses, one raw November night, we were huddled over the gas stove. Mary was trying to toast bread and, Jupiterlike, I was pouring a well-aimed shower of coins into the lap of that Danaän stove, to coax from it a complaisant warmth. No one who has not experienced it can know the joy of an English fireside. When the ponderous penny has dropped, and the eager gas has launched its cheerful roar—then is the moment for scorched shins, shivering backs, and little abortive attempts to mitigate the monotony of the English cuisine.

To us enters our literary friend, partly for hot buttered toast, and partly for companionship. Our literary friend is an authority on Christopher Marlowe and his writings. Being on tour, he has paid a visit to Marlowe's college at Cambridge, he has walked from the Bankside to Shoreditch, and is projecting a pilgrimage to the poet's birthplace, Canterbury. Before taking his leave, our literary friend learns that we are spending our days in Chancery Lane, grubbing among the musty parchments and papers of the Public Record Office, finding here a new fact about John Harvard, and there a lawsuit concerning some property of John Milton's. Thinking at once of the unknown man who destroyed the greatest early genius of the English drama, he shakes his head. Not much chance of finding a trace of that criminal in the Public Record Office. Scholars have ransacked the place in search of him. But Deptford, now—where Marlowe was killed? Why not try Deptford? No telling what you might find there, in some obscure corner.

After our literary friend had gone, I endeavored to think why I ought not to try Deptford. One very good reason that came to me was, I remember, that Peter the Great, Tsar of Muscovy, had tried it: and tsars were notorious for their bad taste—whether it were shown in accidentally beating their children to death, or in fostering revolution with the knout. The story goes that Peter went to Deptford ostensibly to learn shipbuilding as a common workman. But King Charles lodged him and his retinue in Sayes Court, the handsome Deptford mansion of John Evelyn. When the Muscovites came to move out, Evelyn made a bitter complaint to Parliament of the horrors wrought within the house by the nasty nobility, and of the destruction of his cherished hedges by Peter. The potentate, it seems, would seat himself in quest of excitement in a wheelbarrow, and get a powerful gardener to rush him full tilt through a hedge. Evelyn naturally could not be expected to understand what an intoxicated thrill of Tsarility it gave one to smash through those hedges.

Then, too, I reflected that though Deptford, even as late as Peter's time, had been in a condition to be visited, it now was unquestionably a city slum. On picking up the *Evening Standard* I read that health officers were urging the establishment of public baths in Deptford, since it had been estimated that there was one bathroom for every one hundred houses. Finally, where in Deptford should I find an archive—a commodity no doubt scarcer even than bathrooms?

No; the prospect of Deptford was lacking in charm. Instead, I went to the British Museum to find out exactly what was already known of Marlowe's murderer. It took but a very short time to find that nothing was exactly known. Turning to the *Dictionary of National Biography,* I found this:

> In the register of the parish church of St. Nicholas, Deptford, appears the entry, which is ordinarily transcribed thus: 'Christopher Marlowe, slain by ffrancis Archer, 1 June 1593.' Mr. Halliwell-Phillipps read the surname of the assailant as 'Frezer,' *i.e.* Fraser.

Here at once was mystery, full-fledged. The authorities did not agree even on the murderer's name. Some read "Archer," and others "Frezer." Plainly the first step would be to settle the question to my own satisfaction by studying the original writing. But the burial register that contained it was still kept at the church at Deptford where Marlowe was buried. For some moments a bus pilgrimage to Dismal Deptford loomed up unavoidable—but I was spared. From the dim stack a book on Marlowe was produced, whose author had thoughtfully enriched his work with a photographic facsimile of the disputed entry. One careful glance proved beyond a doubt that the "Frezer" reading was right and the "Archer" reading impossible. The scholars and parsons had mistaken the *ff* of *ffrezer* (which was the old way of writing capital *F*) for a capital *A*, owing to the two uprights and the crossbar; and to take *ez* for *ch* in an Elizabethan hand is not so stupid as one might suppose. But "Francis Frezer" was unquestionably the name written by the parish clerk.

So much for the name. What other dim light was there on Marlowe's death? Well, there were two ancient brimstone accounts of the violent and well-merited end of Marlowe, the reputed atheist, which have survived. The first, written by Thomas Beard four years after Marlowe's death, in his *Theatre of Gods Iudgements* (a collection of terrific obituaries), runs as follows:

> Not inferiour to any of the former in Atheisme and impiety, and equall to all in maner of punishment was one of our own nation, of fresh and late memory, called *Marlin* [marginal note: *Marlow*], by profession a scholler, brought up from his youth in the Vniuersitie of Cambridge, but by practise a playmaker, and a Poet of scurrilitie, who by giuing too large a swinge to his owne wit, and suffering his lust to haue the full raines, fell (not without iust desert) to that outrage and extremitie, that hee denied God and his sonne Christ, and not only in word blasphemed the trinitie, but also (as is credibly reported) wrote books against it, affirming our Sauiour to be but a deceiuer, and *Moses* to be but a coniurer and seducer of the people, and the holy Bible to be but vaine and idle stories, and all religion but a deuice of pollicie. But see what a hook the Lord put in the Nosthrils of this barking dogge: It so fell out, that in London streets as he purposed to stab one whome hee ought a grudge vnto with his dagger, the other party perceiuing so auoided the stroke, that withall catching hold of his wrest, he stabbed his owne dagger into his owne head, in such sort, that notwithstanding all the meanes of surgerie that could be wrought, hee shortly after died thereof. The manner of his death being so terrible (for hee euen cursed and blasphemed to his last gaspe, and togither with his breath an oath flew out of his mouth) that it was not only a manifest signe of Gods iudgement, but also an horrible and fearefull terrour to all that beheld him. But herein did the iustice of God most notably appeare, in that hee compelled his owne hand which had written those blasphemies to be the instrument to punish him, and that in his braine, which had deuised the same.

It was to this story that Francis Meres, writing a year later, added the famous embroidery of scandal: "*Christopher Marlow* was stabd to death by a bawdy Seruing man, a riuall of his in his lewde loue." Historians of literature, novelists, and playwrights have seized on this last unsavory morsel of gossip and have served it up under such an ingenious variety of forms that those who have heard nothing else about Marlowe have heard that.

William Vaughan, the author of the second long account, tells a more circumstantial and less expansive tale in his *Golden Grove* (1600):

> Not inferiour to these was one Christopher Marlow by profession a playmaker, who, as is reported, about 7. yeeres a-goe wrote a booke against the Trinitie: but see the effects of Gods iustice; it so hapned, that at Deptford, a little village about three miles distant from London, as he meant to stab with his ponyard one named Ingram, that had inuited him thither to a feast, and was then playing at tables, he quickly perceyuing it, so auoyded the thrust, that withall drawing out his dagger for his defense, he stabbed this Marlow into the eye, in such sort, that his braines comming out at the daggers point, hee shortlie after dyed. Thus did God, the true executioner of diuine iustice, worke the ende of impious Atheists.

It is to be noted here that Vaughan gives the assailant's name as one "Ingram," while the burial register, we remember, reported it as "Francis Frezer." Which was correct? Someone had blundered over this name, but from this distance no one could tell where the age-old mistake lay.

Out of this tangle I took small encouragement. How could I hope to discover anything about so shadowy a criminal? In the first place, he was reputed to have been a serving man; and men of that class do not figure largely in the public records. Secondly, his very name was a matter of doubt. So hopeless it seemed that I gave up all thought of tracking him down, and returned to my other research.

Months passed, and took me far from Chancery Lane. But the magnetic power of the archives, that subtle and incalculable force, drew me back; and somewhere in the unconscious part of memory the names "Ingram" and "Francis Frezer" were still lurking. One day the gods of chance were propitious. I was going through the pages of one of the old index-books to the Close Rolls of the Chancery, searching it for Walter Raleighs, Francis Drakes, and the like. As my eye traveled through the entries for the year 1596, it was suddenly caught and held by the name "Ingram Frizer." In a flash came revelation. Something shouted in my brain that I had my finger on Marlowe's murderer, whose trail I had so long abandoned. The mystery of the name was solved: Vaughan had mentioned the murderer as "Ingram," apparently taking this as his surname, while the parish clerk, though writing "Frezer" correctly, had mistakenly substituted "Francis" as his Christian name.

The date here was 1596, three years after the crime, and Frizer had not been hanged by the neck; on the contrary, here he was, indexed in the Close Rolls of the Chancery. What was he doing there? Referring to the enrolled document, I found it to be merely a deed of bargain and sale, by which Ingram Frizer of London purchased two houses and some land in Buckinghamshire; and in this, of course, there was no clue to the crime. But we had crossed a hot trail. A hazy contradiction of names had leaped into life as Ingram Frizer, a London man of business, living, moving, and having his being three years after killing Marlowe. He challenged me to a chase.

How was I to recover a trace of his crime of 1593? I could not believe that he had not come to some kind of trial for killing Marlowe, even though he had been acquitted. There must have been a record, somewhere. Casting about, I thought first of the great series of ancient Criminal Inquests—those investigations by coroners' courts into questionable deaths—included in the Chancery records. Unfortunately this collection upon examination proved to contain nothing later than the reign of Henry VI.

Baffled here, I had to lead off in a new direction. It occurred to me that although Marlowe was killed at Deptford in Kent, perhaps the case was not tried in Kent. Perhaps Frizer had been indicted for Marlowe's death in the great Court of the Queen's Bench, Westminster, the highest criminal court in the realm. I therefore got out the Queen's Bench Controlment Roll for 35 Elizabeth (1593)—a thick bundle of dark-brown parchments sewn together at the top. For two days I strained my eyes searching in the dim and difficult script for an indictment of Ingram Frizer, and I finished by finding nothing.

Once more I paused and considered. The possibilities of Kent were not yet exhausted. Marlowe's murderer might have been tried by the Justices of Assize, on circuit there. Hope rode high when the bundle of ancient rolls of the South-Eastern Circuit for 1593 was brought out for me. Black with thick dust they were, and appeared not to have been opened for centuries. I thought surely to make a discovery here. But as they slowly passed in dim and fragmentary procession under my eyes hope seemed to pass with them. In the long files of criminals I found no Ingram Frizer.

This was a dark moment. I could see nothing in any direction. While waiting for light, I read over the two old narratives of Marlowe's death once more. Was there a possible clue still hidden there? What was Vaughan's view of the circumstances of the fight? According to him Marlowe, dagger in fist, had attacked Ingram, who drew his own poniard and killed the poet in self-defense. If this were true, could Ingram properly be called a murderer? To freshen up my imagination I made an effort to put myself in his place. Here lay Kit Marlowe, whom I had stabbed to save my life. Was I to look forward quietly to a trial for murder, and then the gallows? But I killed him in self-defense! I thought that I could prove as much to the coroner's jury. And after proving it, what then? Why, then I could appeal to the Queen for a pardon.

A pardon. A clue! A clue which—presto!—turned me back into my natural shape as a researcher. Where would the royal pardons be entered? Of a sudden I recalled having seen them mentioned in a description of the Patent Rolls of the Chancery. This series is made up of copies of the *Litteræ Patentes* or open letters from the sovereign to the subject (the originals are so called from being written upon open sheets of parchment with the Great Seal pendent at the bottom). Among many other kinds of documents, pardons of all sorts were issued through the Chancery as Letters Patent.

Now the index books to the Patent Rolls stand most conveniently on the shelves of the Legal Search Room, just a step down the gloomy corridor from the Round Room where I was working. In a moment I was there, taking down the volume containing 35 Elizabeth (1593), and running my excited finger down the time-faded names noted in the margins.

A dozen rapid leaves, a score or so of names, and treasure-trove!— "Frisar" lay before me like a jewel on the page. I could not believe my good fortune. There beside it was the laconic description of the pardon, clearly written in the customary abbreviated Latin:

> R[egina] xxviij° die Junij con[cessit] Ingramo ffrisar p[er]don[am] de se defend[endo]

This may be put into English roughly as:

> The Queen 28th day of June granted pardon to Ingram ffrisar [for homicide] in self-defense.

In a kind of whirling daze I realized that Marlowe's name was not there. Still, the date was right: four weeks after Marlowe's burial was sufficient time for issuing a pardon. This *must* be the pardon I was after. But before I could rest I must see the document to which this entry was the index. In an unsteady hand I made out the call ticket for Patent Roll 1401, to which the index referred me, only to find that the hands of the Record Office clock pointed to 4:15—too late to see the roll that afternoon! That was another dark moment.

Conquering an absurd fear that the attendants must have guessed my secret from my face, I found my way out from the dark musty halls of the archives to the green quiet of the Rolls Yard, past the reflective eye of the guardian bobby under the massive gateway, and into the narrow rapid roar of Chancery Lane. Law clerks passed like so many hasty puppets. Nothing stood in my mind's eye but the shining hope of finding the first authentic account of the death of Christopher Marlowe. That hope would be dashed or realized precisely at ten o'clock on the morrow, when the fatal roll would be waiting on my table. There would be a pardon, I knew; but suppose it should turn out to be only a bare statement, with no thrilling details? As I faced this staggering doubt in Holborn, I was very nearly juggernauted by a Charing Cross bus.

This would not do. I had no right to risk a violent death, when such a secret would die with me. I must live at least until 10 A.M., and that right rapidly. But my desire to speed the parting minutes fell beneath the inexorability of routine. I had to make my usual way by tube to Paddington with other "season ticketholders" (an Englishman never *commutes*) and take my seat in the customary Beaconsfield train. We were staying then at Jordans Hostel, which lies halfway between Chalfont St. Giles, where Milton wrote, and Beaconsfield, where Chesterton may still be seen from afar off, similarly occupied. On this night of nights the Great Western Railway dropped me in the most ordinary fashion at my little station, and the engine puffed off, remarking, "What*ever* you *may* or *may* not disc*over*, the *world must go on, world-must-go-on, worldmustgoon.*" I walked up past the old Friends' Meeting House, through the orchard to the Hostel, and divulged the tremendous secret to Mary. Then followed an attempt to kill the long evening hours by means of a furious game of badminton with a small boy in the Mayflower Barn (a three-centuries-old affair, affirmed by tradition and at least one eminent scholar to be built from the timbers of the Pilgrim ship). The night which succeeded was long, unusually long for the season. But morning came at length, and with it the London train.

Life goes by contraries. When I approached the Record Office as the bells of St. Clement's were striking ten, I ought, no doubt, to have quickened my steps. Contrariwise, I fell into a kind of fatalistic saunter. If I should find it, well; if not, why, no need to have hurried. . . .

I reached my table. There was the brown roll waiting, as it had waited these three hundred years. Almost calmly I began to unroll the heavy involute of parchment, ten inches wide. But as I noted the length of the average entry my excitement waxed. Faster I rolled—faster, faster—until Frizer's immortal name flashed into view, at the head of a pardon *more than a foot long.*

Surely an angel—perhaps the recording angel—had preserved me for this, or this for me. For me? I cast a furtive glance, half expecting the sharp-eyed double circle of searchers to rise in a body and pounce on my roll—but they were deep in affairs, mostly genealogical, of their own. My eye raced over the pardon—it was written in Latin—and I saw that it quoted in full the details of the inquest held by the Queen's Coroner, William Danby, on "the body of Christopher Morley, lying dead and slain" at Deptford. *Christopher Morley*. Was this Christopher Marlowe the dramatist? My heart skipped a beat. It must be. The same name in a different spelling. Scholars had seen Marlowe's name written "Marlin" and "Marley"; but "Christopher Morley" was a new and modern-sounding form. In passing I realized that the author of *Shandygaff* had here found a great namesake across three centuries.

No matter for the spelling—here was the precious story, the only author-itative and complete story of Kit Marlowe's mysterious death. How did he die? What was the quarrel? Was there a woman in the case? I found the answers to these questions in the findings of sixteen men under oath —the Coroner's jury. Stripped of a little verbiage, here follows a direct translation from the Latin:

". . . When a certain Ingram Frysar, late of London, gentleman, and the aforesaid Christopher Morley and one Nicholas Skeres, late of Lon-don, gentleman, and Robert Poley of London aforesaid, gentleman, on the thirtieth day of May in the thirty-fifth year above mentioned, at Detford Strand aforesaid . . . about the tenth hour before noon of the same day, met together in a room in the house of a certain Eleanor Bull, widow; & there passed the time together & dined & after dinner were in quiet sort together there & walked in the garden belonging to the said house until the sixth hour after noon of the same day & then returned from the said garden to the room aforesaid & there together and in com-pany supped; & after supper the said Ingram & Christopher Morley were in speech & uttered one to the other divers malicious words for the rea-son that they could not be at one nor agree about the payment of the sum of money, that is, *le Reckoninge;* & the said Christopher Morley then lying upon a bed in the room where they supped, & moved with anger against the said Ingram Frysar upon the words as aforesaid spoken be-tween them, and the said Ingram then & there sitting in the room afore-said with his back towards the bed where the said Christopher Morley was then lying, sitting near the bed . . . & with the front part of his body towards the table, & the aforesaid Nicholas Skeres & Robert Poley sitting on either side of the said Ingram in such a manner that the same Ingram Frysar in no wise could take flight: it so befell that the said Christopher Morley on a sudden & of his malice towards the said Ingram afore-thought, then & there maliciously drew the dagger of the said Ingram

which was at his back, and with the same dagger the said Christopher
Morley then & there maliciously gave the aforesaid Ingram two wounds
on his head of the length of two inches & of the depth of a quarter of an
inch; whereupon the said Ingram, in fear of being slain, & sitting in the
manner aforesaid between the said Nicholas Skeres & Robert Poley so
that he could not in any wise get away, in his own defense & for the
saving of his life then & there struggled with the said Christopher Morley
to get back from him his dagger aforesaid; in which affray the same
Ingram could not get away from the said Christopher Morley; and so it
befell in that affray that the said Ingram, in defense of his life, with the
dagger aforesaid of the value of twelve pence, gave the said Christopher
then & there a mortal wound over his right eye of the depth of two inches
& of the width of one inch; of which mortal wound the aforesaid Christopher Morley then & there instantly died; And since that the said Ingram killed & slew the said Christopher Morley aforesaid at Detford
Strand aforesaid . . . in the manner & form aforesaid in the defense and
saving of his own life, against our peace our crown & dignity, as more
fully appears by the tenor of the Record of the Inquest aforesaid which
we caused to come before us in our Chancery by virtue of our writ; We
therefore moved by piety have pardoned the same Ingram Frisar the
breach of our peace which pertains to us against the said Ingram for the
death above mentioned & grant to him our firm peace. . . . Witness the
Queen at Kew on the 28th day of June."

It will be noticed that this pardon, near the end, refers to the record
of the inquest as though it were in the Court of Chancery; and yet I had
searched the whole collection of Chancery Inquests with no result. I felt
that to complete my documentary record I must find that inquest. But
where could it be? I took up the printed description of the Chancery
documents and thrashed through every item. At length, in an obscure
corner of the Miscellany of the Chancery, a title met my eye: "Writs and
Returns, Henry III to Charles II." This looked hopeful, for, as I had just
seen, the inquest had been returned upon a writ into Chancery; and I got
out the Index and Calendar to the Chancery Miscellany. Though the documents well merited the title of "miscellaneous," they had been roughly
grouped together by counties. By going through all the items listed under
Kent, I found at last what I wanted—the indented Coroner's inquest (so
called because two copies were cut apart on a wavy or indented line for
purposes of tallying—whence *indentures*), and the Queen's writ which
summoned the case into Chancery. A comparison showed that this inquest had been copied word for word into the pardon, except for the
jurors' statement that "the said Ingram after the slaying aforesaid, per-

petrated and done by him in the manner aforesaid, neither fled nor withdrew himself. But what goods or chattels, lands or tenements the said
Ingram had at the time of the slaying . . . the said jurors are totally
ignorant."

With all the documents before me, every step in the proceedings was
clear. Ingram Frizer killed Christopher Marlowe on the evening of
Wednesday, May 30, 1593. The inquest was held on Friday, June 1; and
on the same day they buried Marlowe's body. Coroner Danby sent the
record of the inquest into Chancery in obedience to a writ dated June 15.
And Frizer's pardon was granted at Kew on Thursday, June 28.

So much for the new dates. Returning to the scene of the inquest, we
notice that there are two eyewitnesses to the killing, doubtless friends of
Marlowe and Frizer, since they had been feasting with them. Coroner
Danby opens his inquiry. The jury examines Marlowe's body, the dagger
used in the scuffle, the scalp wounds on Frizer's head, and hears the oral
testimony of the two eyewitnesses, Poley and Skeres. Upon deliberation,
the jury brings in its finding of homicide in self-defense.

Two courses are open to us: (*a*) to believe as true the story of Marlowe's attack on Frizer from behind, corroborated in so far as it is by
the wounds on Frizer's head, which wounds must have been inflicted
*before* Marlowe received his deathblow; or (*b*) to suppose that Frizer,
Poley, and Skeres after the slaying, and in order to save Frizer's life on
a plea of self-defense, concocted a lying account of Marlowe's behavior,
to which they swore at the inquest, and with which they deceived the
jury.

The latter seems to me a possible but rather unlikely view of the case.
In all probability the men had been drinking deep—the party had lasted
from ten in the morning until night!—and the bitter debate over the score
had roused Marlowe's intoxicated feelings to such a pitch that, leaping
from the bed, he took the nearest way to stop Frizer's mouth.

We learn that the quarrel which brought on the fight was a dispute
over the reckoning. Money is cause sufficient for a fight; there is no
need to drag a woman into the case. The imaginary object of Marlowe's
so-called "lewde loue," about whom so much has been written, is no-
ticeably absent from the picture, both as a cause and as a witness of the
fray. In spite of the wishes of Francis Meres and his followers, she must
now be returned with thanks to the fertile brain from which she sprang.

Such is the true story of the death of Christopher Marlowe, as I found
it in the records, stripped of scandal, and told by sixteen good men and
true. But was this to be the end? Who could rest content without finding
out more about this Ingram Frizer than his mere name? What manner

of man was he? What's Christopher to him, or he to Christopher? Questionings of this kind urged me along still farther on his trail; and before many days I had run down such a quantity of facts about his position and personal character that through them the killer of Christopher Marlowe will stand out as a living figure.

And as for Marlowe himself, the spelling of his name as "Morley" afforded a pregnant suggestion. It led me to an official letter of the highest importance bearing on the dramatist's early life; but that, as Kipling says, is another story.

Halliwell-Phillipps, great biographer of Shakespeare and a mighty man with the records, spoke once and for all for the Nimrods of the archives: "Which sport is it that elicits the keenest and most genuine enthusiasm—fox-hunting or record-hunting? Undoubtedly the latter.

"For what devotee to field amusements, after galloping day after day for three months in search of a possible fox that does not turn up, would commence another session of the same description with undiminished alacrity? Where is the determined sportsman to be found who would continue to traverse downs and morass if he only winged a miserable sparrow once in a month? Would he persevere for a year or two on the chance of eventually bringing down a woodcock?

"Not a bit of it! The record-hunter is your only true sportsman. Undeterred by hundreds of obstacles—carrying any height of fence—disheartened by no number of failures—merrily henting the stile-a—and, above all, when he once does catch a sight of his bird, never missing it!"

Foxes? Sparrows? Woodcocks? If such small deer stir his blood, picture the high adventure of a chase through a noble forest of parchment three hundred years old—and, at the end of the day, big game.

## Suggestions for Study

1. Summarize the points of difficulty confronting the author at the beginning of his search.
2. How was the confusion of the names "Ingram" and "Frizer" settled?
3. How did the author get the clue that led to unraveling the mystery?
4. Summarize the conclusions arrived at in the search.
5. State the tone of the article and write a thesis sentence for it.
6. Compare the style of this article with that of "Enterprise and Old Iron." What can you infer about the reading group for which each was intended?
7. Define the following words from the article: aberration, pillory, idiosyncrasy, uniformity, archive, propitious, surname, laconic, inquest, writ, alacrity.

## Harnessing Earthworms [6]

### JOHN EDWIN HOGG

And he gave it for his opinion, that whoever could make two ears of corn, or two blades of grass, to grow upon a spot of ground where only one grew before, would deserve better of mankind, and do more essential service to his country, than the whole race of politicians put together.

Jonathan Swift in *Gulliver's Travels*

In 1881, Charles Robert Darwin, the great English scientist, after years of patient study, published a book of 236 pages dealing exclusively with earthworms. In this volume, *The Formation of Vegetable Mould through the Action of Worms,* he makes it clear that nature apparently created the earthworm to be an improver of the soil and to aid the growth of plants. Indeed, he goes so far as to make this statement: "Without the work of this humble creature, who knows nothing of the benefits he confers upon mankind, agriculture, as we know it, would be very difficult, if not wholly impossible."

No machinery of human invention is ever likely to be a substitute for the functions of the earthworm. Every earthworm is an amazing combination of chemist and borer, and has the voracity of a grist mill; it is constantly devouring earth, dead leaves, and other decomposing organic material. Everything it swallows is pulverized in its chickenlike gizzard. From this it extracts its sustenance, adds the end products of its body metabolism, and passes it out in the form of numerous castings. Earthworm castings are a perfect form of soil humus. They are one of the richest plant foods known to civilized man.

Further soil improvements result from aeration through myriads of worm tunnels. Oxidation and nitrification are speeded in soils so ventilated. The various bacteria, an important factor in the formation of humus, are more readily admitted to soils well perforated with wormholes. Every wormhole is also a watering tube through which rain is stored in the ground at a depth of six feet, or more.

By a careful census Darwin estimated that two and a half million earthworms is a moderate infestation for a healthy English acre. That number of worms, he estimated, will annually contribute about eighteen tons of castings to the fertility of the acre. In addition to this valuable donation, fertility is further increased by aeration, the conservation of moisture, and the conversion of many tons of dormant subsoil into rich topsoil available

6. Reprinted by permission of *Nature Magazine.*

for plant growth. Without the work of the worms these desirable soil improvements are inhibited.

The flyleaf record of a copy of Darwin's book, before me as these lines are written, indicates that it has been out of the local public library only fourteen times in the twenty-eight years since the library was established. Nevertheless, anyone with a spark of imagination may read it today to find every basic suggestion for the science of biokinetic farming, the ultra-modern science of harnessing the earthworm to bring agricultural practices into permanent and profitable harmony with the unalterable laws of nature.

No such suggestion was ever acted upon during Darwin's lifetime. And even today politically dominated agricultural science has failed to take advantage of the economic value in the earthworm. Fortunately, however, there are at least two pioneers of science who, many years ago, accepted the work of the world's most outstanding biologist of modern times, to make further research their life's work. One of these gentlemen is Dr. Ehrenfried Pfeiffer, the Holland-Dutch wizard of agriculture, whose book *Bio-Dynamic Farming and Gardening,* recently published at Dornach, Switzerland, has been translated into numerous languages to become a European bestseller—completely uncensored even in the dictator countries. The other is Dr. George Sheffield Oliver, whose experimental farm in Los Angeles County produced the scientific facts for his three-volume work *Our Friend the Earthworm* (an outline of biokinetic methods), which, since its publication in 1937, has rescued hundreds of American farmers from impending bankruptcy and helped their acres to productivity.

Within these space limits it is impossible to discuss the work of both these scientists who, over a period of some thirty years, have pioneered identical fields of biological research with parallel results, each without ever having heard of the other until less than a year ago. Only because Dr. Oliver's Earthworm Farms in California are more accessible to the writer than Dr. Pfeiffer's experimental farm in Holland, this article is restricted to the work of the American.

In 1906, Dr. George Sheffield Oliver, a descendant of James Oliver, inventor of the steel plough, was a prosperous young physician and surgeon in Fort Worth, Texas. He was living at the time on a five-acre estate on the outskirts of the city, and there Darwin's book came to his attention. Being a curious-minded fellow, whose hobby was gardening, he did much reading between the lines, and this suggested some interesting experiments he could easily undertake upon his own property.

To test some of Darwin's statements, Dr. Oliver procured numerous large flower pots, and, for purposes of identification, painted half of them green and the others red. Then in each pair of red and green pots he made simultaneous plantings of flowers and common garden vegetables. In the red pots, however, he had carefully sifted the topsoil to be certain it contained no earthworms or earthworm egg capsules, while in each of the green pots he placed a few earthworms.

Some weeks later he had unquestionable evidence that Darwin was right. The plants in the green pots grew much faster; they were stronger, healthier, and nearly twice the size of those in the red pots. Equally promising was the fact that, while some of the plants in the red pots were damaged by insects, the pests ignored the more luxuriant plants grown in the worm-worked soil.

After many similar experiments, with results always the same, he began experimenting with the propagation of earthworms in artificial culture beds. The effort became a success. He soon found that raising earthworms literally by the billions is largely a matter of making a home for them, feeding them well, and encouraging them to be fruitful. With an abundant supply of earthworms for further experiments, he began "planting" them in his gardens, around his fruit trees, and all over the property. Here he began getting results similar to those of the potted plant experiments—better trees, better flowers, better garden vegetables, faster growth, and a high degree of immunity from attack by insect pests. Such minor pest troubles as he had were duly eliminated by the development and use of several nonpoisonous, insect-repelling sprays.

Eventually the word got about through Fort Worth and Dallas that Dr. Oliver had some magic formula for making things grow. His friends were amazed by the beauty of his trees, the gorgeousness of his flowers, and the great size and superior flavor of strawberries and everything else from his gardens. When they asked how he did it, the physician replied: "It's a secret. Some day, perhaps, I'll reveal it—after I've retired from medical practice."

He did not realize then how close to retirement he really was. When he refused to disclose his gardening secrets, wealthy friends began offering him tempting sums to apply them upon their property. Dr. Oliver finally accepted one such offer, and the job was little more than completed before he had another. Two years later he sold his medical practice, and opened an office in Dallas and another in Fort Worth. The lettering on these office doors read: George Sheffield Oliver—Landscape Engineer.

During the next several years Dr. Oliver went from one large landscaping contract to another and rolled up a comfortable personal fortune beautifying parks, cemeteries, and various other types of public and private estates. With the co-operation of billions of earthworms whose work never faltered, he so improved properties in two years as to give them the appearance of having had at least five years of intensive landscape gardening. All the while he was guarding the secret of how he did it—and hoping that no one with imagination would ever read that musty old book of Darwin's to take a few tips and become his competitor!

About 1920, the fame of the man in Texas who seemed to possess some sort of magic wand for the beautification of landscapes, trickled to the Pacific Coast, and he was lured to Los Angeles with some fat contracts for improving the estates of various motion-picture stars. For the next few years he was more than busy and scarcely interested in jobs calling for an expenditure of less than $10,000. Nevertheless, he found time to establish a ten-acre experimental farm in a remote corner of Los Angeles County. And there, in the field and in the laboratory, where visitors were never permitted behind high-board, barbed-wire-topped fences, the earthworm researches went steadily on year after year—with results such as Darwin never dreamed of!

Secrecy was discarded after 1929, when, amid depression conditions, Dr. Oliver became convinced that putting earthworms to work—harmonizing agricultural practices with the self-enforcing laws of nature—is of outstanding importance in the cure of American agriculture, now suffering from a thousand man-made ills. Today he is recognized by laymen and scientific men alike as the world's greatest living authority on anything pertaining to earthworms, and particularly their applications to the restoration of farm profits and a sound economy for agriculture.

More than 1100 species of earthworms are known to science, and Dr. Oliver is the only scientist who has succeeded in hybridizing various species. He hybridizes them to produce new types peculiarly suited for specific purposes. And if anyone can find a new use for earthworms he will make a worm to make good in that particular job!

The greatest task facing the earthworm today, according to Dr. Oliver, is the restoration of soil fertility by returning this servant of agriculture to the millions of acres in which it has been exterminated, to the untold detriment of mankind. So, to develop a worm that is a sort of coolie soil worker, he has a hybrid that he calls his "soilution worm," a cross between the large, English brandling and the small, native, California orchard worm. The result is a medium-sized creature of prodigious energy, prolific and hardy enough to be in demand for restocking the vast areas in which all native earthworms have been vanquished by the use of strong chemical fertilizers and the poison sprays that kill the earthworms along with the insects (sometimes even the people who eat the poisoned farm products) and insectivorous birds eating the poisoned insects or earthworms.

In recent years export markets for many products of the American farm have been seriously curtailed because of residues of poison on fruits and vegetables. Because of the laxity of American state and local laws instances of people being poisoned by such contaminated foods are an almost daily newspaper topic. But foreign nations are much more fussy. Nearly every European country has enacted laws restricting such American products. These range from embargoes in some countries to milder forms of regulation in others.

For the production of a colorless, odorless, highly volatile oil of great penetrating power, for which the medical profession is finding numerous new uses, Dr. Oliver has a short, thick little worm hybridized and dieted into disgraceful obesity! For the frog farmers, poultrymen, terrapin breeders, and operators of state and private fish hatcheries and game bird farms, for whom earthworms are a partial answer to the problem of nourishing feed at small cost, Dr. Oliver has evolved still another worm. It is a big, ten-inch "meaty" creature of extraordinary vigor.

Being oviparous and hermaphroditic, every adult earthworm is an egg-layer. And by inducing them to lay most of their eggs between layers of damp burlap placed at the proper depth in the compost of culture beds, Dr. Oliver harvests a million earthworm egg capsules about as easily as he gathers a dozen eggs in his henhouse. Packed in damp peat moss, a million earthworm egg capsules make a small package that is easily shipped to any part of the civilized world. Those million egg capsules, after being transferred to suitable soil, will hatch out in about thirty days into from twelve to sixteen million tiny earthworms, which in another ninety days become adult egg-layers. Earthworm egg capsules may also be dried in the sun, held in a dormant stage for as long as eighteen months, and then hatched after being returned to favorable soil.

By the use of several simple mechanical devices, Dr. Oliver also harvests earthworm castings from the compost of culture beds. These go by the hundredweight to the numerous California florists who report them the finest material they have ever discovered for boosting the growth of floral stock and making flowers bloom. For the floral trades he also manufactures a liquid fertilizer made by dripping water through boxes of earthworm castings. The resulting liquid looks like tea. It is odorless and may be stored indefinitely without the slightest deterioration. Plants receiving a small dose of it soon gain a new lease on life.

The poultry on Dr. Oliver's farm—chickens, capons, and ducks—are about the finest, healthiest-looking birds ever seen outside a livestock show. They get that way on a diet that he calls "intensive range"—sprouted grain, earthworms, and earthworm egg capsules. Birds receiving this highly nutritive ration are not only boarded at a cost of about one tenth of a cent each per day, but there are seldom any sick birds, and there is practically no mortality. In five months a Rhode Island Red pullet weighs five and one-half pounds, looks like a two-year-old hen, and is doing the egg-laying work of the two-year-old bird. And when it comes to caponizing young roosters, there is no one quite like a former surgeon for doing it without any slips. Thus Dr. Oliver's capons become eight-pound birds in ninety days—and it costs him about fifteen cents to produce a capon easily marketed for five dollars.

The real tests of Dr. Oliver's biokinetic farming methods, however, have come not from his own experimental farm but from the several hundred farmers in California and practically every other state of the Union where his teachings have had as much as ten years of practical application. Today, without a solitary exception, all those farmers, who from two to ten years ago were tottering on the ragged edge of bankruptcy, are back into sound agricultural profits. By biokinetic processes these farmers are now growing practically everything ever commercially cultivated in the United States. And they are not "retailing their farms" with every sale of produce; with billions of earthworms co-operating with them, soil fertility is being restored faster than crops take it out. For them the renewal of soil fertility is placed on a self-replenishing, perpetual-motion basis at virtually no cost at all. In irrigated areas biokinetic farmers report their enterprises flourishing with much less soil cultivation and half the water bills of neighboring orthodox farms. For them too, are solved certain problems of soil erosion, flood control, and conservation of moisture. Add to these various savings the fact that the biokinetic farmer has little trouble with insect pests, and it would seem that Charles Robert Darwin must be credited with having laid the foundation for a long-delayed and much-to-be-desired revolution that will vastly assist American agriculture.

*Suggestions for Study*

1. Why is Darwin's book referred to in both the first and last sentences of this essay?

2. State in one sentence the idea that this article is presenting.

3. Toward what kind of audience did this writer direct his article? Is the article adapted to that audience?

4. Does the concluding paragraph merely repeat the central idea of the essay, or is it integrated with the exposition?

5. Try to list the sources which the author used in writing the article. What do you suppose was his first move? Try to trace his subsequent moves till all his material was gathered. What probably gave him his first idea to write the article?

6. Define the following words from the article: voracity, pulverize, humus, aeration, myriads, nitrification, infestation, biokinetic, hybridize, prolific, volatile, obesity, terrapin, hermaphroditic.

## C. The Book Review

Contrary to popular opinion, criticism does not mean faultfinding. It really means measuring or evaluating worth; it is the process by which the goodness or badness of anything is determined. An unsupported opinion cannot therefore be a real criticism; criticism begins only when you demonstrate the reasons for your judgment. Nor can it be criticism when only the deficiencies are indicated; true criticism is an impartial, studied analysis to find strength and weakness alike. The critic may point out deficiencies, but if he is true to his calling, he will do so with the intent of being constructive.

Also contrary to public opinion, criticism is not based just upon one's likes or dislikes. These are of course important to the critic, but if he trusts in them alone, he will err. Our tastes shift too rapidly. Today we may like what is distasteful to us tomorrow. As we mature, we outgrow certain works and come to value others which formerly left us unenthusiastic. Shakespeare is not widely read by young folk, nor Peter Rabbit by adults.

Concerning one's personal tastes, there is another point to be observed. We are often entertained or instructed by inferior products. The majority of baseball fans, for example, prefer to see high-scoring games in which extra-base hits, wild base running, and freak plays abound; yet they would agree that the errorless game with a tight pitchers' battle is better baseball. The same applies to literary criticism. One might delight in a Western novel which he would be compelled to say was bad narrative, or be unenthusiastic about an excellently written sonnet by Milton. Recognizing this fact, look for a more solid basis for your criticism than your personal like or dislike. The question then arises: what procedure of evaluation can you follow?

**Principles of Criticism.** As a beginning, define the general and specific purpose of the work you intend to criticize. To determine the general purpose, classify it according to the form of discourse—as description, narration, exposition, argumentation—because this will help you at once to find the author's main intention in writing it. But since not all narrative is written to entertain nor all exposition simply to inform, continue your analysis until you know the author's primary intention. Then place it in its proper category as to type—as informal essay, formal essay, novel, short story, lyric poem, and the like.

But, you may ask, why determine the general purpose at the very beginning? The answer is that one should know the rules before he starts to play a game. If one attends a hockey game, for instance, he expects to see fast action, rough play, quick thinking, and perhaps even a good fight among the players. If, on the other hand, he attends a chess tournament, he expects to see deep thinking, carefully studied play, and individual effort. He would not for a moment condemn the chess tournament because it lacked rough play and fast action; he would even be shocked if he found these two present. Nor would he censure the hockey game for lacking slow and careful maneuvering; he is delighted that these are not present. Likewise in the criticism of literature, a critic first tries to find the rules of the game. What is this work before me intended to do? he asks. What rules will it follow? What type of work is it? He no more thinks of censuring the lyric because it does not tell a story like the novel or short story than he does of censuring the chess tournament for lacking rough play. The lyric is not intended to do that, else it would not be a lyric. He does not try to argue seriously with the idea presented in a pleasing informal essay which is intended only to entertain; such arguing is of import only where a writer is attempting formally to convince the reader that a particular idea is true. Thus the first point for the reader or critic is to determine the general purpose.

You should then ask: what specific purpose has the work? Under the general heading of the novel, for example, one could distinguish a thousand different purposes introduced by the various authors. One may be trying to tell an exciting story, another to make a detailed study of character development, another to achieve psychological effects through unusual style or organization. Obviously then, you must endeavor to see what the author is trying to do, and not criticize a novel of character for lacking a breathtaking plot. One does not condemn *Good-bye, Mr. Chips* because it is not *The Three Musketeers*.

The following selection, taken from Lilo Linke's review of *A Handbook of Freedom,* a group of selections chosen by Jack Lindsay and Edgell Rickword, illustrates how the critic seizes upon the general purpose and the specific purpose:

We ask of a good anthology that it should be a whole library condensed into one volume, and that it should lead us from the reading of those pages we know and cherish to others which we might never have discovered on our own. The *Handbook of Freedom* fulfills both and more. It is not just a series of excerpts in prose and verse. "Our aim was," Rickword says in his introduction, "to show history in its impact on the experience, not as it is reflected in the contemplation." To this end, a record was made of the clamoring voices of the masses offstage, and of the individuals who had the courage to face the hostile limelight on their behalf. . . . From this angle, history is seen from below, and the kings and statesmen are suddenly turned from heroes into the villains of the piece.—*Life and Letters Today,* July, 1939.

One more consideration remains for a critic relative to the purposes of a work. Granting that the work has fulfilled its general and specific purpose, has it accomplished what was worth doing? Sometimes books are excellent in themselves but are useless restatements of what has already been competently written, or they are devoted to trivial subjects. The critic does well then to tell his reader of the contribution made by the new book. For example, T. R. Hay concludes his review of Frank J. Klingberg's *The Morning of America* in this manner:

> The passing of the Virginia Presidents marked the close of an era. The morning of America was ended; the middle period was begun, but the "new American shape was clearly visible." In these present days of uncertainty, when the American tradition, the American way of life, is being subjected to challenges that are tending to change its character if not its spirit, it is important to know something of the forces and traditions which have made the United States great. Dr. Klingberg's book is a worth-while contribution to a knowledge and an understanding of this evolution.—New York *Times Book Review,* May 21, 1941.

THE CRITICISM OF EXPOSITION AND ARGUMENTATION. Having once determined the purposes of a work, turn your attention to content and organization. To illustrate the different ways of considering a work, let us begin with expository and argumentative writings.

*Thesis.* Perhaps as a beginning, the thesis should be analyzed. In judging the skill of the author in presenting the thesis and in keeping to it without violating the principle of unity, ascertain whether it is stated outright and placed conspicuously, whether it is buried, whether it is left to implication, or whether it exists at all. Then question its validity. Is it convincingly presented? Is it supported by accurate facts, or does the writer indulge in opinion and guess? Does he offer documentation or other proof of his assertions? Can you from your own knowledge produce conflicting testimony? It follows naturally that a critic reviews best those books which pertain to subjects which he has personally investigated and understands. You will accordingly do well to review books which fall at least partially within your own range of knowledge.

*Organization.* The structure of a work also demands attention. Some writers are skillful in assisting a reader to grasp the subject matter; others hinder him materially. Watch to see how an author begins his discussion; perhaps he leads gradually to his major points through easy transitions, perhaps he gives an indication of the plan of the work to follow, perhaps he plunges quickly into the middle of things, successfully or unsuccessfully. Then inspect the body of the material for its organization. Is there a noticeable plan? If so, what is its construction? Judge the conclusion for its usefulness. Does it have a summary? Is it necessary? Is any other helpful device employed? These and probably many other questions can be answered concerning the organization.

*Reader.* Because one function of the critic is to act as a link between a book and its readers, he must ascertain for whom the book is intended. Sometimes a discrepancy exists between the intended reader and the reader who can actually understand the presentation. If a physics book which is intended to be light reading for a popular audience employs a complex style, technical vocabulary, and rapid presentation, it will fail to meet its proposed reader; the critic's duty is to point out that failure. Style and vocabulary are important criteria in this connection. The tone should also be observed: is it playful, satirical, pessimistic, pompous, serious, and is it well adapted to effect the purpose?

*Author.* Often a knowledge of the author will enable you to make a better appraisal of a book. This knowledge may first give a clue to the authority with which a man speaks. His achievements, the degrees which he holds, or the honors which have been conferred upon him tell of his authority to speak. This knowledge may also serve to put you on guard against the writer's prejudices. A Republican can scarcely be expected to speak fairly in an election year concerning the Democratic candidate. The critic therefore looks for where this prejudice may color the facts. These prejudices may be of all sorts—political, national, racial, religious, professional.

In addition, whether considering expository, argumentative, or narrative writing, a critic often likes to place a book against a background of other books by the same author in order that he may tell whether the author is improving, failing, or writing in the same old vein. An established writer holds the interests of thousands who eagerly read the reviews of his latest book to see if it measures up to his standard or whether it contains a radical departure from the old style.

*Literary history.* The critic of all types of writing performs an additional service to his readers by seeing a new work in the light of the history of similar writings. He does his best to catalogue a work as genuinely new or as carrying on an old tradition. For example, the critic of automobiles performs a much more valuable service for his public if he knows the history of the automobile industry from the beginning. If a manufacturer presents a new car equipped with an old-style shock absorber, the critic instantly thinks of the old shock absorbers and why they were abandoned; he can thus make a valuable judgment on the new device. Likewise the literary critic will not make the mistake of thinking such tremendous best-sellers as *Anthony Adverse* and *Gone with the Wind* are new forms of the novel; he will immediately recognize their literary type. Then he can look to see whether the book is simply routine or whether it has a unique quality. If he finds that it has a quality which no other book possesses, he defines that quality for the reader.

THE CRITICISM OF NARRATION. If a work is narrative, you must employ other considerations. You are no longer concerned primarily with testing for factual truth or argumentative accuracy, but are endeavoring to apply more suitable standards. Be careful, however, about fixing arbitrary standards on fictional writing. Many students, for example, condemn a novel because it does not have a happy ending, or because it does not move them to tears, or because it does not have exciting action. These are valid means of judgment only if they are related to the purpose of the novel; in themselves they are worthless.

*Purpose.* The determination of purpose is once again the starting point for the criticism. Is the novel primarily to entertain, or does it consider some particular problem? If both purposes are present, which is the dominant one? If a problem is being attacked, the critic must define that problem. The novel may be considering certain psychological quirks of human beings, it may be analyzing character, it may be studying a sociological situation, or it may be presenting any one of a dozen other problems of human life. Thackeray's *Vanity Fair,* for example, deals with a social problem, the human trait of striving for those goals of life which, once attained, are not worth having.

Another general question for the critic is: what is the author's conception of a novel? Does he try to be highly selective in choosing incidents and detail, or does he attempt to be realistic by taking in every available detail, as does a photographic camera? If he shrinks from detailing certain facts of existence, does that limit his work too much? Thackeray, for example, has sometimes been criticized for concentrating on certain aspects of higher social life to the neglect of the seamier side of the life of the masses, that life about which Dickens wrote.

*Tone.* Having determined the purpose and problems of the novel, consider the manner in which the material is treated. Thackeray often employed a bantering tone, quite in keeping with the superficiality of the scene which he was presenting. On much the same theme, another novelist might have used indignation and satire, as Swift did in *Gulliver's Travels,* or religious fervor as Bunyan did in *Pilgrim's Progress.* Is the tone in keeping with the subject? Many critics have objected to Thackeray's informal, discursive manner as impedimentary to the action of the novel. Others have thought it pleasant and fitting. But the critic may wish to consider such a question.

*Character.* In reference to the content of the novel also take into account the three attributes of narrative—character, plot, and setting. Concerning the leading characters, you may ask: Are they stationary, or do they undergo a change of some sort in the course of the action? If they change, does it mean the weakening or the strengthening of their personalities? Do they undergo the change passively, or do they struggle against it? The critic may also test these characters for their trueness to life, and the skill of the author in presenting them. Do the characters really live? If they lack reality, is that lack a defect or an asset? Does the reader feel pity, sympathy, curiosity, or antagonism toward them? Are they real individuals, or representative, type characters? Does the reader have an introspective view of the workings of their minds and the state of their emotions, or does he see them only through their actions? Are they contrasted with each other or with their environment, and to what effect? Finally, you may wish to ask, does the action fit these characters? Does the plot revolve around what they would naturally do, or is it warped to produce a denouement quite foreign to their normal actions?

*Plot.* For a full discussion of plot you must consult the section on narrative in this book, for here we can discuss only a few of its attributes. It is really difficult to discuss plot aside from character; the two are part and parcel of the same thing. Plot is defined as a series of actions arising from a conflict of forces and culminating in a climactic incident followed by a denouement. Because conflict arises through an interplay of forces concerning one or more characters, determine how many characters are involved principally in this conflict and which incidents are necessary to initiate and promote it. As the novel proceeds, is it carefully centered on one plot? The writer may not wish such compression. He may be more ambitious and employ many characters, a subplot or even two, and a shifting setting. If he chooses such a course, how well does he secure his effect? Is the effect lost through his ambitious undertaking? Do the subplots work in well with the main plot, and are they carried along together skillfully? Also, as the plot progresses, observe how well the action is linked together. In the finest examples of plot construction the incidents are so closely intertwined that the removal of any one mars the development of the whole or even destroys it entirely. How well then does one incident give rise to the rest? If such interdependence is lacking, does the plot suffer? Has the author been successful in gaining suspense and climax without a closely constructed series of incidents? If so, by what devices? A critic must also scrutinize the conclusion. According to modern standards, the conclusion should follow naturally from the material preceding it. At the last minute to make a happy or sad ending, the author should not introduce some happening quite foreign to what has gone before, or quite improbable in the light of fact. As a satisfactory concluding action the hero cannot fall off a high cliff and escape unscathed, nor can a deep-dyed villain make a sudden reform. Does the ending then proceed naturally in keeping with the already established nature of the characters and the plot? Finally, the critic may consider the plot in general. Does it present the philosophy of the author, and if so does it prove satisfactory to the reader? Hardy's novels, for example, show the blind striving of men against immutable and incognizant destiny. Defoe's *Robinson Crusoe,* on the other hand, is optimistically romantic in showing man conquering his environment.

*Setting.* The setting, the third element in the novel, usually does not demand as much attention from the critic as do plot and character. Sometimes, however, as in the novels of Hardy, it is a vital force, controlling the characters and giving depth and significance to the action. One can well consider therefore how effectively the setting throws an atmosphere around the action, how it accords with the characters, how it promotes unity of effect, how it adds richness through detail, and how it motivates the action.

SUMMARY. You will probably protest after reading thus far that you lack the range of knowledge and of reading to enable you to make such criticisms as are called for here. In part, you are right. But you do have at your command sufficient intelligence and knowledge to employ some of this material with a fair degree of success. You must also remember that part of your duty as an educated person is the accumulation of knowledge of this sort. Every student should be learning something of the history of his special study, whether it be accounting or farming or teaching. By this study he may in his turn know whether a so-called new idea is really new or whether it is merely an old one revived.

## Book Review I

Dictionary of American History, edited by James Truslow Adams, reviewed by Paul A. Palmer.[7]

This work contains over six thousand articles, nearly twenty-five hundred pages: "the result of the labor of four years and the collaboration of well over a thousand persons." The review must begin with praise. The editor must be complimented on the elaborate system of cross reference, involving generous and discriminating use of *qv's* and *qqv's*, and on the admirable index volume. In organization, certainly, the *Dictionary* is a model work of reference. Mr. Adams must also be congratulated on his success in enlisting the co-operation of the most eminent authorities in their respective specialties. Thus the leading articles on diplomatic history are by Samuel F. Bemis, those on technology and invention by Roger Burlingame, on Indian culture by Clark Wissler, on religious and ecclesiastical history by William W. Sweet, on the period of the Civil War and Reconstruction by J. G. Randall, and on the judiciary and constitutional law by Carl B. Swisher. Among the more distinguished of the longer essays are Carl Becker's "Declaration of Independence," Victor S. Clark's "Manufacturing," and Dexter Perkins's "Monroe Doctrine." Some of the shorter contributions, moreover, such as George Fort Milton's "Lincoln-Douglas Debates," Irving Dilliard's "Comic Strips and Funny Papers," and H. F. Gosnell's "Machine, Party," exemplify a high order of excellence. In one of these briefer articles ("Drinking Habits"), there is information which will interest social historians and may humiliate contemporary dipsomaniacs; namely, that a little more than a century ago the yearly consumption of rum in Wilbraham, Massachusetts (population 2,000), was 8,000 gallons, and the annual consumption of whiskey in Georgia (population 400,000, including slaves) was 2,000,000 gallons. Another very short article ("North Carolina, Governor of, to Governor of South Carolina"), not unrelated to the foregoing, must be quoted in full:

> "It's a damn long time between drinks," said Edward B. Dudley, Governor of North Carolina, to Pierce Mason Butler, chief executive of South Carolina, in 1838, at the home of Mrs. Nancy Anne Jones, about midway between Raleigh and Durham, N. C. About five years later, at a meeting on the state line, not far from Charlotte, Gov. J. M. Morehead said to Gov. J. H. Hammond of South Carolina, "It's a damned long time between drinks."

As well as this reviewer can judge, the accuracy which distinguishes between a gubernatorial "damn" in 1838 and a "damned" in 1843 *(circa)*,

7. Reprinted by permission of the author and the *Kenyon Review*.

is sustained throughout. It is, of course, inevitable that in a work of this scope some errors should escape the attention of the editor and his proof-readers; and of those noted two should be pointed out. George Mason, not James Madison, predicted that the electors would fail to choose a president "nineteen times in twenty" (II, 191). Herbert Croly's *Promise of American Life* was not published in 1900 as stated (IV, 302), but in 1909.

One aware of Mr. Adams's eastern background, his specialized interest and competence in New England history, and his conservative predilections might reasonably (if somewhat meanly) expect to find traces of them in the assignment, coloring, and length of the contributions; but on the whole the work is remarkably free from sectional or partisan bias. Indeed, the generous amount of space and the high level of scholarship devoted to the South, the "Valley of Democracy," and the West mark a real advance in American historiography. As regards partisan prejudice, the assertion in the article entitled "Morals" (IV, 21) that "The Federal Government itself [the cross reference is to the abrogation of the gold clause, 1933] has contributed to this feeling of irresponsibility for contracts by its own failure to fulfill its promises," sounds more like the shriek of Associate Justice McReynolds than the calm tones of an historian; and the reference (V, 207–208) to President F. D. Roosevelt's judicial reorganization plan of February 5, 1937, as a court-packing episode (without quotation marks) is likewise objectionable. But these are exceptional.

Despite its careful organization, its general accuracy and fairness, the *Dictionary* is in two important respects extremely disappointing. In the first place, it lacks a philosophy, a principle of interpretation, to bind its alphabetically-ordered parts into anything like a consistent and coherent whole. As the reflective reader refers to articles here and there or as, following the cross references, he peruses a series of related articles, he may experience considerable confusion. From one contribution he may infer that the influence of climate largely explains regional and national evolution; from another, that the influence of the frontier has been decisive; and from still others, that economic determinism is the key wherewith to unlock the secrets of past, present, and the emerging future. Admittedly, this may be less a criticism of editorial policy than a commentary on the present state of American historical scholarship.

A more serious, at all events a fairer and more pertinent, criticism relates to the failure of the *Dictionary* to fulfill the promise implicit in the Foreword. The editor writes: "A generation ago historians had done the merest spadework. Today our whole culture is their province. . . ." On close scrutiny of the work one is, therefore, amazed to discover that more than half the articles are devoted to politics, government, and war;

about one fourth to economic topics; one fifth to social history; and fewer than five per cent to the arts, literature, and philosophy. For these proportions the editor must be held responsible, and also for the fact that the articles on art, music, drama, and philosophy, although written by qualified scholars, are so brief and perfunctory as to be almost worthless. To take one example, the student who resorts to the *Dictionary* for information relative to the struggles, ideas, and faiths of the so-called "Middle Period" of American history will find nearly a page on the Battle of Gettysburg but not a line on the poetry of Walt Whitman or the novels of Herman Melville. Again, one line is assigned to pragmatism; William James is given about the same amount of space as Jack Johnson; the entry under "Lindbergh Flies across the Atlantic" is about three times as long as the summary paragraph under "Transcendentalism." If, in these cases and others that might be cited, there is any criterion of selection and emphasis, it is clearly journalistic rather than historical.

Useful, even invaluable, as the *Dictionary* will be to political scientists and to those whose main concern is with political, economic, and social history, students of the history of arts and of ideas must continue to turn for reference and guidance to the Beards' *Rise of American Civilization* and *America in Midpassage,* to the incomplete Schlesinger-Fox *History of American Life,* and to the late Professor Parrington's unfinished *Main Currents in American Thought.* This, I fear, is equivalent to saying that a dictionary of American history which shall take "our whole culture as . . . [its] province" remains to be compiled.

*Suggestions for Study*

1. What are the excellences of the *Dictionary?*
2. Is it warped by prejudices?
3. In what two respects is it disappointing?
4. What is its main contribution?
5. Does the reviewer take into account the underlying purpose of the *Dictionary?* How well does the *Dictionary* fulfill its purpose?
6. Does the reviewer's citing of particular details of strength and weakness of the *Dictionary* give you confidence in the justice of his review? Why?
7. Why are the several direct quotations from the work effective?
8. Define the following words from the review: collaboration, discriminating, dipsomaniacs, gubernatorial, predilections, abrogation, implicit, perfunctory, pragmatism.

## Book Review II

Early Victorian England: 1830–1865, edited by G. M. Young, reviewed by Charles Frederick Harrold.[8]

In producing these impressive volumes on Early Victorian England, Mr. G. M. Young and his associates have labored under few of the disadvantages which hampered the efforts of the authors of the preceding volumes in this series, Shakespeare's England and Johnson's England. Indeed, they must have felt embarrassed by the colossal mass of data bequeathed by a self-conscious and journalistic era to a generation already bending under the weight of its own records and researches. But they have borne up nobly, and have sketched in the lineaments of those decades between the first two Reform Acts with admirable regard for scholarship and "human interest." They handle their facts with a fine consciousness of what the reader of today feels most curious about when he thinks of the age of Dickens. They tell us what we want to know of the era in which Soames Forsyte's grandfather was coming to man's estate: how, for instance, the members of the middle class lived on their incomes and accumulated little legacies for their children; where the maid slept and what she wore when she served tea; how the collier's wife provided for her sons and daughters in spite of the public house; in what degree the early Victorian drawing-room was, and was not, a chaos of bric-a-brac; what it meant to spend a week in a great country house; who it was that built the Marble Arch; how the early Victorians spent their holidays; what was involved in emigrating to Canada in 1840; what the advent of the railway meant to the Victorian village and the countryside; what the Victorian gentleman read in the daily press, admired at the Royal Academy, drank after dinner, ate for breakfast, and wore for the ball of the season; how the Victorian family rested on a hierarchy of obligations—of the sons to the father, the daughters to the sons, and of the mother to them all; what they all saw if, and when, they attended a performance at "The Strand" or "Drury Lane"; how London's streets, within two decades, had sprawled outward from the City to the most distant suburbs, filled with ugly and jerry-built structures, and had outpaced the growth of omnibuses until the London clerk spent from two to four hours daily in walking between his rooms in Hammersmith and his stool in Threadneedle Street. All these details and hundreds of others are poured forth in these heavily laden volumes, and are made vivid by no fewer than one hundred and thirty-seven illustrations.

8. Reprinted by permission of the author and the Virginia Quarterly Review.

It is a rich report, notably on the side of social phenomena and economic issues. All of the authors have obviously been conscious of the difficulty of speaking authoritatively about any specific feature of an age which changed with such astonishing rapidity. An era which began with stage coaches and Count D'Orsay, and ended—if it can be said to have ended— with Disraeli "shooting Niagara," is not an age about which to become dogmatic. The essence of such a period cannot be distilled. Yet it is the peculiar disadvantage of any historical symposium, such as the present work, that the underlying unity of the age too often falls between the separate chapters or studies, and the intellectual milieu evaporates in the presence of exuberant data and statistics. This dilemma the editor has tried to meet in a final chapter devoted to portraying the inner quality, or intellectual and emotional life, of the period. But it is an impossible feat to discuss successfully, in one chapter, early Victorian Evangelicalism, Utilitarianism, moral earnestness, metropolitan life, economic and social reform, the Oxford Movement, Chartism, literary taste, education, and social criticism, after the reader has become accustomed to factual and statistical discussion in other and greater proportions. The change in scale is a little disconcerting, and more than a little disappointing. And the effort of the individual contributors to orient their special studies to the main stream of Victorian life and thought does not quite make up the deficiency. But it must be admitted that we have here, in these two admirable volumes, a magnificent, richly illustrated, and very human record of an age that has now become another chapter in the history books. And the record is splendidly authentic: one can visualize the pageant of Hyde Park; one can fairly smell the defective drain under the floor of my lord's dressing-room, by which he is able to predict the weather. And the reader is left with mixed feelings of admiration and dismay for an age unparalleled for rapid change, and for the courage, stupidity, and ingenuity with which it adjusted itself to unprecedented circumstances.

## Suggestions for Study

1. Give an approximate date to the early Victorian period.

2. What problem did the authors of *Early Victorian England* face in compiling their volumes? What does the statement of this problem indicate concerning the fairness of the reviewer?

3. Does the review tell whether or not the volumes make interesting reading? What words show this?

4. What does the list of concrete details in paragraph one indicate concerning the subject matter of the volumes?

5. Why cannot the authors speak with complete authority upon the Vic-

torian scene? By stating this difficulty, does the reviewer imply an adverse criticism? Wherein lies the real weakness of the volumes?

6. What is the value of these volumes?

7. Upon what means of development does the reviewer rely mainly to make an effective review?

8. What features in the review indicate the writer's authority to offer such criticism?

9. Define the following words from the selection: lineaments, orient, advent, hierarchy, dogmatic, essence, symposium, milieu, exuberant, dilemma, authentic.

**Writing the Review.** After measuring the book by such standards as those mentioned above, you are ready to write a criticism. To make this writing vigorous and to the point, you must bear in mind a few other principles. Since any one review obviously cannot consider all the points of judgment just studied, select those which apply most particularly to the book. The structure may be especially good, or especially bad; the adaptation to the reader may be precise or careless; the thesis may be poorly substantiated or adequately proved. But stress whatever strikes you most particularly concerning the book. Second, in giving a judgment, leave no statement unsupported. The reader must always be able to see by what reasoning a critic has arrived at his conclusions. Third, write a review which is applicable to one book only, not to a score. If you abandon the criticism after saying a book is interesting, you are not distinguishing the book at hand from a thousand others. Make direct reference to passages in the book, or select short quotations from it. Writing a good review means writing a review that is concise, persuasive, and unique.

To catch the attention of readers, the review should start vigorously. As the point of interest of the reader lies in the book itself, attention can often be focused by an immediate reference to the book or the subject matter with which it deals. This opening reference may even be the thesis of the review giving the final judgment on the book. However the beginning is made, do not delay long before acquainting the reader with the attitude you are adopting toward the work. Unity is abused by any sudden shifting from high praise to scathing denunciation. Also avoid the use of time-worn adjectives. Such terms as "interesting," "stimulating," "absorbing," mean little to the reader. The critic should try to show in what specific way the work is interesting or stimulating.

Into the introduction can go many details: a statement of the author's purpose, a comparison of the work with other works by the same author, an identification of the work according to its type, a statement of the place of the work in literary history, even pertinent biographical materials on the author.

In writing the body of the review, an immature critic is often satisfied with a summary of the contents, an account of the story, or perhaps a sketch of the author's life. These prolonged summaries are to be avoided. The contents should be stated only with the purpose of providing material for discussion in the review. Similarly, in reviewing a narrative, the critic seldom discloses the entire plot. He may do so if the plot is so bad that he must reveal its outcome to prove his point; but if the plot is good, he gives just enough of it to whet the appetite of his readers and leaves them to find its outcome for themselves. Seldom is much space devoted to an account of the story. The author's life is mentioned only in so far as it is needed for the actual criticism of the book. The reader wants to know about the book itself.

Tone is important for the critic. In the old days critics were savage in their tirades against authors. Francis Jeffrey opened a very famous review of the poet Wordsworth in this manner:

> This will never do. . . . The case of Mr. Wordsworth, we perceive, is now manifestly hopeless; and we give him up as altogether incurable, and beyond the power of criticism. We cannot indeed altogether omit taking precautions now and then against the spreading of the malady;—but for himself, though we shall watch the progress of his symptoms as a matter of professional curiosity and instruction, we really think it right not to harass him any longer with nauseous remedies—but rather to throw in cordials and lenitives, and wait in patience for the natural termination of the disorder. In order to justify this desertion of our patient, however, it is proper to state why we despair of the success of a more active practice.

Such satirical thrusts and savage attacks have for the most part passed away in our century. The modern critic strives to be modest. He is firm in his contentions, but he does not present a know-it-all attitude. Even the poorest and slenderest book demands great labor on the part of its author, and some books are of course the result of a lifetime of study. Thus to set oneself against the writer in a brash and cocksure fashion is not only discourteous—it is foolish.

Two more cautions ought to be given regarding the discussion of an author's ideas. First, they must be treated with the utmost fairness. You must make certain that you understand fully and accurately the statements of the author, and later make sure that you do not warp those ideas in discussing them. Writers commonly complain that they have been misrepresented. Second, beware of being dogmatic in clinging to the principles by which you are judging a work. For many years the tragedies of Shakespeare were denounced because they contain elements of comedy; critics said dogmatically that a dramatist should not mix comedy and tragedy in one play. Now it is believed that Shakespeare mingled the two for a very sound dramatic reason. The student who has not yet formed mature standards must be especially careful about unwarranted positiveness.

The conclusion follows closely the principles for concluding paragraphs which were laid down earlier in the text. It is devoted usually to a restatement of the estimated value of the book.

The review is thus a careful, accurate, and unprejudiced consideration of the work of another. It aims toward moderation of tone, but firmness of judgment. It is well proportioned, stressing the important ideas and excluding or subordinating minor details. It is concise and fast moving, keeping in mind always the demands of the reader. It attempts through careful reasoning to persuade others of the justice of the view which it sets forth. And it is eminently fair in its appreciation of merit and its condemnation of shortcomings.

### Exercise

1. Go to the library, and select four or five technical magazines which pertain to your special interest. Read six or eight reviews in these magazines, and write a short paragraph about each, summarizing the content.

2. Read three reviews of the same book, one review at least being in a technical magazine. The *Book Review Digest* will give you assistance in finding these reviews. Then write a paragraph noting the points at which the reviewers disagree. See if you can account for the disagreement.

## Book Review III

*Abraham Lincoln: The War Years,* by Carl Sandburg, reviewed by Charles A. Beard.[9]

Never yet has a history or biography like Carl Sandburg's *Abraham Lincoln: The War Years* appeared on land or sea. Strict disciples of Gibbon, Macaulay, Ranke, Mommsen, Hegel, or Marx will scarcely know what to do with it. It does not enclose the commonplace in a stately diction appropriate for Augustan pomp. Its pages do not stand out in the cold formalism which marks the work of those historians who imagine that they are writing history as it actually was. Nor are the personalities, events, passions, follies, blind stumblings, ridiculous performances, contradictions, and stupidities of the four years smoothed out to make them fit into "the progressive revelation of the idea of God." The struggle of classes, though more than hinted at, forms no persistent theme employed

9. Reprinted by permission of the author and of the *Virginia Quarterly Review.*

to explain everything from Lincoln's jokes to Jefferson Davis's views in the spring of 1861.

The opening chapters of Mr. Sandburg's first volume do not present, after the fashion of Macaulay, a picture of American society in 1861—the number, posture, interests, and ideologies of the classes whose spokesmen enact the leading roles. Systematists will not discover anywhere in the four volumes "logical" and self-contained "treatments" of finance, taxation, railways, land policies, tariffs, natural resources, labor, and immigration, or the long struggle to curtail the rights of states in the interest of business enterprise. Followers of Lytton Strachey, Gamaliel Bradford, and Freud will look in vain for psychographs of personalities fashioned after their hearts' desires.

But this is not to say that Mr. Sandburg writes "without fear and without research." On the contrary, few if any historians have ever labored harder in preparation for composition. He has traveled widely and searched widely. Great collections of Lincolniana he has scrutinized and used critically. He has examined mountains of newspapers, letters, diaries, pamphlets, stray papers, documents, records, Congressional debates, posters, proclamations, handbills, clippings, pictures, cartoons, and memorabilia, great and small. Work with the paper sources he has supplemented by journeys all over the country, interviews with survivors of the war years and their descendants, and walks over fields and plantations. An indefatigable thoroughness characterizes his preparations and his pages.

In arrangement our author's text is more like a diary or saga than a "systematic presentation." He knows that he cannot tell it all, and says frankly, "the teller does the best he can and picks what is to him plain, moving, and important—though sometimes what is important may be tough reading, tangled, involved, sometimes gradually taking on interest, even mystery, because of the gaps and discrepancies." A few chapter titles from the first volume illustrate the flow: "The Use of Patronage," "December '61 Message," "Opinion Makers," "Expectations of McClellan," "Corruption," "White House Children," "Donelson—Grant—Shiloh." Even without chapters there are excursions and diversions which could be put in or left out. Yet when the four volumes are taken together in bulk, it would seem that they form a realistic history of the great conflict and that all parts and passages are so ordered as to give a sense of verisimilitude.

An air of grave thoughtfulness hangs over the lightest words. The searching, brooding spirit of the laborious historian pervades the treatment of every large problem. With this, that, and many things, specialists will doubtless quarrel more or less gently. Mr. Charles Ramsdell, for example, will not be satisfied with the chapter entitled "War Challenge at Sumter." And yet when I place Mr. Ramsdell's essay on the subject down by the side of Mr. Sandburg's chapter, with the best will in the world, I should not like to say on oath which is the truer, that is, which more closely corresponds to the recorded and unrecorded emotions, thoughts, tempers, and actions in the case. But when specialists have finished dissecting, scraping, refining, dissenting, and adding, I suspect that Mr. Sandburg's work will remain for long years to come a noble monument of American literature.

The scene is viewed mainly from the Northern standpoint. The weight of emphasis is on Northern events and personalities, despite the passages on campaigns and battles. There is a chapter on Jefferson Davis and his government, but orthodox Southerners of the Miss Millie Rutherford school will not like it. They will not see the historical necessity of quoting Andy Johnson's outburst about "an illegitimate, swaggering, bastard, scrub aristocracy" in response to Mr. Davis's reflections on "a common blacksmith or tailor." (See Marx.) And, although Mr. Sandburg cites freely many adverse Southern judgments on Lincoln, he sees that strange figure in the White House undamaged by the animadversions. After all, just what is *the* Southern view of the war years or anything else? Moreover, who, North or South, is fitted to tell the truth, the whole truth, and nothing but the truth?

Yet Lincoln is not portrayed in these pages as the mighty hero, the great wise man who foresaw things perfectly and moved with unerring wisdom to the great end. He is shown as a poor limited mortal, of many moods, tempers, and distempers, stumbling, blundering along, trying this and trying that, telling jokes, bewildered, disappointed, grieved by his fractious wife, weeping now, laughing then, ordering this, canceling that, trying to smooth ruffled personalities, looking upon mankind, like Marcus Aurelius, as composed of little creatures playing and loving, quarreling and fighting, and making up again, all without much rhyme or reason—Lincoln steadfast in his purpose of saving the Union, and, if possible, reducing the area of slavery or getting rid of it entirely.

There may have been men around Lincoln who were greater (whatever that may mean); many of them at least imagined themselves greater; but I am convinced that Mr. Sandburg's pages will dispel any illusions on this score. Even some cold Puritans correctly educated at Harvard, with many misgivings, and reluctantly, came to the conclusion that even they could scarcely have managed things better in the long run. It was hard for cultivated persons to endure his jokes, his uncouth manners, his unexpected sallies, and yet they at last learned that there was something marvelous in him—an Antaeus possessing the divine powers of a Proteus. Linguistic purists who could speak of Lincoln's style as that of a half-educated lawyer finally saw in the rude texture of his sentences a power that none of them could wield. Mr. Sandburg, I feel sure, has given us a fitting sequel to *The Prairie Years,* a truer and more majestic Lincoln than is to be found in the pages of Nicolay and Hay, those apologists to the bourgeois of the Gilded Age.

A week's reading, which nearly finished my dim eyes, carried me along as in a tumultuous flood, amused, entertained, delighted, toward a conclusion which I had long been maturing. Why is it that the formally educated and polished are so often futile in the presence of vast movements of history? Why is it that so many makers of history on a large scale spring from somewhere near the earth of Antaeus and manage to do things on a colossal scale, displaying profound wisdom in the operation? The answer which I had been darkly maturing, Mr. Sandburg has clinched for me. It is that the great philosophies and systems of thought which adepts pile up, teach, and parade, so far as they are valid for life, derive from a few common-sense aphorisms, fables, and maxims evolved by ordinary humanity in its varied efforts to grapple with the stuff of life. Out of the mouths of babes cometh wisdom. Lincoln was the fabulist, the aphorist of the age, strong of will yet supple, facing the storm as a farmer wrestles with the toughness of the soil and the tempests of the seasons, and speaking a language, even in crude jokes, which struck the chords of the primordial that endures at or near the bottom of every civilization and carries on when the top has rotted away.

## Suggestions for Study

1. What means of development does the author use in the two opening paragraphs? Why is reference made to Gibbon, Macaulay, Strachey, and others?

2. What unspoken questions is the reviewer answering in paragraph three as a result of his remarks in the first two paragraphs?

3. Is the biography scholarly?

4. What is Sandburg's purpose in using an unusual manner of presentation? Is the reviewer conscious of and sympathetic with that purpose?

5. Is Sandburg's method of presentation in the main successful?

6. Of what significance in reference to the value of the biography is the word "gently" in paragraph five?

7. Is Sandburg's biography the last word to be said upon Lincoln?

8. Does the reviewer accuse Sandburg of prejudice? From what standpoint is the biography written?

9. What picture of Lincoln emerges from the book as a whole?

10. Why does the reviewer include the last paragraph? Does it have any relation to the rest of the review?

11. Who is Charles A. Beard, the reviewer of the biography?

12. Summarize the value of Sandburg's work as revealed in this review.

13. Define the following words from the review: systematists, curtail, scrutinize, memorabilia, indefatigable, discrepancies, diversions, verisimilitude, animadversions, fractious, Antaeus, Proteus, purists, bourgeois, adepts, aphorisms, maxims, fabulist, primordial.

## Book Review IV

*You Can't Go Home Again,* by Thomas Wolfe, reviewed by Louis B. Salomon.[10]

My feeling about any novel by Thomas Wolfe is that even if it were not good I'd like it. I'd like it for its ebullient, electric vitality, its obvious sincerity, the glowing, almost incandescent poetry of its style, the sense which it gives, however confusedly, of a meaning, a unified current, recognized in the seemingly helter-skelter maze of human life. These qualities light up *You Can't Go Home Again* for me, just as they illuminated *Look Homeward, Angel, Of Time and the River, The Web and the Rock,* and many shorter pieces; but there is no denying that Wolfe's methods, his themes, and to a large extent his material remained the same throughout his work, with the result that his inspiration suffered a gradual diminution of intensity.

That George Webber = Eugene Gant = Tom Wolfe is an equation almost too obvious to mention, in spite of the fact that George is described in *The Web and the Rock* and *You Can't Go Home Again* as short and stocky, while Wolfe was a mountain of a man and Eugene Gant was supposed to be long and rangy. When an author bestows his own personality on a hero and surrounds him with the author's own acquaintances under the transparent disguise of altered names, it makes little difference that he knocks five or six inches off his stature. If you have read *How to Write a Novel,* Wolfe's account of the composing and publishing of *Look Homeward, Angel,* you will find the first half of this last book virtually a retelling of that bit of autobiography. The rest of the story deals with his love affair with "Esther" and its conclusion, with the stock-market crash, and with his travels in Nazi Germany, several chapters of the latter part of the book having, if my memory does not fail me, already appeared as short stories in magazines.

His two principal themes are, as always, man's essential loneliness and the mystic movement of time, like a river that seems ever the same but is

10. Reprinted by permission of the author and of the *Nation.*

constantly shifting. You can't go home again, simply because "home" isn't there; both it and you have changed, and your romanticized memory-picture of it bears no more resemblance to the sordid reality than a sur-realist painting does to an unretouched photograph.

But even themes so universally applicable as these can be overworked, and the pregnant symbolism, the driving power that made *Look Home-ward, Angel* stand out above the common herd of novels like a mountain dawn, has given way to a sprawling looseness of structure that becomes more and more noticeable as the book progresses. There are diversions into long essay passages bound to the narrative by only the most tenuous threads. Nor can this be attributed altogether to the fact that the work is posthumous, not subject to final revision, since the same tendency had already manifested itself all too plainly in *Of Time and the River*.

The very nature of these conventional complaints against Wolfe's art, however, makes them a sort of compliment, a grudging admission that he had something too vitally alive to be judged entirely according to the criteria of form—in short, he irritates us more, because he had the magic power and did not use it precisely as we should have liked, than does the run-of-the-mill writer who obviously was not born with the divine fire. Wolfe belongs to the tribe of Whitman, Emerson, Carlyle,—especially the last. Like Carlyle, he was emotionally disturbed by the stupidity and selfishness of the world, without having any specific formula to offer as a remedy; he had a passion for work and a transcendental scorn for the shackles of form; even his style, with its purple splendor, its heavy lean-ing on apostrophe and impersonation, its ironic ranting against medioc-rity, echoes that "stormy sophist with his mouth of thunder" who preached Cassandra-like warnings to the Victorians. Chapter 29, "The Hollow Men," with its bitter allegory about Standard Concentrated Blots, sounds like an excerpt from *Past and Present*.

And I feel about Wolfe very much as I feel about Carlyle: though I disagree with a great many things he says, I don't know anyone who can say them more splendidly.

## Suggestions for Study

1. Formulate a thesis sentence which will state concisely the reviewer's judgment on *You Can't Go Home Again*.
2. What is the theme of the novel?
3. How does this novel compare with previous novels by the same author? Does such a comparison reveal a significant weakness in this work?
4. Is the content of *You Can't Go Home Again* entirely original, or has the author made use of similar materials before? Has the author drawn upon his own life and experiences for material?

5. Has the reviewer been careful to state at the outset of his criticism the point of view which he has toward the novel, or does he shift the tone during the course of the review? Justify your answer, and in formulating it pay particular attention to the first and last sentences of the review.

6. Why is the comparison of Wolfe to Carlyle inserted in the review? What does that tell about the audience to whom the reviewer was writing?

## D. Biography

One means to success is the ability to see people as they really are, to judge their worth, and to determine how much confidence can be placed in them. Only after years of careful observation of human nature can this ability be acquired, but you can be assisted in the effort by a study of biographical sketches of different kinds.

Consideration is to be taken here of four types of character writing: the character, the character sketch, the biographical sketch, and the autobiography. The character portrays the common traits of a group of similar people; the others pertain only to individuals. The character sketch presents the individual at one specific time in his life. The biographical sketch traces his growth and the influences which molded him. The autobiography analyzes the writer's own life and achievements.

**The Character.** Our modern interest in characterization owes its origin very largely to the "character," a form of writing which dates back to a Greek philosopher, Theophrastus, three hundred years before Christ, who wrote characters to amuse himself and thereby set the form which the character has followed ever since. His major aim was to satirize certain groups of people who, he observed, were addicted to folly. The titles of a few of his sketches will indicate their substance: "The Flatterer," "The Boaster," "The Coward," "The Grumbler," "The Rustic." As a forceful opening sentence he usually employed his thesis, containing a concise definition of the type he was describing. The remainder of the article was devoted to details and illustrations intended to show the many attributes of the group or of a person typical of the group. Modern writers of the character have followed for the most part this same structure and satirical purpose, although sketches of admirable types are not unknown. Usually, however, the stupid, the vicious, or the extravagant have been ridiculed.

Although many characters of the old type are still written today, the form is used most frequently now by historians, sociologists, and the like to portray classes of people. As their purpose is different, they ordinarily discard satire in favor of a scientific, impersonal method. The following sketch by Mark Twain illustrates the older form, and that by Macaulay a historian's use of it.

## The Office Bore

### MARK TWAIN

He arrives just as regularly as the clock strikes nine in the morning. And so he even beats the editor sometimes, and the porter must leave his work and climb two or three pair of stairs to unlock the "Sanctum" door and let him in. He lights one of the office pipes—not reflecting, perhaps, that the editor may be one of those "stuck-up" people who would as soon have a stranger defile his toothbrush as his pipestem. Then he begins to loll—for a person who can consent to loaf his useless life away in ignominious indolence has not the energy to sit up straight. He stretches full length on the sofa a while; then draws up to half length; then gets into a chair, hangs his head back and his arms abroad, and stretches his legs till the rims of his boot heels rest upon the floor; by and by sits up and leans forward, with one leg or both over the arm of the chair. But it is still observable that with all his changes of position, he never assumes the upright or a fraudful affectation of dignity. From time to time he yawns, and stretches, and scratches himself with a tranquil, mangy enjoyment, and now and then he grunts a kind of stuffy, overfed grunt, which is full of animal contentment. At rare and long intervals, however, he sighs a sigh that is the eloquent expression of a secret confession, to wit: "I am useless and a nuisance, a cumberer of the earth." The bore and his comrades—for there are usually from two to four on hand, day and night— mix into the conversation when men come in to see the editors for a moment on business; they hold noisy talks among themselves about politics in particular, and all other subjects in general—even warming up, after a fashion, sometimes, and seeming to take almost a real interest in what they are discussing. They ruthlessly call an editor from his work with such a remark as: "Did you see this, Smith, in the *Gazette?*" and proceed to read the paragraph while the sufferer reins in his impatient pen and listens; they often loll and sprawl round the office hour after hour, swapping anecdotes and relating personal experiences to each other —hairbreadth escapes, social encounters with distinguished men, election reminiscences, sketches of odd characters, etc. And through all those hours they never seem to comprehend that they are robbing the editors of their time, and the public of journalistic excellence in next day's paper. At other times they drowse, or dreamily pore over exchanges, or droop limp and pensive over the chair arms for an hour. Even this solemn silence is small respite to the editor, for the next uncomfortable thing to having people look over his shoulders, perhaps, is to have them sit by in silence and listen to the scratching of his pen. If a body desires to talk private business with one of the editors, he must call him outside, for no hint milder than blasting powder or nitroglycerine would be likely to move the bores out of listening distance. To have to sit and endure the presence of a bore day after day; to feel your cheerful spirits begin to sink as his footstep sounds on the stair, and utterly vanish away as his tiresome form enters the door; to suffer through his anecdotes and die slowly to his reminiscences; to feel always the fetters of his clogging presence; to long hopelessly for a single day's privacy; to note with a shudder, by and by, that to contemplate his funeral in fancy has ceased to soothe, to imagine him undergoing in strict and fearful detail the tortures of the ancient Inquisition has lost its power to satisfy the heart, and that even to wish him millions and millions and millions of miles in Tophet is able to bring only a fitful gleam of joy; to have to endure all this, day after day, and week after week, and month after month, is an affliction that transcends any other that men suffer. Physical pain is a pastime to it, and hanging a pleasure excursion. —*Sketches New and Old.*

## Suggestions for Study

1. State the tone of the sketch. List a number of the specific words which help to establish this tone.

2. List a number of examples to indicate how the author secures concreteness of writing.

3. Divide the sketch into its main parts in order to show its organization.

4. What sentence device enables the author to handle skillfully the very long sentence next to the final sentence?

5. State the purpose and thesis of the sketch.

6. Define the following words from the sketch: defile, loll, affectation, fetters, contemplate, Inquisition, fitful.

# The Country Gentlemen

### T. B. MACAULAY

Of the rent, a large proportion was divided among the country gentlemen, a class of persons whose position and character it is most important that we should clearly understand; for by their influence and by their passions the fate of the nation was, at several important conjunctures, determined.

We should be much mistaken if we pictured to ourselves the squires of the seventeenth century as men bearing a close resemblance to their descendants, the county members and chairmen of quarter sessions with whom we are familiar. The modern country gentleman generally receives a liberal education, passes from a distinguished school to a distinguished college, and has every opportunity to become an excellent scholar. He has generally seen something of foreign countries. A considerable part of his life has generally been passed in the capital; and the refinements of the capital follow him into the country. There is perhaps no class of dwellings so pleasing as the rural seats of the English gentry. In the parks and pleasure grounds, nature, dressed yet not disguised by art, wears her most alluring form. In the buildings good sense and good taste combine to produce a happy union of the comfortable and the graceful. The pictures, the musical instruments, the library, would in any other country be considered as proving the owner to be an eminently polished and accomplished man. A country gentleman who witnessed the Revolution was probably in receipt of about a fourth part of the rent which his acres now yield to his posterity. He was, therefore, as compared with his posterity, a poor man, and was generally under the necessity of residing, with little interruption, on his estate. To travel on the Continent, to maintain an establishment in London, or even to visit London frequently, were pleasures in which only the great proprietors could indulge. It may be confidently affirmed that of the squires whose names were in King Charles's commissions of peace and lieutenancy not one in twenty went to town once in five years, or had ever in his life wandered so far as Paris. Many lords of manors had received an education differing little from that of their menial servants. The heir of an estate often passed his boyhood and youth at the seat of his family with no better tutors than grooms and gamekeepers, and scarce attained learning enough to sign his name to a mittimus. If he went to school and to college, he generally returned before he was twenty to the seclusion of the old hall, and there, unless his mind were very happily constituted by nature, soon forgot his academical pursuits in rural business and pleasures. His chief serious employment was the care of his property. He examined samples of grain, handled pigs, and on market days made bargains over a tankard with drovers and hop merchants. His chief pleasures were commonly derived from field sports and from an unrefined sensuality. His language and pronunciation were such as we should now expect to hear only from the most ignorant clowns. His oaths, coarse jests, and scurrilous terms of abuse were uttered with the broadest accent of his province. It was easy to discern, from the first words which he spoke, whether he came from Somersetshire or Yorkshire. He troubled himself little about decorating his abode, and, if he attempted decoration, seldom produced anything but deformity. The litter of a farmyard gathered under the windows of his bedchamber, and the cabbages and gooseberry bushes grew close to his hall door. His table was loaded with coarse plenty; and guests were cordially welcomed to it. But, as the habit of drinking to excess was general in the class to which he belonged, and as his fortune did not enable him to intoxicate large assemblies daily with claret or canary, strong beer was the ordinary beverage. The quantity of beer consumed in those days was indeed enormous. For beer then was to the middle and lower classes, not only all that beer now is, but all that wine, tea, and ardent spirits now are. It was only at great houses, or on great occasions, that foreign drink was placed on the board. The ladies of the house, whose business it had commonly been to cook the repast, retired as soon as the dishes had been devoured, and left the gentlemen to their ale and tobacco. The coarse jollity of the afternoon was often prolonged till the revelers were laid under the table.

It was very seldom that the country gentleman caught glimpses of the great world; and what he saw of it tended rather to confuse than to enlighten his understanding. His opinions respecting religion, government, foreign countries, and former times having been derived, not from study, from observation, or from conversation with enlightened companions, but from such traditions as were current in his own small circle, were the opinions of a child. He adhered to them, however, with the obstinacy which is generally found in ignorant men accustomed to be fed with flattery. His animosities were numerous and bitter. He hated Frenchmen and Italians, Scotchmen and Irishmen, Papists and Presbyterians, Independents and Baptists, Quakers and Jews. Towards London and Londoners he felt an aversion which more than once produced important political effects. His wife and daughter were in tastes and acquirements below a housekeeper or a stillroom maid of the present day. They stitched and spun, brewed gooseberry wine, cured marigolds, and made the crust for the venison pasty.

From this description it might be supposed that the English esquire of the seventeenth century did not materially differ from a rustic miller or alehouse keeper of our time. There are, however, some important parts of his character still to be noted, which will greatly modify this estimate. Unlettered as he was and unpolished, he was still in some most important points a gentleman. He was a member of a proud and powerful aristocracy, and was distinguished by many both of the good and of the bad qualities which belong to aristocrats. His family pride was beyond that of a Talbot or a Howard. He knew the genealogies and coats of arms of all his neighbors, and could tell which of them had assumed supporters without any right, and which of them were so unfortunate as to be great grandsons of aldermen. He was a magistrate, and, as such, administered gratuitously to those who dwelt around him a rude patriarchal justice, which, in spite of innumerable blunders and of occasional acts of tyranny, was yet better than no justice at all. He was an officer of the trainbands; and his military dignity, though it might move the mirth of gallants who had served a campaign in Flanders, raised his character in his own eyes and in the eyes of his neighbors. Nor indeed was his soldiership justly a subject of derision. In every county there were elderly gentlemen who had seen service which was no child's play. One had been knighted by Charles the First, after the battle of Edgehill. Another still wore a patch over the scar which he had received at Naseby. A third had defended his old house till Fairfax had blown in the door with a petard. The presence of these old Cavaliers, with their old swords and holsters, and with their old stories about Goring and Lunsford, gave to the musters of militia an earnest and warlike aspect which would otherwise have been wanting. Even those country gentlemen who were too young to have themselves exchanged blows with the cuirassiers of the parliament had, from childhood, been surrounded by the traces of recent war, and fed with stories of the martial exploits of their fathers and uncles. Thus the character of the English esquire of the seventeenth century was compounded of two elements which we are not accustomed to find united. His ignorance and uncouthness, his low tastes and gross phrases, would, in our time, be considered as indicating a nature and a breeding thoroughly plebeian. Yet he was essentially a patrician, and had, in large measure, both the virtues and the vices which flourish among men set from their birth in high place, and accustomed to authority, to observance, and to self-respect. It is not easy for a generation which is accustomed to find chivalrous sentiments only in company with liberal studies and polished manners to image to itself a man with the deportment, the vocabulary, and the accent of a carter, yet punctilious on matters of genealogy and precedence, and ready to risk his life rather than see a stain cast on the honor of his house. It is only, however, by thus joining together things seldom or never found together in our own experience, that we can form a just idea of that rustic aristocracy which constituted the main strength of the armies of Charles the First, and which long supported, with strange fidelity, the interest of his descendants.—*History of England,* ch. 3.

*Suggestions for Study*

1. What are the two divisions of this character?
2. What is the author's purpose? Is it satirical like that of some of the older writers of characters?

3. What is his thesis, and where is it stated?

4. Why were the country gentlemen important as a class? Is it good rhetorical practice to state the importance of a subject immediately upon beginning a paper?

5. Why does Macaulay introduce the contrast in paragraph two?

6. What was the Revolution, referred to in paragraph two?

7. Summarize the objectionable traits of the country gentlemen.

8. What attributes of the country gentlemen brighten this picture?

9. What is the major means of paragraph development that enables Macaulay to make this sketch so vivid?

10. Define the following words from the selection: posterity, mittimus, scurrilous, gratuitously, patriarchal, derision, petard.

**The Character Sketch.** The character sketch is a picture of an individual. It sets him apart from any groups to which he may belong, but it does not trace his growth, his backgrounds, or the influences shaping him— these are left to the biography. Its aim is to depict him at some specific point of his life. The writer of the character sketch formulates a strong dominant impression concerning an individual and clarifies it by the selection of pertinent details.

The character sketch may be composed of a description of an individual, or an analysis of his personality, or preferably a combination of the two. In describing the external appearance, the most important procedure consists of stating the leading impression one has of the individual and then presenting such details as will illustrate this best. Although such a description is not as valuable for a character sketch as is an analysis of personality, still it can be useful. Appearances often tell much, or at least arouse suspicions. Unpressed trousers may be a sign of slovenliness; furtive eyes, of thievery; a square chin, of resolution, courage, or stubbornness; a high forehead, of a keen intellect. Sometimes, too, appearances may belie the man. A kindly, warm-hearted old gentleman may often appear to the eye a cross and unapproachable bear. A skillful writer may thus employ a description of external appearance to good advantage in his sketch.

Presenting the personality of a character is more difficult, for you are dealing with intangibles. As a first step, perhaps, classify the individual according to the type to which he belongs—identify him as a hero, villain, tough, spendthrift, idealist, ne'er-do-well, or the like. Then distinguish him from the group. Two devices will assist you: what the character does, and what he says. Any action of his may indicate his character. Ordinarily we think only of great deeds as revealing personality: bravery at the cannon's mouth, heroism in saving lives at a fire, dishonesty in absconding with the funds of a bank, or cowardice in a crucial test of nerve. These do indeed tell a great deal. Macaulay, for example, summarizes very quickly the cruelty of Captain Kidd and the moral anguish of one of his crew by means of such a striking incident: "One of his crew, whom he called a dog, was provoked into exclaiming, in an agony of remorse, 'Yes, I am a dog; but it is you that have made me so.' Kidd, in a fury, struck the man dead." But it is not alone such striking incidents that portray character. Often a small act or a quiet happening will tell quite as much. See, for example, how much you can derive from the following paragraph, taken from Dumas, about the character of the chivalric musketeer Aramis:

> This other musketeer formed a perfect contrast with his interrogator, who had just designated him by the name of Aramis: he was a stout man, of about two- or three-and-twenty, with an open, ingenuous countenance, a black, mild eye, and cheeks rosy and downy as an autumn peach; his delicate mustache marked a perfectly straight line upon his upper lip: he appeared to dread to lower his hands lest their veins should swell, and he pinched the tips of his ears from time to time to preserve their delicate pink transparency. Habitually he spoke little and slowly, bowed frequently, laughed without noise, showing his teeth, which were fine, and of which, as of the rest of his person, he appeared to take great care. He answered the appeal of his friend by an affirmative nod of his head.

For further illustration, study the following paragraph from Thackeray's *Pendennis* to understand the sort of action or incident that is valuable in expressing character:

> Arthur Pendennis's schoolfellows at the Grey Friars School state that, as a boy, he was in no ways remarkable either as a dunce or as a scholar. He never read to improve himself out of school hours, but, on the contrary, devoured all the novels, plays, and poetry on which he could lay his hands. He never was flogged, but it was a wonder how he escaped the whipping post. When he had money he spent it royally in tarts for himself and his friends; he has been known to disburse nine and sixpence out of ten shillings awarded to him in a single day. When he had no funds he went on tick. When he could get no credit he went without, and was almost as happy. He has been known to take a thrashing for a crony without saying a word; but a blow, ever so slight from a friend would make him roar. To fighting he was averse from his earliest youth, as indeed to physic, the Greek Grammar, or any other exertion, and would engage in none of them, except at the last extremity. He seldom if ever told lies, and never bullied little boys. Those masters or seniors who were kind to him, he loved with boyish ardor. And though the Doctor, when he did not know his Horace, or could not construe his Greek play, said that that boy Pendennis was a disgrace to the school, a candidate for ruin in this world, and perdition in the next; a profligate who would most

likely bring his venerable father to ruin and his mother to a dishonored grave, and the like—yet as the Doctor made use of these compliments to most of the boys in the place (which has not turned out an unusual number of felons and pickpockets), little Pen, at first uneasy and terrified by these charges, became gradually accustomed to hear them; and he has not, in fact, either murdered his parents, or committed any act worthy of transportation or hanging up to the present day.

Dialogue provides the other major means of presenting character, for it furnishes an individual an opportunity to speak for himself. In fact, it is so useful that many short story writers reserve it for crucial moments when intensity is required. The ensuing dialogue from Jane Austen's *Pride and Prejudice* will show how vivid the characters, taking part in only a small incident, make themselves by their speech:

Elizabeth Bennet had been obliged, by the scarcity of gentlemen, to sit down for two dances; and during part of that time Mr. Darcy had been standing near enough for her to overhear a conversation between him and Mr. Bingley, who came from the dance for a few minutes to press his friend to join it.

"Come, Darcy," said he, "I must have you dance. I hate to see you standing about by yourself in this stupid manner. You had much better dance."

"I certainly shall not. You know how I detest it, unless I am particularly acquainted with my partner. At such an assembly as this it would be insupportable. Your sisters are engaged, and there is not another woman in the room whom it would not be a punishment to me to stand up with."

"I would not be so fastidious as you are," cried Bingley, "for a kingdom! Upon my honor, I never met with so many pleasant girls in my life as I have this evening; and there are several of them, you see, uncommonly pretty."

"You are dancing with the only handsome girl in the room," said Mr. Darcy, looking at the eldest Miss Bennet.

"Oh, she is the most beautiful creature I ever beheld! But there is one of her sisters sitting down just behind you, who is very pretty, and I dare say very agreeable. Do let me ask my partner to introduce you."

"Which do you mean?" and turning round, he looked for a moment at Elizabeth, till, catching her eye, he withdrew his own, and coldly said: "She is tolerable, but not handsome enough to tempt me; and I am in no humor at present to give consequence to young ladies who are slighted by other men. You had better return to your partner and enjoy her smiles, for you are wasting your time with me."

Be sure to make the character a human being. Do not idealize him excessively; portray his peculiarities or faults as well as his virtues. The final emphasis of the character sketch must always be upon his individuality. Hence, if you can summon specific details and illustrations concerning him as he really is, he will appear vividly to the reader. The thesis should be clearly established, and the details should be chosen with discrimination.

## *Heywood* [11]

### CHRISTOPHER MORLEY

I think Heywood Broun would have been genuinely shocked by some of the tributes printed after his death; for I believe that in the later months of his life he had begun to achieve a way of thinking and feeling in which Privacy is more important than Publicity. Under the apparently naïf exhibitionism, and a sort of intellectual strip-tease which was his armor wherein he trusted, there was a deep humility and a terrified search for certainty. He always took an innocent pleasure in being what used to be known as a Man about Town; and little by little he discovered that the Town that is most interesting is the City of God. In that latter no one is pointed out; there is no consciousness of self; there is, one may believe, the blessing of anonymity and forgetfulness.

I always thought of Heywood as a kind of medieval figure; a strolling friar—how much more becoming a brown robe and knotted cord would have been—a sort of huge Santa Claus. He took his simplicity and kindliness into the most disconcerting slums there are—among night clubs and wisecrackers and Racqueteers—and was everywhere beloved for his drollery and devotion. He was overworked (as Santa Claus always will be) wrapping and delivering innumerable parcels of generosity. Anything that looked to him like cruelty or oppression enlisted his immediate and bewildered and chivalrous anger. The medieval and monkish flavor of his mind was best shown in his love of fables, parables, allegories. Even his love of his hobby, painting, was evidence of that. In a different age he would have been enormously happy coloring rubrics and fanciful bright vignettes on old vellum chronicles. When in 1921 I reprinted his beautiful and satirical little fairy tale *The Fifty-First Dragon* in an anthology of contemporary essays, I said "Heywood Broun is likely, in the next ten or fifteen years, to do as fine work, both imaginative and critical, as any American of his era."

This, in occasional flashing swordstrokes, came to pass; but not as often as one hoped. His profession as daily columnist, his preoccupation as crusader for various causes, his diffusion among sociable and generous

11. Reprinted by permission of the author and the Book-of-the-Month Club.

concerns, increased the temperamental dispersiveness of his mind. He was too humane, too genuinely interested in people, for the savage concentration required by art. His mind, I used to think, was sometimes as disorderly as his person. When he measured himself against anything precise, lucid, articulated, he was likely to fumble. The elementary French grammar that flunked him at Harvard was perhaps symbolic. But where powers of intuition and observation were concerned, whether in poker or politics, he became wise and efficient. Those of us who are relatively average in body or bearing can scarcely guess the handicap imposed upon a mind incarnated in such a conspicuous figure. That beefy and kindly bosom was the broad battleground of the most militant complexes, where opposing troops struggled in briars and thickets. It was surely this, in part, that drove our friend to so many chivalries at once.

Beneath that partly guileful naiveté there was great wisdom and shrewdness in Heywood, and humor of most endearing ricochet. His unshockable tolerance, his sympathy with all kinds of creative experiment, were of the greatest service in our Book-of-the-Month Club meetings—where he never once (in nearly 14 years) arrived on time. This, he said, was to avoid eating too much at the lunch table; but he always ate as much dessert as he could lay hands on, especially raspberry ice cream. In an age increasingly machined and regimented Heywood was an invaluable liaison officer, or commuter, between two worlds, the Flesh and the Spirit; the Serious and the Merry. Few of us will ever know anyone who had more of both. Two of the best things he ever wrote—in his habit of baring his bosom to the moon—were his obituary tributes to Ruth Hale and to his father. In the latter he suggested as a final inscription, *He took and gave much joy in life.* This may well be his own.

## Suggestions for Study

1. For what reason did Heywood Broun come to believe more in privacy than in publicity?

2. What were the medieval traits in his character?

3. Why did he fail to live up to the prediction made about him by Christopher Morley?

4. Summarize the central conception of Heywood Broun in a thesis sentence.

5. Study the eulogy to see by what means the character of Broun is brought out. How does the author secure concreteness of writing?

6. Define the following words from the selection: naïf, exhibitionism, humility, anonymity, allegories, rubrics, vignettes, vellum, diffusion, dispersiveness, humane, lucid, articulated, guileful, ricochet, tolerance, liaison, obituary.

## *Walt Whitman Old and Poor* [12]

### HAMLIN GARLAND

Not till October, 1888, did I cross the river from Philadelphia in search of the poet whose presence had made Camden known throughout the world. The citizens from whom I inquired my way to Mickle Street directed me into a mean section of the town and when I came to the number designated, I could not believe that I had been rightly informed, so dim was the doorplate and so weather-worn the doorway. The street was ugly and narrow, and the house, a two-story frame structure, was such as a day laborer might have owned, and yet the poet's name was there.

In answer to my ring, a small gray man whom I guessed to be Whitman's attendant came clumping down the stairway and received my name impassively. "Wait here," he said, "I'll see if you can come up."

While he went back up the stairs, I studied the faded paper on the walls, and the worn carpet of the hall with growing astonishment. There was nothing to indicate that a poet of world-wide fame was living here. His sordid surroundings filled me with indignation.

From the landing above the man called down, "Walt will see you for a few minutes." He emphasized the brevity of my stay and warned me not to weary the old man.

On entering the door on the left, I found myself in a fairly large, square chamber on the north front of the house, and in the center of it Whitman, standing by his armchair, with a broad white hat on his head, awaited me, a tall man clothed in gray, with a cloud of snowy hair and beard enveloping his face.

Without leaving his place he extended his hand and greeted me pleasantly in a voice rather high in key, mellow and cordial, inviting me to be seated. The grip of his hand was firm and vital.

He was dressed in a loosely fitting gray robe, and his linen shirt with rolling collar unbuttoned at the throat and his cuffs were all equally immaculate. I thought him one of the noblest figures I had ever seen. His head was magnificent in contour, and his profile clean-cut as a coin.

In contrast to his personal order and comeliness, the room was an incredible mess. Beside his chair rose a most amazing mound of manuscripts, old newspapers, and clippings, with many open books lying, face down, at the point where he had laid them aside.

12. From *Roadside Meetings,* by Hamlin Garland (copyright, 1930). Reprinted by permission of The Macmillan Company, publishers.

The furnishings of the room were few and ugly. The bleak windows looked out upon a row of frame tenements whose angular roofs and rude chimneys formed a dreary landscape. It was a melancholy place of confinement for one who had roamed America's open roads and sung its sunlit vistas. No one had prepared me for this bitter revelation of the meager awards which *Leaves of Grass* had won for its author.

In spite of his surroundings Whitman looked the hero of the poems, strong, self-poised, with a certain delicacy of action and speech. His face when turned toward me discovered a pleasant, searching glance. His mouth was hidden in his great beard, but his eyes were smiling and the lines on his brow were level. Nothing querulous showed in voice or word. His speech was nobly pure with nothing of the coarseness I had been led to expect. When he dropped into homely phrase or coined a word, he did so with humorous intonation. It is because some of his interviewers failed to record his smile that so many misinterpretations of his conversation have been recorded. This use of the common phrase now and again lent additional charm to his speech.

He had no word of humor, however. He was grave without being low-spirited or grim, placidly serious in all that he said. He made no reference to his poverty or to his illness, and nothing petulant or self-pitying came into his voice.

Once he rose in order to find some book which he wished to show me, and I perceived that one side of his body was almost useless. He dragged one leg and he used but one arm. In spite of the confusion of his books and papers he seemed to know where to find what he wanted.

The attendant had said "a few minutes," but Walt was interested, I could see that, and so I stayed on with full realization of the value of every additional moment. We talked of his English friends, of his growing acceptance there, and I confidently predicted his acceptance in America. "I can sense a change in the attitude of critics in the last two years," I assured him, and he listened with an eagerness almost pathetic. "I hope you are right," he said.

He asked me about my work in Boston and seemed keenly interested in my praise of *Specimen Days*. "I find it the best introduction to your poetry," I said. "I advise all my pupils to begin by reading it."

"That is very curious," he said musingly. "Most of my readers neglect my prose."

I went on to say, "Your descriptive passages have the magic of setting me in the midst of your landscape. I feel it and see it as you saw and sensed it. I even smell it!"

As I talked he studied me with dim, gray-blue eyes, as if marveling at my youth and fervor. He had laid aside his broad Quaker hat by this time, and I thought the lines of his head the noblest I had ever known. His brow was like that of a serene and kindly philosopher, and his sentences were well chosen and concise. He had no local peculiarity of accent or pronunciation; at least he left no singularity of speech in my memory. My recorded impressions of him were all in harmony with my preconceived notions of his nobility of spirit.

He spoke slowly, choosing the best word for the place with impressive care. There was no looseness of mumbling in his enunciation. Every word came forth clear-cut and musical. He had the effect of compressing sentences into single words, but with his noble voice and subtle inflection there was no excuse for failure to apprehend his thoughts.

"I am a good deal of a Quaker," he said, as if explaining to me his peculiarities of dress. "My ancestors were Quakers, and I delight to recall and to retain certain of their distinctive customs."

One of his "whims," as he called them, was to suffer in silence the sting of the various false reports about him. He would not authorize his friends to go into print to defend him. He reminded me of Grant in this regard. "I prefer to leave all that to time," he said. "Such things clear themselves up, or at worst they deceive only the unthinking whom your explanation would not reach."

Naturally I led the talk toward things literary, and being "moved by the spirit," as he smilingly confessed, he talked freely of his contemporaries and gave me full permission to quote him.

I told him that many good people considered him unduly severe on American literature in general and "certain of our poets in particular, Stedman and Gilder for example."

He became grave. "You refer to a report by a German writer. I do not think Stedman was deceived, though many of his friends think I have the spirit to rasp him. It would have been ingratitude to have said such words even had I thought them, which I do not. I hold Stedman in high regard as a man of decided insight and culture. On personal grounds I owe him much. The traveler you mention either willfully or otherwise *twistified*," here he smiled, "what I said—if I said anything in his presence. I am beset with all kinds of visitors who go away thinking me fair game. It is one of the evils which men of any"—he hesitated— "notoriety must bear patiently.

"As for American literature in general, I have insisted, as all my readers know, on the need of distinctive flavor in our poetry. There is an old Scotch word, Burns uses it occasionally, which expresses exactly what I mean—the word 'race.' A wild strawberry, a wild grape has the racy quality—this distinctive tang. Our poetry lacks *race*. Most of it might have been written in England or on the Continent. I myself like Cooper, Bryant, Emerson, and Whittier because they have this distinctive American quality."

This led me to bring up the work of George W. Cable, Joseph Kirkland, Joel Harris, Mary E. Wilkins, and others of my friends who were getting, it seemed to me, just that flavor he was demanding. "Their books are, in my judgment, forerunners of a powerful native literature."

After a pause he said, "It may be so, but I have not read many of them. Against some of them I *have* read I might bring a grave charge. They have a deplorable tendency toward the *outré*. I call their characters *delirium-tremen characters*. These writers seem not content with the normal man; they must take the exceptional, the diseased. They are not true, not American in the deeper sense at all. To illustrate, in a hunter's camp of twenty men there will always be some who are distorted, unusual, grotesque, but they are not typical of the camp. So in an 'army mess' there are always characters more or less abnormal, men who enjoy distorting their faces and cutting up antics. And yet in all my coming and going among the camps of the Civil War, I was everywhere struck with the decorum—a word I like to use—of the common soldier, his good manners, his quiet heroism, his generosity, even his good, real grammar. These are a few of the typical qualities of the American farmer and mechanic."

All this was said quietly but with deep earnestness, as if he were working the problem out while speaking. Then turning his glance on me, he spoke with decision. "I say that the novel or drama claiming to depict American life is false if it deals mainly or largely with abnormal or grotesque characters. They should be used merely as foils."

This led me to say, "In the early stages of national literature it is natural to deal with the abnormal, the exceptional, because it startles, claims the attention; so it may be that the novelists you speak of may be just in the preparatory stage and that they will pass on to something higher."

He fell into a profound muse, and at last said with deliberate precision as if making a concession which he had not hitherto directly stated, "I don't know but you are right. I can see that the novice would find the exceptional nearest his hand and most noticeable, and it may be that these books are preparatory to a new, indigenous fiction. The public itself, moreover, seems to demand and enjoy such work. It may be as you argue, that the writers and the public will grow toward a higher perception. At any rate I want to utter my protest against such work and to demand that the really heroic character of the common American be depicted in novel and drama."

I forgot his age, his sickness, his drab surroundings as I listened to his musical voice and lofty personal convictions. He appeared a grand and ageless spirit. His sublime faith in the average American was not that of a dreamer, cloistered and bookish; it was the judgment of one who knew the farmer, mechanic, cab driver, miner, street laborer, and roustabout from personal contacts.

"I guess I am aware of our political and literary fraudulencies," he said calmly, "but as things are going on in the States—our time—I am confident of results. I have no sympathy with current pessimistic notions of life, of government, of society."

This serene and buoyant optimism in the midst of old age, poverty, and physical pain filled me with admiration. It was majestic. It was another proof of the grand and simple faith of this indomitable soul who looked into the future with the unswerving gaze of an eagle. He was still of a mind to say, "I know the future will be well, for all that is, is well."

Seeing that my interview was nearing an end, I said, "May I carry from you a friendly message to these young novelists?"

"You may, with this advice and plea: Tell them to go among the common men, as one of them, never looking down upon them. Tell them to study their lives and find out and celebrate their splendid primitive honesty, patience, and what I like to call their heroism. When our novelists shall do that in addition to being true to their time, their art will be worthy all praise from me or any other who is insisting on native anti-class poems, novels, and plays.

"And finally I would say to the young writer, don't depict evil for its own sake. Don't let evil overshadow your books. Make it a foil as Shakespeare did. His evil is always a foil for purity. Somewhere in your play or novel let the sunlight in." Here he raised his superb head and in a grandly suggestive gesture of his arm made his point clear. "As in some vast foundry whose walls are lost in blackness, a scuttle far up in the roof lets the sun and the blue sky in."

As I rose to go I assured him that the circle of his admirers was swiftly widening, and that his influence on our literature was certain to deepen year by year.

"Burroughs tells me the same thing," he said, "and I hope you are both right."

He put on his hat, and rising painfully to his feet gave me his hand at parting. I understood the respect which this formality indicated and was proud of it.

### Suggestions for Study

1. In your own words describe Whitman's appearance.

2. Also in your own words describe the house and neighborhood in which he lived.

3. What effect did poverty and ill health have upon his outlook on life?

4. What was the essence of Whitman's criticism of American literature in general?

5. What is the substance of his advice to American novelists?

6. At the time of the interview, were American critics whole-hearted in acclaiming Whitman?

7. Does Garland show admiration for Whitman as a man and a poet?

8. Does the description of Whitman's appearance prove effective in introducing the reader to the poet's character? Explain. By what means does the author portray Whitman's character?

9. Write a character sketch of Whitman, using your own words and plan of organization.

10. Define the following words from the article: impassively, sordid, mellow, immaculate, comeliness, vistas, querulous, intonation, foil, petulant.

## Sibelius: Close-Up of a Genius [13]

### CARLETON SMITH

Jan Julius Christian Sibelius ranks as the greatest of living symphonists. He may surely be called the most colorful musical man of our day. He is rugged, sturdy, fierce-looking, and every inch a Finn. In his oversized log cabin twenty-eight miles north of Helsinki, he celebrated his seventy-fifth birthday last December 8th by shutting off his telephone and going for a tramp around his snow-covered lake. For over thirty years now he has lived there amid his cypresses and junipers, and with a minimum of interference from the outside world fought his battle to bring symphonies out of the nowhere.

His seventieth birthday in 1935 was a national holiday the like of which Finland had not known in all her long history. Every village square was beflagged and decorated. Two large orchestras and 7,000 of Sibelius' fellow-countrymen crowded into Helsinki's new Messuhalli to do him honor. The President of the Republic was there to present him with a laurel wreath. Microphones were in place to carry the proceedings around the globe. Cablegrams and medals poured in from five continents.

13. From the *American Mercury*, LII (February, 1941), 144. Reprinted by permission of the author and the *American Mercury*.

But the hero of the occasion was in hiding. Not until the very end did he appear—and then only to open his outstretched arms in meaningful thanks.

Ainola, his home—named after his wife, Aino—has been the mecca of foreign visitors for years. Among the more notable pilgrims from America have been the Yale Glee Club, a deputation from the Eastman School of Music, and emissaries of the broadcasting companies. Artists, conductors, journalists, ministers, and maharajahs have made the long trip north to have a word with him. A few have met him, but they departed knowing little of the essential Sibelius. He greets all his visitors with a warm, expansive smile, immediately putting them at ease. In short ejaculations he gives oblique, subtle commentaries on history, sociology, literature—whatever subjects they choose to talk about, except himself. "Sibelius," he says, if you press the point, "is music, not words."

I met him first in Hameenlinna, his birthplace. We had corresponded and I telephoned from Helsinki. Several days later a small white card appeared in my box:

Prof. J. Sibelius<br>
Uusi-Hotelli<br>
14:30, Hameenlinna

The proprietor of a grocery store well stocked with American canned goods directed me to the Uusi-Hotelli (New Hotel). Its sign had fallen down; the reception room stairs were partly gone. Everything was spick-and-span, however, in typical Finnish fashion. A woman appeared from the kitchen. "Professor Sibelius? *Yo, yo!*" Here he was coming toward me, his bald, monolithic head and deep-furrowed brow set atop a massive, powerful frame. "You are very good, very kind to come from America to see me. You, young man! I, very honored. But now you must dinner. What you will drink?"

We sat down at a table loaded with choice food. Sibelius is hospitality personified. "This room; you don't mind, I hope. It is plain. But I like the quiet here and come often. You prefer English . . . but my English is very bad. I know Greek, Latin—classical education, yes—French, Italian, Russian, German, Swedish, Finnish, but not much English. But if you prefer, of course."

Hour after hour he grew more loquacious. "You come now from America? I like America. Very epic, you know. Stirring, grand. I like music from your plains. Those cowboys never get gray hair, do they? Their music, so characteristic of their *mentalité!* I like only not publicity in New York. Too much for me. Sibelius is music, yes?"

In 1914 Sibelius came to the United States, was greeted by ship reporters who did their utmost to convince him he was the coming musical Messiah. During a month's stay he heard concerts in New York and Boston, spent two days at Niagara Falls, conducted his own music in Norfolk, Connecticut, and was made a Doctor of Music *honoris causa* by Yale. I inquired if he'd heard any composers here whom he liked. "*Yo, yo!* One, very musical, very poetic!" he replied with a twinkle in his eye. "I find best American composer—Edgar Allan Poe."

Occasionally he would jump up from the table and rush to the out-of-tune piano to play chords. Whenever the clock struck he could hear the piano strings vibrate in response. "You excuse me," he would say. "Piano speak to me." A small sound stimulates him as well as a big one. Musical ideas, he explained, come to him on a ray of sunshine reflected in the water, falling with a dead leaf, hopping with a bird, or from the wind blowing through tall grass. He spends his hours alone in the woods walking and thinking. Then he does his actual composition.

"Maybe you not like it that everything here is so much Sibelius," he said. "You know all Finland is very much Sibelius. The lakes, the rocks, the trees, my house, my wife—very much Sibelius. You forgive me—it must be so. Otherwise Sibelius not write Sibelius. You understand?"

It was obvious that underneath this warm and hospitable exterior there was a resolute, flintlike character tempered by his struggle with his genius. As he talked his mind was constantly in flight, leaping from topic to topic, making strange fantastic observations, changing the subject with breath-taking suddenness.

We discussed other composers. "This you must say," he emphasized. "Wagner is one of the greatest geniuses in music." This was a strange contradiction because a few minutes earlier he had said he hated Wagnerian music, that it was too literary, that he couldn't remember what it was about without looking in a book. "No! No! Wagner not for Sibelius," he said. "But for others, very good. I find too heavy, too long. Besides, I hate Wagner cult. Once in Bayreuth, I get inside cab and there was sign:

## ON JULY 7, 1883
## WAGNER SAT HERE

I get out and walk."

Of Richard Strauss, his great contemporary, he said, "Strauss is actual; I not. His music has very many clothes, very fine fabrics, bright colors. But I find clothes go out of style. My music abstract—for all times, all places."

He said he preferred Mozart, Verdi, Beethoven. But later at his home I found that he rarely listens to any music except his own. He has three radios and often twirls the dials for hours hunting for Sibelius broadcasts. When he gets one he plays it at maximum volume. Everyone else leaves the room, or the house. "You have to be very good musician to listen to the radio," he says, "or else a very bad one."

Sibelius has very definite notions as to how his music should be played, and is seldom satisfied with performances of it, though he admits he couldn't conduct his greater symphonies himself and make them sound as he conceived them. He left a rehearsal one day when a third trumpet was missing, because he could only hear "that trumpet which wasn't there," and he couldn't stand it. When a famous violinist played his Concerto with the Helsinki symphony and deleted a short passage in the opening movement, Sibelius refused to allow the composition to be played the next winter.

He has a theory as to why his symphonies were first appreciated in England and New England. Here, radio listeners voted him their favorite composer, before Beethoven, Brahms, Tchaikovsky or any other, though his symphonies are not yet understood or accepted in Continental countries. Sibelius says this has to do with ancestral memory. His music harks back to the Eddas, the sagas and the runes. It is a conversation of Odin and Thor in our time. The music maker of the northern spirit, Sibelius gives us a glimpse of what might have been had the upsweep of Mediterranean culture been turned back, had Vikings and Norsemen been allowed to go their own way and express their own thoughts in music.

For fifteen years now he has published no symphony. Any attempt to discover what he is writing meets with an impenetrable barrier. Old cronies think that in his second story workroom at Ainola he has sketched and resketched fifty versions of the long-awaited Eighth Symphony, that he is satisfied with none of them. Others point out that he has palsy—to sign his name now, he must hold his right hand with his left. They say it will never be. Another rumor has it that, being superstitious, he believes he will die when it is published. To all of which he laconically says, "Those who ask me about my symphony do nothing to help me write it."

Sibelius' *Finlandia* and *Valse Triste* have been played from San Francisco to Tiflis, from Stockholm to Santiago. A citizen of the world himself, Sibelius is yet very much a Finn. He has lived through two struggles to the death with his people. He was nearly shot in the war which freed his country. He was under bombardment last year. But wars, even today, are only incidents to Sibelius. The world may collapse about him, but he lives in an unconquerable land. He has sat long on gray rocks, has heard the songs and silences of Earth, Air, and Water. He knows the fire that darts as lightning in the skies and shatters the pines; he knows the cries of the birds as they cross in fog over northern seas. In the long winter nights he has penned their story in sound. And he has told of the yearnings and strivings of the Finns, their stolid response to joy, their unflinching acceptance of death, their hopes for the future.

It was greatly to Sibelius' advantage that he grew up in a relatively isolated country district. He could more easily realize his own powers without waste or distraction. He drew from the public musical life of European capitals just what he needed for nourishment and development, and returned to his own environment to renew his strength.

Sibelius was the eldest son of a country doctor who played the guitar and sang, and died when the young "Janne" was two-and-a-half. "Having lost our father," Sibelius told his friend Ekman, "we children—my sister Linda, myself, and my brother who was three years younger than I— became closely attached to my mother. Widowed at twenty-seven, she was strong, brave, and fortified by a deep religious conviction. She lived only for us, and her mother, Catharina Juliana Borg, widow of Gabriel Borg, the dean of Pyhäjoki, took us to live in her house."

Sibelius spent his summers with his paternal grandmother and aunt at Lovisa or on nearby islands. From time to time he visited his bachelor uncle, an Abo businessman interested in astronomy and music, who was known to take out his violin at two in the morning and play until dawn. Sibelius liked him. Also, he always wanted to know his seafaring uncle who died of yellow fever in Havana and whose name he carried. Educated Finns frequently used the French form of their Christian name. This uncle, when he sailed on his last voyage, left behind a batch of visiting cards with the name *Jean Sibelius*. Twenty-five years later when the young composer started his studies in Helsinki, he used these same cards.

Like all geniuses, Sibelius lived from the beginning according to the laws of his own true being. "If I am asked what interested me most in school," he confesses, "I can say with a clear conscience: nothing." His thoughts always strayed, his head was always in the clouds, and he continually expressed such original and bizarre ideas that his childhood friend, Kajanus, said pointedly that in his normal mood Sibelius was "like the rest of us when we are drunk." As a youngster he was fond of wandering through the woods playing to hobgoblins and witches on his violin. He would stand for hours gazing at the sunset. Even today, at seventy-five, when the wild swans and cranes migrate, his neighbors telephone: "Please tell the Professor the birds are coming," and he goes off to listen to them in flight. The local government often blocks off roads and reroutes traffic so that he will not be disturbed in his meditations.

"At home we all know when he is in the world of music," says Fru Sibelius. "I do not usually speak to him in the morning until he speaks to me. We do not like to disturb his thoughts, to spoil his creative mood. But when he does address me, then we speak of anything. My husband is most disturbed by music. A few bars of a song, a whistle, may snatch him from his work and then everything is spoiled; he must start it all over again. Therefore you never hear music in our home; never singing or whistling, at least unless my husband does it. Once when we were having some redecoration done, one of the painters whistled at his work. I had to go and ask him very humbly not to whistle because it disturbs the professor! The man did not quite understand, and I had to find a simple but vivid example. 'What would you say if you had just painted that wall and some one came and drew a brushful of another color across it, spoiling your work? In the same way the professor is disturbed when you whistle.' The man understood."

The Sibelius' five daughters, too, learned from their earliest childhood to be silent. They never sang or hummed at home, nor do Sibelius' grandchildren, though toward them he is more indulgent.

"It seems in the evening he does not want to rest," his wife says. "He is incredibly alive. There is nothing of an old man's calm in him; you can still see him striving upwards. He lives at a great pace, intensely and energetically. His capacity for work seems unfailing."

Sibelius has no hobbies. His work is everything to him. There was a time when he spent long nights improvising at the piano for his cronies —Kajanus, Gallen-Kallela, the painter, the two Järnefelts, Aho, the author, Saarinen, the architect. The legend is that, while one of these parties was in progress, Kajanus was called to the phone and told he must take the night train to Saint Petersburg to conduct a concert. He rushed off and came back two days later. The party was still going on and, when he rejoined them, Sibelius peered through the dense fog of tobacco smoke and inquired, "Robert, who has been keeping you on the phone so long?"

There is little time now for such conviviality. Sibelius will have a few *kippis* (skoals) whenever a friend joins him. The best wines and champagne are always on the table. But to see him now in starched cuffs and stiff collars, his double-breasted business suit neatly buttoned, his shoes made in Berlin by the ex-Kaiser's bootmaker, it is not easy to picture him as ever having been a careless, wild-haired bohemian.

Sibelius still indulges in an old Finnish custom of topping off his bath by breaking the ice from a bucket of water left outdoors overnight, and pouring its "invigorating" contents over his head. That ritual, however, is only a part of his iron routine. Much of his life is built upon self-imposed discipline, which he sometimes extends to his family. When one of his daughters wanted a divorce, he refused pointblank. He also asked his biographer to remove all reference to his drinking. "What will my grandchildren think?" he demanded.

Sibelius is full of contradictions. Courteous, affable, hospitable, he is also fiercely independent, extremely reserved and jealous of his privacy and solitude. Believing himself to be the greatest composer of all time, he yet refuses to state publicly how his own compositions should be played for fear of offending a powerful conductor. Shy, reticent, loathing self-advertisement, at the same time he is eager to see his name in print and reads every line written about him.

In the luxurious hotels of Helsinki and in the bright lights of his own log cabin, Sibelius becomes a man of the world, an epicure and an aristocrat; in the austere quiet of his woods, he is the mystic—the aloof and solitary dreamer. Ascetic, sparing, economical in his music, he loves excesses, heaping portions, overflowing glasses. Prodigal, open-handed, though in debt, he will always smoke the most expensive Havanas. Once a banker from whom he had borrowed money reproached him, saying, "Look, Jan, I smoke two-for-a-nickel cigars." Sibelius brought a whole box of dollar cigars and broke them on the table. Sibelius could afford them, even if his banker couldn't.

He is proud of his success. "*Yo, yo!* Very great honor for me," he says modestly. "The result of seventy-five years. I very glad. *Yo, yo!*" And then he wrinkles his brow and peers quizzically. "But—you pardon me—Sibelius likes Sibelius!"

*Suggestions for Study*

1. Why was the year 1941 a good year in which to write about Sibelius?
2. What traits of Sibelius' character are emphasized so frequently as to become the central elements in this article?
3. List the separate pieces of information about Sibelius in the order in which they appear in the article. Can you discover a plan in this arrangement? Is it well that the short biographical section appears near the end?
4. What is the effect of the descriptions of Sibelius' eccentricities—to make the man ridiculous or admirable?
5. Explain the meaning of the following words from the selection: bohemian, affable, reticent, epicure, bizarre, stolid, laconically.

**The Biographical Sketch.** The problem of the biographer is more difficult than that of the writer of the character or the character sketch. He must acquaint himself so well with an individual that he makes him a close friend whose thoughts he shares and whose actions he understands. Further he must be aware of the antecedents and growth of the subject so that he may understand the forces of heredity and environment that produced this particular individual.

The subject of the biography may be a prominent person, but very interesting sketches can be written of those who have never made much stir in the world. The important consideration is what is done with the subject, how well he is interpreted. The first step in achieving a successful sketch is to determine the subject's real character from which all his acts radiate consistently. The great characters of fiction, for example, are based upon such central conceptions: Othello as jealous, Macbeth as ambitious, Jaques as melancholic, Uriah Heep as falsely "'umble," Becky Sharp as vain and worldly. These characters live because their humanity has been expressed through a clearly defined central characteristic.

You must be careful, however, not to jump rashly at conclusions concerning an individual. All pertinent information must be assembled before you can make a decision. What did he inherit from his parents and grandparents? What effects did his home life or the life of the community have upon him, intellectually or emotionally? Were his actions as a youth and a man in harmony with his feelings and beliefs, or did he have to force himself into certain acts? Did he experience material and spiritual gain or loss during his life? What were his ideals? Did they accord with his actions? What effect did the realization or frustration of his ambitions have upon him? Consider many such questions before deciding upon a thesis.

Having determined the thesis and the pertinent facts supporting it, be careful in wording the sketch not to insert unnecessary details that may be distracting or dulling to a reader. The sketch considered here is not a cataloguing of dates and accomplishments, such as are found in a *Who's Who;* it is a revelation of the character of an individual. Thus it must center on description, incidents, and dialogue to accomplish that aim. No trivial facts or dates, such as a record of the day of graduation from college, the day of marriage, the day of moving from one city to another, need be cited unless they bear directly upon the interpretation of character. Infinitely more important are the devices which were studied in connection with the character sketch.

The organization of the sketch demands careful attention. The most obvious organization would seem to be a chronological relation of the individual's life from birth to death. Although such a method is useful in skilled hands, it runs the danger of being dull in a short article. The inexperienced writer is likely to have more success if he begins with a character sketch of his subject, an interesting incident concerning him, or some other similar device which will attract attention and arouse interest. He can then proceed to presenting what details and illustrations are required for a full comprehension of the background and growth of the character.

You may gather material concerning the subject of the sketch from several sources. If he is not a prominent person, he can be studied through his letters, the testimony of his friends, or your personal knowledge of him. If he is a man of importance, however, written material on him will be extensive. Biographical dictionaries or other reference works will afford a start. His diaries, letters, and autobiography may produce a rich yield when taken with the oral and written statements of his friends. Very fruitful also are the biographies of him. Every biography—after the first— is to a certain extent dependent on previous researches; each biographer checks his own theories against those held by the others, and so is enabled at times to correct his own work, at times to correct that of his predecessors. You must be sure, however, to establish your own point of view and not merely copy that of other biographers.

The true biographer, let it be remembered, is also an honest man. He pursues his subject with enthusiasm, eager to find all that is important; but he never allows his enthusiasm to blind him to facts. He remains intellectually impartial as he weighs his evidence, and after deriving a conclusion, alters it freely as new testimony arises. He works by the scientific method. His conclusions embrace all the known facts, and never disregard details which he would prefer to ignore.

The biographical sketch may be defined then as a short, impartial attempt to present an individual's life and work in so vivid and accurate a fashion that his beliefs and acts and ambitions blend into a harmonious whole to distinguish him from his fellow men.

## Hu Shih: Sage of Modern China [14]

### MARQUIS W. CHILDS

Of all the men who have been sent from the four corners of the earth to Washington during the past hundred and fifty years to represent their various governments, none, it is a safe surmise, is more representative of his people and his time than the present Ambassador of China. His Excellency Dr. Hu Shih has lived the transformation of his country, its agonies, its torments, its bitterly won achievements, the terror and the shock, the

14. From the *Atlantic Monthly*, CLXVI (October, 1940), 424. Reprinted by permission of the author and the *Atlantic Monthly*.

long, painful travail. And in his short, solid body, in his scholarly, far-ranging mind, in the clear, unwavering humanity of his outlook, is a faith he has finally won to, formed out of the old and the new, the good and the bad.

That is why for America in the present crisis Hu Shih is more than an ambassador. He is a symbol of steadfast courage, of patience, of faith and good will, of intelligence, the virtues that Americans must now draw upon. His hope in the ultimate victory of his nation and the democratic ideal it embodies has never faltered, even though the capital of his country is a beleaguered outpost in the foothills of Tibet, accessible only over a difficult and tortuous road more than a thousand miles from the sea. We of the West who have taken the privileges and prerogatives of democracy so lightly for granted have not a little to learn from this scholar whom China has so generously sent us.

Honors have been heaped upon him by the universities of the world. His published works in English and Chinese fill several shelves. He was instrumental in giving his people a new and simpler language, a democratic tool to replace the complex classical language. But in his life perhaps as much as in his achievements is Hu Shih's contribution.

At twelve he was already a scholar for whom the future seemed to hold great promise. For that matter, before he was three years old he knew 800 characters of the classical language, taught him by his father, who wrote them on slips of pink paper. In his twelfth year his mother, daughter of a peasant farmer, contracted for his marriage to the child of a family that had long been close in friendship. This custom of child engagement went back many centuries. It occurred to no one, least of all to the boy whose future was being signed away, to question it.

Shortly afterward he left his province of Anweih to study the "new learning" in Shanghai. His mother, although she could neither read nor write, had been unsparing in her effort to perfect his education. She paid his teacher three times the usual fee of $2 silver a year so that the classics he memorized were explained to him, while ordinary pupils merely learned them by rote. Kept from play with the village children, at five he had earned the nickname "Shien-seng," the Master.

Shanghai was a vast new world. Hu Shih worked with the extraordinary concentration which has enabled him to excel in so many fields. He read incessantly in the classics of the West. And so impressed was he with the "new learning" that he took a western name. Shih means "fittest," a name taken from the Darwinian phrase "survival of the fittest."

But in his teens came a period of disillusionment, characteristic of a highly precocious adolescent, and typical, too, of the brilliant young Chinese of the time, who felt that progress was hopelessly slow. At the same time, misfortunes overwhelmed his family and he was forced to give up his studies in order to teach English and so support himself and his mother. Hu Shih and his friends wrote gloomy poetry. They drank and dissipated. One rainy night, he relates in his autobiography, when he was deadly drunk, he fought with a policeman and landed in jail.

At home the next morning, a line from the poetry of the great Li Po came into his mind: "Some use might yet be made of this material born in me." Hu Shih stopped teaching, gave up his friends, and after a month of intensive study went to Peking to take the examination for one of the university scholarships in America financed by the Boxer Indemnity fund. He passed the examination, and toward the end of his eighteenth year sailed for San Francisco.

For seven years, first at Cornell and then at Columbia, he studied philosophy, having found that he could not force himself to pursue a course in scientific agriculture. With the culture and the science of the West added to his knowledge of China's ancient wisdom, he went home to fulfill his marriage contract. His bride was a woman with bound feet, virtually illiterate. Why did he go through with this marriage, so contrary to all that he had learned from the time that he signed the contract? The answer is simple. To have failed to live up to the contract would have brought sorrow and disgrace to several people.

Two sons were born to the wife of Hu Shih. Of the loyalty and devotion that have grown up in this marriage there have been many manifestations. When the Japanese were about to take Peking, Hu Shih's wife was alone in their home. She resolved to save what she knew was most precious to her husband—his books and manuscripts. Somehow, Hu Shih says he will never understand how, she managed to have seventy big boxes containing many thousands of volumes transported to the comparative safety of a treaty port. In the confusion and uncertainty of war-torn China that was a minor miracle.

It is hard to realize, in talking with the Ambassador on the verandah of his Washington residence, how far back into the past his roots go. He speaks easily, rapidly, with only a slight accent, developing a line of thought with the careful logic that is a result, in part at least, of his study with Professor John Dewey at Columbia University. Hu Shih's quick sense of humor finds expression in an abrupt, rather startling laugh. His eyes twinkle behind horn-rimmed glasses. Ordinarily his expression is sober. And when he speaks of the sufferings of his countrymen—particularly of the trials of the government at Chungking, where 6,000 civilians were killed in a single air raid—a profound sadness is on his face. It is not despair, not hatred, not fear; only a deep sorrow.

In all his work is his humanitarianism. When he was still a student at Cornell, he started the controversy that was to end with adoption of the pai-hua, the common speech, as the official language of China. There had been lengthy discussions of the need to publish books in the pai-hua, so that learning would be available to a larger proportion of the people. But it was taken for granted that this would be for the common people, with the literary language reserved for the literati. Declaring boldly that the pai-hua should serve for all purposes, Hu Shih began to write poetry in the common speech.

This radical break with the past soon produced a storm of criticism. But it also brought ardent followers who agreed with the young student. It was actually the beginning of a Chinese renaissance, a vast flowering of ideas and hopes expressed in the common language. Hu Shih is called the father of this renaissance. His position has been compared to that of Chaucer and Dante, who first were bold enough to write not in Latin but in the living tongue of the common people. Early in his revolt he wrote a "Pledge Poem" that was his declaration of independence. It began:—

> No more will I lament the Spring,
> No more bewail the Autumn scene—
> Here is my "Pledge song"!

Forswearing the traditional elements of the highly formalized poetry of his native land, he concluded:—

> For poetic materials, have we not at our command this modern world?

In many ways Hu Shih was an innovator. Returning to China after his American studies, he was made professor of Chinese philosophy at Peking National University. There was considerable skepticism about this young upstart who had spent so many years in the materialistic United States. The very first day he walked into the classroom and announced that the course would begin not with the mythical sages, part of the formalized classical learning for nearly 2000 years, but with the first historical events for which there is any substantiating evidence. The effect of this bombshell on the class could scarcely be exaggerated. A young student who was later to become one of Hu Shih's followers has said that it produced almost a physical revolt in the classroom, so sharp was the break with tradition.

The controversy became increasingly bitter. Classical scholars—particularly Lin Shu, who argued that the classical language was eternal—carried the dispute into the field of politics. A demand came for the dismissal of the Minister of Education, the Chancellor of the University, and all the younger professors who had brought back from the West the new science and the new critical scholarship.

It was not that Hu Shih wanted to supplant Chinese culture with the learning of the West. But he knew that China could not isolate itself from the western world. And he believed passionately that China could never become a democracy so long as the culture of the country was confined to a few scholars. It was no use, he realized, superimposing a western political system on a land made up of illiterate peasants plus a hierarchy of priestly scholars. He was quick to rebuke his young compatriots when he saw them embracing western doctrines with the same uncritical belief in which the old gods had been held.

In the period after the May Fourth Movement of 1919, Hu Shih was a restraining influence on young revolutionists who were seizing on western isms and theories. "We should study all 'isms' and 'theories,'" he wrote at this time, "but these are hypothetical solutions. You should not take them as the golden mean." In the same vein a few years later he addressed this warning to young hotheads: "You are ashamed to follow blindly Confucius and Chu Hsi, and you should be ashamed, too, when you blindly follow Marx, Lenin, and Stalin."

Hu Shih had once declared that philosophy was his profession, literature his entertainment, and politics his obligation. The troubled state of China through the twenties compelled him to more active participation. He edited the *Nu Li* weekly (the literal meaning is "Strenuous Effort") to expose corruption and inefficiency. But his friends protested that his appointed task of fusing and creating a new Chinese culture was far more important than any immediate political reform.

Gradually his intellectual interests claimed him again. One of his objectives was to bring about a recognition of the cultural significance of the popular novels written in the pai-hua that every Chinese, rich and poor alike, has read. The scholars had looked down on them, and, although they read these stirring and all too human epics of Chinese life, it was, as they had been written, clandestinely and with a sense of guilt. Now Hu Shih made his countrymen appreciate their real greatness. Furthermore, with the resources of critical scholarship, he cut through the anonymity surrounding their authorship and proved them to be the work of authors of long-established respectability.

At the same time he was working on his *History of Chinese Philosophy,* a monumental work he has never completed. With his teaching, his continuing interest in politics, his keen awareness of world events and world trends, Hu Shih's life was extremely full. He was the modern sage, in the ancient tradition of China but with all the intellectual resources of the twentieth century at his instant command.

Japan's undeclared war, beginning in 1937 with the ruthless attack on civilian Shanghai, had not been entirely unexpected. Chinese leaders were aware of the Japanese ambition to subjugate China, to stamp out all vestiges of modernism and leave nothing but a slave population dependent on Japanese masters and vitiated by the opium habit. Hu Shih knew that his academic life was over, for how long no one could say. There was no hesitation in his response. Completely independent in his political judgments, he had often been critical of General Chiang Kai-shek. Now he offered to serve the leader who had the nation behind him.

It was recognized at once that Dr. Hu Shih's greatest usefulness would be in America, where, because of his numerous friends and his wide knowledge of the country, he could stimulate interest in the Chinese cause. Shortly after the outbreak of the war he returned to this country, and in 1938 he was named Ambassador. It is an assignment that makes heavy demands on him. Besides carrying on all the negotiations inevitably resulting from a long and costly war, he is under constant request to speak in various parts of the country. This past spring he spoke at nine college commencements. When Hu Shih talks to an American audience it is ordinarily not about the immediate problems of his country but about the democratic ideal and the need to guard that ideal in the world today.

Nothing that is happening in Europe or in Asia has shaken his belief in democracy. Realizing the seriousness of the time we are living through, he nevertheless does not subscribe to the present pessimism. Democracy has been tested, he points out, in many countries and under many circumstances. New forms have been worked out, in Australia, in Sweden, in the United States, in Great Britain. The process is a continuous and evolutionary one, and there will inevitably be interruptions, periods of profound pessimism. It is a coincidence and nothing more, in the view of Hu Shih, that democracy should seem to fail at a time when the economic system which we live under is suffering severe dislocation. But democracy, he insists, is not necessarily dependent on capitalism.

It is a striking fact that, under the pressure of war, China has extended rather than suppressed democratic controls. Faced with shortages of essential material, the Chinese have formed industrial co-operatives and by the most heroic efforts have created factories for the production of munitions, clothing, shoes. In Hu Shih's opinion this remarkable development was possible because of the underlying sense of democracy that infuses his whole people.

Primarily, he says, it has been the system of examinations for official position, open to everyone without respect to rank or degree, which has made China a classless nation, democratic in the broadest sense of the word. Education was comparatively inexpensive, and preparation for the examinations, based on the old classical learning, was possible for even very humble citizens. Then, too, as long ago as 200 B.C. the law of primogeniture, under which all property passes to the eldest son, was abolished in China, with the result that estates were not closely held for century after century. Likewise the small palace aristocracy changed with each shift in dynasty.

Even more important, perhaps, was the fact that China, of necessity because of its vast area, has always been a loose federation of semiautonomous provinces. Hu Shih puts especial stress on this. So long as certain minimum requirements were met, there was a wide degree of tolerance. "We have a saying," the Ambassador explains, "that 'Heaven is high and the Emperor is far away.' That expresses the latitude which has been allowed in Chinese life."

It is perhaps not an exaggeration to say that Hu Shih's belief in the democratic ideal, with all that it implies for human enlightenment and human decency, is his religion. He has come by his faith over a long and circuitous course that has led past the shrines of the old gods and the loud persuasion of the new dogmas.

Hu Shih's father, an educated official, held to the rationalist philosophy of Confucius. On the gate of their home, he recalls, was a sign warning away Taoist and Buddhist beggars. His father died when the boy was four years old, and a year later he worked very hard, under his mother's encouragement, to build a paper temple in honor of the great sage. He hung up the scrolls and the tablets, copied from his books, and burned incense sticks, and his mother believed that surely the spirit of Confucius would look down and help the boy to a scholarly career of rich reward.

But the mother of Hu Shih, no longer under the stern, rationalist eye of her husband, lapsed into worship of the old deities and the ancestor rituals. Her favorite, the son remembers, was Kwan-yin, Goddess of Mercy. Once the boy and his mother went on a pilgrimage to a temple dedicated to this benevolent goddess on a mountain top. The mother walked all the way over a stony path in spite of the pain which her bound feet caused her.

As the boy grew older he rebelled against the gaudy idols that he saw around him. The folk versions of Heaven and Hell no longer had power to hold him. In his reading he had come across a brief passage describing a philosopher of the fifth century named Fan Chen, who defended before the whole Imperial Court the theory of the destructibility of the spirit or soul. These sentences summing up Fan Chen's argument made a deep impression on the boy:—

"The body is the material basis of the spirit, and the spirit is only the functioning of the body. The spirit is to the body what sharpness is to a sharp knife. We have never known the existence of sharpness after the destruction of the knife. How can we admit the survival of the spirit when the body is gone?"

The young agnostic suggested to his comrades once that they push some ancient images into the village pool, and this greatly distressed his mother. At Shanghai he absorbed Hobbes, Descartes, Rousseau, Bentham, Kant, the sages and prophets of the West. During the first World War, while he was in the United States, he became an ardent pacifist, a believer in nonresistance. (He describes himself today as an ex-pacifist.) He was an internationalist, a student of Ibsen, John Morley, and Huxley. John Dewey's *How We Think* and *Essays in Experimental Logic* made a lasting impression on him, as did the American temper with its irrepressible optimism.

During his boyhood he had cherished the ancient doctrine of the "Three Immortalities"—Virtue, Service, and Wise Speech. For his own use he translated this into the immortality of the three W's—Worth, Work, and Words. At his mother's death he pondered this simple doctrine and came to the conclusion that it was too narrow, too restricting, ruling out too much of human activity. Finally, as expressed so perfectly in his own analysis of how he arrived at a philosophy of life, this became his faith:—

"As I reviewed the life of my dead mother, whose activities had never gone beyond the trivial details of the home but whose influence could be clearly seen on the faces of those men and women who came to mourn her death, and as I recalled the personal influence of my father on her whole life and its lasting effect on myself, I came to the conviction that *everything* is immortal. Everything that we are, everything that we do, and everything that we say is immortal in the sense that it has its effect somewhere in this world, and that effect in turn will have its results somewhere else and the thing goes on in infinite time and space. . . .

"Fourteen centuries ago a man wrote an essay on 'The Destructibility of the Soul' which was considered so sacrilegious that his Emperor ordered seventy great scholars to refute it, and it was refuted. But five hundred years later a historian recorded a summary of this sacrilegious essay in his great history. And another nine hundred years passed. Then a little boy of eleven chanced upon this brief summary of thirty-five words, and these thirty-five words after being buried for fourteen hundred years suddenly became alive and are living in him and through him in the lives of thousands of men and women."

Only forty-nine years old, Hu Shih is today looked up to as one of the sages of his time, an oracle. Some of the more radical youngsters are inclined to criticize him as a Victorian oldster with pretty antique ideas. But even among the young he is revered for the great contribution that he has made to China. They are discussing and appraising his work as though he were a philosopher of the time of Confucius. The latest study is a thesis by Miss Ya Fen Hsü, submitted for an advanced degree at Smith College. I have found her study, "An Attempt at an Evaluation of Hu Shih's Work and Influence, 1917-1927," very useful in my effort to learn more about the great man China has sent to us.

Instead of the sage's robe Hu Shih wears a common business suit. He is busy at a desk twelve hours or more each day. He goes to the State Department, to the White House, to dinners and lunches and lectures. He has put aside his researches and his philosophy, his teaching and his writing. But in his heart is an unshakable conviction that he will live to see leisure and freedom restored to his country, and, if not he, then his son or his son's son or another man's son's son. That is the faith of a scholar, an ex-pacifist turned ambassador and man of the world.

## Suggestions for Study

1. What is the function of the opening two paragraphs?

2. By what principle does the author select among the factual materials of the life of Hu Shih to present the biographical account in the first third of the sketch?

3. What do the details in paragraph five tell concerning his early training? Select a number of other details throughout the article that provide insight into his character.

4. What do the circumstances of his marriage tell of his character?

5. What contribution did Hu Shih make to the Chinese renaissance?

6. Why was he chosen as the American ambassador?

7. Why does he have faith in democracy in its time of crisis?

8. Why is the sketch concluded with a discussion of his religion? What things characterize his faith?

9. Why does the author not give more of the details of Hu Shih's life?

10. Define the following words from the article: surmise, travail, ultimate, tortuous, accessible, rote, precocious, renaissance, superimposing, hierarchy, hypothetical, clandestinely, ruthless, vestiges, vitiated, autonomous, circuitous, dogma, agnostic, refute.

## Portrait of a Saurian: Samuel Rogers (1763–1855) [15]

### CHARLES FREDERICK HARROLD

Many of us already know the story. No doubt, some of us have let our imaginations attempt (perhaps a little vagrantly) to picture No. 22 St. James Place on a memorable day in early November, 1811, when young Lord Byron, lame and haughty, and newly famous, with "glossy, curling, and picturesque hair," but with subdued and gentle manners, entered the white stone Regency mansion. The owner, whom he had never seen but whose mild and stately poetry he had long loved, had for several years been the talk of London as the arbiter of literary circles, a malignant wit, and a magnificent host. We do not know precisely with what feelings Lord Byron entered. Did he permit himself the ill-bred liberty of gazing curiously at the famous staircase which was later to be adorned with the frieze taken from the Panathenaic procession among the Elgin marbles? Did he look at the mantelpiece executed by Flaxman; at the "cabinet for antiquities" designed, carved, and ornamented by Stothard; at the numerous Etruscan vases; the graceful furniture designed after Greek models by his host? Did he observe the great shadowy paintings on the walls— Raphael's "Madonna and Child," Titian's "Christ Appearing to the Magdalene," or the nearly priceless specimens of Giorgione, Guido, Rubens, Dürer, Gainsborough?

Probably not. The young poet had come, as a humble admirer, to pay his respects to perhaps the most revered poet of the age, Samuel Rogers. Little could he know that, a few years later, in a moment more angry than accurate, he would coin the satiric epithet "beau, bard, and banker" for the gentleman he was about to meet. Mr. Rogers was waiting for him in the drawing-room: a small, slender man, with what Carlyle later called "a pale head, white, bare, and cold as snow," a lugubrious countenance with large "blue eyes, cruel and scornful," glittering with unspoken wit that might cut his pursed lips when uttered. An innate delicacy and unexpected tenderness led him thus to wait alone out of consideration for his guest's lameness, and to conceal two other guests, Moore and Campbell, in the adjoining room until the appointed time. Over the moment that followed, when Byron stood before "the poet Rogers," there must descend a curtain of silence, for no record remains of what the two men said to each other.

Soon Moore and Campbell entered. Rogers was forty-eight but looked nearly sixty, and carried the air of perfect courtesy; Moore, who was

15. Reprinted by permission of the author and the *Sewanee Review*.

thirty-two, was the smallest man of the group, but as handsome and lively as Byron; Campbell, at thirty-four, was the least distinguished and would not have been present had he not unexpectedly "dropped in." The four poets were escorted to the dining room for one of those breakfasts for which Rogers was noted.

Rogers spoke to Byron: would he take some soup?

"No, I never take soup."

"Perhaps some fish?" came blandly from the host.

"No, I never eat fish."

"Certainly some mutton, then."

The same answer: an enigmatic and perplexing refusal.

But our perfect host has perfect poise. "A glass of wine?"

"Thank you, I never taste wine."

While Moore and Campbell conceal their desire to stare in surprise at this refusal, Rogers finds it necessary to ask his guest what he *does* eat.

"I eat nothing but biscuits and soda water."

Our host is not prepared for such an irregular appetite and can supply neither soda water nor biscuits. But Byron takes a plateful of potatoes, mashes them with his fork, drenches them with vinegar, and eats them heartily. The conversation turns upon Walter Scott, who the year before added to his spreading fame by publishing *The Lady of the Lake* and who had recently published *The Vision of Don Roderick*. Comment later drifts to Joanna Baillie, whose latest tragedy, *The Family Legend*, is being played in Edinburgh.

The table talk contrived two things which were frequently happening in Rogers's life: the grouping of celebrated figures of the day into convivial social relationships, and the reconciliation between two of his friends, on this occasion Moore and the newcomer, Lord Byron.[1] For us, who have thus permitted ourselves in imagination to construct the scene from the accounts by Rogers's biographers, Clayden and Ellis, the occasion is peculiarly appropriate for introducing us to his life and significance. It provides for the mention of those features which have lingered in the minds of those few readers who know anything about so forgotten a figure: his literary breakfasts, his cadaverous and wrinkled ugliness, his wealth and ease, the vast number of his friends and connections among the prominent minds of his time, his acid wit, his superb charity, the wide but ephemeral fame of his poetry.

Rogers's ugliness alone would have made him remarkable. It has been

1. Moore, who meets Byron here for the first time, had resented a passage in *English Bards and Scotch Reviewers* as ridiculing the duel between Moore and Jeffrey, and had asked Rogers to invite Byron and him to his house for a reconciliation. There is something of farce not only in the duel but in the matter of reconciliation as well.

the subject of mirth since Lydia White beheld him sitting with the Italian poet, Foscolo, and exclaimed, "Good God! The quick and the dead!"— until Mr. Chesterton not long ago mentioned his "phosphorescent and corpselike brilliancy." Sydney Smith's habitual reference to him as "the departed" was amply ornamented by a French valet who, mistaking Rogers for Moore, threw the company into consternation by announcing "M. Le Mort." There was laughter when one day Rogers emerged last from a visit in the catacombs and Lord Dudley, suddenly shaking him by the hand, said, "Good-bye, Rogers." But the innumerable jokes about his appearance were taken in good part by the fastidious, pale, little man, who simply included them in his store of witty anecdotes with which he regaled his breakfast guests.

His very *tête morte* lent something to the rich simplicity of his famous house, and enhanced the faultless taste with which he had furnished it with antiques. His delicate little figure moved gracefully among the poets, the critics, the dandies, the wits, who regarded his drawing-room as one of the social and literary hubs of the city. And not only at home but abroad he was a familiar figure. His meticulous expression lit up with wit at nearly every country house. Probably no hero or man of genius, from the time of Nelson and Crabbe to that of Tennyson, failed to dine delectably at his table. The company was carefully chosen, according to antipathies and affinities; and the number, rarely exceeding ten, prevented breaking up into groups, made a weary monologue improbable, and permitted a natural informality. Each guest had the whole company for audience. Mackintosh's wonderful talk, Wordsworth's austere pronouncements, Sydney Smith's irrepressible fun, found free play at Rogers's gatherings. The conversation rarely settled upon politics. One would have listened in vain for striking talk on the death of George III, on the Six Acts, the Manchester massacre, the trial of Queen Caroline, the settlement of post-Napoleonic Europe. But the breakfast table grew exciting over the publication of a new poem, the utterance of a crackling epigram, or the moribund Johnsonese of Dr. Parr—"Sir, you are incapable of doing justice to your own argument; you weaken it by diffusion and perplex it by reiteration!"

Even the briefest summary of Rogers's life becomes a record of rich experience and ironic incident. The more than ninety-two years he was to live began on July 30, 1763, at Stoke Newington, in the midst of a wealthy family of bankers. His life was to consist in writing and publishing poetry in the tradition of Gray and Goldsmith; in making leisurely tours to Scotland, France, Italy, Wales; in withdrawing from his position in his father's banking house and settling in London; in years of conversation, art collecting, writing. His father had put on mourning for the "slaughter at Lexington," bidding his family to regard England as a tyrant toward her American colonies; had sheltered Priestley from an angry mob; and had brought up his children in strict Nonconformist principles. The eighteenth century lay full and mellow about Rogers's infancy: he was eating his eighth birthday pudding on the day that Gray died; he saw Haydn play at a concert in a tie-wig and with a sword at his side; he sat near Mary Wollstonecraft at Stoke Newington Chapel; in the Gordon riots he saw cartloads of girls on their way to execution at Tyburn; in 1780 he chatted with Wilkes who came into the office to discuss politics with his father; he and his friend Maltby lifted the knocker at Dr. Johnson's door, then ran in terror lest the Doctor actually appear, and were later assured by Boswell that they would have been received "with all kindness"; he heard Burke compliment Sir Joshua Reynolds on his last discourse at the Royal Academy in 1790; and he saw the deceased John Wesley lying in state in 1791. Yet he lived to recount it to Thackeray, Dickens, and Tennyson. . . .

At eighteen this banker's son read Goldsmith and Gray on the way to work. His first efforts were a Johnsonian essay published in *The Gentleman's Magazine,* and an "Ode to Superstition" in close imitation of Gray. These works, together with letters of introduction from local men of parts, enabled him in 1789 to make a Scotch tour which was particularly rich in literary encounters. He breakfasted with Robertson, heard Blair preach, took coffee with Mrs. Piozzi, and supped with Adam Smith—all in one day. He later realized that the one flaw in the visit was his passing within thirty miles of Dumfries without knowing of the rising genius of Burns. In 1791, during a momentary lull in the French Revolution, he visited Paris. There he dined with Condorcet and Lafayette, attended the opera, looked at paintings, and was told by Diderot: "Never let a Frenchman come nearer to you than this"—the philosopher stretched out his arm in an emphatic manner. Shortly after, while at work on the poem that was to make him "dean of poets," he wandered into Wales, and noted "in a hall . . . a poor blind girl . . . playing on the harp most exquisitely such airs as made Gray put his last hand to the unfinished ode of 'The Bard.'" The chief events that followed were of a similar character: the publication of his *magnum opus—The Pleasures of Memory—,* the meeting with Charles James Fox, in 1798, with whom he had a most admirable friendship, the publication of *Columbus* (1812), *Human Life* (1819), *Italy* (1822 and 1828), the ripening of the friendship with Wordsworth, whom he met in 1803, and the settling at 22 St. James Place into what he called a "life of satisfied desires."

The desires were numerous but they were satisfied in no way more richly than in the success of his poetry. In 1792 his *The Pleasures of Memory* came as a thrilling event to readers living in a period when, as Macaulay said, "poetry had fallen into such decay that Mr. Hayley was considered a great poet." Cowper had published most of his poems and his translations of Homer. The sentimental, abortive Della Cruscan School was only waiting for Gifford's blasting criticism. Tom Moore was a boy of fourteen; Byron was a child of four; Wordsworth was in France drinking the bliss of a false dawn; Coleridge had just gained a medal for a Greek ode at Cambridge and was regarded as a revolutionist; Southey was yet to win a similar distinction at Balliol. Thus it was that Rogers's frail stature loomed magnificently in a Lilliputia between the vanished giants of his father's time and the Romantic titans soon to appear. There was only Cowper to rival him. While the great group of evangelical readers read *The Task,* another group, "polite society," was reading

> Mark yon old mansion frowning through the trees,
> Whose hollow turret woos the whistling breeze.
> That casement, arched with ivy's brownest shade,
> First to these eyes the light of heaven conveyed.
> The mouldering gateway strews the grass-grown court,
> Once the calm scene of many a simple sport;
> When nature pleased, for life itself was new,
> And the heart promised what the fancy drew.

The nostalgia for Goldsmith's sedate and mellow scenes whispered here and was appeased. Thenceforth the author was "the poet Rogers," "the poet of Memory," and held a secure place among contemporary writers. By the time he had settled in London (in 1803) not even the *Lyrical Ballads* had as yet dimmed his lustre. Campbell had imitated both his title and his rhythm in *The Pleasures of Hope.* Romanticism was still struggling—through the cool reception accorded to *Thalaba,* the obscurity of Coleridge, the limited success of Scott's German translations and *The Minstrelsy of the Scottish Border.* Byron was still a boy—at Harrow. From Rogers's momentary position of nearly-unrivalled fame neither the Lake School nor the Cockney School could dislodge him. Wealth, wit, power, and affiliation with Lord and Lady Holland, the champions of Whig policy and eighteenth century classicism, held him in an almost imperial position at Holland House—in a sort of embalmed glory.[2] But

2. Of the triple epithet which Byron fashioned for Rogers—"Beau, bard, and banker"— the first term was scarcely appropriate. Its only claim to truth was the popularity of *The Pleasures of Memory* "among the ladies." There was little of the dandy about Rogers, in the Regency sense of the term; his manners and his general bearing were considered quaintly old-fashioned and "eighteenth-century-ish" by many of his friends in the last years

the tide of Romanticism is irresistibly against him in these first years of the new century; and, in spite of Byron's praise, the year 1814 holds for Rogers an ambiguous aspect: in France, at Auxerre, a learned professor salutes him as the first poet of the age; but A. W. von Schlegel in the same year, in Paris, conversing with Madame de Staël and Benjamin Constant, damns him with faint praise: "Rogers is the only poet of the old school."

Nevertheless his poetry continued to hold a certain public until well into the later years of the century. He was a favorite author of Mrs. Browning. Ruskin wrote to him that he had found renewal and sustenance in *Italy*. Scott wrote humbly and hopefully to him for a short poem to place in his *Minstrelsy*, certain of adding prestige to the book. Additional weight was lent his work by his reputation for poetic integrity. It was known that he spent fourteen years writing *Columbus*, only to have it pounced upon by the *Quarterly* and championed by his readers. He frequently noted that Wordsworth wrote too much, and that he himself spent more time and travail over a distich than Wordsworth spent over a third of the *Prelude*. Still another reason for his fame was the amazing amounts of money he lavished on the publication of his poems. When in 1828 the second part of *Italy* fell stillborn from the press because the younger poets were at last making themselves felt, he "made a bonfire" of the unsold copies and determined on an illustrated edition that should sell in spite of shifts in taste. With nearly staggering prodigality he paid the best English artists—Turner, Flaxman, Stothard, Goodall, Wallis, Daniel, Finden—to aid in bringing out the best possible edition of *Italy*. Ten thousand copies of it appeared in 1830, at a cost of 7,335 £. Within three years the edition had disappeared and brought in a profit. The publication was hailed as a marked event in the history of art. The drawing by Flaxman, the thirty-five by Stothard, the thirty-three by Turner, and the numerous well-executed engravings by other hands were regarded as a great step in a greater introduction of the public to the world of both art and poetry. Rogers's next act was equally bold: he brought out a similar edition of his *Poems*, with the same results.

Meanwhile his acid wit sparkled and hissed at innumerable breakfasts. In 1831 Macaulay found him "the oracle of the circle" at Holland House,

---

of his life. Although he never married he seems to have regretted his decision to live alone. His attitude toward women was more or less formally sentimental, though there is an almost Brummellian letter from him to Maria Edgeworth in which he writes, "I am just now embarking, not for Alexandria, not for Constantinople, nor for Jerusalem, but for Paris, and I am all alone. Now, if you had your wishing cap, we might go together, and how delightful it would be." This was in 1843. Considering his unhandsome face, the extent of his possibilities as a "beau" may be imagined, in spite of this playfully challenging letter, by any imaginative reader.

where even the difficult Lady Holland, with her "Queen Elizabeth airs," bowed before his word, and where he alone was a free man when she was about. He could stand with his back to the chimney-piece without being told by her to stir the fire; other men, including Lord Holland, could not. The only uncertain moments came when Sydney Smith arrived. No party can support two wits at once, at least when one is as fragile as Rogers and the other as explosive and magnetic as Sydney Smith. Conversation appeared to bubble and scintillate as if it rose irresistibly to magic tongues. But the members of this charmed circle knew better. They knew that every wit among them had prepared his "speeches." One gentleman had once seen on another's desk the notes for a conversation which the latter was preparing to toss nonchalantly upon his friends that evening. There was nothing false in this; it was the mode: one read books, recorded good stories, clever remarks, and criticisms in order to throw one's own contribution into the genial and sparkling flow of conversation. Regard for each other's feelings was not one of the cardinal rules of the game. What were Landseer's feelings when he expressed to Rogers his gratitude for the poet's praise of his picture of a Newfoundland dog, and got in reply, "Yes, I thought the ring on the dog's collar well painted"? What were the feelings of the author who presented Rogers with a copy of his work and asked him if he were looking at the contents, and got in reply, as Rogers pointed to the list of subscribers, "No, the discontents"?

But he was at his wickedest when amusing a party by satirizing one of its absent members. At the end of the evening his guests all sought to be the last to leave, in order to forestall the usual acid jokes about those who had just departed, by those who lingered with their host. "Come," said he when one of his dinner guests had just left, "now let us feather honest A—." Whereupon he drew such a ludicrous description of him that all present jumped up, exclaiming, "Let us all go together, and not allow ourselves to be dissected in detail." On the other hand, he charmed his company by the choice of his anecdotes: for example, the story of Adam Smith leaving a party of his friends, saying, "I love your company, gentlemen, but I believe I must leave you—to go to another world"; and of his dying a few hours later, after having burnt sixteen volumes in manuscript on Jurisprudence because he had a mean opinion of posthumous publications. There was also the story of Lord Lauderdale saying to Sheridan, "I should like to use that story of yours," upon which Sheridan replied, "Then I must be on my guard in future, for a joke in your hands is no laughing matter." On the whole, he was well understood, and although many were enraged at his witticisms they almost invariably returned to his drawing-room; for there was an impartiality about his "feathering" that gave all guests much in common and took most of the personal sting away. "They tell me I say ill-natured things," he observed to Sir Henry Taylor in the quiet way of which Sydney Smith usually took too great advantage with noisy mirth. "I have a very weak voice; if I did not say ill-natured things no one would hear what I said."

Moreover, one can afford to express delicate malice about one's acquaintances if one is a munificent friend, or a sort of Maecenas. Campbell defended him by saying, "Borrow 500 £ from him and he will never say a word against you until you want to repay him." Rogers's generosity rescued many of his literary friends from the pinch of circumstances; it saved Sheridan from being removed by bailiffs from his deathbed; it helped Moore in his Bermudan difficulties; it enabled Campbell to invest 500 £ in stock; it reconciled Jeffrey and Moore, Moore and Byron, Parr and Mackintosh; it aided Moxon to set up his publishing house; it aided Richard Cumberland in his numerous predicaments; it procured for Wordsworth (whose poetry he wanted to rewrite) the post of distributor of stamps; secured a pension for shy and troubled Cary, the translator of Dante; helped Ugo Foscolo and Sir Henry Taylor through numerous trying situations; introduced Byron to Holland House (though it brought about the suppression of *English Bards and Scotch Reviewers*); supplied financial advice to Coleridge (whom he thought mad) and to Wordsworth; and sped young Macaulay on his way by what he rarely gave, a compliment. From these acts he no doubt drew a kind of creative satisfaction. On two occasions, however, there must have been a savory ironic pleasure for such a palate as his. When on the death of Southey, Wordsworth accepted the Laureateship, the new Laureate found himself unable to afford Court dress; whereupon Rogers gladly squeezed the bigger man into his own snug clothes. In 1850, when Wordsworth's death left the position again open, and when Rogers himself declined to accept it, he once more drew out the Court dress and fitted it upon Alfred Tennyson. There must have been a twinkle in the old man's eyes and a dry wrinkled smile on his face when he saw his clothes returning to Windsor Palace.

One of Rogers's special characteristics was the passion for collecting, in which he showed discerning taste and great versatility. For he sought not merely *objets d'art* among which to live his days of satisfied desires, but moments and memories as well. Among the "collector's items" in his rooms were the manuscripts of Sterne's sermons and Gray's poems and the agreement between Milton and Samuel Simmons the publisher (April 27, 1667), for the copyright of *Paradise Lost,* glazed and hung upon the wall. There was Roubiliac's clay model for a bust of Pope, by whose side Rogers's father had stood while the artist worked; there was a sketch by

Raphael; there were coins, gems, figurines; there were the best books by the best authors in the best bindings. But among the memories, perhaps more precious to him than all these, was that when he stood in Voltaire's chamber at Ferney and thought of Madame Chatelet; the "five minutes such as I never felt before," in Rousseau's house; the occasion when Crabbe, "delighted at having three thousand pounds in his pocket," could not be prevailed upon to bank them but insisted on "taking them down to show to his son John." He writes ecstatically to Richard Sharp, "Oh, if you know what it is to look upon a lake Virgil has mentioned . . . to see a house in which Petrarch has lived, and to stand upon Titian's grave as I have done, you would instantly pack up and join me." On a visit to William Beckford, he listened to his host read from the manuscript of *Vathek,* and slept "in a bedroom which was approached through a gallery where lights were burned all night, and where there was an illuminated picture of St. Antonio, to which it was reported that Beckford sometimes said his prayers." The collector's point of view, in this double sense, is seen throughout *Italy,* a poetical guidebook to that country, describing the land and retelling its legends and memorable events.

The literary tastes of such a nature are naturally conservative. Rogers, like many of his friends, thought *Childe Harold* doomed to failure for its unprecedented cynicism, violence, and bitterness. He considered the beauty of *Christabel* hopelessly beyond his comprehension. He preferred Schiller to Goethe because the latter failed to "raise the feelings of the reader," though both poets "contained something Satanic." Of Dickens's *Christmas Carol* he said there was "no wit in putting bad grammar into the mouths of all his characters, and showing their vulgar pronunciation by spelling 'are' 'air' . . ." He wanted *Tom Jones* and *Joseph Andrews* Bowdlerized for the family circle. In his later years he observed plaintively, "Except science, nothing is now written with care." Of Wordsworth's blank verse he thought well, but averred that Crowe's was "very perfect." His allegiance was to the eighteenth century, to Gray and Goldsmith, Pope and Johnson, to Beattie's *Minstrel;* he never passed Dryden's house in Gerrard Street without removing his hat. Later he liked Cowper. Thus though he lived through the length of the Romantic generation, though he associated intimately and almost creatively with its greatest poets, he remained to the end a lover of the older tradition, his head filled with the mild witchery of Goldsmith's music, his courtesy and his elegance gently lingering into the broad, blazing day of Macaulay.

Rogers's last years were full of "honor, love, obedience, troops of friends." His house was the gathering place for nearly all English and American men of note. From America came Longfellow, Sumner, Bancroft, Cooper,

Irving, Melville, Webster. He outlived all the major poets of the Romantic school; only Leigh Hunt, Landor, and Barry Cornwall survived him. He was still a "dean among poets," though he knew that his poetry had suffered an eclipse. To the last, however, he kept up his correspondence, and made his usual journeys to Broadstairs for an interlude of quiet, stopping at Canterbury, where in the cathedral the verger always asked him what anthem he would like. In spite of his cadaveric thinness he was remarkably vigorous at eighty-six, when his leg was broken in an accident while he was walking, as was his custom, to his house after a party some distance away. Thereafter, for the six remaining years of his life he was wheeled about in a chair, his wit and his faculties as lively as ever. In these last years, after the sting of Byron's satiric lines on him had healed, the name which Byron had once joyfully applied to him was now doubly applicable—"Tithonus." The death of Sydney Smith, who had called him "the departed," had already given that phrase its own peculiar irony. The more Rogers aged the more attenuated he became. His final years brought out increasingly his physical ugliness and still more increasingly his fame as a wit. The latter, by a curious twist which rumor often takes, assumed impossible proportions, so that "from the Antipodes to the Orkneys," from Hindostan to Canada, he became the godfather to nearly all the bad jokes in existence. "Quashee, who knows nothing of Newton or Milton, grins knowingly at the name of the illustrious banker, and exclaims, 'Him dam funny, dat Sam.'"

He died quietly on December 18, 1855, in the house where for fifty-two years he had fed the greatest men of his time with delectable food and saline wit. With him passed away the last attempt at a skillful ventriloquism which might bring back the voice of Goldsmith. He left behind him the fragrance of eighteenth-century elegance, the memory of graceful dilettanteism and insolent *bon mots,* of generous dinners and breakfasts for the exhilaration of men whose work was to outlive his own.

## Suggestions for Study

1. What is the rhetorical function of the incident concerning Byron?
2. What was the most striking feature of Rogers's appearance?
3. What type of conversation prevailed at his table?
4. What was remarkable about the length of his life?
5. Why did his early efforts in poetry prove highly successful?
6. To whose poetry did his poetry have a resemblance?
7. How long did his popularity last?
8. In what type of conversation did Rogers indulge when at a party?
9. What is meant by calling Rogers a "Maecenas"?
10. Summarize his tastes as a collector and as a literary man.

11. Characterize Rogers in his last years.

12. Peruse the article again, noting when the biographical facts of Rogers's life are presented and in what manner. Why is so much space devoted to Rogers as a social figure? Are more biographical details and facts needed for the sketch? Look again at the introduction. Does it succeed in giving the tone of the article?

13. Define the following words from the sketch: lugubrious, innate, convivial, reconciliation, catacombs, meticulous, delectable, antipathies, affinities, austere, moribund, reiteration, sedate, scintillate, ludicrous, munificent, savory, Bowdlerized, cadaveric, attenuated, saline, dilettanteism.

## *There Was a Young Englishman* [16]

### CLARENCE DAY

In 1766 a young Englishman, a clergyman's son, sailed away to seek his fortune in India. There, in spite of his youth, he was given the command of an unruly province. By the time he was twenty-seven he had "reduced" that province to order, made a fortune by trading, and gone back to England, to live the life of a well-to-do country squire without further toil.

Six of his sons went to India, hoping to repeat his experience. None of them did. Some died in battle, some from the climate, and one died of drink.

One of these active young soldiers, who had himself conquered a province as his father had done, fell in love with and married the most beautiful English girl in Calcutta. A few years later he died, like his brothers. He left a son four years old.

This little boy had some unhappy times after that. His mother carefully dispatched him in charge of a black Indian servant to England, where he was shuttled about from one elderly aunt to another. At the great school that he was then sent away to, he got into trouble because he was nearsighted and not very strong and not at all good at games. Also, one of the boys broke his nose for him, which spoiled his appearance for life. He didn't mind that so much, because he and the fellow who did it were friends; but the masters thrashed him a lot, and, as he was a weakling, he was kicked around and beaten by all the school bullies for years.

After a while his mother, who had married an elderly major, came to England to live. She had become intensely religious; rather harshly so, it seemed to her son; but he loved her, and he loved and admired his stepfather, too.

At college he followed the hounds, drank, and gambled like other

16. From the *Saturday Review of Literature*, XII (June 8, 1935), 12. Reprinted by permission of the *Saturday Review of Literature*.

young men of fashion. He had grown strong, he was now six feet four, and his chest was broad in proportion. He traveled on the Continent, loved a princess, and attended Court Balls. He was a polished young buck in tight fitting trousers strapped under his boots, a long-tailed coat, a high collar, a big cravat tie, and a monocle.

Soon after he was twenty-one and had come into possession of the money which his father had left him, he lost it. A friend of his, a young clergyman, who had a sleek, sanctified exterior and a smooth tongue, wheedled him into making an investment that completely collapsed. Another fellow he knew, a man of good family, fleeced him on a large scale at cards. Years later he pointed out this person to one of his friends. "I have not seen that man," he said, "since he drove me down in his cabriolet to my bankers in the City, where I sold out my patrimony and paid it over to him."

Not wishing to live on his stepfather, he looked around to see what a suddenly poor youth could do. He had already had a try at the law, but he hadn't worked hard at it. He now turned to journalism in his need. He didn't work hard at that either. Although almost penniless, he was still a young man of fashion at heart. It occurred to him that, as he had always liked drawing, art might be his best bet.

It wasn't. His amateur sketches were lifelike, they were full of freshness and fun, but they were far too unstudied to meet the demands of those conventional days. In his more ambitious moments, when he tried his hand at subjects like Hogarth's, his attempts were merely facetious, or prudish and weak. He was a splendid young man in his way, but he was very English, and Art with a capital A brought out an inferior side of him. He sniggered at the nude, for example, and he sentimentalized beauty. Nevertheless he eagerly went over to Paris to paint.

While there he met a pretty Anglo-Irish girl with whom he fell in love.

This girl's mother had been watching and waiting to get her daughter a husband. She urged the youth to find some steady job at once so he could marry. He was vague about this at first. He gave up art and tried to do illustrations, but he sold very few. A man named Charles Dickens, whom nobody had ever heard of before, was writing the adventures of a character whom he called Mr. Pickwick; and the struggling would-be artist made a number of drawings to go with these Pickwick papers. They all were rejected.

He asked his stepfather to help him find some good position, to marry on. The kindly old Major hadn't much money left, owing to the failure of a bank out in India, but he precipitately took what he had and bought a newspaper with it, merely in order to make his stepson its French correspondent.

The girl for whose sake all this was so imprudently done was going to be a wonderful wife for him, the young fellow thought. Perhaps for another husband she might have been; but although he didn't see it, she was narrow-minded, and she had had a bad training. She had been taught to be an artful young girl by her artful Mamma, who was as bad-tempered and vulgar a harridan as ever came out of Ireland. But Mamma could simper and be genteel when she tried; and neither her temper nor her matchmaking wiles were visible to the nearsighted young man. As for the girl, she didn't venture to talk much. He was drawn to her by her singing. She sang simple songs, she made eyes at him, she had lovely white arms, and he married her.

He was only twenty-five, and he didn't find out for some months that he had been cheated again.

It was poverty that opened his eyes. The newspaper on which he was dependent had never been a success, and, under his stepfather's soldierly management, after nine months it collapsed. When his wife's mother found that he was now going downhill financially, and that his family was ruined, she reviled him so loudly and coarsely that she made his home life a hell.

He hunted feverishly for a chance to do bits of ill-paid reviewing. His indolence utterly vanished. He set to work and worked hard, and for longer hours than most men would be able to, trying to sell things to magazine editors who felt lukewarm about him.

His young wife bore him two daughters. When one of these babies died, he wrote his mother, "I think of her only as something charming that for a season we were allowed to enjoy." He added that he could not ask to have her come back to a life of degradation and pain.

At the birth of their third little girl, his wife had an attack of insanity. She never recovered.

The elegant young buck was now down at heel, a hack and a drudge. His mother-in-law screamed tirades at him. His wife became sluggish and dense, like a half-witted child. He worked late into the night trying to support her and his two little girls; and as a matter of honor he felt that he must also pay his stepfather's debts.

After long years of struggle he managed to do this, and more. All England began talking about him, and reading his books. Yet when his first great novel appeared, its tone displeased many critics. It was the work of a man who had mellowed, and who had always had a warm heart, but there was a vein of cynicism in it, and sadness. The man was Thackeray, and the book was *Vanity Fair*.

*Suggestions for Study*

1. State the central conception of Thackeray which is conveyed in this article.
2. Characterize Thackeray's wife and her mother.
3. What facts in Thackeray's life account for the qualities of *Vanity Fair?*
4. Study carefully the facts of Thackeray's life which are included in this article and decide how well chosen they are.
5. By what means does the author secure interest and suspense?
6. Define the following words: sleek, patrimony, harridan, tirades, mellowed.

**The Autobiography.** With a little care and planning an autobiography can be made very attractive. In revealing his own conception of his character and in showing what he regards as significant in his life, the author has freedom to display the full force, charm, or humor of his personality. He has a splendid opportunity to be entertaining and refreshing, and he is under no obligation to be egotistic. Depending upon his purpose and the kind of publication for which he is writing, he can be humorous or serious, amusing or instructive.

However easy the autobiography appears to the inexperienced writer, it presents a peculiar difficulty: material is too plentiful. The incautious student beginning such a paper starts bravely with the date of his birth and plunges boldly into a medley of facts and happenings following that momentous event, soon to lose himself in masses of unimportant details. His paper emerges a mélange of dissociated bits of information concerning a trip here, a vacation there, a part-time job in this store, a full-time job in that, a pet like or dislike, and a thousand and one such odds and ends. He has found the autobiography difficult because he has had the utmost trouble in selecting the important details from the unimportant.

Once again the saving factor for you as a writer is the thesis sentence. If you can get clearly in mind the dominant principle of your life and state that concisely in one sentence, your task is nearly half done. By keeping the thesis ever in mind, you can eliminate all the details which have no bearing upon it and concentrate just on the essentials which are needed to explain it. Upon analyzing yourself, you may find that you are essentially studious, or athletic, or happy-go-lucky, or literary, or scientific, or a combination of several such traits. Your task then is to trace your growth so that this dominant trait will be clearly evident.

As an example of the method which might be used in preparing an autobiography, consider the life of a student who decides that his outstanding characteristic has been an interest in science. This interest he immediately writes down in the form of a thesis sentence. In pursuing the preliminary analysis of his life, he might reason in this way: My father was not a scientist—he was a businessman—but he liked to read about scientific work. For that reason he always kept scientific magazines of a technical and popular sort around the house. My earliest memories are of leafing through the publications of the National Geographic Society, studying the maps and pictures. Later the photographs and drawings of birds in this and other publications began to absorb my interest, and I undertook the identification of the common species of birds in our neighborhood. My joining the Boy Scouts furthered these studies, for we scouts were supposed to observe the phenomena of nature very closely. I even took bird walks at surprisingly early hours in the morning. However, because my family moved to the city about the time I entered high school, I found the opportunity for nature study taken from me, and my interest in it dwindled. Yet I retained a firm desire to be a scientist of some kind. I bought the usual variety of children's chemical sets, tinkered with radio construction, built airplanes, and in general toyed with the many gadgets which high-school boys find fascinating. As yet I do not know what the outcome of all this scientific investigation will be, for I am just a freshman, but it looks at the moment as if my early browsings in the *National Geographic Magazine* are going to bear fruit; geology and geography hold a strong appeal for me, and I may desert my hobbies in chemistry and physics in favor of them.

Having reasoned in this manner, he is ready to write an interesting sketch. He now knows what details in his life will be pertinent to this paper. He will not tell of the summer vacation on Aunt Sue's farm, nor of the trip to Nova Scotia, nor of the time he broke his arm, nor of his liking for going barefoot, unless this point bears directly on the origin and growth of his interest in science. No matter how attractive in themselves, the other bits are ruthlessly discarded. He may, of course, augment the major interest in his life with selected prominent minor interests, particularly if they supplement the major interest. He might, for example, have a genuine liking for literature, perhaps closely associated with his major interest through his liking for biographies of scientists or novels and stories of outdoor life and achievement.

The following outlines are further illustrations of the method by which the student can work in planning his autobiography.

Thesis: The controlling interest in my life has been a love of sports.

I. My parents
   A. My father
      1. A professional baseball player
      2. The owner of a sporting goods store
   B. My mother
      1. The daughter of a professional golfer
      2. A sports enthusiast

II. My earliest memories
   A. In my father's store
      1. Playing with the equipment
      2. Listening to the stories told by customers
   B. At sporting events
      1. At the baseball park
      2. On the golf links

III. The growth of my own interest in sports
   A. In grammar school
      1. Competing in school athletics for physical education training
      2. Playing on a junior softball team
      3. Hunting balls on the golf course
   B. In high school
      1. Participation in school athletics
         a. Football
         b. Baseball
      2. Acquisition of golfing skill
         a. Apprenticeship as a caddy
         b. Promotion to full membership in the club
            (1) Golf lessons from my father
            (2) My first score in the 90's
            (3) Competition in club tournaments

IV. Plans for the future
   A. Those dependent upon my acquisition of further skill in sports
      1. My first choice: to become a professional golfer
      2. My second choice: to become a professional baseball player
   B. Other possible plans
      1. To become a sports writer
      2. To become a high-school or college coach

Thesis: My life thus far has been a constant struggle against poverty.

I. My background
   A. My father's occupations
      1. As a farm hand
      2. As a factory worker
         a. In a tractor factory
         b. In an automobile body factory
   B. Our homes
      1. The first: in a poverty-stricken small town

      2. The second: in the crowded worker's quarter of a large city
        a. Amid conditions conducive to crime
        b. Amid conditions affording little opportunity for physical
          or intellectual growth

II. My struggles as a child
    A. Collecting laundry for my mother to wash
      1. Carrying it long distances
      2. Protecting it from the assaults of neighborhood gangs
    B. Selling newspapers
      1. On the street
      2. On a route

III. School days
    A. Grammar school
      1. Selling newspapers after school
      2. Working for a grocery store on weekends
    B. High school
      1. Working as science laboratory assistant after school hours
      2. Clerking in the grocery on weekends
      3. Working on the automobile assembly line during summer
        vacation

IV. Results
    A. Fostering of self-reliance and independence of character
    B. Creating of a desire to get ahead
      1. My father's ambition for me: to become a white-collar worker
      2. My desire: to become a teacher of science

After having carefully built a framework of this sort, fill in the substance of your paper with all the skill at your command in order that the writing will be appealing. A straightforward chronological sequence of events might well constitute the greater part of the writing, but all the tricks studied in the sections on the character sketch and the biography should be brought into play to render the sketch interesting and penetrating. Short narrative anecdotes, side glances at one's personal habits and traits, concise analyses or descriptions of one's environment, and many other such devices can be woven into the account to advantage. They make the sketch concrete and help remove it from the category of dull facts. The following bits from autobiographical works may give some conception of how this may be done:

> Doubtless, however, either of these stern and black-browed Puritans would have thought it quite a sufficient retribution for his sins, that, after so long a lapse of years, the old trunk of the family tree, with so much venerable moss upon it, should have borne, as its topmost bough, an idler like myself. No aim that I have cherished would they recognize as laudable; no success of mine—if my life, beyond its domestic scope, had ever been brightened by success—would they deem otherwise than worthless,

if not positively disgraceful. "What is he?" murmurs one gray shadow of my forefathers to the other. "A writer of storybooks! What kind of a business in life—what mode of glorifying God, or being serviceable to mankind in his day and generation—may that be? Why, the degenerate fellow might as well have been a fiddler!" Such are the compliments bandied between my great-grandsires and myself, across the gulf of time! And yet, let them scorn me as they will, strong traits of their nature have intertwined themselves with mine.—Hawthorne, *The Customhouse.*

I became convinced, that if I did not put moral courage in the place of personal, or, in other words, undergo any stubborn amount of pain and wretchedness, rather than submit to what I thought wrong, there was an end forever, as far as I was concerned, of all those fine things that had been taught me, in vindication of right and justice. . . .

I had not been long in the school, when this spirit within me broke out in a manner that procured me great esteem. There was a monitor or "big boy" in office, who had a trick of entertaining himself by pelting lesser boys' heads with a hard ball. He used to throw it at this boy and that; make the *throwee* bring it back to him; and then send a rap with it on his cerebellum, as he was going off.

I had borne this spectacle one day for some time, when the family precepts rising within me, I said to myself, "I must go up to the monitor and speak to him about this." I issued forth accordingly, and to the astonishment of all present, who had never witnessed such an act of insubordination, I said, "You have no right to do this." The monitor, more astounded than anyone, exclaimed, "What?" I repeated my remonstrance. He treated me with the greatest contempt, as if disdaining even to strike me; and finished by ordering me to "stand out." "Standing out" meant going to a particular spot in the hall where we dined. I did so; but just as the steward (the master in that place) was entering it, the monitor called to me to come away; and I neither heard any more of standing out, nor saw any more of the ball.—Leigh Hunt, *Autobiography.*

When about sixteen years of age I happened to meet with a book, written by one Tryon, recommending a vegetable diet. I determined to go into it. My brother, being yet unmarried, did not keep house, but boarded himself and his apprentices in another family. My refusing to eat flesh caused an inconveniency, and I was frequently chid for my singularity. I made myself acquainted with Tryon's manner of preparing some of his dishes, such as boiling potatoes or rice, making hasty pudding, and a few others, and then proposed to my brother, that if he would give me, weekly, half the money he paid for my board, I would board myself. He instantly agreed to it, and I presently found I could save half what he paid me. This was an additional fund for buying books. But I had another advantage in it. My brother and the rest going from the printing house to their meals, I remained there alone, and dispatching presently my light repast, which often was no more than a biscuit or a slice of bread, a handful of raisins or a tart from the pastrycook's, and a glass of water, had the rest of the time till their return for study, in which I made the greater progress from that greater clearness of head and quicker apprehension which usually attend temperance in eating and drinking.—Franklin, *Autobiography*.

The writer of autobiography should above all write sincerely and truly about himself. He should try to make the reader conceive of him as a living human being with the frailties, sympathies, and aspirations of other humans. The calendar gives the list of dates; and to the calendar the autobiographer consigns this task. He sees his duty to make a dull listing of dates and chronological details become a living document of his life. He tries to enable the reader to experience life as he has experienced it.

## Autobiography [17]

### T. H. HUXLEY

I was born about eight o'clock in the morning on 4th of May, 1825, at Ealing, which was, at that time, as quiet a little country village as could be found within half-a-dozen miles of Hyde Park Corner. Now it is a suburb of London with, I believe, 30,000 inhabitants. My father was one of the masters in a large semipublic school which at one time had a high reputation. I am not aware that any portents preceded my arrival in this world, but, in my childhood, I remember hearing a traditional account of the manner in which I lost the chance of an endowment of great practical value. The windows of my mother's room were open, in consequence of the unusual warmth of the weather. For the same reason, probably, a neighboring beehive had swarmed, and the new colony, pitching on the window sill, was making its way into the room when the horrified nurse shut down the sash. If that well-meaning woman had only abstained from her ill-timed interference, the swarm might have settled on my lips, and I should have been endowed with that mellifluous eloquence which, in this country, leads far more surely than worth, capacity, or honest work, to the highest places in church and state. But the opportunity was lost, and I have been obliged to content myself through life with saying what I mean in the plainest of plain language, than which, I suppose, there is no habit more ruinous to a man's prospects of advancement.

Why I was christened Thomas Henry I do not know; but it is a curious chance that my parents should have fixed for my usual denomination upon the name of that particular Apostle with whom I have always felt most sympathy. Physically and mentally I am the son of my mother so

17. From *Collected Essays*, Vol. I, by T. H. Huxley. Reprinted by permission of D. Appleton-Century Co., the publishers.

completely—even down to peculiar movements of the hands, which made their appearance in me as I reached the age she had when I noticed them —that I can hardly find any trace of my father in myself, except an inborn faculty for drawing, which unfortunately, in my case, has never been cultivated, a hot temper, and that amount of tenacity of purpose which unfriendly observers sometimes call obstinacy.

My mother was a slender brunette, of an emotional and energetic temperament, and possessed of the most piercing black eyes I ever saw in a woman's head. With no more education than other women of the middle classes in her day, she had an excellent mental capacity. Her most distinguishing characteristic, however, was rapidity of thought. If one ventured to suggest she had not taken much time to arrive at any conclusion, she would say: "I cannot help it, things flash across me." That peculiarity has been passed on to me in full strength; it has often stood me in good stead; it has sometimes played me sad tricks, and it has always been a danger. But, after all, if my time were to come over again, there is nothing I would less willingly part with than my inheritance of mother wit.

I have next to nothing to say about my childhood. In later years my mother, looking at me almost reproachfully, would sometimes say, "Ah! you were such a pretty boy!" whence I had no difficulty in concluding that I had not fulfilled my early promise in the matter of looks. In fact, I have a distinct recollection of certain curls of which I was vain, and of a conviction that I closely resembled that handsome, courtly gentleman, Sir Herbert Oakley, who was vicar of our parish, and who was as a god to us country folk, because he was occasionally visited by the then Prince George of Cambridge. I remember turning my pinafore wrong side forwards in order to represent a surplice, and preaching to my mother's maids in the kitchen as nearly as possible in Sir Herbert's manner one Sunday morning when the rest of the family were at church. That is the earliest indication I can call to mind of the strong clerical affinities which my friend Mr. Herbert Spencer has always ascribed to me, though I fancy they have for the most part remained in a latent state.

My regular school training was of the briefest, perhaps fortunately, for though my way of life has made me acquainted with all sorts and conditions of men, from the highest to the lowest, I deliberately affirm that the society I fell into at school was the worst I have ever known. We boys were average lads, with much the same inherent capacity for good and evil as any others; but the people who were set over us cared about as much for our intellectual and moral welfare as if they were baby farmers. We were left to the operation of the struggle for existence among ourselves, and bullying was the least of the ill practices current among us.

Almost the only cheerful reminiscence in connection with the place which arises in my mind is that of a battle I had with one of my classmates, who had bullied me until I could stand it no longer. I was a very slight lad, but there was a wildcat element in me which, when roused, made up for lack of weight, and I licked my adversary effectually. However, one of my first experiences of the extremely rough-and-ready nature of justice, as exhibited by the course of things in general, arose out of the fact that I—the victor—had a black eye, while he—the vanquished—had none, so that I got into disgrace and he did not. We made it up, and thereafter I was unmolested. One of the greatest shocks I ever received in my life was to be told a dozen years afterwards by the groom who brought me my horse in a stableyard in Sydney that he was my quondam antagonist. He had a long story of family misfortune to account for his position, but at that time it was necessary to deal very cautiously with mysterious strangers in New South Wales, and on inquiry I found that the unfortunate young man had not only been "sent out," but had undergone more than one colonial conviction.

As I grew older, my great desire was to be a mechanical engineer, but the fates were against this and, while very young, I commenced the study of medicine under a medical brother-in-law. But, though the Institute of Mechanical Engineers would certainly not own me, I am not sure that I have not all along been a sort of mechanical engineer *in partibus infidelium*. I am now occasionally horrified to think how very little I ever knew or cared about medicine as the art of healing. The only part of my professional course which really and deeply interested me was physiology, which is the mechanical engineering of living machines; and, notwithstanding that natural science has been my proper business, I am afraid there is very little of the genuine naturalist in me. I never collected anything, and species work was always a burden to me; what I cared for was the architectural and engineering part of the business, the working out of the wonderful unity of plan in the thousands and thousands of diverse living constructions, and the modifications of similar apparatuses to serve diverse ends. The extraordinary attraction I felt toward the study of the intricacies of living structure nearly proved fatal to me at the outset. I was a mere boy—I think between thirteen and fourteen years of age—when I was taken by some older student friends of mine to the first *post-mortem* examination I ever attended. All my life I have been most unfortunately sensitive to the disagreeables which attend anatomical pursuits, but on this occasion my curiosity overpowered all other feelings, and I spent two or three hours in gratifying it. I did not cut myself, and none of the ordinary symptoms of dissection poison supervened, but poisoned I was somehow, and I remember sinking into a strange state of apathy. By way of a last chance, I was sent to the care of some good, kind people, friends of my father's, who lived in a farmhouse in the heart of Warwickshire. I remember staggering from my bed to the window on the bright spring morning after my arrival, and throwing open the casement. Life seemed to come back on the wings of the breeze, and to this day the faint odor of wood smoke, like that which floated across the farmyard in the early morning, is as good to me as the "sweet south upon a bed of violets." I soon recovered, but for years I suffered from occasional paroxysms of internal pain, and from that time my constant friend, hypochondriacal dyspepsia, commenced his half century of cotenancy of my fleshly tabernacle.

Looking back on my "Lehrjahre," I am sorry to say that I do not think that any account of my doings as a student would tend to edification. In fact, I should distinctly warn ingenuous youth to avoid imitating my example. I worked extremely hard when it pleased me, and when it did not—which was a very frequent case—I was extremely idle (unless making caricatures of one's pastors and masters is to be called a branch of industry), or else wasted my energies in wrong directions. I read everything I could lay hands upon, including novels, and took up all sorts of pursuits to drop them again quite as speedily. No doubt it was very largely my own fault, but the only instruction from which I ever obtained the proper effect of education was that which I received from Mr. Wharton Jones, who was the lecturer on physiology at the Charing Cross School of Medicine. The extent and precision of his knowledge impressed me greatly, and the severe exactness of his method of lecturing was quite to my taste. I do not know that I have ever felt so much respect for anybody as a teacher before or since. I worked hard to obtain his approbation, and he was extremely kind and helpful to the youngster who, I am afraid, took up more of his time than he had any right to do. It was he who suggested the publication of my first scientific paper—a very little one—in the *Medical Gazette* of 1845, and most kindly corrected the literary faults which abounded in it, short as it was; for at that time, and for many years afterwards, I detested the trouble of writing, and would take no pains over it.

It was in the early spring of 1846, that, having finished my obligatory medical studies and passed the first M.D. examination at the London University—though I was still too young to qualify at the College of Surgeons—I was talking to a fellow student (the present eminent physician, Sir Joseph Fayrer), and wondering what I should do to meet the imperative necessity for earning my own bread, when my friend suggested that I should write to Sir William Burnett, at that time Director-General for the Medical Service of the Navy, for an appointment. I thought this rather a strong thing to do, as Sir William was personally unknown to me, but my cheery friend would not listen to my scruples; so I went to my lodgings and wrote the best letter I could devise. A few days afterwards I received the usual official circular acknowledgment, but at the bottom there was written an instruction to call at Somerset House on such a day. I thought that looked like business; so at the appointed time I called and sent in my card, while I waited in Sir William's ante-room. He was a tall, shrewd-looking old gentleman, with a broad Scotch accent—and I think I see him now as he entered with my card in his hand. The first thing he did was to return it, with the frugal reminder that I should probably find it useful on some other occasion. The second was to ask whether I was an Irishman. I suppose the air of modesty about my appeal must have struck him. I satisfied the Director-General that I was English to the backbone, and he made some inquiries as to my student career, finally desiring me to hold myself ready for examination. Having passed this, I was in her Majesty's service, and entered on the books of Nelson's old ship, the *Victory,* for duty at Haslar Hospital, about a couple of months after I made my application.

My official chief at Haslar was a very remarkable person, the late Sir John Richardson, an excellent naturalist, and far-famed as an indomitable Arctic traveler. He was a silent, reserved man, outside the circle of his family and intimates; and, having a full share of youthful vanity, I was extremely disgusted to find that "Old John," as we irreverent youngsters called him, took not the slightest notice of my worshipful self either the first time I attended him, as it was my duty to do, or for some weeks afterwards. I am afraid to think of the lengths to which my tongue may have run on the subject of the churlishness of the chief, who was, in truth, one of the kindest-hearted and most considerate of men. But one day, as I was crossing the hospital square, Sir John stopped me, and heaped coals of fire on my head by telling me that he had tried to get me one of the resident appointments, much coveted by the assistant surgeons, but that the Admiralty had put in another man. "However," said he, "I mean to keep you here till I can get you something you will like," and turned upon his heel without waiting for the thanks I stammered out. That explained how it was I had not been packed off to the west coast of Africa like some of my juniors, and why, eventually, I remained altogether seven months at Haslar.

After a long interval, during which "Old John" ignored my existence almost as completely as before, he stopped me again as we met in a casual way, and describing the service on which the *Rattlesnake* was likely to be employed, said that Captain Owen Stanley, who was to command the ship, had asked him to recommend an assistant surgeon who knew something of science; would I like that? Of course I jumped at the offer. "Very well, I give you leave; go to London at once and see Captain Stanley." I went, saw my future commander, who was very civil to me, and promised to ask that I should be appointed to his ship, as in due time I was. It is a singular thing that, during the few months of my stay at Haslar, I had among my messmates two future Directors-General of the Medical Service of the Navy (Sir Alexander Armstrong and Sir John Watt-Reid), with the present President of the College of Physicians and my kindest of doctors, Sir Andrew Clark.

Life on board her Majesty's ships in those days was a very different affair from what it is now, and ours was exceptionally rough, as we were often many months without receiving letters or seeing any civilized people but ourselves. In exchange, we had the interest of being about the last voyagers, I suppose, to whom it could be possible to meet with people who knew nothing of firearms—as we did on the south coast of New Guinea—and of making acquaintance with a variety of interesting savage and semicivilized people. But, apart from experience of this kind and the opportunities offered for scientific work, to me, personally, the cruise was extremely valuable. It was good for me to live under sharp discipline; to be down on the realities of existence by living on bare necessaries; to find out how extremely well worth living life seemed to be when one woke up from a night's rest on a soft plank, with the sky for canopy and cocoa and weevily biscuit the sole prospect for breakfast; and, more especially, to learn to work for the sake of what I got for myself out of it, even if it all went to the bottom and I along with it. My brother officers were as good fellows as sailors ought to be and generally are, but, naturally, they neither knew nor cared anything about my pursuits, nor understood why I should be so zealous in pursuit of the objects which my friends, the middies, christened "Buffons," after the title conspicuous on a volume of the *Suites à Buffon,* which stood on my shelf in the chartroom.

During the four years of our absence, I sent home communication after communication to the "Linnean Society," with the same result as that obtained by Noah when he sent the raven out of his ark. Tired at last of hearing nothing about them, I determined to do or die, and in 1849 I drew up a more elaborate paper and forwarded it to the Royal Society. This was my dove, if I had only known it. But owing to the movements of the ship, I heard nothing of that either until my return to England in the latter end of the year 1850, when I found that it was printed and published, and that a huge packet of separate copies awaited me. When I hear some of my young friends complain of want of sympathy and encouragement, I am inclined to think that my naval life was not the least valuable part of my education.

Three years after my return were occupied by a battle between my scientific friends on the one hand and the Admiralty on the other, as to whether the latter ought, or ought not, to act up to the spirit of a pledge they had given to encourage officers who had done scientific work by contributing to the expense of publishing mine. At last the Admiralty, getting tired, I suppose, cut short the discussion by ordering me to join a ship, which thing I declined to do, and as Rastignac, in the *Père Goriot,* says to Paris, I said to London, *"à nous deux."* I desired to obtain a professorship of either physiology or comparative anatomy, and as vacancies occurred I applied, but in vain. My friend, Professor Tyndall, and I were candidates at the same time, he for the chair of physics and I for that of natural history in the University of Toronto, which, fortunately, as it turned out, would not look at either of us. I say fortunately, not from any lack of respect for Toronto, but because I soon made up my mind that London was the place for me, and hence I have steadily declined the inducements to leave it, which have at various times been offered. At last, in 1854, on the translation of my warm friend Edward Forbes, to Edinburgh, Sir Henry de la Beche, the Director-General of the Geological Survey, offered me the post Forbes had vacated of Paleontologist and Lecturer on Natural History. I refused the former point-blank, and accepted the latter only provisionally, telling Sir Henry that I did not care for fossils, and that I should give up natural history as soon as I could get a physiological post. But I held the office for thirty-one years, and a large part of my work has been paleontological.

At that time I disliked public speaking, and had a firm conviction that I should break down every time I opened my mouth. I believe I had every fault a speaker could have (except talking at random or indulging in rhetoric), when I spoke to the first important audience I ever addressed, on a Friday evening at the Royal Institution, in 1852. Yet, I must confess to having been guilty, *malgré moi,* of as much public speaking as most of my contemporaries, and for the last ten years it ceased to be so much of a bugbear to me. I used to pity myself for having to go through this training, but I am now more disposed to compassionate the unfortunate audiences, especially my ever-friendly hearers at the Royal Institution, who were the subjects of my oratorical experiments.

The last thing that it would be proper for me to do would be to speak of the work of my life, or to say at the end of the day whether I think I have earned my wages or not. Men are said to be partial judges of themselves. Young men may be, I doubt if old men are. Life seems terribly foreshortened as they look back, and the mountain they set themselves to climb in youth turns out to be a mere spur of immeasurably higher ranges when, with failing breath, they reach the top. But if I may speak of the objects I have had more or less definitely in view since I began the ascent of my hillock, they are briefly these: To promote the increase of natural knowledge and to forward the application of scientific methods of investigation to all the problems of life to the best of my ability, in the conviction which has grown with my growth and strengthened with my strength, that there is no alleviation for the sufferings of mankind except veracity of thought and of action, and the resolute facing of the world as it is when the garment of make-believe by which pious hands have hidden its uglier features is stripped off.

It is with this intent that I have subordinated any reasonable, or unreasonable, ambition for scientific fame which I may have permitted myself to entertain to other ends; to the popularization of science; to the development and organization of scientific education; to the endless series of battles and skirmishes over evolution; and to untiring opposition to that ecclesiastical spirit, that clericalism, which in England, as everywhere else, and to whatever denomination it may belong, is the deadly enemy of science.

In striving for the attainment of these objects, I have been but one among many, and I shall be well content to be remembered, or even not remembered, as such. Circumstances, among which I am proud to reckon the devoted kindness of many friends, have led to my occupation of various prominent positions, among which the presidency of the Royal Society is the highest. It would be mock modesty on my part, with these and other scientific honors which have been bestowed upon me, to pretend that I have not succeeded in the career which I have followed, rather because I was driven into it than of my own free will; but I am afraid I should not count even these things as marks of success if I could not hope that I had somewhat helped that movement of opinion which has been called the New Reformation.

## Suggestions for Study

1. What qualities did Huxley acquire from his parents? Why was his endowment of "mother wit" a rather dangerous gift for a scientist?

2. Does the author pass too quickly over his boyhood? Why does he not devote more space to discussing it?

3. For what study did Huxley have a genuine love? How did he combine that love with his studies in natural science, from which he acquired his reputation?

4. How studious did Huxley prove in medical school? What did he later think of his conduct in school?

5. What did he learn of human nature from his relations with Sir John Richardson?

6. What practical knowledge about living did he derive from life on shipboard?

7. How immediate was his success in getting material published in the scholarly journals?

8. Although later a very skillful public speaker, what was the nature of his early public addresses?

9. State Huxley's aims in life. For what reason does he list these instead of pursuing the course of his life further?

10. State the concept concerning himself that Huxley is trying to portray in this autobiographical sketch.

11. Define the following words from the article: portents, mellifluous, quondam, apathy, paroxysms, hypochondria, ingenuous, approbation, frugal, indomitable, churlishness, canopy, inducements, paleontology, alleviation, veracity, clericalism.

## E. The Letter

**The Friendly Letter.** Nearly everyone writes letters to acquaintances, friends, and relatives; yet few ever stop to think how they can make such personal letters interesting. Habitually they put off the task of answering as long as they dare, and finally scrawl a few hurried lines in the hope that their friends, being friends, will excuse the haste.

Since a friendly letter is meant to interest and inform your intimates and so to preserve friendships, careless letter writing is inexcusable. Haste, slovenliness, or carelessness indicates that you do not have the time nor the inclination to treat the correspondent with consideration.

FORM. In a good letter both form and content receive close attention. The form, based on several conventions which may be easily learned, requires the division of the letter into five parts: the heading, the greeting, the body, the close, and the signature.

*Heading.* The heading is usually placed in the upper right-hand corner of the page; to be sure, writers sometimes place it on the left-hand margin at the end of the letter, but this location is not preferred. The heading can take several forms, all correct.

The block form with open punctuation:

> 160 Cross Street
> Detroit, Michigan
> September 23, 1948

The indented form with open punctuation:

> 160 Cross Street
> Detroit, Michigan
> September 23, 1948

The block form with closed punctuation:

> 160 Cross Street,
> Detroit, Michigan,
> September 23, 1948.

The indented form with closed punctuation:

> 160 Cross Street,
> Detroit, Michigan,
> September 23, 1948.

Today the block heading with open punctuation is used more often than the others. In no form of the heading are abbreviations used. It is advisable to write out *street, avenue,* and *place;* the names of states and cities, such as New York, Philadelphia, Washington; and the names of the months. This practice will obviate any confusion. If the writing is not clear, a correspondent who does not know your address may be unable to decide whether you live in Ga., Va., Pa., Ia., or La., in Cal. or Col., in Md. or Mo. Therefore, courtesy and clarity both forbid the use of abbreviations.

*Greeting.* The greeting is placed just below the heading and on the opposite side of the page, even with the left-hand margin. The accepted forms of greeting are:

> Dear Bill,
> Dear Mr. Jones,
> My dear Professor Smith: (a formal usage)

The greeting is usually followed by a comma, although in more formal letters—as to a mere acquaintance—a colon is better. The use of the conventional terms of greeting, "Dear ——" and "My dear ——," depends upon the intimacy of the correspondents. "My dear ——" is commonly thought more formal in the United States. Abbreviations are not used, except Mr., Mrs., and Dr. To write "My dear Prof. Smith" shows lack of good taste.

*Body.* The body of the letter is begun two lines below the greeting. Its structure and the rules for writing it are essentially the same as those studied in this text for other kinds of writing. The rules of rhetoric with their admonitions as to correct paragraphing, sentence structure, and grammar all apply.

*Close.* The close of the letter is placed two lines below the bottom of the last paragraph and is begun near the center of the page. The first word only is capitalized. A comma follows the close. The most commonly used forms are:

> Sincerely yours, ⎱ these two have the greatest degree of formality
> Yours sincerely, ⎰
> Faithfully yours,
> Cordially yours,
> Affectionately yours,

Of course, to one's parents and intimates, other and more appropriate closes are used.

A few other cautions must be made. Keep a neat letter appearance. Let the margins on all sides of the page be straight and wide, and the lines be well spaced and parallel. And above all, be legible. Your correspondent wants to know what you have said to him. Also make sure that the signature at the end of the letter is clear. The correspondent must be able to read the signature, and also he must know who is meant. He may, for example, have ten friends by the name of "Bill."

The envelope is addressed with the same form—block or indented—that is used for the heading. The return address is placed in the upper left-hand corner, and the address just below center on the right-hand side of the envelope.

CONTENT. The writing of the friendly letter is governed by principles very similar to those which govern conversation; the friendly letter is simply the substitution of the written for the spoken word. Conversation, for example, does not ordinarily center upon any one idea for an extended length of time; it progresses by means of a series of topic sentences which have an association in the minds of the speakers but do not have a common idea to which they are related. In like manner the friendly letter has no thesis sentence, except in unusual circumstances. It possesses unity, but that comes through a unity of tone rather than of content. The personality and mood of the writer provide this unity. A conversation is also rarely planned in advance. Two people, when meeting, do not stop to outline their topic of conversation before they speak; they start directly and rely upon their quickness of mind to advance the talk in an interesting and orderly manner. Spontaneity is highly desirable. Likewise a formal outline is seldom made before a friendly letter is written. The writer usually opens with a word of greeting and presses forward to whatever ideas are spontaneously suggested to him. To be sure, some writers pause long enough at the beginning of their task to jot down subjects about which they wish to speak in the letter, for that method may save some time, but seldom do they make a detailed outline. Each writer should perhaps experiment to discover what method he can use to best advantage. Great freedom is therefore given the writer of the letter to move from one subject to another; he must guard only against shifting so rapidly from one topic to another that he bewilders the reader.

The mood of the friendly letter is accordingly informal and conversational. Through such informality, leisure, and chattiness, you can best reveal your personality, which is the essential quality of a friendly letter. Here, in a letter to a friend, is what one of the most famous English letter writers has to say about this art:

> You like to hear from me: this is a very good reason why I should write.—But I have nothing to say: this seems equally a good reason why I should not. Yet if you had alighted from your horse at our door this morning, and at this present writing, being five o'clock in the afternoon, had found occasion to say to me—"Mr. Cowper, you have not spoke since I came in; have you resolved never to speak again?" it would be but a poor reply, if in answer to the summons I should plead inability as my best and only excuse. And this by the way suggests to me a seasonable piece of instruction, and reminds me of what I am very apt to forget, when I have only epistolary business in hand, that a letter may be written upon anything or nothing just as that anything or nothing happens to occur. A man that has a journey before him twenty miles in length, which he is to perform on foot, will not hesitate and doubt whether he shall set out or not, because he does not readily conceive how he shall ever reach the end of it: for he knows that by the simple operation of moving one foot forward first, and then the other, he shall be sure to accomplish it. So it is in the present case, and so it is in every similar case. A letter is written as a conversation is maintained, or a journey performed; not by preconcerted or premeditated means, a new contrivance, or an invention never heard of before—but merely by maintaining a progress, and resolving as a postilion does, having once set out, never to stop till we reach the appointed end.—William Cowper.

There is the method of letter writing. Most people write short notes because they cannot think of any grand events—any inventions "never heard of before"—with which to fill a long letter. Actually their round of daily affairs together with their own thoughts and speculations is of far more interest to their friends than the news of a stranger's going over Niagara Falls in a barrel. Relating these small but interesting bits enables you to move forward easily step by step. Thus you may begin with whatever impulse seizes you and continue in the same impulsive fashion. The following excerpt from a letter by the Reverend Sydney Smith, a famous humorist of the nineteenth century, shows how he followed the whim of the moment to pen a ludicrous and engaging paragraph:

> You are, I hear, attending more to diet than heretofore. If you wish for anything like happiness in the fifth act of life, eat and drink about half what you *could* eat and drink. Did I ever tell you my calculation about eating and drinking? Having ascertained the weight of what I could live upon, so as to preserve health and strength, and what I did live upon, I found that between ten and seventy years of age, I had eaten and drunk forty four-horse wagonloads of meat and drink more than would have preserved me in life and health! The value of this mass of nourishment I considered to be worth seven thousand pounds sterling. It occurred to me that I must, by my voracity, have starved to death fully a hundred persons. This is a frightful calculation, but irresistibly true; and I think, dear Murray, your wagons would require an additional horse each!

Such freedom and informality make a good letter. The writer is natural; only when he forces himself into a mood, humorous or whimsical, does his writing become deadly. Also, because the friendly letter is an informal piece of writing, colloquialism is used freely. *Don't* comes nearer conversation than does *do not*.

The following is a good example of a chatty letter by Charles Lamb, one of the real masters of this form. He is addressing his friend Thomas Manning, who is in the Orient:

> Dear Manning,—When I last wrote you, I was in lodgings. I am now in chambers, No. 4, Inner Temple Lane, where I should be happy to see you any evening. Bring any of your friends, the Mandarins, with you. I have two sitting-rooms; I call them so *par excellence,* for you may stand, or loll, or lean, or try any posture in them; but they are best for sitting; not squatting down Japanese fashion, but the more decorous use of the post—s which European usage has consecrated. I have two of these rooms on the third floor, and five sleeping, cooking, etc., rooms, on the fourth floor. In my best room is a choice collection of the works of Hogarth, an English painter of some humor. In my next best are shelves containing a small but well-chosen library. My best room commands a court in which there are trees and a pump, the water of which is excellent—cold with brandy, and not very insipid without. Here I hope to set up my rest, and not quit till Mr. Powell, the undertaker, gives me notice that I may have

possession of my last lodging. He lets lodgings for single gentlemen. I sent you a parcel of books by my last, to give you some idea of the state of European literature. There comes with this two volumes, done up as letters, of minor poetry, a sequel to "Mrs. Leicester"; the best you may suppose mine; the next best are my coadjutor's; you may amuse yourself in guessing them out; but I must tell you mine are but one third in quantity of the whole. So much for a very delicate subject. It is hard to speak of one's self, etc. Holcroft had finished his life when I wrote to you, and Hazlitt has since finished his life—I do not mean his own life, but he has finished a life of Holcroft, which is going to press. Tuthill is Dr. Tuthill. I continue Mr. Lamb. I have published a little book for children on titles of honor; and to give them some idea of the difference of rank and gradual rising, I have made a little scale, supposing myself to receive the following various accessions of dignity from the King, who is the fountain of honor—As at first, 1, Mr. C. Lamb; 2, C. Lamb, Esq.; 3, Sir C. Lamb, Bart.; 4, Baron Lamb of Stamford; 5, Viscount Lamb; 6, Earl Lamb; 7, Marquis Lamb; 8, Duke Lamb. It would look like quibbling to carry it further, and especially as it is not necessary for children to go beyond the ordinary titles of subregal dignity in our own country, otherwise I have sometimes in my dreams imagined myself still advancing, as 9th, King Lamb; 10th, Emperor Lamb; 11th, Pope Innocent, higher than which is nothing but the Lamb of God. Puns I have not made many (nor punch much) since the date of my last; one I cannot help relating. A constable in Salisbury Cathedral was telling me that eight people dined at the top of the spire of the cathedral; upon which I remarked, that they must be very sharp-set. But in general I cultivate the reasoning part of my mind more than the imaginative.

A word is perhaps needed about the beginning of the letter. Inasmuch as most people seem to be late in answering their personal correspondence, they have the impulse to start every letter with an apology for not having written sooner. If an apology does seem to be called for, it should be offered adroitly without a host of excuses that will not be believed anyway. Here are the openings of several letters from the correspondence of Thomas Moore, which will illustrate how adroitly the apology can be offered:

I am really a very good correspondent. Do you know what the chemists call "latent heat"? This I am full of. It is a property which some bodies have of keeping all their warmth to themselves; or, rather, *in* themselves; which makes them seem not half so warm as other bodies which have all their warmth on the surface. Now this is the case with me; and therefore, whenever you are long without hearing from me, set it down at once to "latent heat," and console yourself with the idea of its being all snug and warm in my heart, instead of lavishing its precious particles through the post-office.—To Miss Godfrey.

You have every reason to be very angry with me—but I really have such an unconquerable aversion to writing letters, that I have often thought Captain Brady's resolution not to answer anything but a *challenge* was the most peaceable way of getting through life. But I feel myself particularly reprehensible in not attending to *your* letter.—To James Corry.

> It is a certain fact, that since I heard from you I have, in my own mind, written you five or six letters, as excellent as ever were penned, though penned they never were. How should they, when I never had a pen in my hand since I sent you off my last little flying reproach? And how could I have a pen in a hand that was never divested of a needle, thread, and thimble, except when I was nursing the sick or conversing with carpenters and upholsterers?—Miss Godfrey to Thomas Moore.

Probably a better method, however, is to open with a word of greeting to the correspondent, like that between friends on the street. Making the correspondent feel he is a valued friend is the way to his heart. Does not the following greeting from Miss Godfrey to Thomas Moore express a real cordiality?

> Rogers gave me the enclosed to get franked to you. I can't resist taking the opportunity to ask after you and Bessy, and little Barbara, and the other little animal;—are you all flourishing in health and happiness? And do your absent friends ever by any accident occupy a stray thought?

A few other words of warning remain. Whenever you receive a letter that contains questions to be answered, be sure to answer those questions so that you will not make a bad impression on the correspondent. If you neglect his questions, he feels irritated and may also believe that his letter has not even been read. It is a good practice to place on the desk before you the letter which you are answering.

Also, do not be afraid of boring your correspondent by writing too long a letter. A major complaint against college students is that they do not write sufficiently long letters. Rambling on to fill space and satisfy a desire for philosophizing is of course poor, for it is boring, but extreme brevity is rather cold. A famous correspondence, probably fictitious, between an English Duke and a Bishop is the ultimate in brevity: "Dear Cork, Please ordain Stanhope, Yours, York"; "Dear York, Stanhope's ordained. Yours, Cork." Thus in a few simple words their business is transacted—but a warm friendship is hardly cultivated.

**The Formal Note.** The formal note is a highly artificial form, written in a set manner. It is used for formal invitations, and has no heading, greeting, or signature. It is written in the third person and the present tense throughout. Contrary to the usual rule for the use of numbers, it requires that all numbers in the date should be written out. The address of the sender and the date of writing are placed below the last line and on the left, with either open or closed punctuation.

> Mr. Archibald Smith requests the pleasure of Mr. and Mrs. Alfred Jones's company at dinner on Saturday evening, January the twenty-fifth, at six-thirty o'clock.
>
> 4 Park Street,
> January the fifteenth.

> Mr. and Mrs. Alfred Jones accept with pleasure the kind invitation of Mr. Archibald Smith to dine on Saturday, January the twenty-fifth, at six-thirty o'clock.
>
> 25 South Avenue,
> January the seventeenth.

> Mr. and Mrs. Alfred Jones regret that a previous engagement prevents their acceptance of Mr. Archibald Smith's kind invitation to dine on Saturday, January the twenty-fifth.
>
> 25 South Avenue,
> January the seventeenth.

## Reading Selections

My dear M.,—I want to know how your brother is, if you have heard lately. I want to know about you. I wish you were nearer. . . . How are my cousins, the Gladmans of Wheathamstead, and farmer Bruton? Mrs. Bruton is a glorious woman.

   Hail, Mackery End—

This is a fragment of a blank verse poem which I once meditated, but got no further. The E.I.H. has been thrown into a quandary by the strange phenomenon of poor Tommy Bye, whom I have known man and mad-man twenty-seven years, he being elder here than myself by nine years and more. He was always a pleasant, gossiping, half-headed, muzzy, dozing, dreaming, walkabout, inoffensive chap, a little too fond of the creature—who isn't at times? but Tommy had not brains to work off an overnight's surfeit by ten o'clock next morning, and, unfortunately, in he wandered the other morning drunk with last night, and with a super-foetation of drink taken in since he set out from bed. He came staggering under his double burthen, like trees in Java, bearing at once blossom, fruit, and falling fruit, as I have heard you or some other traveler tell, with his face literally as blue as the bluest firmament; some wretched calico that he had mopped his poor oozy front with had rendered up its native dye, and the devil a bit would he consent to wash it, but swore it was characteristic, for he was going to the sale of indigo, and set up a laugh which I did not think the lungs of mortal man were competent to. It was like a thousand people laughing, or the Goblin Page. He imagined afterwards that the whole office had been laughing at him, so strange did his own sounds strike upon his *non*sensorium. But Tommy has laughed his last laugh, and awoke the next day to find himself reduced from an abused income of £600 per annum to one-sixth of the sum, after thirty-six years' tolerably good service. The quality of mercy was not strained in his behalf: the gentle dews dropt not on him from heaven. . . .

I have not had such a quiet half hour to sit down to a quiet letter for many years. I have not been interrupted above four times. I wrote a letter the other day in alternate lines, black ink and red, and you cannot think how it chilled the flow of ideas. Next Monday is Whit-Monday. What a reflection! Twelve years ago, and I should have kept that and the following holiday in the fields a-Maying. All of these pretty pastoral delights are over. This dead, everlasting dead desk—how it weighs the spirit of a gentleman down! This dead wood of the desk instead of your living trees! But then, again, I hate the Joskins, *a name for Hertfordshire bumpkins.* Each state of life has its inconvenience; but then, again, mine has more than one. Not that I repine, or grudge, or murmur at my destiny. I have meat and drink, and decent apparel; I shall, at least, when I get a new hat. . . . —Charles Lamb to Thomas Manning, May 28, 1819.

My dear Friend,

At seven o'clock this evening, being the seventh of December, I imagine I see you in your box at the coffeehouse. No doubt the waiter, as ingenious and adroit as his predecessors were before him, raises the teapot to the ceiling with his right hand, while in his left the teacup descending almost to the floor, receives a limpid stream; limpid in its descent, but no sooner has it reached its destination than, frothing and foaming to the view, it becomes a roaring syllabub. This is the nineteenth winter since I saw you in this situation; and if nineteen more pass over me before I die, I shall still remember a circumstance we have often laughed at.

How different is the complexion of your evenings and mine!—yours, spent amid the ceaseless hum that proceeds from the inside of fifty noisy and busy periwigs; mine, by a domestic fireside, in a retreat as silent as retirement can make it; where no noise is made but what we make for our own amusement. For instance, here are two rustics, and your humble servant in company. One of the ladies has been playing on the harpsichord, while I, with the other, have been playing at battledore and shuttle-cock. A little dog, in the meantime, howling under the chair of the former, performed, in the vocal way, to admiration. This entertainment over, I began my letter, and having nothing more important to communicate, have given you an account of it. I know you love dearly to be idle, when you can find an opportunity to be so; but as such opportunities are rare with you, I thought it possible that a short description of the idleness I enjoy might give you pleasure. The happiness we cannot call our own, we yet seem to possess, while we sympathize with our friends who can.... —William Cowper to Joseph Hill, December 7, 1782.

I open my letter to tell you a fact, which will show the state of this country better than I can. The commandant of the troops is *now* lying *dead* in my house. He was shot at a little past eight o'clock, about two hundred paces from my door. I was putting on my greatcoat to visit Madame la Contessa G. when I heard the shot. On coming into the hall, I found all my servants on the balcony, exclaiming that a man was murdered. I immediately ran down, calling on Tita (the bravest of them) to follow me. The rest wanted to hinder us from going, as it is the custom of everybody here, it seems, to run away from "the stricken deer."

However, down we ran, and found him lying on his back, almost, if not quite, dead, with five wounds; one in the heart, two in the stomach, one in the finger, and the other in the arm. Some soldiers cocked their guns, and wanted to hinder me from passing. However, we passed, and I found Diego, the adjutant, crying over him like a child—a surgeon, who said nothing of his profession—a priest, sobbing a frightened prayer—and the commandant, all this time, on his back on the hard, cold pavement, without light or assistance, or anything around him but confusion and dismay.

As nobody could, or would, do anything but howl and pray, and as no one would stir a finger to move him, for fear of consequences, I lost my patience—made my servant and a couple of the mob take up the body—sent off two soldiers to the guard—dispatched Diego to the Cardinal with the news, and had the commandant carried upstairs into my own quarter. But it was too late, he was gone—not at all disfigured—bled inwardly—not above an ounce or two came out.

I had him partly stripped—made the surgeon examine him, and examined him myself. He had been shot by cut balls, or slugs. I felt one of the slugs, which had gone through him, all but the skin. Everybody conjectures why he was killed, but no one knows how. The gun was found close by him—an old gun, half filed down.

He only said "O Dio!" and "Gesu!" two or three times and appeared to have suffered very little. Poor fellow! he was a brave officer, but had made himself much disliked by the people. I knew him personally, and had met with him often at conversazioni and elsewhere. My house is full of soldiers, dragoons, doctors, priests, and all kinds of persons,—though I have now cleared it, and clapt sentinels at the doors. Tomorrow the body is to be moved. The town is in the greatest confusion, as you may suppose.

You are to know that, if I had not had the body moved, they would have left him there till morning in the street for fear of consequences. I would not choose to let even a dog die in such a manner, without succor: —and, as for the consequences, I care for none in a duty.

Yours,

P.S.—The lieutenant on duty by the body is smoking his pipe with great composure.—A queer people this.—Lord Byron to Thomas Moore, December 9, 1820.

Dear Gerald,

Last week, while climbing to the top of Greenhead Ghyll, near Grasmere, I remembered that you were teaching Wordsworth and Coleridge and might like a note in connection with Michael and the "clipping tree." We started up about nine o'clock in the evening, with mist and clouds coming down over the neighboring mountains and with a heavy dew on the bracken around our ankles. In the interests of scholarly exactness, please tell your class that Wordsworth was considerably in error in the opening lines of the poem. For we found that, in spite of his assurances, "You *will* suppose that with an upright path Your feet must struggle." Courage (*cf.* line 6) is too mild a term for the moral spirit with which you have to arm yourself, "for around that boisterous brook The mountains have *not* all opened out themselves, And made a hidden valley of their own" (unless he means a precipitous gorge and not a dale). The truth is that we climbed straight up slippery slopes, hobbled over stones and boulders, and sought in vain for any "opening out," while the "boisterous brook" thundered and roared so as to make conversation impossible. Poor Michael! There is little of the pastoral peace and quiet in Greenhead Ghyll such as a reader might infer from the poem. It is unlikely that the deep gorge has been cut since Wordsworth's day. The wildness, the roar, and the gloom of the place struck me as a curious setting for "A Pastoral Poem." At the opening of the Ghyll, down in the dale (near Grasmere), there is an old house called "Michael's Fold"; but none of the local inhabitants will believe that it has anything really to do with the Michael of the poem. Far up in the Ghyll, however, one is shown a pile of rocks supposed to be the pile left by Michael when he "never lifted up a single stone," . . . another legend which no one can take seriously. Civilization has done its dirty work here as elsewhere: a dam has been built across the brook, and various pipes and metal work damage the primitive wildness of the place. I am sorry to report that the only really pastoral things I saw on my ascent were of the most disagreeable sort, announcing themselves very insistently before I really knew what was in store for me: the carcasses of two dead sheep. "That," thought I, "is the sort of thing that really made up the 'pastoral life' of the dalesmen." Yet there can be no denying that the legendary Michael had before his door one of the most sublime panoramas to be found anywhere: Grasmere vale, Easedale, Langdale Pikes, upland lakes not visible from the lowlands, and a sky magnificent at any hour of the day. The net result of our trip was, for me, an aggravation of a strained ligament in my left knee (one of the by-products of our descent from the top of Helvellyn two days before), so that here in Edinburgh I have been hobbling about painfully on my cane. We didn't leave Grasmere, I might add, before I got you a cane from the same chap from whom I got mine. At Wordsworth's grave I invoked the gods of poetry in your honor and thought of college.

Our two other excursions in the four days we were in Grasmere were to Helvellyn, as I have said, and to Easedale Tarn. The Helvellyn ascent was delightful: the weather was sunny and warm, and the view from the top of the mountain was clear and wide. Easedale Tarn makes a good afternoon's hiking, taking you up Sour Milk Ghyll to a little lake hidden in the pocket of wild peaks and fells, beyond all stone fences and farms, as unchanged, I suppose, as it was in Wordsworth's day.

On our journey to Edinburgh we stopped at Ecclefechan, a shabby, smelly, neglected little stone village, and visited Carlyle's birthplace, now a museum, and his grave. Since none of Carlyle's relatives live near the village, and because the place was so depressing, we went on to Edinburgh at once. Here I have been prowling through the second-hand bookstores, reading in our room, drinking stout at every respectable opportunity, and reading the MS letters of Carlyle, between 1819 and 1830, in the Scottish National Library. As I expected, I am finding nothing in the letters pertinent to my subject, but they are surely quaint to behold, at times a little sad and wretched. Today I had the pleasure of being conducted about the city by Mr. James A. S. Barrett, of Peebles, editor of *Sartor,* a sober, witty old Scotchman, full of anecdotes about Carlyle, Edinburgh, Masson (under whom he studied), and so on.

The length of this letter is no indication that I hope for as long a one from you; but a few lines telling me of your summer and plans would make interesting reading over here in Auld Reekie.—C. F. Harrold to G. D. Sanders.[18]

### Exercises

1. Write one of the following letters:

   A letter of congratulation on a marriage, the birth of a child, graduation from college or high school, the selling of a story to a magazine, or an appointment to a coveted position.

   A letter of thanks for the hospitality shown you during a visit.

   A letter to a friend confined to a sickbed.

   A letter of thanks for a Christmas gift, or other present.

   A letter to a friend asking for advice on what college to attend.

   A letter of advice to a friend in high school who has asked you concerning the college he shall attend.

   A letter home during a summer vacation.

   A letter planning a summer vacation trip.

   A letter of invitation to a friend to spend some time at your home.

   A letter home for money.

   A letter to a son who has written for money.

   A letter to a man who is retiring from his position after a lifetime of service.

2. Write a formal note of invitation, a letter of acceptance, and a letter of regret.

**The Business Letter.** Being more formal than the personal letter, the business letter demands greater precision in both form and content. The recipient of the letter, not being a friend, lacks the indulgence that the writer of a personal letter can expect. Thus care must be exercised to see that form, manuscript appearance, grammar, punctuation, and all the other principles of rhetoric are adhered to. In the last twenty-five years, business houses and institutions have become increasingly aware of the importance of the letter in their work, and correspondingly critical of the letters written to them.

Form. The heading of the business letter is exactly the same as that of the friendly letter; again the block form without punctuation is preferred. The business letter, however, has one item of information not found in the friendly letter: an inside address. Businessmen often do not see the envelopes of letters handled by their secretaries, and so need a record of the addressee. The inside address is placed even with the left-hand margin

18. Reprinted by permission of the author.

of the letter, a space or more below the bottom line of the heading. The style of the inside address should conform to that used in the heading.

> Mr. John Andrews
> 121 Tennessee Drive
> Buffalo, New York

> Dr. George Smith,
>   7 Emory Avenue,
>     Cortland, New York.

Notice that both the closed and open forms of punctuation are correct, although today the open, block form is usually preferred. Simply remember to be consistent. If you have used an open block heading, use the same type of inside address. In addition to the name and address of the receiver, his business title is often given, on the same line as his name or on the line below it:

> Dr. George Smith, Chairman
> Athletic Committee

> Dr. George Smith
> Chairman, Athletic Committee

The greeting of the business letter, placed even with the left-hand margin of the page, differs slightly from that used in the personal letter. Preferred here are:

> Gentlemen:        Dear Mr. Hope:
> Dear Sir:         My dear Mr. Hope: (an extremely formal usage, there-
> Dear Madam:       fore avoided by many companies)
> Mesdames:

In contrast to the usage in friendly letters, the colon always follows the greeting.

Sometimes you may wish to bring a letter to the personal attention of an individual in a firm. You may address this individual directly or, more formally, may write *Attention of Mr.* —— on the same line as the salutation, or on the next line below it.

> Seaboard Shipping Lines
> 145 Front Street
> New York, New York
> Gentlemen:        Attention of Mr. Robert E. Smith
>                 or
> Gentlemen:
>                 Attention of Mr. Robert E. Smith

The close is usually placed in the same position as it is in the friendly letter, although a few firms are now putting it in block form even with the left-hand margin. The conventional business closes are:

| | |
|---|---|
| Yours truly, | Sincerely yours, |
| Yours very truly, | Yours sincerely, |
| Very truly yours, | Cordially yours, |
| Respectfully yours, | Faithfully yours, |

In business letters the signature must be legible. It is correct to make certain by typing the name under the signature.

The envelope should be addressed to correspond with the inside address, and the return address should be placed in the upper left-hand corner. Again either the block or indented styles may be used, with or without punctuation. Simply let them be consistent.

In using the usual 6½″ by 3½″ business envelope, fold the letter first from bottom to top leaving the bottom edge about a quarter of an inch short of the top edge so that when the receiver opens the letter, he will have no trouble in separating the sheets. A triple fold is then made: the left edge is folded two-thirds of the way toward the right edge, which is brought over on top of it. In using the large-size business envelope, one makes a triple fold in the letter, the bottom being folded up and the top brought down over it; thus the creases divide the letter evenly in thirds.

CONTENT. A business letter is based upon the same principles of writing that you have studied previously in this text. It is not a peculiar species boasting rules of its own. To write a good business letter, do as you would do in other types of writing: study the person whom you are addressing, define your purposes, and organize the material most effectively to suit the reader.

Pay special attention to adapting your letter to the reader. If you know his wants, you should be able to phrase your remarks more intelligently. Remember that the business letter aims primarily at showing the reader how he can be served. Even a claim letter, that is, a letter of complaint against an individual or company, performs a service by giving a company the opportunity of rectifying an error and so retaining good will. For that reason the writer of a claim letter takes into account the fact that the recipient will be eager to redeem himself and grieved that he has fallen into error.

Any action which you desire from the reader—the purpose of the business letter is to get action—must be defined sharply and without a waste of words. Make the letter as concise as possible, but never forget to include every bit of information necessary for your reader to take the desired action. Any busy man is annoyed by receiving a letter so incomplete that he must write back to find out what he is expected to do. A great deal has been said and written about the need for conciseness in the business letter. The term conciseness, however, means brevity in wording, not an abbreviation of the subject matter to such an extent that the full meaning is mutilated. Consider the following letter:

> Dear Mr. Jones:
>
> I was a student in your rhetoric class last year. This term I wish to take English by correspondence. Would you please give permission to do so? I would appreciate a prompt reply.
>
> Sincerely yours,

The student writing this letter thought he was being commendably brief. But the instructor had to write back to find out to whom the permission was to be sent, what English course was to be taken, and why the student was desirous of taking correspondence study. The next letter gave most of the needed information. The student, who had failed the rhetoric course, had dropped out of school at the end of the semester, was working in his home town, and hoped to make up his deficiency by the correspondence work. He then enclosed the name and address of the person to whom the permission was to be sent and explained what sort of permission the correspondence administrators desired. The instructor was then finally able to accede to the request. Thus the student was needlessly delayed, and the instructor was put to unnecessary inconvenience.

Complete information must be given. The skillful writer will also add an appeal that will stimulate the reader to the desired action. If you wish to sell the reader a desk, rent him a new apartment, or get him to vote for a new city ordinance, you must stimulate him by indicating how the proposal will be of value to him. If he can see that he will benefit by acceding to your proposal, he will hasten to co-operate.

When you have carefully planned a letter as to the information and appeal needed to get a definite action, begin the actual wording. As in a friendly letter, endeavor to be natural. Simplicity of wording and simplicity of sentence structure appeal most strongly. Those terms which the reader himself uses will please him best. Colloquialisms or slang expressions, however, should not be used; a certain dignity must be preserved if the writer is to be thought well of. Nor should humor or cleverness be indulged in; such tricks are very often misinterpreted, since the humorous remark is thought to be serious.

Diction must be carefully observed. Formerly all sorts of hackneyed expressions were used: abbreviations, stock phrases, clumsy sentence structure. Today the businessman is more careful. He no longer falls back on such clichés as "Yours of the 17th ult. at hand and contents duly noted." Instead he tries to write as he would talk. Here are a few of the hackneyed expressions which he now avoids:

| | |
|---|---|
| as per | our Mr. Jones |
| at an early date | permit me to state |
| at hand | please be advised |
| at your earliest convenience | please find enclosed |
| contents duly noted | recent date |
| beg to state | take pen in hand |
| by return mail | thanking you in advance |
| esteemed favor | your favor |
| has come to hand | yours of the 17th |
| in reply would say | |

Not only are these expressions nonsensical, grammatically poor, or exhausted through use, but they commonly occur in the most important parts of the letter and so weaken the force of the entire writing. The beginning and ending of the letter, like similar parts of the magazine article, make the strongest impression on the reader. Thus the letter should be started with a direct and fresh manner of statement rather than a "Yours at hand" roundabout one. Attention must be stimulated. Likewise at the end, a weak participial construction is poor: "Hoping to hear from you" or "Thanking you in advance." A complete sentence is more forceful: "I thank you for your courtesy."

Whatever kind of letter is written, let it be courteous. The correspondent is pleased if he finds that the difficulties of his side of the transaction are appreciated. It is diplomatic to treat him as a punctilious gentleman and to reveal an interest in him and his affairs. Interest, conciseness, and courtesy will make for pleasant and efficient correspondence.

**The Claim Letter.** The claim letter is written when a complaint is being lodged against a company or individual. Remember that even though inconvenienced in some manner, you should write a courteous letter, setting aside anger during the writing. If the recipient of the letter is treated with consideration, prompt action to remedy the grievance will more likely be forthcoming. No firm or individual likes to make mistakes, and bends every effort to preserve good will by avoiding and rectifying such errors. A courteous, reasonable appeal has the best chance to succeed.

The beginning of the letter should state accurately and fully the circumstances under which the transaction or exchange of services was made. The nature of the business and its date of transaction should be given in full to establish the point of contact with the reader and to put him in possession of the facts so that needless correspondence will not be occasioned. The complaint can then be made. To offer some excuse explaining the difficulty which may have arisen is a courteous gesture and indicates to the reader that the writer is of a reasonable nature. However, such a gesture should not weaken the force of the letter.

To stimulate the reader to action, include in the letter a statement of the inconvenience to which you have been put by the error. Such a statement indicates to the recipient that the complaint is not just imaginary but based on actuality. Having provided the stimulus, then point out the exact action which the firm is to take, so that it may be sure what is expected of it to give satisfaction. The tone of the letter throughout is serious, courteous, forceful, and reasonable.

> Gentlemen:
>
> On February 25, 1946, I ordered the following books from your General Catalogue of 1946:
>
> No. 478　Fowler, H. W. *Dictionary of Modern English Usage*, 1929
> No. 592　Moore, Thomas. *The Epicurean*, 1877
> No. 671　Saintsbury, G. *Short History of French Literature*, 1917
>
> The order was correctly filled for the first two items on this list, but instead of the third, you sent me *Specimens of French Literature*, by G. Saintsbury, number 672 in the Catalogue.
>
> I have returned *Specimens of French Literature* and desire you to rush the correct volume to me, as I have immediate need of it. The delay has already caused me considerable inconvenience.
>
> 　　　　　　　　　　　　　　　　　Yours truly,

**The Letter of Application.** A sales letter tries to sell a product to a consumer, and of course makes that sale the point of action of the letter. Exactly the same is done in the letter of application, except that the writer is selling his own abilities to a firm or individual, and the point of action is to persuade the employer to agree to an interview. As a salesman dare not either overpraise or underrate his product, so an applicant should not be too boastful or too retiring. He steers between extremes. His ability must be shown but not in an impertinent or boastful manner. His tone must be one of confidence. He must state his training, his experience, his desire to work at the position, and his confidence to handle the work; such a letter will be straightforward, but not conceited.

Appearance is extremely important in the letter of application. Many employers cast aside without perusal those letters which are carelessly or sloppily written, and reserve their judgment for neat manuscripts. Thus the margins must be even and wide; the letter is preferably typewritten; all rules of rhetoric are carefully observed; *and all words are spelled correctly.*

The beginning should come directly to the point. As its function is to attract attention, try to ascertain how you can most effectively get into the flow of the reader's thoughts. Obviously, if the thought uppermost in his mind concerns filling a vacancy in his firm, the best way to attract his attention is to apply directly for the position. A simple, clear statement is best, making the application and telling how the applicant learned of the vacancy. It is usually good psychology to get the pronoun "you" in the introductory paragraph and to avoid starting with "I." As the letter must stress throughout that the applicant can be of service to the employer's company, the pronoun "you" is valuable. This advice does not mean that "I" is not to be used in the letter; after all, the applicant is giving his own qualifications. The search for differing ways of saying "I" leads to stilted writing.

Originality of expression aids the introduction, for it makes the letter above the ordinary. To achieve originality, do not, however, act the high-pressure salesman with a blatant "You cannot find a better man than I; select me and your worries are over." The employer has his own ideas on that subject after such a greeting; he never wants to be told outright what to think. Originality rather lies in impressing the employer with the idea that the applicant wishes to work for him and his company. A graceful variation of the theme, "I have long wished to obtain a position in this kind of work," if sincere and not posed, will be effective.

Thus the tone of the introduction is important. It follows closely that the better you know the employer or at least the kind of company for which he works, the better can you phrase the introduction. The old, established firm may prefer a conservative tone; the new firm, seeking a large volume of sales by low prices, may be impressed with a livelier tone. But you should, wherever possible, learn about the employer or the employer's firm.

After you have aroused the interest of the employer, demonstrate, as specifically as possible, your qualifications for the position. Two statements are needed in particular: the amount of actual experience that you have had, and the extent of your education. It is exceedingly important that you consider what qualifications the employer might think desirable. By such consideration you will avoid the common error of inexperienced applicants, that of failing to give pertinent information. The careless applicant is very likely to put down under the heading of experience such generalities as, "For four years I worked in the shops of the Jefferson Tool Company." That is of course insufficient. He must tell exactly what kind of work he did in those four years; for all the employer knows, he might have been sweeping floors as janitor, work which would hardly qualify him for doing specialized machine work. Thus, a concrete and detailed statement enables the employer to see your qualifications to better advantage. The name of the firm, the length of time in its employ, the exact kind of work done, all are to be included. If you have had no experience at all that would aid you—and this condition is less frequent than many young applicants would think—endeavor to show how you are promising material. Indicate why you desire the position, and what aptitude you have shown in work of a similar kind; show a strong probability that you can handle the job.

Under the heading of education, state the schools you have attended, the length of attendance therein, whether a degree has been attained, the general level of your school grades, and a list of subjects which will help you in executing the duties of the job.

The next section of the letter should be devoted to a listing of references—those who can speak for your character, ability, and experience. Usually at least three names are included. The full name and address of each reference should be given. If he and the employer live in the same city, his telephone number should also be listed; many employers like to save time by calling to get an oral recommendation. Always bear in mind a rule of courtesy, that before using a man's name as a reference, you should ask his permission and afterwards thank him for his courtesy in complying with the request. Most men are very willing to give a testimonial, but they do not like to be imposed upon by those who fail to show the common elements of courtesy.

The conclusion clinches the letter. In it you ask for an interview, as you must show your willingness to talk with the employer. At the interview the employer can judge such matters as personal appearance, habits of speech, extent of knowledge; and he can discuss salary, a consideration which is usually not broached in the letter of application. The hackneyed expression, the use of the participle (such as, "Hoping to hear from you,"), and other weak modes of statement must be avoided in the conclusion, which should leave a favorable impression on the employer.

There remain a few other miscellaneous suggestions which may help you. Even though you receive a letter from an employer stating that no positions are available, or that the position has been filled for which an application was made, answer the employer's note, thanking him for his consideration of the letter of application, reasserting the desire to work for him, and expressing the hope that he will keep you in mind should another position become vacant. Such letters create a favorable impression on the employer, and provide an opportunity for you to apply again at a later date in the hope that a new vacancy has been created. Unsolicited letters of application, those which are written with the pious hope that a position is open, sometimes produce excellent results. They have the advantage of coming at a time when the employer is not buried under an avalanche of letters and can give the applicant more careful consideration. The writer of such a letter must be careful, however, to study the qualities, education, and experience which a firm would like to have in its employees and try to meet those qualities as best he can. This study is not so easy as that made by the person who knows what an employer is looking for.

### Exercises

1. Read the following letter, noting the cordial tone inserted in a purely business letter.

Dear Mr. Smith:

Thank you for your order dated April 30 for two volumes. The books are being shipped to you today by express, C.O.D., as requested, with our receipted invoice enclosed.

Perhaps you will find in the enclosed folder some other books to your liking.

Our facilities, of course, are not limited to the books we list. In ordering again, please feel free to order any books you may require including textbooks. On these, when ordered for classroom or similar use, we allow as liberal a discount as our own terms of purchase permit.

This is the first order we have received from you. It is a pleasure to add your name to our list of customers.

Sincerely yours,

2. Having read this example of a pleasant business letter, revise the following letters after noting carefully where the weakness lies in each. They are not all of the same level of ability.

### A

Dear Mr. Thomas:

At a recent meeting of the board of the Y.M.C.A., your name was given to me for personal solicitation. I hesitate to take the time of anyone on such a mission as this, knowing that if you make a contribution you need only be reminded.

Will you therefore kindly indicate whether you are willing to help support the Y.M.C.A.? If you do, enclose your check for whatever sum you desire to contribute. If you don't, please state why.

### B

Gentlemen:

In addition to sending catalog of College of Agriculture and bulletin on Correspondence study, please answer the following by letter:

1. I hold degree with major in biology but no work in Agriculture. Would you permit me to take sufficient work by correspondence between now and

next Sept. so that I could complete requirements for B.S. in Agr. in one year of residence?

2. Hold scholarship to the State U. covering tuition and fees. Can you offer a similar one? I prefer a Northern institution.

3. What is size of your diploma in inches, does it have gold seal with ribbons protruding from underneath and how many signatures? The diploma I now have is the small vest-pocket size unsuitable for framing. I desire a large one suitable for framing. Would you be willing to have large size made for me 20½ × 25 to fit frame my father used for M.D. if I pay cost?

C

Dear Sir:

Referring to yours of February 5th advising of an overcharge made you in connection with ticket purchased by you.

We have pleasure in enclosing draft to your order for $2.95 in adjustment and trust you will overlook agent's unintentional error.

3. Write a business letter on one of the following topics:
- Ordering theater tickets
  Placing an order with a mail-order house or department store
  Writing a bank to seek information concerning your checking account
  Making hotel, train, or steamship reservations
  Requesting a business firm or a governmental agency to send a special bulletin which it publishes
  Requesting an automobile club to send you tour maps

4. Write a claim letter on one of the following themes:
  Requesting your apartment owner to make repairs in your apartment
  Requesting the electric company to adjust an overcharge on the month's bill
  Seeking adjustment from a firm that has put you to needless expense. You ordered a cap and gown for your graduation ceremonies, asking the firm first to send it to your home, but later to send it to your college address; they acknowledged the change of address. Two days before your graduation you had no gown; you wired to the firm to send it immediately, and received word from home that the gown was there. The cost of wiring and mailing was $2. Your letter is to secure reimbursement for the expense to which you were put by their negligence.
  Seeking reimbursement from a railroad. You feel sure that the station agent overcharged you for your ticket which you bought in the Christmas rush.
  Seeking quick action from a firm. You are ready to leave on a camping trip, but your equipment, which you ordered long before, has not arrived.

5. Read the following letters of application, noting the type and amount of information given:

## A

The Eastern Teachers Agency informs me that you are seeking a teacher of English for the coming year. I am making application for that position.

I am a graduate of Harvard University, B.A. 1939. During my course I specialized in English, taking twelve semester hours of composition and thirty-six hours of literature. In addition, I secured twenty hours of Education, sufficient to enable me to hold a teacher's certificate in your state. The remainder of my course of study was devoted to those subjects which would assist me in being a well-rounded teacher: history, sociology, psychology, science, and language. My grade average for the four years was B, an average which placed me well within the top third of my class.

Throughout my schooling I have engaged in many activities outside the classroom. In Newton High School, from which I graduated in 1935, I was a member of the dramatics club and the debating society. I was also awarded the school letter in track and basketball. At Harvard I was a member of the dramatics club and an editor of the *Daily Crimson*. For three years I ran on the track team, winning my letter each year. Thus I feel that my interests are wide enough to enable me to be of assistance to you and to your pupils.

Although I have had no actual experience as a teacher, the grade of A which I received in practice teaching and the keen pleasure which I took in this work seem to indicate that I should be a successful classroom teacher. I have had experience in handling boys of high-school age, as I was assistant scoutmaster of Troop 8 of Newton for three years.

The Eastern Teachers Agency has already sent you my full credentials, which include recommendations by several persons and the record of my school and college work. If there is any way in which I can be of further assistance to you in providing necessary information, please feel free to call on me.

I would like very much to have the pleasure of meeting you and talking over the work in your school. I can call at any time that will be convenient for you.

## B

Mr. W. P. Brown of your home office tells me that you are desirous of employing more automobile salesmen. As I am very much interested in this work and have had considerable experience, I am placing my application with you.

Age: Twenty-three years.

Experience: For three summers I have worked as salesman for the R. E. Edwards Sales Company of Wichita, Kansas, dealers in Whirlwind cars. I have also worked for one year, after school hours, as automobile mechanic for this same firm.

Education: I am a graduate (June, 1940) of the University of Kansas School of Business Administration. I am well grounded in business theory and practice, having studied both economics and accounting.

References: Mr. W. P. Brown, Thunderbolt Automobile Company, Detroit, Michigan.
Mr. R. E. Edwards, Edwards Sales Company, Wichita, Kansas.
Professor J. W. Pound, School of Business Administration, The University of Kansas, Lawrence, Kansas.

However, I desire a personal interview to talk over my qualifications with you. May I call at your convenience?

## C

Your advertisement in the *Free Press* states your need for a salesman in your shoe department. I desire to be considered an applicant for this position.

For many years I have looked forward to making my way in the shoe business. My father was for ten years the owner of a shoe store, and from him I learned at an early age many important facts about the construction, quality, and selling of shoes. During each summer and after school hours, I worked in the store, first as errand boy, and then later for five years as salesman. Thus I have learned both about shoes and about meeting customers.

I am a graduate of Ardmore High School, and this June I hope to receive a B.A. degree from the University of Pennsylvania. I have tried to take those studies which would fit me best for the shoe business. Thus I have pursued a business course and studied such subjects as accounting, bookkeeping, typewriting, and economic geography. However, I have taken work in English composition, French, history, and psychology. My marks have been A and B.

The following men have kindly consented to act as references for me:

Mr. J. L. Turner, 265 Temple Street, Philadelphia, Pennsylvania.

Professor T. D. Smith, Department of Economics, The University of Pennsylvania, Philadelphia, Pennsylvania.

Dr. H. D. Thistlewaite, 4 Ontario Street, Ardmore, Pennsylvania.

May I have a personal interview to present my qualifications more fully? I am free any afternoon after two o'clock.

6. Write a letter of application for a summer position.

Assuming that you are about to graduate from college, write a letter of application for a permanent position.

## F. The Informal Essay

**Definition.** The term *essay* is so broad and has been applied to so many kinds of prose writing that attempting to define it seems futile. One does better, perhaps, to consider two main classifications. These are the formal and the informal essay; even here the division is not exact, for some essays are midway between the two groups. Generally speaking, however, the formal essay is a relatively impersonal, serious piece of prose in which the writer endeavors to explain or prove some thesis. The current magazine articles in a serious vein on politics, war, or economics are good examples of formal essays.

The informal essay, on the other hand, has an entirely different purpose. It aims primarily to entertain rather than to instruct. Whereas the formal essay adopts an impersonal tone, the informal essay is highly personal. By capitalizing upon his beliefs, feelings, and observations, the author hopes to amuse his reader, and he also really asks the reader not to be too serious in considering the matter at hand. He usually adopts a light tone, perhaps even a humorous one, and dwells genially on the different ramifications of his subject. Although he has a definite thesis in mind, plans his writing carefully, and usually has a very specific underlying purpose, he subordinates all these to his primary aim of amusing.

Inasmuch as the formal essay has already been discussed in the chapters on exposition, we shall in this section consider the informal essay. Suppose first that you are a student with a serious, penetrating turn of mind. As you look about you on the ordinary campus scenes and people, you find that your companions and yourself are confronting certain common problems: falling in love, becoming married, making a living, advancing in the world, getting along with each other, keeping in good health, studying, and many similar problems. Such topics naturally interest you. You discuss them frequently with your more serious-minded friends. Is there really such a thing as a true friend, or is everyone out for what he can get for himself? Are riches a satisfactory goal in life, or is something higher demanded, some idealism for example? Is marriage advantageous, or is it just an act of putting one's head in a noose? Will honest effort get one ahead in the world, or does advancement come through "pull" and knowing the right people? Is hard work justified in college, or is it better to slide through one's studies and have a good time making "contacts" and being a good sport? Having talked over such topics many times, you decide to write down your thoughts about them. Being in earnest, you begin without circumlocution and proceed by writing your observations as compactly as you can. In terse, pithy sentences you weigh the pros and cons of your subject and reach certain conclusions. Your writing keeps close to the ground, although at times your enthusiasm for your subject gives a more elevated tone to your work. Thus you express yourself as wisely as you are able on love, marriage, religion, wealth, studies, politics, ambition, wisdom, friendship, and other universal topics. In so doing, you are writing one of the oldest forms of the English essay. Over three hundred years ago in Elizabethan England, Francis Bacon, the renowned politician and scientist, wrote on these subjects with a wisdom that commands our respect today. Through his eyes are seen some of the greatest and most universal problems of human beings.

Suppose now that your mood is lighter. You still have a serious cast of mind, but you are not quite so much in earnest and are willing to be somewhat humorous. Once again you look sharply around the campus and this time are impressed with the oddities of the various students and professors. Bill Diffling, for example, is full of affectation. He wears the latest in clothing—trousers of just the right length, a coat of the most recent cut, a shirt with the latest collar design. Yet you know he has no money, despite his appearance. He rides in the cars of his wealthy friends, but he has no car himself; he attends their parties, but he gives none; he plays on their golf courses, but he belongs to no club himself. Actually he is rather ridiculous, you decide. Many of the co-eds are no better. They play multitudinous tricks on the poor men. Now they give encouragement, now they are coy, now they are scornful; sometimes they play fair, but again they tell the most outrageous prevarications. So it is apparent to you that an observant person can derive great amusement from examining the habits and customs of ordinary people. Hence, as you begin to write this time, you not only discuss the serious aspects of campus life but satirize the scene with the intent of curing some of these evil practices by making them ridiculous. Your manner is now similar to that of the two famous essayists of the early eighteenth century, Addison and Steele. Writing in a beautiful, polished style, these two men dealt with "folly, extravagance, and caprice." Their essays are informal, graceful, humane, and still eminently readable.

Again, suppose that you are no longer concerned quite so much with balancing arguments for and against universal subjects, or with satirizing the manners and customs of your contemporaries, as with examining some of your own foibles. In surveying your likes and dislikes, your peculiarities, and indeed all those things which are of personal importance, you decide that if these were pleasantly presented, they might be of interest to others. You recall, for example, the pleasure you take in returning to your room on a winter's night, taking off your shoes, and curling up in a chair with a good book. Or you dwell on the appeal of an early morning walk, or a mid-week dance, or a breakfast cup of coffee, or sleeping late, or a good play, or various ideas that you fancy. Thus when you write this time, you write of yourself or of various objects and ideas seen through your own eyes. Your personality is of prime importance. Such writing is known as the personal essay, which first flourished in the early nineteenth century with Lamb, Hazlitt, De Quincey, Smith, Hunt, and others. These writers had a special gift of taking the reader into their confidence and revealing to him their innermost thoughts and feelings concerning many subjects in such a manner that even the most trivial objects and ideas assumed importance and absorbing interest. Their whimsicality, humor, beauty of style, and correctness of taste have made them favorites since their day.

Therefore, in these three types of essays—the aphoristic type of Bacon, the periodical type of Addison and Steele, and the personal essay of the early nineteenth century—you have tried the three major forms of the informal essay. As a matter of fact, however, the personal essay is the one which has proved most popular with modern writers. The Baconian essay is somewhat too formal; the writer's personality can be given freer expression through more personal writing. The modern essayists, such as E. V. Lucas, G. K. Chesterton, Agnes Repplier, A. C. Benson, or Christopher Morley, therefore have a primary purpose of entertaining, and feature a light, pleasant, good-humored manner.

## Of Youth and Age

### FRANCIS BACON

A man that is young in years may be old in hours, if he have lost no time; but that happeneth rarely. Generally, youth is like the first cogitations, not so wise as the second; for there is a youth in thoughts as well as in ages; and yet the invention of young men is more lively than that of old, and imaginations stream into their minds better, and, as it were, more divinely. Natures that have much heat, and great and violent desires and perturbations, are not ripe for action till they have passed the meridian of their years: as it was with Julius Cæsar and Septimius Severus; of the latter of whom it is said, *Juventutem egit erroribus, imo furoribus, plenam;* [19] and yet he was the ablest emperor, almost, of all the list; but reposed natures may do well in youth, as it is seen in Augustus Cæsar, Cosmus Duke of Florence, Gaston de Foix, and others. On the other side, heat and vivacity in age is an excellent composition for business. Young men are fitter to invent than to judge, fitter for execution than for counsel, and fitter for new projects than for settled business; for the experience of age, in things that fall within the compass of it, directeth them; but in new things abuseth them. The errors of young men are the ruin of business; but the errors of aged men amount but to this, that more might have been done, or sooner.

Young men, in the conduct and manage of actions, embrace more than they can hold, stir more than they can quiet; fly to the end, without consideration of the means and degrees; pursue some few principles which they have chanced upon absurdly; care not to innovate, which draws

19. He spent a youth full of mistakes, and even of acts of madness.

unknown inconveniences; use extreme remedies at first; and that, which doubleth all errors, will not acknowledge or retract them, like an unready horse, that will neither stop nor turn. Men of age object too much, consult too long, adventure too little, repent too soon, and seldom drive business home to the full period, but content themselves with a mediocrity of success. Certainly, it is good to compound employments of both; for that will be good for the present, because the virtues of either age may correct the defects of both; and good for succession, that young men may be learners, while men in age are actors; and, lastly, good for externe accidents, because authority followeth old men, and favor and popularity youth; but for the moral part perhaps youth will have the pre-eminence, as age hath for the politic. A certain rabbin, upon the text, "Your young men shall see visions, and your old men shall dream dreams," inferreth that young men are admitted nearer to God than old, because vision is a clearer revelation than a dream; and, certainly, the more a man drinketh of the world, the more it intoxicateth; and age doth profit rather in the powers of understanding than in the virtues of the will and affections. There be some have an overearly ripeness in their years, which fadeth betimes; these are, first, such as have brittle wits, the edge whereof is soon turned; such as was Hermogenes the rhetorician, whose books are exceedingly subtle, who afterwards waxed stupid. A second sort is of those that have some natural dispositions, which have better grace in youth than in age; such as is a fluent and luxuriant speech, which becomes youth well, but not age; so Tully saith of Hortensius: *Idem manebat, neque idem decebat.*[20] The third is of such as to take too high a strain at the first, and are magnanimous more than tract of years can uphold; as was Scipio Africanus, of whom Livy saith, in effect, *Ultima primis cedebant.*[21]

*Suggestions for Study*

1. What does Bacon mean by "Natures that have much heat"? By "reposed natures"?
2. What qualities of youth and age should be combined for success in business?
3. What are the weaknesses of young men?
4. What are the weaknesses of aged men?
5. In what do aged men profit more than younger men?
6. What three kinds of men are overripe in their years? What is meant by "brittle wits"?
7. What qualities of a personal essay are lacking in this essay?

20. He remained the same, but it did not befit him equally well.
21. His later life did not live up to the promise of his early years..

8. Characterize Bacon's style, as shown here.

9. Define the following words from the essay: cogitations, perturbations, meridian, compass, innovate, retract, mediocrity, infer, magnanimous.

## The Science of Physic

### JOSEPH ADDISON

I do not remember that in any of my lucubrations I have touched upon that useful science of physic, notwithstanding I have declared myself more than once a professor of it. I have indeed joined the study of astrology with it, because I never knew a physician recommend himself to the public who had not a sister art to embellish his knowledge in medicine. It has been commonly observed in compliment to the ingenious of our profession, that Apollo was a god of verse as well as physic; and in all ages the most celebrated practitioners of our country were the particular favorites of the muses. Poetry to physic is indeed like the gilding to a pill; it makes the art shine, and covers the severity of the doctor with the agreeableness of the companion.

The very foundation of poetry is good sense, if we may allow Horace to be a judge of the art: *Scribendi recte sapere est, et principium, et fons.*[1] And if so, we have reason to believe that the same man who writes well can prescribe well, if he has applied himself to the study of both. Besides, when we see a man making profession of two different sciences, it is natural for us to believe he is no pretender in that which we are not judges of, when we find him skillful in that which we understand.

Ordinary quacks and charlatans are thoroughly sensible how necessary it is to support themselves by these collateral assistances, and therefore always lay their claim to some supernumerary accomplishments which are wholly foreign to their profession.

About twenty years ago, it was impossible to walk the streets without having an advertisement thrust into your hand, of a doctor "who was arrived at the knowledge of the green and red dragon, and had discovered the female fern seed." Nobody ever knew what this meant; but the green and red dragon so amused the people that the doctor lived very comfortably upon them. About the same time there was pasted a very hard word upon every corner of the streets. This, to the best of my remembrance, was

1. The translation is given in the first clause of the sentence.

## TETRACHYMAGOGON

which drew great shoals of spectators about it, who read the bill that it introduced with unspeakable curiosity; and when they were sick, would have nobody but this learned man for their physician.

I once received an advertisement of one "who had studied thirty years by candlelight for the good of his countrymen." He might have studied twice as long by daylight, and never have been taken notice of: but elucubrations cannot be overvalued. There are some who have gained themselves great reputation for physic by their birth, as the "seventh son of a seventh son"; and others by not being born at all, as the "unborn doctor," who, I hear, is lately gone the way of his patients, having died worth five hundred pounds *per annum,* though he was not "born" to a halfpenny.

My ingenious friend Dr. Saffold succeeded my old contemporary Dr. Lilly in the studies both of physic and astrology, to which he added that of poetry, as was to be seen both upon the sign where he lived, and in the bills which he distributed. He was succeeded by Dr. Case, who erased the verses of his predecessor out of the signpost, and substituted in their stead two of his own, which were as follow:

> Within this Place
> Lives Doctor Case.

He is said to have got more by this distich than Mr. Dryden did by all his works. There would be no end of enumerating the several imaginary perfections and unaccountable artifices by which this tribe of men ensnare the minds of the vulgar, and gain crowds of admirers. I have seen the whole front of a mountebank's stage from one end to the other faced with patent certificates, medals, and great seals, by which the several princes of Europe have testified their particular respect and esteem for the doctor. Every great man with a sounding title has been his patient. I believe I have seen twenty mountebanks that have given physic to the Czar of Muscovy. The great Duke of Tuscany escapes no better. The Elector of Brandenburg was likewise a very good patient.

This great condescension of the doctor draws upon him much goodwill from his audience; and it is ten to one, but if any of them be troubled with an aching tooth, his ambition will prompt him to get it drawn by a person who has had so many princes, kings, and emperors, under his hands.

I must not leave this subject without observing that as physicians are apt to deal in poetry, apothecaries endeavor to recommend themselves by oratory, and are therefore, without controversy, the most eloquent persons in the whole British nation. I would not willingly discourage any of the arts, especially that of which I am an humble professor; but I must confess for the good of my native country, I could wish there might be a suspension of physic for some years, that our kingdom, which has been so much exhausted by the wars, might have leave to recruit itself.

As for myself, the only physic which has brought me safe to almost the age of man, and which I prescribe to all my friends, is abstinence. This is certainly the best physic for prevention, and very often the most effectual against the present distemper. In short, my recipe is, "Take nothing."

Were the body politic to be physicked like, particular persons, I should venture to prescribe to it after the same manner. I remember when our whole island was shaken with an earthquake some years ago, there was an impudent mountebank who sold pills, which (as he told the country people) were very good against an earthquake. It may perhaps be thought as absurd to prescribe a diet for the allaying popular commotions, and national ferments. But I am verily persuaded that if in such a case a whole people were to enter into a course of abstinence, and eat nothing but water gruel for a fortnight, it would abate the rage and animosity of parties, and not a little contribute to the cure of a distracted nation. Such a fast would have a natural tendency to the procuring of those ends for which a fast is usually proclaimed. If any man has a mind to enter on such a voluntary abstinence, it might not be improper to give him the caution of Pythagoras in particular: *Abstine a fabis*—Abstain from beans. That is, say the interpreters, meddle not with elections, beans having been made use of by the voters among the Athenians in the choice of magistrates.

## Suggestions for Study

1. What relation does the opening discussion of poetry and medicine have to do with the essay that follows?
2. If a man can write poetry well, what does Addison say we are likely to think concerning the man's professional ability?
3. What is the tone of the essay?
4. Although written two centuries ago, has the essay any timeliness?
5. What specific details does Addison employ to give his essay concreteness?
6. Define the following words from the essay: lucubrations, embellish, charlatans, collateral, supernumerary, distich, artifices, mountebank, apothecary, abstinence, allay.

## *A Little Moral Advice*

SYDNEY SMITH

It is surprising to see for what foolish causes men hang themselves. The most silly repulse, the most trifling ruffle of temper, or derangement of stomach, anything seems to justify an appeal to the razor or the cord. I have a contempt for persons who destroy themselves. Live on, and look evil in the face; walk up to it, and you will find it less than you imagined, and often you will not find it at all; for it will recede as you advance. Any fool may be a suicide. When you are in a melancholy fit, first suspect the body, appeal to rhubarb and calomel, and send for the apothecary; a little bit of gristle sticking in the wrong place, an untimely consumption of custard, excessive gooseberries, often cover the mind with clouds and bring on the most distressing views of human life.

I start up at two o'clock in the morning after my first sleep, in an agony of terror, and feel all the weight of life upon my soul. It is impossible that I can bring up such a family of children, my sons and daughters will be beggars; I shall live to see those whom I loved exposed to the scorns and contumely of the world!—But stop, thou child of sorrow, and humble imitator of Job, and tell me on what you dined. Was not there soup and salmon, and then a plate of beef, and then duck, blanc-mange, cream cheese, diluted with beer, claret, champagne, hock, tea, coffee, and noyeau? And after all this, you talk of the *mind* and the evils of life! These kinds of cases do not need meditation, but magnesia. Take short views of life. What am I to do in these times with such a family of children? So I argued, and lived dejected and with little hope; but the difficulty vanished as life went on. An uncle died, and left me some money; an aunt died, and left me more; my daughter married well; I had two or three appointments, and before life was half over became a prosperous man. And so will you. Everyone has uncles and aunts who are mortal; friends start up out of the earth; time brings a thousand chances in your favor; legacies fall from the clouds. Nothing so absurd as to sit down and wring your hands because all the good which may happen to you in twenty years has not taken place at this precise moment.

The greatest happiness which can happen to any one is to cultivate a love of reading. Study is often dull because it is improperly managed. I make no apology for speaking of myself, for as I write anonymously nobody knows who I am, and if I did not, very few would be the wiser— but every man speaks more firmly when he speaks from his own experience. I read four books at a time; some classical book perhaps on Monday,

Wednesday, and Friday mornings. The *History of France,* we will say, on the evenings of the same days. On Tuesday, Thursday, and Saturday, Mosheim or Lardner, and in the evenings of those days, Reynolds' Lectures, or Burns' Travels. Then I always have a standing book of poetry, and a novel to read when I am in the humor to read nothing else. Then I translate some French into English one day, and retranslate it the next; so that I have seven or eight pursuits going on at the same time, and this produces the cheerfulness of diversity, and avoids that gloom which proceeds from hanging a long while over a single book. I do not recommend this as a receipt for becoming a learned man, but for becoming a cheerful one.

Nothing contributes more certainly to the animal spirits than benevolence. Servants and common people are always about you; make moderate attempts to please everybody, and the effort will insensibly lead you to a more happy state of mind. Pleasure is very reflective, and if you give it you will feel it. The pleasure you give by kindness of manner returns to you, and often with compound interest. The receipt for cheerfulness is not to have one motive only in the day for living, but a number of little motives; a man who from the time he rises till bedtime conducts himself like a gentleman, who throws some little condescension into his manner to superiors, and who is always contriving to soften the distance between himself and the poor and ignorant, is always improving his animal spirits, and adding to his happiness.

I recommend lights as a great improver of animal spirits. How is it possible to be happy with two mold candles ill snuffed? You may be virtuous, and wise, and good, but two candles will not do for animal spirits. Every night the room in which I sit is lighted up like a town after a great naval victory, and in this cereous galaxy and with a blazing fire, it is scarcely possible to be low-spirited, a thousand pleasing images spring up in the mind, and I can see the little blue demons scampering off like parish boys pursued by the beadle.

## Suggestions for Study

1. What is Smith's attitude toward suicide? State his thesis.
2. On what may one often blame a melancholy view of human life?
3. Why should one not despair when faced with misfortune?
4. What suggestions for happiness does Smith offer?
5. By what means does Smith secure concreteness of writing?
6. In what way is this an informal essay? Why can it not be called a formal treatise on morals?
7. Make a topic outline of this essay. This exercise will acquaint you with the logical organization of the writing.

8. Define the following words from the essay; derangement, contumely, claret, hock, legacies, diversity, benevolence, cereous, galaxy.

**Writing the Essay.** As noted already, the real purpose of the informal essay is to entertain. It does not aim to prove anything, but merely sug- gests in an attractive fashion that some things may be true. Usually it is dominated by the personality of the writer; hence it is to prose essen- tially what the lyric is to poetry, a personal expression of the writer. To be read with pleasure, it must be considered a leisurely and conversational form of writing. To be written well, it requires that the author adopt an informal and intimate manner and take the reader as an equal into his confidence to converse on a variety of subjects.

The essay writer, therefore, tries first of all to be himself and to speak naturally. Every man can thus write a fresh and novel essay; no two of us are exactly alike, and if each speaks truly what is within him, he will write refreshingly. To be sure, one who has the fullest personality, the keenest observation, and the widest range of experience and reading is best suited to write an interesting essay, but everyone has ample oppor- tunity. It is not the size and importance of the topic which matters most, but the manner in which it is treated. The essayist may be struck by his manner of going for a walk, by the peculiarity of himself or his friends, or by any one of a thousand things. This observation or experience he links to some sort of generalization and thereby attaches interest and even importance to what seemed before to be trivial. Keenness of observation and the ability to capitalize upon what lies within the range of his own observation are therefore essential qualities of the good essayist.

The author, of course, endeavors to reveal his personality without being boastful or conceited. He has confidence that what he finds of interest will be of interest also to his reader, and indeed without that confidence no essay would be written. He is simply candid with himself and his reader, and so achieves originality.

The informal essayist is not bound by his subject matter quite so rigidly as is the formal essayist. The tone which he assumes—and he must be sure to have unity of tone—gives him freedom to write much as he would talk, striving for spontaneity of ideas and pursuing attractive fancies. He is not confined within the domain of strict logic but can follow wherever his fancy dictates, provided only that he stay within the domain of rea- son. Therefore, he is free to present pet ideas, to cast new light on old subjects, to note unfamiliar scenes, and to play with the intricate psy- chology of mankind, all without feeling the necessity to prove every state- ment and to formulate an absolutely logical chain of conviction.

These remarks, however, must not be construed to mean that the essayist has a free hand to do whatever he likes at any moment in the course of his writing, that he may set his pen to paper with the first thought that occurs to him and follow the dictates of his fancy till he reaches a likely conclusion, that he need not make an outline or plan his essay. Actually, nothing can be farther from the truth. An air of informality and spontaneity comes not from haphazard writing, but from the most careful preparation and skillful execution. Informality is a work of art. It can be attained only by the expenditure of the same time and effort that are given to the writing of a serious treatise. An artistic essay, however formless and even rambling it may appear, is based upon a carefully organized outline, judiciously concealed. In some formal prose writings the introduction enumerates the major points to follow, and the body of the paper considers these in order. But in the informal essay such an apparent structural device is not used. Beginning with the thesis, or an observation closely related to it, the essayist proceeds toward a predetermined goal without seeming to follow an organized plan. Each point ingeniously gives rise to the next by a natural association of ideas. Careful preparation is required in order not to lose sight of the ultimate goal and to retain the interest of the reader. No awkward gaps can be left between ideas, and the shift from one idea to the next must be clearly evident.

A thesis is formulated at the outset. It serves not only as a check against excessive rambling but as a goal toward which to aim. It can be stated outright, or possibly withheld and brought out by implication. Often it is the opening sentence and so provides forcefulness to the beginning. Oliver Goldsmith, a delightful eighteenth-century essayist, made excellent use of it as a vigorous opening sentence from which he could extend his train of thought. Here are the opening paragraphs from several of his essays:

> Foreigners observe that there are no ladies in the world more beautiful, or more ill dressed, than those of England. Our country women have been compared to those pictures where the face is the work of a Raphael, but the draperies thrown out by some empty pretender, destitute of taste, and entirely unacquainted with design.

> Man, when secluded from society, is not a more solitary being than the woman who leaves the duties of her own sex to invade the privileges of ours. She seems, in such circumstances, like one in banishment; she appears like a neutral being between the sexes; and, though she may have the admiration of both, she finds true happiness from neither.

> Animals, in general, are sagacious in proportion as they cultivate society. The elephant and the beaver show the greatest signs of this when

united; but when man intrudes into their communities, they lose all
their spirit of industry, and testify but a very small share of that sagacity
for which, when in a social state, they are so remarkable.

The essayist may also choose to start from that observation which gave
his thoughts their initial impulse, and so proceed toward an ultimate
generalization. Charles Lamb's essay "Old China" follows this plan. It
begins:

> I have an almost feminine partiality for old china. When I go to see
> any great house, I inquire for the china closet, and next for the picture
> gallery. I cannot defend the order of preference, but by saying that we
> all have some taste or other, of too ancient a date to admit of our re-
> membering distinctly that it was an acquired one. I can call to mind
> the first play, and the first exhibition, that I was taken to; but I am not
> conscious of a time when china jars and saucers were introduced into
> my imagination.

Lamb then gradually shifts to a reflection concerning the old days
when he and his sister struggled to find the money to buy such china.
He pictures the pleasures of poverty when each new purchase was a treasured prize. Then he turns to the thought that poverty may have been
enjoyable when he and his sister were young, but now that old age has
crept upon them, they need greater comfort and security. The final note
is struck when he returns to the old china before him. The reader ends
with the feeling that he has been through a very natural and delightful
conversation which arose from a reflection concerning the beautiful old
china in Lamb's possession.

There are, of course, countless other ways of starting the essay. The
principle is that which governs all introductory paragraphs: the reader's
attention must be aroused through interest and curiosity. An impulse
must be provided him. Then he will follow the writer along the main
path or through the by-paths just as long as those paths come in an
orderly fashion.

One other caution must be observed. In a form which tends toward
the general as does the essay, the writer must be especially careful to be
concrete. Illustrations must be frequently interspersed; indeed many successful essays consist almost solely of illustrations designed to explain the
different implications of the thesis.

The informal essay is therefore a brief, informal, conversational piece
of writing, in which the essayist in a personal way expresses himself
freely upon any subject which catches his attention. He has a definite plan
and a definite thesis, but these he conceals so that he can delight and

entertain his reader with the freshness, spontaneity, and informality of his writing.

## Exercise

Write an informal essay on one of the following topics:

The proper time of year for swimming
The habit of smoking
The most suitable clothes to wear to class
Homesickness
Varieties of movies
Social prestige in college
Weather
Mowing the lawn
Spending the week end
Traveling
Hunting
The best kind of conversation
Where and what to eat
Passing courses in college
What a home ought to be
Setting-up exercises
Shaving
Spending the night in a day coach
Death
How to be a gentleman
The cigar-store Indian
Nature at her best
Roadhogs
Love and a uniform
The magazines in the doctor's office

In-laws
City or country?
The church choir
How to be a bore
Cutting classes
Slacks
Absurdities of college life
Candid camera fans
The ingenuity shown in gadgets
Attractive books
Antiques
Weeds
Apartment life
Building a new house
The decay of courtesy among the younger generation
Summer fashions
Where to spend the summer
Driving a truck
Movies or the stage?
Casper Milquetoasts
The practical joker
Missing the train
Ferry boats
Subways

## My Fishpond [22]

### STEPHEN LEACOCK

It lies embowered in a little cup of the hills, my fishing pond. I made a last trip to it just as the season ended, when the autumn leaves of its great trees were turning color and rustling down to rest upon the still black water. So steep are the banks, so old and high the trees, that scarcely a puff of wind ever ruffles the surface of the pond. All around, it is as if the world were stilled into silence, and time blended into eternity.

I realized again as I looked at the pond what a beautiful, secluded spot

22. From the *Atlantic Monthly*, CLVIII (December, 1936), 720. Reprinted by permission of the author and of the *Atlantic Monthly*.

it was, how natural its appeal to the heart of the angler. You turn off a country road, go sideways across a meadow and over a hill, and there it lies—a sheet of still water, with high, high banks, grown with great trees. Long years ago someone built a sawmill, all gone now, at the foot of the valley and threw back the water to make a pond, perhaps a quarter of a mile long. At the widest it must be nearly two hundred feet—the most skillful fisherman may make a full cast both ways. At the top end, where it runs narrow among stumps and rushes, there is no room to cast except with direction and great skill.

Let me say at once, so as to keep no mystery about it, that there are no fish in my pond. So far as I know there never have been. But I have never found that to make any difference. Certainly none to the men I bring there—my chance visitors from the outside world—for an afternoon of casting.

If there are no fish in the pond, at least they never know it. They never doubt it; they never ask, and I let it go at that.

It is well known hereabouts that I do not take anybody and everybody out to my fishpond. I only care to invite people who can really fish, who can cast a line—experts, and especially people from a distance to whom the whole neighborhood is new and attractive, the pond seen for the first time. If I took out ordinary men, especially men near home, they would very likely notice that they got no fish. The expert doesn't. He knows trout fishing too well. He knows that even in a really fine pond, such as he sees mine is, there are days when not a trout will rise. He'll explain it to you himself; and, having explained it, he is all the better pleased if he turns out to be right and they don't rise.

Trout, as everyone knows who is an angler, never rise after a rain, nor before one; it is impossible to get them to rise in the heat; and any chill in the air keeps them down. The absolutely right day is a still, cloudy day, but even then there are certain kinds of clouds that prevent a rising of the trout. Indeed, I have only to say to one of my expert friends, "Queer, they didn't bite!" and he's off to a good start with an explanation. There is such a tremendous lot to know about trout fishing that men who are keen on it can discuss theories of fishing by the hour.

Such theories we generally talk over—my guest of the occasion and I— as we make our preparations at the pond. You see, I keep there all the apparatus that goes with fishing—a punt, with lockers in the sides of it, a neat little dock built out of cedar (cedar attracts the trout), and, best of all, a little shelter house, a quaint little place like a pagoda, close beside the water and yet under the trees. Inside is tackle, all sorts of tackle, hanging round the walls in a mixture of carelessness and order.

"Look, old man," I say, "if you like to try a running paternoster, take this one," or, "Have you ever seen these Japanese leads? No, they're not a gut; they're a sort of floss."

"I doubt if I can land one with that," he says.

"Perhaps not," I answer. In fact, I'm sure he couldn't: there isn't any to land.

On pegs in the pagoda hangs a waterproof mackintosh or two, for you never know—you may be caught in a shower just when the trout are starting to rise. Then, of course, a sort of cellarette cupboard with decanters and bottles, and gingersnaps, and perhaps an odd pot of anchovy paste—no one wants to quit good fishing for mere hunger. Nor does any real angler care to begin fishing without taking just a drop (Just a touch —be careful! Whoa! Whoa!) of something to keep out the cold, or to wish good luck for the chances of the day.

I always find, when I bring out one of my friends, that these mere preparatives or preparations, these preliminaries of angling, are the best part of it. Often they take half an hour. There is so much to discuss— the question of weights of tackle, the color of the fly to use, and broad general questions of theory, such as whether it matters what kind of hat a man wears. It seems that trout will rise for some hats, and for others not. One of my best guests, who has written a whole book on fly fishing, is particularly strong on hats and color. "I don't think I'd wear that hat, old man," he says; "much too dark for a day like this." "I wore it all last month," I said. "So you might, but that was August. I wouldn't wear a dark hat in September; and that tie is too dark a blue, old man."

So I knew that that made it all right. I kept the hat on. We had a grand afternoon; we got no fish.

I admit that the lack of fish in my pond requires sometimes a little tact in management. The guest gets a little restless. So I say to him, "You certainly have the knack of casting!"—and he gets so absorbed in casting farther and farther that he forgets the fish. Or I take him toward the upper end and he gets his line caught on bulrush—that might be a bite. Or, if he still keeps restless, I say suddenly, "Hush! Was that a fish jumped?" That will silence any true angler instantly. "You stand in the bow," I whisper, "and I'll paddle gently in that direction." It's the *whispering* that does it. We are still a hundred yards away from any trout that could hear us even if a trout were there. But that makes no difference. Some of the men I take out begin to whisper a mile away from the pond and come home whispering.

You see, after all, what with frogs jumping, and catching the line in bulrushes, or pulling up a waterlogged chip nearly to the top, they don't really know—my guests don't—whether they have hooked something or not. Indeed, after a little lapse of time, they think they did: they talk of the "big one they lost"—a thing over which any angler gets sentimental in retrospect. "Do you remember," they say to me months later at our club in the city, "that big trout I lost up on your fishpond last summer?" "Indeed I do," I say. "Did you ever get him later on?" "No, never," I answer. (Neither him nor any other.)

Yet the illusion holds good. And besides, you never can tell: there *might* be trout in the pond. Why not? After all, why shouldn't there be a trout in the pond? You take a pond like that and there ought to be trout in it!

Whenever the sight of the pond bursts on the eyes of a new guest he stands entranced. "What a wonderful place for trout!" he exclaims. "Isn't it?" I answer. "No wonder you'd get trout in a pond like that." "No wonder at all." "You don't need to stock it at all, I suppose?" "Stock it!" I laugh at the idea. Stock a pond like that! Well, I guess not!

Perhaps one of the best and most alluring touches is fishing out of season—just a day or two after the season has closed. Any fisherman knows how keen is the regret at each expiring season—swallowed up and lost in the glory of the fading autumn. So if a guest turns up just then I say, "I know it's out of season, but I thought you might care to take a run out to the pond anyway and have a look at it." He can't resist. By the time he's in the pagoda and has a couple of small drinks (Careful, not too much! Whoa! Whoa!) he decides there can be no harm in making a cast or two. "I suppose," he says, "you never have any trouble with the inspectors?" "Oh, no," I answer; "they never think of troubling me." And with that we settle down to an afternoon of it. "I'm glad," says the guest at the end, "that they weren't rising. After all, we had just the same fun as if they were."

That's it: illusion! How much of life is like that! It's the *idea* of the thing that counts, not the reality. You don't need fish for fishing, any more than you need partridge for partridge shooting, or gold for gold mining. Just the illusion or expectation.

So I am going back now to the city and to my club, where we shall fish all winter, hooking up big ones, but losing the ones bigger still, hooking two trout at one throw—three at a throw!—and for me, behind it all, the memory of my fishing pond darkening under the falling leaves. . . . At least it has made my friends happy.

*Suggestions for Study*

1. What does the author gain by his opening description?
2. Why does the author state immediately that no fish are in his pond? Would he have gained anything by withholding his revelation until later?
3. Why are only experts invited to the pond?
4. What traits of human nature are depicted in the essay that make it of humorous significance?
5. What basic idea or thesis is the author trying to portray? What word is of primary importance in understanding this basic idea?
6. What means does the author use to develop his various topic ideas?
7. Although the essay is conversational and informal, do you find an underlying pattern which the author follows?
8. Define the following words from the essay: embowered, pagoda, decanters, retrospect, expiring.

## On the Floor of the Library [23]

### SIMEON STRUNSKY

Unfortunate people who never read detective novels; or, worse still, those who pick up a mystery story and wonder what in the world anyone can see in the book to keep him up till 1:30 in the morning with intermittent trips to the cold meat in the icebox; or, worst of all, those who read the first chapter and then turn to the end to see who did the killing—such unfortunates think they are sufficiently kind when they describe the habit as a mild vice, not so hard on the family as liquor or drugs, but pernicious for the eyesight. They think they are 100 per cent charitable when they tolerate the practice as one form of escape from the realities of a difficult world.

To such outsiders it is not given to understand that the *Mystery of the Chintz Room* or the *Smile of Gautama* is not an escape from the world but an initiation. They simply do not know that a select course in reading from Conan Doyle to Carolyn Wells is a guide to the institutions, culture, and life outlook of the nations from China to Chile. I have set down below a mere fragment of the picture of humanity which may be built up by devoting not more than one evening a fortnight to this field of research hitherto neglected by the sociologists. The list might easily be multiplied by twenty.

(1) The common belief that the British are an open-air people is utterly opposed to the facts. When a member of the British nobility or upper middle classes is found dead in his bed, with a mystic Oriental symbol

23. From *Sinbad and His Friends*, published by Henry Holt & Co. Reprinted by permission of the publishers.

scrawled in blood on the sheets, the mystery is rendered all the more baffling by the fact that all the windows are hermetically sealed, the door is locked from within, the transom has not been opened for years, and the ventilators are choked up—in fact, the plumbers were scheduled to arrive on the morning after the tragedy. If it were not for that grisly Oriental symbol, the obvious conclusion would be that the victim perished for lack of a breath of fresh air. Given such a bedroom—and nearly all fatal bedrooms in our fiction are of this kind—and it is a question which is the greater puzzle: how the murderer managed to get in and escape, or how the victim managed to keep alive until the murderer got at him.

(2) Economy and resourcefulness are not among the virtues of the classes addicted to being murdered in their bedrooms or in their libraries. Twenty years after the tragedy the ghastly stain is still there on the floor. All attempts at erasing the spot in the course of twenty years have failed. What the scrubbing expense must have been, even if we reckon at a much lower rate than the prevailing scale of domestic wages today, is obvious. What the doctor's expenses have been in the way of treatment for nervous derangements inflicted by the ghastly stain on various members of the family is easily calculable. Yet no one in all these twenty years seems to have thought of replacing the bloodstained plank with a new one, at a trifling cost if done by day labor, and for a really insignificant sum if ordered from a collapsible bungalow manufacturer.

(3) Weekend guests in British baronial mansions or in wealthy residences on Long Island drink too much black coffee before going to bed. Then they lie awake all night. That is why about two in the morning they hear that queer, shuffling footfall down the hall to which at the moment they attach no particular meaning and the dread significance of which they realize only next morning when the host is found dead on the library carpet with his eyes fixed in a ghastly stare on the ceiling.

(4) The number of servants who have been in the employ of wealthy families addicted to violent deaths, for a period of forty years and up, and for whose fidelity the survivors can vouch as confidently as for their own husbands and wives, is truly astounding. Here, indeed, my friends, the psychoanalysts, may find the secret of my own passion for the mystery novel. Having in recent years never succeeded in keeping a houseworker for more than a couple of months, it is perfectly comprehensible how all my suppressed desires draw me to these faithful servants who stay forty years and then prefer to be victims of cruel suspicion by the coroner rather than bring disgrace on the family. It is not overstating the case to say that if only I could find a plain cook who will stay with us for forty years, I am perfectly willing to take a chance at being found at the end of

the period upon the floor of my library with the ivory-handled paper cutter through my heart. For that matter, I should welcome an unsuccessful attempt at murder if the assassin is not apprehended until he has found the paper-cutter. As it is, I have to tear the pages open by pulling with both hands from the top.

(5) The victims of foul play in the best British and American families never, absolutely never, cut themselves when shaving, or scrape the skin, or raise a blister. That is how the investigator from Scotland Yard or from his private office in the Equitable Life Building is enabled to detect the cause of death in an almost imperceptible red spot under the chin which the local police have overlooked and which he immediately recognizes as the characteristic bite of the rare South American adder, *Megaloptera Bandanna*. That method, if applied to the average man after he has shaved a second time for the theater, would suggest that he had been done to death by the greater part of the reptilian fauna of the South American forests.

(6) Closely allied to the preceding topic, it appears that the principal occupation of the inhabitants of South America is the manufacture or the jealous preservation of the secret of instantaneously deadly poisons unknown to modern science and leaving no visible after-effects, excepting, of course, the corpse.

(7) Insurance premiums on the lives of the British nobility must be really enormous at Lloyd's. At least one third of the members of the House of Lords are killed every year on the floor of their libraries or at the end of their yew walks close to the abandoned garden pavilion. But it is worse than that. If you have on the one hand the aged Duke of Beaucaire with an income of a million a year, and if you have on the other hand the third son of his fifth younger brother, who was wild at school and has lost himself somewhere on the Rand, and if you have no less than seven lives intervening between the scapegrace nephew and the ducal title, then these seven lives are sure to be wiped out by an earthquake or a fire or a marine disaster, and it only remains for the man who masquerades as the nephew (the real nephew having died of drink in Johannesburg) to come home and finish up the Duke.

(8) Nearly everybody in a mystery novel is a consummate athlete. They escape the vigilance of the detective who is disguised as a taxi-driver, or the pursuing avengers, by getting into a taxicab at one door and leaving by the other while the cab is in motion. This will interest people coming home from the theater who have sometimes tried to open a taxi door from the inside.

(9) The wealth of Burma and Tibet in priceless jewels would be

enough to pay the German indemnity ten times over. An emerald like the Eye of Gautama, a sapphire like the Hope of Asoka, a ruby like the Doom of Dhalatpur—all of them stolen from the forehead of sacred images by European adventurers—would be enough to finance British trade with Russia for the next fifty years. The fields of Burma and Tibet are cultivated entirely by women. The male population consists solely of priests, who are off in the West for the purpose of recovering the hallowed jewels and visiting the vengeance of Brahmaputra on the sacrilegious plunderers. Usually they are disguised as elevator runners at the Savoy or the St. Regis.

People who do not know, think detective fiction is a vice, whereas, it is, like Mr. H. G. Wells, a liberal education.

*Suggestions for Study*

1. What is the tone of the opening paragraph? Is this tone maintained throughout the essay?
2. What criticism of detective stories is implied by the essay?
3. Is the general purpose of the writer to instruct the reader?
4. Who are Conan Doyle and Carolyn Wells?
5. Define the following words from the essay: intermittent, hermetically, imperceptible, ducal, indemnity, hallowed.

# INDEX

# COMMON ABBREVIATIONS USED IN CORRECTING STUDENT MSS.

| | | | |
|---|---|---|---|
| **cap** | capitalize | **sl** | avoid slang |
| **cf** | compare | **sp** | correct the spelling |
| **clar** | make the meaning clear | **stet** | let the original construction stand |
| **coh** | improve the coherence | | |
| **col** | colloquialism; use formal diction | **syl** | correct the division into syllables |
| **D** | improve the diction | **T** | correct the tense |
| **dict** | consult the dictionary | **thought** | make the expression more logical |
| **emp** | make more emphatic | | |
| **euph** | euphony; improve the sound | **tr or ~** | transpose |
| **FW** | avoid fine writing | **trans** | insert proper transitions |
| **G** | correct the grammar | **U** | irrelevant; preserve unity of thought |
| **id** | improve the idiom | **V** | avoid vagueness |
| **il** | illogical; correct | **W** | avoid wordiness |
| **inc** | finish an incomplete construction | **WW** | wrong word; improve diction |
| **K** | awkward; make more graceful | **¶** | begin a new paragraph |
| **lc** | remove capitalization | **no ¶** | do not begin a new paragraph |
| **mar** | leave ample margins | **‖** | make parallel in structure |
| **MS** | make the manuscript neater | **on** | omit |
| **P** | correct the punctuation | **∧** | insert a necessary word or words |
| **quot** | insert quotation marks | | |
| **ref** | make the reference clear | **◠** | no space; bring together |
| **rep** | remove an awkward repetition | **/** | separate |
| **S** | improve faulty sentence structure | **𝔡** | delete |
| | | **?** | some question has been raised |